2015/16

GWASANAETH LLYFRGELL AC ARCHIFAU
POWYS LIBRARY
KT-490-919

CYFEIRLYFR /
REFERENCE

LLANDRINDOD WELLS
LIBRARY

Llyfr i'w ddefnyddio yn y llyfrgell yn unig
This book is for use in the library only

Llyfrgell y Sir/County Library Headquarters
Cefnllys Road, LLandrindod Wells, Powys LD1 5LD

WITHDRAWN
FROM STOCK

THE GUIDE TO

GRANTS FOR INDIVIDUALS IN NEED

FOURTEENTH EDITION

Jennifer Reynolds and Denise Lillya

Additional research by Gabriele Zagnojute

Contributions from Anike Akinola, Emma Weston,
Ian Pembridge and Caroline Field

DIRECTORY OF SOCIAL CHANGE

WITHDRAWN
FROM STOCK

Powys
37218 00017138 4

Published by the Directory of Social Change (Registered Charity no. 800517 in England and Wales)

Head office: 24 Stephenson Way, London NW1 2DP

Northern office: Suite 103, 1 Old Hall Street, Liverpool L3 9HG
Tel: 08450 77 77 07

Visit www.dsc.org.uk to find out more about our books, subscription funding websites and training events. You can also sign up for e-newsletters so that you're always the first to hear about what's new.

The publisher welcomes suggestions and comments that will help to inform and improve future versions of this and all of our titles. Please give us your feedback by emailing publications@dsc.org.uk.

It should be understood that this publication is intended for guidance only and is not a substitute for professional or legal advice. No responsibility for loss occasioned as a result of any person acting or refraining from acting can be accepted by the authors or publisher.

First published 1987
Second edition 1990
Third edition 1992
Fourth edition 1994
Fifth edition 1996
Sixth edition 1998
Seventh edition 2000
Eighth edition 2002
Ninth edition 2004
Tenth edition 2006
Eleventh edition 2009
Twelfth edition 2011
Thirteenth edition 2013
Fourteenth edition 2014

Copyright © Directory of Social Change 1988, 1992, 1994, 1996, 1998, 2000, 2002, 2004, 2006, 2009, 2011, 2013, 2014

All rights reserved. **No part of this book may be stored in a retrieval system or reproduced in any form whatsoever without prior permission in writing from the publisher.** This book is sold subject to the condition that it shall not, by way of trade or otherwise, be lent, re-sold, hired out or otherwise circulated without the publisher's prior permission in any form of binding or cover other than that in which it is published, and without a similar condition including this condition being imposed on the subsequent purchaser.

The publisher and author have made every effort to contact copyright holders. If anyone believes that their copyright material has not been correctly acknowledged, please contact the publisher **who will be pleased to rectify the omission.**

The moral right of the author has been asserted in accordance with the Copyrights, Designs and Patents Act 1988.

ISBN 978 1 906294 95 3

British Library Cataloguing in Publication Data
A catalogue record for this book is available from the British Library

Cover and text design by Kate Bass
Typeset by Marlinzo Services, Frome
Printed and bound by Page Bros, Norwich

FSC www.fsc.org
MIX
Paper from responsible sources
FSC® C023114

LLYFRGELLOEDD POWYS LIBRARIES

Contents

Foreword

Widespread changes to welfare provision brought in under the Welfare Reform Act 2012, coupled with budgetary cuts to services and a rising cost of living, are having a tangible effect on the lives of individuals and families throughout the country. Reforms such as the replacement of council tax benefit with new local schemes, the benefit cap, the 'bedroom tax', the replacement of Disability Living Allowance by Personal Independence Payments, and the significant increase in the use of sanctions have altered the social welfare landscape markedly, and are continuing to do so.

The impact of these changes is significant and the role of charitable funders in providing financial assistance and other sources of support is therefore crucial. It is similarly crucial that the charities and benevolent societies set up to support people in poverty remain responsive to this changing environment by ensuring their funding programmes continue to direct resources to those who need it most.

DSC's *Guide to Grants for Individuals in Need* contributes to this by providing individuals and support workers with a valuable resource to find out about the diverse range of grant schemes available and how to apply for funding. The Guide lists more than 1,900 grantmaking charities with a combined spend on grants of around £268 million a year.

Cripplegate Foundation, an independent charity working in Islington and parts of the City of London, is listed in the Guide for the support it provides to individuals through the Resident Support Scheme. This scheme is run jointly with Islington Council and a network of local charities. It was set up and launched in April 2013, when the government made changes to the Social Fund and passed down to the local level responsibility for providing a safety net to support individuals in severe hardship. Cripplegate Foundation maintained the level of grants expenditure it previously offered through its Grants to Individuals programme and by aligning funds with the Council leveraged over £1.2 million in grants for Islington residents in its first year. In addition to monetary grants the Resident Support Scheme puts a premium on the provision of additional non-financial support, such as training and advice, and links residents to local opportunities that can offer lasting change in their lives.

DSC's *Guide to Grants for Individuals in Need* already plays a vital role in enabling people living in poverty to gain access to the additional support they need. With ongoing welfare reforms, and Government proposals to abolish the Local Welfare Provision Fund from April 2015, the Guide will become an even more valuable tool in the year ahead, with demand on the grant-making charities listed in the Guide likely to increase substantially. Cripplegate Foundation, deeply concerned about the removal of local welfare provision, has come together with over 20 other organisations and bodies to form the 'Keep the Safety Net' campaign. Others similarly concerned about the removal of this support for individuals in need, and the impact it will have on the local and national charities that support them, are urged to join us.

Nicola Steuer
Programme Director, Cripplegate Foundation
www.cripplegate.org.uk

Introduction

Welcome to the fourteenth edition of *The Guide to Grants for Individuals in Need.* The main focus of the book is to list sources of non-statutory help for people in financial need. This edition details more than 1,900 charities with £268 million available in grant awards, compared with 1,400 charities giving £66 million in the first edition (1987).

Grants made by charities in this guide range from £10 food vouchers to larger contributions including grants for domestic items such as washing machines, wheelchairs and house adaptations, although few will cover the whole cost of these. This kind of help does not overcome long-term financial problems, but it can be extremely valuable in helping to meet immediate needs which the state does not currently cover.

This introduction looks at the charities included in this guide and how to locate them, before discussing what help is available from them and how the charities can improve their roles. It looks briefly at other funding sources for individuals, highlighting the need to explore all statutory sources available as well as surveying the relevant reforms in this area. Ashley Wood, formerly of the Gaddum Centre, has again provided a helpful section explaining how to make your application once the relevant charities have been identified; see page xix. We have also tried to highlight some of the key themes that have emerged from this research process in relation to the impact of welfare reforms on grantmakers and how this may affect those wishing to apply for support.

About this guide

We aim to include publicly registered charities (including those in Scotland and Northern Ireland) which give at least £500 a year to individuals in need, although most give considerably more than this.

With a few exceptions, we do not include:

- organisations which give grants solely for educational purposes;
- organisations which give grants to members only and not to dependents;
- individual employer or company welfare funds;
- Friendly Societies;
- local branches of national charities, although they may raise money locally for cases of need;

- organisations only providing services (such as home visiting) rather than cash (or in-kind) grants.

Many of the charities support individuals for educational causes as well. These are all included in the sister guide to this book, *The Guide to Educational Grants*, which includes details of funding opportunities for all forms of education and training up to the end of a first degree, including apprenticeships, personal development and expeditions. Some charities support organisations such as community groups, others have large financial commitments (often providing housing). The entries in this guide concentrate solely on the charities' social welfare grants to individuals in need.

How charities are ordered in this guide

The charities are separated into six sections: five UK-wide sections followed by a local section, broken down into nine countries/regions. The flow chart on page xviii shows how the guide works.

UK-wide charities

The majority of the money in this book is given by the UK-wide charities which are divided into five sections:

1. General charities (page 1)

This section includes charities which operate UK-wide (or at least in more than one country or more than two regions of England) and which are not tied to a particular trade, occupation or disability. These range from those which have very wide objectives, such as 'people in need', 'older people' or 'children and young people', to members of particular ethnic groups. General charities are among the best known and tend to be heavily oversubscribed.

2. Illness and disability charities (page 35)

These charities give grants to people with specific illnesses or disabilities. They can help people (and often their families/carers) who are in financial need as a result of a particular illness or disability. Many of these also give advisory and other support, although for a fuller list of organisations providing these functions please see 'Advice organisations' starting on page 481.

3. Occupational charities (page 57)

This section contains charities that benefit not only the people who worked in the particular trade but also, in many cases, their widows/widowers and dependent children. Membership or previous membership of the particular institute can be required, but many are open to non-members. Length of service can sometimes be taken into account. Many of these charities are members of the Association of Charitable Organisations, an umbrella organisation which represents this area of the sector. There are some occupations which have a number of funds covering the industry, and others which have none.

4. Service and ex-service charities (page 135)

This section contains exceptionally thorough charitable provision for people who have served in the forces, whether as a regular or during national service. This funding is different to the other occupational funds as they support a large percentage of the male population over retirement age (many of them would have undertaken national service). Again, these usually also provide for the widows, widowers and dependent children of the core beneficiaries. Many of these funds have local voluntary workers who provide advice and practical help, and who in turn are backed up by professional staff and substantial resources. SSAFA, formerly known as the Soldiers, Sailors, Airmen and Families Association (Charity Commission no. 210760) is an influential member of this sector, providing the well-used model, and often the initial contact and application form, for many of the regimental funds.

5. Religious charities (page 159)

This section deals with charities that support religious workers, such as members of the clergy, missionaries and so on. Often this support extends to dependents of these workers. Support for people connected to particular faiths (such as Christian, Christian Science and Jewish) are also detailed.

Local charities (page 171)

Included in this section are those charities which only support individuals in Northern Ireland, Scotland or Wales, or just one region of England. Charities which are eligible for two of these chapters have generally been given a full entry in one chapter and a cross reference in the other; charities relevant to three or more of the chapters have generally been included in the national section. Charitable help is unequally distributed across the UK, often with more money available in London and the south east of England than the rest of the UK. However, many of the main cities have at least one large charity able to give over £50,000 a year.

The local section starts with details on how to use this section.

Charities in Northern Ireland

Unfortunately the section for Northern Ireland is very limited, as very little information is available on charities based there at present. It is estimated that there are between 7,000 and 12,000 charities operating in Northern Ireland. The Charity Commission for Northern Ireland, therefore, expects the completion of the registration process to take several years. In the meantime, up-to-date information on the progress of registration can be found on the Charity Commission for Northern Ireland's website: www.charitycommissionni.org.uk.

How grantmaking charities can help

Some charities lament the fact that the people whom they wish to support might refuse to accept charity because of a desire to maintain their independence. A charity holds public money for the benefit of a specific group of people. As such, just as people are encouraged to access any statutory funds they can, they should also be encouraged to accept all charitable money which has been set aside for them.

However, it is not just people who are classified as 'poor' who are eligible for support from grantmaking charities. Formerly known as the 'relief of sickness', this charitable purpose was re-defined under the provisions of the Charities Act 2006, and now comes under the purpose, 'the advancement of health or the saving of lives'.

The Charity Commission guidance 'The advancement of health or the saving of lives' broadened the scope of the previous guidance, 'Charities for the Relief of Sickness' (booklet CC6), meaning a wider range of activities became charitable. The following extract is from the Charity Commission guidance:

> *The advancement of health includes the prevention or relief of sickness, disease or human suffering, as well as the promotion of health. It includes conventional methods as well as complementary, alternative or holistic methods which are concerned with healing mind, body and spirit in the alleviation of symptoms and the cure of illness.*
>
> *The relief of sickness extends beyond the treatment or provision of care, such as a hospital, to the provision of items, services and facilities to ease the suffering or assist the recovery of people who are sick, convalescent, disabled or infirm or to provide comforts for patients.*
>
> *The saving of lives includes a range of charitable activity directed towards saving people whose lives are in danger and protecting life and property.*

The guidance goes on to provide examples of the sorts of charities and charitable purposes which fall within this description, such as:

- charities that provide comforts, items, services and facilities for people who are sick, convalescent, disabled or infirm;
- charities that promote activities that have a proven beneficial effect on health;
- charities set up to assist the victims of natural disasters or war.

These examples focus mainly on the physical aspect of 'relief' rather than on the financial position of people who are living with an illness or disability. This is not because grants for the advancement of health are not means-tested, but simply because these charities exist to relieve a physical need rather than a financial one. There are charitable organisations that exist to carry out either or both charitable purposes; they may either deal exclusively with the financial impact that an illness or disability can have on an individual's life or concentrate on the physical aspect of 'relief', or may address both.

Many charities believe that people should not lose their life savings and standard of living to buy an essential item that they could afford, but would leave them financially vulnerable for the future. Charity Commission guidance differentiates between organisations which attempt to relieve sickness, and organisations for the relief of the sick-poor, which can only support people who are both sick and poor.

Although these are the areas charities *may* support, it would be wrong to believe that any given grantmaking organisation will support all of these needs. Each charity in this guide has a governing document, stating in which circumstances people can and cannot be supported. As mentioned earlier, we have broken down the charities in this guide to aid the reader in identifying those which might be of relevance to them, and we would strongly advise that individuals do not approach a charity for which they are not eligible.

Many charities have complained to us that they receive applications outside their scope which they would like to support but their governing document prevents them from doing so. These applicants have no chance of being supported and only serve to be a drain on valuable resources. Please be aware that it is not the number of charities you apply to which affects your chance of support but the relevance of them.

What types of help can be given?

Charity Commission guidance

The Charity Commission's guidance, *The Prevention or Relief of Poverty for the Public Benefit*, lists what type of help can be given. (Please note that this list should not be seen as comprehensive.) The list is given as follows:

> *Examples of ways in which charities might relieve poverty include:*
>
> *Grants of money in the form of:*
>
> - *weekly allowances for a limited period;*
> - *payments to meet a particular need;*
> - *one-off payments in a crisis or disaster;*
> - *payment of travelling expenses for visiting people, for example in a hospital, convalescent home, children's home, prison or other similar place, particularly where more frequent visits are desirable than payments from public funds will allow;*
> - *payments to meet expenses associated with visiting people (as mentioned above) for example, child-minding, accommodation, refreshments etc.;*
> - *payments to assist in meeting energy and water bills.*
>
> *The provision of items (either outright or, if expensive but appropriate, on loan), such as:*
>
> - *furniture, bedding, clothing, food, fuel, heating appliances;*
> - *washing machines and fridges;*
> - *payment for services, such as: essential house decorating; insulation and repairs; laundering; meals on wheels; outings and entertainment; child-minding; telephone line, rates and utilities*
>
> *The provision of facilities such as:*
>
> - *the supply of tools or books;*
> - *payment of fees for instruction, examination or other expenses connected with vocational training, language, literacy, numerical or technical skills;*
> - *travelling expenses to help recipients to earn their living;*
> - *equipment and funds for recreational pursuits or training intended to bring the quality of life of the beneficiaries to a reasonable standard.*

Charities for the relief of financial hardship might give extra help to people in poverty who are also sick, convalescent, infirm or with disabilities, whether physical or mental. This might include:

Grants of money in the form of:

- *special payments to relieve sickness or infirmity;*
- *payment of travelling expenses on entering or leaving hospitals, convalescent homes, or similar institutions, or for out-patient consultations;*
- *payment towards the cost of adaptations to the homes of people with disabilities; or*
- *payment of telephone installation charges and rentals.*

Charity Commission 2008, as amended December 2011

Note the following information taken from the Commission's website in September 2014:

This guidance is currently under review.

It no longer forms part of our public benefit guidance and should now be read together with our set of 3 public benefit guides. It will remain available to read until we publish replacement guidance.

One-off grants

Some charities will only give one-off cash payments. This means that they will award a single lump sum (say £50) which is paid by cheque or postal order either direct to the applicant, to the welfare agency applying on the person's behalf, or to another suitable third party. No more help will be considered until the applicant has submitted a new application, and charities are usually unwilling to give more than one such grant per person per year.

Recurrent grants

Other charities will only pay recurrent grants. Recurrent payments or grants in kind are disregarded when entitlement to Income Support and Pension Credit are calculated. Although this is a long-standing principle please be aware that the rules may change with the introduction of Universal Credit, so please seek appropriate advice if in doubt.

Some charities will give either one-off or recurrent payments, according to what is more appropriate for the applicant, although some charities which give small recurrent payments may also give one-off grants for irregular expenses.

Grants in kind

Occasionally grants are given in the form of vouchers or are paid directly to a shop or store in the form of credit to enable the applicant to obtain food, clothing or other prearranged items. Some charities still arrange for the delivery of coal.

More commonly, especially with disability aids or other technical equipment, the charity will either give the equipment itself to the applicant (rather than the money) or loan it free of charge or at a low rental price for as long as the applicant needs it. More common items, such as telephones and televisions, can also be given as equipment because the charity can get better trade terms than the individual.

Statutory funding

Whilst there is a wide range of types of grants that can be given and a variety of reasons why they can be made, there is one area that charities cannot support. No charitable organisation is allowed to provide funds which replace statutory funding. The reason for this is that if a charity gives £100, say, to an individual who could have received those funds from statutory sources, then it is the state rather than the individual who is benefiting from the grant. This point is discussed further below in the context of social fund reform.

The effectiveness of grantmaking charities

While some grantmaking charities, particularly national ones, produce clear guidelines, others (often local charities) do not. Based on our experience of researching this publication over the past 20 years, we would like to make some suggestions as to ways in which charities giving grants to individuals, particularly local charities, could seek to encourage greater fairness in funding:

- Local charities could seek to broaden their remit to meet new or more widespread needs. During 2013 the social fund was abolished and replaced by localised provision. We would advise charities to speak to their local authority as well as other local grantmakers in order to define what the local priorities are and see if they can adjust or develop an approach which will ensure that no groups of people will fall beneath the radar of statutory and voluntary bodies. Charities ought to guard their independence closely and should not unduly compromise on their principles in any collaborative enterprise, but they should also consider what can be gained from cooperation, including the sharing of expertise and the potential to influence public services and reduce costs. For any charities considering this route we would recommend the excellent reports produced by Child Poverty Action Group as a starting point: cpag.org.uk/policy-publications.
- If trustees can only meet twice a year, they should aim to cover the peak periods. Although welfare needs arise throughout the year, there are obvious peak times; for example, for fuel needs this is in the winter months.
- Charities should also aim to ensure that needs can be met as rapidly as possible; for example by empowering the clerk or a small number of trustees to make payments up to a certain limit (such as £100).
- They should ensure that they are very well known in their area of benefit. We recommend that each charity (depending on its eligibility restrictions) writes to at least the following places: all welfare agencies (especially Citizens Advice); all community centres and other public meeting points; and the offices of the relevant education authority.

- We would also recommend that grantmaking charities consider developing a website. A website is an accessible way of raising awareness of your work as well as outlining key information such as eligibility criteria, meeting dates and types of grants given. The website does not need to be overly technical and can be as simple as one page of text. There are also many free hosting sites such as Weebly (www.weebly.com) and BT Community Web Kit (www.btck.co.uk) which make expense and professional assistance unnecessary.

The Great Giving campaign and Ineligible Applications report

Over the years DSC has campaigned on a number of fronts for better grantmaking. We believe that grantmakers have a responsibility that extends far beyond providing funding.

The way in which funders operate has a huge impact on the beneficiaries which their funding supports, as well as on the wider voluntary sector.

Our Great Giving campaign has grown out of these long established beliefs. The campaign encompasses four areas: (1) a clear picture of the funding environment; (2) accessible funding for campaigning; (3) an end to hidden small print; and (4) no ineligible applications.

Although the campaign relates mainly to grantmaking charities that support organisations, the four principles of the campaign extend to the charities covered in this guide. We believe that funders have a responsibility to understand the environment in which they are operating. Some funders provide little information about where money is going and what is being supported. Providing a clearer picture will enable better planning and decision-making from funders and policy makers, as well as contributing to the growing body of knowledge about the sector.

We know that most grantmakers receive more applications for funding than they can support. We also know that a significant proportion of those applications are ineligible. In some cases the fault lies with the information provided by the funder, and in some cases the fault lies with the interpretation of that information by the applicant. In our 2010 report on Ineligible Applications we made some recommendations on what grantmakers can do to try and avoid receiving large numbers of ineligible applications:

- Provide comprehensive and accessible information: state what you do and what you want to fund, preferably online if you have a website.
- Ensure your application guidance is clear, concise and as jargon-free as possible: encourage prospective applicants to read it.
- Explain the application procedure clearly: what information will be required, by when and in what form.
- Providing constructive feedback, especially if the application is rejected, this should make it less likely that the applicant submits the same ineligible bid again and again.
- Provide a clear contact point for any queries and instructions on how you prefer to be contacted.
- Keep track of ineligible applications and analyse them periodically to see if there are any patterns. Consider how the information you provide could be changed to reduce their number.

In the current financial climate (which we will touch upon more in the next section) where many grantmakers have experienced a rise in demand for their services, these recommendations are particularly important. Advertising clearly what you do and how you do it, will not only empower individuals to make informed decisions about their applications, it should also limit the number of ineligible applications received and free up vital resources, which will ensure more time can be spent on those individuals the charity exists to support.

Further information on our research into ineligible applications and the Great Giving campaign itself can be found on our website (www.dsc.org.uk).

The impact of welfare reform

April 2013 marked a watershed in the timeline of social security in Britain, with the coalition government's flagship policy of welfare reform bringing about an upheaval of the benefits system and the abolition of the discretionary Social Fund.

Throughout the research process for this guide, we analysed annual reports, accounts and our correspondence with grantmakers in order to gauge the effects and implications the welfare reforms are having on grantmakers and their beneficiaries.

The welfare reforms

In the thirteenth edition of this book we discussed the impending 'seismic shifts' in social security, which would add to challenges already faced by grantmaking charities – those of rising demand, financial difficulties and cuts to statutory funding (Doherty et al. 2013). Since the last *Guide to Grants for Individuals in Need* was published, the welfare reforms we discussed have been implemented. In this edition, we are able to consider the effects of the coalition government's policies on the grantmaking environment in their first year of existence.

The magnitude of the reforms on the statutory welfare system has been unprecedented in the time since Clement Attlee's post-war administration first created the safety net of the welfare system. The reforms found their way into, and indeed, took centre stage, in the broader programme of post-recession austerity – the distribution of which has been seemingly largely unbalanced.

In efforts to 'simplify' the benefits system and to 'make work pay', April 2013 ushered in an overhaul of out-of-work and disability benefits, the piloting of the single-payment Universal Credit, saw some benefits capped, and Housing Benefit adopt an under-occupancy penalty, better known as the bedroom tax. Local authorities assumed responsibility for Council Tax Reduction Schemes and were devolved control of the remnants of the Social Fund under the new guise of Local Welfare Provision. Furthermore, the means of gaining access to the new-look benefits system was made considerably tougher. Those applying for Employment and Support Allowance (ESA) would undergo Work Capability Assessments and Jobseekers could face sanctions if they did not follow a strict code of conduct.

At a time when people were faced with the unfamiliarity of a new benefits system, specialist advice services have had their budgets slashed. Citizens' Advice described the fallout some of its bureaux had experienced:

> *This has meant people face huge delays in being able to access vital services – debt appointments booked two months in advance for example – or simply no access at all.* *Green 2014*

The effect on individuals

Research by the Centre for Welfare Reform found that people in poverty (20% of the population) would bear 36% of cuts, mostly through cuts to the benefit system and local government, on which the burden of more than 50% of all cuts would fall. The report suggests that, by 2015, people who are in poverty will lose on average £2,195 per year in income or services, disabled people will lose £4,410 per year, and people who are in need of social care £8,832 per year. In contrast, people who live neither in poverty nor with a disability will lose on average £467 per year (Duffy 2014).

Despite the disproportionate dispersal of welfare reforms upon those who the grantmaking sector has traditionally served, the evidence we were able to gather from annual reports suggests a continuation of the long-term trends we identified whilst researching the last edition of this guide, rather than a radical overhaul of the grantmaking landscape. Based on the testimonies we were able to gather from annual reports and the figures we obtained from accounts, the impact of many aspects of the welfare reforms has, so far, been limited.

This may, in part, be due to the fact that for a significant portion of the grantmakers in this guide, the most recent annual reports we were able to obtain were those from the 2012/13 financial year, so we were only able to consider the months immediately after the reforms became practice. However, even The Veterinary Benevolent Fund, whose annual report considered 2013 in its entirety, described how it had seen minimal effects on its beneficiaries:

> *The number of beneficiaries requiring help as the result of changes to the benefits system during the year was lower than expected. However, changes to the benefits system are being phased in over a number of years with regional variations so more VBF beneficiaries may come forward for help in the next two years.* *VBF 2013*

Whilst there has not been a uniform rise in demand for assistance across the grantmakers in this guide (in fact, many reported a decrease in applications), the trend of a rising demand in applications from certain demographics – something we identified in the last edition – was apparent.

It would appear that the tough financial situation encountered by younger, working-age people still remains, as debt and high costs of living perpetuate. In comparison with older people, whose pensions have generally been protected (partly due to a pensions system which ensures that state pensions go up by whichever is highest: inflation, annual earnings growth or a 2.5% baseline), the earnings and benefits of working-age adults have lagged behind inflation – the effects of which are clear to see.

Perennial: Gardeners' Royal Benevolent Society described how in 2013 86% of all new cases the charity assisted were below state pension age compared with 52% of new cases in 2008 (Perennial 2013). Furthermore, the 1930 Fund for District Nurses, having noticed a shift in demand from annuities to one-off grants, stated the following in its annual report:

> *This trend has been in place for some time and is a consequence of better pension provision for community nurses. Despite the better pension provision, however, there are still large pockets of individual need within the community nursing population, particularly among younger nurses.* *1930 Fund for District Nurses 2013*

Another persisting trend was the growing complexity of individuals' cases, as personal debt, high costs of living and cuts to public services continue to take their toll on individuals and families. Some grantmakers have seen a knock-on effect on the support services they provide. The Royal National Institute of Blind People (RNIB) described the situation it had encountered:

> *People contacted us with over 466,000 enquiries during the year, and we saw an increasing complexity to these enquiries with people requiring our support to come to terms with the impact that the economic climate and changes to benefit systems and support services are having on living with sight loss.* *RNIB 2013*

While the trend of the increasing complexity of cases is long-term, there were suggestions that some grantmakers had seen this more recently accelerate. BEN – The Automotive Industry Charity, for example, experienced a 5% drop in grants made and a 5% net rise in casework, and calls to its Helpline were up 57% on the previous year. (BEN 2013). For You By You – The Charity for Civil Servants (which in 2013 took steps to broaden its provision to include domestic abuse and mental health services, as well as a more extensive money advice service), stated that:

> *We received over 10,000 applications for help in 2013 (2012: 10,700); and as awareness of our new services grows an increasing proportion of our clients are seeking advice and referrals to specialist organisations, as opposed to grants and allowances.* *Charity for Civil Servants 2013*

So, there is some evidence of the more extensive needs of beneficiaries – unsurprising, perhaps, if the cumulative effects of high costs of living, below-inflation incomes, previous welfare reforms and cuts to specialist advice services are to be considered. There is also evidence of grantmakers picking up the slack as other sources of beneficiaries' support are rescinded further.

Localisation of the Social Fund

It has long been a prerequisite of grantmaking that individuals should exhaust all sources of statutory funding before applying for a grant. In the last edition of this guide we warned of the 'sweeping reform of the discretionary Social Fund', which would abolish the elements of statutory funding most closely supported by the grantmaking sector. Parts of the fund (Community Care grants and Crisis Loans) were integrated into local authorities' Local Welfare Provision without ring-fencing, at a time when local authorities' own budgets were slashed.

A 2013 report published by the Centre for Regional Economic and Social Research found that residents of the poorest local authorities were faring worst, losing up to four times as much per working age adult as those areas least affected (Beatty and Fothergill 2014). Recent research from Sheffield Political Economy Research Institute found that, so far, England has seen a reduction in local authority spending power by £130.06 per person. However, councils in the most deprived areas have experienced the biggest impact, with an average cut of £228.23 per person across the top 10% most deprived local authority areas (Berry and White 2014).

During our research, we came across grantmakers who had taken reactive steps to relieve the pressures faced by their local authorities, in an effort to make fewer resources go further, sometimes at the expense of their own grantmaking programmes.

In April 2013 the Cripplegate Foundation, a grantmaker based in the London borough of Islington, entered into partnership with Islington Council (the council has estimated that funding cuts to essential services will amount to more than £330 million between 2011 and 2015). The product of the partnership – the Islington Resident Support Scheme (RSS) – combined the foundation's former Grants for Residents Scheme with Local Welfare Provision, Discretionary Housing Payments and Islington Council's provision for Council Tax relief. The scheme aims to support the borough's most vulnerable residents over the long and short term and, in addition to making grants, offers referral to other services offering financial, educational, employment or training advice.

Worcester Consolidated Municipal Charity also looked to accommodate the pressures faced by its local authority by acting as an agent for the local authority's Discretionary Welfare Assistance Scheme and, in the first nine months following the scheme's introduction, bought white goods to the value of over £80,000 which, it stated, had decreased the number of grants requested from the local authority (Worcester Consolidated Municipal Charity 2013).

There was also evidence of larger, national organisations taking pre-emptive measures. Buttle UK, for example, has sought to cooperate with outside organisations, including local authorities, in order to absorb some of the blow from government cuts:

> *Buttle UK is working in collaboration with a range of other voluntary sector organisations, to create a database that will be monitoring all of the provisions made by local authorities under these new arrangements, and through the Association of Charitable Officers and London Funders we are actively engaging with local authorities across the UK to try and work with them to minimise the impact of these changes.* Buttle 2013

The government announced in early 2014 its plans to scrap the £178 million funding for Local Welfare Provision, which would essentially remove statutory discretionary funding for individuals in need altogether. However, in September 2014 a successful judicial review case led by the Child Poverty Action Group forced the government to reconsider its decision. A 'new' decision is expected in December 2014 following a public consultation.

During our research for this edition, we have seen instances of grantmakers acting to minimise the widening holes in the statutory safety net. So, as the effects of welfare reform and the possibility of further funding cuts unravel, will the expectation for grantmakers to use their own resources to fill the void left by rescinding state welfare provision increase?

Grantmaking – what the figures tell us

Our headline figures show that in this edition the total amount awarded was £268 million, which means that overall grantmaking has remained at a similar level to the thirteenth edition. This includes the grant totals which we were able to obtain from charities' accounts as well as figures which we obtained by other means. This latter category of figures, which account for around one in five charities, were not available from the Charity Commission, and this is mostly because the charities' incomes or expenditures fell below the threshold at which they were required to submit accounts. For these cases we obtained figures either by speaking directly with charities or viewing their websites (if available). In the minority of instances we relied on experience to give a best estimate of their charitable giving based on their income, total expenditure and past performance. For the remaining 80%, for which data was readily available, we were able to directly compare the grant total for each charity in this edition with their total from the previous edition.

For those charities for which we have given an estimated grant total we erred on the side of caution so as to not upwardly misrepresent the amount of grants available. We were particularly considerate as to whether or not the charities gave solely to individuals for social welfare purposes. In the cases where they also gave to individuals for educational purposes and/or to organisations, we made allowances for these figures, which may have downplayed the headline figure.

The quality of information which we are able to work with as researchers has undoubtedly improved in recent years as more charities have begun to offer more detailed breakdowns of their annual activity in their accounts. Those at the Charity Commission should be lauded for their work in promoting their statement of recommended practice. What this has meant for us is that we have been increasingly able to retrieve more precise figures for grants to individuals from the accounts immediately rather than having a single, opaque figure for 'support', 'charitable activity' or 'grants', which could include a myriad of services beyond grants, as well as grants to organisations. So our information in turn has become more accurate.

Unfortunately, however, some data has remained or become more opaque. For some charities, grantmaking is often lumped in along with a broad sweep of other care services and not distinguished in the accounts. Despite our requests in these instances for a grant total, we were frequently told that this was unavailable.

The Grants for Individuals in Need and Education Survey Results

We sent an e-survey to more than 1,000 of the charities in this book and its sister publication, *The Guide to Educational Grants.* The survey gave us the opportunity to gather the most recent perspective on the environment faced by grantmakers in the time since the reforms ushered in by the Welfare Reform Act 2012 were made practice.

The anecdotal contributions made by some of our respondents served as particularly useful markers in considering the experiences of individual grantmakers.

We have grouped the grantmakers by grantmaking purpose: social welfare; education; and both social welfare and education. This means that we are able to consider the distinct nature of the different groups of grantmaker and can consider the effects different elements of welfare reforms may have had on their experiences.

Have you noticed a change in the number of applications made to you for the support of individuals?

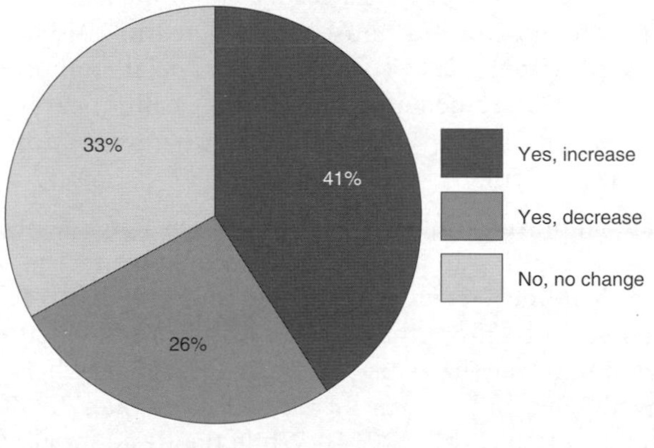

Of our respondents who make grants solely for social welfare purposes, over 40% said that they had noticed an increase in the numbers of applications they had received in recent years. Taking into account the results of the survey we conducted for the thirteenth edition of this guide, in which 39% had noticed an increase (Doherty et. al 2013), this could suggest the beginning of a trend of increased need. This is unsurprising considering the impact unemployment, high rates of inflation, stagnating incomes, the cost of living crisis and the broader programme of austerity has had on individuals in the post-recession years.

A number of charities identified a change in the nature of the applications they had received, even if the volume of applications had not changed. The CILex Benevolent Fund pointed out: 'There has not been a change in numbers but what has changed is the needs of the beneficiaries.'

This was an observation echoed in the comments of other respondents, some of whom had noticed a rise in applications for one-off or smaller grants and for day-to-day essential equipment such as white goods and boiler replacements. This corresponds with the findings of our survey from the thirteenth edition, in which an 'increase in demand for basic, everyday items' was noted. It is unsurprising that, given high costs of living and incomes which have lagged behind inflation, some grantmakers have seen a rise in applications for these kinds of assistance.

Some of our respondents identified specific groups of people as having experienced particular hardship in recent times. Friends of the Elderly, for example, a substantial grantmaker which gave £432,000 in 2012/13 identified that: 'The majority of our target group has been protected from most of the recent changes but people aged 60–62 are now suffering significant hardship.'

This observation was reiterated by the National Benevolent Charity which identified that, from its broad beneficiary group, it has now shifted its focus to the childless, working-age adults in their 50s and 60s. It also identified that the reforms had had a significant impact on people with disabilities. That these specific demographics have, in the experiences of some of our respondents, suffered a distinct hardship seems to reflect the distribution of welfare reforms. Those above the state retirement age have, on the whole, seen their pensions protected in welfare reforms to date, whilst others, and especially those in receipt of more than one kind of benefit, have seen their financial support greatly affected.

The new format for benefits applications, administration and appeals has been identified as having been particularly problematic for some. Independence at Home, a grantmaker for people with long-term illnesses and disabilities stated that: 'Benefits are harder to obtain for those in genuine need and the Social Fund has been eroded.'

This was echoed by other respondents, one of whom made the distinction between the 'marginal' effects of changes to benefits payments and the more severe effects caused by delays or sanctions during assessment and appeals processes. Another respondent has adopted the practice of supporting those whose existing benefits have been cancelled during the process of applying for benefits or when appealing against a decision. This is a point worth revisiting in future editions. Will it increasingly fall to grantmakers to fill the void when those in need cannot access the statutory financial support to which they are entitled? And, with a benefits system which is so difficult to navigate, will it fall increasingly to grantmakers to provide welfare advice and advocacy, especially at a time when public services and referral agencies face further reductions in funding?

Do you find that there are barriers for potential beneficiaries (who would in the past have been referred by an agency) to contact you directly?

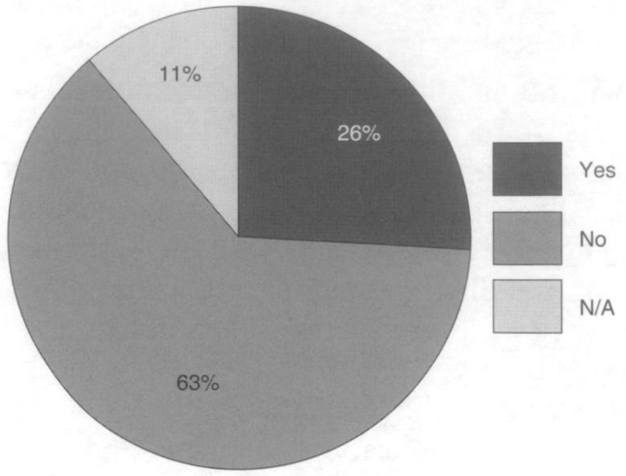

About a quarter of respondents who give purely for social welfare purposes felt that there were barriers for potential beneficiaries who would have previously been referred by an agency. This is compared with 15% who give only for educational purposes and the same percentage of those who give to both. A 'lack of knowledge' of grantmakers and the application process was identified as being the most common reason, followed by embarrassment. This attests to the importance of specialist advice agencies in supporting potential beneficiaries through the application process and as a vital source of outreach to those who are suffering hardship. That 29% of respondents had noticed a decrease in the activities of referral agencies in their area suggests that diminishing resources caused by cuts to funding and, in particular, legal aid, may have had an impact on the capabilities of agencies to refer those in need.

Overall, welfare reforms, at least in their early stages have not had the sweeping effect on grantmakers or their beneficiaries that was expected by some. Though some, such as Independence at Home, have seen an immediate impact from the withdrawal of the Social Fund, it is likely that we are yet to see the full extent of welfare reforms, which was a point made by Hospitality Action:

> *We are waiting to see the full effect of the withdrawal of the Social Fund & the announcement of budget cuts to Local Authorities administering Local Welfare Assistance Schemes.*

There is a possibility that the effects of welfare reforms may remain generally confined to the groups that have already been affected, namely adults below the retirement age and people who are ill or disabled; or, that with the rolling out of Universal Credit by the end of 2017, more cuts to local authority budgets and the introduction of Annual Managed Expenditure, which will come into action in April 2015, more of the grantmaking sector will see the direct effects of welfare reform.

Eligible and ineligible applications report

In the spirit of our Great Giving campaign, we also asked our respondents to disclose the number of applications they had received in the last year, along with the number of ineligible applications they had received. We also asked for the same information from the preceding year. Overall, there had been a 10% rise in the numbers of applications received by the participating grantmakers and the proportion that were considered ineligible remained at around 17%. For some grantmakers, however, this percentage was far higher, with some reporting that ineligible applications made up around 36% of those received.

Welfare reform: a view from the social housing sector

The following piece was contributed by DSC Volunteer Researcher, Caroline Field, who until recently served as Director of Community Engagement at Riverside Housing. She gives an insight into the problems tenants have faced as welfare reforms are rolled out nationwide.

The Government's welfare reforms have now been implemented in many areas and Universal Credit is being extended to more claimants. By 2014, nearly 500,000 people had had their housing benefit reduced because of the removal of the spare bedroom subsidy (commonly called the bedroom tax) by an average of £14.40 per week (DWP 2014). This is starting to have a serious impact on many individuals and may leave many more people in need of financial assistance.

Social landlords are starting to enforce their tenancy agreements routinely, taking action more promptly and offering less room for manoeuvre for tenants. This is resulting in more legal action being taken against tenants and more evictions. An extra 42,905 notices seeking possession to tenants for rent arrears were issued in 2013/14 compared with the previous year: a jump of 21.9% to 239,381. Evictions for rent arrears also jumped 12.9% to 7,131 with an extra 814 households evicted in 2013/14 compared with 2012/13 (Brown 2014). Social landlords take this action reluctantly, but feel they cannot carry the cost of welfare reforms and must take whatever action is available to them.

Private landlords continue to enforce their agreements robustly, resulting in an increase of people contacting the Shelter helpline. Between April 2013 and March 2014, Shelter received more than 7,600 calls from renters at risk of eviction. Over the same period in 2011/12, the helpline received 3,997 callers – an increase of more than 3,900 callers, or of 109% (RT 2014). While the Residential Landlords Association points out that this is much less than 1% of all private tenants, and that private tenancies now last an average of over three years, Shelter reports that 4,000 people are at risk of losing their home through eviction or repossession.

As Universal Credit starts to roll out, the shift to monthly budgeting combined with payment of benefits direct to tenants will have an impact on tenants' ability to pay and to manage their money. The Money Advice Trust states that rent arrears is the fastest growing debt problem in the UK. The economic crisis has seen the number of calls to their National Debtline service from people with rent arrears rise significantly since 2007. From January to October 2013, they received nearly 20,000 calls for help from people with rent arrears, compared with just 8,000 over the same period in 2007 – an increase of 146%. Calls from people with rent arrears have increased 37% over the two years, and 13 % in 12 months – more than any other debt type. The figures also suggest that tenants face a growing number of broader debt problems, with renters now making 57% of total calls to National Debtline, compared with 43% in 2010 (Money Advice Trust 2014). In April 2014, average household debt excluding mortgages, was £6,018, while 483 landlord possession claims are issued and 354 landlord possession orders are made every day (Money Charity 2014).

National debt advice charity the Money Advice Trust reports that more households are becoming susceptible to serious amounts of debt, with a 140% increase in people seeking help for debt-related problems over the seven years from 2007 to 2014 (Money Advice Trust 2014). A study into household budgets has revealed that more people are falling into debt because they can't afford basic household costs such as council tax, energy, water, and telephone bills. National Debtline, the charity's debt advice service, has seen a 'radical' shift in the types of debt problems encountered by the people it helps. More people than ever now require assistance with energy, water, telephone, council tax, and catalogue shopping debts while fewer people report problems with traditional credit products such as bank overdrafts, loans and credit cards (National Debtline 2014).

This may be partly attributable to the rigid application of conditions applied to Job Seekers Allowance (JSA) or Employment Support Allowance (ESA) where those in receipt of the benefit can be sanctioned by having their benefit temporarily stopped if they fail to comply with all the rules. This will do nothing to help tenants with managing their housing costs and household budgets.

The government has a fund for discretionary housing payments (DHP) which can assist people with the difficulties in changing to their new benefits. Money is allocated to local authorities by central government, but on a broadly per capita basis which does not reflect local need – partly because it was not known what local need was going to be. In some parts of the country, mostly in the north of England, some councils are not able to meet demand for DHP, whereas others are either not claiming funds from central government or failing to spend their entire allocation. The Department for Work and Pensions (DWP) made £20 million available in additional discretionary housing payment funds for July 2014 because of 'exceptionally' high demand for emergency help in the wake of the bedroom tax. Inside Housing states that, 'after bids from 86 local authorities, 27 were refused the full funds they had requested, with 18 turned down on the basis that a full award would allow 'excessive buy out' of the policy'. This would mean essentially that the policy wouldn't have the effect of bringing in money to the government from the bedroom tax but rather that the government was subsidising those people who it was intended should be paying, making the policy redundant. Eventually only £12.9 million was allocated, as some councils failed to apply. The impact of welfare reform varies widely depending on local and individual circumstances, and this in turn has an impact on those charities making grants to individuals in need (Apps 2014).

According to a survey of working age social housing tenants affected by the welfare reforms conducted by Ipsos MORI for the National Housing Federation (Ipsos MORI 2013):

- four in ten (40 %) affected by welfare reforms don't have internet access, and 30 % say they would not be confident making a benefit application online;
- nine in ten (92 %) would prefer benefits to be paid direct to their landlord rather than their own accounts;
- two-thirds (68 %) of those who manage money on a short-term basis are not confident about budgeting monthly;
- Universal Credit, which is due to be rolled out nationally by 2017, replaces six existing welfare benefits (including housing benefit) with a single, monthly household payment. People applying for benefits will have to apply via a new online service;
- the Ipsos MORI survey shows that of those social housing tenants who have internet access, half (51 %) admitted they would not be confident making a benefit application online (equivalent to 30% of all respondents).

It is possible that people will eventually come to understand the new system, but the transition is likely to continue to be very difficult for individuals for a while yet, as they learn the skills to manage increased personal debt, the shift to monthly budgeting and the simple difficulty of making an online application for their benefit/s. Grantmaking charities may find demand for their support increases as (and if) the new system unfolds.

Advice for applicants

While there is still a large amount of money available to help applicants, the competition seems likely to remain strong. It is difficult to say how grantmakers will fare in the coming years, but it is unlikely that those who are dipping into reserves can continue to do so indefinitely, and so charities will be looking to ensure that they are making the maximum possible impact with their grants.

For those individuals applying for funding the same basic principles apply – see page xix for Ashley Wood's excellent step-by-step guide. However, in the current climate it is worth bearing a few extra things in mind.

- **Check the latest criteria:** Financial pressures and rising applications have led many charities to tighten up their eligibility criteria or limit the things for which they will give. Make sure that you have the latest guidelines and read them carefully to check that you are eligible to apply and the charity can help with your specific need.

If in doubt, a quick phone call is usually welcomed and can save time for both parties in the long run.

- **Be open and honest when applying:** Take care to fill in any application form as fully as possible and try to be as clear and open as you can. The same applies if you need to write a letter of application. It will help grantmakers to assess your needs quickly and advise you on any other benefits or potential sources of funding for which you may be eligible.
- **Don't just apply to large, well-known charities:** They are likely to be the most oversubscribed, leaving you with less chance of success. Take the time to look for others you may also be eligible to apply for.
- **Apply to all appropriate charities:** Falling average grants may mean that one grantmaker cannot offer enough to cover the full cost of the item or service you need. You may have to consider applying to several and ask for a small contribution from each. If it has not been indicated already for any given charity in this guide whether calls are welcome or not, a quick phone call is usually enough to establish how much they are likely to give for an individual grant.
- **Seek advice:** Some applications require a third-party endorsement. With advice services under increasing pressure, you may find an alternative organisation to contact in this guide; these organisations are listed on page 481. Also consider other impartial professionals who may be able to assist with an application form; for example, a school teacher if the application is on behalf of a child or a medical practitioner such as a GP, consultant or therapist if the application is for a medical item or is related to a medical condition. Others who may be able to help include ministers of religion, social workers, local housing associations or probation officers. A quick telephone call to the grantmaker can determine whether they can be flexible regarding who completes the application in exceptional circumstances.

Other sources of support

Whilst there are many situations in which approaching a charity might be the best option, there is, of course, a limit to the support that they can provide, individually or collectively. There are a number of alternative sources of support that should be considered in conjunction with looking at grantmakers (note that these are beyond the scope of this publication).

Statutory sources

There are some funding opportunities available to individuals from the state. The exact details of these sources vary in different countries in the UK, and in some instances among different local authorities. This area is likely to become ever more confusing in the light of further budget cuts and welfare reforms. Consequently, comprehensive details are beyond the scope of this guide.

However, full details should be available from government departments such as benefits agencies and social services, as well as many of the welfare agencies listed, starting on page 481. The government's website (www.gov.uk) and the DWP website (www.dwp.gov.uk) also have a wealth of information on what is available and how to apply.

There are a number of advice organisations that may also be able to offer advice and support to people who are unsure of their benefit entitlement or who are looking for extra support in the form of a grant. It may prove useful to visit websites such as Turn2Us (www.turn2us.org.uk). These websites can offer advice on both statutory and non-statutory sources of funding to charities working on behalf of individuals and to individuals themselves.

Citizens Advice provides an online advice guide (www.adviceguide.org.uk) and offers useful information on issues relating to statutory benefits and individual entitlement. Local branches of Citizens Advice can also offer people more assistance in this area.

Disaster appeals

In the event of a disaster or other humanitarian crisis the public's reaction is often to help the victims and as quickly as possible and one way to do so is to launch a disaster appeal. These are commonly set up as a public response to a well-publicised disaster, such as the London bombings in July 2005, or the South Yorkshire floods in 2007, where the public wish to show their support. They can also be established in response to a personal misfortune; The Mark Davies Injured Riders Fund, for instance, was established to support injured riders, by the parents of a talented rider killed during the Burghley Horse Trials. For comprehensive advice and guidance on whether to launch an appeal by an existing charity, assist an established charity in its efforts to help with the effects of the crisis, or set up a non-charitable appeal fund, please view the Charity Commission leaflet, CC40 *Disaster Appeals.*

Companies

Many employers are concerned to see former members of staff or their dependents living in need or distress. Few have formal arrangements but a letter or telephone call to the personnel manager should establish if help is possible.

Many large and some of the smaller companies give charitable grants, although most have a policy of only funding organisations. Those that will support individuals have their own charitable foundations or benevolent funds for ex-employees, and therefore are included in this guide.

There has been a growing trend for many prominent utility companies to establish charities which give to individuals who are struggling to pay their utility bills. These charities have continued to grow and have for a number of years provided much relief to the individuals involved, lessening the financial burden on them and ensuring that no legal action will be taken against them for non-payment of bills.

Community foundations

Over recent years, community foundations have established themselves as key community actors. According to UK Community Foundations' website, there are 48 community foundations throughout the UK which distribute around £65 million grants a year and they hold, as at March 2012, £426 million in endowed funds.

Community foundations aim to be cause-neutral and manage funds donated to them by both individuals and organisations, which are then distributed to the local communities which they serve.

Whilst most community foundations only support organisations, some also have funds available for individuals and are therefore included in this guide. The UK Community Foundations' website has a complete list and a map of community foundations (see ukcommunityfoundations.org).

Please note that, like most sources of financial support, funding for individuals is subject to frequent change. Even if your local community foundation is included in this guide it is worth checking the availability on your local community foundation website.

Ministers of religion

There may be informal arrangements within a church, mosque, etc. to help people in need. Ministers of religion are often trustees of local charities which are too small to be included in the guide.

Hospitals

Most hospitals have patient welfare funds, but they are little-known, even within the hospitals and so are not used as frequently as other sources of funds. It may take some time to locate an appropriate contact. Start with the trust fund administrator or the treasurer's department of the health authority.

Local organisations

Rotary Clubs, Lions Clubs, Round Tables and so on are active in welfare provision. Usually they support groups rather than individuals and policies vary in different towns, but some welfare agencies (such as Citizens Advice) have a working relationship with these organisations and keep up-to-date lists of contacts. All enquiries should be made on behalf of the individual by a recognised agency.

Orders

Historic organisations such as the masonic and RAOB (known as Buffs) lodges exist for the mutual benefit of their members and the wider community. Spouses and children of members (or deceased members) may also benefit, but people unconnected with these orders are unlikely to. Applications should be made to the lodge where the parent or spouse is or was a member.

Hobbies and interests

People with a particular hobby or interest should find out whether this offers any opportunities for funding. Included in this guide are a number of sporting associations which exist to relieve people who are in need, but there may be many more which are not registered with the Charity Commission, or have less than £500 a year to give, but are of great value to the people they can help. It is likely that other sports and interests have similar governing bodies wishing to help their members either through making a donation or organising a fundraising event.

Educational support

This guide only deals with grants for the relief of need, ignoring grantmakers which can support individuals for educational purposes. However, many educational charities are prepared to give grants to school children for uniforms, for instance. Receiving financial support for the cost of uniforms would obviously enable parents to spend the money budgeted for that purpose on other needs, so people with children of school age should check for any educational grants available to them. For information on statutory funds, contact your local educational authority or enquire for information at the office of the individual's school. For charitable funding, this guide's sister publication, *The Guide to Educational Grants*, provides information on over 1,400 grantmaking charities (thirteenth edition) giving throughout the UK.

Charity shops

Some charity shops will provide clothing if the applicant has a letter of referral from a recognised welfare agency.

Getting help

Unfortunately, none of these methods can offer a quick fix. Applying for grants can be a daunting experience, especially if you are unfamiliar with the process; it is probably worth starting with the help of a sympathetic advisor. Most branches of Citizens Advice have money advice workers or volunteers trained in money advice work. If you find that you are in financial need try going to the nearest citizens advice bureau and talk to them about your financial difficulties. They may be able to help write an application to an appropriate charity, know of a welfare benefit you could claim or be able to re-negotiate some of your debt repayments on your behalf. They will certainly be able to help you minimise your expenditure and budget effectively.

Acknowledgements

Throughout this introduction, we have commented on the Charity Commission for England and Wales's guidelines and advice. Whilst we are aware that the Charity Commission for England and Wales only has rule over those countries, readers in Northern Ireland and Scotland (as well as the Isle of Man and the Channel Islands) should note that although the exact nature of charitable law differs in these countries, the spirit and guidance remains the same throughout the UK and the Charity Commission's advice should be seen as being just as relevant.

We are extremely grateful to the many people, charity trustees, staff and volunteers, and others who have helped compile this guide. To name them all would be impossible.

A request for further information

The research for this book was done as carefully as we were able, but there will be relevant charities that we have missed and some of the information is incomplete or will become out-of-date. If any reader comes across omissions or mistakes in this guide, please let us know so we can rectify them. A telephone call or e-mail to the Research Department of the Directory of Social Change (0151 708 0136; email: research@dsc.org.uk) is all that is needed. We are also always looking for ways to improve our guides and would appreciate any comments, positive or negative, about this guide, or suggestions on what other information would be useful for inclusion when we research for the next edition.

References

1930 Fund for District Nurses (2013), annual report and accounts 2012/13, Tetbury, 1930 Fund for District Nurses

Apps, P. (2014), 'DWP capped access to discretionary housing fund' [online article], www.insidehousing.co.uk, *Inside Housing*, dated 19 June 2014, accessed 18 September 2014

Beatty, C. and Fothergill, S. (2013), *Hitting the poor places hardest: The local and regional impact of welfare reform*, Sheffield, Centre for Regional Economic and Social Research

BEN (2013), annual report and accounts 2012/13, Sunninghill, BEN – The Automotive Industry Charity

Berry, C. and L. White (2014), *Local authority spending cuts and the 2014 English local elections*, British Political Economy Brief, Sheffield, Sheffield Political Economy Research Institute (SPERI)

Brown, C. (2014), 'Evictions on rise as landlords toughen up' [online article], *Inside Housing*, www.insidehousing.co.uk, dated 13 June 2013, accessed 23 June 2014

Buttle (2013), annual report and accounts 2012/13, London, Buttle UK

Charity for Civil Servants (2013), annual report and accounts 2013, Sutton, The Charity for Civil Servants

Doherty, J., L. Lernelius-Tonks and J. Morris (2013), *The Guide to Grants for Individuals in Need*, London, Directory of Social Change

Duffy, S. (2014), *Counting the Cuts*, www.centreforwelfarereform.org, The Centre for Welfare Reform. accessed 18 September 2014

DWP (2014), *DWP Quarterly Statistical Summary*, Department for Work and Pensions

Green, A. (2014), 'What price advice? Legal aid reform one year on', blogs.citizensadvice.org.uk, Citizens Advice, dated 7 April 2014, accessed 24 September 2014

Ipsos MORI, (2013), *Impact of welfare reform on housing associations – 2012 Baseline report*, Ipsos MORI

Money Advice Trust (2014), 'Rent arrears the fastest growing UK debt problem' [web page], available at: www.moneyadvicetrust.org, accessed 23 June 2014

Money Charity (2014), *Debt statistics – April 2014 summary* [PDF], themoneycharity.org.uk, accessed 23 June 2014

National Debtline (2014). 'Changing Household Budgets' [web page], www.nationaldebtline.org, accessed 23 June 2014

Perennial (2013), annual report and accounts 2013, Leatherhead, Gardeners' Royal Benevolent Society

RNIB (2013), annual report and accounts 2012/13, London, The Royal National Institute of Blind People

RT (2014), 'UK Families living on "knife edge", homeless charity says' [online article], rt.com, dated 22 July 2014, accessed 23 June 2014

VBF (2013), annual report and accounts 2013, London, Veterinary Benevolent Fund

Worcester Consolidated Municipal Charity (2013), annual report and accounts 2013, Worcester, Worcester Consolidated Municipal Charity

Note: all annual reports and accounts are available on the Charity Commission for England and Wales website.

How to use this guide

Below is a typical charity entry, showing the format we have used to present the information obtained from each of the charities.

On the following page is a flowchart. We recommend that you follow the order indicated in the flowchart to look at each section of the guide and find charities that are relevant to you. You can also use the information in the sections 'About this guide' and 'How to make an application' to help inform your applications.

The Fictitious Trust

£24,000 (120 grants)

Correspondent: Ms I M Helpful, Charities Administrator, 7 Pleasant Road, London SN0 0ZZ (020 7123 4567; email: admin@fictitious.org.uk; website: www.fictitious.org.uk).

CC Number: 112234

Eligibility

Children or young people up to 25 years of age who are in need. Preference is given to children of single parent families and/or those who come from a disadvantaged family background.

Types of grants

Small one-off grants of up to £250 for a wide range of needs, including school uniforms, books, equipment and educational trips in the UK and abroad. Grants are also available for childcare costs.

Annual grant total

In 2013 the trust had an income of £25,000 and an expenditure of £27,000. Grants to 120 individuals totaled £24,000.

Other information

The trust also gives relief-in-need grants to individuals.

Exclusions

No grants for private school or university fees.

Applications

On a form available from the correspondent, submitted either directly by the individual or by the parent or guardian for those under 18. Applications are considered in January, April, July and October.

Award and no. of grants

Total amount given during the financial year in question in grants to individuals for education and how many individual grants were made, if this information was available.

Correspondent

The main person to contact, nominated by the trustees.

Charity Commission number

Note: occasionally some of the organisations are not registered charities.

Eligibility

This states who is eligible to apply for a grant. This can include restrictions on age, family circumstances, occupation of parent, subject to be studied, stage of education, ethnic origin, or place of residence.

Types of grants

Specifies whether the charity gives one-off or recurrent grants, the size of grants given and for which items or costs grants are actually given. This section will also indicate if the charity runs various schemes.

Annual grant total

This shows the total amount of money given in grants to individuals in the last financial year for which there were figures available. Other financial information may be given where relevant.

Other information

This contains miscellaneous further information about the charity, including if they give grants to individuals for relief-in-need, or to organisations.

Exclusions

This field gives information, where available, on what the charity will not fund.

Applications

Including how to apply, who should make the application (i.e. the individual or a third party) and when to submit an application.

How to identify sources of help - a quick reference flowchart

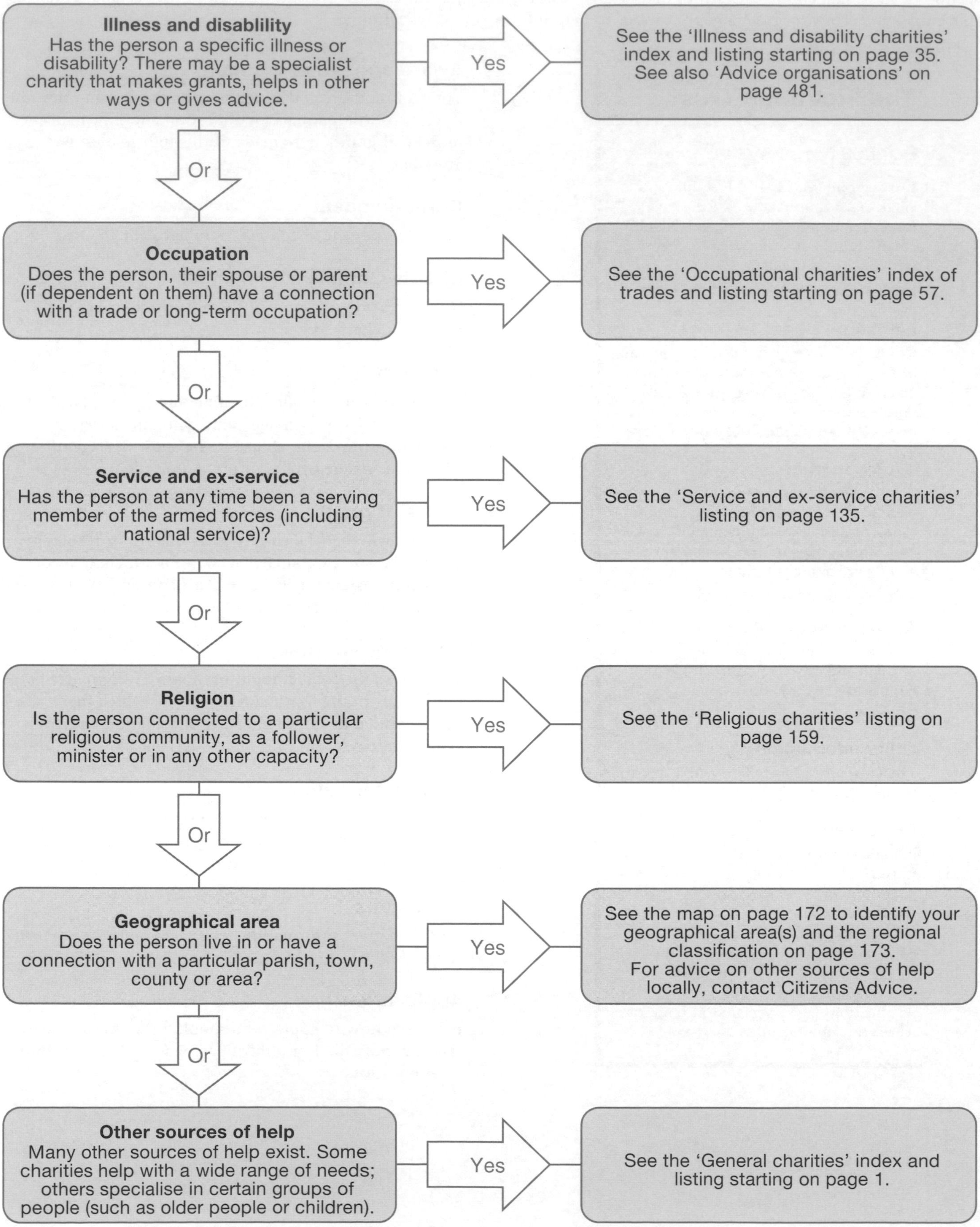

Illness and disablility
Has the person a specific illness or disability? There may be a specialist charity that makes grants, helps in other ways or gives advice.
Yes
See the 'Illness and disability charities' index and listing starting on page 35. See also 'Advice organisations' on page 481.
Or
Occupation
Does the person, their spouse or parent (if dependent on them) have a connection with a trade or long-term occupation?
Yes
See the 'Occupational charities' index of trades and listing starting on page 57.
Or
Service and ex-service
Has the person at any time been a serving member of the armed forces (including national service)?
Yes
See the 'Service and ex-service charities' listing on page 135.
Or
Religion
Is the person connected to a particular religious community, as a follower, minister or in any other capacity?
Yes
See the 'Religious charities' listing on page 159.
Or
Geographical area
Does the person live in or have a connection with a particular parish, town, county or area?
Yes
See the map on page 172 to identify your geographical area(s) and the regional classification on page 173.
For advice on other sources of help locally, contact Citizens Advice.
Or
Other sources of help
Many other sources of help exist. Some charities help with a wide range of needs; others specialise in certain groups of people (such as older people or children).
Yes
See the 'General charities' index and listing starting on page 1.

How to make an application

Once the appropriate charities have been identified, the next stage is the application itself. People often find making applications difficult and those who might benefit sometimes fail to do so because of the quality of the application submitted.

This article gives guidelines both to individuals applying directly and to welfare agencies applying on behalf of individuals on how to make good, clear and relevant applications.

The application form

The first stage in submitting an application is the question of application forms.

Applications on agency letter headings or personal letters direct from the applicant, no matter how well presented, are fairly pointless if the charity being approached has a specific application form which must be completed. This obvious point is often overlooked. It is frustrating when the application is returned with a blank form requesting substantially the same information as has already been submitted. The resulting delay may mean missing a committee meeting where the application would have been considered and a considerable wait until the next one.

Entries in this guide usually indicate when a particular application form is needed, but if there is any doubt the applicant should make a preliminary telephone call to the charity.

Who submits the application?

Again, it is important that an appropriate person sends the application. The guide usually indicates whether an individual in need can apply on his/her own behalf, or whether a third party (professional or otherwise) must apply for them.

In recognition of 'empowerment' of service users, advisory bodies sometimes simply advise families of funds they can approach themselves. However, many charities require applications and forms where appropriate to be completed by, for example, a professional person who is sponsoring the application. Therefore, the individual in need may have to press the agency to make an application on his/her behalf.

The questions

When application forms are used, the questions asked sometimes cause problems, often because they don't appear relevant. Applicants sometimes fail to realise all charities are governed by criteria laid down in their trust deeds and usually specific questions are designed to ensure these criteria are met.

For example, questions concerning date and place of birth are often answered very vaguely. 'Date of birth' is sometimes answered with 'late 50's' or, even worse, 'elderly'. Such a reply reflects the appearance of the person in question and not their age! If the charity can only consider applications for those below a pensionable age, and the request was on behalf of a woman, then the above answers would be too imprecise.

Equally 'Place of birth' is sometimes answered with 'Great Britain' which is not precise enough for funds whose area of benefit is regional or local. It is always better to state the place of birth as well as town and county, even if they are different from the current home address.

Where application forms are not requested, it is essential to prepare clear, concise applications that provide:

1. A description of the person or family and the need which exists

Although applications should be concise, they must provide sufficient detail, such as:

1 The applicant's name, address, place and date of birth

2 The applicant's family circumstances (i.e. married/partners, separated/divorced/single parent, widow/widower, the number and ages of dependent children)

3 The applicant's financial position (i.e. breakdown of weekly income and expenditure and, where appropriate, DWP/housing benefit awarded/refused, savings, credit debts, rent/gas/electricity arrears, etc.)

4 Other relevant information, such as how the need arose (e.g. illness, loss of job, marital separation, etc.) and why other sources (especially DWP/housing departments) have not helped. If applying to a disability charity, applicants should include details of the nature and effects of the disability (although see Medical information below); if applying to a local charity, how long have they lived in the locality.

The application, which says 'this is a poor family who need their gas reconnecting', is unlikely to receive proper consideration. It is also worth mentioning that applications are dealt with in the strictest of confidence, so applicants should aim to provide as much information as is relevant. The form printed after this article may serve as a useful checklist to ensure that all relevant information is included for the particular application.

2. How much money is requested and what it will be used for

This second point appears to cause the most difficulty. Applications are often received without any indication of the amount required or without sufficient explanation as to the desired use of the money.

For example, an applicant may have multiple debts totalling over £1,000. A grant of £100 would clear one of the debts and free much-needed weekly income. So the applicant approaches a suitable charity for a grant of £100. If the applicant explains the situation clearly, trustees can see that a £100 grant in this instance would be an effective use of their charity's resources. However, if it is not made clear, trustees can only guess at the possible benefits of the grant. Because they are unwilling to take undue risks with charitable money, trustees may either turn down an incomplete application or refer it for more information, which inevitably means delays.

Charity and the state

Charities are not supposed to give grants for items that are covered by statutory sources. However, the Big Lottery and increasing reforms to the welfare state have made it much more difficult to say where statutory provision ends and charitable provision begins.

Similarly, means testing under some state provision such as Disabled Facilities Grants regulations can create shortfalls between the amount that statutory sources can and will pay, and the full costs of equipment and adaptations to properties. Sometimes, because of what can and cannot be taken into account, assessments of what families can pay appear unrealistic. Where this is the case it should be stated.

Changes arising from tightening of eligibility criteria and Community Care legislation are creating new areas of unmet need. If individuals are applying to charity because statutory provision is clearly no longer adequate, they should make it clear in the application that they have exhausted all possible statutory sources of funding but they are still left with a shortfall. A supporting reference from a knowledgeable agency may be helpful.

Where the identified need is not met, following any assessment process, applications for alternative or complementary finance should make the reasons clear.

The way that social and health care services are provided is changing. Traditionally, the state assessed an individual's need, and then provided, or arranged for those assessed services to be provided. The change gives those assessed as eligible for services, the money to purchase them themselves by way of an Individual Budget. The aim is to give more independence and choice of services purchased. It is accepted that this is a radical change for many people. Applications to charities, particularly those with social care needs may well have to reflect the services already being purchased from an individual budget, with a cogent argument as to how what is now being applied for is needed and improves quality of life.

Realism

It helps to be realistic. Sometimes families have contributed to their own situation. The applicant who admits this and seems not to expect miracles but rather seeks to plan afresh – even if with fingers crossed – will often be considered more positively than the applicant who philosophises about deprivation and the imperfections of the political regime of the day.

Likewise, the application, which tries to make the trustees feel guilty and responsible for the impending doom which is predicted for the most vulnerable members of the family unless money is given, is unlikely to impress experienced trustees, however sympathetic.

In general, be clear and factual, not moralising and emotional. In effect, a good application attempts to identify the need and promote possible resolutions.

Applications to more than one charity

Where large amounts are being sought, it can take months to send applications one at a time and wait for the outcome of each before applying to another. However, if a number of applications are being sent out together, a paragraph explaining that other charities are being approached should be included together with a commitment to return any surplus money raised. It is also worth saying if any other applications have been successful in contributing to the whole–nothing succeeds like success!

The same application should not be sent off indiscriminately. For example, if somebody is applying to a trade charity on behalf of a child whose deceased father had lengthy service in that particular trade, then a detailed description of the deceased father's service would be highly relevant. If an application for the same child was being made to a local charity, it would not.

Sometimes people who are trustees of more than one charity receive three or four identical letters, none tailored to that particular charity and none indicating that other grantmaking organisations have been approached. The omission of such details and the neglect of explanations raise questions in the minds of trustees, which in the end can result in delays or even refusal.

Timing

When applying to charities, remember the time factor, particularly in cases of urgent need. Committees often sit monthly, or even quarterly. Without knowledge but with 'luck', an application can be received the day before the meeting – but if Murphy's Law operates it will always arrive the day after. For the lack of a little homework, applications may not be considered in time.

From experience, few organisations object to a telephone call being made to clarify criteria, dates of meetings or requests for application forms. So often it seems that applicants leave the whole process to chance, which leads to disillusionment, frustration and wasted time for all concerned.

Savings

When awarding a grant, most trustees take the applicant's savings into account. Some applicants may think this unnecessarily intrusive, but openness and honesty make for a better presented application and saves time. However, sometimes savings may not need to affect trustees' calculations.

For example, if a woman has a motor accident in which she was not at fault but which leaves her permanently disabled, she will receive compensation (often a one-off lump sum) through the guilty party's insurance company based on medical prognoses at the time. If her condition deteriorates faster and further than anticipated, requiring her to obtain an expensive item of equipment, it could well be argued that this should not be paid for out of the compensation awarded. The compensation was paid to cover factors such as loss of earnings potential, a reduced quality of life, reduced ability to easily fulfil basic household tasks and a general loss of future security, not to pay for unexpected and expensive pieces of equipment.

In such circumstances, the applicant should include a paragraph in the application to explain why his/her savings are not relevant to grant calculations.

In conclusion

Two final points should be borne in mind.

1. Be clear

Firstly, social care & health care professionals often resort to the use of jargon when plain English would be more effective. There appears to be two extremes; one to present a report on the basis that the trustees are not very intelligent lay people who need to be educated, or alternatively that they are all psychotherapists who need to be impressed. Usually, this only causes confusion.

2. Medical information

Secondly, medical information should not be presented without an accurate medical diagnosis to support it. Applicants' or social workers' presumptions on medical matters are not relevant. Often what is necessary is to explain why a financial need arises from a particular condition. This may be because of the rarity of the condition or the fluctuating nature of it.

The medical information should be presented by a professional in that field. The task of the applicant or the sponsor is to explain the implications of the condition.

Ashley Wood
Former Assistant Chief Executive
Gaddum Centre

Using the application form template for financial assistance

Over the page is a general-purpose application form. It has been compiled with the help of Gaddum Centre. It can be photocopied and used whenever convenient and should enable applicants (and agencies or persons applying on behalf of individuals) to state clearly the basic information required by most grantmakers.

Alternatively, applicants can use it as a checklist of points to include in the letter. Applicants using this form should note the following things in particular:

1 It is worth sending a short letter setting out the request in brief, even when using this application form.

2 Because this form is designed to be useful to a wide range of people in need, not all the information asked for in the form will be relevant to every application. For example, not all applicants are in receipt of state benefits, nor do all applicants have HP commitments.

   In such cases, applicants should write N/A (not applicable) in the box or on the line in question.

3 If, similarly, you do not have answers for all the questions at the time of applying – for example, if you have applied to other charities and are still waiting for a reply – you should write 'Pending' under the question: 'Have you written to any other charities? What was the outcome of the application?'

4 The first page is relevant to all applications; the second page is only relevant to people applying for school or college fees. If you are applying for clothing or books for a schoolchild then it may be worth filling out only the first page of the form and submitting a covering letter outlining the reasons for the application.

5 Filling out the weekly income and expenditure parts of the form can be worrying or even distressing. Expenditure when itemised in this way is usually far higher than people expect. It is probably worth filling out this form with the help of a professional.

6 You should always keep a copy of the completed form in case the trust has a specific query.

7 This form should not be used where the trust has its own form, which must be completed.

Application form template

Purpose for which grant is sought	**Amount sought from this application** £
Applicant (name)	Occupation/School
Address Telephone no.	
Date of birth / Age	Place of birth
Nationality	Religion (if any)

☐ Single ☐ Married ☐ Divorced ☐ Partnered ☐ Separated ☐ Widow/er

Family details: Name	Age	Occupation/School
Parents/ Partner	......	....
Brothers/Sisters/ Children	......	....
....	......	....
....	......	....
Others (specify)	......	....

Income (weekly)	£ p	**Expenditure** (weekly)	£ p
Father's/husband's wage	......	Rent/mortgage	......
Mother's/wife's wage	......	Council tax	......
Partner's wage	......	Water rate	......
Income Support	......	Electricity	......
Jobseeker's Allowance	......	Gas	......
Employment and Support Allowance	......	Other fuel	......
Pension Credit	......	Insurance	......
Working Tax Credit	......	Fares/travel	......
Child Tax Credit	......	Household expenses (food, laundry etc.).	......
Child Benefit	......	Clothing	......
Housing Benefit	......	School dinners	......
Attendance Allowance	......	Childcare fees	......
Disability Living Allowance	......	HP commitments	......
Universal Credit	......	Telephone	......
Personal Independence Payments	......	TV rental	......
Maintenance payments	......	TV licence	......
Pensions	......	Other expenditure (specify)	......
Other income (specify)	......	....	......
....	......	....	......
....	......	....	......
....	......	....	......
Total weekly income	£	**Total weekly expenditure**	£

Savings £

Debts/arrears
Rent, fuels, loans, HP etc.

Specify in detail	Amount owed
....	£ ....
....	£ ....
....	£ ....
....	£ ....
....	£ ....
Total	£

Has applicant received help from any other source? ☐ YES ☐ NO
(If YES, please include details below)

Sources of grant obtained	Amount
....	£..........
....	£..........

Other sources approached

....

....

Total still required £

Has applicant ever received previous financial help from this charity? ☐ YES ☐ NO If so, when?

Reason for the application

Continue on a separate sheet if necessary

For applications being submitted through a welfare agency

Name of agency ....

Case worker ....

Address..

....

Telephone..

How long has the applicant been known to your department/organisation?..

For all applications

Signature: **Date:**

About the Directory of Social Change

DSC has a vision of an independent voluntary sector at the heart of social change. The activities of independent charities, voluntary organisations and community groups are fundamental to achieve social change. We exist to help these organisations and the people who support them to achieve their goals.

We do this by:

- providing practical tools that organisations and activists need, including online and printed publications, training courses, and conferences on a huge range of topics
- acting as a 'concerned citizen' in public policy debates, often on behalf of smaller charities, voluntary organisations and community groups
- leading campaigns and stimulating debate on key policy issues that affect those groups
- carrying out research and providing information to influence policymakers.

DSC is the leading provider of information and training for the voluntary sector and publishes an extensive range of guides and handbooks covering subjects such as fundraising, management, communication, finance and law. We have a range of subscription-based websites containing a wealth of information on funding from charities, companies and government sources. We run more than

300 training courses each year, including bespoke in-house training provided at the client's location. DSC conferences, many of which run on an annual basis, include the Charity Management Conference, the Charity Accountants' Conference and the Charity Law Conference. DSC's major annual event is Charityfair, which provides low-cost training on a wide variety of subjects.

For details of all our activities, and to order publications and book courses, go to www.dsc.org.uk, call 08450 777707 or email publications@dsc.org.uk

General charities

This section includes all the entries which could not be tied to a particular occupation, disability or locality. It starts with 'Index of general charities' (including, for example, 'Children and young people', and 'Older people') with a separate category for trusts that specifically give grants for holidays. 'Children and young people' contains trusts for people aged 25 or under while 'Older people' contains trusts for people aged 50 or over. This reflects the criteria of some of the trusts in the guide, although not every trust will use these exact limits. We have included refugees and asylum seekers under the 'Ethnic and national minorities in the UK' sections.

The entries under each category are arranged alphabetically, with those trusts which do not fit into any particular category listed at the start of the chapter under 'General'. These charities are listed under 'General' because they can give to a wide range of people, so if individuals are unable to find help from other sources in the guide then they should be able to approach one or more of these. However, note that most of these charities still have restrictions on who they can help. Applicants should not simply send off indiscriminate applications to any charity under the 'General' heading; rather, they should first consider carefully whether they are eligible.

Similarly, within the alphabetically arranged categories following 'General', older people should not apply to all the trusts in the 'Older people' section, for instance, as there may be criteria that will makes them ineligible for support.

Index of general charities

The ACT Foundation

£499,000 (454 grants)

Correspondent: James Kerr, Secretary, 61 Thames Street, Windsor SL4 1QW (01753 753900; fax: 01753 753901; email: info@theactfoundation.co.uk; website: www.theactfoundation.co.uk)

CC Number: 1068617

Eligibility

The trust has the aim of enhancing the quality of life for people in need, particularly those with mental and physical disabilities.

Types of grants

Grants of up to £2,500 are given towards home modifications (where a DFG – Disabled Facilities Grant – has been applied for and has been granted and where there is a shortfall in the funds required) and equipment such as specialised wheelchairs, other mobility aids and medical equipment to assist independent living. Grants are also given towards short-term respite breaks at a registered respite centre. The foundation's website states that grants have been given towards stair lifts, disabled bathroom conversions, motorised wheelchairs, books and equipment for use at specialist colleges, specialist and other furniture and vehicle adaptations.

Annual grant total

In 2012/13 the foundation had an income of £16.8 million and a total expenditure of £13.8 million. A total of £499,000 was awarded in 454 grants to individuals.

A further 109 grants to non-strategic partner organisations totalled £438,000, with one of the foundation's strategic partners, Core Arts education programme, receiving £50,000.

Exclusions

No grants to replace statutory funding or for work, items or services already commenced, purchased or on order. Nor will grants be made towards building alterations where a Disabled Facilities

Grant has not been applied for and has not been awarded.

Applications

Application forms are available to download from the website. Applicants may complete the form themselves or have it completed on their behalf by a third party. If a grant is required for a medical reason, brief details and a medical report should be included as supporting evidence. For applications under £2,500, one quote should be supplied. If the grant is intended for building modifications, a letter of permission from the owner of the property should be attached. Applicants should read the grants terms and conditions on the website. All applications will be acknowledged in writing within one week of being received. The foundation aims to make a decision on all applications within three months. If the application is for an emergency, a faster timescale may be requested.

The Alchemy Foundation

£5,500

Correspondent: R. Stilgoe, Trustee, Trevereux Manor, Limpsfield Chart, Oxted, Surrey RH8 0TL (01883 730600; fax: 01883 730800)

CC Number: 292500

Eligibility

Individuals in need in the UK.

Types of grants

One-off and recurrent grants according to need. Previously the trust has given grants for holidays for children and respite for carers.

Annual grant total

In 2012/13 the foundation had assets of £2.6 million and an income of £282,000. Approximately £11,000 was given in grants to individuals for relief-in-need and educational purposes, distributed through other charities.

Applications

In writing to the correspondent.

Other information

The trust gives grants mostly to organisations, namely for overseas development, social welfare and disability projects.

Al-Mizan Charitable Trust

£24,000 (73 grants)

Correspondent: Zahra Shirzad, Grants Officer, 2 Burlington Gardens, London W3 6BA (email: admin@almizantrust.org.uk; website: www.almizantrust.org.uk)

CC Number: 1135752

Eligibility

British citizens, those granted indefinite leave to remain in the UK and asylum seekers who are living in a condition of social or economic deprivation.
Preference is given to the following groups:

- Orphans (a child who has lost either both parents or one parent who was the main bread-winner in the family)
- Children and young people under the age of 19 years (particularly those in care or who are carers themselves)
- Individuals who are disabled, incapacitated or terminally ill (particularly those who are severely mentally disabled)
- Single parents (particularly divorcees and widows/widowers with children)
- Estranged or isolated senior citizens
- Individuals with severe medical conditions or their families
- Ex-offenders or reformed drug addicts or alcoholics
- Victims of domestic violence and/or physical or sexual abuse
- Victims of crime, anti-social behaviour and/or terrorism

Types of grants

Mainly one-off grants ranging from £24 – £500, with an average grant being £271.Grants are available both for subsistence costs and those which help break the cycle of poverty by encouraging educational attainment and employability.

Annual grant total

In 2012/13 the trust had assets of £141,000 and an income of £209,000. Grants were made totalling £36,000 with £24,000 of that being awarded to 73 individuals for social welfare purposes.

Exclusions

No grants for: general appeals; applicants who are not claiming all available benefits; retrospective funding; expenses relating to the practice or promotion of religion; debt, including council tax arrears; fines or criminal penalties; university tuition fees; gap year trips; building work or construction projects; funeral expenses; gifts (including birthdays and festivals); vehicles; and holidays or recreational outings, unless they serve a medical, social or educational need. No support is given to those who have received a grant in the last twelve months.

Applications

All applications for grant funding must be submitted using the trust's online application system.

Other information

The trust has an informative website and a detailed annual report with case studies.

Anglian Water Assistance Fund

£500,000

Correspondent: The Administrator, Charis Grants, Anglian Water Assistance Fund, PO Box 42, Peterborough PE3 8XH (01733 421060 (Charis Grants); website: www.anglianwater.co.uk/awaf)

Eligibility

The fund can consider helping you if you are in debt with your water and/or sewerage charges to Anglian or Hartlepool Water and you are a current domestic account holder of Anglian or Hartlepool Water.

Types of grants

The fund may be able to help you to clear arrears of domestic water and sewerage charges by offering a number of solutions.

Annual grant total

In 2013/14 the company Anglian Water made a donation to the fund of £6.1 million. The fund in turn made assistance grants of £500,000. These were the figures given in the company's 2013/14 annual accounts. The annual report of the same accounting year stated: 'Our annual contribution to the fund is currently £750,000 and we will increase this by a third to £1 million'. Whichever figure is correct it would appear that the fund is due a significant increase next year (2014/15).

Exclusions

No grants are given towards: fines for criminal offences; education or training needs; medical equipment, aids and adaptations; holidays; debts to central government departments such as tax and national insurance; business debts; overpayment of benefits; accommodation deposits; or catalogue, credit card, personal loan or other forms of unsecured lending. The trust cannot give loans, make payments towards bills, or make any grants in arrears. You are not eligible to apply to the fund if you are already having water and/or sewerage charges deducted from your benefits via the 'Water Direct' scheme.

Check the website for current exclusions before applying.

Applications
The quickest way to apply is through the online application form on the trust's website. Alternatively applicants may download the form or call the trust to receive one in the post. The fund stresses that applicants should ensure that they have included the relevant information necessary to process the application. The fund will need to see evidence of income and water debts, if applicable. If there are arrears of water/sewerage charges, the fund will always look for a full explanation of how the arrears have arisen.

The fund will write to applicants to let them know whether they have been successful or not.

Individuals who receive an award from the trust can apply again after two years. Those who do not receive an award are eligible to re-apply after six months.

Other information
The Anglian Water Assistance Fund (formerly The Anglian Water Trust Fund) is administered by Charis Grants Ltd which also manages the British Gas Energy Trust, EDF Energy Trust, South East Water's Helping Hand and Affinity Water Trust.

The Attlee Foundation

£0

Correspondent: Tania Shaikh-McKenna, Operations Manager, c/o Attlee Youth and Community Centre, 5 Thrawl Street, London E1 6RT (020 7183 0093; email: info@attlee.org.uk; website: www.attlee.org.uk)

CC Number: 1087259

Eligibility
People with disabilities or who are disadvantaged living anywhere in the UK. Priority will be given to applications involving children and young people when funds are low.

Types of grants
One-off grants up to £100 through the 'Tickets Please' programme towards travelling costs for therapeutic support. For example, to attend specialist treatment centres or to maintain family contacts with children or close relatives in hospital, prison or rehabilitation a long way from home within the UK.

Annual grant total
In 2012/13 the foundation had assets of £2.7 million and an income of £119,000. No grants were made to individuals through the 'Tickets Please' scheme.

Exclusions
No grants are given towards funerals, holidays, travel outside the UK, medical equipment, wheelchairs or mobility adaptations.

Applications
At the time of writing the scheme had been suspended; see the foundation's website for updates.

Other information
The foundation also manages a youth centre in the Spitalfields area of East London, which provides open access and inclusive facilities for children, young people and the local community. In 2012/13 £41,000 was spent on the foundation's Family, Children and Youth project.

The Bagri Foundation

£289,000

Correspondent: Mr D. M. Beaumont, Administrator, 80 Cannon Street, London EC4N 6EJ (020 7280 0000; email: enquiries@bagrifoundation.org; website: www.bagrifoundation.org)

CC Number: 1000219

Eligibility
People in need worldwide.

Types of grants
One-off and recurrent grants according to need.

Annual grant total
In 2012/13, the foundation had assets of £14 million, a total income of £151,000 and a total expenditure of £309,000. Grants awarded totalled £289,000.

Applications
In writing to the correspondent.

Barony Charitable Trust

£2,200

Correspondent: Agnes Cunningham, Trustee, Canal Court, 40 Craiglockhart Avenue, Edinburgh EH14 1LT (0845 140 7777)

SC Number: SC021091

Eligibility
People in need through age, ill health, financial hardship or disability who live in Edinburgh and Central Scotland.

Types of grants
One-off grants of around £100, possibly up to £250 in exceptional circumstances. Recent grants have included support for people trying to make a fresh start, the purchase of disability aids such as wheelchairs or hoists and contributions towards the cost of a carer to accompany an individual on holiday.

Annual grant total
In 2012/13, the trust had an income of £3,400 and a total expenditure of £2,400. We estimate the grant total awarded to individuals was approximately £2,200.

Applications
On a form available from the correspondent, submitted preferably through a recognised referral agency such as a GP, health visitor, priest or minister, social worker or care worker. Details of what the money is for, how it will help and any other funding applied for should also be included in the application.

Other information
Note, this trust is linked to the Barony Housing Association and applications from their area of activity receive priority.

British Gas Energy Trust

£10,100,000 (16,675 grants)

Correspondent: Grants Officer, Freepost RRZJ-XBSY-GYRG, British Gas Energy Trust, PO Box 42, Peterborough PE3 8XH (01733 421060; fax: 01733 421020; email: bget@charisgrants.com; website: www.britishgasenergytrust.org.uk)

CC Number: 1106218

Eligibility
Individuals and families who are in poverty, suffering or other distress who are struggling to pay their gas and/or electricity debts. Applications to the trust are welcomed from anyone living within England, Scotland or Wales.

Types of grants
Grants to clear gas and electricity debts and to clear other priority household debts or purchase essential household items such as:

- Boiler replacement
- Energy efficient white goods
- Funeral arrears
- Bankruptcy/DRO/LILA (Scotland) fees. These payments are known as Further Assistance Payments (FAPs)

Annual grant total
In 2012 awards totalled £10.1 million. During the year, 16,675 awards were made to individuals and families, of which 14,211, totalling £8.2 million, were to clear energy debt and 2,464, totalling £1.9 million, were in Further Assistance Payments.

The average amount for energy awards was £642 and for Further Assistance Payments, £569.

At the time of writing this was the most recent financial information available for the trust.

Exclusions

The trust cannot give loans or help with bills or items that have already been paid for. Nor can it help with the following: any household item that is not a 'white good'; fines for criminal offences; overpayments of benefits; educational or training needs; business debts; debts to central government departments, for example, tax and national insurance; catalogues, credit cards, personal loans and other forms of non-secured lending; medical equipment, aids and adaptations; deposits to secure accommodation; and holidays.

Applications

The quickest way to apply is via the trust's online application form. Forms can also be downloaded from the trust's website or requested by email or telephoning the correspondent. A local money advice centre such as Citizens Advice may be able to provide help in completing the form. Supporting documentation is required and the assessment of applications cannot begin without it. Evidence of income can be shown via bank statements, wage slips or benefit letters. All evidence provided must be dated within three months, however, the trust can accept annual benefit letters for work pensions, state pensions, child benefit and Disability Living Allowance (DLA). Applicants are strongly advised to seek money advice before applying to the trust to increase the chance of a successful application. Those in receipt of an award from the trust cannot reapply for two years. Applicants who do not receive an award can reapply if their circumstances change.

Other information

Grants are also made to voluntary organisations working in the field of money advice, debt counselling or energy efficiency advice.

Catholic Clothing Guild

£7,500

Correspondent: Carmel Edwards, Hon Treasurer, 5 Dark Lane, Shrewsbury, Shropshire SY2 5LP (email: carmel.edwards@btinternet.com)

CC Number: 277952

Eligibility

People in need of clothing regardless of denomination in England.

Types of grants

The guild is a small charity which distributes new donated clothing (mainly to children). It may give small money grants when this is not possible, however this is in exceptional circumstances as funding is limited.

Annual grant total

The 2012 accounts were the latest available at the time of writing (August 2014).

In 2012, the guild had an income of £6,500 and a total expenditure of £8,000. We estimate that the total amount of grants awarded to individuals was approximately £7,500.

Applications

Applications should be made by letter or email to their local branch. Telephone calls are not welcomed. Applications must be made through a welfare agency or social services who will also receive the grants. Under no circumstances will applications be accepted by individuals.

Other information

Note: the trust is only able to assist with up to six grants per month due to limited funding.

Coats Foundation Trust

£19,000

Correspondent: Sheila MacNicol, Secretary, Coats Pensions Office, Cornerstone, 107 West Regent Street, Glasgow G2 2BA (01412 076820; email: andrea.mccutcheon@coats.com)

CC Number: 268735

Eligibility

Only applications where no statutory help or help from other charitable organisations is available.

Types of grants

One-off for essential items or services.

Annual grant total

In 2012/13 the trust had an income of just £980 and a total expenditure of almost £75,000. We have estimated the figure for the total welfare grants to individuals to be around £19,000.

Applications

In writing to the correspondent, giving full details of the reason for application, and providing copies of any documents which will back the claim, such as bank statements, payslips, benefit award letters, utility bills, etc. Applicants should also include details of what the extra money is needed for and the cost of the item(s).

Other information

This trust also makes grants to individuals for educational purposes and to organisations.

The Coffey Charitable Trust

£1,000

Correspondent: Christopher Coffey, Trustee, Oaktree House, Over the Misbourne Road, Denham, Uxbridge, Middlesex UB9 5DR (01895 831381; email: coffeytrust@gmail.com)

CC Number: 1043549

Eligibility

People in need in the UK.

Types of grants

Occasional one-off and recurrent grants according to need.

Annual grant total

In 2013/14 the trust had an income of £12,000 and a total expenditure of £6,500. We estimate grants to individuals for educational and social welfare purposes to be around £1,000.

Applications

In writing to the correspondent.

Other information

This trust mainly provides grants to Christian organisations and events.

The Cordwainers' Company Common Investment Fund

£11,000 (70 grants)

Correspondent: The Clerk, Clothworkers' Hall, Dunster Court, Mincing Lane, London EC3R 7AH, (020 7929 1121; fax: 020 7929 1124; email: office@cordwainers.org; website: www.cordwainers.org)

CC Number: 261891

Eligibility

The fund administers a number of small trusts, the eligibility of which varies. Specific trusts exist for people who are blind, people who are deaf and dumb, widows of clergymen, unmarried women in the Church of England, ex-servicemen and widows of those who served in the merchant or armed forces.

Types of grants

Small annual grants in line with the separate trusts' criteria (see above).

Annual grant total

In 2012/13 the trust had assets of £1.8 million and an income of £125,000. Grants were made to around 70 individuals totalling £11,000.

Applications
In writing to the correspondent, supported, if possible, by referrals from welfare or other charitable bodies.

Other information
The trust also makes grants to organisations (£11,500 in 2012/13).

The Dibs Charitable Trust

£5,300

Correspondent: The Administrator, Trustee Department, Coutts, 440 Strand, London WC2R 0QS

CC Number: 257709

Eligibility
People in need.

Types of grants
One-off grants for the relief of immediate distress only, usually ranging from £25 to £250. Grants are not made directly to individuals.

Annual grant total
In 2012/13 the trust had an income of £24,000 and an expenditure of £22,000. We estimate that £5,300 was given in welfare grants to individuals, with funding also awarded to charitable organisations and to individuals with educational needs.

Exclusions
No grants for bankruptcy fees or associated costs, overseas travel, holidays, clothing, funeral expenses or group activities. No pensions or annuities.

Applications
In writing to 212 Business Design Centre, 52 Upper Street, London N1 0QH. Applications should be made through a local social services department or Citizens Advice and are considered throughout the year.

East Africa Women's League (UK) Benevolent Fund

£15,000

Correspondent: Mrs Sheila Heath, Treasurer, Nobles Farm, Gatehouse Rad, Holton-le-Moor, Market Rasen LN7 6AG (email: honsec@eawl.org.uk; website: www.considine.eclipse.co.uk/eawl/eawl.html

CC Number: 294328

Eligibility
People of UK origin who have previously lived and worked in East Africa.

Types of grants
One-off and recurrent grants according to need. Grants range from around £100 to £800.

Annual grant total
In 2013, the charity had income of £15,500 and an expenditure of £22,000.

Applications
In writing to the Treasurer. Members of the fund's subcommittee may visit applicants. The trust does not accept unsolicited applications.

EDF Energy Trust

£1.56 million (2,722 grants)

Correspondent: The Grant Administrator, Freepost RLXG-RBYJ-USXE, PO Box 42, Peterborough PE3 8XH (01733 421060; fax: 01733 421020; email: edfet@charisgrants.com; website: www.edfenergytrust.org.uk)

CC Number: 1099446

Eligibility
Anyone in need in Britain.

Types of grants
Grants to cover the payment of energy bills, to purchase essential energy efficient white goods and cookers, and for Bankruptcy and Debt Relief Order (DRO) fees. The latter two are known as Further Assistance Payments (FAP).

Annual grant total
In 2013 the trust held assets of almost £1.2 million and had an income of £3 million. Grants made to individuals and families totalled more than £1.5 million. Of this total 2,338 grants were made to clear gas and electricity debts and 384 were made in further assistance payments.

The average energy grant was £621 while the average further assistance payment was £266.

Exclusions
The trust cannot help with the following: fines for criminal offences; overpayments of benefits; educational or training needs; debts to central government departments e.g. tax and national insurance; catalogues, credit cards, personal loans and other forms of non-secured lending; medical equipment, aids and adaptations; deposits to secure accommodation; or holidays.

The trust cannot give loans or help with bills or items that have already been bought.

Applications
Online via the website or by requesting an application form from the correspondent or downloading one from the site. Forms can also be obtained from a local advice centre. Applicants must submit relevant financial information: bank statements, wage slips or benefit letters showing income should be dated within the last three months. Annual benefit letters for works pensions, state pensions, child benefit and Disability Living Allowance (DLA) will also be accepted.

All applicants are advised to seek appropriate money or debt advice from an organisation like Citizens Advice before applying in order to maximise their chances of success. The trust's own statistics have previously shown that 'an application submitted with the help of a funded organisation is twice as likely to succeed as an application submitted unaided.'

Those in receipt of an award from the trust cannot reapply for two years. Applicants who do not receive an award can apply again if their circumstances change. Payments for bills will be made directly to the supplier.

Other information
A total of £379,000 was awarded in grants to organisations 'to increase independent money advice services and education for the prevention and relief of poverty.'

Family Action

£419,000 (1,607 grants)

Correspondent: Grants Service, 501–505 Kingsland Road, Dalston, London E8 4AU (020 7254 6251 – Tuesday, Wednesday and Thursday ONLY between 2 pm and 4 pm; email: grants.enquiry@family-action.org.uk; website: www.family-action.org.uk)

CC Number: 264713

Eligibility
Assistance from Family Action is primarily targeted at families and individuals living on low incomes, particularly those living on benefits.

Types of grants
Clothing, fuel bills, household needs such as beds and cookers and so on are most commonly requested. Help can also be given for more varied needs.

Annual grant total
In 2012/13 the charity held assets of £12.9 million and had an income of £18.5 million. A total of £419,000 was awarded in 1,607 grants to individuals.

Exclusions
Funds are not available for council tax arrears, debts (except utility bills), fines, funeral expenses, gifts, items already covered by statutory funds, private school fees, rent arrears or payments, repayment of Social Fund or other loans, bankruptcy or items already purchased.

Applications
The Family Action Welfare Grants Programme is not currently accepting applications. The charity is hoping to reopen the grants programme in January 2015. Check the charity's website for further details.

Other information
The charity was formerly known as Family Welfare Association.

The Fielding Charitable Trust

£1,000

Correspondent: Richard Fielding, Trustee, West Hall, Longburton, Sherborne, Dorset DT9 5PF (01963 210234)

CC Number: 1091521

Eligibility
People in need in the UK. Preference is given to older people and people with disabilities.

Types of grants
One-off and recurrent grants according to need.

Annual grant total
In 2012/13, the trust had an expenditure of £4,200. We estimate the grant total awarded to individuals was approximately £1,000 as the trust also awards grants to organisations and to individuals for educational purposes.

Applications
In writing to the correspondent.

Elizabeth Finn Care

£4 million (3,797 grants)

Correspondent: Elizabeth Finn, Grants Committee, Hythe House, 200 Shepherds Bush Road, London W6 7NL (020 8834 9200; fax: 020 8834 9299; email: info@elizabethfinn.org.uk; website: www.elizabethfinncare.org.uk)

CC Number: 207812

Eligibility
People who are British or Irish and have a professional or similar background or connection, and their dependents. Applicants must have a low income and have less than £4,000 in savings.

Types of grants
Recurrent grants are made towards daily living expenses. One-off grants are also available towards needs such as car expenses, household items, house repairs and adaptations, specialist equipment and help with nursing/residential fees. All grants are means-tested.

Annual grant total
In 2012/13 the charity made grants to 3,797 individuals totalling £4 million.

Exclusions
The charity will not give grants for healthcare costs, computer equipment, holidays, educational costs, debts, legal fees or funeral expenses.

Applications
Applicants should contact the charity to enquire about whether they are eligible via the online enquiry form on the website. A grants leaflet containing eligibility information is also available to download via the charity's website. If the charity thinks it may be able to help, an application form will be issued. This may be submitted either directly by the individual, through a third party such as a social worker or through an organisation such as Citizens Advice or other welfare agency.

Other information
If at any stage the charity cannot help, it will try to signpost applicants to other possible sources of funding.

The David Fogwill Charitable Trust

£7,700

Correspondent: Alex Fogwill, Trustee, 53 Brook Drive, Corsham, Wiltshire SN13 9AX (01249 713408)

CC Number: 1062342

Eligibility
People in need who are involved in Christian outreach projects or ministry.

Types of grants
One-off and recurrent grants up to £1,000. Support costs are usually paid to the organisations to which the Christian outreach worker is contracted.

Annual grant total
In 2012/13 the trust had an income of £20,000 and a total expenditure of £16,000. We estimate that grants to individuals totalled £7,700, with funding also awarded to Christian organisations.

Applications
In writing to the correspondent. Applications can be submitted directly by the individual or family member and should include details of the Christian activity and the organisation involved. Applications are considered in January and July.

Fund for Human Need

£13,000 (128 grants)

Correspondent: A. J. Hickox, Langdale, 1 Duffield Lane, Woodmancote, nr. Emsworth PO10 8PZ (01243 375417)

CC Number: 208866

Eligibility
Grants are available to refugees, asylum seekers, people who are homeless and anybody attempting to get over a short-term hurdle.

Types of grants
One-off and recurrent grants of up to £100 each. Grants are generally distributed via other organisations and charities.

Annual grant total
In 2012/13 the fund had an income of £20,000 and a total expenditure of £21,000.

Applications
Applications may be made in writing to the correspondent, including details of financial circumstances, however, the majority of applications are made through intermediary organisations.

Other information
Grants are also made to organisations.

The R. L. Glasspool Charity Trust

£1.1 million (4,463 grants)

Correspondent: The Grants Team, Second Floor, Saxon House, 182 Hoe Street, Walthamstow, London EH17 4QH (020 8520 4354; fax: 020 8520 9040; email: application@glasspool.org.uk (for application requests only); website: www.glasspool.org.uk)

CC Number: 214648

Eligibility
People in need who are on a low income.

Types of grants
One-off grants for white goods, beds and bedding, other household goods, clothing (including school uniform, where other sources are not available) baby needs (if not eligible for a Sure Start Maternity Grant), travel expenses for hospital visits to family members, and as contributions towards equipment and adaptations for people with disabilities (where there has been a recommendation from an occupational health therapist). Grants are paid to the referring agency.

Only in very exceptional circumstances may grants be given for flooring, educational computer equipment or televisions or vocational materials and training.

Annual grant total

In 2012/13 the trust managed to help more individuals than ever, awarding almost £1.1 million in grants to 4,463 individuals.

Exclusions

No grants for loans or debts, bursaries, project funding, research or educational grants, bankruptcy and Debt Relief Order Fees, holidays, outings, respite costs, household repairs, rent in advance or deposits, funeral costs or headstones, removal costs, or equipment and adaptations that should be funded by statutory services.

Apart from in exceptional circumstances, the trust does not normally make more than one grant per individual/family. The trust will not make a grant where funding is available from another source, particularly statutory funds.

Applications

The trust has an automated application request and submitting process. To request an application form, a blank email should be sent to application@glasspool.org.uk by an organisation acting on behalf of the individual. An application form will be sent to your mailbox within an hour. Application forms should be completed and returned to the trust by email. Once your application form is accepted, you will be issued with an automated reference number. Only when you have been issued with a reference number will the Grants Team have access to your application, they will then contact you within two to three weeks. Do not contact the trust during this time.

Under no circumstances does the trust accept applications directly from individuals. Applications must be made by an eligible organisation, which must be either: a statutory healthcare, social care or advice service; a charity that directly provides, or is contracted to provide, a statutory healthcare, social care or advice service; Citizens Advice; a prison or probation service (NOMS); or a tenancy support worker employed either by a local authority, industrial and provident society or a housing association which is registered with the Housing Corporation. The referring agency must have its own bank account and be prepared to administer the grant on behalf of the trust.

The application form is designed for applying by email only and will be rejected if received by post.

Other information

The trust is one of the few charities which operates nationally with no restrictions on its type of beneficiary. Note the following from the trust's website:

> Given the volume of applications that we receive and the limited funds available we are unable to assist in every case. The discretionary nature of the grants means we do not provide specific reasons for rejecting an application. We do not provide feedback on applications received on an individual basis and do not have the resources to enter into correspondence regarding this.

Lady Hewley's Charity (formerly known as the Lady Hewley's Trust)

£109,000

Correspondent: Neil Blake, Administrator, Military House, 24 Castle Street, Chester CH1 2DS

CC Number: 230043

Eligibility

Present or retired ministers of the United Reformed, Congregational and Baptist churches and their widows who are in need. This is a national trust, although preference is given to applicants whose ministry is in the northern counties of England.

Types of grants

Welfare grants to a maximum of about £1,000 (unless outside the scope of social security payments).

Annual grant total

In 2012/13 the trust had assets of £15.5 million and an income of almost £362,000. Grants to individuals totalled £167,000, of which £109,000 was for welfare needs. Grants made to specific groups of beneficiaries were broken down as follows:

Retired ministers	£51,000
Widows	£41,000
Ministers	£14,400
Daughters	£2,800

Exclusions

No grants will be given when local authority funds are available.

Applications

Applications are invited through contact with respective churches at both local church, regional and province levels. Individual applications are considered twice a year and grants are made according to an individual's personal and financial circumstances.

The Margaret Jeannie Hindley Charitable Trust

£10,200

Correspondent: The Trustees, Marshalls Solicitors, 102 High Street, Godalming, Surrey GU7 1DS (01483 416101)

CC Number: 272140

Eligibility

Relief of poverty and distress among people in 'reduced or destitute circumstances'. In practice priority is given to people living in the Godalming area.

Types of grants

Some recurrent grants of £40 to £50 each month are made. One-off grants up to £750 are more usual.

Annual grant total

In 2012/13 the trust had an income of £17,600 and a total expenditure of £21,000. We estimate that grants to individuals totalled £10,200, with funding also awarded to local organisations.

Applications

In writing to the correspondent. The trustees meet regularly throughout the year to consider applications.

The Hoper-Dixon Trust

£6,800

Correspondent: The Provincial Bursar, The Dominican Council, Blackfriars, St Giles, Oxford OX1 3LY (01865 288231; email: enquiries@hoperdixon.org.uk; website: www.hoperdixon.org.uk)

CC Number: 231160

Eligibility

People in need connected with, or resident in or near, any house or pastoral centre under the direction of the Dominicans of the English Province Order of Preachers.

Types of grants

One-off and recurrent grants according to need, normally ranging from £100 to £1,000. Recent grants have been given to assist with: medical expenses not covered by public funds; help for those unable to work due to sickness or injury; help with unexpected expenses; relocation expenses and basic household equipment for those setting-up a new home; help for pilgrims going to Lourdes, both those who are sick and those caring for them; and the costs of attending a funeral for a close family member.

Annual grant total

In 2012/13 the trust had an income of £17,600 and a total expenditure of £13,800. We estimate that grants to individuals totalled £6,800, with funding also awarded for educational purposes.

Applications

Applications are normally made by a Dominican Friar for the benefit of someone connected with the Order or living in the neighbourhood of a house of the Order. A list of Dominican houses and contact details is available from the English Province of the Order of Preachers website.

Third-party welfare organisations applying on behalf of an individual should contact the trust in writing or by email to enquire about possible eligibility.

The Houston Charitable Trust

£7,600

Correspondent: G. A. Houston, Trustee, Pednor Chase, Pednor, Chesham, Buckinghamshire HP5 2SY

CC Number: 1083552

Eligibility

People in need and those seeking funding for educational purposes, or for reasons relating to the advancement of the Christian faith. In practice, grants are available worldwide.

Types of grants

One-off and recurrent grants according to need.

Annual grant total

In 2012/13 the trust had assets of £504,000 and an income of £129,000. Grants to individuals totalled £10,600, of which welfare grants amounted to £7,600. A further £3,000 was awarded to individuals for purposes relating to the advancement of the Christian faith.

The majority of grants were given to organisations, however, with Christian institutions receiving £89,000 and welfare charities another £36,000.

Applications

In writing to the correspondent, though the trust has previously stated: 'unsolicited applications are not supported as the funds are already committed for the foreseeable future.'

The Johnston Family Trust

£24,000

Correspondent: B. J. S. Parsons-Smith, Administrator, Aspen Cottage, Apse Manor Road, Shanklin PO37 7PN (01512 366666)

CC Number: 207512

Eligibility

'Members of the upper and middle classes (and widows and daughters of such people) who, through no fault of their own, have fallen into impoverished circumstances.' Assistance is limited to men over 50 and women over 40.

Types of grants

Recurrent grants of around £650 a year and one-off grants of around £100 each for TV licences and birthday gifts.

Annual grant total

In 2013 the trust had an income of £20,000 and a total expenditure of £27,000. We estimate that grants to individuals totalled £24,000.

Applications

In writing to the correspondent. Applications are considered throughout the year.

The William Johnston Trust Fund

£29,000 (21 grants)

Correspondent: B. J. S. Parsons-Smith, Administrator, Aspen Cottage, Apse Manor Road, Shanklin PO37 7PN (01512 366666)

CC Number: 212495

Eligibility

Older people in need who live in the UK.

Types of grants

Recurrent grants paid twice annually, usually in June and December. One-off grants towards, for example, TV licences. Birthday gifts are also awarded.

Annual grant total

In 2013 the fund held assets of £1.2 million and had an income of £42,000. Grants to 21 individuals totalled £29,000.

Applications

In writing to the correspondent. Applications can be submitted directly by the individual or family member and are considered throughout the year.

St Jude's Trust

£0

Correspondent: Roger Millman, Administrator, Druces LLP, Salisbury House, London Wall, London EC2M 5PS (020 7216 5525; fax: 020 7628 7525; email: r.millman@druces.com)

CC Number: 222883

Eligibility

People in need through disability or disadvantage.

Types of grants

One-off and recurrent grants according to need.

Annual grant total

In 2012/13 the trust had assets of £992,000 and an income of £34,000. Grants to 28 organisations totalled £24,000. No grants were made to individuals during the year.

Applications

In writing to the correspondent. Our research indicates that applications are considered twice a year. Acknowledgements are not given.

Other information

Grants are given to both organisations and individuals.

Kilcreggan Trust

£2,900

Correspondent: The Secretary, Manton Grange, Preshute Lane, Manton, Marlborough, Wiltshire SN8 4HQ (01672 514050)

CC Number: 1017264

Eligibility

People in need in England and Wales.

Types of grants

One-off and recurrent grants according to need.

Annual grant total

In 2012/13 the trust had an income of £4,300 and a total expenditure of £11,700. We estimate that welfare grants to individuals totalled £2,900, with funding also awarded to organisations and to individuals for educational purposes.

Applications

In writing to the correspondent.

The McKenna Charitable Trust

£0

Correspondent: John Boyton, Trustee, Ingenious Media plc, 15 Golden Square, London W1F 9JG (020 7319 4000)

CC Number: 1050672

Eligibility

People in need in England and Wales, with a preference for supporting the educational needs and support of people with disabilities.

Types of grants

One-off grants are occasionally made to individuals, according to need.

Annual grant total

In 2012/13 the trust had an income of £30,000 and an expenditure of £122,000. It had assets of £218,000. Grants were made to eight organisations totalling £119,000. There were no grants made to individuals during the year.

Applications

In writing to the correspondent although the charity has stated that it does not consider or respond to unsolicited applications.

Motability

£18,700,000

Correspondent: Customer Services Team, Warwick House, Roydon Road, Harlow, Essex CM19 5PX (0300 456 4566; website: www.motability.co.uk)

CC Number: 299745

Eligibility

People who receive one of the following benefits: Higher Rate Mobility Component of Disability Living Allowance (HRMC DLA); Enhanced Rate of the Mobility Component of Personal Independence Payment (ERMC PIP); War Pensioners' Mobility Supplement (WPMS); or Armed Forces Independence Payment (AFIP).

Types of grants

Assistance can be given towards 'the best value suitable solution that meets basic mobility needs'. This can include: vehicle advance payments; supplying and fitting adaptations, for instance hand controls to enable somebody with a lower body disability to drive an automatic car or hoists to load electric wheelchairs into estate cars; driving lessons for people who are disabled, or whose children or spouses are disabled, especially people aged 16 to 24; or wheelchair accessible vehicles for customers who wish to get in a car while seated in their wheelchair.

Annual grant total

In 2012/13 the trust had net assets of £11.1 million (excluding pension liability) and had an income of £28.9 million. Grants were made totalling £18.7 million. The majority of funding for grants, almost £17 million, was provided by the Department for Work and Pensions and administered by Motability. More than £1.7 million was raised and distributed independently by Motability.

Applications

Potential applicants should contact the customer services team on 0300 456 4566. The trust usually requests that potential applicants have their national insurance number to hand.

Note the following from the Motability website:

> If Motability is able to provide financial help, you are expected to contribute as much as you can afford towards a vehicle solution that will meet your mobility needs. There is a lot of demand for financial help and we try to ensure that the available money is used to help as many people as possible to become or remain mobile.

At times there may be waiting lists for some of the schemes; for more information, see the Motability website or contact the customer services team.

Municipal General Charities for the Poor

£7,300 (61 grants)

Correspondent: Michael Gamage, Clerk, Payne and Gamage Solicitors, 48 Lombard Street, Newark, Nottinghamshire NG24 IXP (01636 640649)

CC Number: 217437

Eligibility

People who live in the parishes of Coddington, Collingham, Farndon, Hawton, Holme, Langford, Newark and Winthorpe and are in need by reason of youth, age, ill-health, disability, financial hardship or other disadvantage.

Types of grants

One-off grants of £200–£300 are mainly given towards household items such as cookers, washing machines, furniture and other household equipment. Christmas gifts of £75 each are also available.

Annual grant total

At the time of writing (August 2014) the latest financial information available was from 2012. In 2012 the charity had assets of £989,000 and an income of £31,000. Grants to 11 individuals totalled £3,500 and further £3,800 was awarded in Christmas gifts to 50 people.

Applications

Application forms are available from the correspondent. They should be submitted through a social worker, Citizens Advice or other welfare agency. Awards are normally considered in February, May, August and November and must include details of the particular need.

Other information

The charity also makes grants to organisations and is responsible for the administration of a number of charitable funds.

Natlas Trust

£20,000

Correspondent: Joel Adler, Trustee, 32 Brampton Grove, London NW4 4AQ (020 7427 6532)

CC Number: 1019856

Eligibility

People in need living in the UK or the State of Israel.

Types of grants

One-off and recurrent grants according to need.

Annual grant total

In 2012/13 the trust held assets of £579,000 and had an income of £107,000. We estimate that grants to individuals totalled around £20,000, with the majority of funding awarded to organisations.

Applications

In writing to the correspondent.

Newby Trust Ltd

£129,000 (386 grants)

Correspondent: Annabel Grout, Secretary, Hill Farm, Froxfield, Petersfield, Hampshire GU32 1BQ (01730 827557; email: info@newby-trust.org.uk; website: www.newby-trust.org.uk)

CC Number: 227151

Eligibility

People in the UK with welfare or medical needs. Beneficiaries are generally in receipt of welfare benefits, such as Income Support and Disability Living Allowance or living on a low wage.

Types of grants

One-off grants of £10 to £200, for items such as mobility aids, household essentials, furnishings, clothing, school uniforms and footwear.

Annual grant total

In 2012/13, the trust had assets of £17.2 million and an income of £409,000. Grants were made to 386 individuals totalling £129,000, of which £83,000 was given for welfare purposes and £46,000 in medical grants.

Exclusions

The trust does not provide full funding for larger items, such as washing machines, but can make a contribution to the overall costs. No grants are given to pay debt arrears or bankruptcy fees.

Applications

Social Services, NHS Trusts or registered charities may apply online on behalf of individuals in need. Applications made directly by the individual are not accepted. Cheques are payable to the sponsoring organisation. Full guidelines are available on the trust's website.

Other information

Grants are also given to organisations for education, training and research purposes.

The Osborne Charitable Trust

£2,000

Correspondent: John Eaton, Administrator, 57 Osborne Villas, Hove, East Sussex BN3 2RA (01273 732500; email: john@eaton207.fsnet.co.uk)

CC Number: 326363

Eligibility

People in need in the UK and overseas.

Types of grants

One-off and recurrent grants according to need and one-off grants in kind.

Annual grant total

In 2012/13 the trust had an income of £8,200 and a total expenditure of £8,400. We estimate that around £2,000 was made in grants to individuals for social welfare purposes.

Exclusions

No grants for religious or political purposes.

Applications

This trust does not respond to unsolicited applications.

Other information

The trust also makes grants to individuals for educational purposes.

Professionals Aid Council

£80,000 (361 grants)

Correspondent: Finola McNicholl, Administrator, 10 St Christopher's Place, London W1U 1HZ (020 7935 0641; email: admin@pcac.org.uk; website: www.professionalsaid.org.uk)

CC Number: 207292

Eligibility

Professionals with a strong educational background (degree level or equivalent). Applicants must be resident in the UK and have less than £10,000 in savings.

Types of grants

Weekly and one-off grants according to need including living expenses, furniture, white goods, essential repairs and household adaptations, clothing, respite care, residential and nursing home fees.

One-off grants were made for TV licences, telephone rental charges, household insurance, road tax and car insurance, etc.

Annual grant total

In 2012 the charity had assets of £2.15 million and an income of £122,000. During the year weekly grants were made to 164 beneficiaries and 197 one-off grants were also made, altogether totalling £80,000.

These were the latest accounts available at the time of writing (July 2014).

Exclusions

No grants for private medical fees, vet bills or pet insurance, debts, mortgage repayments or utility bills or electronic equipment.

Applications

By completing the initial enquiry form online or writing to the correspondent. Grants are means tested.

Other information

The organisation also offers advice and assistance. Grants are also made for educational purposes.

The J. C. Robinson Trust No. 3

£12,500

Correspondent: Christine Howe, Barnett Wood Bungalow, Blackboys, Uckfield, East Sussex TN22 5JL

CC Number: 207294

Eligibility

The elderly and disadvantaged as well as the training and community spirit of young people in England.

Types of grants

Grants range from £50 to £1,000 according to need.

Annual grant total

In 2012/13 the trust had an income of £32,000. Grants to individuals and organisations totalled £25,000 but further details were not disclosed in the annual report.

Applications

In writing to the correspondent, including supporting documents giving evidence of need, such as a letter from a doctor or social worker. Applications should usually be made through an organisation such as Citizens Advice or through a third party such as a social worker.

Mrs L. D. Rope's Second Charitable Settlement

£20,000 (22 grants)

Correspondent: Crispin Rope, Trustee, Crag Farm, Boyton, Near Woodbridge, Suffolk IP12 3LH

CC Number: 275810

Eligibility

People in need, with a preference for people who are resident in Suffolk.

Types of grants

One-off and recurrent grants ranging from £50 to £10,000. Grants are given for the relief of poverty and for the support of religion and education. Almost all grants are made to charities or organisations with which the trust has long-term connections or at the recommendation of members of the late founders' families.

Annual grant total

In 2012/13 the trust made 93 grants totalling £177,000, 22 of which were made to individuals. The total income of the trust was £140,000, and total expenditure was £181,000. The trust's assets were £630,000.

Applications

The trust does not invite unsolicited applications. The 2012/13 accounts note that individual grants were made to those whose circumstances were 'known to the trustees.'

Mr William Saunders Charity for the Relief of Indigent Gentry and Others

£4,600

Correspondent: St Andrew Trustees Ltd, Speechly Birch???am LLP, 6 St Andrew Street, London EC4A 3LX (020 7427 6400)

CC Number: 212012

Eligibility

'Indigent gentry, tutors, governesses, merchants and others'; and their dependents, who are on low incomes and live throughout England and Wales.

Types of grants

Annuities for individuals on low incomes.

Annual grant total

In 2012/13 the charity had an income of £12,700 and a total expenditure of £9,300. We estimate that pensions to individuals totalled £4,600, with funding also awarded to local organisations that provide care for people in need.

Applications

In writing to the correspondent.

The Severn Trent Water Charitable Trust Fund

£1.8 million (2,192 grants)

Correspondent: Grants Officer, 12–14 Mill Street, Sutton Coldfield, West Midlands B72 1TJ (01213 557766; email: office@sttf.org.uk; website: www.sttf.org.uk)

CC Number: 1108278

Eligibility

People with water or sewage services by Severn Trent Water or by companies or organisations which operate on behalf of Severn Trent, who are in financial difficulty and unable to pay their water charges.

Types of grants

One-off grants are given to clear or reduce water and/or sewage debt. Further assistance can be given through the purchase of essential household items or by the payment of other priority bills and debts. These grants are limited and will normally only be given if an application shows either that it will help the individual maintain a future sustainable weekly budget, or it will make an important and significant difference to the individual's quality of life. Generally, grants are paid directly to the appropriate organisation.

Annual grant total

In 2012/13 the fund held assets of £1.8 million and had an income of £4.4 million. Financial assistance to 2,192 individuals and families totalled £1.8 million and was distributed as follows:

Water debts	£1.78 million
Other household needs	£39,000
Bankruptcy orders	£9,500
Electricity	£6,400
Rent	£1,900
Gas	£600
Council tax	£300

During the year, no grants were made for telephones.

Exclusions

No grants are made for court fines, catalogue debts, benefits/tax credit overpayments, personal loans or other forms of borrowing. No retrospective grants are given. Grants are usually one-off and applicants cannot reapply within two years of receipt.

Applications

On a form available online or to download from the trust's website. Applications can be submitted at any time by the individual or through a money advice centre, Citizens Advice or similar third party, to: Severn Trent Trust Fund, FREEPOST RLZE-EABT-SHSA, Sutton Coldfield B72 1TJ.

Applicants may receive a telephone call or visit as part of the application process. Unsuccessful applicants may reapply after six months.

Other information

The fund also made grants totalling £260,000 to organisations which provide free debt advice and debt counselling services.

The Skinners' Benevolent Trust (formerly the Hunt and Almshouse Charities)

£27,000 (58 grants)

Correspondent: Grants Administrator, Skinners Hall, 8 Dowgate Hill, London EC4R 2SP (020 7213 0562; fax: 020 7236 6590; email: charitiesadmin@skinners.org.uk; website: www.skinnershall.co.uk)

CC Number: 1132640

Eligibility

The Skinners' Benevolent Trust aims to support individuals living on a very low income, who have been cut off in some way from society and who are trying to re-build their lives. They provide grants for essential household items that cannot be paid for from statutory funds.

Adults who fall into one (or more) of the following priority areas can apply: living with **mental health issues;** in recovery from **substance/alcohol use;** victims of **domestic violence.** Also, adults who are in receipt of a **state retirement pension** and/or have some kind of **disability or chronic illness.** Applicants must live in one of the designated geographical areas (certain London and Kent boroughs). For a complete list of these (and all criteria and eligibility) refer to the trust's website.

Types of grants

One-off grants of up to £250 towards essential household items such as white goods, furniture or furnishings.

Annual grant total

In 2012/13 grants were awarded to 32 people for an essential household item, while 26 beneficiaries continued to receive regular payments. Total grant expenditure was £27,000.

Exclusions

We cannot help with applications made by individuals or organisations providing one-off support or advice; applicants who have received a grant from the charity in the previous two years; general financial assistance, including debt and utility costs; mobility or computer equipment; building work; items that have already been purchased; applications on behalf of children; applications that fall outside our criteria.

Applications

On a form available from the correspondent. Applications must be supported by a medical professional or someone working within a recognised social care agency, such as Social Services, disability information and support organisations, housing support agencies or local charities. This person should have a personal and ongoing knowledge of the applicant's circumstances and the ability to receive and monitor any grant. Applications are considered on a monthly basis. Applicants should already have applied to their local welfare scheme (where available and if eligible) and have received a decision.

Other information

The trust has an informative website.

The Henry Smith Charity (UK)

See entry on page 164

The St Martin-in-the-Fields' Christmas Appeal Charity

£810,000 (2,520 grants)

Correspondent: Craig Norman, Clerk to the Trustees, St Martin-in-the-Fields, 6 St Martin's Place, London WC2N 4JH (020 7766 1138; email: vrfapplications@smitf.org.; website: www.stmartin-in-the-fields.org/charity/vicars-relief-fund)

CC Number: 261359

Eligibility

People in need or hardship. Priority is given to those who are in danger of becoming homeless, those who are currently homeless, destitute and/or vulnerable, and those attempting to establish or maintain a tenancy.

Types of grants

One-off grants up to £250 to have a positive impact and help alleviate distress or avert a crisis. Grants from the Vicar's Relief Fund are given to pay arrears (if they put someone at risk of homelessness) and towards deposits for a more permanent home (for those in temporary accommodation). They are also available for beds, furniture and other household items such as cookers and fridges. The 'VRF' can fund clothing and ordinary living expenses for those who are destitute or homeless.

Annual grant total

In 2012/13 the charity held assets of £1.6 million and had an income of £2.1 million. Grants totalled more than £1.7 million, £810,000 of which was given to individuals through the Vicar's Relief Fund. The average grant was around £200.

More than half of the charity's grants expenditure (£900,000) was awarded to The Connection at St Martin's-in-the-Field, a charity which supports homeless people in central London, giving them 'the skills and confidence they need to rebuild their lives.'

Exclusions

There are no grants for holidays, course fees, recurring costs, holidays, respite breaks, school trips, IT equipment, medical treatment, TV's and TV licences, childcare expenses, toys, books and play equipment, administrative charges, fines and professional fees, structural renovations or specialist equipment such as wheelchairs.

Applications

An application form and a list of guidelines can be requested from the correspondent. Forms must be requested and submitted on behalf of the individual by agencies such as social services, probation services, Citizens Advice or other welfare organisations.

Note: The charity can no longer accept applications that have been handwritten or faxed and cannot send application forms to anyone other than a support worker.

Other information

The charity receives around 400 applications for help from the fund each month which means that sometimes even eligible applications are refused. The charity tries to ensure that the fund's resources are prioritised and fairly distributed across the UK; therefore, the charity expects that applications are made only as a last resort.

The St Vincent de Paul Society (England and Wales)

£50,000

Correspondent: Elizabeth Palmer, Chief Executive, St Vincent de Paul Society, 9 Larcom Street, London SE17 1RX (020 7703 3030; email: info@svp.org.uk; website: www.svp.org.uk)

CC Number: 1053992

Eligibility

Anyone in need in England and Wales. Although predominantly a Catholic charity, it is completely non-denominational in its operation. Grants are only offered following a visit from a member of the society.

Types of grants

Material assistance is given in the provision of furniture, food, appliances, clothes, fuel and small financial disbursements. Friendship to anyone in need is a fundamental principle of the society; financial relief is incidental to this. During the year over 500,000 visits were made to 90,000 individuals and families across England and Wales.

Annual grant total

The society is not primarily a grantmaking organisation and will only make financial assistance through the family support and befriending schemes. In 2012/13 the total expenditure in this area was £1.7 million; however, the trust does not publish separate grant figures. In previous years grants have amounted to around £50,000.

Exclusions

There are no grants available for education.

Applications

In writing to the correspondent at any time. Applications can be submitted directly by the individual or through any third party, such as advice centres or probation services. The application should detail the nature of the request and relevant background information. A contact address and telephone number for the person requiring assistance must be provided to enable staff to arrange a visit as well as, if applicable, the contact details of the person making the application.

Other information

There are around 1,050 parish groups in England and Wales, with around 10,000 members who raise and distribute income locally. The society runs six children's camps, seven holiday homes, four residential premises, as well as support centres and programmes. Considerable support is given to developing countries by SVP members in India, Sudan, South Sudan, Guyana, Grenada and Romania.

Mary Strand Charitable Trust

£54,000

Correspondent: Lynda Walker, Trustee, c/o Universe Media Group, Alberton House, 30 St Mary's Parsonage, Manchester M3 2WJ (01612 141200; email: lynda.walker@totalcatholic.com)

CC Number: 800301

Eligibility

People who are in need due to poverty, sickness or old age.

Types of grants

One-off and recurrent grants, towards items like household goods, essential travel costs and clothing.

Annual grant total

The 2012 accounts were the latest available at the time of writing (August 2014).

In 2012 the trust had assets of £467,000, an income of £75,000 and a total expenditure of £117,000. Grants awarded to individuals for welfare purposes totalled £54,000.

Applications

In writing to the correspondent, to be submitted either directly by the individual or through a local priest, charity or welfare agency.

Other information

The trustees publish a column in each edition of The Universe, a weekly Catholic newspaper. The column contains details of deserving causes with names changed to preserve anonymity, and appeals are made for specific requirements. Donations from readers are received in answer to these appeals and then distributed.

Grants are also paid to organisations (£48,000 in 2012).

The Talisman Charitable Trust

£82,500 (67 grants)

Correspondent: Philip Denman, Trustee, Lower Ground Floor Office, 354 Kennington Road, London SE11 4LD (020 7820 0254; website: www.talismancharity.org)

CC Number: 207173

Eligibility

People in the UK who are living on a very low income.

Types of grants

One-off and recurrent grants according to need.

Annual grant total

In 2012/13 the trust had assets of £9.4 million and an income of £199,000.

Grants were made to 67 individuals totalling £82,500 and were distributed as follows:

Housing	46	£51,000
Disablement or disability	12	£24,000
Child poverty	3	£3,000
Small means or hardship	4	£3,000
Health	2	£2,000

Grants were also made to organisations totalling £59,500 and to 12 individuals for educational purposes totalling £19,500.

Applications

In writing to the correspondent through a social worker, Citizens Advice or similar third party.

Applications should be on headed paper and include the individual's full name and address, a summary of their financial circumstances, what is needed and how much it will cost. A brief history of the case and a list of any other charities approached should be included as well. Supporting evidence such as medical documentation, a letter from the applicant's school and written quotations would also be helpful. Applications are considered throughout the year. Only successful applications will receive a reply.

Other information

This trust was previously called The Late Baron F. A. d'Erlanger's Charitable Trust.

The Three Oaks Trust

£66,000 (341 grants)

Correspondent: The Trustees, The Three Oaks Family Trust Co. Ltd, 65 Worthing Road, Horsham, West Sussex RH12 1TD (email: contact@thethreeoakstrust.co.uk; website: www.thethreeoakstrust.co.uk)

CC Number: 297079

Eligibility

People and families in need who live in West Sussex. There is a particular focus on people with a physical or mental disability (including learning difficulties), and on low-income families, single parents and the long-term sick.

Types of grants

One-off grants of up to £150 towards basic furnishings, clothing, washing machines, fridges, telephone connections and so on.

Annual grant total

In 2012/13 the trust held assets of £6.7 million and had an income of £231,000. 341 grants to individuals totalled £66,000.

Exclusions

No funding for gap year work or similar activities.

Applications

Direct applications by individuals will not be considered. Applications can only be made through Crawley and Horsham Social Services and Citizens Advice and other invited local agencies. Details of the agency to which any cheque should be made payable should be included in the application. Unsuccessful applicants will not be contacted.

The trustees have noted in their 2012/13 report that:

> In the case of long-term difficulties, the trustees are more likely to be sympathetic to a request if the person or family on behalf of whom the request is being made, is able to reflect on whether there are any changes they could make to prevent the same problems reoccurring.

Further guidelines are offered on the trust's website.

Asylum seekers

Asylum Seekers Support Initiative – Short Term (ASSIST)

£65,000

Correspondent: Welfare Payments Team, c/o Victoria Hall Methodist Church, 60 Norfolk Street, Sheffield, South Yorkshire S1 2JB (01142 754960; email: admin@assistsheffield.org.uk; website: www.assistsheffield.org.uk)

CC Number: 1100894

Eligibility

Asylum seekers who live in Sheffield.

Types of grants

Small weekly grants for food and basic living expenses, usually £20 per person.

Annual grant total

In 2012/13, the charity had assets of £122,000 and an income of £169,000. Grants were made totalling £65,000.

Applications

Preliminary contact should be made with the charity.

Other information

This charity also provides advice and information and runs awareness-raising activities.

Carers and volunteers

The Andrew Anderson Trust

£25,000

Correspondent: Andrew Anderson, Trustee, 1 Cote House Lane, Bristol BS9 3UW (01179 621588)

CC Number: 212170

Eligibility

People who are, or were, involved in charitable activities, and their dependents, who are in need.

Types of grants

One-off and recurrent grants according to need.

Annual grant total

In 2012/13 the trust had assets of £11.1 million and an income of £284,000. Grants to individuals for welfare and education totalled £49,000.

Applications

The trust states that it rarely gives to people who are not known to the trustees or who have not been personally recommended by people known to the trustees. Unsolicited applications are therefore unlikely to be successful.

Other information

Grants are also given to organisations.

Carers Trust

£51,000

Correspondent: The Administrator, 32–36 Loman Street, London SE1 0EH (0844 800 4361; fax: 0844 800 4362; email: info@carers.org; website: www.carers.org)

CC Number: 1145181

Eligibility

Unpaid carers in the UK, especially those who live near a Carers Trust centre.

Types of grants

One-off grants. Carers can apply for grants, usually of up to £400, to purchase equipment that will have a direct and long-term impact, not only on their caring role, but on their overall quality of life.

Annual grant total

In 2012/13 the trust had assets of £5.6 million and an income of £8.3 million. During the year a total of £103,000 was awarded in grants to 397 individuals. We estimate the annual total of welfare grants to be around £51,000. The trust also makes grants for educational purposes.

Applications

Applications are made via your local Carers Trust centre, a list of which is available on the trust's website. Direct applications will not be considered.

Other information

The trust was formed by the merger of The Princess Royal Trust for Carers and Crossroads Care in April 2012 and acts as a resource body, providing advice, information and support for carers.

Grants were also paid to institutions, totalling £725,000, and to the trust's 'Network Partners', amounting to more than £1.3 million.

The Margaret Champney Rest and Holiday Fund

£16,800

Correspondent: Gillian Galvan, Administrator, The Gate House, 9 Burkitt Road, Woodbridge IP12 4JJ (01394 388746; email: ogilviecharities@btconnect.com; website: www.ogilviecharities.org.uk/Grants/Rest-and-holiday-fund/Funding-for-Holidays-for-Carers.html)

CC Number: 211646

Eligibility

Carers, particularly those caring for a severely disabled relative, who need a break away from the person they are caring for. The fund's website notes that in exceptional circumstances assistance may be given 'where the carer and cared for wish to holiday together, provided they are husband and wife or partners, or an adult child caring for an aged parent or vice versa.'

Types of grants

Generally one-off grants of between £200 and £300 towards recuperative breaks. 'The primary aim is to give a complete break to a carer while the person cared for is receiving respite care.'

Annual grant total

In 2013 the fund had an income of £12,600 and a total expenditure of £17,000. We estimate that grants to individuals totalled about £16,800.

Exclusions

Grants are not available towards regular family holidays.

Applications

Applications should be made via a social worker, community nurse or similar professional agency. They are considered at any time and should include the professional's name, job title and name and address of the organisation they represent as well as the name of the applicant and a brief summary of their circumstances. Candidates should also include full details of weekly income and expenditure, details of other agencies being approached for funding, who will care for the person while the break is being taken and the proposed holiday venue, date and likely costs.

An income and expenditure form may be downloaded from the fund's website.

Children and young people

Active Foundation

£50

Correspondent: The Secretary, Unit G, 41 Warwick Road, Solihull B92 7HS (01217 074260)

CC Number: 1076709

Eligibility

Children, people who are disadvantaged and people with disabilities.

Types of grants

One-off and recurrent grants according to need. Grants made in previous years have included those towards the purchase of equipment, wheelchairs, hoists and so on, activity holidays for children and adolescents being treated for various chronic illnesses and hospital transportation costs for a girl who had a kidney transplant.

Annual grant total

In 2012/13 the foundation had no income and a total expenditure of £200. We estimate that grants to individuals totalled £50. Grants are also made to organisations and the foundation also helps to provide educational and sporting opportunities for children who have special needs.

Applications

In writing to the correspondent.

Ann Beaumont's Educational Foundation

£7,500 (59 grants)

Correspondent: Rose Welham, Correspondent, 55 Castle Road, Hadleigh, Ipswich IP7 6JP (email: rosewelham55@aol.com)

CC Number: 310397

Eligibility

Students under the age of 25 years who are in need of financial assistance and live in the parish of Hadleigh.

Types of grants

Grants to help with course books, equipment or educational trips for people at school, college, university or those starting work.

Annual grant total

In 2012/13 the charity had assets of £1.3 million, an income of £43,500 and made 59 grants to individuals totalling £7,500.

Applications

In writing to the correspondent, together with evidence of the cost of the books or equipment required. Applications are considered four times a year.

Other information

9 grants were made to organisations during the year.

Brad's Cancer Foundation

See entry on page 46

Buttle UK – Small Grants Programme

£2.6 million (11,654 grants)

Correspondent: Alan Knowles, Director of Finance and Administration, Buttle UK, Audley House, 13 Palace Street, London SW1E 5HX (020 7798 6227; email: info@buttleuk.org; website: www.buttleuk.org)

CC Number: 313007

Eligibility

Children under 18 years old living with parents or careers and estranged, orphaned and vulnerable young people under 20 years of age and living independently. The trust prioritises people facing exceptional difficulties or crisis, particularly living in severe poverty or facing domestic violence, drug and alcohol misuse, estrangement, illness, distress, abuse, neglect, behavioural or mental health issues.

Types of grants

One-off grants of about £230, for a range of essential household items or services which are critical to the well-being of a child. During the last year 83% of the grants were provided for cookers, fridges, washing machines and children's beds and bedding. Financial support is available for items of furniture, household equipment, baby necessities, clothing. A full list of eligible and ineligible items can be found on the trust's website.

Annual grant total

In 2012/13 the trust had assets of £46.1 million and both an income and a total charitable expenditure of around £4.6 million. A total of 11,654 grants were awarded totalling around £2.6 million.

Exclusions

The trust cannot help:

- People over 21 years of age
- Families and young people not normally resident in the UK or who are non-EU residents on a student or work visa
- Parents who are not the main carer for the child
- Children who are subject to a child protection plan or who are looked after by a local authority
- Young people leaving care who can access funding under the provisions of The Children (Leaving Care) Act 2000

Applications

Applications can be made online on the trust's website and should be completed by a statutory or voluntary organisation who supports the family or the individual and is capable of assessing their needs and can also administer a grant on behalf of the trust.

Contact details for applicants resident in:

England: Audley House, 13 Palace Street, London SW1E 5HX, infor@buttleuk.org, 020 7828 7311

Scotland: PO Box 5075, Glasgow G78 4WA, annmariep@buttleuk.org, 01505 850437

Wales: PO Box 2528, Cardiff CF23 0GX, wales@buttleuk.org, 02920 541996

Northern Ireland: PO Box 484, Belfast BT6 0YA, nireland@buttleuk.org, 02890 641164

Further information and guidelines are available on the trust's website.

Other information

Grants are also distributed through the BBC Children in Need Emergency Essentials Programme.

The trust also runs a School Fee Grants scheme for schoolchildren.

Children Today Charitable Trust

£291,000

Correspondent: Aydin Djemal, Company Secretary, The Moorings, Rowton Bridge, Christleton, Chester CH3 7AE (01244 335622; fax: 01244 335473; email: info@children-today.org.uk; website: www.children-today.org.uk)

CC Number: 1137436

Eligibility

Children and young people under 25 who have a disability.

Types of grants

Grants of up to £1,000 to provide vital, life-changing specialist equipment, such as wheelchairs, walking aids, trikes, educational toys, communication aids, lifting and posturepaedic sleep equipment and specially designed sensory equipment like fibre optic sprays.

Annual grant total

In 2012/13 the trust held assets of £178,000 and had an income of £897,000. Equipment grants to individuals totalled £291,000.

Applications

Application forms are available from the correspondent. Grants are only given for specialised pieces of equipment for individual children (not groups or schools), and applications must be made by the individual applying, their parent, or legal guardian. Applications must include: a reference from a professional, for example, a teacher, social worker, doctor or occupational therapist; the applicant's basic financial information; and a pro forma invoice or a quotation from the supplier of the equipment. The charity aims to deal with all applications within 28 days of receipt.

Only one application in any 12 month period.

Other information

If you wish to apply for computer equipment, the charity works in partnership with the Aidis Trust, and encourages applicants to contact them directly (Telephone 0808 800 0009 Mon-Fri 9am-5pm).

The Family Fund

£34,600,000 (64,020 grants)

Correspondent: Sarah Duff, Grant Services Manager, Unit 4, Alpha Court, Monks Cross Drive, Huntington, York YO32 9WN (01904 621115; fax: 01904 652625; email: info@familyfund.org.uk; website: www.familyfund.org.uk)

CC Number: 1053866

Eligibility

Families who are caring at home for a child or young person aged 17 or under who is severely disabled or seriously ill. Eligible families must show evidence of their entitlement to one of the following: child tax credit, working tax credit, income based job seekers allowance, income support, incapacity benefit, employment and support allowance, housing benefit and pension credit. If you do not receive any of the above, further information may be needed to complete your application. Applicants must have permanent legal residency in the UK and have lived in the UK for six months.

Types of grants

The help given must be related to the child's care needs. The top three types of grant in 2012/13 by total spend were holidays and outings (£14 million), computers (£5.7 million) and white goods (£4.4 million). Grants were also awarded towards: clothing and bedding; driving lessons; hospital visiting expenses; recreation and home entertainment; furniture; and floor covering. The fund is not always able to meet the full cost of every item requested due to limited funding.

Annual grant total

In 2012/13 the fund made grants totalling £34.6 million to 64,020 families.

The number of families helped was distributed across the UK as follows:

Country	No of families
England	50,719
Scotland	5,515
Wales	4,830
Northern Ireland	2,956

Exclusions

The fund cannot provide items which are the responsibility of statutory agencies, such as medical or educational equipment or small items for daily living, such as bath aids, which are the responsibility of social services. No funding is given for general household bills, utility bills, mortgage or rent payments or household repairs. No grants for families receiving NASS payments. The fund cannot help foster carers.

Applications

Applications can be made by parents, carers or by young people aged 16 and 17 on their own behalf. Application forms and guidance notes are available to download from the fund's website or may be obtained by contacting the fund. You should tell the fund what you need to make a difference to your child/young person/family, making sure to put requests in order of importance. The application should be accompanied by photocopies of supporting documents and should be sent by post.

If you are making an application on behalf of more than one disabled child, complete an additional child form for each child you are applying for.

The fund tries to help families raising a disabled or seriously ill child or young person once every year. If you have been helped by the fund before, the decision letter confirming the grant should state when you are eligible to re-apply, which is usually after 12 months, but may be longer. If you have applied before, you may be able to reapply through your Family Fund online account. The fund may consider early applications in certain circumstances.

For first time applicants, the trust may arrange a home visit or a follow-up telephone call and applications are typically assessed in three to four months. For applicants who are reapplying a decision may be made in two to six weeks. All time scales are approximate and not guaranteed. The time taken to deal with applications depends on the volume of applications and funding available at any one time.

Applicants are advised to always check the fund's website before applying as an increased demand has seen some funds close early in recent years.

Other information

The fund is funded entirely by the government administrations of England, Northern Ireland, Scotland and Wales, and works within guidelines agreed by the trustees.

Note the following from the fund's website: 'As the Family Fund has limited funding, and is unable to help all families caring for a disabled child or young person we use our own disability criteria to determine whether a child is eligible.' To meet the criteria for funding, the child or young person must have additional complex needs, or have a serious or life threatening illness AND there must be evidence that their additional needs impact on the family's choices and their opportunity to enjoy ordinary life. The child or young person must also require a high level of support in three or more of the following areas: the physical environment; education; communication; access to social activities; personal care, supervision and vigilance; specialist resources, including ICT, required; and medical or therapeutic treatment and condition management. The child or young person's condition must be long-term or life limiting. A full list of criteria is available on the fund's informative and comprehensive website.

The Family Fund also runs a travel insurance policy for families with disabled or seriously ill children. The policy is open to families with children below the age of 18 and to those with a young person between the ages of 18 and 23 who is in full-time education at the time of the family break. More information is available in a media pack, which can be downloaded from the website.

Happy Days Children's Charity

£516,000

Correspondent: Mandy Bilbrough, Holidays and Residential Trip Organiser, Clody House, 90–100 Collingdon Street, Luton, Bedfordshire LU1 1RX (01582 755999; email: mandy@happydayscharity.org; website: www.happydayscharity.org)

CC Number: 1010943

Eligibility

Children and young people aged 3 to 17 years (inclusive) who have special needs i.e. children who are sick, disabled, abused, neglected and/or disadvantaged by poverty and children who have a terminal illness. The charity can only assist families with an income of less than £25,000 a year (including all benefits but not DLA or carer's allowance).

Types of grants

One-off two to four night respite break holidays in the UK. All funding is paid directly to the providers. The charity offers funding for one suitable adult, which may be a parent, guardian or a trusted adult (such as a nurse or carer). In special circumstances, the charity may choose to make alternative arrangements.

Annual grant total

In 2012/13 the charity held assets of £287,000 and had an income of £920,000. More than 11,000 children benefitted from holidays, trips and activities, which amounted to £516,000.

Exclusions

No extra adults are funded.

Applications

On a form available to download from the website or from the correspondent. Applications may be submitted by a family member (a parent, guardian, grandparent or sibling) or by a GP, consultant, nurse or social worker.

Enclosed with the application should be: a photograph of the child; a copy of all benefits received (income support, child benefits, tax credits, DLA, carer's allowance award, etc.); a copy of wage slips or self-employed accounts; a letter from the child's GP, hospital consultant or paediatrician addressed to Happy Days; details of weekly income and expenditure; and a respite break holiday destination list. Applicants should ensure that the form is completed with a signature. Telephone enquiries are welcomed.

Note: due to a long waiting list, it may take up to a year to 16 months before funding becomes available. Applications for children with terminal illnesses may be fast-tracked.

Other information

Grants are also made to groups of children and young people who have special needs for day trips and holidays.

Lifeline 4 Kids (Handicapped Children's Aid Committee)

£60,000

Correspondent: The Appeals Team, Administrator, 215 West End Lane, West Hampstead, London NW6 1XJ (020 7794 1661; fax: 020 8459 8826; email: appeals@lifeline4kids.org; website: www.lifeline4kids.org)

CC Number: 200050

Eligibility

Children and young people with disabilities under the age of 19.

Types of grants

Cash grants are never given. The charity will purchase specific requested items or equipment on behalf of the individual.

The charity's website explains:

For the individual child we provide the full spectrum of specialised equipment such as electric wheelchairs, mobility aids and varying items including specialised computers and sensory toys. We are able to give emergency and welfare appeals immediate approval within the authorised limits of our welfare sub-committee. No appeal is too large or too small for us to consider.

Annual grant total

In 2013 the charity had an income of £58,000 and an expenditure of £122,000. Full accounts were not available at the time of writing (August 2014); however we estimate that around £60,000 was awarded in grants to individuals.

Exclusions

Funding is not normally provided for:

- Building or garden works
- Fridges or cookers, ovens
- Carpets, floor covering
- Washing machines
- Clothing
- Shoes (unless specialist)
- Childcare costs
- Transport expenses
- Tuition fees
- Driving lessons
- Recreational activities or holidays

Applications

Initially, in writing (preferably by email) to the correspondent, indicating any specific requirements and including brief factual information (such as the child's name, date of birth and health condition as well as indicating specific requirements, the cost of the help sought and family contact details. If appropriate, an application form will then be sent out (specify whether email or post option is preferred). The form contains questions relating to the child's medical condition and requires backup information from health professionals together with a financial statement of the applicant.

Applications are considered monthly, although urgent cases can be dealt with more quickly.

Other information

The trust also supplies equipment and items for schools, children's hospices, respite care homes and clubs for children who have a disability or are underprivileged.

The charity notes that they have been inundated with applications for iPads. Candidates are reminded that funding can only be considered for the iPad 2 16GB for a child over the age of five subject to specific circumstances (mainly where request is supported by the child's school). For more details see the Lifeline 4 Kids website or contact the charity.

School-Home Support (SHS) Service UK

£18,000

Correspondent: Welfare Fund Coordinator, Cityside House, 40–42 Adler Street, Whitechapel, London E1 1EE (020 7426 5025 (on Thursdays and Fridays only); email: welfarefund@shs.org.uk; website: www.schoolhomesupport.org.uk)

CC Number: 1084696

Eligibility

Children and families in need working with SHS practitioners.

Types of grants

One-off payments for essential living costs and basic household items. Grants may be made for food, white goods, school uniforms, furniture and so on.

Annual grant total

In 2012/13 the charity held assets of £546,000 and had an income of £3.6 million. Our research suggests that about £18,000 is available in grants each year from the welfare fund of the charity, usually broken down into monthly budgets.

Applications

Applications must be made on behalf of families by their SHS practitioner. For more information contact the welfare fund coordinator by telephone (Mondays and Fridays only) or by email. The trustees meet four times a year.

Other information

SHS works with over 750 schools around the country helping to get children with complex needs and difficult backgrounds into school and ready to learn. Provision of human resources and services is the main activity of the charity.

Eliza Shepherd Charitable Trust

£1,000

Correspondent: Carol Shepherd, Trustee, Southview Cottage, Islington Road, Islington, Alton, Hampshire GU34 4PR (01420 520375)

CC Number: 1064464

Eligibility

Children and young people who are in need.

Types of grants

Grants awarded according to need.

Annual grant total

In 2012/13, the trust had an income of £2,000 and a total expenditure of £2,100. We estimate that the total amount of grants awarded to individuals was approximately £1,000 as the trust also awards grants to organisations.

Applications

In writing to the correspondent.

S. C. Witting Trust

£5,000 (50 grants)

Correspondent: The Administrator, Friends House, 173 Euston Road, London NW1 2BJ

CC Number: 237698

Eligibility

Individuals in need in England either under the age of 16 or over the age of 60.

Types of grants

One-off grants.

Annual grant total

In 2013 the trust gave 50 grants of £100.

Exclusions

No grants towards debts or loans.

Applications

Applications:

- Must be made in writing by social workers or equivalent
- The applications must give a short case history, reasons for need and amount needed
- Applications are considered monthly and unsuccessful applications will not be acknowledged unless a stamped address envelope is provided
- No telephone calls
- No emails

Other information

Grants are also made to individuals for educational purposes.

Ethnic and national minorities in the UK

Prisoners of Conscience Appeal Fund

£81,500 (130 grants)

Correspondent: The Grants Officer, PO Box 61044, London SE1 1UP (020 7407 6644; fax: 020 7407 6655; email: info@prisonersofconscience.org; website: www.prisonersofconscience.org)

CC Number: 213766

Eligibility

Prisoners of conscience and/or their families, who have suffered persecution for their beliefs. The fact that the person is seeking asylum or has been a victim of civil war is not sufficient grounds in itself.

Types of grants

One-off grants ranging from £350 to £500 for the provision of food, clothing, toiletries, travel costs, basic furniture, counselling/therapy sessions, family reunion costs, medical needs which are not supplied by the NHS such as orthopaedic beds or repairs to wheelchairs and PLAB or some vocational conversion courses.

Family reunion grants are also available for costs involved with bringing close dependents to join prisoners of conscience in the UK such as flights and visa and DNA testing costs.

Annual grant total

In 2013 relief grants made in the UK for 130 individuals and families totalled £81,500 with bursaries for 12 individuals totalling an additional £46,000.

Exclusions

No support is given to people who have used or advocated violence or supported a violent organisation.

Applications

Application forms are available from the correspondent and should be submitted by a third party such as human rights organisations, refugee groups, solicitors and organisations in the UK and overseas, from large NGOs to small refugee community organisations. Applicants who do not know of a third party organisation that they can submit an application through should contact the fund for advice. Applications should include evidence of identification of the applicant and of costs.

Family reunion grants are considered for times a year in January, April, July and October and applications should be submitted by the preceding month. Other grants are considered.

Other information

The fund was initially established in 1962 as the relief arm of Amnesty International, but is now a charity in its own right. It is the only agency in the UK making grants specifically to prisoners of conscience – individuals who have been persecuted for their conscientiously-held beliefs, provided that they have not used or advocated violence. Grant recipients include political prisoners, human rights defenders, lawyers, environmental activists, teachers and academics who come from many different countries such as Burma, Zimbabwe, Sri Lanka, Tibet, Iran, Cameroon and Eritrea.

The charity's aim is to raise and distribute money to help them and/or their families rehabilitate themselves during and after their ordeal. Financial grants cover general hardship relief, furniture, medicines, travel costs, family reunion costs, education, requalification and resettlement costs and medical treatment and counselling after torture.

The Pusinelli Convalescent and Holiday Home

£5,200

Correspondent: David Leigh, Administrator, Leigh Saxton Green, 4–7 Manchester Street, London W1U 3AE (020 7486 5553; email: enquiries@lsg-ca.co.uk)

CC Number: 239734

Eligibility

People who are or were German citizens and their dependents. Applicants must live in Greater London, Essex, Hertfordshire, Kent or Surrey.

Types of grants

Grants of up to £500 for families who would not otherwise be able to have a holiday.

Annual grant total

In 2012/13, the home had an income of £6,800 and a total expenditure of £5,400. We estimate that the total amount of grants awarded to individuals was approximately £5,200.

Applications

Applications should be made to the correspondent directly from the individual or from any welfare agency on their behalf.

The Society of Friends of Foreigners in Distress

£15,000

Correspondent: Valerie Goodhart, Trustee, 68 Burhill Road, Hersham, Walton-on-Thames KT12 4JF (01932 244916; email: vkgoodhart@gmail.com)

CC Number: 212593

Eligibility

People living in London or its surrounding area who are from countries which are not in the Commonwealth, the USA or which were not once part of the British Empire.

Types of grants

Pensions and one-off grants can be awarded for electrical goods, clothing, living costs, household bills, food, travel expenses and repatriation, furniture and equipment for disabilities.

Annual grant total

In 2012/13 the society had an income of £12,500 and a total expenditure of £18,500. We estimate that grants to individuals totalled around £15,000.

Applications

In writing to the correspondent at any time. Applications should be submitted by a social worker, Citizens Advice or other welfare agency.

Tollard Trust

£1,100

Correspondent: Jacqueline Carlyle Clarke, Trustee, Tollard Green Farm, Tollard Royal, Salisbury, Wiltshire SP5 5PX (01725 516323)

CC Number: 327369

Eligibility

People in need who live in Bournemouth, Poole and elsewhere in Dorset and live in their own homes, with a particular focus on the elderly and those with disabilities. Applicants should be, or should have been: chemists; members of the clergy; ex-services and service people; farmers; legal professionals; masons; medical professionals; musicians; research workers; seafarers and fishermen; and textile workers and designers.

Grants are also available for older people from Asia and Africa who are disabled or in financial need.

Types of grants

Recurrent grants, typically of around £100, towards items, services or facilities.

Annual grant total

In 2012/13 the trust had an income of £7,100 and a total expenditure of £1,200. We estimate that grants for individuals totalled £1,100, the majority of which were distributed through other charities.

Exclusions

No grants are made for education and training, including expeditions or scholarships.

Applications

Grants are made once a year, usually in November. Most grants are in answer to requests from charities, for example, Salvation Army, Pramacare, RUKBA, Greenhill, McDougall and other local charities. Only very occasionally are grants made directly to individuals.

Assyrians

The Assyrian Charity and Relief Fund of UK

£100

Correspondent: Revd Henry Shaheen, Administrator, 277 Rush Green Road, Romford RM7 0JL (01708 730122; email: henry.andrew.shaheen@gmail.com)

CC Number: 1050419

Eligibility

People of Assyrian descent living in UK or worldwide who are in need, hardship or distress.

Types of grants

The fund offers food, medicine and temporary shelter to people in need. One-off and recurrent grants are made usually ranging between £10 and £400.

Annual grant total

In 2013/14 the trust had both an income and a total expenditure of £200. We estimate that social welfare grants to individuals totalled £100.

Exclusions

No grants are available for business people, political organisations, those already settled in Europe, America, Australia and Canada or those financially secure.

Applications

In writing to the correspondent, submitted through a social worker, Citizens Advice, welfare agency or other charity.

Belgians

Royal Belgian Benevolent Society

£1,000

Correspondent: Michel Vanhoonacker, Trustee, 8 Northumberland Avenue, London WC2N 5BY (020 7127 4292; email: events@blcc.co.uk)

CC Number: 233435

Eligibility

Belgian nationals who live in Britain, and their close dependents.

Types of grants

Previously grants were given in the range of £300–£2,000.

Annual grant total

In 2013 the society had an income of £1,300 and a total expenditure of £2,300. We estimate that support to individuals for welfare needs totalled around £1,000.

Applications

The correspondent has informed us that the scheme is on hold and applications are not accepted for the foreseeable future. For the time being enquiries to the society are not welcomed.

Other information

Note: the scheme is currently on hold and applications are not invited.

Grants are also made for educational purposes.

Dutch

The Netherlands' Benevolent Society

£14,500 (18 grants)

Correspondent: Bernadijn van Acker, Administrator, PO Box 858, Bognor Regis PO21 9HS (01932 355885; fax: 01932 355885; email: info@koningwillemfonds.org.uk; website: www.koningwillemfonds.org.uk)

CC Number: 213032

Eligibility

People in need who are Dutch nationals or of Dutch extraction and living in the UK. Assistance may also be given to widows, widowers and dependents of Dutch nationals.

Types of grants

One-off grants ranging between £100 to £1,000 and regular allowances of £80 per month. In the past grants have included payments for: debts to allow someone to make a 'fresh start'; essential home repairs; clothing; basic living items; and the costs of a training course where they lead to employment.

Annual grant total

In 2012 the trust had assets of £859,000 and an income of over £,44,000. Grants were made to 18 individuals (of 34 applications received) totalling £14,500. The 2012 accounts were the latest available at the time of writing (August 2014).

Exclusions

Beneficiaries must not have access to financial help from other sources.

Applications

On a form available from the society administrator. Applications are usually made through churches, the Netherlands Embassy, the Netherlands Consulates, the Department of Work and Pensions regional offices or welfare charities. They are considered every month, except in August, at the trustees' monthly meeting, although emergency cases may be considered sooner. Information of the individual's financial situation, including details of any social security benefits, should be included.

Germans

The German Society of Benevolence

£6,200

Correspondent: David Leigh, Administrator, Leigh Saxton Green, 4–7 Manchester Street, London W1U 3AE (email: info@gwc-london.org.uk)

CC Number: 247379

Eligibility

Older people in need who are, or were, citizens of Germany, and their dependents. Applicants must live in Greater London, Essex, Hertfordshire, Kent or Surrey.

Types of grants

Small one-off and recurrent grants for heating, clothing and other needs.

Annual grant total

In 2012/13 the society had an income of £8,200 and a total expenditure of £6,400. We estimate that grants to individuals totalled £6,200.

Applications

Applications are considered from individuals or from agencies acting on their behalf.

Indians

India Welfare Society

£3,500

Correspondent: Suresh Gupta, President, 11 Middle Row, London W10 5AT (020 8969 9493; email: iwslondon@hotmail.com; website: www.indiawelfaresociety.org)

CC Number: 286800

Eligibility

Members of the Indian community, who have membership with the society, and are in need.

Types of grants

One-off and recurrent grants according to need for hardship and welfare purposes only.

Annual grant total

In 2013, the society had an income of £8,500 and a total expenditure of £7,000. We estimate that the total amount of grants awarded to individuals was approximately £3,500 as the society also awards grants for other charitable purposes.

Applications
In writing to the correspondent.

Swiss

The Swiss Benevolent Society

£19,500

Correspondent: Petra Kehr Cocks, Welfare Officer, 79 Endell Street, London WC2H 9DY (020 7836 9119; fax: 020 7379 1096; email: info@swissbenevolent.org.uk; website: www.swissbenevolent.org.uk)

CC Number: 1111348

Eligibility
Swiss citizens who are experiencing hardship and are temporarily or permanently resident in the consular district of London. In special cases, those living in other parts of the UK may also receive assistance.

Types of grants
Monthly pensions and one-off grants towards holidays, heating costs, travel to and from day centres, therapies, household equipment, telephone and TV licences, for example.

Annual grant total
In 2013 the society had an income of £57,000 and a total expenditure of £50,000. Grants to individuals totalled £19,500.

Applications
In writing to the welfare officer including proof of nationality. Applications can be submitted directly by the individual, through an organisation such as Citizens Advice or via any third party. They are considered at any time.

Other information
The trust has a welfare officer who also supports beneficiaries through: providing advice, counselling and support; offering advocacy with various agencies; co-ordinating overall care; and arranging visits from volunteers to homes, hospitals and nursing homes.

Zimbabweans

The Rhodesians Worldwide Assistance Fund

£15,000

Correspondent: The Administrator, PO Box 213, Lingfield, Surrey RH7 6WW (email: ian@12buzz.com; website: zrwaf.com)

CC Number: 802274

Eligibility
People formerly resident in Zimbabwe who are in need, and their widows and dependents.

Types of grants
One-off grants are given to meet short-term needs. Recent grants have paid for riser recliner chairs, stair lifts, specialised wheelchairs, furniture and rental deposits.

Annual grant total
In 2012/13 the fund had an income of £12,500 and a total expenditure of £33,000. We have estimated total grants to individuals for social welfare purposes to be in the region of £15,000.

Exclusions
No grants are given for education, debts, business expenditure, house repairs, motor vehicles, legal expenses, foreign travel or medical expenses.

Applications
On a form available from the correspondent or to download from the fund's website. Applicants will need to prove their former residence in Zimbabwe and their right to remain in the UK. Applications can be submitted directly by the individual or through another charity or close relative. Trustees meet four times a year to consider applications, though urgent cases can be dealt with between meetings.

Zimbabwe Rhodesia Relief Fund

£10,000

CC Number: 326922

Eligibility
Zimbabweans living worldwide who are distressed or sick.

Types of grants
One-off and recurrent grants of around £70 to £300.

Annual grant total
In 2012/13 the fund had an income of £18,000 and a total expenditure of £22,000. We estimate that grants to individuals totalled £10,000, with Zimbabwe-based charitable organisations also receiving funding.

Exclusions
Grants are not given for educational purposes or for travel.

Applications
In writing to the correspondent. Applications should be made through somebody known to the charity and include proof of past or present Zimbabwean citizenship.

Holidays

The Family Holiday Association

£660,000 (2,092 grants)

Correspondent: Paula Wilkinson, Grant and Project Officer, 3 Gainsford Street, London SE1 2NE (020 3117 0651; fax: 020 7323 7299; email: grantofficer@familyholidayassociation.org.uk; website: www.fhaonline.org.uk)

CC Number: 800262

Eligibility
Families who are referred by social workers, health visitors or other caring agencies as desperate for a holiday break. Applicants must be on a low income, not have had a holiday within the past four years (unless there are exceptional circumstances) and have at least one child aged between 3 and 18.

Types of grants
Day trips, short breaks and week-long holidays. Holidays are generally for holiday parks in the UK such as Haven or Butlins. Breaks include accommodation, linen rental (where available), entertainment passes and holiday insurance (subject to medical conditions). The charity may also make a contribution towards holiday expenses.

Annual grant total
In 2012/13 the charity held assets of £860,000 and had an income of £1.2 million. Holidays for a record number of 2,092 families amounted to £660,000.

Exclusions
The Family Holiday Association regrets that it is not in a position to help families with no recourse to public funds or those in receipt of foster care payments.

Applications
Through the online application form or on a paper form available to download from the association's website. The association does state that online applications are processed much faster. Applications can be submitted from 1 November for holidays in the following year. The association usually has enough applications to commit all its funds by December. Applications must be referred by a welfare agency or voluntary organisation.

Note the following from the charity's website: 'All communications and payments relating to the family's application will be through the referring agent.' The referring agent must be prepared to assist families with every stage of the application and holiday booking process.

The Victoria Convalescent Trust

£97,000

Correspondent: Mrs A. J. Perkins, The Grants Co-ordinator, 11 Cavendish Avenue, Woodford Green, Essex IG8 9DA (020 8502 9339)

CC Number: 1064585

Eligibility

People in medical need of convalescence, recuperative and respite care in England and Wales. Preference is given to people living in Surrey and Croydon.

Types of grants

Grants of up to £400 for services and equipment; and up to £900 for recuperative holidays and respite care.

Annual grant total

In 2013 the trust had an income of £119,000 and a total expenditure of £141,000. Grants to individuals totalled £97,000 of which, more than £87,000 was for convalescence and respite purposes.

Applications

On a form available from the correspondent. Applications must be submitted through a social worker, a health care worker or a welfare agency or another professional worker and will be considered every month. Medical and social reports supporting the need for a break must be provided.

Other information

Occasionally, support is given to women living in Greater London for vital equipment and services.

Vitalise

See entry on page 40

Homelessness

Housing the Homeless Central Fund

£44,000 (225 grants)

Correspondent: The Clerk to the Trustees, 2A Orchard Road, Sidcup DA14 6RD (email: hhcfund@gmail.com)

CC Number: 233254

Eligibility

People who are either homeless or have serious accommodation problems. Priority may be given to expectant parents or those with children.

Types of grants

One-off grants of £100 to £300 for household items and fuel bills. Recent grants have paid for cots and beds, clothing, and rent arrears.

Annual grant total

In 2012/13 the fund held assets of £343,000 and had an income of £58,000. Individuals received 225 grants, totalling £44,000.

Exclusions

No recurrent grants are given or grants for holidays, medical apparatus, funeral expenses, travel costs, vehicles, educational expenses, structural improvements to property, rent deposits, toys, computers or televisions.

Applications

Guidelines and application forms should be requested by and will be sent to a third party organisation, on headed paper and enclosing an sae. Decisions are usually made within a week, although no grants are made in March or December. Note: telephone calls will not be accepted and applications must be made through a representative of a recognised third party organisation for example Citizens Advice, social services or another welfare organisation.

Older people

Age Sentinel Trust

£11,600

Correspondent: Francesca Colverson, Head of Fundraising, Longreach, Clay Lane, Chichester PO19 3PX (020 8144 4774; email: agesentineltrust@googlemail.com; website: agesentinel.org.uk)

CC Number: 1133624

Eligibility

People over 60, who are living on a low income. Priority is given to people with dementia, particularly Alzheimer's disease, and those with other debilitating illnesses.

Types of grants

One-off and recurrent grants to help people through a financial crisis or to pay for services, such as emergency home repairs, access improvements, maintenance and gardening costs.

Annual grant total

In 2012/13, the trust had an income of £50,000 and a total expenditure of £54,000. The trust awarded £23,000 to both organisations and individuals and we estimate that £11,600 of that total was awarded directly to individuals.

Applications

On a form available from the correspondent.

Aid for the Aged in Distress (AFTAID)

£38,500

Correspondent: Susan Elson, Trustee, Begbies Chettle Agar, Epworth House, 25 City Road, London EC1Y 1AR (0870 803 1950; fax: 0870 803 2128; email: info@aftaid.org.uk; website: www.aftaid.org.uk)

CC Number: 299276

Eligibility

UK citizens who are over 65, reside in the UK, are living on a low income and have minimal savings.

The trust's accounts state that, 'an increasing number of applications that are received are having to be declined as they fall outside the charity's remit and criteria. Unfortunately, this creates additional administration costs and a drain on resources.'

Types of grants

Emergency grants for essential items to facilitate the beneficiary to maintain their independence in the familiar surroundings of their home, for example heating appliances, bedding, cookers, washing machines or other white goods, essential furniture and carpets. Grants are also made towards more expensive items such as a stair lift, walk-in shower, motorised scooter and so on. Applications can sometimes be considered towards costs for an elderly carer to enjoy a respite break.

Grants are paid directly to the supplier of the goods or services.

Annual grant total

In 2012 the charity held assets of £383,000 and had an income of £64,000. Grants for elderly people totalled £38,500 with 'grant vetting, approval and support costs' totalling £19,500. The 2012 accounts were the latest available at the time of writing (August 2014).

Exclusions

Grants cannot be made for any ongoing payments, arrears or debts of any kind.

Applications

On a form available through the charity's website. Applicants will initially need to fill in an online form which will automatically issue the application form by return email.

Applications can be made directly by the individual or through a welfare organisation and should include written support from a social worker, doctor or similar professional of the official care services who are personally aware of the beneficiary's situation.

Barchester Healthcare Foundation

£38,000 (59 grants)

Correspondent: Grants Management Team, Suite 201, Second Floor, Design Centre East, Chelsea Harbour, London SW10 0XF (0800 328 3328; fax: 020 7352 2229; email: info@bhcfoundation.org.uk; website: www.bhcfoundation.org.uk)

CC Number: 1083272

Eligibility

Older people over the age of 65 and adults over the age of 18 with a physical or mental disability living in England, Scotland and Wales. In 2014 the main focus is on the elderly.

Types of grants

One-off grants of between £100 and £5,000 can be given according to need. The foundation specifies that applications encouraging the person's mobility, independence and improved quality of life are favoured. Awards have previously been made for specialist equipment, electric wheelchairs, riser/recliner chairs, stair lifts, mobility scooters, computers and other I.T. equipment, holidays and respite breaks, outings, transportation, home security, disability related house and car adaptations or repairs, household goods (where related to medical condition) and so on.

Annual grant total

At the time of writing (August 2014) the latest financial information available was from 2012. In 2012 the foundation had assets of £60,000 and an income of £167,000. Grants to 59 individuals totalled £38,000.

Exclusions

Grants are not made:

- Retrospectively
- To candidates who have received a grant within the previous three years
- For services offered in a care home operated by Barchester Healthcare or by any other company
- Towards home repairs and alterations not related to disability/medical condition
- For basic household items (white goods, furniture, carpets) not related to disability/medical condition
- For daily living costs (rent, utility bills, clothing and so on)
- To repay debts

Applications

Applications can be filled in online on the foundation's website or a form can be downloaded and submitted to the correspondent. All applications must be supported by a third party sponsor, for example, a health or social care professional, social worker or charity representative. The trustees meet quarterly, although applications can be dealt with between meetings.

Applicants can expect a response within ten weeks; however the foundation is unable to acknowledge the receipt of postal applications.

Other information

Support is also given in grants to small community groups and local charities (£59,000 to 57 organisations in 2012).

The Percy Bilton Charity

£145,000 (1,062 grants)

Correspondent: Tara Smith, Administrator, Bilton House, 7 Culmington Road, Ealing, London W13 9NB (020 8579 2829; fax: 020 8579 3650; website: www.percybiltoncharity.org.uk)

CC Number: 1094720

Eligibility

People who are on a low income and are either over 65 years old, have a physical or learning disability, or are receiving hospital or other medical treatment for a long-term illness (including mental illness).

Types of grants

One-off grants of up to £200 for specific essential items only. For example, laundry equipment, cooking and heating appliances, basic furniture, beds and bedding, floor coverings, clothing and footwear, and other essential household items.

Annual grant total

In 2012/13 the charity held assets of £21.8 million and had an income of £765,000. A total of £145,000 was awarded in 1062 grants to individuals. The charity also distributed 2,010 Christmas food parcels, amounting to £44,000.

Organisations were awarded a further £452,000 in 189 grants.

Exclusions

No payments are made towards items costing over £200, travel expenses, sponsorship, holidays, respite care, educational grants, computer equipment or software, house alterations and maintenance (including adaptations for disabled facilities), debts, dishwashers, reimbursement of costs for articles already purchased, garden fencing or clearance, motor vehicle purchase or expenses, nursing and residential home fees, funeral expenses, removal expenses, medical treatment or therapy, and course fees including driving or IT lessons. No repeat grants within a 12 month period.

Applications

On a form available from the correspondent to be submitted by a social worker, community psychiatric nurse or occupational therapist, including a covering letter on local or health authority headed paper. The correspondent should be contacted by telephone to request an application form which will be sent by email. A full list of guidelines is available from the charity's website. Applicants should wait for four weeks before contacting the charity to check the progress of an application.

Note: the charity is unable to respond to applications made by anyone other than a social worker or occupational therapist or to requests which fall outside the charity's funding criteria. Applicants should also ensure that they have applied to all statutory sources and any appropriate specialist charities (e.g. employment related funds and armed forces funds) before approaching the charity. Successful applicants should not reapply within 12 months of receiving a grant.

Monica Eyre Memorial Foundation

£1,500

Correspondent: Michael Bidwell, Trustee, 5 Clifton Road, Winchester, Hampshire SO22 5BN

CC Number: 1046645

Eligibility

People in need, particularly older people and people with disabilities/special needs in the UK.

Types of grants

Grants are made to enable people with low-mobility in residential care to get a holiday with essential carer support.

Annual grant total

In 2012/13 the trust had an income of £5,500 and a total expenditure of £5,000. We estimate the grant total for individuals for social welfare purposes was around £1,500.

Applications

In writing to the correspondent.

Other information

The trust also makes grants to organisations and to individuals for educational purposes.

Friends of the Elderly

£432,000 (1,278 grants)

Correspondent: Supporting Friends Team, 40–42 Ebury Street, London SW1W 0LZ (020 7730 8263; fax: 020 7259 0154; email: info@supportingfriends.fote.org.uk; website: www.fote.org.uk)

CC Number: 226064

Eligibility

Men and women who live in England and Wales aged 60 or over (over 50 for homeless people), with low income and with limited savings (£3,000 maximum savings for individuals, £4,500 for couples) are eligible for support. The trust cannot help people living in residential care or those living in Scotland.

Types of grants

One-off grants are given for essential items such as basic furniture, flooring and household appliances. The charity can also assist with utility bills, household repairs and adaptations and mobility aids.

The charity also distributes allowances, on a monthly or twice yearly basis, to support older people on low incomes in maintaining their independence. Payments of regular allowances are arranged to suit the individual. The charity maintains contact with recipients of regular payments through telephone calls, letters, and cards and presents at birthdays and Christmas.

Annual grant total

In 2012/13 the charity held assets of £32.7 million and had an income of £29.2 million. Welfare grants to 1,278 elderly individuals totalled £432,000. Of these grants, 963 people received one-off payments and 315 were in receipt of regular allowances.

Exclusions

Unfortunately, the charity can only help applicants living in England or Wales and cannot help those living in residential care. Grants are not available for items already purchased, council tax, rent arrears or care homes fees.

Applications

On a form available to download from the charity's website. Applications should be made through a third party organisation such as social services, Citizens Advice, Age UK or another welfare agency. The role of the referral organisation is to assist with the application process, providing confirmation of the applicant's circumstances and supporting the purchase of the required item or service. The charity aims to respond within two weeks of receiving the application. Unsuccessful applicants may be signposted to other possible sources of funding.

The charity welcomes enquiries from potential applicants.

Other information

The charity offers a range of care and support options for its elderly beneficiaries through residential homes, community nursing, befriending schemes and dementia support. A main aim of the charity is to reduce the level of isolation amongst elderly people, which is something its 'Phoning Friends' telephone service aspires to do.

In 2012/13 the charity helped older people to claim almost £97,000 in benefits they were eligible for through its provision of welfare advice and assistance. 2,251 isolated older people also benefitted from attending a social event or holiday organised by grassroots organisations supported by the charity.

Home Warmth for the Aged

£19,000

Correspondent: William Berentemfel, Administrator, 19 Towers Wood, South Darenth, Dartford DA4 9BQ (01322 863836; email: w.berentemfel@btinternet.com)

CC Number: 271735

Eligibility

People of pensionable age, at risk from the cold in winter who have no resources other than their state pension/income support and have savings of less than £4,000.

Types of grants

Provision of heating appliances, bedding, clothing and solid fuel. Grants are also available to pay fuel debts where the supply has been disconnected; these are one-off grants only, typically ranging between £90 and £250.

Annual grant total

In 2012/13 the trust had an income of £15,900 and an expenditure of £19,500. We estimate that grants to individuals totalled £19,000.

Exclusions

No grants are made to people who have younger members of their family living with them.

Applications

On a form available from the correspondent, to be submitted only through social workers, doctors, nurses, etc. to whom grants are returned for disbursement. If there is an armed forces connection, applications should be made through SSAFA (see service section of this guide). Applications made directly by individuals are not considered. Applications are considered monthly.

Independent Age

£597,000

Correspondent: Advice Service, 6 Avonmore Road, London W14 8RL (0800 319 6789; fax: 020 7605 4201; email: advice@independentage.org; website: www.independentage.org)

CC Number: 210729

Eligibility

People who are over the state retirement age who are lonely or isolated and find themselves in financial need. Preference is given to individuals who will benefit most from long-term support.

Types of grants

One-off grants are made towards, for example, unexpected, emergency expenses and items which it is often difficult to budget for. The charity has previously stated that 'there is no definitive list of what and how much is awarded, and each grant is considered individually, on the basis of need.' Grants may be made for things like household repairs and maintenance; white goods; convalescence and respite care; spectacles and dental treatment. Parcels of clothing and toiletries are also distributed to those entering hospital and warm packs are given to help older people through the cold winter months.

Annual grant total

In 2013 the charity spent £597,000 (excluding staff and non-staff support costs) on the provision of grants and other services for older people.

As part of its activities during the year, the charity supported beneficiaries with 1,456 grants for one-off emergencies, distributed 2,569 emergency packs (bedding packs, hospital packs, warm packs) and gave 695 members each a Christmas pack.

Exclusions

Grants are only available to existing beneficiaries.

Applications

Financial assistance is given as part of a holistic service whereby a caseworker will work with the individual to assess and help address their issues. Initial contact should be made through the advice line (0845 262 1863) or by emailing advice@independentage.org.

The charity is no longer taking on new commitments for regular payments. note the following from its 2013 annual report: 'Independent Age is not commencing any new regular payments going forward; it will only continue to manage the existing regular payment commitments.'

Other information

The charity provides information, advice and practical help through its network of staff and dedicated volunteers across the UK. The website also offers a range of helpful publications relevant to older people.

The broader range of services now offered by the charity is in part due to the merger with two other older people's charities, Counsel and Care and Universal Beneficent Society.

The Heinz, Anna and Carol Kroch Foundation

£80,000 (664 grants)

Correspondent: Beena Astle, Administrator, PO Box 462, Teddington TW11 1BS (020 8977 5534; fax: 01524 262721; email: hakf50@hotmail.com)

CC Number: 207622

Eligibility

People who are older, have a chronic illness, have fled domestic situations or are homeless and are in financial hardship.

Types of grants

One-off grants typically ranging from £100 to £500 towards hospital travel costs, household bills, furniture, other hospital expenses, clothing, food, medical and disability equipment, living costs, home adaptations, help in the home and so on.

Annual grant total

In 2012/13 the foundation held assets of £5.7 million and had an income of £178,000. A total of £80,000 was awarded in 664 grants to individuals.

Exclusions

No grants for education or holidays.

Applications

In writing to the correspondent. Most applications are submitted through other charities and local authorities. Applications should include full financial information including income and expenditure, what the grant will be used for and a why it is needed. Applicants should also state if they have approached any other charities for financial assistance and how successful they have been to date. Applications are considered monthly.

Morden College

£204,000

Correspondent: Major-General David Rutherford-Jones, Clerk, Clerk's House, 19 St German's Place, Blackheath, London SE3 0PW (020 8463 8330; email: TheClerk@mordencollege.org; website: www.mordencollege.org)

CC Number: 215551

Eligibility

People in need who are aged over 50, from a professional or managerial background, who have retired from paid employment either on medical grounds or because they have reached the statutory retirement age.

Types of grants

One-off grants and quarterly allowances.

Annual grant total

In 2012/13 the charity held assets of £208.3 million and had an income of £10.8 million. A total of £204,000 was awarded in grants and outpensions to individuals.

Exclusions

The charity does not give for nursing home top up fees or any services or products which should be funded by statutory authorities.

Applications

On a form available from the correspondent, online or to download from the charity's website. Applications must include details of the applicant's income and expenditure as well as their employment history. Applicants are means tested to ensure they are in need of assistance.

Other information

Morden College is the general title used for the administration of Sir John Morden's Charity and Dame Susan Morden's Charity. Sir John Morden's Charity provides grants and accommodation for the elderly. Dame Susan Morden's Charity is primarily concerned with the advancement of religion by assisting the Church of England with the upkeep of their churches and associated activities.

The charity runs a care home for beneficiaries no longer capable of living independently as well as accommodation for independent and supported living.

The National Benevolent Charity

£217,000 (198+368 grants)

Correspondent: Dawn Swirczek, Administrator, National Benevolent Institution, Peter Herve House, Eccles Court, Tetbury, Gloucestershire GL8 8EH (01666 505500; fax: 01666 503111; email: office@thenbc.org.uk; website: www.thenbc.org.uk)

CC Number: 212450

Eligibility

The National Benevolent Charity assists people who have fallen into poverty, through no fault of their own, and who cannot escape that poverty because of age, illness, disability or some other substantial reason.

To be eligible for financial assistance an applicant must:

- Be in receipt of all state benefits and have applied to any trade or professional charity/charities that support any medical condition from which they may suffer
- Have been resident in the UK for at least 24 months
- Live in their own (owned or rented) home
- Have less than £10,000 in assets (excluding their home) if a single person and less than £15,000 if a couple
- Have a disposable income after certain expenses (such as rent or council tax) of less than £8,000 per year if a single person and less than £12,000 if a couple

Only in exceptional circumstances people under state retirement age will be assisted, for example, if they are in receipt of long-term sickness benefits or Disability Living Allowance (DLA).

Types of grants

The following information was provided by the charity:

> Assistance is available by two methods, and occasionally both. First, single payments can be made to meet urgent needs, such as the cost of replacing appliances, property repairs, the purchase of clothing, etc. Although there is no upper limit, only rarely will a single payment be more than £500. Second, regular weekly payments can made, for 12 or maybe 24 months, sometimes longer, to help someone through a difficult time in their life.

In 2012 the regular payments were at £15 per week for a single person and up to £20 per week for a couple (for those who are not in receipt of the state retirement pension at £20 for singles and £25 for couples).

Annual grant total
At the time of writing (August 2014) the latest financial information available was from 2012. In 2012 the charity had assets of £10.6 million and an income of £782,000. Grants were made totalling £217,000. Out of that sum £148,000 was paid in regular assistance to 198 people and further £69,000 was paid in 170 one-off grants.

Exclusions
Grants are not available for nursing home, social or private healthcare fees. Repayments of debts will not normally be considered.

Applications
Application forms are available to download from the website or can be collected from the charity's office at Peter Herve House or by calling 01666 505500. Applications should be supported by one or more referees, for example, a doctor, nurse, social worker, local clergyman or an advice worker. Financial documentation (bank, benefit statements and so on) will need to be provided, together with any other information relating to health, disability or different exceptional circumstances. The Welfare Committee meets to consider application every couple of months. In special cases urgent requests may be considered.

Other information
The charity also operates residential properties in Tetbury, Westgate-on-Sea and Old Windsor, providing accommodation for people over 50 who are in financial need.

Note the following from the charity's website: 'Each year The National Benevolent Charity receives many more applications for financial assistance than it has funds available for distribution. For the time being, preference is given to applicants who do not meet the qualifications of other benevolence charities.'

NBFA (National Benevolent Fund for the Aged)

£72,000

Correspondent: Cherry Bushell, Executive Director, 32 Buckingham Palace Road, London SW1W 0RE (020 7828 0200; email: info@nbfa.org.uk; website: www.nbfa.org.uk)

CC Number: 243387

Eligibility
For TENS pain relief machines applicants must be over 65, on a low income (up to £190 individual income per week), must have received relevant medical advice and must not be fitted with a pacemaker.

For away breaks applicants must be over 65, on a low income, not have been on holiday for three years or more, and to be mobile enough to get on and off a coach.

For telephone alarms applicants must be over 60, on a low income and have no access to any other alarm system or provider.

Types of grants
Short (five-day) breaks, pain relief equipment and low-cost emergency telephone alarms.

Annual grant total
In 2012/13 the fund had an income of £72,000 and a total expenditure of £163,000. During this financial year, the fund spent £72,000 (direct costs) on the provision of holidays and emergency alarms for beneficiaries.

Applications
For away breaks and pain relief machines applicants should contact the trust by phone. Application forms for TENS pain relief machines are available to download from the charity's website, though applicants must consult their physiotherapist for advice before submitting an application.

The Nottingham Aged Persons' Trust

See entry on page 314

The Roger Pilkington Young Trust

£47,000 (83 grants)

Correspondent: Ben Dixon, Trustee, c/o Everys Solicitors, Magnolia House, Church Street, Exmouth, Devon EX8 1HQ (01395 264384; email: law@everys.co.uk)

CC Number: 251148

Eligibility
People over 60 years of age whose income has been reduced through no fault of their own, but prior to application was enough for them to live in a 'reasonable degree of comfort'.

Types of grants
Monthly pensions of about £45 for single people and £60 for married couples/civil partners.

Annual grant total
In 2012/13, the trust had assets of £1.4 million and an income of £62,000. Grants were made to 71 individuals and 12 couples/civil partners totalling £47,000.

Applications
On a form available from the correspondent, after the pensions are advertised.

Other information
Grantmaking is a small part of this charity's activities.

Most of their income goes towards sourcing emergency accommodation and catering facilities where there is no alternative provision. They also provide Christian pastoral and practical support; and access to specialist advice and counselling, in relation to the full range of welfare issues, including problems with debt; alcohol and drugs; benefit and employment issues; stress and family and relationship difficulties; sickness and bereavement.

The Florence Reiss Trust for Old People

£4,900

Correspondent: Dr Stephen Reiss, Trustee, 94 Tinwell Road, Stamford, Lincolnshire PE9 2SD (01780 762710)

CC Number: 236634

Eligibility
Women over 55 and men over 60 who are in need. Priority is given to those who live in the parishes of Streatley in Berkshire and Goring-on-Thames in Oxfordshire.

Types of grants
One-off and recurrent grants according to need.

Annual grant total
In 2012/13, the trust had an income of £9,900 and a total expenditure of £9,900. We estimate that the total grants given to individuals was approximately £4,900 as the trust also gives donations to organisations concerned with the welfare of the elderly.

Applications
In writing to the correspondent.

The Stanley Stein Deceased Charitable Trust

£21,000

Correspondent: Michael Lawson, Trustee, Burwood House, 14–16 Caxton Street, London SW1H 0GY (020 7873 1000; email: michael.lawson@williamsturges.co.uk)

CC Number: 1048873

Eligibility
People over the age of 75 who are experiencing financial hardship or have

health problems, particularly disability, visual or hearing impairment.

Types of grants

One-off and recurrent grants are given according to need. The trust can also help with the provision of equipment and facilities, as well as counselling and advice.

Annual grant total

In 2012/13 the trust had an income of £11,700 and an expenditure of £45,000. We estimate that grants to individuals for welfare purposes totalled around £21,000.

Applications

On a form available from the correspondent.

Other information

Grants are given for both education and welfare causes.

Tancred's Charity for Pensioners

£22,000

Correspondent: Andrew Penny, Clerk, Forsters, 31 Hill Street, London W1J 5LS (020 7863 8522; email: andrew.penny@forsters.co.uk)

CC Number: 229936

Eligibility

Men and women aged 50 or over who are UK citizens and clergy of the Church of England or Church in Wales, or who have been commissioned officers in the armed forces.

Types of grants

Annual pensions of around £2,250 a year are paid quarterly to a limited number of beneficiaries.

Annual grant total

In 2013 the charity had an income of £23,000 and a total expenditure of £28,000. Pensions to individuals totalled £22,000. At the year's end, the charity was assisting ten pensioners, all of whom were retired clergymen.

During 2013, two one-off grants of £500 and £1,000 were approved by the trustees.

Applications

In writing to the correspondent. Individuals may apply at any time, but applications can only be considered when a vacancy occurs, which is approximately once a year.

Other information

The charity is administered along with the Tancred's Educational Foundation.

WaveLength

£68,000

Correspondent: Anny Mills, Applications Officer, 159a High Street, Hornchurch, Essex RM11 3YB (Freephone: 0800 018 2137; fax: 01708 620816; email: info@w4b.org.uk; website: www.wavelength.org.uk)

CC Number: 207400

Eligibility

People who are confined to their bed, largely housebound, elderly or disabled and in financial need.

Types of grants

The provision of radios and televisions. Recently, the charity has moved towards replacing long-term rentals of television sets with donations (1,500 TVs were donated in in 2012/13) as it 'seeks to find a more effective way of meeting its objectives.'

The charity does not provide television licences unless the applicant is in receipt of, or is applying for, equipment from the charity. The charity expects applicants to make provision for any subsequent licences.

Annual grant total

In 2012/13 the charity had an income of £275,000 and a total expenditure of £221,000. During this financial year, the charity spent £68,000 (direct costs) on the provision of radio sets, TV rental and licences to beneficiaries.

Exclusions

No grants to: individuals applying on their own behalf; grantmaking bodies; statutory bodies; top up funding on under-priced contracts.

Applications

On a form available directly from the correspondent or to download from the website. Applications must be submitted through a third party such as a social worker, Citizens Advice, religious organisation or other welfare agency. Applicants must be UK residents and should provide evidence such as passport, birth certificate or citizenship document.

Note: we recommend that third parties applying on behalf of an applicant read the extensive guidelines (available from the charity's website) before an application is submitted.

Other information

The charity was known as the Wireless for the Bedridden Society until 2010.

In special circumstances, the charity may choose to supply equipment to other organisations. In the past, partners have included Women's Aid and the Helen Bamber Foundation.

Williamson Memorial Trust

£2,500

Correspondent: Colin Williamson, Trustee, 6 Windmill Close, Ashington, Pulborough, West Sussex RH20 3LG (01903 893649)

CC Number: 268782

Eligibility

People who are over 65 years of age.

Types of grants

One-off grants of between £20 and £100, given as gifts rather than maintenance. Grants are mainly given at Christmas.

Annual grant total

In 2012/13 the trust had both an income of £9,300 and a total expenditure of £10,000. Grants are made for education and welfare purposes to individuals and organisations. We estimate the total of grants awarded to individuals for social welfare purposes was around £2,500.

Applications

Due to a reduction of its funds and the instability of its income, the trust regrets that very few new applications will be considered to ensure it can meet its existing commitments. Support will generally only be given to cases known personally to the trustees and to those individuals the trust has existing commitments with.

Orders

Catenian Benevolent Association

£65,000 (32 grants)

Correspondent: Mark Allanson, Trustee, 2nd Floor, 1 Park House, Station Square, Coventry CV1 2FL (02476 224533; email: contact@thecatenians.com; website: www.thecatenians.com)

CC Number: 214244

Eligibility

Members of the association and their dependents who are in need.

Types of grants

One-off and recurrent grants according to need. Loans are also available.

Annual grant total

In 2012/13 the fund held assets of £8.7 million and had an income of £243,000. Grants to 32 individuals totalled £65,000, with a further £195,000 paid to individuals in non-secured loans.

Applications

In writing to the correspondent. Trustees meet to consider applications four times a year, though urgent applications may be considered between meetings.

Grand Charitable Trust of the Order of Women Freemasons

£6,600

Correspondent: The Administrator, 27 Pembridge Gardens, London W2 4EF (020 7229 2368; website: www.owf.org.uk)

CC Number: 1059151

Eligibility

Women freemasons who are in need.

Types of grants

One-off and recurrent grants to help towards medical, household and living expenses.

Annual grant total

In 2012/13 the trust held assets of £764,000 and had an income of £159,000. Grants were made to individuals totalling £6,600.

The trust's grantmaking activities mainly focused on funding for organisations, with The Adelaide Litten Charitable Trust, which owns sheltered housing properties, receiving £49,000, and outside charities a further £93,000.

Applications

In writing to the correspondent, usually through the local lodge. The trustees meet regularly throughout the year to consider applications.

Other information

The trust is administered through The Order of Women Freemasons which was established as 'The Honourable Fraternity of Antient Masonry' in 20 June 1908. 'Its first Grand Master and driving force was a man – the Rev. Dr. William Frederick Cobb. However, since 1912, the Grand Masters have all been women.' The group altered its name in 1958 to avoid confusion with a similarly named organisation, and has kept it ever since.

The Grand Charity (of Freemasons under the United Grand Lodge of England)

£3.5 million (1,527 grants)

Correspondent: Mike Martin, Senior Masonic Relief Grants Officer, Freemasons Hall, 60 Great Queen Street, London WC2B 5AZ (020 7395 9293; fax: 020 7395 9295; email: mmartin@the-grand-charity.org; website: www.grandcharity.org)

CC Number: 281942

Eligibility

Any freemason, past or present (under the United Grand Lodge of England) in need, their widows, and their immediate dependents.

As a general guide, almost anyone in receipt of pension credit or another means-tested benefit is likely to be eligible; however, assets and capital (not including the home) will be taken into account.

Queries regarding eligibility should be directed towards your Lodge Almoner, Provincial Grand Almoner or the Freemasonry Cares helpline (080003560 90).

Types of grants

Grants are usually made for essential daily living costs and are expected to last for a minimum period of 12 months. In certain circumstances, one-off grants may be made for specific items. Emergency grants may also be made in 'exceptional' circumstances.

Annual grant total

In 2012/13 the charity had assets of £64.5 million and an income of £13.7 million. Masonic relief grants totalled £3.5 million. Of 2,173 applications, 1,527 were successful.

Exclusions

There is no limit to the number of grants an individual may receive over their lifetime, although usually only one grant per year will be made.

Applications

Applicants should first contact their Lodge Almoner or Provincial Grand Almoner who will provide support throughout the application process. Applications can be submitted at any time and a decision is usually reached within four to eight weeks of receipt. The charity has now adopted the use of a joint application form with the Royal Masonic Trust for Girls and Boys and the Masonic Samaritan Fund. The form is designed to make it easier for an applicant to seek support from more than one charity for different types of need at the same time. Details on required supporting documentation can be found on a checklist attached to the form.

For further information on emergency grants, the visiting brother should contact the Director of Masonic Relief Grants.

Current grant recipients will receive a review form prior to the anniversary of the initial application.

Other information

The charity also manages the Relief Chest Scheme. Each 'relief chest' is used to accumulate funds collected by a Lodge, Chapter or Province for charitable purposes. These are then used by the individual Lodges to distribute grants to charities and individuals in need. Applications for these funds should be made through the relevant Lodge, Chapter or Province.

In 2002, the charity took over responsibility for the Transferred Beneficiaries Fund, which makes regular payments to former beneficiaries of the Royal Masonic Benevolent Institution Annuity Fund. This fund is not open to new applications for assistance.

Practical help and financial support for individuals in times personal distress and for local charities is also given independently of the Grand Charity by individual lodges and Provincial Grand Lodges. Addresses are available from the correspondent.

The separate entries for the Royal Masonic Benevolent Institution and the New Masonic Samaritan Fund in this *Guide* may be helpful. There is also the Masonic Trust for Girls and Boys, which helps children of any age (including adopted children and step-children) of Freemasons under the United Grand Lodge of England. (See entry in *The Guide to Educational Grants,* also published by DSC).

The Grand Lodge of Antient, Free and Accepted Masons of Scotland

£155,000

Correspondent: The Trustees, c/o Freemasons Hall, 96 George Street, Edinburgh EH2 3DH (01312 255577; email: curator@grandlodgescotland.org; website: www.grandlodgescotland.com)

SC Number: SC001996

Eligibility

Members and their dependents, and the widows and dependents of deceased members.

Types of grants

One-off and recurrent grants according to need.

Annual grant total

In 2012/13 the trust had an income of £1.3 million. About £155,000 is given in welfare grants each year.

Applications

On a form available from the correspondent, or by direct approach to the local lodge.

Other information

The trust also runs care homes for older people. £25,000 in educational grants were given during the year.

The New Masonic Samaritan Fund

£3.9 million

Correspondent: The Secretary, 60 Great Queen Street, London WC2B 5AZ (020 7404 1550; fax: 020 7404 1544; email: info@msfund.org.uk; website: www.msfund.org.uk)

CC Number: 1130424

Eligibility

Freemasons, their families, dependents and widows or surviving partners who are in both financial and medical need.

Types of grants

One-off grants towards medical, respite, mobility and dental care. Grants have recently been awarded towards, for example, stairlifts, 'wetroom' installations, home care and dentures.

Annual grant total

In 2012/13 the fund held assets of £60.3 million and had an income of £4.25 million. Grants to individuals totalled £3.9 million.

During the year, 1,211 applications were approved.

Exclusions

No grants can be made towards treatment which has already been provided privately, or which can be made through the NHS without undue delay or hardship.

Applications

Potential applicants should initially contact the fund by phone. An Almoner or Visiting Brother will be appointed to assist with every application. Application forms will be sent to the Almoner/Visiting Brother. Once completed and returned a decision is usually made within four weeks.

Other information

> In each of the last five years nearly 50% of the grants made by the MSF have been in support of the wives, widows and dependents of Freemasons.

To access the MSF Counselling Careline, simply call 020 7404 1550. One of the team will assess the caller's eligibility and will then provide a freephone number through which the helpline can be accessed.

The Royal Antediluvian Order of Buffaloes, Grand Lodge of England War Memorial Annuities

£21,000 (81 grants)

Correspondent: The Secretary, Grove House, Skipton Road, Harrogate, North Yorkshire HG1 4LA (01423 502438; email: hq@raobgle.org.uk; website: www.raobgle.org.uk)

CC Number: 220476

Eligibility

Members of the order who are elderly or who have disabilities and their dependents.

Types of grants

Annuities, though the Grand Lodge may have other charitable funds available for one-off grants.

Annual grant total

In 2012/13 the trust held assets of £203,000 and had an income of £29,000. Grants to individuals totalled £21,000.

Applications

Applications should be made through the member's lodge. All assistance originates at the local lodge level; if its resources are inadequate, the lodge may then seek assistance at provincial or ultimately national level. For dependents of deceased members it is necessary to state the lodge to which the member belonged. If its name and number is known the correspondent will probably be able to identify a current local telephone number or address. If only the place is known this may still be possible, but not in all cases (particularly when the lodge concerned does not belong to this Grand Lodge group).

Other information

This fund was established by the Grand Lodge of England as a tribute to members of the order who died during the First World War.

The Grand Lodge also runs two convalescent homes; one in Harrogate and the other in Paignton.

Royal Masonic Benevolent Institution

£53,000

Correspondent: David Innes, Chief Executive, Royal Masonic Benevolent Institution, 60 Great Queen Street, London WC2B 5AZ (020 7596 2400; fax: 020 7404 0724; email: enquries@rmbi.org.uk; website: www.rmbi.org.uk)

CC Number: 207360

Eligibility

Freemasons (usually over 60 years of age, unless unemployed due to incapacity) of the English Constitution (England, Wales and certain areas overseas) and their dependents.

Types of grants

Christmas gifts and annuities.

Annual grant total

In 2012/13 annuities and grants amounted to £53,000.

Applications

On a form available from the correspondent, usually submitted through the lodge of the relevant freemason. Applications are considered every month.

Other information

The institution has a team of welfare visitors covering the whole of England and Wales and also runs 17 homes catering for around 1,000 older freemasons.

Politics

Conservative and Unionist Agents' Benevolent Association

£48,000

Correspondent: Sally Smith, The Hon. Secretary, Conservative Campaign Headquarters, Millbank Tower, 30 Millbank, London SW1P 4DP (020 7984 8172; email: sally.smith@conservatives.com)

CC Number: 216438

Eligibility

Individuals in need who are, or have been, Conservative and Unionist Agents, or Women Organisers, and their dependents. Support is also given to the dependents of deceased Conservative or Unionist Agents or Women Organisers.

Types of grants

Recurrent grants to help with living costs. One-off grants are given towards, for example, roof repairs, emergency plumbing, replacement kitchen equipment, stair-lifts, bathrooms suitable for those with disabilities, and new boilers. Support towards funeral costs, night nursing expenses and emergency medical care may also be given.

Annual grant total

In 2012/13 the association had assets of over £2.7 million and an income of £94,000. Grants were made totalling £58,000. We estimate that around £10,000 was given in educational grants leaving approximately £48,000 for relief-in-need purposes.

Applications

Initial telephone calls are welcomed and application forms are available on request. Applications can be made either directly by the individual, or through a member of the management committee or local serving agent. All beneficiaries are allocated a 'visiting agent'.

Other information

The majority of the association's grants are made for relief-in-need purposes but some help is given to the children of deceased members for the costs of education.

Prisoners/ ex-offenders

The Aldo Trust

£7,000

Correspondent: c/o NACRO, Coast Cottage, 90 Coast Road, West Mersea, Colchester CO5 8LS (01206 383809; fax: 01206 383809; email: owenwheatley@btinternet.com)

CC Number: 327414

Eligibility

People in need who are being held in detention pending their trial or after their conviction. The applicant must still be serving the sentence. Applicants must have less than £25 in private cash.

Types of grants

Grants up to a maximum of £10 a year towards any needs except toiletries and training shoes.

Annual grant total

In 2012 the trust had an income of £33,000 and a total charitable expenditure of £28,700. This was the latest financial information available at the time of writing. The charity supports individuals and organisations for both social welfare and educational purposes. We estimate that grants to individuals for social welfare purposes totalled around £7,000.

Applications

On a form available from the correspondent. Applications must be made through prison service personnel (for example, probation, chaplaincy, education), and should include the name and number of the prisoner, age, length of sentence and expected date of release. No applications direct from prisoners will be considered. Applicants may apply once only in each twelve-month period, and applications are considered monthly.

Other information

NACRO also offers a fund for people on probation; see separate entry in this guide.

The Michael and Shirley Hunt Charitable Trust

£15,000 (102 grants)

Correspondent: D. S. Jenkins, Trustee, Ansty House, Henfield Road, Small Dole, West Sussex BN5 9XH (01903 817116)

CC Number: 1063418

Eligibility

Prisoners and their relatives and dependents, such as their spouses and children.

Types of grants

One-off and recurrent grants for prisoners' families' welfare needs and for travel expenses for prisoners on care leave.

Annual grant total

In 2012/13 the trust had assets of £6 million and an income of £277,000. Grants to 102 individuals totalled £15,000.

A further £50,000 was awarded to charitable organisations.

Applications

In writing to the correspondent. Applications can be made directly by the individual or, where applicable, through a third party such as Citizens Advice, probation service or a social worker.

Other information

The trust also supports animal welfare causes.

The National Association for the Care and Resettlement of Offenders (NACRO)

£25,000

Correspondent: Finance and Corporate Services Director, Unit 4, Park Place, 10–12 Lawn Lane, London SW8 1UD (020 7840 7200; fax: 020 7840 7240; email: helpline@nacro.org.uk; website: www.nacro.org.uk)

CC Number: 226171

Eligibility

Ex-offenders and their partners and families.

Types of grants

One-off grants only, usually of around £50. Only one grant can ever be made to an individual.

Annual grant total

Our research tells us that grants usually total around £50,000 each year. Grants are given for both educational and welfare purposes. We estimate that welfare grants to individuals totalled £25,000.

Applications

Either directly by the individual or through the Probation Service, social service department, Citizens Advice or registered charity. Applications are considered every two months.

Other information

NACRO runs a resettlement advice service to provide information and advice for ex-offenders, their families and people who work with them. Its helpline can be contacted by calling 020 7840 1212 or by emailing helpline@nacro.org.uk.

SACRO Trust

£3,400

Correspondent: The Trust Fund Administrator, 29 Albany Street, Edinburgh EH1 3QN (01316 247270; fax: 01316 247269; email: info@national.sacro.org.uk; website: www.sacro.org.uk)

SC Number: SC023031

Eligibility

People living in Scotland who are subject to a license/court order or who have been released from prison and are in the process of rehabilitation.

Types of grants

Grants are usually to a maximum of £300, although applications for larger sums can be considered. Grants given include those for electrical goods, clothing, furniture, driving lessons and education and training.

Annual grant total

In 2012/13 the trust had an income of £5,300 and awarded 50 grants totalling £7,400. We estimate grants to individuals for social welfare purposes to be around £3,400. The trust also gives grants for educational purposes.

Exclusions

No grants are made where financial help from other sources is available.

Applications

On a form available from the correspondent. Applications can only be accepted if they are made through a local authority, voluntary sector worker, health visitor or so on. They are considered every two months. No payment can be made directly to an individual by the trust; payment will be made to the organisation making the application. Other sources of funding should be sought before applying to the trust.

Other information

The Sacro Trust is related to the Sacro organisation which provides 'community-based support to help offenders re-integrate into society and live stable, independent lives.' The organisation runs criminal justice, youth justice and mediation services, and also conducts research and policy work.

The Paul Stephenson Memorial Trust

£0

Correspondent: Pauline Austin, Administrator, The New Bridge, 27A Medway Street, London SW1P 2BD (020 7976 0779)

CC Number: 295924

Eligibility

People who have served at least two years of imprisonment and are near the end of their sentence or have been released recently.

Types of grants

One-off grants of up to £100. Grants can be in cash or in kind for a particular need of the applicant or their immediate family, such as home furnishings, clothing, tools for work or assistance with college expenses.

Annual grant total

In 2012 the trust had an income of £2,000 and a total expenditure of £0. This was also the case the previous year.

The 2012 accounts were the latest available at the time of writing.

Exclusions

Grants are not given for recreational activities, setting up small businesses or becoming self-employed, or for existing debts.

Applications

On a form available from the correspondent, which must be submitted via a probation officer, prison education officer or voluntary associate. Applicants should mention other trusts or organisations that have been applied to and other grants promised or received, including any statutory grants. Trustees usually meet twice a year.

Quakers

Open Wing Trust

£4,000

Correspondent: Jennifer Kavanagh, Clerk, Flat 2, 44 Langham Street, London W1W 7AU (email: online contact form; website: www.openwing.org.uk)

CC Number: 1149773

Eligibility

Individuals over the age of 18 who are living in England and Wales at the beginning of their career and those contemplating a radical re-orientation of their life's work or the deepening of an existing vision. The trustees advise: 'We expect applicants to be in a process of inner change leading to a socially engaged commitment to working with those in need.'

Types of grants

One-off grants according to need. Trustees will consider funding specific living costs such as food and rent, training programmes, or offering support during voluntary work or an internship.

Annual grant total

The trust's website states: 'We expect to fund up to three small one-off grants a year, with an individual maximum of £2,000 (total available each year is £4,000).'

Exclusions

No re-applications for further funding will be considered within five years of an initial grant. No grants for organisations or to fund specific work. Applications made on behalf of others will not be accepted.

Note: The trust's website states: We will not fund holidays or unspecified thinking time.

Applications

Via the online application form. Applications should be submitted directly by the individual. They should be accompanied by two supporting letters: one from somebody who has known the applicant for at least five years, and the other from somebody who has a connection with the application (for example, work or study) and has known the applicant for at least two years. Applicants will need to demonstrate commitment to their purpose, and that they are in need of financial support to make it feasible. Consult the guidance notes on the trust's website before applying to ensure that your application is in line with the aims and values of the trust.

The trustees expect to meet twice a year to consider applications, but can make decisions between meetings. Suitable applicants will be invited to meet the trustees.

The Westward Trust

£6,000

Correspondent: Alison Ironside, Trustee, 17 Green Meadow Road, Birmingham B29 4DD (01214 751179)

CC Number: 260488

Eligibility

Quakers in need who live in the UK.

Types of grants

One-off and recurrent grants can be given according to need.

Annual grant total

In 2012/13 the trust had an income of £9,000 and a total expenditure of £12,200. We estimate that about £6,000 was given to individuals.

Applications

In writing to the correspondent.

Other information

Grants are also made to organisations, particularly Quaker charities or projects in which members of the Religious Society of Friends are involved.

Vegetarian

The Vegetarian Charity

£5,000

Correspondent: Susan Lenihan, Grants Secretary, 56 Parliament Street, Chippenham, Wiltshire SN14 0DE (01249 443521; email: grantssecretary@vegetariancharity.org.uk)

CC Number: 294767

Eligibility

Children and young people under the age of 26 who are vegetarian or vegan and are sick or in need.

Types of grants

One-off and recurrent grants to relieve poverty and sickness, usually ranging from £250 to £1,000.

Annual grant total

In 2012/13 the charity had assets of £1.1 million and an income of £50,000. Grants paid during the year to individuals and organisations totalled £22,500; a further breakdown was not available. We estimate that grants to individuals for social welfare purposes was around £5,000.

Applications

On a form available from the correspondent, including details of any other grants received, a CV, covering letter and three references. Applications are considered throughout the year.

Other information

Grants are also made to organisations which promote vegetarianism among young people and to vegetarian children's homes.

Victims of crime or injustice

The Heinz, Anna and Carol Kroch Foundation

See entry on page 24

Sic Point Foundation

£88,000 (123 grants)

Correspondent: Susan Cohen, Executive Director, 25–26 Enford Street, London W1H 1DW (020 3372 8881; email: info@sixpointfoundation.org.uk; website: www.sixpointfoundation.org.uk)

CC Number: 1143324

Eligibility

UK resident Holocaust survivors and Jewish refugees who have experienced Nazi persecution. To be eligible there must also be financial disadvantage which is measured as an income of under £10,000 per year (excluding pensions and social security payments) and assets of under £32,000 (excluding a primary residence and vehicle).

Types of grants

One-off grants for home improvements, medical needs, accessibility and other items that enhance quality of life.

Annual grant total

In 2012/13 the foundation held assets of £4 million and had an income of £830,000. Individuals received 123 grants totalling £88,000, with organisations receiving a further £911,000.

Exclusions

No reimbursement for goods or services already purchased.

Applications

Individuals or people acting on behalf of them should contact the foundation to discuss an application. Enquiries can be made in writing, by telephone or email, or through the submission of an online enquiry form. There may be a home visit from a social worker experienced in assessing Holocaust survivors and refugees. Grants are usually processed through the foundation's partner, the Association of Jewish Refugees.

Women

Frederick Andrew Convalescent Trust

£23,000 (41 grants)

Correspondent: Karen Armitage, Clerk to the Trustees, Andrew and Co., St Swithin's Court, 1 Flavian Road, Nettleham Road, Lincoln LN2 4GR (01522 512123; email: info@factonline.co.uk; website: www.factonline.co.uk)

CC Number: 211029

Eligibility

Women who have been in paid employment at some time.

Types of grants

Grants of up to £1,000 for convalescence and domestic help, and up to £600 for therapy. Types of therapy covered include: physiotherapy, occupational therapy, speech therapy, chiropody and podiatry and counselling.

Annual grant total

In 2012 the trust had assets of £1.7 million and had an income of £74,000. Grants to individuals totalled £23,000.

At the time of writing (August 2014) this was the most recent financial information available for the trust.

Applications

An initial assessment form must be completed and returned to the correspondent. The form is available from the trust's website. The trust responds to every application.

Bircham Dyson Bell Charitable Trust – The Crossley Fund

£600

Correspondent: Helen D'Monte, Senior Trust Manager, Bircham Dyson Bell, 50 Broadway, Westminster, London SW1H 0BL (020 7227 7000; fax: 020 7222 3480; email: helendmonte@bdb-law.co.uk)

CC Number: 803150

Eligibility

Single women, including widows, of at least 50 years of age, who are in need.

Types of grants

Grants of £4 per week towards rent, paid in quarterly instalments.

Annual grant total

In 2012/13 the trust had assets of £49,000 and an income of £36,000. Payments to individuals from the Crossley Fund totalled £600.

Applications

Note the following from the trust's annual report:

> The Trustees continue to support the existing Crossley Fund beneficiaries. However they have decided reluctantly that as matters stand they must try to meet their existing commitments and have closed the fund to new applicants. They will review the position from time to time according to their resources and the number of beneficiaries.

Other information

The trust was established in 1989 by a London law firm, Bircham Dyson Bell, with general charitable objectives. In 1997, the trustees also became responsible for the administration of the 'Crossley Fund'.

The trust has previously stated: 'We get lots of inappropriate applications; we can only help older people with rent.'

The Eaton Fund for Artists, Nurses and Gentlewomen

£120,000 (359 grants)

Correspondent: Anne Murray, Administrator, PO Box 528, Fleet GU51 9HH (020 3289 3209; email: admin@eatonfund.org.uk; website: www.eatonfund.org.uk)

CC Number: 236060

Eligibility

Artists, including painters, potters, sculptors and photographers but not performing artists; nurses, including SRN, SEN, medical carers and dental nurses who are in employment or retired; and women over 18, who are in need of financial assistance.

Types of grants

One-off grants for artist's materials and equipment; picture framing for an exhibition; wheelchairs; and the setting up of a new home due to disability, family breakdown or homelessness.

Annual grant total

In 2012/13, the fund had assets of £8.2 million and an income of £158,000. Grants were made to 359 individuals totalling £120,000.

Exclusions

Grants are not given for educational fees, recurring expenses such as mortgage repayments, rent, fuel or phone bills, special diets, care home fees, private treatments or to clear debt.

Applications

On a form available from the correspondent or to download from the website. Forms can be submitted directly by the individual but the fund also asks that a supporting letter from an appropriate third party, such as a doctor or social worker, be included. Any relevant documents like invoices or quotations should also be sent in with the form. They are considered six times a year and applicants will be notified of the decision within a month of the application deadline. For more information on specific application deadlines see the 'calendar' section of the fund's website.

The fund advises that an application is more likely to be successful where:

- Detailed background information is given about the applicant and their specific need
- Applicants have also applied to other charities for assistance when requesting sums of more than £400

The Arthur Hurst Will Trust

£16,000

Correspondent: Official Solicitor and Public Trustee, Victory House, 30–34 Kingsway, London WC2B 6EX (020 3681 2759; fax: 020 3681 2762)

CC Number: 207991

Eligibility

Women and members of the clergy who are in need and who have been forced to give up their work because of ill health. The trust also supports widows and children of clergymen.

Types of grants

One-off grants according to need.

Annual grant total

In 2012/13 the trust had an income of £209,000 and a total expenditure of £233,000. Payments to beneficiaries totalled £32,000. Grants can be paid either directly to the individual or through another organisation and are also given for educational purposes. We estimate that grants for social welfare purposes totalled around £16,000.

Applications

Applications can be submitted directly by the individual or, where applicable, through a social worker, Citizens Advice, a welfare agency or another third party. Applications can be considered at any time, although there is not always available funding to make payments.

Note: the trust's Charity Commission record lists Elizabeth Finn Care as its contact; however, the trust's receipts and payments accounts were signed by Suzanne Marks for the Public Trustee on 14/10/2013. We have, therefore, listed the Public Trustee as the correspondent.

The Morris Beneficent Fund

£27,000

Correspondent: Simon Jamison, Treasurer and Secretary, No. 10 Evendons Centre, 171 Evendons Lane, Wokingham RG41 4EH (01189 798653)

CC Number: 256473

Eligibility

'Distressed gentlewomen' recommended by members of the fund. Grants generally go to older women.

Types of grants

Recurrent grants according to need.

Annual grant total

Grants and annuities usually total around £25,000 each year; however, in 2012 the fund gave gifts to the value of £27,000 to individuals. Annuities for the year totalled almost £25,000 and occasional gifts a further £2,000. At the end of 2012 eight ladies were receiving annuities and two beneficiaries were receiving occasional gifts.

At the time of writing (August 2014) this was the most recent financial information available for the fund.

Applications

On an application form supplied by a member. No unsolicited applications will be considered.

Other information

The trustees decide each year how many annuitants can be supported, though this number rarely exceeds 20 as the trustees prefer to raise the level of grants rather than awarding a larger number of smaller annuities.

The Perry Fund

£25,000

Correspondent: William Carter, Clerk to the Trustees, 7 Waterloo Road, Wolverhampton WV1 4DW

CC Number: 218829

Eligibility

The focus of activity remains granting of annuities to ladies who find it extremely difficult to manage on their very low pension In granting special needs payments, the trustees have looked at a wide range of ladies from all sorts of social backgrounds and from all ethnic origins and all ages.

Types of grants

Annuities of around £3,000 are paid and some one-off grants.

Annual grant total

In 2012 grants of around £25,000 were made, to seven regular annuities at £3,000 each (not always for the whole year), and nine one-off payments totalling £6,000. Total income was £30,000, and total expenditure was £28,000. This was the most recent information available at the time of writing (July 2014).

Applications

On a form available from the correspondent. Applications can be submitted directly by the individual or through a third party such as a social worker, nursing home manager or welfare organisation. The trustees usually meet twice a year to consider applications.

The Royal Society for the Relief of Indigent Gentlewomen of Scotland

£1.1 million

Correspondent: The Secretary and Cashier, 14 Rutland Square, Edinburgh EH1 2BD (01312 292308; fax: 01312 290956; email: info@igf.org; website: www.igf.org)

SC Number: SC016095

Eligibility

Single women, widows or divorcees in need who are over 50 years of age, of Scottish birth, background or education, and have (or whose husband, ex-husband or father had) a professional or business background. Those prevented from pursuing a career by devoting their lives to the care of relatives may also be considered. Applicants need not live in Scotland.

The income and capital limits for admission to the roll and the level of annuities and other grants paid are regularly reviewed. Details of current income and ceilings are available from the Secretary and Cashier.

Types of grants

Annuities, paid in quarterly instalments, of around £1,100 a year, or less if the beneficiary is under 60 years of age and receives help from DWP. Beneficiaries may also receive one-off grants for TV licences, telephone rental, holidays, nursing, property maintenance and so on.

Annual grant total

In 2013/14 the society had assets of £40.2 million and an income of £1.6 million. Grants were made totalling £1.1 million and were distributed as follows:

Principal grants	£841,000
Supplementary grants	£124,000
Winter grants	£109,000
Extra	£47,000
Welcome grants	£14,000
Other grants	£7,000

792 principal grants (annuities) were awarded during the year.

Exclusions

The society is unable to support ladies who are separated or currently in a civil partnership.

Applications

On a form available from the correspondent, to be submitted directly by the individual or through a social worker, Citizens Advice or other welfare agency or third party. Application deadlines are end of March and September for consideration in May and November. Details of applicant's age, current financial position, personal family background and a copy of the divorce document (if appropriate) are required.

Other information

The society also provides regular home visiting, counselling and assistance with application forms.

Sawyer Trust

£68,000

Correspondent: John Pooley, Trustee, PO Box 797, Worcester WR4 4BU (email: info@sawyertrust.org; website: www.sawyertrust.org)

CC Number: 511276

Eligibility

Women over 50 who are in need through financial hardship, sickness or poor health. If there are surplus funds, men over 50 in similar circumstances may also receive assistance.

Types of grants

One-off grants up to £500. Recent grants have been awarded for household items and fittings, removal costs, telephone bills, travel costs and rent arrears. The trust states that they will consider a wide range of assistance but do not pay cash directly to applicants.

Annual grant total

In 2012/13 the trust held assets of £2.1 million and had an income of £70,000. Grants to individuals totalled £68,000.

Exclusions

Luxury goods or services; parties or outings; shortfall on insurance claims, except in certain circumstances; legal expenses; credit card debt or ongoing costs.

Applications

On an application form available to download from the trust's website or by requesting one by writing to the correspondent. Applications may be completed by the applicant or someone else on their behalf, and must be supported by an accredited third party; for example, Citizens Advice, a housing association, or a charitable organisation recognised by the trust. Written evidence in the form of a bank statement must be presented as evidence of applicant's circumstances. Applications must be posted. Trustees meet monthly to consider applications.

The Society for the Assistance of Ladies in Reduced Circumstances

£565,000

Correspondent: The General Secretary, Lancaster House, 25 Hornyold Road, Malvern, Worcestershire WR14 1QQ (0300 365 1886; email: info@salrc.org.uk; website: www.salrc.org.uk)

CC Number: 205798

Eligibility

Women who live completely alone, have savings less than £8,000, receive a means tested benefit, and are not eligible for help from any other charity.

Types of grants

Monthly payments towards day-to-day living expenses, TV licences and telephone rental charges. Beneficiaries are sent birthday and Christmas cards. The society can also advise on other sources of funding.

Annual grant total

In 2013 the society had an income of £914,000 and a total expenditure of £861,000. Monthly payments to women in need totalled £565,000 for the year.

On average, 416 women were in receipt of payments each month.

Exclusions

No grants for education, care or nursing home fees, holidays, repayment of debts or funeral expenses. The Trust is unable to assist students or women who work 16 hours or more a week.

One-off grants for essential needs are no longer available.

Applications

On a form available from the correspondent. Applications can be submitted directly by the individual or through a third party such as Citizens Advice or a social worker. All details of employment history should be supplied. The society requests that the following documentation is provided: a copy of the applicant's most recent council tax bill; copies of the most recent notifications, letters and calculations of any statutory benefits, tax credits or state or occupational pensions received; payslips covering the past three months (if applicable); and statements from all bank accounts. If all documentation is supplied, a firm decision may be confirmed in a few days. It is advised that applicants view the society's website for a detailed list of requirements.

Potential applicants can call the helpline for an informal chat (0300 365 1886, Mon-Fri 9am-1pm and 2pm to 4.30 pm) or complete an enquiry form on the society's website, if help is required.

Other information

Grants are also made to organisations though none were awarded in 2012/13.

The society has an informative website.

St Andrew's Society for Ladies in Need

£51,000

Correspondent: Maureen Pope, Administrator, 20 Denmark Gardens, Ipswich Road, Holbrook, Ipswich, Suffolk IP9 2BG (01473 327408; email: mpope1@btinternet.com; website: standrewssociety.btck.co.uk/)

CC Number: 208541

Eligibility

Single women from a well-educated, professional or semi-professional background who are now living alone in reduced circumstances. Applicants must be retired or unable to work and of British nationality. Preference is given to elderly women who are over 80 years of age.

Types of grants

Recurrent grants, up to a maximum of £20 a week to help with daily living expenses, are paid each quarter. Priority is given to ladies who are trying to maintain their own homes but grants are also given to those struggling with nursing home fees. One-off special grants are also available for heating, the cost of moving house, domestic appliances, furniture, disability aids, holidays and convalescence.

Annual grant total

In 2012 the society held assets of £1.4 million and had an income of £86,000. Grants were made to individuals totalling £51,000. The vast majority of this was given in regular grants with just £4,800 awarded in one-off special grants to meet particular short-term needs. The 2012 accounts were the latest available at the time of writing (August 2014).

Exclusions

No grants to younger women and non-retired ladies who are able to work. No assistance with the discharge of debts.

Applications

On a form available from the correspondent, to be submitted either directly by the individual or through a social worker, Citizens Advice, other welfare agency or somebody with power of attorney. They should include as much background detail as possible, such as education, occupation and so on. Applications are considered at quarterly committee meetings, though urgent cases can be dealt with between meetings.

WRVS Benevolent Trust

£15,000

Correspondent: Hon. Secretary, PO Box 567, Tonbridge TN9 9LS (07894 060 517; email: wrvsbenevolenttrust@hotmail.co.uk; website: www.wrvs-benevolent-trust.co.uk)

CC Number: 261931

Eligibility

Past or present members of the Women's Royal Voluntary Service (WRVS) who have given at least five years of service and are in need.

Types of grants

One-off grants ranging from £50 to £6,000. Recent grants have been made for washing machines, replacement windows, moving costs, carbon monoxide alarms, car tax, nursing home top up fees and dry rot treatment.

Annual grant total

In 2013 this charity had an income of £47,000 and total expenses of £25,000. We estimate that grants to individuals for social welfare purposes were around £15,000.

Applications

On an application form available to download from the website. Applications can be considered year round.

Illness and disability charities

There are many charities for people with illnesses or disabilities. The entries in this section are only for those that give financial help from their own resources. There are many others that do not have a large enough income to do this but may be the starting point for getting financial help. For this reason we have a list of organisations which provide advice and support on page 481.

This section starts with an index of illness or disability. The entries are arranged alphabetically within each category, with those trusts supporting more than one illness or disability listed at the start of the chapter.

Local disability charities are not included in this section but are listed in the relevant local section of the book. Northern Irish, Scottish and Welsh disability charities are also listed in the relevant locality rather than in this section.

Index of illness and disability funds

The ACT Foundation

See entry on page 1

Active Foundation

See entry on page 14

Barchester Healthcare Foundation

See entry on page 22

The Birchington Convalescent Benefit Fund

£0 (11 grants)

Correspondent: Michael Locke, Administrator, Church Society, Dean Wace House, 16 Rosslyn Road, Watford WD18 0NY (01923 235111; fax: 01923 800362; email: admin@churchsociety.org; website: www.churchsociety.org)

CC Number: 249574

Eligibility

Children under the age of 18 who are chronically ill or recovering from surgery or long-term illness.

Types of grants

One-off grants of £200 towards part-payment of convalescent holidays for children.

Annual grant total

In 2013, income was £125; however in this particular year the trustees do not appear to have made any awards. We consider that grantmaking will resume in the future.

Exclusions

Grants are rarely given for expensive or overseas holidays. Grants are not given for reasons other than holidays. Grants are not given to allow ill parents to have a break from their children.

Applications

On a form available from the correspondent or to download from the website. Applications should be made through a third party, for example, a doctor, social worker or hospital staff. Details of the sponsor of the application, type of illness or surgery, financial status and type and cost of the holiday needed should be included. Decisions on grant awards are made in February, April and June.

Other information

The fund is managed by the Church Society. Those awarded a grant also receive a complimentary children's bible.

Caudwell Children

£2.9 million

Correspondent: Applications Manager, Minton Hollins Building, Shelton Old Road, Stoke-on-Trent, Staffordshire ST4 7RY (0845 300 1348; fax: 01782 600639; email: applications@caudwellchildren.com; website: www.caudwellchildren.com)

CC Number: 1079770

Eligibility

People under 18 with a disability or serious illness who live in the UK. Household income/salary (not including benefits) should be less than £45,000 gross per annum.

Types of grants

One-off and recurrent donations for mobility, sensory and sports equipment; therapy, treatment and family holidays.

Annual grant total

In 2012 the charity had assets of £6.2 million and an income of £5.5 million. Grants totalled £2.9 million.

At the time of writing this was the most recent financial information available for the trust.

Exclusions

No grants for: building works, fixtures and fittings; gardening and the making safe of gardens; respite care; dolphin therapy/faith healing; computers (unless specifically designed for people with special needs); iPads; motor vehicle purchase/adaptations; equipment repair or maintenance; domestic appliances; non-specialist furniture, decoration, clothing or bedding; private education; speech or occupational therapy; or legal costs.

Applications

Application forms are available to download from the website or from the correspondent. The charity uses different application forms depending upon what is being applied for. Financial details must be included. The application process can, during busy periods, take up to six months and applicants may be visited by a trustee.

Other information

The charity provides family support services, equipment, treatment and therapies for disabled children and their families across the UK. It also runs the Enable Sport programme for talented disabled athletes and the Destination Dreams holiday for children fighting life threatening conditions. More details of all of the charity's activities are available from its informative website.

Clevedon Forbes Fund

£40,000 (127 grants)

Correspondent: Margaret Barker, Trustee, The Dower House, Church Walk, Wrington, Bristol BS40 5QQ (01934 862435; email: wendy@clevedonforbes.org; website: www.clevedonforbes.org)

CC Number: 249313

Eligibility

People of limited means who are recovering from surgery or who are in need of a break due to illness or trauma. Grants are also available for carers to have a holiday from caring for someone who is sick or who has disabilities. The majority of grants are given to individuals living in the South West but those living further afield will be considered.

Types of grants

One-off grants to those in need.

Annual grant total

In 2012/13 the trust had assets of £1.6 million and an income of £70,500. 127 grants were made to individuals totalling £40,000.

Exclusions

Grants are not made for capital goods. Individuals cannot apply for another grant until a three year period has elapsed.

Applications

Applications need to be made through a professional in the statutory or voluntary sector, such as a social worker or welfare officer. Application forms are available on the fund's website or directly from the correspondent.

The trustees are currently (January 2014) encouraging referees to apply to the fund during the winter months even if the proposed holiday is to be taken much later in the year.

Other information

A Christian gospel booklet is sent out to people receiving a grant unless there is a specific request to the contrary.

Equipment for Independent Living

£33,000

Correspondent: June Sutherland, Honorary Secretary, 10 Pembroke Walk, London W8 6PQ

CC Number: 228438

Eligibility

People over 16 who are disabled in the UK and overseas.

Types of grants

One-off grants towards disability equipment enabling people to obtain mobility, independence and earning power. Awards are usually in the range of £100 to £1,000.

Annual grant total

In 2013 the trust had an income of £25,000 and a total expenditure £35,000. We estimate grants to be in the region of £33,000.

Exclusions

Normally grants are not made towards: medical equipment; course fees and materials; welfare expenditure of a non-capital nature, such as a holiday or moving expenses; equipment which is supplied by the NHS or social services; equipment running costs; building adaptations and decorating; household equipment (unless specially adapted for the person's disability); or private treatment, home care fees or computers (unless they are used as a speech aid or to enable the individual to earn their living).

Funds are not normally granted to cases submitted by other charities which have much larger resources than the trust.

Applications

Applicants must be referred in the first instance by a professional person involved with their welfare, for example, a social worker, occupational therapist or specialist nurse. The professional person should write to the Honorary Secretary describing the applicant's circumstances and saying what equipment is needed and why. If appropriate, a full application form will then be sent out.

Applications can be submitted at any time and are considered in January, April, July and October.

The Farrell Trust

£10,300

Correspondent: Trust Administrator, PO Box 531, Letchworth Garden City SG6 9ES (email: ftcharity@yahoo.co.uk; website: www.farrelltrust.org.uk)

CC Number: 257667

Eligibility

People who have physical or mental health problems, older people and those on low incomes. Grants are also occasionally made to carers.

Types of grants

Grants of between £50 and £200 are given towards holidays and respite breaks for disabled people and their carers. Grants cannot be paid directly to the applicant.

Annual grant total

In 2012/13 the trust had an income of £4,600 and a total expenditure of £10,500. We estimate that grants to individuals totalled £10,300.

Exclusions

Successful applicants may not reapply for three years.

Applications

On an application form available from the trust's website. Applications may be completed by the individual or an advocate, a friend, family member or carer.

Evidence of income support and Disability Living Allowance or immediate and urgent need must be provided along with the application form. It is recommended that applicants attach a letter of support from a doctor, social worker, occupational therapist or minister of religion.

Applications that do not contain sufficient evidence will not be considered.

Other information

The trust was officially formed in 1968 by Pamela Farrell who, having lost her husband to Multiple Sclerosis, saw the need for specially designed accommodation for married couples, one of whom has a disability. The trust built 18 houses on two residential developments, which 'have allowed many families to stay together and retain their independence', and later acquired more properties as specially adapted holiday homes. The holiday properties were eventually handed over to the John Grooms Charity (CC no. 212463) in October 1998 as the trust turned its focus to grantmaking.

The trust has an informative website.

Foundations Independent Living Trust

£696,000 (488 grants)

Correspondent: Gayle Dawkes, Grants and Customer Service Assistant, Bleaklow House, Howard Town Mill, Glossop, Derbyshire SK13 8HT (0845 864 5210; email: info@filt.org.uk; website: https://www.filt.org.uk)

CC Number: 1103784

Eligibility

People who are elderly, vulnerable, disabled and/or have health conditions, who own their home or rent from a private landlord.

Types of grants

Grants for repairs, minor adaptations, home improvements, heating and insulation measures.

Annual grant total

In 2012/13 the trust held assets of £70,000 and had an income of £830,000. A total of £696,000 was awarded in 488 grants to beneficiaries.

Applications

Via a local home improvement agency. Applications cannot be made directly to the trust but enquires are welcome. Local home improvement agencies are listed on the trust's website.

Gardening for Disabled Trust

£20,000

Correspondent: The Secretary, PO Box 285, Tunbridge Wells, Kent TN2 9JD (email: info@gardeningfordisabledtrust.org.uk; website: www.gardeningfordisabledtrust.org.uk)

CC Number: 255066

Eligibility

Members of the trust who wish to participate in gardening regardless of age or disability.

Types of grants

One-off grants according to need to help towards tools, raised beds, paving, labour and greenhouses.

Annual grant total

In 2012 the trust had an income of £21,000 and a total expenditure of £31,000. At the time of writing (August 2014) these were the most recent figures available for the trust and, due to its low income, it was not requested to submit its accounts to the Charity Commission. We estimate that around £20,000 was given in grants to individuals, some of which was distributed through other organisations.

Exclusions

No grants to pay for a gardener for general maintenance or for clearing or fencing.

Applications

In writing to the correspondent detailing the work they would like done and an estimate of the cost of tools, materials and labour (if necessary). Applications can be submitted through the online contact form on the website. If labour is required the applicant should provide original copies of two quotes. Applicants should also include a note from their GP, social worker or occupational therapist describing their disability. Applications are considered monthly.

The N. and P. Hartley Memorial Trust

£2,000

Correspondent: Virginia Watson, Trustee, 24 Holywell Lane, Leeds LS17 8HA

CC Number: 327570

Eligibility

People who are disabled, older or terminally ill. Priority is firstly given to those living in West Yorkshire, secondly to individuals living in the north of England and thirdly to those elsewhere in the UK and overseas.

Types of grants

One-off grants towards, for example, specialist equipment for people with disabilities.

Annual grant total

Grants to individuals total between £3,000 and £4,000 each year.

Applications

In writing to the correspondent, preferably through a social worker, Citizens Advice or other welfare agency, for consideration twice yearly. Applications from previous beneficiaries are welcomed.

Other information

The trust also makes a number of grants to organisations and to individuals for educational purposes.

Independence at Home

£286,000 (1,006 grants)

Correspondent: Kate Williams, Chief Executive, 4th Floor, Congress House, 14 Lyon Road, Harrow HA1 2EN (020 8427 7929; fax: 020 8424 2937; email: iah@independenceathome.org.uk; website: www.independenceathome.org.uk)

CC Number: 245259

Eligibility

People who are substantially disabled or severely ill and who live at home or who wish to do so.

Types of grants

Grants ranging between £100 and £750 towards specific additional costs associated with living at home with a disability, including equipment and adaptations. Grants can be made towards almost any expense which is not covered by statutory provision and which is related to a disabled person living at home.

Annual grant total

In 2013/14 the trust had assets of £4.5 million and an income of £336,000. Grants were made to 1,006 individuals totalling £286,000

Exclusions

No grants are made to people living in residential care. Grants are not made towards medical treatment or therapies; funeral expenses; debts and arrears; leisure equipment such as televisions; motor vehicles (although we may be able to help towards the cost of adaptations); telephone rental or call charges; or TV licenses. Only one grant can be held in any 12 month period.

Applications

Applications must be accompanied by a letter of referral from an occupational therapist, specialist nurse, social worker or a trained worker from a charity that is supporting the applicant. The letter should describe the applicant's circumstances, confirm the medical diagnosis and explain what sort of help is required. The application form and guidance notes are downloadable from the website. Applications should be submitted by post and are considered on an ongoing basis. The trust accepts informal contact to prior to applications being made.

The League of the Helping Hand (LHH)

£122,000

Correspondent: The Secretary, LHH, P. O. Box 342, Burgess Hill RH15 5AQ (01444 236099; email: secretary@lhh.org.uk; website: www.lhh.org.uk)

CC Number: 208792

Eligibility

People who have a physical disability, learning difficulty or mental health problem and are in financial need. Those who care for somebody who is disabled, elderly or ill may also be eligible.

Types of grants

One-off and recurrent payments. Grants ranging between £50 and £250 are awarded towards essential household items, specialist equipment and carers' breaks. Quarterly gifts are available to help with daily living costs, the beneficiaries of which also receive newsletters, birthday and Christmas cards and, where possible, an annual personal visit from the Secretary.

Annual grant total

In 2012/13 the trust held assets of £2.5 million and had an income of £151,000. Grants to individuals totalled almost £122,000 and were distributed as follows:

One-off gifts	£61,000
Quarterly gifts	£50,000
Christmas gifts	£4,600
Holidays	£3,500
Visits	£2,500

Exclusions

No help is given for debts, business costs, holidays, tenancy deposits, building works, mobility scooters, wheelchairs, medical, dental or therapeutic treatments; or for education-related items.

Applications

On a form available to download from the trust's website. Applications must be submitted through a social worker, carers' support centre, Citizens Advice or other welfare body. If it is not possible to download the form, the correspondent should be contacted directly. An sae must be enclosed. The trustees meet every three weeks to consider applications, although emergency needs can be dealt with more quickly. Telephone enquiries are welcome.

Note: applications submitted directly by individuals will not be considered.

Other information

The charity states that:

> The League of the Helping Hand (LHH) was founded in 1908 by Miss Edith Ashby who wanted to address the suffering of those who had very little to live on. She was adamant from the first that all help should be given in the most kindly and friendly way possible.

Mobility Trust

£150,000

Correspondent: Anne Munn, Chief Executive, 17b Reading Road, Pangbourne, Reading, Berkshire RG8 7LR (01189 842588; fax: 01189 842544; email: mobility@mobilitytrust.org.uk; website: www.mobilitytrust.org.uk)

CC Number: 1070975

Eligibility

People with severe physical disabilities due to accident or disease.

Types of grants

The trust provides powered wheelchairs or scooters for people who are unable to obtain such equipment through statutory sources or afford it themselves. If someone is unable to walk at all and requires a powered wheelchair they should apply to their local NHS Wheelchair Service before making an application to the trust.

Annual grant total

In 2012/13 the trust had an income of £293,000 and an expenditure of £297,000.

Financial information was available on the Charity Commission's website at the time of writing (October 2014); however, further information required by the Commission had not yet been submitted by the trust.

Applications

Applications must be submitted in the first instance by a letter directly by the individual or through a social worker, medical advisor or other welfare agency. The letter should explain why the person needs the equipment, detailing any disabilities and their cause. If there is a possibility of helping the person they will be sent a form to complete.

The Florence Nightingale Aid-in-Sickness Trust (FNAIST)

£290,000 (329 grants)

Correspondent: Ann Griffiths, Grants and Funding Manager, Independent Age, 6 Avonmore Road, London W14 8RL (020 7605 4244; email: ann.griffiths@fnaist.org.uk or fnaist@independentage.org.uk; website: www.fnaist.org.uk)

CC Number: 211896

Eligibility

People who are in poor health, convalescent or have disabilities. Preference will be given to people with professional, secretarial, or administrative qualifications or experience.

Types of grants

One-off grants are available for convalescence or respite care, medical equipment and other aids, sensory equipment, communications aids, telephone installation (or mobile phones in rare cases), computers and software, drug storage units, electric beds, household aids (for example, washing machines) and other needs to improve individuals' independent living. Partial funding may be provided where a large grant is requested.

Annual grant total

In 2013 the trust had assets of £9.7 million and an income of £341,000. Grants were made to 329 individuals totalling £290,000. The grants were given in the following categories:

Aid purposes	161
Respite/convalescent breaks	120
Mobility equipment	35
Miscellaneous	13

Exclusions

Grants are not available for:

- House alterations, adaptations, improvements or maintenance
- Car purchase or adaptations
- Holidays, exchange visits or nursing home fees
- Debts or repayments
- General clothing
- Stairlifts
- General house furnishing

Under normal circumstances, grants can only be given to any one household at intervals of three years.

Applications

Application forms are available to download from the trust's website or can be requested from the correspondent. They should be submitted by Citizens Advice, other charities, a social worker, an occupational therapist, doctor, health centre worker or a similar professional with a medical background. Candidates should provide a brief medical history of the applicant and proof of the need for assistance. Applications are considered monthly, although urgent requests can be dealt with between meetings.

React (Rapid Effective Assistance for Children with Potentially Terminal Illnesses)

£429,000 (1,212 grants)

Correspondent: Grants Administrator, St Luke's House, 270 Sandycombe Road, Kew, Surrey TW9 3NP (020 8940 2575; fax: 020 8940 2050; email: react@reactcharity.org; website: www.reactcharity.org)

CC Number: 802440

Eligibility

Financially disadvantaged families caring for a child under 18 years living with a potentially terminal illness.

Types of grants

Grants in kind and one-off grants. They can be made towards domestic or medical equipment not available through a health authority such as for example, wheelchairs, hoists or adjustable beds, educational equipment which will aid a child's development at home or in hospital (sensory toys, communication and speech aids or computers), domestic equipment which will improve the child's quality of life (such as beds, white goods or soft furnishings) and hospital expenses (travel, food or related costs). Week long breaks at React holiday homes can also be offered and assistance may also be given with funeral expenses and memorial headstones. The charity says it can consider most requests; however, if you would like to check whether or not a specific item fits the criteria, the charity can be contacted by phone.

Annual grant total

In 2012/13 the charity held assets of £337,000 and had an income of £799,000. Charitable expenditure totalled £429,000 and was distributed as follows:

Medical	253	£137,000
Domestic	283	£96,000
Mobile home holidays	300	£69,000
Funeral expenses	52	£44,000
Travel and subsistence	170	£29,000
Educational	66	£25,000
Home adaptations	52	£24,000
Respite holidays	36	£5,400

Exclusions

No retrospective grants (except in exceptional circumstances). No grants towards trips overseas, structural building works, private treatment or the purchase of vehicles.

Applications

On a form available from the correspondent or to download from the website. Potential applicants can also ask their nurse, carer or social worker if they have a blank form available. Forms must be completed and signed by a parent/guardian and endorsed by a medical or social care professional. Supporting letters are welcome and sponsors must specifically endorse the items requested. Where applicable, quotes or exact prices for specific items should be supplied. Families are required to declare financial details and should disclose those of any other applications that have been made. The charity aims to respond to every application within 48 hours.

Other information

The charity has holiday homes in seven locations around the country. Unfortunately, they are not wheelchair adapted; however, in cases where this is a problem, the charity may be able to make alternative arrangements. See the website for more details.

Reuben Foundation

£36,000

Correspondent: Patrick O'Driscoll, Trustee, 4th Floor, Millbank Tower, 21–24 Millbank, London SW1P 4QP (020 7802 5014; fax: 020 7802 5002; email: contact@reubenfoundation.com; website: www.reubenfoundation.com)

CC Number: 1094130

Eligibility

Persons from disadvantaged background who are in need, hardship or distress as a result of local, national or international disorder or due to social or economic circumstances.

Types of grants

One-off grants according to need, generally for healthcare and educational and training purposes.

Annual grant total

At the time of writing (August 2014) the latest financial information available was from 2012. In 2012 the foundation had assets totalling £66.5 million and an income of £3.9 million. Grants to 20 individuals totalled £73,000 given for both educational and medical purposes. We estimate that about £36,000 was awarded in healthcare support.

Applications

The foundation has stated that grants are made by invitation only and that suitable causes are identified 'through the existing trustees' contacts and by building new relationships with a range of charitable organisations and intermediaries.'

Contact the foundation with inquiries about applications.

Other information

The foundation was established in 2002 as an outlet for the philanthropic giving of billionaire property investors David and Simon Reuben. The foundation was endowed by the brothers with a donation of $100 million (£54.1 million), with the income generated to be given to a range of charitable causes, particularly in the fields of healthcare and education.

Most of the support is given to organisations (over £2 million to 415 bodies in 2012). Grants are also made to individuals for educational costs.

The SF Group Charity

£40,000

Correspondent: Brenda Yong, Charitable Fund Manager, FREEPOST NAT13205, Nottingham NG8 6ZZ (email: brenda.yong@sfcharity.co.uk; website: www.sfcharity.co.uk)

CC Number: 1104927

Eligibility

Severely disabled people of all ages. This can include people with significant sensory, physical and intellectual impairments and those with complex and challenging behavioural needs. The charity's website states that it is only able to accept applications from applicants in the counties of Nottinghamshire, Leicestershire, Derbyshire, Warwickshire and the West Midlands (primarily areas covered by the postcodes starting NG, LE, DE, CV, B, WS, WV, DY and some starting with S). There is a postcode searcher on the website.

Payments for or towards specific items or services which will make a 'positive' difference to the quality of life of individuals or groups.

Types of grants

Applications are treated on their merit. The majority of grants given are around £1,000. Previously, grants have been given for special clothing, footwear, mattresses and beds, indoor/outdoor wheelchairs, mobility scooters, kitchen equipment, a Meywalker and structural amendments to houses and living areas. Grants may be given for ordinary household items if it can be shown that they will have an impact on alleviating the disability rather than improving general family circumstances. Grants for UK holidays may also be considered, but applications should be submitted 6–12 months in advance of proposed holiday dates.

Annual grant total

In 2012 the charity had assets of £207,000 and an income of £92,000. Direct charitable expenditure totalled £98,000. The charity makes grants both to organisations and to individuals, though a breakdown of grants was not available in the accounts. We estimate that grants to individuals totalled £40,000.

At the time of writing (August 2014) this was the most recent financial information available for the charity.

Exclusions

No grants for: debts; education and course fees; debts; motor vehicle purchase or expenses; nursing and residential home fees; funeral expenses; removal expenses; driving lessons; items already purchased; therapies such as swimming with dolphins and hyperbaric therapy; alternative therapies such as reflexology, acupuncture and faith healing, i-Pads, or major home improvements.

Applications

Applications are welcomed from individuals, professional workers and representatives of organisations. Where the request is from a private individual, a detailed letter of support from a professional (such as a family doctor, a hospital consultant, a social worker, a teacher or a worker from a community or disability organisation) is essential. If applying for specialist seating, manual or powered wheelchairs, the letter must be from an occupational therapist or physiotherapist.

Applicants should first complete a short preliminary enquiry form. This can be done online at www.sfgroup.com, or by completing the form attached to the charity's information leaflet which can be requested by phone or email. The Fund Manager will make contact within two weeks of receiving the application to discuss the request in more detail.

Other information

The charity is also known as the Tishie Yong Foundation for the Disabled.

Vitalise

£190,000

Correspondent: The Bookings Team, 212 Business Design Centre, Upper Street, London N1 0QH (0303 3030145; fax: 020 7288 6899; email: bookings@vitalise.org.uk; website: www.vitalise.org.uk)

CC Number: 295072

Eligibility

Adults with physical disabilities and carers who might not otherwise be able to afford a break. Applicants must be aged 18 or over and must not have been on a break for over 12 months or have savings of more than £23,000. In exceptional circumstances, the charity may consider those who have been on a break in the previous 12 months. Applicants must not qualify for statutory funding.

Types of grants

Financial assistance towards the cost of a break at a Vitalise Centre. Assistance rarely covers the entire cost of a break. In 2012/13 the Joan Brander Memorial Fund was able to subsidise every break by £340.

Annual grant total

In 2012/13 the charity held assets of £6 million and had an income of £7.3 million. A total of £190,000 was expended from the Joan Brander Memorial Fund and helped to subsidise breaks for 363 individuals and families.

Exclusions

Grants do not cover associated costs; for example, transport to and from the centre.

Applications

Both an online application form and a downloadable form are available on the website. Applications require a letter of support from a social worker or healthcare professional.

Provisional bookings must be made before completing the application form.

Other information

While the charity can only provide a limited number of grants, it also offers advice on other funding options for potential guests.

Bruce Wake Charity

£56,000 (39 grants)

Correspondent: Peter Hems, Trustee, c/o Grant Thornton UK LLP, Regent House, 80 Regent Road, Leicester LE1 7NH (01162 471234; email: wake@webleicester.co.uk; website: www.brucewaketrust.co.uk)

CC Number: 1018190

Eligibility

People who are disabled (predominantly wheelchair-users) in the UK.

Types of grants

The trustees will consider grant applications related to the provision of leisure activities for the disabled, but favour particularly applications whereby the potential beneficiaries meet one or all of the following criteria:

- The potential beneficiaries are physically disabled wheelchair users
- Improved access for wheelchair users is proposed
- A sporting or leisure activity involving disabled wheelchair users is proposed

Annual grant total

In 2012/13, the charity had assets of £8.8 million, which generated an income of £193,000. Grants were made to individuals totalling £90,000, of which £34,000 was paid through Leicester Charity Link and 39 grants totalling £56,000 were paid directly by the charity.

Applications

In writing through a charitable organisation or equivalent recognised body. Applications should include all appropriate financial information. They are considered quarterly.

Other information

Grants were made to 149 organisations totalling £348,000.

Aids/HIV

Eileen Trust

£63,000

Correspondent: Linda Haigh, Finance Manager, Alliance House, 12 Caxton Street, London SW1H 0QS (020 7808 1172)

CC Number: 1028027

Eligibility

People who have contracted HIV through NHS treatment, for example, following transfusions or a needlestick injury. It provides financial support in the form of small regular payments or one-off payments to affected individuals and their dependents.

Types of grants

Financial help is given in three ways: regular monthly payments of £150 to £800 (in 2012/13) to contribute to meeting the additional costs of living with HIV, or assist those who have been bereaved; single payments of £670 to £5,000 (in 2012/13) in response to specific requests for help; and winter payments of £1,000 (supplementary to regular payments).

Annual grant total

In 2012/13 the trust held assets of £190,000 and had an income of £84,000. Grants and payments to individuals totalled more than £63,000 and were distributed as follows:

Regular payments	£35,000
Winter payments	£16,000
Grants	£12,700

Applications

Applications for assistance are received in the main via the trust's case worker and from time to time by direct approach.

George House Trust

See entry on page 253

The Terrence Higgins Trust Hardship Fund

£329,000

Correspondent: Terence Higgins Trust, 314–320 Gray's Inn Road, London WC1X 8DP (020 7812 1600; fax: 020 7812 1601; email: info@tht.org.uk; website: www.tht.org.uk)

CC Number: 288527

Eligibility

People in the UK who have HIV and are in severe financial need.

Types of grants

One-off emergency grants.

Annual grant total

In 2012/13 Terence Higgins Trust held assets of £6.5 million and had an income of £20.1 million. Through its Hardship Fund, the trust awarded £329,000, supporting 2,300 people living in 'the most severe poverty and destitution.'

Exclusions

No grants for council tax, rent, holiday expenses, air fares or funeral costs.

Applications

Applications are made via the trust's network of offices and referral agencies, a list of which can be found on the THT website. Application enquiries to the correspondent can also be made by telephone and email.

Other information

Terence Higgins Trust is the largest HIV and sexual health charity in Europe. Its Hardship Fund is supported by the Elton John AIDS Foundation and the MAC AIDS Fund.

The trust offers a range of services for people affected by HIV, such as: advice services, including benefits advice (which supported 4,300 people in 2012/13) and counselling services (supported 500 people in London alone during 2012/13). In 2012/13 more than 8,000 people benefitted from the trust's Long Term Condition Management (LTCM) services, which support people to live healthily with their condition.

THT also runs myHIV.org.uk, a website containing self-management tools, a community forum and information.

Amongst its other work, the trust runs the national HIV prevention programme, HIV Prevention England.

JAT

£5,000

Correspondent: Janine Clements, Director, JAT, 2A Dunstan Road, London NW11 8AA (07546 429885; website: www.jat-uk.org)

CC Number: 327936

Eligibility

Jewish people with HIV/AIDS.

Types of grants

One-off grants are available from the trust, which may share the cost of major items with other agencies. Past grants have been given towards the costs of Passover food, travel expenses for respite care, washing machines, cookers, moving costs and so on.

Annual grant total

The total for grants to individuals generally does not exceed £5,000 per year.

Exclusions

No grants are given towards rent, mortgage arrears, luxury items or repayments of loans, debts or credit cards.

Applications

On a form available from the correspondent. All referrals must be through a professional person such as a social worker, health visitor and so on. A referral must accompany every application and be on headed paper including client's name, date of birth, detailed breakdown of weekly income, details and nature of request, name, position and signature of referrer and details of whom the cheque should be made payable to. First applications require symptomatic proof of HIV diagnosis from the applicant's doctor.

Other information

The trust was established to provide support and advice for Jewish people affected by HIV. The trust provides 'confidential, non-judgemental' support services for its beneficiaries.

The Macfarlane Trust

£2.7 million

Correspondent: Linda Haigh, Finance Manager, Alliance House, 12 Caxton Street, London SW1H 0QS (020 7233 0057; fax: 020 7808 1169; email: admin@macfarlane.org.uk; website: www.macfarlane.org.uk)

CC Number: 298863

Eligibility

People with haemophilia who as a result of receiving contaminated blood products are living with HIV, and their dependents. No other people are eligible. The trust is in contact with those known to have haemophilia and to be HIV positive through infected blood products and therefore any further eligibility to register with the trust seems unlikely. Assistance is also given to the bereaved spouses or partners of an infected beneficiary.

Types of grants

One-off and recurrent grants are available towards the additional costs associated in living with HIV. Grants can be given towards health-related needs such as convalescence, respite, travel, clothes, medical care and specialist equipment. Grants are also given to primary beneficiaries towards winter fuel costs (payments of either £500 or £250) and towards supplementing the costs of children who are dependents. Payments to ensure that widows and dependents have a household income of at least £19,000 per year are also awarded.

Annual grant total

In 2012/13 the trust held assets of £4.6 million and had an income of £2.2 million. Grants to individuals totalled £2.7 million and were distributed as follows:

Widows payments and dependents	£1.1 million
Discretionary top up payments	£981,000
Dependents supplement payments	£310,000
One-off grants	£160,000
Winter payments	£113,000

Applications

On an application form available from the correspondent, although requests by letter or telephone are also considered. A medical report and supporting letter from a doctor or similar medical professional are required. Applicants must be registered with the trust in order to apply.

Other information

Note the following from the trust's latest annual report:

> By far the majority of our funding is committed to regular payments to beneficiaries; we regard the retention and increase of these as our top priority. After our commitments to management costs, to enable us to run the Trust, we are currently only able to allocate a small grants budget, which is inadequate for the level of demand from our beneficiaries. Unfortunately, following the introduction of the MFET Ltd payments, and the publication of the Archer Report, the Macfarlane Trust's overall allocation was reduced significantly and this has impacted on our ability to make financial grants.

The trust offers benefits and financial advice and through its informative website, signposts to other helpful organisations. On its website, the trust also has online community resources to which its beneficiaries can login.

Alzheimer's disease

The Margaret and Alick Potter Charitable Trust

See entry on page 212

Arthritis and rheumatism

Arthritis Action (Arthritic Association Treating Arthritis Naturally)

£7,100

Correspondent: Graham Weir, Company Secretary, 1 Upperton Gardens, Eastbourne, East Sussex BN21 2AA (0800 652 3188 (freephone), 01323 416550 (general); email: info@arthriticassociation.org.uk; website: www.arthriticassociation.org.uk)

CC Number: 292569

Eligibility

People who have arthritis or a related condition, and are in financial need. Grants are only available to members of the Arthritic Association, those who are undertaking a dietary programme with the association and towards treatments associated with the programme.

Types of grants

One-off grants in kind for consultation fees, dietary supplements and remedial therapy:

> Every member following the association's Gold Programme is entitled to a free physical assessment and two free treatments. Thereafter, they are eligible to apply for a non-means-tested grant to assist with subsequent fees for consultations with independent and regulated health practitioners. Grants to members include reimbursement of these fees and payments made direct to associated practitioners in respect of consultations with members.

Annual grant total

In 2012/13 the association had assets of £6.7 million and an income of £537,000. Grants totalled £8,100, of which £7,100 was paid to members to help with consultation fees and about £1,000 was given in research grants to universities.

Applications

Application forms are available from the correspondent. They can be submitted directly by the individual or through a social worker, Citizens Advice or other welfare agency. Our research suggests that requests are normally considered in January, March, July and October.

Other information

Arthritis Action works to promote natural dietary treatments for arthritis, makes grants for research in this area and provides information on foods, postural management and mineral supplements.

The association states that they 'are the only UK-based charity to have developed a self-management programme which provides direct support through a healthy eating plan supported by a course of physical therapy.'

Strongbones Children's Charitable Trust

£112,000

Correspondent: April Fitzmaurice, Grants Officer, Unit B9 Seedbed Centre, Davidson Way, Romford RM7 0AZ (01708 750599; email: grantsofficer@strongbones.org.uk; website: www.strongbones.org.uk)

CC Number: 1086173

Eligibility

Young people under the age of 21 with scoliosis, brittle bone disease, bone cancer, arthritis or any other condition of the bone.

Types of grants
One-off grants of around of £250 – £1,000 for medical equipment, mobility aids, sensory equipment, specially adapted wheelchairs and trikes, furniture, computers/software, clothes, social activities, hospital travel and toys.

Annual grant total
In 2012/13 the trust held assets of £57,000 and had an income of £316,000. Grants to individuals totalled £112,000.

Exclusions
Holidays abroad, driving lessons, debts and bills, equipment where there has not been an assessment by an NHS physiotherapist, household appliances and furniture (excluding washing machines/dryers for incontinence).

Applications
Applicants may apply using the trust's online application form. Applications should include details of the child's condition and why a grant is needed. The trust also requires that forms are signed and accompanied by a cover letter from the child's NHS consultant, physiotherapist, GP, school nurse or social worker. Applications for funding over £1,000 should be accompanied by a quote. Decisions can take up to three months. Families can only receive one grant in any 12 month period and unsuccessful applicants may reapply at a later date.

Other information
The trust also owns homes which it uses to provide respite holidays for children and their families. Information on these homes and the trust's activities is available on its website.

Ataxia

Ataxia UK (formerly Friedreich's Ataxia Group)

£46,000

Correspondent: Susan Millman, Chief Executive, Ground Floor, Lincoln House, 1 – 3 Brixton Road, London SW9 6DE (020 7582 1444; email: office@ataxia.org.uk; website: www.ataxia.org.uk)

CC Number: 1102391

Eligibility
People who are in need and have Cerebellar Ataxia (Friedreich's Ataxia and spinocerebellar).

Types of grants
A number of Cornberg Grants are available towards the costs of specialist equipment and home adaptations. The Jerry Farr Travel Fellowship awards a maximum of £3,500 to fund a travel experience for one Ataxia sufferer each year.

Annual grant total
In 2012/13 the charity had assets of £890,000 and an income of £990,000. Grants to individuals totalled £46,000 and were distributed as follows:

Cornberg (Assistance and Adaptation Grants)	£38,000
General welfare	£7,700
Jerry Farr Travel Scholarship	£300

Exclusions
People may apply only if they have not received a grant from the charity in the past three years.

Applications
For more information and to find out if you are eligible for a Cornberg Grant, contact the helpline on 0845 644 0606 or email helpline@ataxia.org.uk. Closing dates for rounds of applications are displayed on the website.

Application forms for the Jerry Farr Travel Scholarship can be downloaded from the website.

Note: The charity is no longer accepting applications for general welfare grants.

Other information
Much of the charity's expenditure contributes towards research of Cerebellar Ataxia; in 2012/13 a total of £375,000 was contributed in research grants to external institutions and towards the charity's own research activities.

The charity also runs centres providing information, a helpline, services and advocacy for people affected by the illness. You can contact the helpline by calling 0845 644 0606 or emailing helpline@ataxia.org.uk.

Blindness/ partial sight

Action for Blind People

£11,500 (21 grants)

Correspondent: Anita M. South, Administrator, Action House, 53 Sandgate Street, London SE15 1LE (020 7635 4800; email: central@actionforblindpeople.org.uk; website: www.actionforblindpeople.org.uk)

CC Number: 205913

Eligibility
Registered blind or partially sighted people who are in need and live within the boundaries of the charity's action areas. Applicants will need to show that they have exhausted other funding options.

Types of grants
Grant assistance is available for holiday breaks (excluding travel costs) and assistive software technology, such as SuperNova, ZoomText, HAL and JAWS.

Annual grant total
In 2012/13 the charity had assets of £21.5 million and a consolidated income of £21.5 million. Grants were made to 21 individuals totalling £11,500 which was given in grants to facilitate independent living and provision of assistive technology software.

Exclusions
If applying for a holiday grant, the applicant must not have had a holiday in the last five years.

Applications
On a form available from the correspondent. Applications for assistance will only be accepted from people living within an action team area, supported by an action coordinator. A list of action areas can be found on the charity's website or by calling the national freephone helpline on 0800 915 4666.

Note: grants are usually paid directly to the service or product supplier.

Other information
Following a review of its services in 2007, the charity has limited its grants programme to holiday and software grants and is only available to clients who live within the boundaries of the charity's 'action teams', which are all based in England (call 0303 123 9999 to check the boundaries). As a result it now gives far less in direct grants than it has done in previous years. However, the charity does provide help and advice on a wide range of issues including applying for benefits, housing, aids and adaptations, finding a job and accessing local services.

In 2009 the charity finalised an Association Agreement with the Royal National Institute for the Blind (RNIB), making it part of the RNIB Group. *(See the RNIB entry for further information on their activities).*

Blind Children UK (formerly National Blind Children's Society)

£3,000

Correspondent: Phillippa Caine, Administrator, Hillfields, Reading Road, Burghfield Common, Reading, Berkshire RG7 3YG (0800 781 1444; email: services@blindchildrenuk.org; website: www.nbcs.org.uk)

CC Number: 1051607

Eligibility

People aged up to 25 years in full-time education who are (or are eligible to be) registered blind or partially sighted and live in the UK.

Types of grants

One-off grants towards IT equipment or sensory/recreational equipment for use in the home to aid with the individual's learning and development.

Annual grant total

In 2012 the society had assets of £679,000 and an income of £1 million. Grants for equipment totalled almost £3,000 and there were no grants for other purposes made this year. The 2012 accounts were the latest available at the time of writing (August 2014).

Applications

On a form available from the correspondent, for consideration at monthly meetings. Applications can be submitted either by the individual with a supporting letter, or via a social worker, welfare agency or qualified teacher of people who are visually impaired. They are considered on a monthly basis.

Other information

Grants are also made to organisations in support of groups of children with visual impairments.

Gardner's Trust for the Blind

£38,000

Correspondent: Angela Stewart, 117 Charterhouse Street, London EC1M 6AA (020 7253 3757)

CC Number: 207233

Eligibility

Registered blind or partially-sighted people who live in the UK.

Types of grants

One-off grants for domestic household tools and for educational purposes. The trust also gives grants in the form of pensions.

Annual grant total

In 2012/13 the trust had assets of almost £3.3 million and an income of £94,000. Education and trade grants totalled £13,000 and music grants £1,000. General aid grants and annual grantees totalled £38,000.

Exclusions

No grants for holidays, residential or nursing home fees or for loan repayments.

Applications

In writing to the correspondent. Applications can be submitted either directly by the individual or by a third party, but they must also be supported by a third party who can confirm the disability and that the grant is needed. They are considered in March, June, September and December and should be submitted at least three weeks before the meeting.

Other information

Grants are also given for educational purposes.

The Royal Blind Society for the UK

£18,000

Correspondent: Grants Co-ordinator, 6 St John's Parade, Alinora Crescent, Goring-by-Sea, Worthing, West Sussex BN12 4HJ (01903 245379; email: grants@royalblindsociety.org; website: www.royalblindsociety.org.uk)

CC Number: 1131623

Eligibility

People who are registered blind or partially sighted and on a low income.

Types of grants

General grants are provided to blind and partially sighted people on low incomes for a wide range of purposes.

Annual grant total

In 2013 (a 15-month accounting period), the society had assets of £796,000 and an income of £1.6 million. Grants to individuals totalled £9,400 and a further £8,600 was spent on grants from restricted funds.

The society also provided holidays and breaks for more than 2,400 beneficiaries, with £1.1 million spent providing breaks over fifteen months.

Applications

On a form available from the correspondent or to download from the website. Applications must be submitted through a professional welfare worker who knows the applicant well, for example, a social worker or similar welfare advisor. They are considered on a quarterly basis. The society offers informal advice on the application process and applicants should contact the grants co-ordinator on 01903 245379 for assistance.

Other information

The society's objects are to relieve persons who are blind or partially sighted and in charitable need. It has done this by providing holidays to blind and partially sighted people in the society's two hotels to break social isolation, financial support by way of small grants and providing the services of dedicated family support workers to visually impaired children and their families.

The Family Support Service is a national initiative that aims to support every child diagnosed with a serious eye condition, providing tailored care, guidance, and encouragement to them and their families using a national network of family support workers.

Holidays and breaks are offered that have been designed to specifically accommodate visually impaired and disabled people and their families. Holidays are tailored to suit individual needs and interests. For more information see www.royalblindsociety.org/holidays

Merger with Eyeless Trust

The society's website states:

> The Royal Blind Society for the United Kingdom which has been helping Blind and Partially Sighted people for 150 years has announced a merger with The Eyeless Trust. The Eyeless Trust was created by the late Lillian Ramsay MBE and has, in the 20 years since its formation, worked tirelessly throughout the United Kingdom to support children with particular congenital visual impairments, and their families, through dedicated Family Support Workers.
>
> For a number of years the two charities have worked closely together with the Royal Blind Society providing holidays and activity days for children supported by the Eyeless Trust at its hotels. The two charities have also shared some administrative and fundraising support.
>
> The newly enlarged Royal Blind Society will continue the work of The Eyeless Trust as the Children and Families Division of the Royal Blind Society. The two charities will use the positive synergy between the two organisations, not only to increase the number of visually impaired children supported, but also to offer a wider range of services to blind and partially sighted children and their families.

Note: On 12 May 2014 the following information was posted on the trust's website by Gareth Holmes, author at the society:

> The Royal Blind Society has announced that it has placed its East Preston based

Bradbury Hotel and Belmont Hotels on the property market, following long-term falling demand and financial pressure.

Eileen Harding, the charity's Chief Executive Officer, said of the announcement: This was an extremely hard decision to make. Everyone at The Royal Blind Society understands that the hotels are a special place for many guests. And that the Royal Blind Society staff have been central to that.

Mrs Harding went on to say: A big priority for us now is to partner with an organisation in the regions to ensure we can offer alternative holiday accommodation when the sales have been completed. We tried to keep the hotels open for as long as possible as a specialist provision, but the sad fact is that only 10% of our rooms are used and we are unable to afford the on-going costs.

For further, current information visit the society's website.

The Royal National Institute of Blind People (RNIB)

£60,000

Correspondent: Grants Team, Information Resource Team, RNIB, 105 Judd Street, London WC1H 9NE (Helpline: 0303 123 9999; email: InfoResourceTeam@rnib.org.uk.; website: www.rnib.org.uk)

CC Number: 226227

Eligibility

Registered or certified blind and partially-sighted people who live in the UK and receive a means-tested benefit (excluding tax credits). Applicants must have been rejected for funding by their local authority for the items needed and must have savings of less than £6,000.

Types of grants

One-off grants of up to £400, though the charity has strict guidelines on how much it will give for certain items. Grants are only available for carpets and flooring (for health and safety reasons), essential adaptations, repairs or redecorations, white goods, cookers, microwaves, furniture, talking kitchen or labelling equipment, and (only in exceptional circumstances) washer dryers and tumble dryers.

Priority is given to items essential for day-to-day living.

Annual grant total

Grants to individuals usually total around £60,000 per year.

Exclusions

Emergency grants are not available. No grants for recreational needs, educational costs, nursing home fees, the costs of medical treatment, telephone installation, employment needs or repeatedly accruing debts. Successful applicants cannot reapply within three years.

Applications

Application forms are available to download from the website. Applications must be supported by a professional who knows the personal circumstances of the applicant, such as a social worker, occupational therapist, health care visitor or a worker from a local society for the blind. Applicants must not use a GP, family member or friend as their support. Applications are considered throughout the year.

Note: if the total amount required exceeds the maximum grant amount (£400) then the rest of the funding must be secured before an application to RNIB is submitted.

Other information

The RNIB provides a number of services for blind and partially sighted people, including a telephone helpline (listed above). The charity also offers financial guidance, including information on benefits and welfare as well as advice on other sources of funding, both statutory and from other organisations.

Bowel conditions

The National Association for Colitis and Crohn's Disease (Crohn's and Colitis UK)

£73,000

Correspondent: Caroline Hardy, Administrator, 4 Beaumont House, Beaumont Works, Sutton Road, St Albans AL1 5HH (01727 830038; email: enquiries@crohnsandcolitis.org.uk; website: www.crohnsandcolitis.org.uk)

CC Number: 1117148, SC038632

Eligibility

People in need who have ulcerative colitis, Crohn's Disease or related inflammatory bowel diseases (IBD). Candidates must have been resident in the UK for at least six months and be on a low income. Carers may also be supported.

Types of grants

One-off grants of up to £300 to meet special needs which have arisen as a direct result of the illness. Support can be given for washing machines, dryers, refrigerators, telephone installation, clothing, beds and bedding, recuperative holidays and so on.

No more than three grants in any six year period can be given to each applicant.

Annual grant total

At the time of writing (August 2014) the latest financial information available was from 2012. In 2012 the charity had assets of £3 million and an income of £3.6 million. Personal grants totalled £75,000 and were awarded to 237 individuals. Some support is given to individuals in education therefore we estimate that social welfare grants totalled around £73,000.

Exclusions

Recurring household bills or debts cannot be considered.

Applications

Application forms are available to download from the charity's website. The form has two extra sections, one of which should be completed by a doctor to confirm the individual's illness and one to be filled in by a social worker (or health visitor, district nurse, CAB advisor and so on). Completed applications should be sent to the personal grants fund secretary at: PO Box 334, St Albans, Herts AL1 2WA. Applications are normally considered every six to eight weeks.

Payments are usually made to the service provider, shop or other agency, not the applicant.

Other information

Grants are also made for educational purposes and to institutions for research. Occasionally local grants are made to hospitals. The main role of the charity is to provide information and advice to people living with IBD.

Further information on grants can be obtained from Julia Devereux (telephone: 0800 011 4701 or 01727 759654; email: julia.devereux@crohnsandcolitis.org.uk).

Brittle bones

The Brittle Bone Society

£46,000

Correspondent: Patricia Osborne, Chief Executive, 30 Guthrie Street, Dundee DD1 5BS (01382 204446; fax: 01382 206771; email: contact@brittlebone.org; website: www.brittlebone.org)

CC Number: 272100

Eligibility

Children and others with osteogenesis imperfecta (brittle bones) or similar disorders. Only members of the society are eligible for funding.

Types of grants

Grants in the range of £200 to £5,000 towards wheelchairs and other specialist equipment. This could include home alterations, assistance with holiday costs and laptops for children who are unable to attend school for a prolonged period. The society orders equipment directly from the manufacturer and once received, the successful applicant is responsible for its insurance and maintenance.

The society notes that it will often not be able to fund the cost of whole items but will help raise the remaining funds on the applicant's behalf by applying to other trusts and grantmaking bodies.

Annual grant total

In 2012/13 the society held assets of £348,000 and had an income of £363,000. Grants to individuals totalled £46,000 and were distributed as follows:

Wheelchair purchase	£33,000
Welfare and equipment	£13,000
Wheelchair repairs	£2,900
Holidays	–

Exclusions

The society does not usually fund higher education, white goods or building works.

Applications

Contact the society by phone or email to make an initial enquiry and to receive an application via email or post. Health and social care professionals can request an application form on a client's behalf. The application form should include formal quotes for costs and a supporting letter from an occupational therapist, social worker or other professional as appropriate. The letter of support should confirm you have osteogenesis imperfecta, and state the need and suitability of the item for which you are requesting financial assistance.

Other information

The society also provides advice and support for people affected by osteogenesis imperfecta and works with children's medical institutions across the country.

Although the society does not offer advice on benefits rights directly, it can refer people seeking assistance to relevant organisations.

Cancer and Leukaemia

Miss Ada Oliver

£2,500

Correspondent: The Trustees c/o Marshalls Solicitors, c/o Marshalls Solicitors, 102 High Street, Godalming, Surrey GU7 1DS (01483 416101)

CC Number: 234456

Eligibility

People who have cancer or rheumatism and are in financial need. Preference is given for people living in Surrey.

Types of grants

Monthly and one-off grants of up to £100 are given for a variety of needs. Recent grants have been given for settling rent arrears, nursing home fees and necessities.

Annual grant total

In 2012/13 the charity had an income of £3,800 and a total expenditure of £5,300. We estimate that the total amount of grants awarded to individuals was £2,500 as the trust also gives grants to organisations.

Applications

In writing to the correspondent, including details of income and circumstances. Applications can be submitted throughout the year by a social worker, Citizens Advice or other welfare agency on behalf of the individual.

Brad's Cancer Foundation

£13,500

Correspondent: Susan Bartlett, Administrator, 14 Crosslands Meadow, Riverview Park, Colwick, Nottingham NG4 2DJ (01159 400313; email: mick@brads.org.uk; website: www.brads.org.uk)

CC Number: 1103797

Eligibility

Teenagers who have cancer and related illnesses throughout the East Midlands region.

Types of grants

The provision of financial assistance to teenagers and their families, including grants towards equipment. Awards are often of £500 or under.

Annual grant total

In 2012/13 the foundation had an income of £47,000 and a total expenditure of £19,800. Note that the charitable expenditure varies each year. In the past about £13,500 has been awarded to children and young people annually.

Applications

In writing to the correspondent.

Other information

Grants are also made to organisations, in particular, Teenage Cancer Trust.

CLIC Sargent

£1 million (5,107 grants)

Correspondent: Grants Department, Horatio House, 77–85 Fulham Place, London W6 8JA (020 8752 2878; website: www.clicsargent.org.uk)

CC Number: 1107328

Eligibility

Children and young people aged 24 and under who are living in the UK and are receiving treatment for cancer.

Types of grants

Grants of up to £250, though grants up to £500 may be approved for families who have an exceptional need. In addition there is an automatic grant of £170 which is made to every family as soon as a young person or child is diagnosed to help with immediate financial needs. Other types of grants, such as compassionate crisis or community support grants, may also be available to some. The need for financial support must be related to the child's illness and for the additional expenses incurred.

Annual grant total

In 2012/13 the charity made 5,107 grants totalling just over £1 million.

Exclusions

No grants are made for the costs of treatment, medical equipment, therapies or school fees.

Applications

Through a health or social care professional, such as a CLIC Sargent Social Worker.

Other information

Details of other financial support and services offered by the charity (including welfare advice) are available from a CLIC Sargent care professional. Alternatively, call 0300 330 0803 or visit the website for more information, advice and support.

CLIC Sargent was formed in 2005 following a merger between CLIC and Sargent Cancer Care for Children.

The Leukaemia Care Society

£11,400 (81 grants)

Correspondent: Monica Izmajlowicz, Chief Executive, One Birch Court, Blackpole East, Worcester WR3 8SG (01905 755977; email: care@leukaemiacare.org.uk; website: www.leukaemiacare.org.uk)

CC Number: 259483

Eligibility

People with leukaemia and allied blood disorders. Financial support is open to all patients and carers who are no more than four years post-diagnosis or, if there has been bereavement, no more than two years after this.

Types of grants

Grants in the form of vouchers for a choice of three supermarkets.

Annual grant total

In 2012/13 the society held assets of £1.4 million and had an income of £894,000. 81 grants towards individuals' general living costs totalled £11,400.

Exclusions

No repeat grants to individuals.

Applications

Applicants should first call the CARE Line on 0808 801 0444 to discuss their case and request the necessary forms. Applications usually take 14–30 days to complete. All applicants will be requested to complete an income and expenditure sheet and must provide proof of diagnosis such as a letter from their consultant.

Other information

The society also provides a signposting service in respect of welfare rights and other charities and organisations that may be able to offer grants and additional advice in areas such as debt management.

Macmillan Grants

£8.5 million (30,611 grants)

Correspondent: Grants Department, 89 Albert Embankment, London SE1 7UQ (080880800 00; fax: 020 7840 7841; website: www.macmillan.org.uk)

CC Number: 261017

Eligibility

People, of any age, who have cancer, or who are still affected by the illness, and are in financial need.

To qualify, applicants must not have capital savings of more than £8,000 per couple, or £6,000 for a single person. Household weekly disposable income (after housing costs) must not exceed: £170 for a single person, £289 for a couple, £85 for each child and £119 for each additional adult (when their income is relevant to the request). Certain benefits such as Disability Living Allowance and Attendance Allowance do not count as disposable income. These are general conditions, but Macmillan does take into account individual circumstances.

Types of grants

One-off grants of around £250 on average towards costs arising from cancer or its treatment: including travel to hospital, heating, clothing, furnishings, convalescence in the UK and so on.

Annual grant total

In 2012 the charity had assets of almost £54.5 million and an income of £155.7 million. Macmillan grants to 30,611 individuals totalled £8.5 million.

At the time of writing (August 2014) this was the most recent financial information available for the charity.

Exclusions

No grants for daily expenses, private medical care or holidays outside the UK.

Applications

On a form available from the correspondent. No direct applications can be made; they must be made through a Macmillan or community nurse, health or social worker, hospital social worker or a health professional from another welfare charity and be supported by a short medical report from a second professional such as your doctor, consultant or Macmillan nurse. Welfare workers can receive more information about the scheme by calling Macmillan Support Line on 0808 808 0000. Applications are usually processed on the day they are received and, if successful, payments are sent out within three working days.

Macmillan advises that the grant request must demonstrate a clear link to the impact of cancer and its treatment. Comprehensive application guidance notes are available on the website.

Other information

Grants to patients are only one feature of the charity's work. Others include funding Macmillan Nurses (who are skilled in providing advice and support on symptom control and pain relief), Macmillan buildings for in-patient and day care, and financing an education programme for professionals in palliative care. The fund also gives grants to three associated charities.

The charity now offers support in the form of its financial guidance service, which can help you understand everything from 'mortgages to pensions and insurance to savings'. You can speak to a financial guide by calling the Support Line or by emailing the team on financialguidance@macmillan.org.uk.

The Shona Smile Foundation

£1,100

Correspondent: Sue Gill, Trustee, 18 The Combers, Kesgrave, Ipswich IP5 2EY (email: sue_gill@sky.com; website: www.shonasmile.org)

CC Number: 1110177

Eligibility

Children and young people under the age of 18 who have one of the forms of rhabdomyosarcoma.

Types of grants

Cash donations towards, for example, everyday items, something that the child/young person wants or needs or helping to fulfil a dream of his/her choosing.

Annual grant total

In 2012/13 the foundation had an income of £2,600 and a total expenditure of £1,300. We estimate that grants to individuals totalled £1,100.

Applications

In writing to the correspondent.

Cerebral palsy

The Nihal Armstrong Trust

£18,000

Correspondent: Rahil Gupta, Trustee, 111 Chatsworth Road, London NW2 4BH (020 8459 6527; email: info@nihalarmstrongtrust.org.uk; website: www.nihalarmstrongtrust.org.uk)

CC Number: 1107567

Eligibility

Children living in the UK, up to and including the age of 18, with cerebral palsy. Applicants must be in receipt of means tested benefits and be able to provide supporting evidence.

Types of grants

Grants up to £1,000 towards equipment, communication aids or a particular service that will benefit children with cerebral palsy. Items/services must not be available from the local authority.

Annual grant total

In 2012/13 the trust had an income of £16,700 and a total expenditure of £20,000. We estimate that grants to individuals totalled £18,000.

Exclusions

The trust does not fund holidays, refurbishment costs or household appliances. Grants are not available as part-funding for equipment or services that cost more than £1,000.

Applications

Applications can be made via the trust's website and must be supported by a doctor, school, social worker, health visitor, speech, occupational therapist or physiotherapist. Trustees meet three times a year, with application deadlines falling one week before each quarterly meeting. See the trust's website for specific dates.

The trustees prefer to receive applications via the website where possible. Individuals who are sending information on equipment/services or suppliers' estimates, can forward any documents to the address provided in the 'contacts' section. A short list of supporting documents required is available on the trust's website.

Other information

The trust is managed by a small group of trustees who between them, have a wealth of experience relating to families who care for someone with cerebral palsy. The trust states it "is keen to make life easier for these families" and encourages individuals to apply.

Make A Child Smile

£2,300

Correspondent: John Somerset-How, Director, Purbeck Cottage, Westergate Street, Westergate, West Sussex PO20 3QS (01243 276693; email: j.somerset-how@sky.com; website: www.makeachildsmile.info)

CC Number: 1062275

Eligibility

Children with cerebral palsy.

Types of grants

One-off grants to support children with cerebral palsy through conductive education.

Annual grant total

In 2012/13 the charity had an income of £23,000 and a total expenditure of £24,000. Grants totalled £9,400. Salaries totalled £13,300. The charity gives grants to individuals and organisations to help towards the costs of buying therapy, services or equipment. No breakdown of the grants was given and we have estimated that grants to individuals whose parents/guardians/carers are financially disadvantaged is in the region of £2,300.

Applications

On an application form available from the correspondent. Requests for applications should be made online, via email or in writing. Applicants are visited upon submission of the application form.

Other information

The charity is also known as the UK Network for Conductive Education.

Cystic fibrosis

The Cystic Fibrosis Holiday Fund

£97,000 (80 grants)

Correspondent: Rachael Hutson, Secretary, 1 Bell Street, London NW1 5BY (020 7616 1300; fax: 020 7616 1306; email: info@cfholidayfund.org.uk; website: www.cfholidayfund.org.uk)

CC Number: 1088630

Eligibility

Children and young people up to the age of 25 who are diagnosed with cystic fibrosis, and their families.

Types of grants

Grants of around £250–£450 to enable children with cystic fibrosis to go on holidays or short trips (this may also include the child's family).

Annual grant total

At the time of writing (August 2014) the latest financial information available was from 2012. In 2012 the fund had assets of £99,000 and an income of £145,000. Holiday grants totalled £97,000.

Exclusions

People who have received grants within the previous two years cannot be assisted. The fund is usually unable to cover full costs and will not make retrospective grants.

Applications

Application forms can be downloaded from the fund's website, requested from the correspondent or completed line. A medical report form will be sent to applicants to be completed by their doctor/medical consultant. Applications are assessed by the fund's medical advisory panel which meets quarterly (see the website for the date of the next deadline or contact the correspondent). Note that the approval procedure can take a few months so applicants should leave enough time before their proposed holiday when applying.

Cystic Fibrosis Trust

£167,000 (281 grants)

Correspondent: Jackie Rice, Support Service Manager, 11 London Road, Bromley, Kent BR1 1BY (020 8464 7211; email: enquiries@cftrust.org.uk; website: www.cftrust.org.uk)

CC Number: 1079049

Eligibility

People in need who have cystic fibrosis.

Types of grants

One-off grants towards: household items that will directly benefit the health of the person with cystic fibrosis; assistance for those setting-up home for the first time (maximum grant of £300); the first annual prescription prepayment certificate; the cost of a holiday (maximum grant of £300, mainly for adults as the charity tends to refer children to the Cystic Fibrosis Holiday Fund); help at home or items that may facilitate an earlier discharge from hospital or prevent a hospital stay; costs during a hospital stay for a transplant or assessment (this may include carer's costs and is limited to £250); and help with funeral costs (maximum grant of £750). See the trust's guidelines for more details as in some cases, a separate application form may be required.

Annual grant total

In 2012/13 the trust held assets of £11.9 million and had an income of £9.7 million. A total of £167,000 was awarded in 281 grants to individuals.

Exclusions

Computers, cars, driving lessons, major home improvements, debts or to meet ongoing costs. Holiday grants are only awarded to people who have not had a holiday in the last two years (other than under exceptional circumstances).

Applications

Application forms are available from the correspondent or can be downloaded from the website. Applications must be supported by a social worker or other professional and should state whether the applicant has applied to other charities and the outcome, the general financial circumstances and the reason for the application. The trust strongly advises that individuals or their health professionals contact the welfare grants officer before submitting an application.

The trust has produced an application guideline document which is available on the website.

Other information

The trust also provides confidential advice, support and information on all aspects of cystic fibrosis in the form of factsheets and dedicated helplines for general and welfare benefits advice.

The trust also has a Helpline (0300 373 1000).

Deafblind

Sense, the National Deaf-Blind and Rubella Association

£0

Correspondent: Krystyna Cieslik, Assessment and Advice Officer, Sense, 101 Pentonville Road, London N1 9LG (01215 259137; fax: 0300 330 9251; email: krystyna.cieslik@sense.org.uk; website: www.sense.org.uk)

CC Number: 289868

Eligibility

People who are deaf-blind or multi-sensory impaired, and their families.

Types of grants

One-off emergency grants only, in exceptional circumstances. Grants range between £50 and £100, though more may be awarded in specific cases. Part-funding for more expensive items may be available.

Annual grant total

In 2012/13 the charity held assets of £46 million and had an income of £80 million.

Applications

Note the following statement: 'As a charity, Sense does not provide grant funding to individuals'

However, applications for the Richmond Trust can be made through the charity:

> The Richmond Trust is a small grant-awarding trust for deafblind people and their families . . . The Richmond Trust meets twice a year so there may be a delay between application and any communication from the trust. Applications for grants can be made via Sense's Information and Advice Service or through Krystyna Cieslik.

Other information

Sense provides a complete range of support and services for people with dual sensory impairments, or a sensory impairment and another disability (and their families) including holidays.

Dystonia

The Dystonia Society

£246 (1 grant)

Correspondent: Angie Brown, Helpline and Support Manager, The Dystonia Society, 1st Floor, 89 Albert Embankment, London SE1 7TP (0845 458 6211; fax: 0845 458 6311; email: angie@dystonia.org.uk; website: www.dystonia.org.uk)

CC Number: 1068595

Eligibility

People living with Dystonia in the UK.

Types of grants

One-off and recurrent grants according to need.

Annual grant total

In 2012/13 the society had assets of £506,000 and an income of £721,000. During the year only one grant was made – £246 to an individual (£27,000 to six individuals in 2011/12).

Exclusions

No grants for medical treatment or other therapies, or for items or services available from the NHS.

Applications

On a form available from the correspondent. Application forms must be endorsed by a health or social care professional who has known the applicant for at least two years.

Grants do not usually exceed £300, except in special circumstances.

Haemato-logical disorders

Roald Dahl's Marvellous Children's Charity

£91,000 (323 grants)

Correspondent: Richard Piper, Chief Executive, 81A High Street, Great Missenden, Buckinghamshire HP16 0AL (01494 890465; fax: 01494 890459; email: enquiries@roalddahlcharity.org; website: www.roalddahlcharity.org)

CC Number: 1137409

Eligibility

The pilot programme is open to any family in the UK in which:

- There is a child or children with a serious long-term health condition ('affected child or children')
- The affected child or children are eligible to receive High Rate DLA (the Care component) or the Enhanced Rate for 6 of the 12 activities in the PIP or an has equivalent level of need
- At least one affected child has yet to reach their 21st birthday
- Some form of support would help improve the emotional or psychological state of some or all of the family members (not necessarily the affected child/children)
- There are serious financial constraints that mean the family cannot access such support
- The family has never received a grant from the Stronger Families Programme

Types of grants

During the pilot period the maximum amount for a grant is £500. There is a preliminary list of things that the charity may support on the website.

Annual grant total

In 2012/13 the charity held assets of £1.4 million and had an income of £707,000. The charity gave grants totalling £91,000, helping 323 families.

A further £368,000 was given in project and research grants and in funding for specialist children's nurses.

Exclusions

The charity does not expect to fund: debts or repayment of utility bills, rent, etc.; trips outside the UK for medical treatment or holidays; educational fees; car seats, walkers, bicycles, pushchairs or mobility chairs; specialist furniture, fittings or household appliances; beds, cots, bedding or clothing; living expenses when a child is admitted to hospital away from the hometown; travel expenses to and from hospital.

Applications

At the time of writing (August 2014) the charity is running a new pilot grants programme – the Stronger Families Programme. The pilot stage of the programme is set to run until October 2014, with plans to 'roll out the new style programme from November 2014' after any refinements have been made.

Applications for the pilot programme must be made through established 'Applicant Officers' such as a social worker, healthcare professional or a charity representative. For more information, refer to the grant application guidance on the website.

Other information

Note: all information applies to the pilot programme which is in progress at the time of writing.

Haemophilia

The Haemophilia Society (The Tanner Fund)

£4,000

Correspondent: Liz Carroll, Chief Executive, First Floor, Petersham House, 57A Hatton Garden, London EC1N 8JG (020 7831 1020; fax: 020 7405 4824; email: info@haemophilia.org.uk; website: www.haemophilia.org.uk)

CC Number: 288260

Eligibility

People with haemophilia and related bleeding disorders, and their families.

Types of grants

One-off hardship grants up to £200 for items relating to applicants' medical problems, such as bedding, fridges to store treatment, floor coverings and washing machines.

Annual grant total

In 2012/13 the society had assets of £803,000 and an income of £875,000. Grants made to individuals through the Tanner Fund totalled £4,000.

Exclusions

No grants are given for debts, holidays, motor vehicles or ongoing bills such as gas or electricity.

Applications

On a form available from the correspondent. Applications must be completed in conjunction with a medical professional or a social worker. They are considered as received. Note that each family may only make one application a year.

Other information

The society, founded in 1950, is the UK's 'only national independent charity for all people affected by bleeding disorders', with centres across the country. The organisation's central activities include the provision of information, advocacy with the government and the NHS, as well as providing support to sufferers of bleeding disorders in making informed decisions regarding treatment.

The society also has a helpline: 0800 018 6068.

Huntingdon's disease

The Huntington's Disease Association

£12,000

Correspondent: Nicholas Heath, Trustee, Suite 24, Liverpool Science Park IC1, 131 Mount Pleasant, Liverpool L3 5TF (01513 315444; fax: 01513 315441; email: info@hda.org.uk; website: www.hda.org.uk)

CC Number: 296453

Eligibility

People with Huntington's disease, their immediate families and those at risk, who live in England or Wales.

Types of grants

One-off grants only, typically of up to £350, although each application is considered on merit. Grants have been for clothing, furniture, domestic equipment (e.g. washing machines and cookers) and flooring.

Annual grant total

In 2012/13 the association had assets of £996,000 and an income of £1.8 million. Expenditure for welfare grants to individuals tends to vary each year and in past years has totalled around £12,000.

Exclusions

No grants towards equipment or services that should be provided by statutory services. Support will not be given for the payment of debts, loans, bills, funeral expenses, holidays or travel.

Applications

On a form available from the correspondent. Applications should be submitted through a Regional Care Adviser or other professional. Requests are processed monthly. Full guidance notes are available on request.

Liver

The Ben Hardwick Fund

£15,000

Correspondent: Anne Auber, 12 Nassau Road, Barnes, London SW13 9QE (020 8741 8499)

CC Number: 1062554

Eligibility

Children with primary liver disease, and their families, who are in need.

Types of grants

One-off and recurrent grants, usually ranging between £150 and £500, to help with costs which are the direct result of the child's illness, such as hospital travel costs, in-hospital expenses, telephone bills and childminding for other children left at home.

Annual grant total

In 2012/13 the fund had an income of £4,200 and a total expenditure of £19,700.

Applications

In writing to the correspondent, usually through a hospital social worker or other welfare professional. Applications are considered at any time.

Other information

The fund also makes grants to organisations.

Meningitis

Meningitis Trust

£126,000

Correspondent: Grants Financial Officer, Fern House, Bath Road, Stroud GL5 3TJ (01453 768000; email: info@meningitisnow.org; website: www.meningitis-trust.org)

CC Number: 803016

Eligibility

People in need who have meningitis or who have disabilities as a result of meningitis.

Types of grants

One-off and recurrent grants towards respite care, sign language lessons, specialist aids and equipment, travel and accommodation costs, therapeutic activities, re-education and special training, and funeral expenses and headstones.

Annual grant total

In 2012/13 the trust had assets totalling £1.3 million and an income of over £2.6 million. Grants for educational and welfare purposes totalled £251,000 and we have estimated the welfare grants figure to be around £126,000.

Exclusions

Usually no grants will be given towards domestic bill arrears, clothing, bedding and furniture.

Applications

On a form available from the correspondent or downloaded from the website, where criteria is also posted. An initial telephone call to the grants financial officer on 01453 769043 or the 24-hour helpline on 0800 028 1828 to discuss the application process is welcomed. Applications should be submitted through a third party and are reviewed on a monthly basis.

Other information

The trust runs a 'family day' for children who have meningitis and their families. The day includes arts, crafts and music for children and gives parents an opportunity to meet the trust's staff and other families. The trust also supports a range of professional counselling, home visits, therapy and information services. The trust has an informative website.

Mental illness

The Matthew Trust

£20,000

Correspondent: Annabel Thompson, Director, PO Box 604, London SW6 3AG (020 7736 5976; fax: 020 7731 6961; email: amt@matthewtrust.org; website: www.matthewtrust.org)

CC Number: 294966

Eligibility

The trust is currently running four projects with the aims of: supporting children under 16 who have mental health problems; providing breaks for child carers; supporting young people aged 16–25 who have mental health problems; and enabling people with mental health problems who are over 60 through projects, with a view to promoting their inclusion in the wider community.

The priorities of the charity may change so applicants are advised to consult the website before applying.

Types of grants

One-off grants of between £50 and £250 towards counselling or medical bills; the provision of equipment and furniture to make a flat liveable; the provision of security equipment; and the provision of personal clothing items. The trust also helps with second chance learning and skills training; travel costs for prison visits; respite breaks; and debt support in special circumstances.

Annual grant total

In 2012/13 the trust held assets of £270,000 and had an income of £49,000. Grants to individuals totalled £20,000.

Applications

In writing to the correspondent through a professional agency such as a social worker, probation officer, community care worker or GP. The professional representative should also include their name and contact details on the application. Applications should include: the name, address, age and gender of the applicant; the health and age of other close family members; a summary of the mental health problem; the applicant's present circumstances; the type of support required, including costs where applicable; if the applicant has received support from the trust previously; and details of any other organisations which have been approached for support. Applications may be posted or emailed.

Note: The Matthew Trust is a 'last-stop' agency and will only consider applications when all other avenues of statutory and voluntary funding have been exhausted and then only where a care programme has been established.

Motor neurone

The Motor Neurone Disease Association

£811,000

Correspondent: Support Services, MND Association, David Niven House, 10–15 Notre Dame Mews, Northampton NN1 2BG (01604 611802; email: support.services@mndassociation.org; website: www.mndassociation.org)

CC Number: 294354

Eligibility

People with motor neurone disease, living in England, Wales and Northern Ireland.

Types of grants

i) Top-up of respite care (usually £500–£2,000).

ii) Equipment rental.

iii) Building adaptations.

Annual grant total

In 2012/13 the trust held assets of £5.6 million and had an income of £13.3 million. Grants to individuals totalled £811,000.

Applications

On a form available online or to download from the website. Applications must be submitted through a health or social care professional. In addition to stating what is requested, applications should include details of why the need is not met by statutory sources and where any payments should be made.

Other information

The trust has a network of association branches which can offer information about the grants available. Further information is available on the trust's website.

Multiple sclerosis

Multiple Sclerosis Society

£1.6 million

Correspondent: The Grants Team, MS National Centre, 372 Edgware Road, Cricklewood, London NW2 6ND (020 8438 0700; fax: 020 8438 0701; email: grants@mssociety.org.uk.; website: www.mssociety.org.uk)

CC Number: 1139257

Eligibility

People with multiple sclerosis and their families and carers, living in the UK. People living in Scotland or Northern Ireland may be subject to other conditions, contact MS Society Scotland (01313 354050) or MS Society Northern Ireland (02890 802803) for full details.

Types of grants

One-off grants towards: home and car adaptations; mobility aids, wheelchairs and other specialised equipment; driving lessons for a person with MS or their carer; activities for adult carers, including hobbies or courses; and grants for young carers to help with things like music lessons, school trips and sports equipment.

The society runs a short breaks and respite care grant programme. Grants are considered for:

- Respite care, in the home or at a care centre or similar
- An activity (or series of activities), short break or holiday for someone with MS and/or their carer/family
- Salary costs for a professional carer needed to help someone with MS, or their carer, have a break in the home or elsewhere
- Associated costs such as travel, accommodation and disability equipment hire
- Some alternative or complementary therapies

The society in England, Wales and Northern Ireland has two funds which offer grants to carers:

Carers Grant Fund has three age categories:

- Young carers (aged 15 and under) can apply for a one-off grant of up to £300
- 'Transitional' carers (aged 16–24) can apply for a one-off grant of £300 (leisure) or £1,000 (personal development)

- Adult carers (aged 25 and over) can apply every five years for grants of up to £300 (leisure) and £1,000 (personal development)

Short Breaks and Activities Fund: Carers can apply for grants towards the costs of short breaks, holidays, activities, and respite care.

For more information about both funds, visit the website or contact the London grants team.

Annual grant total

In 2012 the society held assets of £18.2 million and had an income of £25.4 million. Grants given in support of individuals totalled £1.6 million.

At the time of writing (August 2014) this was the most recent financial information available.

Exclusions

Applicants with more than £16,000 in savings are not eligible for regular grants and those with more than £8,000 in savings are expected to contribute towards the cost of the item. For a short break or activity grant you are not eligible if you have more than £23,000 in savings.

Grants cannot be made for purchases already made; any ongoing or long-term financial commitments (such as living costs and bills); loans, debt assistance or legal fees; or paying for treatments.

Applications

On a form available from the correspondent or a local MS Society branch. For more information and to apply, those living in England, Wales or Northern Ireland should contact the London team on 020 8438 0700. For those living in Scotland, call 01313 354050 to speak to the grants team in Edinburgh.

Applicants should send their completed forms to their local branch, where trained volunteers will look at your application confidentially. If the branch cannot give you a grant for the full amount, and you can't make up the difference yourself, they may send your application to the grants team in London or Edinburgh. They will consider a top-up grant.

The teams can also advise on other sources of funding that may be available to you.

Other information

The society has a freephone helpline (0808 800 8000), free information booklets on all aspects of living with MS for people with, and affected by, MS and a network of branches, manned by volunteers, across the UK offering local support to people with MS.

Muscular dystrophy

Joseph Patrick Trust

£103,000 (130 grants)

Correspondent: Robert Meadowcroft, Secretary, c/o Muscular Dystrophy Group, 61A Southwark Street, London SE1 0BU (020 7803 4800; fax: 020 7401 3495; email: jptgrants@muscular-dystrophy.org; website: www.muscular-dystrophy.org/how_we_help_you/financial_support)

CC Number: 294475

Eligibility

People with muscular dystrophy or an allied neuromuscular condition.

Types of grants

On average about 150 one-off grants of between £200 and £1,250 are made each year to partially fund the purchase of wheelchairs (powered and manual), scooters, electric beds, trikes, computers, vehicle adaptations, riser chairs, mobile arm supports, portable aids, therapy equipment and so on. Discretionary payments can be made for funeral expenses and other emergencies.

Annual grant total

In 2012/13, the trust had assets of £364,000 and received an income of £155,000. The total amount awarded in grants was £103,000. Of these awards, 68 were for adults and 62 were for children.

Exclusions

Grants are not given for: holidays, household adaptations, building works or domestic appliances; equipment which has already been bought; recurring costs (e.g. wheelchair repairs); the purchase or lease of vehicles, vehicle deposits, maintenance or repair of vehicles. No grants are given outside the UK.

Applications

On a form available from the correspondent or to download from the website. Applications can also be completed online but remember to send supporting documentation on by post as well.

Completed forms can be submitted directly by the individual or via a third party and should be supported by an assessment and quotation for the equipment requested, confirming the need and suitability of the equipment. The assessment must be carried out by an appropriately qualified professional, such as a physiotherapist, occupational therapist, social worker, etc. The assessment must be on headed paper.

For guidance on what to include in the assessment check the trust website.

Applications are considered six times a year. Grants are only be made payable to the supplier.

Neurological disorders

Cerebra for Brain Injured Children and Young People

£476,000

Correspondent: Christopher Jones, Chief Executive, 2nd Floor, Lyric Building, King Street, Carmarthen SA31 1BD (0800 328 1159; email: grants@cerebra.org.uk; website: www.cerebra.org.uk)

CC Number: 1089812

Eligibility

Children and young people aged 16 or under who have a neurodevelopmental disorder or condition. The condition may be of a physical nature, a learning disability or both.

Examples of the types of conditions covered include: cerebral palsy; autistic spectrum disorders; seizure disorders; ADHD; traumatic brain injury; acquired brain injury; Down's syndrome; hydrocephalus; and conditions caused in utero.

This list is by no means exhaustive and applicants who are unsure as to whether they fit the criteria should contact Cerebra directly.

Types of grants

One-off grants of up to a maximum of 80% of the cost or £400, whichever is the lowest amount, of equipment or resources that would improve quality of life and which are not available from statutory agencies like social services or the NHS. Examples of grants made include those towards touch screen computers, specialist car seats, power wheelchairs, therapies, trampolines, sensory toys, and tricycles and quadricycles.

For anything where there is a medical need the trust asks that potential applicants check with them as they may be able to help.

Annual grant total

In 2012 the charity had assets of £965,000 and an income of £4.2 million. Grants totalled £476,000.

These were the latest accounts available at the time of writing (September 2014).

Exclusions
Grants are not given for: driving lessons; motorised vehicles such as quad bikes and motorbikes; anything that could be considered a home improvement such as paint for decorating, conservatories, carpet or other flooring; garden landscaping; household items such as vacuum cleaners, washing machines, wardrobes, standard beds (special beds may be considered); vehicle purchase or maintenance; assessments; general clothing; treatment centres outside the UK; Lycra suits; holidays; and educational items such as home tutors, standard teaching materials or the son-rise programme.

Applications
Application forms and guidance notes can be downloaded from the Cerebra website. Grants are all paid directly to the assistance provider. All applications must be accompanied by financial statements and two references: one from a medical professional and the other from someone who knows your child professional, for example a teacher or social worker. Further guidelines on references are contained within the application form.

Other information
The trust also provides other support services such as telephone counselling and a wills and trust voucher scheme.

Parkinson's disease

Parkinson's UK

£93,000

Correspondent: Sarah Day, Company Secretary, 215 Vauxhall Bridge Road, London SW1V 1EJ (020 7932 1327; email: enquiries@parkinson's.org.uk; website: www.parkinson's.org.uk)

CC Number: 258197

Eligibility
People with Parkinson's disease, with under £10,000 in individual savings or under £15,000 in joint savings.

Types of grants
One-off grants to people with Parkinson's through the Mali Jenkins Fund. The fund can provide grants up to the following amounts:

Equipment or home adaptations	£1,500
Respite breaks	£1,000
Professional fees (such as bankruptcy and Debt Relief Order costs)	£1,000
Other items e.g. domestic appliances or household goods	£500

Applicants who are applying for more than the total amounts shown may be eligible for some of the funding. They will need to show how the difference will be met, for example from personal contributions or from another charity.

Annual grant total
In 2012 the charity had an income of £24 million and assets of £19.4 million. Grants to individuals totalled £93,000.

These were the latest accounts available at the time of writing (September 2014).

Exclusions
No support for ongoing costs; regular payments, such as utility bills or insurance costs; debt relief or legal costs; retrospective funding; holidays; items for which statutory funding is available e.g. through social services or the NHS; items that are the responsibility of a care home or nursing home to provide for a resident; business costs; or funeral costs.

Applications
Application forms and guidance notes can be obtained on the website or by calling the helpline. Applications should be accompanied by a supporting letter from an appropriate professional.

If the application is for equipment or a home adaptation the letter must be from an occupational therapist, physiotherapist or speech and language therapist, as appropriate. Two price quotes should also be supplied to show that the cost is reasonable and the item represents value for money.

For respite and other items, a supporting letter from any of the following may be suitable: a Parkinson's UK information and support worker; the applicant's GP; a Parkinson's nurse; a social worker; or other professional that knows the applicant well.

Forthcoming application deadlines will be advertised online.

Polio

The British Polio Fellowship

£240,000

Correspondent: Ted Hill, Administrator, Unit A, Eagle Office Centre, The Runway, South Ruislip, Middlesex HA4 6SE (0800 018 0586; email: tedhill@britishpolio.org.uk; website: www.britishpolio.org.uk)

CC Number: 1108335

Eligibility
People in need who have been disabled through poliomyelitis (polio) and live in the UK.

Types of grants
Welfare grants of up to £500 are given for scooters, electric or manual wheelchairs, riser/recliner chairs, specialist beds and mattresses; household aids and equipment to enable independence; and home and car adaptations. Support may occasionally be given for essential home improvement and crisis prevention.

Grants of up to £100 are awarded each autumn to help with heating costs for those who are not eligible for state assistance.

The average holiday grant is £300, though it may not exceed £500. Call or email holidays@britishpolio.org.uk for more information and to request an application form.

Annual grant total
In 2012 the fellowship had an income of £1.5 million and a total expenditure of £974,000. It had £4.1 million in assets which mainly consisted of investments and fixed assets and was therefore not available for distribution. Around £240,000 was made in grants to individuals for social welfare purposes.

The 2012 accounts were the latest available at the time of writing.

Exclusions
No grants are given for hospital expenses, household bills or home carers. Statutory sources such as social services' Social Fund must be approached before approaching the fellowship.

Applications
Welfare and heating grant forms are available from the correspondent or a local branch welfare officer. Applications should be submitted by the individual or by an appropriate third party on their behalf and include a medical certificate or doctor's note stating polio-disability. Welfare applications are considered throughout the year. Heating grants are awarded once a year in the autumn.

Holiday grant forms are available from the correspondent or by emailing holidays@britishpolio.org.uk. They are assessed every other month.

Other information
The fellowship has over 50 local branches and provides support and advice on a wide range of issues affecting people disabled through polio.

Renal

The British Kidney Patient Association

£326,000 (574 grants)

Correspondent: Fiona Armitage, Administrator, 3 The Windmills, St Mary's Close, Turk Street, Alton GU34 1EF (01420 541424; email: info@britishkidney-pa.co.uk; website: www.britishkidney-pa.co.uk)

CC Number: 270288

Eligibility

Dialysis patients and their families on low incomes; transplant patients and those receiving conservative care if health and quality of life is being seriously affected by their renal condition.

Types of grants

One-off grants can be given for all kinds of need caused by the condition, including car insurance and tax, gas/electric/water bills, telephone installation, TV licenses, and domestic goods such as washing machines and carpets.

Grants can also be made to cover the costs of hospital visits, such as travel expenses, car tax and insurance. The association may fund holidays, or part of the costs of a holiday.

Grants of up to £1,500 can be awarded towards the cost of a basic holiday in the UK or overseas. Applicants interested in such grants should refer to the BKPA website for more information.

Annual grant total

In 2012 the association had assets of £3 million, an income of £1.7 million and made grants totalling £652,000 in patient grants for both welfare and educational purposes. Approximately £326,000 was given in grants for welfare purposes. In 2012 a record 1148 individuals and families were awarded grants. Approximately 574 grants were given for welfare.

These were the latest set of accounts available at the time of writing (August 2014).

Exclusions

Grants are not made for: telephone bills; court fines; improvements to a patient's home; credit card and loan repayments; medical equipment; and council tax payments.

Applications

Applications are available to download from the BKPA website. Forms must be submitted by a renal social worker or member of the patient's renal team.

Other information

The association also makes grants to hospitals and supports the Ronald McDonald Houses at the Alder Hey Children's Hospital, Liverpool, Bristol Royal Hospital for Children, Evelina Children's Hospital, London and the Royal Hospital for Sick Children, Yorkhill which provide support for the families of young renal patients attending the units at these hospitals.

It also funds non-laboratory research and provides support services, information and advice to kidney patients, amongst other projects.

Spinal injury

ASPIRE (Association for Spinal Injury Research Rehabilitation and Reintegration) Human Needs Fund

£262,000

Correspondent: The Aspire Grants Officer, ASPIRE National Training Centre, Wood Lane, Stanmore, Middlesex HA7 4AP (020 8420 6707; fax: 08432905334; email: grants@aspire.org.uk; website: www.aspire.org.uk)

CC Number: 1075317

Eligibility

People in the UK and Ireland who have a spinal cord injury and are in need. Priority is given to re-establishing independent mobility.

Types of grants

One-off grants to help towards the purchase of specialist equipment such as wheelchairs and computers. The charity states that it will rarely offer full funding, but will offer part-funding and assistance with securing the remainder.

Annual grant total

In 2012/13 the charity held assets of £3.3 million and had an income of £4.6 million. Grants to individuals totalled £262,000.

Exclusions

Grants from the fund are solely for people with acquired non progressive spinal cord injury. The charity states that it is unlikely to fund applications for holidays, standing wheelchairs, house adaptations, passive exercise equipment, vehicles or secondary functions on wheelchairs, including standing functions and cosmetic features, for reasons that could be met by other means.

ASPIRE will not fund repairs, maintenance, insurance, replacement of parts or contracts for equipment, or equipment already purchased or ordered.

Only one application per applicant per five year period, unless the previous provision is insufficient due to a change in medical circumstances.

Applications

On a form available from the charity's website. Each application requires a supporting statement from an occupational therapist or medical consultant to explain why the specialist equipment is appropriate. The charity may request additional information or supporting evidence prior to considering an application. Completed applications will usually be considered within six weeks of receipt. A full list of guidelines is available on the website, where there is also additional information in the form of a grants brochure.

Other information

ASPIRE also provides a range of services for eligible individuals and has programmes in the areas of housing, independent living, sports development and assistive technology. See the charity's informative website for a full list of its activities.

Spinal muscular

Spinal Muscular Atrophy Support UK (formerly known as The Jennifer Trust for Spinal Muscular Atrophy)

£25,000

Correspondent: Doug Henderson, Managing Director, The Jennifer Trust for Spinal Muscular Atrophy, 40 Timothy's Bridge Road, Stratford Enterprise Park, Stratford-upon-Avon CV37 9NW (01789 267520; fax: 01789 268371; email: office@jtsma.org.uk; website: www.jtsma.org.uk)

CC Number: 1106815

Eligibility

People diagnosed as having the genetic condition spinal muscular atrophy. Note that the trust cannot give grants to people with any other condition.

Types of grants

One-off grants of up to £300 for urgent welfare needs and equipment.

Annual grant total
In 2012/13 the trust had assets of £267,000 and an income of £625,000. Welfare and equipment grants totalled £25,000.

Exclusions
No grants towards vehicles or their adaptations.

Applications
Enquiries should be made with the trust's outreach workers.

Other information
The trust is also known as Spinal Muscular Atrophy UK The Jennifer Trust.

Individual financial grants are only one of the ways in which the trust provides support. For more information, contact the trust and request an information pack or visit the website.

Sports injuries

RFU Injured Players Foundation

£554,000 (154 grants)

Correspondent: Katie Lister, Administrator, Rugby House, Twickenham Stadium, 200 Whitton Road, Middlesex TW2 7BA (0800 783 1518; email: katielister@rfu.com; website: www.rfuipf.org.uk)

CC Number: 1122139

Eligibility
People who are seriously injured playing sport under the auspices of the Rugby Football Union.

Types of grants
Small grants of up to £2,000 per year and large grants of up to £20,000 (or higher in exceptional circumstances) for a variety of needs.

Grants are commonly given for home improvements to provide disability access, medical equipment and mobility aids, exercise and therapy equipment, communication aids, respite care and travel expenses.

Annual grant total
In 2012/13 the foundation held assets of £6.4 million and had an income of £1.8 million. A total of £554,000 was awarded to individuals; £426,000 in 97 large grants and a further £128,000 in 57 small grants.

The largest single grant to an individual amounted to £20,000 whereas small grants were all for £2,000 or less.

Exclusions
No grants for general household expenses such as food, clothing, utility bills or vehicle fuel costs.

Applications
Application forms for both small and large grants may be downloaded from the website. Large grants application forms are also available from Katie Lister and can be submitted in advance, so that the charity can pledge funds, enabling the purchase to be planned. Applicants are advised to attach an estimate or invoice proving costs.

All applications will be acknowledged within five working days. Decisions on small grants are made within 14 working days. Decisions normally take between six to eight weeks for large grants of less than £20,000 and for those over £20,000, up to three months.

Contact by applicants to discuss any aspect of the application process is welcomed by the foundation.

Other information
The foundation is notified of players who receive injuries through the RFU's Injury Reporting process. When someone is catastrophically injured, the RFU Injured Player Welfare Officer will contact the family of the person involved and offer initial help with travel and other expenses to visit the player in hospital and support them through their recovery and rehabilitation.

Long-term support also includes a pastoral contact programme, through which clients are visited by the foundation on a regular basis.

The Rosslyn Park Injury Trust Fund

£6,900

Correspondent: Diane McIntier, Secretary, 102 Halfway Street, Sidcup, Kent DA15 8DB (020 8302 4082; email: bridihalfwayst@talktalk.net; website: www.rosslynpark.co.uk/information/injury-trust-fund)

CC Number: 284089

Eligibility
Young people who have a disability or are in poor health as a result of an injury suffered while playing sports (amateur sports). Their dependents may also receive help.

Types of grants
One-off grants for computers, special care, medical equipment, computers and disability aids. The fund has a list of recent beneficiaries on its website.

Annual grant total
In 2013 the fund had an income of £10,800 and a total expenditure of £7,100. We estimate that grants to individuals totalled £6,900.

Applications
In writing to the correspondent. Applications can be submitted by either the individual or through social services and are considered as they are received.

Other information
The fund's website tells the story of how it was founded: 'In 1981 the head boy of Llandovery College was playing as the captain of his team in the Rosslyn Park Schoolboy Sevens Competition. During the game he fell awkwardly in a tackle leaving him quadriplegic. At the time of this tragic injury there was very limited accident insurance available for schoolboys playing sport and that fact, coupled with the public sympathy felt for the player, led to the setting up on 2 December 1981 of the registered charity now known as Rosslyn Park Injury Trust Fund.'

Royalties from the book 'The Final Whistle: The Great War in Fifteen Players' support the fund.

Stroke

Stroke Association

£150,000

Correspondent: The Welfare Secretary, Stroke Association House, 240 City Road, London EC1V 2PR (020 7566 0300; fax: 020 7490 2686; email: grants@stroke.org.uk; website: www.stroke.org.uk)

CC Number: 211015

Eligibility
People who have had a stroke and are in need. Applicants must have less than £3,000 in savings and their income must not exceed their expenditure by more than £50.

Types of grants
One-off grants of up to £300 to help improve the individual's quality of life. Grants are available towards: specialised respite care or family holidays within the UK; white goods; cooking equipment; energy bills (but not arrears); installation of telephones or other telecommunications; beds and bedding; medical or disability aids; armchairs; driving assessments or lessons; and travel costs for, for example, hospital visits.

Annual grant total
In 2012/13 the association held assets of £14.9 million and had an income of £31.1 million. Welfare grants to individuals totalled £150,000.

Exclusions

The association will not fund private medical costs; labour costs (other than the installation of white goods) including item removal and structural alteration costs; nursing home fees (other than respite care); computer equipment or televisions; debts; and rent or bills arrears.

Applications

On a form available from a regional correspondent to be completed by a social worker, health professional or Stroke Association staff member on the individual's behalf. Regional correspondent email addresses are listed on the charity's website. Applicants should ask their health or social care professional to contact the association by email using their professional email account to receive an application form. People who are in touch with one of the charity's Life After Stroke services should ask their co-ordinator. Awards are means-tested, taking into account the total household income.

Other information

The association runs a range of services for people recovering from strokes, including advice and information, communication and stroke prevention services. It also has a Stroke Helpline (0303 3033 100). A full list of services is available on the charity's website.

Tuberous sclerosis

Tuberous Sclerosis Association Benevolent Funds

£4,800

Correspondent: David Vaughan, Trustee, 3 Clos-Y-Deri, Llanedi, Pontarddulais, Swansea SA4 0XW (01214 456970; email: social@tuberous-sclerosis.org; website: www.tuberous-sclerosis.org)

CC Number: 1039549

Eligibility

People in need who have tuberous sclerosis complex and their families and carers. Membership is usually required, forms for which are available to download from the website.

Types of grants

Grants are administered through the TSA Support Fund and can help with home adaptations; household essentials such as washing machines, carpets and flooring; short holidays with family, family visits or days out; or a holiday for a carer. The fund can also help with travel costs for those wishing to attend TSA events or for those needing to attend TSC clinics.

The Janet Medcalf Memorial Award is awarded three times a year, with each awardee receiving £300.

Note: 'The amounts awarded from the Support Fund will vary depending on individual circumstances and needs. Whether your application is successful will depend on the availability of funds, the amount you need and on what you need the money for.'

Annual grant total

In 2012/13 the funds had assets of £3.6 million and an income of £402,000. Grants to individuals totalled £4,800 and were distributed as follows:

Benevolent grants	£2,100
Family days and weekends	£1,800
The Janet Medcalf Memorial Award	£900

Exclusions

The fund cannot help with costs of things that have already been ordered or paid for, recurrent or long-term costs (including living costs and bills) or costs associated with debt. There are no grants available for things which are the responsibility of a statutory service. Applicants must not reapply within one year of a successful application being made.

Applications

On a form available to download from the website along with a monitoring form. Applications should include evidence (photocopies) of any benefits you receive and quotes for the item(s) you wish to purchase. Forms should be returned to: TSA Support Fund, CAN Mezzanine, 32–36 Loman Street, London SE1 0EH (for residents of England, Wales and Northern Ireland) or TSA Support Fund, PO Box 8728, Airdrie (for residents of Scotland).

The fund will contact you within three weeks of receipt of application and may request a reference from a health/social care or education professional. The fund aims to notify applicants of a decision within six weeks of receipt.

Note the following from the website: 'We do not want to misinform you at any point so we recommend that your first contact should be from a support group or charity in the country where you live.' If at any point you require assistance to complete your form, your local TSA Adviser can help you.

Other information

The fund supports research into the causes and management of tuberous sclerosis. It also provides education and information about the condition.

Occupational charities

This section contains the following parts.

An index of particular trades or professions. The categories of trades/ professions are listed alphabetically.

After the index, the charities themselves are arranged alphabetically within each trade/profession. Charities include both independent charities and benevolent funds associated with trade unions or professional bodies.

Trusts included are those that support both members of the occupation listed and their dependents. Individuals should also check for any trade unions listed that cover their area of work as unions will sometimes have resources available for workers in their sector who are not members. When a possible occupation has been identified, go to the relevant page and read the entries carefully. Being a member of a profession is not necessarily enough, there may well be other criteria that make individuals ineligible.

We have grouped together certain occupations to make relevant trusts easier to identify. For instance, dance, magic, music, painting, theatre and writing have all been placed under Arts, as there are some trusts that support arts generally (which would give to a number of these categories) and some that will give only to one specific branch. Paid work is not essential for all trusts: for instance, there are trusts for certain amateur sportspeople.

We have placed all medical and health workers in the same category, as again there are trusts that support these workers generally and some that will only support certain areas. The exceptions to this are the trusts that support carers, which have been included in the general section under the 'Carers and volunteers' category (see page 13). The category 'Food, drink and provision trades' (see page 88) contains many different individual roles within the industry. In this edition, trusts concerning clergy and missionaries have been listed in the 'Religious charities' chapter (see page 159). Please also note that trusts such as the Hull Fishermen's Trust Fund, which support a particular occupation but only give in a particular locality, are included in the relevant local section of this guide.

Index of occupational charity funds

Accountancy

The AIA Educational and Benevolent Trust

£3,900

Correspondent: Tim Pinkney, Administrator, Staithes 3, The Watermark, Metro Riverside, Tyne and Wear NE11 9SN (01914 930272; fax: 01914 930278; email: trust.fund@aiaworldwide.com; website: www.aiaworldwide.com)

CC Number: 1118333

Eligibility

Fellows and associates of the institute, and their close dependents, who are in need.

Types of grants

One-off grants according to need.

Annual grant total

In 2012 the trust had an income of £2,000 and a total expenditure of £8,000. We estimate that social welfare grants to individuals totalled £3,900. Grants are also given to those wishing to undergo education and training in accountancy.

At the time of writing (August 2014) this was the most recent financial information available for the trust.

Applications

On a form available from the trust's website which should be printed and posted to the correspondent.

Applications are received on an ongoing basis.

The Chartered Accountants' Benevolent Association

£683,000

Correspondent: Donna Cooper, Grants Co-ordinator, 8 Mitchell Court, Castle Mound Way, Rugby CV23 0UY (0800 107 6163(24hr helpline); email: donna.cooper@caba.org.uk; website: www.caba.org.uk)

CC Number: 1116973

Eligibility

Chartered Accountants' Benevolent Association (CABA) provides advice and practical support to current and former ICAEW chartered accountants and their families; ICAEW chartered accountants; retired ICAEW chartered accountants; spouses and life partners; active ACA students; those living overseas. Visit the website for full information.

Types of grants

One-off and recurrent grants towards daily living costs, respite care, household essentials and so on. The association also provides interest-free loans.

Annual grant total

In 2012 the association held assets of £86.2 million, £242,000 of which represented permanent endowment or restricted funds. It had an income of almost £1.8 million. Financial assistance to individuals totalled £683,000 (excluding support costs and including four loans totalling almost £28,000). The 2012 accounts were the latest available at the time of writing (August 2014).

Applications

Initial contact can be made by calling the 24 hour helpline or by using the live chat feature on the association's website.

Other information

The association offers a wide range of support and advice on issues such as accessing state benefits, debt and financial problems and stress management. Services are free and only the direct financial support is means tested.

The Chartered Certified Accountants' Benevolent Fund

£15,000 (14 grants)

Correspondent: Hugh McCash, Honorary Secretary, 2 Central Quay, 89 Hydepark Street, Glasgow G3 8BW (01415 344045; fax: 01415 344151; email: hugh.mccash@accaglobal.com; website: www.accaglobal.com/gb/en/member/membership-benefit/benevolent-fund/apply-assistance.html)

CC Number: 222595

Eligibility

Members, and former members, of the ACCA, and their dependents.

Types of grants

Grants in 2012/13 ranged from £150 to £3,000. Recurrent grants are available to help with stairlifts, telephone bills, holidays, TV rental and so on; one-off grants in tragic circumstances to help beneficiaries get back on their feet; and low-interest or interest-free loans on property.

Annual grant total

In 2012/13 the fund held assets of £3 million and had an income of £177,000. Grants to 14 individuals totalled £15,000.

Exclusions

Grants are not available for the education of children.

Applications

On a form available from the correspondent or downloadable from the website. Applications can be submitted directly by the individual or through a social worker, Citizens Advice, welfare agency or other third party. They are considered at meetings held every two or three months.

The Chartered Institute of Management Accountants Benevolent Fund

£82,000 (46 grants)

Correspondent: Caroline Aldred, Secretary, CIMA, 26 Chapter Street, London SW1P 4NP (020 8849 2221; email: benevolent.fund@cimaglobal.com; website: www.cimaglobal.com)

CC Number: 261114

Eligibility

Past and present CIMA members and their dependents anywhere in the UK and the world.

Types of grants

One-off grants for specific needs such as television licence/rental, telephone rental, motor insurance/tax, disability aids, some repairs and necessary household items such as fridges, cookers and so on. Grants are also made for medical bills for members outside the UK. Regular grants are also made to help meet basic living costs. Interest free loans may be provided in exceptional circumstances.

Annual grant total

In 2013 the fund had assets of £2.1 million and an income of £106,000. Grants to 46 individuals totalled £102,000, mostly for welfare purposes.

Exclusions

No grants to enhance property, for investment in business ventures, or for private medical care: though, assistance may be given to members living outside the UK who do not have access to state-funded medical treatment or medical insurance and have large medical bills.

Applications

On a form available from the correspondent or to download from the website. Applications can be submitted directly by the individual or through a recognised referral agency (Citizens Advice, doctor, social worker and so on), or through a third party. They are considered monthly/as necessary.

Other information

The fund can also signpost people to relevant services and provide support from a welfare officer.

Educational grants are also made for dependent children. CIMA have another charity, the General Charitable Trust, which funds the advancement of education in accountancy and related topics.

The Institute of Financial Accountants' and International Association of Book-Keepers' Benevolent Fund

£7,500

Correspondent: The Secretary, IFA and IAB Benevolent Fund, Beighton Business Centre, 52A High Street, Sheffield S20 1ED (01473 327361; email: secretary@ifaiabbenfund.org.uk; website: www.ifaiabbenfund.org.uk)

CC Number: 234082

Eligibility

Past and present members of the institute or the association, their dependents, and all current IFA and IAB students.

Types of grants

Grants, usually one-off, 'where there is a critical situation that affects daily life'.

Annual grant total

In 2012/13 the fund had an income of £22,000 and a total expenditure of £16,500. We estimate that social welfare grants to individuals totalled £7,500, with funding also awarded to individuals for educational purposes.

Exclusions

No recurrent or ongoing payments are made where they could be considered to 'be in lieu of a steady income'.

Applications

On a form available from the correspondent or to download from the website. Applications can be submitted directly by the individual or on their behalf by a family member. Details of income and expenditure, as well as any relevant supporting evidence (for example, bank statements, pay slips, tax return forms, proof of rent or mortgage payments) should be included. Every application is considered on its merits.

Other information

The trustees may choose to support the educational needs of those who are pursuing professional qualifications of the IFA or IAB when the fund has surplus income.

Advertising and marketing

NABS

£231,000

Correspondent: Support Team, 6th Floor, 388 Oxford Street, London W1C 1JT (0800 707 6607; email: support@nabs.org.uk; website: www.nabs.org.uk)

CC Number: 1070556

Eligibility

People who work or have worked in advertising, marketing, marketing services and related industries, and their dependents.

Types of grants

One-off and recurrent grants according to need. The trustee's report for 2012 stated that their aim is:

> To provide fast, critical, short-term financial support combined with practical help, e.g. debt advice, support from our careers department, access to other charities, etc., with the aim of getting people back on their feet and able to support themselves as quickly as possible.

Annual grant total

In 2012 the charity had both assets and an income of £4 million. Grants totalling £231,000 were made to individuals for social welfare purposes. The 2012 accounts were the latest available at the time of writing.

Applications

On a form available by calling the helpline or by emailing the correspondent. Completed forms, which should include a career history, financial information and references, are considered monthly.

Other information

The charity provides a wide range of services for members of the industry, including a telephone helpline, career coaching and workshops, a flatshare scheme and a working parents programme. It also owns Peterhouse, a comprehensive retirement complex containing a registered care home.

Agriculture and related rural issues

Forest Industries Education and Provident Fund

£3,800

Correspondent: Jane Karthaus, Trustee, Woodland Place, West Street, Belford, Northumberland NE70 7QA (01668 213937; email: jane.karthaus@gmail.com; website: www.confor.org.uk/AboutUs/Default.aspx?pid=150)

CC Number: 1061322

Eligibility

Members of the Forestry and Timber Association (or Confor) and their dependents who are in need, hardship or distress (for example, illness, death or injury). Members must have been involved with the association for at least one year.

Types of grants

One-off grants are made towards expenses for those experiencing hardship.

Annual grant total

At the time of writing (August 2014) the latest financial information available was from 2012. In 2012 the fund had an income of £7,100 and an expenditure of £7,900. We estimate that welfare grants totalled around £3,800.

Exclusions

Retrospective funding is not given.

Applications

Application forms are available from the fund's website or can be requested from the correspondent.

Other information

Anyone can join Confor who has an interest in trees, woodlands or timber. Grants are also made for educational purposes.

The Gamekeepers Welfare Trust

£4,400 (23 grants)

Correspondent: Philip Holt, Administrator, High Park Farm, High Park, Kirkbymoorside, York YO62 7HS (01751 430100; email: gamekeeperwtrust@binternet.com; website: thegamekeeperswelfaretrust.com)

CC Number: 1008924

Eligibility

Gamekeepers and those in similar occupations who are in need, and their dependents.

Types of grants

One-off and recurrent grants according to need.

Annual grant total

The latest accounts available were for 2012. During the year, the trust had assets of £144,000 and an income of £27,500. Grants to 23 individuals totalled £4,400. A further £8,400 was given to organisations of which, £7,200 was for educational purposes.

Applications

On a form available from the correspondent or the website. Applications can be made at any time.

The Royal Agricultural Benevolent Institution

£2.22 million (12,267 grants)

Correspondent: Head of Welfare, Shaw House, 27 West Way, Oxford OX2 0QH (01865 724931; fax: 01865 202025; email: grants@rabi.org.uk; website: www.rabi.org.uk)

CC Number: 208858

Eligibility

Farmers, farm managers, farm workers and their dependents. Applicants should usually have less than £10,000 in savings. Retired applicants must normally be aged at least 65 and have worked full time in the industry for at least ten years. These qualifications may be waived if the applicant has been forced to give up work due to illness or disability.

There is an emergency fund available for working farmers and farm workers who are experiencing exceptionally difficult circumstances of a temporary nature.

Types of grants

One-off grants and regular financial assistance. Grants can be given towards white goods, disability equipment, TVs and licences, telephone rental, lifelines, help in the home, care home fees, replacement boilers and so on. Emergency relief is available for essential domestic expenses in times of financial difficulty. Emergency grants have also been made in the past to assist farmers who have struggled with flooding and the foot and mouth outbreak.

The institution can also pay for temporary help on the farm if the individual or an immediate dependent is seriously ill or has an accident. Grants may also be made through the Gateway

Project which offers vocational training grants to enable farmers and their immediate family to gain qualifications to enable them to increase the farm income.

Annual grant total

In 2013 the institution had assets of more than £61 million and had an income of £6.3 million. Grants totalled £2.2 million.

Exclusions

No grants can be given towards business debts and expenses, medical expenses or private education costs.

Applications

Enquiries can be made by telephoning the helpline on 0300 303 7373 or by letter or email to the correspondent either directly by the individual or through a social worker, Citizens Advice or other third party.

All new applicants for regular assistance will be visited by one of the institution's regional welfare officers. The grants committee meets every six weeks to consider applications, though emergency needs can be fast-tracked.

Other information

The institution also operates two residential homes, one in Bury St Edmunds and one in Burnham on Sea and also associated sheltered flats for older members of the farming community.

The RABI Welfare Team 'are fully trained in all complexities of the state benefits system' and can advise people on pension credits and other state entitlements. There is a flyer about the Welfare Department and the work they do on the institution's informative website.

RSABI (Royal Scottish Agricultural Benevolent Institution)

£446,000 (527 grants)

Correspondent: The Welfare Manager, The Rural Centre, West Mains of Ingliston, Newbridge, Edinburgh EH28 8LT (01314 724166; fax: 01314 724156; email: rsabi@rsabi.org.uk; website: www.rsabi.org.uk)

SC Number: SC009828

Eligibility

People who have been engaged for at least ten years, full-time in a land-based occupation in Scotland, and their dependents. Applicants should be either retired or unable to work, on a low income and have limited savings (£12,000 for a single applicant, £16,000 for couples) or be facing a crisis due to ill-health, accident or bereavement, for example.

Qualifying occupations include: agriculture, aquaculture, crofting, forestry, fish-farming, games keeping, horticulture, rural estate work and other jobs that depend on the provision of services directly to these industries.

Types of grants

Recurring payments ranging between £700 and £900 (or between £1,100 and £1,400 in case of partnered/joint beneficiaries) made twice a year on a bi-annual basis to those on limited income and little or no savings. The charity can provide help with fuel and heating expenses, TV licences and seasonal bonuses and so on to older people and those who are unable to work. RSABI welfare staff ensure that individuals receive their full entitlements to any other benefits due and will help and advise with other difficulties such as care services, housing or similar matters.

One-off grants to help individuals meet a particular crisis in their lives can be given towards home repairs and modifications, disability aids, essential transport costs, car tax or insurance and respite breaks. Supermarket gift cards are also offered (£25–£75 per person).

There are 'Essential needs packages' up to £250 available to assist with the costs of household appliances, furniture, floor covering and other home necessities.

Annual grant total

In 2012/13 the charity had assets of £10.3 million and an income of £654,000. Grants to individuals totalled around £446,000. Out of this sum £364,000 was made in basic benefit grants and £81,000 was paid in single grants.

Exclusions

Grants are not made to help with business expenses or to cover loans, overdrafts or debt repayments.

Applications

Preliminary application forms are available from the correspondent or can be downloaded from the website. They can be submitted directly by the individual or through a third party (such as a social worker or Citizens Advice) and are considered at any time. Applicants will be assigned a welfare officer to complete a more detailed form as part of the application process.

Candidates are also encouraged to contact the charity to discuss their application.

Other information

Grants are carefully tailored to match the needs of individual applicants.

RSABI operates GATEPOST – a confidential listening and support service for Scotland's farming and land-based community. Call 0300 111 4166 – Monday-Friday, 9am-5pm.

The Rural, Agricultural and Allied Workers' Benevolent Fund

£5,000

Correspondent: Fund Administrator, Food and Agriculture, UNITE, 128 Theobald's Road, Holborn, London WC1X 8TN (020 7611 2500)

Eligibility

Rural and agricultural members of the organisation (now a trade group within Unite the Union).

Types of grants

One-off grants with an average value of £150. In some cases recurrent support may be given.

Annual grant total

The amount varies, but usually never more than £5,000 per year.

Exclusions

This fund does not award grants to individuals who are not current union members within the agricultural section.

Applications

Potential applicants should contact their local branch official.

The Timber Trades Benevolent Society

£104,000

Correspondent: Ivan Savage, General Manager, Masons Croft, 19 Church Lane, Oulton, Stone ST15 8UL (084489222 05; email: info@ttbs.org.uk)

CC Number: 207734

Eligibility

People who have worked for a minimum of ten (or five in exceptional circumstances) years for a firm selling timber commercially, such as timber merchants, importers or exporters or agents and their dependents. Note the society does not cover carpenters or joiners.

Types of grants

Grants have been awarded towards heating installation, adaptation of cars for disabled use, domestic appliances, phone rentals, TV rental or licences, hampers, funeral costs house repairs or essential car maintenance. Winter fuel grants (£300 in 2013) are also made. Regular allowances are paid quarterly (£150 per quarter).

Annual grant total

In 2013 the society had an income of £305,000 and a total expenditure of £254,000. Grants to individuals amounted to £104,000 and were distributed as follows:

Regular payments	£34,000
Winter fuel payments	£32,000
Telephone rental	£12,900
Christmas gifts	£12,800
TV rentals and licences	£4,500
One-off grants	£4,100
Spring gifts	£3,000
Holidays	£400

Exclusions

No grants are made towards care or nursing home fees. The society will not support furniture manufacturers and carpenters servicing the building trade.

Applications

On a form available from the correspondent. Applications can be submitted directly by the individual or through a social worker, Citizens Advice, welfare agency or other third party. They are considered on a regular basis.

Airline pilots

The British Airline Pilots' Association Benevolent Fund (BALPA)

£22,000

Correspondent: Antoinette Girdler, Administrator, BALPA House, 5 Heathrow Boulevard, 278 Bath Road, West Drayton UB7 0DQ (020 8476 4029; email: balpa@balpa.org)

CC Number: 229957

Eligibility

Serving and retired commercial pilots, flight engineers and navigators who are or have been members of BALPA, and their dependents.

Types of grants

One-off and recurrent grants and interest-free loans. The fund prefers to give grants for specific needs such as electricity bills, school books for children and so on.

Annual grant total

In 2012/13 the fund had assets of £1.5 million and an income of £36,000. The fund made grants of approximately £44,000 and gave around £15,000 in interest-free loans.

Exclusions

Grants are not given for school fees.

Applications

In writing to the correspondent requesting an application form. Applications are considered quarterly.

The Guild of Air Pilots Benevolent Fund

£1,400

Correspondent: Chris Spurrier, Trustee, Derwent, Fox Lane, Eversley Cross, Hook, Hampshire RG27 0NQ (01252 877653; fax: 020 7404 4035; email: gapan@gapan.org; website: www.gapan.org)

CC Number: 212952

Eligibility

Members of the guild and those who have been engaged professionally as air pilots or air navigators in commercial aviation and their dependents.

Types of grants

One-off and recurrent grants ranging between £250 and £2,000. Loans can also be made to assist in the rehabilitation of people after accidents or to enable them to regain licences. The fund does not grant money for the repayment of debts or long-term expenses such as school fees or prolonged medical care.

Annual grant total

In 2012/13 the fund had assets of £708,000 and an income of £84,000. Educational grants totalling approximately £14,000 were made and a further £1,400 was given in welfare grants.

Exclusions

Training and higher education are not usually supported.

Applications

On a form available from the website, including details of the individual's financial situation and proof of an aviation career. Applications are considered in January, April, July and October. The fund has helpers and visitors who can assist applicants fill in the form. The trust attaches great importance to the comments and recommendations of helpers.

Other information

The fund works closely with the other aviation trusts for individuals (both military and civilian). If an applicant has approached another such trust, they should say so in their application to this fund.

Antiques

The British Antique Dealers' Association Benevolent Fund

£7,000

Correspondent: Mark Dodgson, Administrator, 20 Rutland Gate, London SW7 1BD (020 7589 4128; fax: 020 7581 9083)

CC Number: 238363

Eligibility

Members and former members of the association who are in need, and their dependents.

Types of grants

One-off or recurrent grants ranging from £100 to £2,000 for needs such as assistance with household bills.

Annual grant total

In 2013, the fund had an income of £8,500 and a total expenditure of £7,500. We estimate that the total amount of grants awarded to individuals was approximately £7,500.

Applications

On a form available from the correspondent. Applicants should provide two references from members or former members of the association. Applications are considered on a regular basis.

Architecture

The Architects' Benevolent Society

£600,000 (314 grants)

Correspondent: Robert Ball, Chief Executive, 43 Portland Place, London W1B 1QH (020 7580 2823; fax: 020 7580 7075; email: help@absnet.org.uk; website: www.absnet.org.uk)

CC Number: 265139

Eligibility

People engaged or formerly engaged in the practice of architecture, and their dependents. This includes (but is not limited to) architects, assistants, technicians and technologists and landscape architects.

Types of grants

Recurrent monthly grants, one-off grants and interest-free loans.

Annual grant total

In 2012/13 the society held assets of £20.3 million and had an income of

£1.3 million. Grants and gifts to 314 individuals totalled £600,000.

Exclusions

No educational grants.

Applications

A short application form is available from the correspondent or to download from the website. Applications can be submitted directly by the individual or through a social worker, Citizens Advice or other welfare agency. Once received, the society will arrange a visit by one of their welfare officers. Applications are considered throughout the year.

Other information

The society's trained welfare officers can offer support and information on various issues, including those relating to the state benefits system.

Arts

The Artists' General Benevolent Institution

£416,000 (137 grants)

Correspondent: Brad Feltham, Secretary, Artists' General Benevolent Institution, Burlington House, Piccadilly, London W1J 0BB (020 7734 1193; email: agbi1@btconnect.com; website: www.agbi.org.uk)

CC Number: 212667

Eligibility

Professional artists, i.e. painters, sculptors, illustrators, art teachers at A-level or above, who live in England, Wales and Northern Ireland who have earned their living (or a major part of it) from art and cannot work due to accident, illness or old age. Widows and orphaned children of artists are also eligible for assistance.

Types of grants

One-off and recurrent grants to artists who through old age, illness or accident are unable to work and earn. Grants cover a wide range of items and uses, such as domestic and utility bills, repair of equipment or replacement of worn-out items, help to cover costs of car replacements, visits to family and friends and respite care. Recent grants have been awarded towards the costs of home adaptations for an artist who gave up work to care for her terminally ill husband and towards the studio rent of artists who, due to injury, could not resume work for a period of time.

Annual grant total

In 2012/13 the institution had an income of £448,000 and a total expenditure of £599,000. Grants to 137 professional artists in need amounted to £416,000.

Exclusions

The fund cannot help with career or legal difficulties, loss of earnings due to poor sales, etc., expenses associated with exhibitions, or (except in exceptional circumstances) student fees.

Applications

Applications should initially be in writing, including a full CV listing all training, qualifications, exhibitions in professional galleries and teaching experience (if any) at GCSE, A-level or above. They can be submitted directly by the individual, through a recognised referral agency such Citizens Advice, or by a doctor, social worker, etc. The secretary visits most potential beneficiaries in order to carry out an assessment and to collect original works, as well as letters from two referees and a doctor or consultant (if applicable). The council meets to consider applications regularly throughout the year. Enquiries from potential applicants are welcomed.

The Entertainment Artistes' Benevolent Fund

£93,000 (79 grants)

Correspondent: Giles Cooper, Chair, Brinsworth House, 72 Staines Road, Twickenham, Middlesex TW2 5AL (020 8898 8164; email: giles.copperl@eabf.org.uk; website: www.eabf.org.uk)

CC Number: 206451

Eligibility

Entertainment artistes and people associated with the entertainment professions (professional performers in variety, pantomime, revue, circus, concert party, cabaret, clubs, television, radio, making of records and light entertainment in general), and their dependents.

Types of grants

Regular top-up pensions and one-off grants for gas, electricity and fuel bills, medical and nursing needs, television licenses and rentals, household repairs, maintenance and telephone bills, traveling expenses, funeral costs and food vouchers. Personal loans and support in debt crisis may also be available.

Annual grant total

In 2013 the fund had assets of £7.5 million and an income of £2.4 million. Grants and pensions totalled around £93,000. Recurrent grants were given to 40 families totalling £65,000 and single payments were made to 39 individuals totalling £28,000. One-off grants were made in: Greater London (31%); South East (23%); North West (14%); South West (9%); Midlands (8%); Scotland (6%); and Yorkshire and Humberside, North East and Rest of the world (Australia) (3%).

Applications

Application forms are available from the correspondent. They can be made directly by the individual or through a social worker/welfare agency. Requests for support are considered every couple of months.

Other information

The fund also has its own residential and nursing care home for older entertainment artistes and supports its residents.

Equity Trust Fund (formerly Equity Trust Fund)

£77,000 (96 grants)

Correspondent: Kaethe Cherney, Company Secretary, Plouviez House, 19–20 Hatton Place, London EC1N 8RU (020 7831 1926; email: kaethe@equitycharitabletrust.org.uk; website: www.equitycharitabletrust.org.uk)

CC Number: 328103

Eligibility

Professional performers (under Equity or ITC contracts), stage managers and directors, and their dependents.

Types of grants

One-off grants for almost any welfare need.

Annual grant total

In 2012/13 the fund had assets of £9.9 million and an income of £462,000. Grants were made to 96 individuals, for welfare and benevolence needs totalling £77,000.

Exclusions

No grants to amateur performers, musicians or drama students.

Applications

Download from the website or email Rosalind@equitycharitabletrust.org.uk Welfare grants are available at any time during the year, dependent upon the Trustees meetings.

Other information

The trust has an informative website.

Grand Order of Water Rats Charities Fund

£50,000

Correspondent: Mike Martin, Administrator, 328 Gray's Inn Road, London WC1X 8BZ (020 7407 8007; email: charities@gowr.net; website: www.gowr.net)

CC Number: 292201

Eligibility

People, and their dependents, who have been involved in a theatrical profession for at least seven years and are in need.

Types of grants

One-off and recurrent grants according to need.

Annual grant total

In 2012 the fund had assets of almost £1.7 million and an income of £105,000. Grants totalled £50,000.

These were the latest set of accounts available at the time of writing (September 2014).

Exclusions

No grants are given towards students' fees, education, taxes, overdrafts, credit card bills or bank loans.

Applications

In writing to the correspondent.

The Evelyn Norris Trust

£25,000

Correspondent: Kaethe Cherney, Acting Secretary, Plouviez House, 19–20 Hatton Place, London EC1N 8RU (020 7831 1926; fax: 020 7242 7995; email: kaethe@equitycharitabletrust.org.uk; website: www.equitycharitabletrust.org.uk/evelynnorris.php)

CC Number: 260078

Eligibility

Members or ex-members of the concert or theatrical profession who are older, sick, disabled or in need.

Types of grants

One-off grants of up to £700 towards convalescence or recuperative holidays following illness, injury or surgery.

Annual grant total

In 2013 the trust had an income of £33,000 and a total expenditure of £43,000. At the time of writing (August 2014) the trust's accounts for the year were not yet available to view from the Charity Commission. In recent years, grants to individuals have totalled £25,000.

Exclusions

No grants for student/education course fees.

Applications

Application forms are available to download from the website, though the trust advises potential applicants to at first call or email to discuss eligibility details and the application process. Applications are considered monthly and can be submitted directly by the individual or through a social worker, Citizens Advice, welfare agency or any third party. Applications should include any relevant financial or personal information.

Other information

In past years, grants have also been made to residential homes.

The Royal Opera House Benevolent Fund

£132,000 (51 grants)

Correspondent: Cheng Loo, Secretary, Benevolent Fund, Royal Opera House, Covent Garden, London WC2E 9DD (020 7212 9128; email: ben.fund@roh.org.uk; website: www.roh.org.uk/about/benevolent-fund)

CC Number: 200002

Eligibility

People who work, or have worked, for the Royal Opera House or Birmingham Royal Ballet, and their widows, widowers, partners or children. Applicants do not have to have contributed to the fund in order to receive help.

Note: In previous years, it has been required that applicants have an annual income of no more than £10,000 if single and £15,000 if married; though this is not currently stated on the trust's website or in its accounts, such limits may still apply.

Types of grants

Grants range from £50 per month to £3,000 as a one-off grant. Monthly allowances are towards food and clothing. One-off grants have been given towards essential building repairs, second-hand furniture, hoist, glasses, dentures, cash flow problems, home equipment, medical costs and MOT repairs. Interest-free loans are also available.

Annual grant total

In 2012/13 the fund held assets of £7.2 million and had an income of £140,000. A total of £132,000 was awarded in 51 grants to individuals and was distributed as follows:

Monthly allowances	35	£118,000
Other grants	16	£14,200

Applications

On a form available from the correspondent, providing details of income and expenditure. They should be submitted directly by the individual for consideration on receipt.

Other information

The fund continues to support FirstAssist, a counselling and legal advice service for employees, as well as the ROH Occupational Health Unit.

The Scottish Artists' Benevolent Association

£20,000

Correspondent: Lesley Nicholl, Secretary, 2nd Floor, 5 Oswald Street, Glasgow G1 4QR (01412 487411; fax: 01412 210417)

SC Number: SC011823

Eligibility

Scottish artists in need and their dependents.

Types of grants

Regular or one-off grants according to need and single payments can also be made to cover emergency situations. Grants are mainly given to people who are older or in poor health.

Annual grant total

In 2012/13 the association had an income of £31,000 and an expenditure of £26,000. We estimate that grants to individuals totalled around £20,000.

Applications

On a form available from the correspondent to be submitted directly by the individual.

The Show Business Benevolent Fund

£25,000

Correspondent: Mandy Barnes, President, Caledonian Suite, 70 West Regent Street, Glasgow G2 2QZ (01412 550508; email: info@ssbf.co.uk; website: www.ssbf.co.uk)

SC Number: SC009910

Eligibility

Members of The Show Business Association who are in need, and their dependents, including widows/widowers.

Types of grants

One-off and recurrent grants towards, for example, clothing, fuel, living expenses, funeral costs, TV rental and licences and holidays to Blackpool.

Annual grant total

In 2012/13 the fund had an income of £47,000 and an expenditure of £36,000. We estimate that grants to individuals totalled around £25,000.

Applications

In writing to the correspondent.

Dance

The Dance Teachers' Benevolent Fund

£8,000

Correspondent: Elizabeth Claxton, Trustee, Rostrons, Yare House, 62–64 Thorpe Road, Norwich NR1 1RY (01603 619166; email: info@dtbf.co.uk; website: www.dtbf.co.uk)

CC Number: 278899

Eligibility

Dance teachers or ex-dance teachers who are experiencing short or long-term hardship. Applicants are normally expected to be a registered member of one of the recognised examining bodies, or to have acquired a minimum of eight years' experience as a professional dance teacher.

Types of grants

Grants for clothing, household items, medical treatment and so on. Recurrent grants may be given to applicants living on a low income and loans may also be considered.

Annual grant total

In 2012/13 the fund had an income of £25,000 and an expenditure of £27,000. We estimate that grants to individuals totalled £8,000.

Applications

On a form available from the correspondent. Forms can be submitted by the individual or any third party and are considered all year.

Other information

The fund was founded in 1979 by a group of dance teachers drawn from all the major dance bodies. As it relies entirely on donations for income, the fund has organised numerous fundraising galas and events since its formation.

The International Dance Teachers' Association Ltd Benevolent Fund

£7,500 (17 grants)

Correspondent: Keith Holmes, Secretary, International House, 76 Bennett Road, Brighton, East Sussex BN2 5JL (01273 685652; fax: 01273 674388; email: info@idta.co.uk; website: www.idta.co.uk)

CC Number: 297561

Eligibility

Members and former members of the association, other dancers, former dancers, teachers or former teachers of dance, employees or former employees of the association, and their dependents who are affected by hardship. Support is mainly given in cases where individuals are unable to teach or work due to sickness, injury or disability.

Types of grants

According to our research, one-off grants ranging from £100 to £5,000 are available. Support is of a benevolent nature for people in need during times of crisis or ill health rather than to develop career.

Annual grant total

At the time of writing (August 2014) the latest available financial information was from 2012. In 2012 the fund had assets of £99,000 and an income of £40,000. Grants were made to 17 individuals totalling £7,500.

Applications

Applications are available from the correspondent.

Other information

The fund also organises various dancing events and may sponsor dance related organisations.

The Royal Ballet Benevolent Fund

£82,000

Correspondent: Clementine Cowl, Charity Manager, Royal Opera House, Covent Garden, London WC2E 9DD (01273 234011; email: info@rbbf.org.uk; website: www.rbbf.org.uk)

CC Number: 207477

Eligibility

People who have been employed in a ballet or contemporary dance company as a dancer, dance teacher, choreographer, choreologist or as an independent dance artist for at least five years. In certain circumstances, the fund may consider people who do not fit this criteria, for instance people who have had their careers prematurely ended by injury.

Types of grants

One-off grants and regular payments are available to relieve any form of hardship. This includes financial assistance to older people on a low income, aids for people with a disability, help with the transition from dance to another career, or specialist surgery/therapy for injured dancers. Typical grants cover items such as supplementary pensions; disability equipment and adaptations; medical treatment and care.

Annual grant total

In 2012/13 the fund held assets of £4.5 million and had an income of £241,000. Grants and allowances totalled £82,000.

Exclusions

There are no grants available for students training to be dancers. The fund cannot help dancers whose careers have not been within ballet and contemporary dance companies, for example dancers whose main career has been in musical theatre.

The fund does not normally pay off credit card debts.

Applications

On a form available from the correspondent or to download from the website. Applications should be submitted directly by the individual along with a professional CV. The form may be completed by someone else on behalf of the applicant but the applicant must sign. An assessment of the applicant's income based on earnings from work or benefits and an assessment of the applicant's expenditure should be submitted as supporting evidence. Confirmation of the applicant's professional details must be provided by at least one referee. The trustees meet to consider applications four times a year.

The trustees welcome informal enquiries to discuss an application prior to the submission of a formal application.

Other information

The fund offers non-financial assistance in the form of advice services and home visits.

There is an informative website, with links to other agencies offering similar assistance.

Music

The Concert Artistes' Association Benevolent Fund

£20,000

Correspondent: Pamela Cundell, Trustee, 13 Holmdene Avenue, London NW7 2LY (020 8959 3154; email: office@thecaa.org)

CC Number: 211012

Eligibility

Members of the association, and their dependents, who are in need. Applicants must have held their membership for at least two years (or five years if over 40 at the time of joining).

Types of grants

One-off and recurrent grants according to need. Grants have previously been given towards the payment of household bills, dentures, hearing aids, glasses, disability equipment and electrical goods. Monthly grants may also be distributed to pensioners.

Annual grant total

In 2012/13 the fund had an income of £23,000 and a total expenditure of £22,000. We estimate that grants to individuals totalled around £20,000.

Applications

On a form available from the correspondent to be submitted directly by the individual. Applications are considered on an ongoing basis.

The English National Opera Benevolent Fund

£23,000

Correspondent: Humayun Ahmed, Administrator, ENO Benevolent Fund, London Coliseum, 38 St Martin's Lane, London WC2N 4ES (020 7845 9252; email: hahmed@eno.org)

CC Number: 211249

Eligibility

People who are or have been employed by the English National Opera and/or Sadler's Wells Companies and are in need.

Types of grants

Applicants for recurrent grants must be over 58 years old and payments are normally towards telephone, TV and insurance costs. One-off support is considered on a case by case basis. Grants normally range between £150 and £3,000. Loans are also available. Medical/dental treatment is not normally supported, except where delay would affect a performing career. The fund will help with payments for treatment which is not generally available through the NHS.

Annual grant total

In 2012/13 the fund had an income of £13,300 and a total expenditure of £24,000. We estimate that grants to individuals totalled around £23,000.

Applications

Submitted directly by the individual on a form available from the correspondent, to be considered quarterly.

The Incorporated Association of Organists' Benevolent Fund

£7,000

Correspondent: Michael Whitehall, Hon Secretary and Treasurer, 180 Lynn Road, Wisbech, Cambridgeshire PE13 3EB (01945 463826; email: michael@whitehalls.plus.com; website: www.iaobf.com)

CC Number: 216533

Eligibility

Organists and/or choirmasters who are members/former members of any association or society affiliated to the Incorporated Association of Organists and their dependents who are in need.

Types of grants

One-off and recurrent grants according to need.

Annual grant total

In 2013 the fund had an income of £19,500 and a total expenditure of £15,700. We estimate that social welfare grants to individuals totalled £7,000. Funding is also awarded to dependents of members or former members of the IAO to assist with pipe-organ course or examination fees.

Applications

On a form available to download from the website or from the correspondent. Applications can be made by the individual but should be countersigned by the secretary of the applicant's local organists' association. They should be submitted by 31 March for consideration at the trustees' annual meeting in May. In urgent cases the secretary may obtain approval at other times.

ISM Members' Fund (The Benevolent Fund of The Incorporated Society of Musicians)

£80,000 (61 grants)

Correspondent: Caroline Aldred, Head of Members Fund Operations, 10 Stratford Place, London W1C 1AA (020 7629 4413/020 7313 9310; email: membership@ism.org/caroline@ism.org; website: www.ism.org)

CC Number: 206801

Eligibility

Members and former members of the fund and their dependents who are in need.

Types of grants

One-off and recurrent grants according to need.

Annual grant total

In 2012/13 the fund had assets of £3.3 million and an income of £123,000. Grants were made to 61 individuals and totalled almost £80,000.

Exclusions

No grants towards professional training.

Applications

On a form available from the correspondent, to be submitted directly by the individual at any time. An initial informal discussion with the primary contact would be beneficial. Applications are considered by a committee who assess the needs of each applicant and decide on the nature and amount of financial support given.

Other information

The fund provides an outsourced telephone counselling service which is available to all members and their families.

The Musicians Benevolent Fund

£1.4 million

Correspondent: Help and Advice Team, 7–11 Britannia Street, London WC1X 9JS (0800 082 6700 (Helpline); email: help@helpmusicians.org.uk; website: www.helpmusicians.org.uk)

CC Number: 228089

Eligibility

The fund can help if: you are a working professional musician; you are retired and your principal career was in music; you work in a related music profession; or (in some circumstances) if you are a dependent or partner of a musician. Additionally, you must: be able to show that you are in need of financial help; be a UK citizen or have spent the majority of your working life as a musician in the UK (at least three years); and be resident in the UK at the time of application. Financial help is not normally given to people with savings of more than £16,000. For older and retired musicians, this limit is £20,000, however.

The fund defines a professional musician as:

> Someone who has earned their living substantially from music for a significant portion of their working life. We define 'working life' to be from the start of a career (i.e. the end of formal education, usually minimum age 18) to state pension age, or to the age at which a crisis occurs. This would normally be more than three years.

To qualify, you must be directly involved in the production of music, or in work for which the main qualification is a high level of music training.

Types of grants

Support is given to professional musicians who are facing an unexpected crisis, a long-term illness or disability, or to help cope with retirement. The type of support given depends on the personal circumstances of the applicant. Contact the fund or see its informative website for more details.

Annual grant total

In 2013 the charity had net assets of £56.9 million and an income of £4.1 million. Financial support through crisis/continuing care grants totalled £1.4 million.

Exclusions

The fund is not able to assist amateur musicians or people whose paid musical work is clearly secondary to another career.

Applications

Contact the fund by calling the helpline or emailing. If the fund feels it can help, you will be asked to complete a simple form, providing details of you, your finances and the problem you are facing. You will be asked to provide details of a musical referee who can vouch for your career and status as a professional musician, as well as some evidence of finances, such as bank statements. Once the fund has received all the paperwork, it will aim to give a decision within ten days and, if it is able to offer you support, will try to arrange a visit to your home within eight weeks of agreeing to help, in order to better assess your application and personal needs. In a 'real emergency' a response may be made more quickly.

In the case of the fund being unable to help, it will try to signpost you in the direction of somebody who can.

Other information

The following information is taken from the fund's annual report: 'The charity supports musicians with a mix of advice, guidance and financial support . . . This support falls into three categories:

- Musicians at the point of entering the profession
- Musicians in their working lives who hit a serious crisis, illness or accident
- Musicians in retirement or later life

The fund's trained team can offer advice on a range of issues, including welfare advice, and can help put you in touch with other sources of support, such as debt advice services or medical specialists. Part of the way it offers support is through its successful home visiting scheme. The fund also runs a Talent Programme and the Music Students Health Scheme for young musicians, more details of which are available on the website.

Organists' Charitable Trust

£1,000

Correspondent: The Trustees, 10 Stratford Place, London W1C 1BA (020 8318 1471; email: secretary@organistscharitabletrust.org; website: www.organistscharitabletrust.org)

CC Number: 225326

Eligibility

Organists, and their dependents, who are in financial difficulties.

Types of grants

One-off grants ranging between £500 and £1,000.

Annual grant total

Accounts for the year 2012 were the latest available at the time of writing (August 2014).

In 2012, the trust had an income of £12,000 and a total expenditure of approximately £2,500. We estimate that grants for social welfare purposes totalled around £1,000.

Applications

On a form available from the correspondent. Applications can be submitted directly by the individual or through a third party such as a social worker. They are considered at any time. Repeat applications are welcomed.

The Performing Rights Society Members' Benevolent Fund (PRS Members' Fund)

£401,000

Correspondent: John Logan, General Secretary, 29–33 Berners Street, London W1T 3AB (020 7306 4067; email: john.logan@prsformusic.com; website: www.prsformusicfund.com)

CC Number: 208671

Eligibility

Songwriters and composers of music who are or were members of the Performing Rights Society, and their dependents (including of deceased members), who are in need and/or unable to work because of old age, illness, accident or disability. Members must have held membership for seven years or more.

Types of grants

The fund offers a variety of grants and loans:

- Special needs grants – one-off grants to help the elderly or people with disabilities towards, for example, essential property repairs or the replacement of domestic equipment
- Winter heating grants – to elderly and vulnerable beneficiaries
- Holiday scheme – to provide help to elderly members who would otherwise be unable to afford a holiday
- Short-term loans – to help with an unexpected financial crisis
- Emergency help – usually towards the replacement of essential domestic appliances
- Regular grants – of up to £20 per week to help with general living expenses, including food and medication, are given to members who are receiving benefits but still cannot maintain basic standards of living. Help may also be given towards telephone and TV rental, TV licences or gas and heating bills. Persons in receipt of regular grants also receive a Christmas hamper, and in some cases a Christmas bonus

Annual grant total

At the time of writing (September 2014) the latest financial information available from the Charity Commission was from 2012. In 2012 the fund held assets totalling £9 million and had an income of £732,000. Grants to beneficiaries totalled £401,000. The trustees' annual report from 2012 further specifies that there were 530 weekly grants made, 123 Christmas hampers awarded, 50 older and vulnerable members were helped with winter heating costs totalling £19,348 and payments for repairs/

replacements of furniture and appliances reached £11,800.

The fund's website notes that in 2013 over 1,200 awards were made totalling around £428,000.

Exclusions

The fund will not help:

- With the cost of buying a home
- To promote any commercial venue
- Composers who do not have any other employment
- Towards payments as an advance against future royalties

Applications

Application forms can be downloaded from the fund's website or requested from the correspondent. They can be submitted by the individual, through a social worker, Citizens Advice or other welfare agency, by next of kin or by an associate. In cases of claims based on illness, a medical or GP's report is required. The trustees met monthly.

All applications are means tested in line with DWP income and savings criteria. Recipients of regular support are paid a visit by the fund at least once a year.

Other information

As well as offering financial assistance the fund can make referrals for specialist financial advice as well as provide specialist health assessments in conjunction with their partners, the British Association for Performing Arts Medicine. The fund also provides sheltered accommodation and from 2013 runs a career counselling service.

The Royal Society of Musicians of Great Britain

£540,000

Correspondent: Penny Ryan, Accountant, 10 Stratford Place, London W1C 1BA (020 7629 6137; fax: 020 7629 6137; email: enquiries@royalsocietyofmusicians.co.uk; website: royalsocietyofmusicians.co.uk/)

CC Number: 208879

Eligibility

Current, former or beginning professional musicians and their families who are in need because of illness, accident or age. Membership of the society is not a requirement, although some priority may be given.

Types of grants

One-off and recurrent grants from £50 to £5,000. Loans of musical instruments are also available.

Annual grant total

In 2012/13 the society had assets of £17.7 million and an income of £851,000. Grants made to individuals totalled £540,000. The majority of grants (77%) were given to non-members. The society also has a number of restricted funds.

Exclusions

Grants are not given to students or people whose only claim for relief arises from unemployment.

Applications

In writing to the correspondent. Enquiries from welfare organisations are welcomed as is the identification of need from any concerned individual. Normally, applications will need to be supported by a member of the society (a copy of the current membership list is supplied to applicants). Requests for assistances are considered monthly.

Other information

The society is a charity for musicians, run by musicians. Specialist advice is also available from honorary officers, which include medical consultants. If unable to help, the society may refer applicants to other relevant organisations.

Painting

The Eaton Fund for Artists, Nurses and Gentlewomen

See entry on page 31

Theatre

The Actors' Benevolent Fund

£529,000

Correspondent: The General Secretary, 6 Adam Street, London WC2N 6AD (020 7836 6378; fax: 020 7836 8978; email: office@abf.org.uk; website: www.actorsbenevolentfund.co.uk)

CC Number: 206524

Eligibility

Professional actors and theatrical stage managers who are unable to work because of an accident, sickness or old age.

If you are a dancer, a singer or a variety performer or if you are a member of the theatrical profession and have children under 19 there are other charities which may be able to help. Phone the office for advice.

Types of grants

Weekly allowances; grants paid monthly, in summer and at Christmas; hampers; and Winter heating grants. During the year the fund also provided assistance with general household expenses, the cost of replacing household equipment, mobility aids, physiotherapy, osteopathy, the shortfall of nursing home fees and holiday and funeral costs.

Annual grant total

In 2013 the fund had assets of £21.4 million and an income of £923,000. Financial support for nearly 220 individuals, of whom 185 received regular payments, totalled £529,000.

Exclusions

No grants are available to students. Grants are unlikely to be made for credit card debts, loans or private dental or medical treatment, which should be covered by the NHS, although the trust will consider such applications.

Applications

On a form available from the correspondent or online or to download from the fund's website. Applications should be submitted directly by the individual and include a detailed CV and, if appropriate, the applicant's Spotlight link, Equity number or IMDB entry. If applying due to ill health or an accident, a recent doctor's letter giving details of the individual's condition should be included. It may also be helpful to include any Benefit Agency letters which confirm the level of benefits received. Applications are considered on the last Thursday of each month and forms should be submitted by the Friday before a meeting.

In cases of emergency, where potential beneficiaries need their application to be considered before the next scheduled meeting contact the fund's office on 020 7836 6378 for advice.

Other information

The Actors' Benevolent Fund also provides advice on welfare and debt and supports its beneficiaries through visits, telephone calls and birthday cards.

The fund occasionally approaches other theatrical charities on behalf of applicants, if given permission to do so. There is a list of charities with which the fund has links available on its helpful website.

The Actors' Charitable Trust (TACT)

£137,500 (102 grants)

Correspondent: Robert Ashby, General Secretary, The Actors Charitable Trust, 58 Bloomsbury Street, London WC1B 3QT (020 7636 7868; email: robert@tactactors.org; website: www.tactactors.org)

CC Number: 206809

Eligibility

Children (aged under 21) of professional actors who are in financial need. Note: the trust cannot help those who have solely worked in variety, amateur dramatics or as an extra.

Types of grants

One-off and recurrent grants for help with essential furnishings, utility bills (where this will benefit the children), holidays, childcare costs, clothing and special equipment. Additional grants at Christmas and crisis grants are also available.

Annual grant total

In 2012/13 the trust had assets of £6.3 million and an income of £515,000. Grants for educational and welfare purposes were made to 127 families, with 203 children between them, totalling £275,000.

Exclusions

Grants are not usually given for private school fees; however, the trust may consider making a grant if private education would be beneficial to the child i.e. due to special educational needs or family situation. TACT does not pay independent school fees.

Applications

On a form available from the correspondent or to download from the website. Applications can be considered at any time and can be submitted either by the individual or a parent. Telephone and email enquiries are welcomed.

The Royal Theatrical Fund

£205,000

Correspondent: Sharon Lomas, Secretary, West Suite, 2nd Floor, 11 Garrick Street, London WC2E 9AR (020 7836 3322; fax: 020 7379 8273; email: admin@trtf.com; website: www.trtf.com)

CC Number: 222080

Eligibility

People who have professionally practised or contributed to the theatrical arts (on stage, radio, film or television or any other medium) for a minimum of seven years, who are in need, and the dependents of such people.

Types of grants

Monthly allowances and one-off grants towards domestic bills, shortfalls in nursing and residential fees, car tax, stairlifts, computers, insurance, TV licences and so on.

Annual grant total

In 2012/13 the fund held assets of £6.8 million and had an income of £552,000. Grants to individuals totalled more than £205,000 and were distributed as follows:

Monthly allowances	£76,000
One-off grants/gifts	£71,000
Nursing home/residential/ convalescent/home care	£48,000
Birthday and Christmas gifts	£10,200

Exclusions

No grants are made to students or towards courses or projects.

Applications

On an application form available from the correspondent. Alternatively in writing to the correspondent, making sure to include: a letter outlining your financial difficulties and how the fund may be able to help; any other relevant information; a letter of support from your GP or hospital, or a current medical certificate; and a full CV or details of your theatrical career. Applications can be submitted at any time. The welfare committee meets on the first Wednesday of each month (except August) to consider applications. Telephone enquiries are welcome.

Other information

In cases where the fund cannot assist, the Welfare Committee may choose to refer the applicant to another suitable fund or organisation.

The fund also works to provide advice relating to state benefits and emotional support for beneficiaries who are lonely or isolated.

The Theatrical Guild

£25,000

Correspondent: Laura Hannon, Office Manager, The Theatrical Guild, 11 Garrick Street, London WC2E 9AR (020 7240 6062; email: admin@ttg.org.uk; website: www.ttg.org.uk)

CC Number: 206669

Eligibility

People who work, or have retired from, either backstage or front-of-house in a professional theatre. Financial support may be given where accident, ill health or other circumstances have prevented the applicant from working. In special cases, support may be given to working members of the profession and to one-parent families who are prevented from accepting a job due to the cost of childcare.

Types of grants

One-off and recurring grants are typically given for bills, equipment, special medical needs and re-training costs. Applicants typically seek help when they are unable to work through accident, ill health, emergency or some other reason.

Annual grant total

In 2012 the trust had assets of £1.3 million and an income of £137,000. Grants to 64 beneficiaries totalled £50,000 and are given for both social welfare and educational purposes. A breakdown of grants was not available from the accounts. We estimate that welfare grants to individuals totalled around £25,000.

At the time of writing (August 2014) these were the most recent accounts available for the trust.

Exclusions

No grants are given for the repayment of credit card debt. Help cannot be given to help drama students, amateur performers or anyone who hasn't worked or doesn't currently work in professional theatre.

Applications

Application forms can be downloaded from the website or can be requested by calling or emailing the office. Applications can be submitted either directly by the individual, through a third party such as a social worker or through an organisation such as Citizens Advice. They are considered monthly, with the exception of August and December. Those seeking emergency assistance should contact the office directly by email or phone.

Other information

The Guild also offers counselling, welfare support and educational sponsorship.

Writing

The Authors' Contingency Fund

£17,000

Correspondent: Sarah Baxter, Contracts Advisor and Literary Estates, 84 Drayton Gardens, London SW10 9SB (020 7373 6642; fax: 020 7373 5768; email: SBaxter@societyofauthors.org; website: www.societyofauthors.org)

CC Number: 212406

Eligibility

Professional authors in the UK and their dependents. Grants are also made to professional poets and their dependents and female journalists.

Types of grants

One-off grants usually of between £500 and £750, to relieve a temporary financial emergency.

Annual grant total

In 2012 the fund had an income of £17,200 and a total expenditure of £18,700. We estimate that social welfare grants to individuals totalled £17,000.

At the time of writing (August 2014) this was the most recent financial information available for the fund.

Exclusions

The trust cannot help with the following:

- Grants to cover publication costs
- Grants to authors who are in financial difficulty through contributing towards publication costs
- Tuition fees
- General support whilst writing a book

Applications

On a form available from the correspondent or to download from the website, including information about the applicant's circumstances and career history. Applications can be submitted directly by the individual and are considered on receipt. The assessment process usually takes around three weeks.

Other information

The fund, in conjunction with the John Masefield Memorial Trust, makes grants to British poets and administers the Margaret Rhondda Awards to support women journalists.

Francis Head Award

£13,000

Correspondent: Sarah Baxter, Contracts Advisor and Literary Estates, 84 Drayton Gardens, London SW10 9SB (020 7373 6642; fax: 020 7373 5768; email: sbaxter@societyofauthors.org; website: www.societyofauthors.org)

CC Number: 277018

Eligibility

Professional writers (writing in the English language) who were born in the UK and are over the age of 35. The focus of the trust is primarily on those who are temporarily unable to support themselves or their dependents due to illness or accident, although the trust's website does state that 'the terms of the trust are reasonably wide.'

Types of grants

Emergency grants usually ranging from £1,000 to £2,000.

Annual grant total

In 2012 charity had an income of £22,000 and a total expenditure of £22,000. We estimate that grants totalled £13,000.

At the time of writing (August 2014) this was the most recent financial information available for the charity.

Exclusions

No grants are given to cover publication costs, tuition fees or general maintenance whilst writing a book. Support is also unavailable to authors who are in financial difficulty because they have invested money in publication costs.

Applications

On a form available from the correspondent or to download from the trust's website. Applications can be submitted directly by the individual and should include a covering letter explaining the circumstances prompting the application. A decision is usually made within three weeks.

Peggy Ramsay Foundation

£50,000

Correspondent: G. Laurence Harbottle, Trustee, Hanover House, 14 Hanover Square, London W15 1HP (020 7667 5000; fax: 020 7667 5100; email: laurence.harbottle@harbottle.com; website: www.peggyramsayfoundation.org)

CC Number: 1015427

Eligibility

Writers for the stage who have been produced publicly, are 'of promise' and are in need of time to write which they cannot afford, or are in need of other assistance. Applicants must live in the British Isles (including Republic of Ireland and the Channel Islands).

Adaptations of plays intended for younger audiences may be accepted in special circumstances.

Types of grants

One-off grants. Individual grants never ordinarily exceed a standard commissioning fee. Grants are sometimes made for equipment, such as laptops, and for expenditure which makes writing possible.

Annual grant total

In 2012 the foundation had assets of £5.2 million and an income of £255,000. Grants to 53 individuals totalled £101,000. Grants were made to individuals for educational purposes as well.

These were the latest accounts available at the time of writing (July 2014).

Exclusions

The foundation does not support production costs or any project that does not have a hold a direct benefit to individual playwrights or writing for the stage or fees for training courses. No grants are made for writing not intended for the theatre. The trustees will not accept as qualification books for musicals, pantomime scripts, puppet plays, foreign language plays, translations of school plays.

Applications

Apply by writing a short letter to the correspondent, submitted with a CV directly by the individual. Applicants should also provide answers to the following questions:

- When and where was the first professional production of a play of yours
- Who produced the play which qualifies you for a grant
- When and where was your qualifying play produced, what was its run and approximate playing time and has it been revived
- For that production were the director and actors all professionals engaged with Equity contracts
- Did the audience pay to attend

Scripts and publicity material must not be included. Trustees meet quarterly although applications are dealt with between meetings. Applicants will usually receive a decision in six to eight weeks.

Other information

Grants were also made to organisations totalling £22,000.

The Royal Literary Fund

£1.4 million (210 grants)

Correspondent: Eileen Gunn, Chief Executive, 3 Johnson's Court, off Fleet Street, London EC4A 3EA (020 7353 7159; email: eileen.gunn@rlf.org.uk; website: www.rlf.org.uk)

CC Number: 219952

Eligibility

Authors of published work of literary merit and their dependents. The work must be written in English. Books stemming from a parallel career as an academic or practitioner are not eligible.

Types of grants

One-off (outright) grants, instalment grants and pensions. Instalment grants and pensions are awarded over a three and five year period respectively.

Pensions are reviewed for renewal after the five year period

Recent examples of beneficiaries (from the fund's annual report) include: (a) 'A poet and translator was suffering from ME, which slowed his progress as a writer. He survived on benefits and help from his family. The committee decided to make him an annual grant for three years.' (b) 'An award winning poet who suffered from mental health problems and addiction to drugs and alcohol was now in recovery and living in supported accommodation on benefits. The committee made him a grant.'

Annual grant total

In 2012/13 the fund had assets of over £134 million and an income of £3.2 million. Grants and pensions totalled £1.4 million.

Exclusions

No grants for projects or work in progress. The trust does not make loans. Books stemming from a previous academic or practitioner career do not count.

Applications

On a form available from the correspondent. Application forms request details of all income and expenditure, and a member of staff will subsequently arrange to meet with new applicants at their homes. Applicants are asked to supply copies of their published work which is then read by two members of the committee who decide on the question of literary merit. When requesting an application form applicants are asked to provide a list of their publications, including names of publishers, dates and whether they were the sole author. If this is approved, a grant/pension may be made based on an assessment of need.

Other information

One grant was paid to the Royal Society of Literature (£10,000).

The Society of Authors Pension Fund

£18,000 (10 grants)

Correspondent: The General Secretary, c/o The Society of Authors, 84 Drayton Gardens, London SW10 9SB (020 7373 6642; fax: 020 7373 5768; email: info@societyofauthors.org; website: www.societyofauthors.org)

CC Number: 212401

Eligibility

Authors over 65 who have been a member of the Society of Authors for at least ten years.

Types of grants

Annual grants of £1,800 which are paid in quarterly instalments.

Annual grant total

In 2012 the fund had assets of £539,000 and an income of £26,000. Grants were made to ten individuals totalling £18,000. The 2012 accounts were the latest available at the time of writing (August 2014).

Applications

In writing to the correspondent when vacancies are announced in the society's journal.

Atomic energy

UBA Benevolent Fund

£54,000

Correspondent: Elaine Price, Fund Manager and Secretary, Unit CU1, Warrington Business Park, Long Lane, Warrington WA2 8TX (01925 633005; fax: 01925 633455; email: info@ubabenfund.com; website: www.tnibf.org)

CC Number: 208729

Eligibility

Past and present members of the non-industrial staff of UKAEA, Amersham International plc and British Nuclear Fuels plc (or any successor organisation) and their dependents, who are in need. (Where single status has been adopted, all employees are eligible.) People who left the company as industrial employees are not eligible. Applicants do not need to have been a subscriber to the fund.

Types of grants

Allowances of between £5 and £20 per week. One-off grants are given for most purposes, except where this would affect state benefits. Interest-free loans are also available. Grants are given towards furniture, disability aids (stair lifts, wheelchairs, alarms and so on), holidays, nursing home fees, Christmas grants, television licences and sets, repairs, fuel bills (to prevent disconnection), telephone bills, removal costs, debts (in some cases), minor repairs and child minding.

Annual grant total

In 2012/13 the fund held assets of £3 million and had an income of £74,000. Welfare grants and allowances to individuals totalled £54,000 and a further £23,000 was given in interest-free loans.

Exclusions

Grants are not given for private health care (excluding convalescence and residential home fees) or private education.

Applications

On a form available from the correspondent. Applications may be channelled through the network of local representatives, located at or near the organisations' sites; direct to the fund's office; or through other charities or similar bodies. They are considered every two months from January onwards.

Banking, finance and insurance

The Bank Workers Charity

£870,000

Correspondent: The Clerk, Pinners Hall, 105–108 Old Broad Street, London EC2N 1EX (0800 023 4834; email: info@bwcharity.org.uk; website: www.bwcharity.org.uk)

CC Number: 313080

Eligibility

Current and ex-employees of banks in the UK and their dependents.

Types of grants

Regular grant payments for those on limited incomes; limited help with residential and nursing home fees; contributions towards the cost of wheelchairs, scooters, mobility aids and domestic appliances; carer's respite breaks and some family holidays; in special cases, assistance with telephone bills and TV licenses; grants towards house repairs and maintenance.

Annual grant total

In 2012/13 the charity had assets of £46.5 million and an income of £1.6 million. Grants totalled £1.1 million broken down as follows:

- Families – £470,000
- Retirees – £400,000
- Child education – £244,000

Exclusions

No grants for non-priority debts, private medical fees or home improvements, except when essential repairs are needed to ensure independent living, safety and security. People who have worked in the insurance or stock broking industries cannot be helped.

Applications

On a form available from the correspondent or to download from the website. Once the form has been received it will be reviewed by staff. Additional contact may be required to obtain further information or clarification. The trustees meet quarterly to consider new cases.

Other information

The charity also provides support in three main areas: home, money and wellbeing. They have client advisors who offer information, advice and guidance covering a range of issue as well as offering independent and confidential counselling.

The Chartered Institute of Loss Adjusters Benevolent Fund

£0

Correspondent: The Secretariat, 51–55 Gresham St, London EC2V 7HQ (020 7337 9960; email: info@cila.co.uk; website: www.cila.co.uk)

CC Number: 210559

Eligibility

Members of the institute and their dependents who are 'distressed through sickness or other misfortune'.

Types of grants

One-off and recurrent grants according to need. In 2012/13 the fund made no grants.

Annual grant total

In 2012/13 the fund had no income and made no grants to individuals.

Applications

In writing to the correspondent. If a member passes away, the fund notifies his/her partner of the financial assistance available.

The Alfred Foster Settlement

£14,000

Correspondent: Graham Prew, Administrator, Barclays Bank Trust Co. Ltd, Executorship and Trustee Service, Osborne Court, Gadbrook Park, Rudheath, Northwich CW9 7UE (01606 313118)

CC Number: 229576

Eligibility

Employees and former employees of banks and their dependents who are in need.

Types of grants

One-off grants according to need.

Annual grant total

In 2012/13 the charity had an income of £39,000 and a total expenditure of £29,000. Grants were given to individuals totalling £28,000 and we estimate the total given in welfare grants was approximately £14,000.

Applications

By the employee's bank, to their local regional office or directly to the correspondent.

Other information

The charity also makes grants to individuals for educational purposes.

The Insurance Charities

£481,000

Correspondent: Annali-Joy Thornicroft, Secretary, 20 Aldermanbury, London EC2V 7HY (020 7606 3763; fax: 020 7600 1170; email: info@theinsurancecharities.org.uk; website: www.theinsurancecharities.org.uk)

CC Number: 206860

Eligibility

Children of people who have spent at least five years working in the insurance industry in UK or Eire. Adult children of insurance people can be considered where personal resources are insufficient to meet reasonable expenditure.

Types of grants

Ongoing grants and interest-free or low interest loans towards day-to-day expenses and one-off grants towards special needs such as domestic appliances, disability aids and property maintenance. Help is also given to students on first degree courses.

Annual grant total

In 2012/13 the charities had assets of £30.1 million and an income of £1.8 million. Grants were made to 259 individuals totalling £962,000. This is the net figure after deducting £95,000, the contribution made by the Paul Golmick Fund towards grants.

Applications

An initial form can be completed online or downloaded from the website.

Other information

The charities also make grants to past and present employees of the insurance industry experiencing financial hardship.

The Paul Golmick Fund is administered by the charities and was set up to promote the maintenance and education of children and young people under the age of 24, but primarily under the age of 18, who reside in the UK or Republic of Ireland and who have at least one parent or guardian with service to the insurance industry.

The Lloyd's Benevolent Fund

£191,000

Correspondent: Raymond Blaber, Secretary, c/o Lloyd's Benevolent Fund, 1 Lime Street, London EC3M 7HA (020 7327 6453; email: raymond.blaber@lloyds.com)

CC Number: 207231

Eligibility

People who work or have worked in the Lloyd's insurance market and their dependents, anywhere in the world.

Types of grants

One-off or recurrent grants can be given towards relieving general hardship.

Annual grant total

In 2012/13 the fund held assets of £9.8 million and had an income of £291,000. Grants to 30 beneficiaries totalled £191,000.

Exclusions

No assistance for underwriting members of Lloyd's. School fees or medical costs will not be covered.

Applications

On a form available from the correspondent. Applications can be submitted by the individual or through a social worker, Citizens Advice, other welfare agency or other third party. They are considered throughout the year.

UNITE the Union Benevolent Fund

£94,000

Correspondent: Steven Skinner, Trustee, Unite, 128 Theobald's Road, London WC1X 8TN (020 7611 2500; email: stephen.skinner@unitetheunion.org; website: www.unitetheunion.org/member_services/unite_the_union_benevolent_fun.aspx)

CC Number: 228567

Eligibility

Members, former members, employees or ex-employees of the union and their dependents.

Types of grants

One-off grants of between £100 and £1,000 to people who have fallen on hard times through being absent from work through prolonged sickness, retirement through ill-health, family bereavements or a change in domestic circumstances. Grants have included payment towards a riser/recliner for person with back problems, help to somebody dismissed while on sick leave, heating grants for older people, Christmas bonuses for people who are elderly or have young children, and general assistance with bills.

Annual grant total

In 2012 the fund had an income of £183,000 and a total expenditure of £216,000. It had assets of £1.1 million which mainly consisted of investments and was therefore not available for distribution. Grants totalling £94,000 were made to individuals for social welfare purposes.

The 2012 accounts were the latest available at the time of writing.

Exclusions

Help with legal fees, educational grants and credit card bills is not usually available.

Applications

On a form available from the correspondent or to download from the website. Relevant supporting documents such as doctor's letters, bank statements, payslips, etc., should also be attached to the application. Applications are considered every other month.

Book retail

The Book Trade Charity

£119,000

Correspondent: David Hicks, Chief Executive, The Foyle Centre, The Retreat, Abbots Road, Kings Langley, Hertfordshire WD4 8LT (01329 848731; email: david@btbs.org; website: www.booktradecharity.org)

CC Number: 1128129

Eligibility

People in need who have worked in the book trade in the UK for at least one year (normally publishing/distribution/book-selling), and their dependents. Priority will be given to people who are chronically sick, redundant, unemployed or over 50 years of age.

Types of grants

One-off grants of up to £1,000 and recurrent grants of around £1,300 a year. Grants are normally to supplement weekly/monthly income and for recuperative holidays. Other support is given in a variety of ways, for example, assistance with telephone and television rental, medical aid, aids for disabled people and house repairs/redecoration. Grants are also given to help retrain people from the book trade who have been made redundant.

Annual grant total

In 2013 this charity had assets of £5.7 million consisting for the most part of land and buildings and therefore not available for grant giving. Its income was £508,000 and grants were made totalling £123,000 of which £119,000 was awarded in social welfare grants (including £10,000 in medical costs).

Applications

On a form available from the correspondent. Applications can be submitted by the individual or through a recognised referral agency (social worker, Citizens Advice, doctor and so on). They are considered as they arrive.

Brewing

E. F. Bulmer Benevolent Fund

£65,000 (252 grants)

Correspondent: James Greenfield, Administrator, Fred Bulmer Centre, Wall Street, Hereford HR4 9HP (01432 271293; email: efbulmer@gmail.com; website: www.efbulmer.co.uk)

CC Number: 214831

Eligibility

Former employees of H P Bulmer Holdings plc (before it was acquired by Scottish and Newcastle plc) or its subsidiary companies for a period of not less than one year, or their dependents, who are in need. Grants are occasionally made to other individuals in need in Herefordshire.

Types of grants

One-off grants, typically up to £500, are awarded according to need. Some top-up pensions are made from a historic list but the fund is not considering new pension applicants.

Annual grant total

In 2012/13 the fund held assets of £12.2 million and had an income of £368,000. Grants totalled £242,000 and were distributed as follows:

Grants to organisations	72	£177,000
Pension supplements	156	£31,000
One-off grants to H P Bulmer pensioners	55	£19,100
One-off grants to other individuals	41	£15,300

Financial assistance to 252 individuals totalled more than £65,000.

Applications

Initial enquiries should be made to the administrator, preferably by email. Applications should be made through a recognised organisation such as social services, Citizens Advice or other reputable organisations. Applicants are encouraged to consider the information noted on the fund's website before applying. The fund aims to inform eligible applicants of their outcome as soon as possible after a Trustee's meeting. Ineligible applicants will not receive a reply.

Other information

The fund maintains the Fred Bulmer centre which provides facilities and accommodation for other charities.

Building trade

Builders' Benevolent Institution

£57,000

Correspondent: The Secretary, 12 Shepherds Walk, Chestfield, Kent CT5 3NB (01227 791623; email: bbi@fmb.org.uk)

CC Number: 212022

Eligibility

Those who are or who have been master builders (employers in the building industry), and their dependents. Applicants with less than ten years' experience are not eligible, nor are those who have been employees.

Types of grants

Mostly pensions and Christmas vouchers. Occasionally, the charity distributes one-off grants towards the cost of necessary items such as home alterations and urgent house repairs. The charity notes that the average length of time over which beneficiaries receive support is around 15 years.

Annual grant total

In 2013 the charity had assets of £1.1 million and an income of £73,000. Grants were made totalling approximately £57,000 and were distributed as follows:

Pensions	£51,000
Christmas gift vouchers	£4,200
Temporary relief	£1,300

Applications

On a form available from the correspondent, submitted directly by the individual, through a social worker, Citizens Advice, other welfare agency or third party. Applications are considered throughout the year.

The Chartered Institute of Building Benevolent Fund

£47,000

Correspondent: Franklin MacDonald, Secretary, Englemere, Kings Ride, Ascot, Berkshire SL5 7TB (01344 630780; fax: 01344 630777; email: fmacdonald@ciob.org.uk; website: www.ciob.org.uk)

CC Number: 1013292

Eligibility

Members of the institute and their dependents who are in real need.

Types of grants

One-off and recurrent grants towards, for example, computer equipment for a housebound individual, help for a family in general financial hardship and continuing support for a member following redundancy and ill-health.

Note: the fund cannot allocate grants for academic study but it may be able to help members who are in circumstances of hardship to obtain specialised, skill-based training.

Annual grant total

In 2013 the fund had both an income and total expenditure of £110,000. It had assets of £1 million mainly consisting of investments and was therefore not available for distribution. Grants made to individuals for social welfare purposes totalled £47,000.

Applications

In writing to the correspondent. Applications are considered as they arrive. Informal enquiries via email are welcomed.

Other information

A significant part of the charitable expenditure is spent on providing practical advice, information and advocacy. The fund also provides a guide called 'Fresh Start' which offers information for members coping with unemployment or redundancy and is available to download from the website.

The Lighthouse Club

£453,000 (339 grants)

Correspondent: Peter Burns, Administrator, Armstrong House, Swallow Street, Stockport, Cheshire SK1 3LG (01614 290022; email: peterb@cooksonhardware.com; website: www.lighthouseclub.org)

CC Number: 1149488

Eligibility

People, or dependents of people, who work or have recently worked in the construction industry, or in an industry associated with construction (e.g. civil engineering, demolition or design), in the UK or Republic of Ireland. Applicants should usually have worked in the industry for at least two years, although not necessarily consecutively.

Types of grants

Recurrent grants to help towards living costs for those in need through accident, disability or ill-health and for those in need because a member of their family (who was in the construction industry) has died or has a fatal illness. One-off grants are also available towards essential items or services, such as a new bed, a replacement washing machine, funeral costs and school uniforms.

Annual grant total

In 2013 the fund had assets of £484,000 and an income of £847,000. Grants were made to 339 individuals totalling £453,000. Of those helped 175 received regular support while 164 received one-off support.

Exclusions

The maximum length of time for recurrent grants to be given is five years.

Applications

In the first instance contact the administrator or a branch welfare officer (a list of local branches is available on the fund's website) to receive a copy of the application form.

Other information

The Lighthouse Club now provides a 24x7 construction industry helpline, which can be contacted by calling 0845 605 1956. The charity's 2013 accounts state that it can help to access advice on a range of matters including:

- Occupational health and wellbeing issues as an employee or an employer (Through our partners Constructing Better Health)
- Support and advice for sufferers of stress and addiction related illness
- Advice on matters ranging from divorce to employment
- Advice on specific tax related issues concerning employment within the construction sector (Through our partners RIFT)
- Help to manage and reschedule debt
- Help to understand the benefits system and entitlement, especially if caring for others
- Support on career changes, especially after accident or injury preventing return to your original job

Scottish Building Federation Edinburgh and District Charitable Trust

£22,000

Correspondent: Fiona Watson, Administrator, Scott-Moncrieff (Secretaries and Treasurers), Exchange Place 3, Semple Street, Edinburgh EH3 8BL (01314 733500; email: charity@scott-moncrieff.com; website: www.scott-moncrieff.com/charitable_trusts/page7.html)

SC Number: SC029604

Eligibility

People in reduced circumstances who have been involved with the building trade in the City of Edinburgh or the Lothians.

Types of grants

One-off grants according to need.

Annual grant total

In 2013 the trust had an income and expenditure of almost £48,000. Funding is also provided for educational purposes. We estimate that grants awarded to individuals for social welfare purposes was around £23,000.

Applications

On an application form available from the correspondent's website www.scott-moncrieff.com/services/charities/charitable-trusts/scottish-building-federation-edinburgh Details of employment in the trade must be included.

Caravan

The National Caravan Council (NCC) Benevolent Fund

£5,000

Correspondent: Sara-Jane Amey, Trustee, PO Box 1421, Woking GU22 2ND (email: info@nccbf.org.uk; website: www.nccbf.org.uk)

CC Number: 271625

Eligibility

People in need who are, or have been, employed in the caravan industry, and their dependents.

Types of grants

Normally one-off grants ranging from £200 to £2,500, although occasionally recurrent grants may be given. Smaller grants have been given to help with maintenance or unexpected bills, and larger ones have been made to help provide the likes of building adaptations or heating.

Annual grant total

In 2012/13 the fund had an income of £7,300 and a total expenditure of £6,000. We estimate that grants to individuals totalled £5,000.

Applications

On a form available from the correspondent including details of employment within the caravan industry. Applications can be submitted directly by the individual or through an appropriate third party.

Other information

The fund was established in 1976 by six key caravan industry leaders, 'initially to help those current, past or retired employees who have been involved with the caravan industry.' In 2010, the fund changed its status so it could support people in need from outside the caravan industry.

Through a partnership with Happy Days Children's Charity (1010943), the fund owns a touring caravan and a caravan holiday home which it uses to give disadvantaged children and their families the opportunity to enjoy a holiday experience.

Caring

The Care Professionals Benevolent Fund

£8,800 (19 grants)

Correspondent: Shaun Turner, Administrator, Bacchus, The Village, Prestbury, Cheshire SK10 4DG (0845 601 9055; email: info@thecareworkerscharity.org.uk; website: www.cpbenevolentfund.org.uk)

CC Number: 1132286

Eligibility

Current and former employees of the care profession (who work/have worked in a registered domiciliary, residential care, or supported living service) and their dependents who are in need. Current workers must have worked in the care industry for one continuous year. Former workers must have worked in the industry for a total of three continuous years out of the past five; six continuous years in the past ten years; or more than ten years' service during their lifetime. Applicants must have limited savings and resources.

Types of grants

Assistance takes the form of:

- Essential need – items essential for everyday living which, due to a recent unforeseen loss of income, cannot otherwise be afforded (this does not include items considered a luxury, for example, televisions or computer equipment). If you are affected by a long-term illness or have reduced mobility, items considered essential for your wellbeing, such as a mobility scooter or daily living aids
- Crisis – if you are of a working age and have been affected by an unforeseen circumstance such as bereavement, illness, injury or emergency rehousing then assistance can be given towards funeral payments, essential household items and health and safety property repairs

Annual grant total

In 2012 the fund had assets of £110,000 and an income of £64,000. Grants to individuals totalled £8,800

At the time of writing (August 2014) this was the most recent financial information available for the fund.

Exclusions

No grants are given for debts or arrears (apart from in exceptional cases where the applicant has been referred by a welfare agency who can confirm that the situation has arisen from a recent life-changing circumstance or an unforeseen loss of income, and that all other sources of support have been exhausted). Nor are grants given for: bankruptcy or debt relief order fees; statutory sick pay shortfall; future payments or bills; reimbursement for items already purchased; education-related costs such as school fees, fees for educational courses, student maintenance and student loan repayments; most private medical treatments; or shortfalls in care fees.

Applications

On an application form available to download from the website. Applicants must complete an online entitlement check and send the results report along with their application. Applications should also include supporting evidence such as a letter from your ex-employer to confirm your length of service, three months' bank statements and evidence to suggest the reason for your application. Detailed guidelines on completing the application form are also available on the website.

At the time of writing (August 2014) the fund's website states that: 'At present applications are taking 6–8 weeks to be assessed. If your application is of an extremely urgent nature then please contact the office in the first instance before applying.'

Ceramic

The Ceramic Industry Welfare Society

£7,000

Correspondent: The Secretary, Unity Trades Union, Hillcrest House, Garth Street, Stoke-on-Trent ST1 2AB (01782 272755)

CC Number: 261248

Eligibility

People in need who are or have been employed in the ceramics industry, or widows of former employees.

Types of grants

Recurrent grants are fixed at £45 per six week period depending on the circumstances of the applicant as confirmed by the society's representative through a personal visit.

Annual grant total

In 2013 the society had an income of £4,000 and a total expenditure of £7,200. We estimate that grants to individuals totalled £7,000.

Exclusions

No grants are payable beyond 12 months of the date of retirement.

Applications

In writing to the correspondent.

Chartered surveyors

Lionheart (The Royal Institution of Chartered Surveyors Benevolent Fund)

£610,000

Correspondent: Dawn Shirley, Office Administrator, Surveyor Court, Westwood Way, Coventry CV4 8BF (0845 603 9057; fax: 02476 474701; email: info@lionheart.org.uk; website: www.lionheart.org.uk)

CC Number: 261245

Eligibility

Members and former members of the Royal Institution of Chartered Surveyors or organisations it has merged with and their dependents. Applications are welcome from people in the UK and those living overseas. Applicants should visit the website for current eligibility criteria and are advised to contact one of the charity's support officers if in any doubt as to their suitability to apply for a grant. Support officers can also help with information and advice on the charity's other services.

Types of grants

One-off and recurrent grants and loans are given towards: essential domestic appliances, furnishings, re-decorations and property repairs; living expenses; care in the community, residential and nursing care; respite care and holidays; and medical aids, adaptations and equipment for children with disabilities and the elderly. Additional financial help is also available for those most in need at Christmas.

Annual grant total

In 2013/14 the charity had assets of £17.4 million and an income of £1.8 million. Grants to individuals for social welfare purposes totalled £610,000 excluding support costs.

Applications

On a form available to download from the website. Evidence of RICS membership or details of the member of whom the applicant is a dependent should be provided. Applications are considered quarterly, although urgent cases can be considered between meetings.

Other information

The charity offers confidential advice, counselling, befriending, information and help in kind to members of the profession and their dependents on a range of social welfare, financial, employment and property-related matters. A helpline is operated on 0845 603 9057.

Chemical engineers

The Chemical Engineers Benevolent Fund

£16,500

Correspondent: Jo Downham, Finance Manager, c/o The Institution of Chemical Engineers, Davis Building, 165–189 Railway Terrace, Rugby, Warwickshire CV21 3HQ (01788 578214; email: jdownham@icheme.org.uk; website: www.icheme.org/about_us/benevolent_fund.aspx)

CC Number: 221601

Eligibility

Current and former chemical engineers and their immediate dependents. This includes all chemical engineers worldwide, not simply members or former members of the Institution of Chemical Engineers.

Types of grants

One-off and recurrent grants, and loans, for example, towards medical treatment, special equipment, nursing home fees, special education needs and general expenses.

Annual grant total

In 2012 the fund had assets of £331,000 and an income of £50,000. Grants to individuals totalled £16,500.

At the time of writing (August 2014) this was the most recent financial information available for the fund.

Exclusions

There are no grants available for students.

Applications

In writing to the correspondent, to be submitted either directly by the individual or through a third party such as a social worker, Citizens Advice or other welfare agency or another third party. Applications should include proof of employment as a chemical engineer, such as a passport descriptor or company document.

Civil service

Assist Fund (formerly known as the Century Benevolent Fund)

£55,000

Correspondent: The Administrator, Po Box 62849, London SE1P 5AE

CC Number: 251419

Eligibility

Employees and ex-employees of the Government Communications Bureau and its associated organisations, and their dependents.

Types of grants

One-off or recurrent grants and loans towards telephone bills, house repairs and so on.

Annual grant total

In 2012/13 the fund had an income of £203,000 and an expenditure of £91,000. Grants to individuals usually total between £50,000 and £60,000 each year.

Exclusions

There are no educational grants available.

Applications

In writing to the correspondent, although applications are often made by word of mouth. Applications are generally considered four times a year, but exceptions can be made in urgent cases.

For You By You – The Charity for Civil Servants

£2.9 million (4,400 grants)

Correspondent: The Help and Advisory Team, Fund House, 5 Anne Boleyn's Walk, Cheam, Sutton, Surrey SM3 8DY (0800 056 2424; fax: 020 8240 2401; email: help@foryoubyyou.org.uk; website: www.foryoubyyou.org.uk)

CC Number: 1136870

Eligibility

Serving, former and retired staff of the Civil Service and associated organisations, and their dependents, who are in need.

Types of grants

Grants, loans and allowances according to need. Grants have been given towards: essential household bills; utilities; household appliances; childcare; other daily living expenses; relief of priority debts, such as council tax or rent arrears; home adaptations; heating repairs; funeral expenses; hospital visiting costs; nursing home fees; and mobility equipment such as hoists, ramps, mobility scooters, walking aids and wheelchairs.

Annual grant total

In 2013 the charity held assets of more than £38.9 million and had an income of £8.2 million. Financial support to more than 4,400 individuals totalled £2.9 million and was distributed as follows:

Reduced/low incomes	£1.3 million
Debt	£561,000
Poor/inappropriate living arrangements	£545,000
Bereavement	£211,000
Illness	£186,000
Immobility	£89,000
Emergency situations	£24,000

During the year, £94,000 was distributed in loans to 12 beneficiaries.

A further £2,000 was awarded towards community projects.

Exclusions

The charity does not help employees of the NHS, local/county councils or the armed forces. Funding is not available towards: items that have already been bought or bills that have already been settled; non-priority debt, such as a payday loan; purchasing a property; education costs; and legal expenses or fines. Grants are not normally awarded to cover medical costs.

Applications

By completing the online application form. The charity runs a freephone help service (0800 056 2424, open every working day, 8.30am-5pm) which provides advice and information as well as assistance with completing applications.

Other information

The charity runs services to give advice on, for example, money issues, stress and depression, carers' support, domestic abuse and mental wellbeing. It has also entered into a pilot service with Relate, which aims to provide counselling on relationship breakdowns. More details of the full range of services are available on the website.

The Overseas Service Pensioners' Benevolent Society

£152,000 (102 grants)

Correspondent: David Le Breton, Secretary, 138 High Street, Tonbridge, Kent TN9 1AX (01732 363836; fax: 01732 365070; email: bensoc@ospa.org.uk; website: www.ospa.org.uk)

CC Number: 235989

Eligibility

Retired members of the Overseas Service Pensioners' Association, and their dependents, who are in need. In certain circumstances those with other relevant service in the Overseas Civil Service or in a former British dependent (colonial) territory can be supported as well as the dependents of such people.

Types of grants

Grants of up to £1,500 are usually paid quarterly to help with general living expenses. Occasionally, single grants are given for special needs and towards holidays. All cases are reviewed annually.

Annual grant total

In 2013 the society had an income of £71,000 and an expenditure of around £152,000. During the year 102 cases of support have been recorded. Holiday and one-off grants totalled £12,500.

The society notes that over half of the beneficiaries are Zimbabwe Public Service pensioners, or their dependents, living mainly in Zimbabwe and South Africa.

Exclusions

Grants are not normally made for residential care or nursing home fees.

Applications

Application forms can be requested from the correspondent. They can be submitted directly by the individual or by a third party, such as a close relative or legal representative.

Prospect Benevolent Fund

£92,000 (90 grants)

Correspondent: The Finance Officer, New Prospect House, 8 Leake Street, London SE1 7NN (020 7902 6600; fax: 020 7902 6667; email: enquiries@prospect.org.uk; website: www.prospect.org.uk)

Eligibility

Members and retired members of the union (and the former Institution of Professional Civil Servants), and their dependents, who are experiencing financial problems.

Types of grants

Generally one-off grants with recurrent grants not exceeding £1,500. The trustees aim to relieve immediate problems and often point applicants to other channels and agencies for long-term solutions. Grants are usually sent to the applicant, but for speed and/or reliability, some awards are sent direct to the utility/body owed money. Occasionally this is processed through an agency or second party (such as a welfare officer, debt counsellor, branch officer or relative).

The fund also makes death benefit grants to dependents of a deceased member (except retired members) which is equal to five times the higher national rate annual subscription. In 2014 this sum was £1,042.20.

Annual grant total

In 2013 the fund held assets of £567,000 and had an income of £65,000. Grants were made to 90 individuals totalling £92,000. Support consisted of £13,000 in 12 general grants and £79,000 in 78 death grants.

Exclusions

The fund does not make loans.

Applications

Application forms are available from the correspondent. They can be submitted directly by the individual or through the employer's welfare officers or branch representatives. Applications are considered throughout the year and generally are processed quickly.

Public and Commercial Services Union Benevolent Fund

£130,000

Correspondent: Gavin Graham, Administrator, PCS Member Benefits, Freepost BFH 1003, 160 Falcon Road, London SW11 2LN (020 7801 2810 or 020 7801 2601, option 3; fax: 020 7801 2852; email: membenefits@pcs.org.uk; website: www.pcs.org.uk/en/about_pcs/member_benefits/finance/benevolent_fund.cfm)

Eligibility

Members and associate members of the union who are suffering severe financial hardship, through sickness, family troubles or other problems. Applications will be rejected if the individual is not a fully paid-up member, or associate member, of the union. Candidates must have been members for at least six months.

Types of grants

One-off grants to a maximum of £500 in any 12 month period.

Annual grant total

Previously around £130,000 has been distributed in benevolence services.

Exclusions

Grants are not given for:

- Private debts and credit card overdrafts
- Medical treatment
- Education costs
- Legal expenses
- Strike action

Loans are not provided.

Applications

Application forms are available from the correspondent or can be downloaded from the Public and Commercial Services Union website. Completed applications should be submitted either directly by the individual/family member, or through a third party (such as a union representative) and may be emailed or posted. They are reviewed weekly.

Clayworking

Institute of Clayworkers Benevolent Fund

£1,500

Correspondent: Francis Morrall, Trustee, British Ceramic Confederation, Federation House, Station Road, Stoke-on-Trent, Staffordshire ST4 2SA (01782 571846; email: francism@ceramfed.co.uk)

CC Number: 212300

Eligibility

People in the clay-working industry, namely current and former employees of the British Ceramic Confederation member companies and members and ex-members of the institute, and their dependents. Applicants will normally be unable to work due to ill-health or an accident.

Types of grants

Recurrent pensions and one-off grants, usually of £250. Our research indicates that in exceptional cases where applicants have been identified by other charitable bodies as being in extreme need, larger grants may be given.

Annual grant total

At the time of writing (September 2014) the latest financial information available was form 2012. In 2012 the fund had an income of £2,500 and a total expenditure of £1,700. We estimate the annual total of grants to be around £1,500.

Applications

In writing to the correspondent. Applications should include age, length of service, date of termination of employment (if applicable), brief description (two or three sentences) of circumstances leading to application, and brief testimonial (a sentence or two) from a supervisor/manager, if appropriate. Our research suggests that the fund only accepts applications made through a former employer and not usually those made directly by the individual. Requests may be made at any time.

Clergy

Gibbons Charity

£11,000

Correspondent: Don Woolford, Administrator, The Swallows, Station Road, Admaston, Telford, Shropshire TF5 0AW (01952 243846; email: don.woolford@btinternet.com)

CC Number: 215171

Eligibility

Widows, widowers, spouses, divorced partners and children of Shropshire Church of England clergy (and retired clergy) who face hardship.

Types of grants

One-off and recurrent grants according to need.

Annual grant total

In 2013, the charity had an income of £6,500 and a total expenditure of £11,100. We estimate that the total amount of grants awarded to individuals was approximately £11,000, however this figure is unusual based on previous giving. Grants have usually totalled £2,000–£3,000 in the past.

Applications

In writing to the correspondent.

The Rehoboth Trust

£14,000

Correspondent: Shakti Singh Sisodia, Trustee, 71 Rydal Gardens, Hounslow TW3 2JJ (020 8893 3700)

CC Number: 1114454

Eligibility

Christian ministers or retired ministers who are in need in the UK and abroad.

Types of grants

Grants given according to need.

Annual grant total

In 2012 the trust had an income of £28,000 and a total expenditure of £29,000. We estimate that grants to individuals totalled £14,000. The 2012 accounts were the latest available at the time of writing.

Applications

In writing to the correspondent.

Other information

Grants are also made to organisations.

The Wells Clerical Charity

£3,500

Correspondent: The Ven. Nicola Sullivan, Trustee, 6 The Liberty, Wells, Somerset BA5 2SU (01749 670777; email: general@bathwells.anglican.org)

CC Number: 248436

Eligibility

Clergy of the Church of England who have served in the historic archdeaconry of Wells and their dependents who are in need.

Types of grants

One-off grants according to need.

Annual grant total

In 2012 the charity had an income of £8,700 and a total expenditure of £7,300. We estimate that grants to individuals for social welfare purposes totalled around £3,500. These were the latest accounts available at the time of writing (July 2014).

Applications

In writing to the correspondent.

Other information

Grants are also made for educational purposes.

Clothing and textiles

The Bespoke Tailors' Benevolent Association

£93,000 (50 grants)

Correspondent: Elizabeth Fox, Administrator, 65 Tierney Road, London SW2 4QH (07831 520801; email: Elizabeth.Fox@ukgateway.net)

CC Number: 212954

Eligibility

Journeyman tailors, tailoresses and their near relatives who were employed in the bespoke (made to measure) tailoring trade. Preference is given to past and present members of the institute but help can be given to other eligible applicants.

Types of grants

Small one-off grants and regular allowances. Previously, allowances have been in the region of£20 a week.

Annual grant total

In 2013, the charity had an income of £121,000 and total assets of £2,800,000. During the year, the charity provided grants of approximately £93,000 to 50 beneficiaries.

Applications

On a form available from the correspondent. Applications should preferably be submitted through a social worker. However, those submitted directly by the individual or through another third party will be considered.

Other information

In late 2012 the Tailors Benevolent Institute and the Master Tailors Benevolent Association merged to form the Bespoke Tailors Benevolent Association.

The City of London Linen and Furnishings Trades Association

£500

Correspondent: Geoffrey Blake, Trustee, 69a Langley Hill, Kings Langley, Hertfordshire WD4 9HQ (01923 262857)

CC Number: 211522

Eligibility

Members and former members of the association and their dependents.

Types of grants

One-off grants according to need. The association can also contribute towards the cost of a holiday at one of the Textile Benevolent Association holiday homes.

Annual grant total

In 2012 the association had an income of £1,000 and a total expenditure of £815. The 2012 accounts were the latest available at the time of writing (August 2014). Grants are awarded to individuals for both social welfare and educational purposes.

Applications

In writing to the correspondent.

Other information

The association states that grants are mainly for the relief of need; education grants are of secondary importance.

The Cotton Industry War Memorial Trust

£116,000 (190 grants)

Correspondent: Peter Booth, Administrator, Stable Barn, Coldstones Fold Farm, Bewerley, Harrogate HG3 5BJ (01423 711205; email: ciwmt@btinternet.com)

CC Number: 242721

Eligibility

People in need who have worked in the cotton textile industry in the north west of England. This includes weaving, spinning and dyeing. Cotton industry workers who were badly injured while fighting for HM Forces in wartime may also be eligible.

Types of grants

Convalescence arrangements are made for people who are in poor health or who have suffered injury due to their work in the cotton textiles industry. The trust makes arrangements for beneficiaries' convalescence at commercial hotels in Blackpool. One-off grants may also be awarded for specific needs.

Annual grant total

In 2013 the trust held assets of £6.6 million and had an income of £313,000. The trust arranged convalescence for 190 individuals through its Convalescent Scheme, totalling £116,000. A further £257,000 was awarded to organisations.

Exclusions

People who have worked with clothing, footwear, hosiery and other man-made fabrics are not eligible.

Applications

On a form available from the correspondent. Note that the correspondent cannot send forms directly to applicants, only to employers, trade unions, SSAFA or similar welfare agencies for them to pass on to potential beneficiaries. Applicants must show that they have worked in the textile industry and provide medical evidence if claiming assistance due to employment injury or disability. Applications are considered quarterly.

Other information

The trust gives substantial grants to educational bodies to assist eligible students in furthering their textile studies, to other bodies which encourage recruitment into or efficiency in the industry and to organisations furthering the interests of the industry by research and so on.

The Fashion and Textile Children's Trust

£67,000

Correspondent: Anna Pangbourne, Director, Office 1 and 2, J411/412 The Biscuit Factory, 100 Clements Road, London SE16 4DG (0300 123 9002; fax: 020 7691 9356; email: anna@ftct.org.uk; website: www.ftct.org.uk)

CC Number: 257136

Eligibility

Children and young people under 18 years whose parents work or have worked in the UK fashion and textile retailing and manufacturing industry.

Types of grants

See the trust's website for full details of grants available. The trust concentrates its grant giving on 'the essential costs of education'. However, it also makes some welfare grants to children from particularly poor backgrounds for items such as disability equipment, clothing, bedding and shoes.

Annual grant total

In 2012/13 the trust had assets of £7.9 million and an income of £456,000. Grants were made to individuals totalling £282,000 broken down as follows:

School fees	£215,000
Welfare/general assistance	£67,000

Exclusions

No grants are given towards childcare, study/travel abroad; overseas students studying in Britain; student exchange; or people starting work. No grants are available for those in higher education.

Applications

On a form available from the correspondent or an initial enquiry form from the trust's website. Applications can be submitted at any time either directly by the individual or through a third party such as a social worker, teacher or Citizens Advice. Applicants are encouraged to call the trust in the first instance to discuss an application.

The Feltmakers Charitable Foundation

£8,900

Correspondent: Maj. J. T. H. Coombs, Clerk to the Trustees, Post Cottage, The Street, Greywell, Hook, Hampshire RG29 1DA (01256 703174; email: jcpartnership@btopenworld.com; website: www.feltmakers.co.uk)

CC Number: 259906

Eligibility

Employees or former employees of the hat trade who are in need.

Types of grants

Annual pensions.

Annual grant total

In 2012/13 the foundation had assets of £496,000 and an income of £44,000. Support for pensioner hatters totalled £9,400 of which, pensions amounted to £8,900.

A further £21,000 was awarded to 14 charitable organisations.

Applications

Applicants must be nominated in the first place by their employer or former employer, or in exceptional circumstances by a welfare organisation.

Other information

The foundation supports current and historical research into felt making and the general promotion of the trade. During 2012/13, the foundation contributed £5,600 in support of the Feltmakers' Design Awards.

Footwear Friends

£70,000 (204 grants)

Correspondent: Gabi O'Sullivan, Secretary, Footwear Benevolent Society, 5th Floor, 15–16 Margaret Street, London W1W 8RW (020 7323 2362; email: info@footwearfriends.org.uk; website: www.footwearfriends.org.uk)

CC Number: 222117

Eligibility

People who are working or have worked in the boot trade and footwear industry, usually for a minimum of five years, and their dependents.

Types of grants

One-off grants and recurrent payments. Grants are available for, for example, hardware, appliances, furnishings, special equipment for people with disabilities or essential repairs. Funding is also available towards convalescent holidays. Recurrent grants may be paid once every six months, or seasonally at Christmas and mid-year.

Annual grant total

In 2012/13 the society held assets of £1.1 million and had an income of £134,000. Financial assistance to 204 individuals totalled more than £70,000.

Christmas grants	£18,700
Mid-year grants	£17,200
One-off grants	£16,400
Half yearly allowances	£7,500
December bonus grants	£4,800
Christmas grants	£4,800
Provision for potential grants	£900
Holiday grants	£300

Applications

On a form available from the correspondent or to download from the society's website. Applications can be completed by the individual or a third party. If completed by the individual, it must be verified by someone who has known the applicant for some time, who works in a professional capacity and is not related to the applicant; or a third party acting on behalf of the applicant, for example a welfare adviser.

Other information

Also known as the Footwear Benevolent Society and formerly as The Boot Trade Benevolent Society.

Johnson Charitable Trust

£19,200

Correspondent: Yvonne Monaghan, Trustee, Johnson Service Group plc, Johnson House, Abbots Park, Monks Way, Preston Brook WA7 3GH (01928 704600; email: enquiries@johnsonplc.com)

CC Number: 216974

Eligibility

Employees and ex-employees of the Johnson Group plc and their dependents.

Types of grants

One-off and recurrent grants according to need.

Annual grant total

In 2012/13 the trust held assets of £1.6 million and had an income of £48,000. Allowances, gifts and Christmas hampers to individuals totalled £19,200 and were distributed as follows:

Widows/widowers allowance and gifts	£9,900
Christmas hampers	£9,300

A further £300 was given towards a pensioners' lunch.

Applications

In writing to the correspondent.

The Sydney Simmons Pension Fund

£1,750

Correspondent: Jonathan Westbrooke, Trustee, Furniture Makers' Hall, 12 Austin Friars, London EC2N 2HE (02072565558; email: clerk@furnituremakers.org.uk; website: www.furnituremakers.org.uk)

CC Number: 252677

Eligibility

People in need who are or have been employed in the carpet trade.

Types of grants

One-off grants usually in the range of £300 to £500.

Annual grant total

In 2012 the trust had an income of £4,500 and a total expenditure of £3,500. We estimate the total awards given to individuals to be £1,750. This information was the most recent available at the time of writing (January 2014).

Applications

On a form available from the correspondent.

Other information

The fund also makes grants to organisations.

The Textile Benevolent Association (1970)

£13,000

Correspondent: Sandra O'Hara, Administrator, 72a Lee High Road, Lewisham, London SE13 5PT (020 8852 7239; fax: 020 8463 0303)

CC Number: 261862

Eligibility

People in need who are employees and former employees of: wholesalers and retailers engaged in the textile trade; and of manufacturers in the trade which distribute to retailers as well as manufacture. The wives, widows, husbands and widowers of such people can also benefit.

Types of grants

Grants are towards holidays, winter fuel bills, clothing, cookers, washing machines and so on.

Annual grant total

The total amount of grants awarded for the year to individuals was approximately £13,000 based on previous giving.

Applications

On a form available from the correspondent, usually via employers, doctors or social services.

Coal industry

The Coal Industry Social Welfare Organisation

£1 million

Correspondent: Vernon Jones, Secretary, The Old Rectory, Rectory Drive, Whiston, Rotherham, South Yorkshire S60 4JG (01709 728115; fax: 01709 839164; email: mail@ciswo.org.uk; website: www.ciswo.org.uk)

CC Number: 1015581

Eligibility

Widows and families of miners who have died as a result of industrial accident or disease (mainly pneumoconiosis). Help is also available to mineworkers and their dependents who are experiencing financial difficulties.

Types of grants

- General hardship grants towards, for example, buying a motorised wheelchair, specialist equipment and home adaptations
- Grants to the dependents of miners who have died as a result of their work
- Grants to miners who are in hospital as a result of their work, up to a maximum amount per year
- Grants up to a maximum amount for miners who have to travel to an outpatients centre as a result of an accident at work

Annual grant total

In 2013 the trust held assets of £34.3 million (£20 million of which represents endowment funds) and an income of £3 million. Grants were made totalling just over £1 million and were distributed as follows:

Hardship grants	£392,000
Regulation cases	£384,000
Education grants	£218,000
Special needs	£49,000
Social intervention fund	£19,500
Durham project	£10,000
Christmas voucher scheme	£4,000
Other grants	£2,000

Applications

In writing to the correspondent for consideration by the trustees. The trust usually sends one of its own social workers to visit the individual to assess their needs and assist with the application form.

Other information

The trust also operates a number of convalescence homes throughout the UK and a comprehensive social work service.

From January 2010 the Coal Industry Benevolent Trust merged with the Coal Industry Social Welfare Organisation who now administer the trust.

The Coal Trade Benevolent Association

£168,000 (308 grants)

Correspondent: Nicholas Ross, Secretary, Unit 6 Bridge Wharf, 156 Caledonian Road, London N1 9UU (020 7278 3239; email: coalbenev@btconnect.com; website: www.coaltradebenevolentassociation.org)

CC Number: 212688

Eligibility

Non-manual workers of the coal industry in England and Wales who have worked in the production or distribution sectors and allied trades, and their dependents.

Types of grants

Weekly payments to supplement low income and help with telephone costs, televisions, respite holidays, birthday and Christmas cheques and shopping vouchers. One-off grants are also available towards capital items such as stairlifts, special bathrooms, washing machines, carpets and other items. Winter fuel payments (£50 in 2013) are made in December. Further special fuel payments have been distributed to regular beneficiaries during periods of exceptionally cold weather.

Annual grant total

In 2013 the association had an income of £237,000 and a total expenditure of £349,000. Grants to 308 beneficiaries amounted to £168,000.

Applications

On a form available from the correspondent for consideration throughout the year.

Other information

CTBA supports a network of volunteer case visitors in branches across the country. These volunteers act as the association's way of keeping in touch with its beneficiaries, with individuals receiving personal visits at least twice a year.

Commerce

The George Drexler Foundation

£41,000

Correspondent: Jonathan Fountain, 35–43 Lincolns Inn Fields, London WC2A 3PE (020 7869 6080; email: georgedrexler@rcseng.ac.uk)

CC Number: 313278

Eligibility

Former employees of the Ofrex Group and their dependents.

Types of grants

One-off and recurrent grants of £1,000 to £10,000.

Annual grant total

In 2012/13 the foundation had assets of £6.1 million and an income of £269,000. Grants to individuals to relieve poverty totalled £41,000; to individuals for educational purposes totalled £140,000 and for educational grants to organisations totalled £84,500.

Exclusions

No support for medical electives, volunteering or gap year projects.

Applications

On a form available from the correspondent, submitted directly by the individual, enclosing an sae. Applications should be submitted in May for consideration in June/July.

Other information

The foundation also provides educational grants to people in need who have a direct link with commerce, that is, who have owned and run their own commercial business. Applicants whose parents or grandparents have this link can also be supported. This does not include professional people such as doctors, lawyers, dentists, architects or accountants. No exceptions can be made.

The Ruby and Will George Trust

£26,000 (20 grants)

Correspondent: Damien Slattery, 125 Cloverfield, West Allotment, Newcastle upon Tyne NE27 0BE (01912 664527; email: admin@rwgt.co.uk; website: www.rwgt.co.uk)

CC Number: 264042

Eligibility

People in need who have been or who are employed in commerce, and their dependents. Preference is given to people who live in the north east of England.

Types of grants

One-off or recurrent grants for items which are needed but cannot be afforded, usually related to sickness and disability, for example, wheelchairs, washing machines and clothes. Grants usually range from between £250 and £5,000.

Annual grant total

In 2012/13 the trust had assets of £3.4 million and an income of £69,000. Grants are given to individuals both for educational and welfare purposes. In this accounting year £51,500 was given to 40 individuals and we estimate the total for welfare grants was around £26,000.

Applications

The trust has an online application process, 'though those without access to the internet can still submit a paper-based application'. Applicants will need to prove their commerce connection and their income and expenditure. Two references are required.

The trust considers applications four times a year, usually in January, May, July and October. Applications should be submitted two weeks in advance. Note: upcoming deadline dates can be found on the trust's website.

H. J. Rawlings Trust

£6,500

Correspondent: The Administrator, Liverpool Charity and Voluntary Services, 151 Dale Street, Liverpool L2 2AH (01512 275177; website: www.charitycheques.org.uk)

CC Number: 265690

Eligibility

People in need, with a preference for current and former employees of John Holt and Company (Liverpool) Ltd and their dependents.

Types of grants

One-off and recurrent grants according to need.

Annual grant total

In 2012/13 the trust held assets of £968,000 and had an income of £34,000. Grants totalled £35,000, of which £6,500 was received by individuals for welfare needs, with the remainder awarded to local organisations.

Applications

In writing to the correspondent.

Commercial travellers

The CTBI – The Salespeople's Charity

£463,000 (249 grants)

Correspondent: Mandi Leonard, Secretary, 2 Fletcher Road, Ottershaw, Chertsey, Surrey KT16 0JY (01932 429636; email: sec.ctbi@ntlworld.com; website: www.ctbi.org)

CC Number: 216538

Eligibility

People in the UK who are in need and have worked as a sales representative/agent promoting or selling to the trade for at least five years, and their dependents. Applicants must have been employed for a minimum of six months in each of these years. Sales must be business to business and involve the representative leaving their office and visiting client sites.

Types of grants

Recurrent grants and gifts in kind. One-off grants are also given towards respite breaks, disability aids, home adaptations, TV licences and for critical one-off payments.

Annual grant total

In 2013 the charity had an income of £613,000 and a total expenditure of £558,000. Grants to 249 beneficiaries totalled £463,000 and were distributed as follows:

Quarterly benefit, birthday and Christmas payments	£379,000
Hampers and food vouchers	£33,000
Gifts	£18,400
One-off grants	£17,700
TV licences, phones, etc.	£14,000
Respite	–

Exclusions

No help is given to those engaged in 'van sales', retail, telesales or general selling to the public.

Applications

On a form available from the correspondent or to download from the website. Applications should include evidence of employment in commercial sales and be submitted either directly by the individual or through a third party. The trustees meet five times a year to consider applications, though emergency payments can be made quickly in cases of extreme hardship.

UCTA Samaritan Benefit Fund Society

£79,000

Correspondent: Peter Brennan, Trustee, The Cottage, Dairy House Lane, Dunham Massey, Altrincham WA14 5RD (01612 653462; email: pjbfca@gmail.com)

CC Number: 1071037

Eligibility

Commercial travellers and their dependents in the UK who are in need.

Types of grants

One-off and recurrent grants according to need.

Annual grant total

In 2012 the society had assets of £208,000 and an income of £92,000. It made grants totalling £79,000. This was the latest financial information available at the time of writing.

Applications

On a form available from the correspondent.

Other information

The society continues to locate potential beneficiaries using the internet and the diligence of the trustees.

Cooperative

The National Association of Co-operative Officials (NACO) Benevolent Fund

£2,800

Correspondent: Lynne Higginbottom, Administrator, 6A Clarendon Place, Hyde, Cheshire SK14 2QZ (01613 517900; fax: 01613 666800; email: info@naco.coop; website: www.naco.coop)

CC Number: 262269

Eligibility

Members and former members of the association, and their dependents, including widows and children of deceased members, who are in need.

Types of grants

One-off grants up to a maximum of £1,000. Additional grants of up to £2,500 are available to a spouse/civil partner (or other nominated person) upon the death of a member whilst in membership to help with bereavement costs and funeral expenses.

Annual grant total

In 2013 the fund had an income of £5,300 and a total expenditure of £3,000. Note that financial figures vary each year. We estimate that about £2,800 was awarded in grants to individuals.

Applications

Application forms are available to download from the fund's website. They can be submitted directly by the individual including details of personal finance. Applications are considered at executive meetings, dates of which are available online.

Coopers

William Alexander's Coopers' Liverymen Fund

£1,000

Correspondent: Adrian Carroll, Clerk, Coopers Hall, 13 Devonshire Square, London EC2M 4TH (020 7247 9577; email: clerk@coopers-hall.co.uk; website: www.coopers-hall.co.uk/coopers)

CC Number: 234614

Eligibility

Members of the Coopers' Company, their widows and other dependents, who are in need.

Types of grants

Money can be given to supplement relief or assistance provided out of public funds, in the form of one-off grants and Christmas grants.

Annual grant total

In 2012/13, the fund had an income of £4,500 and a total expenditure of £1,100. We estimate that the total amount of grants awarded to individuals was approximately £1,000.

Exclusions

No funds are available for education. Funds must not be applied directly in relief of taxes, rates or other public funds.

Applications

In writing to the correspondent.

Corn exchange

The Bristol Corn Trade Guild

£4,500

Correspondent: Richard Cooksley, Administrator, Portbury House, Sheepway, Portbury, Bristol BS20 7TE (01275 373539; fax: 01275 374747; email: cooksleyandco@btconnect.com; website: www.bcfta.org.uk/theguild.php)

CC Number: 202404

Eligibility

People who have a connection with the corn, grain, feed, flour and allied trades and are in need. Dependents of such people are also eligible. Current and former members of the Bristol Corn and Feed Trade Association may be favoured.

Types of grants

One-off grants generally between £200 and £800 can be given towards medical equipment or specialist treatment, repairs and household essentials, also as food vouchers. Recurrent grants can be made for utility bills.

Annual grant total

In 2013 the guild had an income of £5,500 and a total expenditure of £4,800.We estimate that grants totalled around £4,500.

Applications

In writing to the correspondent. Applications can be submitted directly by the individual or through a social worker, Citizens Advice or other welfare agency.

Other information

Members and former members of the Bristol Corn and Feed Trade Association are also invited to various activities organised by the guild, for example, sporting events or Christmas lunch.

The Corn Exchange Benevolent Society

£43,000 (36 grants)

Correspondent: Richard Butler, Secretary, 20 St Dunstan's Hill, London EC3R 8HL (020 7283 6090; email: richard.butler@baltic-charities.co.uk; website: www.baltic-charities.co.uk)

CC Number: 207733

Eligibility

Members of the society and their dependents who are in need. Limited funds are also available for non-members who work or have been engaged in any aspect of grain trading in England and Wales (corn, grain, seed, animal feed stuffs, pulses, malt, flour or granary-keeping trades) and their dependents.

Types of grants

Quarterly grants are available to help towards day-to-day living costs. Recent one-off grants have been awarded towards school uniforms, funeral expenses, hospital visit travel expenses, help with motor purchase, car insurance, roof tiling, shower installation, bathroom refurbishment and general living expenses. Christmas gifts are made to all beneficiaries. In 2013 special grants were also paid towards heating costs during periods of cold weather.

Annual grant total

In 2013 the society had an income of £95,000 and a total expenditure of £94,000. Grants to individuals totalled £43,000. Of this, £18,900 was given in quarterly payments, with the remaining £24,000 awarded in special grants to beneficiaries.

Applications

On a form available from the correspondent or to download from the website. Applications can be submitted directly by the individual or through a social worker, Citizens Advice or other welfare agency. Applicants are required to provide full details of income and expenditure.

Initial approaches by phone, email or in writing are also welcomed.

Customs and excise

The North West Customs and Excise Benevolent Society

£0

Correspondent: Brian Roberts, Trustee, First Floor, VAT Process Owner Team (VPOT), Regian House, Liverpool, Merseyside L75 1AD (03000 587869; email: brian.roberts@hmrc.gsi.gov.uk)

CC Number: 225008

Eligibility

Serving or retired members of HM Revenue and Customs within the Merseyside area who are in need, and their dependents.

Types of grants

One-off grants according to need.

Annual grant total

In 2013 the society had an income of £3,000. For the past three years there has been no charitable expenditure, although in the past it has reached around £1,500.

Applications

Potential applicants should contact the correspondent either in writing or by telephone.

Driving instructors

The Driving Instructors' Accident and Disability Fund

£90

Correspondent: Dean Scott Mayer, Trustee, Leon House, 233 High Street, Croydon CR0 9XT (0206868010)

CC Number: 328419

Eligibility

Driving instructors, former driving instructors and members of the Driving Instructors' Association who have been injured or disabled and their dependents.

Types of grants

Small one-off grants.

Annual grant total

In 2012/13 we estimate that grants to individuals totalled around £90. Total expenditure tends to vary, and in the past five years has ranged between £3 and £380.

Applications

In writing to the correspondent.

Electrical

The Electrical Industries Charity

£291,000 (696 grants)

Correspondent: Charitable Services Team, Electrical Industries Charity, 36 Tanner Street, London SE1 3LD (0800 652 1618; website: www.electricalcharity.org)

CC Number: 1012131

Eligibility

Employees and former employees of the UK electrical and electronic industries and allied sciences, including mechanical engineering, and their dependents. There are no age limits.

Types of grants

Grants are available for a wide range of needs, including home repairs, disability adaptations, mobility equipment and everyday essentials such as heating and food. In certain cases, the charity may also be able to offer financial assistance for carers' respite breaks.

Annual grant total

In 2012/13 the charity held assets of £5.9 million and had an income of £1.7 million. Grants to individuals totalled £291,000.

Exclusions

Grants are not normally given to cover the costs of private medical care, educational fees, bankruptcy fees, nursing/residential fees or for headstones or funeral plaques.

Applications

Application forms and a list of guidelines are available to download from the website or by calling the charity's helpline. Applicants must provide the latest letter/statement from the benefits or pensions office or their current payslip, copies of their latest bank statements from current and savings accounts and, if a specific item is required, two or three estimates. Medical equipment normally requires an occupational therapy assessment, which can be discussed at a later date. Enquiries are welcomed.

Other information

The Electrical Industries Charity was formerly known as the Electrical and Electronics Industries Benevolent Association (EEIBA).

The Institution of Engineering and Technology Benevolent Fund (IET Connect)

£568,000

Correspondent: Christine Oxland, Chief Executive, Napier House, 24 High Holburn, London WC1V 6AZ (0845 685 0685 (UK only) +44 (0)20 7344 5498 (worldwide); email: ietconnect@theiet.org; website: www.ietconnect.org)

CC Number: 208925

Eligibility

Members and former members, including those of the Institution of Electrical Engineering and the Institution of Engineering and Technology, and their dependents.

Types of grants

One-off grants have been awarded towards: essential living costs; counselling sessions; boiler, fridge, washing machine or car breakdown repairs; home repairs for storm or flood damage; equipment such as walkers, wheelchairs and stairlifts; home adaptations to aid mobility and independence such as ramps, bathroom conversions and alarm installations; communication aids; and respite care and breaks for carers.

Those struggling to pay their IET membership can contact the IET membership department directly on +44 (0)1438 765 678.

The fund is moving away from giving recurrent grants, as the latest accounts note: 'The preference is now to give a larger initial sum, where appropriate, to get the person or family 'back on their feet' and into a good position to resolve their personal situation and move forward.'

Annual grant total

In 2012/13 the fund held assets of £20.7 million and had an income of £1.2 million. Grants to individuals amounted to £568,000

Exclusions

The fund is unable to fund items retrospectively.

Applications

On a form available from the correspondent.

Other information

The fund has reformulated its policies and is now pursuing a more preventative strategy through its activities. Note the following from the fund's 2012/13 accounts:

> Whilst IET Connect will always provide financial help where needed to members and their dependents the emphasis is continuing to be directed at offering preventative support. Where appropriate, and certainly for people of working age, the aim is for the financial assistance to be seen as a short-term prop, until employment can be found and independence regained.

RTRA Benevolent Fund

£500

Correspondent: Jan Bray, Administrator, Retra House, St John's Terrace, 1 Ampthill Street, Bedford MK42 9EY (01234 269110; fax: 01234 269609; email: retra@retra.co.uk)

CC Number: 1002444

Eligibility

Support to previous members of the RTRA trade association who are experiencing financial difficulties due to death, loss of business or other unforeseen circumstances. People in need who are directly connected with the electronic and electrical retailing industry are also assisted.

Types of grants

One-off or recurrent grants, generally in the range of £250–£1,000, to provide short-term support.

Annual grant total

In 2012/13 the fund had an income of £3,200 and a total expenditure of £600. We estimate that grants to individuals totalled about £500. The charitable expenditure varies.

Applications

In writing to the correspondent at any time. Applications should be submitted either directly by individual/family member, through an organisation (such as Citizens Advice or other welfare agency) or via a member of RTRA.

Other information

Assistance is often given in conjunction with other organisations supporting the industry.

Engineering

The Chartered Institution of Building Services Engineers' Benevolent Fund

£35,000 (49 grants)

Correspondent: Janet Wigglesworth, Chief Executive's Secretary, CIBSE, Delta House, 222 Balham High Road, London SW12 9BS (020 8675 5211; fax: 020 8673

3302; email: benfund@cibse.org; website: www.cibse.org)

CC Number: 1115871

Eligibility

Members and former members of the fund and their dependents (on death of the member), who are in need.

Types of grants

Regular payments to supplement pensions and other income sources. One-off grants towards the cost of special equipment such as stair lifts or equipment which will enable the individual to work from home and major one-off bills such as essential repairs to the home. Help may also be given in the form of waived CIBSE subscriptions.

Annual grant total

In 2012 the fund held assets of nearly £474,000 and had an income of £57,000. Grants to 49 individuals totalled £35,000. The 2012 accounts were the latest available at the time of writing (August 2014).

Exclusions

Private health care or education.

Applications

In writing or by contacting the helpline. Applications can be submitted at any time either directly by the individual or through a social worker, Citizens Advice or other welfare agency. An almoner will visit the applicant to obtain details. Applications are considered on receipt.

The Worshipful Company of Engineers Charitable Trust Fund

£630 (2 grants)

Correspondent: Anthony Willenbruch, Clerk, The Worshipful Company of Engineers, Wax Chandlers' Hall, 6 Gresham Street, London EC2V 7AD (020 7726 4830; fax: 020 7726 4820; email: clerk@engineerscompany.org.uk; website: www.engineerstrust.org.uk)

CC Number: 289819

Eligibility

Professional engineers who have been engaged in engineering at chartered engineer level in industry and commerce and who are in need. Existing members of the Worshipful Company of Engineers, retired members, or their spouses, widows/widowers, children, orphans and others dependents.

Types of grants

Grants are generally of up to £1,000 and can be given for various welfare purposes.

Annual grant total

In 2013 the trust had assets of £1.3 million, an income of £85,000 and a total charitable expenditure of around £33,000, distributed in grants to individuals and organisations. Relief of poverty grants totalled £7,300, of which two grants were given to individuals totalling £630. The amount of grants awarded to individuals varies each year.

Applications

In writing to the correspondent by post or email at any time. Applications should provide as much detail about the individual's circumstances as possible.

Other information

The trust also awards annual prizes for excellence in engineering and supports engineering research. Support can be given to organisations concerned with engineering or organisations in the city of London that further the interest of the history, traditions and customs of the city.

The Guild of Benevolence of The Institute of Marine Engineering Science and Technology

£120,000

Correspondent: Anthony Muncer, Chair, Aldgate House, 33 Aldgate Street, London EC3N 1EN (020 7382 2644; fax: 020 7382 2670; email: guild@imarest.org; website: www.imarest.org/guild)

CC Number: 208727

Eligibility

Past and present members of the institute and guild, certified marine engineers, past and present employees of the institute or guild, and the dependents of the above.

Types of grants

Regular weekly grants of around £25 are given to supplement a low income. One-off grants, to a maximum of £4,000, are also available for disability aids, debt relief, reasonable nursing home fees, funeral costs, home maintenance and respite care. All regular beneficiaries receive a Christmas gift of £100.

Annual grant total

In 2012/13 the trust had an income of £110,000 and a total expenditure of £203,000. Grants to individuals totalled £120,000.

Exclusions

There are no grants for educational costs.

Applications

On a form available from the correspondent or to download from the website. Evidence of service or qualifications as a marine engineer must be produced if not already a member of the Institute of Marine Engineers, as well as full disclosure of financial situation. Applicants should expect a visit by a guild representative who will assess their needs and assist in completing the application form. Applications are considered by trustees every eight weeks, though in cases of emergency can be considered between meetings.

Other information

The guild originated from a fund set up in 1912 by the Institute to help families of the engineer officers lost when the RMS Titanic sank on 15 April 1912. Its role has since developed to help more generally the relief of hardship of marine engineers and their dependents. The Marine Engineers Benevolent Fund (MEBF) was incorporated into the guild in 1989 and the regular and one-off grants previously payable from the MEBF were transferred to the guild.

The guild is a constituent charity of the Merchant Navy Welfare Board (MNWB) and receives referrals from a number of charities including SSAFA, Royal British Legion, the Officers' Association, Occupational Benevolent Funds Association and Royal Merchant Navy Schools Foundation, as well as local social services.

The Benevolent Fund of the Institution of Civil Engineers Ltd

£512,000

Correspondent: Kris Barnett, Chief Executive, 30 Mill Hill Close, Haywards Heath, West Sussex RH16 1NY (01444 417979; fax: 01444 453307; email: benfund@ice.org.uk; website: www.bfice.org.uk)

CC Number: 1126595

Eligibility

Past and present members of the institution, and their dependents in the UK and overseas. The dependents of former members of the Institution of Municipal Engineers.

Types of grants

One-off grants and loans towards: essential domestic appliances, furnishings, re-decorating and repairs to property; residential and nursing home care; building and contents insurance aids, adaptations and equipment to promote independence; respite care and holidays; and Christmas and Easter gifts.

Monthly payments may be made to those on very low incomes.

A small number of grants are also available to student members of the fund to help with living costs and course materials.

Annual grant total

In 2013 the fund had assets of £14.5 million, (a significant part of which is designated permanent endowment and cannot be spent on grantmaking), and an income of £1.1 million. Grants were made to 139 individuals in the UK and 18 overseas, totalling £532,000, including support for eight students. There is no breakdown in the accounts for grant purposes but most funding is awarded for social welfare. We have estimated that the amount awarded to individuals for educational purposes was around £20,000.

Applications

On a form available from the correspondent. Applications can be submitted directly by the individual or through a social worker, Citizens Advice or other welfare agency, or through a close relative, solicitor or similar third party. They should include information about the individual's income, expenditure and capital and can be submitted at any time. Most applicants will be visited by one of the fund's volunteer visitors.

Other information

The fund owns properties in West Sussex and has nomination rights to the Hanover Housing Association which it uses to help (ex-)members and their families who are facing difficult circumstances and need somewhere to live.

It also runs a 24-hour helpline (0800 587 3428) which offers support and advice on a wide range of issues including, stress management, debt problems, childcare and substance abuse.

The Benevolent Fund of the Institution of Mechanical Engineers (IMechE) – known as Support Network

£240,000

Correspondent: Maureen Hayes, Casework and Support Officer, 1 – 3 Birdcage Walk, Westminster, London SW1H 9JJ (020 7304 6816; fax: 020 7973 1262; email: info@supportnetwork.org.uk; website: www.supportnetwork.org.uk)

CC Number: 209465

Eligibility

Past and present members of the institution, and their dependents, who are in need. Former members must have paid subscription fees for at least five years. Priority is given to those on low incomes who qualify for means-tested state benefits.

Types of grants

One-off grants and loans are available towards a variety of needs, including house repairs and adaptations, medical equipment, domestic appliances, beds and bedding, furniture, respite care, holidays and carer's breaks. Recurrent grants are also available to help with living expenses.

Annual grant total

In 2013 the fund had assets of £20.7 million and an income of £1.4 million. All grants to individuals were listed as relief of poverty and totalled £294,000. Although educational/training grants are not separately listed, this may be because most of the criteria for educational/training grants appear to include a financial qualification as well. We have estimated the social welfare grants to total around £240,000. There were also 287 money advice recipients.

Exclusions

No grants are given for school fees, business ventures, private medical treatment or the payment of debts.

Applications

Applicants should first contact the fund, by phone, letter, email or fax. If they are eligible they will be asked to complete an application form and meet with one of the fund's volunteer visitors. Applications are considered by the grants committee every two months.

Other information

The support network offers a range of support and advice services which also includes student grants, sheltered housing and residential care, help with job seeking and telephone helplines. Visit the website to find out more.

The Institution of Plant Engineers Benevolent Fund

£13,500

Correspondent: Grants Administrator, 22 Greencoat Place, London SW1P 1DX (020 7630 1111)

CC Number: 260934

Eligibility

Members/former members of the institution, and their dependents living in England, Scotland and Wales.

Types of grants

One-off grants according to need. Most grants are given to people who are financially stressed through serious illness, unemployment or bereavement. For example, support for a young member no longer able to work due to multiple sclerosis.

Annual grant total

The 2012 accounts were the latest available at the time of writing (August 2014).

In 2012, the fund had an income of £15,000 and a total expenditure of £14,000. We estimate that the total amount of grants awarded to individuals was approximately £13,500.

Applications

In writing to the correspondent. Applications can be submitted directly by the individual or by a relative or close friend. They are considered in March, July and November.

The ISTRUCTE (Institution of Structural Engineers') Fund

£72,000 (21 grants)

Correspondent: Dr Susan Doran, Secretary, International HQ, 47–58 Bastwick Street, London EC1V 3PS (020 7235 4535; fax: 020 7235 4294; email: benfund@istructe.org; website: www.istructe.org)

CC Number: 1049171

Eligibility

Members of the institution and their dependents who are in financial difficulties due to circumstances such as: unemployment; illness, accident or disability; family problems; difficulties during retirement; or bereavement.

Types of grants

One-off and recurrent grants and loans up to a maximum of £10,000 per year towards, for example, home repairs, household equipment, property adaptations, disability equipment, carers' breaks and daily living costs for those on very modest incomes.

Annual grant total

In 2013 the fund had assets of £2.3 million and an income of £163,000. Grants were made to 21 individuals totalling £72,000.

Exclusions

No grants for private health care. If the fund settles debts for a beneficiary, it will not usually pay any subsequent debts. The fund will not normally help members' children over the age of 21.

Applications

On a form available by emailing the correspondent which can be submitted by the individual or an appropriate third party. The fund likes to visit applicants before any grant is made.

Note: In cases of genuine emergency, the fund can pay up to £500, as a loan, normally within days.

The Matthew Hall Staff Trust Fund

£210,000 (199 grants)

Correspondent: Mrs P. R. Pritchard, Administrator, AMEC, Booths Hall, Chelford Road, Knutsford WA16 8QZ (01565 683281)

CC Number: 1019896

Eligibility

Former employees of Matthew Hall (1992) plc who are over the age of 65, suffering financial hardship and have completed at least two years of service, and their dependents. The spouses of deceased former employees who had completed between two and ten years of service are also eligible.

Types of grants

One-off and recurrent grants according to need.

Annual grant total

In 2012/13 the fund held assets of £2.4 million and had an income of £50,000. A total of £210,000 was made in 199 grants to former employees.

Applications

In writing to the correspondent. Trustees meet at least twice a year, normally in July and December, to consider applications.

Other information

The trust was founded using a gift from Bertram Baden, the then owner of the company.

Environ-mental health

Environmental Health Officers Welfare Fund

£3,000

Correspondent: Graham Jukes, Chief Executive, Chadwick Court, 15 Hatfields, London SE1 8DJ (020 7928 6006; fax: 020 7827 5862; email: membership@cieh.org; website: www.cieh.org)

CC Number: 224343

Eligibility

Past and present members of Chartered Institute of Environmental Health Officers, Association of Public Health Inspectors or The Guild of Public Health Inspection and their dependents, who are in need.

Types of grants

One-off and recurrent grants according to need.

Annual grant total

In 2013 the fund had an income of £208 and a total expenditure of £3,000. Grants to individuals accounted for all expenditure.

Applications

Initial enquiries should be made by telephone or through the contact form on the CIEH website. Applications should then be forwarded through the regional or branch secretary.

Estate workers

Midhurst Pensions Trust

£36,000

Correspondent: Anina Cheng, Administrator, 4th Floor, Swan House, 17–19 Stratford Place, London W1C 1BQ (020 7907 2100; email: charity@mfs.co.uk)

CC Number: 245230

Eligibility

People in need who have been employed by the Third Viscount Cowdray, Lady Anne Cowdray, any family company or on the Cowdray Estate, and their dependents.

Types of grants

One-off grants typically in the range of £25 to £2,000.

Annual grant total

In 2012/13 the trust held assets of £4.5 million and had an income of £91,000. Payments to pensioners totalled £36,000.

Applications

In writing to the correspondent.

Other information

Grants are also awarded to charitable organisations, though none were made during 2012/13.

Farriers

The Worshipful Company of Farriers Charitable Trust 1994

£2,700

Correspondent: The Clerk, 19 Queen Street, Chipperfield, Kings Langley, Herts WD4 9BT (01923 260747; fax: 01923 261677; email: theclerk@wcf.org.uk; website: www.wcf.org.uk/charity)

CC Number: 1044726

Eligibility

Registered farriers, their widows and dependents who are in need.

Types of grants

One-off and recurrent grants according to need. Grants are usually given to people who are unable to work through injury or sickness.

Annual grant total

In 2012/13, the trust had assets of £1.52 million and an income of £56,000. Grants were made to individuals totalling £2,700.

Applications

In writing to the clerk. Applications are considered eight times a year.

Fire service

The British Fire Services Association Members Welfare Fund

£14,000

Correspondent: David Stevens, Secretary and Treasurer, 9 Brooksfield, South Kirkby, Pontefract, West Yorkshire WF9 3DL (01977 650245; email: welfare.bfsa@btinternet.com)

CC Number: 216011

Eligibility

Fire-fighters and ex-fire-fighters who have held BFSA membership, and their dependents.

Types of grants

Members, ex-members and their dependents. Assistance may be in the form of one-off grants to aid the purchase of mobility items, electrical appliances, furniture or repairs. Alternatively the Management Committee of the Fund may consider long-term maintenance grants, to those on limited income.

Annual grant total

In 2012 the fund had an income of £22,000 and total expenditure of £21,000. This was the latest information available at the time of writing (July 2014).

Applications

In writing to the correspondent, including details of income and expenditure and a record of fire service employment. Applicants are usually visited at home by a representative of the fund to assess their needs.

Fire Fighters Charity

£241,000

Correspondent: John Parry, Chief Executive, The Fire Fighters Charity, Level 6, Belvedere, Basing View, Basingstoke, Hampshire RG21 4HG (01256 366566; fax: 01256 366599; email: info@firefighterscharity.org.uk; website: www.firefighterscharity.org.uk)

CC Number: 1093387

Eligibility

The charity's website states that it can assist:

- Serving Fire and Rescue Service (FRS) personnel
- Former FRS personnel (having served for at least five years before retiring, being made redundant after two years, or retired because of illness or injury)
- Works fire fighter or former works fire fighter that meets the criteria determined by the Trustees
- Employee of The Fire Fighters Charity
- Former employee of The Fire Fighters Charity (with at least five years' service or retired on the grounds of illness or injury)
- Any person engaged on, or assisting in the management or provision of a Fire Services Youth Scheme
- Any dependant of any person falling within the above categories

Types of grants

The charity looks to assist its beneficiaries by providing practical solutions to meet beneficiary need. The majority of these solutions are one-off and the type of solution can vary depending on the need, in some cases this may be a monetary solution in the form of a grant or the charity may assist practically by purchasing the solution (for example equipment or home adaptations that are required due to disability/ill health). Assessments are made under either a health or general category and the cost of the solution can vary according to the needs of the beneficiary.

Annual grant total

In 2012/13 the charity held assets of £26.7 million and had an income of £7.5 million. Beneficiary support expenses were distributed as follows:

One-off solutions	£230,000
Continuing support	£10,000
Wreaths	£400

Exclusions

The charity cannot finance private medical care, pay off debts or cover funeral or repatriation costs. The charity does not provide loans to beneficiaries, pay university/educational fees or residential care nursing fees. Statutory provision must be exhausted in the first instance.

Applications

Note the following from the charity's accounts:

> Over recent years the charity has sought to move away from making grants and the level of assistance in this manner has now substantially reduced. This has taken place alongside the introduction of the Beneficiary Support Service. The grant application process has now ceased, however, a small number of beneficiaries will require ongoing support from grants, but this is now administered through the Beneficiary Support Service.

To access any of the charity's services, call the support service on 0800 389 8820 (Mon-Fri, 9am-5pm). Textphone/ Minicom users should call 0800 783 7610.

Other information

The charity also runs rehabilitation and recuperation programmes at various residential sites.

For more information, or to access self-help factsheets, visit the charity's informative website.

Food, drink and provision trades

The Bakers' Benevolent Society

£8,900

Correspondent: Suzanne Pitts, Clerk to the Society, The Mill House, 23 Bakers Lane, Epping, Essex CM16 5DQ (01992 575951; fax: 01992 561163; email: bbs@bakersbenevolent.co.uk; website: www.bakersbenevolent.co.uk)

CC Number: 211307

Eligibility

People in need who have worked in the baking industry and its allied trades and are now retired and their dependents and widows.

Types of grants

Recurrent grants to top-up a low income. One-off grants are also available towards items such as mobility aids, lifelines and telephone rental, and household essentials.

Annual grant total

In 2012/13 the society had assets of £1.4 million and an income of £451,000. Grants and pensions to individuals totalled £8,900.

Applications

On a form available from the correspondent to be submitted either directly by the individual or a family member or through an appropriate welfare agency. Applications should include details of occupational history, age and financial circumstances. Applications are considered upon receipt.

Other information

> The Bakers' Benevolent Society is an Almshouse Charity that was founded in 1832 and has had Sheltered accommodation in Epping, Essex for more than 30 years.

Barham Benevolent Foundation

£11,900 (15 grants)

Correspondent: Michael Cook, Trustee, 8 Stumps End, Bosham, Chichester, West Sussex PO18 8RB (01243 573993; email: michael_cook@btconnect.com)

CC Number: 249922

Eligibility

People who have been employed in the dairy business, and possibly their dependents, who are in need.

Types of grants

One-off grants according to need. In some circumstances the foundation will pay for holiday accommodation for employees, their close relations and former employees of the milk business.

Annual grant total

In 2012/13 the foundation held assets of £5.1 million and had an income of £144,000. Of £67,000 distributed in grants, welfare payments to 15 individuals totalled £11,900, with the remainder received by institutions and individuals for educational purposes.

Applications

In writing to the correspondent.

Other information

Most funding given by the foundation goes towards supporting education relating to the dairy industry.

The Benevolent (formerly The Wine and Spirits Trades' Benevolent Society)

£338,000 (561 grants)

Correspondent: Pam Jarrett, Office Manager, 39–45 Bermondsey Street, London SE1 3XF (020 7089 3888; fax: 020 7089 3889; email: pam.jarrett@thebenevolent.org.uk; website: www.thebenevolent.org.uk)

CC Number: 1023376

Eligibility

People living in England, Northern Ireland or Wales who have worked for more than five years, directly or indirectly, in the buying, selling, producing or distributing of wines and spirits, and their dependents.

Types of grants

Regular beneficial grants towards general living expenses of up to £65 paid monthly and one-off grants of up to £250 for a variety of items, including cookers, fridges, other household furniture, structural repairs, respite breaks, electric scooters and stairlifts. The society also makes Christmas gift donations and gives grants towards TV licence fees.

Annual grant total

In 2013 the society had assets of £5.3 million and an income of £2 million. Grants to individuals totalled £340,000 and were broken down as follows:

Beneficial grants	391	£274,000
Discretionary grants	118	£57,000
TV License scheme	52	£7,000

Exclusions

No grants are given towards business equipment.

Applications

On a form available from the correspondent. Applications can be submitted directly by the individual, or through a social worker or welfare agency. They are considered throughout the year and should include history of employment within the drinks industry. All new beneficiaries are visited by the society's welfare officer before a regular donation is made.

Other information

The society, formerly known as 'The Wine and Spirits Trades' Benevolent Society', also provides sheltered housing and offers personal welfare support and advice.

Butchers' and Drovers' Charitable Institution (BDCI)

£221,000 (94 grants)

Correspondent: Tina Clayton, Administrator, Butchers' and Drovers' Charitable Institution, 105 St Peter's Street, St Albans, Hertfordshire AL1 3EJ (01727 896094; email: info@bdci.org.uk; website: www.bdci.org.uk)

CC Number: 296990

Eligibility

People in the UK, who work or have worked in any aspect of the meat industry whether wholesale, retail or otherwise, and their close family members. Applicants will normally have worked within the industry for at least ten years and will often be retired or medically certified unfit to work.

Types of grants

Pensions, one-off grants and loans. The average value of one-off grants in 2012 was £900, although up to £2,000 could be awarded in special circumstances. Awards can be made towards heating bills, mobility aids, white goods, house repairs, clothing and so on. Grants of up to £50 a week are made to top up nursing home fees.

Annual grant total

At the time of writing (August 2014) the latest financial information available was from 2012. In 2012 the charity had assets of £9.9 million and an income of £671,000. Grants to individuals totalled £221,000 and can be broken down as follows:

One-off grants	£109,000
Pensions	£108,000
Nursing home top-up	£4,600

Applications

Application forms can be requested from the correspondent or downloaded from the charity's website. They can be submitted directly by the individual or through a third party, such as a social worker, Citizens Advice or other welfare agency. Preference is given to candidates who can provide details of meat trade connections verified in writing by existing meat traders or by production of other documents. Requests are considered at bi-monthly meetings. Decision is normally reached within the following ten days after the meeting.

Other information

The charity also provides residential accommodation to those in need.

The Fishmongers' and Poulterers' Institution

£18,400

Correspondent: Roy Sully, Secretary, Butchers' Hall, 87–88 Bartholomew Close, London EC1A 7EB (020 7600 4106; fax: 020 7606 4108; email: fpi@butchershall.com; website: www.butchershall.com)

CC Number: 209013

Eligibility

People in need who are, or have been, involved in the processing, wholesale and retail fish and poultry trades for at least ten years, and their dependents.

Types of grants

Pensions and one-off grants. In 2012 one-off grants were given for needs such as the purchase of white goods, replacement windows and assistance with care costs.

Annual grant total

In 2012 the institution had assets of £574,000 and an income of £32,000. Grants to individuals totalled £18,400, of which £16,400 was given in pensions and £2,000 in one-off grants.

At the time of writing (August 2014) this was the most recent financial information available for the institution.

Applications

On a form available from the correspondent. Applications can be submitted directly by the individual or through a third party. The institution points out in its 2012 annual report that many applications are received through intermediary bodies such as the Royal British Legion or Care and Repair agencies. They are considered three times a year.

The Sir Percival Griffiths' Tea-Planters Trust

£7,000

Correspondent: Stephen Buckland, Trustee, Duncan Lawrie Ltd, Wrotham Place, High Street, Wrotham, Sevenoaks, Kent TN15 7AE (020 7201 3065)

CC Number: 253904

Eligibility

People who are or have been involved in tea planting in India, live in the UK and are in need. Dependents of such people are also eligible.

Types of grants

Our research suggests that one-off and recurrent grants of up to £3,000 are available to help with general living expenses. Single payments include those for assistance with medical equipment, electrical goods and so on.

Annual grant total

At the time of writing (August 2014) the latest financial information available was from 2012. In 2012 the trust had an income of £9,100 and a total expenditure of £7,200. We estimate that grants to individuals totalled around £7,000.

Applications

Application forms are available from the correspondent. They should include details of career in India (dates, tea garden and so on) and can be submitted at any time either directly by the individual or through a third party, such as a social worker, Citizens Advice, or another welfare agency.

GroceryAid

£2.5 million

Correspondent: Gillian Barker, Director General, Unit 2, Lakeside Business Park, Swan Lane, Sandhurst, Berkshire GU47 9DN (01252 875925; fax: 01252 890562; email: info@groceryaid.org.uk; website: www.groceryaid.org.uk)

CC Number: 1095897

Eligibility

To qualify for assistance applicants must: have worked for a minimum of ten years in the UK grocery industry (including food manufacturing, wholesaling and retailing in all its aspects and the retail off-licence trade); have no more than £12,000 in savings/capital (excluding property); and be able to demonstrate a degree of financial hardship.

Full-time and part-time workers are eligible and the grant can transfer to spouses or long-term partners in the event of the beneficiary's death. The charity also notes that:

> For those in the industry who have worked for some time but perhaps not quite long enough to qualify for our ongoing support, or who do not qualify within our financial parameters, we are sometimes able to provide one-off grants. These applications are judged on their own individual merit.

Types of grants

Annual grants of £830, paid quarterly (roughly £16 per week). Grants are also provided for one-off items such as white goods, telephones, telephone response systems, televisions and mobility equipment. Emergency grants for specific financial problems such as house repairs, boiler replacement and household equipment are also available.

Annual grant total

In 2012/13 the charity held assets of £12.4 million and had an income of £8.4 million. Quarterly grants were made totalling £1.8 million, with a further £742,000 spent on the provision of goods and services. Charitable expenditure was distributed as follows:

Quarterly payments	£1.8 million
Christmas hampers	£192,000
Basic essentials	£132,000
One-off payments	£130,000
Emergency assistance	£104,000
Mobility	£94,000
Welfare Helpline	£45,000
Birthday vouchers and TV licences	£22,000
Telephone response systems	£13,000
Beneficiary outings	£10,000

Applications

On a form available from the correspondent or to download from the website. Applications can be submitted directly by the individual, through a social worker, Citizens Advice, other welfare agency, or via a third party such as a relative. Applications are considered throughout the year. Applicants will be visited, if possible, by a welfare assessor who will carry out a more detailed assessment of their needs.

Other information

In February 2012 the Caravan and the Sweet Charity, the charity for the confectionary trade, merged to form GroceryAid.

A welfare helpline (0808 802 1122) is also operated for all staff from the grocery industry, whether or not they are eligible for financial help from the charity.

The Benevolent Society of the Licensed Trade of Scotland

£142,000

Correspondent: Chris Gardner, Chief Executive, 79 West Regent Street, Glasgow G2 2AW (01413 533596; fax: 01413 533597; email: chris@bensoc.org.uk; website: www.bensoc.org.uk)

SC Number: SC005604

Eligibility

Members of the society and people who have been employed full time in the licensed trade in Scotland for at least three years.

Types of grants

Annual pensions usually of up to £640. Each pensioner also receives a substantial Christmas and holiday gift. One-off grants are also available for temporary emergencies.

Annual grant total

In 2012/13 the society had an income of £409,000 and a total expenditure of £366,000. Grants and donations to individuals totalled £142,000.

Applications

On a form available from the correspondent, who can be contacted in writing, by telephone or email, or through the website. Applications can be made directly by the individual or through a social worker, Citizens Advice or other welfare agency. The BEN can offer help to applicants who need assistance to complete an application.

Licensed Trade Support and Care

£426,000

Correspondent: Helpline Team, Heatherley, London Road, Ascot, Berkshire SL5 8DR (0808 801 0550; fax: 01344 884703; email: helpline@supportandcare.org.uk; website: www.supportandcare.org.uk)

CC Number: 230011

Eligibility

People in need who are working, or have worked, in the licensed drinks industry, including their spouses/partners and dependent children. To qualify for assistance applicants should have worked in the trade for a minimum of five years continuously at some time in their working lives.

Types of grants

Recurrent grants are given to those on a very low income to help with utility bills, food costs and hospital travel expenses. One-off grants are also made towards: urgently needed equipment, such as household appliances and mobility aids; household improvements like door widening, stair-lifts and ramps; convalescent care and nursing costs for those recovering from illness; winter fuel grants and funeral expenses.

Annual grant total

In 2013 the charity had assets of £54 million and an income of £18.5 million. Welfare grants to individuals totalled £426,000.

Exclusions

No grants for: education related costs such as fees for educational courses, student maintenance, and student loan repayments; top up fees for residential care; or private medical treatments.

Applications

On a form available to download from the website, including proof of employment, personal details, personal history and full financial circumstances. Applications can be submitted either directly by the individual or through a social worker, Citizens Advice or other welfare agency. Enquiries about the application process are welcome and if necessary a volunteer may visit the applicant to help complete the application.

Other information

The charity also operates two schools in Brighton and Ascot and offers bursaries to students whose parents have worked in the licensed drinks industry amounting to around £492,000 in 2013.

The National Association of Master Bakers, Confectioners and Caterers Benevolent Fund

£10,000

Correspondent: The Secretary, 21 Baldock Street, Ware, Hertfordshire SG12 9DH (01920 468061; fax: 01920 461632; email: info@craftbakersassociation.co.uk; website: www.craftbakersassociation.co.uk)

CC Number: 206691

Eligibility

Former master bakers and their families who are in need.

Types of grants

Quarterly grants to help towards living costs such as gas, electricity and telephone bills. One-off grants are also available for specific items such as wheelchairs and household adaptations.

Annual grant total

In 2013 the fund had an income of £22,000 and a total expenditure of £16,900. We estimate that grants to individuals totalled around £10,000, with funding also awarded to organisations.

Exclusions

No grants are given for business debt or towards nursing home fees.

Applications

On a form available from the correspondent, to be submitted by the individual or through a recognised referral agency such as a social worker, Citizens Advice or doctor. Applications are usually considered on a monthly basis.

The National Federation of Fish Friers Benevolent Fund

£2,200

Correspondent: The General Secretary, New Federation House, 4 Greenwood Mount, Meanwood, Leeds LS6 4LQ (01132 307044; fax: 01132 307010; email: mail@federationoffishfriers.co.uk; website: www.federationoffishfriers.co.uk)

CC Number: 229168

Eligibility

Members or former members of the federation and their dependents (whether subscribers to the fund or not).

Types of grants

One-off grants in the range of £150 to £300 for necessities and convalescent holidays in the UK.

Annual grant total

In 2013, the fund had an income of £1,100 and a total expenditure of £2,400. We estimate that the total amount of grants awarded to individuals was approximately £2,200.

Exclusions

No grants are available for debts due to poor business practice or to organisations.

Applications

On a form available from the correspondent. Applications can be submitted by the individual, through a recognised referral agency (such as a social worker, Citizens Advice or AFF Associations/branches) or by the individual's family, and are considered throughout the year.

Other information

The fund maintains several convalescent homes.

The Provision Trade Charity

£42,000

Correspondent: Mette Barwick, Secretary, 17 Clerkenwell Green, London EC1R 0DP (020 7253 2114; fax: 020 7608 1645; email: secretary@ptbi.org.uk; website: www.ptbi.org.uk)

CC Number: 209173

Eligibility

People in need in the provision and allied trade, and their dependents. Applicants are normally retired and must have been employed in the trade for a number of years.

The provision trade covers the following: bacon, pork, canned meat/fish and dairy products.

Types of grants

Recurrent grants are issued quarterly. Summer and winter gifts and one-off grants can also be awarded where appropriate. One-off grants may also be issued to assist with special purchases or home improvements.

Annual grant total

In 2013 the charity had assets of £863,000 and an income of £67,000. Grants totalled £42,000.

Exclusions

The charity does not provide loans.

Applications

On a form which can be downloaded from the website. Applications may be returned by email or post. Applications are usually considered in February, May, August and November. They can be submitted directly by the individual or through a social worker, Citizens Advice, other welfare agency or through a relation or friend. Prospective beneficiaries are visited by the trust's welfare visitor.

Other information

This charity was founded as the Cheesemonger's Benevolent Institution in 1835 'for pensionary relief of indigent or incapacitated members of the Provision Trade and their widows'. The charity is also referred to as 'PTBI'.

Furnishing trade

The Furniture Makers

£140,000 (129 grants)

Correspondent: Damilola Bamidele, Grants and Education Manager, 4th Floor, Furniture Makers' Hall, 12 Austin Friars, London EC2N 2HE (020 7256 5954; email: welfare@furnituremakers.org.uk; website: www.furnituremkrs.co.uk/default.aspx)

CC Number: 1015519

Eligibility

Current and former employees of the furnishing industry and their dependents who are in financial need. Applicants must have worked in the industry for a minimum of two years.

Types of grants

One-off grants averaging around £500 towards the purchase of scooters, recliner chairs, TV licences, the installation of walk-in showers, central heating and telephone lines. Help is also given towards the payment of rent arrears, interior decorating costs and holidays. Quarterly annuities range between £10 and £20 per week.

The Edenfield Holiday Scheme enables beneficiaries with ten years' experience in the industry to take respite breaks or holidays.

Annual grant total

In 2012/13 the charity held assets of £7.5 million and had an income of £542,000. Welfare grants to individuals totalled £140,000 and were distributed as follows:

Weekly grants	£119,000
One-off grants	£19,600
Edenfield grants (holidays)	£1,200

A further £37,000 was awarded in student bursaries and for other needs.

Applications

An application form is available to download from the charity's website. Once completed, forms should be posted or emailed to the correspondent. The charity welcomes enquiries.

Other information

In February 2012 the Furnishing Industry Trust and the charity of the Furniture Makers Company merged to form the Furniture Makers.

Gas engineering

The Institution of Gas Engineers Benevolent Fund

£2,000

Correspondent: Kristina Parkin, Administrator, IGEM House, High Street, Kegworth, Derbyshire DE74 2DA (01509 678167; email: lesley@igem.org.uk; website: www.igem.org.uk)

CC Number: 214010

Eligibility

Members and ex-members of the Institution of Gas Engineers, and their dependents. Note that other people in the gas industry who have no such connection with the institution are not eligible.

Types of grants

One-off and recurrent grants according to need.

Annual grant total

In 2012 the trust had an income £12,000 and a total expenditure of £4,300. Grants were made totalling approximately £4,000 which was split between educational and welfare grants.

These were the latest set of accounts available at the time of writing (August 2014).

Applications

In writing to the correspondent.

Hairdressing

The Barbers' Amalgamated Charity

£9,500

Correspondent: Colonel P. J. Durrant, Clerk, The Worshipful Company of Barbers, Barber-Surgeons' Hall, 1A Monkwell Square, Wood Street, London EC2Y 5BL (020 7606 0741; fax: 020 7606 3857; email: clerk@barberscompany.org; website: www.barberscompany.org)

CC Number: 213085

Eligibility

Poor, generally older, members of the medical, barber or hairdressing professions and their dependents.

Types of grants

Annual pensions to those in need.

Annual grant total

In 2012/13 the charity had an income of £14,700 and a total expenditure of £9,800. We estimate that grants to individuals totalled £9,500.

Applications

In writing to the correspondent directly by the individual or via a family member, or through an organisation such as Citizens Advice or other welfare agency. Applications are considered throughout the year.

Hair and Beauty Benevolent

£100,000

Correspondent: The Secretary, 11 The Leys, Chesham Bois, Amersham, Bucks HP6 5NP (01494 729358; email: info@habb.org; website: www.habb.org)

Eligibility

Members and former members of the hairdressing and beauty industries and their dependents.

Types of grants

One-off and recurrent grants to those in need. Grants have been made for house adaptations, mobility aids, TV licences and holidays. In some cases regular financial assistance may be given.

The HABB children's welfare fund also provides one-off and recurrent grants. Grants have been made for monthly pocket money to children from low-income families as well as one-off grants for specialist equipment, holidays, school uniforms, bedding and Christmas/birthday payments.

Annual grant total

The fund is not registered with the Charity Commission and so limited financial information was available. The website notes that the fund needs '£150,000 a year to meet our existing commitments to beneficiaries and to take new requests for assistance on board.' We estimate that each year, grants to individuals total around £100,000. The fund currently supports more than 100 adults and children.

Exclusions

No assistance with non-priority debts or bankruptcy fees. The trust cannot help those who have not worked in the profession since 1970.

Applications

In writing, by email or by telephoning the fund. In order to process the application the fund will need to know: what help is needed, why the help is needed, the applicant's length of involvement in the industry and when they last worked in the industry. If it was the applicant's partner who worked in the industry, this information should be provided on them. After this initial enquiry HABB will notify eligible applicants, who can then download an application form from the website which should be returned along with copies of bank statements and proof of work in the industry.

Applications are decided on the second Tuesday of each month. All applicants will be informed of the decision in writing. Regular beneficiaries will have their cases reviewed annually.

Other information

The fund has been sponsored by a number of corporate partners including well-known names such as L'Oréal, Wella and Schwarzkopf.

Horticulture

Gardeners' Royal Benevolent Society (Perennial)

£500,000

Correspondent: Sheila Thomson, Director of Services, 115 – 117 Kingston Road, Leatherhead, Surrey KT22 7SU (0800 093 8543, 07901556108; email: info@perennial.org.uk; website: www.perennial.org.uk)

CC Number: 1155156, SC040180

Eligibility

People who are, or have been, employed or self-employed in the horticultural industry in the UK and their spouses/

partners, widows/widowers, immediate dependents. This includes qualified and unqualified gardeners, nursery workers, landscapers, garden centre employees, arboriculturists, people running their own small businesses and others in the industry who are in necessitous circumstances, such as financial difficulties, illness, disability and so on.

Types of grants

The charity offers the following help:

- One-off grants towards a variety of needs, including support for mobility aids, property adaptations, property maintenance, domestic appliances, bills, furniture and fittings, personal items, funeral expenses, travel and other costs linked to training, holidays and personal care. In certain circumstances grants may also be available for debt clearance
- Regular quarterly allowances payable on a long-term basis (in some cases for life)
- Assistance and top-up for care home fees ranging from £10 to £100 per week

Annual grant total

In 2013 the charity had assets of £45.1 million, an income of £3.8 million and spent £1.6 million in assisting the beneficiaries. Grants for welfare purposes totalled around £500,000, including regularly paid benefits, support for heating in winter, grants from the Good Samaritan Fund and Children's Fund.

The biggest part of the charity's expenditure is spent in providing advice and advocacy services, including debt advice.

Exclusions

Help is not available for maintaining council or other rented property. Grants are not usually awarded where statutory provision is available.

Applications

Initial contact should be made to the charity via phone, email or post, either directly by the individual or through a third party/any welfare organisation. All applicants requiring financial assistance are visited by a caseworker, usually within ten days, who will make an initial assessment and fill in an application form with the prospective client (or their parent if the applicant is the child of a horticulturalist).

Other information

In 2010 this charity merged with the Royal Fund for Gardeners' Children. From 2014 the charity had a change in its legal status – became a company limited by guarantee and was registered with the Charity Commission. It continues to be registered with the Office of the Scottish Charity Regulator.

The charity also provides advice, advocacy and support on welfare rights, entitlement to benefit, accommodation issues and debt advice. To access help get in touch with the charity: general advice at 0800 210 0547, services@perennial.org.uk; debt advice at 0800 294 4244, debtadvice@perennial.org.uk.

Grants are also available to individuals for education and training purposes.

Hotel and catering

Hospitality Action

£507,000 (808 grants)

Correspondent: Grants and Advisory Team, 62 Britton Street, London EC1M 5UY (020 3004 5507; fax: 020 7253 2094; email: help@hospitalityaction.org.uk; website: www.hospitalityaction.org.uk)

CC Number: 1101083

Eligibility

Former and current workers in the hospitality industry in the UK. The individuals or the company they work for would need to have been involved in the direct provision of food, drink or accommodation away from home. Individuals must have worked in the industry for one continuous year in the past five years or have worked for seven continuous years in their lifetime. Applicants must have limited savings.

Types of grants

Grants offered are: essential needs grants; crisis grants; top-up grants; and winter fuel grants.

Annual grant total

In 2013 the charity held assets of £8.5 million and had an income of £1.1 million. 808 grants to individuals, the majority of which were for under £1,000, totalled £507,000. Grants can be broken down as follows:

Essential needs grants	£314,000
Top up grants	£87,000
Short-term crisis grants	£52,000
Christmas grants	£20,000
Winter fuel grants	£11,000
Family members' scheme	£8,600
Other grants	£7,200
TV and phone grants	£7,200

Exclusions

Funding is not available towards the following:

- Education related costs such as private school fees, fees for educational courses, student maintenance, and student loan repayment
- Most private medical treatments
- Residential Care fee shortfalls
- Legal costs
- Property repairs/adaptations where equity release is a viable option

The charity cannot consider a grant for an item until all statutory sources of funding have been tried.

Only one grant per applicant in any twelve month period.

Applications

On a form available from the website. The individual's NI number, work history, reason for application, payee details and quotes (if applicable) should be included. The form must be signed. The charity will notify the applicant of the decision in writing. Detailed guidance notes are available from the website.

Note: 'All applications for financial assistance need to be supported by an independent third party who can confirm the applicant's need and financial situation. See application guidance notes for more details on who can support different types of request.'

Other information

Hospitality Action runs The Ark Foundation Programme which offers seminars on drugs and alcohol misuse. The organisation has a membership scheme for retirees of the hospitality industry.

The Sir John Edwin and Arthur Mitchell Fund

£33,000

Correspondent: Ms H. Woodall, Administrator, Mitchells and Butlers, 27 Fleet Street, Birmingham B3 1JP (01214 984129; website: www.mbtrusts.org.uk)

CC Number: 528922

Eligibility

Employees and former employees of Mitchells and Butlers, Six Continents and Bass Companies, in brewing, licensed retailing or catering.

Types of grants

Recurrent and one-off grants to pay essential bills or buy essential household items, assistance with property deposits, home adaptations for people with disabilities, convalescent and respite breaks, wheelchairs and aids, counselling, etc.

Annual grant total

In 2012/13 the fund held assets of £1.3 million. Its income was £43,000 (2012: £45,000) and total grant expenditure for the year amounted to £33,000 (2012: £32,000). Grants were made during the course of the financial year to The Licensed Trade Charity to fund former employees of Mitchells and Butlers and also grants were made directly to former employees of the company.

Exclusions

Top-up fees for residential care, private medical treatment or retrospective funding of items/services already purchased.

Applications

Applications are made through Licensed Trade Support and Care, part of the Licensed Trade Charity, who provide support to current and former brewery and licensed trade workers where it is needed. An application can be made by contacting the helpline on 01344 898550, by contacting the trust by email or downloading an application form and guidelines directly from the website.

Applicants may receive a visit by a member of the welfare team in order to assess their needs and also, if necessary, provide help with the application process.

Other information

The fund supplies money to beneficiaries through the umbrella welfare organisation Licenced Trade Support and Care (LTSC). LTSC provide a holistic support service offering benefit, housing and debt advice as well as financial assistance.

Jewellery

The British Jewellery, Giftware and Finishing Federation Benevolent Society

£40,000 (63 grants)

Correspondent: Lynn Snead, Secretary, Federation House, 10 Vyse Street, Hockley, Birmingham B18 6LT (01217 454613; email: lynn@teg.co.uk; website: www.batf.uk.com)

CC Number: 208722

Eligibility

People in financial need or who have a disability who have worked in the industries covered by the federation, and their dependents. Eligible trades are jewellery manufacture and distribution, giftware, surface engineering and travel goods and fashion accessories industries.

Types of grants

One-off grants and loans are given towards the provision of essential items such as cookers, washing machines, fridges, freezers, bedding, telephone rental, television licence fees and household repairs. Recurrent grants are also paid to those on a low income. Typically, grants range from £100 to £350.

Annual grant total

In 2013 the society had assets of £716,000 and an income of £90,000. Grants were made to 63 individuals totalling £40,000.

Applications

On a form available from the correspondent. Applications can be submitted either directly by the individual or through a social worker, Citizens Advice, welfare agency or other third party. Applications are considered quarterly.

The Silversmiths and Jewellers Charity

£58,000

Correspondent: Julie Griffin, Administrator, PO Box 61660, London SE9 9AN (020 8265 9288; email: info@thesjcharity.co.uk; website: www.tsjc.org.uk)

CC Number: 205785

Eligibility

People in need who are, or have been, employed in any sector of the gold and silversmithing trade or the jewellery trade, and their dependents.

Types of grants

Quarterly payments of £135, summer gifts of £50, Christmas gifts of £150 and Christmas hampers are given to regular grantees. One-off grants are also made for special needs such as domestic goods, furniture, bedding and hospital travel costs.

Annual grant total

In 2013 the charity had an income of £158,000 and a total expenditure of £137,000. It has assets of £1.7 million which mainly consisted of investments and are therefore not available for distribution. Grants totalling were made to individuals for social welfare purposes.

Applications

On a form available from the correspondent. Applications can be submitted directly by the individual or through a social worker, Citizens Advice or other welfare agency.

Other information

This charity was previously known as the Goldsmiths', Silversmiths' and Jewellers' Benevolent Society.

Laundry

Johnson Charitable Trust

See entry on page 80

The Worshipful Company of Launderers Benevolent Trust

£3,300 (5 grants)

Correspondent: Terence Winter, Clerk, Launderers' Hall, 9 Montague Close, London SE1 9DD (020 7378 1430; fax: 020 7378 9364; email: clerk.launderers@btconnect.com; website: www.launderers.co.uk)

CC Number: 262750

Eligibility

Existing and retired members of the laundry industry and their dependents.

Types of grants

Grants can be paid annually (towards fuel bills); bi-annually (fuel bills and a summer grant); or monthly (towards general living expenses).

Annual grant total

In 2012/13 the trust had assets of £562,000 and an income of £45,000. Grants totalled £21,000, of which £3,300 was given in monthly grants to five individuals from the General Fund.

Applications

In writing to the correspondent.

Other information

The trust is made up of three portfolios: The General Fund; The Arthur Kennedy Fund; and The Launderers' and Cleaners' Education Trust. The Launderer and Cleaners' Education Fund offers the Travelling Scholarship, which is available once every two years.

Leather

Leather and Hides Trades' Benevolent Institution

£70,000

Correspondent: Karen Harriman, Secretary, 143 Barkby Road, Leicester LE4 9LG (01162 741500; email: karenharriman@btconnect.com; website: www.lhtbi.org.uk)

CC Number: 206133

Eligibility

People who work or have worked in the leather trade (i.e. in the production of leather or in the handling of hide and skin) for ten years or more. Applicants are usually over 60, though people under 60 may also be considered. Bereaved spouses are also eligible to apply.

Types of grants

Annuities of between £240 and £1,240 a year (paid quarterly). Grants towards residential or nursing home fees, special one-off payments for equipment and Christmas hampers.

Annual grant total

In 2012 the charity had assets of £761,000 and an income of £53,000. Annuities (paid to 70 beneficiaries) and grants were made totalling £70,000. This was the latest financial information available at the time of writing.

Applications

On a form available from the correspondent or through the charity's website. Applications can be submitted directly by the individual or through a social worker, Citizens Advice or other welfare agency. Applications can be considered at any time.

Note: Recurrent grants are subject to annual review.

Legal

The Barristers' Benevolent Association

£95,000

Correspondent: Janet South, Administrator, 14 Gray's Inn Square, London WC1R 5JP (020 7242 4761; email: susan@the-bba.com; website: www.the-bba.com)

CC Number: 1106768

Eligibility

Past or present practising members of the Bar in England and Wales, and their spouses, former spouses and dependents. No grants to those who when qualified went straight into commerce.

Types of grants

Assistance may be provided by way of grant or loan, or a combination of the two. Grants range from small amounts of cash, regular food vouchers, and payment of specific bills such as TV licences, car tax, telephone bills or the purchase of equipment or medicine not available from the NHS.

Annual grant total

In 2012 the charity had assets of £9.5 million and an income of £635,000. £189,000 was given in grants and it is assumed that approximately £95,000 was given to individuals for welfare purposes.

These were the latest set of accounts available at the time of writing (July 2014).

Applications

On a form available from the correspondent, which requires applicants to set out their personal circumstances. They are considered at monthly meetings of the management committee.

Other information

Grants are also made for educational purposes.

The Chartered Institute of Legal Executives' Benevolent Fund

£3,700

Correspondent: Valerie Robertson, Charities and CSR Officer, The Chartered Institute Of Legal Executives, Kempston Manor, Manor Drive, Kempston, Bedford MK42 7AB (01234 845763; email: vrobertson@cilex.org.uk; website: www.cilex.org.uk)

CC Number: 295527

Eligibility

Members and former members of the institute (including associates, fellows and student members), and their families or dependents. Help is particularly aimed at those who have become unemployed through old age, illness or other circumstances.

Types of grants

One-off grants ranging between £100 and £1,000 can be given for specific purposes, for example, utility bills (such as telephone or fuel), nursing/residential care, medical equipment and so on. Grants can also be made to members who are unable to pay their membership subscriptions through redundancy or illness and so on.

Annual grant total

In 2013 the fund had assets of £187,000 and an income of £3,500 generated through donations and investment. Grants for assistance totalled £3,700.

Applications

Further details on the application procedure can be requested from the correspondent or accessed on the institute's website (for registered members). Applications should be submitted directly by the individual or a dependent and can be considered at any time.

Other information

The fund also offers information, practical advice and advocacy services.

The United Law Clerks Society

£5,000

Correspondent: John Dungay, Innellan House, 109 Nutfield Road, Merstham, Surrey RH1 3HD (01737 643261; email: john_a_dungay@hotmail.com)

CC Number: 277276

Eligibility

People employed or who were employed by any person of the legal profession in England, Scotland and Wales, and their dependents.

Types of grants

One-off and recurrent grants according to need, mainly to pensioners and people who are sick. Recurrent grants are usually for £5 to £10 a week, but can be for up to £720 a year. One-off grants can be for up to £500 or £600 a year, for example, towards cookers, roof repairs, special chairs/beds and so on.

Annual grant total

In 2012/13 the society had an income of £700 and a total expenditure of £5,400. Both income and expenditure have fallen consistently from around £5,000 and £22,000 respectively in the last five years.

Exclusions

No grants for students.

Applications

On a form available from the correspondent at any time. Applications can be submitted either directly by the individual, through a third party such as a social worker, or through an organisation such as Citizens Advice or other welfare agency.

Librarians

The Chartered Institute of Library and Information Professionals (CILIP) Benevolent Fund

£11,500 (20 grants)

Correspondent: Eric Winter, Secretary, CILIP Benevolent Fund, 7 Ridgmount Street, London WC1E 7AE (020 7255 0648; email: eric.winter@cilip.org.uk; website: www.cilip.org.uk)

CC Number: 237352

Eligibility

Members and former members of the CILIP and their dependents. This includes former members of the Library Association and the Institute of Information Scientists who may not have chosen to become members of CILIP.

Types of grants

One-off grants only for 'unusual or unexpected expenses that may be causing anxiety and hardship'. Grants are given towards, for example, urgent house repairs, household equipment, unexpectedly large heating bills, overdrafts or debts that have accumulated due to illness and so on. Interest-free loans are also available.

Annual grant total

In 2013 the fund held assets of £138,000 and had an income of £29,000. Welfare grants to 20 individuals totalled £11,500.

Exclusions

No grants to students. The fund is not able to offer recurrent grants or pension top-ups.

Applications

Applicants should either write to or telephone the correspondent and outline their difficulties. A visit will then be arranged to discuss the circumstances in more detail. The trustees meet three or four times a year to consider applications, though urgent requests can be dealt with more quickly.

Market research

The Market Research Benevolent Association

£12,200 (28 grants)

Correspondent: Danielle Scott, Secretary and Treasurer, 11 Tremayne Walk, Camberley, Surrey GU15 1AH (0845 652 0303; email: info@mrba.org.uk; website: www.mrba.org.uk)

CC Number: 274190

Eligibility

People who are or have been engaged in market research and their dependents.

Types of grants

Generally one-off grants for people in need. Interest-free loans are also available. Funding has been given towards the costs of wheelchairs and other medical equipment, convalescence and other medical expenses, and emergency house and car repairs.

Annual grant total

In 2012/13 the association held assets of £514,000 and had an income of £30,000. We estimate that grants to individuals amounted to £4,000, with funding also awarded to organisations.

A further £8,200 was given in loans converted to grants.

Applications

Applicants should contact the correspondent by phone or by email to be assigned to an MRBA Regional Manager and sent an application form. The regional manager will then contact the applicant and offer assistance throughout the application process. When completed, the application form will be the subject of a summary report which will then be reviewed by the MRBA Committee, which meets every six weeks. The regional manager will then inform the applicant on whether and how the association is able to assist. Urgent cases can be fast-tracked.

Other information

The association also provides advice as well as debt and bereavement support.

Match manufacture

The Joint Industrial Council and the Match Manufacturing Industry Charitable Fund

£600

Correspondent: Rachel Perks, Administrator, Republic Technologies Ltd, Sword House, Totteridge Road, High Wycombe, Buckinghamshire HP13 6DG (01494 533300)

CC Number: 260075

Eligibility

People who are or have been involved in the manufacture of matches, and their dependents.

Types of grants

One-off grants towards, for instance, medical expenses, dental and optical expenses, home security, removal costs (to sheltered accommodation) and winter fuel costs. Christmas grants are also available.

Annual grant total

This fund has been relatively inactive over the past number of years, with neither income or expenditure rising above £1,400 per year. In 2012 it had no income and an expenditure of £1,300. We estimate that social welfare grants to individuals totalled around £600. Grants are also given to individuals for educational purposes.

At the time of writing (August 2014) this was the most recent financial information available for the fund.

Applications

In writing to the correspondent, directly by the individual. Applications are considered throughout the year.

Media

The Chartered Institute of Journalists Orphan Fund

£15,000

Correspondent: Dominic Cooper, Administrator, 2 Dock Offices, Surrey Quays Road, London SE16 2XU (020 7252 1187; fax: 020 7232 2302; email: memberservices@cioj.co.uk; website: www.cioj.co.uk)

CC Number: 208176

Eligibility

Orphaned children of institute members who are in need, aged between 5 and 22 and in full-time education.

Types of grants

Monthly grants (plus birthday/Christmas/summer holiday payments).

Annual grant total

In 2012 the fund had assets of £1.8 million and an income of £86,000. Grants to individuals totalled £30,000 for both welfare and education. We have estimated that grants to individuals for social welfare purposes totalled £15,000. These were the latest accounts available at the time of writing (July 2014).

Applications

In writing to the correspondent.

Other information

This fund also gives grants for educational purposes.

The Cinema and Television Benevolent Fund

£621,000 (6,134 grants)

Correspondent: Welfare Department, 22 Golden Square, London W1F 9AD (0800 138 2522; email: welfare@ctbf.co.uk; website: www.ctbf.co.uk)

CC Number: 1099660

Eligibility

People who have worked behind the scenes in the cinema, film and commercial television industries in the UK for two years in any capacity, i.e. production, exhibition, distribution, administration or transmission of film or commercial television. Help is also available to dependents.

Applicants should have less than £10,000 in savings, must be in receipt of all state benefits applicable to their situation, must have received debt counselling from CAB or one of the large free debt advice agencies and must have exhausted statutory options. If applicable, a Disabled Facilities Grant (DFG) must have been applied for from the local authority.

Types of grants

Recurrent payments and one-off grants for a wide range of needs, for example, towards white goods, televisions, disability aids/special equipment, disability adaptations and home repairs.

Annual grant total

In 2012/13 the fund held assets of £31.6 million and had an income of £3.6 million. A total of 6,134 grants were awarded to individuals, amounting to £621,000. The following are the grants categories with distributions totalling more than £20,000:

Regular monthly grants	£301,000
Support to Glebelands and Broccoli Cloisters residents	£97,000
Other grants	£46,000
Christmas gifts and hampers	£34,000
Birthday grants (vouchers)	£29,000
Telephone rentals and payments	£29,000

Categories with awards amounting to less than £20,000 were cold weather grants, household appliances, television licences, assistance with utility bills, wheelchairs and mobility, assistance with rent and mortgages and medical. Loans totalling £1,000 were also awarded.

Exclusions

The fund is not able to assist individuals who have been employed solely by the BBC on a full-time basis. No grants for educational purposes (except in exceptional circumstances).

Applications

On a form available from the website or welfare department. Applications are considered on an ongoing basis and should be submitted either directly by the individual or through a third party such as a social worker. Supporting documents must be submitted. These include an up-to-date CV, any documentation that proves employment (such as a payslip), DWP letters showing government benefits, local authority letters showing housing and council tax benefits, letters/bills from creditors, any other relevant paperwork and documentation relating to other funding sources, for example DFG applications.

Other information

The fund owns and manages a home for the elderly at Glebelands, which gives priority to those who have worked in the world of film, cinema and television. For more information contact the fund or go to the Glebelands website (www.glebelands.org).

The Grace Wyndham Goldie (BBC) Trust Fund

£1,200

Correspondent: Cheryl Miles, Secretary, BBC, Room M1017, Broadcasting House, Cardiff CF5 2YQ (02920 322000; website: www.bbc.co.uk/charityappeals/grant/gwg.shtml)

CC Number: 212146

Eligibility

Employees and ex-employees worldwide engaged in broadcasting or an associated activity, and their dependents.

Types of grants

One-off grants to help relieve continuing hardship not covered by aid from other sources.

Annual grant total

In 2012 the trust had assets of £1.2 million and an income of £49,000. Grants totalling £26,700 were made of which £22,500 were for educational purposes and £1,200 were for social welfare. The 2012 accounts were the most recent available at the time of writing (July 2014).

Exclusions

Grants are not given for medical, nursing or care home fees, funeral expenses or holidays.

Applications

On a form available from the correspondent. As the income of the fund is limited, and to ensure help can be given where it is most needed, applicants must be prepared to give full information about their circumstances.

The Guild of Motoring Writers Benevolent Fund

£10,000

Correspondent: Elizabeth Aves, Administrator, 23 Stockwell Park Crescent, London SW9 0DQ (020 7737 2377; website: www.gomw.co.uk)

CC Number: 259583

Eligibility

Motoring writers, photographers and historians who are in need and are, or have been, members of the guild. Their dependents may also be supported.

Types of grants

One-off and recurrent grants according to need. For example, to help with short-term financial difficulties following redundancy or injury. Grants are also available to retired members for stair lifts, orthopaedic beds, interim nursing costs and so on.

Annual grant total

In 2012 the fund had an income of £12,800 and a total expenditure of £10,600. We estimate that social welfare grants to individuals totalled £10,000.

At the time of writing (August 2014) this was the most recent financial information available for the fund.

Applications

In writing to the correspondent at any time. Applications can be made either directly by the individual through a third party.

The Newspaper Press Fund (Journalists' Charity)

£300,000 (150–200 grants)

Correspondent: David Ilott, Director and Secretary, Dickens House, 35 Wathen Road, Dorking, Surrey RH4 1JY (01306 887511; fax: 01306 888212; email: enquiries@journalistscharity.org.uk; website: www.journalistscharity.org.uk)

CC Number: 208215

Eligibility

Practising and former journalists and their dependents who are in need because of sickness, accident or other unforeseen circumstances. There are no age restrictions.

Types of grants

One-off grants normally in the range of £250 and £500 but all cases are decided on their merits. Regular payments on a weekly and monthly basis may be provided. Medical fees are only supported in exceptional circumstances.

Annual grant total

In 2013 the charity had assets and income of £1.5 million and a total expenditure of £2.3 million. At the time of writing (August 2014) full accounts were not available. Normally around 150–200 awards are made each year totalling around £300,000.

Exclusions

The charity states that its 'aim is to give financial support in times of need however [they] cannot subsidise those who, in the long term, find it difficult to make a living from journalism unless through illness or other misfortune.' Grants are not offered to subsidise an existing lifestyle. Awards are not generally given towards holidays (although support may be given for convalescence or respite breaks) and will not be provided for credit card debts, bank loans, legal costs or fines.

Applications

Application forms can be requested from the correspondent using an online form on the charity's website. They can be submitted directly by the individual or a family member. Applications should include details of the career in journalism and are considered monthly. The consideration process may take two to six weeks.

Other information

The charity also runs residential and care homes in Dorking.

NUJ Extra

£89,000

Correspondent: Lena Calvert, Administrator, Headland House, 308–312 Gray's Inn Road, London WC1X 8DP (020 7843 3700; fax: 020 7837 8143; email: lenac@nuj.org.uk; website: www.nujextra.org.uk)

CC Number: 1112489

Eligibility

Members and former members of the National Union of Journalists and the dependents of deceased members. Applicants must have paid at least one year's full subscription to the NUJ. Note: current members are only eligible for short-term assistance.

Types of grants

One-off grants are given for: urgent bills, mainly rent and utilities; wheelchairs; beds; domestic goods; medical equipment; and minor home adaptations. Bills or rent payments will generally be made directly to the supplier or landlord. Recurrent grants of up to £175 a week are available to top up the income of those living on a state pension and/or other benefits. Christmas bonus grants are also made.

Annual grant total

In 2013 the charity held assets of £2.3 million and had an income of £45,000. Grants to individuals totalled £89,000.

Exclusions

No grants for legal expenses, private medical treatment or private education. Help is unlikely to be available for consumer debts. Members who left owing the union contributions are not eligible for help.

Applications

On a form available from the correspondent or to download from the website. Applications can be submitted by the individual or through an NUJ welfare officer or other third party. Applicants are required to provide details of their personal income and expenditure. They are considered throughout the year.

Other information

NUJ Extra is an amalgamation of charities previously known as National Union of Journalists Members in Need Fund and National Union of Journalists Provident Fund.

Medicine and health

The 1930 Fund for District Nurses

£28,000

Correspondent: Mia Duddridge, Administrator, The Trust Partnership, 6 Trull Farm Buildings, Tetbury, Gloucestershire GL8 8SQ (01285 841900; fax: 01285 841576; email: 1930fund@thetrustpartnership.com; website: www.1930fundfornurses.org)

CC Number: 208312

Eligibility

Qualified nurses who have worked in the community as a district nurse, community nurse, school nurse, health visitor, community midwife or community psychiatric nurse. Those applying for monthly or quarterly payments must hold a bank account solely in their own name.

Types of grants

One-off grants typically ranging from £100 to £300 for a variety of needs, including bathroom and kitchen equipment, household essentials, mobility aids, spectacles, dentures and specialist equipment. The fund also provides recurrent grants to help with living expenses, which are paid monthly or quarterly.

Annual grant total

In 2012/13 the fund held assets of £1.8 million and had an income of £68,000. Recurrent and one-off welfare grants totalled £28,000.

Exclusions

No grants are given for care home fees, educational fees, private healthcare, payment of debt, payment of rent/council tax or for expenses incurred before the grant is received.

Successful applicants of one-off grants may not reapply within a year.

Applications

On a form available from the correspondent or to download from the website. Applications can be submitted directly by the individual or through a family member, social worker, Citizens Advice or other welfare agency. They are considered at quarterly meetings. Applicants are required to supply evidence of having worked as a nurse, such as copies of any nursing certificates or qualifications and, if applicable, a recent payslip. A third party applying on behalf of a nurse should include a letter of endorsement from an approved authority. If the application is for home adaptations, repairs or the purchase of specific items, a copy of the invoice or quote must be supplied.

The fund welcomes enquiries.

Other information

The fund, which was founded in 1930 by a Mr Ernest Cook, has an informative website.

Ambulance Services Benevolent Fund

£25,000 (30 grants)

Correspondent: Simon Fermor, Secretary, Cherith, 150 Willingdon Road, Eastbourne, East Sussex BN21 1TS (01323 721150; email: enquiries@asbf.co.uk; website: www.asbf.co.uk)

CC Number: 800434

Eligibility

Present and former ambulance men/women, who have been employed by the NHS ambulance services, and their dependents. If retired, it must be for age or medical reason. People who only served for a couple of years before seeking other employment for the rest of their working life are not considered.

Types of grants

One-off grants of £100 to £1,000 are awarded to relieve genuine hardship, poverty or distress, or to assist medically.

Annual grant total

In 2012/13 the fund had assets of £428,000 and a revenue income of £54,000. Grants were made to 30 individuals totalling £25,000. Total income was £203.204, but this includes legacies and donations of £150,000.

Exclusions

No grants for items which have already been purchased.

Applications

Applications should be made through a third party, although if it is a particularly confidential matter applications can be accepted directly from the individual.

Third parties should write to the correspondent setting out the issue, how the need arose, the applicant's personal details, their length of service, any dependents they have and any other relevant information needed to complete the picture. Applicants applying directly can download an application form from the website.

BMA Charities Trust Fund

£34,000 (38 grants)

Correspondent: Marian Flint, Principal Officer, BMA House, Tavistock Square, London WC1H 9JP (020 7383 6142; email: info.bmacharities@bma.org.uk; website: bma.org.uk/about-the-bma/who-we-are/charities)

CC Number: 219102

Eligibility

Medical doctors, medical students and their dependents who are in financial need due to illness or unemployment, whether or not they are BMA members. All beneficiaries must be in receipt of their full state benefit entitlement.

Types of grants

One-off grants for specific items in times of crisis, such as disability equipment, rent, utility bills, travel expenses and retraining costs. Applicants who are in work can normally only apply for assistance with paying for GMC retention fees or medical defence insurance. For medical students in immediate need, there is a maximum grant amount of £500.

Annual grant total

In 2013 the fund had an income of £327,000 and a total expenditure of £265,000. Grants to individuals from the Hastings Fund amounted to £34,000. Of the 38 beneficiaries who received grants 19 were refugee doctors, ten were other doctors and nine were medical students.

During the year, a further £141,000 was awarded to 77 beneficiaries from the Medical Education Fund and £30,000 to two external charities.

Exclusions

The fund does not help with legal fees, private medical treatment or career development projects. There are no general grants for 'living costs'.

Applications

On a form available from the correspondent, to be submitted at any time. Two personal references are required, one of which must be from a doctor. Trustees meet to consider applications four times a year.

Other information

The BMA Charities Trust Fund incorporates the Hastings Benevolent Fund and the Medical Education Fund.

The fund can make referrals to its licensed money advisor for those applicants who are troubled by debt.

The British Dental Association Benevolent Fund (BDA Benevolent Fund)

£172,000

Correspondent: Elizabeth Rickarby, General Manager, 64 Wimpole Street, London W1G 8YS (020 7486 4994 or 020 8340 8354; email: generalmanager@dentistshelp.org; website: www.bdabenevolentfund.org.uk)

CC Number: 208146

Eligibility

Dentists resident in the UK who are or have been on the UK dental register and their dependents. Students at UK dental schools who are members of the association can also be supported.

Types of grants

One-off grants towards food and clothing, school uniforms, payment of bills or debts, household expenses (such as heating, lighting and repairs), Christmas gifts, for respite care and nursing home fees and to help meet specific needs, for examples washing machines, fridges, other household items, TV licences or funeral costs. Regular grants are available to supplement income and interest-free loans may be offered to relieve difficulties with a limited time span.

Annual grant total

In 2013 the fund had assets of £5.6 million and an income of 308,000. Grants were made totalling £172,000. In addition, a further £191,000 was paid in interest-free loans.

Exclusions

Help is not usually given with private medical fees or private school fees. The fund does not generally help people with a considerable amount of capital. Grants will not be made to replace the statutory support.

Applications

Application forms can be requested from the correspondent. They are considered upon receipt and can be submitted directly by the individual or through a third party, such as a social worker, Citizens Advice or other welfare agency. All new applicants are visited by the officer of the fund. Emergency grants can be made within a couple of days.

The Cameron Fund

£156,000

Correspondent: David Harris, Administrator, Flat 6 Christchurch, Kew Road, Richmond TW9 2AU (020 7388 0796; email: secretary@cameronfund.org.uk; website: www.cameronfund.org.uk)

CC Number: 261993

Eligibility

Present or former general practitioners, their families and dependents that are in need.

Types of grants

One-off and recurrent grants towards essential living costs, nursing home fees and so on. Each application is considered on its own merits. Occasionally support may be offered in the form of an interest-free loan.

Annual grant total

In 2013 the fund had an income of £356,000 and assets of almost £5.7 million. Grants were made totalling £156,000 to individuals for welfare purposes.

Exclusions

No grants can be made towards items which should be provided through statutory sources. Educational grants are only given to families previously supported by the fund.

Applications

On a form available from the correspondent or to download from the website. Applications should include information detailing assets, debt, income and expenditure. Additional information is often requested to ensure utmost accuracy.

Referrals from Local Medical Committees and other organisations or individuals who may know of someone who might benefit from support are also welcome. A trustee will usually visit the applicant before agreeing a grant and beneficiaries are reviewed annually.

Applicants must ensure that they have begun the process of claiming State and Local Authority benefits.

Other information

The fund also offers financial, legal and career advice as well as counselling.

Cavell Nurses' Trust

£420,000 (621 grants)

Correspondent: Kate Tompkins, Chief Executive, Grosvenor House, Prospect Hill, Redditch, Worcestershire B97 4DL (01527 595999; email: admin@cavellnursestrust.org; website: www.cavellnursestrust.org)

CC Number: 210571

Eligibility

Working and retired nurses, midwives and healthcare assistance together with student nurses suffering hardship, through illness, disability, accidents and family breakdowns. Applicants should hold no more than £4,000 in savings.

Types of grants

One-off and recurrent grants towards, for example, household repairs and equipment, current utility and telephone bills, specialist aids, convalescence and respite breaks. Regular grants range from £10 to £30 per week.

Annual grant total

In 2013 the trust had assets of £3.3 million and had an income of £517,000. Grants to individuals totalled £420,000. In the year 413 one-off grants were awarded with a further 208 individuals receiving regular grants.

Exclusions

No grants for debt repayment, holidays, bankruptcy fees, funeral expenses, educational costs or nursing home fees.

Applications

An initial short eligibility form must be completed first to see if your application is likely to be funded, which is available on the trust's website. A member of the welfare team will then contact you to discuss your circumstances and application.

Other information

Previously known as NurseAid.

Chartered Physiotherapists' Benevolent Fund

£101,000 (63 grants)

Correspondent: Jennifer Jeffcoat Carey, Administrator, Chartered Society of Physiotherapy, 14 Bedford Row, London WC1R 4ED (020 7306 6642; email: mbf@csp.org.uk; website: www.csp.org.uk)

CC Number: 219568

Eligibility

Members, past members, assistant members and student members of the society.

Types of grants

One-off grants and recurrent grants (of £150 per month in 2013) to help with living expenses, household repairs, heating bills and road tax (where car use is essential).

Annual grant total

In 2013 the fund had assets of £2 million and an income of £169,000. Grants were made to 63 individuals totalling £101,000.

Exclusions

No grants towards payment of debts or when statutory help is available. Grants cannot be made to those who hold capital exceeding the maximum figure used by the Department of Work and Pensions to decide on benefit eligibility.

Applications

On a form available from the correspondent. Applications should be submitted directly by the individual or by a third party such as a carer or partner. Applications are considered in January, April, July and October.

The Benevolent Fund of the College of Optometrists and the Association of Optometrists

£108,000

Correspondent: David Lacey, Administrative Secretary, PO Box 10, Swanley, Kent BR8 8ZF (01322 660388; email: davidlacey293@btinternet.com)

CC Number: 1003699

Eligibility

Current and retired members of the optical profession and their dependents.

Types of grants

Regular monthly payments to elderly or ill members towards bills and other living expenses. One-off grants are occasionally given towards costly items of expenditure such as house repairs, wheelchairs and holidays. Christmas grants are also given. For younger practitioners unable to work, the fund may assist with professional fees. Grants usually range from £20 to £200.

Annual grant total

In 2012/13, the fund had assets of £1.3 million, an income of £70,000 and a total expenditure of £125,000. Grants to individuals totalled £108,000.

Exclusions

No grants to students.

Applications

Application forms are available from the correspondent and a financial form must be completed. Applications are considered all year round and applicants are usually visited by a member of the profession.

The Eaton Fund for Artists, Nurses and Gentlewomen

See entry on page 31

The Ethel Mary Fletcher Fund for Nurses

£2,200

Correspondent: H. Campbell, Vice-President, Cricket Green Medical Practice, Room 2, 2nd Floor, 75–79 Miles Road, Mitcham, Surrey CR4 3DA (020 8685 1945; email: enquiries@rbna.org.uk; website: www.rbna.org.uk)

CC Number: 209887

Eligibility

Registered, or retired, state nurses over 40 years of age who are sick and disabled and who live in the UK.

Types of grants

Pensions are given.

Annual grant total

In 2012 the fund had an income of £3,800 and an expenditure of £2,400. Grants totalled approximately £2,200.

These were the latest set of accounts available at the time of writing (August 2014).

Applications

On a form available from the correspondent. Applications are considered quarterly.

Institute of Healthcare Management Benevolent Fund

£100,000

Correspondent: The Administrator, John Snow House, 59 Mansell Street, London E1 8AN (020 7265 7321; fax: 020 7265 7301; email: enquiries@ihm.org.uk; website: www.ihm.org.uk)

CC Number: 208225

Eligibility

Current and former members and former staff of the institute, and their dependents.

Types of grants

Our research suggests that the fund may offer emergency one-off grants (usually around £200), monthly grants (according to circumstances), special Christmas and summer holiday grants with emphasis on dependent children (usually paid to people receiving regular grants), and top-up nursing/residential home fees or similar support.

Annual grant total

At the time of writing (August 2014) the latest financial information available was from 2012. In 2012 the fund had an income of £8,300 and a total expenditure of £105,000, which is exceptionally high. We estimate that financial support to individuals totalled around £100,000. Note that in previous years the expenditure has been of around £12,000 a year.

Exclusions

Generally grants are not given to students but some educational grants may be given to members of the institute only; this does not extend to their dependants.

Applications

Applications should be submitted through a regional representative on the national council of the institute and are considered upon receipt.

Junius S. Morgan Benevolent Fund

£217,000 (104 grants)

Correspondent: Shirley Baines, Grant Administrator, Rathbone Trust Company Ltd, 1 Curzon Street, London W1J 5FB (020 7399 0110; email: grantadmin@juniusmorgan.org.uk; website: www.juniusmorgan.org.uk)

CC Number: 1131892

Eligibility

Registered nurses and auxiliaries (including midwives and retired nurses) who have practised in the UK for a minimum of five years and find themselves in financial hardship due to illness, death of a family supporter, marriage breakdown, unforeseen expenditure or debt, and so on.

Types of grants

One-off grants of up to £1,500 and recurrent payments for a variety of purposes, including electricity and fuel bills, telephone charges, household renewal costs (decorating, furniture or furnishings), television rental and licence fees, home adaptations and repairs to those with disabilities, and so on.

Annual grant total

In 2013 the fund had assets of £2.5 million and an income of £344,000. Grants were made to 104 individuals totalling £217,000. The average grant was of £1,417 per person.

Exclusions

Grants are not normally given towards educational fees, residential/nursing home fees, holidays or respite care, funeral costs, bankruptcy fees and to carers or student nurses.

Applications

Applications may be submitted online on the fund's website or are available to download together with full application guidelines. All requests must be supported by an independent third party (such as a social worker, care worker, Citizens Advice, GP and so on) who is acting in a professional capacity. Applications should also include three months of recent bank statements and a copy of the most recent statement of the applicant's savings account. Awards are considered on a fortnightly basis and applicants will be notified of a decision in writing.

Other information

Grants may also be made to organisations.

The NHS Pensioners' Trust

£65,000 (250 grants)

Correspondent: Frank Jackson, Director, PO Box 456, Esher KT10 1DP (01372 805760; email: nhsptinfo@gmail.com; website: www.nhspt.org.uk)

CC Number: 1002061

Eligibility

i) Any person who has retired from service in any capacity in the NHS in England, Wales or Scotland; ii) Any person who has retired from service in England, Wales or Scotland for any of the related health service organisations or caring professions prior to the creation of the NHS; and iii) Any person who is the wife, husband, widow, widower or other dependent of those specified above.

Types of grants

Grants of up to £350, for general upkeep to ease financial difficulty in cases of hardship, including the cost of disabled living, aids and equipment, repairs to the home and fuel bills. Larger grants can be considered in particular circumstances. Grants are one-off, but individuals can reapply in the following year.

Annual grant total

In 2012/13 the trust held assets of £934,000 and had an income of £34,000. Grants to 250 individuals totalled

£65,000. The trust spent a further £5,600 on the provision of advice services.

Exclusions

No grants are paid for top-up fees in nursing or residential accommodation.

Applications

On a form available from the correspondent following receipt of an sae. Applications containing supporting information and/or the backing of social work agencies will be processed more quickly. A trust representative may follow up applications to verify information.

Other information

Advice services are also available from the trust.

Pharmacist Support

£254,000 (164 grants)

Correspondent: Grants Officer, 5th Floor, 196 Deansgate, Manchester M3 3WF (0808 168 2233; email: info@pharmacistsupport.org; website: www.pharmacistsupport.org)

CC Number: 221438

Eligibility

Pharmacists and their families, pre-registration trainees and those retired from the profession. Support is also available to pharmacists no longer on the register of the RPSGB or General Pharmaceutical Council such as those taking a break from pharmacy, on maternity leave or those who have been removed from the register (for whatever reason). Not available in Northern Ireland.

Types of grants

The charity offers four types of grants:

- Health and wellbeing grants are given to support 'mental or physical quality of life.' Funding is typically given for respite care, counselling and therapies, convalescence, home help during convalescence, particular disability aids and for contributions towards residential and nursing home fees
- One-off grants are awarded for unexpected expenses such as essential car or home repairs, winter fuel bills or the purchase of a washing machine, for example
- Recurrent grants act as 'top-ups' for those on very low incomes who 'are finding it difficult to make ends meet without getting into debt.' Recipients of these grants are often widows/widowers or retired pharmacists
- Student hardship grants are for pharmacy students who are facing extreme financial hardship due to unforeseen circumstances such as family issues, ill health or bereavement

Interest-free loans are also available.

Annual grant total

In 2013 the charity held assets of £14.5 million and had an income of £899,000. Financial assistance was given to 164 individuals (29 of whom received recurrent grants) totalling £254,000.

Assistance is also given to pharmacists dealing with issues of addiction through the Health Support Programme. In 2013 grants paid directly from the charity to assist individuals through recovery totalled £29,000, with a further £17,300 paid to the charity's partner, Action on Addiction, to fund their support services for individuals.

Exclusions

There are no grants available for pharmacy technicians or pharmacy assistants. Support is not available in Northern Ireland.

Applications

On a form available for download from the charity's website, or by contacting the correspondent. Applications will be considered year round and can be submitted either directly by the individual or through a social worker, Citizens Advice, other welfare agency, or other third party on behalf of an individual. The charity recommends that applicants make contact informally before applying in order to discuss eligibility and needs.

Other information

Pharmacist Support, formerly known as the Royal Pharmaceutical Society's Benevolent Fund, offers a range of services, information and specialist advice for pharmacists, former pharmacists and their families.

In partnership with Action on Addiction, the charity runs its Health Support Programme, which seeks to support pharmacists who are dealing with addiction and dependency issues through the provision of qualified addiction specialists. Those requiring more information on the Health Support Programme should call 0808 168 5132.

To talk to a trained volunteer about any work or home-related issues (including stress, bullying, ill health, financial worries, bereavement and anxiety about exams), call the 'Listening Friends' telephone helpline on 0808 168 5133.

General enquiries can be made by calling 0808 168 2233.

The Queen's Nursing Institute

£122,000 (120 grants)

Correspondent: Joanne Moorby, Welfare and Grants Officer, 1A Henrietta Place, London W1G 0LZ (020 7594 1400; email: mail@qni.org.uk; website: www.qni.org.uk)

CC Number: 213128

Eligibility

Queen's Nurses (district nurses who were trained by the QNI between 1887 and 1967) and community nurses who have worked in the community for a minimum of three years. The majority of beneficiaries are community nurses who are no longer able to work because of illness, age or disability.

Types of grants

One-off and recurrent grants ranging from help with household essentials, building repairs and adaptations to specialist aids and equipment.

Annual grant total

In 2013 the institute had assets of £8.7 million and an income of £890,000. Grants were made to 120 individuals totalling £122,000 in providing welfare support.

Exclusions

No grants for residential or nursing home fees, debt, medical treatment costs or funeral expenses.

Applications

On a form available from the correspondent or to download from the website. Applications are accepted from individuals themselves, their friends, family or professionals and voluntary organisations supporting them. An application form detailing eligibility, health and housing status, income, savings and expenditure must be completed.

The RCN Foundation

£186,000 (412 grants)

Correspondent: Michael Pearce, Administrator, Welfare Service, 20 Cavendish Square, London W1G 0RN (0345 408 4391; email: michael.pearce@rcn.org.uk; website: www.rcnfoundation.org.uk)

CC Number: 1134606

Eligibility

Registered or retired nurses, midwives, HCAs and health visitors in the UK, who are experiencing financial difficulties for one of the following reasons:

- During a period of ill health when full contractual sick pay has ceased

- Following ill health retirement
- During retirement (60+)
- Following a relationship breakdown, if there are children
- During a dispute with an employer

Types of grants

The foundation's website states:

> Through our Benevolent Funding, we provide vital support to help members of the nursing team get their lives and careers back on track in times of need.
>
> The list below outlines several examples of how the RCN Foundation can assist:
>
> - Rental payment where there is a shortfall in Housing Benefit entitlement
> - Respite break following a period of illness or caring for a sick relative
> - Payment of a utility service, such as gas or water, during a period of reduced income
> - Short-term childcare costs when a relationship has broken down and this facilitates remaining at work
> - Funding for disability equipment needed due to illness
> - Costs of essential household items when fleeing domestic violence.
>
> This list is by no means exhaustive; please contact us to find out if we can help you.
>
> If you wish to apply for funding, please contact us to request an application form by calling 020 7647 3882 or by emailing rcnfoundation@rcn.org.uk.

Annual grant total

In 2012/13 the foundation had assets of £26.9 million and an income of £3.2 million. Grants made for education and training totalled 299,000. Benevolent fund grants (social welfare) totalled £186,000. Grants for individuals totalled £350,000. We consider that all of thc benevolent fund grants were awarded to individuals and the total awarded to individuals for educational purposes was £231,000 (the figure given for bursaries).

Exclusions

No grants to repay consumer debts; for private medical treatment; for awards for family members; or for top-up fees for care homes.

Applications

If you wish to apply for funding, contact the foundation to request an application form by calling 020 7647 3882 or by emailing: rcnfoundation@rcn.org.uk. The aim is to process applications within 20 days.

Other information

Previously known as The Royal College of Nursing Benevolent Fund, the purpose of the foundation is to enable nurses and nursing to improve the health and wellbeing of the public through:

- Benevolent funding
- Education and training bursaries
- Supporting the development of clinical practice and the improvement of care
- Developing practice to enable people and communities to make positive choices about their own health and wellbeing
- Promoting research.

The Royal College of Midwives Trust

£192,000

Correspondent: Clifford Crisp, Administrator, Royal College of Midwives, 15 Mansfield Street, London W1G 9NH (020 7312 3535; fax: 020 7312 3536; email: info@rcm.org.uk; website: www.rcm.org.uk)

CC Number: 275261

Eligibility

Midwives, former midwives and student midwives who are in need. Preference is given to those who are members of the RCM or who have served as members of staff with the RCM or RCM Trust Ltd for at least five years.

Types of grants

Usually one-off grants for emergency or other unexpected needs (typically £50 to £200). Grants are given, for instance, towards the cost of a wheelchair, removal expenses, furniture, disability chairs, personal items and childcare costs.

The trust's website notes that 'unfortunately, the fund is not large enough to provide regular financial support, nor can it act as a top-up for low salaries or student midwives' bursaries, although it is able to advise on other sources of help.'

However, Christmas grants are routinely paid to long-standing elderly midwife members on low incomes.

Annual grant total

In 2013 the trust had assets of almost £6.9 million and an income of £2.95 million. Support to members amounted to £192,000.

Exclusions

Dependents of those eligible are unable to receive grants.

Applications

On a form available from the correspondent or to download from the website. Applications should be submitted either directly by the individual or through a third party such as a nursing organisation.

Other information

The trust engages in a range of other activities such as providing information, advice and support to members as well as running educational programmes and conferences and undertaking campaigning work. Total charitable expenditure amounted to almost £2.8 million in 2013.

The Royal Medical Benevolent Fund

£413,500

Correspondent: The Senior Case Manager, 24 King's Road, Wimbledon, London SW19 8QN (020 8540 9194; email: info@rmbf.org; website: www.rmbf.org)

CC Number: 207275

Eligibility

Assists GMC-registered, UK resident doctors and their recognised dependents who, through illness or disability are in financial hardship, through the provision of grants, loans and advice services.

Types of grants

This fund assists doctors, medical students and their dependents. Help ranges from financial assistance in the form of grants and interest-free loans to a telephone befriending scheme for those who may be isolated and in need of support. Assistance is tailored to the individual's needs. Support includes:

- One-off grants to help with costs such as home adaptations or specialist vehicles for those with disabilities
- Interest free loans or grants to help where eligible applicants are in financial need
- Specialist money and debt management advice to renegotiate debts and secure all eligible state benefits
- Back-to-work support such as paying childcare or retraining costs
- Support for medical students in exceptional financial hardship
- Support for refugee doctors retraining in the UK

For more detailed information on eligibility for financial help check the financial support section of the fund's website or talk to one of the fund's case workers on 020 8540 9194.

Annual grant total

In 2012/13 the fund had assets of £29 million and an income of £1.9 million. According to the statement of financial activities for 2013/14, grants were made to individuals totalling £827,000 for educational and welfare purposes. We estimate that social welfare grants to individuals totalled around £413,000.

Exclusions

The following are excluded:

- Private health care and medical insurance/fees
- Legal fees
- Inland revenue payments
- Debts to relatives or friends
- Private education

Applications

For an application pack and further information, email the correspondent at: help@rmbf.org or telephone the case workers' team on: 020 8540 9194. Applications should be submitted either directly by the individual or through a social worker, Citizens Advice, other welfare agency, medical colleague or other medical and general charities.

Two references are required (at least one of which should be from a medical practitioner). All applicants are visited before a report is submitted to the case committee. Income/capital and expenditure are fully investigated, with similar rules applying as for those receiving Income Support. Applications are considered bi-monthly.

Other information

Every year the RMBF helps hundreds of doctors, medical students and their dependents in a variety of ways.

Voluntary visitors liaise between beneficiaries and the office. The fund has an informative website.

The Royal Medical Foundation

£61,500 (35 grants)

Correspondent: Helen Jones, RMF Office, Epsom College, College Road, Epsom, Surrey KT17 4JQ (01372 821010; email: rmf-caseworker@epsomcollege.org.uk; website: www.royalmedicalfoundation.org)

CC Number: 312046

Eligibility

Medical practitioners (registered with the GMC) and their dependents who are in need.

Types of grants

One-off grants, monthly pensions and maintenance grants of £500 to £15,000. Previous applications have included support for doctors with debt problems, fall-out from divorce or suspension, re-training expenses, practical financial support during/after rehabilitation, help with essential domestic bills, respite breaks, home alterations for the elderly or people with disabilities and nursing home fees.

Annual grant total

In 2012/13 the foundation gave grants to individuals totalling £98,000, which were broken down as follows:

Short-term or one-off grants for urgent assistance	29	£45,000
Financial assistance with educational expenses	9	£34,000
Regular payments to medical practitioners and their widows/widowers	4	£15,500
Other grants	2	£650

Applications

On a form available from the correspondent, for consideration throughout the year. Applications can be submitted either by the individual or a family member, through a third party such as a social worker or teacher, or through an organisation such as Citizens Advice or a school. The trust advises applicants to be honest about their needs. All applicants are means tested.

Other information

The Royal Medical Foundation is a charity founded by Dr John Propert in 1855 and administered by an Act of Parliament. Its original objects were to provide an asylum for qualified medical practitioners and their spouses and to found a school for their sons.

Today the foundation's aims and objectives are to assist registered doctors and their families who are in financial hardship. Practical assistance is given in three ways:

- Provision of regular payments to their widows, widowers and their children
- Provision of one-off grants when emergency help is required and
- In exceptional circumstances, assistance with school fees for sons or daughters of registered doctors enabling them to maintain educational stability at times of distress caused by illness, bereavement or financial need in their family

The foundation is managed by a board of directors drawn from various professions and is located at Epsom College.

The Society for Relief of Widows and Orphans of Medical Men (The Widows and Orphans)

£30,000

Correspondent: Charlotte Farrar, Secretary, Lettsom House, 11 Chandos Street, Cavendish Square, London W1G 9EB (01837 83022; email: info@widowsandorphans.org.uk; website: www.widowsandorphans.org.uk)

CC Number: 207473

Eligibility

Support is given in the following order of priority: (i) necessitous dependents of deceased members of the society (ii) necessitous members of the society (iii) necessitous dependents of members of the society (iv) necessitous medical practitioners not being members of the society and their dependents.

Types of grants

Our research suggests that one-off and recurrent grants from £500 to £3,000 and holiday gifts are available to help families in times of hardship. Support can be given towards household items, home repairs and alterations, debt repayments, disability aid, utility bills, also holiday expenses and so on.

Annual grant total

At the time of writing (August 2014) the latest financial information available was from 2012. In 2012 the society had assets of £5.1 million and an income of £169,000. Grants to 78 individuals totalled £60,000. It is estimated that £30,000 was distributed in welfare grants. All grant recipients, except for one orphan, were regular practitioners or their dependents. We estimate that relief in need awards totalled around £30,000.

Exclusions

Grants are not normally made towards nursing home fees, loans, long-term assistance or second degrees.

Applications

Application forms (separate for different types of applicants) can be found on the society's website or requested from the correspondent. They can be submitted directly by the individual or a family member and are usually considered in February, May, August and November. Note that applications **must** be submitted via post.

Other information

Support is also given for educational needs.

The Society of Chiropodists Benevolent Fund

£23,000

Correspondent: Honorary Secretary, 1 Fellmongers Path, Tower Bridge Road, London SE1 3LY (020 7234 8635; email: hb@scpod.org)

CC Number: 205684

Eligibility

Members/former members of the society or one of its constituent bodies and their dependents.

Types of grants
One-off grants according to need, usually ranging from £50 to £1,000. Interest-free loans may also be made in appropriate cases.

Annual grant total
In 2012 the fund had assets of £867,000 and an income of £27,000. Grants to individuals totalled £15,500 and included Christmas grants of £190 to 57 members or dependents. A further £7,600 was expended on paying the annual subscription fees of 21 members who were experiencing financial difficulties and has been included in the grant total.

At the time of writing (August 2014) these were the most recent accounts available for the fund.

Applications
On a form available from the correspondent, to be submitted directly by the individual or through a third party.

The Society of Radiographers Benevolent Fund

£2,100

Correspondent: Benevolent Fund Secretariat, 207 Providence Square, Mill Street, London SE1 2EW (020 7740 7200; email: info@sor.org; website: www.sor.org)

CC Number: 326398

Eligibility
Past and present members of the society and their dependents, with a possible preference for people who are in ill health, elderly or incapacitated.

Types of grants
One-off grants towards, for example, stairlifts, re-training, orthopaedic beds, house adaptations, car repairs, healthcare travel costs, long-term residential care, computer equipment and washing machines.

Annual grant total
In 2012/13 the fund had an income of £11,300 and a total expenditure of £2,300. We estimate that welfare grants to individuals totalled £2,100.

Exclusions
There are no grants available for further education.

Applications
Applicants must complete an application form and a financial circumstances form, both of which are available on request from the correspondent or to download directly from the fund's website. Applications can be submitted by the individual or through a third party such as a colleague or relative.

The Trained Nurses Annuity Fund

£13,000

Correspondent: Ms H. M. Campbell, The Princess Royal House T.A.C, Stonecot Hill, Sutton, Surrey SM3 9HG (020 8335 3691; email: enquires@rbna.org; website: www.rbna.org.uk)

CC Number: 209883

Eligibility
Nurses aged 40 or over who are disabled and have at least three years' service. Applications are made through third-party organisations such as Citizens Advice, SSAFA or Care of the Elderly.

Types of grants
Annuities and occasionally one-off grants. Each year beneficiaries of recurrent grants send a short report explaining whether their financial circumstances have changed and whether they are still in need of assistance. Annuities are paid twice-yearly in July and December.

Annual grant total
In 2012 the fund had an income of £16,400 and a total expenditure of £13,200. This was the latest information at the time of writing (July 2014).

Exclusions
No grants for education or house improvements.

Applications
On a form available from the correspondent. These should normally be submitted by doctors or social workers along with a doctor's certificate or by the individual. Referrals may also be made through a third party such as Citizens Advice, Age UK, SSAFA, etc. Applications are considered at quarterly executive meetings and payments are made in July and December.

Metal trades

The Institution of Materials, Minerals and Mining – Benevolent Fund

£37,000

Correspondent: The Honorary Secretary, The Member's Benevolent Trust, 1 Carlton House Terrace, London SW1Y 5DB (020 8299 4905; email: mbt@iom3.org; website: www.iom3.org)

CC Number: 207184

Eligibility
Members of the institute and former members and their dependents who are in need.

Types of grants
One-off and recurrent grants in the range of £250 and £3,500. One-off grants in kind are also made. Grants are for general household needs, furniture, security installations, medical aids and adaptations, clothing, respite breaks and school uniforms.

Annual grant total
In 2013 the fund had assets of over £1.4 million, an income of £75,000 and made grants totalling £37,000.

Applications
On a form available from the correspondent for consideration at any time.

London Metal Exchange Benevolent Fund

£5,000

Correspondent: Philip Needham, Administrator, The London Metal Exchange Ltd, 56 Leadenhall Street, London EC3A 2DX (020 7264 5555)

CC Number: 231001

Eligibility
People in need who are members of, or have been connected with, the London Metal Exchange, and their dependents.

Types of grants
One-off and recurrent grants according to need.

Annual grant total
In 2013/14 the fund had an income of £1,000 and a total expenditure of £5,700. We estimate total grants to the in the region of £5,000.

Applications
On a form available from the correspondent.

Rainy Day Trust

£115,000 (162 grants)

Correspondent: Nicola Adams-Brown, Administrator, British Home Enhancement Trade, 10 Vyse Street, Hockley, Birmingham B18 6LT (01212 371130; fax: 01212 371133; email: rainyday@brookehouse.co.uk; website: www.rainydaytrust.org.uk)

CC Number: 209170

Eligibility
People who are in need and have worked in the hardware/DIY, housewares, pottery and glass, brushware, builders merchants, garden supply and allied trades – normally for at least five years. The majority of beneficiaries are over 60 years old but younger individuals may also be eligible for assistance. The spouse or widower of an employee can also apply.

Types of grants
One-off grants towards, for example, mobility equipment and installation, travel expenses to see distant relatives, TV licences, nursing home and residential care fees, funeral expenses, food hampers at Christmas, household equipment and so on. Recurrent grants for healthcare costs.

Annual grant total
In 2013 the trust had assets of £1.8 million and an income of £139,000. Grants were made to 162 individuals totalling £115,000. These were broken down as follows:

Quarterly pensions	£82,000
Other grants	£22,000
Christmas hamper/grants	£4,500
Telephone grants	£3,800
Holiday grants	£1,400
Funeral grants	£700
TV licence grants	£600

Exclusions
No grants are given to children, or to people working in the steel and motor industries.

Applications
On a form available from the correspondent or the trust's website. Applications are considered at any time.

Mining

Mining Institute of Scotland Trust

£12,500

Correspondent: The Secretary, 14/9 Burnbrae Drive, Edinburgh EH12 8AS

SC Number: SC024974

Eligibility
Members or former members of the Mining Institute of Scotland and their dependents.

Types of grants
One-off and recurrent hardship grants of up to £1,000 a year. Widows of members can receive Christmas and summer holiday grants.

Annual grant total
The trust has about £25,000 available to give in grants each year, for both education and social welfare purposes.

Applications
In writing to the correspondent, in the first instance, to request an application form.

Other information
Schools are also supported.

Motor industry

Ben – The Automotive Industry Charity

£642,000 (2,303 grants)

Correspondent: Welfare Team, Lynwood, Rise Road, Sunninghill, Ascot SL5 0AJ (01344 876770; fax: 01344 622042; email: careservices@ben.org.uk; website: www.ben.org.uk)

CC Number: 297877

Eligibility
People from the UK or Republic of Ireland employed or formerly employed in the motor or allied industries and their dependents. Applicants must have less than £5,000 in savings and be in financial difficulty.

Types of grants
Most grants for household items or essential bills are of less than £500, though grants up to £1,500 are available for larger items such as disability adaptations or specialist equipment. In the past year, the charity has made grants towards essential household items, wheelchairs, adaptations and help towards children's costs such as essential school trips, clothing and specialist equipment.

Annual grant total
In 2012/13 the charity held assets of £19.6 million and had an income of £12.9 million. A total of 2,303 grants were awarded to individuals, amounting to £642,000. Of this number, 2,236 grants, totalling £602,000, were one-off and 67 grants, totalling £40,000, were recurrent.

Exclusions
The charity cannot assist with top up fees for people in care homes, property repairs or improvements (except heating and adaptations for a disabled person), private education costs, private medical costs and medications, or costs associated with bankruptcy.

Applications
Applicants should at first telephone or email the correspondent, providing basic background information. An application form will then be sent, which can be submitted directly by the individual or through a social worker, Citizens Advice or other welfare agency. Once the form has been completed and returned, your circumstances will be considered and the charity will see how best it can help. The next step is a telephone call or a meeting to discuss what the charity thinks it may be able to do to help. Once it has received all the information it needs, decisions on most grants can be made in a few days. For larger grants (over £1,000), however, decisions can take up to a month. The charity can also let you know if there are any other organisations which may be able to help.

Other information
BEN offers free support and advice on a broad range of issues through its welfare team, who operate from three offices across the country.

The charity also runs care centres, more details of which are available from its informative website.

The Society of Motor Manufacturers and Traders Charitable Trust Fund

£6,200

Correspondent: Jenny Wallbank, Administrator, SMMT, 71 Great Peter Street, London SW1P 2BN (020 7344 9267; email: charitabletrust@smmt.co.uk; website: www.smmt.co.uk)

CC Number: 209852

Eligibility
People in need who held 'responsible positions' in the motor industry, and their dependents.

Types of grants
One-off and recurrent grants according to need.

Annual grant total
In 2013 the fund had an income of £199,000 and a total expenditure of £56,000. Payments due to BEN for beneficiaries totalled £6,200.

Applications
In writing to the correspondent.

Other information
During the year, grants were not given directly to individuals by the fund, but rather, they were made payable to BEN (Motor and Allied Trades Benevolent Fund), 'to cover the cost of specific contributions to a number of its

beneficiaries.' The fund's annual report states that:

> Since 1990 under an informal arrangement, BEN have assisted in the administration of trust beneficiaries' income payments. This relationship arose as BEN was able to provide an existing structure within which the suitability for payment of prospective SMMT Charitable Trust Fund beneficiaries could be assessed.

The fund also seeks to help 'young persons where such assistance would enable them to gain employment in the automotive sector.' Therefore, in 2013 the Foyer Federation, a charity that focuses on youth development, received £41,000 from the fund towards an automotive project for 30 beneficiaries. The fund's annual report states that 'the trustees were very pleased with the results of the 2013 Foyer Federation project, and have since agreed to make a further grant to the Federation for a continuation of the project into 2014.'

Vehicle Builders and Repairers Association Benevolent Fund

£2,000

Correspondent: David C. Hudson, Administrator, c/o Vehicle Builders' and Repairers' Association Ltd, Belmont House, Gildersome, Leeds LS27 7TW (01132 538333; fax: 01132 380496; email: vbra@vbra.co.uk; website: www.vbra.co.uk)

CC Number: 225924

Eligibility

Present and former members, and employees of members, of the Vehicle Builders and Repairers Association who are in need, and their dependents. Applicants must have been a member or employee of a member for at least five years.

Types of grants

One-off and recurrent grants according to need.

Annual grant total

In 2013 the fund had an unusually low income of £134 and a total expenditure of £2,200. We estimate that grants to individuals totalled £2,000.

Applications

On a form available from the correspondent.

Other information

The fund is also known as the H T Pickles Memorial Benevolent Fund.

Naval architecture

Royal Institution of Naval Architects

£32,000 (1,740 grants)

Correspondent: Trevor Blakeley, Chief Executive, 8–9 Northumberland Street, London WC2N 5DA (020 7235 4622; fax: 020 7259 5912; email: hq@rina.org.uk; website: www.rina.org.uk)

CC Number: 211161

Eligibility

Members and their dependents who are in need.

Types of grants

One-off grants for a variety of needs.

Annual grant total

In 2012/13 the charity had assets of £9.2 million and an income of £8.2 million. Grants were made totalling £32,000. Grantmaking is a very small part of this charity's activities.

Applications

In writing to the correspondent, to be considered as they arrive.

Other information

The Royal Institution of Naval Architects is an internationally renowned professional institution whose members are involved at all levels in the design, construction, maintenance and operation of marine vessels and structures. Members of RINA are widely represented in industry, universities and colleges, and maritime organisations in over ninety countries. The charity also runs training schemes and bursaries.

Newsagents

The National Federation of Retail Newsagents Convalescence Fund

£10,800

Correspondent: Michael Jenkins, Administrator, Yeoman House, Sekforde Street, Clerkenwell Green, London EC1R 0HF (020 7017 8855; email: michael@nfrn.org.uk; website: www.nfrn.org.uk)

CC Number: 209280

Eligibility

Members of the federation and their spouses. Other people in the retail newsagency trade who are not members of the federation are not eligible.

Types of grants

One-off grants for convalescent holidays.

Annual grant total

In 2013 the fund had an income of £13,800 and a total expenditure of £11,300. We estimate that grants to individuals totalled around £10,800.

Applications

In writing to the correspondent or by contacting the NFRN helpline on 0800 121 6376 (020 7017 8880 from a mobile phone) or emailing helpline@nfrn.org.uk. Applications can be submitted directly by the individual, through a third party such as a social worker or through a district office of the federation. They are considered at any time.

NewstrAid Benevolent Society

£766,000

Correspondent: Sinead Flood, Welfare Manager, Suites 1&2, Thremhall Estate, Start Hill, Bishop's Stortford CM22 7TD (01371 874198; fax: 01371 873816; email: sinead@newstraid.org.uk; website: www.newstraid.org.uk)

CC Number: 1116824

Eligibility

People and their immediate dependents, who have been employed in newspaper and magazine distribution in the UK and who have fallen on hard times. Distribution means people who deal with newspapers and magazines from the time they leave the printing press until they reach the reader. All applications are assessed on their merits but the charity states that applicants should have normally been connected with the trade for a minimum of ten years.

Types of grants

Annual payments and one-off grants for various items including household appliances, special chairs, mobility aids, small repairs and disability equipment. The charity offers interest free loans to home owners in respect of costly repairs, repayable on the sale of their property.

Annual grant total

In 2013 the charity had assets of £8.6 million and an income of £1.8 million. £766,000 was given in grants to individuals for welfare purposes.

Exclusions

No grants for private medicine or school or college fees.

Applications

Initial contact should be made by calling the welfare team or by submitting an enquiry form available to download from the website. The application will then be followed up by a telephone call from the welfare team.

Other information

In 2012 there was a one-off payment of £200 to all beneficiaries to celebrate the 200th birthday of Charles Dickens.

Patent agents

The Incorporated Benevolent Association of the Chartered Institute of Patent Attorneys

£21,000

Correspondent: Derek Chandler, Trustee, 95 Chancery Lane, London WC2A 1DT

CC Number: 219666

Eligibility

British members and former members of the institute, and their dependents.

Types of grants

One-off and recurrent grants or loans according to need.

Annual grant total

In 2012/13 the association had assets of £864,000 and an income of £48,500. Grants to individuals totalled £21,000 and were made for social welfare purposes only.

Applications

In writing to the correspondent, marked 'Private and Confidential'. Applications can be submitted at any time. Where possible, grants are provided via a third party.

Other information

The association also makes grants for educational purposes.

Pawnbrokers

Pawnbrokers' Charitable Institution

£120,000

Correspondent: K. Way, Administrator, 184 Crofton Lane, Orpington BR6 0BW (01689 811978)

CC Number: 209993

Eligibility

Pawnbrokers in need who have been in the business for at least five years, and their dependents. Help is primarily given to people over 60 but assistance may also be available to younger people if there is sufficient need.

Types of grants

Regular payments, Christmas gifts, equipment and one-off grants to meet emergency needs for those on a low income who cannot manage on a state pension.

Annual grant total

In 2012/13 the institution had an income of £100,000 and an expenditure of £126,000. Grants made totalled approximately £120,000.

Accounts had been received by the Charity Commission but were not available to view at the time of writing (September 2014).

Applications

On a form available from the correspondent.

Petroleum

BP Benevolent Fund

£23,000 (19 grants)

Correspondent: Peter Darnell, Fund Administrator, BP Benevolent Fund Trustees Ltd, 4 Woodside Close, Shermanbury, Horsham RH13 8HH (01403 710437; email: peter.darnell@uk.bp.com)

CC Number: 803778

Eligibility

Former employees of BP plc or subsidiary or associated companies and the dependents of such persons.

Types of grants

One-off and recurrent according to need and vouchers. Occasional hardship grants up to a maximum of £750.

In 2012 grants were paid for a variety of reasons including: personal bankruptcy costs; replacement cookers; funeral costs; mobility aids; clothing and household expenses.

Annual grant total

In 2012 the fund had assets of over £1.1 million and an income of £38,000. Of 31 applications received, awards were made to help 14 individuals. Of these five occasional hardship grants were paid totalling £2,000; nine other grants totalled £21,000.

The fund also provides interest free loans. They approved nine new loans totalling £37,000 in 2012.

The 2012 accounts were the latest available at the time of writing (August 2014).

Applications

In writing to the correspondent.

Police

St George's Police Children Trust (formerly St George's Police Trust)

£317,000 (407 grants)

Correspondent: Michael Baxter, Administrator, St Andrews, Harlow Moor Road, Harrogate, North Yorkshire HG2 0AD (01423 504448; website: www.thepolicetreatmentcentres.org/en/cat/stgeorgehome.aspx)

CC Number: 1147445

Eligibility

Children in full time education with at least one parent who was a member of a police force covered by the trust (see 'Other Information'), and who is now deceased or incapacitated due to their work. Young people not in full time education who have lost a police officer parent, but who are unable to earn their own living as a result of having special needs, may also be eligible.

Normally, to be eligible the police officer parent must have donated to the trust while serving.

Types of grants

One-off and recurrent grants towards living costs, holidays, clothing, birthday, Christmas gifts and the like.

Annual grant total

In 2013 the trust had assets of £11.5 million, an income of £909,000 and a total expenditure of £458,000. Grants to 407 children and young people totalled £317,000 excluding support costs.

Applications

On an application form available to download from the website. Applications should be submitted via the police force in which the parent served. This is usually done through the police federation office, the occupational health and welfare department or occasionally the force benevolent fund. Applications are considered as they arrive.

Other information

The following information is taken from the 2013 annual report of St George's Police Children Trust (Charity no. 1147445):

> The St George's Police Children Trust was founded by Catherine Gurney OBE, who also founded the Police Treatment Centres. The trust is based at and operates from offices at St Andrews, the Police Treatment Centre in Harrogate and the two charities have a number of trustees in common.
>
> During 2013 St George's Police Trust changed its name to better represent the aims of the charity to St Georges Police Children Trust. A new more child friendly and up to date logo was designed for promotion and marketing purposes.

The trust covers the following police forces: Cheshire; Cleveland; Cumbria; Derbyshire; Durham; Greater Manchester Police; Humberside; Lancashire; Lincolnshire; Merseyside; Northumbria; North Wales; North Yorkshire; Nottinghamshire; Police Service of Scotland; South Yorkshire; Staffordshire; West Mercia; and West Yorkshire.

Metropolitan Police Benevolent Fund

£151,000 (49 grants)

Correspondent: William Tarrant, Administrator, Charities Section, 10th Floor, Metropolitan Police Services, Empress State Building, Empress Approach, London SW6 1TR (020 7161 1667; email: william.tarrant@met.police.uk)

CC Number: 1125409

Eligibility

Current and former officers if the Metropolitan Police and their dependents, who are in need due to illness, injury, financial difficulties and so on.

Types of grants

Generally one-off grants according to need. Support can be given for bereavement expenses, building repairs and alterations, furniture and other household necessities, payment of debts and so on. Interest free loans are also offered.

Annual grant total

At the time of writing (August 2014) the latest financial information available was from 2012. In 2012 the fund had assets of £3.7 million and an income of £2 million. Charitable activities totalled £1.8 million and can be broken down as follows:

Metropolitan Police Convalescent Home Fund	£1.3 million
Metropolitan and City Police Orphans Fund	£326,000
Officers and former officers (and their dependents)	£151,000

A further £385,000 was provided in 36 loans.

Applications

In writing to the correspondent directly by the individual. Applications are considered throughout the year.

Other information

Since 2008 the fund has been an amalgamation of four former charities (Metropolitan Police Convalescent Home Fund, Metropolitan Police Widows' and Widowers' Fund, Metropolitan Police Relief Fund and Metropolitan Police Combined Fund).

Grants are also made to organisations supporting police officers and their families. Officers are also allowed free access to Flint House – the police rehabilitation centre in Goring.

Metropolitan Police Civil Staff Welfare Fund

£21,000

Correspondent: William Tarrant, Administrator, Charities Section, Metropolitan Police Service, 10th Floor (East), Empress State Building, Lillie Road, London SW6 1TR (020 7161 1667; email: william.tarrant@met.police.uk)

CC Number: 282375

Eligibility

Members and past members of the Metropolitan Police Staff and the Metropolitan Police Authority and their families and dependents who, through poverty, hardship or distress, are in need.

Types of grants

One-off grants ranging between £100 and £3,000. Loans, which in 2012/13 ranged between £400 and £4,700, are also available.

Annual grant total

In 2012/13 the fund held assets of £272,000 and had an income of £40,000. Welfare grants to individuals totalled £21,000. Loans amounted to a further £33,000.

Exclusions

Grants are unlikely to be made towards private healthcare, private education fees, legal costs, business debts or bills that have already been paid.

Applications

On a form available from the correspondent. Applications should be submitted directly by the individual or, where applicable, through a social worker, Citizens Advice or other welfare agency.

Northern Ireland Police Fund

£1.71 million

Correspondent: The Secretary, Maryfield Complex, 100 Belfast Road, Holywood BT18 9QY (02890 393556; fax: 02890 393555; email: admin@nipolicefund.org; website: www.nipolicefund.org)

Eligibility

Serving and retired police officers in Northern Ireland, and their dependents, who have been directly affected by terrorist violence whether on or off-duty. This includes those with serious physical and/or psychological injuries which would be considered sufficiently serious to warrant the award of an IOD Band 2 medical discharge, as determined by an occupational physician. The applicant must also be able to demonstrate that the IOD was a result of the individual being the directly intended target of terrorist attack. Applications are also considered from the families of officers who have committed suicide if a causal link can be established between a direct attack on the officer and their subsequent death.

Types of grants

Regular grants to those on a very low income (£11,273 or below in 2010/11) paid in two annual instalments, usually in April and September. The fund also administers a number of separate schemes for one-off grants including:

- Disability support scheme – to provide equipment or household items which would improve the applicant's quality of life
- Bereavement support scheme – to provide financial support to the dependents and parents of officers who have lost their lives as a direct result of terrorist violence
- Disability adaptations scheme – for those seriously injured who need specialist equipment or adaptations to their homes
- Prostheses/wheelchair grants
- Carers respite breaks – for the primary carers of officers, ex-officers, parents and the widows of murdered officers

- Chronic pain management scheme – for pain management programmes
- Psychological support scheme – to help with the costs of counselling and treatment

In general unless the applicant has no or a negative disposable income grants will not be awarded for items costing £150 or less. Grants from the disability or bereavement schemes are capped at a maximum of £7,000.

Annual grant total

According to the NIPF website:

> Its remit is to provide support to those police officers injured as a result of terrorist violence, and their families, and the widows, children and parents of officers killed in terrorist incidents. The Fund has an annual budget of £1.8m per year for the provision of these services.

In 2011/12 grants totalled £1.7 million.

Despite a request for more current information, at the time of writing (August 2014), this was the most recent information we were able to obtain for the fund.

Exclusions

Once an application has been approved the applicant must wait 12 months before re-applying. Applicants cannot re-apply for the same item if their first request has been declined nor can applications be split into separate parts to avoid the capping of awards.

Applications

In the first instance applicants should contact the fund to discuss eligibility. Once this has been established an assessment will follow. The fund publishes detailed eligibility criteria, limits and application information on their website. Ensure you consult the criteria for the relevant fund before applying.

Other information

The fund was established in 2001 following the Patten Report into policing in Northern Ireland.

Police Dependants' Trust

£750,000

Correspondent: Chief Executive, 3 Mount Mews, High Street, Hampton, Middlesex TW12 2SH (020 8941 6907; fax: 020 8979 4323; email: office@pdtrust.org; website: www.pdtrust.org)

CC Number: 251021

Eligibility

Dependents of current police officers or former police officers who have died from injuries received in the execution of duty. Police officers or former police officers incapacitated as a result of injury received in the execution of duty, or their dependents.

Types of grants

One-off grants in the range of £280 to £21,000, averaging about £2,300 each. Grants are available for specialist equipment, disability aids, clothing, holidays (including support for accompanying professional carers) and funeral expenses. Residential care grants may also be considered to assist with incidental expenses. Annual maintenance grants are given to help incapacitated officers and police dependents enjoy a reasonable standard of living.

Annual grant total

In 2012/13 the trust had assets of £24.9 million and an income of over £1 million. Grants to 190 individuals totalled £890,000 (excluding support costs) and were distributed as follows:

Special purpose grants	£839,000
Children support grants	£51,000

There was no breakdown given of the percentage of educational grants and welfare grants. We have estimated the educational grants to be around £140,000.

Applications

On a form available from the correspondent, to be submitted through one of the force's welfare officers. Applications are generally considered every two months although urgent decisions can be made between meetings.

Post office

The Rowland Hill Memorial And Benevolent Fund

£338,000

Correspondent: Mary Jeffery, Manager, Room 412, Royal Mail, 185 Farringdon Road, London EC1A 1AA (0800 232 1762; email: rowland.hill.fund@royalmail.com; website: www.rowlandhillfund.org)

CC Number: 207479

Eligibility

People in need who have been employed by the Royal Mail, Post Office, Parcelforce Worldwide, Romec or associated companies, for at least six months (full or part-time, not casual); retired employees in receipt of a Royal Mail pension; and people who no longer work for Royal Mail or Post Office and have not yet retired, but will receive a Royal Mail pension when they do. If none of the above apply, you must be able to prove that you were employed by Royal Mail or Post Office Ltd. The direct dependents of such people may also be eligible for assistance. Applicants must have less than £12,000 in savings.

Types of grants

One-off grants of up to £5,000 but usually less than £1,000 for disability aids, house adaptations, hospital travel costs, funeral expenses, medical equipment, essential household items and increasingly, personal debt. Beneficiaries must be experiencing financial hardship due to unforeseen circumstances. Recurrent cost of living grants and help with nursing home fees are also available to older people.

Loans are available to Royal Mail Group employees to help short-term crises and are repaid from salary.

Annual grant total

In 2012/13 the fund held assets of £4 million and had an income of £564,000. Grants to individuals totalled almost £338,000 and were distributed as follows:

Lump sum grant payments	£297,000
Cost of living grants	£33,000
Home fees	£7,500

Applications

Call the free 24 hour helpline operated by Royal Mail (0800 688 8777, selecting option 1, then option 4). A trained advisor will conduct a telephone assessment (approximately 40 minutes in length) to discuss what you are applying for as well as details of income, expenditure and any savings and documentary evidence that supports your application. This includes recent bank statements, details of Royal Mail service, medical evidence and cost estimates, if appropriate. They will then, with your agreement, prepare a report of the case to the fund for consideration.

People applying through a third party such as a social worker or Citizens Advice may apply via telephone or in writing to the correspondent, including as much background information and supporting documentation as possible. The fund also accepts SSAFA Form A and will ask for bank statements.

Other information

The fund's sister organisation is POOBI, the Post Office Orphans Benevolent Institution, which helps Royal Mail families with children who are in need. They can be contacted by calling 020 7354 7130.

The National Federation of Sub-Postmasters Benevolent Fund

£122,000 (49 grants)

Correspondent: George Thomson, General Secretary, Evelyn House, 22 Windlesham Gardens, Shoreham-by-Sea, West Sussex BN43 5AZ (01273 452324; fax: 01273 465403; email: benfund@nfsp.org.uk; website: www.nfsp.org.uk)

CC Number: 262704

Eligibility

Serving or retired sub-postmasters/sub-postmistresses, full-time employees of the NFSP, and the dependents of the above in the event of a breakdown in health, bereavement or domestic distress.

Types of grants

One-off and recurrent grants according to need. Support can be given for a wide range of requirements, for example towards installing equipment in the post office to help the applicant work, holiday expenses for people with disability or those convalescing, for home or car adaptations, specific items or equipment to aid medical conditions or disability, and so on.

Annual grant total

At the time of writing (August 2014) the latest financial information available was from 2012. In 2012 the fund had assets of £1.1 million and an income of £66,000. Grants totalled £122,000, including 18 one-off grants and 31 beneficiaries receiving recurrent assistance.

Applications

Application forms are available from the fund's website or can be requested from the correspondent. They can be submitted directly by the individual or through another welfare charity. Applications are usually considered quarterly, but emergency cases can be dealt with as they arise.

Other information

The fund also provides access to a one on one counselling service with qualified counsellors who offer counselling and emotional support following a traumatic incident in life (such as illness or trauma reaction after an attack/raid) as well as on other issues affecting sub-postmasters, their immediate family members and sub-post office staff.

Printing

The GPM Charitable Trust

£5,000

Correspondent: Keith Keys, Administrator, 43 Spriggs Close, Clapham, Bedford MK41 6GD (07733 262991; email: gpmcharitabletrust@tiscali.co.uk; website: www.gpmtrust.org)

CC Number: 227177

Eligibility

Workers, former workers and their dependents in the printing, graphical, papermaking and media industries.

Types of grants

Grants for household essentials, mobility aids, respite or convalescent breaks, goods services or facilities. Loans for individuals are also available.

Annual grant total

In 2012/13 the trust had an income of £8,100 and an expenditure of £23,000. We estimate that the trust gave grants to individuals for social welfare purposes to the value of £5,000. Further grants were afforded to organisations.

The trust also worked with the Bookbinders Charitable Society on a refurbishment project for sheltered accommodation.

Applications

On a form available to download from the trust's website, or from the correspondent, to be returned by email or post.

Other information

Formed in 2001, the trust brought together the former Lloyd Memorial and NATSOPA (National Society of Operative Printers and Assistants) trusts. The Sheridan Trust, a Manchester-based printing charity, joined in 2010.

The Printing Charity (Printers' Charitable Corporation)

£449,000

Correspondent: Henry Smith, Grants Officer, First Floor, Underwood House, 235 Three Bridges Road, Crawley, West Sussex RH10 1LS (01293 649368; fax: 01293 542826; email: henry@theprintingcharity.org.uk; website: www.theprintingcharity.org.uk)

CC Number: 208882

Eligibility

People who have worked for at least three years in the printing profession, graphic arts or allied trades and their dependents who are in need. A list of eligible trades can be found on the charity's website.

Types of grants

One-off grants of about £800–£900 and recurrent payments of up to £25 per week. Assistance can be given for mobility aids, home repairs and adaptations, household items, nursing or care home top-ups, respite grants for carers, convalescence, bankruptcy fees, people with hearing/sight difficulties, travel costs to and from the hospital, additional care not provided by the NHS, also emergency relief for people affected by natural disasters.

Annual grant total

In 2013 the charity had assets of £36.4 million and an income of £1.6 million. Grants to individuals totalled £449,000 and can be broken down as follows:

Regular financial assistance	£256,000
One-off grants	£184,000
Nursing home grants	£8,900

Applications

Application forms and guidelines are available from the charity's website. Further information on the application process can also be received by contacting the correspondent. Assistance is means tested so applicants should be prepared to make a full declaration of their finances, including state benefits and funding from other charitable sources. Applications can be made by individuals directly or through a welfare agency.

The charity advises potential applicants to contact them before submitting an application.

Other information

The charity also provides sheltered homes for older people at Basildon and Bletchley and gives education and training help to individuals.

Probation

The Edridge Fund

£50,000 (149 grants)

Correspondent: The Secretary, Edridge Applications, 4 Chivalry Road, London SW11 1HT (020 3397 7025; email: office@edridgefund.org; website: www.edridgefund.org)

CC Number: 803493

Eligibility

Members, and ex-members, of the probation service and CAFCASS who are (or were) eligible to be members of

NAPO and their bereaved partners, spouses and dependents.

Types of grants

Financial and welfare support, generally in a one-off grant, to alleviate cases of distress and hardship. Applications are assessed individually and grants are designed to help towards the applicant's specific requirements.

Annual grant total

In 2012 the fund had assets of £175,000 and an income of £62,000. Grants to individuals totalled £50,000.

During the year, the fund received 178 applications, of which 149 were successful. This was the latest financial information available at the time of writing.

Applications

On a form available from the correspondent, a local representative or to download from the fund's website. The fund prefers to receive applications via email. If the applicant is sending the application from a home email, it must be sent to office@edridgefund.org. If it is being sent from the applicant's probation, prison or CAFCASS address, it can be sent securely to edridge.applications@edridge.cjsm.net (this address cannot be used from a home email address). Applicants wishing to send a handwritten scanned copy, must send a.pdf file; otherwise, handwritten applications must be sent by ordinary post.

Applications are usually dealt with by the trustees within three weeks; however, in 'extreme' cases of emergency, decisions can be made much more quickly.

Note: If applicants do not wish their local representative to be aware of their application it should be stated clearly on their form. If an applicant has not received an email or letter of acknowledgement within five working days of submitting their application, the fund should be contacted through its voicemail.

Property and Facilities

Sears Group Trust

£126,000 (139 grants)

Correspondent: Hilary Brookes, Administrator, c/o Capita Employee Benefits, Hartshead House, 2 Cutlers Gate, Sheffield S4 7TL (01142 737331)

CC Number: 1022586

Eligibility

Employees, former employees and their dependents of any company that is, or has been, associated with Sears Ltd, who are in financial need.

Types of grants

One-off and recurrent grants according to need. Recurrent grants are made to top up low incomes and paid in two instalments, usually in June and December. Recent one-off grants have been awarded towards respite care, decorating, window repairs, televisions and kitchen appliances. The trust also owns a number of pieces of mobility equipment which may be gifted or loaned to individuals. Entitlement to recurrent grants is reviewed every three years.

Annual grant total

In 2012/13 the trust held assets of £9.8 million and had an investments income of £378,000. Individuals received a total of £126,000 in 139 grants; 117 of which were annual grants, the remaining 22 one-off. Organisations received a further £7,000.

Exclusions

No grants for bankruptcy or funeral costs.

Applications

Initial contact should be made with the correspondent who will arrange for a visit from one of the trust's welfare visitors. The visitor will assess the applicant and make a recommendation to the trustees. Trustees meet to consider applications two to three times per year; however, applications can be processed between meetings.

Other information

In 2012/13 the trust's welfare visitors made more than 1,400 home calls to pensioners and former Sears employees, to whom they were able to offer advice on applications for statutory benefits.

Public relations

iprovision (formerly The Institute of Public Relations Benevolent Fund)

£2,200 (3 grants)

Correspondent: Ruth Ritchie, iprovision Administrator, c/o CIPR Public Relations Centre, 52–53 Russell Square, London WC1B 4HP (020 8144 5536; email: administrator@iprovision.org.uk; website: www.cipr.co.uk/iprovision)

CC Number: 242674

Eligibility

Members of the institute and dependents of members or deceased members.

Types of grants

One-off and recurrent grants according to need as well as interest free loans. Grants can cover white goods, daily living expenses, unexpected one-off costs, and help can be given towards the costs of respite breaks, etc.

Annual grant total

In 2012 the fund had assets of £756,000 and an income of £53,000. Grants totalled £2,200.

At the time of writing (August 2014) these were the most recent accounts available for the fund.

Exclusions

No grants for CIPR annual subscriptions, business costs or debts.

Applications

Initially contact the administrator in writing, by phone or by email outlining your situation, how you think iprovision could help you. The administrator will then contact you personally, so make sure to include your contact details. You will be asked to complete the application form which is available to download from the website and will be asked to provide some financial details. The trustees meet to consider applications every three months though, if the need is urgent, decisions may be made between meetings.

Note: if you are contacting the administrator by post, mark your envelope 'Private and Confidential'.

Public sector

City of London Benevolent Association

£5,000

Correspondent: Philippa Sewell, City of London, Town Clerk's Department, PO Box 270, Guildhall, London EC2P 2EJ (020 7332 1425; email: philippa.sewell@cityoflondon.gov.uk; website: www.cityoflondon.gov.uk)

CC Number: 206643

Eligibility

People in need who are, or have been, members of the Court of Common Council, and their dependents.

Types of grants

One-off grants according to need.

Annual grant total

In 2012/13 the charity had an income of £10,000 and a total expenditure of £6,000.

Applications

Initial contact should be made with the administrator.

There For You (UNISON Welfare)

£708,000

Correspondent: Julie Grant, Head of UNISON Welfare, UNISON Centre, 130 Euston Road, London NW1 2AY (020 7121 5620; email: thereforyou@unison.co.uk; website: www.unison.org.uk/welfare)

CC Number: 1023552

Eligibility

Financial help given to UNISON members and in certain circumstances former members of NALGO can apply. Partners/dependents of deceased members can apply in their own right.

Types of grants

One-off grants for individuals experiencing unforeseen difficulties such as redundancy, illness, bereavement or relationship breakdown. Recent awards have been given to help with household bills, travel costs, childcare, school uniforms, winter fuel costs, furniture, domestic appliances, funeral expenses, disability aids and so on. Emergency grants are available when there is a crisis and money is needed quickly. For example, if an individual has been forced to leave their home and is in need of food and temporary shelter. Weekly grants for up to 12 weeks may be considered if the applicant is in a temporary period of reduced income, especially if they have considerable debt.

Funding is also available for holidays, convalescence and respite breaks under the charity's 'Wellbeing Breaks' scheme.

Annual grant total

In 2013 the charity had assets of £5.8 million, an income of £1.2 million and a total expenditure of £1.3 million. Grants were made totalling £708,000 and can be broken down as follows:

Short-term weekly assistance	£134,000
Priority debt	£101,000
Household – white goods and furniture	£82,000
Special payments e.g. rent deposits, hospital travel	£61,000
Utilities costs	£55,000
Household maintenance and services	£44,000
Funeral expenses	£45,000
Bankruptcy	£39,000
Wellbeing breaks	£35,000
Clothing	£37,000
Priority payments	£28,000
Disability, health, medical	£27,000
Emergency crisis payments	£12,000
Other debt e.g. childcare	£7,000

Exclusions

Assistance will not normally be given where the applicant has savings of £3,000 or more. Grants are generally not given for educational costs, private medical treatment, legal fees, car purchase or income lost due to industrial action.

Applications

Individuals should first contact their branch welfare officer or secretary who will help them to fill in an application form. Applications are usually processed within two weeks, though urgent requests can be dealt with more quickly, sometimes within 48 hours. People who are having difficulty contacting their local branch may submit the form, available from the website, directly to the national office.

Note that there are separate application forms for welfare grants and wellbeing breaks.

Other information

The charity, previously known simply as UNISON Welfare, provides support and advice on a variety of issues including personal debt and state benefits.

Public transport

The Worshipful Company of Carmen Benevolent Trust

£1,400

Correspondent: Michael Breeze, Hon. Secretary, Five Kings House, 1 Queen St Place, London EC4R 1QS (020 7489 8289; fax: 020 7236 3313; email: carmencompany@btconnect.com; website: www.thecarmen.co.uk)

CC Number: 1050893

Eligibility

People based in the UK who have worked in the transport industry (for example, HGV drivers or bus drivers) and their dependents.

Types of grants

One-off grants usually in the region of £50 to £500, where the grant will make an exceptional difference to the individual, for example, to a disabled person who needed computer equipment.

Annual grant total

In 2012/13 the trust had assets of £1.3 million and an income of £109,000. Grants totalled £58,000, the majority of which was given to organisations. £2,900 was given in five one-off payments to individuals. The trust makes grants for educational purposes as well as for social welfare, though a breakdown of the individual grants distributed was not available in the accounts. We estimate that social welfare grants to individuals totalled £1,400.

Exclusions

The trust cannot help with holidays or bankruptcy fees.

Applications

In writing to the correspondent. Note, this trust only occasionally makes grants to individuals. The trustees meet at least twice each year.

The Transport Benevolent Fund

£538,000 (3,418 grants)

Correspondent: Vicky Jennings, Secretary, Transport Benevolent Fund, New Loom House, 101 Back Church Lane, London E1 1LU (0300 333 2000; fax: 0870 831 2882; email: help@tbf.org.uk; website: www.tbf.org.uk)

CC Number: 1058032

Eligibility

Employees and former employees of the public transport industry who are in need (often due to being sick, disabled or convalescent), their partners and dependents. Only members of the benevolent fund are supported.

Types of grants

Grants are for unexpected one-off situations, where help is not available from other sources. They can be given towards medical equipment, complementary medical treatments (up to a maximum of £250 per twelve month period) and other needs.

Loans are only available to beneficiaries of the Staff Welfare Fund who are able to make repayments through regular deductions from their salary.

Annual grant total

In 2012/13 the fund had an income of £2.6 million and a total expenditure of £2.5 million. Grants to individuals amounted to £538,000. The majority of grants were made from the Transport Benevolent Fund, with £9,000 also paid from the Transport for London Staff Welfare Fund. Grants were distributed as follows:

Hardship	3,274	£513,000
Medical equipment and mobility aids	87	£20,000
Convalescence	56	£5,000
Medical treatment	1	–

A further £873,000 was spent on the provision of services.

Exclusions

The fund is not normally able to assist with dental or optical treatment, funeral costs, short-term absence from work (generally less than two weeks), replacement of possessions or medical operations. Continuing support is not offered except in particular cases (e.g. loans of medical equipment).

Applications

By writing to or emailing the fund with a description of your claim outlining your need, how it arose and how much you are asking for. Applications are considered monthly or when required.

Other information

The fund's website states that:

> The Transport Benevolent Fund (TBF) was founded in 1923 by the predecessors of Transport for London (TfL) to relieve cases of necessity among its members and to meet their needs for convalescence or surgical equipment. The needs of staff today take a very different form, but there is still need, hardship and distress among those who work in the public transport industry (or are retired from it) and TBF is still there to help when things are not going so well.

TBF also manages the TfL Staff Welfare Fund.

Legal and financial advice are also offered to beneficiaries, including in the areas of debt management and bankruptcy.

Quarrying

The Institute of Quarrying Educational Development and Benevolent Fund

£36,000 (6 grants)

Correspondent: Benevolent Fund Secretary, McPherson House, 8a Regan Way, Chetwynd Business Park, Chilwell, Nottingham NG9 6RZ (01159 729995; email: mail@quarrying.org; website: www.quarrying.org)

CC Number: 213586

Eligibility

Members or former members of the Institute of Quarrying and/or their dependents.

Types of grants

One-off grants ranging from £100 to £2,500. No recurrent grants are made although most beneficiaries successfully reapply each year.

Annual grant total

In 2012/13 the fund held assets of £1 million and had an income of £27,000. Grants totalling £36,000 were made to six long-term beneficiaries.

Exclusions

People who are involved in the quarrying industry but are not members of the institute cannot be considered.

Applications

On a form available from the correspondent. Applications may be submitted at any time.

Other information

The fund also supports projects which advance the education and research of quarrying.

Railways

Associated Society of Locomotive Engineers and Firemen (ASLEF) Hardship Fund

£13,000

Correspondent: Mick Whelan, General Secretary, ASLEF, 77 St John Street, Clerkenwell, London EC1M 4NN (020 7324 2400; fax: 020 7490 8697; email: info@aslef.org.uk; website: www.aslef.org.uk)

Eligibility

Members of ASLEF, and their dependents, who are in need.

Types of grants

One-off grants can be given according to need.

Annual grant total

During the year the fund had an income of £87,000 in contributions from over 17,000 members. Grants to individuals totalled £13,000.

Applications

In writing to the correspondent.

The Railway Benefit Fund

£308,000 (607 grants)

Correspondent: Daniel Jaszczak, Executive Director, Electra Way, Crewe CW1 6HS (email: info@railwaybenefitfund.org.uk; website: www.railwaybenefitfund.org.uk)

CC Number: 206312

Eligibility

Active and retired members of the British Railway Board, its subsidiaries and related organisations, and their spouses and children.

Types of grants

One-off and recurrent grants of £100 to £1,500 for funeral costs, disabled facilities, property repairs, utility bills, medical care, long-term sickness and childcare. Grants are categorised as follows:

- Single benevolent grants are one-off grants provided to meet specific needs, for example to provide scooters for the disabled or to meet outstanding bills
- Annuities are paid quarterly to people on a low income
- Residential care grants are paid monthly to 'top up' care home fees
- Grants from the Webb Fund are paid quarterly to assist the parents of underprivileged children
- Childcare grants are one-off payments given towards clothing, footwear, school projects and the initial costs of entering higher education

Annual grant total

In 2012 the fund had assets of £3.3 million, an income of £468,000 and made grants totalling £311,000 to individuals for both welfare and education. Grants for welfare totalled £308,000 and were broken down as follows:

Benevolent grants	342	£206,000
Annuities	177	£85,000
Webb Fund grants	24	£10,500
Residential care grants	2	£5,300
Other grants	62	£1,600

The 342 single benevolent grants were broken down again into various needs:

Funeral expenses	46	£58,000
Equipment for disabled people	42	£43,000
Minor house repairs	37	£42,000
Debts and arrears	53	£31,000
Household equipment	55	£29,000
Convalescence	14	£7,100
Other	95	£19,200

These were the latest set of accounts available at the time of writing (July 2014).

Applications

On a form available from the correspondent. Applications can be submitted either directly by the individual or a family member or through a third party such as a social worker, teacher or Citizens Advice. Applicants must be able to provide verification of railway service.

The Railway Housing Association and Benefit Fund

£84,000

Correspondent: Anne Rowlands, Chief Executive, Railway Housing Association and Benefit Fund, Bank Top House, Garbutt Square, Darlington DL1 4DR (01325 384641; fax: 01325 384641; email: info@railwayha.co.uk; website: www.railwayha.co.uk)

CC Number: 216825

Eligibility

People who are working or who have worked in the railway industry, and their dependents, in England, Scotland and Wales.

Types of grants

One-off grants towards house repairs, care attendants, respite care, essential household items, aids and adaptations and general financial assistance.

Annual grant total

In 2012/13 the association held £26.1 million in assets and had an income of £5.9 million. Grants to individuals totalled £84,000.

Applications

The association has transferred the administration of its grants to the Railway Benefit Fund and potential applicants should contact them directly at: Electra Way, Crewe Business Park, Crewe, Cheshire CW1 6HS – 01270 251316. However, the association is happy to help and advise any individual who wishes to discuss their case prior to making an application.

Other information

The association's primary concern is the management of affordable accommodation for the benefit of older people in need.

RMT (National Union of Rail, Maritime and Transport Workers) Orphan Fund

£150,000

Correspondent: Collin Sharpe, Administrator, Unity House, 39 Chalton Street, London NW1 1JD (020 7529 8291; fax: 020 7387 4123; email: c.sharpe@rmt.org.uk; website: www.rmt.org.uk)

Eligibility

Children of deceased members of the union who are under the age of aged 22.

Types of grants

Grants are made of £12 per week per child under the age of 16 and £12.75 per week per child continuing to receive full-time education between the ages of 16 and 22, payable on the member's death.

Annual grant total

Generally around £150,000 is distributed in grants each year.

Applications

Application forms are available from the local union branch or to download from the union's website. For children over the age of 16 in full-time education an education certificate should also be attached. Applications should be made through the local union branch and must be endorsed by the branch secretary. Grants are made quarterly, in March, June, September and December.

Other information

The fund also provides accident, retirement, death and demotion benefits and grants for union members or their widows/widowers. More details are available on the website.

Removal trade

Removers Benevolent Association

£6,100

Correspondent: The Grants Officer, The British Association of Removers, Tangent House, 62 Exchange Road, Watford, Hertfordshire WD18 0TG (01923 699480; fax: 01923 699481; email: rba@bar.co.uk; website: www.bar.co.uk)

CC Number: 284012

Eligibility

People in need who are or have been employed for a minimum of two years by a member or former member of the British Association of Removers Ltd, and their dependents.

Types of grants

One-off grants, usually in the range of £250 to £750, to help those experiencing a temporary period of financial difficulty due to an illness or other difficulties. Occasionally, recurrent grants may be given.

Annual grant total

At the time of writing (August 2014) the latest financial information available was from 2012. In 2012 the association had an income of £13,400 and a total expenditure of £6,200. We estimate that grants totalled about £6,100.

Applications

In writing to the correspondent. Applications should be made by a member of the company the employee has worked for on behalf of the candidate. They are considered upon submission.

Retail trade

Retail Trust

£878,000

Correspondent: Grants Manager, Marshall Hall, Marshall Estate, Hammers Lane, London NW7 4DQ (0808 801 0808; email: helpline@retailtrust.org.uk; website: www.retailtrust.org.uk)

CC Number: 1090136

Eligibility

People in need who have worked in the retail, wholesale, manufacturing and distribution trades for at least two years if still in the trade, two continuous years if retired, and five continuous years for former retail employees who have moved on to other trades. Dependents and widows/widowers of the above are also eligible.

Applicants who are unsure if they qualify should contact the support line.

Types of grants

One-off and recurrent grants towards disability aids and adaptations; funeral costs; the prevention of homelessness (rent, mortgage arrears and rent deposits); council tax arrears; essential household furniture; food vouchers; the prevention of fuel poverty; (in exceptional cases) bankruptcy and Debt Relief Order fees; and respite breaks. Grants are paid directly to suppliers or other responsible organisations, such as social services, on behalf of applicants.

Annual grant total

In 2012/13 the trust held assets of £31.3 million and had an income of £9.7 million. Grants to individuals totalled £878,000.

Exclusions

No grants are given for private medical treatment, legal fees, most personal debts or for items purchased prior to the application.

Applications

On a form available to download from the website or to complete online. Applications should be submitted either directly by the individual or through a social worker, Citizens Advice or other welfare agency. Applications may be posted or emailed to the correspondent. Case workers who are completing the application on behalf of an individual should, in addition, email a covering letter. On average, applications take four weeks to process if all required documentation is supplied, though in some cases this make take longer.

Other information

Retail Trust runs a helpline for its beneficiaries (freephone 0808 801 0808) which in 2012/13 was contacted more than 23,000 times.

The trust also has sheltered and extra-care accommodation in locations across England as well as a care home in Scotland. See the trust's informative website for more details.

Road haulage

The Road Haulage Association Benevolent Fund

£7,600

Correspondent: Alistair Morrow, Secretary, Road Haulage Association, Roadway House, The Rural Centre, Newbridge EH28 8NZ (01313 334900; email: a.morrow@rha.uk.net; website: www.rha.uk.net)

CC Number: 1082820

Eligibility

Current and former members and employees/ex-employees of members, of the association, and their dependents.

Types of grants

One-off grants according to need.

Annual grant total

In 2012 the fund had assets of £887,000 and an income of £57,000. Expenditure on 'charitable cases' totalled £7,600, all of which we believe was given in support of individuals.

At the time of writing (August 2014) this was the most recent financial information available for the fund.

Exclusions

Grants are not usually awarded towards holidays (unless there are exceptional circumstances).

Applications

On a form available from the correspondent, to be submitted directly by the individual or through a social worker, Citizens Advice or other third party. Applications are considered throughout the year.

School inspectors

HM Inspectors of Schools' Benevolent Fund

£4,000

Correspondent: Clive Rowe, Administrator, Hassocks House, 58 Main Street, Newtown Linford, Leicester LE6 0AD (01530 243989)

CC Number: 210181

Eligibility

Present and retired HM Inspectors of schools in England and Wales and their dependents who are in need or distress.

Types of grants

One-off grants of £500 to £5,000 and loans of up to £10,000.

Annual grant total

In 2013 the fund had an income of £16,600 and a total expenditure of £25,000. We estimate that grants to individuals amounted to around £4,000, with loans also available.

Applications

In writing to the correspondent, either directly by the individual or through a third party such as a friend or colleague. Applications are considered as they arise, should include the applicant's financial situation and, for example, arrangements for repaying loans.

Other information

The fund also provides pastoral support, including advice, for its beneficiaries and at the time of writing is working with the Institute of Education at University of London to create an online archive to highlight the work of HMIS.

Science

The Benevolent Fund administered by the Institute of Physics

£20,000

Correspondent: Simon Kellas, Head of Governance, Institute of Physics, 76–78 Portland Place, London W1B 1NT (020 7470 4830; email: simonkellas@iop.org; website: www.iop.org)

CC Number: 209746

Eligibility

Physicists and members of their family in need, whether members of the institute or not.

Types of grants

One-off and recurrent grants according to need.

Annual grant total

In 2013 the fund held assets of £1.4 million and had an income of £27,000. Grants to seven individuals totalled £20,000.

Applications

In writing to the correspondent, marked 'Private and confidential'. The committee meets periodically through the year although emergency cases can be considered more urgently.

Other information

The fund also provides free access to legal advice; see the Institute of Physics website for details.

John Murdoch's Trust

£4,000

Correspondent: The Trust Administrator, c/o The Royal Bank of Scotland plc, Trust Administrator, Eden Lakeside, Chester Business Park, Wrexham Road, Chester CH4 9QT (01244 625810)

SC Number: SC004031

Eligibility

People in need who are over the age of 50 and have pursued science, in any of its branches, either as amateurs or professionals.

Types of grants

Our research suggests that yearly allowances and one-off grants, on average of about £200 to £1,000, are offered. Awards are given for general relief-in-need purposes not for scientific needs.

Annual grant total

In 2012/13 the trust had an income of £40,000 and an expenditure of 34,000. Our research indicates that the annual total of grants varies but is usually in the range of about £4,000 a year.

Applications

Application forms are available from the correspondent. Grants are normally considered twice a year.

The Royal Society of Chemistry Benevolent Fund

£160,000

Correspondent: Nicola Cranfield, Administrator, Thomas Graham House, Science Park, Milton Road, Cambridge CB4 0WF (01223432484; website: www.rsc.org)

CC Number: 207890

Eligibility

People who have been members of the society for the last three years, or ex-members who were in the society for at least ten years, and their dependents, who are in need.

Types of grants

Regular allowances, one-off grants and loans. Recent grants have been towards essential home maintenance; help with transport costs, household equipment and furniture, school uniforms, care breaks, medical expenses, Christmas bonuses and funeral costs.

Annual grant total

In 2012 the fund had assets of £92 million, an income of £49 million and gave grants totalling £320,000 for both educational and welfare purposes.

These were the latest set of accounts available at the time of writing (August 2014).

Exclusions

Anything which should be provided by the government or local authority is ineligible.

Applications

In writing or by telephone in the first instance, to the correspondent. Applicants will be requested to provide a financial statement (forms supplied by the secretary) and include a covering letter describing their application as fully as possible.

Other information

The society also provides advice and guidance services.

The charity stated the following in its annual report for 2012:

> The approximate value of grants made by the RSC was £0.32m, which is not material in relation to the total expenditure and therefore no analysis of grants is provided in the notes to the accounts, and no grant making policy is disclosed.

The Worshipful Company of Scientific Instrument Makers

£4,000

Correspondent: The Clerk, Glaziers Hall, 9 Montague Close, London SE1 9DD (020 7407 4832; email: theclerk@wcsim.co.uk; website: www.wcsim.co.uk)

CC Number: 221332

Eligibility

Members and past members of the company and their dependents.

Types of grants

One-off grants according to need. Grants have been used for bereavement and funeral costs.

Annual grant total

Welfare grants totalled around £4,000 based on the charity's previous grantmaking activities. The latest accounts were not available at the time of writing (October 2014), as they had yet to be submitted to the Charity Commission.

Applications

In writing to the correspondent.

Other information

The majority of the charity's charitable work is concerned with educational scholarships.

Seafaring and fishing

The Baltic Exchange Charitable Society

£92,000 (37 grants)

Correspondent: Richard Butler, Secretary, Baltic Exchange Charitable Society, Nordic House, 20 St Dunstan's Hill, London EC3R 8HL (020 7283 6090; fax: 020 7283 6133; email: richard.butler@baltic-charities.co.uk)

CC Number: 277093

Eligibility

Employees and ex-employees and their dependents of member companies of the Baltic Exchange as well as companies in the oilseeds trade. Help is usually given to retired or elderly people and occasionally to younger people who find themselves in a difficult situation.

Types of grants

One-off grants usually in the range of £50 to £10,000. Grants have recently been awarded towards physiotherapy, replacement of damaged furniture, plumbing, a new boiler, removal costs, a contribution to care home fees, grave maintenance, an alarm system, a stair-lift and other mobility expenses. Fuel payments were also made during exceptionally cold weather. Recurrent grants are paid quarterly to help with living expenses. In 2013 Christmas gifts were distributed to all beneficiaries. Loans may also be offered.

Annual grant total

In 2013 the society had an income of £168,000 and a total expenditure of £230,000. Grants to 37 individuals totalled £92,000; of which, £69,000 was awarded in quarterly payments and £23,000 in special one-off grants.

Applications

On a form available from the correspondent. Applications can be submitted at any time.

Other information

At the end of the year, outstanding loans to beneficiaries amounted to £347,000.

The Corporation of Trinity House, London

£27,800 (33+ grants)

Correspondent: Graham Hockley, Secretary, Trinity House, Tower Hill, London EC3N 4DH (020 7481 6914; email: graham.hockley@thls.org; website: www.trinityhouse.co.uk)

CC Number: 211869

Eligibility

Mariners and their dependents.

Types of grants

The charity operates 18 almshouses at Walmer, Kent and makes provision for regular payments to up to 60 annuitants. Other direct support is made through occasional one-off grants to former seafarers and their dependents.

Annual grant total

The charity's significant assets are no reflection of the money available for grantmaking which is a very small part of its activities.

In 2012/13 the charity had assets of £166 million and an income of £7.9 million. Grants were made to 33 retired seafarers in financial need at a rate of £676 per year. This totalled £22,300. A further £10,500 was awarded in grants to individuals, some of which was distributed for educational purposes. We estimate this to be around £5,000.

Applications

Enquiries regarding welfare grants can be made via email to the secretary.

Other information

The following information is taken from the charity's website: 'The safety of shipping, and the well being of seafarers, have been our prime concerns ever since Trinity House was granted a Royal Charter by Henry VIII in 1514.'

Today there are three distinct functions:

- The General Lighthouse Authority (GLA) for England, Wales, the Channel Islands and Gibraltar. The remit is to provide Aids to Navigation to assist the safe passage of a huge variety of vessels through some of the busiest sea-lanes in the world
- A charitable organisation dedicated to the safety, welfare and training of mariners
- A Deep Sea Pilotage Authority providing expert navigators for ships trading in Northern European waters

The charity also makes grants to organisations and to individuals for educational purposes. In this accounting year, the charity made awards to organisations totalling £3.4 million.

Fawcett Johnston Charity

£2,000

Correspondent: Lisa Douglas, Administrator, The Town Hall, Senhouse Street, Maryport CA15 6BH (01900 813205; email: maryport.council@talk21.com)

CC Number: 208326

Eligibility

Grants for poor and destitute sailors and ship carpenters and their dependents who live in Maryport, Cumbria.

Types of grants

One-off and recurrent according to need.

Annual grant total

In 2012 the charity had an income of £2,500 and a total expenditure of £2,100. We estimate that social welfare grants to individuals totalled £2,000.

At the time of writing (August 2014) this was the most recent financial information available for the charity.

Applications

In writing to the correspondent.

Fishermen's Mission

£62,000 (1,852 grants)

Correspondent: David Dickens, Secretary and Chief Executive, Fishermen's Mission Head Office, Mather House, 4400 Parkway, Fareham, Hampshire PO15 7FJ (01489 566910; email: enquiries@rnmdsf.org.uk; website: www.fishermensmission.org.uk)

CC Number: 232822

Eligibility

Commercial fishermen, including retired fishermen, and their wives and widows who are experiencing unforeseen tragedy or hardship.

Types of grants

Immediate one-off payments to widows of fishermen lost at sea. There are also other individual grants to alleviate cases of hardship (e.g. provision of basic furniture for impoverished older fishermen). Grants are almost always one-off.

Annual grant total

In 2012/13, the mission held assets of £9 million and recorded an income of £3 million. Welfare payments were made totalling around £62,000.

Applications

In writing to the correspondent or the local superintendent, either directly by the individual or through a social worker, Citizens Advice or other welfare agency. Record of sea service and names of fishing vessels and/or owners is required.

Other information

Grantmaking is a small part/area of this mission's activities. They also have a team of welfare staff who provide advice and assistance to fishing communities throughout the UK. In addition they assist injured or ill fishermen and where appropriate arrange for them to receive enhanced medical attention, and finally, source emergency accommodation and catering facilities where there is no alternative provision.

The Honourable Company of Master Mariners and Howard Leopold Davis Charity

£87,500

Correspondent: The Clerk, HQS Wellington, Temple Stairs, Victoria Embankment, London WC2R 2PN (020 7836 8179; email: info@hcmm.org.uk; website: www.hcmm.org.uk)

CC Number: 1127213

Eligibility

British Master Mariners, navigating officers of the merchant navy, and their wives, widows and dependents who are in need.

Types of grants

One-off and quarterly grants according to need.

Annual grant total

In 2013 the charity had assets of £3.7 million and an income of £98,000. Grants to individuals totalled £175,000. We estimate that grants for social welfare purposes totalled around £87,500.

Applications

In writing to the correspondent. Applications can be submitted directly by the individual, through a social worker, Citizens Advice, or other welfare agency, or by a friend or relative. They are considered quarterly.

Other information

This trust is an amalgamation of four separate funds: the Education Fund, the Benevolent Fund, the London Maritime Institution and the Howard Leopold Davis Fund.

The London Shipowners' and Shipbrokers' Benevolent Society

£33,000 (9 grants)

Correspondent: Richard Butler, Secretary, 20 St Dunstan's Hill, London EC3R 8HL (020 7283 6090; email: richard.butler@baltic-charities.co.uk)

CC Number: 213348

Eligibility

Shipowners and shipbrokers and their dependents.

Types of grants

Annual cost of living grants, paid quarterly. One-off grants at Christmas and during periods of cold weather.

Annual grant total

In 2013 the society had an income of £36,000 and a total expenditure of £61,000. Grants to nine individuals amounted to more than £33,000. Of this, £14,800 was distributed in quarterly payments to beneficiaries and £18,500 was awarded in special grants.

Applications

On a form available from the correspondent. Applications can be submitted at any time either directly by the individual or a family member, through a third party such as a social worker, or through an organisation such as Citizens Advice or other welfare agency. The applicant must provide full details of income and expenditure.

Other information

The society can also provide advice and counselling.

The Marine Society and Sea Cadets

£643,000

Correspondent: Claire E. Barnett, 202 Lambeth Road, London SE1 7JW (020 7654 7011; fax: 020 7928 8914; email: info@ms-sc.org; website: www.ms-sc.org)

CC Number: 313013

Eligibility

Professional seafarers, active and retired, who are in need.

Types of grants

Bursaries, scholarships, one-off grants and loans. Interest-free loans rather than grants are given where the need is short-term and the applicant expects to be earning again.

Annual grant total

In 2012/13 the charity had assets of £21.8 million and an income of £14.4 million. Grants to individuals totalled £1.2 million, although the charity states that 'individual grants given are small and not material within the overall total.'

Exclusions

Recurrent grants are not made.

Applications

In writing to the correspondent in the first instance, requesting an application form.

Other information

Grants are also made to sea cadet units.

Nautilus Welfare Fund

£180,000 (250+ grants)

Correspondent: Mike Jess, Secretary, Trinity House Hub, Webster Avenue, Mariner's Park, Wallasey CH44 0AE (01513 468840; email: welfare@nautilusint.org; website: www.nautiluswelfarefund.org)

CC Number: 218742

Eligibility

Former seafarers with significant career at sea, and their dependents.

Types of grants

One-off grants towards household items, medical expenses, home repairs and adaptations, removal expenses, essentials for independent living or mobility aids. Regular payments of up to £12 a week are normally paid in quarterly instalments to supplement state/employment pensions.

Annual grant total

In 2013 the fund had assets of £22.7 million and an income of £4.2 million. Grants were made totalling £180,000, of which £147,000 was given in regular awards to 250 merchant mariners and the remaining £33,000 was distributed in one-off grants.

Applications

Application forms are available from the fund's website or the correspondent. They can be submitted directly by the individual or through a third party, such as SSAFA. Proof of sea-service, medical and birth certificates, also details of income and expenditure, bills and so on are required to support the application. Requests for funding are normally processed within two weeks. Candidates will usually be visited by the fund's own caseworker from local area or a person from SSAFA.

Other information

The fund also manages the Mariners Park welfare complex in Wallasey, which accommodates independent older seafarers and their dependents in bungalows and flats and older seafarers and their dependents assessed for residential or nursing care in the Mariners Park Care Home. The management and maintenance of this site takes up a large proportion of the fund's income.

The fund is continually developing its holistic welfare service offering advice and other services suited to each individual beneficiary's needs.

There are caseworkers based in Merseyside, Hull/Grimsby (01482 595296) and Southampton/Portsmouth (02380 206769).

The Royal Liverpool Seamen's Orphan Institution

£151,000 (50 grants)

Correspondent: Linda Gidman, Administrator, 2nd Floor, Tower Building, 22 Water Street, Liverpool L2 1BA (01512 273417; email: enquiries@rlsoi-uk.org; website: www.rlsoi-uk.org)

CC Number: 526379

Eligibility

Children of deceased British merchant seafarers, who are of pre-school age or in full-time education (including further education). Help can also be given to seafarers who are at home caring for their family alone.

Types of grants

Maintenance grants.

Annual grant total

In 2013 the charity had assets of £3 million and an income of £279,000. Grants to individuals totalled £303,000 and is given for both welfare and educational purposes. 101 grants were made to individuals in total.

Applications

On a form available from the correspondent or to download from the website, to be considered at any time.

Other information

The Royal Liverpool Seamen's Orphan Institution's most recent accounts from 2013 stated the following:

> In 2013 the charity came to an arrangement with the Royal Merchant Navy Education Foundation whereby they would in future take over the support of beneficiaries in further education. This has resulted in transferring 20 beneficiaries over to the Royal Merchant Navy

Education Foundation leaving a total of 81 beneficiaries for the Royal Liverpool Seamen's Orphan Institution to support as of 31 December 2013.

Sailors' Society

£9,000

Correspondent: Welfare Fund Manager, 350 Shirley Road, Southampton SO15 3HY (02380 515950; fax: 02380 515951; email: welfare@sailors-society.org)

CC Number: 237778

Eligibility

Merchant seafarers and their dependents who are in need.

Types of grants

Emergency grants to ease financial hardship.

Annual grant total

In 2012 the society had assets of £13.5 million and an income of £3.3 million. Educational grants to individuals totalled £1,000. Welfare grants awarded to individuals totalled £9,000. The accounts for 2012 were the latest available online.

Applications

In the first instance a short application should be sent by email to welfare@sailors-society.org.

Other information

The society maintains a network of Chaplains at the various key ports around the world who carry out ship visiting routines and minister to seafarers. It also provides centres and clubs for seafarers and associated maritime workers at strategic seaports.

Sailors' Children's Society

£286,000

Correspondent: Deanne Thomas, Chief Officer, Francis Reckitt House, Newland, Cottingham Road, Hull HU6 7RJ (01482 342331; fax: 01482 447868; email: info@sailorschildren.org.uk; website: www.sailorschildren.org.uk)

CC Number: 224505

Eligibility

Seafarers children who are in full-time education and the families are in severe financial difficulties. Grants can also be given if the seafarer is in a two-parent family but is permanently disabled. Usually, the only source of income for the family are state benefits.

Types of grants

(i) Monthly child welfare grants designed to boost income and enable families to provide basic essentials. (ii) A clothing grant payable per child twice a year, in August and January, to help children start off the new school year and to buy a new winter coat. (iii) Christmas grants to help to buy a special Christmas present. (iv) Educational holiday grants. (v) Ad hoc grants to help with the purchase of essential items such as children's beds, cookers, etc. (vi) Holiday Caravan Scheme: the society provides a week's free holiday to families in one of the seven caravans it owns around the coast.

Annual grant total

In 2012/13 the society had assets of £1.9 million, an income of £570,000 and gave grants totalling £321,000 broken down as follows:

Child welfare grants	£198,000
Clothing grants	£74,000
Special grants	£35,000
Holiday travel grants	£14,000

Applications

On a form available from the correspondent, with details about children, income and expenditure, including copies of relevant certificates, for example, birth certificates and proof of seafaring service. Applications can be submitted directly by the individual or through a social worker, Citizens Advice, other welfare agency, or through seafaring organisations. Applications are considered every other month, beginning in February.

Other information

Previously known as Sailors' Families' Society.

The society has an informative website.

Seamen's Hospital Society

£146,000 (390 grants)

Correspondent: Peter Coulson, General Secretary, 29 King William Walk, Greenwich, London SE10 9HX (020 8858 3696; fax: 020 8293 9630; email: admin@seahospital.org.uk; website: www.seahospital.org.uk)

CC Number: 231724

Eligibility

Current or retired merchant seafarers and fishermen who are in need, and their dependents. Applicants must be seafarers with significant service at sea, except where accident or illness has interrupted intended long-term commitment. They may have worked anywhere in the UK and be of any nationality.

Types of grants

One-off grants can be given towards medical treatment and disability aids/equipment (such as wheelchairs, riser recliner chairs, stair lifts and installation of disabled access), household essentials (white goods, beds, carpets), home repairs and alterations, maintenance costs, utility bills, holidays, convalescence and respite breaks, clothing, priority debts, sometimes funeral expenses and other.

Annual grant total

At the time of writing (August 2014) the latest financial information available was from 2012. In 2012 the society had assets of £7.8 million and an income of £462,000. Grants were made to 390 individuals totalling £146,000, consisting of £133,000 in general grants to 300 beneficiaries and £13,000 in physiotherapy support to 90 people.

Exclusions

Grants are not normally given towards study or retraining costs. Our research suggests that members and former members of the Royal Navy are not eligible. Otherwise, the society states that 'there are no rigid rules about what you can get a grant for. We look at each case individually and assess the overall situation.'

Applications

Application forms are available to download from the society's website or can be requested from the correspondent. They should be completed in conjunction with a caseworker, such as representatives from SSAFA, Shipwrecked Mariners' Society, Citizens Advice or the Fishermen's mission. If you are not already in contact with a caseworker contact the society to arrange assistance. Candidates will need to include full information of sea service and specify details of the support required. The society welcomes informal contact prior to submitting applications to discuss eligibility, need and so on.

Other information

The society supports Dreadnought patients at Guys and St Thomas' Hospital in London as well as running various regional health and fitness programmes for seafarers. It also helps to fund the Seafarers Advice and Information Line (SAIL) (0845 741 3318, admin@sailine.org.uk), which provides advice and information on a wide range of issues.

Grants are also made to other maritime charitable institutions with the same or similar objects (£328,000 in 2012).

The Shipwrecked Fishermen and Mariners' Royal Benevolent Society

£1.5 million (2,313 grants)

Correspondent: The Grants Team, 1 North Pallant, Chichester, West Sussex PO19 1TL (01243 787761; fax: 01243 530853; email: grants@shipwreckedmariners.org.uk; website: www.shipwreckedmariners.org.uk)

CC Number: 212034

Eligibility

Fishermen, mariners and their widows and dependents, who are on a low income, especially those who are over 60 or in poor health. Priority is given to widows with young children. There is a minimum sea service of five years for one-off grants and ten years for regular payments, although this is reviewed periodically to reflect employment patterns. Applicants must be in receipt of all the state benefits they are entitled to.

Types of grants

Mainly regular grants of £676 a year (usually to people aged over 60). One-off grants are available for those who do not qualify for regular support for help towards white goods, beds and bedding, household repairs, rent deposits, utility bill arrears, bankruptcy charges and as contributions towards the installation of stairlifts and electrically powered vehicles. Immediate grants are given to widows and children left in need following the death of a serving fisherman or mariner. Death benefit grants are also given to the widows of life members of the society. Where appropriate, financial assistance may be offered to survivors of shipwrecks landed on the coasts of the UK or Ireland.

Annual grant total

In 2012/13 the society held assets of £25.1 million and had an income of £1.8 million. A total of 2,313 grants were awarded, amounting to almost £1.5 million. Most of these grants were given as regular payments.

Exclusions

Applications for assistance are only accepted from eligible applicants residing in the UK and Ireland.

Applications

On a form available from the correspondent or to download from the website. Applications can be submitted by the individual or through a third party and are considered on a weekly basis.

Other information

The society is one of the largest maritime charities in the UK and administers grants on behalf of some other funds such as the Royal Seamen's Pension Fund, the Hull Fishermen's Trust Fund and a subsidiary charity, the Fleetwood Fishing Industry Benevolent Fund. It manages the payment of grants from Trinity House, London, a fellow maritime charity.

The society also has an extensive network of Honorary Agents, who conduct case work, fundraising activities and distribute grants to beneficiaries around the country.

Secretaries

The Chartered Secretaries' Charitable Trust (formerly known as The Institute of Chartered Secretaries and Administrators' Benevolent Fund)

£68,000 (122 grants)

Correspondent: Elizabeth Howarth, Charities Officer, 16 Park Crescent, London W1B 1AH (020 7580 4741; fax: 020 7323 1132; email: icsacharities@icsa.org.uk; website: www.icsa.org.uk/about-us/charitable-trust)

CC Number: 1152784

Eligibility

Members and former members of the institute and their dependents who are in need, living in UK, Eire and associated territories.

Types of grants

Weekly allowances and regular support according to need, for example towards telephone line rental, white goods, house repairs, rental for emergency alarm systems and TV rental and licences. One-off grants are given for specific items and services, often paid directly to the supplier, including those for clothing, clearance of debts, decorating, property repairs. Loans are also considered.

Annual grant total

Welfare grants totalled around £68,000 based on the fund's previous grantmaking activities. No financial information was available from the Charity Commission's website at the time of writing (October 2014).

Applications

On a form available from the correspondent or to download from the website, indicating full current income and expenditure details. Institute members (volunteers) visit beneficiaries where necessary. Applications can be made throughout the year. Contact the correspondent if assistance in making the application is required. Applicants may be visited by a volunteer.

Other information

The Institute of Chartered Secretaries and Administrators' Benevolent Fund became a linked charity to the Chartered Secretaries' Charitable Trust. Accounts for this new charity were not due at the Charity Commission at the time of writing.

Self-employed and small businesses

The Prime Charitable Trust

£5,400

Correspondent: Pauline Weller, Administrator, Federation of Small Businesses, Sir Frank Whittle Way, Blackpool FY4 2FE (01253 336000; email: admin@prime-charitable-trust.co.uk; website: www.prime-charitable-trust.co.uk)

CC Number: 328441

Eligibility

Members or former members of the National Federation of Self-Employed and Small Businesses Ltd and their family and dependents, who due to illness or incapacity are unable to maintain themselves.

Types of grants

One-off and recurrent grants according to need.

Annual grant total

In 2012/13 the trust had an income of £6,600 and a total expenditure of £5,600. We estimate that social welfare grants to individuals totalled £5,400, though expenditure tends to vary each year. In 2010/11, for example, total expenditure was just over £500.

Applications

In writing to the correspondent.

Social workers

The Social Workers' Benevolent Trust

£31,000 (73 grants)

Correspondent: The Honorary Secretary, 16 Kent Street, Birmingham B5 6RD (email: swbt@basw.co.uk; website: www.basw.co.uk)

CC Number: 262889

Eligibility

Social workers who hold a professional social work qualification and are experiencing financial difficulties, and their dependents. Unqualified social workers may also be considered depending upon the nature and length of their employment.

Types of grants

One-off grants up to a maximum £500 are given for specific debts and other needs.

Annual grant total

In 2012/13 the trust held assets of £211,000 and had an income of £39,000. Grants to individuals totalled £31,000. Of 95 applications received, 73 were successful.

Exclusions

No grants for: daily living costs; social work training; private health care; private education; or private social care.

Applications

On a form available from the correspondent or to download from the website. Applications should be submitted directly by the individual and are considered bi-monthly.

Solicitors

The Solicitors' Benevolent Association Ltd

£812,000

Correspondent: John Platt, Administrator, 1 Jaggard Way, London SW12 8SG (020 8675 6440; email: sec@sba.org.uk; website: www.sba.org.uk)

CC Number: 1124512

Eligibility

Solicitors who are or have been on the Roll for England and Wales and have practised, and their dependents, who are in need.

Types of grants

One-off and recurrent grants and interest-free loans (if sufficient equity is available). They can be used for a wide range of essential everyday needs, including food and heating.

Annual grant total

In 2012 the charity had assets of £16.7 million and an income of £1.9 million. During the year grants and loans were made to 349 individuals. Grants totalled £1 million and loans advanced totalled £612,000, with welfare grants totalling £812,000.

Grants were broken down as follows:

Living allowances	£475,000
Supplementary, leisure, special and miscellaneous grants	£322,000
Educational support	£218,000
Nursing home fees	£16,000

These were the latest set of accounts available at the time of writing (August 2014).

Exclusions

Solicitors who have been considered to have brought the profession into disrepute are not eligible but assistance may be available to their dependents.

Applications

On a form available from the website.

Sport

The Mark Davies Injured Riders' Fund

£23,000

Correspondent: Rosemary Lang, Chief Co-ordinator, Lancrow Farmhouse, Penpillick Hill, Penpillick, Cornwall PL24 2SA (01726 813156; email: rosemary@mdirf.co.uk; website: www.mdirf.co.uk)

CC Number: 1022281

Eligibility

People injured in horse-related accidents (excluding professional and amateur jockeys and those injured in the horse racing industry) and their carers.

Types of grants

One-off cash grants and grants in kind according to need. Grants to beneficiaries vary from less than £100 to more than £40,000, depending on need. Assistance has recently been given in the form of travel expenses, physiotherapy, adapted motor cars, house adaptations and home and stable help.

Annual grant total

In 2013 the fund held assets of £445,000 and had an income of £96,000. Beneficial payments to individuals totalled £23,000.

Applications

In writing to the correspondent at any time. All applicants are visited by a local fund volunteer to discuss their medical and financial needs. A report is then made to the trustees, who will consider whether or not to award a grant.

Other information

The fund's annual report states that:

> Many of the MDIRF applicants do not require financial assistance, they need medical, legal or financial advice or to talk over problems arising from accidents. The MDIRF has access to experts in every field prepared to give their time voluntarily to advise and discuss difficulties faced by accident victims.

The fund has also published helpsheets for riders on its informative website.

The Francis Drake Fellowship

£1,700

Correspondent: Joan Jupp, Administrator, 24 Haldane Close, London N10 2PB (020 8883 8725)

CC Number: 248302

Eligibility

Widows, dependents and orphans of members of the fellowship who have died.

Types of grants

One-off and recurrent grants according to need. There is a sliding scale of grants depending on surplus income. If after general household/living expenses (excluding food, clothing, etc.,) the applicant has a surplus of under £70 per week, grants are £550; if the surplus income is between £70 and £90, grants are £450; between £90 and £110, grants are £350; between £110 and £130, grants are £200; and for incomes over £130, grants are £50.

Annual grant total

In 2012 this charity had an income of £2,900 and a total expenditure of £3,800. We estimate that the total awarded to individuals for social welfare purposes was around £1,700. The latest accounts available at the time of writing (July 2014) were for 2012.

Applications

In writing to the correspondent, requesting an application form. Applications should be submitted through the bowling club's Francis Drake Fellowship delegate. Applications are accepted two years after the date of the member's death.

The Rugby Football League Benevolent Fund

£78,000

Correspondent: Steve Ball, Administrator, Red Hall, Red Hall Lane, Leeds, West Yorkshire LS17 8NB (0844 477 7113; email: rfl@rfl.uk.com; website: www.rfl.uk.com)

CC Number: 1109858

Eligibility

People who play or assist, or who have played or assisted, in the game of Rugby League in the UK or for a team affiliated to an association primarily based in the UK and their dependents. Beneficiaries should be in hardship or distress, in particular, as a result of injury through playing or training, or when travelling to or from a game or training session.

Types of grants

Hardship grants, also donations towards special vehicles and repairs, home improvements, furniture, wheelchairs, gym equipment, computers, hotel accommodation, travel, physiotherapy, home appliances, educational courses and Christmas presents.

Annual grant total

In 2012 the fund had assets of £453,000 and an income of £221,000. Grants to 89 beneficiaries totalled £87,000. Grants were made to individuals for education totalling £9,400; and to individuals for social welfare purposes totalling £78,000.

The 2012 accounts are the latest available at the time of writing.

Applications

In the case of serious injury applicants should notify the RFL Operations Department (Tel. 0844477713 Ext. 6), who will then contact Dave Phillips, the RFL Benevolent Fund Welfare Officer.

Other information

Grants are also made for educational purposes.

Cricket

The Hornsby Professional Cricketers Fund Charity

£49,000 (46 grants)

Correspondent: Revd Michael Vockins, Administrator, Birchwood Lodge, Birchwood, Storridge, Malvern, Worcestershire WR13 5EZ (01886 884366)

CC Number: 235561

Eligibility

Former professional cricketers and their dependents who are in need.

Types of grants

Recurrent grants of around £240, paid monthly, and special payments at Christmas (£700 in 2012/13), in mid-summer or for heating allowance. One-off payments may be given to help with a particular or urgent need. Assistance may also be given towards medical costs and special equipment such as electric wheelchairs and stairlifts.

Annual grant total

In 2012/13 the charity held assets of £447,000 and had an income of £44,000. Almost £49,000 was awarded in payments, which were distributed as follows:

Monthly allowances	9	£25,000
Winter allowances	11	£6,800
Summer allowances	11	£6,300
Heating allowance	7	£6,000
Special grants	3	£3,100
Former WHMF recipients	5	£1,500

Applications

In writing to the correspondent. Applications can be submitted either directly by the individual or by the county cricket club.

Football

The Football Association Benevolent Fund

£31,000 (51 grants)

Correspondent: Richard McDermott, Secretary, Wembley Stadium, Wembley, PO BOX 1966, London SW1P 9EQ (0844 980 8200; email: richard.mcdermott@thefa.com)

CC Number: 299012

Eligibility

People who have been involved in Association Football in any capacity, such as players and referees, and their dependents, who are in need. The fund interprets people involved in football as broadly as possible, although it tends not to support professional footballers, passing their details on to the occupational benevolent funds which they can apply to.

Types of grants

One-off and recurrent grants ranging from £250 to £2,000 are given to meet any need.

Annual grant total

In 2012 the fund had assets of £4 million and had an income of £72,000. Individuals received 48 grants, totalling £31,000. This was the latest financial information available at the time of writing.

Applications

On a form available from the correspondent. Applications should be made through the County Football Associations. They are considered on a regular basis.

Institute of Football Management and Administration Charity Trust

£1,500

Correspondent: Graham Mackrell, Trustee, The Camkin Suite, 1 Pegasus House, Tachbrook Park, Warwick CV34 6LW (01926 831556; fax: 01926 429781; email: ifma@lmasecure.com)

CC Number: 277200

Eligibility

Members or former members of the institute (formerly the Football League Executive Staffs Association) who have worked for a Football League or Premier League Club and who are in need, and their widows/widowers.

Types of grants

One-off grants in particular cases of need, and Christmas vouchers.

Annual grant total

In 2012/13, the trust had an income of £2,000 and a total expenditure of £1,700. We estimate that the total amount of grants awarded to individuals was approximately £1,500.

Applications

In writing to the correspondent. Applications can be submitted directly by the individual or through a family member, friend or colleague.

The League Managers Benevolent and Community Fund Trust

£25,000

Correspondent: The Trustees, League Managers Association, National Football Centre, Newborough Road, Needwood, Burton upon Trent DE13 9PD (01283 576350; fax: 01283 576351; email: lma@lmasecure.com; website: www.leaguemanagers.com)

CC Number: 1016248

Eligibility

Members of the League Managers Association who are in need and their wives, widows and children.

Types of grants
One-off and recurrent grants according to need.

Annual grant total
In 2012 the trust had an income of £8,300 and an unusually high total expenditure of £61,000. At the time of writing (August 2014) these were the most recent figures available for the trust and, due to its low income, it was not required to submit its accounts to the Charity Commission. We estimate that grants to individuals totalled £25,000.

Applications
In writing to the correspondent. Applications are considered throughout the year.

Other information
The trust also helps to raise funds for a number of charitable causes.

Professional Footballers' Association Accident Insurance Fund

£2.2 million

Correspondent: Darren Wilson, Director of Finance, 20 Oxford Court, Bishopsgate, Manchester M2 3WQ (01612 360575; email: info@thepfa.co.uk; website: www.givemefootball.com)

Eligibility
Members or former members of the association in England and Wales who require medical treatment as a result of a specific injury or illness which results in their permanent and total disability to play professional football.

Types of grants
Grants are to provide private medical treatment for all members and for members unable to claim under the terms of the PFA accident insurance policy due to the nature/circumstances of the injury. Grants are also given to meet operation costs which may not be covered by the insurance and free places are available at Lilleshall Rehabilitation Centre. Grants are also available to former members for treatment on injuries received as a result of their playing career.

Annual grant total
Direct expenditure (excluding support costs and legal and professional fees) totalled almost £2.2 million in 2012/13 and can be broken down as follows:

Insurance premiums	£950,000
Medical fees and grants	£650,000
Permanent total disability	£382,000
Lilleshall costs	£168,000
Other costs	£24,000

Applications
On a form available from the correspondent. Completed applications should be returned directly by the individual or by a family member/social worker on their behalf. There are no deadlines and applications are considered as they are received.

Other information
The fund contributes to ensure that all Premier League and Football League contracted players are covered under the PFA's Accident and Sickness Insurance Scheme.

Professional Footballers' Association Benevolent Fund

£519,000 (555 grants)

Correspondent: Darren Wilson, Director of Finance, 20 Oxford Court, Bishopsgate, Manchester M2 3WQ (01612 360575; email: info@thepfa.co.uk; website: www.thepfa.com/thepfa/finance)

CC Number: 1056012

Eligibility
Current and former members of the association in England and Wales who are experiencing financial hardship and are on a low income, and their dependents.

Types of grants
One-off grants in the range of £50 to £2,000 to help relieve financial hardship. Where appropriate, general advice regarding financial management and options concerning further education may be offered. There is also funding available in the event of the death of any member whilst under contract, up to a maximum of £1 million.

Annual grant total
In 2012/13 the fund held assets of £18 million and had an income of £1.3 million. A total of £519,000 was awarded in 555 grants to individuals.

Exclusions
No grants are made for cars, holidays or to set up businesses. Loans are not available to former members and there are no recurrent grants.

Applications
On a form available from the correspondent. Completed applications should be returned directly by the individual or by a family member/social worker on their behalf. There are no deadlines and applications are considered as they are received.

The Referees' Association Members' Benevolent Fund

£5,800

Correspondent: The Clerk to the Trustees, Unit 12, Ensign Business Centre, Westwood Way, Westwood Business Park, Coventry CV4 8JA (02476 420360; fax: 02476 677234; email: ra@footballreferee.org; website: www.footballreferee.org)

CC Number: 800845

Eligibility
Members and former members of the association in England and their dependents who are in need.

Types of grants
One-off and recurrent grants to relieve an immediate financial need such as hospital expenses, convalescence, clothing, living costs, household bills, medical equipment and help in the home.

Annual grant total
In 2012/13 the fund had an income of £12,600 and a total expenditure of £6,000. We estimate that grants to individuals totalled £5,800.

Applications
On a form available from the correspondent. Applications should be submitted directly by the individual for consideration at any time.

Golf

PGA European Tour Benevolent Trust

£299,000 (22 grants)

Correspondent: Jonathan Orr, Administrator, PGA Building, Wentworth Drive, Virginia Water, Surrey GU25 4LX (01344 840400; email: cduffain@europeantour.com; website: www.europeantour.com/tourgroup/benevolenttrust/index.html)

CC Number: 327207

Eligibility
Members and former members of the PGA European Tour and other people whose main livelihood is, or has been, earned by providing services to professional golf, and their dependents.

Types of grants
One-off or recurrent grants according to need. In 2012 grants ranged from £1,600 to £50,000.

Annual grant total

At the time of writing (August 2014) the latest financial information available was from 2012. In 2012 the trust had assets of £1.1 million and an income of £35,000. A total of £299,000 was awarded to 22 individuals (to 9 existing and 13 new beneficiaries).

Applications

In writing to the correspondent at any time. Applications can be submitted directly by the individual or through a social worker, Citizens Advice, other welfare agency or another third party.

Horse racing

The Injured Jockeys Fund

£690,000 (414 grants)

Correspondent: Lisa Hancock, Chief Executive, 1 Victoria Way, Newmarket, Suffolk CB8 7SH (01638 662246; fax: 01638 668988; email: Contact form on website; website: www.injuredjockeys.co.uk)

CC Number: 1107395

Eligibility

Jockeys who have suffered through injury, and their families. Applicants must hold (or have held) a licence to ride under the Rules of Racing, be in financial need and have obtained all state aid to which they are entitled.

Types of grants

One-off and recurrent grants to assist with medical care and to help alleviate financial problems and stress. Grants have included help with medical treatment and equipment, contributions to private medical insurance, wheelchairs, holidays, televisions and emergency cash. Assistance may also be given to help with the cost of education where children have special needs. Interest-free mortgage advances are available.

Annual grant total

In 2012/13 the fund held assets of £33.6 million and had an income of £3.2 million. Grants to 414 injured jockeys totalled £690,000. The major grants categories were as follows:

Regular payments	£242,000
Discretionary grants	£145,000
Physiotherapy and care costs	£95,000
Medical, consultancy and operational	£79,000
Expenses for homes	£52,000
TV and Sky	£33,000
Grants for motoring, tax and insurance	£30,000

Smaller grants totals were also awarded towards holidays and a further £1,600 was given to organisations.

Applications

On a form available from the correspondent. The fund has nine almoners who cover the whole of the UK and visit potential beneficiaries to assess their needs.

Other information

IJF also runs Oaksey House in Berkshire, 'a rehabilitation centre for jockeys past and present, the racing workforce, other sports men and women and those from the local community.' Jack Berry House in Malton, North Yorkshire – the fund's second rehabilitation centre – is due for completion in October 2014.

Racing Welfare

£254,000

Correspondent: Jan Byrd, Administrator, 83 Queensway, Mildenhall, Bury St Edmunds, Suffolk IP28 7JY (01638 560763; email: info@racingwelfare.co.uk; website: www.racingwelfare.co.uk)

CC Number: 1084042

Eligibility

People in need who are, or have been, employed in the thoroughbred horse-racing and breeding industry, and their dependents. Applicants must have worked in the industry for at least five years (with the exception of anyone who has had a work related accident and/or is under 25 years old).

The charity has estimated the overall number of people working in the industry at 18,600.

Types of grants

One-off and recurrent grants and small interest-free loans according to need. Throughout the years the majority of funding has been given in the form of quarterly benefits to the elderly on minimum income; however the trustees' annual report from 2012 notes that 'these payments are increasingly viewed as a blunt instrument with more specific financial grants being the preferred method to address individual need.' Support can be given to help with disability aids and equipment, house adaptations, bedding, clothing, food, medical expenses, car adaptations, drugs rehabilitation, retraining and so on. Grants have also been given in response to sudden, unexpected events such as family deaths, disease diagnoses, assaults or loss of employment.

Annual grant total

At the time of writing (August 2014) the latest financial information available was from 2012. In 2012 the charity had assets of £21 million and an income of £1.9 million. Grants were made to individuals totalling £228,000. The trustees specify that £91,000 was spent in quarterly payments. New loans were made totalling £11,700.

Applications

Application forms are available from a welfare officer at most racing centres or from the correspondent. Candidates are normally visited by the welfare officer before the application is considered by the trustees. Individuals are encouraged to get in touch with the charity to discuss their application and available help.

Payments are normally paid directly to service providers rather than individuals.

Other information

The charity's main activity is provision of support and guidance through its welfare officers based all over the country who offer information and advice on financial issues, diet and nutrition and housing. There is a 24-hour helpline (0800 630 0443) offering the same advice. It also expands its housing services, runs a holiday scheme for its elderly and disabled beneficiaries, continues to fund sporting events and sports centre memberships for those in need, and has a life skills programme at the Northern Racing College and British Racing School for young people between the ages of 16 and 19.

Small number of grants may be made to organisations that offer services to people who work in, or are retired from, racing (£106,000 in 2012).

Motor sport

The Auto Cycle Union Benevolent Fund

£54,000 (58 grants)

Correspondent: Roy Hanks, Benevolent Fund Chair, ACU House, Wood Street, Rugby, Warwickshire CV21 2YX (01788 566400; email: dw@acu.org.uk; website: www.acu.org.uk)

CC Number: 208567

Eligibility

Past and present members of the Auto Cycle Union, and their dependents, who are in need through accident, illness or hardship in England, Scotland or Wales.

Types of grants

One-off and recurrent grants. Loans may also be available.

Annual grant total

In 2013 the fund held assets of £2.4 million and had an income of

£115,000. Grants to 58 individuals totalled £54,000.

Applications

On a form available from the local ACU officer or centre. Applications should be made directly by the individual and include details on current income and expenses. They are considered monthly. In very special circumstances the committee has the power to make emergency payments pending full information.

Other information

A full list of ACU clubs and centres is available on the website.

British Motorcycle Racing Club Benevolent Fund

£8,800

Correspondent: Mike Dommett, CEO, Unit D2, Seedbed Centre, Davidson Way, Romford, Essex RM7 0AZ (01708 720305; fax: 01708 720235; website: www.bemsee.net/ben-fund)

CC Number: 213308

Eligibility

Members of the club and their dependents who are in need, with a particular focus on those who have been injured whilst riding.

Types of grants

One-off grants towards subsistence, travel and, as is the case most often, towards medical care and equipment costs.

Annual grant total

In 2013 the fund had both an income and a total expenditure of £9,000. We estimate that grants to individuals totalled £8,800.

Applications

In writing to the correspondent. Applications can be submitted at any time, either directly by the individual or through a third party such as a spouse or friend.

British Racing Drivers Club (BRDC) Benevolent Fund

£35,000

Correspondent: The Trustees, c/o Rawlinson and Hunter, Eighth Floor, 6 New Street Square, London EC4A 3AQ (020 7842 2000; email: chris.hawley@rawlinson-hunter.com; website: www.brdc.co.uk)

CC Number: 1084173

Eligibility

Members of the BRDC and their families and dependents or persons involved with motor racing generally and their families and dependents.

Types of grants

One-off and recurrent grants according to need.

Annual grant total

In 2012/13 the fund had an income of £21,000. Total expenditure was £38,000. Assets in the previous year (2011/12) were £500,000, but accounts were not required, so not shown, by the Charity Commission for 2012/13. The fund generally supports five or six people a year.

Applications

On a form available from the correspondent including details of income and expenditure, assets and liabilities. Applications can be submitted directly by the individual, by an organisation such as Citizens Advice or through a third party such as a social worker. There are no deadlines and applications are considered at trustee meetings.

Other information

During 2008/09 the British Racing Drivers Club (BRDC) Benevolent Fund merged with the British Motoring Sport Relief Fund and the assets of the latter have been transferred under the control of the trustees of the BRDC Benevolent Fund.

The fund's website states that the fund administrator is 'fully conversant with the benefits available from statutory or voluntary bodies' which illustrates the fund's ability to help beyond the provision of financial assistance.

The Grand Prix Mechanics Charitable Trust

£4,000

Correspondent: Fiona Miller, Administrator, Rawlinson and Hunter, Eighth Floor, 6 New Street Square, New Fetter Lane, London EC4A 3AQ (020 7842 2000; fax: 01896 820264; email: email@gpmechanicstrust.com; website: www.gpmechanicstrust.com)

CC Number: 327454

Eligibility

Past and present Grand Prix mechanics and their dependents who are in need.

Types of grants

One-off and recurrent grants towards medical costs, bills and living expenses and so on.

Annual grant total

In 2012/13 the trust had an income of £249,000 and an expenditure of £151,000. Welfare grants totalled around £4,000 based on the trust's previous grantmaking activities. Accounts had been submitted to the Charity Commission at the time of writing (October 2014) but had not yet been uploaded onto its website for viewing.

Applications

In writing to the correspondent or via the online contact form.

Other information

During 2011/12 a £25,000 grant was made to BEN, the automobile industry charity.

Snooker and billiards

The Professional Billiards and Snooker Players Benevolent Fund

£3,000

Correspondent: Simon Brownell, Administrator, World Snooker Ltd, Suite 2.1, Albert House, 111–117 Victoria Street, Bristol BS1 6AX (01173 178216; email: simon.brownell@worldsnooker.com; website: www.worldsnooker.com/page/AboutBenevolentFund)

CC Number: 288352

Eligibility

Current or retired professional snooker or billiards players who are members of the World Professional Billiards and Snooker Association and their dependents, who are in need.

Types of grants

One-off grants and interest-free loans according to need. Trustees currently prioritise one-off payments on the death of players, payments to cover the private medical insurance policies of those who are ill or have suffered an injury related to the sport and the provision of loans for specific purposes to be repaid over a set period of time.

Annual grant total

In 2012/13 the fund had an income of £84 and a total expenditure of £4,500. We estimate that grants to individuals totalled £3,000.

Applications

On an application form available from the correspondent, including personal and financial details and medical evidence where appropriate. Applicants for loans will be asked to identify how the loan will be repaid.

Stationery

The British Office Supplies and Services Federation Benevolent Fund

£50,000 (250 grants)

Correspondent: The Trustees, 2 Villiers Court, Meriden Business Park, Copse Drive, Coventry CV5 9RN (01676 526048; email: info@bossfederation.co.uk; website: www.bossfederation.co.uk)

CC Number: 279029

Eligibility

Applications are welcome from those who work or have worked in the stationery, office products and office machines sector, and their dependents.

Types of grants

One-off grants according to need are given towards, for example, wheelchairs or property repair. Regular quarterly payments are also made.

Annual grant total

In 2013 the fund had an income of £68,000 and a total expenditure of £57,000. Grants made to individuals for social welfare purposes usually total around £50,000.

Applications

On a form available from the correspondent. Applications can be submitted directly by the individual or through a relevant welfare agency or third party. Applicants will usually be visited by one of the fund's volunteers who will assess their needs and offer support.

Other information

This fund was previously known as The British Office Systems and Stationery Federation Benevolent Fund.

Stock Exchange

The Stock Exchange Benevolent Fund

£683,000

Correspondent: James Cox, Secretary, 10 Paternoster Square, St Pauls, London EC4M 7DX (020 7797 1092/3120; fax: 020 7374 4963; email: stockxbf@yahoo.co.uk; website: www.sebf.co.uk)

CC Number: 245430

Eligibility

Members and ex-members of the Stock Exchange and their dependents.

Types of grants

Annuities and one-off grants according to need. Recent grants have been made for medical equipment, motor repairs and household essentials.

Annual grant total

In 2013 the fund held assets of £22.4 million and had an income of over £652,000. Grants were made totalling £683,000, of which £455,000 was given in pensions to 78 individuals and £218,000 in one-off grants to 12 beneficiaries.

Applications

On a form available from the correspondent or to download from the website. Applications are considered quarterly, on the first Tuesday of March, June, September and December, although emergency grants can be made between meetings. Forms should be submitted two months before the next meeting.

Other information

The fund tries to keep in regular contact with its beneficiaries and is there to offer advice and support if needed.

Stock Exchange Clerks Fund

£82,000 (53 grants)

Correspondent: A. Barnard, Administrator, 1–5 Earl Street, London EC2A 2AL (020 7797 4373 or 01245 322985)

CC Number: 286055

Eligibility

Former members of the fund and former employees of the London Stock Exchange or member firms of the London Stock Exchange, who are in need, and their dependents.

Types of grants

Monthly payments to help with living costs. One-off grants towards medical equipment, mobility costs, household goods and funeral expenses. Most beneficiaries also receive a Christmas food parcel.

Annual grant total

In 2013 the fund had an income of £38,000 and assets of £1.2 million. Grants totalled just over £82,000.

Applications

On a form available from the correspondent. Applications can be submitted at any time by the individual or through a third party. New applicants are visited by the Funds Liaison Officer who will then make a report to the trustees.

Any information concerning individuals who were previously employed in the industry and who may be in need of assistance can be given in complete confidence to either the correspondent or any of the trustees.

Tax inspectors

The Benevolent Fund of the Association of Her Majesty's Inspectors of Taxes

£1,900

Correspondent: Jim Ferguson, Trustee, Room 1/72, HM Revenue and Customs, 100 Parliament Street, London SW1A 2BQ (020 7147 2807)

CC Number: 207206

Eligibility

Current and former tax inspectors and other senior officers in the Inland Revenue who are members of the association, and their dependents, who are ill or in other necessitous circumstances.

Types of grants

One-off and recurrent grants of up to £500 for people on sick leave to help towards the cost of medical equipment, hospital travel and medicines.

Annual grant total

In 2012/13 the fund had an income of £6,700 and a total expenditure of £2,400. We estimate that social welfare grants to individuals totalled £1,900.

Exclusions

Clerical grade inspectors are not normally eligible.

Applications

In writing to the correspondent at any time. Applications can be submitted directly by the individual.

Teaching

Church School Masters and Mistresses' Benevolent Institution

£9,900

Correspondent: The Trustees, 3 Kings Court, Harwood Road, Horsham RH13 5UR (01403 250798; email: info@cssbi.org.uk; website: www.cssbi.org.uk)

CC Number: 207236

Eligibility

Current or former teachers/lecturers and those in teacher training who are members of the Church of England or another recognised Christian denomination and their dependents who are in need.

Types of grants

One-off grants according to need.

Annual grant total

In 2012/13 the institution had assets of £2.5 million and an income of £35,000. Grants totalled £19,800. We estimate that of this, £9,900 was distributed in welfare grants to individuals, with the remainder awarded to individuals for educational purposes.

Applications

On a form available to download from the website to be submitted directly by the individual or a family member. Applications are considered upon receipt.

Other information

Since the first meeting in 1857 when a benevolent fund was established, the CSSBI has supported Church of England teachers who 'fell on hard times'. Today the CSSBI is actively looking for those individuals from all Christian denominations who would benefit from support.

The Headmasters' Association Benevolent Fund

£8,500

Correspondent: Andrew Smetham, Trustee, The Water Barn, Water Meadow Lane, Wool, Wareham BH20 6HL (01929 463727)

CC Number: 260303

Eligibility

The widows and dependents of deceased secondary school headmasters who were members of the association. Help is also given to secondary school headmasters and ex-headmasters who are, or were, members of the association and are in urgent need of assistance. Eligibility is restricted to those who were members of the former association prior to its amalgamation with the Association of Headmistresses in 1978.

Types of grants

One-off and recurrent grants according to need. Loans are also available.

Annual grant total

In 2012 the fund had an income of £18,600 and a total expenditure of £9,000. This was the latest financial information available at the time of writing. We estimate that grants to individuals totalled £8,500.

Applications

In writing to the correspondent. Applications are considered as they arrive.

IAPS Charitable Trust

£5,600 (4 grants)

Correspondent: Richard Flower, Secretary, 11 Waterloo Place, Warwick Street, Leamington Spa CV32 5LA (01926 887833, 01926461508; email: rwf@iaps.org.uk; website: https://www.iaps.org.uk/about/our-charities)

CC Number: 1143241

Eligibility

Members, retired members and the dependents of current, retired or deceased members of Independent Association of Prep Schools (IAPS). Support may also be given to association employees or, with the consent of the directors, anyone connected with education.

Types of grants

One-off grants are available according to need to relieve general hardship.

Annual grant total

In 2013/14 the trust had assets of £710,000 and an income of £67,000. Grants to individuals totalled £11,200. The amount awarded solely for welfare purposes was not specified in the accounts; however it is noted that four individuals were given benevolent grants. We estimate that hardship grants totalled around £5,600. Individual grants are made from restricted funds.

The trustees' annual report from 2013/14 notes that 'the charity has an ambition to increase the funds available for bursaries and in particular to be able to support bursaries for younger pupils.'

Applications

In writing to the correspondent. Applications are considered at termly meetings, although urgent cases can be decided in between.

Other information

In 2012 the IAPS Benevolent Fund and the IAPS Bursary Trust, and in 2013 the IAPS Orchestra Trust merged with the trust allowing to extend its work.

The trust also supports organisations and gives educational grants to school pupils and teachers. In 2013/14 grants to institutions totalled £38,000.

The trust is also known as 'itrust'.

The National Association of Schoolmasters Union of Women Teachers (NASUWT) Benevolent Fund

£331,000 (1,027 grants)

Correspondent: Andrew Sladen, Administrator, NASUWT, Hillscourt Education Centre, Rose Hill, Rednal, Birmingham B45 8RS (01214 536150 (8.30am -5.30pm); email: legalandcasework@mail.nasuwt.org.uk; website: www.nasuwt.org.uk)

CC Number: 285793

Eligibility

Members, former members and their dependents (including of deceased members) who have fallen on hard times because of illness, bereavement, an accident or loss of employment through dismissal or redundancy. Members should have paid a subscription to the union. Note that candidates should have less than £5,000 in savings and investments (though this limit may be waived in extenuating circumstances).

Types of grants

One-off and recurrent grants or interest-free loans can be given according to need. Support is given in monthly grants of £86, holiday grants (£200 for adults and £125 for dependents under the age of 18), convalescence grants of £500, living expenses, for specific needs (for example, household equipment or council tax arrears), also in educational support to schoolchildren (£125 for those under the age of 16 and £150 for those aged over 17). Grants have also been given to people with terminal illnesses to visit relatives, for the services of an occupational therapist to assess disability home conversion needs, for a purchase of a converted vehicle for a member who is paralysed and a monthly grant to a member's widow with no occupational pension.

Annual grant total

At the time of writing (August 2014) the latest financial information available was from 2012. In 2012 the fund had assets of £2 million and had an income of £290,000. Grants to 1,027 individuals totalled £331,000. The accounts further specify that benevolent loans converted to grants totalled £2,700. A total of £7,300 was allocated for provision of benevolent loans.

Exclusions

Support is not available for:

- Private health care or dental treatment
- Private school fees or educational courses
- Assistance with curriculum-based field trip
- Legal fees
- House purchase
- Repayment money owed to friends or family
- Repayment of student loans or student living expenses

Assistance is not given if it would affect the applicant's entitlement to means-tested state benefits.

Applications

Potential applicants should either contact their local association secretary or the correspondent to arrange a meeting with a benevolence visitor. The visitor will complete an application form with the individual and submit a recommendation to the benevolence committee. The committee normally meets monthly to consider new applications; however emergency cases can be processed more quickly.

Other information

Grants totalling £18,000 were also made to 24 NASUWT Federations during the year.

The fund also provides members with access to a money advice service through Payplan, see the website for further details.

The Ogilvie Charities

£1,000

Correspondent: Gillian Galvan, General Manager, The Gate House, 9 Burkitt Road, Woodbridge, Suffolk IP12 4JJ (01394 388746; fax: 01394 388746; email: ogilviecharities@btconnect.com; website: www.ogilviecharities.org.uk)

CC Number: 211778

Eligibility

People who are, or have been, teachers or governesses in England and Wales, and children resident in any London borough who are in need, hardship or distress by assisting with the cost of holidays or days out in the country; accompanied by or unaccompanied by other family members.

Types of grants

One-off grants of £100 to £250.

Annual grant total

In 2013 the charities had an income of £59,000 and total expenses of £35,000. The accounts were not available for viewing. Grants awarded to individuals usually total around £1,000.

Applications

In writing to the correspondent, to be submitted through a social worker, Citizens Advice or other welfare agency. The referring agency may telephone the trust if there are doubts about their client's eligibility. Applications can be considered at any time.

Other information

The charity makes grants mainly to organisations.

Recourse

£64,000

Correspondent: Julian Stanley, Group Chief Executive, Teacher Support Network, 40a Drayton Park, London N5 1EW (020769727535; email: enquires@recousre.org.uk; website: www.recourse.org.uk)

CC Number: 1116382

Eligibility

People working in adult, further and higher education who have less than £6,000 in savings. Applicants must have work or have worked in further or higher education for at least two days a week and for at least one term.

Types of grants

Grants for energy bills, mortgage repayments, food, council tax, childcare costs, house repairs, special needs equipment, care home fees, clothing, white goods, furniture and removal costs.

Annual grant total

In 2013 the charity had an income of £490,000. We estimate that grants totalling £64,000 were awarded during the year based on previous giving.

Exclusions

No grants for student teachers, student loans, private school fees, educational course fees, school trips, unsecured debts, house purchases or private medical treatment.

Applications

Applicants should contact the charity by phone or email in the first instance for an application form. The charity will also provide financial advice.

Other information

Recourse also offers information and advice, telephone counselling and online coaching.

The Association of School and College Leaders Benevolent Fund

£8,900 (28 grants)

Correspondent: Carole Baldam, Secretary, 130 Regent Road, Leicester LE1 7PG (01162 991122; fax: 01162 991123; email: carole.baldam@ascl.org.uk)

CC Number: 279628

Eligibility

Current or former members of the association and their dependents (including dependents of deceased members). Retired employees of the association are also supported.

Types of grants

One-off and recurrent grants are available according to need. Support can be given in cases of serious accident, redundancy, chronic illness, disability or other unexpected circumstances. Single payments are usually made towards treatment or equipment relating to disability or illness and to help with general household needs. Low interest loans are available as well. The trustees also organise holiday gifts and social interactions to elderly beneficiaries.

Annual grant total

At the time of writing (August 2014) the latest financial information available was from 2012. In 2012 the fund had assets of £516,000 and an income of £57,000. Grants totalled £8,900 and were made to 28 beneficiaries.

Applications

In writing to the correspondent. Candidates are normally paid personal visits by the trustees to assess the case.

Other information

The association was previously known as The Secondary Heads Association Benevolent Fund.

Schoolmistresses' and Governesses' Benevolent Institution

£128,000

Correspondent: Sarah Brydon, Director and Secretary, SGBI Office, Queen Mary House, Manor Park Road, Chislehurst, Kent BR7 5PY (020 8468 7997; email: sarah.brydon@sgbi.net)

CC Number: 205366

Eligibility

Women who work, or have worked, as a schoolmistress, matron, bursar, secretary or librarian in the private sector of education. Self-employed teachers may also receive assistance.

Types of grants

All types of help including annuities and one-off grants towards telephone bills, TV licences, household items, clothing, medical needs, holidays and mobility equipment. Grants typically range from £50 to £500. Loans may also be available.

Annual grant total

In 2012/13 the trust held assets of £3.9 million and had an income of £1.2 million. Grants to individuals totalled £128,000 and were distributed as follows:

Annuities	£92,000
General cash grants	£12,100
Household expenses	£7,000
General needs	£5,500
Mobility	£4,500
Holiday and occupational	£3,200
Telephone	£2,100
Television	£1,600
Medical	£300
Clothing	£50

Applications

On a form available from the correspondent, to be submitted at any time directly by the individual or family member. Applications are considered monthly.

Other information

The institution arranges annual visits to beneficiaries from its case manager. 'The beneficiaries are considered to be members of The SGBI 'family' and the visits by the case manager are intended to strengthen the links and encourage a sense of 'belonging.'

Queen Mary House, a residential home which can accommodate around 40 ladies, is run by the institution.

The Society of Schoolmasters and Schoolmistresses

£5,000

Correspondent: Sarah Brydon, Administrator, Queen Mary House, Manor Park Road, Chislehurst, Kent BR7 5PY (020 8468 7997; email: sarah.brydon@sgbi.net; website: www.sossandsgbi.org.uk)

CC Number: 206693

Eligibility

Schoolmasters or schoolmistresses (employed/retired) of any independent or maintained school who have ten years of continuous service, and their dependents.

Types of grants

One-off and recurrent grants up to a maximum of £600 per year. Grants are normally made to retired schoolmasters or schoolmistresses who have no adequate pension, but exceptions can sometimes be made for younger teachers.

Annual grant total

In 2013 the society had an income of £9,000 and a total expenditure of £6,300. We estimate that around £5,000 was made in grants to individuals for social welfare purposes.

Applications

On a form available from the correspondent. Applications can be submitted directly by the individual. They are considered quarterly.

Teacher Support Network

£99,000

Correspondent: Grants Team, 40A Drayton Park, London N5 1EW (England – 0800 056 2561, Wales – 0800 855 088; email: enquiries@teachersupport.info; website: www.teachersupport.info)

CC Number: 1072583

Eligibility

Serving, former and retired teachers or lecturers, and their dependents who live in a household with less than £4,000 in savings and realisable assets and own no more than one home. All candidates should have been assessed by a Teacher Support Network Group debt counsellor and not received more than £3,000 in financial assistance from the group over the last seven years from the date of the application.

Types of grants

One-off grants of between £300 to £3,000 are aimed to help with short-term financial emergencies, including due to illness or injury. Support is given towards a range of needs, for example clothing, removal costs, rent, council tax, utility bills, special needs equipment, funeral costs, also to help stay in or get back to work. Assistance towards household repairs will be considered for those who have retired. Payments are normally made to third parties/service providers, not the applicants.

Annual grant total

At the time of writing (August 2014) the latest financial information available was from 2012. In 2012 the charity had assets of £4.3 million and an income of £1.8 million. A total of £99,000 was awarded in welfare grants.

The charities main focus continues to be help with mortgage repayments, council tax arrears or other items that are fundamentally important to the daily functioning of teachers and their families.

Exclusions

Student teachers are not eligible for financial support and student loans are not made. Grants are not given for private school fees, educational course fees, school trips, unsecured debts, house purchases, care home fees, holidays, white goods, furniture or private medical treatment. Assistance is not generally awarded for non-priority debt.

Applications

Applicants are invited to contact the grants team to discuss their needs and the application procedure. Applications can be made online directly by the individual and are considered once a week, usually on Wednesdays. They are means-tested so financial information is needed, alongside other supporting documentation proving the need (such as bank statements for the last three months, three quotes for the service required or bills/evidence of arrears).

Other information

Grantmaking is just one aspect of the work of this trust. In 1999, it established Teacher Support Line (formerly Teacherline), 'providing day-to-day support for teachers in both their personal and professional lives'. Services include: coaching, counselling, advice, information and financial assistance. Individuals may also be signposted to other bodies for help.

Telecom-munications

The BT Benevolent Fund

£687,000

Correspondent: Mike Pearce, Accountant, Room 323, Reading Central Telephone Exchange, 41 Minister Street, Reading RG1 2JB (0845 602 9714; fax: 01189 590668; email: benevolent@bt.com; website: www.benevolent.bt.com)

CC Number: 212565

Eligibility

People who work, or have worked, for British Telecom or its predecessors (GPO/Post Office Telephones), and their dependents.

Types of grants

One-off grants are given towards: household appliances, disability aids, home adaptations, convalescence, carer's breaks, funeral costs and debt arrears, especially when there is a risk of eviction and small children are involved. Weekly grants are also available to older former employees, and their dependents, who are living on a low income. Recipients of weekly grants are also eligible to receive a £100 one-off Christmas grant.

Annual grant total

In 2012 the fund had assets of £2.8 million and an income of £842,000.

Weekly grants were paid to 204 recipients, with a total annual value of £199,000. Single grants totalled £488,000.

The 2012 accounts were the latest available at the time of writing (August 2014).

Applications

On a form available from the correspondent. Applications are considered when received and can be submitted either directly by the individual or through a third party such as a welfare agency.

Other information

The fund also operates a 'contact scheme' to provide advice and support for BT pensioners who are over 75 years old.

Tobacco

The Tobacco Pipe Makers and Tobacco Trade Benevolent Fund

£214,000

Correspondent: The Administrator, The Tobacco Pipe Makers and Tobacco Trade Benevolent Fund, Forum Court, 83 Copers Cope Road, Beckenham, Kent BR3 1NR (020 8663 3050; fax: 020 8663 0949; email: info@tobaccocharity.org.uk; website: www.tobaccocharity.org.uk)

CC Number: 1135646

Eligibility

People who have been engaged for a substantial period of time in the manufacture, wholesale or retail sections of the tobacco industry and their dependents, who are in need. Both full-time and part-time workers are eligible for assistance. Applicants should have no more than £12,000 in savings/capital (not including property).

Types of grants

Recurrent payments and one-off grants, mainly for household items, television licences and house repairs. Grants are also given to help with winter fuel costs and at birthdays and Christmas.

Annual grant total

In 2012/13 the fund held assets of £6 million and had an income of £433,000. Grants to individuals totalled £214,000 and were distributed as follows:

Pensions and General Relief	£91,000
One-off grants	£40,000
Maintenance grants	£33,000
Welfare assistance	£19,400
TV rentals and licences	£14,700
Christmas and birthday gifts	£14,700
House insurance	£1,100

Applications

Application forms are available from the correspondent or to download from the website. They can be submitted directly by the individual or through a social worker, Citizens Advice, welfare agency or other third party. Applicants are asked to provide details of the length of their service in the tobacco trade, financial position and whether they own their own home. Applications are considered regularly throughout the year.

Other information

The fund was formed in April 2010 as a result of a merger between the Tobacco Trade Benevolent Association, the Worshipful Company of Tobacco Pipe Makers and Tobacco Blenders Benevolent Fund. The fund works alongside other charities such as GroceryAid, the Royal British Legion and SSAFA to help achieve its objectives.

Beneficiaries are visited regularly and are provided with a point of contact.

Travel agents

Thomas Cook Pensioners' Benevolent Fund

£0

Correspondent: Stephen Harvey, Administrator, 71 Station Street, Rippingale, Bourne, Lincolnshire PE10 0SX (01778440683)

CC Number: 1030497

Eligibility

Retired former employees of Thomas Cook and their dependents and the dependents of deceased former employees who are in need.

Types of grants

One-off grants to alleviate hardship, for example, the replacement of worn out electrical equipment or modifications to property to accommodate disability or immobility.

Annual grant total

In 2012/13 the fund had an income of £35 and had no expenditure. There has been no expenditure from the fund since the 2009/10 financial year.

Applications

In writing to the correspondent. If eligible the individual will be required to complete a claim form.

Other information

If eligibility is established for an individual, the fund would consider an application in conjunction with another charity or organisation.

The Guild of Registered Tourist Guides Benevolent Fund

£12,000

Correspondent: Elizabeth Keatinge, Administrator, c/o GRTG, The Guild House, 52D Borough High Street, London SE1 1XN (01980 623463; fax: 01908 625597; email ekeatinge.lake@talk21.com)

CC Number: 211562

Eligibility

Institute registered (blue badge) guides who are in need and have been qualified for at least one year and former and retired guides who have been qualified for five years or more. The dependents of guides qualified for at least five years may also be eligible for support.

Types of grants

One-off grants to relieve need and enable a guide to work. Grants can be up to £700, but are normally between £300 and £400.

Annual grant total

In 2012 the fund had both an income and a total expenditure of £17,800. We estimate that grants to individuals totalled £12,000.

At the time of writing (August 2014) this was the most recent financial information available for the fund.

Exclusions

Grants are not given for debts or private hospital care.

Applications

In writing to the correspondent, including the tourist board with which the applicant was registered, whether any statutory bodies have been approached and details of the specific need. Applications can be made directly by the individual or through a third party. They can be considered at any time. Each trustee has a portfolio of clients and is responsible for checking how the beneficiaries are getting on, sometimes through home visits.

Lifeline The ABTA Charitable Trust

£42,000

Correspondent: Grants Administrator, 3rd Floor, 30 Park Street, London SE1 9EQ (020 3117 0547; fax: 020 3117 0581; email: apatel@abtalifeline.org.uk; website: www.abtalifeline.org.uk)

CC Number: 295819

Eligibility

People who are or have been employed by ABTA members, ABTA itself or other organisations within the industry who are engaged in the sale of ABTA products, and their dependents. In exceptional circumstances the parent of someone working in travel may be helped. Both the parent and the person applying on behalf of the parent will have to be assessed.

Types of grants

One-off and recurrent grants and loans unrestricted in size. Grants have been given for holidays, disability aids, bills, redecorating costs, school uniforms, and so on.

The trust advises on its webste that:

> Whilst we do not help with paying off debts, in exceptional circumstances we may be able to help with priority debts (rent, mortgage, utility bills). But first you must seek guidance from the Citizens Advice Bureau. The CAB can help you plan and budget according to your needs, and provide advice on how to tackle the debts that you have.

Annual grant total

In 2013 the fund had assets of £556,000 and an income of £97,000. Grants were made to 26 individuals totalling £42,000.

Exclusions

The fund generally does not have any restrictions in relation to its grant criteria, except it cannot help with costs arising from the failure of a company.

Applications

On a form available from the correspondent or to download from the website. Applications should be submitted either directly by the individual, through a third party such as a social worker, or through an organisation such as Citizens Advice. They are considered every twelve weeks, although urgent applications can be considered between meetings. There are detailed guidelines available on the Lifeline website, read these carefully to ensure that you attach the correct supporting documentation with your application.

United Nations

British Association of Former United Nations Civil Servants Benevolent Fund

£6,600

Correspondent: John Miller, Clerk and Treasurer, 4 Roebuck Rise, Purley on Thames, Reading, Berks RG31 6TP (01189 422783; email: jbmiller83@gmail.com; website: www.bafuncs.org/benevolent.html)

CC Number: 297524

Eligibility

Former employees of the United Nations organisation or its specialised agencies, and their dependents who are in need. Applicants must be resident in the UK, but do not have to be UK nationals.

Types of grants

One-off grants, grants in kind and loans of between £100 and £500. Grants can be made towards a wide range of needs, including health and convalescence needs, help in the home, living costs, electrical goods, furniture, aids for older people or those who are disabled and assistance towards hospital visits. Loans include those to people who are recently widowed, prior to establishing their pension rights.

Annual grant total

In 2013, the fund had an income of £12,700 and a total expenditure of £6,800. We estimate that the total amount of grants awarded to individuals was approximately £6,600.

Applications

On an application form available from the fund's website. Applications are normally referred to appropriate BAFUNCS registered welfare officer for immediate follow-up. Applications are considered throughout the year.

Other information

The fund is also known by its short title, 'BAFUNCS Benevolent Fund'.

Veterinary

Veterinary Benevolent Fund

£185,000 (49+ grants)

Correspondent: Vanessa Kearns, Administration Manager, British Veterinary Association, 7 Mansfield Street, London W1G 9NQ (020 7908 6385; fax: 020 7980 4890; email: info@vetlife.org.uk; website: www.vetlife.org.uk)

CC Number: 224776

Eligibility

Veterinary surgeons who are or have been on the register of the Royal College of Veterinary Surgeons (RCVS) and are ordinarily resident in the UK, and their dependents.

Types of grants

Regular monthly payments for people living on a low income and one-off grants up to a maximum of £1,000 towards TV licences, telephone line rental, additional heating costs, car tax and insurance, holidays, medical equipment, disability aids and so on. The fund has previously noted an increasing trend towards providing more one-off support with less demand for recurrent grants. Short-term, interest-free loans may also be made to tide beneficiaries over in times of crisis.

Annual grant total

In 2013 the fund had assets of £6.6 million and an income of £541,000. Grants to beneficiaries totalled £185,000 comprising £137,000 in regular payments to 49 individuals and around £47,000 in special gifts, usually at Christmas time. A further £1,000 was paid in loans to two people.

Exclusions

No grants towards:

- Anyone before they have qualified and are on the RCVS register
- The cost of studying veterinary medicine as a second degree
- Business or partnership debt
- Mandatory training courses
- Indemnity insurance
- Private education
- Private medical care or care home fees
- Repaying loans to family and friends
- Improvements and repairs to rented property
- Support to individuals simply because they are unemployed

Applications

Application forms are available from the VBF office or can be downloaded from www.vetlife.org.uk and should be submitted with three months of recent bank statements and other supporting documentation (such as a copy of a letter from the DWP with details of any state benefits received, recent mortgage/rent statement and copies of letters from creditors regarding arrears, if there are outstanding debts). Two references are required. A decision may be made immediately or VBF may request that one of their representatives make a home visit before a decision is reached. In any case, the outcome will usually be known within two weeks of receipt of the completed form.

Other information

Alongside the benevolent fund the charity also runs a helpline, health programme and the Vetlife website. The fund owns four bungalows at Burton near Christchurch (Dorset) which are available 'for deserving veterinary surgeons and their families.'

Watch and clock makers

The National Benevolent Society of Watch and Clock Makers

£140,000 (155 grants)

Correspondent: Anne Baker, Secretary, 18a Westbury Road, New Malden, Surrey KT3 5BE (020 8288 9559; email: sec@nbswcm.org; website: www.nbswcm.org)

CC Number: 206750

Eligibility

Members of the UK watch and clock trade and their widows/widowers and dependents who are in need. Generally grants are given to those with an income below £15,000 although the trustees have the discretion to act outside this guideline if the circumstances permit.

Types of grants

Help is usually offered in the form of quarterly grants (£150 per quarter in 2013), Christmas payments (£200) and 'heating' gifts (£100 in March 2013).

Annual grant total

In 2012/13 the society held assets of £2.9 million and had an income of £106,000. Grants to individuals totalled almost £140,000 and were distributed to 155 beneficiaries as follows:

Grants in aid	£90,000
Heating and seasonal gifts	£48,000
Television licence fee	£1,200

Applications

Applications for grants should be made by contacting the secretary, providing the applicant's full name, address, telephone number and any relevant details. The secretary will then send an application form. Completed forms should be submitted by individuals or, if they require assistance, through a family member, social worker, welfare agency or Citizens Advice.

Service and ex-service charities

Unlike other occupations, the service/ex-service charities have been given their own section in this guide as there are many more charities available and they can support a large number of people. This branch of the sector is committed to helping anyone who has at least one day's paid service in any of the armed forces, including reserves and those who did National Service, and their husbands, wives, children, widows, widowers and other dependents.

These charities are exceptionally well organised. Much of this is due to the work of SSAFA, which has an extensive network of trained caseworkers around the country who act on behalf of SSAFA and other service charities. Many of the trusts in this section use the same application procedures as SSAFA and assist a specified group of people within the service/ex-service community, while others (such as Royal British Legion) have their own procedures and support the services as a whole.

Although many service benevolent funds rely on trained SSAFA volunteer caseworkers to prepare applications, some do have their own volunteers. Alternatively, some funds ask applicants to write to a central correspondent. In such cases, applicants may like to follow the guidelines in the article 'How to make an application' earlier in this guide. Most entries in this section state whether the applicant should apply directly to the trust or through a caseworker. If in doubt, the applicant should ring up the trust concerned or the local SSAFA office.

Some people may prefer to approach their, or their former spouse's, regimental or corps association. Each corps has its own entry in this guide and the regimental associations are listed at the end of this section. Many of them have their own charitable funds and volunteers, especially in their own recruiting areas. In other cases they will work through one of the volunteer networks mentioned above. Again, if in doubt or difficulty, the applicant should ring up the regimental/corps association or the local SSAFA office.

SSAFA is much more than just a provider of financial assistance, providing advice, support and training. It can assist members of the service and ex-service communities on many issues, ranging from how to replace lost medals to advice on adoption. Its website (www.ssafa.org.uk) is an excellent source of reference for the members of the community, giving a wide range of useful information and links. Local SSAFA offices can generally be found in the local telephone directories (usually under Soldiers', Sailors' & Airmen's Families Association – Forces Help) or advertised in such places as Citizens Advice, doctor's waiting rooms or libraries. Alternatively, the central office is based at: 4 St Dunstan's Hill, London EC3R 8AD (0845 241 7141); e-mail: info@ssafa.org.uk; Website: www.ssafa.org.uk).

ABF The Soldiers' Charity (also known as The Army Benevolent Fund)

£4.18 million (6,040 grants)

Correspondent: The Director of Grants and Welfare, Mountbarrow House, 6–20 Elizabeth Street, London SW1W 9RB (0845 241 4833; email: info@soldierscharity.org; website: www.soldierscharity.org)

CC Number: 211645

Eligibility

Members and ex-members of the British Regular Army and the Reserve Army (TA) and their dependents who are in need. Serving TA soldiers must have completed at least one year's satisfactory service, and former TA soldiers should have completed at least three years' satisfactory service.

Types of grants

Grants are made in the following areas: debt relief; mobility assistance and home modifications; annuities and care home fees; war widow and family financial support; and holidays.

Annual grant total

In 2012/13 the fund had assets of £45 million, an income of £12.9 million and a total expenditure of £14.7 million. Grants to individuals totalled over £5.2 million the majority of which was made in welfare grants. We have estimated that £1.09 million was given in educational awards comprising £711,000 in Individual Recovery Plan grants for retraining and £379,000 for bespoke employment advice. This leaves £4.18 million awarded for welfare purposes. Grants to organisations totalled £2.8 million.

Applications
The fund does not deal directly with individual cases. Soldiers who are still serving should contact their regimental or corps association, who will then approach the fund on their behalf. Former soldiers should first contact SSAFA or the Royal British Legion. Applications are considered at any time, but all are reviewed annually in July.

Enquiries may be made directly to the fund to determine the appropriate corps or regimental association. See also, in particular, the entries for SSAFA and the Royal British Legion.

Other information
The charity also gives grants to individuals for educational purposes and to organisations.

Airborne Forces Security (ABFS) Fund

£120,000 (199 grants)

Correspondent: Tracy Miller, Controller, Regimental Headquarters, The Parachute Regiment, Merville Barracks, Colchester, Essex CO2 7UT (01206 817079; email: tracy.miller904@mod.uk)

CC Number: 206552

Eligibility
Serving and former members of the Parachute Regiment, the Glider Regiment and other units of airborne forces, and their dependents.

Types of grants
One-off grants are given according to need, including: clothing, bedding, furniture and household essentials; rent, living expenses, removals; educational needs; monthly allowances; rehabilitation; and so on.

Annual grant total
At the time of writing (August 2014) the latest financial information available was from 2012. In 2012 the fund had assets of £5.5 million and an income of £327,000. Grants were made to 199 individuals totalling £120,000.

Exclusions
Grants are not normally given for repayment of private loans, legal proceedings or fines, and purchase of private cars.

Applications
In writing to the correspondent. Applications are usually made through the Army Benevolent Fund, SSAFA or the Royal British Legion.

AJEX Charitable Foundation

£45,500

Correspondent: Ronald Shelley, Trustee, Shield House, Harmony Way, Hendon, London NW4 2BZ (020 8202 2323; fax: 020 8202 9900; email: headoffice@ajex.org.uk; website: www.ajex.org.uk)

CC Number: 1082148

Eligibility
Jewish ex-servicemen and women, and their dependents, who are in need.

Types of grants
One-off and recurrent grants according to need. Special grants are also made to cover emergencies and exceptional circumstances. Examples of special grants include the cost of stair lifts and electric motor scooters.

Annual grant total
In 2012 the foundation held assets of almost £1.8 million and had an income of £174,000. Grants to individuals for social welfare purposes were made totalling £45,500. The 2012 accounts were the latest available at the time of writing (August 2014).

Applications
On a form available from the correspondent, to be returned directly by the individual or through a third party. Evidence of service in the British army and of Jewish religious status is required.

Other information
The foundation's website provides the following information: AJEX – The Association of Jewish Ex-Servicemen and Women spans some eighty years. Its membership includes over 4,000 individuals who served in the British Army, either during or after the Second World War.

In the 21st century, AJEX has a very important role, focusing on three main areas: remembrance for the sacrifices of the past; help for those in need in the present; and education for the future.

ATS and WRAC Benevolent Fund

£244,000 (371 grants)

Correspondent: The Benevolence Secretary, ATS and WRAC Association Benevolent Fund, Gould House, Worthy Down, Winchester SO21 2RG (01962 887612; fax: 0300 400 1938; email: benfund@wracassociation.co.uk; website: www.wracassociation.co.uk)

CC Number: 206184

Eligibility
Former members of the Auxiliary Territorial Service during the Second World War and members of the Women's Royal Army Corps who served up to April 1992, who are in need, and their dependents.

Types of grants
One-off grants generally up to £600, though requests for larger grants may be considered. The fund can also help with making up the shortfall for nursing home fees (2012/13 – £35 per week) and supports some annuitants who receive regular payments throughout the year.

Note the following from the fund's 2012/13 annual report: 'There is no minimum service requirement that would bar an applicant from receiving help, although the Trustees do set guidelines based on service to ensure that the funds continue to meet demand.'

Annual grant total
In 2012/13 the fund held assets of £6.1 million and had an income of £326,000. Grants to 371 individuals amounted to £244,000 and were distributed as follows:

Benevolent Fund	355	£223,000
Princess Royal's Memorial Fund	16	£21,000

During the year, of 420 applications received, 355 met the criteria for assistance.

Applications
All applications for financial assistance should go through the Soldiers, Sailors, Airman and Families Association (SSAFA) or the Royal British Legion caseworkers who will visit the applicants and submit whatever forms are necessary. Grants are distributed through these agencies.

Other information
If you feel that you might qualify for financial assistance, apply to your local Royal British Legion or SSAFA office in the first instance.

The Black Watch Association

£75,000

Correspondent: The Trustees, 6 Atholl Crescent, Perth PH2 6ST (01738 623214; email: bwassociation@btconnect.com; website: www.theblackwatch.co.uk)

SC Number: SC016423

Eligibility
Serving and retired soldiers of the regiment, their wives, widows and families.

Types of grants

One-off grants towards rent arrears, clothing, household equipment, funeral expenses and mobility aids. Support is also given towards holidays for widows and dependent children and former members of the regiment in necessitous circumstances.

Annual grant total

In 2013 the association had an income of £153,000 and an expenditure of £165,000. Grants totalled approximately £75,000 for welfare purposes.

Exclusions

No grants towards council tax arrears, loans or large debts.

Applications

On an application form to be completed by a caseworker from SSAFA (19 Queen Elizabeth Street, London SE1 2LP; Tel: 0845 130 0975; Website: www.ssafa.org.uk). Applications are considered throughout the year.

Blind Veterans UK

Correspondent: Ian Whitehead, Director of Finance and IS, 12–14 Harcourt Street, London W1H 4HD (020 7723 5021; fax: 020 7262 6199; email: enquiries@blindveterans.org.uk; website: www.blindveterans.org.uk)

CC Number: 216227

Eligibility

Eligibility for membership takes into account both military service and sight loss:

- All applicants must have served at any time in the Regular or Reserve UK Armed Forces, or in the Merchant Navy during World War Two, or in the Polish/Indian Forces under British Command
- The trust uses its own criteria for the level of sight loss required to receive help and the charity's doctors will assess this. The website advises that 'it doesn't matter how or when your sight loss was caused, or whether you were on active service at the time'

Types of grants

Grants are given to allow applicants to develop their independence by a combination of training, rehabilitation, holiday and respite care. An annual support grant is given to all beneficiaries and further assistance is available for specific needs, such as help in the garden, a domestic help allowance, healthcare needs, nursing home fees, also for specialist equipment, computers and other technology, reading aid, mobility support and so on. The charity will also help with retraining and employability issues.

Annual grant total

In 2012/13 the charity held assets of £145 million and had an income of £24 million. A total of about £22 million was spent on charitable activities. The amount awarded in grants to individuals was not specified, as the trust has informed us that they do not record these figures separately. Grants may have been awarded out of any of the following categories of charitable expenditure:

Category	Total expenditure*
Care centre activities	£10.9 million
Independent living assistance	£4.5 million
Welfare services	£3.3 million
Housing provision	£2.4 million
Recruitment of beneficiaries and communications	£654,000

**Note these figures denote total charitable expenditure less staff costs and depreciation.*

The trustees' annual report from 2012/13 states that in 2013/14 they plan to 'process 500 grants to 1,800 members and other beneficiaries to the value of £1.2 million.'

Exclusions

The charity can only assist those with a severe level of sight loss.

Applications

Application forms are available on the charity's website or from the admissions department. The application must include details of the applicant's service (including service number and dates of service) and details of their ophthalmic consultant. On receipt the trust will contact the respective service office and ophthalmic consultant for reports. The process can take about ten weeks.

All applicants are encouraged to get in touch with the charity to discuss their needs (free line 0800 389 7979).

Other information

The charity was previously known as St Dunstan's. Its activities cover four main areas: help and training for independent living; care centre activities; welfare services; and housing provision. Lifelong support and advice are offered to beneficiaries and their families. There are three centres in Brighton, Sheffield and Llandudno which provide rehabilitation and training to individuals learning to cope with blindness. The Brighton and Llandudno centres also serve as nursing, residential and respite care centres.

This charity also administers the Diana Gubbay Trust which exists for the benefit of men and women in the Emergency Services (Police, Fire and Ambulance) who suffer severe loss of sight whilst on duty. The ophthalmic criteria are the same as for Blind Veterans UK.

British Limbless Ex-Service Men's Association (BLESMA)

£392,000

Correspondent: Linda Williams, Membership Grants Assistant, Frankland Moore House, 185–187 High Road, Chadwell Heath, Romford, Essex RM6 6NA (020 8590 1124; fax: 020 8599 2932; email: headquarters@blesma.org; website: www.blesma.org)

CC Number: 1084189

Eligibility

Serving and ex-serving members of HM or auxiliary forces who have lost a limb or eye or have a permanent loss of speech, hearing or sight, and their widows/widowers. Despite the association's name, it serves members of both sexes.

Types of grants

One-off and recurrent grants towards, for example, wheelchairs and Electric Propelled Vehicles, stair lifts, car adaptations and gardening costs.

Annual grant total

In 2013 the association had assets of £23.4 million and an income of £3.4 million. Welfare grants were made totalling £392,000.

Applications

On a form available from the correspondent. Applications can be submitted at any time, either directly by the individual or through their local BLESMA representative, SSAFA, Citizens Advice or similar welfare agency.

Other information

The association provides permanent residential and respite accommodation through its two nursing and residential care homes at Blackpool and Crieff in Perthshire.

The Burma Star Association

£142,000 (235 grants)

Correspondent: Glynis Longhurst, Treasurer, 34 Grosvenor Gardens, London SW1W 0DH (020 7823 4273; email: burmastar@btconnect.com; website: www.burmastar.org.uk)

CC Number: 1043040

Eligibility

People who were awarded the Burma Star Campaign Medal (or the Pacific Star with Burma clasp) during the Second

World War, and their immediate dependents, who live in the UK, Republic of Ireland or other Commonwealth country.

Types of grants

One-off grants usually in the range of £200 to £1,000 towards: top-up fees for nursing, care and residential homes; respite care and holidays; domestic goods; debts; disability aids; funeral expenses; repairs and adaptations; travel costs; mobility aids and so on.

Annual grant total

In 2013 the association had assets of £977,000 and an income of £145,000. Grants to 235 individuals totalled around £142,000 and can be broken down as follows:

Nursing and residential homes	£78,000
Repairs	£21,000
Stairlifts and riser-recliner chairs	£15,200
Debts	£7,400
Aid for veterans overseas	£5,000
Local benevolence work	£3,800
Household goods	£3,100
Wheelchairs/EPVs	£3,000
Personal aids	£1,900
Communication aids	£1,400
Respite care	£1,300

Exclusions

No grants are available towards private medical treatment, headstones or plaques. The association does not give loans.

Applications

On an application form available from the correspondent or a local branch officer. Applications can be made by the individual or through a third party. They should either be sent directly to the correspondent or submitted via branches of the association or other ex-service organisations. Grants are made through the local branches, SSAFA, the Royal British Legion or other ex-service organisations after investigation and completion of an application form giving full particulars of circumstances and eligibility (including service particulars verifying the award of the Burma Star). Applications are considered throughout the year.

Other information

The association has 73 branches across the UK and 7 overseas, which offer support and advice to their local members and make small grants where possible. The contact details for local branch officers can be obtained from the correspondent.

The Commandos' Benevolent Fund

£35,000

Correspondent: Michael Copland, Honorary Treasurer, Old Pinkneys, Lee Lane, Maidenhead SL6 6PE (01628 630375; email: mandlcopland@yahoo.co.uk; website: commandosbenevolentfund.org.uk/)

CC Number: 229631

Eligibility

People who served with the Army Commandos during the Second World War, and their dependents. Unfortunately service with any other commando group does not make people eligible for help from this fund.

Types of grants

One-off grants towards, hospital transport, household bills, stair-lifts, flooding costs, holidays, respite breaks, removal expenses, home adaptations, medical costs, funeral expenses and so on. The fund states that it will consider all applications on a case by case basis.

Annual grant total

In 2012 the fund had an income of £39,000 and a total expenditure of £45,000. Grants to individuals totalled £35,000.

At the time of writing (August 2014) this was the most recent grants information available for the fund.

Applications

In writing, with service details, to the Assistant Secretary, PO Box 104, Selby, Yorkshire YO8 5YY: or on a form available from the website. Applications can be submitted directly by the individual or through a social worker, Citizens Advice or other welfare agency such as SSAFA. Applications should include appropriate documentation such as estimates for goods or services. Applications are considered as soon as possible after receipt.

W. J. and Mrs C. G. Dunnachie's Charitable Trust

£80,000

Correspondent: Trust Administrator, c/o Low Beaton Richmond, Sterling House, 20 Renfield Street, Glasgow G2 5AP (01412 218931; fax: 01412 484411; email: murdoch@lbr-city.demon.co.uk)

SC Number: SC015981

Eligibility

People who are in poor health or who have a disability as a result of their service during the Second World War.

Types of grants

One-off and recurrent grants according to need.

Annual grant total

In 2012/13 the trust had an income of £85,000 and a total expenditure of £93,000. We estimate that grants to individuals totalled £80,000.

Applications

In writing to the correspondent at any time. Most applications are submitted via SSAFA or through a regimental association.

The Hampshire and Isle of Wight Military Aid Fund (1903)

£19,000

Correspondent: Lt Col Colin Bulleid, Secretary, Serle's House, Southgate Street, Winchester, Hampshire SO23 9EG (01263 852933; email: secretary@hantsMAF.org; website: www.hantsmaf.org)

CC Number: 202363

Eligibility

Members, or former members, of the British Army (whether regular, territorial, militia, yeomanry or volunteer), and their dependents, who are in need, and who are, or were:
a) Members or former members of any Regiment or Corps raised in Hampshire.
b) Members or former members of The Princess of Wales's Royal Regiment (Queen's and Royal Hampshire's) who were resident in Hampshire at the time of their enlistment.

Territorial Army soldiers must have had at least four years of service with a TA unit in Hampshire or operational service.

Types of grants

One-off grants for services or items such as:

- Rent arrears
- Debts/bankruptcy
- Repairs/heating
- Nursing home fees
- Funeral costs
- Respite care/holiday
- Removals/house deposit
- Travel costs

Or for meeting physical needs through modifications to the home or an electrically powered vehicle. Beneficiaries have received help with:

- Stair-lifts
- Riser chairs/beds
- EPVs

- Showers
- White goods
- Carpets

Annual grant total

In 2012 the fund had an income of over £40,000 and a total expenditure of £53,000. This was the latest financial information available at the time of writing (August 2014). Based on previous research we estimate that grants to individuals totalled around £19,000.

Applications

The fund should not normally be approached directly. The following information is taken from the charity's website:

> Access to assistance from the Hampshire and Isle of Wight Military Aid Fund is via a report from either SSAFA or The Royal British Legion.
>
> You can find the contact details for your regional office on their websites: www.ssafa.org.uk/or www.britishlegion.org.uk
>
> If you are living Hampshire at the moment, use the contact details below:
>
> **Hampshire SSAFA** Tel: 02380 704978 email: secretary@hampshiressafa.org.uk
>
> **The Royal British Legion Regional Office Hampshire** Tel: 02380 620900 Fax: 02380 620900 email: hampshire@britishlegion.org.uk.

Other information

The fund also distributes grants and monthly allowances on behalf of the Army Benevolent Fund for nursing home top up fees and support for individuals on a low income staying in their own homes.

Help for Heroes

£900,000 (6,810 grants)

Correspondent: Grants Team, Administrator, 14 Parker's Close, Downton Business Park, Downton, Salisbury, Wiltshire SP5 3RB (01980 844354; email: grants@helpforheroes.org.uk; website: www.helpforheroes.org.uk)

CC Number: 1120920, SC044984

Eligibility

Current and former members of the armed forces who have been wounded or injured while serving, and their dependents.

Types of grants

Grants towards equipment, facilities or services to assist the individual's rehabilitation. Individuals are supported through Quick Reaction Fund (QRF) and Individual Recovery Plan (IPR). Support towards specialist sports equipment can also be given from the Battle Back Fund. Help can be provided towards accessibility aids, travel costs, specialist equipment or similar needs. QRF support is aimed to be provided within 72 hours in urgent cases.

Annual grant total

In 2012/13 the charity had assets of £107.8 million and an income of £29.4 million. During the year a total of 6,810 individuals were supported in the following categories:

IPR	£900,000
QRF	£500,000
Battle Back	£400,000

We estimate that around £900,000 was awarded for welfare needs.

Applications

Candidates are encouraged to contact the correspondent to discuss their needs and application procedure.

Other information

The charity works with the armed forces and other military charities. Funding is also given for training and educational needs and to organisations working for the benefit of members of the armed forces.

Individuals and their families or carers are also welcomed to visit one of the 'support hubs' to receive further advice and support on a range of welfare issues. For more details and contact information of the recovery centres see the website.

Lloyd's Patriotic Fund

£49,000 (100+ grants)

Correspondent: Suzanna Nagle, Secretary, Lloyd's Patriotic Fund, Lloyd's, One Lime Street, London EC3M 7HA (020 7327 6144; fax: 020 7327 5229; email: communityaffairs@lloyds.com; website: www.lloyds.com)

CC Number: 210173

Eligibility

Ex-servicemen and women of the Royal Navy, the Army, Royal Marines and Royal Air Force who are in need, and their dependents.

Types of grants

One-off grants, on average of about £300, can be given for essential domestic items, electric wheelchairs, home adaptations and 'exceptional' expenses. In deserving cases grants may also be given for debt relief and help with utility bills.

Annual grant total

In 2012/13 the fund had assets of £1.7 million and an income of £1.3 million. Grants to individuals and organisations for welfare purposes totalled £330,000. Out of that sum continuing annuities totalled £9,200 and £40,000 was given to SSAFA to support over 100 individuals.

Note that in this year the fund received a major donation from the council of Lloyd's. Normally the income varies and in the past few years has ranged from £83,000 to £477,000.

Exclusions

Note, new annuity payments are no longer considered. Existing recipients will continue to be assisted.

Applications

Applications should be made through the local SSAFA branch, using their application form.

Other information

Grants are also given for educational purposes (in 2012/13 a total of £7,500).

The fund works with SSAFA and other partners through which funds are administered. Various military organisations are supported, with a particular focus on those who help people with disabilities or individuals facing poverty, illness and hardship.

The Nash Charity

£15,000

Correspondent: Steve Walbourne, Trustee, Peachey and Co., 95 Aldwych, London WC2B 4JF (020 7316 5200; fax: 020 7316 5222)

CC Number: 229447

Eligibility

Ex-service personnel who have been wounded or disabled during wartime.

Types of grants

Grants are usually paid through social services, Citizens Advice or other welfare agencies to purchase specific items.

Annual grant total

In 2012/13 the charity had an income of £13,000 and a total expenditure of £18,000.

Applications

In writing to the correspondent at any time. Applications can be submitted directly by the individual or through an appropriate third party.

The Not Forgotten Association

£656,000

Correspondent: Col. Piers Storie-Pugh, Chief Executive, 4th Floor, 2 Grosvenor Gardens, London SW1W 0DH (020 7730 2400; fax: 020 7730 0020; email: info@nfassociation.org; website: www.nfassociation.org)

CC Number: 229666

Eligibility

Service and ex-service men and women who are disabled or suffering from some form of ill health. Applicants must have served in the Armed Forces of the Crown (or Merchant Navy during hostilities).

Types of grants

The association does not give financial grants directly to applicants; rather it gives help in kind in the following areas: televisions and licences for those with restricted mobility or who are otherwise largely housebound, holidays for both groups and individuals (accompanied by carers if required), day outings to events and places of interest. The association is now including more activity and adventure breaks and outings, in light of more recent military conflicts.

Annual grant total

In 2012/13 the association had an income of £1.1 million and a total expenditure of £1.3 million. Assistance to individuals totalled £656,000 and was distributed as follows:

Holidays	£247,000
Televisions	£175,000
Entertainment	£164,000
Outings	£70,000

Almost 11,000 people benefitted directly from the association's charitable activities.

Exclusions

The association cannot help wives, widows or families (unless they are themselves ex-members of the forces or they are acting as carers).

Applications

Applications should be submitted through SSAFA, Royal British Legion, Combat Stress or the Welfare Service of the Service Personnel and Veterans' Agency. These agencies will complete the common application form on behalf of the applicant and then make the appropriate recommendation to the association, with the applicant's income and expenditure details and degree of disability. Applications are considered throughout the year. Successful applicants may reapply after three years.

Other information

The association organises two flagship events for war pensioners – its annual Garden Party at Buckingham Palace and a Christmas Party at St James' Palace.

The Officers' Association

£1.38 million (828 grants)

Correspondent: Kathy Wallis, Assistant Benevolent Secretary, Benevolence Department, 1st Floor, Mountbarrow House, 6–20 Elizabeth Street, London SW1W 9RB (020 7808 4163; email: hboscawen@officersassociation.org.uk; website: www.officersassociation.org.uk)

CC Number: 201321

Eligibility

Officers who have held a commission in HM Forces, their widows and dependents. Officers on the active list will normally be helped only with resettlement and employment.

Types of grants

One-off and recurrent grants according to need. Cash grants are made for specific items such as disability equipment, property repairs, convalescence, holidays or to help set up a new home following a family crisis. Regular allowances are given mainly to older people who are living on a low income. Help is also given towards residential care and nursing home fees.

Limited assistance may be given for education or training needs in exceptional circumstances.

Annual grant total

In 2012/13 the association had assets of £16.7 million and an income of £3.1 million. Grants were made to 828 individuals totalling £1.38 million and were given almost exclusively for relief-in-need purposes.

Applications

On a form available from the Benevolence Secretary or downloaded from the website. Applications can be submitted either directly by the individual or via a third party. The association has a network of honorary representatives throughout the UK who will normally visit the applicant to discuss their problems and offer advice.

Other information

The association has a residential home at Bishopsteignton, South Devon, for ex-officers (male and female) over the age of 65 who do not need special care. There is also a small estate of 12 bungalows in Leavesden specially designed for disabled officers and their families.

The association provides a series of advice leaflets on finding accommodation in residential care or nursing homes, how to get financial assistance and how to find short-term convalescence accommodation and sheltered accommodation for older people who are disabled. It also has an employment department to help ex-officers up to the age of 60 find suitable employment. This service is open to officers just leaving the services and to those who have lost their civilian jobs.

The association has an informative website.

For applicants in Scotland: See entry for the Officers' Association Scotland.

Officers' Association Scotland

£116,000 (83 grants)

Correspondent: Welfare Team, Administrator, New Haig House, Logie Green Road, Edinburgh EH7 4HR (01315 501575/1581; fax: 01315 575819; email: oasadmin@oascotland.org.uk; website: www.oascotland.org.uk)

SC Number: SC010665

Eligibility

Those who have held a Sovereign's Commission with embodied service in HM Naval, Military or Air Forces, and their dependents who are in need. Ex-officers who were commissioned into the Reserve, Auxiliary, or Territorial Forces are also eligible. Applicants must be resident in Scotland at the time of their initial application, have been members of a Scottish regiment or intend to settle in Scotland.

Types of grants

Recurrent grants of about £380 per quarter. One-off grants are also made and in the past have been used to fund things such as home repairs, respite breaks, mobility aids and so on.

Annual grant total

In 2013/14 the association had assets of £6.3 million and an income of £308,000. Grants to individuals totalled £116,000, including £92,000 in annual payments to 62 beneficiaries and £24,000 in 21 one-off awards.

Applications

Potential beneficiaries can contact the correspondent to discuss eligibility. Alternatively, applications can be initiated by sending your personal and service details to the association via the online contact form on the association's website, by email or in writing. Applications are passed to the local SSAFA branch who will contact you to progress the application.

Other information

The association runs a 'friendship visits programme' to provide company for retired officers and their dependents who are feeling isolated. It also offers support and advice to officers making the transition from service to civilian employment and for the rest of their working lives.

The REME Benevolent Fund

£340,000

Correspondent: William Barclay, Corps Secretary, REME Benevolent Fund, Regimental Headquarters REME, Box H075, Hazebrouck Barracks, Arborfield RG2 9NH (01189 763220; email: REMERHQ-CorpsSec@mod.uk)

CC Number: 246967

Eligibility

Members and former members of the REME who are in need, and their immediate dependents.

Types of grants

One-off grants usually up to £1,000 for any need, however in exceptional circumstances larger grants may be made. Annuities and help with nursing home fees are also available.

Annual grant total

In 2013 the fund had assets of £571,000 and an income of £678,000. Grants were made to individuals totalling £340,000 and were distributed as follows:

Grants in aid – Individuals	£312,000
Annuity allowances	£19,800
Nursing home fees	£3,300
Erskine and Queen Alexandra' Hospitals	£4,400

475 applications were received for grant in aid support, with 330 (69%) of applicants assisted. The average grant made was £603.

Exclusions

No grants for medical expenses, funeral expenses, litigation costs or debts.

Applications

On a form available from the correspondent or a local branch of SSAFA or the Royal British Legion. Grants are only made through a third party (e.g. SSAFA/RBL), and applications made direct will be referred to a welfare agency for investigation. Applications are screened immediately on receipt and are either rejected on sight, referred back for more information or to a committee which meets every four weeks.

Other information

The fund also makes grant to other service organisations.

The Royal Air Force Benevolent Fund

£15,000,000

Correspondent: Michael Neville, Administrator, 67 Portland Place, London W1B 1AR (0800 169 2942; email: info@rafbf.org.uk; website: www.rafbf.org)

CC Number: 1081009

Eligibility

Past and present members of the RAF or WRAF, including National Service, or partners, widows, widowers or dependent children (under 18).

Types of grants

Almost all types of assistance can be considered in the form of grants or loans. Grants are given for essential living costs, such as utility bills or essential household items; welfare breaks; sickness maintenance grants; funeral costs; and emergency needs.

Annual grant total

In 2012 the charity had assets of £125 million, an income of £17 million and gave grants for welfare purposes totalling £15 million.

These accounts were the latest available at the time of writing (July 2014).

Exclusions

No grants for private medical costs or for legal fees.

Applications

On a form available directly from the correspondent or on their website via an online application form. Applications can be submitted by the individual or through an ex-service welfare agency such as RAFA or SSAFA. The fund runs a free helpline which potential applicants are welcome to call for advice and support on the application process. Applications are considered on a continual basis.

Other information

The charity provides advice and assistance on a range of issues including benefits and debt advice and relationships. The fund maintains a short-term care home in Sussex and a further three homes in Northumberland, Avon and Lancashire which are operated jointly with the RAFA. They may also be able to help with purchasing a house. They also have two holiday homes available at reduced rates for beneficiaries.

The Royal Air Forces Association

£46,000

Correspondent: Welfare Director, 117½ Loughborough Road, Leicester LE4 5ND (01162 665224; fax: 01162 665012; email: welfare@rafa.org.uk; website: www.rafa.org.uk)

CC Number: 226686

Eligibility

Serving and former members of the Royal Air Force (including National Service), and their dependents. The widows and widowers and dependents of those that have died in service, or subsequently, are also eligible for assistance.

Types of grants

Small, one-off grants when all other sources of funding have been exhausted. Recent grants have been awarded for gas and electricity bills, clothing, bedding, electrical goods, furniture and hospital travel costs. The trust may also assist with nursing, convalescent and respite care costs.

Annual grant total

In 2012 the association had assets of over £22.3 million, an income of £9.3 million and a total expenditure of £7 million. Welfare grants were made totalling £46,000. Other welfare support totalled over £1.3 million. The 2012 accounts were the latest available at the time of writing (August 2014).

Exclusions

Credit card debts are not eligible, nor are medical fees.

Applications

On a form available from the relevant area welfare officer. They are contactable on the numbers below. Confirmation of RAF service is required. Applications may be submitted directly by the individual, or through SSAFA, Royal British Legion or other welfare agency.

Northern Area	Michael Grell	01772 426930
North East	Karen Leahair	01347 847525
Eastern Area	Paul Davies	01162 688784
South West	Glenford Bishop	01392 462088
South East	Sue Smith	020 8286 6667
Midlands	Tracey Khan	01214 499356
Scotland and Overseas	Mike McCourt	01312 255221
Wales	Barbara Howells	01495 249522
Northern Ireland	Sarah Waugh	02890 325718

Other information

The association provides support and advice on state benefits, including war pensions. It also manages two sheltered housing complexes, a residential home and three respite care homes.

Royal Artillery Charitable Fund

£750,000

Correspondent: Lt Col. I. A. Vere Nicoll, Secretary, Artillery House, Royal Artillery Barracks, Larkhill, Salisbury, Wiltshire SP4 8QT (01980 845233, 01980 845698; fax: 01980 634020; email: rarhq-racf-welfare-sec@mod.uk; website: www.theraa.co.uk)

CC Number: 210202

Eligibility

Current or former members of the Royal Artillery and their dependents.

Types of grants

According to our research, one-off and recurrent grants of £250–£700 are given for essential needs, for example, household bills, kitchen and domestic equipment, rent, water rates, nursing home fees, disability equipment, clothing, council tax and utility or power bills.

Annual grant total

At the time of writing (July 2014) the latest financial information available was from 2012. In 2012 the fund had assets of £14.2 and an income of £1.1 million. Individual grants totalled £799,000 distributed to 1,772 people. Most of the support is given for general welfare needs, therefore we estimate the total of grants in need to be around £750,000.

Exclusions

Grants are not given towards income tax, loans, credit card debts, telephone bills, legal fees or private medical treatment.

Applications

Applications should be made through a SSAFA (details of local branches can be found in telephone directories or from Citizens Advice) or other organisations, such as the Royal British Legion or Earl Haig Fund in Scotland (see separate entry), Officers Association, Royal Artillery Association or other regimental charities. Applications can be considered at any time.

Other information

Grants are also given to organisations (£217,000 in 2012) and for educational purposes.

The fund is the sole corporate trustee of the Royal Artillery Charitable Fund (Permanent Endowment), the Royal Artillery Benevolent Fund, the Royal Artillery Association and the Kelly Holdsworth Artillery Trust.

The Royal British Legion

£14,200,000 (25,926 grants)

Correspondent: Welfare Services, 199 Borough High Street, London SE1 1AA (Helpline: 0808 802 8080 (8am-8pm, 7 days a week); email: info@britishlegion.org.uk; website: www.britishlegion.org.uk)

CC Number: 219279

Eligibility

Serving and ex-serving members of the armed forces and their wives, partners, widows, children and other dependents in England, Wales, Ireland as well as any country overseas (for Scotland see the entry for the Earl Haig Fund Scotland in the Scotland section of the guide).

Types of grants

Following a standard assessment of the beneficiary's financial situation, the Legion makes grants to individuals, either financial or by the provision of goods or services. Grants can be given for any purpose within the scope of the Royal Charter, which governs the Legion. Financial assistance offered by the Legion includes an Immediate Needs Scheme, help for homelessness and a Property Repair Loan Scheme.

Annual grant total

In 2013 the charity held assets of £286.7 million and had an income of £124.6 million. Welfare grants to 25,926 individuals totalled £14.2 million.

Exclusions

No assistance with business debts, legal expenses, loans or medical care.

Applications

Call the charity's helpline which will be able to put you in contact with your local welfare representative. An income and savings assessment may be required as part of the application process.

Note: Most charities for ex-servicemen and women co-operate together in their work and the Royal British Legion may also be approached through other service organisations and vice versa.

Other information

The Royal British Legion is one of the largest providers of charitable help for individuals in the country and is financed mainly by gifts from individuals, especially through its annual Poppy Day collection.

It provides a comprehensive service for advising and helping ex-servicemen and women and their dependents (though for ex-service women, wives, widows and dependents, see also the entry for Royal British Legion Women's Section). Direct financial assistance is but one aspect of this work. There are over 3,000 branches of the Royal British Legion, all of which can act as centres for organising whatever help the circumstances may require. Support is available to all who served in the forces, whether in war or peace-time, as regulars or those who have done national service.

The Legion manages six cares homes in locations around the country and is dedicated to supporting the recovery of soldiers and ex-soldiers. It has pledged '£50 million over ten years, to support the Defence Recovery Capability programme for wounded, injured and sick Armed Forces men and women.' As part of the programme, in conjunction with the MoD and Help for Heroes, the Legion has taken the lead with the running of PRCs (Personnel Recovery Centres) in Edinburgh and Germany and has so far committed £27 million towards the operation of the Battle Back Centre – a sports and outdoor activity facility based at Lilleshall. Financial support has also been given to PRCs managed by Help for Heroes at Catterick, Colchester and Tidworth.

There are four break centres operated by the Legion, through which it facilitates holidays for serving and former service personnel and their families. It also provides adventure holidays for young people from service families.

Former members of the armed forces can seek support in their transition from military to civilian life through the Legion's website civvystreet.org, which 'gives beneficiaries and their partners information, advice and guidance on careers, skills and self-employment.'

More information on services provided can be found on the Legion's informative website or by calling the helpline.

Royal Commonwealth Ex-Services League

£1.7 million

Correspondent: Christopher Warren, Secretary General, Haig House, 199 Borough High Street, London SE1 1AA (020 3207 2413; website: www.commonwealthveterans.org.uk)

CC Number: 231322

Eligibility

Ex-servicemen and women of the crown, their widows or dependents, who are living outside the UK. There are currently member organisations in over 40 countries throughout the world.

Types of grants

All types of help can be considered. Grants are one-off, usually ranging from £100 to £500 and renewable on application. Grants are generally for medically related costs such as hearing aids, wheelchairs, artificial limbs, food or repairs to homes wrecked by floods or hurricanes and so on.

Annual grant total

In 2013 the league held assets of £2.5 million and had an income of £1.7 million. Total welfare expenditure was £1.7 million. The league assisted in 2,211 individual cases, of which 727 received assistance directly from the charity's own funds, with the remainder receiving funds administered by the league but from other charities.

This total also includes grants made to local member organisations for benevolence work. Including these local cases takes the total number of individuals helped both directly and indirectly up to 12,121.

Applications

Considered daily on receipt of applications from member organisations or British Embassies/High Commissions, but not directly from individuals. Applications should include proof of military service to the crown.

Other information

The league has members or representatives in most parts of the world through whom former servicemen or their dependents living abroad can seek help. The local British Embassy or High Commission can normally supply the relevant local contact. In a Commonwealth country the local ex-service association will probably be affiliated to the league. The league's annual report, available from the Charity Commission or from the league, gives an interesting breakdown and analysis of funds allocated according to location.

The Royal Corps of Signals Benevolent Fund (formerly known as The Royal Signals Benevolent Fund)

£420,000 (673 grants)

Correspondent: Col. Terrance Canham, Administrator, RHQ Royal Signals, Griffin House, Blandford Camp, Blandford Forum, Dorset DT11 8RH (01258 482081; email: RSIGNALSHQ-RegtSec@mod.uk; website: www.royalsignals.org/rsbf)

CC Number: 284923

Eligibility

Members and former members of the Royal Signals, regular or territorial volunteer reserve, and their widows and other dependents.

Types of grants

One-off and recurrent grants according to need. Grants are given towards priority debts, such as rent and utilities, mobility aids, white goods, household repairs and Christmas allowances. Applications for amounts up to £600 may be decided between the funding committee meetings.

Annual grant total

In 2013 the fund had assets of £9.6 million and an income of £1.5 million. 556 grants were made during the year totalling £320,000. The fund also administered 117 grants from the Army Benevolent Fund, which totalled £100,000.

Exclusions

The fund does not distribute loans.

Applications

Applications should be made through SSAFA or another charitable organisation and are considered as required.

Other information

The fund also gives grants to other service charities (£44,000 in 2013).

The fund is an amalgamation of the Royal Signals Association Fund, the Royal Signals Officers Fund and the Royal Signals Corps Fund.

The Royal Logistics Corps Association Trust Fund

£626,000 (1,624 grants)

Correspondent: Regimental Treasurer, The RLC Association Trust, Dettingen House, The Princess Royal Barracks, Deepcut, Camberley, Surrey GU16 6RW (01252 833334; email: regttreasurer@rhqtherlc.org.uk; website: www.rascrctassociation.co.uk)

CC Number: 1024036

Eligibility

People in need who have at any time served in or with the former RASC or the former RCT, including people who served and are now serving in the Royal Logistics Corp. Members of the women's services and the dependents of any of the above are also eligible.

Types of grants

One-off grants towards wheelchairs and other mobility aids, house repairs, utility bills, bathroom conversions, house adaptations and so on.

Annual grant total

In 2013 the trust had an income of £2.7 million and a total expenditure of £2.1 million. The following statement is taken from the trust's annual report: 'In 2013 over 2,100 benevolent or welfare cases were considered of which 1,624 received grants totalling £625,976.'

Exclusions

No grants for repayment of general debts or loans.

Applications

Applications should be made through SSAFA, the Royal British Legion, Poppyscotland or a similar welfare organisation. Grants are made to the sponsoring organisation rather than directly to the individual. Applications can be made at any time, though requests for larger amounts need to be considered by the executive committee, making them longer to process.

Other information

The trust supports the activities of the RLC, the largest Corps in the Army totalling some 13,000 regular and 4,500 TA soldiers. It also funds and manages the fraternal activities of the Associations of the RLC and its predecessor corps with 80 branches.

The trust's annual report states: 'The main activity of the trust in 2013 was the continuing promotion of efficiency of the RLC and the provision of welfare and benevolence support to its dependencies, adjusting its policies and working practices to accommodate the Form Corps Association.'

In 2013 trustees set a budget of just over £2 million to provide support in the areas of 'benevolence, sport and adventurous training, heritage, bands and the headquarters messes, plus a range of regimental and association activities to promote the efficiency of the corps.'

Royal Military Police Central Benevolent Fund

£101,000

Correspondent: Col Jeremy Green, The Regimental Secretary, RHQ RMP, Defence College of Policing and Guarding, Postal Point 38, Southwick, Fareham, Hampshire PO17 6EJ (02392 284406; email: rhqrmp@btconnect.com)

CC Number: 248713

Eligibility

People who are serving or have served in the Royal Military Police corps, or any of its predecessors, and their dependents.

Types of grants

One-off cash grants typically up to £1,000, though larger grants may be available. Grants have been made towards heating, funeral expenses, household furniture, debts, clothing and bedding, mobility aids, holidays, medical needs, special chairs, removals and other needs. Christmas grants are distributed to people who have received an individual benefit grant and are over 80 years of age. These grants remained at £85 in 2012/13 but were due for review.

Annual grant total

In 2012/13 the fund held assets of £3.5 million and had an income of £349,000. Grants to individuals totalled more than £101,000 and were distributed as follows:

Individual grants	£54,000
Army Benevolent Fund	£18,600
Christmas grants	£12,700
Annuities	£10,400
Nursing home fees	£5,700

Another £104,000 was awarded to military organisations.

Applications

In writing to the correspondent. All applications are passed to the Royal British Legion or SSAFA, who will visit applicants to verify eligibility and financial need.

Royal Naval Benevolent Trust

£2.5 million

Correspondent: The Grants Administrator, Castaway House, 311 Twyford Avenue, Portsmouth PO2 8RN (02392 690112; fax: 02392 660852; email: rnbt@rnbt.org.uk; website: www.rnbt.org.uk)

CC Number: 206243

Eligibility

Serving and ex-serving men and women of the Royal Navy and Royal Marines (not officers) and their dependents.

Types of grants

The grants vary in amount from under £100 up to several thousand pounds with the average being about £550 and go towards a variety of needs, including rent and mortgage payments, food, clothing, fuel, childcare, medical treatment, disability aids, respite and recuperative holidays, household goods and repairs, removal expenses, debts and training for a second career.

Annual grant total

In 2012/13 the trust had assets of almost £34 million and an income of £5.3 million. Single grants amounted to over £1.5 million and regular charitable payments to an additional £1 million (these figures include support costs which have not been broken down).

Applications

On a form available from the correspondent, to be submitted through a social worker, welfare agency, SSAFA, Royal British Legion or any Royal Naval Association branch. Applications are considered twice a week.

Other information

The trust pays over 1,200 annuities of up to £16 a week to older beneficiaries. They cost about £1 million a year including support costs.

The trust also runs a residential and nursing home for older ex-naval men (not women) namely, Pembroke House, Oxford Road, Gillingham, Kent.

The trust has an informative website.

The Royal Naval Reserve (V) Benevolent Fund

£2,000

Correspondent: Valerie Stamper, Administrator, MP 3.4, NCHQ, Leach Building, Whale Island PO2 8BY (02392 623570)

CC Number: 266380

Eligibility

Members or former members of the Royal Naval Volunteer Reserve, Women's Royal Naval Volunteer Reserve, Royal Naval Reserve and the Women's Royal Naval Reserve, who are serving or have served as non-commissioned rates. The fund also caters for wives, widows and young children of the above.

Types of grants

One-off grants only, ranging from £50 to £350. Grants have been given for gas, electricity, removal expenses (i.e. to be near children/following divorce); clothing; travel to visit sick relatives or for treatment; essential furniture and domestic equipment; help on bereavement. Schoolchildren from poor families may very occasionally receive help for clothes, books or necessary educational visits, and help can also go to eligible children with aptitudes or disabilities which need special provision.

Annual grant total

In 2013 the fund had an income of £5,100 and a total expenditure of £4,900. We estimate that around £2,000 was made in grants to individuals social welfare purposes.

Applications

In writing to the correspondent directly by the individual or through the local reserve division, Royal British Legion, SSAFA or Royal Naval Benevolent Trust, which investigates applications.

The Royal Navy and Royal Marines Children's Fund

£361,000

Correspondent: Monique Bateman, Director, Castaway House, 311 Twyford Avenue, Stamshaw, Portsmouth PO2 8RN (02392 639534; fax: 02392 677574; email: rnchildren@btconnect.com; website: www.rnrmchildren'sfund.org)

CC Number: 1075015

Eligibility

Young people under 25 who are in need and are the dependent of somebody who has served, or is serving, in the Royal Navy, Royal Marines, the Queen Alexandra's Royal Naval Nursing Service or the former Women's Royal Naval Service.

Types of grants

One-off and recurrent grants ranging between £20 and £20,000 for general welfare needs including, help in the home, hospital travel expenses, respite care, specialist equipment, house adaptations and childcare. Assistance is also available to children who had been traumatised by death or family break-up.

Annual grant total

In 2012/13 the fund had assets of £9.1 million and an income of £1.27 million. The sum of £732,500 was given in grants to individuals or families for educational and welfare purposes.

The average grant per child in this accounting year was £674.

Applications

On a form available from the correspondent or to download from the website. Applications can be submitted directly by the individual or through the individual's school/college, SSAFA, Naval Personal, social services or other third party. They can be submitted at any time and are considered on a monthly basis, though urgent cases can be dealt with between meetings.

The Royal Navy Officers' Charity

£270,000

Correspondent: Commander Michael Goldthorpe, Director, 70 Porchester Terrace, London W2 3TP (020 7402 5231; email: rnoc@arno.org.uk; website: www.arno.org.uk/home)

CC Number: 207405

Eligibility

Officers, both active service and retired, of the Royal Navy, Royal Marines, QARNNS and WRNS and their respective reserves, of the equivalent rank of Sub-Lieutenant RN and above, and their spouses, former spouses, families and dependents, who are in need. There are no age limits.

Types of grants

One-off grants and recurrent payments. Grants have been awarded towards nursing home fees, the provision of disability or mobility aids, the replacement of household goods, home repairs and to supplement inadequate incomes. Educational grants may be given to complete a particular stage of a child's education (not school fees).

Annual grant total

In 2013 the society had assets of £12.9 million and had an income of £470,000. 222 benevolence grants to individuals totalled £270,000.

Exclusions

The society does not make grants for school fees or medical care, except in very exceptional circumstances.

Applications

On a form available from the correspondent. Applications can be submitted either directly by the individual, or through a third party such as a social worker or Citizens Advice and are considered monthly.

Other information

The society was founded on 16 May 1739 by a group of naval officers suffering from unreasonable treatment by the Admiralty. The benevolent function of the society emerged later and became its sole purpose in 1791.

In 2008, the Association of Royal Navy Officers Charitable Trust transferred its assets to the society and the charity changed its name from the Royal Naval Benevolent Society for Officers.

The Royal Observer Corps Benevolent Fund

£41,000 (47 grants)

Correspondent: The Secretary, 120 Perry Hall Road, Orpington, Kent BR6 0EF (01689 839031; fax: 01689 839031; email: info@rocbf.org.uk; website: www.rocbf.org.uk)

CC Number: 209640

Eligibility

All former members of the Royal Observer Corps who are in need, hardship or distress. Length of service is not a consideration, except that the person for whom the application has been made must have served long enough to have received their Royal Observer Corps official number. Eligibility also extends to their widows, widowers and dependents.

Types of grants

Almost all types of grants can be considered. Typically the fund can provide financial help for mobility aids, debt relief, essential home repairs or modification and respite care.

Annual grant total

In 2012 the trust had assets of £915,000 and an income of £36,000. Grants to 47 individuals were made totalling around £41,000. The 2012 accounts were the latest available at the time of writing (August 2014).

Exclusions

Grants are not given towards debts or arrears owed to government bodies.

Applications

By direct contact with the fund or through SSAFA, the Royal British Legion or the Royal Air Forces Association. Applications are considered on receipt and normally a decision is given within days.

Sister Agnes Benevolent Fund

£93,000 (12 grants)

Correspondent: PA to the Chief Executive, King Edward VII Hospital, Beaumont Street, London W1G 6AA (020 7486 4411; email: info@kingedwardvii.co.uk; website: www.kingedwardvii.co.uk)

CC Number: 208944

Eligibility

People who have served in the armed forces, regardless of rank or length of service, who are uninsured and are either inpatients or outpatients at King Edward VII's Hospital Sister Agnes, and their spouses, ex-spouses, widows and widowers.

Types of grants

Means tested grants for up to 100% of hospital fees. In some cases, consultant fees may also be covered.

Annual grant total

In 2012/13, the fund had assets of £751,000 and an income of £103,000. Grants were made to 12 individuals totalling £93,000.

Applications

On a form available from the correspondent or to download from the website, including evidence of service and financial details.

Note: Uninsured service personnel, their spouses, ex-spouses, widows and widowers are all eligible for a 20% subsidy on their hospital bill (this is not means-tested). To claim, eligible individuals need to notify the hospital when booking their procedure.

Other information

The Sister Agnes Benevolent Fund is a restricted fund of King Edward VII's Hospital Sister Agnes. It was established in 1979 by an anonymous donation, to be held upon trust.

SSAFA

£12,800,000

Correspondent: Head of Welfare and Volunteer Advice, 4 St Dunstan's Hill, London EC3R 8AD (0845 241 7141; email: Online form; website: www.ssafa.org.uk)

CC Number: 210760

Eligibility

Service and ex-service men and women and their immediate dependents who are in need.

Types of grants

One-off grants are available for a variety of needs, for example, electrically powered vehicles, white goods, household items, holidays and carers' breaks.

Annual grant total

In 2012 the trust held assets of £9.2 million and had an income of £50.4 million. Grants for welfare purposes totalled £12.8 million, of which £721,000 was paid from charity funds and more than £12 million on behalf of service funds and other charities.

Grants are disbursed by caseworkers who work throughout the SSAFA branch network. In 2012 caseworkers dealt with 40,645 cases of which 17,873 (44%) received financial assistance. The charity also estimates that a further £3.9 million was secured for and paid directly to individuals from other sources.

Exclusions

The trust does not assist with legal issues, private medical care costs, educational grants and anything the state has a statutory duty to provide.

Applications

Contact should normally be made by letter direct to the honorary secretary of the local branch. The appropriate address can usually be obtained from the SSAFA website, Citizens Advice, the local telephone directory (under SSAFA) and most main post offices. In case of difficulty, the local address can be obtained from the correspondent.

Other information

SSAFA operates throughout the UK and in garrisons and stations overseas. It is concerned with the welfare of service and ex-service men and women and their families and provides a wide range of advice and support services. All SSAFA branches are empowered to give immediate help without reference to higher committees. Also, because of their extensive coverage of the UK, they act as agents for service and other associated funds. Indeed, SSAFA is much more of a caseworking organisation than a benevolent fund.

A residential home is maintained on the Isle of Wight for older ex-service personnel and their dependents. Eligible men and women can be accepted from any part of the UK. SSAFA also manages cottage homes for ex-service men and women and their spouses, some purpose-built for people with disabilities, for which residents pay no rent but make a modest maintenance payment.

Two SSAFA Norton Homes provide short-term accommodation so that families can stay nearby whilst visiting a loved one at Selly Oak Hospital in Birmingham or the Defence Medical Rehabilitation Centre at Headley Court, Surrey. The houses are designed as 'homes from home' and are both located in secure and peaceful environments.

Stepping Stone homes are provided for service families facing relationship difficulties or marital breakdown who need somewhere to live while they consider their future.

Support services for serving and ex-service prisoners, with the aim of reducing re-offending and helping prisoners resettle into society, are also available.

SSAFA provides a confidential telephone support line for serving personnel which is staffed all year round and is outside the chain of command (UK: 0800 731 4880; Germany: 0800 182 7395; Cyprus: 800 91065; Falkland Islands #6111; Rest of the world: +44 (0)1980 630854). It also continues to grow and develop its health and social care services for serving personnel around the world with specialist health centres in Leicester and Nottingham. It also provides family support groups and adoption services.

For further information on all of the services listed here, and more, go to the trust's website or visit a local branch.

St Andrew's Scottish Soldiers Club Fund

£500

Correspondent: The Administrator, The Royal Scottish Corporation, 22 City Road, London EC1Y 2AJ (020 7240 3718, 0800 652 2989 (UK helpline); email: info@scotscare.com; website: www.scotscare.com)

CC Number: 233297

Eligibility

Serving and former Scottish soldiers, and their dependents, who are in need.

Types of grants

One-off grants according to need.

Annual grant total

In 2012/13 the fund had an income of £2,400 and an expenditure of almost £600. We estimate that around £500 was given in grants to individuals. Note that the charitable expenditure varies each year.

Applications

In writing to the correspondent. Applications are usually made through an ex-service body such as SSAFA or the Royal British Legion.

The WRNS Benevolent Trust

£302,000

Correspondent: Sarah Ayton, General Secretary, Castaway House, 311 Twyford Avenue, Portsmouth, Hampshire PO2 8RN (02392 655301; fax: 02392 679040; email: grantsadmin@wrnsbt.org.uk; website: www.wrnsbt.org.uk)

CC Number: 206529

Eligibility

Ex-Wrens and female serving members of the Royal Navy (officers and ratings) who joined the service between 3 September 1939 and 1 November 1993 who are in need.

Types of grants

The following information is taken from the trust's website:

> *Amenity Grants*
>
> Regular installments to help towards the payment of bills, clothing or perhaps household goods.
>
> *Care Enhancement Grants*
>
> Where an ex-Wren is living in a Care Home, assistance may be considered towards any shortfall in top-up fees, or to a supplement to help eke out the meagre State Personal Expenses Allowance. On occasion, we can also consider assistance with fees incurred where an individual receives care in their own home.
>
> All Regular Grants are reviewed on an annual basis, which means we are kept informed of the individual's welfare and can reassess their needs as required.
>
> *One-off Grants*
>
> As well as the regular grants detailed above we award many 'one-off' grants. These can be to help with arrears or debts, removal or travel costs, convalescence care, education, household goods and repairs, medical aids and in some cases, funerals.
>
> There is an upper ceiling on these grants so if the total cost is beyond that, we trawl other eligible charities for their help. For example, we may be unable to meet the full cost of a stair-lift or motorised scooter but an amount is pledged and the outstanding balance met by approaching other charities; the money is always raised somehow.

Refer to the trust's very helpful and informative website for full, current details of the range of grants.

Annual grant total

In 2013 the trust had assets of £4 million and an income of £509,000. Welfare grants including pensions totalled £302,000 with a further £3,300 being given for educational purposes.

Exclusions

People who deserted from the service are not eligible.

Applications

Applications can be made direct to the correspondent, or through SSAFA.

Other information

The following information is taken from the trust's informative and helpful website:

> The charity was established in 1942 to help in cases of hardship among the thousands of women who served in the Women's Royal Naval Service. A member is anyone who served in the Women's Royal Naval Service and transferred to the Royal Navy before 1 November 1993, or anyone who has served in the WRNS since 3 September 1939. This amounts to 143,000 women and there are currently 50,000 members.
>
> The trust assists approximately 350 former Wrens and their families each year and in 2013 spent over £300,000 on annual and one-off grants. Over the last seven decades it has helped more than 12,000 women.
>
> All trustees are former Wrens including our current Service and Royal Navy and Royal Marines representatives.

Grants are mostly made in the form of pensions, or for relief in need.

Service and regimental funds

Royal Engineers' Association

£372,000

Correspondent: Lt Col Neil Jordan, Deputy Controller, Brompton Barracks, Dock Road, Chatham, Kent ME4 4UG (01634 822982; email: benevolence@reahq.org.uk; website: www.reahq.org.uk)

CC Number: 258322

Eligibility

Past or present members of the corps, and their dependents, who are in need.

Types of grants

One-off and recurrent grants. Grants are given for a wide range of purposes including mobility aids and walk-in showers. Regular weekly allowances are made to around 140 people and Christmas cards and monetary gifts are sent out in November to around 1,200 people who are resident in elderly people's homes, hospitals and homes for the mentally infirm and to those in receipt of weekly pensions. Annuities for top-up fees for nursing homes are given in exceptional circumstances.

Annual grant total

In 2012 the association had assets of £10.3 million and an income of £1.1 million. Awards to individuals totalled £372,000 and were distributed as follows:

Grants	£264,500
Weekly allowances	£86,000
Christmas grants	£21,500

The 2012 were the latest available at the time of writing (August 2014).

Exclusions

No grants for private education, private medical fees, court or legal fees or debts.

Applications

On a form available from the correspondent, to be submitted through SSAFA or The Royal British Legion. Applications for less than £500 will be considered at any time, while cases requiring over £500 are considered at monthly committee meetings.

Other information

Grants are also made to other affiliated charities, for example in 2012 SSAFA (£7,500) and Combat Stress and Veterans Aid (£2,500 each).

Army

The Household Division Charity

£60,000

Correspondent: Major William Style, Treasurer, Household Division Funds, Horse Guards, Whitehall, London SW1A 2AX (email: londist-so3accounts@mod.uk)

CC Number: 1138248

Eligibility

Current and former members of the Household Division, and their dependents, who are in need.

Types of grants

One-off and recurring grants according to need.

Annual grant total

In 2012/13 the charity held assets of £5.9 million some of which is permanent endowment and cannot be spent on grant giving. It had an income of £444,000 and charitable expenditure totalled £239,000. The charity awards grants to individuals and organisations for both social welfare and educational purposes. We estimate grants to individuals for social welfare purposes to be around £60,000.

Applications

In writing to the correspondent. Applications may be submitted by the individual or by a third party such as a representative from SSAFA, Citizens Advice or other welfare organisation.

Other information

The trustees annual report for 2012/13 states:

> The trustees review financial commitments regularly. The Household Division is recognised by the nation as setting an international standard of excellence. With a legacy spanning 360 years, the Household Division Charity is driven primarily to generate even greater levels of military efficiency. Resources are allocated for the promotion of 'esprit de corps' based on optimal physical and mental fitness, breadth of knowledge, competence and experience to develop courage and professional effectiveness in the face of any danger. In support of this objective, funds are allocated to further education opportunities for individuals and groups, often abroad. Resources spent on welfare and memorialisation reinforce the sense of special unity that binds all members, serving and retired, able-bodied and injured, and their families including the bereaved.

Irish Guards Charitable Fund

£65,000 (69 grants)

Correspondent: The Lieutenant Colonel, Regimental Headquarters, Irish Guards, Wellington Barracks, Birdcage Walk, London SW1E 6HQ (020 7414 3293; email: igwebmaster@btconnect.com; website: www.helpforirishguards.com)

CC Number: 247477

Eligibility

Serving and retired officers of the Irish Guards and their dependents who are in need.

Types of grants

One-off grants according to need

Annual grant total

In 2013 the fund held assets of £2 million and had an income of £360,000. A total of 69 grants were awarded to individuals, amounting to £65,000.

A further £51,000 was given in 17 grants to organisations.

Applications

In writing to the correspondent.

The Parachute Regiment Afghanistan Trust (formerly known as The Afghanistan Trust)

£112,000 (96 grants)

Correspondent: Elisabeth Condie, Administrator, RHQ Para, Merville Barracks, Circular Road South, Colchester, Essex CO2 7UT (01206 817074; email: secretary@paracharity.org; website: afghanistantrust.org/)

CC Number: 1121647

Eligibility

Soldiers of the Parachute Regiment injured in Afghanistan and families and dependents of the Regiment's soldiers killed or injured in Afghanistan.

Types of grants

Three types of grant are available to meet immediate needs, medium-term and long-term needs:

- Immediate needs grants – where there is a need for an immediate provision of funds (less than 24 hours)
- Medium-term grants – where needs are not immediate but will require further consideration and support, for example Motability deposits or adaptations, specialist equipment, family support or assistance to the bereaved

- Long-term grants – in cases where soldiers require longer-term assistance and are unable to remain in the Regiment. Help may include mobility support, home adaptations, etc.

Annual grant total

In 2012 the trust had assets of £1.15 million and an income of £837,000. Grants totalled £112,000 and were made to 96 individuals.

This was the latest set of accounts available at the time of writing (August 2014).

Applications

Applications can originate through the Battalion welfare network. Direct applications may also be made in writing to the correspondent.

Other information

Grants are also made to other service charities.

Service and regimental funds

Royal Navy and Royal Marines

Royal Marines Charitable Trust Fund
RM Corps Secretary, Building 32, HMS Excellent, Whale Island, Portsmouth PO2 8ER (tel: 02392 547225; fax: 02392 547207; website: www.rmctf.org.uk)

Royal Naval Association
General Secretary, Room 209, Semaphore Tower (PP70), HM Naval Base, Portsmouth, Hampshire PO1 3LT (tel: 02392 723747; fax: 02392 723371; email: admin@royalnavalassoc.com; website: www.royal-naval-association.co.uk)

Women's Royal Naval Service Benevolent Trust
General Secretary, Castaway House, 311 Twyford Avenue, Portsmouth, Hampshire P02 8RN (tel: 02392 655301; fax: 02392 679040; email: generalsecretary@wrnsbt.org.uk; website: www.wrnsbt.org.uk)

Merchant Navy

Merchant Navy Welfare Board
Welfare Officer, 8 Cumberland Place, Southampton SO15 2BH (tel: 02380 337799; fax: 02380 634444; email: enquiries@mnwb.org.uk; website:)

Royal Alfred Seafarers Society
Weston Acres, Woodmansterne Lane, Banstead, Surrey SM7 3HB (tel: 01737 353763; fax: 01737 362678; email: enquiries@royalalfred.org.uk; website: www.royalalfredseafarers.com)

Royal Air Force

Princess Mary's Royal Air Force Nursing Services Trust
RAF Naphill, High Wycombe, Buckinghamshire HP14 4UE (tel: 01494 497297)

Royal Air Force Disabled Holiday Trust
Administrator, 67 Portland Place, London W1B 1AR (tel: 020 7307 3303; email: admin@rafdht.org.uk)

Royal Air Forces Ex-POW Association Charitable Fund
Welfare Officer, 4 Barn Close, Hartford, Huntingdon, Cambridgeshire PE29 1XF (tel: 01672 870529; email: rafexpowassn@gmail.com)

Royal Observer Corps Benevolent Fund
Secretary, 120 Perry Hall Lane, Orpington BR6 0EF (email: info@rocbf.org.uk; website: www.rocbf.org.uk)

Army

The Adjutant General's Corps Regimental Association
Secretary, Gould House, Worthy Down, Winchester SO21 2RG (tel: 01962 887435; website: www.rhqagc.com)

Afghanistan Trust, the Parachute Regiment
Secretary, RHQ PARA, Merville Barracks, Circular Road South, Colchester CO2 7UT (tel: 01206 817074; website: www.afghanistantrust.org)

Argyll and Sutherland Highlanders' Regimental Association
Secretary, The Castle, Stirling FK8 1EH (tel: 01786 475165)

Army Air Corps Fund (post Sept 1957)
Headquarters Army Air Corps, Middle Wallop, Stockbridge, Hampshire SO20 8DY (tel: 01264 784426; email: AACHQ-RHQ-RegtSec@mod.uk)

Army Physical Training Corps Association
Regimental Secretary, Fox Lines, Queen's Avenue, Aldershot, Hampshire GU11 2LB (tel: 01252 787161; email: raptchq-reg-sec@mod.uk; website: www.raptassociation.org.uk)

Ayrshire Yeomanry
(See Yeomanry Benevolent Fund)

Bedfordshire and Hertfordshire Regiment
(See Royal Anglian Regiment Benevolent Charity)

Berkshire Yeomanry
(See Yeomanry Benevolent Fund)

Berkshire and Westminster Dragoons
(See Yeomanry Benevolent Fund)

Blues and Royals Association
Honorary Secretary, Home HQ, Household Cavalry, Combermere Barracks, Windsor SL4 3DN (tel: 01753 755132; email: rhq-d.regsec@householdcavalry.co.uk)

Border Regiment
(See Duke of Lancaster's Regiment)

Buckinghamshire, Berkshire & Oxfordshire Yeomanry
(See Yeomanry Benevolent Fund)

Cambridgeshire Regiment
(See Royal Anglian Regiment Benevolent Charity)

Cameronians (Scottish Rifles)
(See King's Own Scottish Borders Association)

Cheshire Regiment
(See Mercian Regiment Benevolent Fund)

Cheshire Yeomanry
(See Yeomanry Benevolent Fund)

Coldstream Guards Association
Assistant Regimental Adjutant, Wellington Barracks, Birdcage Walk, London SW1E 6HQ (tel: 020 7414 3263)

Connaught Rangers Association
Applications should be forwarded directly to the ABF The Soldiers' Charity, see page 135.

Corps of Army Music Trust
Corps Secretary, Kneller Hall, Kneller Road, Twickenham TW2 7DU (tel: 020 8744 8652)

County of London Yeomanry (3rd)
(See Yeomanry Benevolent Fund)

Derbyshire Yeomanry
(See Yeomanry Benevolent Fund)

Devonshire and Dorset Regiment
(See the Rifles – Exeter)

Devonshire Regiment
(See the Rifles – Exeter)

Dorset Regiment
(See the Rifles – Exeter)

Dragoons:
1st King's Dragoon Guards
(See Queen's Dragoon Guards Benevolent Fund)

2nd (Queen's Bays)
(See Queen's Dragoon Guards Benevolent Fund)

3rd Carabiniers (Prince of Wales's Dragoon Guards)
(See Royal Scots Dragoon Guards Association)

4th/7th Royal Dragoon Guards
(See Royal Dragoon Guards Benevolent Fund)

5th Royal Inniskilling Dragoon Guards
(See Royal Dragoon Guards Benevolent Fund)

2nd Royal Scots Greys
(See Royal Scots Dragoon Guards Association)

3rd Dragoon Guards
(See Royal Scots Dragoon Guards Association)

6th Dragoon Guards
(See Royal Scots Dragoon Guards Association)

25th Dragoon Guards
(See Royal Scots Dragoon Guards Association)

Westminster Dragoons
(See Yeomanry Benevolent Fund)

Duke of Albany's Seaforth Highlanders
(See Queens Own Highlanders (Seaforth and Camerons) Regimental Association)

Duke of Cornwall's Light Infantry
(See the Rifles – Bodmin)

Duke of Edinburgh's Royal Regiment
(See the Rifles – Salisbury)

Duke of Lancaster's Regiment
Secretary, Fulwood Barracks, Preston PR2 8AA (tel: 01772 260362; fax: 01772 260583; email: INFHQ-KINGS-LANCS-RegtSec@mod.uk)

Duke of Wellington's Regiment
(See Yorkshire Regiment)

Durham Light Infantry
(See the Rifles – Durham)

East Anglian Regiment
(See Royal Anglian Regiment Benevolent Charity)

East Lancashire Regiment
(See Duke of Lancaster's Regiment)

East Yorkshire Regiment
(See Yorkshire Regiment)

Essex Regiment
(See Royal Anglian Regiment Benevolent Charity)

Fife and Forfar Yeomanry
(See Yeomanry Benevolent Fund)

Fusiliers Aid Society (Fallen Fusiliers)
City of London Headquarters, HM Tower of London, London EC3N 4AB (tel: 020 3166 6906; (email: asstregsec@thefusiliers.org; website: www.thefusiliers.org)

Glasgow Highlanders
(See Royal Highland Fusiliers Benevolent Association)

Gloucestershire Regimental
(See the Rifles – Gloucester)

The Gordon Highlanders' Association
Home HQ The Highlanders, St Luke's, Viewfield Road, Aberdeen AB15 7XH (tel: 01224 318174; email: highlandersaberdeen@btinternet.com)

Green Howards
(See Yorkshire Regiment)

Grenadier Guards Association
General Secretary, Wellington Barracks, Birdcage Walk, London SW1E 6HQ (tel: 020 7414 3285; email: assnnco@grengds.com; website: www.grengds.com)

The Gurkha Welfare Trust
PO Box 2170, 22 Queen Street, Salisbury SP2 2EX (tel: 01722 323955; fax: 01722 343119; email: info@gwt.org.uk; website: www.gwt.org.uk)

Hampshire and Isle of Wight Military Aid Fund
Secretary, Serles House, Southgate Street, Winchester SO23 9EG (tel: 01962 852933; email: secretary@hantsMAF.org)

Herefordshire Light Infantry Regiment
(See the Rifles – Shrewsbury)

Highland Light Infantry
(See Royal Highland Fusiliers Benevolent Association)

Highlanders (Seaforth, Gordons & Camerons) Regiment
(See Highlanders Regimental Association)

The Highlanders Association
Regimental Secretary, HHQ The Highlanders, Cameron Barracks, Inverness IV2 3XE

Honourable Artillery Company Benevolent Fund
Armoury House, City Road, London EC1Y 2BQ (tel: 020 7382 1537; fax: 020 7382 1538; email: hac@hac.org.uk; website: www.hac.org.uk)

Hussars:

3rd The King's Own
(See Queen's Royal Hussars)

7th Queen's Own
(See Queen's Royal Hussars)

8th King's Royal Irish
(See Queen's Royal Hussars)

10th Royal Hussars
(See King's Royal Hussars Welfare Fund)

11th Hussars
(as above)

14th King's Hussars
(as above)

14th/20th King's Hussars
(as above)

20th Hussars
(as above)

23rd Hussars
(as above)

26th Hussars
(as above)

13th/18th Royal (Queen Mary's Own)
(See Light Dragoons Charitable Trust)

15th/19th King's Royal Hussars Regiment
(See Light Dragoons Charitable Trust)

The Queen's Own Hussars
(See Queen's Royal Hussars)

Queen's Royal Irish Hussars
(See Queen's Royal Hussars)

Imperial Yeomanry
(See Yeomanry Benevolent Fund)

Indian Army Association
c/o Royal Commonwealth Ex-Services League, Haig House, 199 Borough High Street, London SE1 1AA (tel: 020 3207 2413)

Inns of Court and City Yeomanry
(See Yeomanry Benevolent Fund)

Intelligence Corps Association
Building 200, Chicksands, Shefford, Bedfordshire SG17 5PR

Irish Guards Association
RHQ Irish Guards, Wellington Barracks, Birdcage Walk, London SW1E 6HQ (tel: 020 7414 3295; email: igalondonbranch@gmail.com)

King's Royal Hussars Association
Unit Welfare Officer, KRH, Aliwal Barracks, Tidworth SP9 7BB (tel: 01980 656839; email: info@krh.org.uk)

King's Regiment Liverpool/Manchester
(See Duke of Lancaster's Regiment)

King's Own Royal Border Regimental Association
(See Duke of Lancaster's Regiment)

King's Own Royal Regiment
(See Duke of Lancaster's Regiment)

King's Own Scottish Borderers Association
(See the Royal Regiment of Scotland)

King's Own Yorkshire Light Infantry Regiment
(See the Rifles – Pontefract)

King's Royal Rifle Corps
(See the Rifles – Winchester)

King's Shropshire Light Infantry
(See the Rifles – Shrewsbury)

Labour Corps
Applications should be forwarded directly to the ABF The Soldiers' Charity, see page 135.

Lancashire Fusiliers
(See Fusiliers Aid Society)

Lancashire Regiment (Prince of Wales's Royal Volunteers) Regiment
(See Duke of Lancaster's Regiment)

Lancers:

9th/12th/27th Royal Lancers
(See 9th/12th Royal Lancers (Prince of Wales) Charitable Association)

16th, 5th, 17th & 21st Lancers
(See Queen's Royal Lancers)

9th Queen's Royal Lancers
(See 9th/12th Royal Lancers (Prince of Wales) Charitable Association)

Leinster Regiment (for those resident in UK)
Applications should be forwarded directly to the ABF The Soldiers' Charity, see page 135.

The Life Guards Association Charitable Trust
Honorary Secretary, Combermere Barracks, Windsor SL4 3DN (tel: 01753 755229;email: LG.RegSec@householdcavalry.co.uk)

Light Dragoons Regimental Association Charitable Trust
Fenham Barracks, Newcastle upon Tyne NE2 4NP (tel: 01912 393138; email: mail@lightdragoons.org.uk; website: www.lightdragoons.org.uk)

Light Infantry
(See the Rifles – appropriate local office)

London Irish Rifles Regimental Association Benevolent Fund
Connaught House, 4 Flodden Road, Camberwell, London SE5 9LL (email: webmaster@londonirishrifles.com)

London Regiment
Applications should be forwarded directly to the ABF The Soldiers' Charity, see page 135.

London Scottish Regiment Benevolent Fund
95 Horseferry Road, Westminster, London SW1P 2DX (tel: 020 7630 0411)

Lothian & Border Horse
(See Yeomanry Benevolent Fund)

Lovat Scouts
(See Yeomanry Benevolent Fund)

Loyal Regiment (North Lancashire)
(See Duke of Lancaster's Regiment)

Machine Gun Corps
Applications should be forwarded directly to the ABF The Soldiers' Charity, see page 135. (For Heavy Branch Machine Gun Corps see **Royal Tank Regiment Association and Benevolent Fund**)

Manchester Regiment Aid Society and Benevolent Fund
(See Duke of Lancaster's Regiment)

Mercian Benevolent Fund
Whittington Barracks, Lichfield, Staffordshire WS14 9TJ (tel: 01543 434353;

Middlesex Regiment (Duke of Cambridge's Own)
(See Princess of Wales's Royal Regiment)

Military Provost Staff Corps Association
(See Adjutant General's Corps Regimental Association)

North Staffordshire Regiment
(See Mercian Benevolent Fund)

Northamptonshire Regiment
(See Royal Anglian Regiment Benevolent Charity)

Northamptonshire Yeomanry Association (1st and 2nd Regiments)
(See Yeomanry Benevolent Fund)

Nottinghamshire and Derbyshire Regiment
(See Mercian Benevolent Fund)

'Old Contemptibles'
Applications should be forwarded directly to the ABF The Soldiers' Charity see page 135.

Oxfordshire and Buckinghamshire Light Infantry
(See the Rifles – Winchester)

Oxfordshire Yeomanry
(See Yeomanry Benevolent Fund)

Parachute Regiment
(See Airborne Forces Security Fund)

Post Office Rifles
Applications should be forwarded directly to the ABF The Soldiers' Charity see page 135.

Prince of Wales Leinster Regiment Association
Secretary, 7 Nethercombe House, Ruthin Road, Blackheath, London SE3 7SL

Prince of Wales's Own (West & East Yorkshire) Regiment
(See Yorkshire Regiment)

Princess of Wales's Royal Regiment Benevolent Fund
Benevolence Secretary, Howe Barracks, Canterbury, Kent CT1 1JY (tel: 01227 817971; email: jim.reynolds334@mod.uk)

Queen Alexandra's Royal Army Nursing Corps Association
Secretary, AMS Headquarters, Slim Road, Camberley, Surrey GU15 4NP (tel: 01276 412754; email: regtsecqaranc@hotmail.com; website: www.qarancassociation.org.uk)

Queen's Dragoon Guards
Regimental Secretary, Maindy Barracks, Whitechurch Road, Cardiff CF14 3YE (tel: 02920 781213; fax: 02920 781384; email: adminofficer@qdg.org.uk; website: www.qdg.org.uk)

Queen's Lancashire Regiment
(See Duke of Lancaster's Regiment)

Queen's Own Buffs, The Royal Kent Regiment
(See Princess of Wales's Royal Regiment)

Queen's Own Cameron Highlanders' Regiment
(See Queen's Own Highlanders (Seaforth and Camerons) Regimental Association)

Queen's Own Highlanders (Seaforth and Camerons) Regimental Association

RHQ HLDRS, Cameron Barracks, Inverness IV2 3XD (tel: 01463 224380; email: rhqthehighlanders@btopenworld.com; website: www.qohldrs.co.uk)

Queen's Own Yorkshire Dragoons

(See Yeomanry Benevolent Fund)

Queen's Regiment

(See Princess of Wales's Royal Regiment)

Queen's Royal Hussars

Regimental Secretary, Regent Park Barracks, Albany Street, London NW1 4AL (tel: 020 7756 2273; email: regsec@qrhussars.co.uk)

Queen's Royal Lancers

Regimental Secretary, HHQ, QRL Lancer House, Prince William of Gloucester Barracks, Grantham, Lincolnshire NG31 7TJ (tel: 01159 573195; email: qrlregsec@gmail.com; website: www.qrlassociation.co.uk)

Queen's Royal Surrey Regiment

(See Princess of Wales's Royal Regiment)

Reconnaissance Corps

(See Royal Armoured Corps War Memorial Benevolent Fund)

Rifle Brigade

(See the Rifles – Winchester)

The Rifles

Main Office: Benevolence Secretary, Peninsula Barracks, Romsey Road, Winchester, Hampshire SO23 8TS (tel: 01962 828530/01962 828126; email: benevolence@the-rifles.co.uk)

Regional offices:

Bodmin – The Keep, Victoria Barracks, Bodmin, Cornwall PL31 1EG (tel: 01208 72810; email: bodmin@the-rifles.co.uk)

Durham – Elvet Waterside, Durham City, Durham DH1 3BW (tel: 01913 865496: email: durham@the-rifles.co.uk)

Exeter – Wyvern Barracks, Exeter, Devon EX2 6AR (tel: 01392 492434; email: exeter1@the-rifles.co.uk and exeter2@the-rifles.co.uk)

Gloucester – Custom House, 31 Commercial Road, Gloucester, Gloucestershire GL1 2HE (tel: 01452 522682; email: regimental-secretary@rgbw.army.mod.uk)

London – 52–56 Davies Street, London W1K 5HR (tel: 020 7491 4936; email: london@the-rifles.co.uk)

Oxford – Edward Brooks Barracks, Cholswell Road, Shippon, Abingdon, Oxon OX13 6JB (email: oxford@the-rifles.co.uk)

Salisbury – The Wardrobe, 58 The Close, Salisbury, Wiltshire SP1 2EX (tel: 01722 414536; email: salisbury@the-rifles.co.uk)

Shrewsbury – Copthorne Barracks, Shrewsbury, Shropshire SY3 8LZ (tel: 01743 262425; email: shrewsbury@the-rifles.co.uk)

Taunton – 14 Mount Street, Taunton, Somerset TA1 3QE (tel: 01823 333434; email: taunton@the-rifles.co.uk)

Yorkshire – Minden House, Wakefield Road, Pontefract, West Yorkshire WF8 4ES (tel: 01977 703181; email: yorkshire@the-rifles.co.uk)

Ross-Shire Buffs, Duke of Albany's Seaforth Highlanders

(See Queen's Own Highlanders (Seaforth and Camerons) Regimental Association)

Royal Anglian Regiment Benevolent Charity

RHQ Royal Anglian Regiment, The Keep, Gibraltar Barracks, Bury St Edmunds IP33 3RN (tel: 01284 752394; email: RHQRANGLIAN-ChfClk@mod.uk; website: www.royalanglianregiment.com)

Royal Armoured Corps War Memorial Benevolent Fund

c/o RHQ Royal Tank Regiment, Stanley Barracks, Bovington Camp, Wareham, Dorset BH20 6JB (tel: 01929 403444; email: regtlsec@royaltankregiment.org; website: www.royaltankregiment.com)

Royal Army Chaplains' Department Association

Ramillies, Marlborough Lines, Andover SP11 8HJ (tel: 01264 382104 email: ArmyCG-FIN@mod.uk)

Royal Army Dental Corps Association

RHQ RADC, HQ AMS, The Former Army Staff College, Slim Road, Camberley, Surrey GU15 4NP (tel: 01276 412753; email: RADCRHQ@hotmail.com; website: www.radc-association.org.uk)

Royal Army Ordnance Corps Charitable Trust

(See Royal Logistics Corps Association Trust)

Royal Army Pay Corps

Secretary, RHQ AGC Centre, Winchester, Hampshire SO21 2RG (tel: 01962 887436; email: info@rapc.co.uk; website: www.rapc.co.uk)

Royal Army Veterinary Corps Benevolent Fund

Secretary, RHQ RAVC, HQ AMD, The Former Army Staff College, Slim Road, Camberley, Surrey GU15 4NP (tel: 01276 412749; email: regtsecravc@hotmail.com; website: www.ravc-association.org)

Royal Berkshire Regiment

(See the Rifles – Salisbury)

Royal Dragoon Guards Benevolent Fund

3 Tower Street, York YO1 9SB (email: hhq@rdgmuseum.org.uk)

Royal Dublin Fusiliers

Applications should be forwarded directly to the ABF The Soldiers' Charity, see page 135.

Royal Electrical and Mechanical Engineers (REME) Association & Benevolent Fund

RHQ REME (H075), Hazebrouck Barracks, Arborfield RG2 9NJ (tel: 01189 763220; email: REMERHQ-CorpsSec@mod.uk)

Royal Engineers Association
Ravelin Building, Brompton Barracks, Chatham ME4 4UG (tel: 01634 847005; email: info@reahq.org.uk; website: www.reahq.org.uk)

Fusiliers Aid Society
City of London Headquarters, HM Tower of London, London EC3N 4AB (tel: 020 3166 6906; (email: asstregtsec@mod.uk; website: www.thefusiliers.org)

Royal Gloucestershire Hussars
(See Yeomanry Benevolent Fund)

Royal Gloucestershire, Berkshire & Wiltshire Regiment
(See the Rifles – Gloucester)

Royal Green Jackets
(See the Rifles – Winchester)

Royal Hampshire Regiment
(See Princess of Wales's Royal Regiment)

Royal Highland Fusiliers Benevolent Association
518 Sauchiehall Street, Glasgow G2 3LW

Royal Inniskilling Fusiliers
(See Royal Irish Regiment Benevolent Fund)

Royal Irish Fusiliers
(See Royal Irish Regiment Benevolent Fund)

Royal Irish Rangers
(See Royal Irish Regiment Benevolent Fund)

Royal Irish Regiment Benevolent Fund
RHQ The Royal Irish Regiment, St Patrick's Barracks, Ballymena, BFPO 808, Northern Ireland (tel: 02825 661381; fax: 02825 661378; email: benfund@royalirishregiment.co.uk; website: www.royalirish.easynet.co.uk)

Royal Irish Rifles
(See Royal Irish Regiment Benevolent Fund)

9th/12th Royal Lancers (Prince of Wales) Charitable Association
Regimental Secretary, TA Centre, Wigston, Leicestershire LE18 4UX (tel: 01162 785425; email: admin@delhispearman.org.uk; website: www.delhispearman.org.uk)

Royal Lincolnshire Regiment
(See Royal Anglian Regiment Benevolent Charity)

Royal Logistic Corps Association Trust
RHQ The RLC, Dettingen House, The Princess Royal Barracks, Deepcut, Camberley, Surrey GU16 6RW (tel: 01252 833334; email: regttreasurer@rhqtherlc.org.uk)

Royal Military Academy Sandhurst Band
Applications should be forwarded directly to the ABF The Soldiers' Charity, see page 135.

Royal Munster Fusiliers Charitable Fund
Applications should be forwarded to the ABF The Soldiers' Charity, see page 135.

Royal Norfolk Regimental Association
(See Royal Anglian Regiment Benevolent Charity)

Royal Northumberland Fusiliers
(See Fusiliers Aid Society)

Royal Regiment of Fusiliers (post 1968)
(See Fusiliers Aid Society)

Royal Regiment of Scotland
Regimental Secretary, The Castle, Edinburgh EH1 2YT

Royal Scots Benevolent Society
Henderson Loggie, 34 Melville Street, Edinburgh EH3 7HA)

Royal Scots Dragoon Guards Association
The Castle, Edinburgh EH1 2YT

Royal Scots Fusiliers
(See Royal Highland Fusiliers Benevolent Association)

Royal Sussex Regiment
(See Princess of Wales's Royal Regiment)

Royal Tank Regiment Association and Benevolent Fund
RHQ Royal Tank Regiment, Stanley Barracks, Bovington, Dorset BH20 6JA (tel: 01929 403331; email: regtlsec@royaltankregiment.org; website: www.royaltankregiment.com)

Royal Ulster Rifles Benevolent Fund
(See Royal Irish Regiment Benevolent Fund)

Royal Warwickshire Regimental Association
Area Headquarters, St John's House, Warwick CV34 4NF (tel: 01926 491653; email rrfhqwark@btconnect.com:)

Royal Welsh Fusilier Comrades' Association
Secretary, RHQ The Royal Welsh, Maindy Barracks, Cardiff CF14 3YE (tel: 02920 781207; fax: 02920 781357; email: rhgroyalwelsh@hotmail.co.uk)

Royal Welsh Benevolent Fund
Secretary, RHQ The Royal Welsh, Maindy Barracks, Cardiff CF14 3YE (tel: 02920 781207; fax: 02920 781357; email: rhgroyalwelsh@hotmail.co.uk)

Scots Guards Association
2 Clifton Terrace, Edinburgh EH12 5DR (tel: 01313 371084)

Seaforth Highlanders' Regiment
(See Queens Own Highlanders (Seaforth and Camerons) Regimental Association)

Sharpshooters Yeomanry
(See Yeomanry Benevolent Fund)

Sherwood Foresters
(See Mercian Regiment Benevolent Fund)

Sherwood Rangers Yeomanry
(See Yeomanry Benevolent Fund)

Small Arms School Corps Comrades' Association
HQ SASC, Land Warfare Centre, Imber Road, Warminster, Wiltshire BA12 0DJ (tel: 01985 222487)

Somerset Light Infantry
(See the Rifles – Taunton)

South Lancashire Regiment (Prince of Wales's Volunteers)
(See Duke of Lancaster's Regiment)

South Staffordshire Regiment
(See Mercian Regiment Benevolent Fund)

Special Air Service Association
PO Box 35051, London NW1 4WF (tel: 020 7756 2408; email: assn@marsandminerva.co.uk)

Staffordshire Regiment
(See Mercian Regiment Benevolent Fund)

Staffordshire Yeomanry
(See Yeomanry Benevolent Fund)

Suffolk Regiment
(See Royal Anglian Regiment Benevolent Charity)

Sussex Regiment
(See Princess of Wales's Royal Regiment)

Ulster Defence Regiment Benevolent Fund
Applications should be submitted through one of four regional contact centres of Aftercare Service: www.aftercareservice.org

Welsh Guards Afghanistan Appeal
RHQ Welsh Guards, Wellington Barracks, Birdcage Walk, London SW1E 6HQ (tel: 020 7414 3291; email: DINF-FtGds-WG-OffMgr@mod.uk)

Welsh Guards Benevolent Fund
RHQ Welsh Guards, Wellington Barracks, Birdcage Walk, London SW1E 6HQ (tel: 020 7414 3291; email: DINF-FtGds-WG-OffMgr@mod.uk)

West Riding Regiment
(See Yorkshire Regiment)

West Yorkshire Regimental Association
(See Yorkshire Regiment)

Wiltshire Regiment
(See the Rifles – Salisbury)

Women's Royal Army Corps Benevolent Fund
Gould House, Worthy Down, Winchester SO21 2RG (tel: 01962 887570; email: sue.hatton@wracassociation.org.uk; website: www.wracassociation.org.uk)

Worcestershire Regiment
(See the Mercian Regimental Benevolent Fund)

Worcestershire & Sherwood Foresters Regiment
(See the Mercian Regimental Benevolent Fund)

Yeoman of the Guard – Queen's Bodyguard
(See Yeomanry Benevolent Fund)

Yeoman Warders
(See Yeomanry Benevolent Fund)

Yeomanry Benevolent Fund
Honorary Secretary, 9 Ambleside, St Annes Road, Godalming, Surrey GU7 1LP (tel: 01483 421625; email: checkven@aol.com) This fund covers all Yeomanry Regiments.

York and Lancaster Regiment
(See Yorkshire Regiment)

Yorkshire Hussars
(See Yeomanry Benevolent Fund)

Yorkshire Regiment
RHQ, 3 Tower Street, York YO1 9SB (tel: 01904 461013;email: RHQYORKS-OffrRec@mod.uk)

All-service funds

Funds marked with a (*) also have an entry in the main 'Service and ex-service charities' section on page 135.

***Association of Jewish Ex-servicemen and Women (AJEX)**
Shield House, Harmony Way, London NW4 2BZ (tel: 020 8208 2323)

Fund dedicated to the welfare of Jewish veterans and their dependents.

British Korean Veterans (1981) Relief Fund
c/o Royal British Legion, 199 Borough High Street, London SE1 1AA (tel: 020 3207 2133)

Fund for the relief of distress amongst men and women who served with the British Forces during the Korean Campaign between June 1950 and July 1954, who are holders of, or entitled to, the British Korean Medal or United Nations Medal, their widows and dependents. Applicants need not be members of the British Korean Veterans Association to qualify for assistance.

***British Limbless Ex-Service Men's Association (BLESMA)**
General Secretary, 185–187 High Road, Chadwell Heath, Romford RM6 6NA (tel: 020 8590 1124; fax: 020 8599 2932; email: ChadwellHeath@blesma.org; website: www.blesma.org)

To promote the welfare of all those of either sex who have lost a limb or limbs, or one, or both eyes, whilst in service or as a result of service in any branch of her Majesty's Forces or auxiliary Forces and to assist needy dependents of such limbless ex-Servicemen and women. It will also help those ex-Servicemen and women who suffer amputation of a limb or limbs after service.

***Burma Star Association**
Benevolence Secretary, 34 Grosvenor Gardens, London SW1W 0DH (tel: 020 7823 4273; email: burmastar@btconnect.com; website: www.burmstar.org.uk)

Grants for men and women who served with his Majesty's or Allied Forces or in the Nursing Services during the Burma campaign and are Burma Star medal holders.

Canadian Veterans' Affairs

Welfare Officer, Department of Veterans' Affairs, Canadian High Commission, MacDonald House, 1 Grosvenor Square, London W1K 4AB (tel: 020 7258 6339)

Support for Canadian veterans, and their widows and dependents, living in the UK.

Chindits Old Comrades Association

Capt. B K Wilson, Secretary & Welfare Officer, c/o The TA Centre, Wolsley House, Fallings Park, Wolverhampton WV10 9QR

The aim of the association is to provide advice and aid (including, in appropriate cases, financial aid) to people who served in Burma with the Chindit Forces in 1943 and 1944, and their widows.

Ex-Services Mental Welfare Society (Combat Stress)

Tyrwhitt House, Oaklawn Road, Leatherhead KT22 0BX (tel: 0800 138 1619; email: contactus@combatstress.org.uk; website: www.combatstress.org.uk)

The society is the only organisation specialising in helping those of all ranks of the armed services and merchant navy suffering from combat related psychological injury caused by the traumatic events they have experienced in service. Remedial treatment is offered at three centres in Surrey, Shropshire and Ayrshire. The society also has a network of welfare officers who visit at home or hospital, and can help with war pensions and appeals. Information packs on request.

The Far East Prisoners of War (FEPOW) Trust Funds

c/o Royal British Legion, 199 Borough High Street, London SE1 1AA (tel: 020 3207 2133)

Support for people who were FEPOW and their spouses, widows/widowers and dependents from the Far East Prisoner of War Fund and the FEPOW Central Welfare Fund.

Forces Pensions Society

68 South Lambeth Road, London SW8 1RL (tel: 020 7820 9988; email: memsec@forpen.co.uk; website: www.forcespensionsociety.org)

This society provides advice on all aspects of Armed Forces Pensions Schemes. No financial assistance is given.

Irish Ex-Service Trust

c/o Royal British Legion, 199 Borough High Street, London SE1 1AA (tel: 020 3207 2030)

This is a government fund for those ex-service persons of the British Armed Forces who are resident in Northern Ireland or the Republic of Ireland, and their dependents. The trust makes one-off and recurrent grants for a variety of needs, particularly in those cases that might not normally be considered by other trusts/welfare organisations.

Joint Committee of the Order of St John and British Red Cross

c/o Royal British Legion, 199 Borough High Street, London SE1 1AA (tel: 0845 772 5725)

Help is available mainly by grants administered through other voluntary organisations, for War Pensioners and their widows/widowers, primarily those disabled in the first and Second World wars and the subsequent recognised conflicts, but not including Falklands War, the Gulf War 1990/91 or service in Northern Ireland.

*Lloyd's Patriotic Fund

c/o Welfare Department, SSAFA Forces Help, 19 Queen Elizabeth Street, London SE1 2LP (tel: 0800 731 4880)

The fund aims to help former members of the armed forces and their dependents who are in need. Grants will be given to a limited number of cases for one-off single grants for those with chronic illness or living in poverty, or in need of respite holidays.

National Ex-Prisoners of War Association

59 Pinkwell Lane, Hayes UB3 1PJ (tel: 07968 991714; website: www.prisonerofwar.org.uk)

To relieve poverty and sickness among members of all ranks of the forces or nursing services and who during such service were prisoners of war in any theatre of war, and their widows and dependents.

Normandy Veterans Association Benevolent/ Welfare Fund

General Secretary, 53 Normandy Road, Cleethorpes, South Humberside DN35 9JE (tel: 01472 600867)

The purpose of the fund is to give practical help to members, and to dependents of veterans, whose circumstances require it.

*"Not Forgotten" Association

4th Floor, 2 Grosvenor Gardens, London SW1W 0DH (tel: 020 7730 2400; fax: 020 7730 0020; email: info@nfassociation.org; website: www.nfassociation.org)

Provides recreational facilities for wounded service and disabled ex-service men and women as follows: TV sets (applicants whose mobility is severely restricted), TV licences, holidays, day outings and, for those confined to care homes, in-house entertainments.

Please note: the Association is unable to make cash grants, undertake welfare casework or assist widows.

*Officers' Association

First Floor, Mountbarrow House, 6–20 Elizabeth Street, London SW1W 9RB (tel: 0845 873 7153; website: www.officersassociation.org.uk)

The association awards regular and one-off financial help and advice to those in distress at home. Help is also provided towards care home third party shortfalls. Advice papers are also available on Care in the Community Legislation, Pension Credit and associated benefits, and accommodation e.g. Care Homes and sheltered accommodation.

*Officers' Association Scotland

New Haig House, Logie Green Road, Edinburgh EH7 4HR (tel: 01315 572782; website: www.poppyscotland.org.uk)

The association aims to relieve distress among all those who have at any time held a Sovereign's Commission with embodied service in HM Naval, Military, or Air Forces, and among their wives, widows, husbands, widowers, children and dependents. This includes ex-officers who were commissioned into the Reserve, Auxiliary, or Territorial Forces. Applicants must be resident in Scotland at the time of their initial application or have been members of a Scottish Regiment. Financial assistance is available through the Benevolence Service and help to ex-officers looking for employment is given through the Employment Service.

*Poppyscotland (Earl Haig Fund Scotland)

New Haig House, Logie Green Road, Edinburgh EH7 4HR (tel: 01315 572782; fax: 01315 575819; email:enquiries@poppyscotland.org.uk; website: www.poppyscotland.org.uk)

Head of Charitable Services: Gary Gray; Benevolence Secretary: Capt. Jim Macfarlane.

To relieve financially all ex-servicemen and women in need residing in Scotland, and their dependents. Poppyscotland also assists Merchant Seamen who have served in a war environment and Polish ex-Servicemen provided, in both cases, they are resident in Scotland. Grants may be given either following an annual review or as an individual one-off payment.

Prisoners Families Fund

c/o Welfare Department, SSAFA Forces Help, 19 Queen Elizabeth Street, London SE1 2LP (tel: 0800 731 4880)

This fund makes grants for essential household items and children's clothing where a prisoner's family is struggling as a result of imprisonment.

The corporation provides financial help to widows, children and other dependents of officers and men of the Armed Forces who are in need, in the form of continuing allowances and grants, including education grants or bursaries.

Special Forces Benevolent Fund

c/o Brig Roger Dillon, D Group, 23 Grafton Street, London W1S 4EY (tel: 020 7318 9200)

Grants and pastoral support to 1939–1945 members of Special Operations Executive and their dependents.

Veterans Aid

40 Buckingham Palace Road, London SW1W 0RE (tel: 0800 012 6867; email: info@veterans-aid.net; website: www.veterans-aid.net)

This organisation provides advice and assistance to homeless or 'pending' homeless ex-service personnel and their families in the UK and overseas. Help can be given in the form of food, clothing and shelter. Assistance is also given with drug, alcohol and gambling addictions and issues around mental health.

War Widows Association of Great Britain

c/o Royal British Legion, 199 Borough High Street, London SE1 1AA (tel: 0845 241 2189; website: www.warwidowsassociation.org.uk)

The association, formed in 1971 to improve conditions for all service widows and their dependents, works with government departments and service and ex-service organisations to help with all matters of its members' welfare. The association does not make grants.

Religious charities

Christian

The Acorn Foundation

£36,000

Correspondent: Michael Wood, Administrator, 14 Jordans Way, Jordans, Beaconsfield, Buckinghamshire HP9 2SP (01494 870171)

CC Number: 1068004

Eligibility

People in need who live in the UK.

Types of grants

Grants are given according to need.

Annual grant total

In 2012/13 the foundation held assets of £2 million and had an income of £102,000. Grants totalled £93,000, of which £36,000 was awarded to individuals for welfare needs. Organisations also received funding.

Applications

Grants are made in partnership with a number of local authorities.

Other information

The foundation also works to promote the Christian faith.

The Alexis Trust

£4,300 (44 grants)

Correspondent: Prof. Duncan Vere, Trustee, 14 Broadfield Way, Buckhurst Hill, Essex IG9 5AG (020 8504 6872)

CC Number: 262861

Eligibility

Members of the Christian faith.

Types of grants

Grants of between £50 and £100 are available, mostly for Christian-based activities.

Annual grant total

In 2012/13, the trust had assets of £496,000 and a total income of £38,000. Expenditure was £37,000 and the total amount of grants awarded to individuals was £4,300.

Applications

In writing to the correspondent.

Other information

In 2012/13, the trust awarded £32,000 worth of grants to charitable organisations and institutions.

Frances Ashton's Charity

£68,000 (65 grants)

Correspondent: Georgina Fowle, Administrator, Beech House, Woolston, North Cadbury, Somerset BA22 7BJ (fax: 01732 520159)

CC Number: 200162

Eligibility

Serving and retired Church of England clergy, or their widows/widowers, who are in need.

Types of grants

One-off grants of between £150 and £880. The trust has a number of areas of priority including emergency, medical or care needs.

Annual grant total

In 2013 the charity had assets of £1.8 million and an income of £75,000. Grants totalled £68,000.

Exclusions

Grants are not given towards property purchase, school fees or higher education costs (unless the child is disabled), parochial expenses, credit card debts and loans, general living expenses, sabbatical expenses or office furniture/equipment.

Applications

On a form available from the correspondent, to be submitted directly by the individual by 1 June each year. They are considered in September.

Archdeaconry of Bath Clerical Families Fund

£6,000

Correspondent: The Trustees, The Bath and Wells Diocesan Board of Finance, The Old Deanery, Wells, Somerset BA5 2UG (01749 670777)

CC Number: 230676

Eligibility

Widows and children of clergymen who have died and who last served in the deaneries of Bath, Chew Magna and Portishead.

Types of grants

One-off and recurrent grants according to need.

Annual grant total

In 2012/13 the fund had an income of £3,200 and a total expenditure of £7,400. We estimate that around £6,000 was made in grants to individuals for social welfare purposes.

Applications

In writing to the correspondent.

The Bible Preaching Trust

£11,000

Correspondent: Richard Mayers, Secretary and Treasurer, 5 The Crescent, Egham, Surrey TW20 9PQ (email: richard.mayers@tesco.net)

CC Number: 262160

Eligibility

Ministers of the Evangelical Christian faith who are in need. Theological students may occasionally benefit.

Types of grants

Usually one-off grants ranging from £250 to £2,000.

Annual grant total

In 2012/13, the trust had an income of £7,700 and a total expenditure of £11,200. We estimate the grant total to be £11,000.

Exclusions

Funding is not given for social causes, group projects, or to any person who cannot agree to the trust's doctrinal statement.

Applications

Either by recommendation or by letter: application forms and trust deed extracts are then sent out. Trustees' meetings are held every four months at which applications will be considered. 'Mass-targeting' applications or those outside the terms of the trust may not be answered.

Buckingham Trust

£9,000

Correspondent: Tina Clay, Trustee, 17 Church Road, Tunbridge Wells, Kent TN1 1LG (01892 774774)

CC Number: 237350

Eligibility

People in need who are missionaries or Christian workers, or people with some Christian connection. Applicants must be known to the trustees.

Types of grants

One-off and recurrent grants according to need.

Annual grant total

In 2012/13 the trust had assets of £729,000 and an income of £222,000. Grants were made totalling £193,000, of which £105,000 was given to charities, £79,000 to churches and the remaining £9,000 to individuals.

Applications

In writing to the correspondent. However, the trust has previously stated that its funds are fully committed each year and not given to new applicants.

Other information

This trust also makes grants to organisations and Churches.

The Chasah Trust

£9,200

Correspondent: Richard Collier-Keywood, Trustee, Glydwish Hall, Fontridge Lane, Etchingham, East Sussex TN19 7DG (01435 882768)

CC Number: 294898

Eligibility

Missionaries who are known to the trustees, or are a contact of the trustees.

Types of grants

One-off and recurrent grants to support Christian work.

Annual grant total

In 2012/13 the trust had an income of £27,000 and a total expenditure of £33,000. Grants to individuals totalled £9,200. A further £24,000 was awarded to religious organisations.

Applications

In writing to the correspondent.

Christadelphian Benevolent Fund

£115,000

Correspondent: Kenneth Smith, Treasurer, Westhaven House, Arleston Way, Shirley, Solihull, West Midlands B90 4LH (01217 137100)

CC Number: 222416

Eligibility

Members of the Christadelphian body who are experiencing difficult times.

Types of grants

One-off and recurrent grants according to need. Interest-free loans are also available.

Annual grant total

In 2013 the trust held assets of £2.3 million and had an income of £293,000. Grants to individuals totalled £115,000 and were distributed as follows:

Compassionate grants	£40,000
Fuel aid	£28,000
Regular grants	£17,900
Water aid	£14,100
Annual holiday scheme	£12,600
Christmas bounty	£2,800

A further £107,000 was paid to Christadelphian Care Homes.

Applications

In writing to the correspondent. Compassionate grants are given to individuals on the basis of representations made by the ecclesia of which those individuals are members.

The Church of England Pensions Board

£116,000

Correspondent: Lee Marshall, Administrator, 29 Great Smith Street, London SW1P 3PS (020 7898 1802; email: pensions@churchofengland.org; website: www.cofe.anglican.org/about/cepb)

CC Number: 236627

Eligibility

Retired clergy and licensed lay workers of the Church of England, their widows, widowers and dependents.

Types of grants

Allowances for those participating in the retirement housing scheme and to clergy widows and widowers to supplement their low income. The standard of 'low income' is reviewed annually. Our research suggests that no new grants are made for assistance with private nursing or retirement care.

Annual grant total

In 2013 the board had assets of £112.2 million and an income of £22.8 million. A total of £116,000 was awarded in grants.

Applications

Application forms can be requested from the correspondent.

Other information

The trust's main concern is the administration of the pension scheme and the provision of supported housing and nursing care. It operates seven such complexes across the country. The trust also runs a retirement housing scheme which offers mortgages and loans to assist those vacating 'tied' housing.

The trust is known by a number of working names: Bishop Morley College, Church Workers Pension Augmentation Fund, Clergy (Widows and Dependents) Pensions Augmentation Fund, Clergy Pensions Augmentations Fund, Clergy Retirement Housing Trust, Clergy Widows and Dependents Pensions Augmentation Fund, Suffolk Clergy Housing Trust and The Rev Joshua Case Trust.

The Clergy Rest Fund

£26,000 (24 grants)

Correspondent: Hugh MacDougald, Administrator, Winckworth and Sherwood Solicitors, Minerva House, 5 Montague Close, London SE1 9BB (020 7593 5000; website: www.wslaw.co.uk)

CC Number: 233436

Eligibility

Church of England clergy who are in need.

Types of grants

One-off grants ranging from £500 to £1,500 for a variety of needs.

Annual grant total

In 2013 the fund had an income of £43,000 and a total expenditure of £49,000. Grants were made to 24 individuals totalling £26,000.

Applications

In writing to the correspondent.

Other information

The fund also makes grants to institutions connected with the Church of England.

The Collier Charitable Trust

£7,000

Correspondent: Michael Blagden, Secretary, Cherry Tree Cottage, Old Kiln Lane, Churt, Farnham, Surrey GU10 2HX (01428 717534)

CC Number: 251333

Eligibility

Retired Christian missionaries and teachers in the UK and overseas.

Types of grants

One-off and recurrent grants of around £300 each. The trust may also provide accommodation.

Annual grant total

In 2013 the trust had an income of £22,000 and total expenditure of £89,000. Our research indicates that generally grants to individuals take up between 5–10% of the total charitable expenditure, with grants to organisations getting priority. We have estimated that around £7,000 was given in grants to individuals.

Applications

In writing to the correspondent.

Other information

Grants are also made to organisations, mostly those which are known to the trustees.

The Deakin and Withers Fund

£29,000

Correspondent: Grants Team, c/o South Yorkshire Community Foundation, Unit 3 – G1 Building, 6 Leeds Road, Sheffield S9 3TY (01142 424294; fax: 01142 424605; email: grants@sycf.org.uk; website: www.sycf.org.uk)

CC Number: 221932

Eligibility

Single women in the UK, whether divorced, unmarried or widowed, who are in reduced circumstances and who are members of the Church of England or of a church having full membership of the Council of Churches for Britain and Ireland. Grants are not given to ladies under 40 years of age and beneficiaries are usually over 55 years.

Types of grants

Annuities of around £500 paid in December.

Annual grant total

In 2012/13 the fund held assets of £197,000 and had an investment income of £57,000. Grants were awarded totalling £29,000.

Applications

On a form available from the correspondent to be submitted directly by the individual, through a third party such as a social worker, or through an organisation such as Citizens Advice or other welfare agency.

If there is a surplus of income, the trustees will consider any new applications that have been received.

Other information

In 2008 the Deakin Institute and the Withers Pension amalgamated and became the Deakin and Withers Fund.

The fund is linked with South Yorkshire Community Foundation.

The Four Winds Trust

£4,600

Correspondent: Simon Charters, Trustee, 64 Station Road, Drayton, Portsmouth PO6 1PJ (email: simoncharters1965@gmail.com)

CC Number: 262524

Eligibility

Evangelists, missionaries and ministers, including those who have retired, and their widows, widowers and other dependents who are in need.

Types of grants

One-off and recurrent grants according to need.

Annual grant total

In 2012/13 the trust had assets of £853,000 and an income of £40,000. Grants were made totalling £27,000, of which £4,600 was distributed to individuals.

Charitable and religious organisations received £21,000 and a further £1,500 was given in other gifts and donations.

Applications

In writing to the correspondent, although the trust states that it does not consider unsolicited applications.

The Fund for the Support of Presbyters and Deacons

£200,000

Correspondent: Benefits Section, Methodist Church House, 25 Marylebone Road, London NW1 5JR (020 7486 5502; email: stipends@methodistchurch.org.uk; website: www.methodist.org.uk)

CC Number: 1132208

Eligibility

Retired ministers and deacons of the Methodist church who are in need, and their dependents. Grants can also be made to enable ministers and deacons who are in need as a result of illness or impairment to continue to work where otherwise they would have to retire.

Types of grants

One-off grants to meet all kinds of needs including unexpected household expenditure (for example, the replacement of boiler/cooker/washing machine), gardening costs, property maintenance and repairs, bills, recarpeting, redecorating and medical needs (such as stair lifts, mobility scooters, opticians and dental costs). Grants of up to £3,000 are also available for residential care fees.

Annual grant total

In 2012/13 the fund had an income of £450,000 and a total expenditure of £635,000. A breakdown of grants was not available though in previous years, grants to individuals have totalled around £200,000.

Applications

In writing to the correspondent at any time.

Other information

The fund also makes grants to the Methodist Ministers' Housing Society.

The I. W. Griffiths Trust

£48,000

Correspondent: Lord Brian Griffiths of Fforestfach, Trustee, 18 Royal Avenue, London SW3 4QF (020 7774 4015)

CC Number: 1090379

Eligibility

People who are, or have been, engaged in Christian mission and are in need.

Types of grants

One-off and recurrent grants according to need.

Annual grant total

In 2012 the trust had assets of £124,000 and an income of £40,000. Grants were made totalling £48,000.

These were the latest accounts available at the time of writing (September 2014).

Applications

In writing to the correspondent.

The Hounsfield Pension

£3,900

Correspondent: Godfrey Smallman, Administrator, Wrigleys Solicitors, Fountain Precinct, Balm Green, Sheffield S1 2JA (01142 675594; fax: 01142 763176)

CC Number: 221436

Eligibility

Unmarried women, widows and widowers who are over 50 years old, live in England or Wales, are members of the Church of England and have never received parochial relief or public assistance. The charity tries to keep the numbers of male and female beneficiaries as equal as possible.

Types of grants

Grants are fixed annually and are paid in two instalments.

Annual grant total

In 2012/13 the charity had an income of £5,000 and a total expenditure of £4,100. We estimate that grants to individuals totalled £3,900.

Exclusions

Applicants must reside in England or Wales.

Applications

In writing to the correspondent. Only a limited number of pensions are available, and places become available at irregular intervals.

H. E. Knight Charitable Trust

£1,500

Correspondent: Aubrey Curry, Trustee, 14 Bramley Gardens, Whimple, Exeter EX5 2SJ (01404 822295)

CC Number: 283549

Eligibility

Individuals involved in missionary Christian work and spiritual teaching in the UK.

Types of grants

Ongoing support for Christian workers. Grants of up to £500 are awarded.

Annual grant total

In 2012/13, the trust had an income of £2,400 and a total expenditure of £3,100. We estimate that the total amount of grants awarded to individuals was approximately £1,500. The trust also awards grants to other voluntary organisations that support and facilitate religious activities.

Applications

In writing to the correspondent. Note, the trust has stated that the majority of its funds go to missionaries known to the trustees and, as such, other applicants are unlikely to be successful. The trust does not accept unsolicited applications.

The Leaders of Worship and Preachers Trust

£11,000

Correspondent: Adrian J. Needham, Executive Officer, Unit 35 First Floor Offices, Orbital 25 Business Park, Dwight Road, Watford, Hertfordshire WD18 9DA (01923 231811; email: lwptoffice@lwpt.org.uk; website: www.lwpt.org.uk)

CC Number: 1107967

Eligibility

Preachers and leaders of worship who are in need, and their dependents.

Types of grants

One-off and recurrent grants towards the cost of care, mobility equipment and other aids.

Annual grant total

In 2012/13 the trust had assets of £272,000 and an income of £2.9 million. Grants were made totalling £11,000.

Applications

Applicants should contact the trust to request an application form.

The Lind Trust

£20,000

Correspondent: Gavin Wilcock, Trustee, Drayton Hall, Drayton, Norwich NR8 6DP

CC Number: 803174

Eligibility

Individuals engaged in 'Christian and youth based work.'

Types of grants

One-off and recurrent grants according to need.

Annual grant total

In 2012/13 the trust had assets of £22 million and an income of £2.6 million. Grants and donations were made totalling £53,000, the great majority of which were made to organisations.

Applications

In writing to the correspondent at any time. The trust commits most of its money early, giving the remaining funds to eligible applicants.

Ministers' Relief Society

£18,000

Correspondent: Alan Lathey, Trustee, 2 Queensberry Road, Penylan, Cardiff CV23 9JJ

CC Number: 270314

Eligibility

Protestant ministers, their widows and dependents who are in need. Children of deceased ministers must be under 21 and of 'genuine evangelical and protestant convictions' to be eligible.

Types of grants

One-off and recurrent grants according to need. Recent grants have been given to: ministers who are retired or disabled, and their widows, and have inadequate income or savings; specific emergencies, such as serious illness, removal costs, enforced resignation or dismissal by congregation; and candidates and students seeking vocational training in the ministry.

Annual grant total

In 2012 the society had an income of £25,000 and a total expenditure of £20,000. The 2012 accounts were the latest available at the time of writing. We estimate grants to individuals for social welfare purposes were in the region of £18,000.

Applications

On a form available from the correspondent, to be submitted directly by the individual.

The Mylne Trust

£7,000

Correspondent: Paul Jenkins, Secretary, PO Box 530, Farnham GU9 1BP (email: admin@mylnetrust.org.uk; website: www.mylnetrust.org.uk)

CC Number: 208074

Eligibility

Members of the Protestant faith who have been engaged in evangelistic work, including missionaries and retired missionaries, and Christian workers whose finances are inadequate. Married ordinands with children are also supported when all other sources of funding have failed to cover their needs.

Types of grants

Annual and one-off grants for living costs and training expenses.

Annual grant total

In 2012/13 grants were made totalling £14,000. The charity gives for both educational and social welfare purposes and we estimate the total awarded to individuals for welfare purposes was around £7,000.

Applications

The trust states the following on its website:

> The trust has reviewed and, in 2013, changed its policy and procedure for making grants. Most grants are now being handled with partners already in Christian mission work. (Applications based on earlier procedures, using the old application forms, will no longer be considered by the trust.)
>
> *Worldwide except Africa*
>
> In principle, the only grant applications that will be considered by direct application to the trust are those from candidates for mission work who are studying or planning to study within the UK. Such applicants are invited to contact the Clerk to the Mylne Trust at admin@mylnetrust.org.uk requesting a current application form.

There are special arrangements for applicants who are based in Africa. For more information see the charity's website.

Other information

Applicants are advised to visit the charity's helpful website.

The Nazareth Trust Fund

£1,800

Correspondent: Dr Robert Hunt, Trustee, Barrowpoint, 18 Millennium Close, Salisbury, Wiltshire SP2 8TB (01722 349322)

CC Number: 210503

Eligibility

The trust gives support to individuals known to the trustees who promote the Christian faith and/or are Christian missionaries.

Types of grants

One-off grants ranging between £100 and £750.

Annual grant total

In 2012/13, the fund had assets of £37,400, an income of £38,200 and the grant total awarded to individuals was £1,800.

Exclusions

No support for individuals not known to the trustees.

Applications

In writing to the correspondent, although the trust tends to only support individuals and organisations personally known to the trustees.

Other information

Grants are also made to organisations (£40,200 in 2012/13).

The Paton Trust

£1,600

Correspondent: Trust Administrator, c/o Alexander Sloan, Chartered Accountants, 38 Cadogan Street, Glasgow G2 7HF (01412 048989)

SC Number: SC012301

Eligibility

Ministers of the Established Church of Scotland who are elderly or in poor health.

Types of grants

One-off grants up to £100. Grants are given to ministers who are in need of a convalescence break and to ministers who are retiring to provide them with a holiday at the time of retirement.

Annual grant total

In previous years grants have totalled around £1,600 although the total figure does tend to fluctuate.

Applications

On a form available from the correspondent. Applications are considered throughout the year and should be submitted directly by the individual.

Lady Peel Legacy Trust

£700

Correspondent: Christine Ruge-Cope, Administrator, 21 Chace Avenue, Potters Bar, Hertfordshire EN6 5LX

CC Number: 204815

Eligibility

Priests in the Anglo-Catholic tradition who, due to ill health or age, have had to resign their work or livings.

Types of grants

One-off or recurrent grants according to need.

Annual grant total

In 2012/13 although income had increased slightly to £7,500, total expenditure was down to £1,700. We estimate grants for individuals for social welfare purposes was around £700.

Applications

In writing to the correspondent. The closing dates for applications are 1 April and 1 November each year. Telephone contact is not invited.

The Podde Trust

£4,500 (19 grants)

Correspondent: Peter Godfrey, Trustee, 68 Green Lane, Hucclecote, Gloucester GL3 3QX (01452 613563; email: thepodde@gmail.com)

CC Number: 1016322

Eligibility

Individuals involved in Christian work in the UK and overseas.

Types of grants

One-off and recurrent grants.

Annual grant total

In 2012/13 the trust had assets of £2,000 and an income of £44,000. The trust awards grants for charitable purposes including the advancement of religion, education and the relief of poverty. There were 38 grants to individuals totalling £8,900 but no breakdown of the purposes. We estimate grants for social welfare purposes to be around £4,500. A further £36,500 was given to 40 organisations.

Applications

In writing to the correspondent. Note: the trust states that it has very limited resources, and those it does have are mostly already committed. Requests from new applicants therefore have very little chance of success.

The Pyncombe Charity

£10,000

Correspondent: Rita Butterworth, Administrator, Wingletye, Lawford, Crowcombe, Taunton TA4 4AQ (01984 618388; email: joeandrita@waitrose.com)

CC Number: 202255

Eligibility

Serving Anglican clergy under 70 years of age and their immediate families who are resident with them, who are in financial need resulting from a serious illness, an injury or special circumstances.

Types of grants

Small one-off grants.

Annual grant total

In 2012/13 the charity had an income of £16,600 and an expenditure of £13,400. We estimate that grants to individuals totalled £10,000.

Exclusions

No grants towards educational expenses.

Applications

Applications must be made through the diocesan bishop on a form available from the correspondent. Applications should be submitted by April. No direct applications can be considered and the charity has told us the majority of the direct applications received are ineligible. Note: it is important that the financial impact of the applicant's circumstances is clearly stated and quantified in the application.

Other information

The charity also makes donations to Pyncombe Educational Foundation and towards the repairs and maintenance of Poughill parish church.

The Retired Ministers' and Widows' Fund

£30,000 (45 grants)

Correspondent: Bill Allen, Secretary, 7 Wendover Lodge, Church Street, Welwyn AL6 9LR (01438 489171; email: willallen@tinyonline.co.uk)

CC Number: 233835

Eligibility

Retired ministers, and ministers' widows of Presbyterian, Independent (including Unitarian, Free Christian, Congregational and the United Reformed) and Baptist churches, who live in England and Wales and are on a low income. In 2012/13 this was defined as those with an income (not including state benefits) of less than £5,200 (£7,800 for married couples) and savings not exceeding £40,000. The savings limit for one-off grants is £10,000, although any of these limits may be disregarded in exceptional circumstances, such as when an application is made by a resident of a nursing home.

Types of grants

Biannual payments totalling £580 a year for widows and single ministers and £800 a year for married ministers. Gifts are given at Christmastime. One-off grants of up to £375 may also be awarded to help in an emergency. Priority will be given to those already registered with the charity.

A maximum of two one-off grants may be received in a four year period by any single beneficiary.

Annual grant total

In 2012/13 the fund held assets of £686,000 and had an income of £36,000. Welfare grants, including Christmas gifts, to 45 individuals totalled £30,000.

Applications

On a form available from the correspondent. Applications can be submitted by the individual but should be signed by a local minister.

Other information

This fund has its origins in 1733.

Retired Missionary Aid Fund

£596,000

Correspondent: Roger Herbert, Secretary, 64 Callow Hill Road, Alvechurch, Birmingham B48 7LR (01214 452378; website: www.rmaf.co.uk)

CC Number: 211454

Eligibility

Retired missionaries from the Christian Brethren Assemblies who are in need. Help may also be given to their dependents.

Types of grants

Quarterly grants, birthday gifts and Christmas hampers.

Annual grant total

In 2012/13 the fund held assets of £1.4 million and had an income of £479,000. Grants to individuals totalled more than £596,000 and were distributed as follows:

Gifts to retired missionaries	£566,000
Earmarked gifts for retired missionaries	£18,000
Gift vouchers and Christmas hampers	£11,000
Funeral grant	£1,500

Applications

The fund only gives support to its members, who should make their circumstances known to the correspondent.

George Richards' Charity

£23,000

Correspondent: Dr Paul Simmons, Administrator, Flat 96, Thomas More House, Barbican, London EC2Y 8BU (020 7588 5583)

CC Number: 246965

Eligibility

Church of England clergy who are in need and their widows and dependents. Preference is given to older people and those in poor health.

Types of grants

One-off and recurrent grants for heating expenses, household costs, travel, education, clothing, Christmas gifts and medical care. Pensions are available for those who have been forced to retire early from active ministry and are on a low income.

Annual grant total

In 2012 the charity had an income of £22,000 and a total expenditure of £25,000. This was the latest financial information available at the time of writing.

Exclusions

No grants for repaying debt.

Applications

On a form available from the correspondent, including details of all sources of income. Applications should be submitted directly by the individual. They are usually considered twice a year.

The Henry Smith Charity (UK)

£1.13 million

Correspondent: Kindred Team, 6th Floor, 65–68 Leadenhall Street, London EC3A 2AD (020 7264 4970; fax: 020 7488 9097; website: www.henrysmithcharity.org.uk)

CC Number: 230102

Eligibility

Individuals are eligible to register as kindred if they are direct descendants, or adoptees, of one of the kindred previously registered (with certain date restrictions). The onus is on the individual to prove their descent. Note the following from the charity's website: 'From June 2013, following agreement with the Charity Commission, the previous requirement for descendants of kindred to be born to married parents no longer applies.'

Clergy grants are only made to ordained clergy of the Church of England. Priority is given to those with dependents.

Types of grants

The charity manages two funds for the benefit of individuals:

Kindred grants: One-off and recurrent grants for kindred who are in financial need. Grants have included: regular financial support to kindred of retirement age on low incomes, general financial assistance to those on low incomes, grants to students, training to equip young people for employment, and grants for white goods.

Poor clergy fund: Grants are awarded to fund emergency or exceptional costs which cannot be afforded by family incomes.

Annual grant total

In 2013 the charity had assets of £785 million and an income of £10.6 million. Grants to individuals totalled more than £1.1 million, of which £649,000 was given to poor kindred and £481,000 to poor clergy.

Applications

For Kindred grants: To register or to apply for assistance, the Kindred Team can be contacted by email: kindred@henrysmithcharity.org.uk, or telephone: 020 7264 4979 or 020 7264 4980. A helpful list of FAQs is available from the website and should be read before any contact is made.

For Clergy grants the charity's website states that:

> Grants are made by the Diocesan Bishops, from a budget provided by the Charity. The Poor Clergy Fund is not therefore open to applications made directly to the Charity from individual clergy. Grants are only made to ordained clergy of the Church of England and there are specific further guidelines set down by the Charity against which Diocesan Bishops may consider individual clergy for a grant.

Other information

The Poor Clergy Fund now has two strands, the first of which is for individuals. The second strand is known as the Surplus of the Poor Clergy Fund and makes grants for projects which promote Christianity.

The charity also makes a large number of grants to organisations (almost £26 million in 2013), a lot of which is further distributed to individuals.

The Society for the Relief of Poor Clergymen

£25,000

Correspondent: The Treasurer, SRPC, 312 Waterside Court, Millpond Place, Carshalton, Surrey SM5 2JT (020 3652 0551; email: treasurer@srpc-aid.com; website: srpc-aid.com/)

CC Number: 232634

Eligibility

Evangelical ordained ministers and accredited lay workers and their dependents or widows/widowers in the Church of England and the Church in Wales.

Types of grants

One-off grants for illness or financial support when it can be shown that it has caused distress and hardship to the individual or family.

Annual grant total

In 2013 the society had an income of £23,000 and a total expenditure of £28,000. We estimate that grants to clergymen in need totalled £25,000.

Exclusions

Grants are not given towards school fees or normal travel expenses.

Applications

On a form available to download from the website. Applications can be submitted directly by the individual or through a third party without the knowledge of the individual and in confidence if the individual is not inclined to apply. Completed forms should be returned by email to secretary@srpc-aid.com or by post to The Secretary, SRPC, c/o CPAS, Unit 3, Sovereign Court One, Sir William Lyons Road, University of Warwick, Science Park, Coventry CV4 7EZ. Trustees meet to consider applications two to three times a year.

Sons and Friends of the Clergy

£1.2 million

Correspondent: The Rt Revd Graeme Knowles, The Registrar, 1 Dean Trench Street, Westminster, London SW1P 3HB (020 7799 3696; fax: 020 7222 3468; email: enquiries@clergycharities.org.uk; website: www.clergycharities.org.uk)

CC Number: 207736

Eligibility

The following information is taken from the charity's informative website:

> The charity is able to give financial help to clergy of the Anglican Communion who work in Great Britain, Ireland and the Diocese in Europe, and to Anglican clergy missionaries who are working abroad, provided they are sponsored financially by a UK-based missionary society. We can also assist such clergy in retirement, as well as their widows/widowers, their separated or divorced spouses/civil partners and their dependent children under the age of 25. In certain circumstances help can also be given to the unmarried elderly daughters of such clergy. Limited assistance in the form of book grants may be given to ordinands who are training for the ordained ministry.

Types of grants

Full details, including examples and criteria of the types of grants this charity will fund are set out on its very helpful website; the following information is taken from the 'Grants' section of the site:

> Set out below are some of the areas in which the charity can consider help. These areas are given as a guide only and are by no means exhaustive. The Registrar and his staff will gladly discuss any particular cases to see whether and, if so, how we may be able to help with any problem. If we are unable to help, we may be able to suggest other charities or trusts that may be able to provide what is needed. Please email, or telephone: 020 7799 3696 for a confidential discussion.

Examples of funding include: bereavement expenses; children's car seats; child maintenance; clothing; contact grants for maintaining contact with children after separation or divorce; counselling; debts; financial management courses; heating expenses; holidays; hospital travel; medical expenses; nursing home fees; ordinands; removals and resettlement for clergy/retired clergy; retirement housing; and sabbaticals and retreats.

Annual grant total

In 2013 the charity had assets of £86 million and an income of £3.7 million. Grants to 1,264 individuals totalled £1.9 million broken down as follows:

General welfare	£532,500
Holidays	£356,500
Resettlement and house expenses	£224,000
University maintenance	£292,500
Education expenses	£194,000
School fees	£146,000
School clothing	£87,000
Christmas	£76,000
Debt	£53,000
Ordinand book grants	£48,000
Bereavement	£19,500

This breakdown includes £40,000 which went to organisations.

Social welfare grants totalled £1.2 million and educational grants totalled £757,000.

Exclusions

Exclusions are given on the charity's website as follows:

> Grants for any one purpose will not normally be awarded more frequently than annually. Holiday grants, however, will not normally be awarded more frequently than once every two years.
>
> Grants are not normally made:
> - To augment stipends or pensions
> - In connection with the purchase of a house or flat
> - In connection with the purchase or maintenance of motor vehicles (save in limited circumstances for applicants with disabilities)
> - For the cost of fares or freight in connection with removals to or from the United Kingdom
> - To reimburse litigation costs or other legal costs
>
> Help for separated or divorced spouses can only be considered if the ordained spouse is still in Holy Orders.
>
> The charity does not make loans.

Applications

Note the following information taken from the charity's website when making an application:

> If you feel that you are eligible for consideration, please write to us or email us with the necessary details and request an application form.

> Please provide the address to which the form should be sent as application forms are not sent out electronically.
>
> Please then complete the application form **fully** in accordance with the instructions on it and return it to us with all necessary supporting documentation referred to in the form as soon as possible. Failure to complete the form fully or to send all the supporting documentation invariably causes delay in processing the application.
>
> For school fee cases, applications should be submitted as early as possible, ideally a term before the grant is required.

Other information

The following is taken from the charity's website:

> The charity now known as the Corporation of the Sons of the Clergy was founded in 1655 by a group of merchants in the City of London and clergymen who were all sons of the cloth. During the Commonwealth, persecution of clergy who had remained loyal to the Crown was widespread and many who had been deprived of their livings by Cromwell were destitute. The charity's foundation dates from a recognition by a body of sons of clergymen that action was required to meet a pressing need among clergy families for charitable help. The charity's present name is often felt to be a misleading one, but it is in fact an accurate description of its founding fathers.

The trustees' annual report for 2013 states:

> January 2013 saw the beginning of the new charity – the Sons and Friends of the Clergy. This entity came as the culmination of many years of negotiation between the Friends of the Clergy Corporation and the Corporation of the Sons of the Clergy.
>
> The landscape of our work is constantly changing as new demands and expectations are placed upon the clergy and their dependents. The bringing together of the two charities, along with the continued generosity of those who support our work, has ensured that we have the capacity to adapt to this changing context. The end of 2013 saw the beginning of our grappling not only with the changing circumstances affecting our beneficiaries but also with a fresh exploration of the most productive and generous ways in which we might help them. This has involved us, staff and trustees alike, in examining once again the definition of poverty as it affects those we wish to help. How this will develop is our work for the coming year, but we note that 2013 saw a steady rise in both the number of cases we considered and also in the total amount of grants awarded. So we continue to explore ways in which we may respond to the challenge for clergy and their dependents in the financial complexities of our age.

The Foundation of Edward Storey

£156,000

Correspondent: Timothy Burgess, Clerk to the Trustees, Storey's House, Mount Pleasant, Cambridge CB3 0BZ (01223 364405; email: info@edwardstorey.org.uk; website: www.edwardstorey.org.uk)

CC Number: 203653

Eligibility

'Financially unsupported' (i.e. single, separated, divorced or widowed) women who fall into either of two qualifying categories:

a) Women over 40 living within the county of Cambridgeshire

b) Widows, ex-wives or dependents of Church of England clergy; women priests, deacons or deaconesses of the Church of England; clergywomen, missionaries, or other women with a close professional connection with the Church of England.

Types of grants

Recurrent grants and pensions (which are annually reviewable and renewable). Pensions are occasionally available (only to those over 60). Some grants are issued with contractual terms of repayment.

Annual grant total

In 2012/13 the foundation held assets of £13.9 million and had an income of £1.4 million. Grants to individuals totalled £156,000 and were distributed as follows:

Parish grants	£82,000
Clergy widow pensions	£27,000
Clergy widow grants	£24,000
Parish pensions	£22,000

Applications

On an application form available from the correspondent. Applications can be submitted directly by the individual or a family member (if sponsored by a suitable third party), through a third party such as a social worker, Diocesan Widows' Officers, Diocesan Visitors, clergy and so on, or through an organisation such as Citizens Advice or other welfare agency. Applicants may be visited by the foundation's case officer. Applications are considered on a regular basis.

Other information

The trust also manages sheltered accommodation and a residential home based across four different sites.

The Thornton Fund

£7,500

Correspondent: Dr Jane Williams, Trustee, 93 Fitzjohn Avenue, Barnet, Hertfordshire EN5 2HR (020 8440 2211; email: djanewilliams@dsl.pipex.com)

CC Number: 226803

Eligibility

Ministers and ministerial students of the Unitarian church and their families who are in need.

Types of grants

One-off grants ranging from £250 to £1,500. Recent grants have been given towards convalescence, counselling, replacement of equipment not covered by insurance and taxis for somebody unable to drive for medical reasons.

Annual grant total

In 2012 this charity had an income of £19,000 and a total expenditure of £21,000. This was the most up to date information available at the time of writing (July 2014). We estimate grants awarded to individuals for social welfare purposes to be around £7,500.

Applications

In writing to the correspondent through a third party such as a minister. They are considered on an ongoing basis.

Other information

The fund occasionally makes grants to the general assembly of Unitarian and Free Christian Churches for special projects.

Torchbearer Trust Fund

£39,500

Correspondent: Phil Burt, Secretary, Capernwray Hall, Carnforth, Lancashire LA6 1AG (01524 733908; fax: 01524 736681; email: info@capernwray.org.uk; website: www.capernwray.org.uk)

CC Number: 253607

Eligibility

People engaged in full-time Christian missionary work. Preference is given to students and former students of Torchbearer Bible schools.

Types of grants

One-off and recurrent grants according to need.

Annual grant total

In 2012/13 the trust had assets of £157,000 and an income of £72,000. Grants for individuals totalled £79,000. No breakdown was given in the accounts of the amount for educational grants and that for relief in need. We have taken the welfare figure as £39,500.

Applications
In writing to the correspondent.

Other information
Grants are also available for missionary work.

Arthur Townrow Pensions Fund

£111,000 (150 grants)

Correspondent: P. I. King, Secretary, PO Box 48, Chesterfield, Derbyshire S40 1XT (01246 238086; website: www.townrowfund.org.uk)

CC Number: 252256

Eligibility
Women in need who are unmarried or widows, over 40 years of age and live in the Chesterfield and North-East Derbyshire areas. The fund specifies that the applicant should be 'of good character' and be a member of the Church of England or a Protestant dissenting church that acknowledges the doctrine of the Holy Trinity. Applicants should have an income of £8,000 or less.

Types of grants
Recurrent grants of £60 a month (£720 per annum). One half of the pensions granted must be paid to unmarried women and widows living in Chesterfield, Bolsover and north east Derbyshire. The remaining grants may be paid anywhere in England but only to eligible unmarried women over the age of 40.

Annual grant total
In 2012/13 the fund held assets of £3.6 million and had an income of £154,000. Grants to 150 individuals totalled £111,000.

Applications
On a form available from the correspondent. Applications should be submitted either directly by the individual or through a third party.

Other information
Arthur Townrow was a flour-miller in Chesterfield who left a bequest to be used to support widows and spinsters who are on low incomes.

The Widows' Fund

£44,000

Correspondent: Diane Naylor, Administrator, Jardine Lloyd Thompson, St James House, 7 Charlotte Street, Manchester M1 4DZ (01619 314400)

CC Number: 248657

Eligibility
Protestant ministers over 60 and their widows, widowers and children who are in need. Ministers who have been prevented from continuing in their ministries due to poor health or disability may also qualify for assistance.

Types of grants
Recurrent grants to supplement a low income and one-off emergency grants for specific purposes.

Annual grant total
In 2012 the fund had assets of £710,000 and an income of £33,000. Grants were made totalling £44,000, of which £42,000 was given in annuities and £2,000 in benevolent grants. The 2012 accounts were the latest available at the time of writing (August 2014).

Applications
In writing to the correspondent.

Christian Science

The Morval Foundation

£63,000

Correspondent: Tricia Cullimore, Secretary, Meadow Brook, Send Marsh Road, Ripley GU23 6JR

CC Number: 207692

Eligibility
Older Christian Scientists living in the UK who are members of The Mother Church, The First Church of Christ, Scientist in Boston, USA.

Types of grants
Monthly grants to allow older Christian Scientists to continue living independently in their own homes and one-off grants according to need.

Annual grant total
In 2012/13 the foundation held assets of £1.6 million and had an income of £53,000. Grants to individuals totalled £63,000 and were distributed as follows:

Monthly grants	£51,000
One-off grants	£12,000

Applications
On a form available from the correspondent, to be submitted directly by the individual for consideration at any time.

Other information
The foundation administers three funds; the Morval Fund, the Ruston Bequest and the New Chickering Fund.

Jewish

Carlee Ltd

£0

Correspondent: The Secretary, 32 Paget Road, London N16 5NQ

CC Number: 282873

Eligibility
Jewish people in need, including Talmudical scholars, widows and their families.

Types of grants
One-off and recurrent grants according to need.

Annual grant total
For a few years grants have only be made to organisations; however in the past awards have also been made to individuals.

Applications
In writing to the correspondent.

Other information
The main area of activity is grantmaking to organisations.

Chasdei Tovim Me'oros

£8,700

Correspondent: Yoel Bleier, Trustee, 17 Durlston Road, London E5 8RP (020 8806 2406)

CC Number: 1110623

Eligibility
People of the Jewish faith who are in need.

Types of grants
Grants given according to need.

Annual grant total
In 2012/13, the trust had an income of £19, 900 and a total expenditure of £18,000. We estimate that the total amount of grants awarded to individuals was approximately £8,700. The trust also awards grants to organisations.

Applications
In writing to the correspondent.

Closehelm Ltd

£56,000

Correspondent: A. Van Praagh, Trustee, 30 Armitage Road, London NW11 8RD (020 8201 8688)

CC Number: 291296

Eligibility
People, particularly those of the Jewish faith, who are in need.

Types of grants
Grants and loans are given to needy families for housing, medical and other costs.

Annual grant total
In 2012/13 the charity held assets of £2.8 million and had an income of £395,000. We estimate that grants to individuals for social welfare needs totalled £56,000, with funding also awarded to individuals for educational purposes. A further £126,000 was given in grants to organisations.

Applications
In writing to the correspondent.

The Engler Family Charitable Trust

£6,700

Correspondent: J. Engler, Trustee, Motley Bank, South Downs Road, Bowdon, Altrincham WA14 3HB (email: jengleruk@yahoo.co.uk)

CC Number: 1108518

Eligibility
Members of the Jewish faith living in England or Wales, with a particular focus on young people and the elderly.

Types of grants
Grants given according to need.

Annual grant total
In 2012/13 the trust had an income of £7,100 and a total expenditure of £13,600. We estimate that grants to individuals totalled £6,700, with funding also awarded to Jewish organisations across England and Wales.

Applications
In writing to the correspondent.

Finnart House School Trust

£23,000

Correspondent: Jamie Wood, Clerk to the Trustees, Radius Works, Back Lane, London NW3 1HL (07804 854905; email: info@finnart.org; website: www.finnart.org)

CC Number: 220917

Eligibility
Young people of the Jewish faith who are in need through sickness or disadvantage. Priority is given to people over 16, although all applicants are considered.

Types of grants
Grants of between £100 and £1,000 to provide care or education.

Annual grant total
In 2012/13 the trust had assets of £4.9 million and an income of £136,000. Grants were awarded to individuals in need totalling £23,000 and scholarship grants totalled £92,000.

Exclusions
Only members of the Jewish faith can be supported.

Applications
On a form available from the correspondent. Applications must be submitted through a social worker or social welfare organisation and are considered three or four times a year. For information about the School Hardship Fund contact by email, telephone or letter.

Other information
This trust also gives grants for educational purposes and to organisations which work with children and young people of the Jewish faith who are in need.

Gur Trust

£9,000

Correspondent: The Administrator, 206 High Road, London N15 4NP (020 8801 6038)

CC Number: 283423

Eligibility
People connected to the Jewish Orthodox faith in the UK.

Types of grants
One-off and recurrent grants according to need.

Annual grant total
In 2012/13 the trust had an income of £43,000 and a total expenditure of £39,000. Recent accounts were not available to view at the time of writing (August 2014). We estimate that welfare grants to individuals totalled around £9,000.

Applications
In writing to the correspondent. 'Funds are raised by the trustees. All calls for help are carefully considered and help is given according to circumstances and funds then available.'

Other information
Grants are also made to organisations and to individuals for educational purposes.

The Jewish Aged Needy Pension Society

£20,000

Correspondent: Sheila Taylor, Secretary, 34 Dalkeith Grove, Stanmore, Middlesex HA7 4SG (020 8958 5390)

CC Number: 206262

Eligibility
Members of the Jewish community aged 60 or over, who have known better circumstances and have lived in the UK for at least ten years or are of British nationality.

Types of grants
Up to 60 pensions of up to £10 per week for all kinds of need.

Annual grant total
In 2012 the society had an income of £13,400 and a total expenditure of £21,000.

Applications
In writing to the correspondent. Applications are considered quarterly.

Kupath Gemach Chaim Bechesed Viznitz Trust

£260,000

Correspondent: Saul Weiss, Trustee, 171 Kyverdale Road, London N16 6PS (020 8442 9604 or 0781 125 3203)

CC Number: 1110323

Eligibility
Members of the Jewish faith who are in need.

Types of grants
One-off and recurrent grants according to need.

Annual grant total
In 2012/13 the trust had an income of £356,000 and a total expenditure of £343,000. Welfare grants to individuals amounted to £260,000, with a further £80,000 awarded to Jewish organisations.

Applications
In writing to the correspondent.

Mercaz Torah Vechesed Ltd

£10,000

Correspondent: Joseph Ostreicher, Trustee, 28 Braydon Road, London N16 6QB (020 8880 5366)

CC Number: 1109212

Eligibility
Members of the Orthodox Jewish community who are in need.

Types of grants
One-off grants.

Annual grant total
In 2012/13 the charity had an income of £594,000 and a total expenditure of £500,000. Grants totalled £485,000, the majority of which was distributed to Jewish organisations. We estimate that grants to individuals amounted to £10,000.

Applications
In writing to the correspondent.

MYA Charitable Trust

£200

Correspondent: Myer Rothfeld, Trustee, Medcar House, 149a Stamford Hill, London N16 5LL (020 8800 3582)

CC Number: 299642

Eligibility
Individuals in need who are Jewish, worldwide.

Types of grants
One-off and recurrent grants according to need.

Annual grant total
In 2012/13 the trust had assets of £1.2 million and an income of £247,000. Grants to individuals totalled £520. We estimate that welfare grants to individuals totalled £200, with funding also awarded to individuals for educational purposes.

Most of the grants made by the trust are awarded to organisations; in 2012/13 these totalled £112,000.

Applications
In writing to the correspondent.

The Chevras Ezras Nitzrochim Trust

£199,000

Correspondent: Hertz Kahan, Trustee, 53 Heathland Road, London N16 5PQ

CC Number: 275352

Eligibility
Jewish people who are in need due to sickness, disability, financial hardship or unemployment. The trust focuses on those living in the Greater London area, although help can also be given to individuals living further away.

Types of grants
One-off and recurrent grants are available according to need. Support is also given in provision of food items, medical supplies and clothing.

Annual grant total
At the time of writing (August 2014) the latest financial information available was from 2012. In 2012 the trust had assets of £13,400 and an income of £263,000. Grants to individuals totalled £199,000.

Applications
In writing to the correspondent. Applications can be made at any time.

Other information
Grants are also made to organisations for advancement of religion, relief of poverty and educational purposes (£50,000 in 2012).

NJD Charitable Trust

£10,000

Correspondent: Alan Dawson, Administrator, St Brides' House, 10 Salisbury Square, London EC4Y 8EH (020 7842 7306; email: info@igpinvest.com)

CC Number: 1109146

Eligibility
Members of the Jewish faith who are in need.

Types of grants
One-off and recurrent grants according to need.

Annual grant total
In 2012/13 the trust had an unusually low income of £142 and a total expenditure of £64,000. In previous years grantmaking activities have accounted for all expenditure. We believe the majority of grants were awarded to organisations. We have estimated that welfare grants to individuals totalled £10,000. Grants are also given for educational purposes.

Applications
In writing to the correspondent. Applications are considered throughout the year.

Norwood (formerly Norwood Ravenswood)

£55,000

Correspondent: Julian Anthony, Company Secretary, Broadway House, 80–82 The Broadway, Stanmore, Middlesex HA7 4HB (020 8809 8809; email: info@norwood.org.uk; website: www.norwood.org.uk)

CC Number: 1059050

Eligibility
People with learning disabilities and children and families in need. Beneficiaries are mostly Jewish although one-quarter of their clients are of mixed faith. This is a national trust but concentrates on London and the south east of England.

Types of grants
According to need, but no regular allowances. Grants towards the celebration of Jewish religious festivals, social need and occasional holidays.

Annual grant total
In 2012/13, the charity had assets of £41.4 million and an income of £33 million. Grants total about £55,000 each year.

Applications
Grants are recommended by Norwood staff. Initial contact should be made by phone or emailing socialwork@norwood.org.uk.

Other information
Grants are made in conjunction with a comprehensive welfare service. Norwood provides a range of social services for Jewish children and families, including social work, day facilities, residential and foster care.

Toras Chesed (London) Trust

£0

Correspondent: Aaron Langberg, Trustee, 14 Lampard Grove, London N16 6UZ (020 8806 9589; email: ari@toraschesed.co.uk)

CC Number: 1110653

Eligibility
Members of the Jewish faith who are in need.

Types of grants
One-off and recurrent grants according to need.

Annual grant total
In 2012/13 the trust had an income of £337,000 and a total expenditure of £358,000. Grants totalling £323,000 were awarded in educational grants to individuals and organisations. We believe that no grants were awarded to individuals for social welfare purposes.

Applications
In writing to the correspondent for consideration by the trustees.

The Benjamin Winegarten Charitable Trust

£7,500 (3 grants)

Correspondent: Benjamin Winegarten, Trustee, 25 St Andrew's Grove, London N16 5NF (020 8800 6669)

CC Number: 271442

Eligibility

People involved in the advancement of the Jewish religion and religious education who are in social need.

Types of grants

One-off and recurrent grants according to need.

Annual grant total

In 2012/13 the trust held assets of £963,000 and had an income of £135,000. Welfare grants to three individuals totalled £7,500, with 19 charitable organisations receiving a further £108,000.

Applications

In writing to the correspondent.

The ZSV Trust

£652,000 (600 grants)

Correspondent: Z. V. I. Friedman, Trustee, 12 Grange Court Road, London N16 5EG

CC Number: 1063860

Eligibility

Jewish people in need, particularly older people, refugees, orphans and families in distress.

Types of grants

One-off and recurrent grants according to need. Most of the trust's funds are spent on providing food parcels. Other recent grants have been given towards medical assistance, clothing, shoes and weddings.

Annual grant total

In 2012 the trust had assets of £54,000 and an income of £678,000. Grants to around 600 families totalled over £652,000 and were broken down as follows:

Food parcels	£371,000
Relief of poverty	£94,000
Endowments to poor brides	£89,000
Families undergoing stress	£53,000
House repairs and utilities	£29,000
General donations	£6,900
Youth activities	£6,600
Clothing and shoes	£4,200

The 2012 accounts were the latest available at the time of writing (August 2014).

Applications

In writing to the correspondent. Individuals need to apply through social services or are often recommended by Rabbis or other community leaders.

Local charities

This section lists local charities that give grants to individuals for welfare purposes. The information in the entries applies only to welfare grants and concentrates on what the charity actually does rather than on what its governing document allows it to do.

Almost all of the charities listed have a grant-making potential of £500 a year for individuals, but most give considerably more than this.

Regional classification

We have divided the UK into nine geographical areas, as numbered on the map on page 172. Scotland, Wales and England have been separated into areas or counties in a similar way to previous editions of this guide. On page 173, we have included the 'Geographical areas' list which shows the unitary and local authorities within each such area or county. (Please note: not all of these unitary or local authorities have a grantmaking charity included in this guide.)

The Northern Ireland section has not been subdivided into smaller areas. Within the other sections, the charities are ordered as follows.

Scotland:

- Firstly, the charities which apply to the whole of Scotland, or at least two areas in Scotland.
- Secondly, Scotland is sub-divided into five areas. The entries which apply to the whole area, or to at least two unitary authorities within, appear first.
- The rest of the charities in the area are listed in alphabetical order of unitary authority.

Wales:

- Firstly, the charities which apply to the whole of Wales, or at least two areas in Wales.
- Secondly, Wales is sub-divided into three areas. The entries which apply to the whole area, or to at least two unitary authorities within, appear first.
- The rest of the charities in the area are listed in alphabetical order of unitary authority.

England:

- Firstly, the charities which apply to the whole area, or at least two counties in the area.
- Secondly, each area is sub-divided into counties. The entries which apply to the whole county, or to at least two towns within it, appear first.
- The rest of the charities in the county are listed in alphabetical order of parish, town or city.

London:

- Firstly, the charities which apply to the whole of Greater London, or to at least two boroughs.
- Secondly, London is sub-divided into the boroughs. The entries are listed in alphabetical order within each borough.

In summary, within each county or area section, the charities in Scotland and Wales are arranged alphabetically by the unitary or local authority which they benefit, while in England they are listed by the city, town or parish and in London by borough.

To be sure of identifying every relevant local charity, look first at the entries under the heading for your:

- Unitary authority for people in Scotland and Wales
- City, town or parish under the relevant regional chapter heading for people living in England
- Borough for people living in London

People in London should then go straight to the start of the London chapter, where charities which give to individuals in more than one borough in London are listed.

Other individuals should look at the sections for grantmakers which give to more than one unitary authority or town before finally considering those at the start of the chapter that make grants across different areas or counties in your country or region.

For example, if you live in Liverpool, first establish which region Merseyside is in by looking at the map on page 172. Then having established that Merseyside is in region 5, look at the 'Geographical areas' list on page 173 and see on which page the entries for Merseyside start. Then look under the heading for Liverpool to see if there are any relevant charities. Next check the charities which apply to Merseyside generally. Finally, check under the heading for the North West generally.

Having found the grantmakers covering your area, please read any other eligibility requirements carefully. While some charities can and do give for any need for people in their area of benefit, most have other criteria which potential applicants must meet.

1
2
3
4
5
6
7
8
9

Geographical areas

Northern Ireland

The Belfast Association for the Blind

£8,000

Correspondent: R. Gillespie, Hon. Secretary, 30 Glenwell Crescent, Newtownabbey, County Antrim BT36 7TF (02890 836407)

IR Number: XN45086

Eligibility

People who are registered blind in Northern Ireland. Consideration may also be given to those registered as partially sighted.

Types of grants

One-off grants of towards holidays, house repairs, visual aids and so on. Grants are also given for educational purposes.

Annual grant total

We have no current information for this charity. We know that previously around £16,000 was given in grants to individuals for both social welfare and educational purposes.

Applications

In writing to the correspondent through a social worker. Applications are considered throughout the year.

Other information

Grants are also made to organisations.

The Belfast Central Mission

£15,000

Correspondent: Janet Sewell, Community Services Manager, Grosvenor House, 5 Glengall Street, Belfast BT12 5AD (02890 241917; fax: 02890 240577; email: jsewell@belfastcentralmission.org; website: www.belfastcentralmission.org)

IR Number: XN46001

Eligibility

Children, young people and the elder who are in need and live in Greater Belfast.

Types of grants

One-off gifts of food parcels and toys at Christmas to children, families and older people. Our research shows that around 3000 toy parcels and 1600 food parcels are distributed every Christmas. Short breaks and holidays for elderly people are offered each year.

Annual grant total

According to our research, approximately £15,000 worth of donations and gifts in kind are available annually.

Applications

Application forms are available from the correspondent. Grants are normally decided in October and November.

Other information

This charity also runs advice centres and residential homes. It organises social gatherings and companionship to older people and runs a mentoring scheme for young people who have been residents of BCM's Supported Housing Project.

The Belfast Sick Poor Fund

£5,000

Correspondent: Grants Officer, c/o Bryson House, 28 Bedford Street, Belfast BT2 7FE (02890 325835; fax: 02890 439156)

Eligibility

Families in Northern Ireland with children aged under 18 who are in poor health or who have a disability and are in receipt of benefits or on a low income and who are in need.

Types of grants

One-off grants ranging from £50 to £200 for necessities and comforts.

Annual grant total

Grants usually total about £5,000 each year.

Applications

In writing to the correspondent by a social worker or other health professional. The fund cannot accept self-referrals. Applications should include: background information on the applicant with a breakdown of needs; why the request is being made; how a grant will benefit the applicant; details of income and expenditure on a weekly or monthly basis; and details of other sources of financial assistance and outcomes of any applications.

Other information

The fund derives its income from BBC Children in Need who have been a long-term sponsor.

Church of Ireland Orphans and Children Society for Counties Antrim and Down

£70,000

Correspondent: The Administrator, Church of Ireland House, 61–67 Donegall Street, Belfast BT1 2QH (02890 828830; email: office@diocoff-belfast.org; website: connor.anglican.org)

Eligibility

Orphaned children who live in the counties of Antrim or Down and who are members of the Church of Ireland.

Types of grants

Annual grants of up to £500 and one-off bereavement grants of £1,000 to a family on the death of a parent.

Annual grant total

Around £70,000 is available each year. No other information was available at the time of writing (August 2014).

Exclusions

No grants to applicants living outside the beneficial area.

Applications

Applications can be made at any time through the clergy of the parish in which the individual lives. Direct applications cannot be considered.

The Community Foundation for Northern Ireland

Correspondent: Grant Programmes Team, Community House, Citylink Business Park, Albert Street, Belfast BT12 4HQ (02890 245927; email: info@communityfoundationni.org; website: www.communityfoundationni.org)

IR Number: XN 45242

Eligibility

People in need in Northern Ireland. The foundation manages a number of funds providing support to local organisations, communities and individuals. Specific eligibility criteria will vary for separate funds.

Types of grants

Grants from David Ervine and the Women's Fund may provide support to individuals (the applicants are strongly advised to consult the website to ensure that the funding is available to individuals at a particular time when they wish to apply).

The Thomas Devlin Foundation operates solely for the benefit of people leaving school and developing their career in the arts field.

Annual grant total

In 2013 grants to individuals were only made from the Thomas Devlin Foundation for education in the arts.

Applications

Applications can be made online on the foundation's website. The standard application form consists of two parts – one is completed in the first instance and the second is emailed to the applicant to be filled in within the following two weeks and returned along with supporting documentation.

Like with all community foundations, funds are likely to open and close at short notice. See the website for latest updates before starting an application.

Other information

Grants are largely made to community groups and organisations and most funds will not fund individuals. Occasionally new funds aimed specifically at individuals may open.

The Londonderry Methodist City Mission

£1,500

Correspondent: Fund Administrator, Mission Office, Clooney Hall Centre, 36 Clooney Terrace, Londonderry, Derry BT47 6AR (02871 348531; fax: 02871 348531; email: office@clooneyhall.org.uk; website: www.methodistcitymission.com)

Eligibility

People in need who live in Derry/Londonderry and the surrounding area.

Types of grants

One-off grants according to need up to £500 per application.

Annual grant total

Our research suggests that grants usually total around £1,500.

Applications

In writing to the correspondent. Applications can be submitted directly by the individual/family member or through a third party (such as a social worker, Citizens Advice or other welfare agency). References are required to support applications made directly by individuals.

Other information

The charity has a specific interest in the homeless and runs a hostel for homeless men over the age of 18.

The Presbyterian Old Age Fund, Women's Fund and Indigent Ladies Fund

£149,000 (93 grants)

Correspondent: The Secretary, Presbyterian Church in Ireland, Assembly Buildings, 2–10 Fisherwick Place, Belfast BT1 6DW (02890 322284; fax: 02890 417303; email: bsw@presbyterianireland.org; website: www.pcibsw.org)

Eligibility

Needy, elderly (over 60 years of age) or infirm members of the Presbyterian Church in any part of Ireland. Applicants will normally be living at home, have an income of less than £12,000/17,500 euro per year, be in receipt of some type of state benefit, have less than £16,000/20,000 euro in savings, have no significant support from their family members and have medical needs requiring extra expenditure (some, albeit not all, of the above criteria need to be satisfied).

Types of grants

Annual grants were of £1,360 paid in quarterly instalments. Special gifts of £340 were sent to every beneficiary in the run up to Christmas. One-off grants are also made to help in cases of immediate financial need.

Support can be given for equipment, services or activities, including travel allowances to visit relatives or attend a funeral, household equipment, clothing and beddings, specialist medical or disability aids, home security, heating appliances and boilers, home insulation, respite care and a wide range of other needs.

Annual grant total

In 2013 a total of 93 people were assisted (41 in Old Age Fund, 36 in Women's Fund and 16 in Indigent Ladies' Fund) totalling £149,000 (£62,000 from Old Age Fund, £59,000 from Women's Fund and £28,000 from Indigent Ladies' Fund).

Exclusions

Requests normally covered by statutory sources are not supported.

Applications

In writing to the correspondent. Applications should be supported by a minister and are usually considered in January, April, June and October.

Other information

The Church's Board of Social Witness runs a full social care programme spanning family and childcare, older people's services, criminal justice, learning difficulties, mental health and disability.

The Presbyterian Orphan and Children's Society

£266,000

Correspondent: Paul Gray, Administrator, Glengall Exchange, 3 Glengall Street, Belfast BT12 5AB (02890 323737; email: paulgray1866@gmail.com; website: www.presbyterianorphanandchildren'ssociety.org)

IR Number: XN45522

Eligibility

Children aged 23 or under who are in full or part-time education, living in Northern Ireland and Republic of Ireland, usually in single parent families. One parent must be a Presbyterian.

Types of grants

Regular grants paid each quarter. Depending on financial resources, a summer grant and Christmas grant is paid to each family. Exceptional grants, such as education expenses, funeral costs, basic clothing/furnishings, debt repayments and grants for general household expenditure are also available.

Annual grant total

In 2012 the charity had assets of £9 million and an income of £691,000. Grants were made to individuals totalling £533,000. Grants are also made for educational purposes.

The society gives around 3000 regular grants, 1500 special grants and 120 exceptional grants each year.

These were the latest accounts available at the time of writing (August 2014).

Applications

Applications are made by Presbyterian clergy; forms are available from the correspondent or to download from the website.

The Retired Ministers' House Fund

£150,000

Correspondent: Ian McElhinny, Secretary, Presbyterian Church in Ireland, Assembly Buildings, 2–10 Fisherwick Place, Belfast BT1 6DW (02890 417220 or 02890 322284; email: info@presbyterianireland.org; website: www.presbyterianireland.org)

Eligibility

Retired members and servants of the Presbyterian Church in Ireland, and those contemplating retirement. Applicants will generally be over the age of 60. Applications from widows or dependents of ministers and missionaries will also be considered.

Preference is given to those: over the age of 60; intending to repay loan in less than five years; requiring less than maximum available (£50,000); willing to make regular repayments; and having limited resources.

Types of grants

Provision of rented accommodation, equity sharing arrangements and loans for purchase of property (or, in exceptional circumstances, property improvements).

Annual grant total

Generally about £150,000 a year may be spent on charitable activities, although this varies annually.

Exclusions

The fund does not distribute one-off grants.

Applications

In writing to the correspondent. Applications are considered as they arrive.

The Royal Ulster Constabulary – Police Service of Northern Ireland Benevolent Fund

£800,000

Correspondent: The Administrator, Police Federation for Northern Ireland, 77–79 Garnerville Road, Belfast BT4 2NX (02890 764215; email: benevolentfund@policefedni.com; website: www.rucgc-psnibenevolentfund.com)

IR Number: XN 48380

Eligibility

The fund aims to provide assistance to: serving police officers; injured and disabled officers; ex members/pensioners; ex members who are not pensionable; widows/widowers; partners/dependents of any of the above; parents of deceased single officers. Eligibility relates to financial hardship. By visiting applicants, representatives can obtain an understanding of the individual's circumstances, financial and otherwise. The representative will require a detailed financial report for presentation to the committee. All cases are treated as confidential. 'The bottom line is simply that a case of need must be identified.'

Types of grants

One-off and recurrent grants and loans according to need. The fund offers a wide range of assistance including adventure holidays for children, short breaks for widows, convalescence for injured officers and financial help when required.

Annual grant total

Around £800,000 per year to individuals for social welfare purposes.

Exclusions

No grants for NHS treatment. Loans will not be provided for cases of personal debt.

Applications

Initial contact should be made with the central point of contact who will advise the applicant on which of the police organisations is most appropriate to offer support in their circumstances. Contact may be made by calling 02890 768686 or emailing office@northernirelandpolicefamilyassistance.org.uk with a brief outline of your circumstances. All applicants will be visited by a fund representative in order to prepare a case to present to the committee at their monthly meeting.

Other information

The Benevolent Fund also owns a number of holiday apartments on the Antrim Coast and in Co. Fermanagh. They are available on a weekly basis throughout the year, to widows/pensioners and retired ex-members. Eligibility and booking information on the holiday apartments can be found on the website.

The Society for the Orphans and Children of Ministers and Missionaries of the Presbyterian Church in Ireland

£15,000

Correspondent: Paul Gray, Assembly Buildings, 210 Fisherwick Place, Belfast BT1 6DW (02890 323737)

Eligibility

Children and young people aged under 26 who are orphaned and whose parents were ministers, missionaries or deaconesses of the Presbyterian Church in Ireland.

Types of grants

One-off grants of £300 to £2,000 for general welfare purposes.

Annual grant total

Grants to individuals for educational and welfare purposes total about £30,000.

Applications

On a form available from the correspondent. Applications should be submitted directly by the individual in March for consideration in April.

Other information

The trust also gives educational grants to the children of living ministers and missionaries.

The Sunshine Society Fund

£5,000

Correspondent: David Mahaffy, PA, Bryson Charitable Group, Bryson House, 28 Bedford Street, Belfast BT2 7FE (02890 325835; fax: 02890 439156)

Eligibility

Families in Northern Ireland with children aged under 18 who are ill, disabled or facing financial hardship.

Types of grants

One-off grants for necessities and comforts. Only a small number of grants (no more than 20) are made each year.

Annual grant total

Around £5,000 is available each year for grants.

Applications

In writing to the correspondent by a social worker or other health care professional. Applications should include: background information on the applicant with a breakdown of needs; why the request is being made; how a grant will benefit the applicant; details of income and expenditure on a weekly or monthly basis; and details of other sources of financial assistance and outcomes of any applications.

Scotland

General

The Adamson Trust

£35,000 (79 grants)

Correspondent: Edward Elworthy, Administrator, PO Box 26334, Crieff, Perthshire PH7 9AB (email: edward@elworthy.net; website: www.theadamsontrust.co.uk/index.html)

SC Number: SC016517

Eligibility

Children aged 17 or under who have a physical or mental disability.

Types of grants

Grants range from £150 to £5,000 and are given to help with the cost of a holiday or respite break. Grant recipients must take the trip before their 18th birthday.

Annual grant total

In 2013/14 the trust made 79 grants to individuals totalling £35,000, and a further 31 grants to organisations, amounting to £49,000.

Exclusions

No grants can be given towards the costs of accompanying adults.

Applications

On a form available from the correspondent, to be returned with: details of the planned holiday; booking confirmations (if possible); and information about the child beneficiary. Supporting evidence such as a letter from the child's GP, hospital or health professional should also be attached. All applications are considered by the trustees four times a year in February, May, August and November with closing dates of 30 November, 31 March, June and 30 September respectively.

Other information

The trust also makes grants to schools and organisations.

The Aged Christian Friend Society of Scotland

£1,000

Correspondent: Trust Administrator, Johnston Smillie Ltd, 2 Roseburn Terrace, Edinburgh EH12 6AW (01313 177377; fax: 01313 134377; email: mail@jsca.co.uk)

SC Number: SC016247

Eligibility

Christians in need living in Scotland who are over the age of 65.

Types of grants

Annual pensions, usually of about £200 a year.

Annual grant total

At the time of writing (September 2014) the latest financial information available was from 2012. In 2012 the society had an income of £239,000 and an expenditure of £328,000. Most of the society's expenditure is spent on running the Colinton Cottages. Our research suggests that about £1,000 is given in grants to individuals.

Applications

In writing to the correspondent providing full details of the need.

Other information

The society is now a company limited by guarantee. Its principal activity is the provision of housing for older people in Scotland.

The Airth Benefaction Trust

£12,000

Correspondent: Douglas Hunter, Trust Administrator, HBJ Gateley Wareing, Exchange Tower, 19 Canning Street, Edinburgh EH3 8EH (01312 282400; fax: 01312 229800; email: info@gateleyuk.com)

SC Number: SC004441

Eligibility

People in need in Edinburgh.

Types of grants

Recurrent grants and pensions.

Annual grant total

In 2013 the trust had an income of £10,000 and a total expenditure of £12,600. We estimate that grants to individuals totalled £12,000.

Applications

On a form available from the correspondent to be submitted either directly by the individual or through a third party such as a social worker. These should be returned no later than 30 September for consideration in December. Beneficiaries are invited to reapply each year.

The Avenel Trust

£5,500

Correspondent: Mrs A. Cameron, Trustee, Duich, Dolphinton Road, West Linton, Peeblesshire EH46 7HG

SC Number: SC014080

Eligibility

Children in need under 18 and students of nursery nursing living in Scotland.

Types of grants

One-off grants of £10 to £500 are given for safety items such as fireguards and safety gates, shoes, clothing, bedding, cots and pushchairs, money for bus passes, recreational activities for young carers and washing machines.

Annual grant total

In 2012/13 the trust had an income of £24,000 and an expenditure of £23,000. Grants are awarded to individuals and organisations for both social welfare and educational purposes. We estimate grants to individuals for social welfare purposes to be around £5,500.

Exclusions

Grants are not given for holidays or household furnishings.

Applications

Applications are considered every two months and should be submitted through a tutor or third party such as a social worker, health visitor or teacher. Applicants are encouraged to provide as much information about their family or individual circumstances and needs as possible in their applications.
Applications can only be accepted from people currently residing in Scotland.

The Benevolent Fund for Nurses in Scotland

£200,000

Correspondent: A. Davidson, Liaison Officer, 1 Lufra Bank, Edinburgh EH5 1BS (07584 322257; email: admin@bfns.org.uk; website: www.bfns.org.uk)

SC Number: SC006384

Eligibility

Current and former nurses, midwives or student nurses who have worked, were trained in or have otherwise substantial connection with Scotland and are experiencing financial difficulties.

Types of grants

Quarterly grants to applicants with limited income due to illness or disability, or those with minimal level of their pension. One-off grants towards general welfare needs, furnishing or home adaptations are also given.

Annual grant total

In 2013 the fund had an income of £213,000 and an expenditure of £202,000. We estimate that grants to individuals totalled around £200,000.

Applications

Application forms are available from the correspondent and can be submitted by the individual directly or through a recognised referral agency (such as a social worker, Citizens Advice, doctor and so on). They are considered upon receipt. The trust may decide to visit potential beneficiaries.

The Biggart Trust

£6,500

Correspondent: Andrew S. Biggart, Trustee, Maclay Murray and Spens, 1 George Square, Glasgow G2 1AL (0330 222 0050; fax: 0330 222 0053)

SC Number: SC015806

Eligibility

People in need, with a preference for those related to the founders of the trust and their descendants.

Types of grants

One-off and recurrent grants (half-yearly), which in previous years have ranged from £600 to £1,100.

Annual grant total

In 2012/13 the trust had an income of £11,100 and a total expenditure of £13,200. We estimate that grants to individuals totalled £6,500, with funding also awarded to organisations.

Applications

In writing to the correspondent, directly by the individual.

The Blyth Benevolent Trust

£2,000

Correspondent: Trust Administrator, Bowman Solicitors, 27 Bank Street, Dundee DD1 1RP (01382 322267; fax: 01382 225000)

SC Number: SC017188

Eligibility

Women aged over 60 and in need. Preference is given to people who are blind or partially-sighted with the surname Bell or Blyth, and who live in or are connected with Newport-on-Tay, Fife or Dundee.

Types of grants

Annuities paid twice a year. A Christmas bonus may be paid, if funds permit.

Annual grant total

In 2012/13 the trust had an income of £3,100 and a total expenditure of £2,300. We estimate that grants to individuals totalled £2,000.

Applications

In writing to the correspondent to be submitted either directly by the individual or, where applicable, through a third party such as a social worker, or through an organisation such as Citizens Advice or other welfare agency.

The Buchanan Society

£25,000

Correspondent: The Trustees, 1F Pollokshields Square, Glencairn Drive, Pollokshields, Glasgow G41 4QT

SC Number: SC013679

Eligibility

Only people with the following surnames: Buchanan, McAuslan (any spelling), McWattie or Risk.

Types of grants

Pensions for older people in need. One-off grants can also be given.

Annual grant total

In 2012 the society had an income of £57,000. It is assumed that £25,000 was provided in welfare grants during the year. Around 70 people are supported annually. Grants are also made for educational purposes.

These were the latest accounts available at the time of writing (August 2014).

Applications

On a form available from the correspondent, to be submitted either directly by the individual or a family member, or through a third party such as a social worker or teacher.

Other information

The Buchanan Society is the oldest Clan Society in Scotland having been founded in 1725. Grantmaking is its sole function.

Challenger Children's Fund

£55,000

Correspondent: Mr T. Sellar, Trustee, Challenger Children's Fund, Suite 353, 44/46 Morningside Road, Edinburgh EH10 4BF (07531 580414; email: info@ccfscotland.org; website: www.ccfscotland.org)

SC Number: SC037375

Eligibility

The trust aims to help any child in Scotland under the age of 18 years living with a disability through a physical impairment of the musculoskeletal, neurological or cardio-respiratory system of the body

The following conditions on their own, however, are not accepted: psychiatric disorders, learning disabilities, behavioural disorders, development delay, Down's Syndrome, autism, visual or hearing impairment, cancer, diabetes, epilepsy, HIV, back pain and chronic fatigue syndrome. If they are associated with a physical disability, however, consideration will be given.

Types of grants

One-off grants up to £500. More may be granted in some circumstances. Grants can be given towards anything which is not provided by statutory sources but is required to meet the special needs of the child. Items include clothing, apparatus, equipment, household appliances such as washing machines, furniture, travel and home or garden adaptations. In the case of a holiday grant, if it is essential that a child must be accompanied, consideration will be given to the cost.

Annual grant total

In 2012/13 the trust had an income of £76,000 and a total expenditure of £63,000. We estimate that grants to individuals totalled around £55,000

Exclusions

Grants cannot be made retrospectively. Only one application per year.

Applications

On a form which can be obtained from the correspondent or on the website. Applications should be sponsored by a social worker, GP, health visitor, district nurse or therapist. Trainee workers and community care assistants may also apply, but a qualified person must countersign the application. Grants are given to the agency sponsoring the application or the company the purchase(s) are being made from. They cannot be given direct to the child or child's family. Applications can be submitted once a year.

The Craigcrook Mortification

£30,000 (23 grants)

Correspondent: Fiona Watson, Manager, Charity Accounting Services, Scott-Moncrieff, Exchange Place, 3 Semple Street, Edinburgh EH3 8BL (01314 733500; email: fiona.watson@scott-moncrieff.com; website: www.scott-moncrieff.com/charities/charitable-trusts/craigcrook-mortification)

SC Number: SC001648

Eligibility

People in need who are over 60 and were born in Scotland or have lived there for more than ten years.

Types of grants

Pensions of between £1,000 and £1,500 per annum payable in half-yearly instalments. One-off payments are not available.

Annual grant total

The trust's webpage states: 'At present there are 23 pensioners who each receive between £1,000 and £1,500 per annum payable in half-yearly instalments.'

Exclusions

Assistance is not normally given to those living with relations or in nursing homes.

Applications

On a form available from the correspondent or to download from the website. Applications should be supported by a minister of religion, doctor, bank manager, lawyer or similar professional.

Other information

The trust has limited capacity to take on new applicants.

E. McLaren Fund for Indigent Ladies (formerly known as The McLaren Fund for Indigent Ladies)

£72,000

Correspondent: The Trustees, BMK Wilson, Second Floor, 90 St Vincent Street, Glasgow G2 5UB (01412 218004; fax: 01412 218088; email: rmd@bmkwilson.co.uk)

SC Number: SC004558

Eligibility

To provide relief to widows and unmarried women in need, with preference for widows and daughters of officers of certain Scottish regiments.

Types of grants

One-off grants, annual pensions, holidays and Christmas gifts according to need. Annual pensions total £500 per pensioner.

Annual grant total

In 2013 the trust had assets of £2.5 million and an income of £100,000. Grants and pensions totalled £72,000.

Applications

On a form available from the correspondent. Applications to be made throughout the year for consideration when the trustees meet in March, July and December. Beneficiaries' payments are reviewed annually at the discretion of the trustees. All applicants will be visited.

The Educational Institute of Scotland Benevolent Fund

Correspondent: The General Secretary, Educational Institute of Scotland, 46 Moray Place, Edinburgh EH3 6BH (01312 256244; fax: 01312 203151; email: enquiries@eis.org.uk; website: www.eis.org.uk)

SC Number: SC007852

Eligibility

Members of the institute suffering from financial hardship due to unexpected illness, long-term health problems or a sudden change in financial circumstances, their widows/widowers and dependents. Applicants must have held a full membership for at least one year prior to application.

Types of grants

One-off and recurrent grants towards, for example, daily living costs, television licences, telephone rental, hairdressing and holidays. Emergency grants may also be available to members who have had an arrestment on their salary, who face eviction, or who have had their gas or electricity cut off.

Annual grant total

In 2012/13 the fund had an income of £223,000 and a total expenditure of £127,000.

Applications

On a form available from a local Benevolent Fund Correspondent. Individual contact details are available from the EIS website. The correspondent may arrange a visit to discuss an application and can offer help to applicants completing the form.

Faculty of Advocates 1985 Charitable Trust

£61,000

Correspondent: Gaynor Adam, Secretariat Officer, Advocate's Library, Parliament House, Edinburgh EH1 1RF (01312 265071)

SC Number: SC012486

Eligibility

1. Widows, widowers, children or former dependents of deceased members of the Faculty of Advocates. 2. Members of the faculty who are unable to practise by reason of permanent ill health.

Types of grants

Single grants, annuities or loans appropriate to the circumstances.

Annual grant total

In 2012/13, the trust had an income of £186,000 and a total expenditure of £121,000. Grants totalled approximately £61,000.

Applications

The trust is regularly publicised among members and applications are often informal, by word of mouth via a trustee. Alternatively applications may be made in writing to the correspondent.

The Hugh Fraser Foundation (Emily Fraser Trust)

£30,000

Correspondent: Heather Thompson, Partner, Turcan Connell, Princes Exchange, 1 Earl Grey Street, Edinburgh EH3 9EE (01312 288111; email: ht@turcanconnell.com)

SC Number: SC009303

Eligibility

People in need who work or worked in the drapery, printing, publishing, bookselling, stationery and newspaper and allied trades and their dependents. The trustees consider applications particularly from individuals who are or were in the employment of House of Fraser Ltd, Scottish Universal Investments Ltd and Paisleys.

Types of grants

One-off grants of £100 to £4,000.

Annual grant total

In 2012/13 the trust had an income of £2.3 million and a total expenditure of £1.9 million. We estimate that grants to individuals totalled around £30,000, with funding mainly awarded to organisations.

Applications

In writing to the correspondent. The trustees meet on a quarterly basis, normally in January, April, July and October. Applications should be received three months before the meeting.

Note: the foundation's focus is on making grants to charitable organisations and only rarely, and in exceptional circumstances, will the trustees consider applications from individuals and their dependents.

The Glasgow Society of the Sons and Daughters of Ministers of the Church of Scotland

£28,000

Correspondent: Fiona Watson, Manager, Charity Accounting Services, Scott-Moncrieff, Exchange Place, 3 Semple Street, Edinburgh EH3 9BL (01314 733500; website: www.scott-moncrieff.com/services/charities/charitable-trusts/glasgow-society-of-the-sons-and-daughters)

SC Number: SC010281

Eligibility

Children of ministers of the Church of Scotland who are in need, particularly students and the children of deceased ministers.

Types of grants

One-off and recurrent grants according to need. Annual grants are made with an extra payment prior to Christmas.

Annual grant total

In 2012/13 the charity had an income of £55,000. About £28,000 a year is given in welfare grants to individuals.

Applications

On a form available from the correspondent or downloaded from the website. Applications from children of deceased ministers may apply at any time.

Other information

Educational grants are also made.

The Douglas Hay Trust

£45,000

Correspondent: John D. Ritchie, Secretary and Treasurer, Barstow and Millar, Midlothian Innovation Centre, Pentlandfield, Roslin, Midlothian EH25 9RE (01314 409030; fax: 01314 409872; email: johndritchie@btinternet.com; website: www.douglashay.org.uk)

SC Number: SC014450

Eligibility

Children aged under 18 who are physically disabled and live in Scotland.

Types of grants

One-off grants ranging from £40 to £500 towards shoes, clothes, bedding, home improvements, holidays, computers, equipment and education.

Annual grant total

In 2012/13 the trust had an income of £37,000 and a total expenditure of £53,000. We estimate grants to be in the region of £45,000.

Applications

On a form available from the website or by contacting the correspondent. They should be submitted through a social worker, medical practitioner or other welfare agency. Applications are considered monthly.

The Anne Herd Memorial Trust

£12,000

Correspondent: The Trustees, 27 Bank Street, Dundee DD1 1RP

SC Number: SC014198

Eligibility

People who are blind or partially sighted who live in Broughty Ferry (applicants from the city of Dundee, region of Tayside or those who have connections with these areas and reside in Scotland will also be considered).

Types of grants

Grants are usually given for educational equipment such as computers and books. Grants are usually at least £50.

Annual grant total

In 2012/13 the trust had an income of £40,000. The trust gives approximately £25,000 a year in grants for education and welfare.

Applications

In writing to the correspondent, to be submitted directly by the individual in March/April for consideration in June.

June and Douglas Hume Memorial Fund

£4,000

Correspondent: Jennifer McPhail, Grant Programmes Executive, Empire House, 131 West Nile Street, Glasgow G1 2RX (01413 414964; fax: 01413 414972; email: jennifer@foundationscotland.org.uk; website: www.foundationscotland.org.uk)

SC Number: SC022910

Eligibility

Terminally ill patients who wish to spend their final days in their own home. Priority will be given to applicants from the West of Scotland and in particular the Helensburgh area.

Types of grants

One-off grants of up to £1,000 to assist patients with specialist equipment, as well as any house modifications necessary to accommodate such equipment. Grants may be used for bath and stair lifts, reclining beds and chairs, wheelchairs and walking frames, for example.

Annual grant total

In 2012/13 the fund had an expenditure of £4,000.

Applications

Applicants should contact Jennifer McPhail on 01413 414964 in the first instance and an application form will be sent out to applicants where funds are available. Applications completed by the applicant must be accompanied by a reference from a GP or consultant. Alternatively the application may be filled out directly by a medical professional. Applications are considered as they are received.

Other information

The fund is administered by Foundation Scotland.

William Hunter Old Men's Fund

£10,000

Correspondent: The Trustees, c/o Edinburgh Chamber of Commerce, Ground Floor, Capital House, 2 Festival Square, Edinburgh EH3 9SU (01312 212999; fax: 01312 615056)

SC Number: SC010842

Eligibility

Older men in need who were born in Scotland and are of Scottish parentage and who are/were merchants, manufacturers or master tradesmen.

Types of grants

Recurrent grants paid twice a year of £370 for people under 80, and £385 for those over 80.

Annual grant total

In 2012/13 the fund had an income of £13,700 and a total expenditure of £36,000. Our research tells us that grants usually total around £10,000, though grants expenditure for this financial year may have been higher.

Applications

In writing to the correspondent.

George Jamieson Fund

£100

Correspondent: The Administrator, Wilsone and Duffus, 7 Golden Square, Aberdeen AB10 1EP (01224 651700; email: info@key-moves.co.uk; website: www.key-moves.co.uk)

SC Number: SC007537

Eligibility

Widows and single women who are in need and live in the city of Aberdeen or the counties of Aberdeen and Kincardine.

Types of grants

Recurrent grants.

Annual grant total

Expenditure usually totals £100–£200.

Applications

In writing to the correspondent. Applications can be submitted directly by the individual or through a social worker, Citizens Advice or other welfare agency. Applications should include details of the individual's circumstances and are considered on a regular basis.

Jewish Care Scotland

£1,000

Correspondent: The Trustees, The Walton Community Care Centre, May Terrace, Giffnock, Glasgow G46 6LD (01416 201800; fax: 01416 202409; email: admin@jcarescot.org.uk; website: www.jcarescot.org.uk)

SC Number: SC005267

Eligibility

Jewish people in need living in Scotland.

Types of grants

One-off grants of £50 to £750 towards clothing, food, household goods, rent, holidays, equipment, travel and education.

Annual grant total

In 2012 the charity had an income of £720,000 and a total expenditure of £817,000. Educational grants to individuals usually total around £18,000 and social welfare grants around £1,000. In this financial year, however, the trustees have declared that there were no grants or donations made. We have retained the entry here as grants may well be made again in the near future. The 2012 accounts were the latest available at the time of writing (July 2014).

Applications

In writing to the correspondent.

Other information

The board also helps with educational costs and friendship clubs, housing requirements, clothing, meals-on-wheels, counselling and so on.

Key Trust

£9,000

Correspondent: The Trustees, c/o Key Housing, 70 Renton Street, Glasgow G4 0HT (0141–342 1890; fax: 0141–342 1891; email: info@keyhousing.org)

SC Number: SC006093

Eligibility

People living in Scotland who are in need due to age, ill health or disability.

Types of grants

One-off grants according to need. Grants have been given to help people setting up home, for example, towards furnishings such as carpets and to enable people to gain independence and 'experience more out of life'.

Annual grant total

In 2012/13 the trust had an income of £20 and a total expenditure of £11,300. We estimate that grants to individuals totalled £9,000; however, expenditure seems to vary significantly each year and in previous years has been far less (£300 in 2011/12).

Applications

On a form available from the correspondent, submitted either directly by the individual or through a social worker, Citizens Advice or other welfare agency.

John A. Longmore's Trust

£12,000

Correspondent: Robin D. Fulton, Trustee, Turcan Connell, Princes Exchange, 1 Earl Grey Street, Edinburgh EH3 9EE (01312 288111; fax: 01312 288118)

SC Number: SC007336

Eligibility

People who live in Scotland and have an incurable disease.

Types of grants

Annuities of around £330 are paid in two instalments. One-off grants of up to £1,000 to improve the quality of life on a day-to-day basis. Equipment sought can be either fixed or moveable such as a wheelchair.

Annual grant total

In 2012/13 the trust had an income of £23,000 and a total expenditure of

£13,100. We estimate that grants to individuals totalled £12,000.

Exclusions

No grants are given towards holidays or house decoration.

Applications

On a form available from the correspondent, to be returned with a covering letter detailing income and expenses of the household and a breakdown of how the grant will be used. Applications are considered in the third week of every month and should be submitted by the 16th of the month. Note: in recent years the trust has suffered from an income deficit and, therefore, may not be in a position to consider new applications.

The Agnes Macleod Memorial Fund

£3,300

Correspondent: Linda Orr, Secretary, Nurses Cottage, Hallin, Waternish, Isle of Skye IV55 8GJ (email: linda@m-orr.freeserve.co.uk; website: www.clan-macleod-scotland.org.uk)

SC Number: SC014297

Eligibility

Women in need who are over 60, living in Scotland and were born with the name Macleod or whose mothers were born Macleod.

Types of grants

To provide monetary grants or donations of gift vouchers when benefits from the state are either not sufficient or not appropriate. Grants range from £100 to £250 and are one-off.

Annual grant total

In 2012/13 the fund had an income of £3,600 and a total expenditure of £3,700. We estimate that grants to individuals totalled £3,300.

Applications

In writing to the correspondent. Advertisements are also put in newspapers. Applications are considered in May and November. Doctors, social workers, Citizens Advice, other welfare agencies, health visitors, ministers and priests may also submit applications on behalf of an individual.

The George McLean Trust

£7,000

Correspondent: Grants Administrator, Blackadders Solicitors, 30–34 Reform Street, Dundee DD1 1RJ (01382 229222; fax: 01382 342220; email: enquiries@blackadders.co.uk)

SC Number: SC020963

Eligibility

People in need who are living with a mental or physical disability and reside in Fife and Tayside. Older people may also qualify for assistance.

Types of grants

Grants typically range between £100 to £1,000 and are made towards convalescence, hospital expenses, electrical goods, clothing, holidays, travel expenses, medical equipment, nursing fees, furniture, disability aids and help in the home.

Annual grant total

In 2012/13 the trust had an income of £47,000 and a total expenditure of £36,000. We estimate that grants to individuals totalled £7,000, with a further £28,000 awarded to local organisations.

Exclusions

No grants are made towards debts.

Applications

On a form available from the correspondent. Applications can be submitted directly by the individual or through any third party. They are considered monthly.

Other information

Roughly 20% of the trust's expenditure goes to individuals, with much of the rest going to local charitable organisations. This is flexible, however, as the trustees consider where funding is needed most.

Annie Ramsay McLean Trust for the Elderly

£3,000

Correspondent: The Trustees, Blackadders Solicitors, 30–34 Reform Street, Dundee DD1 1RJ (01382 229222; fax: 01382 342220; email: toni.mcnicoll@blackadders.co.uk)

SC Number: SC014238

Eligibility

Elderly people aged 60 or over, who live in Fife and Tayside.

Types of grants

One-off and recurrent grants of £100 to £1,000 towards needs such as convalescence, travel expenses, furniture, clothing, medical and disability equipment, electrical goods, holidays, nursing home fees, help in the home, household items, electrically operated chairs, motorised scooters and so on.

Annual grant total

In 2012/13, the trust had an income of £48,400 and a total expenditure of £46,600. We estimate that the total amount of grants awarded to individuals was approximately £3,000. The trust awards most of its grants to organisations.

Exclusions

No grants are given towards debts.

Applications

On a form available from the correspondent. Applications can be submitted directly by the individual or thorough any third party. They are considered monthly.

North of Scotland Quaker Trust

£5,000

Correspondent: The Trustees, Quaker Meeting House, 98 Crown Street, Aberdeen AB11 6HJ

SC Number: SC000784

Eligibility

People who are associated with the Religious Society of Friends in the North of Scotland Monthly Meeting area, namely Aberdeen City, Aberdeenshire, Moray, Highland, Orkney, Shetland, Western Isles and that part of Argyll and Bute from Oban northwards.

Types of grants

One-off and recurrent grants according to need.

Annual grant total

In 2013 the trust had an income of £23,500 and an expenditure of £21,500.

We estimate grants to individuals for social welfare purposes to be around £5,000.

Exclusions

No grants are given to people studying above first degree level.

Applications

In writing to the correspondent.

Other information

Grants are also given for educational purposes.

The Nurses' Memorial to King Edward VII Edinburgh Scottish Committee

£60,000

Correspondent: The Trustees, Johnston Smillie Ltd, Chartered Accountants, 2 Roseburn Terrace, Edinburgh EH12 6AW

SC Number: SC023963

Eligibility

Nurses with a strong connection to Scotland (including nurses who have worked in Scotland, or Scottish nurses working outside Scotland) who are retired, ill or otherwise in need. Retired nurses are given priority.

Types of grants

One-off and monthly grants towards accommodation charges, domestic bills and to supplement inadequate income.

Annual grant total

In 2013 the trust had an income of £82,000 and a total expenditure of £89,000. Between 50 and 60 nurses are usually supported each year, with grants totalling around £60,000.

Applications

Details of present financial and other circumstances are required on a form available from the correspondent. The information given should be confirmed by a social worker, health visitor, doctor or similar professional.

Poppyscotland (The Earl Haig Fund Scotland)

£771,000

Correspondent: The Trustees, New Haig House, Logie Green Road, Edinburgh EH7 4HR (01315 501557; fax: 01315 575819; email: enquiries@poppyscotland.org.uk; website: www.poppyscotland.org.uk)

SC Number: SC014096

Eligibility

People in Scotland who have served in the UK Armed Forces (regular or reserve) and their widows/widowers and dependents.

Types of grants

Annual and one-off grants to overcome financial difficulties of varying complexity.

Annual grant total

In 2012/13 the fund had an income of £4.4 million and assets of almost £9.9 million. Grants made totalled around £771,000 and were given to 1,500 individuals.

Exclusions

Grants are not normally given towards non-priority debt, headstones or the replacement of medals. Loans are not available.

Applications

In writing to the correspondent.

Other information

Poppyscotland is in many respects the Scottish equivalent of the benevolence department of the Royal British Legion in the rest of Britain. Like the legion, it runs the Poppy Appeal, which is a major source of income to help those in need. There is, however, a Royal British Legion Scotland, which has a separate entry in this guide. The two organisations share the same premises and work together.

In 2006 the Earl Haig Fund Scotland launched a new identity – 'Poppyscotland' – and is now generally known by this name.

Radio Forth Cash for Kids

£200,000

Correspondent: Rachel Smith, Manager, Radio Forth, Forth House, Forth Street, Edinburgh EH1 3LE (01314 751332; email: cashforkids@radioforth.com; website: www.forthonline.co.uk)

SC Number: SC041421

Eligibility

Children under the age of 18 who suffer from sickness, have a disability or are disadvantaged and live in Edinburgh, Fife and the Lothians.

Types of grants

Grants are given according to need. Support could be given towards clothing, travel costs for medical reasons, hospital expenses and medical and disability equipment and so on.

Annual grant total

Grants have previously totalled around £200,000.

Exclusions

Generally holidays are not funded except for in exceptional circumstances.

Applications

Application forms are available from the correspondent or to download from the charity's website. A letter of support is required from a GP, health visitor, social worker, occupational therapist or other professional involved with the child who can support the claim. Applications need to be accompanied by at least three monthly bank statements from the child's parents/guardians. Trustees meet several times a year to consider requests which should be submitted at least a month in advance to the meeting (specific dates of the meetings can be requested from the correspondent). All applicants are notified of the outcome.

Other information

The charity is a part of Bauer Radio's Cash for Kids Charities (Scotland) and serves the East Central Scotland and Edinburgh area.

Groups and small charities are also supported.

Radio Tay Cash for Kids

£75,000

Correspondent: Lynda Macfarlane, Charity Co-ordinator, Cash for Kids, 6 North Isla Street, Dundee DD3 7JQ (01382 423263 or 01382 423285; email: lynda.macfarlane@radiotay.co.uk; website: www.tayfm.co.uk)

Eligibility

Children and young people aged under 18 who are in need and live within Radio Tay's transmission area (Dundee, Angus, Perth and North East Fife).

Types of grants

One-off grants of £50 to £5,000 for a range of needs.

Annual grant total

The Radio Tay website states that all funds raised go towards helping children in the Radio Tay transmission area, with a focus on 'improving quality of life, personal development & the fulfilment of aspirations.' Around 27,000 children are assisted each year, with funding also available for organisations.

Exclusions

Grants are not made to pay salaries or rent.

Applications

On a form available from the correspondent. Applications must be submitted with a letter of reference from a social worker, doctor, minister or health visitor. Grants are awarded quarterly, typically in February, May, August and November, with applications to be submitted by the previous month.

The Royal Society for Home Relief to Incurables, Edinburgh

£130,000 (200 grants)

Correspondent: Fiona Watson, Manager, Charity Accounting Services, Scott-Moncrieff, Exchange Place 3, Semple Street, Edinburgh EH3 8BL (01314 733500; fax: 01314 733535; email: fiona.watson@scott-moncrieff.com; website: www.scott-moncrieff.com/services/charities/charitable-trusts/royal-society-for-home-relief-to%20incurables)

SC Number: SC004365

Eligibility

People throughout Scotland (normally under retirement age) who have earned a livelihood (or been a housewife) but are no longer able to continue due to an incurable illness. The society will normally consider those who have ceased employment within the last ten years.

Types of grants

Allowances are given quarterly (totalling £540 per year) to provide extra help.

Annual grant total

At the time of writing (August 2014) the latest financial information available was from 2012. In 2012 the society had an income of £146,000 and an expenditure of £144,000. The society states that currently about £130,000 is available for distribution each year. Over 200 individuals are supported annually.

Exclusions

One-off grants are not provided. The society is unable to support individuals suffering from alcoholism or drug abuse, mental illness, those with learning difficulties, primary epilepsy, blindness or visual impairment and birth deformities, where these are **main illnesses**.

Applications

Application forms are available to download from the Scott-Moncrieff website. The trustees meet four times a year to consider requests. A support statement from the applicant's social worker or health care professional would assist the trustees.

The Royal Society for the Relief of Indigent Gentlewomen of Scotland

See entry on page 32

Sailors' Orphan Society of Scotland

£50,000

Correspondent: Joyce Murdoch, Administrator, 18 Woodside Crescent, Glasgow G3 7UL (01413 532090; fax: 01413 532190; website: www.sailorsorphansociety.co.uk)

SC Number: SC000242

Eligibility

Dependents of seafarers who are or may be in a position of need either through disadvantage or through death or incapacity of one or both of their parents, and to provide support to disadvantaged young people within seafaring communities in Scotland.

Children must be under 16 or in full-time education if over 16.

Types of grants

Monthly grants of around £80 per child as well as two additional payments in July and December. One-off grants may also be paid at the trustees' discretion.

Annual grant total

In 2012/13, the trust had an income of £49,000. Grants usually total about £50,000.

Applications

On an application form available to download from the website. Applications should include a reference from a third party who can confirm the disadvantage suffered or the death or incapacity of a parent.

ScotsCare

£398,000 (1,000+ grants)

Correspondent: Willie Docherty, CEO, 22 City Road, London EC1Y 2AJ (020 7240 3718; email: info@scotscare.com; website: www.scotscare.com)

CC Number: 207326

Eligibility

Scottish people, and their children and widows, who are in need, hardship or distress and live within a 35-mile radius of Charing Cross. Beneficiaries are usually in receipt of state benefits.

Types of grants

The trust gives weekly allowances to older people, one-off grants to people unable to improve their circumstances, help with respite holidays, outings and social events, household essentials, sheltered housing and help to come off benefits.

Annual grant total

In 2012/13 the organisation had assets of £49 million and an income of £2.2 million. Grants to over 1,000 individuals totalled £398,000 of which £375,500 was given for welfare purposes.

Exclusions

No grants are made for debts or for items that have already been purchased.

Applications

On a form available to download from the website or from the organisation directly.

Other information

The organisation also runs a helpline: 0800 652 2989.

The Scottish Artists' Benevolent Association

See entry on page 64

The Scottish Association of Master Bakers' Benevolent Fund

£15,000

Correspondent: Grants Administrator, Atholl House, 4 Torphichen Street, Edinburgh EH3 8JQ

SC Number: SC010444

Eligibility

Members or ex-members of the Scottish Association of Master Bakers and their families who are in need. Other members of the Scottish baking industry may also be supported.

Types of grants

One-off grants of up to £700 towards electrical goods, household repairs, repayment of small debts and so on.

Annual grant total

In 2012 the association had an income of £20,000 and a total expenditure of £16,700. We estimate that grants to individuals totalled £15,000.

At the time of writing (August 2014) this was the most recent financial information available for the association.

Applications

On a form available from the correspondent.

The Scottish Chartered Accountants' Benevolent Association

£120,000

Correspondent: Robert Linton, Administrator, Robert Linton and Co., c/o ICAS 2nd Floor, 7 West Nile Street, Glasgow G1 2PR (01413 011788; email: scaba@robertlinton.co.uk)

SC Number: SC008365

Eligibility

Members of the Institute of Chartered Accountants of Scotland who are in need, and their dependents.

Types of grants

One-off and recurrent grants for a variety of needs. Previously grants have been given for hospital travel costs, house repairs, general living expenses, mobility aids, retraining and home help.

Annual grant total

In 2012 the association had an income of £128,000 and an expenditure of £140,000. Grants usually total about £120,000 each year.

These were the latest accounts available at the time of writing (August 2014).

Applications

An initial letter or telephone call should be made to the correspondent.

Other information

Grants are also given for educational purposes.

The Scottish Cinematograph Trade Benevolent Fund

£15,000

Correspondent: The Administrator, Grant Thornton UK LLP, Scottish Legal Life Building, 95 Bothwell Street, Glasgow G2 7JZ (01412 230000; email: info@sctbf.co.uk; website: www.sctbf.co.uk)

SC Number: SC001786

Eligibility

People in need who are/have been working in the cinema industry in Scotland for at least two years.

Types of grants

One-off and recurrent grants for general living costs, household essentials, 'Aid Call' systems and convalescence.

Annual grant total

In 2013 the fund had an income of £6,200 and an expenditure of £27,000. Our research suggests that in previous years grants have totalled about £15,000.

Applications

In writing to the correspondent. Applications can be submitted either directly by the individual or through a third party, for example, a social worker, Citizens Advice or other welfare agency.

Other information

The fund also offers advice on state benefits and pensions and employs a welfare visitor.

Scottish Grocers' Federation Benevolent Fund

£8,500

Correspondent: John Drummond, Chief Executive, Federation House, 222–224 Queensferry Road, Edinburgh EH4 2BN (01313 433300; fax: 01313 436147; email: info@scottishshop.org.uk; website: www.scottishshop.org.uk/about/benevolent-fund)

SC Number: SC014216

Eligibility

Past members or employees of the grocery trade in Scotland who are in need.

Types of grants

One-off grants or recurrent grants, distributed quarterly, usually totalling around £900 a year.

Annual grant total

In 2012 the fund had an income of £19,800 and a total expenditure of £8,900. Though the website states that 'Around £14,000 is distributed annually', we estimate that during this financial year social welfare grants to individuals totalled £8,500.

At the time of writing (August 2014) this was the most recent financial information available for the fund.

Applications

On a form available from the correspondent or to download from the website. Applicants are then visited to assess the most appropriate form of help.

Other information

Each beneficiary has an almoner appointed to them so that any special needs can be met and their welfare can be monitored.

The Scottish Hide and Leather Trades' Provident and Benevolent Society

£10,000

Correspondent: David Ballantine, Trust Administrator, c/o Mitchells Roberton Solicitors, George House, 36 North Hanover Street, Glasgow G1 2AD (01415 523422; fax: 01415 522935; email: info@mitchells-roberton.co.uk)

SC Number: SC004504

Eligibility

People of retirement age who have worked in the Scottish hide and leather trades.

Types of grants

The society exists principally to provide pensions to its members. It also pays pensions to the widows and widowers of members who have survived their pensionable spouse. Donations equivalent to the annual pensions are also paid to people who have been employed in the trades but who are not members. Very occasionally one-off payments of about £100 to £200 are made for specific purposes, usually for the replacement of household equipment, such as a washing machine, fridge and so on.

Annual grant total

In 2013 the society had an income of £10,500 and a total expenditure of £10,100. We estimate that grants to individuals totalled £10,000.

Applications
Most applicants have been recommended by other members of the society or local organisations.

The Scottish Hydro Electric Community Trust

Correspondent: The Trust Secretary, Inveralmond House, 200 Dunkeld Road, Perth PH1 3AQ (01738 512616; website: shect.org/)

SC Number: SC027243

Eligibility
Members of the local community living in the Scottish Hydro Electric supply area. Grants can be given for domestic properties and properties used for not-for-profit community projects. Domestic properties must be the sole residence of the applicant.

Types of grants
The trust offers help to customers faced with high charges (normally in excess of £3,000) for an electricity connection within the Scottish Hydro-Electric Distribution area, particularly those in rural areas. Grants are awarded at the trustees' discretion and range from a few hundred pounds to a few thousand; however the usual level is 30% of the connection cost and will not cover more than 50%. Connections or upgrades for renewable energy installations are also considered.

Annual grant total
In 2012/13 the trust had an income of £111,000 and an expenditure of £84,000. The amount of grants was not specified.

Exclusions
Applications for holiday homes or second homes will not be considered. Applications for retrospective connections may only be considered in exceptional circumstances.

Applications
Firstly applicants should obtain a quotation for the electricity supply from the local Scottish Hydro Electric Power Distribution depot (or other authorised agent). Application forms can be completed online on the trust's website or downloaded and posted to the trust or to the quotation provider (who will then forward it to the trust on behalf of the individual). It is also requested to provide information of the applicants' financial circumstances and details of the need, including costs. The trustees meet quarterly, normally in January, March, May and October.

Other information
Grants are also given to community ventures for electricity connections.

Scottish Nautical Welfare Society

£115,000

Correspondent: Gail Haldane, Administrator, 937 Dumbarton Road, Glasgow G14 9UF (01413 372632; fax: 01413 372632; email: gvsa@hotmail.com)

SC Number: SC032892

Eligibility
Active, retired and disabled seafarers with ten years in service who are in need and their widows.

Types of grants
Recurrent quarterly grants of £156.

Annual grant total
In 2012/13, the trust had an income of £123,000 and we estimate that grants totalled £115,000.

Applications
In writing to the correspondent.

Other information
This society was established in April 2002 as an amalgamation of Glasgow Aged Seaman Relief Fund, Glasgow Seaman's Friend Society and Glasgow Veteran Seafarers' Association.

Scottish Prison Service Benevolent Fund

£15,000

Correspondent: The Governor, HMP Glenochil, King O Muirs Road, Glenochil FK10 3AD,

SC Number: SC021603

Eligibility
Scottish prison officers, both serving and retired, and their families who are in need.

Types of grants
One-off and recurrent grants according to need.

Annual grant total
In 2012/13 the trust had an income of £21,000. About £18,000 is distributed in grants annually.

Applications
In writing to the correspondent.

Scottish Secondary Teachers' Association Benevolent Fund

£7,500

Correspondent: The General Secretary, West End House, 14 West End Place, Edinburgh EH11 2ED (01313 137300; fax: 01313 468057; email: info@ssta.org.uk; website: www.ssta.org.uk)

SC Number: SC011074

Eligibility
Members and retired members of the association and, in certain circumstances, their dependents and families who are in need. Spouses and partners of deceased members are also supported.

Types of grants
One-off and recurrent grants (generally limited to a period of six months) to help members through a period of long-term illness or other difficulty. The association notes on its website that support is most often given 'in cases of financial hardship but can also be used to meet for requests where the member is not actually experiencing financial difficulties but for whom additional funds would be useful'; one example includes a grant for a member to visit an ill friend at hospital.

Annual grant total
In 2013 the fund had an income of £9,400 and an expenditure of £7,700. We estimate that about £7,500 was given in grants to individuals.

Applications
In writing to the correspondent. Applications can be submitted directly by the individual or through a third party. Applicants are asked to provide details of their financial circumstances.

The Scottish Solicitors' Benevolent Fund (incorporating The Scottish Law Agents' Society Benevolent Fund)

£20,000

Correspondent: Michael Sheridan, Secretary, c/o Sheridans Solicitors, 166 Buchanan Street, Glasgow G1 2LW (01413 323536; fax: 01413 533819; email: secretary@slas.co.uk; website: www.slas.co.uk)

SC Number: SC000258

Eligibility

People in need who are or were members of the solicitor profession in Scotland and their dependents. Typical dependents include solicitors unable to practise due to ill health, and the spouses and children of deceased solicitors who have been unable to make adequate provision for their families.

Types of grants

One-off and recurrent grants according to need. A standard award is £500 for a period of six months.

Annual grant total

No accounts have been provided to the Office of the Scottish Charity Regulator since 2009/10 when the fund had an income of £21,000. However, the fund has been advertising on the Scottish Law Agents Society website since then.

Applications

On a form available to download from the fund's website, including financial details and two referees.

Dr John Robertson Sibbald Trust

£9,500

Correspondent: Andrew Dalgleish, Consultant, Brodies LLP, 15 Atholl Crescent, Edinburgh EH3 8HA (01312 283777; fax: 01312 283878)

SC Number: SC001055

Eligibility

Adults living in Scotland who have an incurable disease and who are in financial need.

Types of grants

Usually £140 a year payable in two instalments in May and November. Occasional one-off grants are given in exceptional circumstances.

Annual grant total

In 2012/13, the trust had an income of £4,500 and a total expenditure of £10,000. We estimate that the total amount of grants awarded to individuals was approximately £9,500.

Applications

On a form available from the correspondent. Applications should be accompanied by a certificate from a surgeon or physician giving full details of the disease and certify that in their opinion it is incurable. As much background information about the applicant as possible is also required which can be in the form of a letter from a social worker or friend describing the family circumstances and giving other personal information. Applications should be submitted by 15 November for consideration in late November/early December.

The Miss M. O. Taylor and Alexander Nasmyth Funds

£10,000

Correspondent: The Administrator, Royal Scottish Academy, The Mound, Edinburgh EH2 2EL (01312 256671; fax: 01312 206016; email: info@royalscottishacademy.org; website: www.royalscottishacademy.org)

SC Number: SC007352 and SC004198

Eligibility

Scottish artists of established reputation, mainly in painting, sculpture, architecture or engraving, who are in need. To be eligible you must have had some previous experience of success in the profession, namely, have exhibited and sold work with a recognised gallery or institution.

Types of grants

One-off payments of up to £1,000. Grants are means tested.

Annual grant total

The Nasmyth Fund is registered separately from the Taylor Fund which is held as fund within the Royal Scottish Academy (RSA). The Nasmyth Fund generally has an income of about £9,000 and an expenditure of around £8,000, although this may vary. In 2011/12, which was the latest financial information available at the time of writing (September 2014), the RSA had a total grant expenditure of £109,000; however, this covers other funding programmes too.

We estimate that grants to individuals from both funds combined will usually exceed £10,000.

Applications

Application forms are available from the correspondent. Awards are made once a year and the deadline is usually early June, check the website for the exact date.

Mrs S. H. Troughton Charitable Trust

£2,400

Correspondent: Anina Cheng, Trust Administrator, 4th Floor, Swan House, 17–19 Stratford Place, London W1C 1BQ (020 7907 2100; email: charity@mfs.co.uk)

CC Number: 265957

Eligibility

People in need who receive a pension and live on the estates of Ardchattan in Argyll, and Blair Atholl.

Types of grants

One-off and recurrent grants ranging from £400 to £600.

Annual grant total

In 2012/13 the trust had an income of £14,500 and a total expenditure of £17,000. In previous years, grants to organisations have accounted for the majority of the trust's charitable expenditure. We estimate that grants to individuals totalled £2,400.

Exclusions

Grants are not given to people whose income is £1,000 above their personal allowance for income tax.

Applications

In writing to the correspondent at any time by the individual or, where applicable, via a third party such as a social worker or through an organisation such as Citizens Advice or other welfare agency. Unsuccessful applications will not be acknowledged.

The trust has stated that funds are fully committed until the end of 2014 and it will not be in a position to consider any new applications until after this point.

The Eliza Haldane Wylie Fund

£14,900

Correspondent: Shona Brown, Trust Administrator, Balfour and Manson LLP, 54–66 Frederick Street, Edinburgh EH2 1LS (01312 001200; fax: 01312 001300)

SC Number: SC011882

Eligibility

People in need who are related to or associated with Eliza Haldane Wylie or her family, or are 'gentlefolk of the middle class'.

Types of grants

Small one-off payments.

Annual grant total
In 2012/13 the fund had an income of £16,600 and a total expenditure of £15,100. We estimate that grants to individuals totalled £14,900.

Applications
In writing to the correspondent.

Aberdeen and Perthshire

The Neil Gow Charitable Trust

£12,000

Correspondent: Trust Administrator, c/o Miller Hendry, 10 Blackfriars Street, Perth PH1 5NS (01738 637311; fax: 01738 638685; email: info@millerhendry.co.uk)

SC Number: SC012915

Eligibility
People in need who live in the district of Perth and Kinross or the immediate neighbourhood.

Types of grants
Annuities of around £90 each, paid quarterly.

Annual grant total
In 2012/13 the trust had an income of £11,800 and a total expenditure of £13,100. We estimate that grants to individuals totalled £12,000.

Applications
In writing to the correspondent.

Grampian Police Diced Cap Charitable Fund

£20,000

Correspondent: The Secretary, Grampian Police, Queen Street, Aberdeen AB10 1ZX (email: secretary@dicedcap.org; website: www.dicedcap.org)

SC Number: SC017901

Eligibility
People in need who live in the Grampian police force area.

Types of grants
One-off and recurrent grants to improve the health and well-being of any deserving persons.

Annual grant total
In 2012/13 the fund had an income of £158,000. Grants usually total about £50,000, although most of this is given to organisations. We estimate that around £20,000 each year is given to individuals for social welfare purposes.

Applications
In writing to the correspondent.

The Gertrude Muriel Pattullo Trust for Handicapped Boys

£2,400

Correspondent: Private Client Team, Blackadders Solicitors, 30–34 Reform Street, Dundee DD1 1RJ (01382 229222; fax: 01382 342220; email: dundee@blackadders.co.uk)

SC Number: SC015505

Eligibility
Boys aged 18 or under who are living with a physical disability and have resided in the city of Dundee or the county of Angus.

Types of grants
Gifts in kind and one-off cash grants. In the past, grants have been given for electrical goods, clothing, hospital expenses, holidays, medical and disability equipment, travel expenses, furniture, nursing fees and home help.

Annual grant total
In 2012/13 the trust had an income of £5,000 and a total expenditure of £5,100. We estimate that grants to individuals totalled £2,400, with funding also awarded to local organisations.

Exclusions
No grants are given towards repayment of debts.

Applications
On a form available from the correspondent at any time. Applications can be submitted directly by the individual or, where applicable, through a social worker, Citizens Advice or other welfare agency.

The Gertrude Muriel Pattullo Trust for Handicapped Girls

£2,600

Correspondent: Private Client Team, Blackadders Solicitors, 30–34 Reform Street, Dundee DD1 1RJ (01382 229222; fax: 01382 342220; email: dundee@blackadders.co.uk)

SC Number: SC011829

Eligibility
Girls aged 18 years or under who have physical disabilities and live in the city of Dundee or the county of Angus.

Types of grants
One-off grants ranging from £100 to £500 have been given for electrical goods, clothing, hospital expenses, holidays, medical and disability equipment, travel expenses, furniture, nursing fees and home help.

Annual grant total
In 2012/13 the trust had an income of £6,500 and a total expenditure of £5,400. We estimate that grants to individuals totalled £2,600, with funding also awarded to local organisations.

Exclusions
No grants are given for the repayment of debts.

Applications
On a form available from the correspondent at any time. Applications can be submitted directly by the individual or through a social worker, Citizens Advice, or other welfare agency. Applications are considered monthly.

The Gertrude Muriel Pattullo Trust for the Elderly

£2,500

Correspondent: Private Client Team, Blackadders Solicitors, 30–34 Reform Street, Dundee DD1 1RJ (01382 229222; fax: 01382 342220; email: dundee@blackadders.co.uk)

SC Number: SC004966

Eligibility
Older people, generally pensioners, especially those living with a disability, resident in the city of Dundee and county of Angus.

Types of grants
One-off grants for general welfare purposes. Funding is available towards, for example, medical services, appliances and comforts not available from the NHS, home nursing and holidays. The trust also assists with the provision of accommodation, furnishings and clothing.

Annual grant total
In 2012/13, the trust had an income of £4,600 and a total expenditure of £5,200. We estimate that grants to individuals totalled £2,500, with funding also awarded to local organisations.

Exclusions
No grants are given for debt repayment.

Applications
On a form available from the correspondent at any time. Applications can be submitted either directly by the individual or through a third party such as a social worker.

Aberdeen and Aberdeenshire

Aberdeen Indigent Mental Patients' Fund

£1,200

Correspondent: Trust Administrator, Peterkins Solicitors, 100 Union Street, Aberdeen AB10 1QR (01224 428000)

SC Number: SC003069

Eligibility
People who live in Aberdeen and are, or have been, mentally ill on their discharge from hospital.

Types of grants
One-off and recurrent grants according to need.

Annual grant total
In 2013/14 the fund had an income of £4,600 and an expenditure of £1,400. We estimate that around £1,200 has been awarded in grants to individuals.

Applications
In writing to the correspondent.

The Aberdeen Widows' and Spinsters' Benevolent Fund

£40,000

Correspondent: Trust Administrator, c/o Raeburn Christie Clark and Wallace, 12–16 Albyn Place, Aberdeen AB10 1PS (01224 332400; fax: 01224 332401)

SC Number: SC002057

Eligibility
Widows and unmarried women over 60 years of age who live in the city or county of Aberdeen; in cases of special need and where surplus income is available, those between 40 and 60 are considered.

Types of grants
Generally yearly allowances of up to £360 paid in two instalments in June and December.

Annual grant total
In 2012/13 the fund had an income of £59,000 and a total expenditure of £49,000. Grants usually total around £40,000.

Applications
On a form available from the correspondent.

James Allan of Midbeltie Trust

£65,000

Correspondent: Michael Macmillan, Administrator, Burnett and Reid, 15 Golden Square, Aberdeen AB10 1WF (01224 644333; fax: 01224 632173; email: mdcmillan@burnett-reid.co.uk)

SC Number: SC003865

Eligibility
Widows who live in Aberdeen and are in need.

Types of grants
Recurrent yearly allowances of around £300 a year payable in two instalments in May and November.

Annual grant total
In 2012/13, the trust had an income of £71,000 and we estimate that grants totalled £65,000.

Applications
On a form available from the correspondent. Applications can be submitted either directly by the individual, through a third party such as a social worker or through an organisation such as Citizens Advice or another welfare agency. Applications are usually considered in April and October.

Braemar Charitable Trust

£1,000

Correspondent: Wiliam Meston, Trustee, Coilacriech, Ballater, Aberdeenshire AB35 5UH (01339 755377)

SC Number: SC007892

Eligibility
People in need who live in the parish of Braemar.

Types of grants
Grants of about £25 each are given for a variety of purposes, including medical equipment.

Annual grant total
In 2012/13, the trust had an income of £1,200 and an expenditure of £1,000. We estimate that the total amount of grants awarded to individuals was approximately £1,000.

Applications
In writing to the correspondent: normally in November for consideration in December. The trust requires information about the applicant detailing their personal circumstances, age, etc.

Dr John Calder Trust

£1,000

Correspondent: Clive Phillips, Administrator, St Machar's Cathedral, 18 The Chanonry, Aberdeen AB24 1RQ

SC Number: SC004299

Eligibility
People in need who live in the parish of Machar or within the city of Aberdeen. Preference will be given to widows left with young children, where sufficient support cannot be obtained from the parish council.

Types of grants
A major part of the funding is provided in educational grants, although relief in need grants can also be considered.

Annual grant total
In 2012/13 the trust had an income of £15,000 and a total expenditure of £7,400. We estimate that under £1,000 was awarded in welfare support to individuals.

Applications
The trust has previously stated that funds were fully committed and that this situation was likely to remain so for the medium to long-term.

Other information
The trust also gives grants for educational purposes and to organisations.

The George, James and Alexander Chalmers Trust

£50,000

Correspondent: Trust Administrator, c/o Storie Cruden and Simpson Solicitors, 2 Bon Accord Crescent, Aberdeen AB11 6DH (01224 587261; fax: 01224 580850; email: info@storiecs.co.uk)

SC Number: SC008818

Eligibility
Women living in Aberdeen who have fallen on hard times as a result of misfortune and not through any fault of their own.

Types of grants
Recurrent grants of about £450 a year, payable in half-yearly instalments.

Annual grant total
In 2012/13 the trust had an income of £148,000. Our research tells us that grants usually total around £50,000.

Applications
On a form available from the correspondent.

Other information
Regular grants are also made to organisations.

The Gordon Cheyne Trust Fund

£18,900

Correspondent: Trusts Administrator, Raeburn Christie Clark and Wallace, 12–16 Albyn Place, Aberdeen AB10 1PS (01224 332400; fax: 01224 332401)

SC Number: SC012841

Eligibility
Widows and daughters of deceased merchants, shopkeepers and other businessmen who are elderly natives of Aberdeen or who have lived there for at least 25 years.

Types of grants
Annual allowances of around £400 are paid twice yearly.

Annual grant total
In 2012/13 the trust had an income of £24,000 and a total expenditure of £29,000. Grants to individuals totalled £18,900.

Applications
On a form available from the correspondent via a social worker, Citizens Advice or other welfare agency.

The Crisis Fund of Voluntary Service Aberdeen

£40,000

Correspondent: Crisis Fund Administrator, Voluntary Service Aberdeen, 38 Castle Street, Aberdeen AB11 5YU (01224 212021; fax: 01224 580722; email: info@vsa.org.uk; website: www.vsa.org.uk)

SC Number: SC012950

Eligibility
People in Aberdeen who are facing extreme hardship.

Types of grants
Immediate grants ranging from about £50 to £150 for emergency needs such as food, beds and bedding, clothing and essential household items.

Annual grant total
Grants usually total about £40,000 each year.

Applications
On an application form available from the correspondent. Applications should be submitted through a social worker or other professional welfare agency.

The Donald Trust

£25,000

Correspondent: Trusts Administrator, Raeburn Christie Clark and Wallace, 12–16 Albyn Place, 52–54 Rose Street, Aberdeen AB10 1PS (01224 332400; fax: 01224 332401; email: info@raeburns.co.uk)

SC Number: SC0158844

Eligibility
People in need who 'belong to' the city of Aberdeen and former county of Aberdeen. 'Advanced age, lack of health, inability to work, high character and former industry are strong recommendations.'

Types of grants
An annuity of around £400 a year, paid in two instalments.

Annual grant total
In 2013 the trust had an income of £37,000 and a total expenditure of £34,000. We estimate that annuities totalled around £25,000.

Exclusions
Generally, people under the age of 60 are not eligible.

Applications
On a form available from the correspondent. Applications should be submitted through a third party such as a social worker. They are considered twice a year.

Garden Nicol Benevolent Fund

£7,500

Correspondent: Alan Innes, Trust Administrator, c/o Peterkins, 100 Union Street, Aberdeen AB10 1QR (01224 428000; fax: 01224 644479)

SC Number: SC007140

Eligibility
Women in need who 'having been in a position of affluence have, by circumstances beyond their control, been reduced to comparative poverty'. Applicants must both have been born and be living in the city or county of Aberdeen.

Types of grants
One-off and recurrent grants according to need.

Annual grant total
In 2012/13 the fund had an income of £9,400 and a total expenditure of £7,600. We estimate that grants to individuals totalled £7,500.

Applications
In writing to the correspondent.

John Harrow's Mortification

£1,600

Correspondent: Trust Administrator, Peterkins Solicitors, 100 Union Street, Aberdeen AB10 1QR (01224 428000; email: maildesk@peterkins.com)

SC Number: SC003617

Eligibility
People in need who live in the parishes of Old Machar and Denburn, Aberdeen and attend the church in Denburn or St Machar Cathedral.

Types of grants
About £800 is given to the ministers of each parish at Christmas for distribution to older people.

Annual grant total
Our research tells us that grants usually total around £1,600 each year.

Applications
Applications are made via the ministers of the parishes of Old Machar and Denburn, not directly to the trust.

The Jopp Thomson Fund

£16,000

Correspondent: Trust Administrator, Ledingham Chalmers LLP, 52–54 Rose Street, Aberdeen AB10 1HA (01224 408408; fax: 01224 408400; email: mail@ledinghamchalmers.com)

SC Number: SC009106

Eligibility
People in need through age, ill health or disability. Preference is given for widowed and single women living in Aberdeenshire and those whose name or maiden name is Thomson or Middleton.

Types of grants
Annuities of around £500 paid in two instalments to each beneficiary to be used at their discretion.

Annual grant total
In 2012/13 the trust had an income of £24,000 and an expenditure of £19,300.

Previously around £16,000 has been awarded in grants.

Applications

Application forms are available from the correspondent. They can be submitted directly by the individual or through a third party and are considered in April each year.

Other information

This fund is an amalgamation of the Henry John Jopp Fund and the Jessie Ann Thomson Fund.

The Mary Morrison Cox Fund

£14,400

Correspondent: The Trustees, 18 Bon-Accord Crescent, Aberdeen AB11 6XY (01224 573321)

SC Number: SC007881

Eligibility

People in need who live in the parish of Dyce, Aberdeen. Preference is given to older people and people living with disabilities.

Types of grants

One-off grants, ranging from £100 to £400, to help with general living expenses.

Annual grant total

In 2012/13 the fund had an income of £13,600 and a total expenditure of £14,600. We estimate that grants to individuals totalled £14,400.

Applications

The trust has a list of potential beneficiaries to whom it sends application forms each year, usually in November. In order to be added to this list, applicants should contact the trust.

Miss Caroline Jane Spence's Fund

£25,000

Correspondent: Trust Administrator, c/o Mackinnons, 14 Carden Place, Aberdeen AB10 1UR (01224 632464; fax: 01224 632184; email: aberdeen@mackinnons.com)

SC Number: SC006434

Eligibility

Widows or unmarried females living within the city or county of Aberdeen who are in need.

Types of grants

Recurrent grants are made.

Annual grant total

In 2012/13 the trust had an income of £95,000 and an unusually high total expenditure of £141,000. In previous years grants to individuals have totalled around £25,000.

Exclusions

No grants are made where statutory funding is available.

Applications

On a form available from the correspondent. Applications can be submitted either directly by the individual, or through a social worker, Citizens Advice or other welfare agency or other third party. Applications are considered in November, January and April.

Other information

Grants are also made to organisations.

The Fuel Fund of Voluntary Service Aberdeen

£0

Correspondent: Gail Chandler, Administration Coordinator, 38 Castle Street, Aberdeen AB11 5YU (01224 212021; fax: 01224 580722; email: info@vsa.org.uk; website: www.vsa.org.uk)

SC Number: SC012950

Eligibility

People living in Aberdeen who need help in maintaining a warm home, particularly older people, people with a disability and families with young children.

Types of grants

One-off grants of around £30.

Annual grant total

Our research tells us that grants usually total around £500 each year. In 2012/13, however, the OSCR record of the Voluntary Service Aberdeen, stated that it had made no expenditure on grants or donations during the year.

Applications

On an application form available from the correspondent. Applications should be submitted through a social worker or other professional welfare agency.

Angus

Charities Administered by Angus Council

£40,000

Correspondent: Sarah Forsyth, Administrator, Angus Council, Angus House, Orchardbank Business Park, Angus DD8 2AL (01307 476269)

SC Number: SC025065

Eligibility

Residents of Arbroath, Brechin, Carnoustie, Forfar, Kirriemuir, Montrose, Kettins, Carmyllie and Arbirlot (particularly older people and people who are in need).

Types of grants

One-off grants generally of £30 or more.

Annual grant total

The council administers over 100 charitable trusts – the largest of which is Strangs Mortification. Each year income from investments total around £40,000 which is used to pay grants to individuals in need in the Forfar area.

Applications

On a form available from the correspondent, any social work or housing office or Forfar Resource Store.

Other information

Over 100 charitable trusts are administered by Angus Council including: Brechin Charitable Funds, Arbroath Charitable Funds, Forfar Charitable Funds, Forfar Landward Charities, Carnoustie Charitable Funds and Kirriemuir Charitable Funds.

The Boyack Fund

£900

Correspondent: Trust Administrator, Hodge Solicitors, 28 Wellmeadow, Blairgowrie, Perthshire PH10 6AX (01250 874441; fax: 01250 873998; email: info@hodgesolicitors.co.uk)

SC Number: SC004998

Eligibility

Pensioners in need who live in Monifieth by Dundee.

Types of grants

Grants of around £50 a year.

Annual grant total

In 2013 the fund had both an income and a total expenditure of £1,000. We estimate that grants to individuals totalled £900.

Applications

On a form available from the correspondent, to be submitted directly by the individual or a family member. Applicants must state how long they have lived in Monifieth and will be means tested. Anyone with significant assets/income will be excluded.

The Colvill Charity

£8,000

Correspondent: Trusts Administrator, Thorntons Law LLP, Brothockbank House, Arbroath DD11 1NJ (01241 872683; fax: 01241 871541; email: arbroath@thorntons-law.co.uk)

SC Number: SC003913

Eligibility

People who are in need and live in the town of Arbroath and the parish of St Vigeans and the surrounding area.

Types of grants

Annual grants of up to about £100 are given to older people. Special one-off grants of up to about £250 are also available for specific medical or household needs.

Annual grant total

In 2012/13 the charity had an income of £35,000 and a total expenditure of £43,000. Our research tells us that grants to individuals usually total £8,000 per year, though the total for grants may have been higher during this financial year.

Applications

On a form available from the correspondent to be submitted directly by the individual or through a social worker, Citizens Advice or other welfare agency. Applications can be made at any time, though requests for regular grants are usually assessed once a year.

The St Cyrus Benevolent Fund

£1,000

Correspondent: The Trustees, Scotston of Kirkside, St Cyrus, Montrose, Angus DD10 0DA

SC Number: SC004237

Eligibility

People who are sick, infirm and in need and live in the parish of St Cyrus, Montrose only.

Types of grants

One-off grants of £25 to £100 are given as well as gift vouchers and grants in kind. Grants given include those towards clothing, food, travel expenses, medical equipment and disability equipment. Parcels are distributed at Christmas time.

Annual grant total

In 2012/13 the charity had an income of £1,100 and a total expenditure of £1,200. We estimate that around £1,000 was made in grants to individuals for social welfare purposes.

Applications

In writing to the correspondent. Recommendation by social worker, minister, doctor, nurse or similar is essential. The trust stated: 'An individual may make a direct application in the first instance but it will be thoroughly checked through the usual type of referee'. Applications are considered at any time.

Other information

The trust also makes grants to organisations for medical equipment and welfare.

The Angus Walker Benevolent Fund

£5,700

Correspondent: T. Duncan and Co. Solicitors, 192 High Street, Montrose DD10 8NA (01674 672533)

SC Number: SC008129

Eligibility

People in need who live in Montrose.

Types of grants

One-off grants.

Annual grant total

In 2012/13 the fund had an income of £21,000 and a total expenditure of £5,900. We estimate that grants to individuals totalled £5,700.

Applications

By formal application via a trustee, local district councillors, the minister of Montrose Old Church or the rector of St Mary's and St Peter's Episcopal Church, Montrose.

Dundee

Broughty Ferry Benevolent Trust

£31,000

Correspondent: The Trustees, 12 Tircarra Gardens, Broughty Ferry, Dundee DD5 2QF

SC Number: SC010644

Eligibility

People in need living in Broughty Ferry, Dundee, who are not in residential care.

Types of grants

One-off grants according to need.

Annual grant total

In 2012/13, the trust had an income of £30,000 and a total expenditure of £32,000. We estimate that the total amount of grants awarded to individuals was approximately £31,000.

Applications

On a form available from the correspondent. Applications can be submitted either directly by the individual or through a social worker, Citizens Advice or other welfare agency.

The Mair Robertson Benevolent Fund

£4,300

Correspondent: The Trustees, 144 Nethergate, Dundee DD1 4EB

SC Number: SC007435

Eligibility

Older women living in Dundee and Blairgowrie who are suffering from financial hardships.

Types of grants

One-off grants of up to about £300.

Annual grant total

In 2012/13 the fund had an income of £9,200 and a total expenditure of £8,800. We estimate that grants to individuals totalled £4,300.

The fund also gave to charities based locally in Blairgowrie and Dundee.

Applications

On a form available from the correspondent. Applications can be submitted directly by the individual or, where applicable, through a social worker, Citizens Advice, other welfare agency or other third party.

Petrie's Mortification

£5,000

Correspondent: The Administrator, Thorntons Solicitors, Whitehall House, 33 Yeaman Shore, Dundee DD1 4BJ (01382 229111; fax: 01382 202288)

SC Number: SC003464

Eligibility

Aged, infirm and indigent individuals over 55 years of age belonging to, or settled in, Dundee.

Types of grants

One-off and recurrent according to need.

Annual grant total

In 2012/13 the trust had an income of £4,300 and a total expenditure of £5,300.

Applications
In writing to the correspondent. Applications can be submitted either directly by the individual, or through a social worker, Citizens Advice or other welfare agency, or another third party.

The Margaret and Hannah Thomson Trusts

£8,000

Correspondent: Trust Manager, Thorntons Solicitors, Whitehall House, 33 Yeaman Shore, Dundee DD1 4BJ (01382 229111; fax: 01382 202288; email: dundee@thorntons-law.co.uk)

SC Number: SC000276

Eligibility
Firstly, people in need who live in Dundee and were wounded during the Second World War, and their spouses. Secondly, ex-employees (or their dependents) of the carpet making industry in Dundee who were employed for at least 20 years and are in need of financial assistance for whatever reason.

Types of grants
Recurrent grants of £360 per year.

Annual grant total
In 2012/13 the trust had an income of £34,000 and a total expenditure of £28,000. Grants were made in previous years totalling around £8,000; however, as more recent annual incomes have increased, the total of grants made to individuals may have also risen.

Applications
In writing to the correspondent. Applications can be submitted either directly by the individual or through a social worker, Citizens Advice or other welfare agency.

Moray

Hospital Master For Auchray

£500

Correspondent: Grants Administrator, Moray Council, Council Headquarters, High Street, Elgin IV30 1BX (01343 543451)

SC Number: SC019016

Eligibility
Older people or people who are infirm and were in business in the burgh of Elgin and who are now in financial need.

Types of grants
Help with council house rent.

Annual grant total
In 2012/13, the trust had an income of £2,700 and an expenditure of £500.

Applications
On an application form available from the correspondent to be submitted by the individual or family member. There are no deadlines for applications.

Other information
The council also administers various small charities (under £500 grant total) for residents of the following areas: Kirkmichael, Inveravon, Mortlach, Keith and Aberlour (Keith/Dufftown Poor Funds and Keith Nursing Fund); Dufftown (Watt Bequest); Lossiemouth; the parishes of Boharm, Deskford, Dibble, Knockando, Rothes and Speymouth; and the burgh of Cullen. Further details are available from the correspondent.

Perth and Kinross

The Anderson Trust

£8,400

Correspondent: Trusts Administrator, Miller Hendry, 10 Blackfriars Street, Perth PH1 5NS (01738 637311; fax: 01738 638685; email: info@millerhendry.co.uk)

SC Number: SC008507

Eligibility
Women in need who live in the parish of Kinnoull or Perth and who belong to the established Church of Scotland.

Types of grants
Grants are limited to a maximum of £500 per person each year.

Annual grant total
In 2012/13 the trust had an income of £7,600 and a total expenditure of £8,600. We estimate that grants to individuals totalled £8,400.

Applications
On a form available from the correspondent at any time.

Mrs Agnes W. Carmichael's Trust (incorporating Ferguson and West Charitable Trust)

£2,500

Correspondent: Alison Hodge, Administrator, Watson and Lyall Bowie, Union Bank Building, Coupar Angus, Blairgowrie PH13 9AJ (01828 628395)

SC Number: SC004415

Eligibility
People with disabilities or other health problems, older people and other defined groups of people in need.

Types of grants
Grants of £50 to £250.

Annual grant total
In 2012/13 the trust had an income of £4,600 and total expenditure of £4,630. We estimate that the trust awards approximately £2,500 to individuals. It also gives grants to local organisations.

Applications
On a form available from the correspondent. Applications should give details of the individual's financial circumstances. Deadlines are in November and applications are considered in December.

Other information
The trust also supports older people's organisations.

The Guildry Incorporation of Perth

£31,000

Correspondent: Lorna Peacock, Secretary, 42 George Street, Perth PH1 5JL (01738 623195)

SC Number: SC008072

Eligibility
People in need who live in Perth.

Types of grants
One-off and recurrent grants usually ranging between £100 and £500.

Annual grant total
In 2012/13 the guild had an income of £227,000. In previous years around £80,000 was given in grants to individuals, of which approximately £31,000 was given for welfare purposes, namely weekly pensions (£18,000); quarterly pensions (£8,500); and coal allowances (£4,800).

Applications
Application forms can be requested from the correspondent. They are considered at the trustees' meetings on the last Tuesday of every month.

Scones Lethendy Mortifications

£6,000

Correspondent: The Treasurer, King James VI Hospital, Hospital Street, Perth PH2 8HP (01738 624660)

SC Number: SC015545

Eligibility
People in need who live in the burgh of Perth and are poor descendants of Alexander Jackson, or with the surname Jackson and other people who are in need (Jackson Mortifications)

Types of grants
Grants usually of around £65 a quarter.

Annual grant total
This appears to be a historic trust which our research tells us usually gives around £6,000 each year. Total expenditure does tend to vary on an annual basis, however.

Applications
On a form available from correspondent. Both trusts have a waiting list to which applications would be added, although successful applicants are judged on need rather than when they applied.

Other information
Another similar trust is the Cairnie Mortification: Recurrent grants lasting for ten years can be given to two young men, starting when they are near the age of 14. Priority is given to those who are direct descendants of Charles Cairnie or any of his five brothers, otherwise grants can be given to people with the surname Cairnie.

Central

Clackmannanshire

The Clackmannan District Charitable Trust

£1,000

Correspondent: Trusts Administrator, Legal and Administration, Clackmannanshire Council, Greenfield House, Alloa FK10 2AD (01259 452108; email: adminservices@clacks.gov.uk; website: www.clacksweb.org.uk)

SC Number: SC011479

Eligibility
People in need who have lived in Clackmannanshire for 12 consecutive months preceding the application being considered or who have lived in Clackmannanshire for three years at some time in the past and continuously for the six consecutive months preceding the application being considered.

Types of grants
Assistance is mainly given for essential household goods such as electric cookers, washing machines, beds and bedding.

Annual grant total
Grants usually total about £1,000 each year.

Applications
On a form available either directly from the correspondent, at community access points or to download from the website. Applications can be submitted at any time but are only considered in March and September.

The Spittal Trust

£12,400

Correspondent: Finance and Corporate Services, Kilncraigs, Greenside Street, Alloa FK10 1EB (01259 450000; fax: 01259 452117; email: corporatedevelopment@clacks.gov.uk; website: www.clacksweb.org.uk/community/spittaltrust)

SC Number: SC018529

Eligibility
People in need who are of a 'deserving character' and have lived in Alloa for at least ten years immediately before applying to the trust.

Types of grants
Small, one-off grants for essential household goods such as for example, beds, bedding, electric cookers and washing machines.

Annual grant total
In 2012/13 the trust had an income of £1,400 and a total expenditure of £12,600. We estimate that grants to individuals totalled £12,400.

Applications
On a form available to download from the from the Clackmannanshire council website or from reception at the Council office. The trust also requires proof of income and, if necessary, evidence of any medical conditions. Application deadlines are at the end of February, May, August and November for consideration in March, June, September and December. Exact dates of trustee meetings are advertised on the website.

Falkirk

The Anderson Bequest

£7,500

Correspondent: J. W. Johnston, Trustee, 13 Register Street, Bo'ness, West Lothian EH51 9AE (01506 822112)

SC Number: SC011755

Eligibility
People in need who live in Bo'ness.

Types of grants
Annual grants, normally of around £150 per year.

Annual grant total
In 2012/13 the fund had an income of £23,500 and an unusually high total expenditure of £29,000. Our research tells us that usually around £7,500 is given in grants to individuals each year.

Applications
In writing to the correspondent.

Falkirk Temperance Trust

£500 (1 grant)

Correspondent: Bryan Smail, Chief Finance Officer, Falkirk Council, Municipal Buildings, Falkirk FK1 5RS (01324 506337; email: bryansmail@falkirk.gov.uk)

SC Number: SC001904

Eligibility
Individuals who have alcohol, drug or other substance abuse problems and live in the former burgh of Falkirk.

Types of grants
One-off grants according to need, usually ranging from £500 to £2,000. In 2013/14 a grant was made to the social

worker of a recovering heroin addict to enable her to purchase carpets for the concrete floors in her flat.

Annual grant total

In 2013/14 the trust had an income of £2,000 and made one grant of £500. There were no administration costs.

Applications

In writing to the correspondent at any time giving details of the specific funding required and what it is for. Applications can be made directly by the individual or family member or by a third party such as Citizens Advice or a social worker.

Other information

The trust exists mainly to assist organisations operating within Falkirk whose work deals with alcohol and other forms of substance abuse and addiction.

The Shanks Bequest

£1,000

Correspondent: Hillary McArthur, Administrator, Finance Services, Falkirk Council, Municipal Buildings, West Bridge Street, Falkirk FK1 5RS

Eligibility

People in need who live in Denny.

Types of grants

There is a list of beneficiaries, which is updated each year, who receive a share of the income (about £40) as a Christmas gift.

Annual grant total

Grants usually total around £1,000 per year.

Applications

In writing to the correspondent.

Other information

Falkirk Council also administers other small trusts for individuals in need who live in the Falkirk area. Further details from the correspondent above.

Fife

The Bruce Charitable Trust

£15,000

Correspondent: Elizabeth Calderwood, Secretary, c/o Pagan Osborne, 106 South Street, St Andrews KY16 9QD (01334 475001; fax: 01334 476322)

SC Number: SC014927

Eligibility

People who are older, in need, infirm or distressed who live in the burgh of Cupar.

Types of grants

One-off grants of up to £400.

Annual grant total

In 2012/13 the trust had an income of £19,800 and a total expenditure of £35,000. We estimate that grants to individuals totalled £15,000, with funding also awarded to local organisations.

Applications

In writing to the correspondent including the applicant's date of birth, postal address and reason for request. Applications should be made by an organisation such as Citizens Advice or through a third party such as a social worker.

Other information

The trust also funds local organisations and charities, youth groups, cultural, educational and recreational facilities.

Charities Administered by Fife Council (West Fife Area)

£4,000

Correspondent: Linda Purdie, Team Leader, Fife Council, Fife House, North Street, Glenrothes, Fife KY7 5LT (0845 155 5555)

Eligibility

The beneficial area differs from charity to charity, the largest of which are the McGregor Bequest and the Wildridge Memorial Fund. The majority refer only to Dunfermline, but smaller ones exist for Aberdour, Culross, Lochgelly, Limekilns, Kincardine, Ballingry and Tulliallan.

Types of grants

Generally one-off grants to people in need. Grants may be made in cases of emergency, for fuel payments, groceries and so on.

Annual grant total

Grants usually total around £4,000 per year.

Applications

Applications should be made to one of the eight local panels in the communities. A list of local service centres can be found on the council website (www.fifedirect.org.uk).

Other information

In late 2012, the administrators of the charities at Fife Council were working in conjunction with the Office of the Scottish Charity Regulator to rationalise and merge the charities.

The Fleming Bequest

£20,000

Correspondent: Elizabeth Calderwood, Trust Administrator, Pagan Osborne, 106 South Street, St Andrews, Fife KY16 9QD (01334 475001; fax: 01334 476322; email: elcalderwood@pagan.co.uk)

SC Number: SC016126

Eligibility

People living in the parish of St Andrews and St Leonards in the town of St Andrews who are older, in poor health or in financial difficulty.

Types of grants

One-off grants, up to around £300. Grants are awarded towards clothing, carpets, fridge/freezers, special chairs and other essential household needs.

Annual grant total

In 2012/13 the trust had an income of £15,800 and an expenditure of £27,000. We estimate that grants to individuals totalled around £20,000.

Applications

In writing to the correspondent preferably through a social worker, Citizens Advice or similar welfare agency. Applications are considered at any time and should include details of the applicant's postal address, date of birth and reason for the request.

The St Andrews Welfare Trust

£10,000

Correspondent: Elizabeth Calderwood, Trust Administrator, Pagan Osborne, 106 South Street, St Andrews, Fife KY16 9QD (01334 475001; fax: 01334 476322)

SC Number: SC008660

Eligibility

People in need who live within a four mile radius of St Andrews.

Types of grants

One-off grants of up to £400 are given towards carpeting, cookers, clothing, fireguards and so on.

Annual grant total

Our research tells us that around £10,000 is given to individuals and about £4,000 to organisations each year.

Exclusions

No grants for educational purposes, such as gap year projects.

Applications

In writing to the correspondent through a social worker, Citizens Advice or other welfare agency. Applications should include applicant's date of birth, postal address and reason for request and are considered throughout the year.

Other information

Grants are also given to playgroups and senior citizen Christmas teas.

Stirling

The George Hogg Trust

£15,000

Correspondent: Secretary, Tayview, Main Street, Killin, Perthshire FK21 8UT

SC Number: SC001890

Eligibility

People who live in Killin and are in need.

Types of grants

One-off and recurrent grants according to need. For example, a recent grant of £200 was given towards an electric wheelchair.

Annual grant total

In 2012/13 the income of the trust was £14,000 and the charitable expenditure was £19,000.

Applications

In writing to the correspondent via a third party such as a local doctor or minister. There are no deadlines and applications are normally considered at the Annual General Meeting.

Edinburgh, the Lothians and Scottish Borders

The Blackstock Trust

£11,000

Correspondent: Trust Secretary, Pike and Chapman, 36 Bank Street, Galashiels TD1 1ER (01896 752379)

SC Number: SC014309

Eligibility

People who are elderly or sick and live in the counties of Roxburgh, Berwick and Selkirk.

Serving and retired British police officers and their dependents who have been injured or incapacitated while serving as a police officer

Types of grants

Financial assistance (usually up to £500) for accommodation, maintenance or welfare, short holiday breaks, respite care and the provision of amenities.

Annual grant total

In 2012/13 the trust had an income of £26,000 and a total expenditure of £25,000. We estimate that grants to individuals totalled £11,000, with funding also awarded to Scottish organisations with similar charitable purposes.

Applications

In writing to the correspondent, including details of financial position (income and capital).

Capital Charitable Trust

£16,000

Correspondent: The Administrator, Aitken Nairn W.S., 7 Abercromby Place, Edinburgh EH3 6LA (01315 566644; email: reception@aitkennairn.co.uk)

SC Number: SC004332

Eligibility

People in need who live in the Edinburgh and Lothians area.

Types of grants

Small, one-off grants of about £10 to £20 for clothes, decorating, household goods and other general welfare needs.

Annual grant total

At the time of writing (September 2014) the latest financial information available was from 2011/12. In 2011/12 the trust had an income £18,200 and a total expenditure of £24,000. In the past grants have totalled about £16,000.

Applications

Our research shows that application forms can be obtained from the Lothian Regional Council Social Work Departments and other responsible bodies who will forward them to the correspondent. Applications are not accepted directly from the individual.

The Robert Christie Bequest Fund

£40,000

Correspondent: Trust Administrator, Gibson McKerrell Brown LLP, 14 Rutland Square, Edinburgh EH1 2BD (01312 288319; email: enquiries@g-m-b.co.uk)

SC Number: SC000465

Eligibility

People over 60 who are in need, live in Edinburgh or Midlothian and have an acutely painful disease.

Types of grants

Annual allowances are given according to need.

Annual grant total

In 2012/13 the fund had an income of £116,000 and a total expenditure of £111,000. We estimate that grants to individuals totalled around £40,000.

Applications

On a form available from the correspondent. Applications can be submitted directly by the individual or through a social worker, Citizens Advice or other welfare agency. Applications are usually considered twice a year.

The Ecas (Access/ Holiday Fund)

£25,000

Correspondent: Grants Administrator, Ecas, Norton Park, 57 Albion Road, Edinburgh EH7 5QY (01314 752344; fax: 01314 752341; website: www.ecas-edinburgh.org)

SC Number: SC014929

Eligibility

People who are long-term and significantly disabled through impairment of the musculoskeletal, neurological or cardio-respiratory systems of the body, living in Edinburgh and the Lothians.

Unfortunately, people with the following conditions do not fall within the fund's eligibility criteria: psychiatric disorders, learning difficulties, behavioural disorders, developmental delay, Down's syndrome, autism, visual or hearing impairment, cancer, diabetes, epilepsy, HIV, back pain and chronic fatigue syndrome.

Types of grants

One-off grants up to a maximum of £500. Only in exceptional circumstances will larger grants be considered. Recent grants have been given for washing machines, fridge-freezers, cookers, lap tops, furniture, car adaptations, sheds and flooring. The fund also awards grants towards holidays and may contribute towards the cost of an accompanying carer or partner.

Annual grant total
In 2012/13 the trust had an income of £225,000 and a total expenditure of £336,000. We estimate that grants to individuals totalled £25,000.

Exclusions
There are no grants available for bills, debts, wheelchairs, scooters or small pieces of domestic equipment. Funding is not given to pay for items which have already been bought.

People with following conditions on their own do not meet the criteria for participation in Ecas activities: psychiatric disorders, learning difficulties, behavioural disorders, developmental delay, Down's syndrome, autism, visual or hearing impairment, cancer, diabetes, epilepsy, HIV and back pain.

Applications
On a form available from the correspondent or to download from the website. Applications must be supported by a social worker or health care professional. A short GP report may also be required. Applications can be made at any time but individuals should allow around six weeks (12 weeks for holiday applications) for the administration of any grant. Applicants who are in receipt of Income Support, Housing Benefit or Pension Credit and Disability Allowance may have their applications fast tracked.

Any application for funds for maintenance or repair for battery-packs, power-chairs or scooters must be accompanied by evidence of third party insurance.

Applications requesting computer equipment will be asked to contact Ecas for assessment.

Note: The trust tends to purchase items and holidays directly from the supplier. If an item is eligible for only part-funding, Ecas will not release funds until the rest of the money has been raised.

Other information
Ecas also runs classes – ranging from art and craft, to yoga, swimming and ICT – as well as a 'facilitated friendship' scheme and the Ecas Befriending Project, all of which aim to improve the quality of life for people living with physical disabilities.

Edinburgh Voluntary Organisations' Trust

£68,000 (1,015 grants)

Correspondent: Janette Scappaticcio, EVOT Trust Administrator, 14 Ashley Place, Edinburgh EH6 5PX (01315 559100; fax: 01315 559101; email: janette.scappaticcio@evoc.org.uk; website: www.evoc.org.uk)

SC Number: SC031561

Eligibility
Individuals in need who live in the city of Edinburgh and the Lothians. Priority is given where there is a serious illness of the individual or in the family.

Types of grants
One-off grants of up to £150 where they will be of real benefit to the family or individual. For example, grants are given for a specific need such as clothing and household essentials.

Annual grant total
In 2012/13, the trust held assets of £4.2 million and had an income of £144,000. Grants were made totalling £101,000, of which £68,000 was given to individuals and £33,000 to organisations. Of that £68,000, £20,300 was constituted by distributions made on behalf of Ponton House to the value of £8,800 and BBC Children in Need to the value of £11,500.

Exclusions
No grants for electrical equipment, white goods, holidays (except in special circumstances), students' fees/equipment or the repayment of debt.

Applications
On a form available from the website. Applications should be submitted through a local authority, hospital or voluntary sector agency. They are considered monthly.

Other information
The Edinburgh Voluntary Organisations' Council (EVOC) previously administered a number of small trust funds which have now been amalgamated into a new fund, EVOT.

The Merchant Company Endowments Trust (formerly known as The Edinburgh Merchant Company Endowments Trust)

Correspondent: The Secretary and Chamberlain, The Merchant Hall, 22 Hanover Street, Edinburgh EH2 2EP (01312 209284; fax: 01312 204842; email: info@mcoe.org.uk; website: www.mcoe.org.uk)

SC Number: SC002002

Eligibility
'Decent, indigent men and women' who are over the age of 55 and have lived or worked in the city of Edinburgh or in Midlothian. Help may also be given to younger individuals who are certified on medical grounds as unable to earn their living.

Types of grants
Assistance can be given in the form of a cash grant, bi-annual pension, gift or appliance, as well as provision and care support.

Annual grant total
In 2012/13 the trust had an income of £826,000 and an expenditure of £450,000.

Applications
On a form available from the correspondent. The trust employs an almoner who assesses need and reports to the trust prior to any grant being made.

Other information
The trust also provides almshouse accommodation.

The John Watt Trust

£400

Correspondent: Fiona Marshall, Associate, MHD Law, 45 Queen Charlotte Street, Leith, Edinburgh EH6 7HT (01315 550616; fax: 01315 531523; email: fiona.marshall@mhdlaw.co.uk)

SC Number: SC011575

Eligibility
People over 55 who have the name Watt; or who were born in the parish of South Leith; or who live in the parish of South Leith and have done so for at least ten years prior to their application; or are in need who were born in or have constantly lived in the city of Edinburgh or any part of Midlothian.

Types of grants
Annual grants of £100 paid in half yearly instalments.

Annual grant total
Grants usually total around £400 each year.

Applications
Prospective applicants must respond to an advertisement in the local press or through the local Leith churches, but more information can be gained from the correspondent. Applications are generally requested in November for consideration in January.

Other information
The trust has a visitor who visits the pensioners throughout the year and reports to the trustees on their state of health and needs.

Edinburgh

Alexander Darling Silk Mercer's Fund

£22,000

Correspondent: Gregor Murray, Secretary and Chamberlain, The Merchant Company, The Merchants' Hall, 22 Hanover Street, Edinburgh EH2 2EP (01312 209284; fax: 01312 204842; email: gregor.murray@mcoe.org.uk; website: www.mcoe.org.uk)

SC Number: SC036724

Eligibility
Unmarried or widowed women, over 55, who live in Edinburgh or who have worked in Edinburgh in the manufacture or sale of textile garments for ladies and children. Preference is given to women bearing the surname Darling, Millar, Small or Scott and to women born in the town of Lanark. Unfortunately, women who have only been involved in the manufacture and sale of textiles for men do not qualify for these grants.

Types of grants
Recurrent grants every six months to support living costs. The fund also helps with the cost of white goods for qualifying people over the age of 55.

Annual grant total
In 2012/13 the fund had an income of £47,000 and a total expenditure of £41,000. We estimate that grants to individuals totalled £22,000.

Applications
Applications should be made in writing to the secretary of the Merchant Company, either directly by the individual or through a third party such as a social worker or Citizens Advice. Every written application is followed up by a visit by the almoner, during which a declaration regarding the applicant's financial circumstances is required.

The Edinburgh Royal Infirmary Samaritan Society

£19,000

Correspondent: The Administrator, 21 Walker Street, Edinburgh EH3 7HX

SC Number: SC004519

Eligibility
Patients of NHS hospitals in Edinburgh who are in need.

Types of grants
Specific sums of money for clothing, bills, travel expenses or other help for the families and dependents of patients while in these hospitals or on leaving. Grants range between £5 and £150.

Annual grant total
In 2012/13 the society had an income of £19,400 and a total expenditure of £21,000. We estimate that grants to individuals totalled £19,000.

Applications
Through a medical social worker based at Edinburgh Royal Infirmary Social Work Department on an application form. Applications are considered fortnightly.

The Edinburgh Society for Relief of Indigent Old Men

£30,000

Correspondent: Trust Secretary, c/o Lindsays, Caledonian Exchange, 19A Canning Street, Edinburgh EH3 8HE (01312 291212; fax: 01312 295611; email: edinburgh@lindsays.co.uk)

SC Number: SC005284

Eligibility
Older men of good character resident in Edinburgh, who usually have no pension apart from statutory sources, have capital of £3,000 or less and are experiencing hardship or disability. Under exceptional circumstances, men under 65 will be considered.

Types of grants
Monthly payments, normally of around £50.

Annual grant total
In 2012/13 the society had an income of £47,000 and a total expenditure of £56,000. Grants usually total around £30,000.

Applications
In writing to the correspondent.

EMMS International – Hawthornbrae Trust

£18,000 (25 grants)

Correspondent: The Administrator, 7 Washington Lane, Edinburgh EH11 2HA (01313 133828; fax: 01313 134662; email: info@emms.org; website: www.emms.org)

SC Number: SC032327

Eligibility
People resident within the Edinburgh City Boundary who are recovering from an illness and are of 'good character' who have insufficient funds to pay for a holiday for themselves.

Types of grants
Grants of up to £300 for adults and £150 for children (under 16) for recuperative holidays. Grants to one family will not exceed £900.

Annual grant total
In 2013 the fund has an income of £17,000. Grants totalling £14,000 were made to 25 beneficiaries.

Exclusions
The trust cannot give grants towards spending money.

Applications
On a form available from the correspondent. Applications must be sponsored by a social worker, health visitor or minister and be supported by a medical reference from a GP. Applications are considered throughout the year on a first come first served basis and usually take up to six to eight weeks to process.

Other information
Grants are not paid to individuals but to sponsoring agencies or accredited guesthouses or travel agents.

EMMS International also runs a bursary scheme for medical students undertaking electives in mission schools and hospitals.

Leith Benevolent Association Ltd

£500

Correspondent: The Trustees, 7 North Forth Street, Leith EH6 4EY (fax: 01314 670099; email: applications@leithbenevolentassociation.co.uk; website: www.leithbenevolentassociation.co.uk)

SC Number: SC011276

Eligibility

People in financial need who live in Leith.

Types of grants

One-off grants, usually of £10 to £15 per person.

Annual grant total

Grants to individuals total around £500 a year.

Applications

On an application form available to download from the website. Applications are considered in September and February and should be received no later than the end of July and December preceding each meeting.

Other information

Grants are mainly given to organisations.

The William Brown Nimmo Charitable Trust

£20,000

Correspondent: Grants Administrator, MHD Law LLP, 45 Queen Charlotte Street, Leith, Edinburgh EH6 7HT (01315 550616; fax: 01315 531523; email: fiona.marshall@mhdlaw.co.uk)

SC Number: SC001671

Eligibility

Older women living on a low income who were born, and permanently live, in Leith or Edinburgh.

Types of grants

Annual grants of around £165.

Annual grant total

Grants total about £20,000 each year. The trust usually accepts several new beneficiaries a year, but this is dependent on available income and existing beneficiaries failing to re-qualify for a grant. In 2012/13 the trust had an income of £38,000 and a total expenditure of £34,000.

Applications

On a form only available from 1 June from the correspondent. They should be returned by 31 July for consideration in September/October. Applicants are visited.

Police Aided Clothing Scheme (Edinburgh)

£20,000

Correspondent: The Administrator, Divisional Co-Ordination Unit, St Leonard's Police Station, 14 St Leonard's Street, Edinburgh EH8 9QW (01316 625792; email: EdinburghDCU@scotland.pnn.police.uk)

SC Number: SC011164

Eligibility

Underprivileged children between the ages of 5 and 18 who live in the area administered by City of Edinburgh Council. In exceptional circumstances adults may be assisted.

Types of grants

In kind gifts of socks, shoes, sweatshirts, coats and jackets or other clothing/footwear.

Annual grant total

In 2012/13 the charity had an income of £89,000 and a total expenditure of £78,000. Each year about £20,000 is spent to support individuals in need. We have been informed that the amount is not set and may be higher, depending on need.

Exclusions

The charity does not make cash grants and does not provide assistance towards school uniforms.

Applications

Initial enquiries should be made in writing or by phone to the Custodiers Department of the police service. All applicants are visited in their homes by a police officer in uniform to complete an application.

The Surplus Fire Fund

£8,000

Correspondent: Janette Scappaticcio, Trust Administrator, 1st Floor, 14 Ashley Place, Edinburgh EH6 5PX (01315 559109; fax: 01315 559101; email: janette.scappaticcio@evoc.org.uk; website: www.evoc.org.uk)

SC Number: SC018967

Eligibility

People in the Edinburgh City area who have been affected by a fire.

Types of grants

One-off payments. Grants fall into two categories:

- Personal injury or death – for people suffering physical or psychological injury, or the dependents of people who have lost their lives or suffered injury, in connection with fires in the area
- Domestic damage – grants to compensate for damage (other than structural damage) to domestic premises and household contents caused by a fire

Annual grant total

In 2012/13 the fund had an income of £29,000 and a total expenditure of £16,700. We estimate that grants to individuals totalled £8,000, with funding also awarded to organisations with similar purposes.

Applications

At the time of writing (early September 2014) the fund was in the process of being transferred to the administration of the Edinburgh Voluntary Organisations Council and was not accepting applications. The Council expected that it would be able to begin accepting applications via an electronic application form on the website in around two months (from the time of writing). Potential applicants should at first contact the correspondent to confirm the fund's status before making an application.

Midlothian

The Cockpen Lasswade and Falconer Bequest

£0

Correspondent: Bob Atack, Administrator, Corporate Resources, Midlothian Council, Midlothian House, Buccleuch Street, Dalkeith, Midlothian EH22 1DN (01312 713161; email: atackb@midlothian.gov.uk)

Eligibility

People in need who live in Cockpen, Bonnyrigg and Lasswade and the immediate adjoining district.

Types of grants

Grants can be given for medical, surgical or convalescent expenses which are not covered by the NHS.

Annual grant total

Our research suggests that grants usually total about £1,000 annually; however the amount may vary. In 2012/13 no grants were made.

Applications

In writing to the correspondent. Applications can be made at any time. They will need to be supported by a local health visitor, medical practitioner, district nurse, parish minister or bank manager.

Charities Administered by Midlothian Council

Correspondent: Bob Atack, Administrator, Corporate Resources, Midlothian Council, Midlothian House, Buccleuch Street, Dalkeith EH22 1DN (01312 713161; email: atackb@midlothian.gov.uk)

Eligibility

There are various bequests administered by Midlothian Council. Most of them are small (under £500) and therefore do not warrant individual entries in this guide. The following entry gives basic details about the bequests. Further information and eligibility criteria are available from the correspondent.

Types of grants

One-off grants according to need.

Annual grant total

The council stated in a financial report dated 31 March 2013 that 'in relation to some of the bequests, difficulty has been experienced in meeting the criteria and therefore, no disbursements have been made for some time.'

Applications

In writing to the correspondent. Applications can be submitted directly by the individual or family member.

Other information

The following funds are available:

(a) The Ainslie, Sir Samuel Chisholm and Fraser Hogg Bequests – Eligibility: Poor people who live in the parish of Dalkeith – Types of grants: Individual disbursements

(b) The Cockpen, Lasswade and Falconer Bequest – Eligibility: People in need who live in the former burghal areas of Bonnyrigg and Lasswade, and in the immediate surrounding district – Types of grants: Individual disbursements for medical or convalescent expenses not covered by the NHS

(c) The John and Margaret Haig Bequest – Eligibility: People in need over the age of 70 who live in the former Bonnyrigg Burghal Ward – Types of grants: Individual disbursements.

(d) The Stair Bequest – Eligibility: Elderly people in need who live in the parish of Cranston – Types of grants: Logs for the poor

(e) The Tod Bequest – Eligibility: Poor people in need who live in Loanhead or Polton – Types of grants: One-off payments

(f) The Mrs E. W. Yorkston Bequest – Eligibility: Poor young people belonging to the former burghal area of Lasswade who have an infectious disease or have suffered from one and are now convalescing – Types of grants: Grants to help with the cost of a suitable rest in the country or at a convalescent home.

Scottish Borders

Christie Fund

£500

Correspondent: The Trustees, Iain Smith and Partners, 11 – 13 Murray Street, Duns TD11 3DF (01361 882733; fax: 01361 883517)

SC Number: SC000957

Eligibility

People in need in Duns Parish.

Types of grants

One-off grants to a usual maximum of £200. Funds are available to help with specific items where the applicant does not have access to other means of funding.

Annual grant total

The trustees appear to award grants every few years after income has built up.

Applications

In writing to the correspondent at any time, through a social worker, Citizens Advice or other welfare agency. Applications should include full details of the assistance needed, stating why funding is unavailable from other sources.

The Elizabeth Hume Trust

£2,500

Correspondent: J. Brown, Administrator, 26 Whitehall Road, Chirnside, Duns, Berwickshire TD11 3UB

SC Number: SC005995

Eligibility

People in need who live in the parish of Chirnside.

Types of grants

Grants can be given according to need at the trustees' discretion.

Annual grant total

At the time of writing (August 2014) the latest financial information available was from 2012. In 2012 the trust had an income of £3 and an expenditure of £10,400. We estimate that relief-in-need grants to individuals totalled around £2,500.

Applications

In writing to the correspondent. Applications can be made either directly by an individual or through a third party, such as a family member, social worker or teacher, also through an organisation, for example Citizens Advice, school or church.

Other information

Grants can also be made to organisations and for social welfare purposes.

Roxburghshire Landward Benevolent Trust

£500

Correspondent: The Trustees, Alderwood, Main Street, St Boswells, Roxburghshire TD6 0AP

SC Number: SC008416

Eligibility

People in need who live in the Landward area of the former Roxburgh County Council.

Types of grants

One-off grants up to £500. Grants are normally given to assist people with health and social problems where government assistance is not available. Financial help can be towards travel to hospital, respite care, equipment such as wheelchairs, and the purchase of domestic equipment.

Annual grant total

In 2012/13 this trust had an income of £6,400 and a total expenditure of £5,600. Grants to individuals generally total around £500. The trust also makes grants to organisations.

Exclusions

No grants to settle debts or to duplicate state aid.

Applications

In writing to the correspondent. Applications can be submitted directly by the individual, through a social worker, Citizens Advice or other welfare agency, or through other third party on behalf of an individual. They are considered in April and October. Applicants will be visited by a trustee before any decision to make a payment is made.

Glasgow and West of Scotland

The Association for the Relief of Incurables in Glasgow and the West of Scotland

£125,000

Correspondent: Trust Administrator, BMK Wilson Solicitors, 90 St Vincent Street, Glasgow G2 5UB (01412 218004; fax: 01412 218088; email: bmkw@bmkwilson.co.uk)

SC Number: SC014424

Eligibility

People over 18 years of age in financial need with long-term illnesses who are living at home. Applicants must be living in Glasgow or the West of Scotland.

Types of grants

Quarterly pensions. One-off grants of up to £350 for specific needs, such as telephone installation, washing machines and cookers.

Annual grant total

In 2013 the association had an income of £172,000 and a total expenditure of £152,000. We estimate that grants to individuals totalled £125,000.

Exclusions

No grants given to clear debts or towards holidays.

Applications

Applications must be made through a social worker, Citizens Advice or another welfare agency on a form available from the correspondent. GP must confirm medical condition. Applications are considered quarterly with deadlines 14 days prior to each meeting.

Merchants House of Glasgow

£1,000

Correspondent: David Ballantine, Collector and Clerk, 7 West George Street, Glasgow G2 1BA (01412 218272; fax: 01412 262275; email: theoffice@merchantshouse.org.uk; website: www.merchantshouse.org.uk)

CC Number: SC008900

Eligibility

Pensioner members of the House who are in need and live in Glasgow and the West of Scotland.

Types of grants

Recurrent pensions are paid to help elderly people who are facing hardship.

Annual grant total

In 2012 the trust had an income of £2 million. Grants totalled £430,000, the majority of which were given to organisations. A very small amount, which we estimate to be around £1,000, is given as pensions to members of the Merchants House.

At the time of writing (August 2014) this was the most recent financial information available for the trust.

Applications

In writing to the correspondent at any time.

Other information

The Merchants House administers several funds in trust, including the Inverclyde Bequest Fund for Seamen, RNVR Club (Scotland) Memorial Trust and the Commercial Travellers of Scotland Benevolent Fund for Widows and Orphans.

James Paterson's Trust

£18,000

Correspondent: Trust Administrator, Mitchells Roberton Solicitors, George House, 36 North Hanover Street, Glasgow G1 2AD (01415 523422; fax: 01415 522935; email: info@mitchells-roberton.co.uk)

SC Number: SC017645

Eligibility

Women who have worked in factories or mills in the Glasgow area, consisting of the district of the City of Glasgow and the contiguous districts of Dumbarton, Clydebank, Bearsden and Milngavie, Bishopbriggs and Kirkintilloch, East Kilbride, Eastwood and Renfrew.

Types of grants

Grants are given to pay primarily for short-term convalescent accommodation and occasionally for medical expenses and private accommodation in any private hospital. Grants are usually one-off payments of around £250.

Annual grant total

In 2012/13 the fund had an income of £31,000 and a total expenditure of £20,000. We estimate that grants totalled around £18,000.

Applications

In writing to the correspondent. Applications can be submitted directly by the individual or through a social worker, Citizens Advice or other welfare agency. They are considered throughout the year.

Lord Provost's Children's Fund

£500

Correspondent: The Trustees, Glasgow City Council, Social Services Department, Wheatley House, 25 Cochrane Street, Glasgow G1 1HL (01412 870555)

SC Number: SC042267

Eligibility

Children and young people under 18 years of age living in the Glasgow City Council area.

Types of grants

One-off grants according to need.

Annual grant total

In 2012/13 the fund had an income of £214,000 and a total expenditure of over £65,000. The fund's accounts were not available to view. In the past the previous Provost charities made grants totalling around £500 per year.

Applications

Applications are made via a social worker.

Other information

The fund is one of three funds created to rationalise a number of smaller funds administered by Glasgow City Council Social Services department. The other funds are the Lord Provost's Fund for Vulnerable Citizens and the Lord Provost's Fund for Older People, which can also be found in this guide.

Lord Provost's Fund for Elderly People

£500

Correspondent: The Trustees, Glasgow City Council, Social Work Services, Wheatley House, 25 Cochrane Street, Glasgow G1 1HL (01412 870555)

SC Number: SC042269

Eligibility

Older people in the Glasgow district council area who are in financial need.

Types of grants

One-off grants according to need.

Annual grant total

In 2012/13 the fund had an income of £519,000 and a total expenditure of over £6,000. The charity's accounts were not available to view. In the past the previous Provost charities made grants totalling around £500 per year.

Applications

Applications are made through social workers to those already in contact with the department.

Other information

The fund is one of three funds created to rationalise a number of smaller funds administered by Glasgow City Council Social Services department. The other funds are the Lord Provost's Fund for Vulnerable Citizens and the Lord Provost's Children's Fund, which can also be found in this guide.

Radio Clyde Cash for Kids

£709,000 (28,237 grants)

Correspondent: Lesley Allan, Grants Officer, Radio Clyde Cash for Kids, 3 South Avenue, Clydebank Business Park, Glasgow G81 2RX (01412 041025; email: lesley.cashforkids@radioclyde.com or cashforkids@radioclyde.com; website: www.clydecashforkids.com)

SC Number: SC003334

Eligibility

Children under the age of 16 who are in need by reason of ill-health, disability, financial hardship or other disadvantage and live within the geographical areas to which Radio Clyde broadcasts (west central and south-west Scotland).

Applications are accepted from families in the following local authority areas: Argyll and Bute, Dumfries and Galloway, East Ayrshire, East Dunbartonshire, East Renfrewshire, Glasgow, Inverclyde, North Ayrshire, North Lanarkshire, Renfrewshire, South Ayrshire, South Lanarkshire and West Dunbartonshire.

Types of grants

Christmas family grants of £25 per child. Awards are intended to help pay for Christmas presents, Christmas dinner or winter clothing. Grants are normally paid to a third party supporter, usually a social work department, health centre, housing association, recognised voluntary organisation or a person in authority such as a headteacher, doctor or member of the clergy.

Annual grant total

In 2013 the charity had an income of £1.1 million and a total expenditure of £1.3 million. Grants and donations totalled just over £1 million. The correspondent has informed us that a total of £709,000 was awarded to 28,237 vulnerable children across Glasgow and the west.

Applications

Applications can be made online on the charity's website. After completing the form applicants should print the confirmation page and pass it to their referee for an endorsement. All applications should be referred by a third party such as Citizens Advice, housing association, social work department, a headteacher, GP or member of the clergy. The referee must be willing to accept payment on behalf of the applicant. Applicants are usually notified of the decision by email.

Applications tend to open for a month in early October, check the website for the exact dates.

Other information

Details of the scheme are broadcast on Radio Clyde in the run up to Christmas. Grants are also awarded to groups organising a trip to the pantomime or Christmas parties with Santa, and to organisations or for various projects for the benefit of children (including summer, special and community grants) throughout the year A total of 103,839 vulnerable children were supported through these schemes in 2013.

Mairi Semple Fund for Cancer Relief and Research

£5,400

Correspondent: M. Sinclair, Trustee, 4 Barrhill, Glenbarr, Tarbert, Argyll PA29 6UT

SC Number: SC000390

Eligibility

People who live in Kintyre or the Island of Gigha and are suffering from cancer.

Types of grants

Provision of equipment and/or domestic nursing help, assistance with hospital travel costs for patients or relatives and the provision of measures to enable the 'greater privacy, quietness and dignity' of hospitalised patients with terminal cancer.

Annual grant total

In 2012/13 the fund had an income of £10,000 and a total expenditure of £11,000. We estimate that grants to individuals totalled £5,400, with funding also awarded to projects relating to cancer research.

Exclusions

No grants are given to students for research.

Applications

In writing through the doctor, nurse or church minister of the patient, at the relevant address: (i) Minister, Killean and Kilchenzie Church, Manse, Muasdale, Tarbert, Argyll; (ii) Doctor, The Surgery, Muasdale, Tarbert, Argyll; (iii) Nurse, The Surgery (same address as (ii)).

Argyll and Bute

The G. M. Duncan Trust

£1,000

Correspondent: Mary McCallum, Senior Accountant Assistant, Argyll and Bute Council, Witchburn Road, Campbeltown, Argyll PA28 6JU (01586 555236)

Eligibility

People in need who live in the burgh of Campbeltown.

Types of grants

Vouchers to be exchanged for groceries or goods at a local shop.

Annual grant total

Grants usually total about £1,000 each year.

Applications

In November each year an advert is published in the local press inviting applications. Successful applicants receive their voucher in early December.

Glasgow Bute Benevolent Society

£8,000

Correspondent: The Administrator, 70 Garscadden Road, Glasgow G15 6QJ

SC Number: SC016182

Eligibility

People in need who live in Bute, particularly the elderly. The length of time a person has lived in Bute and how long they have been connected with the area is taken into consideration.

Types of grants

Our research suggests that the society does not award grants as such – suitable applicants are admitted to the Society's Roll of Pensioners and receive a pension payable half-yearly and a Christmas bonus payment. The half-yearly pension is usually of about £50 and the value and availability of the bonus depends on income available.

Annual grant total

At the time of writing (August 2014) the latest financial information was from 2012. In 2012 the society had an income of £9,500 and an expenditure of £8,500. We estimate that support to individuals totalled around £8,000.

Exclusions

People in receipt of parochial help are not supported, unless in extraordinary circumstances.

Applications
Application forms are available from the correspondent. Candidates should provide a supporting recommendation by a minister of religion, doctor, solicitor or other responsible person.

Other information
Small grants for educational purposes may be made on rare occasions.

Dumfries and Galloway

Elizabeth Armstrong Charitable Trust

£400

Correspondent: Kenneth Hill, Senior Partner, 38 High Street, Langholm, Dumfries and Galloway DG13 0JH (01387 380428; email: office@sandjlangholm.co.uk)

SC Number: SC002180

Eligibility
People in need living in Canonbie in Dumfriesshire.

Types of grants
One-off and recurrent grants according to need.

Annual grant total
In 2013/14 we estimate that grants to individuals totalled around £400.

Applications
In writing to the correspondent.

Samuel Elliot Bequest

£500

Correspondent: The Trustees, Dumfries and Galloway Council, Corporate Finance, Carruthers House, English Street, Dumfries DG1 2HP (01387 260031; fax: 01776 704819)

SC Number: SC004899

Eligibility
Older people who are in need and live in the burgh of Lockerbie and the parishes of Dryfesdale and Johnstone.

Types of grants
Recurrent grants according to need.

Annual grant total
Grants usually total around £500 each year.

Applications
In writing to the correspondent.

The Holywood Trust

£73,000

Correspondent: Richard Lye, Trust Administrator, Hestan House, Crichton Business Park, Bankend Road, Dumfries DG1 4TA (01387 269176; fax: 01387 269175; email: funds@holywood-trust.org.uk; website: www.holywood-trust.org.uk)

SC Number: SC009942

Eligibility
Young people aged 15 to 25 living in the Dumfries and Galloway region, with a preference for people who are mentally, physically or socially disadvantaged.

Types of grants
The trust supports a large number of individual young people throughout Dumfries and Galloway who benefit from small grants to improve their lives. Grants of up to £500 are generally provided. The majority of grants are around £200.

Annual grant total
In 2012/13 the trust had assets of £10.5 million and an income of almost £2 million. Grants to individuals totalled £99,000. Grants were made to 386 young people in 2012/13 and were broken down as follows:

Personal welfare (clothing, basic household items)	26%
Student expenses	25%
Personal challenge (volunteering abroad, excelling in sport and music)	22%
Personal development	17%
Other	10%

We believe that social welfare grants to individuals totalled £73,000.

Exclusions
No grants are given towards carpets or accommodation deposits.

Applications
Forms are available from the correspondent, or can be downloaded from the trust's website. Applications are considered at least four times a year. The trust welcomes supporting statements from third parties.

Other information
The Trust also provides the HANDY (Holywood Assistance to Needy and Disadvantaged Youngsters) Fund, which has been established to provide for individual welfare payments to disadvantaged children and young people who are referred by third party professional staff who are aware of their family circumstances (education officials, social workers, health visitors, staff of voluntary sector organisations). Awards of up to £100 per child per year will be considered. View the website for more information.

Lockerbie Trust

£7,600

Correspondent: The Administrator, Farries Kirk and McVean, Dumfries Enterprise Park, Heathhall, Dumfries DG1 3SJ (01387 252127; fax: 01387 250501)

SC Number: SC019796

Eligibility
People in need who live in Lockerbie.

Types of grants
One-off grants are up to £500. Annual payments may be considered but only in exceptional circumstances.

Annual grant total
In 2012/13 the trust had an income of £17,500 and an expenditure of £15,400. We estimate that about £7,600 was awarded in grants to individuals.

Exclusions
According to our research, educational grants are not awarded where Scottish Office grants are available.

Applications
Application forms can be requested from the correspondent. They can be submitted directly by the individual. Candidates should note that the availability of grants from other sources will be taken into account in assessing applications. Generally grants are decided quarterly, in February, June, August and November.

Other information
Organisations and groups or societies are also supported.

The Henry McDonald Trust

£700

Correspondent: The Administrator, Dumfries and Galloway Council, Council Headquarters, English Street, Dumfries DG1 2DD (030 3333 3000; fax: 01387 260034; email: contact@dumgal.gov.uk; website: www.dumgal.gov.uk)

Eligibility
Mothers and babies or young children who live in Stranraer and are in need. Assistance will only be given to people who have exhausted all other sources of funding.

Types of grants
One-off grants up to about £500. In the past grants have been given for furniture and hospital travel costs.

Annual grant total
According to our research around £700 is available for distribution to eligible beneficiaries.

Applications
On a form available from the correspondent. Applications can be submitted directly by the individual or through a third party, such as a social worker. Our research indicates that applications not submitted through a social worker will usually be asked to undertake an interview to help the fund assess the individual's level of need.

Other information
The fund has recently been absorbed into the Stranraer Common Good Fund but the criteria and income available has not changed. The Stranraer Common Good Fund makes grants for organisations and projects in the Stranraer area.

The James McKune Mortification

£500

Correspondent: John McMyn, Trustee, Blawearie, Kirkbean, Dumfries DG2 8DW

SC Number: SC011893

Eligibility
People in need who are natives of the parish of Kirkbean and have lived there for 20 years.

Types of grants
Annual pensions of £30 a year.

Annual grant total
Our research tell us that grants usually total around £500 a year.

Applications
On a form available from the correspondent. Applications should be submitted directly by the individual before 31 January for consideration in March.

The Nivison Trust

£0

Correspondent: S. Hinton-Smith, Trustee, Dumfries and Galloway District Council, Carruthers House, English Street, Dumfries DG1 2HP

SC Number: SC019380

Eligibility
People in need who live in Sanquhar.

Types of grants
Quarterly payments of £20.

Annual grant total
Usually about £1,000, however the trust has told us that they are not currently accepting applications as they are allowing reserves to build up. There has been no expenditure since at least 2009/10.

Applications
Usually in writing to the correspondent but see 'Annual grant total' section.

John Primrose Trust

£2,000

Correspondent: The Trustees, 1 Newall Terrace, Dumfries DG1 1LN

SC Number: SC009173

Eligibility
People in need with a connection to Dumfries and Maxwelltown by parentage or by living there.

Types of grants
Grants of £100 to £150 are given twice a year to 10 to 20 older people.

Annual grant total
In 2012/13 the trust had an income of £14,700 and a total expenditure of £5,700. The trust awards grants to both individuals and organisations for educational and social welfare purposes. We estimate grants to individuals for social welfare purposes to be around £2,000.

Applications
On an application form available from the correspondent, to be considered in June and December.

East Ayrshire

Miss Annie Smith Mair Bequest

£5,000

Correspondent: c/o Head of Democratic Services, East Ayrshire Council, Council Headquarters, London Road, Kilmarnock KA3 7BU (01563 576093; email: admin@east-ayrshire.gov.uk; website: www.east-ayrshire.gov.uk)

SC Number: SC021095

Eligibility
People in need who live, or were born in, Newmilns.

Types of grants
One-off grants usually in the range of £50 to £1,000, towards clothing, household essentials, minor house or garden maintenance work/adaptations, mobility and personal aids, short breaks and small donations for living expenses.

Annual grant total
In 2012/13 the charity had an income of £286 and a total expenditure of £5,100. We estimate that grants to individuals totalled £5,000.

Applications
On a form available from the correspondent or from the East Ayrshire Council website. Applications can be made directly by the individual or through a GP, social worker, Citizens Advice or other welfare agency.

Note: if an application is being made on health grounds alone, a GP's certification of need will also be required.

Other information
The charity is administered by East Ayrshire Council and in recent years, has aided more than 100 people through its grantmaking activities.

The Archibald Taylor Fund

£12,500

Correspondent: Gillian Hamilton, Administrative Officer, East Ayrshire Council, Council Headquarters, London Road, Kilmarnock KA3 7BU (01563 576093; email: admin@east-ayrshire.gov.uk; website: www.east-ayrshire.gov.uk/Home.aspx)

SC Number: SC019308

Eligibility
People in need of special nursing, convalescent treatment at the coast or in the country; or a holiday during convalescence. Applicants must be in financial need.

Types of grants
Grants are given for the provision of special nursing or convalescent treatment and convalescent holidays of up to three weeks. Previous awards have ranged from £250 to £1,000.

Annual grant total
In 2012/13 the charity had an income of £2,600 and a total expenditure of £13,300. We estimate that grants to individuals totalled £12,500.

Applications
On a form available from the correspondent or to download from the East Ayrshire website, for consideration throughout the year. Applications can be made either directly by the individual, or through a social worker, Citizens Advice or other third party such as a GP. The following should be submitted with the application: details of the proposed holiday and cost, household income, employer's certificate of earnings and/or a benefit award letter and a declaration by the applicant's GP.

Completed forms should be returned to: Head of Democratic Services, East Ayrshire Council Headquarters, London Road, Kilmarnock KA3 7BU.

East Renfrewshire

The Janet Hamilton Memorial Fund

£200

Correspondent: Finance Department, East Renfrewshire Council, Council Headquarters, Eastwood Park, Rouken Glen Road, Giffnock, Glasgow G46 6UG (01415 773001)

SC Number: SC019475

Eligibility

People who are chronically sick or infirm, who live in the former burgh of Barrhead and are of pensionable age.

Types of grants

Postal orders of £15, distributed at Christmas.

Annual grant total

In 2012/13 the fund had an income of £550 and a total expenditure of £200.

Applications

Directly by the individual on a form available from the correspondent. A signature from a doctor confirming the person's state of health is necessary, as well as a signed copy of his/her life certificate. Grants are distributed in early December.

Glasgow

The Glasgow Care Foundation

£146,000

Correspondent: The Secretary, Fifth Floor, 30 George Square, Glasgow G2 1EG (01412 483535; email: info@glasgowcarefoundation.org; website: www.glasgowcarefoundation.org)

SC Number: SC000906

Eligibility

Residents of Glasgow who have lived in the city for a minimum of five years and are in need by reason of age, ill-health, disability, financial hardship or other disadvantage.

Types of grants

Pensions, holidays and one-off grants for a variety of needs. Recent grants have included beds and mattresses, white goods, carpets, curtains and blinds, cots, furniture, clothing, soft furnishings, small electrical goods and decorating materials. Food vouchers and toys are also distributed to families at Christmas.

Annual grant total

In 2012/13 the foundation had an income of £324,000 and a total expenditure of £305,000. We estimate that grants to individuals totalled £146,000, with local organisations also receiving funding.

Exclusions

People who are living in care are not eligible.

Applications

Applications can be made online, only through a recognised agency working in the community such as social services. Note the following for online applications: 'If applying online for the first time, you will need to register first to obtain a unique password which you can then use in subsequent online applications. If you have already registered and have been given a password then you can go directly to complete the online application form.' The foundation's welfare officers visit and investigate all cases. Any previous successful applications to the foundation will be taken into account.

Other information

The foundation was formerly known as the City of Glasgow Society of Social Service.

Incorporation of Bakers of Glasgow

£500

Correspondent: Iain Paterson, Clerk, Trades Hall, 85 Glassford Street, Glasgow G1 1UH (01415 531605; fax: 01413 322613; email: iain.paterson@tradeshouse.org.uk; website: www.tradeshouse.org.uk)

SC Number: SC014018

Eligibility

People who are members of the incorporation and their dependents.

Types of grants

One-off and recurrent grants according to need.

Annual grant total

Grants to individuals total about £500 each year.

Applications

In writing to the correspondent.

Other information

The exact date on which the Incorporation of Bakers was founded is uncertain but it is known that the Incorporation existed long prior to its first official mention in 1556.

Today the incorporation is engaged in works of charity and benevolence. Christmas and holiday gifts are paid to numerous needy pensioners and the incorporation provides prizes for students of baking and allied subjects at Glasgow College of Food Technology. Grants are also made to organisations.

The Andrew and Mary Elizabeth Little Charitable Trust

£45,000

Correspondent: Ronnie Munton, Trust Administrator, Low Beaton Richmond Solicitors, Sterling House, 20 Renfield Street, Glasgow G2 5AP (01412 218931; fax: 01412 484411; email: gabrielle@lbr-law.co.uk)

SC Number: SC011185

Eligibility

People in need whose sole source of income is income support, disability benefit or pension, who live in the city of Glasgow.

Types of grants

One-off and recurrent grants according to need.

Annual grant total

In 2012/13 the trust had an income of £62,000 and a total expenditure of £66,000. Typically grants to individuals account for 80% of the trust's charitable expenditure and grants to organisations the remaining 20%. Therefore, we estimate that individuals received a total of £45,000.

Applications

In writing to the correspondent, to be submitted through social services. Applications should include financial details and are considered monthly.

Lord Provost's Fund for Vulnerable Citizens

£500

Correspondent: The Trustees, Glasgow City Council, Social Work Services, Wheatley House, 25 Cochrane Street, Glasgow G1 1HL (01412 870555)

SC Number: SC042268

Eligibility

People in need who live in Glasgow.

Types of grants

One-off and recurrent grants of up to £300.

Annual grant total

In 2012/13 the fund had an income of £1.7 million and a total expenditure of over £60,000. The fund's accounts were not available to view. In the past the previous Provost charities made grants totalling around £500 per year.

Applications

Applications are made through social workers working in the Glasgow City Council area.

Other information

The fund is one of three funds created to rationalise a number of smaller funds administered by Glasgow City Council Social Services department. The other funds are the Lord Provost's Children's Fund and the Lord Provost's Fund for Older People, which can also be found in this guide.

The Trades House of Glasgow

£45,000

Correspondent: The Clerk, Administration Centre, North Gallery – Trades Hall, 85 Glassford Street, Glasgow G1 1UH (01415 531605; website: www.tradeshouse.org.uk)

SC Number: SCO40548

Eligibility

People in need who live in Glasgow, especially those receiving only a pension.

Types of grants

One-off grants of between £5 and £5,000.

Annual grant total

In 2012/13 this charity had an income of £12.8 million and a total expenditure of £793,000. Grants and donations totalled £182,500 and were awarded to both organisations and individuals for social welfare, education and other charitable purposes. We estimate grants to individuals for social welfare purposes totalled around £45,000.

Applications

In writing to the correspondent.

Other information

Guilds and Craft Incorporations are the Scottish equivalent of the craft guilds or livery companies, which developed in most of the great cities of Europe in the Middle Ages. Over the years many of the House's political and legal duties have been transferred to other bodies, but the charitable functions and concern for the future of Glasgow remain. The assistance of the needy, the encouragement of youth and support for education, particularly the schools and the further education colleges in developing craft standards, are now its chief objects.

The Trades House also operates the Drapers Fund which distributes £50,000 annually to children-in-need who are under the age of seventeen. To apply write supplying as much detail as possible highlighting the circumstances of the individual/organisation concerned to: The Manager, The Drapers Fund, The Trades House of Glasgow, Trades Hall, 85 Glassford Street, Glasgow G1 1UH.

The Ure Elder Trust

£13,000

Correspondent: The Administrator, Maclay Murray and Spens LLP, 1 George Square, Glasgow G2 1AL (0330 222 0050; fax: 0330 222 0053)

SC Number: SC003775

Eligibility

Widows in need who live in Glasgow, especially Govan.

Types of grants

Annual grants paid twice a year plus a bonus at Christmas.

Annual grant total

At the time of writing (August 2014) the latest financial information available was from 2012. In 2012 the trust had an income £9,400 and a total expenditure of £13,100. We estimate that just under £13,000 was awarded in grants to individuals.

Applications

Application forms are available from the correspondent. They can be submitted directly by the individual or through a third party and are normally considered in April and October.

Inverclyde

Gourock Coal and Benevolent Fund

£4,300

Correspondent: Mr S. Baldwin, Trustee, 38 Taymouth Drive, Gourock, Renfrewshire PA19 1HJ

SC Number: SC009881

Eligibility

People in need who live in the former burgh of Gourock. There is a preference for older people, especially people who live on their own.

Types of grants

Gas and electricity vouchers are available and coal deliveries can also be made.

Annual grant total

In 2012/13, the fund had an income of £3,700 and a total expenditure of £4,500. We estimate that the total amount of grants awarded to individuals was approximately £4,300.

Applications

In writing to any minister or parish priest in the town, or the local branch of the WRVS (not to the correspondent). Applications are normally considered in December and can be submitted either directly by the individual or through a social worker, Citizens Advice or other welfare agency.

The Lady Alice Shaw-Stewart Memorial Fund

£250

Correspondent: The Trustees, Inverclyde Council, Municipal Buildings, Greenock, Inverclyde PA15 1JA (01475 717171)

SC Number: SC019228

Eligibility

Female ex-prisoners recommended by the probation officer in the Inverclyde Council area.

Types of grants

On average one-off grants total about £200 each and are given for general welfare purposes, such as electrical goods, holidays and driving lessons.

Annual grant total

Grants have decreased to around £250 a year.

Applications

In writing to the correspondent. Applications should be submitted by a probation officer on behalf of the individual.

Other information

The council administers about 20 other small trusts for people living in Greenock, Gourock, Inverkip and Kilmacolm.

Mrs Mary Sinclair's Trust

£500

Correspondent: The Trustees, Neill Clerk and Murray Solicitors, 3 Ardgowan Square, Greenock PA16 8NW (01475 724522)

SC Number: SC002535

Eligibility

Older seafarers who were born or sailed out of Greenock, their widows and children, who are in need.

Types of grants

A twice yearly pension to each beneficiary of £12.

Annual grant total

In 2012/13 the trust had an income of £3,800. Grants generally total around £500 a year.

Applications

Application forms can be obtained from the correspondent.

South Ayrshire

The James and Jane Knox Fund

£0

Correspondent: Bill Grant, Trustee, South Ayrshire Council, County Buildings, Wellington Square, Ayr KA7 1DR (0300 123 0900)

SC Number: SC008856

Eligibility

Older men in need, preferably bachelors, in the parish of Monkton and Prestwick.

Types of grants

One-off and recurrent grants for the provision of comforts.

Annual grant total

In 2013/14 the fund had no charitable expenditure.

Applications

In writing to the correspondent directly by the individual with as much information as possible. Applications are considered as and when required.

Other information

South Ayrshire Council administers a number of smaller trusts, details of which can be obtained from the correspondent.

The Loudoun Bequest

£0

Correspondent: Bill Grant, Trustee, South Ayrshire Council, County Buildings, Wellington Square, Ayr KA7 1DR (0300 123 0900)

SC Number: SC017166

Eligibility

People in need who live in Monkton and Prestwick.

Types of grants

Gifts of coal to individuals who meet the criteria.

Annual grant total

In 2013/14 the trust had no charitable expenditure.

Applications

In writing to the correspondent directly by the individual, providing detailed information.

West Dunbartonshire

Lennox Children's Trust

£9,000

Correspondent: The Administrator, c/o Citizens Advice, Bridgend House, 179 High Street, Dumbarton G82 1NW (01389 744690; fax: 01389 768019)

SC Number: SC023740

Eligibility

Children who are in need through poverty, neglect, behavioural or psychological disorders, physical or mental disability, and who live in the Dunbartonshire area.

Types of grants

One-off and recurrent grants according to need. Grants have been given for disability aids, educational and medical equipment and toys.

Annual grant total

In 2012/13 the trust had an income of £3,100 and total expenditure of £9,500. We estimate that grants to individuals totalled £9,000.

Applications

On a form available from the correspondent, to be submitted by a third party with a connection to the child.

Highlands and Islands

Lady McCorquodale's Charity Trust

£6,000

Correspondent: Anina Cheng, Administrator, 4th Floor, Swan House, 17–19 Stratford Place, London W1C 1BQ (020 7907 2100; email: charity@mfs.co.uk)

CC Number: 268786

Eligibility

People who are in need, with a preference for older people.

Types of grants

One-off and recurrent grants are given for day-to-day needs, such as clothing and food.

Annual grant total

In 2012/13 the trust had an income of £15,700 and a total expenditure of £18,100. As the trust's main focus is to offer funding for other charitable institutions, we estimate that individuals received a total of £6,000 from around £18,000 distributed.

Applications

In writing to the correspondent. Applications can be submitted either directly by the individual or, where applicable, via a social worker, Citizens Advice or other third party.

Dr Sutherland Fund for the Poor (Charlotte Sutherlands Trust)

£1,800

Correspondent: The Administrator, Murdoch Stewarts, Suite 4/2, Merchants House, 7 West George Street, Glasgow G2 1BA (01414 122234)

SC Number: SC006694

Eligibility

People in need who live in the parishes of Olrig – Caithness, Kirkwall and St Ola in the Orkney Isles.

Types of grants

Our research suggests that typically grants of around £50 each are awarded to relieve poverty.

Annual grant total

In 2012/13 the fund had an income of £1,500 and an expenditure of £2,000. We have estimated the annual total of grants to individuals to be around £1,800.

Applications

According to our research, grants are not given on application. The fund's administrators write to the relevant social work departments and ask for a list of eligible beneficiaries, who the administrators then contact.

Highland

Dr Forbes Inverness Trust

£10,000

Correspondent: David Hewitson, Secretary and Treasurer, Munro and Noble Solicitors, 26 Church Street, Inverness IV1 1HX (01463 221727; fax: 01463 225165; email: legal@munronoble.com)

SC Number: SC005573

Eligibility

People with a medical or similar need who live in the former burgh of Inverness or immediately surrounding areas to the south of the Beauly/Inverness Firth.

Types of grants

Generally one-off grants to help with the cost of medical treatment and equipment, convalescence, food, clothing and travel expenses to visit sick relatives. Help has also been given with holidays for people who, from a medical point of view, would benefit from it.

Annual grant total

In 2012/13 the trust had an income of £9,400 and a total expenditure of £10,300. We estimate that grants to individuals totalled around £10,000.

Applications

On a form available from the correspondent, can be submitted by the individual or through a recognised referral agency (such as a social worker, Citizens Advice or a doctor) or other third party. Forms are considered throughout the year and must be signed by the applicant's doctor. Supporting letters can also help the application.

The Highland Children's Trust

£10,000

Correspondent: The Administrator, 105 Castle Street, Inverness IV2 3EA (01463 243872; email: info@hctrust.co.uk; website: www.hctrust.co.uk)

SC Number: SC006008

Eligibility

Children and young people in need who are under 25 and live in the Highlands.

Types of grants

One-off grants of £50 to £500 are available for the following purposes:

- Student hardship funding
- School or educational trips
- Family holidays
- Educational items for children with special educational needs

Annual grant total

This trust awards grants to individuals totalling around £20,000 for both education and welfare purposes. We estimate grants for social welfare totalled £10,000.

Exclusions

Grants are not given for postgraduate study, to pay off debts, nor to purchase clothing, footwear, food, furniture or cars and so on.

Applications

On a form available from the correspondent or downloaded from the website, where criteria and guidelines are also posted. They can be submitted at any time either directly by the individual or through a social worker, Citizens Advice or other welfare agency.

Applications must include details of income and savings.

Shetland Islands

Shetland Charitable Trust

£422,000

Correspondent: Ann Black, Chief Executive, 22–24 North Road, Lerwick, Shetland ZE1 0NQ (01595 744994; email: mail@shetlandcharitabletrust.co.uk; website: www.shetlandcharitabletrust.co.uk)

SC Number: SC027025

Eligibility

People who are vulnerable due to age, ill health, disability or financial hardship and have been resident in Shetland for more than a year.

Types of grants

One-off hardship grants are made from the social assistance fund. Christmas grants.

Annual grant total

In 2012/13 the trust had an income of £11 million and assets of £226 million. Grants to individuals and organisations: £416,000 in Christmas grants and £5,500 in social assistance grants.

£29,000 was also paid in grants from the Arts Grants Scheme which makes grants to both individuals and organisations; however, a breakdown was not available.

Applications

Applications for Christmas grants tend to open in September of each year; check the website before contacting the trust to ensure applications are being accepted. Applicants for the social assistance grants should contact the duty social worker on 01595 744400.

Other information

Grants are also given to organisations.

Western Isles

The William MacKenzie Trust

£15,000

Correspondent: Trust Administrator, Mann Judd Gordon, 26 Lewis Street, Stornoway, Isle of Lewis HS1 2JF (01851 702335)

SC Number: SC001598

Eligibility

People who are older or in poor health and live in Stornoway.

Types of grants

One-off grants to enable individuals to continue living in their own homes. Grants have been given for house adaptations, reclining chairs and domestic equipment such as washing machines.

Annual grant total

In 2012/13 the trust had both an income and a total expenditure of £38,000. We estimate that grants to individuals totalled £15,000, with organisations also receiving funding.

Applications

In writing to the correspondent. Applications can be submitted directly by the individual or, where applicable, through a social worker, Citizens Advice or other welfare agency.

Wales

General

Children's Leukaemia Society

£32,000 (121 grants)

Correspondent: Elaine Churchill, Trustee, 384 Coed-Y-Gores, Llanedeyrn, Cardiff CF23 9NR (020920250132; email: childrensleukaemiasociety@hotmail.co.uk; website: www.childrensleukaemiasociety.co.uk)

CC Number: 1008634

Eligibility

Children under 16 who are in need and have leukaemia. Grants are made to those living in south Wales and the West Country.

Types of grants

Gifts for children who are undergoing chemotherapy, usually in the form of an Argos voucher. The provision of holidays for children and their families following treatment.

Annual grant total

In 2012/13 the society held assets of £290,000 and had an income of £83,000. Payments for holidays and gifts to children totalled £32,000; 51 holidays were funded and 70 gifts given. The total number of gifts includes 'special circumstances' gifts for terminally ill children.

Applications

In writing to the correspondent.

Other information

The society owns holiday homes and upgrades caravans for use as holiday accommodation for children and their families, though none were upgraded in 2012/13.

LATCH Welsh Children's Cancer Charity

£254,000

Correspondent: Ian Rogers, Trustee, LATCH Office, Children's Hospital for Wales, Heath Park, Cardiff CF14 4XW (02920 748858/9 or 01633 601398; fax: 02920 748868; email: info@latchwales.org; website: www.latchwales.org)

CC Number: 1100949

Eligibility

Children who have cancer and leukaemia (including tumours) and have been referred to the Paediatric Oncology Unit at The Children's Hospital for Wales.

Types of grants

One-off and recurrent grants for children and their families who are in need of financial assistance towards, for example, travel costs to and from hospital, subsistence grants for daily expenses, utility bills, specialist equipment and other household needs (such as washing machines), childcare costs, car repairs, holidays and outings or other needs.

Annual grant total

In 2013 the charity had assets of £4 million and an income of £1 million. Grants were made totalling £254,000.

Applications

Applications should be made through one of the LATCH social workers who can submit applications for consideration by the trust. More information on support given is available from other organisations, such as respite care.

Other information

The charity also supports the development of the specialist medical care at the oncology unit. Children and their families can also be provided on-site accommodation, advocacy and information services and emotional support.

The Welsh Rugby Charitable Trust

£326,000

Correspondent: Edward Jones, Hon. Secretary, 55 West Road, Bridgend CF31 4HQ (01656 653042; email: ehjones100@googlemail.com; website: www.wrct.org.uk)

CC Number: 502079

Eligibility

People who have been severely injured whilst playing rugby union football in Wales, and their dependents.

Types of grants

One-off grants to help injured players regain their independence. Grants can be made towards cars, wheelchairs, hoists, domestic aids and gifts in summer (for a holiday break) and at Christmas.

Annual grant total

In 2012/13 the trust had an income of £283,000 and a total expenditure of £345,000. Grants to individuals amounted to £326,000 and were distributed as follows:

Relief of injured players	£275,000
Summer grants	£33,000
Christmas gifts	£18,000

Applications

In writing to the correspondent, including the circumstances of the injury and the effect it has on the applicant's career. Information on the financial position before and after the accident should also be included. Applications are considered every two months (or sooner in emergency cases) and can be submitted either directly by the individual or by a club representative.

Players who have been seriously injured but not permanently disabled are usually visited by the trust to assess the degree of need before any grant is made.

The Widows, Orphans and Dependents Society of the Church in Wales (WODS)

£85,000 (70 grants)

Correspondent: Louise Davies, Head of Finance, 39 Cathedral Road, Cardiff CF11 9XF (02920 348228; email: louisedavies@churchinwales.org.uk; website: www.churchinwales.org.uk)

CC Number: 503271

Eligibility

Widows, orphans and dependents of deceased clergy of the Church in Wales only, who are living on a low income. Each year the society sets minimum income levels which each diocesan committee should aim to achieve. In 2013 these levels were set at £14,050 for widows, £13,450 for dependents and £2,550 for orphans.

Types of grants

One-off grants in the form of birthday, Christmas and Easter bonuses.

Annual grant total

In 2013 the society held assets of £703,000 and had an income of £89,000. Individuals received 70 grants totalling £85,000.

Applications

In writing to the correspondent. Applications should be made through one of the six diocesan committees of the Church in Wales. Details of the applicant's financial situation should be included.

Mid-Wales

Ceredigion

The Margaret and Alick Potter Charitable Trust

£1,000

Correspondent: Dr Beryl Thomas, Trustee, 31 North Parade, Aberystwyth, Dyfed SY23 2JN (01970 623808; email: marquetry@msn.com)

CC Number: 1088821

Eligibility

People with all types of dementia (as well as Alzheimer's disease) and their families who live in North Ceredigion.

Types of grants

Grants are given according to need.

Annual grant total

The trust has an average annual income of around £5,000 although total expenditure varies. In 2012/13 total expenditure was £2,000.

Applications

In writing to the correspondent.

Other information

The trust also makes grants to local organisations.

Powys

The Brecknock Welfare Trust

£1,000

Correspondent: Gail Rofe, Administrator, Brecon Town Council, The Guildhall, High Street, Brecon, Powys LD3 7AL (01874 622884; email: brecon.guildhall@btinternet.com)

CC Number: 240671

Eligibility

People in need who live in the town of Brecon.

Types of grants

One-off grants in kind according to need, such as electrical goods, clothing, medical and disability equipment and furniture.

Annual grant total

In 2012 the trust had an income of £1,700 and an expenditure of £1,400. This was the latest financial information available at the time of writing. We estimate that around £1,000 was made in grants to individuals for social welfare purposes.

Exclusions

Grants are in kind and no cash awards are made.

Applications

In writing to the correspondent. Applications should be submitted through a recognised referral agency (such as a social worker, Citizens Advice or doctor and so on).

The Llanidloes Relief-in-Need Charity

£1,200

Correspondent: Elaine Lloyd, Administrator, Woodcroft, Woodlands Road, Llanidloes, Powys SY18 6HX (01686 412636; email: elainellloyd@gmail.com)

CC Number: 259955

Eligibility

People in need who live in the communities of Llanidloes and Llanidloes Without only.

Types of grants

One-off grants for people in need.

Annual grant total

In 2013/14 the charity had an income of £240 and an expenditure of £2,700. Grants totalled approximately £2,500 and were split between educational and welfare purposes.

Applications

In writing to the correspondent. Applications should be made through social service, doctors, Citizens Advice or churches.

The Montgomery Welfare Fund

£3,500

Correspondent: Wendy Davies, Administrator, 15 Lymore View, Montgomery, Powys SY15 6RJ (01686 668734)

CC Number: 214767

Eligibility

People in need who live permanently in the ecclesiastical parish of Montgomery (not the county).

Types of grants

One-off grants ranging from £25 to £100. Reapplications can be made. Grants cover a wide range of needs.

Annual grant total

In 2012/13, the fund had an income of £3,700 and a total expenditure of £3,600. We estimate that the total amount of grants awarded to individuals was approximately £3,500.

Exclusions

No grants to pay rates, tax or other public funds.

Other information

Grants can also be given to individuals for education, 'development in life' and so on.

The Visual Impairment Breconshire (Nam Gweledol Sir Brycheiniog)

£1,700

Correspondent: Carol Wothers, Administrator, 23 Pen y Fan Close, Libanus, Brecon, Powys LD3 8EJ (01874 625590; website: www.visualimpairment.breconshire.powys.org.uk)

CC Number: 217377

Eligibility

Blind and partially-sighted people living in Brecknock.

Types of grants

One-off grants at Christmas and for special equipment/special needs, for example, cookers and talking books.

Annual grant total

Our research tells us that grants average around £1,700 a year, though the actual grant figure tends to fluctuate quite widely.

Applications

In writing to the correspondent, to be considered when received.

Other information

This charity also runs activities, provides resources and makes grants to organisations.

North Wales

The Corwen College Pension Charity

£1,400

Correspondent: Diane McCarthy, Diocesan Secretary, The Diocese of St Asaph, Diocesan Office, High Street, St Asaph, Denbighshire LL17 0RD (01745 582245; email: dianemccarthy@churchinwales.org.uk)

CC Number: 248822

Eligibility

Needy widows or widowers of clergy of the Church in Wales who have held office in the district of Merionydd in Gwynedd or the communities of Betws Gwerfil Goch, Corwen Gwyddelwern, Llandrillo, Llangar and Llansantffraid Glyndyfrdwy (all in Clwyd).

Types of grants

Recurrent grants according to need.

Annual grant total

In 2012 the charity had an income of £3,100 and a total expenditure of £1,500. We estimate that social welfare grants to individuals totalled £1,400.

At the time of writing (August 2014) this was the most recent financial information available for the charity.

Applications

In writing to the correspondent, for consideration in February.

The North Wales Police Benevolent Fund

£2,300

Correspondent: Mel Jones, Administrator, North Wales Police Federation, 311 Abergele Road, Old Colwyn, Colwyn Bay LL29 9YF (01492 805404)

CC Number: 505321

Eligibility

Members and former members of the North Wales Police Force, former members of previous forces amalgamated to form the North Wales Police, and their families and immediate dependents who are in need.

Types of grants

One-off and recurrent grants according to need. Grants are also made at Christmas.

Annual grant total

In 2012/13 the trust had an income of £5,000 and a total expenditure of £2,500. We estimate that grants to individuals totalled £2,300.

Applications

In writing to the correspondent. Applications are considered quarterly, although urgent applicants can be considered as they arrive.

The North Wales Psychiatric Fund

£9,500

Correspondent: Hilary Owen, Administrator, Bryn y Neuadd Hospital, Aber Road, Llanfairfechan, Gwynedd LL33 OHH (01248 682573)

CC Number: 235783

Eligibility

People in North Wales who are mentally ill and are under the care of a social worker or health professional.

Types of grants

One-off grants for clothes, furniture, holidays and learning courses.

Annual grant total

In 2013 the fund had an income of £3,300 and a total expenditure of £9,800. We estimate that grants to individuals totalled £9,500.

Exclusions

There are no grants available for the payment of debts.

Applications

In writing to the correspondent through a social worker or health professional, including details of income and other possible grant sources. Applications are considered throughout the year.

The Evan and Catherine Roberts Home

£4,300

Correspondent: Ken Owen, Trustee, Ael Y Garth, 81 Bryn Avenue, Old Colwyn, Colwyn Bay LL29 8AH (01492 515209)

CC Number: 244965

Eligibility

People over the age of 60 who live within a 40-mile radius of the Bethesda Welsh Methodist Church in Old Colwyn, with preference for members of the Methodist Church. Those living in parts of Conwy, Denbighshire, Flintshire and Gwynedd are eligible.

Types of grants

One-off grants ranging from £50 to £150.

Annual grant total

In 2012/13 the trust had an income of £1,400 and a total expenditure of £4,400. We estimate that grants to individuals totalled £4,300

Applications

On a form available from the correspondent.

Elizabeth Williams Charities

£6,700

Correspondent: Alison Alexander, Administrator, Arfon Cottage, 19 Roe Parc, St Asaph, Denbighshire LL17 0LD (01745 583798; email: alison.alexander@btinternet.com)

CC Number: 216903

Eligibility

People in need who live in the communities of St Asaph, Bodelwyddan, Cefn and Waen in Denbighshire.

Types of grants

One-off grants, generally between £50 and £100, are given as Christmas bonuses for people who are older, to families with parents suffering serious illnesses and for particular needs.

Annual grant total

In 2012/13 the charities had an income of £7,000 and a total expenditure of £6,900. We estimate that grants to individuals totalled £6,700.

Exclusions

Grants are not given for aid that can be met specifically by public funds, for private education or if the grant would affect a claimant's benefit from the DWP.

Applications

In writing to the correspondent, to be submitted either directly by the individual or, where applicable, through a social worker, Citizens Advice or other welfare agency. Applications can also be submitted via a trustee. They are generally considered in November, although specific cases can be considered at any time.

Anglesey

Anglesey Society for the Welfare of Handicapped People

£5,000

Correspondent: Robert Jones, Administrator, 8 Gorwel Deg, Rhostrehwfa, Llangefni, Anglesey

CC Number: 218810

Eligibility

People living in Anglesey who have tuberculosis or any other disease, illness or disability.

Types of grants

One-off or recurrent grants according to need.

Annual grant total

In 2013, the trust had an income £2,800 and a total expenditure of £5,200. We estimate the grant total to be £5,000.

Applications

In writing to the correspondent.

Other information

The trust also makes grants to organisations.

Conwy

Conwy Welsh Church Acts Fund

£2,500

Correspondent: Catherine Dowber, Financial Administrator, Head of Financial Services, Conwy County Borough Council, Bodlondeb, Conwy LL32 8DU (01492 576201; email: welshchurchactsfund@conwy.gov.uk; website: www.conwy.gov.uk/doc.asp?cat=2972&doc=14371)

Eligibility

People in need living in the County Borough of Conwy.

Types of grants

One-off grants ranging from £50 to £2,000, for the relief of poverty and sickness, elderly people, the blind and visually impaired, the advancement of religion, the advancement of literature and the arts, medical and social research, those on probation, and the relief of emergencies and disasters.

Annual grant total

Our research tells us that the fund generates approximately £10,000 per annum for distribution, which is divided between individuals (for both welfare and educational purposes) and organisations.

Exclusions

Grants are not made to individuals for sport or tuition fees.

Applications

On a form available from the correspondent, to be submitted directly by the individual or through a third party. The closing date for applications is the first week in May or October, for consideration in June/July or November/December respectively.

Other information

The fund has its origins in The Welsh Church Act of 1914.

There is a page about the fund on the Conwy County Borough Council website.

Denbighshire

The Freeman Evans St David's Day Denbigh Charity

£1,000 (2 grants)

Correspondent: Medwyn Jones, Town Clerk, Denbigh Town Council, Town Hall, Crown Square, Denbigh LL16 3TB (01745 815984; email: townclerk@denbightowncouncil.gov.uk)

CC Number: 518033

Eligibility

People in need who are older, in poor health or who have a disability and live in Denbigh and Henllan.

Types of grants

One-off grants according to need, including towards disability aids, furniture, travel costs, home adaptations, Christmas gifts and so on.

Annual grant total

In 2012/13 the charity had assets of £1.4 million and an income of £33,000. Two individuals were awarded grants directly totalling about £1,000, including dyslexia assessment fee and assistance for purchasing a car with a winch. Some individual support is channelled through Citizens Advice or similar agencies.

Applications

In writing to the correspondent. Applications can be made either directly by the individual or through a third party, such as a social worker, Citizens Advice or other welfare agency. The trustees meet regularly throughout the year to consider applications.

Other information

Most awards are made to organisations (about £35,000 in 2012/13). Grants are also given for educational purposes.

Flintshire

Flintshire Welsh Church Acts Fund

£1,000

Correspondent: Trevor Jones, Community Cohesion Officer, Policy, Performance and Partnerships, Flintshire County Council, County Hall, Mold, Flintshire CH7 6NB (01352 702613; email: trevor.jones@flintshire.gov.uk)

CC Number: 504476

Eligibility

People who are sick or who have disabilities and are living in Flintshire.

Types of grants

One-off and recurrent grants, ranging between £100 and £500.

Annual grant total

In 2012/13 the fund had an income of £25,000 and a total expenditure of £24,000. Our research tells us that social welfare grants to individuals have previously totalled around £1,000. Grants are also given to organisations and for educational purposes.

Applications

On a form available from the correspondent. Applications are considered quarterly.

Other information

This trust was previously listed as County Council of Clwyd Welsh Church Acts Fund.

Gwynedd

The Freeman Evans St David's Day Ffestiniog Charity

£40,000

Correspondent: William Maldwyn Evans, Trustee, NatWest Bank plc, Meirionnydd Business Centre, Bridge Street, Dolgellau, Gwynedd LL40 1AU (01341 421242; email: maldevans@aol.com)

CC Number: 518034

Eligibility

People who are older, in poor health or who have disabilities and live in the districts of Blaenau Ffestiniog and Llan Ffestiniog as they were prior to the 1974 reorganisation.

Types of grants

One-off and recurrent grants for home adaptations, specialist chairs, stair-lifts, electric wheelchairs and phone lifelines.

Annual grant total

In 2013/14 the charity had an unusually low income of £4 and a total expenditure of £48,000. We estimate that grants to individuals totalled £40,000.

Applications

Applications can be submitted in writing directly by the individual or, where applicable, through a recognised referral agency such as a social worker, minister of religion, councillor, Citizens Advice or doctor. Applications are considered by the trustees twice a year, though urgent cases can be dealt with between meetings.

Wrexham

The Jones Trust

£21,000

Correspondent: Patricia Williams, Secretary, 33 Deva Way, Wrexham LL13 9EU (01978 261684)

CC Number: 229956

Eligibility

People who are sick, convalescing, disabled or infirm in the county of Wrexham.

Types of grants

Grants for respite care in residential and nursing homes and convalescence. Grants for appliances and surgical aids not readily available through the health service are also considered.

Annual grant total

In 2013 the trust had assets of £1 million and an income of £38,000. Grants to individuals totalled £21,000.

Applications

In writing to the correspondent.

Ruabon and District Relief-in-Need Charity

£1,600

Correspondent: James Fenner, Administrator, 65 Albert Grove, Ruabon, Wrexham LL14 6AF (01978 820102; email: jamesrfenner@tiscali.co.uk)

CC Number: 212817

Eligibility

All people who are considered to be in need who live in the county borough of Wrexham, which covers the community council districts of Cefn Mawr, Penycae, Rhosllanerchrugog and Ruabon.

Types of grants

One-off and recurrent grants. Previously grants have been made towards installation of a telephone, heating costs, children's clothing, cookers, furniture, musical instruments, electric wheelchairs, clothing for adults in hospital, travel costs for hospital visits and books and travel for university students.

Annual grant total

In 2013 the charity had an income of £3,300 and an expenditure of £3,400. Grants for welfare totalled approximately £1,600.

Exclusions

Grants are not given for instigating bankruptcy proceedings. Loans are not given.

Applications

In writing to the correspondent either directly by the individual or a family member, through a third party such as a social worker or teacher, or through an organisation such as Citizens Advice or a school. Applications are considered on an ongoing basis.

The Wrexham and District Relief in Need Charity

£18,000

Correspondent: Frieda Leech, Clerk, Holly Chase, Penypalmant Road, Minera, Wrexham LL11 3YW (01978 754152; email: clerk.wpef@gmail.com)

CC Number: 236355

Eligibility

People in need who live in the former borough of Wrexham or the communities of Abenbury, Bersham, Bieston, Broughton, Brymbo, Esclusham Above, Esclusham Below, Gresford, Gwersyllt and Minera in Wrexham.

Types of grants

One-off or recurrent grants according to need typically ranging from £40 to £500. Grants have been given towards the costs of maternity necessities, household equipment, wheelchairs, clothing and a stairlift, for example.

Annual grant total

In 2013 the charity had an income of £18,400 and a total expenditure of £18,700. We estimate that grants to individuals totalled £18,000.

Applications

In writing to the correspondent. Applications should be submitted directly by the individual, or by a third party, and should include full details of the applicant's weekly income and expenditure together with the cost of the item required where applicable. Applications are considered throughout the year.

South Wales

Gwalia Housing Trust

£15,000

Correspondent: Trust Administrator, 7–13 The Kingsway, Swansea SA1 5JN (01792 488140; email: ght@gwalia.com; website: www.gwaliatrust.org.uk)

CC Number: 700822

Eligibility

Tenants of Gwalia who are supported by a neighbourhood housing officer or floating support worker and clients of Gwalia Care and Support who are supported by a floating support worker.

Types of grants

One-off grants for housing related needs such as furniture and white goods. Tenants of Gwalia can apply for grants of up to £500, which can also be given for carpets (if there is no other flooring is in the property). Individuals who are under the Gwalia Care and Support Scheme can apply for a grant of up to £300.

Annual grant total

In 2012/13 the trust had assets of £2.5 million and an income of £136,000. Grants totalled £30,000. We estimate that grants to individuals totalled around £15,000.

Applications

Via the online application form on the trust's website which may also be printed and sent to the correspondent. All applications must have a letter of support from and must be signed off by either the neighbourhood housing officer or a floating support worker.

Other information

The trust provides housing for people in necessitous circumstances, particularly older people, students and those living with disabilities.

The trust also makes grants through its Community Development Fund. Grants of up to £750 are available to assist communities living in Gwalia's residential or non-residential accommodation and who are identified as being in need of financial assistance to improve their quality of life or living environment.

Local Aid for Children and Community Special Needs

£1,000

Correspondent: Denise Inger, Trustee, 89 Clase Road, Morriston, Swansea SA6 8DY (01792 405041; website: www.localaid.co.uk)

CC Number: 1104585

Eligibility

People with special needs/learning difficulties, between the ages of 3 and 30, who live in Swansea or Neath Port Talbot.

Types of grants

One-off grants or grants in kind ranging from £50 to £150 for specialist equipment such as a specialist bed, chair or bike, or towards the costs of travel.

Annual grant total

In 2012/13 the charity had an income of £190,000 and a total expenditure of £163,000. Our research tells us that grants are only occasionally made to individuals in need and in previous years have totalled an estimated £1,000.

Exclusions

No grants are given for items which should be funded by statutory sources.

Applications

In writing to the correspondent, including confirmation that the amount requested is not available from statutory sources. Applications should be submitted through a social worker, Citizens Advice or other welfare agency or professional. They are considered quarterly.

Other information

The majority of expenditure is allocated to funding the charity's own projects working with children with disabilities.

Cardiff

The Cardiff Caledonian Society

£9,500

Correspondent: Cathy Rogers, Administrator, 9 Llandinam Crescent, Cardiff CF14 2RB (02921 405800)

CC Number: 257665

Eligibility

People of Scottish nationality and their families, who live in Cardiff or the surrounding district and are in need.

Types of grants

One-off grants are given for clothing, food, household bills, travel expenses and furniture. Support may be given to people who are homeless, disabled or affected by hardship.

Annual grant total

In 2012/13 the fund had an income of £15,500 and a total expenditure of £19,800. The trustees award grants to individuals for both educational and welfare purposes.

Applications

In writing to the correspondent. Applications can be submitted directly by the individual or through a social worker, Citizens Advice or other welfare agency at any time. Applications are considered on a regular basis.

Cardiff Citizens Charity

£1,800

Correspondent: Liza Kellett, Chief Executive, The Community Foundation in Wales, Unit 9 Coopers Yard, Curran Road, Cardiff CF10 5NB (02920 536590; email: mail@cfiw.org.uk; website: www.cfiw.org.uk)

CC Number: 206549

Eligibility

People in need who live in the city of Cardiff.

Types of grants

One-off grants in the range of £100 to £400 for funeral expenses, clothes, specialist computer software, household appliances and so on.

Annual grant total

In 2012/13, the charity had an income of £4,000 and a total expenditure of £2,000. We estimate that the total amount of grants awarded to individuals was approximately £1,800.

Exclusions

No grants are made for educational purposes.

Applications

On a form available from the correspondent, to be submitted through a recognised referral agency (such as a social worker, Citizens Advice or doctor) or other third party. Evidence of weekly/monthly expenditure must be submitted. Trustees meet twice yearly to consider applications.

Other information

This charity was formerly known as the Cardiff Charity for Special Relief. The charity is now administered by the Community Foundation in Wales.

The Duffryn Trust

£2,600

Correspondent: Mr D. C. Williams, Trustee, 89 Cyncoed Road, Cardiff CF23 5SD (02920 484554)

CC Number: 1031718

Eligibility

People in need with a preference for those who live in Cardiff.

Types of grants

One-off and recurrent grants according to need.

Annual grant total

In 2012/13 the trust had an income of £5,200 and a total expenditure of £5,400. We estimate that grants to individuals totalled £2,600, with funding also awarded to Christian organisations.

Applications

In writing to the correspondent.

Other information

The trust supports evangelical churches and missionary organisations.

Carmarthenshire

The Megan and Trevor Griffiths Trust Fund

£800

Correspondent: Janet Griffiths, Honorary Secretary, 46 Partridge Road, Roath, Cardiff CF24 3QX (email: mtgtrust@googlemail.com)

CC Number: 328684

Eligibility

People with physical or mental disabilities. Preference is given to people living in the former administrative county of Carmarthen (Carmarthenshire and parts of Ceredigion and Pembrokeshire).

Types of grants
Small grants are available for goods or services that cannot be obtained through statutory agencies, and specifically to promote independence. This can include IT equipment, electrical goods, hospital expenses, respite care, holidays, special toys/instruments, fees for training courses and disabled and therapeutic equipment. Grants are one-off and usually limited to £100.

Annual grant total
In 2012/13 the fund had an income of £1,700 and a total expenditure of £1,300. Previously grants to individuals have totalled around £800.

Exclusions
Grants are not given for the payment of debts, property repairs or towards white goods and furniture.

Applications
In writing to the correspondent. Applications must be supported by a third party, preferably a professional, for example, a social worker, family doctor or occupational therapist. Application deadlines usually are in mid-October and at the end of May.

Other information
The trust has rarely supported applications from outside Carmarthenshire and has previously stated that they have sufficient numbers of worthy applicants from Carmarthenshire and surrounding counties in South Wales.

Merthyr Tydfil

Merthyr Mendicants

£3,000

Correspondent: Allen Lane, Administrator, 4 Georgetown Villas, Georgetown, Merthyr Tydfil, Mid Glamorgan CF48 1BD (01685 373308)

CC Number: 208105

Eligibility
People in need who live in the borough of Merthyr Tydfil.

Types of grants
One-off grants according to need. Grants have been given towards medical equipment not available from the National Health Service (providing it is recommended by a medical authority); Christmas parcels; holidays for children; telephone helplines for incapacitated people; and help with domestic equipment such as cookers, refrigerators, washing machines, bedding and beds.

Annual grant total
In 2012 the trust had an income of £13,300 and a total expenditure of £13,100. This was the latest financial information available at the time of writing. We estimate that social welfare grants to individuals totalled £3,000. Grants are also given to organisations and for educational purposes.

Applications
In writing to the correspondent, including information on any other sources of income. Applications can be submitted directly by the individual or through a social worker, Citizens Advice or other welfare agency.

Monmouthshire

Llandenny Charities

£1,000

Correspondent: Dr Graham Russell, Trustee, Forge Cottage, Llandenny, Usk, Monmouthshire NP15 1DL (01633 432536; email: gsrussell@btinternet.com)

CC Number: 223311

Eligibility
People over 65 and in need who are in receipt of a state pension, live in the parish of Llandenny and have lived there for more than one year.

Types of grants
Pensions to people receiving a state pension.

Annual grant total
In 2013 this charity had an income of £2,700 and a total expenditure of £2,300.

Applications
In writing to the correspondent, to be submitted directly by the individual. Applications should be submitted by 15 January for consideration in February.

Other information
Grants are also awarded for educational purposes.

Monmouth Charity

£2,500

Correspondent: Andrew Pirie, Trustee, Pen-y-Bryn, Oakfield Road, Monmouth NP25 3JJ (01600 716202)

CC Number: 700759

Eligibility
People in need who live within an ten-mile radius of Monmouth and neighbourhood.

Types of grants
One-off grants usually up to a maximum of £500.

Annual grant total
In 2012/13 the charity had an income of £9,400 and an expenditure of £9,100. Grants are made for both educational and welfare purposes and to individuals and organisations. We estimate the grant total for individuals for social welfare purposes to be around £2,500.

Applications
The trust advertises in the local press each September/October and applications should be made in response to this advertisement for consideration in November. Emergency grants can be considered at any time. There is no application form. Applications can be submitted directly by the individual or through a social worker, Citizens Advice or other welfare agency.

Monmouth Support Fund

£800

Correspondent: Philip Bly, Trustee, Marshall House, 8 The Gardens, Monmouth, Monmouthshire NP25 3HF (01600 719787; email: philip.bly@dsl.pipex.com)

CC Number: 223790

Eligibility
People in need, hardship or distress who live in Monmouth.

Types of grants
One-off grants of up to £60, including those towards winter heating costs.

Annual grant total
In 2013 fund had an income of £1,300 and an expenditure of £900. We estimate the annual total of grants to be around £800.

Applications
In writing to the correspondent. Our research suggests that applications should be made by 1 January and are considered in the same month. Applications can be submitted directly by the individual, through a social worker, Citizens Advice, other welfare agency or a member of the clergy.

Other information
The trust was previously known as Monmouth Relief-in-Need Charity.

The Monmouthshire County Council Welsh Church Act Fund (formerly known as the Monmouthshire Welsh Church Acts Fund)

£0

Correspondent: Joy Robson, Head of Finance, Monmouthshire County Council, Innovation House, PO Box 106, Magor, Caldicot (01633 644657; website: www.monmouthshire.gov.uk)

CC Number: 507094

Eligibility

People living in the boundaries of Monmouthshire County Council who are in need. Grants are also given to discharged prisoners and their families.

Types of grants

Grants of money or payment for items, services or facilities. Accommodation can be provided to older people who need it because of infirmities or disabilities. People who are visually impaired may also be given access to charitable homes and holiday homes.

Annual grant total

In 2012/13 the fund had assets of £4.65 million and an income of £77,000. Grants were not made to individuals in need this year.

Applications

On a form available from the correspondent or downloaded from the website, which can be submitted at any time. Applications are considered seven times a year.

Other information

The fund also makes grants to organisations.

Pembrokeshire

Haverfordwest Freemen's Estate

£8,300

Correspondent: The Clerk, R. K. Lucas and Son, The Tithe Exchange, 9 Victoria Place, Haverfordwest, Pembrokeshire SA61 2JX (01437 762538)

CC Number: 515111

Eligibility

Hereditary freemen of Haverfordwest aged 18 years and over.

Types of grants

One-off grants according to need.

Annual grant total

In 2012/13 the estate had an income of £18,300 and a total expenditure of £16,700. We estimate that grants to individuals totalled £8,300, with funding also awarded to local organisations.

Applications

Freemen must be enrolled by the chair of the local authority. The honour is hereditary being passed down through the male or female line.

The William Sanders Charity

£5,400

Correspondent: Julia Phillips, Administrator, 11 Freemans Walk, Pembroke, Dyfed SA71 4AS

CC Number: 229182

Eligibility

Widows and unmarried women in need who live within a five mile radius of the parish of St John's, Pembroke Dock.

Types of grants

Christmas grants typically ranging from £25 to £40. They are available in November and December each year.

Annual grant total

In 2012/13 the charity had an income of £9,700 and a total expenditure of £5,600. We estimate that grants to individuals totalled £5,400.

Applications

In writing to the correspondent directly by the individual or a family member.

The Tenby Relief-in-Need and Pensions Charity

£25,000 (120 grants)

Correspondent: Clive Mathias, Clerk to the Trustees, Lewis Lewis and Co., County Chambers, Pentre Road, St Clears, Carmarthen SA33 4AA (01994 231044; email: clive@lewislewis.co.uk)

CC Number: 231233

Eligibility

Older people in need who live in the community of Tenby.

Types of grants

Pensions of £17 a month to help relieve financial difficulties. Most beneficiaries will also receive a small Christmas bonus of £20. Usually, once a grant has been agreed it will be paid indefinitely.

Annual grant total

In 2013 the charity held assets of £742,000 and had an income of £34,000. Grants to 120 individuals totalled £25,000.

Applications

On a form available from the correspondent, to be submitted directly by the individual or a family member.

William Vawer

£2,000

Correspondent: R. K. Lucas, Trust Administrator, R. K. Lucas and Son, 9 Victoria Place, Haverfordwest, Pembrokeshire SA61 2JX (01437 762538; fax: 01437 765404)

CC Number: 213880

Eligibility

People in need who live in the town of Haverfordwest.

Types of grants

Pensions to existing pensioners. Other grants to those in need, hardship or distress.

Annual grant total

In 2012/13, the trust had an income of £8,000 and a total expenditure of £2,200. We estimate that the total amount of grants awarded to individuals was approximately £2,000.

Applications

In writing to the correspondent.

Swansea

The Swansea and District Friends of the Blind

£5,000

Correspondent: John Allan, Secretary, 3 De La Beche Street, Swansea SA1 3EY (01792 655424; email: allan.john@btconnect.com)

CC Number: 211343

Eligibility

People who are registered blind and live in Swansea.

Types of grants

One-off grants which, in the past, have gone towards visual impairment aids such as talking watches, computers and the like. Gifts are also distributed at Christmas and Easter.

Annual grant total

In 2012/13 the charity had an income of £7,300 and a total expenditure of £51,000. We estimate that through the distribution of welfare grants, Christmas and Easter gifts, the charity gave around £5,000 to individuals in need.

Applications

In writing to the correspondent. Applications are considered on a regular basis.

Other information

The majority of the charity's funding goes towards the provision of information, advice and support services for registered blind people. It also arranges events and outings, particularly in summer and at Christmas.

Torfaen

The Cwmbran Trust

£25,000

Correspondent: Kenneth Maddox, Meritor HVBS (UK) Ltd, Grange Road, Cwmbran, Gwent NP44 3XU (01633 834040; email: cwmbrantrust@meritor.com)

CC Number: 505855

Eligibility

People in need living in the town of Cwmbran, Gwent.

Types of grants

One-off and recurrent grants are awarded for a wide variety of educational and welfare purposes, such as stair-lifts, home-study courses, computer equipment, wheelchairs, holidays, debt clearance, removal costs, building renovation, funeral costs and respite care. Grants usually range between £125 to £2,500.

Annual grant total

In 2013 the trust had assets of £2.3 million and an income of £89,000. Grants were made to 43 individuals totalling £32,000 for educational and welfare purposes. There are three interest free loans outstanding. The majority of funding for individuals appears to be for social welfare purposes and we estimate social welfare grants awarded to individuals to be around £25,000.

Applications

In writing to the correspondent. Applications can be submitted directly by the individual or through a social worker, Citizens Advice, welfare agency or other third party. Applications are usually considered in March, May, July, October and December.

Other information

The trust also makes grants to organisations.

Vale of Glamorgan

The Cowbridge with Llanblethian United Charities

£22,000

Correspondent: Clerk to the Trustees, 66 Broadway, Llanblethian, Cowbridge, Vale of Glamorgan CF71 7EW (01446 773287)

CC Number: 1014580

Eligibility

People in need who live in the town of Cowbridge with Llanblethian.

Types of grants

The provision of items, services or facilities that will reduce the person's need.

Annual grant total

In 2012/13 the charity had both an income and total expenditure of £24,000. Based on previous grant giving, we estimate that the total amount of grants awarded to individuals for social welfare purposes was in the region of £22,000 and for educational purposes was approximately £1,300.

Applications

In writing to the correspondent. Applications can be submitted directly by the individual or through a welfare agency.

Other information

Grants are also made for educational purposes.

The Neale Trust Fund for Poor Children

£0

Correspondent: David Ward Jenkins, Trustee, Lanby, 16 White House, Barry CF62 6FB (01446 730204; email: dwjnx@btinternet.com)

CC Number: 225652

Eligibility

Schoolchildren in need who live in the district of Barry and are aged 16 or under.

Types of grants

One-off grants of up to £500 each for: clothes; shoes; educational, medical or disability equipment; and travel expenses.

Annual grant total

In 2012/13 the charity had an income of £700 and no expenditure. On average, about £750 is available each year to distribute in grants, although spending does tend to fluctuate.

Exclusions

No grants are given for video/computer equipment.

Applications

In writing to the correspondent, who will then send out a form to be completed. The need for support has to be shown by the applicant. Applications are considered in January and September according to availability of funds or in special cases by home visit of the secretary. Applications can be made through the social services, Citizens Advice or local childcare officer, or directly by the individual. The trust does not accept unsolicited applications.

North East

General

The Christina Aitchison Trust

£1,000

Correspondent: Revd Roger Massingberd-Mundy, Trustee, The Old Post Office, The Street, West Raynham, Fakenham NR21 7AD

CC Number: 1041578

Eligibility

People who are blind or have any ophthalmic disease or disability, and people who have a terminal illness and who are in need.

Types of grants

One-off and recurrent grants to relieve blindness, ophthalmic disease or disability, and terminal illness.

Annual grant total

In 2012/13 the trust had an income of £1,900 and an expenditure of £2,200. Grants totalled approximately £2,000 and were split between educational and welfare purposes.

Applications

On a form available from the correspondent.

Other information

Grants are also given to individuals and organisations concerned with education, equitation, sailing and music.

Mrs E. L. Blakeley-Marillier Charitable Fund

£14,300

Correspondent: Karyna Squibb, Trust Administrator, Wollen Michelmore, Carlton House, The Terrace, Torquay, Devon TQ1 1BS (01803 213251; fax: 01803 296871; email: karyna.squibb@wollenmichelmore.co.uk; website: www.wollenmichelmore.co.uk)

CC Number: 207138

Eligibility

Ladies over 55 who are in need and are not of the Roman Catholic faith or members of the Salvation Army. Preference is given to women from the counties of Yorkshire and Devon and in particular the towns of Scarborough and Torquay.

Types of grants

Annuities of a maximum £520 per year are paid in two instalments. Grants will not be given if the effect is to reduce income support or other benefits, or to reduce debt.

Annual grant total

In 2012/13 the fund had an income of £2,800 and a total expenditure of £14,500. We estimate that annuities to individuals totalled £14,300.

Applications

On a form available from the correspondent to be submitted directly by the individual including a general financial overview. Applications are usually considered in November and May.

The Charity of Miss Ann Farrar Brideoake

£50,000

Correspondent: Alan Ware, Trustee, Cowling Swift and Kitchin, 8 Blake Street, York YO1 8XJ (01904 625678; fax: 01904 620214)

CC Number: 213848

Eligibility

Communicant members of the Church of England living within the dioceses of York, Liverpool and Manchester, who are in need. This includes clergy and retired clergy.

Types of grants

Recurrent grants are given to help in 'making ends meet'. Support is given towards household outgoings, domestic equipment, holidays, children's entertainment and so on as well as special medical needs. One-off payments are made in special circumstances and debt relief can be supported in exceptional circumstances.

Annual grant total

In 2012/13 the charity held assets of £2.1 million and had an income of £73,000. Grants to individuals totalled £50,000.

Applications

On a form available from the correspondent, to be countersigned by the local vicar as confirmation of communicant status. Applications should be submitted in April or May for consideration in July/August.

Lord Crewe's Charity

£23,000 (Around 20 grants)

Correspondent: Clive Smithers, Manager and Clerk, Rivergreen Centre, Aykley Heads, Durham DH1 5TS (01913 837398; email: enquiries@lordcrewescharity.co.uk; website: www.lordcrewescharity.org.uk)

CC Number: 1155101

Eligibility

Necessitous clergy, their widows and dependents who live in the dioceses of Durham and Newcastle. Grants may be given more generally to people in need who live in the area of benefit, with preference to people resident in parishes where the charity owns land or has the right of presentation to the benefice.

Types of grants

One-off and recurrent grants are given according to need in specific instances of hardship and to assist clergy moving out of church housing on retirement.

Annual grant total

At the time of writing (August 2014) financial information was not yet available following the change in the charity's legal status. Previously around 20 welfare grants have been given totalling about £23,000.

Exclusions

Applicants who are not members of clergy are not supported and the trustees ask not to be contacted by people who do not fit the criteria.

Applications for church buildings and church projects are not supported either (projects except in the very small number of parishes in which the charity holds property or has rights of presentation.).

Applications

The charity's website states that there is no 'application form or an open application procedure for grants.' 'The charity works directly with its beneficiaries and with a number of partner organisations.' The application round opens in March and continues until July. Grants are considered in the first two weeks of August and the outcome is communicated to the applicant by the end of the month. Consult the website for the latest updates on awards.

Other information

From 2014 the charity has become a charitable incorporated organisation and changed its registered charity number (previously 230347).

Small annual grants are made to organisations and support is also given for welfare purposes. Payments are made to Lincoln College of Oxford to be applied in scholarships, fellowships and hardship grants. No other institution can be supported in the same way.

The Olive and Norman Field Charity

£11,500

Correspondent: John Pelter, Chair, British Red Cross Society, Carrick House, Thurston Road, Northallerton DL6 2NA (01609 772186; email: olive&norman@redcross.org.uk)

CC Number: 208760

Eligibility

People who are in poor health, convalescent or who have disabilities and live in the former North Riding of Yorkshire (now the counties of Durham and North Yorkshire and the unitary authorities of Darlington, Hartlepool, Middlesbrough, Redcar and Cleveland, Stockton-on-Tees and York).

Types of grants

One-off grants, usually in the range of £100 to £350, are given towards electric goods, convalescence, medical equipment, furniture and disability equipment.

Annual grant total

In 2013 the charity had an income of £27,000 and a total expenditure of £20,000. At the time of writing the charity's accounts were not available from the Charity Commission and so a breakdown of grants was not available. In previous years, however, grants to individuals have totalled an estimated £11,500.

Exclusions

The charity is unable to assist with debt, computer equipment (unless there is a specific medical need) or house renovations.

Applications

On a form available from the correspondent or social services. Applications should be submitted either through a social worker, Citizens Advice or other welfare agency. Applications are usually considered in February, April, June, September and December.

The Greggs Foundation

£195,000

Correspondent: David Carnaffan, Grants Manager, Fernwood House, Clayton Road, Jesmond, Newcastle upon Tyne NE2 1TL (01912 127626; email: greggsfoundation@greggs.co.uk; website: www.greggsfoundation.org.uk)

CC Number: 296590

Eligibility

People in need who live in the north east of England (Northumberland, Tyne and Wear, Durham and Teesside). Priority is given to children and families.

Types of grants

Grants up to £150 and are given for essential items such as white goods, furniture, baby equipment, flooring, clothing and school uniforms.

Annual grant total

In 2013 the foundation held assets of £11.2 million and had an income of £1.8 million. Hardship grants to individuals totalled almost £195,000. Of this, 1,005 grants were made directly from the foundation, amounting to £104,000. A further £91,000 was given in block grants directly to social organisations to make grants on the foundation's behalf.

Various other causes received a total of £1.2 million (excluding supporting costs).

Exclusions

Grants are not given to cover debts, bankruptcy fees, holidays, funeral expenses, medical equipment, overseas expeditions, computer equipment or sponsorship.

Applications

The foundation now uses an online application form. In exceptional circumstances, if you cannot use the online form, contact the trust to make other arrangements. Applications should be made through a welfare agency, such as social services, probation services, Citizens Advice, victim support, health, disability and housing associations, or other similar organisations. Applications submitted directly by the individual will not be considered. The foundation asks that applicants do not send any additional information as this will not be considered.

Applications received by Friday at 4pm will be processed in the following week. If the applicant does not receive a reply after three weeks it can be assumed that the application has been unsuccessful.

Other information

Through the Hardship Fund, the Greggs Foundation administers funds on behalf of a number of other local charitable trusts, including the Brough Benevolent Association, the Barbour Trust, the 1989 Willan Trust, the Chrysalis Trust, the Hadrian Trust, the Joicey Trust, the Sir James Knott Trust and the Rothley Trust.

Note: only one form from each applicant should be submitted to the joint trusts, as the payment will be made from joint funds.

Lady Elizabeth Hastings' Non-Educational Charity

£128,000

Correspondent: Andrew Fallows, Clerk, Carter Jonas, 82 Micklegate, York YO1 6LF (01904 558212; email: leh.clerk@carterjonas.co.uk; website: www.ladyelizabethhastingscharities.co.uk)

CC Number: 224098

Eligibility

Clergy working in the parish of Burton Salmon, in the county of north Yorkshire, the ecclesiastical parishes of Thorp Arch, Collingham with Harewood, Bardsey with East Keswick and Shadwell, in the county of west Yorkshire and the ecclesiastical parish of Ledsham with Fairburn in the counties of north and west Yorkshire, and their dependents.

Types of grants

One-off grants averaging around £880 per person are given for welfare purposes.

Annual grant total

In 2012/13 the charity held assets of £15.2 million and had an income of £517,000. A total of 145 clergy and their dependents received a combined £128,000 in grants from the Non-Educational Charity. In addition, the charity made yearly payments, grants to churches and grants to the poor which totalled around £31,000.

Applications

In writing to the correspondent.

Other information

The trust is managed by and derives its income from the Lady Elizabeth Hastings Estate Charity.

The John Routledge Hunter Memorial Fund

£3,000

Correspondent: Mary Waugh, Administrator, Dickinson Dees (Solicitors), One Trinity, Broad Chare, Newcastle upon Tyne NE1 2HF (01912 799000)

CC Number: 225619

Eligibility

People who live in Northumberland and Tyne and Wear (north of River Tyne) who have (or recently have had) chest, lung or catarrhal complaints.

Types of grants

Grants of £200 to £500 towards a two or three week recuperative holiday in a hotel in Lytham St Annes or Southport (including rail travel expenses, bed, breakfast, evening meal and £25 in cash). Holidays are taken between Easter and September.

Annual grant total

The 2011/12 accounts were the latest available at the time of writing (August 2014).

In 2011/12, the fund had an income of £13,000 and a total expenditure of £6,000. We estimate that the total amount of grants awarded to individuals was approximately £3,000. The fund also awards grants to organisations.

Applications

On a form available from the correspondent, supported by a certificate signed by a doctor. Applications should be submitted directly by the individual and are considered from January to April.

Hylton House Fund

£2,000

Correspondent: Barbara Gubbins, Chief Executive, County Durham Community Foundation, Victoria House, St John's Road, Meadowfield Industrial Estate, Durham DH7 8XL (01917 806344; fax: 01917806344; email: info@cdcf.org.uk; website: www.cdcf.org.uk)

CC Number: 1047625–2

Eligibility

People in the North East (County Durham, Darlington, Gateshead, South Shields, Sunderland and Cleveland) with cerebral palsy and related disabilities, and their families and carers. Applicants (or their family members, if the applicant is aged under 18) must be on income support or a low income or have a degree of disability in the family, which creates a heavy financial demand.

Types of grants

Grants of up to £500 towards: holidays and respite support for carers of up to two weeks in the UK or abroad; education, training and therapy; training and support for carers and self-help groups (if there is no statutory support available); domestic equipment (maximum award £250); aids and equipment, particularly specialist clothing, communication and mobility aids; travel costs to allow applicants and their carers to attend a specific activity, specialist centre or hospital if no alternative transport is available; respite support to pay for an employed carer in the home or for visiting a specialist centre where care is provided; costs of setting up home (unless this is a SCOPE or local authority-led move); debts, if it can be proved that they were incurred by the disability.

Annual grant total

Grants usually total around £4,000. We estimate grants to individuals for social welfare purposes to be around £2,000.

Exclusions

No grants for: legal costs; ongoing education; medical treatment; decorating and/or refurbishment costs (unless the work is due to the nature of the applicant's disability); motor vehicle adaptations; motor insurance, deposits or running costs; televisions or DVD players; assessments, such as the costs involved in the Scope Living Options Schemes; or retrospective funding. Only one grant can be held in each financial year starting in April.

Applications

On a form available from the correspondent downloaded from the website. All applications must include a reference from a social worker or professional adviser in a related field, with a telephone number and the individual's permission for them to be contacted about an application. A full breakdown of costs should also be included. For specialist equipment and therapy, confirmation from an occupational therapist/doctor/physiotherapist or other professional advisor that the equipment is suitable, is also required.

Appeals are considered in January, April, July and October and should be received before the start of the month. They can be considered between these dates within a month of application if the need is urgent, but the applicant will need to request this and provide a reason why an exception to the usual policy needs to be made.

The Leeds Jewish Welfare Board

£4,000

Correspondent: Liz Bradbury, Chief Executive, 311 Stonegate Road, Leeds LS17 6AZ (01132 684211; fax: 01132 034915; email: theboard@ljwb.co.uk; website: www.ljwb.co.uk)

CC Number: 1041257

Eligibility

Primarily people of the Jewish faith who live in Leeds or North and West Yorkshire.

Types of grants

Grants may be given as part of a 'support package'. They are rarely given as a one-off without a full assessment of the situation. Loans may also be given and depending on individual circumstances may be part-grant/part-loan. A flexible approach together with budgeting advice is offered. The majority of grants are given to families with children. These may be for clothes, bedding requirements and so on. Grants are also given at Jewish festivals such as Passover. Counselling and meals-on-wheels services along with a comprehensive range of services and resources are also offered to children, families and older people primarily, but not exclusively, of the Jewish faith.

Annual grant total

In 2012/13 the charity had assets of £5.8 million and an income of £3.4 million. Each year a small amount is reserved for grantmaking purposes. In 2012/13 we estimate that grants to individuals totalled £4,000.

The organisation also spent over £3.2 million on its various other charitable services; providing activities and support for the elderly, children and their families, and people with physical and mental health problems from the Jewish community.

Applications

Applications for help can be made at any time by individuals, welfare agencies, friends or relatives. The charity can respond quickly in urgent cases. The applicant will be seen by a caseworker who will assess the application and gather the relevant information.

Other information

The organisation was established in 1878 as a voluntary Board of Guardians, with its main purpose being, according to the charity's website, 'to hand out funds to the needy to prevent them from having to enter the workhouse'. These days, the Leeds Jewish Welfare Board employees more than 100 staff and has hundreds of volunteers, who provide support in the community.

The North East Area Miners Social Welfare Trust Fund

£0

Correspondent: Vincent B. Clements, Regional Manager, Coal Industry Social Welfare Organisation, 6 Bewick Road, Gateshead, Tyne and Wear NE8 4DP (01914 777242; email: vincent.clements@ciswo.org.uk; website: www.ciswo.org.uk)

CC Number: 504178

Eligibility

People in need living in Durham, Northumberland and Tyne and Wear who are employed by the coal industry, or who have not been employed since retirement or redundancy from the coal industry.

Types of grants

One-off grants according to need.

Annual grant total

In 2012/13 the trust had an income of £106,000 and a total expenditure of £474,000. No grants were made to individuals in the year.

The trust continued to help miners and people from former mining communities to afford convalescent holidays spending £122,000 to assist individuals in the year.

Applications

In writing to the correspondent. Applications can be submitted directly by the individual or through a social worker, Citizens Advice or other welfare agency. They are usually considered four times a year.

Other information

The trust also makes grants to organisations.

The Northern Ladies Annuity Society

£142,000 (589 grants)

Correspondent: Jean Ferry, Secretary, MEA House, Ellison Place, Newcastle upon Tyne NE1 8XS (01912 321518)

CC Number: 1097222

Eligibility

Single, unmarried and widowed ladies in need, who live or have lived for a number of years in Northumberland, Tyneside, Wearside, County Durham or Cumbria. At present only those over the state retirement age are considered. The applicant should have an annual income of less than £8,000 and savings of no more than £10,000.

Types of grants

Annuities of £1,300/£975/£650/£325 (depending on circumstances) paid quarterly. One-off grants are also available for those in receipt of an annuity for expenses such as holidays, domestic appliances, household items and other unexpected costs. Christmas hampers are also distributed to most annuitants. The society has also distributed fuel grants during recent spells of cold winter weather.

Note: individuals not already in receipt of an annuity are ineligible for any other form of help from the society.

Annual grant total

In 2012/13 the society held assets of £7.2 million and had an income of £255,000. More than £142,000 was awarded in 589 grants which were distributed as follows:

Annuities (full and half)	426	£126,000
Hampers (special grants)	122	£6,400
Holiday (special grants)	21	£5,300
General (special grants)	20	£4,800

Exclusions

The society does not give one-off grants to non-annuitants, nor support to students, and will ignore any such requests for assistance.

Applications

Applications to become an annuitant should be made on a form available from the correspondent. Completed forms can be submitted directly by the individual or through a third party such as Citizens Advice or a social worker. Applications are considered monthly.

Other information

In 2012/13 the society spent a further £76,000 on providing subsidised accommodation for ladies at 31 properties.

The Rycroft Children's Fund

£17,000

Correspondent: Robert Newman, Secretary, 4th Floor, The Chancery, 58 Spring Gardens, Manchester M2 1EW (01613 003740; email: robert.newman@chanceryaccounts.co.uk; website: www.rycroftchildren'sfund.co.uk)

CC Number: 231771

Eligibility

Children in need who live in Cheshire, Derbyshire, Greater Manchester, Lancashire, Staffordshire, South and West Yorkshire. There is a preference for children living in the cities of Manchester and Salford and the borough of Trafford. Applicants should be aged 18 or under.

Types of grants

One-off grants according to need.

Annual grant total

In 2012/13 the fund had an income of £31,000 and an expenditure of £38,000. Grants totalled £34,000, of which we estimate £17,000 was given to individuals.

Exclusions

Grants are not given to individuals for education, overseas travel, individual holidays or computers.

Applications

On a form available from the correspondent to be submitted either directly by the individual or, where applicable, through a social worker, Citizens Advice or other welfare agency. Details of the applicant's available income and contributions from other sources must be included. Applications can be made at any time.

The SF Group Charity

See entry on page 40

Sherburn House Charity

£167,000

Correspondent: Stephen Black, Administration Manager, Ramsey House, Sherburn Hospital, Durham DH1 2SE (01913 722551; fax: 01913 720035; email: admin@sherburnhouse.org; website: www.sherburnhouse.org)

CC Number: 217652

Eligibility

People in 'extreme social and financial need' who live in the North East of England between the rivers Tweed and Tees.

Types of grants

One-off grants according to need.

Annual grant total

In 2012/13 the charity held assets of £29.3 million and had an income of £2.5 million. Almost 1,000 relief in need grants totalled £167,000. Of this amount, just over £1,000 was awarded to residents of the charity's care homes.

In other grants, £1,100 was given for educational purposes and a further

£381,000 was received by 148 organisations.

Exclusions

Applicants must wait two years before reapplying. No grants are awarded for floor covering (apart from in exceptional circumstances), central heating, driving licences, telephones or telephone arrears, specialist medical equipment, funeral expenses or holidays (apart from in exceptional circumstances) or where there is an apparent surplus of income over expenditure.

Applications

At the time of writing, the charity's preferred method of application-making via its online form had been disabled. However, a form is also available to download from the website. Applications must be made through a welfare agency such as social services, probation services, Citizens Advice or other organisation. The applicant must disclose weekly household income and expenditure, explaining any excess of income over expenditure. Applications are normally assessed on a monthly basis.

Note: if a grant is successful, only one item will be awarded. Cheques are paid to the welfare agency on behalf of the applicant. Agencies have one month to use a grant before it is withdrawn. A full list of application guidelines is available to download from the website.

Other information

The charity also runs residential care, sheltered housing and independent accommodation for elderly people, more details and application packs for which are available from its informative website.

Wright Funk Fund

£3,000

Correspondent: Grants Team, County Durham Community Foundation, Victoria House, Whitfield Court, St John's Road, Meadowfield Industrial Estate, Durham DH7 8XL (01913 786340; fax: 01913 782409; email: info@cdcf.org.uk; website: www.cdcf.org.uk)

CC Number: 1047625

Eligibility

Families in Darlington and County Durham.

Types of grants

Hardship grants of up to £250 to help keep families together or to support families in crisis. Our research tells us that past grants have been made for domestic equipment such as fridges, washing machines and cookers; carpets and bedding; support for carers; and, in exceptional circumstances, household bills.

Annual grant total

Grants usually total in excess of £3,000 to £5,000 each year.

Exclusions

The fund does not assist with bankruptcy fees or debt and will not make retrospective grants.

Applications

On a form available to download from the website. Applications can be completed by the individual or by a representative on the applicant's behalf, if necessary. A reference from a social worker or professional advisor in a related field should also be attached. Forms must be completed and signed. Guidance notes can also be downloaded from the County Durham Foundation's website. A telephone interview with a representative of the foundation may be conducted to determine eligibility. The grants team can be contacted for additional guidance.

Yorkshire Water Community Trust

£681,000 (1,698 grants)

Correspondent: Trust Officer, Freepost BD3074, Bradford BD3 7BR (0845124 24 26; fax: 01274 262265; email: info@ywct.org.uk; website: www.ywct.org.uk)

CC Number: 1047923

Eligibility

People who are in arrears with Yorkshire Water and have at least one other priority debt, such as gas or electricity, council tax, rent or mortgage repayments. Council and housing association tenants whose water charges are included with their rent may also apply.

Types of grants

No cash grants are given. One-off payments are made to Yorkshire Water and credited to the applicant's account. The average award in 2012/13 was £402.

Annual grant total

In 2012/13 the trust had an income of £749,000 and a total expenditure of £745,000. An overall amount of £681,000 was awarded in 1,698 grants to individuals.

Exclusions

Successful applicants may not reapply within two years.

Applications

On a form available from the correspondent or to download from the trust's website. Although applications can be submitted directly by the individual or a friend or relative, the trust prefers them to be submitted by a social worker, Citizens Advice or other welfare agency. Council and housing association tenants must apply through their landlord. The trust asks that as much information is provided as is possible. Applicants must attach proof of household income in the form of wage slips or a confirmation of benefits, as well as proof of debts. Applications are considered quarterly.

A full list of guidance notes is available on the trust's website. Enquiries are welcomed.

Other information

The trust's 2012/13 annual report states:

> During 2012–13 the Trust Officers sent out 4,771 application forms to individuals advice centres which was an increase of 50% on the previous year. Over 2,000 applications for assistance were received back. The majority of individual requests for Application Forms originated from Yorkshire Water staff, with other requests from various advice agencies and individuals direct.

County Durham

Bull Piece Charity

£1,000

Correspondent: Robert Cummings, Secretary

CC Number: 237477

Eligibility

People in need who live in Hamsterley, South Bedburn, Lynesack and Softley.

Types of grants

Recurrent gifts of £30, usually made at Christmas.

Annual grant total

In 2012/13 the charity had an income of £2,800 and a total expenditure of £1,400. We estimate that grants usually total around £1,000.

Applications

Applications by word of mouth (or in writing) to a representative of the Parish Council.

County Durham Community Foundation

£84,000

Correspondent: Barbara Gubbins, Chief Executive, Victoria House, Whitfield Court, St John's Road, Meadowfield Industrial Estate, Durham DH7 8XL

(01913 786340; email: info@cdf.org.uk; website: www.cdcf.org.uk)

CC Number: 1047625

Eligibility

People in need who live in County Durham and Darlington.

Types of grants

Usually one-off grants of between £50 to £2,000. Visit the foundation's website for further details. Individuals can only hold one grant per each financial year starting in April.

Annual grant total

In 2012/13 the foundation held assets of £9.6 million and had an income of £3.9 million. Grants for individuals totalled over £167,500 and we estimate the total grants for welfare purposes to be £84,000.

Exclusions

No grants are made towards medical treatment, nursing care or anything which is the responsibility of Social Services or the NHS. Grants are not made retrospectively.

Applications

Applicants can either: use a form available from the correspondent or the website; or write to the correspondent including their name, address, how they fit the criteria, what is needed and why, costs, when the grant is needed, details of income and savings, details of why the need can't be met, where any other money will be coming from (if not requesting the full amount), names of other organisations approached and details of how a cheque should be made payable to (unless directly to the provider, such as a residential home, rather than to the applicant). In all cases, applications must include a reference from a professional third party, such as a GP, community nurse or social worker. The foundation will give a decision within one month, although this can be sooner if the request is particularly urgent. As with all community foundations, fund may open and close at short notice so check the website before beginning any application.

Other information

Grants are also made to organisations.

The Ferryhill Station, Mainsforth and Bishop Middleham Aid-in-Sickness Charity

£1,000

Correspondent: Zoe Whent, Trustee, Dunelm, Mainsforth Village, Ferryhill, County Durham DL17 9AA (01740 652434)

CC Number: 500190

Eligibility

People in need who are in poor health, convalescent or who have disabilities and live in the parishes of Ferryhill Station, Mainsforth and Bishop Middleham.

Types of grants

One-off grants ranging from £250 to £1,000 towards medical care and equipment, holidays for people with disabilities (and their carers) and for special needs arising from disability or illness.

Annual grant total

In 2012/13 the charity had both an income and an expenditure of £2,100. We estimate that social welfare grants to individuals totalled £1,000, with funding also awarded to organisations.

Applications

In writing to the correspondent, either directly by the individual or via a third party such as a district nurse, social worker, Citizens Advice or other welfare agency. Applications are considered on a regular basis.

The Ropner Centenary Trust

£16,700 (29 grants)

Correspondent: Alan Theakston, Trustee, 15 The Green, High Coniscliffe, Darlington, County Durham DL2 2LJ (01325 374249)

CC Number: 269109

Eligibility

Present and former maritime employees who are in need, and their dependents. Preference is generally given to people living in the North East of England and particularly those who have worked for Ropner Shipping Company Ltd.

Types of grants

One-off and recurrent grants according to need.

Annual grant total

In 2012/13 the trust had assets of £1 million and an income of £35,000. 29 individuals received grants totalling £16,700.

Applications

In writing to the correspondent. Applications are considered annually, although urgent requests can be dealt with between meetings.

Other information

Grants are also paid to organisations with similar aims (£12,000 in 2012/13).

The Sedgefield Charities

£5,000

Correspondent: John Hannon, Clerk, East House, Mordon, Sedgefield, County Durham TS21 2EY (01740 622512; email: east.house@btinternet.com)

CC Number: 230395

Eligibility

People in need who live in the parishes of Bishop Middleham, Bradbury, Cornforth, Fishburn, Mordon, Sedgefield and Trimdon in County Durham.

Types of grants

One-off grants, including those for furnishings, bedding, medical requisites, mobility aids, hospital travel costs, travel for the disabled, living expenses and respite care.

Annual grant total

In 2013 the charity had an income of £15,500 and a total expenditure of £20,200. The charity gives to individuals and organisations and awards grants for both educational and social welfare purposes. We estimate the amount awarded to individuals for social welfare purposes was around £5,000.

Applications

In writing to the correspondent. Applications can be submitted directly by the individual or through a social worker, Citizens Advice, welfare agency or other third party such as a carer or relative. They are considered as they arise.

East Yorkshire

The Joseph and Annie Cattle Trust

£11,000 (20 grants)

Correspondent: Roger Waudby, Administrator, PO Box 23, Hull HU12 0WF (01964 671742; fax: 01482 211198)

CC Number: 262011

Eligibility

Primarily people who live in the Hull or East Riding of Yorkshire area and are in need. Preference is given to people who are older, disabled or disadvantaged, particularly children who are dyslexic.

Types of grants

One-off grants of £200 to £500 for needs such as travel expenses, furniture, medical and disability equipment, electric goods and help in the home.

Annual grant total

In 2012/13 the trust had assets of £8.3 million and an income of £459,000. Grants for educational and welfare purposes were made to 39 individuals totalling £21,500.

Applications

In writing to the correspondent, only via a welfare organisation, for consideration on the third Monday of every month. Note, if applicants approach the trust directly they will be referred to an organisation, such as Disability Rights Advisory Service, or social services.

Other information

Grants are also made to organisations (£305,000 – 2012/13).

The Leonard Chamberlain Trust

£2,500

Correspondent: Alison Nicholson, Secretary, 4 Bishops Croft, Beverley, North Humberside HU17 8JY (01482 865726)

CC Number: 1091018

Eligibility

Applicants must live within the area of benefit: East Riding of Yorkshire, particularly Hull and Selby.

Types of grants

One-off grants according to need.

Annual grant total

In 2013 the charity had assets of £6 million which figure includes mainly permanent endowment and is not available for grant giving. It had an income of almost £182,000 and total expenses of £71,000. Grants awarded to individuals for social welfare purposes totalled £2,500 and for educational purposes totalled £9,500.

Applications

In writing to the correspondent.

Other information

The trust's main purpose is the provision of housing for residents in the area of benefit who are in financial need and it also makes a small number of grants for religious and educational purposes.

The Hesslewood Children's Trust (Hull Seamen's and General Orphanage)

£21,000

Correspondent: Rex Booth, Secretary to the Trustees, 1 Canada Drive, Cherry Burton, East Yorkshire HU17 7RQ (01946 550474)

CC Number: 529804

Eligibility

People under 25 and in need who are native to, or have family connections with, the former county of Humberside and North Lincolnshire. Students who have come to the area to study are not eligible.

Types of grants

One-off and recurrent grants, typically up to £1,000, according to need. Grants have been given for specified short periods of time at special schools, holiday funding for individuals and youth organisations in the UK and overseas, and for musical instruments and special equipment for children who are disabled.

Annual grant total

In 2012/13 the trust had assets of £2.6 million and an income of £85,000. Grants made to or on behalf of individuals totalled £31,500 of which £21,000 was awarded in welfare grants.

Exclusions

Loans are not made.

Applications

On a form available from the correspondent. Applications can be made either directly by the individual or through the individual's school/college/welfare agency or another third party on their behalf. Applicants must give their own or their parental financial details, the grant required, and why parents cannot provide the money. If possible, a contact telephone number should be quoted. Applications must be accompanied by a letter from the tutor or an educational welfare officer (or from medical and social services for a disability grant). The deadlines are 16 February, 16 June and 16 September.

Other information

Grants are also made to organisations.

The Hull Aid in Sickness Trust

£26,000 (43 grants)

Correspondent: Dawn Singleton, Clerk to the Trustees, 34 Thurstan Road, Beverley, Hull HU17 8LP (01482 860133; email: haist@thesingletons.karoo.co.uk)

CC Number: 224193

Eligibility

People in need, on a low income, who live in the city and county of Kingston upon Hull and are sick, disabled, infirm or convalescent.

Types of grants

One-off and recurrent grants, to aid and improve quality of life. This can include grants for electrical goods, medical and disability equipment, food and living costs and so on.

Annual grant total

In 2012/13 the trust had assets of £1,100,000 and an income of £47,000. Grants were made totalling £40,000, of which around £26,000 was given in grants to individuals.

Exclusions

No grants are given towards debts or where funds are available from public funds.

Applications

On a form available from the correspondent, to be submitted directly by the individual or through a social worker, Citizens Advice, other welfare agency or other third party. Applications must be supported by a doctor's certificate or similar. The trustee's may send a visitor to the applicant for the purpose of preparing a report to support the application.

Other information

Grants of £1,000 or more were made to 14 organisations in the year.

Humberside Police Welfare and Benevolent Fund

£10,500

Correspondent: The Administrator, Humberside Police, Queens Gardens, Hull HU1 3DJ (08456060 222; email: webmail@humberside.pnn.police.uk; website: www.humberside.police.uk)

CC Number: 503762

Eligibility

Serving and retired officers of the Humberside Police and retired officers from other forces who live in Humberside, and their partners and dependents; and civilian employees of Humberside Police Authority, retired civilian employees and their partners and dependents.

Types of grants

One-off and recurrent grants of up to £500. Loans are also available.

Annual grant total

In 2013 the fund had an income of £14,800 and a total expenditure of £11,100. We estimate that grants to individuals totalled £10,500.

Applications

In writing to the correspondent at any time, either through the branch/ divisional representative or the headquarters.

The Nafferton Feoffee Charity Trust

£1,000

Correspondent: Margaret Buckton, Trustee, South Cattleholmes, Wansford, Driffield, East Yorkshire YO25 8NW (01377 254293)

CC Number: 232796

Eligibility

People in need who live in the parish of All Saints Nafferton with St Mary's Wansford.

Types of grants

One-off grants in the range of £100 to £250. Recent grants have been given for hospital travel costs, heating expenses and food vouchers. Bursaries are also available to local students.

Annual grant total

In 2013 the trust had assets of £1.7 million and an income of £56,000. During this accounting year, the trust awarded grants to eight individuals totalling £2,130 with organisations receiving the remaining £18,120 grant expenditure. We estimate that £1,000 was awarded to individuals for social welfare purposes.

Exclusions

The trust stated that the parish only consists of 3,000 people and every household receives a copy of a leaflet outlining the trust's work. People from outside this area are not eligible to apply.

Applications

In writing to the correspondent at any time, directly by the individual.

Other information

Grants are also made to organisations and to individuals for educational purposes.

Robert Towries Charity

£1,200

Correspondent: Debbie Ulliot, The Cottage, Carlton Lane, Aldbrough, Hull HU11 4RA (01964 527255; email: roberttowerytrust@googlemail.com)

CC Number: 222568

Eligibility

People in need who live in Aldbrough and Burton Constable.

Types of grants

One-off and recurrent grants for food and fuel.

Annual grant total

In 2012/13 the charity had an income of £10,500 and a total expenditure of £4,800. The charity makes grants to individuals and organisations for both educational and social welfare purposes. We estimate the total figure for grants awarded to individuals for social welfare purposes was around £1,200.

Applications

In writing to the correspondent directly by the individual.

Aldbrough

Aldbrough Poor Fields

£400

Correspondent: Sarah Greenwood, Clerk, 2 The Cottage, Elstronwick, Hull HU12 9BP (01964 670828; email: clerk@aldbroughparishcouncil.co.uk)

CC Number: 222569

Eligibility

People aged over 65, widows and disabled children who are in need and live in Aldbrough village.

Types of grants

Vouchers are given towards food and fuel at Christmas. Gifts in kind are also made.

Annual grant total

Total expenditure averages at around £400 each year.

Applications

In writing to the correspondent for consideration in November.

Barmby on the Marsh

The Garlthorpe Charity

£4,500

Correspondent: John Burman, c/o Hepstonstalls Solicitors, 7–15 Gladstone Terrace, Goole, North Humberside DN14 5AH (01405 765661)

CC Number: 224927

Eligibility

People in need who live in the parish of Barmby on the Marsh.

Types of grants

One-off grants according to need.

Annual grant total

In 2012/13 the charity had an income of £8,200 and a total expenditure of £6,300. We estimate that grants to individuals totalled £4,500.

Applications

In writing to the correspondent.

Other information

The charity uses one sixth of its income to fund the maintenance and repair of the church in the ecclesiastical parish of St Helen, Barmby on the Marsh.

Bridlington

The Bridlington Charities (Henry Cowton)

£0

Correspondent: Andrew Mead, Administrator, 118 St James Road, Bridlington, North Humberside YO15 3NJ (01262 403333)

CC Number: 224609

Eligibility

People in need who live in the parish of Bridlington and Bridlington Quay.

Types of grants

Grants of between £50 and £210 for the purchase of fuel (gas, coal, electricity). Payment is made direct to the suppliers. One-off grants towards school clothing can also be made.

Annual grant total

In 2012 the charities had assets of £168,000 and an income of £53,000 (most of which comes from rents payable on land that the charity owns). In this financial year the trustees were involved in a dispute with one of the charity's tenants and as a result, no charitable payments were made. We assume grants will resume when the dispute is settled.

The 2012 accounts were the latest available at the time of writing (August 2014).

Exclusions

No loans or grants for meals or paid help.

Applications

In writing to the correspondent, usually for consideration in February, May, August and November. Applications can be submitted through a social worker, Citizens Advice or other welfare agency. The charities' field officers visit the applicants and report to the trustees in writing.

Other information

Some money is usually made available for local organisations. The charity is registered as 'Henry Cowton'.

Kingston upon Hull

The Charity of Miss Eliza Clubley Middleton

£14,000

Correspondent: Trust Administrator, Rollits, Rowntree Wharf, Navigation Road, York YO1 9WE (01904 625790; fax: 01904 625807)

CC Number: 229134

Eligibility

Poor women of the Catholic faith who have lived in the Hull area for more than ten years.

Types of grants

Grants are distributed twice a year, at Christmas and in the summer. The typical average value of any individual grant is less than £75.

Annual grant total

In 2012/13 the charity had an income of £6,400 and a total expenditure of £18,000.

Applications

A list of current beneficiaries is circulated to all local priests each year. They then recommend any additions or note changes in circumstances.

The 'Mother Humber' Memorial Fund

£13,500

Correspondent: Malcolm Welford, Secretary, 5 Summerfield Close, Driffield, East Yorkshire YO25 5YS (01377 256212)

CC Number: 225082

Eligibility

People in need who live in the city of Kingston upon Hull.

Types of grants

One-off grants ranging from £50 to £500.

Annual grant total

In 2012/13 the fund held assets of £488,000 and had an income of £34,000. We estimate that grants to individuals totalled £13,500, with funding also awarded to local organisations.

Exclusions

No grants are made for educational appeals and sponsorship, for example Duke of Edinburgh Award students, the payment of debts, the payment of wages or administration expenses.

Applications

On a form available from the correspondent to be submitted through a social worker, Citizens Advice or other welfare agency.

The Joseph Rank Benevolent Fund

£63,000 (470 grants)

Correspondent: Debby Burman, Clerk to the Trustees, Artlink Centre, 87 Princes Avenue, Hull HU5 3QP (01482 225542; email: info@josephrankfund.org.uk; website: www.josephrankfund.org.uk)

CC Number: 225318

Eligibility

Men aged 65 or over and women aged 60 or over, who are retired and have lived in Hull for at least ten of the last 15 years. If the applicant is married, their partner must also meet these age limits. Applicants should be on a low income and have no more than £6,000 in savings.

Types of grants

Recurrent grants of £30 per quarter to single people and £60 per quarter to married couples.

Annual grant total

In 2013 the fund held assets of £3.4 million and had an income of £115,000. A total of £63,000 was awarded in 470 grants to individuals; 412 of which were paid to single beneficiaries, the remaining 58 to married couples.

A further £4,100 was donated to local charities.

Applications

On a form available from the correspondent. Applications are considered throughout the year.

Wilmington Trust

£2,500

Correspondent: Graham Wragg, Trustee, 16 Caledonia Park, Hull HU9 1TE (01482 223050)

CC Number: 250765

Eligibility

People in need who live in Kingston upon Hull (east of the river Hull).

Types of grants

Our research suggests that one-off grants ranging from £50 to £100 can be provided towards various needs, including clothing, furniture, white goods and other household items, unforeseen emergencies and, particularly, for holidays benefiting the applicant's health.

Annual grant total

At the time of writing (August 2014) the latest financial information available was from 2012. In 2012 the trust had an income of £7,000 and a total expenditure of £5,300. We estimate the annual total of grants to individuals to be around £2,500.

Applications

Application forms are available from the correspondent. Applications must be made through Citizens Advice, social workers or members of the clergy. The trustees usually meet twice a year to consider grants, although decisions can also be made between the meetings.

Other information

The trust also makes grants to local organisations.

Newton on Derwent

Newton on Derwent Charity

£3,000

Correspondent: The Administrator, FAO, Grays Solicitors, Duncombe Place, York YO1 7DY (01904 634771)

CC Number: 529830

Eligibility

People who are sick, older or in need who live in the parish of Newton on Derwent.

Types of grants

One-off grants according to need.

Annual grant total

In 2013 the charity had an income of £13,200 and an expenditure of £12,300. We estimate that welfare grants to individuals totalled around £3,000.

Applications

In writing to the correspondent.

Other information

This charity has been given a dispensation by the Charity Commission from publishing the names of its trustees.

Ottringham

The Ottringham Church Lands Charity

£1,500

Correspondent: Mary Fairweather, Trustee, South Field, Chapel Lane, Ottringham, Hull, East Yorkshire HU12 0AA (01964 626908; email: maryfairweather@hotmail.com)

CC Number: 237183

Eligibility

People in hardship and/or distress who live in the parish of Ottringham.

Types of grants

Normally one-off grants, but recurrent grants may be considered.

Annual grant total

Income was £10,400 but expenditure only £3,000 in the year 2012/13. The charity also gives grants for educational purposes.

Exclusions

No grants are given which would affect the applicant's state benefits.

Applications

In writing to the correspondent at any time. Applications can be submitted either directly by the individual, through a third party such as a social worker or teacher, or through an organisation such as Citizens Advice or a school.

North Yorkshire

Bedale Welfare Charity (The Rector and Four and Twenty of Bedale)

£9,000

Correspondent: John Winkle, Administrator, 25 Burrill Road, Bedale, North Yorkshire DL8 1ET (01677 424306; email: johnwinkle@awinkle.freeserve.co.uk)

CC Number: 224035

Eligibility

People who live in the parishes of Aiskew, Bedale, Burrill with Cowling, Crakehall, Firby, Langthorne and Rand Grange and are in need, hardship or distress. Necessitous children and young people, older people suffering from illness or people with disabilities are particularly supported.

Types of grants

One-off grants, usually ranging from £40 to £500, can be given for various items and services according to need.

Annual grant total

In 2012/13 the charity had an income of £15,300 and a total expenditure of £27,000, which is the highest in the past five years. Note that the expenditure varies every year. Most of the grants are distributed in relief-in-need grants and to organisations. We estimate that social welfare support to individuals totalled around £9,000.

Applications

Application forms are available from the correspondent. They can be submitted at any time either directly by the individual or through a third party, such as a social worker or teacher.

Other information

Grants are also made to organisations and can be given for educational purposes.

The Gargrave Poor's Lands Charity

£11,200

Correspondent: The Trustees, Kirk Syke, High Street, Gargrave, Skipton, North Yorkshire BD23 3RA

CC Number: 225067

Eligibility

People in need who live in Gargrave, Bank Newton, Coniston Cold, Flasby, Eshton or Winterburn.

Types of grants

One-off and recurrent grants for debt relief, travel to hospital, household equipment, furniture, respite care, electrical goods and essential repairs. Christmas gifts are also made each year to permanent residents who are poor, older, disadvantaged or disabled.

Annual grant total

In 2012/13 the trust had assets of £411,000 and an income of £44,500. Grants for social welfare purposes were made totalling £11,200 and were distributed as follows:

Christmas distribution	£4,500
Hardship relief	£6,700

Applications

On a form available from the correspondent. Applications can be submitted at any time.

Goldsborough Poor's Charity

£1,200

Correspondent: Len Clarkson, Trustee, 25 Princess Mead, Goldsborough, Knaresborough, North Yorkshire HG5 8NP (01423 865102; email: lenandelsie@gmail.com)

CC Number: 502912

Eligibility

Elderly people who live in Coneythorpe (or near Knaresborough), Flaxby or Goldsborough. Most recipients tend to be widows or widowers.

Types of grants

Recurrent grants are given to supplement pensions or low incomes.

Annual grant total

In 2013/14 the charity had an income of £1,500 and an expenditure of £1,400. We have estimated the annual total of grants to individuals to be around £1,200.

Applications

In writing to the correspondent. Applications can be submitted either directly by the individual or through a third party, for example, a social worker,

Citizens Advice or other welfare agency. Grants are awarded twice a year.

Reverend Matthew Hutchinson Trust (Gilling and Richmond)

£2,500

Correspondent: Christine Wiper Gentry, Administrator, 3 Smithson Close, Moulton, Richmond, North Yorkshire DL10 6QP (01325 377328)

CC Number: 220870/220779

Eligibility

People who are in need and live in the parishes of Gilling and Richmond in North Yorkshire.

Types of grants

One-off grants according to need. Recent grants have been given towards medical care, telephone rental, a violin, running shoes and children's nursery fees.

Annual grant total

This charity has branches in both Gilling and Richmond, which are administered jointly, but have separate funding. In 2013 the combined income of the charities was £25,500 and their combined expenditure was £11,700.

Applications

In writing to the correspondent. Applications can be submitted directly by the individual or through a trustee, social worker, Citizens Advice or other welfare agency.

Other information

Grants are also made to organisations including local schools and hospitals.

The Purey-Cust Trust

£1,300 (17 grants)

Correspondent: Nicholas McMahon Turner, Trustee, Stockton Hermitage, Malton Road, York YO32 9TL (01378 34730; email: pureycusttrust@hotmail.com; website: www.pureycrusttrust.org.uk)

CC Number: 516030

Eligibility

People with medical needs who live in York and the surrounding area.

Types of grants

One-off grants ranging between £100 and £1,500, for healthcare equipment, specialist medical equipment and medical education.

Annual grant total

In 2012/13, the trust had assets of £2.56 million, an income of £56,000 and a total expenditure of £26,200. The total grants awarded to individuals was £1,300 with the remainder awarded to local organisations and the City of York Council.

Exclusions

The trust tries to assist with one-off grants for specific purposes rather than ongoing routine costs, such as rent, rates and salaries.

Applications

On a form which is available on the trust's website. Applications may be emailed or posted. Applications must show evidence of the medical need and can be submitted directly by the individual or through a social worker, Citizens Advice, other welfare agency or third party. Applications are considered throughout the year.

The Rowlandson and Eggleston Relief-in-Need Charity

£1,000

Correspondent: Peter Vaux, Administrator, Clowbeck Farm, Barton, Richmond DL10 6HP (01325 377236; email: petervaux@brettanbymanor.co.uk)

CC Number: 515647

Eligibility

People in the parishes of Barton and Newton Morrell who are in need.

Types of grants

One-off grants usually in the range of £100 to £500. Recent grants have been given towards funeral expenses, medical equipment, disability aids and lifeline telephone systems for older people.

Annual grant total

In 2013/14 the charity had an income of £4,500 and a total expenditure of £3,100. We estimate that around £1,000 was given to individuals for social welfare purposes.

Applications

In writing to the correspondent including details of circumstances and specific need(s). Applications may be submitted directly by the individual or through a social worker, Citizens Advice or other third party.

Other information

This charity also provides other facilities and make grants to individuals for educational purposes.

York Dispensary Sick Poor Fund

£1,500

Correspondent: The Secretary, 1 St Saviourgate, York YO1 8ZQ (01904 558600)

CC Number: 221277

Eligibility

People living in York and the surrounding districts who are suffering from both poverty and ill-health.

Types of grants

Our research suggests that one-off grants are given for specific needs, such as clothing, domestic equipment or holidays.

Annual grant total

At the time of writing (September 2014) the latest financial information available was from 2012. In 2012 the fund had an income of £21,000 and a total expenditure of £15,900, which is a bit lower than in the previous years. Grants to individuals make up a small proportion of the total expenditure. We estimate the annual total of such grants to be around £1,500.

Applications

In writing to the correspondent. Applications should, preferably, be made through social services or a similar welfare agency, although direct application is possible. Requests are considered twice a year, normally in March and October.

Other information

The fund aims to meet those needs which fall outside the responsibilities of the NHS or other statutory sources. Most support is given to various organisations, with some receiving annual payments.

Carperby-cum-Thoresby

The Carperby Poor's Land Charity

£1,400

Correspondent: David Brampton, Trustee, The Bastal House, Carperby, Leyburn, North Yorkshire DL8 4DD

CC Number: 502524

Eligibility

People in need who live in the parish of Carperby-cum-Thoresby.

Types of grants

One-off and recurrent grants are given according to need.

Annual grant total

In 2012 the charity had an income of £1,500 and a total expenditure of £1,500. We estimate that social welfare grants to individuals totalled £1,400.

At the time of writing (August 2014) this was the most recent financial information available for the charity.

Applications

In writing to the correspondent, with details of the financial need. Applications can be submitted directly by the individual or through a social worker, Citizens Advice or other welfare agency. They are usually considered quarterly.

Danby

The Joseph Ford's Trust

£500

Correspondent: Liz Sheard, Trustee, 28 West Lane, Danby, Whitby YO21 2LY (01287 660416)

CC Number: 514043

Eligibility

People who live within the original parish of Danby and are blind, aged or in poverty or misfortune.

Types of grants

One-off or recurrent grants according to need.

Annual grant total

In 2012/13 the trust had an income of £530 and a total expenditure of £560. We estimate that social welfare grants to individuals totalled around £500.

Applications

In writing to the correspondent or any other trustee, at any time.

Knaresborough

The Knaresborough Relief-in-Need Charity

£10,000

Correspondent: Mike Dixon, Administrator, 9 Netheredge Drive, Knaresborough, North Yorkshire HG5 9DA (01423 863378; email: thedixongang@btinternet.com)

CC Number: 226743

Eligibility

People in need who live in the parish of Knaresborough, with a preference for people who have lived there for at least five years or twenty years for a pension.

Types of grants

Pensions of £30 a year and occasional one-off grants of up to £5,000.

Annual grant total

Grants total around £10,000 annually. Pensions are also paid to around 200 individuals.

Applications

In writing to the correspondent.

Lothersdale

Raygill Trust

£2,500

Correspondent: Roger Armstrong, Armstrong Wood and Bridgman, 12–16 North Street, Keighley, West Yorkshire BD21 3SE (01535 613660; email: mail@awbclaw.co.uk)

CC Number: 249199

Eligibility

Those in need who live in the ecclesiastical parish of Lothersdale, with a preference for the elderly, disabled and young people.

Types of grants

One-off grants are available to assist with the cost of living. Grants to assist with educational needs are also available.

Annual grant total

In 2012/13 the trust had an income of £11,700 and a total expenditure of £10,400. We estimate that £2,500 was granted to individuals on welfare grounds. The trust also made grants to organisations in the Lothersdale area, and to individuals for educational purposes.

Applications

In writing to the correspondent. Applications can be submitted directly by the individual or through a third party or welfare agency.

Northallerton

The Grace Gardner Trust

£1,200

Correspondent: The Secretary, c/o Town Hall, High Street, Northallerton, North Yorkshire DL7 8QR (01609 776718; email: enquiries@northallertontowncouncil.gov.uk)

CC Number: 511030

Eligibility

Older people, people with disabilities or those who are disadvantaged who live within the boundary of Northallerton parish.

Types of grants

One-off grants of up to £200 according to need including those for electric goods, home improvements, travel expenses, furniture and disability equipment.

Annual grant total

In 2012/13 the trust had an income of £5,400 and a total expenditure of £2,500.

Applications

In writing to the correspondent including details of age and place of residence. Applications can be submitted directly by the individual or through a recognised referral agency (such as social worker, Citizens Advice or doctor) at any time.

Other information

The trust also makes grants to local organisations for day trips.

Scarborough

The Scarborough Municipal Charity

£6,500

Correspondent: Elaine Greening, Administrator, Flat 2, 126 Falsgrave Road, Scarborough YO12 5BE (01723 375256; email: scar.municipalcharity@yahoo.co.uk)

CC Number: 2177793

Eligibility

People who have live in the borough of Scarborough for at least five years and are in need, hardship or distress. Retired people are provided accommodation.

Types of grants

Small one-off grants according to need. The awards can range between £250 and £1,500 but usually are modest. Support can be given towards livings costs, specific essential items, services and travel expenses.

Annual grant total

The latest financial accounts were not available to view at the time of writing (July 2014). In 2013 the charity had an income of £181,000 and a total expenditure of 119,000. In the past five years grants to individuals have totalled on average around £13,100. We estimate that about £6,500 is awarded in individual grants for welfare purposes each year.

Exclusions

In exceptional circumstances support may be given to someone resident outside the area of benefit or living in the borough temporarily.

Applications

Application forms are available from the correspondent. Our research suggests that they are considered quarterly.

Other information

The trustees are responsible for both the almshouse and the relief in need branches of the charity. The majority of the trust's expenditure is spent in direct charitable activities maintaining the almshouses and providing services to the tenants.

St Margaret

Robert Winterscale's Charity

£900

Correspondent: Richard Watson, Administrator, Crombie Wilkinson, 17–19 Clifford Street, York YO1 9RJ (01904 624185; email: r.watson@crombiewilkinson.co.uk)

CC Number: 224230

Eligibility

People over 60 years of age who have lived in the ancient parishes of St Margaret's and St Denys for more than five years and are in need.

Types of grants

Biannual pensions totalling about £25 a year.

Annual grant total

In 2012 the charity had an income of £1,700 and a total expenditure of £1,000. We estimate that social welfare grants to individuals totalled £900.

At the time of writing (August 2014) this was the most recent financial information available for the charity.

Applications

On a form available from the correspondent. Applications can be submitted directly by the individual, through an organisation such as Citizens Advice or through a third party such as a social worker. Applications are considered on a regular basis.

West Witton

The Smorthwaite Charity

£5,000

Correspondent: Geoff Clarke, Trustee, Pen Cottage, Main Street, West Witton, Leyburn, North Yorkshire DL8 4LX (01969 624393)

CC Number: 247681

Eligibility

Older people in need who live in West Witton.

Types of grants

Annual grants ranging from £100 to £150.

Annual grant total

In 2012/13 the charity had an income of £14,000 and a total expenditure of £18,500. We estimate that grants to individuals totalled around £5,000.

Applications

The charity usually advertises in the local post office. Most applications tend to be submitted by word of mouth and through conversations with the trustees rather than through a formal application process.

Other information

Much of the charity's expenditure goes towards the upkeep of the rental properties it owns in the area.

York

Norman Collinson Charitable Trust

£16,000 (84 grants)

Correspondent: Dianne Hepworth, Clerk to the trustees, 30 Main Street, Wetwang, Driffield YO25 9XJ (01377 236262; website: www.normancollinsoncharitabletrust.org.uk)

CC Number: 277325

Eligibility

People in need in the City of York, or from within a 20 mile radius of the City.

Types of grants

One-off grants for essential costs.

Annual grant total

In 2012 the trust had an income of £39,000 and made grants totalling £35,000. 84 grants totalling £16,000 were made to individuals, the remainder was distributed in small grants to organisations. This was the latest financial information available at the time of writing.

Exclusions

Rent arrears or holidays.

Applications

Applications and detailed guidance notes can be downloaded from the trust's website. Applications are considered by the trustees at monthly meetings, usually on the second Tuesday. Applications should be received by the first Tuesday for consideration in the month. Applications should be completed by a third party. Grants will not be made directly to beneficiaries.

In exceptional circumstances emergency applications up to £250 can be considered outside the monthly trust meeting.

Other information

Grants are distributed through partner agencies in the local area, for example: Leeds and York PFT, City of York Council, NYCC, Ryedale Citizens Advice and Horton Housing.

The Charity of St Michael-le-Belfrey

£4,800

Correspondent: Christopher Goodway, Clerk, Grays Solicitors, Duncombe Place, York YO1 7DY (01904 634771)

CC Number: 222051

Eligibility

People in need who live in the parish of St Michael-le-Belfrey, York.

Types of grants

One-off and recurrent grants ranging from £50 to £500. Quarterly pensions are available to older people as well as one-off payments to relieve special needs.

Annual grant total

In 2013 the charity had an income of £7,800 and a total expenditure of £9,800. We estimate that grants to individuals totalled £4,800, with funding also awarded to organisations.

Exclusions

No grants for the purposes of education.

Applications

On a form available from the correspondent. Evidence of financial circumstances will be required. Applications can be submitted directly by the individual or through a social worker, Citizens Advice, other welfare agency or other third party.

The Charity of Jane Wright

£3,200

Correspondent: Diane Grayson, Clerk, Harland and Co., 18 St Saviourgate, York YO1 8NS (01904 655555; email: cjw@harlandsolicitors.co.uk)

CC Number: 228961

Eligibility

People in need who live in the city of York.

Types of grants

One-off grants and vouchers according to need.

Annual grant total

In 2012/13 the charity held assets of £1.4 million and had an income of £64,000. 'Miscellaneous individual grants' totalled £3,200. During the year, no one-off grants were made for school uniforms or to residents of the charity's almshouses.

A further £11,100 was awarded in relief-in-need grants to York College and Blueberry Academy.

Applications

Applications must be made directly or via recognised welfare agencies. They are considered at or between trustees' meetings.

Other information

The charity was founded on 21 December 1675 by Jane Wright who was born in York. Although she lived and died as a wealthy businesswoman in Whitechapel, London, she left her estate to benefit the poor in her hometown. In the present day, the charity also manages 11 almshouse flats.

York Children's Trust

£4,000

Correspondent: Margaret Brien, Administrator, 29 Whinney Lane, Harrogate HG2 9LS (01423 504765)

CC Number: 222279

Eligibility

Young people under the age of 25 living within a 20 mile radius of the city of York.

Types of grants

One-off grants according to need.

Annual grant total

In 2012 this trust had assets of £2.1 million and an income of £92,000. During the year grants totalled £49,000 for both individuals and organisations. £32,000 was paid to organisations. Individuals were awarded a total of £17,000 of which £4,000 was for social welfare and medical grants. The 2012 accounts were the latest available at the time of writing (August 2014).

Applications

On a form available from the correspondent. Trustees meet to consider applications four times a year. More urgent grants of up to £300 may be awarded between meetings.

Other information

The trust was established through the amalgamation of five existing charities: St Stephen's Orphanage, Blue Coat Boys' and Grey Coat Girls' Schools, The William Richard Beckwith Fund, The Charity of Reverend A.A.R. Gill and The Matthew Rymer Girls Education Fund. Grants are also made to organisations and to individuals for educational purposes.

York City Charities

£280

Correspondent: Richard Watson, Clerk, Crombie Wilkinson, 17–19 Clifford Street, York YO1 9RJ (01904 624185; email: r.watson@crombiewilkinson.co.uk)

CC Number: 224227

Eligibility

People in need who live within the pre-1996 York city boundaries (the area within the city walls).

Types of grants

One-off grants of between £50 and £200 according to need. Previously grants have been given towards furniture and to people on probation to set up a new home.

Annual grant total

In 2013 the charity had assets of £1.2 million and an income of £237,000. Grants made to individuals totalled £580. The charity has both restricted and endowments funds. We estimate that welfare support totalled around £280.

Applications

In writing to the correspondent. Applications should be submitted by a doctor, occupational nurse, headteacher, social worker, Citizens Advice or other third party or welfare agency, if applicable. The trustees meet quarterly.

Other information

Most of the charitable expenditure is allocated for the maintenance of almshouses (£189,000 in 2013).

York Moral Welfare Charity

£1,200

Correspondent: Carole Money, Administrator, c/o York CVS, 15 Priory Street, York YO1 6ET (01904 621133; email: carole.money@yorkcvs.org.uk)

CC Number: 216900

Eligibility

Women and girls under the age of 50, who live in York and who are in need.

Types of grants

Generally one-off grants, between £50 and £100, to help with essential household items, fuel bills, furnishings, baby equipment and children's clothes.

Annual grant total

In 2012/13, the charity had an income of £3,600 and a total expenditure of £2,800. We estimate that the total amount of grants awarded to individuals was approximately £1,200.

Exclusions

No grants for education or travel costs.

Applications

On a form available from the correspondent. Applications should be made through a recognised agency and include details of the individual's income. They are considered on an ongoing basis.

Other information

Grants (usually up to £250) may also be made to local organisations which operate with similar aims.

Northumberland

The Eleemosynary Charity of Giles Heron

£6,000

Correspondent: George Benson, Trustee, Brunton House, Wall, Hexham, Northumberland NE46 4EJ (01434 681203)

CC Number: 224157

Eligibility

People in need who live in the ancient parish of Simonburn.

Types of grants

One-off grants ranging from £100 to £500.

Annual grant total

In 2012/13 the charity had an income of £13,600 and a total expenditure of £24,000. Grants are made for both educational and welfare purposes and to both individuals and organisations. We estimate grants to individuals for social welfare purposes to be around £6,000.

Applications

In writing to the correspondent directly by the individual.

Morpeth Dispensary

£2,500

Correspondent: Michael Gaunt, Trustee, 15 Bridge Street, Morpeth, Northumberland NE61 1NX (01670 512336)

CC Number: 222352

Eligibility

People who are sick and poor and live in or around Morpeth.

Types of grants

Grants are one-off and range from £40 to £300 including those for new washing machines, household bills, cookers, decorating costs, clothing, furniture and so on.

Annual grant total

In 2012 the charity had an income of £3,500 and an expenditure of £2,900. Grants average around £2,500 per year.

These were the latest accounts available at the time of writing (August 2014).

Applications

In writing to the correspondent at any time through a third party such as a social worker, GP, Citizens Advice or other welfare agency. Applications must include detail of the applicant's age, whether a single parent, whether on benefits, their address and any details regarding health matters. Grants are made directly to the third party, not the applicant.

Other information

Grants are also made to organisations to provide additional help at Christmas, for instance a trip to the theatre at Christmas for those individuals meeting the eligibility criteria.

Berwick-upon-Tweed

Berwick-upon-Tweed Nursing Amenities Fund

£200

Correspondent: Alan Patterson, Administrator, Greaves West and Ayre, 1–3 Sandgate, Berwick-upon-Tweed, Northumberland TD15 1EW (01289 306688; fax: 01289 307189; email: ajp@gwayre.co.uk)

CC Number: 230711

Eligibility

People who are sick, poor or in need and live in the borough of Berwick-upon-Tweed.

Types of grants

One-off grants up to £200.

Annual grant total

In 2013/14 the fund had an income of £1,200 and an expenditure of £300. We estimate that about £200 was given in grants. Bear in mind that the expenditure varies each year, although in the past five years has not reached over £1,000.

Applications

In writing to the correspondent. Applications should be made through a social worker, Citizens Advice or other welfare agency and can be submitted at any time.

South Yorkshire

The Aston Charities

£4,100

Correspondent: Jim Nuttall, Clerk, 3 Rosegarth Avenue, Aston, Sheffield S26 2DB (01142 876047)

CC Number: 225071

Eligibility

People in need who live in Aston, Aughton or Swallownest, with a preference for older people.

Types of grants

One-off and recurrent grants according to need. Grants have previously been made towards the cost of holidays for a single parent family and an unemployed couple and their three children. Help has also been given towards installing a telephone for an older couple. The trust does not normally give cash grants instead it pays the supplier of the services.

Annual grant total

In 2013 the charities had an income of £19,800 and a total expenditure of £12,600. We estimate that grants to individuals totalled £4,100, with funding also awarded for educational purposes and to organisations.

Exclusions

The charity does not make loans or give to profit-making concerns.

Applications

In writing to the correspondent or any trustee, directly by the individual or through a social worker, Citizens Advice or other welfare agency. Applications are considered quarterly.

The Brampton Bierlow Welfare Trust

£1,200

Correspondent: Jill Leece, Administrator, Newman and Bond, 35 Church Street, Barnsley S70 2AP (01226 213434)

CC Number: 249838

Eligibility

People in need who live in Brampton Bierlow and West Melton, and those parts of Wentworth and Elsecar within the ancient parish of Brampton Bierlow.

Types of grants

One-off grants from £100 to £250 for necessities and comforts. Christmas grocery vouchers are also distributed.

Annual grant total

In 2013 the trust had an income of £10,400 and a total expenditure of £5,000. We estimate that social welfare grants to individuals totalled £1,200. Grants are also given to organisations and to individuals for educational purposes.

Applications

Applications in writing to the correspondent can be submitted by the individual and are considered at any time.

The Cantley Poor's Land Trust

£15,000 (147 grants)

Correspondent: Margaret Jackson, Clerk to the Trustees, 30 Selhurst Crescent, Bessacarr, Doncaster, South Yorkshire DN4 6EF (01302 530566)

CC Number: 224787

Eligibility

People in need who live in the ancient parish of Cantley with Branton.

Types of grants

One-off grants ranging from £50 to £500 including those towards electric goods, clothing, medical equipment, furniture and disability equipment.

Annual grant total

In 2012/13 the trust had an income of £102,000. Grants totalled just over £104,000.

Exclusions

Restrictions apply to the relief of rates, taxes and repeat grants.

Applications

On a form available from the correspondent, to be submitted directly by the individual or through a welfare agency. Applications are considered on a monthly basis.

The Fisher Trust

£1,000

Correspondent: Jennifer Laister, Trustee, 77 Woodburn Drive, Chapeltown, Sheffield S35 1YT (01142 462293)

CC Number: 226355

Eligibility

Unitarian and Roman Catholic widows and unmarried women in need who are over 45 and live in and around Sheffield.

Types of grants
Annual allowances of £100 to £150 to help supplement low incomes.

Annual grant total
Grants usually total about £1,000 each year.

Applications
On a form available from the correspondent, to be submitted via the applicant's minister. Applications are normally considered in April.

Rebecca Guest Robinson (The Robinson Bequest)

£800

Correspondent: John Armitage, Trustee, 10 St Mary's Gardens, Worsbrough, Barnsley, South Yorkshire S70 5LU (01226 290179)

CC Number: 247266

Eligibility
People who live in the villages of Birdwell and Worsbrough, near Barnsley, and are in need. Preference is given to children, young people and older people.

Types of grants
Modest one-off grants, usually ranging between £50 and £250. According to our research, support could be given towards clothing, household equipment, disability aids, holidays and childcare.

Annual grant total
In 2012/13 the charity had an income of £2,300 and an expenditure of £1,600. We estimate that the annual total of grants to individuals was around £800.

Exclusions
Grants are not normally made where the statutory support could be obtained.

Applications
Application forms are available from the correspondent. They can be submitted directly by the individual or a family member.

Other information
Local organisations are also supported.

The Sheffield West Riding Charitable Society Trust

£2,500

Correspondent: Malcolm Fair, Diocesan Secretary, Diocesan Church House, 95–99 Effingham Street, Rotherham S65 1BL (01709 309100; email: malcolm.fair@sheffield.anglican.org; website: www.sheffield.anglican.org)

CC Number: 1002026

Eligibility
Clergymen of the Church of England in the diocese of Sheffield who are in need. Also their widows, orphans or distressed families, and people keeping house, or who have kept house, for clergymen of the Church of England in the diocese or their families.

Types of grants
One-off and recurrent grants of £100 to £1,000.

Annual grant total
In 2013 the trust had an income of £12,700 and a total expenditure of £4,700. We estimate grants to individuals for social welfare purposes was around £2,500.

Applications
On a form available from the correspondent.

Other information
Welfare grants are also made to the clergy, house-keepers and disadvantaged families in the diocese.

Armthorpe

Armthorpe Poors Estate Charity

£2,500

Correspondent: Tracey Ellis, 6 The Lings, Armthorpe, Doncaster, South Yorkshire DN3 3RH (01302 355180)

CC Number: 226123

Eligibility
People who are in need and live in Armthorpe.

Types of grants
One-off and recurrent grants of £50 to £500 towards items such as mobility aids, aids for people with visual difficulties, hospital visiting and care of older people.

Annual grant total
In 2012/13 the charity had both an income and total expenditure of £10,000. The charity gives to both individuals and organisations for educational and social welfare purposes. We estimate the total grants given to individuals for social welfare purposes was around £2,500.

Applications
Contact the clerk by telephone who will advise if a letter of application is needed. Applicants who live outside Armthorpe will be declined.

Barnsley

The Barnsley Tradesmen's Benevolent Institution

£500

Correspondent: David Bishop Richards, Administrator, 9 Kensington Road, Barnsley, South Yorkshire S75 2TX (01226 281929)

CC Number: 246313

Eligibility
Merchants and traders, their widows and children, who are in need and have lived in the old borough of Barnsley for at least seven years.

Types of grants
Recurrent grants are given towards general daily living expenses such as food, medical care and equipment and travel to and from hospital.

Annual grant total
Generally this trust gives grants totalling around £1,800 a year, however, the past two financial years have seen lower overall spending by the fund – £1,400 in 2011/12 and £540 in 2012/13.

Applications
In writing to the correspondent, either directly by the individual or through a third party such as Citizens Advice or other welfare agency. Applications are considered monthly.

The Fountain Nursing Trust

£4,800

Correspondent: The Administrator, Newman and Bond Solicitors, 35 Church Street, Barnsley, South Yorkshire S70 2AP (01226 213434; fax: 01226 213435; email: info@newmanandbond.co.uk)

CC Number: 224507

Eligibility
People in need who are in poor health, convalescent, infirm or have a disability and live in the urban district of Darton, Barnsley.

Types of grants
One-off and recurrent grants are available according to need. Our research shows that in the past grants have included those for medical equipment and expenses, nursing fees or help at home. The trust aims to address those needs which cannot be covered by the NHS or other statutory sources.

Annual grant total
In 2012/13 the trust had an income of £100 and an expenditure of £5,100, which is the highest in the past five years. We estimate the annual total of grants to be around £4,800. Bear in mind that the grant figure tends to fluctuate and is generally about £1,000.

Applications
In writing to the correspondent.

Beighton

Beighton Relief-in-Need Charity

£1,500

Correspondent: Diane Rodgers, Trustee, 41 Collingbourne Avenue, Sothall, Sheffield S20 2QR (01142 692875; email: beigtonrelief@hotmail.co.uk)

CC Number: 225416

Eligibility
People in need who live in the former parish of Beighton.

Types of grants
One-off grants according to need. Recent grants have been given towards bath lifts and childcare seats for people who are disabled. Winter fuel grants of £15 per household were also given to older people.

Annual grant total
In 2013 this charity had an income of £6,700 and a total expenditure of £6,500. It gives to both individuals and organisations for social welfare and educational purposes. We estimate that grants for social welfare purposes awarded to individuals totalled around £1,500.

Applications
In writing to the correspondent. Applications can be submitted directly by the individual or through a social worker, Citizens Advice, other welfare agency or a third party such as a relative, neighbour or trustee.

Bramley

The Bramley Poor's Allotment Trust

£1,400

Correspondent: Marian Houseman, Administrator, 9 Horton Rise, Rodley, Leeds LS13 1PH (01132 360115)

CC Number: 224522

Eligibility
People in need who live in the ancient township of Bramley, especially people who are elderly, poor and sick.

Types of grants
One-off grants between £40 and £120.

Annual grant total
In 2013 the trust had an income of £3,900 and a total expenditure of £3,000. Grants given to individuals for welfare purposes totalled approximately £1,400.

Applications
In writing to the correspondent. The trust likes applications to be submitted through a recognised referral agency (social worker, Citizens Advice, doctor, headmaster or minister). They are considered monthly.

Doncaster

The John William Chapman Charitable Trust

£30,000

Correspondent: Rosemarie Sharp, Secretary to the Trust, Jordans, 4 Priory Place, Doncaster DN1 1BP (email: info@chapmantrust.org; website: chapmantrust.org/)

CC Number: 223002

Eligibility
People in need who live in the metropolitan borough of Doncaster.

Types of grants
One-off grants in kind, not cash, up to the value of £500 towards fridges, cookers, washing machines, beds, cots, carpets and clothing.

Annual grant total
In 2012/13 the trust held assets of £3.7 million and had an income of £187,000. Grants to individuals totalled £30,000, with a further £43,000 awarded to organisations.

Exclusions
No repeat grants. No grants are given towards wardrobes, cupboards, drawers, living room suites, TVs, Hi-Fis, video players, educational course fees, funeral expenses, external work to a property, payment of debts (including rent bonds), decorating materials, toys, removal expenses, baby high chairs or gates, structural repairs or heating in tenanted property.

Applications
On a form available from the correspondent or to download from the trust's website. Applications must be accompanied by a letter from a social worker, GP or welfare agency as well as evidence of any loans or refusals from statutory services. Applicants who complete an online form must also supply documentary evidence on paper. The trust visits applicants before consideration of their application.

Note: only one application can be accepted in any 12 month period, except in exceptional circumstances. Incomplete applications will be returned and may not be considered in the intended month's allotment.

Epworth

Epworth Charities

£150

Correspondent: Katie-Jo Hardacre, Administrator, 34 Low Street, Haxey, Doncaster, South Yorkshire DN9 2LE (01427 330267; email: katesowerby@hotmail.com)

CC Number: 219744

Eligibility
People in need who live in Epworth.

Types of grants
One-off and recurrent grants in the range of £50 and £250 are given to relieve a specific need.

Annual grant total
In 2012/13 the charity had an income of £2,200 and an expenditure of £390, which is the lowest in the past five years. We estimate the annual total of grants to individuals for welfare purposes to be around £150.

Applications
In writing to the correspondent. Applications can be made directly by the individual and are considered on an ongoing basis.

Other information
Grants are also made for educational purposes.

Finningley

The Sir Stuart and Lady Florence Goodwin Charity

£3,000

Correspondent: Grants Administrator, Bassetlaw District Council, Finance Department, Queen's Buildings, Potter Street, Worksop, Nottinghamshire S80 2AH (01909 533296; email: democratic.services@bassetlaw.gov.uk)

CC Number: 216902

Eligibility

People over 60 who are need and live in the former rural district of East Retford. Consideration may be given to younger applicants.

Types of grants

One-off grants to improve quality of life. Recent grants have been given for medical equipment such as nebulisers, access ramps, walk-in baths and mobility scooters.

Annual grant total

In 2012/13 the charity had an income of £9,700 and a total expenditure of £3,600.

Applications

In writing to the correspondent. Applications can be submitted directly by the individual or through a third party such as Age Concern or social services. Grants will only be made to the person raising the invoice, not the individual.

Rotherham

The Common Lands of Rotherham Charity

£5,000

Correspondent: Ann Louise Ogley, Administrator, Barn Cottage, 66 Moorgate Road, Rotherham, South Yorkshire S60 2AU (01709 365032)

CC Number: 223050

Eligibility

People in need who live in Rotherham. Preference is usually given to older people.

Types of grants

One-off and recurrent grants according to need.

Annual grant total

In 2013, the charity had an income of £17,000 and a total expenditure of £8,000. We estimate that the total amount of grants awarded to individuals was approximately £5,000. The charity also awards grants to organisations.

Applications

In writing to the correspondent following advertisement in September.

The Stoddart Samaritan Fund

£12,600

Correspondent: Peter Wright, 7 Melrose Grove, Rotherham, South Yorkshire S60 3NA (01709 376448)

CC Number: 242853

Eligibility

People in need who have medical problems and would benefit from financial assistance to help their recovery. Applicants must live in Rotherham and the surrounding area.

Types of grants

One-off grants to assist people recovering from medical problems.

Annual grant total

In 2012/13 the fund had an income of £14,500 and a total expenditure of £12,800. We estimate that grants to individuals totalled £12,600.

Applications

On a form available from the correspondent, to be submitted by the applicant's doctor. Applications are considered on a regular basis.

Sheffield

Sir George Franklin's Pension Charity

£5,200

Correspondent: Rachel Heath, Clerk, 2nd Floor, Fountain Precinct, Balm Green, Sheffield S2 3QE (01142 231726)

CC Number: 224883

Eligibility

People in need aged 50 and over who live in the city of Sheffield.

Types of grants

Annual allowances of £350 paid half-yearly in June and December.

Annual grant total

In 2012/13 the charity had an income of £7,300 and a total expenditure of £5,400. We estimate that grants to individuals totalled £5,200.

Applications

On a form available from the correspondent. Vacancies arise infrequently and are publicised locally. Applications should only be made in response to this publicity. Speculative applications will not be successful.

Other information

The charity is named after Sir George Franklin (1853–1916), who once served as Lord Mayor of Sheffield and Pro-Chancellor of the University of Sheffield.

Sir Samuel Osborn's Deed of Gift Relief Fund

£2,400

Correspondent: Sue Wragg, Fund Manager, South Yorkshire Community Foundation, Unit 3 – G1 Building, 6 Leeds Road, Attercliffe, Sheffield S9 3TY (01142 424294; fax: 01142 424605; email: grants@sycf.org.uk; website: www.sycf.org.uk/apply_for_a_grant/sir_samuel_osborn__s_deed_of_gift_relief_fund)

CC Number: 1140947

Eligibility

Residents of Sheffield, with some preference for those with a connection to the Samuel Osborn Company.

Types of grants

One-off grants for people with disabilities, affected by hardship or suffering from medical conditions. Grants can be for short breaks, medical equipment and 'any other comforts associated with poor health'.

Annual grant total

In 2012/13, the fund had assets of £9.1 million and an income of £1.2 million. Grants administered to individuals totalled £4,800 and we estimate that £2,400 of that was awarded for welfare purposes.

Exclusions

Grants are not given for medical items available from the NHS.

Applications

On a form available to download from the fund's website. The community foundation welcomes informal approaches about applications prior to submitting. Applicants with a connection to the Osborn company should include written evidence. Decisions should be made within 12 weeks.

Note that only one grant per applicant per year is permitted.

Other information

The fund is now administered by the South Yorkshire Community Foundation. Grants are also made for educational purposes.

Teesside

John T. Shuttleworth Ropner Memorial Fund

£33,000

Correspondent: Brenda Dye, Grants Manager, County Durham Community Foundation, Victoria House, St Johns Road, Meadowfield Industrial Estate, Durham DH7 8XL (01913 786340; fax: 01913 782409; email: brenda@cdcf.org.uk; website: www.cdcf.org.uk)

CC Number: 1047625

Eligibility

Sick, elderly or disabled individuals and their carers in the Tees Valley area who are in need of respite care, or who need temporary support following hospitalisation, bereavement or because of dependency treatment. Applicants must live in Stockton, Thornaby-on-Tees, Redcar, Middlesbrough, Hartlepool or Darlington. Applicants must also have exhausted all statutory options before applying and must not have savings of more than £16,000. Priority will be given to first time applicants.

Types of grants

Grants of up to £1,000 for recuperative or respite care, home help assistance, bereavement related costs, travel and accommodation for individuals (and for their families) undergoing dependency treatment at a clinic or centre away from their place of residence.

Annual grant total

The fund has the capacity to distribute around £33,000 per year.

Exclusions

Only one grant per family per financial year. Retrospective grants will not be made. No grants for medical equipment or treatment, or nursing care.

Applications

On an application form available to download from the Durham Community Foundation website. A reference and covering note on headed paper or a compliments slip must also be included from your GP, community nurse or social worker who is willing to discuss your request. When the fund's resources are spent for the year, the fund closes. Visit the community foundation's website for re-opening dates.

The Teesside Emergency Relief Fund

£10,000

Correspondent: Linda Leather, Client Case Officer, Tees Valley Community Foundation, Wallace House, Falcon Court, Preston Farm Industrial Estate, Stockton-on-Tees TS18 3TX (01642 260860; email: info@teesvalleyfoundtion.org; website: www.teesvalletfoundation.org)

CC Number: 1111222–3

Eligibility

People in need who live in county borough of Teesside area in the areas of Hartlepool, Middlesbrough, Redcar and Cleveland and Stockton on Tees.

Types of grants

Grants of up to £500 for items needed to relieve immediate hardship. Grants are paid directly to the referring organisation to administer on the applicants behalf. Shop vouchers may also be provided. Typically grants are provided for beds/mattresses, bedding, towels, mini fridge, microwave or mini oven/hob, kitchen essentials such as pots, pans and crockery, clothing, shoes, blankets, assistance with gas/electric and in exceptional circumstances money for food

Annual grant total

For the 2013/14 year the fund was expected to distribute £10,000.

Accounts are incorporated into Tees Valley Community Foundation. and their total income was £550,000 with a total spend of £960,000.

Exclusions

No grants for non-essential items such as TVs, DVD players, stereos, etc. or for replacement mattresses soiled through bed wetting. No grants are paid to alleviate debts.

Applications

On a form available to download from the website. Applications should be supported by a social worker, health visitor, welfare officer, GP, probation officer, local tenancy office or other welfare agency representative. Proof of household income must also be attached – this includes benefit confirmation letters, benefit books or payslips. Applications are considered on a regular basis.

Hartlepool

The Furness Seamen's Pension Fund

£11,600

Correspondent: Heather O'Driscoll, Administrator, Waltons Clark Whitehill, Oakland House, 38–42 Victoria Road, Hartlepool, Cleveland TS26 8DD (01429 234414; fax: 01429 231263; email: heather.odriscoll@waltonscw.co.uk)

CC Number: 226655

Eligibility

Seamen in need who are 50 or over and live in the borough of Hartlepool or the former county borough of West Hartlepool, or who had their permanent residence there during their sea service. All applicants must have served as seamen for at least 15 years and with some part of the sea service in vessels registered in Hartlepool, West Hartlepool or the Port of Hartlepool, or vessels trading to/from any of these ports.

Types of grants

Quarterly pensions.

Annual grant total

In 2012/13 the fund had an income of £10,700 and a total expenditure of £11,800. We estimate that pensions totalled £11,600.

Applications

On a form available from the correspondent. Advertisements are placed in the Hartlepool Mail when vacancies are available.

Middlesbrough

The Lady Crosthwaite Bequest

£60

Correspondent: Richard Cross, Administrator, Strategic Resources, PO Box 506, Middlesbrough, Cleveland TS1 9GA (01642 729556)

CC Number: 234932

Eligibility

Pensioners in need who live in the former county borough of Middlesbrough.

Types of grants

According to our research, small grants are given at Christmas and for occasional day trips (via the social services and community councils) together with one-off lump sums to organisations.

Annual grant total

In 2012/13 the charity had an income of £1,700 and a total expenditure of £60. The expenditure has been the same for a few years.

Applications

In writing to the correspondent. Applications should be made through social services.

Middleton

Ralph Gowland Trust

£750

Correspondent: Joan Staley, Trustee, 38 Hill Terrace, Middleton-in-Teesdale, Barnard Castle, County Durham DL12 0SL (01833 640542)

CC Number: 701019

Eligibility

People in need aged 60 or over who live in the parish of Middleton in Teesdale.

Types of grants

One-off and recurrent grants according to need.

Annual grant total

In 2012/13 the trust had both and income and total expenditure of £1,000. We estimate that around £750 was made in grants to individuals for social welfare purposes.

Applications

In writing to the correspondent.

Tyne and Wear

Charity of John McKie Elliott Deceased (The John McKie Elliot Trust for the Blind)

£220

Correspondent: Robert Walker, Trustee, 6 Manor House Road, Newcastle upon Tyne NE2 2LU (01912814657; email: bobwalker9@aol.com)

CC Number: 235075

Eligibility

People who are blind or have a visual impairment and live in Gateshead or Newcastle upon Tyne.

Types of grants

One-off and recurrent grants can be given according to need for specific equipment, items or services.

Annual grant total

At the time of writing (August 2014) the latest financial information available was from 2012. In 2012 the charity had an income of £1,300 and an expenditure of £470. Both the income and the charitable expenditure vary. We estimate that educational grants totalled around £220.

Applications

In writing to the correspondent.

Other information

The trust also gives educational grants.

The Sunderland Guild of Help

£10,000

Correspondent: Norman Taylor, Chair, 4 Toward Road, Sunderland, Tyne and Wear SR1 2QG (01915 672895 (only on Wednesdays 9.30am–4pm); email: info@guildofhelp.co.uk; website: www.guildofhelp.co.uk)

CC Number: 229656

Eligibility

People in need who live in Sunderland.

Types of grants

Support is given for the advancement of health and the relief of poverty. In special circumstances, refurbished goods have been given to those most in need in the form of beds, washing machines and fridges.

Annual grant total

In 2012/13 the guild had an income of £10,300 and a total expenditure of £14,000. We estimate that grants to individuals totalled £10,000.

Exclusions

New goods or goods made to order cannot be supplied. Applications requesting money or loans will be rejected.

Applications

Applications can only be considered if they are submitted through a social worker or professional familiar with the guild's system. They should include an income and expenditure statement and are considered throughout the year.

Other information

The guild administers funds including the Sunderland Queen Victoria Memorial Fund 1901 and the Sunderland Convalescent Fund.

In addition, the guild also acts as an enabling charity through its premises on Toward Road, Sunderland where other small charities are provided with accommodation at rents that reflect their charitable status.

The Sunderland Orphanage and Educational Foundation

£12,000

Correspondent: Peter Taylor, McKenzie Bell, 19 John Street, Sunderland SR1 1JG (01915 674857)

CC Number: 527202

Eligibility

Young people under 25 who are resident in or around Sunderland who have a parent who is disabled or has died, or whose parents are divorced or legally separated.

Types of grants

Grants are given to children for clothing and living expenses. Grants are also made to students.

Annual grant total

In 2012/13 the trust had an income of nearly £24,000 and a total expenditure of over £24,000. The foundation makes grants to individuals for both education and welfare purposes. We estimate the total paid in welfare grants to be around £12,000.

Applications

Applications should be made in writing to the correspondent. They are considered every other month.

The Thomas Thompson Poor Rate Gift

£4,400

Correspondent: Carol Farquhar-Johnston, Newcastle City Council Civic Centre, Newcastle upon Tyne NE1 8QH (01912 116287; email: carol.s.farquhar-johnston@newcastle.gov.uk)

CC Number: 253846

Eligibility

People in need who live in Byker.

Types of grants

One-off grants for items such as washing machines, furniture and cookers. Grants have also been given to replace Christmas presents and children's bikes which have been stolen.

Annual grant total

In 2012/13 the organisation had an income of £4,300 and a total expenditure of £4,500. We estimate that £4,400 was given in grants to individuals.

Applications

In writing to the correspondent, for consideration throughout the year. Grants to replace stolen property are usually submitted through Victim Support.

The Tyne Mariners' Benevolent Institution

£99,000 (146 grants)

Correspondent: Janet Littlefield, Administrator, Hadaway and Hadaway, 58 Howard Street, North Shields, Tyne and Wear NE30 1AL (01912 570382; email: janetl@hadaway.co.uk)

CC Number: 229236

Eligibility

Former merchant seamen who live in Tyneside (about five miles either side of the River Tyne) and their widows. Applicants must be: (a) at least 55 years old and have served at least five years at sea; (b) under the age of 55, but unable to work owing to ill-health; or (c) the widows of such people.

Types of grants

Recurrent grants of around £40 per calendar month and Christmas gifts.

Annual grant total

In 2013 the institution held assets of £1.2 million and had an income of £344,000. Pensions and Christmas gifts to individuals totalled £99,000.

Applications

On a form available from the correspondent, to be submitted either directly by the individual or through a social worker, Citizens Advice or other welfare agency. Applications can be considered at any time.

Other information

The institution also administers and maintains the Master Mariners Homes in Tynemouth, providing 30 homes for beneficiaries.

Gateshead

The Gateshead Relief-in-Sickness Fund

£1,000

Correspondent: Victoria Spark, Administrator, Thomas Magnay and Co., 8 St Mary's Green, Whickham, Newcastle on Tyne NE16 4DN (01914 887459)

CC Number: 234970

Eligibility

People who are in poor health, convalescent or who have disabilities and live in the borough of Gateshead.

Types of grants

One-off grants towards providing or paying for items, services or facilities, which will alleviate need or assist with recovery, and are not readily available from other sources. Recent grants have been given to adapt a bathroom for a boy with learning and physical disabilities and for computers and talking typewriters for people who are registered blind.

Annual grant total

Grants are given to both individuals and organisations and total around £2,000 each year.

Applications

In writing to the correspondent. Applications can be submitted directly by the individual or through a social worker, Citizens Advice or other welfare agency.

Horton

Houghton-le-Spring Relief in Need Charity

£3,100

Correspondent: Brian Scott, 28 Finchale Close, Houghton-le-Spring, Tyne and Wear DH4 5QU (01915 841608; email: rectorstmichaels@btinternet.com)

CC Number: 810025

Eligibility

People in need living in the parishes of Bournmoor, South Biddick and West Rainton in County Durham, the parishes of Hetton and Warden Law in Tyne and Wear, and those parts of the borough of Sunderland and the parish of Framwellgate Moor, which formerly constituted part of the ancient parish of Houghton le Spring.

Types of grants

One-off and recurrent according to need.

Annual grant total

In 2012/13 the charity had an income of £1,600 and a total expenditure of £3,200. We estimate that grants to individuals totalled £3,100.

Applications

In writing to the correspondent.

Newcastle upon Tyne

The Non-Ecclesiastical Charity of William Moulton

£36,000

Correspondent: George Jackson, Clerk to the Trustees, 10 Sunlea Avenue, North Shields NE30 3DS (01912 510971; email: jgeorgelvis@blueyonder.co.uk)

CC Number: 216255

Eligibility

People in need who have lived within the boundaries of the city of Newcastle upon Tyne for at least the past 12 months.

Types of grants

Grants typically range between £50 and £200 for general household/personal needs such as washing machines, cookers, furniture, clothing and so on.

Annual grant total

In 2013 the charity held assets of £1.3 million and had an income of £84,000. Financial assistance to individuals totalled £36,000 and was distributed as follows:

Payments, gifts and donations	£31,000
Mothers' Union holiday grants	£5,000

Exclusions

No grants are given for education, training or rent arrears.

Applications

On a form available from the correspondent. Applications should be submitted through a social worker, Citizens Advice or other welfare agency and are considered monthly.

Other information

The charity also makes grants to local organisations though none were awarded during 2013.

The Town Moor Money Charity

£75,000 (318 grants)

Correspondent: Richard Grey, Hon. Treasurer, Moor Bank Lodge, Claremont Road, Newcastle upon Tyne NE2 4NL (01912 615970; email: admin@freemenofnewcastle.org; website: www.freemenofnewcastle.org)

CC Number: 248098

Eligibility

Freemen of Newcastle upon Tyne, Northumberland and Durham and their widows and children who are in need.

Types of grants

One-off and recurrent grants according to need. Grants are means-tested and paid in June and December.

Annual grant total

In 2012/13 the charity held assets of £150,000 and had an income of £28,000. Individuals received 318 grants totalling £75,000.

Applications

Application forms are available in April and October from the senior steward of the appropriate company. They are usually considered in May and November.

Sunderland

The George Hudson Charity

£19,500

Correspondent: Peter Taylor, Secretary, 19 John Street, Sunderland SR1 1JG (01915 674857; fax: 01915 109347; email: enquires@mckenzie-bell.co.uk)

CC Number: 527204

Eligibility

People under the age of 18 whose father has died or is unable to work and are living in Sunderland, with first preference to children of seafarers or pilots belonging to the Port of Sunderland, and in second preference to those born and resident in the ancient township of Monkwearmouth.

Types of grants

The trust gives pocket money, Christmas bonuses and clothing vouchers.

Annual grant total

In 2012/13 the charity had assets of £558,000 and an income of £41,000. £11,200 was given in monthly allowances and Christmas bonuses to 53 children. £8,100 was given in clothing and footwear grants. £200 was also spent on confectionery for beneficiaries. Management and administration costs were relatively high at £13,000.

Applications

On a form available from the correspondent. Applications are considered every other month.

The Mayor's Fund for Necessitous Children

£200

Correspondent: The Children's Services Finance Manager, Financial Resources, Room 2.86, Civic Centre, Sunderland SR2 7DN (01915 531826)

CC Number: 229349

Eligibility

Children in need (under 16, occasionally under 19) who are in full-time education, live in the city of Sunderland and whose family are on a low income.

Types of grants

Grants of about £25 for the provision of school footwear, paid every six months.

Annual grant total

In 2012/13 the fund had an income of £100 and a total expenditure of £400. We estimate that around £200 was given in grants to individuals for social welfare purposes.

Exclusions

No grants are made to asylum seekers.

Applications

Applicants must visit the civic centre and fill in a form with a member of staff. The decision is then posted at a later date. Proof of low income is necessary.

Other information

The fund also makes grants to individuals for educational purposes.

Tynemouth

The Charlton Bequest and Dispensary Trust

£0

Correspondent: Roy King, Trustee, 50 The Broadway, North Shields NE30 2LQ (01912 575297)

CC Number: 1055160

Eligibility

People who are sick, poor, have disabilities or who are convalescent and live in the former county borough of Tynemouth (now part of North Tyneside County Borough). Preference may be given to people resident at one of the trust's almshouses.

Types of grants

Grants to pay for items, services or facilities which are calculated to alleviate the suffering or assist the recovery of eligible people who do not have funds readily available to them from other sources.

Annual grant total

In 2012/13 the trust had assets of £1.8 million and an income of £72,000. There were no individual awards made and the charitable expenditure was allocated for the provision of accommodation.

The trustees' annual report from 2012/13 reassures that 'the trust will continue to consider and make grants available to the sick and needy in 2013/14 in accordance with the terms of the trust deed.'

Applications

In writing to the correspondent.

Other information

This trust was formed from the North Shields and Tynemouth Dispensary and the County Borough of Tynemouth Nursing Association. It is primarily concerned with the provision of apartments for older people in poor health.

Wallsend

Wallsend Charitable Trust

£2,000

Correspondent: The Secretary, North Tyneside Council, 16 The Silverlink North, Newcastle upon Tyne NE27 0BY (01916 437006)

CC Number: 215476

Eligibility

People over 60 who are on or just above state benefit income levels and live in the former borough of Wallsend.

Types of grants

One-off grants ranging between £10 to £500 to help meet extra requirements including, washing machines, fridge-freezers, carpets, home decoration, safety and security measures and medical equipment.

Annual grant total

In 2013 the trust had an income of £38,000 and a total expenditure of £19,400. The majority of the trust's charitable expenditure was given to organisations with similar objects, totalling £16,600. We believe that grants to individuals may have totalled as much as £2,000.

Exclusions

The trust will not help with continuing costs such as residential care or telephone rentals and will not help a person whose income is significantly above state benefit levels. Applicants must have exhausted all statutory avenues such as DWP, social services department and so on.

Applications

In writing to the correspondent either directly by the individual or through a social worker, Citizens Advice or other welfare agency or third party, such as a friend or relative. Applications are considered quarterly in April, July, September and December. They must include details of the purpose of the grant and an estimate of the cost.

Other information

Grants are given to organisations provided that the majority of members meet the same criteria as apply to individuals.

This trust is also known as the Victor Mann Trust.

West Yorkshire

Bradford and District Wool Association Benevolent Fund

£3,500

Correspondent: Sir James Hill, Chair, Sir James (Wool) Ltd, Unit 2 Baildon Mills, Northgate, Baildon, Shipley, West Yorkshire BD17 6JX (01274 532200)

CC Number: 518439

Eligibility

Former workers in the wool trade in Bradford and district or their spouses, who are in need. Preference is given to those who are elderly or disabled.

Types of grants

Normally recurrent grants up to a maximum of £200 towards heating, electricity and telephone costs. Special cases (such as the need for mobility aids, for example) are considered.

Annual grant total

The 2012 accounts were the latest available at the time of writing (August 2014).

In 2011/12, the fund had an income of £3,000 and a total expenditure of £3,500. We estimate that the total amount of grants awarded to individuals was approximately £3,500.

Applications

In writing to the correspondent either directly by the individual or through a relative or friend. Applications are considered at any time.

Mary Farrar's Benevolent Trust Fund

£7,400

Correspondent: Peter Haley, Administrator, P. Haley and Co., Poverty Hall, Lower Ellistones, Saddleworth Road, Greetland, Halifax HX4 8NG (01422 376690)

CC Number: 223806

Eligibility

Women of limited means over 55 years of age, who are native to the parish of Halifax, or have lived there for more than five consecutive years.

Types of grants

Pensions, paid quarterly.

Annual grant total

In 2012/13 the fund had an income of £4,900 and a total expenditure of £7,600. We estimate that pensions totalled £7,400.

Exclusions

A maximum 6 grants are available each year for married women and widows.

Applications

On a form available from the correspondent. Applications can be submitted by the individual, through a recognised referral agency (such as a social worker, Citizens Advice, or doctor) or another third party such as a relative, friend, minister of religion or trustee.

Huddersfield and District Army Veterans' Association Benevolent Fund

£10,500

Correspondent: Sarah Lamont, Administrator, 10 Belton Grove, Huddersfield HD3 3RF (01484 310193)

CC Number: 222286

Eligibility

Veterans of the army, navy and air force who are in need, aged over 60 years, and who were discharged from the forces 'with good character' and live in Huddersfield and part of Brighouse.

Types of grants

One-off and recurrent grants according to need.

Annual grant total

In 2013 the fund had an income of £25,000 and a total expenditure of £23,000. Grants to individuals totalled £10,500.

Applications

In writing to the correspondent, or on a form published in the fund's applications leaflet. The leaflet is available from doctor's surgeries, local libraries and so on.

Other information

The fund also provides social activities and trips to members of the forces in the Huddersfield area, spending £6,000 in 2013. It also has a welfare officer who can provide assistance with health and family problems and advice regarding funeral arrangements.

The Lucy Lund Holiday Grants

£400

Correspondent: Beverley Goldsmith, Administrator, Teachers Assurance, Tringham House, Deansleigh Road, Bournemouth BH7 7DT

CC Number: 236779

Eligibility

Present and former teachers who need a recuperative holiday. Preference is given to female teachers and particularly those from the former west riding of Yorkshire. No grants are given to dependents or students.

Types of grants

One-off grants for recuperative holidays.

Annual grant total

In 2013 the trust had an income of £2,100 and a total expenditure of £1,400. This expenditure is unusually high when compared to figures from previous years. We believe grants to individuals usually average around £400.

Applications

On a form available from the correspondent to be submitted by the individual.

Sir Titus Salt's Charity

£1,400

Correspondent: Norman Roper, Trustee, 6 Carlton Road, Shipley, West Yorkshire BD18 4NE (01274 599540)

CC Number: 216357

Eligibility

People in need who are over the age of 75 and live in Shipley, Baildon, Saltaire, Nab Wood and Wrose of Bradford.

Types of grants

Food vouchers paid once a year, available from Shipley Information Centre. On average 300 grants of £5 each are made every year.

Annual grant total

In 2012/13 the charity had an income of £1,600 and a total expenditure of £1,500. We estimate that social welfare grants to individuals totalled around £1,400.

Applications

Applications should be made through the Shipley Information Centre to be considered in November/December each year.

West Yorkshire Police (Employees) Benevolent Fund

£2,300

Correspondent: Pat Maknia, Administrator, West Yorkshire Police Finance Department, PO Box 9, Wakefield WF1 3QP (01924 292841)

CC Number: 701817

Eligibility

Employees and ex-employees of the West Yorkshire Police Force or the West Yorkshire Metropolitan County Council under the direct control of the chief constable who are in need, and their widows, orphans and other dependents.

Types of grants

One-off and recurrent grants according to need.

Annual grant total

In 2012/13 the fund had an income of £3,100 and a total expenditure of £2,500. We estimate that grants to individuals totalled £2,300.

Applications

In writing to the correspondent. Trustee meetings are held every three months, although urgent cases can be considered at any time.

Baildon

The Butterfield Trust

£1,000

Correspondent: Revd Canon John Nowell, Trustee, The Vicarage, Church Hill, Baildon, Shipley BD17 6NE (01274 594941)

CC Number: 216821

Eligibility

People in need who live in the parish of Baildon.

Types of grants

One-off grants for emergencies.

Annual grant total

In 2013 the trust had an income and total expenditure of £3,000. We estimate that around £1,000 was made in grants to individuals for social welfare purposes.

Applications

In writing to the correspondent. Decisions can be made immediately.

Bingley

The Bingley Diamond Jubilee Relief-in-Sickness Charity

£350

Correspondent: John Daykin, Administrator, Weatherhead and Butcher, 120 Main Street, Bingley BD16 2JJ (01274 562322; email: info@wandb.uk.com)

CC Number: 508248

Eligibility

People who live in the parish of Bingley (as constituted on 14 February 1898) who are sick, convalescent, have disabilities or are infirm.

Types of grants

Emergency payments or annual grants.

Annual grant total

In 2013 the charity had an income of £1,500 and a total expenditure of £700. We estimate that around £350 was made in grants to individuals for social welfare purposes.

Applications

In writing to the correspondent through a social worker, Citizens Advice, other welfare agency or a third party. For specific items, estimates of costs are required. The trustees meet in February and November. A subcommittee of trustees can deal promptly with emergency payments.

Other information

The charity also makes grants to local organisations.

The Samuel Sunderland Relief-in-Need Charity

£4,400

Correspondent: John Daykin, Clerk, Weatherhead and Butcher Solicitors, 120 Main Street, Bingley BD16 2JJ (01274 562322; email: info@wandb.uk.com)

CC Number: 225745

Eligibility

People who live in the former parish of Bingley (as constituted on 14 February 1898) and are in need, hardship or distress.

Types of grants

Emergency payments and annual grants (including Christmas gifts).

Annual grant total

In 2013 the charity had an income of £8,400 and a total expenditure of £8,900. We estimate that grants to individuals totalled £4,400, with local organisations also receiving funding.

Exclusions

The charity stresses that it only accepts applications from individuals residing within the boundary of the former parish of Bingley. Applications from those living elsewhere will not be considered.

Applications

In writing to the correspondent through a social worker, Citizens Advice, other welfare agency or any other third party on behalf of the individual. When specific items are required estimates of the cost must be provided. General applications should be submitted before 1 February and are usually considered in mid to late February. Applications for Christmas gifts must be submitted by 1 November and are usually considered on the first Thursday in November. Urgent applications from eligible persons can be considered throughout the year.

Other information

The charity also makes grants to local organisations.

Bradford

The Bradford Tradesmen's Homes

£7,200

Correspondent: Colin Askew, Administrator, 44 Lily Croft, Heaton Road, Bradford BD8 8QY (01274 543022; email: admin.bth@btconnect.com)

CC Number: 224389

Eligibility

Unmarried women over the age of 60 who have lived in Bradford metropolitan district for at least seven years who are not in employment and are in need.

Types of grants

Pensions of £65 per quarter. plus a Christmas grant.

Annual grant total

In 2012/13 the charity had assets of £990,000 and an income of £208,000. Grants to individuals totalled £7,200. Of this, pensions amounted to £1,000 and a further £6,200 was awarded in Christmas gifts to residents of the charity's almshouses.

Applications
On a form available from the correspondent. Applications can be submitted directly by the individual or, where applicable, through a social worker, Citizens Advice, other welfare agency, doctor, clergy or other third party. Applicants will be visited before an award is made and they must provide the names of two referees. Applications are considered throughout the year.

Other information
Bradford Tradesmen's Homes was first established in 1865, with the purpose of building and maintaining 30 homes for elderly tradesmen. Housing is still a priority for the trust and in 2012/13 £112,000 was spent on running its 45 almshouses for elderly men and women.

Children's Charity Circle Bradford and District

£500

Correspondent: Julie Cadman, Administrator, 14 Oakwood Drive, Bingley, West Yorkshire BD16 4AH (01274 561204)

CC Number: 230279

Eligibility
Children in need under 16 who live in Bradford.

Types of grants
One-off grants usually of £100 towards disability equipment, holidays, bedding and clothing.

Annual grant total
Grants to individuals generally total around £500 a year. Grants are also made to organisations.

Exclusions
No grants are given towards domestic bills or electrical goods.

Applications
In writing to the correspondent through a social worker, Citizens Advice or other welfare agency. They are considered monthly. Individuals should not apply directly.

The Moser Benevolent Trust Fund

£4,600

Correspondent: Donald Stokes, Trustee, 33 Mossy Bank Close, Queensbury, Bradford, West Yorkshire BD13 1PX (01274 817414)

CC Number: 222868

Eligibility
People in need who are 60 or over and have lived or worked in the former county borough of Bradford for at least three years.

Types of grants
On average around ten recipients receive pensions of around £400 a year.

Annual grant total
In 2012/13 the trust had an income of £6,200 and a total expenditure of £4,800. We estimate that grants to individuals totalled £4,600.

Applications
In writing to the correspondent. Applicants should include details of income and assets and are accepted at any time.

Other information
The fund is named after Jacob Moser, Lord Mayor of Bradford from 1910–11. In 1898, the mayor and his wife, Florence, donated £10,000, to establish a 'Benevolent Fund for the Aged and Infirm Workpeople of Bradford', and served the city as well-respected philanthropists throughout their lives.

Joseph Nutter's Foundation

£10,700

Correspondent: John Lambert, Secretary, 2 The Mews, Gilstead Lane, Bingley BD16 3NP (01274 688666; email: john@bradfordtextilesociety.org.uk)

CC Number: 507491

Eligibility
People aged 16 or under who live in the metropolitan district of Bradford and have suffered the loss of a parent.

Types of grants
One-off grants of around £100 to £200 are given towards clothing, bedding, beds and household equipment which specifically benefit the child, such as cookers, fires and washing machines. Other needs may occasionally be considered on an individual basis.

Annual grant total
In 2012/13 the foundation had an income of £19,200 and a total expenditure of £10,900.

Applications
In writing to the correspondent at any time. Applications can be submitted directly by the individual or family member.

Paul and Nancy Speak's Charity

£8,000

Correspondent: Malcolm Dixon, Secretary, 10 The Orchards, Bingley, West Yorkshire BD16 4AZ (01274 770878)

CC Number: 231339

Eligibility
Women in need who are over the age of 50 and live in Bradford.

Types of grants
Regular allowances of £500 a year, paid quarterly.

Annual grant total
In 2013 the charity had an income of £3,400 and a total expenditure of £8,500. We estimate that grants to individuals totalled £8,000.

Applications
In writing to the correspondent.

Calderdale

The Community Foundation for Calderdale

£18,000

Correspondent: Grants Department, The 1855 Building (first floor), Discovery Road, Halifax, West Yorkshire HX1 2NG (01422 438738; fax: 01422 350017; email: grants@cffc.co.uk; website: www.cffc.co.uk)

CC Number: 1002722

Eligibility
People in need who live in Calderdale.

Types of grants
One-off grants of up to £130 and occasionally small loans to meet urgent needs, such as household equipment, clothing and food which cannot be readily funded from other sources. People over 60 can apply for grants of up to £250 towards a short break away from home.

Annual grant total

In 2012/13 grants were awarded to 343 individuals totalling £37,000. We estimate grants to individuals for social welfare purposes totalled around £18,000.

Applications

Individuals should apply through a referring agency, such as Citizens Advice, on an application form available from the website. Grants will only be awarded to individuals in the form of a cheque; cash is not given.

Other information

The foundation also gives to organisations and to individuals for educational purposes.

The Halifax Society for the Blind

£4,500

Correspondent: Lindsay Dyson, Administrator, Halifax Society for the Blind, 34 Clare Road, Halifax, West Yorkshire HX1 2HX (01422 352383; email: halifaxblindsociety@gmail.com; website: www.sightsupportcalderdale.co.uk)

CC Number: 224258

Eligibility

People in need who are registered blind or partially sighted and live in Calderdale. Applicants should have savings of no more than £4,000 and a 'disposable' household weekly income of no more than £120 (after paying rent/mortgage, council tax and utilities bills).

Types of grants

One-off grants of cash up to £250 or equipment according to need. Grants have been given towards beds, school equipment, televisions and decorating costs.

Annual grant total

In 2012/13 the society held assets of £1.6 million and had an income of £75,000. Grants to individuals totalled £4,500.

Applications

Application forms are available from the correspondent and can be submitted when they are supported by a social worker or a rehabilitation officer. Members can also self-refer by discussing their needs with the HSB manager. Applications are considered on a regular basis.

Other information

The society has 390 members, runs five social centres and a resource centre and operates a minibus service.

The Halifax Tradesmen's Benevolent Institution

£22,000

Correspondent: Anthony Wannan, Administrator, West House, Kings Cross Road, Halifax HX1 1EB (01422 352517; email: anthony.wannan@bm-howarth.co.uk)

CC Number: 224056

Eligibility

People in need aged 60 or over who have been self-employed or a manager of a business for at least seven years and live in the parish of Halifax and the surrounding area, and their dependents. Applicants should have no income other than a pension and have only modest savings.

Types of grants

Pensions, which in recent years have amounted to around £550 per annum.

Annual grant total

In 2012/13 the charity had an income of £16,400 and a total expenditure of £24,000. We estimate that pensions to individuals totalled £22,000.

Applications

In writing to the correspondent, to be considered quarterly.

Dewsbury

Dewsbury and District Sick Poor Fund

£11,100

Correspondent: John Alan Winder, 130 Boothroyd Lane, Dewsbury, West Yorkshire WF13 2LW (01924 463308)

CC Number: 234401

Eligibility

People who are sick and in need who live in the county borough of Dewsbury and the ecclesiastical parish of Hanging Heaton.

Types of grants

One-off grants according to need for household goods and holidays to aid recuperation after illness. Vouchers are also available for food, clothing and the purchase of medical aids.

Annual grant total

In 2013 the fund had an income of £3,700 and a total expenditure of £11,300. We estimate that grants to individuals totalled £11,100.

Applications

In writing to the correspondent including details of illness and residential qualifications. Applications can be submitted either directly by the individual, through a third party such as a social worker or through an organisation such as Citizens Advice.

Halifax

The Goodall Trust

£3,800

Correspondent: Andrew Buck, Administrator, 122 Skircoat Road, Halifax HX1 2RE (01422 255880; email: atbuck@tiscali.co.uk)

CC Number: 221651

Eligibility

Widows and unmarried women who are in need and live in the present Calderdale ward of Skircoat or the parts of the parishes of St Jude and All Saints (Halifax) which are within the ancient township of Skircoat.

Types of grants

Recurrent grants are given according to need.

Annual grant total

In 2013 the trust had an income of £3,900 and a total expenditure of £4,100. We estimate that grants to individuals totalled £3,800.

Applications

On a form available from the correspondent. Applications should be submitted by mid-September either directly by the individual; by a relative, friend or neighbour; or through a welfare agency. They are considered in October.

Charity of Ann Holt

£12,200

Correspondent: G. D. Jacobs, Oak House, 9 Cross Street, Oakenshaw, Bradford, West Yorkshire BD12 7EA (01274 679835; email: oakey9uk@yahoo.co.uk)

CC Number: 502391

Eligibility

Single women over the age of 55, who have lived in Halifax for at least five years, and are in need.

Types of grants

Pensions of around £200 a year, paid in quarterly instalments until the recipient dies, moves out of the area or relocates to a residential home.

Annual grant total
In 2012/13 the charity had an income of £15,100 and a total expenditure of £12,400. We estimate that grants to individuals totalled £12,200.

Applications
In writing to the correspondent, directly by the individual. Applicants will need to be prepared to provide two referees who are not relations, such as a vicar, ex-employer or someone else they have known for a number of years.

Horbury

St Leonard's Hospital – Horbury

£1,200

Correspondent: Ian Whittell, Administrator, 31 New Road, Horbury, Wakefield, West Yorkshire WF4 5LS (01924 272762)

CC Number: 243977

Eligibility
People in need, hardship or distress who live in the former urban district of Horbury.

Types of grants
One-off grants usually ranging from £20 to £200. Recent grants have been given towards adaptations, convalescence, nursing, renovation and repairs to homes for disabled access and helping people who are homeless or experiencing marital problems.

Annual grant total
In 2013, the charity had an income of £3,500 and a total expenditure of £3,500. We estimate that the total amount of grants awarded to individuals was approximately £1,200.

Exclusions
No grants are made towards maintenance of equipment already paid for. No loans are made although recurrent grants are considered if necessary.

Applications
In writing to the correspondent. Applications can be submitted directly by the individual, through a social worker, Citizens Advice or other welfare agency or through a church member. They are considered at any time and the trustees can act quickly in urgent cases.

Other information
Grants may also be made to local organisations.

Horton

John Ashton (including the Gift of Hannah Shaw).

£2,600

Correspondent: Gordon Doble, Trustee, Upper Beck House, 22 Hammerton Drive, Hellifield, Skipton BD23 4LZ (01729 851329)

CC Number: 233661

Eligibility
People in need who are over 65 and live alone in the Great Horton area of Bradford.

Types of grants
Small grants, according to need.

Annual grant total
In 2013, the charity had an income of £3,200 and a total expenditure of approximately £2,800. We estimate that the total amount of grants awarded to individuals was approximately £2,600.

Applications
On a form available from the correspondent to be submitted directly by the individual or through a family member for consideration in June and December.

Huddersfield

The Beaumont and Jessop Relief-in-Need Charity

£1,000

Correspondent: Leslie Chadwick, Trustee, 35 Westcroft, Honley, Holmfirth HD9 6JP (01484 662880; email: lesbuk@gmail.com)

CC Number: 504141

Eligibility
People in need who are over 65 and live in the ancient township of Honley (near Huddersfield).

Types of grants
One-off grants ranging from £60 to £500 towards, for instance, Winged Fellowship holidays, heating grants (nominated by doctors), medical equipment, spectacles, transport to luncheon clubs and so on.

Annual grant total
In 2012/13, the charity had an income of £3,900 and a total expenditure of £2,000. We estimate that the total amount of grants awarded to individuals was approximately £1,000. The charity also awards grants to local organisations.

Applications
In writing to the correspondent, indicating the purpose of the grant. Applications can be submitted directly by the individual or through a social worker, Citizens Advice, other welfare agency or other third party (nurses or doctors). Applications are considered throughout the year.

The Charles Brook Convalescent Fund

£14,400

Correspondent: Carol Thompson, Administrator, Mistal Barn, Lower Castle Hill, Almondbury, Huddersfield HD4 6TA (01484 532183)

CC Number: 229445

Eligibility
People who are convalescing and live within the old Huddersfield Health Authority catchment area.

Types of grants
One-off grants for special foods, medicines or appliances, household goods such as washing machines and fridges, floor coverings, cleaning services, clothing, bedding and holidays for convalescence.

Annual grant total
In 2012/13 the fund had an income of £14,400 and a total expenditure of £14,600. We estimate that grants to individuals totalled £14,400.

Exclusions
No loans.

Applications
On a form available from the social work department at Royal Infirmary, Huddersfield and St Luke's Hospital, Huddersfield. Applications must be submitted through a social worker and include details of weekly income/expenditure and family situation. Applications sent directly to the correspondent cannot be considered.

The H. P. Dugdale Foundation

£53,000 (45 grants)

Correspondent: T. J. Green, Administrator, Bank Chambers, Market Street, Huddersfield HD1 2EW (01484 648482)

CC Number: 200538

Eligibility
People in need who live in the county borough of Huddersfield (comprising the urban districts of Colne Valley, Kirkburton, Meltham and Holmfirth).

People who have previously lived in the area for a period of ten consecutive years are also eligible for assistance.

Types of grants

One-off and recurrent grants according to need.

Annual grant total

In 2012/13 the foundation had assets of £1.3 million and an income of £65,000. Grants were made totalling approximately £53,000, and were distributed as follows:

Regular payments	35	£42,000
Christmas gifts	-	£8,000
One-off payments	10	£3,200

Applications

Application forms are given to local organisations such as social services and churches. They are then submitted by or on behalf of the individual. The trustees meet twice a year to consider applications.

Keighley

The Beamsley Trust

£0

Correspondent: Mary Hamilton, Administrator, Central Hall, Alice Street, Keighley, West Yorkshire BD21 3JD (01535 665258; email: enquiries@craventrust.org.uk; website: www.craventrust.org.uk)

CC Number: 1045419

Eligibility

People resident within the Craven area who are in need, hardship or distress. The area of benefit includes Settle, Skipton and Barnoldswick and is bordered by Sedbergh to the north, Keighley to the east, Denholme and Hurst Green to the South and Ingleton to the west, see the map on the website for the exact area.

Types of grants

Grants generally ranging from £100 to £1,500 for 'items, services or facilities which help to reduce their difficulties'.

Annual grant total

A list of grants made on the trust's website suggests that no grants we made directly to individuals during 2012/13; however, the trust's objects include 'the relief of financial need among people resident in the area' and the trust accepts applications for individuals through its website.

Exclusions

No grants for students, foreign travel or rates, taxes or other public funds. The trust cannot commit itself to repeat or renew a grant.

Applications

On a form available from the website, preferably to be submitted through a referral agency or a referee such as Citizens Advice, social services, or a vicar or doctor. Supporting evidence such as copies of bank statements, correspondence or notices should be provided. After your application is submitted, and before the trustees meet, a telephone call or visit will be arranged. Applications are considered at trustee meetings which are held twice a year. Applications should be considered a month before the meeting (see the website for exact deadlines).

Bowcocks Trust Fund for Keighley

£3,000

Correspondent: Alistair Docherty, 17 Farndale Road, Wilsden, Bradford BD15 0LW (01535 272657)

CC Number: 223290

Eligibility

People in need who live in the municipal borough of Keighley as constituted on 31 March 1974.

Types of grants

One-off grants according to need.

Annual grant total

In 2012/13 the trust had an income of £9,200 and a total expenditure of £13,000. Grants are given for educational and social welfare purposes and to both individuals and organisations. We estimate grants to individuals for social welfare purposes totalled around £3,000.

Applications

Initial telephone calls are welcomed. Applications should be made in writing to the correspondent by a third party.

The William and Sarah Midgley Charity

£2,300

Correspondent: Eileen Proctor, Administrator, 7 Lachman Road, Trawden, Colne, Lancashire BB8 8TA (01282 862757; email: eileenproctor@talktalk.net)

CC Number: 500095

Eligibility

People who are in need, hardship or distress and live in Barcroft, Lees and Cross Roads in the former borough of Keighley, West Yorkshire.

Types of grants

Our research suggests that Christmas hampers are normally given to older people in the area. Occasional one-off cash grants and gifts in kind have also been made for electrical goods, clothing, food, travel expenses, medical and disability equipment and furniture.

Annual grant total

In 2013/14 the charity had an income of £4,800 and an expenditure of £2,500. We estimate that around £2,300 was awarded in grants to individuals.

Applications

In writing to the correspondent.

Leeds

The Bramhope Trust

£0

Correspondent: Bryan Bundey, Trustee, 4 The Sycamores, Bramhope, Leeds LS16 9JR (01132 678534)

CC Number: 504190

Eligibility

People in need within the parish of Bramhope.

Types of grants

Gifts of varying amounts are given to organisations and individuals.

Annual grant total

In 2012/13, the trust had assets of £907,000 and an income of £36,000. Grants were given totalling £27,000, although it appears that none of this was awarded directly to individuals.

Applications

In writing to the correspondent directly by the individual or through a doctor. Applications are considered throughout the year.

Other information

The trust also gives grants to churches and other voluntary organisations in Bramhope. In 2012/13, these grants totalled £27,000.

Chapel Allerton and Potter Newton Relief-in-Need Charity

£1,900

Correspondent: Christopher Johnson, Trustee, 6 Grosvenor Park, Leeds LS7 3QD (01132 680600)

CC Number: 245504

Eligibility

People who live within the parishes of Chapel Allerton and Potter Newton, Leeds.

Types of grants
One-off grants between £5 and £150 are given mainly for white electrical goods. Support can also be given to assist with arrears of fuel bills, rent (where housing benefit is not available), telephones (where required by people who are sick or housebound), also to replace cookers beyond repair and to provide food in emergencies when social security is not available.

Annual grant total
In 2013 the charity had an income of £2,600 and an expenditure of £2,100. We estimate that grants to individuals totalled around £1,900.

Exclusions
According to our research, grants for furniture are not made, as there are two local furniture stores organised by churches.

Applications
Applications must be made through the Leeds or Chapeltown Citizens Advice, a social services department, probation officer, health visitor or other referral agency. The trustees usually meet in March but applications can be dealt with at any time.

The Community Shop Trust

£54,000 (432 grants)

Correspondent: The Trustees, Unit 4, Clayton Wood Bank, West Park Ring Road, Leeds LS16 6QZ (01132 745551; fax: 01132 783184; email: info@leedscommunitytrust.org; website: www.leedscommunitytrust.org)

CC Number: 701375

Eligibility
People in need who live in the Leeds area. Families with children are usually given preference.

Types of grants
One-off grants for emergency assistance for electrical and kitchen appliances, beds, bedding, carpets, removals and so on. Christmas grants are issued as grocery vouchers one to two weeks before Christmas. Holiday grants to enable families to go on holiday together. 'Kosy Kids' grants for improving a child's bedroom. 'Keen Kids' grants for education, sport and music.

Annual grant total
In 2012 the trust made grants to 435 families totalling £56,000, broken down as follows:

Type of grant	Cases	Items	Amount
Emergency grants	232	347	£40,000
Christmas grants	181	181	£10,500
Holidays	20	20	£4,000
Kosy Kids	2	10	£1,000
Totals	435	558	£56,000

Nearly all grants were for social welfare purposes but included in these items are the cost of two computers and five school uniforms which we have taken to be educational grants and estimated the total at £1,600. The 2012 accounts were the latest available at the time of writing (August 2014).

Applications
In writing to the correspondent through a social worker, Citizens Advice or other welfare agency. Potential applicants are then sent an application form to complete. For this reason the initial letter must give details of the personal circumstances. Decisions on emergency grant applications are usually made within two days.

Other information
The trust is also known as the Leeds Community Trust. It runs two shops and distributes the profits to local charities, groups and individuals in need, particularly people in vulnerable situations.

Kirke Charity

£2,500

Correspondent: Bruce Buchan, Trustee, 8 St Helens Croft, Leeds LS16 8JY (01924 465860)

CC Number: 246102

Eligibility
People in need who live in the ancient parishes of Adel, Arthington or Cookridge.

Types of grants
One-off grants, generally of around £100.

Annual grant total
In 2012/13 the charity had an income of £9,200 and an expenditure of £5,200. Grants usually total around £5,000 for both education and welfare purposes.

Applications
Applications can be submitted directly by the individual or through a social worker, Citizens Advice or other welfare agency.

The Leeds Tradesmen's Trust

£4,500

Correspondent: Grants Team, 1st Floor, 51A St Paul's Street, Leeds LS1 2TE (01132 422426; email: info@leedscf.org.uk)

CC Number: 1096892

Eligibility
People over 50 who have carried on business, practised a profession or been a tradesperson for at least five years (either consecutively or in total) and who, during that time, lived in Leeds or whose business premises (rented or owned) were in the city of Leeds. Grants are also given to self-employed business/professional people who 'have fallen upon misfortune in business'; normally older people. Widows and unmarried daughters of the former are also eligible.

Types of grants
Quarterly pensions, normally of £10 to £500 a year, plus Christmas grants and spring fuel grants only to those already receiving a pension.

Annual grant total
In 2012/13 pensions totalled £4,500.

Applications
Enquiries should be made to the Leeds Community Foundation's grants team by telephone or email.

Other information
Community Foundation for Leeds took over the administration of the trust in April 2013.

The Metcalfe Smith Trust

£15,100

Correspondent: Geoff Hill, Secretary, c/o Voluntary Action Leeds, Stringer House, 34 Lupton Street, Hunslet, Leeds LS10, 2QW (email: secretary@metcalfesmithtrust.org; website: www.metcalfesmithtrust.org.uk)

CC Number: 228891

Eligibility
Adults and children who live in Leeds and have 'a physical disability, long-term illness or a mental health difficulty'.

Types of grants
One-off grants ranging from £250 to £2,500 towards items or services that will significantly improve quality of life. Grants are given towards, for example, disability equipment, computers, respite breaks, heating costs, small items of furniture and course fees.

Annual grant total

In 2012/13 the trust had assets of £707,000 and an income of £29,000. Grants to individuals totalled £15,100 and were distributed as follows:

Relief in need	£14,700
Emergency fund	£500

A further £4,000 was given in grants to organisations.

Exclusions

No support is given for individuals outside the area of benefit, general appeals, recurrent grants, fundraising initiatives or research costs.

Applications

Application forms are available on request by completing the 'application request form' on the trust's website. Individual applications must be supported by a social worker or local welfare organisation. They are considered twice a year, normally in May and October/November. See the website for dates of application deadlines and trustees' meetings. Emergency grants of up to £100 can be made at any time and applicants can use the online application form.

Other information

The trust's annual report states that: 'The Metcalfe Smith Trust was established in 1867, by a Victorian banker and benefactor, John Metcalfe Smith, who built Cookridge Convalescent Hospital, in memory of his father, for the benefit of people living and working in the Borough (as it was then) of Leeds.'

Radio Aire and Magic 828's Cash For Kids

£390,000

Correspondent: Katy Winterschladen, Regional Charity Manager, 51 Burley Road, Leeds LS1 3LR (01132 835555; email: katy.winterschladen@bauermedia.co.uk; website: www.radioaire.co.uk/charity)

Eligibility

Children under the age of 18 who live in Leeds and West Yorkshire, particularly those who are underprivileged, have a sickness or disability.

Types of grants

One-off grants for children in need. A large part of the charity's activity is the provision of Christmas gifts to local children who might otherwise not receive anything. Grants have also been made for specialist medical equipment, surgery and therapy, mobility aids, beds and bedding, day trips, kitchen appliances and so on.

Annual grant total

In 2013 the charity raised over £975,000 to support more than 20,000 local children in Leeds and West Yorkshire. This amount included a contribution of £829,000 towards the annual Christmas appeal which provided gifts to over 15,000 local children. We have estimated that grants to individuals totalled around £390,000.

Applications

Application forms are available from the correspondent. Our research suggests that candidates should attach payslips or other evidence of income and bank statements for the last three months. The trustees normally meet four times a year to consider applications.

Other information

Grants are also made to local organisations with similar aims. Funds are not restricted but the charity has previously told us that in practice approximately 60% of funds raised are distributed to organisations and the remaining 40% distributed to individual appeals each year.

Sandal Magna

The Henry and Ada Chalker Trust

£1,000 (90 grants)

Correspondent: The Trustees, Beaumont Legal, Beaumont House, 1 Paragon Avenue, Wakefield, West Yorkshire WF1 2UF (0845 122 8100)

CC Number: 224808

Eligibility

People in need who live in Sandal Magna, with a preference for elderly residents.

Types of grants

Recurrent grants of around £10 a year are distributed in the first week of December.

Annual grant total

Grants to individuals total around £1,000 each year. Approximately 90 grants are awarded.

Applications

On a form available from the correspondent. As this is a recurrent grant new applications are stockpiled until there is a vacancy on the current list.

The Sandal Magna Relief-in-Need Charity

£300

Correspondent: Martin J. Perry, Administrator, 50 Dukewood Road, Clayton West, Huddersfield HD8 9HF (01484 860594; email: marpam@fsmail.net)

CC Number: 810052

Eligibility

People in need who live in the old parish of Sandal Magna (this includes Sandal, Walton, Crigglestone, Painthorpe and West Bretton).

Types of grants

One-off grants of about £50 to £300 are made each year to six to ten individuals. Recent grants have been used for the purchase of a second-hand washing machine, decorating materials, bedding for a child and a safety gate for the stairs.

Annual grant total

In 2012 this charity had an income of £1,800 and total expenses of £683. Expenditure varies from £3,600 to £700. This year's expenditure is the lowest for five years. Grants are awarded to both individuals and organisations. The 2012 accounts were the latest available at the time of writing (August 2014).

Applications

In writing to the correspondent. Applications can be sent directly by the individual or through a social worker, Citizens Advice or other welfare agency.

Todmorden

Todmorden War Memorial Fund

£1,000

Correspondent: Stephen Ormerod, Trustee, 2 Maitland Close, Todmorden, West Yorkshire OL14 7TG (07941 195488)

CC Number: 219673

Eligibility

Veterans of the First and Second World Wars who are sick or in need and live in the former borough of Todmorden, and their dependents.

Types of grants

Grants are mostly one-off; recurrent grants are very occasionally given. TV licences are given to First and Second World War families. Food vouchers, medicine, medical comforts, bedding, fuel, domestic help and convalescence expenses are also given.

Annual grant total

In 2013 the fund had an income of £4,200 and a total expenditure of £6,500. We estimate that around £3,000 was made in grants to individuals for social welfare purposes.

Applications

In writing to: Mrs M Gunton, Case Secretary, 8 Walton Fold, Todmorden, Lancashire OL14 5TE. Applications must be through a welfare agency or similar organisation and they are considered monthly.

Other information

The fund also makes grants to organisations.

Wakefield

The Brotherton Charity Trust

£2,100

Correspondent: Christopher Brotherton-Ratcliffe, Trustee, PO Box 374, Harrogate HG1 4YW

CC Number: 221006

Eligibility

People in need who are over 60 years old and live in Wakefield.

Types of grants

Annual pensions.

Annual grant total

In 2013 the trust had an income of £3,200 and a total expenditure of £2,300. We estimate that pensions totalled £2,100.

Applications

On a form available from the correspondent. When vacancies arise an advert is placed in the Wakefield Express and a waiting list is then drawn up. Applications can be made directly by the individual or family member.

North West

General

The Cotton Districts Convalescent Fund and the Barnes Samaritan Charity

£21,000

Correspondent: Nicholas Stockton, Secretary, c/o Cassons Chartered Accountants, Rational House, 64 Bridge Street, Manchester M3 3BN (0845 337 9409; fax: 0845 337 9408; email: manchester@cassons.co.uk; website: www.cotton-districts.co.uk)

CC Number: 224727

Eligibility

People in need who have a severe/long-term illness, are convalescent or who have a disability and live in: the counties of Lancashire and Greater Manchester; the districts of Craven, North Yorkshire and High Peak, Derbyshire; the districts of Macclesfield and Warrington in Cheshire; and the district of Calderdale, West Yorkshire.

Types of grants

The charity makes grants to enable a subsidised convalescent holiday of one week to be taken at hotels in Blackpool and St Annes. Applicants are expected to pay an amount towards the cost of a week's half-board holiday, with the charity paying the difference. Alternatively, the charity may instead make a contribution of £200 towards the costs of a holiday elsewhere in the UK. Consideration will be given to making a grant towards the costs of a special needs holiday proposed by the applicant (for example where nursing or other care is required).

Monthly grants not exceeding £45 per month are also available towards living costs for those who are in poor health, convalescent or who have a disability.

Annual grant total

In 2012 the charity had an income of £43,000 and a total expenditure of £36,000. At the time of writing (August 2014) this was the most recent financial information available for the charity and its accounts were not yet available to view on the Charity Commission. In previous years, payments to beneficiaries have totalled £21,000.

Applications

In writing to the secretary, providing details of your financial and medical circumstances. The application should be accompanied by a supporting letter from a sponsor, such as a doctor or social worker, confirming these medical and financial circumstances.

Note: the trust has previously stated that due to a lack of income, future grantmaking will be limited.

Other information

This trust was previously known as The Cotton Districts Convalescent Fund.

George House Trust

£107,000 (484 grants)

Correspondent: Rosie Robinson, Joint Chief Executive, 75–77 Ardwick Green North, Manchester M12 6FX (01612 744499; fax: 01612 743355; email: info@ght.org.uk; website: www.ght.org.uk)

CC Number: 1143138

Eligibility

People with HIV who live in the north west of England.

Types of grants

One-off grants ranging from £20 to £150 to help with essential items and household bills. Cheques are generally paid to the supplier but if this is not possible, the applicant may receive a cheque or other suitable form of payment directly. Other types of grants are available for people who use the trust's services.

Annual grant total

In 2012/13 the trust held assets of £1.2 million and had an income of £747,000. Welfare grants to 484 individuals totalled £107,000.

Exclusions

No grants are made to people without original proof of HIV diagnosis. Normally no more than one payment per person can be made each year.

Applications

Applications should be made in writing through the trust's website or on a form available from the office (those living outside Manchester can have one sent to their home). Evidence that the individual has been diagnosed HIV positive, such as a copy of a letter from the consultant at an HIV testing clinic, should be enclosed with the form. The letter must include the applicant's date of birth. Applicants should post this evidence to the George House address, even if the application is made via the website. Where applicable, copies of bills or written estimates for goods must also be forwarded to the trust's office. If funding is a matter of emergency (i.e. people with no money for food or gas) then it is worth contacting the trust as it may be able to make a small grant straight away.

Other information

The trust's activities range from raising HIV awareness through its information and community services, to providing advice, counselling and support for people affected by HIV and AIDS.

The Grant, Bagshaw, Rogers and Tidswell Fund

£12,700

Correspondent: Lawrence Downey, Administrator, Ripley House, 56 Freshfield Road, Formby, Liverpool L37 3HW (01704 879330; email: lawrencedowney@btconnect.com)

CC Number: 216948

Eligibility

Older people in need who live, or were born in, Liverpool, the Wirral, Ellesmere Port or Chester.

Types of grants

Small pensions are paid half-yearly. Occasional one-off grants may also be given.

Annual grant total

In 2012/13 the fund had an income of £14,100 and a total expenditure of £12,900. We estimate that grants to individuals totalled £12,700.

Applications

On a form available from the correspondent. Applications should be returned by 28 February and 30 October for consideration in April and December respectively.

Gregson Memorial Annuities

£2,900

Correspondent: Alison Houghton, Trustee, Brabners Chaffe Street, Horton House, Exchange Flags, Liverpool L2 3YL (01516 003000; fax: 01512 273185; email: alison.houghton@brabnerscs.com)

CC Number: 218096

Eligibility

Female domestic servants who have been in service for at least ten years in Liverpool, Southport, Malpas and the surrounding area and who cannot work now for health reasons.

Types of grants

Annuities of about £300 a year, payable in two six-monthly instalments.

Annual grant total

In 2012/13, the trust had an income of £3,300 and a total expenditure of £3,000. We estimate that the total award granted to individuals was approximately £2,900.

Applications

Applications in writing to the correspondent are considered throughout the year.

The Lancashire Infirm Secular Clergy Fund

£119,000 (92 grants)

Correspondent: Revd Peter Stanley, Trustee, St Joseph's Presbytery, Harpers Lane, Chorley PR6 0HR (01257 262713)

CC Number: 222796

Eligibility

Catholic secular clergy of the dioceses of Liverpool, Salford and Lancaster who are unable, through age or infirmity, to attend to their duties of office and are in need.

Types of grants

Annual grants mostly of £1,300 each although smaller grants of around £600 are also available.

Annual grant total

In 2012/13 the fund held assets of £3.4 million and had an income of £112,000. Grants to infirm clergy totalled £119,000.

Applications

On a form available from the correspondent, to be submitted directly by the individual.

The North West Police Benevolent Fund

£123,000 (43 grants)

Correspondent: Jackie Smithies, Secretary, Progress House, Broadstone Hall Road South, Reddish, Stockport SK5 7DE (01613 554420; fax: 01613 554410; email: jsmithies@gmpf.polfed.org; website: www.nwpbf.org)

CC Number: 503045

Eligibility

Serving and retired officers of Cheshire Constabulary, Greater Manchester Police, Lancashire Constabulary, Merseyside Police and previous police forces amalgamated within the constituent forces, together with their dependents, who are in a condition of need and hardship. Former officers of the above forces may be considered at the trustees' discretion.

In 2011 the fund was joined by National Crime Agency (NCA) (previously known as Serious Organised Crime Agency – SOCA). From September 2013 Cumbria Constabulary also became a member.

Types of grants

One-off or recurrent grants and interest-free loans are given for convalescence, medical and disability equipment (but not for private health care) or to help in other cases of need arising from unforeseen circumstances.

In the event of death of a serving police officer a grant of £5,000 is paid to the dependent family.

Orphaned children of the police officers are supported through the St George's Police Children's Trust (see a separate entry).

Annual grant total

In 2013 the fund had assets of £5.7 million and an income of over £2 million. Grants were made totalling around £123,000. Support was given in the following categories:

Serving officers	£55,000
Deaths	£40,000
Pensioners	£21,000
Attendance at convalescent homes (serving officers)	£3,500
Attendance at convalescent homes (pensioners)	£3,300
Christmas grants (pensioners and widows)	£250

In 2013 there were 85 applications for assistance, of which 43 were approved as grants (including eight death grants) and 35 as interest-free loans. Most applications were received from Merseyside (26) and GMP (23) followed by Cheshire (17) and Lancashire (16). A lower number of applications was received from N.C.A. (2) and Cumbria (1).

Exclusions

No grants available for private health, education or legal fees.

Applications

Application forms are available from the correspondent. They are usually made through a force welfare officer or a member of the management committee. Our research suggests that requests for assistance are generally considered each month and should be submitted by the second Wednesday in January or by the first Wednesday in any other month.

Other information

The fund does not give grants to organisations but does contribute to other police funds and convalescent homes. Members are also able to use the police treatment centres or holiday lodges. See the website for further details.

Roundhouse (formerly Cockshot) Foundation

£2,500

Correspondent: Michelle Rothwell, Trustee, Belle Isle, Windermere, Cumbria LA23 1BG (01539 447087; email: cockshotfoundation@belleisle.net)

CC Number: 1104085

Eligibility

People in need, hardship or distress resident in the counties of Cumbria, Lancashire and Greater Manchester.

Types of grants

On-off and recurrent grants according to need.

Annual grant total

In 2012/13 the foundation had an income of £4,300 and a total expenditure of £10,300. The foundation gives to organisations and individuals for both educational and social welfare purposes. We estimate the total awarded to individuals for social welfare purposes was around £2,500.

Applications

In writing to the correspondent.

The SF Group Charity

See entry on page 40

United Utilities Trust Fund

£4.7 million

Correspondent: The Secretary, FREEPOST RLYY-JHEJ-XCXS, Sutton Coldfield B72 1TJ (0845 179 1791; email: contact@uutf.org.uk; website: www.uutf.org.uk)

CC Number: 1108296

Eligibility

People in need who live in the area supplied by United Utilities Water (predominantly the north west of England).

Types of grants

Payments for water and/or sewerage charges due to United Utilities Water. The trust can also help with water or sewerage charges which are collected by other companies or organisations on behalf of United Utilities Water. In certain cases, the trust can also consider giving some help to meet other essential bills, household needs or priority debts. Payments are made directly to the supplier.

Annual grant total

In 2012/13 the trust had an income of £5 million and a total expenditure of £5.5 million. Grants and further assistance to individuals and families totalled £4.7 million.

During the year, the trust received 8,057 applications and was able to provide assistance in 4,883 cases.

Exclusions

No grants for court fines, catalogue debts, credit cards, personal loans or other forms of borrowing; statutory loans/benefit overpayments/tax credit overpayments now being reclaimed. The fund cannot make payments towards bills already paid or purchases already made.

The trust will not normally consider more than one application from the same person.

Applications

Application forms and full guidelines are available from the website. Money advisers and other referral agents may use the online application process. All applicants may use the offline application form. Applicants may receive a phone call or a home visit as part of the assessment process. All applications will be acknowledged and applicants will be issued with a reference number which they must use when making enquiries regarding the application. Successful applicants may not reapply for a period of two years, while unsuccessful applicants may apply again after six months.

For grants towards bankruptcy fees a separate application form is required; call 0845 179 1791 to request one.

Other information

The trust states on its website that: 'One of the Trust's aims is to help people out of immediate financial difficulties and wherever possible through debt counselling/money advice to encourage and help financial stability in the future.' In 2012/13 grants totalling £288,000 were awarded towards debt counselling services.

Cheshire

The Cheshire Provincial Fund of Benevolence

£20,000

Correspondent: Peter Carroll, Trustee, Ashcroft House, 36 Clay Lane, Timperley, Altrincham, Cheshire WA15 7AB (01619 806090; email: enquiries@cheshiremasons.co.uk)

CC Number: 219177

Eligibility

Freemasons of Cheshire and their dependents who are in need.

Types of grants

One-off and recurrent grants according to need.

Annual grant total

In 2012/13 the fund had assets of £4.1 million and an income of £248,000. Grants were made totalling £198,000, of which £137,000 was given to masonic institutions. We estimate that welfare grants to individuals totalled around £20,000. Funding was also awarded to non-masonic charitable organisations.

Applications

In writing to the correspondent.

Other information

Freemasons in Cheshire have also supported the Teddies for Loving Care Appeal (TLC), which provides teddies for children visiting A&E departments in Cheshire hospitals. On average around 12,000 bears are donated every year.

John Holford Charity

£11,000

Correspondent: Kerris Owen, Clerk to the Trustees, Parish Office, St Peter's Church, The Cross, Chester CH1 2LA (07794654212; email: jholfordcharity@gmail.com; website: www.johnholfordcharity.org)

CC Number: 223046

Eligibility

People in need who live in the parishes of Astbury, Clutton, Congleton and Middlewich.

Due to local authority changes the list of eligible parishes has been extended and now also includes: Alsager, Brereton, Church Lawton, Eaton, Goostrey, Holmes Chapel, Hulme Walfield, Mow Cop, North Rode, Odd Rode, Rode Heath, Sandbach, Smallwood, Swettenham and Wheelock.

Types of grants

One-off and recurrent grants for a variety of needs, ranging from £100 to £2,500.

Annual grant total

At the time of writing (September 2014) the latest financial information available was from 2012. In 2012 the charity had an income of £65,000 and an expenditure of 63,000. Full accounts could not be viewed, but in the past five years grants to individuals and organisations totalled £23,000 on average. We estimate that about £11,000 is given to individuals.

Exclusions

According to our research, grants are not given for education or medical treatment.

Applications

Applications can be made online on the charity's website. Alternatively an application form can be downloaded from the website or requested from the correspondent. They can be submitted by the individual or through a social worker, carer, Citizens Advice, other welfare agency or also a relative. Two letters of support are required. Requests are considered on a regular basis.

Other information

Organisations are also supported.

The Ursula Keyes Trust

£37,000 (60 grants)

Correspondent: c/o Dot Lawless, Administrator, Baker Tilly, The Steam Mill Business Centre, Steam Mill Street, Chester CH3 5AN (01244 505100; fax: 01244 505101; website: www.ursula-keyes-trust.org.uk)

CC Number: 517200

Eligibility

People in need, especially those with a medical condition, who live in the area administered by Chester District Council and in particular those within the boundaries of the former City of Chester and the adjoining parishes of Great Boughton and Upton.

Types of grants

One-off grants towards, for example, washing machines for families in need or computers for children with disabilities.

Annual grant total

In 2012 the trust had assets of £5 million and had an income of £314,000. Grants to 60 individuals totalled £37,000.

A further £131,000 was given in grants to organisations.

At the time of writing (August 2014) this was the most recent financial information available for the trust.

Exclusions

No grants to repay debts or loans or to reimburse expenditure already incurred.

Applications

In writing to the correspondent. A summary form is available to download from the website and should be submitted along with your application. Applications must be supported by a social worker, a doctor (if relevant) or another professional or welfare agency.

Applications are usually considered at the end of January, April, July and October and should be received at least four weeks in advance to be certain of consideration at any particular meeting.

Wilmslow Aid Trust

£500

Correspondent: Dr Iain Duncan, Trustee, 41 Stanneylands Road, Wilmslow, Cheshire SK9 4ER (01625 533384)

CC Number: 253340

Eligibility

People in need who live in Wilmslow and the surrounding neighbourhood, particularly those who suffer from ill-health or disability.

Types of grants

One-off grants are given according to need. Our research suggests that support can be provided for items, such as replacement beds and bedding after a house fire, fridge/freezers for single parents, removal costs due to bankruptcy, heating system repairs, furniture, clothing, decorating materials and so on.

Annual grant total

In 2012/13 the trust had an income of £1,600 and an expenditure of £1,200. We estimate the annual total of grants to individuals to be around £500.

Applications

In writing to the correspondent. Applications should be submitted through a welfare agency, church, social worker or Citizens Advice. They need to include the individual's address, income and full details and purpose of the requested assistance.

Other information

The trust also gives grants to organisations.

Chester

Chester Municipal Charities

£40,000

Correspondent: John Catherall, Administrator, PO Box 360, Tarporley CW6 6AZ (01829 759416; email: info@chestermunicipalcharities.org)

CC Number: 1077806

Eligibility

Residents of Chester who are in need due to age, ill health, disability or financial hardship.

Types of grants

Mainly one-off grants for relief-in-need.

Annual grant total

In 2012 the charity had assets of £10 million and an income of £426,000. Grants to both organisations and individuals totalled £159,000. Grants for welfare purposes usually total around £40,000 each year.

These were the latest accounts available at the time of writing (July 2014).

Applications

On a form available from the correspondent.

Other information

The charity also manages almshouses.

The Chester Parochial Charity

£14,900

Correspondent: Kerris Owen, Clerk, Parish Office, St Peter's Church, The Cross, Chester CH1 2LA (07794 654212; email: cprncharity@gmail.com)

CC Number: 1001314

Eligibility

People in need who live in the city of Chester.

Types of grants

One-off grants, usually ranging from £50 to £1,000, are given for furniture, washing machines, cookers, electrical items, clothing, school uniform, carpets, and so on. A supermarket vouchers scheme is also available to help low-income families, mainly over the Christmas period.

Annual grant total

In 2012/13 the charity had an income of £34,000 and a total expenditure of £24,000. At the time of writing (August 2014) the charity's accounts were not yet available to view on the Charity Commission; however, the charity's record tells us that trustees awarded grants to the sum of £14,900.

Applications

On a form available from the correspondent. Applications can be made directly by the individual, through a recognised referral agency or through a third party such as a family member. All applicants will be visited by a trustee who will then report back to the subcommittee for a final decision. Applications are considered at any time.

Congleton

The Congleton Town Trust

£5,000

Correspondent: Joanne Money, Clerk, c/o Congleton Town Hall, High Street, Congleton CW12 1BN (01260 291156; email: info@congletontowntrust.co.uk; website: www.congletontowntrust.co.uk)

CC Number: 1051122

Eligibility

People in need who live in the town of Congleton (this does not include the other two towns which have constituted the borough of Congleton since 1975).

Types of grants

Grants in the range of £200 to £3,000 are given to individuals in need or to organisations that provide relief, services or facilities to those in need.

Annual grant total

In 2012 the trust had an income of £24,000 and a total expenditure of £20,000. These were the latest accounts available at the time of writing (July 2014). We estimate grants to individuals for social welfare purposes totalled around £5,000.

Applications

On a form available from the correspondent or downloaded from the trust's website, to be submitted directly by the individual or a family member. Applications are considered quarterly, on the second Monday in March, June, September and December.

Other information

The trust also administers several smaller trusts and makes grants to organisations.

Frodsham

Frodsham Nursing Fund

£3,200

Correspondent: Joan Pollen, Trustee, 22 Fluin Lane, Frodsham WA6 7QH (01928 731043; email: andrewfaraday@hotmail.com)

CC Number: 503246

Eligibility

People in need who are sick, convalescent or living with disabilities and are resident in the town of Frodsham.

Types of grants

One-off grants according to need. Past grants have been given for items such as bedding, clothing, medical aids, heating and other domestic appliances. Temporary relief may also be provided to those caring for somebody who is sick or disabled.

Annual grant total

In 2013/14 the fund had an income of £3,000 and a total expenditure of £3,500. We estimate that social welfare assistance for individuals totalled around £3,200; however, the fund's expenditure tends to fluctuate widely from year to year.

Applications

In writing to the correspondent, either directly by the individual or on their behalf by a doctor, nurse or social worker. Applicants should briefly state their circumstances and what help is being sought.

Macclesfield

Macclesfield and District Relief-in-Sickness Charity

£5,000

Correspondent: Peter Womby, Trustee, Oak Crescent, Leek Old Road, Sutton, Macclesfield, Cheshire SK11 0JA (01260 252220)

CC Number: 501631

Eligibility

People who are sick, convalescent, disabled or infirm who live in Macclesfield, the rural district of Macclesfield and the urban district of Bollington.

Types of grants

One-off grants only for necessary items such as washing machines, telephone installation, removals or specialist wheelchairs and especially for health-related items that would improve the quality of the applicant's situation.

Annual grant total

In 2012/13, the charity had an income of £6,600 and a total expenditure of £5,000.

Applications

Applications must be made through a local social services office, doctor's surgery or other welfare agencies and they should verify the need of the applicant.

Mottram St Andrew

United Charities

£200

Correspondent: Ronald Taylor, Trustee, The Farmhouse, Moss Lane, Mottram St Andrew, Macclesfield, Cheshire SK10 4QZ (01625 585039)

CC Number: 217145

Eligibility

People in need who live in the parish of Mottram St Andrew.

Types of grants

On average 35 one-off grants ranging from £35 to £250 reviewed annually; recurrent grants according to need. Recent grants have been given in cases of illness and death, for travel to and from hospital and Christmas bonuses to pensioners.

Annual grant total

In 2013, the charity had an income of £2,900 and a total expenditure of £600. We estimate that the total amount of grants awarded to individuals was approximately £200. The charity also provides services for the advancement of health or saving lives.

Applications

In writing to the correspondent or to individual trustees. Applications can be submitted directly by the individual or through a social worker, Citizens Advice, other welfare agency or other third party. They are considered in November and should be received by early November.

Widnes

The Knight's House Charity

£150

Correspondent: Jennifer Turton, Administrator, Halton Borough Council, Municipal Building, Kingsway, Widnes, Cheshire WA8 7QF (0303 333 4300)

CC Number: 218886

Eligibility

People in need who live in Widnes.

Types of grants

One-off grants for kitchen appliances, clothing, carpets, and decorating materials. Second-hand furniture and beds may also be provided through an informal partnership with a separate organisation, Justice and Peace.

Annual grant total

In 2012/13 the charity had an income of £11,000 and an unusually low expenditure of £170. We estimate that grants to individuals totalled £150.

Applications

On a form available from the correspondent.

Other information

The charity also makes grants to organisations.

Wilmslow

The Lindow Workhouse Trust

£2,300

Correspondent: Jacquie Bilsborough, Administrator, 15 Westward Road, Wilmslow SK9 5JY

CC Number: 226023

Eligibility

People in need who live in the ancient parish of Wilmslow.

Types of grants
One-off grants to help with, for example, fuel bills, equipment repairs, property repairs. Any cases of real need are considered.

Annual grant total
In 2013 the charity had an income of £6,000 and a total expenditure of £4,600. We estimate the total amount of grants awarded to individuals for social welfare purposes was around £2,300.

Exclusions
No grants are made towards relief of rates, taxes or other public funds.

Applications
In writing to the correspondent at any time. Applications can be submitted either directly by the individual or a family member, through a third party such as a social worker or teacher, or through an organisation such as Citizens Advice or a school.

Wybunbury

The Wybunbury United Charities

£1,500

Correspondent: Barnabas Pettman, Administrator, 12 Lyndhurst Grove, Stone, Staffordshire ST15 8TP (01785 819677; fax: 01785 819677)

CC Number: 227387

Eligibility
People in need who live in the 18 townships of the ancient parish of Wybunbury as it was in the 1600s and 1700s. The townships are Basford, Batherton, Blakenhall, Bridgemere, Chorlton, Checkley-cum-Wrinehill, Doddington, Hatherton, Hough, Hunsterson, Lea, Rope, Shavington-cum-Gresty, Stapeley, Walgherton, Weston, Willaston and Wybunbury.

Types of grants
The three administering trustees for each township are responsible for distribution of grants. Some make annual payments to individuals in need but funds are also kept in most townships to cover emergency payments for accidents, bereavement or sudden distress.

Annual grant total
The 2012 accounts were the latest available at the time of writing (August 2014).

In 2012, the charity had an income of £5,000 and a total expenditure of £5,500. We estimate that the total amount of grants awarded to individuals was approximately £1,500.

Applications
By direct application to one of three administering trustees.

Other information
The charity also awards grants for educational purposes and to organisations.

Cumbria

Barrow Thornborrow Charity

£4,300

Correspondent: Fred Robinson, Trustee, The Parrock, Stankelt Road, Silverdale, Carnforth LA5 0TW (email: fredrob906@gmail.com)

CC Number: 222168

Eligibility
People who are disabled or sick and live, or were born in, the former county of Westmorland, the former county borough of Barrow, the former rural districts of Sedbergh and North Lonsdale, or the former urban districts of Dalton-in-Furness, Grange and Ulverston.

Types of grants
One-off grants towards items, services or facilities which are calculated to alleviate suffering and assist recovery and are not available from other sources. In previous years grants have been awarded for household equipment, travel expenses in cases of hospitalisation, clothing, computer aids and assistance with essential property repairs.

Annual grant total
In 2013 the charity had an income of £5,000 and a total expenditure of £4,500. We estimate that grants to individuals totalled £4,300.

Applications
In writing to the correspondent including details of the applicant's circumstances. Applications can be submitted through a social worker, Citizens Advice or other welfare agency.

Cumbria Community Foundation

£28,000

Correspondent: The Grants Team, Cumbria Community Foundation, Dovenby Hall, Cockermouth, Cumbria CA13 0PN (01900 825760; fax: 01900 826527; email: enquiries@cumbriafoundation.org; website: www.cumbriafoundation.org)

CC Number: 1075120

Eligibility
People resident in Cumbria. Other restrictions can apply, such as geographical and age-related restrictions, depending on the fund being applied to.

Types of grants
One-off and recurrent grants for various welfare needs, equipment, fuel bills, household adaptations and independent living and homelessness.

Annual grant total
In 2012/13 the foundation made 97 grants to individuals totalling £55,000. We have estimated that grants to individuals for social welfare purposes to be around £28,000.

Applications
The foundation administers numerous funds that give grants to individuals, they have differing eligibility criteria and application forms. Applicants should check the website for full details of each scheme, and how to apply.

Other information
The trust administers funds for both individuals and organisations, some of which may open and close regularly. In this accounting year, total grants to organisations was in the region of £2 million.

The Cumbria Constabulary Benevolent Fund

£8,000

Correspondent: Federation Representative, Cumbria Constabulary Police Headquarters, 1 The Green, Carleton Hall, Penrith, Cumbria CA10 2AU (01768 217073; fax: 01708 217425)

CC Number: 505994

Eligibility
Members and former members of the Cumbria Constabulary in need, and their widows and dependents.

Types of grants
One-off cash grants ranging from £250 to £750, usually for the purchase of medical equipment.

Annual grant total
The 2012 accounts were the latest available at the time of writing (August 2014).

In 2012, the fund had an income of £185,000 and a total expenditure of £15,000. We estimate that the total amount of grants awarded to individuals was approximately £8,000. The fund also awards grants to organisations.

Applications
In writing to the correspondent directly by the individual or family member. Applications are considered within 14 days.

The Jane Fisher Trust

£3,800

Correspondent: Steven Marsden, Secretary, Livingstons Solicitors, 9 Benson Street, Ulverston, Cumbria LA12 7AU (01229 585555; fax: 01229 584950; email: s.paling@livingstons.co.uk)

CC Number: 225401

Eligibility
People in need over 50 and people who are disabled, who have lived in the townships of Ulverston and Osmotherley or the parish of Pennington for at least 20 years.

Types of grants
Small monthly payments. No lump sum grants have been made for many years.

Annual grant total
In 2012/13 the trust had an income of £2,600 and a total expenditure of £4,000. We estimate that grants to individuals totalled £3,800.

Applications
On a form available from the correspondent. Applications are considered when they are received. They must include details of income, capital, age, disabilities, marital status and how long the applicant has lived in the area.

Lakeland Disability Support

£6,000

Correspondent: Brenda Robinson, Trust Secretary, 46 Victoria Road North, Windermere, Cumbria LA23 2DS (01539 442800)

CC Number: 1102609

Eligibility
People with physical disabilities who live in South Lakeland, Cumbria.

Types of grants
Grants ranging from £200 to £5,000 towards, for example, the cost of respite care, garden access, special education, or equipment such as electric scooters, special chairs or computers.

Annual grant total
In 2013 the charity had an income of £45,000 and a total expenditure of £24,000. Grants to individuals totalled £6,000, with a further £16,600 awarded to local organisations.

Exclusions
No grants for long-term care provision.

Applications
On a form available from the correspondent. Applications may be made by the individual or a third party and should be accompanied by a reference from a carer, doctor or social worker. Applications are considered quarterly in March, June, September and December. Successful applicants should wait for 12 months before reapplying.

Ambleside

The Ambleside Welfare Charity

£23,000

Correspondent: Michael Johnson, Clerk to the trustees, 11 The Green, Bolton-le-Sands, Carnforth LA5 8FD (01539 431656; email: lakesparish@fsmail.net)

CC Number: 214759

Eligibility
People in need who live in the parish of Ambleside, especially those who are ill.

Types of grants
One-off and recurrent grants according to need. Help is also given to local relatives for hospital visits.

Annual grant total
In 2013 the charity had an income of £51,000 and a total expenditure of £33,000. Welfare donations amounted to £23,000.

Applications
In writing to the correspondent.

Agnes Backhouse Annuity Fund

£15,000

Correspondent: James Hamilton, Trustee, Temple Heelis Solicitors, 1 Kent View, Kendal, Cumbria LA9 4DZ (01539 723757)

CC Number: 224960

Eligibility
Unmarried women (including widows) aged over 50 who live in the parish of Ambleside.

Types of grants
Recurrent grants, usually of around £50.

Annual grant total
In 2012 the fund had an income of £22,000 and a total expenditure of £15,500. We estimate that annuities totalled £15,000.

At the time of writing (August 2014) this was the most recent financial information available for the fund.

Applications
In writing to the correspondent.

Carlisle

Carlisle Sick Poor Fund

£6,100

Correspondent: Lynne Rowley, Administrator, 15 Fisher Street, Carlisle, Cumbria CA3 8RW (01228 674507)

CC Number: 223124

Eligibility
People living in Carlisle and its neighbourhood who are in financial hardship due to ill health.

Types of grants
One-off grants of up to £200 are given towards bedding, food, fuel, medical aids and equipment, convalescence, holidays and home help.

Annual grant total
At the time of writing (August 2014) the latest financial information available was from 2012. In 2012 the fund had an income of £8,500 and an expenditure of £12,400. We have estimated the annual total of grants to individuals to be around £6,100.

Applications
Application forms are available from the correspondent.

Other information
Support is also given to local organisations providing care and relief to people who are sick and in need.

Cockermouth

The Cockermouth Relief-in-Need Charity

£100

Correspondent: Revd Wendy Sanders, Trustee, Parish Administration, Christ Church Rooms, South Street, Cockermouth, Cumbria CA13 9RU (01900 829926)

CC Number: 221297

Eligibility
People in need who live in Cockermouth.

Types of grants
One-off grants typically in the range of £25 to £35.

Annual grant total

In 2012 the charity had an income of £2,000 and a total expenditure of £200. This was the latest financial information available at the time of writing. We estimate that social welfare grants to individuals totalled £100. Funding is also given to organisations.

Applications

In writing to the correspondent. Applications can be made directly by the individual or family member.

Crosby Ravensworth

The Crosby Ravensworth Relief-in-Need Charities

£2,200

Correspondent: George Bowness, Trustee, Ravenseat, Crosby Ravensworth, Penrith, Cumbria CA10 3JB (01931 715382; email: gordonbowness@aol.com)

CC Number: 232598

Eligibility

People in need who have lived in the ancient parish of Crosby Ravensworth for at least 12 months. Preference is given to older people.

Types of grants

One-off and recurrent grants. Grants include coal vouchers, usually of around £30, to senior citizens and a basket of fruit (or other gift) to people who have been in hospital. Grants can also be given to local students entering university if they have been educated in the parish.

Annual grant total

In 2012 the charities had an income of £13,600 and a total expenditure of £8,800. We estimate that social welfare grants to individuals totalled £2,200. Grants are also awarded to individuals for educational and training purposes and to organisations.

At the time of writing (August 2014) this was the most recent financial information available for the charities.

Applications

In writing to the correspondent; to be submitted directly by the individual including details of the applicant's financial situation. Applications are normally considered in February, May and October.

Kirkby Lonsdale

The Kirkby Lonsdale Relief-in-Need Charity

£1,000

Correspondent: Mary Quinn, Trustee, 19 Fairgarth Drive, Kirkby Lonsdale, Carnforth, Lancashire LA6 2DT (01524 271258)

CC Number: 224872

Eligibility

People in need who live in the parish of Kirkby Lonsdale.

Types of grants

One-off grants of £30, usually given just before Christmas.

Annual grant total

Grants usually total around £1,000.

Applications

In writing to the correspondent directly by the individual, or by a third party on his or her behalf. Applications are considered in early December.

Workington

The Bowness Trust

£500

Correspondent: Richard Atkinson, Trustee, Milburns Solicitors, Oxford House, 19 Oxford Street, Workington, Cumbria CA14 2AW (01900 67363; fax: 01900 65552)

CC Number: 502323

Eligibility

People in need who live in Workington and live at home (not in institutions).

Annual grant total

In 2012/13 the trust had an income of £7,000 and a total expenditure of £800. We estimate that the total amount of grants awarded to individuals was £500.

Applications

In writing to the correspondent.

Greater Manchester

J. T. Blair's Charity

£16,500

Correspondent: Anne Hosker, Director of Finance, Gaddum Centre, Gaddum House, 6 Great Jackson Street, Manchester M15 4AX (01618 346069; website: www.gaddumcentre.co.uk)

CC Number: 221248

Eligibility

People over 65 who live in Manchester and Salford and are in need.

Types of grants

Weekly pensions of up to £10 are paid at four-weekly intervals.

Annual grant total

In 2012/13 the charity had an income of £17,100 and a total expenditure of £16,700. We estimate that grants to individuals totalled £16,500.

Applications

On a form available from the correspondent, to be submitted by a social worker or other professional person. The trustees meet three or four times a year. Applicants should contact the charity for specific deadlines. Those in receipt of a pension are visited at least once a year.

Lawrence Brownlow Charity (The Brownlow Trust)

£1,500

Correspondent: Edward Hill, Trustee, 24 Exford Drive, Bolton BL2 6TB (01204 524823; email: brownlow.trust@ntlworld.com)

CC Number: 223414

Eligibility

People in need who live in the ancient townships of Darcy Lever, Haulgh and Tonge, in Bolton. Support is mainly given to the elderly, the infirm and children/young people.

Types of grants

Our research indicates that one-off grants can be given for a variety of purposes, including household bills, living costs and help at home.

Annual grant total

In 2012/13 the charity had an income of £3,600 and an expenditure of £1,700. We have estimated the annual total of grants to individuals to be around £1,500.

Applications

In writing to the correspondent. Applications can be submitted either directly by the individual or through a third party, for example, a social worker, Citizens Advice or another welfare agency. Grants are usually considered in November.

The Community Foundation for Greater Manchester (working name Forever Manchester)

£3,700

Correspondent: The Awards Team, 2nd Floor, 8 Hewitt Street, Manchester M15 4GB (01612 140940; email: enquiries@communityfoundation.co.uk; website: forevermanchester.com/)

CC Number: 1017504

Eligibility

People in need who live in Greater Manchester.

Types of grants

Grants are usually one-off. Funds for individuals include the Stockport Fund, which supports individuals that contribute positively to the quality of life of people in Stockport, and the Seed Fund, which supports individuals who have community ideas.

Annual grant total

Grants totalling £7,400 were made to individuals in 2012/13 for welfare and education. Grants to individuals for welfare purposes totalled approximately £3,700.

Applications

Visit the foundation's website or contact the foundation for details of grant funds that are appropriate for individuals to apply for.

Other information

The Community Foundation for Greater Manchester manages a portfolio of grants for a variety of purposes which are mostly for organisations, but there are a select few which are for individuals. Funds tend to open and close throughout the year as well as new ones being added, and others being spent out. Check the website for information on current schemes.

The Manchester District Nursing Institution Fund

£18,000

Correspondent: Anne Hosker, Director of Finance, Gaddum Centre, Gaddum House, 6 Great Jackson Street, Manchester M15 4AX (01618 346069; email: info@gaddumcentre.co.uk; website: www.gaddumcentre.co.uk)

CC Number: 235916

Eligibility

People with health related needs in the cities of Manchester and Salford and the borough of Trafford.

Types of grants

One-off grants. It is important that the request is directly related to the health issue of the applicant and not to a general condition of poverty.

Annual grant total

In 2013 the fund had an income of £25,000 and a total expenditure of £29,000. In previous years grants have also been made to voluntary organisations as well as to individuals. We estimate that grants to individuals totalled £18,000.

Exclusions

No grants for funeral expenses, taxes, bills, debts or fines.

Applications

On a form available from the correspondent which must be completed by a sponsor from a recognised social and/or health agency. The trustees meet monthly and the deadline for any meeting is the first Wednesday of the month.

The Mellor Fund

£2,000

Correspondent: Gillian Critchley, Trustee, 95 Salisbury Road, Radcliffe, Manchester M26 4NQ (01617 668086)

CC Number: 230013

Eligibility

People who are sick or in need and live in Radcliffe, Whitefield and Unsworth.

Types of grants

One-off grants towards fuel, food and clothing, domestic necessities, medical needs, recuperative breaks and so on. Recurrent grants are generally not given.

Annual grant total

In 2013 the fund had an income of £5,300 and a total expenditure of £2,900. We estimate that around £2,000 was made in grants to individuals for social welfare purposes.

Applications

In writing to the correspondent. Applications can be submitted directly by the individual or through a social worker, Citizens Advice, other welfare agency or a relative, and should include brief details of need, resources, income and commitments. Applications are considered when received.

The Pratt Charity

£500

Correspondent: Anne Hosker, Director of Finance, Gaddum Centre, Gaddum House, 6 Great Jackson Street, Manchester M15 4AX (01618 346069; email: info@gaddumcentre.co.uk; website: www.gaddumcentre.co.uk)

CC Number: 507162–1

Eligibility

Women over 60 who live in or near Manchester and have done so for a period of not less than five years.

Types of grants

Grants are given towards education, health and relief of poverty, distress and sickness.

Annual grant total

The Gaddum Centre administers and considers applications made to the Pratt Charity. The accounts of the Pratt Charity were not available because they are not consolidated into Gaddum Centre's accounts, as the trustees consider that the amounts in the accounts are not significant.

We estimate that around £500 was made in grants to individuals for social welfare purposes.

Applications

In writing to the correspondent via a social worker.

Other information

The charity is administered by the Gaddum Charity.

Bolton

The Bolton and District Nursing Association

£1,000

Correspondent: David Wrennall, Trustee, Bolton Guild of Help (Inc.), Scott House, 27 Silverwell Street, Bolton BL1 1PP (01204 524858)

CC Number: 250153

Eligibility

People who are sick, convalescing, have disabilities or who are infirm and live in the area of Bolton Metropolitan Borough Council.

Types of grants

One-off grants for items and services, such as the provision of medical equipment, disability equipment and convalescence.

Annual grant total

In 2013 the trust had an income of £3,200 and a total expenditure of £1,800. We estimate that around £1,000 was made in grants to individuals for social welfare purposes.

Applications

On a form available from the correspondent. Applications can be submitted directly by the individual or through a third party such as a social worker, health visitor or welfare agency. Initial telephone enquiries are encouraged to establish eligibility.

The Bolton Poor Protection Society

£1,000

Correspondent: The Trustees, Bolton Guild of Help, Scott House, 27 Silverwell Street, Bolton BL1 1PP

CC Number: 223099

Eligibility

People in need who live in the former county borough of Bolton.

Types of grants

One-off grants for emergencies and all kinds of need, ranging from £25 to £50.

Annual grant total

In 2013 the charity had an income of £1,300 and a total expenditure of £1,500. We estimate that around £1,000 was made in grants to individuals for social welfare purposes.

Applications

Initial telephone enquiries are encouraged to establish eligibility. Application forms are sent out thereafter.

The Louisa Alice Kay Fund

£40,000 (205 grants)

Correspondent: Tracey Wallace, Secretary, Bolton Guild of Help (Inc.), Scott House, 27 Silverwell Street, Bolton BL1 1PP

CC Number: 224760–1

Eligibility

People in need who live in Bolton.

Types of grants

One-off grants for emergencies and relief-in-need, mostly for replacing household equipment and furniture.

Annual grant total

In 2013 grants were made to 205 individuals totalling £40,000 and were distributed in the following areas:

Washing machines	£15,000
Cookers	£12,300
Fridges/freezers	£6,500
Beds/furniture	£5,000
Other assistance	£1,500

Applications

On a form available from the correspondent. Applications can be submitted either directly by the individual or a family member, through a third party such as a social worker, or through an organisation such as Citizens Advice or other welfare agency. Applicants will sometimes be interviewed before a grant is awarded.

Other information

The fund is the main subsidiary of the Bolton Guild of Help Incorporated.

Bury

The Bury Relief-in-Sickness Fund

£1,500

Correspondent: Gill Warburton, Trustee, The Royal Bank of Scotland plc, PO Box 26, 40 The Rock, Bury, Lancashire BL9 0NX (01617 978040)

CC Number: 256397

Eligibility

People living in the metropolitan borough of Bury who are in poor health, convalescent or have disabilities.

Types of grants

One-off grants towards convalescence, medical equipment and necessities in the home which are not available from other sources.

Annual grant total

In 2013, the fund had an income of £3,500 and a total expenditure of £1,700. We estimate that the total amount of grants awarded to individuals was £1,500.

Applications

In writing to the correspondent.

Denton

The Denton Relief-in-Sickness Charity

£1,100

Correspondent: Mary Goodliffe, Trustee, Apartment 44, Enfield Court, Garside Street, Hyde SK14 5GU (01613 660586)

CC Number: 223597

Eligibility

People in need who are sick, convalescent, infirm or have disabilities and live in the parish of Denton (Tameside).

Types of grants

One-off grants ranging from £250 to £500. Awards are given to address medical needs not covered by the NHS or other statutory sources.

Annual grant total

In 2013 the charity had an income of £11,100, which is considerably higher than in the previous years, and an expenditure of £2,400. We estimate that grants to individuals totalled around £1,100.

Applications

In writing to the correspondent. Applications can be submitted directly by the individual or through a third party, for example, Citizens Advice or a social worker.

Other information

Grants are given to individuals and organisations.

Golborne

The Golborne Charities – Charity of William Leadbetter

£6,000

Correspondent: Paul Gleave, Administrator, 56 Nook Lane, Golborne, Warrington WA3 3JQ (01942 727627; email: p.gleave56@hotmail.com)

CC Number: 221088

Eligibility

People in need who live in the parish of Golborne as it was in 1892.

Types of grants

One-off grants between £50 and £80 but occasionally up to £250. Grants are usually cash payments, but are occasionally in kind, for example for food, bedding, fireguards, clothing and shoes. Also help with hospital travel and necessary holidays.

Annual grant total

In 2013/14 the charity had an income of £6,500 and a total expenditure of £8,000. We estimate that grants to individuals for educational purposes were around £2,000 and for social welfare purposes around £6,000.

Exclusions

Loans or grants for payments of rates are not made. Grants are not repeated in less than two years.

Applications

In writing to the correspondent through a third party such as a social worker or a teacher, or via a trustee. Applications are considered at three-monthly intervals. Grant recipients tend to be known by at least one trustee.

Manchester

The Crosland Fund

£10,200

Correspondent: John Atherden, Administrator, Manchester Cathedral, Victoria Street, Manchester M3 1SX (01618 332220)

CC Number: 242838

Eligibility

People affected by hardship who live in the City of Manchester.

Types of grants

One-off grants are given quarterly, usually to the sum of £40 to £50. Grants are typically given for basic necessities such as clothing, food, bedding, furniture, repairs and household materials. Children's Christmas presents may also be given.

Annual grant total

In 2012/13 the fund had an income of £6,900 and a total expenditure of £10,400. We estimate that welfare grants to individuals totalled £10,200.

Applications

In writing to the correspondent. Applications must be submitted through a recognised organisation, for example, a social worker, Citizens Advice or other welfare agency. They are considered in February, May, August and November.

The Dr Garrett Memorial Trust

£3,900

Correspondent: Anne Hosker, Director of Finance, Gaddum Centre, Gaddum House, 6 Great Jackson Street, Manchester M15 4AX (01618 346069; email: info@gaddumcentre.co.uk; website: www.gaddumcentre.co.uk)

CC Number: 1010844

Eligibility

Families or groups in need who live in Manchester.

Types of grants

Grants are given towards the cost of convalescence or holidays for individual families and groups.

Annual grant total

In 2012/13 the trust had an income of £10,900 and a total expenditure of £8,000. We estimate that grants to individuals totalled £3,900, with funding also awarded to local organisations.

Exclusions

Applicants should not have had a funded holiday during the past three years.

Applications

On a form available from the correspondent which should be completed by a sponsor from a recognised social or health agency. Applications must be submitted by the end of April each year.

Other information

The trust also provides information and advice on a range of social and health care issues.

The Manchester Relief-in-Need Charity and Manchester Children's Relief-in-Need Charity

£42,000

Correspondent: Anne Hosker, Director of Finance, Gaddum Centre, Gaddum House, 6 Great Jackson Street, Manchester M15 4AX (01618 346069; email: info@gaddumcentre.co.uk; website: www.gaddumcentre.co.uk)

CC Number: 224271 and 249657

Eligibility

People in need who live in the city of Manchester and are over 25 (Relief-in-Need) or under 25 (Children's Relief-in-Need).

Types of grants

One-off grants for domestic appliances, furniture, clothing, heating and fuel bills, and other general necessities. Cheques are made out to the supplier of the goods or services.

Annual grant total

In 2012/13 the charities had a combined income of £82,000. Welfare grants to individuals totalled £42,000; Manchester Relief-in-Need awarded 207 grants amounting to £33,000 and the Manchester Children's Relief-in-Need an estimated £9,000.

Exclusions

Debts are very rarely paid and council tax and rent debts are never met. Normally an individual may only receive one grant in any 12 month period.

Applications

On a form available from the correspondent which should be completed by a sponsor from a recognised social or health related agency. The trustees meet during the last week of every month. Applications must be received by the 15th of the month.

Other information

Grants are also made to organisations.

New Mills

John Mackie Memorial Ladies' Home

£4,400

Correspondent: David Wellens, Trustee, Axholme, Woodbourne Road, New Mills, High Peak, Derbyshire SK22 3JX (01663 742246; email: dhw111@hotmail.com)

CC Number: 215726

Eligibility

Widows, unmarried women and divorcees, who are members of the Church of England, are over 50 and are in need. Applicants must have a connection with the parish of New Mills.

Types of grants

Christmas gifts in the region of £60 to around 80 individuals. Applicants will not receive help if they re-marry.

Annual grant total

In 2013 the trust had an income of £3,700 and a total expenditure of £4,600. We estimate that grants to individuals totalled £4,400.

Applications

In writing to the correspondent, with (i) evidence of the birth, marriage and death of the applicant's husband, (ii) references from three house owners, confirming her character, respectability and needy circumstances, (iii) proof that she has a small income and (iv) evidence that she is a member of the Church of England. Applications can be submitted either directly by the individual or through a third party. They are considered throughout the year.

Oldham

The Sarah Lees Relief Trust

£3,500

Correspondent: Catherine Sykes, Trustee, 10 Chew Brook Drive, Greenfield, Oldham OL3 7PD (01457 876606)

CC Number: 514240

Eligibility

People living in Oldham who are sick, convalescent, infirm, or have disabilities.

Types of grants

One-off grants up to £500 and gifts in kind.

Annual grant total

In 2012/13 the trust had an income of £4,500 and a total expenditure of £3,600. We estimate that grants to individuals totalled £3,500

Exclusions

No grants for items, services or facilities that are readily available from other sources.

Applications

In writing to the correspondent through a social worker or other recognised welfare agency. Trustees meet three times a year, but urgent requests will be considered in between meetings.

Oldham United Charity

£1,000

Correspondent: Phil Higgins, Administrator, c/o Oldham M. B. Council, Level 14, Civic Centre, West Street, Oldham OL1 1UT (01617 703000; email: phil.higgins1234@outlook.com)

CC Number: 221095

Eligibility

People in need who live in the metropolitan borough of Oldham.

Types of grants

One-off grants according to need. Recent grants have been mainly for medical needs, for example, wheelchairs and washing machines for people who are incontinent. Some grants are given to students towards educational expenses.

Annual grant total

In 2012/13, the charity had an income of £3,400 and a total expenditure of £3,900. We estimate that the total amount of grants awarded to individuals was approximately £1,000. The charity also awards grants for educational purposes and to organisations.

Applications

In writing to the correspondent. Grants are usually considered quarterly.

Rochdale

The Norman Barnes Fund

£4,500

Correspondent: Rochdale MBC, Finance Services, Floor 2, Number One Riverside, Smith Street, Rochdale OL16 1XU (01706 924707; email: jim.murphy@rochdale.gov.uk; website: www.rochdale.gov.uk/the_council/charitable_trusts.aspx)

CC Number: 511646

Eligibility

People over the age of 60 who live in Rochdale, Castleton, Norden or Bamford.

Types of grants

One-off grants according to need. There is no limit to the number of applications or the amount that can be applied for.

Annual grant total

In 2012/13 the fund had an income of £12,600 and a total expenditure of £9,200. We estimate that grants to individuals totalled £4,500, with funding also awarded to local organisations.

Exclusions

No payments for tax, council tax, or other statutory payments, except where relief or assistance is already provided out of public funds.

Applications

On an application form available to download from the Rochdale council website or by contacting the correspondent. It is recommended that applicants include a supporting comment from a doctor, social worker, Age UK representative or some other relevant professional. Requests for items or services should include written quotations. Standard items like fridges or cookers will be ordered directly by the trustees. For grants greater than £250, the support of an officer of Rochdale Council's Social Services Department is required.

Heywood Relief-in-Need Trust Fund

£3,800

Correspondent: Heywood Phoenix Trusts, Heywood Township Office, The Phoenix Centre, Church Street, Heywood, Lancs OL10 1LR (fax: 01706 924185; email: phoenixtrusts@hotmail.co.uk)

CC Number: 517114

Eligibility

People in need who live in the former municipal borough of Heywood. In exceptional cases applications may be considered from those who are only temporarily located within the borough.

Types of grants

One-off grants usually ranging from £50 to £400. Grants have been given to help with fuel arrears, clothing and furniture.

Annual grant total

In 2012/13 the fund had an income of £5,500 and a total expenditure of £3,900. We estimate that grants to individuals totalled £3,800.

Exclusions

No grants to pay council tax, public funds or other taxes. No repeat grants.

Applications

In writing to the correspondent. Applications should be supported by a social worker, health visitor or similar professional.

The Middleton Relief-in-Need Charity

£900

Correspondent: The Administrator, c/o Township Management Service, Middleton Public Library, Long Street, Middleton, Manchester M24 6DU (email: middletonreliefinneed@hotmail.com)

CC Number: 200079

Eligibility

People in need who live in the former borough of Middleton. In exceptional circumstances people who are only temporarily resident in the area may be considered.

Types of grants

One-off grants (typically £200) for emergencies, for example, travel expenses to visit people in hospital or similar institutions, fuel bills, television licence fees, arrears, holidays for disadvantaged families and general household necessities.

Annual grant total
In 2012/13 the charity had an income of £1,600 and a total expenditure of £1,900. We estimate that social welfare grants to individuals totalled £900, with funding also awarded to organisations.

Exclusions
No grants for rates, taxes or other public funds. No repeat grants.

Applications
On an application form available from the correspondent. Made by individual application or through social workers, health visitors, victim support schemes and Citizens Advice. All applications must include supporting information from, for example, a social worker, health visitor or other professional.

The Nurses' Benefit Fund

£600

Correspondent: Susan Stoney, Clerk, The Old Parsonage, 2 St Mary's Gate, Rochdale OL16 1AP (01706 644187; email: law@jbhs.co.uk)

CC Number: 222651

Eligibility
Nurses or any other person formerly in the employment of Rochdale District Nursing Association and any retired or district nurse living in the borough of Rochdale.

Types of grants
Recurrent grants paid either once or twice a year.

Annual grant total
Grants average around £1,100 a year. Grants are given to both individuals and organisations.

Applications
In writing to the correspondent.

The Rochdale Fund for Relief-in-Sickness

£13,500

Correspondent: Susan Stoney, Clerk, The Old Parsonage, 2 St Mary's Gate, Rochdale OL16 1AP (01706 644187; email: law@jbhs.co.uk; website: www.rochdalefund.org.uk)

CC Number: 222652

Eligibility
People living in the borough of Rochdale (including Wardle, Littleborough, Middleton, Heywood, Norden, Birtle, Milnrow and Newhey) who are in poor health, convalescent or who have disabilities. Help may also be given to those whose physical or mental health is likely to be impaired by poverty, deprivation or other adversity.

Types of grants
One-off grants according to need. The trustees will consider any requests for items which will make life more comfortable or productive for the individual. For example, recent grants have been given towards wheelchairs, hoists, IT equipment, house adaptations, special leisure equipment, medical aids, washing machines, cookers, clothing, beds, bedding and respite breaks.

Annual grant total
In 2012/13 the fund had assets of £1.3 million and an income of £50,000. Grants were made totalling about £30,000, of which £17,300 was awarded to organisations and £13,500 was given to specific families.

Exclusions
Grants are not given for the payment of debts, including utility bills, council tax and Inland Revenue payments or to help with hardship not directly related to, or caused as a result of, sickness.

Applications
On a form available from the correspondent or to download from the website. Applications can be made either directly by the individual (if no other route is available) or through a social worker, Citizens Advice, other welfare agency or other third party such as a doctor. Whether completed by the individual or a third party all applications must be supported by a letter from a recognised body such as Social Services, Doctor, etc.

Other information
The fund's website states that they may also make grants to organisations, 'both statutory and voluntary, to assist them in providing equipment, services or facilities which may alleviate the suffering, or promote the recovery of, persons who qualify.'

Rochdale United Charity

£7,400

Correspondent: Saddleworth Parish Council, Civic Hall, Lee Street, Uppermill, Oldham OL3 6AE (01457 876665; website: parishcouncil.saddleworth.org/contact.html)

CC Number: 224461

Eligibility
People in need who live in the ancient parish of Rochdale (the former county borough of Rochdale, Castleton, Wardle, Whitworth, Littleborough, Todmorden and Saddleworth).

Types of grants
One-off grants typically ranging from £50 to £250. Grants have been awarded for the provision of domestic appliances such as fridges and cookers, medical aids and equipment, telephones, televisions or radios for the lonely or housebound and towards the costs of arranging recuperative holidays.

Annual grant total
In 2012/13 the charity had an income of £14,300 and a total expenditure of £15,000. We estimate that grants to individuals totalled £7,400, with local organisations also receiving funding.

Exclusions
No grants for the relief of rates, taxes or other public funds. No recurrent grants.

Applications
On a form available from the correspondent, to be submitted through a social worker, GP, health visitor, Citizens Advice or other welfare agency. Applications are usually considered quarterly.

Salford

The Booth Charities

£1,500 (19 grants)

Correspondent: Jonathan Aldersley, Clerk, c/o Butcher and Barlow LLP, 3 Royal Mews, Gadbrook Park, Northwich, Cheshire CW9 7UD (01606 334309 email: jaldersley@butcher-barlow.co.uk)

CC Number: 221800

Eligibility
People who are retired, over 60, on a basic pension, live in the city of Salford and are in need.

Types of grants
Annual pensions of up to £105 and one-off grants towards TV licences.

Annual grant total
In 2012/13 the charities held assets of £31.8 million and generated an income of £964,000. The charities' main area of activity is providing grants to organisations. In the year they made grants totalling £358,000, of which £1,500 was paid in grants to individuals. 14 individuals received pensions during the year and five received assistance with TV licence fees.

Applications
On a form available from the correspondent. Applications for one-off grants must be made by social services, ministers of religion, doctors and so on.

Distribution meetings are held regularly throughout the year.

City of Salford Relief of Distress Fund

£0

Correspondent: Keith Darragh, Administrator, Salford City Council: Social Services, Crompton House, 100 Chorley Road, Swinton, Manchester M27 6BP (01617 278875; email: Martin.Anglesey@salford.gov.uk)

CC Number: 251658

Eligibility

People in need who live in the city of Salford.

Types of grants

According to our research, one-off grants of up to £250 are available to families and individuals. Higher amounts may be considered depending on the circumstances. Support could be given for clothing, convalescence/holidays, furniture, special equipment for those with special needs, for bedding and so on. Previous grants have also included funds for a memorial to a young person's father, a grant to enable a family to partially equip their home after a fire and a holiday for a family where the mother had terminal cancer.

Annual grant total

In 2013/14 the fund had an income of about £100. No grants were made during the year, however in the past the expenditure have totalled around £1,000.

Exclusions

Grants are not considered where assistance is required to help with the local authority rent or council tax arrears.

Applications

Our research suggests that application forms should be submitted by a city of Salford social worker, who must be prepared to attend a meeting with the trustees to present the case.

Stockport

Sir Ralph Pendlebury's Charity for Orphans

£2,100

Correspondent: Stephen Tattersall, Administrator, Lacy Watson and Co., Carlyle House, 107–109 Wellington Road South, Stockport SK1 3TL

CC Number: 213927

Eligibility

Orphans who have lived, or whose parents have lived, in the borough of Stockport for at least two years and who are in need.

Types of grants

Our research suggests that recurring payments, usually of £5 or £6 a week, plus clothing allowances twice a year are available. Support can also be given for holidays. The main priority for the charity is relief-in-need.

Annual grant total

At the time of writing (August 2014) the latest financial information available was from 2012. In 2012 the charity had an income of £7,800 and a total expenditure of £4,400. We estimate that around £2,100 was awarded in grants for welfare purposes.

Applications

In writing to the correspondent. Applications should be made by a parent/guardian.

Other information

Grants are also made for educational purposes.

Sir Ralph Pendlebury's Charity for the Aged

£4,200

Correspondent: Stephen Tattersall, Administrator, Lacy Watson and Co., Carlyle House, 107–109 Wellington Road South, Stockport, Cheshire SK1 3TL

CC Number: 213928

Eligibility

People above pensionable age who have lived in the borough of Stockport for at least two years and are in necessitous circumstances.

Types of grants

Small grants to elderly people.

Annual grant total

At the time of writing (August 2014) the latest financial information available was from 2012. In 2012 the charity had an income of £7,100 and an expenditure of £8,600. We have estimated the annual total of grants to individuals to be around £4,200.

Applications

In writing to the correspondent.

Other information

Grants may also be made to organisations.

Isle of Man

The Manx Marine Society

£5,000

Correspondent: Capt. R. K. Cringle, 10 Carrick Bay View, Ballagawne Road, Colby, Isle of Man IM9 4DD (01624 838233)

Eligibility

Seafarers, retired or disabled seafarers and their widows, children and dependents, who live on the Isle of Man. Young Manx people under 18 who wish to attend sea school or become a cadet are also eligible.

Types of grants

One-off and recurrent grants of up to £400 according to need.

Annual grant total

About £5,000 a year is awarded to individuals for social welfare purposes.

Applications

On a form available from the correspondent. Applications are considered at any time and can be submitted either by the individual, or through a social worker, Citizens Advice or other welfare agency.

Other information

The trustees also award grants for educational purposes.

Lancashire

The Accrington and District Helping Hands Fund

£4,400

Correspondent: The Secretary, Tithe Cottage, 4 Grindleton Road, West Bradford, Clitheroe BB7 4TE (01200 422062)

CC Number: 222241

Eligibility

People living in the former borough of Accrington, Clayton-le-Moors and Altham, who are in poor health and either supported by benefits or on a low income.

Types of grants

One-off grants usually ranging from £100 to £300 towards the cost of: (i) special foods and medicines, medical comforts, extra bedding, fuel and medical and surgical appliances; (ii) the provision of domestic help; (iii)

convalescence (iv) the provision of mobile physiotherapy service. Grants are usually paid directly to the supplier.

Annual grant total

In 2013 the fund had an income of £14,000 and a total expenditure of £4,600. We estimate that grants to individuals totalled £4,400.

Applications

On a form available from the correspondent submitted either directly by the individual or through a social worker, Citizens Advice or other welfare agency. Applications should include evidence of income and state of health, as well as estimates of what is required.

Baines's Charity

£7,500

Correspondent: Duncan Waddilove, Administrator, 2 The Chase, Normoss Road, Blackpool, Lancashire FY3 0BF (01253 893459)

CC Number: 224135

Eligibility

People in need who live in the ancient townships of Carleton, Hardhorn-cum-Newton, Marton, Poulton-le-Fylde and Thornton.

Types of grants

One-off grants ranging from £100 to £250. 'Each case is discussed on its merits.'

Annual grant total

In 2013 the charity had an income of £17,000 and a total expenditure of £18,000. Grants are made to individuals and organisations for both welfare and educational purposes. We estimate the amount paid in grants to individuals for welfare purposes was £4,000.

Applications

On a form available from the correspondent, either directly by the individual, or through a social worker, Citizens Advice or other welfare agency. Applications are considered upon receipt.

James Bond/Henry Welch Trust

£4,300

Correspondent: Jane Glenton, The Clerk to the Trustees, c/o Democratic Services, Lancaster City Council, Town Hall, Dalton Square, Lancaster LA1 1PJ (01524 582068)

CC Number: 222791

Eligibility

People in need who live in the area covered by Lancaster City Council and have diseases of the chest/lung and early forms of phthisis. Children with disabilities and other special needs are also eligible.

Types of grants

One-off and recurrent grants, typically ranging from £100 to £500, towards, for example, computer equipment, household essentials and holidays.

Annual grant total

In 2012/13 the trust had an income of £9,800 and an expenditure of £8,800. We estimate that grants to individuals totalled £4,300, with funding also awarded to local organisations.

Applications

The trust's home visitor will visit the individual and complete the form. Applications can be submitted at any time.

Daniel's and Houghton's Charity

£15,000

Correspondent: Helen Ryan, Brabners Chaffe Street LLP, 7–8 Chapel Street, Preston PR1 8AN (01772 823921; fax: 01772 201918)

CC Number: 1074762

Eligibility

People in need who live in Lancashire with preference given to those living in Preston, Grimsargh, Broughton, Woodplumpton, Eaves, Catforth, Bartle, Alston and Elston.

Types of grants

One-off and recurrent grants according to need.

Annual grant total

In 2012/13 the charity held assets of £690,000 and had a total income of £27,000. Grants paid during the year totalled £18,000.

Exclusions

No grants are given for items or services where statutory funds are available.

Applications

In writing to the correspondent.

Other information

Grants are also made to organisations.

The Foxton Dispensary Charity

£20,000

Correspondent: Robert Dunn, Clerk, PO Box 227, Lytham St Annes FY8 9BJ (01253 722277; email: clerk@foxtoncharity.co.uk; website: www.foxtoncharity.co.uk)

CC Number: 224312

Eligibility

People in need who are in poor health, convalescent or who have a disability and live in the urban district of Poulton-le-Fylde and the county borough of Blackpool.

Types of grants

One-off grants towards food and other necessities such as household equipment.

Annual grant total

In 2013 the charity had an income of £22,000 and total expenses of £28,000. We estimate grants to be in the region of £20,000.

Applications

On a form available from the correspondent or through the website. Applications should be made via a doctor, healthcare professional or social services department. They are considered on an ongoing basis. All applicants are visited by one of the trustees before a grant is made.

The Goosnargh and Whittingham United Charity

£4,300

Correspondent: John Bretherton, Clerk to the Trustees, Lower Stanalea Farm, Stanalea Lane, Goosnargh, Preston PR3 2EQ (01995 640224)

CC Number: 233744

Eligibility

Older people in need who live in the parishes of Goosnargh, Whittingham and Barton.

Types of grants

One-off and recurrent grants are given according to need.

Annual grant total

In 2013 the charity had an income of £8,000 and a total expenditure of £4,600. We estimate that grants to individuals totalled £4,300.

Applications

In writing to the correspondent, to be submitted directly by the individual or family member.

The Harris Charity

£1,400

Correspondent: David Ingram, Secretary, Richard House, 9 Winckley Square, Preston PR1 3HP (01772 821021; fax: 01772 259441; email: harrischarity@mooreandsmalley.co.uk; website: theharrischarity.co.uk/)

CC Number: 526206

Eligibility

People in need under 25 who live in Lancashire, with a preference for the Preston district.

Types of grants

One-off grants of £100 to £5,000 for electrical goods, travel expenses and disability equipment.

Annual grant total

In 2012/13 the charity had assets of £3.5 million, an income of £181,000 and made grants totalling 53,000, of which £2,800 was awarded to individuals. We estimate that £1,400 of this was for social welfare purposes.

Exclusions

No grants for course fees or to supplement living expenses.

Applications

On an application form downloaded from the website, where guidance and criteria can also be found. Applications are considered during the three months after 31 March and 30 September and must be submitted before these dates either directly by the individual or a third party on behalf of the individual (social worker, Citizens Advice and so on).

Other information

The original charity known as the Harris Orphanage Charity dates back to 1883. A new charitable scheme was established in 1985 following the sale of the Harris Orphanage premises in Garstang Road, Preston. The charity also supports charitable organisations that benefit individuals, recreation and leisure and the training and education of individuals.

Lancashire County Nursing Trust

£11,000

Correspondent: Hadyn Gigg, Trustee, Plumpton House, Great Plumpton, Preston PR4 2NJ (01772 673618; email: hadyngigg@yahoo.co.uk)

CC Number: 224667

Eligibility

Retired nurses who are in need and have been employed in Lancashire, south Cumbria or Greater Manchester. Grants are also given to people who are in need in the area but it is important to note that most of the trust's income is for the benefit of nurses and only a relatively small amount is available for others.

Types of grants

One-off grants, usually ranging from £100 to £300. Support for retired nurses can be for any purpose but funding for people who are sick and in need is generally focused on medical care, holidays and equipment.

Annual grant total

In 2013 the trust had an income of £16,100 and a total expenditure of £12,900. We estimate grants to individuals for social welfare purposes to be in the region of £11,000.

Applications

In writing to the correspondent. Applications can be submitted directly by the individual or through a social worker, Citizens Advice, nursing authority or other welfare agency.

The Lancashire Football Association Benevolent Fund

£600

Correspondent: David Burgess, Trustee, The County Ground, Thurston Road, Leyland, Preston, Lancashire PR25 2LF (01772 624000; fax: 01772 624700; email: info@lancashirefa.com; website: www.lancashirefa.com)

CC Number: 247179

Eligibility

People in need who are members of clubs associated with Lancashire Football Association and players or officials injured during, or travelling to or from, matches organised by the association.

Types of grants

One-off grants ranging from £100 to £300 towards, for example, hospital expenses, living costs and household bills.

Annual grant total

Grants average around £600 a year. The trustees appear to save income for a number of years until they can pay around this amount in grants.

Applications

On a form available from the correspondent. Applications can be submitted directly by the individual or through a personal representative or a friend.

Peter Lathom's Charity

£0 (2 grants)

Correspondent: Christine Aitken, Administrator, 13 Mallard Close, Aughton, Ormskirk, Lancashire L39 5QJ (01515 202717)

CC Number: 228828

Eligibility

People in need living in West Lancashire.

Types of grants

One-off grants in November/December.

Annual grant total

In 2013 this charity had assets of £1.4 million, an income of £53,000 and a total expenditure of £47,000. Educational grants awarded to individuals totalled £5,500. There were no welfare grants made in the year due to a lack of applications.

Applications

On a form available from the correspondent.

Other information

Grants are also given for education.

The Shaw Charities

£1,000

Correspondent: Mrs E. Woodrow, Administrator, 99 Rawlinson Lane, Heath Charnock, Chorley, Lancashire PR7 4DE (01257 480515; email: woodrows@tinyworld.co.uk)

CC Number: 214318

Eligibility

People over 60 who are on a low income and live in Rivington, Anglezarke, Heath Charnock and Anderton, Lancashire.

Types of grants

Recurrent grants at Easter and Christmas. Grants range from £15 to £20.

Annual grant total

In 2012/13 the charity had an income of £7,000 and a total expenditure of £2,500. We estimate that around £1,000 was made in grants to individuals for social welfare purposes.

Applications

On a form available from the correspondent to be submitted by the individual for consideration in March and November.

Other information

Grants for the purchase of books by undergraduates are also given through the Shaw's Educational Endowment.

Blackpool

The Blackpool Ladies' Sick Poor Association

£27,000

Correspondent: Patricia Dimuantes, Administrator, 22 James Avenue, Blackpool FY4 4LB (01253 353592)

CC Number: 220639

Eligibility

People in need who live in Blackpool.

Types of grants

Food vouchers are distributed monthly. Special relief grants can be made for immediate needs such as rent, second-hand cookers and washers, clothing, heaters, fireguards, stair gates and so on.

Annual grant total

In 2012/13 the association held assets of £406,000 and had an income of £32,000. Grants to individuals totalled more than £27,000 and were distributed as follows:

General relief	£18,600
Special relief	£8,900

Applications

Applications must include proof of extreme hardship and must be in writing via health visitors, social workers, Citizens Advice or other welfare agencies such as Age Concern, MIND and so on. Health visitors and social workers can write to the association's treasurer directly, otherwise letters should be sent to the correspondent. Applications are considered all year round, excluding August.

Other information

The association occasionally makes grants to organisations with similar objectives.

The Swallowdale Children's Trust

£22,000 (210 grants)

Correspondent: Alexa Alderson, Administrator, 13 Newlands Avenue, Blackpool FY3 9PG

CC Number: 526205

Eligibility

People who live in the Blackpool area and are under the age of 25. Orphans are given preference.

Types of grants

One-off grants are given for a wide variety of needs, including hospital expenses, clothing, food, travel expenses, medical equipment, nursing fees, furniture, disability equipment and help in the home.

Annual grant total

In 2012/13 the trust held assets of £999,000 and had an income of £40,000. During the year, the trust awarded 210 hardship grants to individuals, totalling £22,000. Grants amounting to £10,400 were made to Lancashire Outward Bound and to Life Education Centres, with the aim of assisting young people 'to achieve a more positive approach to life.' No grants were awarded to individuals to assist in education.

Applications

On a form available from the correspondent, with the financial details of the individual or family. Applications must be made through a social worker or teacher. They are considered every two months.

Caton-with-Littledale

The Cottam Charities

£25,000

Correspondent: Emma Edwards, Administrator, Blackhurst Swainson Goodier Solicitors, 3 and 4 Aalborg Square, Lancaster LA1 1GG (01524 32471; email: eje@bsglaw.co.uk)

CC Number: 223936 and 223925

Eligibility

People in need who are over 50 and have lived in the parish of Caton-with-Littledale for at least five years.

Types of grants

One-off grants ranging from about £100 to £140.

Annual grant total

Our research tells us that grants from the charities usually total £25,000 each year.

Applications

In writing to the correspondent directly by the individual or family member by mid-November for consideration in November/December each year. Applicants must reapply each year.

Darwen

The W. M. and B. W. Lloyd Trust

£15,000

Correspondent: John Jacklin, Trustee, Gorse Barn, Rock Lane, Tockholes, Darwen, Lancashire BB3 0LX (01254 771367)

CC Number: 503384

Eligibility

People in need who live in the old borough of Darwen in Lancashire. Preference is given to single parents.

Types of grants

One-off and recurrent grants according to need. Educational grants are given priority over social or medical grants.

Annual grant total

In 2012/13 the trust had an income of £95,000 and a total expenditure of £63,000. We estimate grants to individuals for social welfare purposes to be around £15,000.

Applications

On a form available from the correspondent, only through a social worker, Citizens Advice, other welfare agency, doctor or health visitor. Applications are considered quarterly in March, June, September and December. Applicants are advised to enquire about the other funds (detailed in this entry) administered by the trustees and available to people living in Daren.

Other information

Grants are made to both individuals and organisations for educational and social welfare purposes.

The trustees also administer the following funds:

- The Peter Pan Fund for the benefit of people with mental disabilities
- The Darwen War Memorial and Sick Poor Fund, originally to help war widows and dependents after the 1st World War and the sick poor of Darwen
- The Darwen Disabled Fund which was originally designed to assist with the social welfare of people with physical disabilities in Darwen
- The Ernest Aspin Donation, which supports individuals wanting to take part in sporting activities and in particular training and educating young people in sport
- The T P Davies Fund which is for the benefit of the residents of Darwen
- Darwen Probation Volunteers Fund supporting people in Darwen who have come under the probation and after care service, and their families

Lancaster

The Gibson, Simpson and Brockbank Annuities Trust

£3,400

Correspondent: Emma Edwards, Administrator, Blackhurst Swainson Goodier Solicitors, 3 and 4 Aalborg Square, Lancaster LA1 1GG (01524

32471; fax: 01524 386515; email: eje@bsglaw.co.uk; website: www.bsglaw.co.uk)

CC Number: 223595

Eligibility

Unmarried women or widows in need (with an income of less than £1,000 from sources other than their state pension), who are over 50 years old and have lived in Lancaster for the last three years.

Types of grants

Quarterly grants.

Annual grant total

In 2013 the trust had an income of £8,400 and a total expenditure of £3,600. We estimate that grants to individuals totalled £3,400.

Applications

On a form available from the correspondent to be submitted directly by the individual. Applications are usually considered every three months.

The Lancaster Charity

£2,100

Correspondent: Philip Oglethorpe, Clerk to the Trustees, William Penny's, Regent Street, Lancaster LA1 1SG (01524 842663; email: lancastercharity@btconnect.com; website: www.lancaster-charity.org.uk)

CC Number: 213461

Eligibility

People over 60 who are in need and have lived in the old city of Lancaster for at least three years. People under 60 may be considered if they are unable to work to maintain themselves due to age, accident or infirmity.

Types of grants

Top-up pensions according to need.

Annual grant total

In 2013, the charity had assets of £1.9 million and an income of £186,000. During the year, payments totalling £2,100 were made to pensioners. The majority of income is spent on maintaining the charity's almshouses.

Applications

On a form available from the correspondent. Applications are considered when vacancies occur.

Littleborough

The Littleborough Nursing Association

£500

Correspondent: Marilyn Aldred, Trustee, 26 Hodder Avenue, Shore, Littleborough OL15 8EU (01706 370738; email: marilyn41@talktalk.net)

CC Number: 222482

Eligibility

People in need who are sick, convalescent, disabled or infirm and live in the former urban district of Littleborough.

Types of grants

Recurrent grants according to need.

Annual grant total

Our research tells us that grants to individuals usually total around £500 each year. Grants are also given to organisations in Littleborough.

Exclusions

Grants are not given for costs which are normally covered by the DWP or NHS.

Applications

In writing to the correspondent for consideration in October. Applications can be submitted directly by the individual or through a social worker, Citizens Advice, other welfare agency or other third party.

Lowton

The Lowton United Charity

£2,000

Correspondent: John Naughton, Secretary, 51 Kenilworth Road, Lowton, Warrington WA3 2AZ (01942 741583)

CC Number: 226469

Eligibility

People in need who live in the parishes of St Luke's and St Mary's in Lowton.

Types of grants

One-off grants at Christmas and emergency one-off grants at any time.

Annual grant total

Grants total about £4,000 a year. About half of grants are given at Christmas for relief-in-need purposes and the rest throughout the year. Educational grants are also made.

Applications

Usually through the rectors of the parishes or other trustees.

Nelson

Nelson District Nursing Association Fund

£4,500

Correspondent: Joanne Eccles, Administrator, Democratic and Legal Services, Pendle Borough Council, Nelson Town Hall, Market Street, Nelson, Lancashire BB9 7LG (01282 661654; email: joanne.eccles@pendle.gov.uk)

CC Number: 222530

Eligibility

Sick or poor people who live in Nelson, Lancashire.

Types of grants

One-off grants according to need, ranging from £50 to £500.

Annual grant total

In 2012/13, the fund had an income of £4,400 and a total expenditure of £4,900. We estimate that the total amount of grants awarded to individuals was approximately £4,500.

Applications

In writing to the correspondent. Applications can be submitted directly by the individual or through a social worker, Citizens Advice or other welfare agency. All applicants will be visited by the association's welfare officer as part of the assessment process.

Pendle

The Fort Foundation

£1,800

Correspondent: Edward Fort, Trustee, Fort Vale Engineering Ltd, Calder Vale Park, Simonstone Lane, Simonstone, Burnley BB12 7ND (01282 440000)

CC Number: 1028639

Eligibility

Young people in Pendle Borough and district, with a preference for those undertaking courses in engineering.

Types of grants

One-off grants of £50 to £1,000.

Annual grant total

In 2012/13 the foundation had an income of £305,000 and a total expenditure of £94,000. It had assets of £517,000. Grants made to individuals for social welfare purposes totalled £1,000.

Exclusions

Grants are not made for fees.

Applications
In writing to the correspondent, directly by the individual. Applications are considered at any time.

Other information
Grants are primarily made to organisations.

Merseyside

Channel – Supporting Family Social Work in Liverpool

£12,500

Correspondent: Rebecca Black, Trustee, 38 Brick Kiln Lane, Rufford, Ormskirk L40 1SZ (01704823408; email: beccavblack@hotmail.com)

CC Number: 257916

Eligibility
Families with young children, elderly people or people with disabilities who live in Liverpool and are in need.

Types of grants
One-off grants of no more than £100 for childcare, clothing, food, furniture and kitchen equipment.

Annual grant total
In 2012/13 the charity had an income of £11,000 and a total expenditure of £12,700. We estimate that welfare grants to individuals totalled £12,500.

Applications
Applications can only be made through a social worker, health worker or voluntary agency, who should contact the correspondent for advice on funding, an application form and guidelines. Applications are considered on an ongoing basis.

The Girls' Welfare Fund

£2,500

Correspondent: Mrs S. M. O'Leary, Trustee, West Hey, Dawstone Road, Heswall, Wirral CH60 4RP (email: gwf_charity@hotmail.com)

CC Number: 220347

Eligibility
Girls and young women (usually aged 15 to 25) who are in need and were born, educated and live in Merseyside. Applications from other areas will not be acknowledged.

Types of grants
One-off and recurrent grants according to need. Grants range from £50 to £750.

Annual grant total
In 2013 the fund had an income of £9,800 and a total expenditure of £10,700. We estimate that grants to individuals for social welfare purposes totalled around £2,500.

Exclusions
Grants are not made to charities that request funds to pass on and give to individuals.

Applications
By letter to the correspondent or via email (including full details of what is needed and for what purpose). Applications can be submitted directly by the individual or through a social worker, Citizens Advice or another welfare agency. Applications are considered quarterly in March, June, September and December.

Other information
The fund also gives grants to organisations benefiting girls and young women on Merseyside, and to eligible individuals for leisure, creative activities, sports, arts and education.

The Liverpool Caledonian Association

£12,000

Correspondent: Ian Fisher, Secretary, 72 Cambridge Road, Crosby, Liverpool L23 7TZ (01519 243909)

CC Number: 250791

Eligibility
People of Scottish descent, or their immediate family, who are in need and who live within a 15-mile radius of Liverpool Town Hall. The association states: 'generally speaking we do not welcome applications from people who have fewer than one grandparent who was Scots born'.

Types of grants
Regular monthly payment of annuities, heating grants and a limited number of Christmas food parcels. The usual maximum grant is £50.

Annual grant total
In 2012 the association had an income of £11,000 and a total expenditure of £15,000. This is the most recent information available at the time of writing (July 2014).

Exclusions
Holidays are generally excluded.

Applications
In writing to the correspondent either directly by the individual, through a social worker, Citizens Advice, or other welfare agency or through any other third party. Applications are considered at any time and applicants will be visited.

The Liverpool Ladies' Institution

£3,400

Correspondent: David Anderton, Trustee, 15 Childwall Park Avenue, Childwall, Liverpool L16 0JE (01517 229823; email: d.anderton68@btinternet.com)

CC Number: 209490

Eligibility
Single women in need who were either born in the city of Liverpool or live in Merseyside. Preference is given to women who are members of the Church of England, and to older women.

Types of grants
Recurrent grants.

Annual grant total
In 2013 the charity had an income of £3,400 and a total expenditure of £3,500. We estimate that grants to individuals totalled £3,400.

Applications
On a form available from the correspondent. Applications should be submitted, at any time, through a social worker, Citizens Advice or other welfare agency. The charity has stated that it receives a lot of inappropriate applications.

The Liverpool Merchants' Guild

£832,000

Correspondent: Trusts and Estates Team, Moore Stephens, 110–114 Duke Street, Liverpool L1 5AG (01517 031080; fax: 01517 031085; email: info@liverpoolmerchantsguild.org.uk; website: www.liverpoolmerchantsguild.org.uk)

CC Number: 206454

Eligibility
People over 50 who have been employed in a professional, supervisory or clerical capacity (or self-employed people) and their dependents who live in Merseyside (or who have lived there for a continuous period of at least 15 years) and are in need or distress.

Types of grants
Annual pensions of £200 upwards, paid twice yearly. One-off grants of up to £5,000 for items of exceptional expenditure, for example equipment or adaptations to support independent living.

Annual grant total

In 2012 the guild had assets of £31.2 million, £24 million of which represents permanent endowment and is not available for grantmaking. There is also a restricted legacies fund of £1 million included in the assets figure. The guild's income was £1.2 million and grants were made totalling £832,000 which included £735,000 given in 331 pensions and £96,000 given in grants. The 2012 accounts were the latest available at the time of writing.

Exclusions

Manual workers and their dependents.

Applications

On a form available from the correspondent or to download from the website. Applications must be countersigned by two unrelated referees and include all relevant supporting documentation. They can be submitted at any time and are considered every three months.

Note: Applicants wishing to apply for a one-off grant will need to fill in the standard application form and a supplementary grants form (also available on the website).

Other information

The Liverpool Merchants' Guild was instituted in the year 1880 for the purpose of taking over and managing a fund bequeathed by the will of Catherine Wright, of Liverpool, who died in the month of September 1868.

Catherine Wright by her will bequeathed the sum of £10,000 to the trustees for the purpose of founding an institution to be called Wright's Institution, the object of which was to grant pensions to persons who had been unable to make adequate provision for their declining years.

The name was changed in 1880 to Liverpool Merchants' Guild and in 2006 a Royal Charter was granted replacing the original of 1914.

The Liverpool Provision Trade Guild

£6,200

Correspondent: The Secretary, KBH Accountants Ltd, 255 Poulton Road, Wallasey CH44 4BT (01516 388550)

CC Number: 224918

Eligibility

Members of the guild and their dependents who are in need. If funds permit, benefits can be extended to other members of the provision trade in Merseyside who are in need and their dependents.

Types of grants

Recurrent grants of £400 to £900 paid monthly, half-yearly or annually.

Annual grant total

In 2012/13 the guild had an income of £3,700 and a total expenditure of £6,400. We estimate that grants to individuals totalled £6,200.

Applications

In writing to the correspondent, directly by the individual. Meetings are held in May and December to discuss applications.

Merseyside Jewish Community Care

£20,000

Correspondent: Lisa Dolan, Chief Executive, Shifrin House, 433 Smithdown Road, Liverpool L15 3JL (01517 332292; email: info@mjccshifrin.co.uk; website: www.merseysidejewishcommunitycare.co.uk)

CC Number: 1122902

Eligibility

People of Jewish faith who live in Merseyside and are in need due to poverty, illness, old age, social disadvantage, disability or mental health problems.

Types of grants

Small one-off grants and loans to help towards medical equipment, respite breaks and basic essentials such as food and clothing. Grants are only paid on the provision of receipts for the goods/services purchased or are simply made directly to the supplier.

Annual grant total

In 2012/13 the trust had assets of £1.9 million and an income of £282,000. 'Relief grants' were made totalling £20,000, for basic essentials such as food and clothing.

Applications

By letter or telephone to the correspondent, directly by the individual.

Other information

Merseyside Jewish Community Care provides a care and welfare service for Jewish people in Merseyside.

Birkenhead

Birkenhead Relief-in-Sickness Charities

£1,500

Correspondent: Barb Warrilow, Administrator, Wirral CVS, Unit 30, Woodside Business Park, Birkenhead, Wirral CH41 1EL (01516 475432; email: barb@wirralcvs.org.uk)

CC Number: 217686

Eligibility

People in need through long-term sickness, who are on a low income and live in the old county borough of Birkenhead. Applicants should have tried to obtain a social fund loan before approaching the trust.

Types of grants

One-off grants to a usual maximum of £250. Grants are given for essential items such as clothing, electrical appliances, furniture (for example beds), travel costs and household items (for example bedding, towels).

Annual grant total

In 2012/13, the charity had an income of £2,300 and a total expenditure of £1,800. We estimate that the grant total given to individuals was approximately £1,500.

Applications

Applications must be submitted through a recognised referral agency (such as a social worker, Citizens Advice or doctor) or other third party, and are considered throughout the year. A doctor's note will be needed to back up the claim if the applicant is not in receipt of Disability Living Allowance. An appointment will be made with the claimant, or a member of the family if they are unable to attend, to discuss the claim.

The Christ Church Fund for Children

£4,200

Correspondent: Robert Perry, Trustee, 28 Beresford Road, Prenton CH43 1XG

CC Number: 218545

Eligibility

Children in need up to the age of 17 whose parents are members of the Church of England and who live in the county borough of Birkenhead. Preference is given to children living in the ecclesiastical parish of Christ Church, Birkenhead.

Types of grants

Grants for any kind of need, but typically for bedding, furniture, clothing and trips.

Annual grant total
In 2012/13 the fund had an income of £3,800 and a total expenditure of £4,400. We estimate that social welfare grants to individuals totalled £4,200.

Applications
In writing through a recognised referral agency (for example, a social worker or Citizens Advice) or other third party. Applications are usually considered quarterly (around January, April, September and December), but emergency applications can be considered at any time.

Higher Bebington

The Thomas Robinson Charity

£1,000

Correspondent: Charles Van Ingen, Administrator, 1 Blakeley Brow, Wirral, Merseyside CH63 0PS

CC Number: 233412

Eligibility
People in need who live in Higher Bebington.

Types of grants
One-off grants of £50 to £500. Grants can also be made for educational purposes.

Annual grant total
In 2013 the charity had an income of £4,000 and a total expenditure of £2,300. We estimate that around £1,000 was made in grants to individuals for social welfare purposes.

Applications
In writing to: The Vicar, Christ Church Vicarage, King's Road, Higher Bebington, Wirral CH43 8LX. Applications can be submitted directly by the individual or a family member, through a social worker, or a relevant third party such as Citizens Advice or a school. They are considered at any time.

Other information
The charity also makes grants to individuals for educational purposes.

Liverpool

The Charles Dixon Pension Fund

£6,600

Correspondent: Richard Morris, Trustee, The Society of Merchant Venturers, Merchants' Hall, The Promenade, Clifton Down, Bristol BS8 3NH (01179 738058; fax: 01179 735884; email: enquiries@merchantventurers.com)

CC Number: 202153

Eligibility
Merchants who are married men, widowers or bachelors of good character, who are practising members of the Church of England, and widows of pensioners who are in reduced circumstances. Applicants must live in Bristol, Liverpool or London and must be over 60 years of age.

Types of grants
Pensions, usually between £500 and £2,000 a year.

Annual grant total
In 2012/13 the fund had an income of £8,900 and a total expenditure of £6,800. We estimate that welfare grants to individuals totalled £6,600.

Applications
On a form available from the correspondent. Applications can be submitted directly by the individual or, where applicable, through a social worker, Citizens Advice, other welfare agency or a third party such as a clergyman. They are dealt with as received.

Liverpool Corn Trade Guild

£5,300

Correspondent: Ian Bridge, Trustee, 1A St Johns Road, Southport PR8 4JP (01704 565596)

CC Number: 232414

Eligibility
Members of the guild and their dependents who are in need. If funds permit benefits can be extended to former members and their dependents. Membership is open to anyone employed by any firm engaged in the Liverpool Corn and Feed Trade.

Types of grants
One-off and recurrent grants according to need. Loans may also be provided.

Annual grant total
At the time of writing (August 2014) the latest financial information available was from 2012. In 2012 the charity had an income of £5,800 and an expenditure of £5,500, which is the lowest in the past five years. We estimate that grants to individuals totalled around £5,300.

Applications
In writing to the correspondent. Applications can be made directly by the individual.

Liverpool Wholesale Fresh Produce Benevolent Fund

£10,000

Correspondent: Thomas Dobbin, Secretary, 207 Childwall Road, Liverpool L15 6UT (01517 220621)

CC Number: 1010236

Eligibility
People in need, who are or have been associated with the Liverpool fruit trade either as importers or wholesalers, and their families.

Types of grants
One-off and recurrent grants usually ranging from £50 to £80.

Annual grant total
In 2012/13, the fund had an income of £5,200 and a total expenditure of £32,600. We estimate that the total amount of grants awarded to individuals was approximately £10,000. The fund also awards grants to organisations and provides other types of finance.

Applications
In writing to the correspondent.

Other information
The fund has stated that it now predominantly makes grants to local charities in Merseyside due to a dwindling number of applications from individuals connected with the fresh produce trade.

The Ann Molyneux Charity

£9,000

Correspondent: John Wilson, Trustee, Liverpool Seafarers Centre, 20 Crosby Road South, Liverpool L22 1RQ (0300 8008085; email: john.wilson@liverpoolseafarers.org.uk)

CC Number: 229408

Eligibility
Seafarers and their widows living in the city of Liverpool. Preference for men who sailed from the city for most of the last five years that they were at sea. Applicants must be in receipt of benefits.

Types of grants
Pensions of £200 a year (paid quarterly).

Annual grant total
Previously grants have totalled on average about £20,000 a year.

Applications

On a form available from Liverpool Parish Church and Our Lady and St Nicholas. Applications should be accompanied by seafarer's books, details of income and a testimonial from a person of good standing in the community.

The Pritt Fund

£15,500

Correspondent: Liverpool Law Society, The Cotton Exchange Building, Second Floor, Edmund Street, Liverpool L3 9LQ (01512 366998; website: www.liverpoollawsociety.org.uk)

CC Number: 226421

Eligibility

Solicitors or clerks of solicitors, who are in need and have practised in the city of Liverpool or within the area of Liverpool Law Society, and their dependents.

Types of grants

One-off and recurrent grants according to need.

Annual grant total

In 2012/13 the fund had an income of £14,200 and a total expenditure of £15,800. We estimate that grants to individuals totalled £15,500.

Applications

On a form available from the correspondent.

Lydiate

The Charity of John Goore

£1,400

Correspondent: Edward Bostock, Third Floor, Stanley Buildings, 43 Hanover Street, Liverpool, Merseyside L1 3DN (01512 322444; fax: 01512 322445; email: info@cfmerseyside.org.uk; website: www.cfmerseyside.org.uk/John-Goore-Fund---Individuals)

CC Number: 238355

Eligibility

People in need living in the parish of Lydiate only.

Types of grants

Grants of up to £500 to alleviate some of the difficulties faced by people with a physical or mental disability, for example, small home improvements, travel to community activities/facilities and specialist equipment. Grants of up to £250 are also available to local carers for respite breaks, travel expenses and additional costs of living incurred as a direct result of being a carer.

Annual grant total

In 2012/13 the charity had an income of £6,600 and a total expenditure of £6,500. We estimate that social welfare grants to individuals totalled around £1,400. Grants are also awarded to individuals for educational purposes and to organisations.

Exclusions

No grants for payment of debts.

Applications

Applications should be made through the Community Foundation for Merseyside. Forms are available from the foundation's website and can be filled out electronically and returned to applications@cfmerseyside.org.uk.

Applications should include a letter of support from the person being cared for (if appropriate). Applications for home improvements should include details of the service provider, the quote received and the amount requested.

Sefton

Southport and Birkdale Provident Society

£11,000 (90 grants)

Correspondent: Ian Jones, Treasurer, 12 Ascot Close, Southport PR8 2DD (01704 560095)

CC Number: 224460

Eligibility

People in need who live in the metropolitan borough of Sefton.

Types of grants

One-off grants in kind only after social services have confirmed that all other benefits have been fully explored. Grants have been awarded towards clothing, bedding, cookers, washing machines and other basic household needs.

Annual grant total

In 2013 the society had an income of £30,000 and a total expenditure of £20,000. Grants to individuals amounted to £11,000.

During the year, the society received 122 applications of which 16 were declined, 9 cancelled and 97 were agreed and paid. Of these, seven were from organisations who received a total of £8,700.

Exclusions

No cash payments. Grants are not given for education, training experience, rental deposits, personal debt relief or hire purchase. Medical services are not supported.

Applications

In writing to the correspondent with as much information on family background and the reasons for the request as possible. Applications should be submitted through social services. They are considered at any time.

Wirral

The Conroy Trust

£1,800

Correspondent: Tom Bates, Administrator, 22 Waterford Road, Prenton, Wirral CH43 6UU (01516 522128)

CC Number: 210797

Eligibility

People in need who live in the parish of Bebington.

Types of grants

Bi-monthly payments to regular beneficiaries and one-off grants for special needs. Grants usually range from £50 to £300.

Annual grant total

In 2012 the trust had an income of £5,100 and a total expenditure of £3,700. This was the latest financial information available at the time of writing. We estimate that social welfare grants to individuals totalled £1,800, with funding also awarded to organisations.

Exclusions

No grants are made for educational purposes.

Applications

In writing to the correspondent directly by the individual.

The John Lloyd Corkhill Trust

£10,000

Correspondent: Michelle Jafrate, Administrator, 5 Broadway, Greasby, Wirral, Merseyside CH49 2NG (01516 784428; email: jlct.wirral@tiscali.co.uk)

CC Number: 216371

Eligibility

People with lung conditions who live in the metropolitan borough of Wirral.

Types of grants

Mostly for equipment (such as nebulisers). Help is also given towards services and amenities, for example holidays and occasionally to buy domestic appliances such as fires, washing machines and so on.

Annual grant total

Previously grants have totalled on average about £5,000 a year.

Applications

Applicants are generally referred by their social worker or doctor and have a low income. Supporting medical evidence must be supplied. Applications are considered in June and December.

The Maud Beattie Murchie Charitable Trust

£13,000

Correspondent: Anthony Bayliss, Duncan Sheard Glass, Castle Chambers, 43 Castle Street, Liverpool L2 9TL (01512 431209)

CC Number: 265281

Eligibility

Retired members of Beattie stores who are in need and people in need who live in the Wirral.

Types of grants

One-off and recurrent grants according to need. Grants to organisations are mostly recurrent.

Annual grant total

In 2012/13 the trust had an income of £29,000. Total spending was £30,000, with grants made of around £26,000 split between individuals and organisations.

Exclusions

No grants for educational purposes.

Applications

Applications should be made through Wirral Social Services. They are usually considered in June and December.

The West Kirby Charity

£13,500

Correspondent: Jane Boulton, Administrator, 14 Surrey Drive, Wirral CH48 2HP (01516 254794)

CC Number: 218546

Eligibility

People in need who have lived in the old urban district of Hoylake (Caldy, Frankby, Greasby, Hoylake, Meols and West Kirby) for at least three years. Preference is given to older people and people who have a disability.

Types of grants

Pensions of about £20 a month. Christmas gifts and one-off grants are also made to non-elderly locals.

Annual grant total

In 2012 the charity had an income of £12,000 and a total expenditure of £12,000. This was the latest information at the time of writing (July 2014).

Applications

On a form available from the correspondent. Applications are usually considered quarterly.

Midlands

General

The Beacon Centre for the Blind

£1,000

Correspondent: Phil Thomas, Company Secretary, Wolverhampton Road East, Wolverhampton WV4 6AZ (01902 886781; email: enquiries@beacon4blind.co.uk; website: www.beacon4blind.co.uk)

CC Number: 216092

Eligibility

People who are registered blind or partially sighted and live in the metropolitan boroughs of Dudley (except Halesowen and Stourbridge), Sandwell and Wolverhampton, and part of the South Staffordshire District Council area.

Types of grants

One-off grants up to £250 towards socials and outings, holidays, and talking books and newspapers. Grants for specific items of equipment can be given to those who are visually impaired.

Annual grant total

In 2012/13 the charity had assets of £8.6 million, an income of £2.1 million and a total expenditure of £2.4 million. Grantmaking is a small part of the charity's activities. 7 grants were made to individuals totalling £1,900. We estimate that around £1,000 was awarded to individuals in need. Grants are also awarded for educational purposes.

Applications

In writing to the correspondent stating the degree of vision and age of the applicant, and their monthly income and expenditure. Applications can be submitted through a social worker or a school, and are considered throughout the year.

Other information

The charity provides domiciliary care for up to 71 elderly blind and partially sighted people who attend the day centre each week to participate in therapeutic activities. The charity also provides a gym, outreach and a talking newspaper.

The Birmingham and Three Counties Trust for Nurses

£10,000

Correspondent: David Airston, Administrator, 16 Haddon Croft, Halesowen B63 1JQ (01216 020389; email: ruthmadams_45@msn.com)

CC Number: 217991

Eligibility

Nurses on any statutory register, who have practiced or practice in the city of Birmingham and the counties of Staffordshire, Warwickshire and Worcestershire.

Types of grants

One-off or recurrent grants according to need. Grants are given to meet the costs of heating, telephone bills, cordless phones for the infirm, household equipment, household repairs, car repairs, electric scooters, wheelchairs, medical equipment and personal expenses such as spectacles and clothing. Grants are also made for convalescent care, recuperative holidays and to clear debt.

Annual grant total

In 2012/13 the trust had an income of £5,300 and a total expenditure of £14,000. Previous grants have mostly been made for welfare purposes.

Applications

On a form available from the correspondent. Applications can be submitted either directly by the individual or through a friend, relative or a social worker, Citizens Advice or other welfare agency. Details of financial status including income and expenditure, reasons for application, and health status, where relevant, should be included. Applications are considered throughout the year. Applicants are visited by a trustee (where distance allows) for assessment. Supportive visiting continues where considered necessary.

The Charities of Susanna Cole and Others

£4,000

Correspondent: Peter Gallimore, Trustee, 19 Oak Tree House, 153 Oak Tree Lane, Bournville, Birmingham B30 1TU (01214 714064)

CC Number: 204531

Eligibility

Quakers in need who live in parts of Worcestershire and most of Warwickshire and are 'a member or attendee of one of the constituent meetings of the Warwickshire Monthly Meeting of the Society of Friends'. Preference is given to younger children and retired people on an inadequate pension.

Types of grants

One-off and recurrent grants according to need. Help may be given with domestic running costs, rent or accommodation fees, convalescence, recreation and home help, and to those seeking education or re-training.

Annual grant total

In 2012 the charity had an income of £12,000 and a total expenditure of £8,500. Grants are made for welfare and educational purposes. We estimate grants to individuals for social welfare purposes to be around £4,000. The 2012 accounts were the only ones available at the time of writing (July 2014).

Applications

In writing to the correspondent via the overseer of the applicant's Quaker meeting. Applications should be received by early March and October for consideration later in the same months.

The J. I. Colvile Charitable Trust

£3,000

Correspondent: John Hankey, Administrator, 4 Park Lane, Appleton, Abingdon, Oxfordshire OX13 5JT (01865 862668)

CC Number: 1067274

Eligibility

People in need who are resident in Gloucestershire, west Oxfordshire and south Warwickshire. Help is regularly given to ex-servicemen and their families via, for example, SSAFA.

Types of grants

One-off grants ranging from £250 to £500.

Annual grant total

Grants usually total around £3,000 per year.

Applications

In writing to the correspondent. Applications can be submitted directly by the individual or family member, or by an organisation such as Citizens Advice. They are considered as necessary.

Other information

Grants are also made to youth training projects.

Baron Davenport's Charity

£376,000 (1,572 grants)

Correspondent: Kate Slater, Charity Administrator, Portman House, 5–7 Temple Row West, Birmingham B2 5NY (01212 368004; email: enquiries@barondavenportscharity.org; website: www.barondavenportscharity.org)

CC Number: 217307

Eligibility

Widows, unmarried women and divorcees aged over 60 and in need; women and children abandoned by their partners; and people under 25 whose fathers have died. Exceptions may be made for younger widows with limited income and school-age children living at home who are in financial need. Applicants must have lived in the West Midlands, Shropshire, Staffordshire, Warwickshire or Worcestershire area within a 60 mile radius of Birmingham Town Hall for at least five years. Applicants must have a net income of less than £178 per week and savings that do not exceed £10,000.

Types of grants

Recurrent grants (at the time of writing), of £260 (for ladies living in rented accommodation) and £290 (for owner occupiers), paid twice annually. Note: grants are paid directly into beneficiaries' bank or building society accounts; applicants must have an account in their own name to be eligible.

Small one-off grants are available for single mothers on low incomes for essential household items. Those under the age of 25, whose fathers have died, are also eligible for small grants towards essential items.

Annual grant total

In 2013 the charity held assets of £33.8 million and had an income of £1.2 million. Grants totalled £1 million; of which, £376,000 was distributed in 1,572 grants to individuals.

A further 402 grants, amounting to £630,000, were awarded to almshouses, hospices and children's charities in Birmingham and the West Midlands.

Exclusions

Applications will not be accepted from those in receipt of Low/High Rate Attendance Allowance; Middle/High rates of Disability Living Allowance or Mobility Allowance (or car allowance).

Applications

Except for emergency cases, applications should be made through local authority social services departments or recognised welfare agencies, although direct applications from individuals may also be considered. Application forms are available from the correspondent or to download from the website.

Applications for the Spring distribution should be submitted by 15 March, and for the Autumn distribution, 15 September. Grants are paid in May and November respectively. No more than one application should be submitted within twelve months.

Applications for one-off grants can be submitted at any time and are considered approximately every month. Enquiries are welcomed.

Other information

The trust and CVS regard as fatherless those whose fathers have died, and in some cases children abandoned by their fathers. For emergency needs, see the separate entries in: Shropshire, Staffordshire, Warwickshire, Worcestershire, and West Midlands.

The W. E. Dunn Trust

£51,000 (333 grants)

Correspondent: David Corney, Trustee, The Trust Office, 30 Bentley Heath Cottages, Tilehouse Green Lane, Knowle, Solihull B93 9EL (01564 773407)

CC Number: 219418

Eligibility

People who are in need and live in the West Midlands, particularly Wolverhampton, Wednesbury, north Staffordshire and the surrounding area. Preference is given to people who are very old or very young, who the trust recognises as possibly being the least able to fund for themselves.

Types of grants

One-off grants usually ranging from £50 to £200.

Annual grant total

In 2012/13 the trust had assets of £4.5 million and an income of £330,000. Grants totalling almost £53,000 were distributed to 337 individuals in the following areas:

Clothing and furniture	145	£21,000
Domestic equipment	125	£21,000
Radio, TV and licences	39	£5,900
Social and welfare	20	£2,700
Education	4	£1,900

Exclusions

Grants are not made to settle or reduce debts already incurred.

Applications

Applications should be made in writing via a social worker, Citizens Advice or other welfare agency. The trustees meet on a regular basis to consider applications.

Other information

Grants are also made to 176 organisations (£153,500 in 2012/13).

Frimley Fuel Allotments (formerly known as The Frimley Fuel Allotments Charity)

£57,000 (193 grants)

Correspondent: Kim Murray, Hon. Secretary, 2A Hampshire Road, Camberley GU15 4DW (01276 23958; email: ffa.office@googlemail.com; website: www.frimleyfuelallotments.org.uk)

CC Number: 231036

Eligibility

People in need who live in the parish of Frimley. Priority is given to people who are older or who have a disability, and those who care for them.

Types of grants

One-off grants.

Annual grant total

In 2013 the trust had assets of £1.7 million and an income of £133,000. Grants totalled £57,000, of which £39,000 was awarded as standard grants to individuals with a further £18,000 paid in heating grants.

Applications

On a form available from the secretary or a local Citizens Advice, church or social services centre. Applications for the Christmas heating grants should be returned to the respective social service centre by mid-November and can be made directly by the individual. Applications for other grants can be made at any time and are considered on a regular basis.

Other information

Grants are also made to local organisations (£36,000 in 2013).

The Fund for the Forgotten

See entry on page 457

Francis Butcher Gill's Charity

£18,000

Correspondent: Anna Chandler, Administrator, Freeth Cartwright, Cumberland Court, 80 Mount Street, Nottingham NG1 6HH (01159 015562; fax: 01159 015500; email: anna.chandler@freethcartwright.co.uk)

CC Number: 230722

Eligibility

Unmarried or widowed women aged over 50 in need, who are regular attendees of Protestant Christian worship, or who would be were they not prevented by bodily infirmity. Applicants must also be of good standing and live in Nottinghamshire, though those living in Derbyshire or Lincolnshire may also be considered.

Types of grants

Pensions of £350 per quarter are given to a fixed number of pensioners. One-off grants may also occasionally be available for items such as gas fires.

Annual grant total

In 2012/13 the charity had an income £15,000, and a total expenditure of £21,000.

Applications

On a form available from the correspondent. Applications should be submitted either through a doctor or member of the clergy or directly by the individual supported by a reference from the one of the aforementioned. Applications can be submitted at any time for consideration in March and October, or at other times in emergency situations. For pensions, applications will only be considered as a vacancy arises.

The Edmund Godson Charity

£2,000

Correspondent: Freya Villis, Trustee, 30 Hemingford Road, Cambridge CB1 3BZ (07866267692; email: fv221@cam.ac.uk)

CC Number: 227463

Eligibility

People in need who wish to emigrate and who currently live in and around Woolwich, Charlton, Shooters Hill, Eltham, Abbey Wood and Plumstead in southeast London, Shinfield near Reading, Leominster in Herefordshire and Tenbury in Worcestershire.

Types of grants

One-off grants according to need.

Annual grant total

In 2012/13 the charity had an income of £11,500 and a total expenditure of £8,100. As the charity mainly makes grants to organisations, we estimate that grants to individuals totalled £2,000.

Applications

Directly by the individual on a form available from the correspondent. Details of the proposed destination, occupation, emigration eligibility and financial circumstances should be given. Note that most grants in recent years have been made to organisations, rather than to individuals.

Jordison and Hossell Animal Welfare Charity

£1,000

Correspondent: Sally Reid, Trustee, Whitestones, Haselor, Pelham Lane Alcester, Warwickshire B49 6LU (01789 488942; email: sallyreid@me.com)

CC Number: 515352

Eligibility

People in the Midlands who are on low incomes and are in need of financial assistance in meeting vets' bills for their pets.

Types of grants

One-off grants of up to £500 towards vets' bills.

Annual grant total

In 2012/13, the charity had an income of £2,000 and a total expenditure of £1,300. We estimate that the total amount of grants awarded to individuals was approximately £1,000.

Exclusions

No grants for vets' bills for larger animals such as horses and farm animals.

Applications

In writing to the correspondent. Applications must be made by the vet in question or a third party such as Citizens Advice, rather than by the individual. The charity does not deal with the applicant directly. Evidence that the beneficiary is on benefits is required.

Melton Mowbray Building Society Charitable Foundation

£5,800

Correspondent: Martin Reason, Trustee, Melton Mowbray Building Society, Leicester Road, Melton Mowbray LE13 0D3 (01664 414141; fax: 01664 414040; email: m.reason@mmbs.co.uk; website: www.mmbs.co.uk/index.cfm?id=167&navid=98)

CC Number: 1067348

Eligibility

Individuals in need who live within a 30 mile radius of Melton Mowbray.

Types of grants

One-off grants in the range of £100 and £250, to provide, for example: opportunities for children from disadvantaged backgrounds; means of preparing young people for adult life; and help for those suffering from disabilities.

Annual grant total

In 2012/13 the foundation had an income of £16,700 and a total expenditure of £17,600. We estimate that grants to individuals totalled £5,800, with local organisations receiving around £11,600.

Exclusions

No grants are made for circular appeals or for projects of a high capital nature.

In the interest of fairness, successful applicants cannot reapply within 12 months of receiving a grant.

Applications

In writing to the correspondent to be submitted either directly by the individual or a family member, through a third party such as a social worker or teacher, or, where applicable, through an organisation such as Citizens Advice or a school. Applications should include details of the cash value sought, the nature of the expense, the reason for application and the location of the applicant. Applications are considered at meetings held on a quarterly basis.

Other information

On its website the foundation pledges to 'commit at least 33% and up to 50% of the annual contribution made by the

Melton Mowbray Building Society to either kickstart a community project within the catchment area or to establish an enduring activity or initiative for the benefit of the community.'

The Melton Mowbray Building Society has a helpful page about the foundation on its website.

Thomas Monke (formerly known as Thomas Monke's Charity)

£2,000

Correspondent: Christopher Kitto, Administrator, 29 Blacksmiths Lane, Newton Solney, Burton-on-Trent, Staffordshire DE15 0SD (01543 267995)

CC Number: 214783

Eligibility

Young people under the age of 25 who live in Austrey, Measham, Shenton and Whitwick.

Types of grants

One-off and recurrent grants according to need.

Annual grant total

In 2013 the charity had an income of £4,200 and an expenditure of £4,000. Grants totalled around £2,000.

Applications

Application forms are available from the correspondent.

Other information

Grants are also made for educational purposes.

The Newfield Charitable Trust

£17,200 (73 grants)

Correspondent: David Dumbleton, Clerk, Rotherham and Co. Solicitors, 8–9 The Quadrant, Coventry CV1 2EG (02476 227331; fax: 02476 221293; email: d.dumbleton@rotherham-solicitors.co.uk)

CC Number: 221440

Eligibility

Girls and women (under 30) who are in need of care and assistance and live in Coventry or Leamington Spa.

Types of grants

'The relief of the physical, mental and moral needs of, and the promotion of the physical, social and educational training of' eligible people. Most grants are under £500 towards things such as clothing, electrical goods, holidays, travel expenses and furniture.

Annual grant total

In 2012/13 the trust had assets of almost £1.5 million and an income of £53,000. During the year, the trustees received a total of 146 applications, from which 139 applicants were awarded. Grants totalled nearly £35,000 and were distributed as follows:

Educational	10	£3,800
Clothing	56	£13,800
General	73	£17,200

Exclusions

No grants for arrears or utility bills.

Applications

Write to the correspondent for an application form. Applications are accepted from individuals or third parties such as social services, Citizens Advice, school/college, etc. A letter of support/reference from someone not a friend or relative of the applicant (such as school, social services, etc.) is always required. Details of income/expenditure and personal circumstances should also be given. Applications are considered eight times a year.

The Norton Foundation

£11,600 (126 grants)

Correspondent: The Administrator, Richard Perkins and Company, 50 Brookfield Close, Hunt End, Redditch B97 5LL (01527 544446; email: correspondent@nortonfoundation.org; website: www.nortonfoundation.org)

CC Number: 702638

Eligibility

Young people under 25 who live in Birmingham, Coventry or Warwickshire and are in need of care, rehabilitation or aid of any kind, 'particularly as a result of delinquency, maltreatment or neglect or who are in danger of lapsing or relapsing into delinquency'.

Types of grants

One-off grants of up to £500 are given towards clothing, household items and holidays.

Annual grant total

In 2012/13 the trust had assets of £4.4 million and an income of £119,000. Grants were made totalling £96,000, of which £13,000 was given in individual grants, £24,000 was awarded in discretionary grants and the remaining £60,000 was given to organisations. Grants to individuals were distributed as follows:

Household	104	£9,900
Clothing	22	£1,700
Education and training	13	£1,270

Applications

By a letter which should contain all the information required as detailed in the guidance notes for applicants. Guidance notes are available from the correspondent or the website. Applications must be submitted through a social worker, Citizens Advice, probation service, school or other welfare agency. They are considered quarterly.

The Pargeter and Wand Trust

£6,500

Correspondent: Marcus Fellows, Trustee, BCOP, 1st Floor, 40B Imperial Court, Kings Norton Business Centre, Pershore Road South, Birmingham B30 3ES (01214 597670; email: marcus.fellows@bcop.org.uk)

CC Number: 210725

Eligibility

Women who have never been married, are aged over 55 and live in their own homes. There is a preference for those living in the West Midlands area, but other areas of the country are considered.

Types of grants

Small annuities of around £300 are paid quarterly and reviewed annually. Smaller, one-off grants, usually in the range of £50 to £150, are also available.

Annual grant total

In 2012/13 the trust had an income of £11.200 and a total expenditure of £6,600. We estimate that grants to individuals totalled £6,500.

Applications

Applications should be made via Age UK.

Pedmore Sporting Club Trust Fund

£6,800

Correspondent: The Secretary, Nicklin and Co. LLP, Church Court, Stourbridge Road, Halesowen, West Midlands B63 3TT (email: psclub@pedmorehouse.co.uk; website: www.pedmoresportingclub.co.uk)

CC Number: 263907

Eligibility

People in need who live in the West Midlands.

Types of grants

One-off grants have included those for medical care equipment, travel to and from hospital, wheelchairs, other access aid and IT equipment. Money is normally paid directly to the service/item provider, not the individual. Christmas and Easter parcels are given to senior citizens.

Annual grant total

At the time of writing (August 2014) the latest financial information available was from 2012. In 2012 the trust had assets of £284,000 and an income of £42,000. Grants to individuals totalled £6,800.

Exclusions

The trust is unable to help with general living costs.

Applications

Our research indicates that candidates for the holiday food parcels should be recommended by a member of the sporting club. Other applications can be made in writing to the correspondent. The trustees meet quarterly and might interview the candidates.

Other information

Grants are mainly made to organisations, preferably local (£50,000 in 2012).

The Persehouse Pensions Fund

£9,400

Correspondent: Clive Wheatley, Administrator, 12A Oakleigh Road, Stourbridge, West Midlands DY8 2JX (01384 379775; email: clive.wheatley@virginmedia.com)

CC Number: 500660

Eligibility

Elderly or distressed people belonging to the upper or middle classes of society who were born in the counties of Staffordshire or Worcestershire, or people who have lived in either county for ten years or more, and have been 'reduced to poverty by misfortune'.

Types of grants

Mainly pensions, but occasional one-off grants.

Annual grant total

In 2012/13 the fund had an income of £12,300 and a total expenditure of £9,600. We estimate that welfare grants to individuals totalled £9,400.

Applications

On a form available from the correspondent; to be submitted directly by the individual.

The Roddam Charity

£1,800

Correspondent: Stuart Barber, Administrator, Merewood, Springfields, Newport TF10 7EZ (01952 814628; email: bougheyroddamha@btinternet.com)

CC Number: 213892

Eligibility

People in need who live in the TF10 postcode area who are sick, convalescent, disabled or infirm. The beneficial area includes the parishes of Newport, Chetwynd, Church Aston, Chetwynd Aston, Woodcote, Moreton, Sambrook, Tibberton, Edgmond and Lilleshall in Shropshire and Forton in Staffordshire.

Types of grants

One-off grants in the range of about £50 to £200. Grants are made to help with items, services or facilities that are not readily available from other sources and which will relieve the suffering or assist the recovery of individuals in poor health and people living with disabilities.

Annual grant total

In 2012/13 the charity had an income of £3,700 and a total expenditure of £3,800. We estimate that social welfare grants to individuals totalled £1,800, with funding also awarded to organisations.

Exclusions

No grants for rates, taxes or other public funds.

Applications

On a form available from the correspondent to be submitted directly by the individual. Applications are usually considered quarterly.

The SF Group Charity

See entry on page 40

Richard Smedley's Charity

£3,000

Correspondent: Maurice Ward, Robinsons Solicitors Co., 21–22 Burns Street, Ilkeston, Derbyshire DE7 8AA (01159 324101; email: maurice.ward@robinsons-solicitors.co.uk)

CC Number: 221211

Eligibility

People in need who live in the parishes of Breaston, Dale Abbey, Draycott with Church Wilne, Heanor, Hopewell, Ilkeston, Ockbrook and Risley (all in Derbyshire) and of Awsworth, Bilborough, Brinsley, Greasley and Strelley (all in Nottinghamshire).

Types of grants

One-off grants generally in the range of £50 to £350 are given towards items such as furniture, washing machines, mobility aids, clothing and carpets.

Annual grant total

In 2013, the charity had an income of approximately £9,000 and a total expenditure of £5,000. We estimate that grants to individuals for social welfare purposes totalled £3,000.

Applications

On an application form available from the correspondent; to be submitted either directly by the individual or through a social worker, Citizens Advice or other welfare agency. Applications can be submitted at any time and are usually considered quarterly.

Other information

Grants are also made to organisations.

The Snowball Trust

£14,600 (28 grants)

Correspondent: Ian Smedley, Trustee, The Barn, Wood End Lane, Fillongley, Coventry CV7 8DB (01676 542255; email: i.smedley@btinternet.com)

CC Number: 702860

Eligibility

Children and young people under 21 who are in poor health or who have a disability and live in Coventry and Warwickshire.

Types of grants

One-off grants mainly for medical equipment and disability aids. The Charity Commission's record notes that the trust's policy is, 'to grant sums of money for the provision of moveable equipment and other resources for qualifying individuals or organisations'.

Annual grant total

In 2012/13 the trust had an income of £29,000 and a total expenditure of £30,000. Grants to individuals totalled £14,600.

Applications

On a form available from the correspondent; to be submitted either by the individual or through a third party such as a special school, social worker or other welfare agency. Applications should include a firm quote for the equipment to be supplied, a letter of support from the individual's school and/or a medical professional, and confirmation of the parents'/guardians' financial need.

Other information

The trust also makes grants to organisations (14,800 in 2012/13).

The Edwin John Thompson Memorial Fund

£0

Correspondent: David Thompson, Trustee, Albrighton Hall, High Street, Albrighton, Wolverhampton WV7 3JQ (01902 372036)

CC Number: 213690

Eligibility

People in need who live in the County Borough of Dudley or any other local district, area or administrative unit within a radius of fifteen miles from Dudley Town Hall.

Types of grants

One-off and recurrent grants according to need.

Annual grant total

In 2012/13 the fund had assets of £700,000 and an income of £26,000. Grants were made totalling £18,700, the majority of which (£12,700) was given to organisations. During the year one individual benefitted from a grant of £6,000, which we believe was given for educational purposes.

Applications

In writing to the correspondent.

The Eric W. Vincent Trust Fund

£2,100 (25 grants)

Correspondent: Janet Stephen, Clerk, PO Box 6849, Stourbridge DY8 9EN (email: vttrust942@gmail.com)

CC Number: 204843

Eligibility

People in need living within a 20-mile radius of Halesowen.

Types of grants

Grants of around £100 can be made for clothing, furniture, hospital travel expenses, equipment and holidays.

Annual grant total

In 2012/13, the fund had assets of £1.38 million and an income of £44,400. Grants were made to 25 individuals totalling £2,100.

Exclusions

The trust does not make loans or give grants for gap year projects or to pay off debts.

Applications

The trustees normally meet bi-monthly. Applications should be in writing through a health professional, social worker, Citizens Advice or other welfare agency. Applications will not be considered if they are not made through a relevant third party. Details of financial circumstances must be included.

Other information

Small grants (£1,000 or less) are also made to organisations (this totalled £26,500 in 2012/13).

The Anthony and Gwendoline Wylde Memorial Charity

£2,000

Correspondent: Kirsty McEwen, Clerk, 3 Waterfront Business Park, Dudley Road, Brierley Hill, West Midlands DY5 1LX (0845 111 5050; email: kirsty.mcewen@higgsandsons.co.uk; website: www.wyldecharity.weebly.com)

CC Number: 700239

Eligibility

People in need with a preference for residents of Stourbridge (West Midlands) and Kinver (Staffordshire).

Types of grants

One-off grants in the range of £50 and £500.

Annual grant total

In 2012/13, the charity had an income of £47,000 and a total expenditure of £42,000. Full accounts were not available at the time of writing (September 2014); however previously grants to individuals for both educational and social welfare purposes have totalled about £4,000.

Exclusions

No grants are made towards bills or debts.

Applications

In writing to the correspondent. Applications can be submitted directly by the individual or a family member and are considered on an ongoing basis.

Other information

Most support is given to organisations.

The Jonathan Young Memorial Trust

£14,000 (56 grants)

Correspondent: John Young, Trustee, 3 Hardwick Road, The Park, Nottingham NG7 1EP (01159 470493; email: info@jonathan-young-trust.co.uk; website: www.joanthan-young-trust.co.uk)

CC Number: 1067619

Eligibility

People who are living with a disability and would benefit from access to computer technology. The trust operates primarily within the East Midlands (Nottinghamshire, Derbyshire, Leicestershire, Lincolnshire and South Yorkshire) but will occasionally consider applications from further afield. Grants are occasionally made to those who are disadvantaged by reasons other than disability.

Types of grants

Grants of £200 to £500 towards the cost of computer equipment.

Annual grant total

In 2013 the trust had an income of £10,000 and a total expenditure of £15,000. Grants were made of around £14,000.

Exclusions

The trust does not make grants for general living expenses, course or college fees, disability aids, such as wheelchairs, or any non-electronic items.

Applications

In writing to the correspondent, either directly by the individual, carer or parent or through a welfare organisation such as social services or Citizens Advice. Applications should include:

- Name, address, telephone number and age
- Background information
- The nature and extent of the disability
- Financial information – income/expenditure and how much can be contributed towards the equipment
- Why a computer would be beneficial
- The specific equipment needed, including any software and a quotation if possible

For individuals applying directly, a supporting letter from a GP, social worker, teacher or similar should be included. Applications are considered in April and October.

Derbyshire

Alfreton Welfare Trust

£2,300

Correspondent: Celia Johnson, Administrator, 30 South Street, Swanwick, Alfreton, Derbyshire DE55 1BZ (01773 609782)

CC Number: 217114

Eligibility

People in need who live in the former urban district of Alfreton in Derbyshire, namely, the parishes of Alfreton, Ironville, Leabrooks, Somercotes and Swanwick.

Types of grants
One-off grants of up to £200. Our research indicates that previous grants have included travel expenses to hospital, provision of necessary household items and installation costs, recuperative holidays, relief of sudden distress (such as theft of pension or purse, funeral costs, or marital difficulties), telephone installations and to cover outstanding bills. Support can also be given to people with disabilities (including help to buy wheelchairs and so on).

Annual grant total
In 2012/13 the trust had an income of £2,500 and an expenditure of £2,400. We have estimated the annual total of grants to individuals to be around £2,300.

Exclusions
Grants are not given to organisations and groups or for educational purposes.

Applications
In writing to the correspondent. Applications can be made directly by the individual and are considered throughout the year.

The Dronfield Relief-in-Need Charity

£1,000

Correspondent: Dr Tony Bethell, Trustee, Ramshaw Lodge, Crow Lane, Unstone, Dronfield, Derbyshire S18 4AL (01246 413276)

CC Number: 219888

Eligibility
People in need who live in the ecclesiastical parishes of Dronfield, Holmesfield, Unstone and West Handley.

Types of grants
One-off grants, up to a value of £100, towards household needs (such as washing machines), food, clothing, medical appliances (such as a nebulizer) and visitors' fares to and from hospital.

Annual grant total
This charity gives around £1,000 a year in grants to individuals for welfare purposes.

Exclusions
No support for rates, taxes and so on.

Applications
In writing to the correspondent through a social worker, doctor, member of the clergy of any denomination, a local councillor, Citizens Advice or other welfare agency. The applicants should ensure they are receiving all practical/financial assistance they are entitled to from statutory sources.

Other information
Grants are also given to local organisations.

The Margaret Harrison Trust

£3,000

Correspondent: Alexandra Mastin, Trustee, 5 The Avenue, Darley Dale, Matlock DE4 2HT (01629 732931)

CC Number: 234296

Eligibility
'Gentlewomen of good character' aged 50 or over who have lived within a 15-mile radius of St Giles Parish Church, Matlock for at least five years.

Types of grants
Small quarterly pensions.

Annual grant total
In 2012 the trust had an income of £5,000 and an expenditure of £4,000. Grants usually total around £3,000 per year.

These were the latest set of accounts available at the time of writing (August 2014).

Applications
On a form available from the correspondent.

The Sawley Charities

£1,300

Correspondent: Monica Boursnell, Trustee, 35 Weston Crescent, Long Eaton, Nottingham NG10 3BS (01159 726727)

CC Number: 241273

Eligibility
People over 60 years of age in need who have lived in the parishes of Sawley and Wilsthorpe in Derbyshire for at least six years. Normally only state pensioners are considered.

Types of grants
One-off cash grants, usually of around £15 each, towards heating costs.

Annual grant total
In 2013, the charity had an income of £2,900 and a total expenditure of £2,700. We estimate that the total amount of grants awarded to individuals was approximately £1,300.

Applications
On an application form available from the correspondent. Applications can be submitted directly by the individual or family member and should be received by September for consideration in October/November.

Other information
Grants are also made to welfare organisations.

Woodthorpe Relief-in-Need Charity

£25

Correspondent: Michael Scott, Clerk, 8 Wigley Road, Inkersall, Chesterfield, Derbyshire S43 3ER (01246 474457)

CC Number: 244192

Eligibility
People in need, hardship or distress who live in the ancient parishes of Barlborough, Staveley and Unstone.

Types of grants
According to our research, one-off grants of up to £750 can be given for general purposes such as fuel, beds, washing machines, furnishings, mobility chairs and so on.

Annual grant total
In 2013 the charity had an income of approximately £6,700 and a total expenditure of £25, which is exceptionally low. In previous years the charitable spending has been above £1,000 on average.

Applications
In writing to the correspondent.

Other information
Local organisations may also be supported.

Buxton

The Bingham Trust

£16,000

Correspondent: Roger Horne, Trustee, Blinder House, Flagg, Buxton, Derbyshire SK17 9QG (01298 83328; email: binghamtrust@aol.com; website: www.binghamtrust.org.uk)

CC Number: 287636

Eligibility
People in need, primarily those who live in Buxton. Most applicants from outside Buxton are rejected unless there is a Buxton connection.

Types of grants
One-off grants ranging from £200 to £1,500. Grants are made for a wide variety of needs, for example, to relieve poverty, to further education and for religious and community causes.

Annual grant total
In 2012/13 the trust had assets of £4.3 million and an income of £180,000. Grants to individuals for welfare and

education totalled £32,000. There was no breakdown of how much was awarded in educational/social welfare grants and we estimate the total of welfare grants to be around £16,000.

Exclusions

No grants are made for debts or businesses.

Applications

On a form available from the correspondent or to download from the website. Applications should include a supporting letter from a third party such as a social worker, Citizens Advice, doctor or minister. They are considered during the first two weeks of January, April, July and October and should be received before the end of the previous month.

Other information

The trust mainly makes grants to organisations.

Chesterfield

The Chesterfield General Charitable Fund

£2,200

Correspondent: Michael Hadfield, Trustee, The Warren, 404 Old Road, Chesterfield, Derbyshire S40 3QF (01246 566655; email: kmfp2@gmx.co.uk)

CC Number: 511375

Eligibility

People in need who live in the parliamentary constituency of Chesterfield.

Types of grants

One-off and recurrent grants usually ranging from £200 to £800.

Annual grant total

In 2012/13 the fund had an income of £5,500 and a total expenditure of £4,600. We estimate that grants to individuals totalled £2,200, with local organisations also receiving funding.

Applications

In writing to the correspondent, directly by the individual. Applications are considered quarterly.

The Chesterfield United Charities (formerly known as Chesterfield Municipal Charities)

£750

Correspondent: David Jones, Administrator, Shipton Halliwell and Co., 23 West Bars, Chesterfield, Derbyshire S40 1AB (01246 232140)

CC Number: 217112

Eligibility

People who are in need and live in the areas administered by North East Derbyshire District Council or Chesterfield Borough Council.

Types of grants

One-off grants and regular payments of around £100 made twice a year.

Annual grant total

In 2013 the charities had an income of £110,000 and a total expenditure of £94,000. During the year, we estimate that £750 was distributed in grants to individuals.

Applications

In writing to the correspondent.

Other information

Chesterfield United Charities was formed in October 2011 after three charities – Chesterfield Municipal Charities, Louisa Lucas Memorial Homes and the Eustace Edmunds Gift – were brought together. The United Charities now consists of an almshouses branch and a relief-in-need branch.

The charities' spent £79,000 on the running of its two almshouses at St Helen's Close and Louisa Lucas Memorial Homes during 2013.

Clay Cross

The Eliza Ann Cresswell Memorial

£1,100

Correspondent: Dr Christine Fowler, Trustee, Blue Dykes Surgery, Eldon Street, Clay Cross, Chesterfield, Derbyshire S45 9NR (01246 866771; fax: 01246 861058)

CC Number: 230282

Eligibility

People in any kind of need who live in the former urban district of Clay Cross (now the civil parish of Clay Cross), particularly needy families with young children.

Types of grants

Usually one-off grants in whole or part payment of a particular need, for example heating costs, housing, debts, replacement of bedding and damaged furniture, removal costs, and holidays.

Annual grant total

In 2012 the charity had an income of £2,400 and a total expenditure of £2,200. We estimate that social welfare grants to individuals totalled £1,100, with funding also awarded to organisations.

At the time of writing (August 2014) this was the most recent financial information available for the charity.

Exclusions

The charity does not give cash directly to applicants nor does it usually pay the full amount of a debt unless any repayment is beyond the individual's means.

Applications

In writing to the correspondent. A description of the person's financial position, the gaps in statutory provision, what contribution the applicant can make towards the need and what help can be given to prevent the need for future applications should be included. Applications are considered throughout the year. Grants are given on the recommendation of social workers, health visitors, probation officers, home nurses, doctors, clergy and welfare organisations (for example Citizens Advice), and are paid through these bodies.

Derby

The Derby City Charity

£500

Correspondent: Lindsay Kirk, Administrator, Derby City Council, Constitutional Services, 5th Floor, Saxon House, Friary Street, Derby DE1 1AN (01332 643656; email: lindsay.kirk@derby.gov.uk)

CC Number: 214902

Eligibility

People under 25 who live in the city of Derby and are in need.

Types of grants

One-off grants only according to need.

Annual grant total

In 2012/13 the charity had an income of £3,600 and an expenditure of £1,800. We estimate that around £750 in grants was given to individuals for education.

Applications

On a form available from the correspondent on written request. Applications can be submitted either through a relevant third party such as a social worker, Citizens Advice or other welfare agency, or directly by the individual. The trustees meet at least twice a year to consider applications.

Other information

The charity also gives grants to individuals for educational purposes.

The Liversage Trust

£20,000

Correspondent: Yvonne Taylor, Administrator, London Road, Derby DE1 2QW (01332 348199; fax: 01332 349674; email: info@liversagetrust.org; website: www.liversagecourt.org/charitable-grant-giving)

CC Number: 1155282

Eligibility

Grants are made to subsidise almshouse residents, subsidise Liversage Court residents, local people in need and organisations. Subsidies for almshouse residents include Christmas bonuses and winter fuel allowances.

Types of grants

Cash grants for the relief of poverty, usually limited to a maximum of £150 although most grants are of between £30/£40 and £150. Grants can be made towards clothing, food or consumer durables.

Annual grant total

The trust incorporated and re-registered with the Charity Commission in January 2014, therefore no accounts were available at the time of writing. However, grants usually total around £20,000 per year.

Exclusions

Usually only one grant per applicant within a two-year period, although trustees do have discretion in cases of crisis.

Applications

On a form available from the trust's website or the correspondent. Applications should be submitted through a recognised referral agency such as a social worker, Citizens Advice or doctor. They are considered throughout the year.

Other information

The trust's main concern is the management of almshouses and the care home, Liversage Court.

Glossop

The Mary Ellen Allen Charity

£3,500

Correspondent: Philip Sills, Administrator, 1 Bowden Road, Glossop, Derbyshire SK13 7BD (01457 865685)

CC Number: 512661

Eligibility

People over 60 who are in need and live in the former borough of Glossop (as it was in 1947). There is a preference for those who have lived in the area for at least five years in total.

Types of grants

About 15 one-off grants a year in the range of £50 to £500.

Annual grant total

In 2012/13 the charity had an income of £4,200 and a total expenditure of £7,100. We estimate that grants to individuals totalled £3,500, with funding also awarded to local organisations.

Applications

In writing to the correspondent through a social worker, Citizens Advice or other welfare agency where applicable, or directly by the individual. Applications can be submitted at any time for consideration in January, April, July and October.

Ilkeston

The Old Park Ward Old Age Pensioners Fund

£1,200

Correspondent: J. Dack, Administrator, 3 Knole Road, Nottingham NG8 2DB (01159 132118)

CC Number: 201037

Eligibility

People over 65 who are in need and live in the Old Park ward of the former borough of Ilkeston.

Types of grants

One-off cash grants, usually at Christmas time.

Annual grant total

In 2012/13 the fund had an income of £13,700 and a total expenditure of £14,600. In previous years social welfare grants to individuals have totalled an estimated £1,200.

Applications

In writing to the correspondent.

Other information

The majority of the fund's income is spent on providing recreational facilities and events such as dancing, bingo, a monthly Sunday lunch club and other outings.

Matlock

The Ernest Bailey Charity

£1,100

Correspondent: The Chief Executive, Derbyshire Dales District Council, Town Hall, Bank Road, Matlock DE4 3NN (01629 761100; email: legal@derbyshiredales.gov.uk)

CC Number: 518884

Eligibility

People who are sick, poor, elderly, in distress and in need and live in Matlock (this includes Bonsall, Darley Dale, South Darley, Tansley, Matlock Bath and Cromford).

Types of grants

Most applications have been from local groups, but individuals in need and those with educational needs are also supported. Each application is considered on its merits. Grants to individuals are one-off and usually to a maximum of £250.

Annual grant total

In 2012/13 the charity had an income of £2,600 and an expenditure of £2,500. Grants totalled approximately £1,100 for welfare purposes.

Applications

On a form available from the correspondent. Applications are considered in October and must be returned by the end of September. They can be submitted directly by the individual and/or can be supported by a relevant professional. Applications should include costings (total amount required, funds raised and funds promised). Previous beneficiaries may apply again, with account being taken of assistance given in the past.

Spondon

The Spondon Relief-in-Need Charity

£22,000

Correspondent: Lynn Booth, Secretary and Treasurer, PO Box 5073, Spondon, Derby DE21 7JZ (01332 678533; email: info@spondonreliefinneedcharity.org; website: www.spondonreliefinneedcharity.org)

CC Number: 211317

Eligibility

People in need who live in the ancient township of Spondon.

Types of grants

One-off grants in kind up to the value of £500, including those towards electric goods, white goods, clothing, furniture, disability equipment, carpets, childcare and so on. Christmas goodwill gifts are also made.

Annual grant total

In 2013 the charity had assets of £683,000, an income of £30,000 and a total expenditure of £26,000. Grants are made for educational and welfare purposes. In this accounting year, social welfare grants totalled £22,000 and provided for: carpets; furniture/bedding; school trips; and white goods. All grants were under £1,000.

Exclusions

The charity does not contribute towards domestic debts and so on.

Applications

On a form available from the correspondent. Each form must be accompanied by a letter of support from a sponsor such as a doctor, health authority official, social worker, city councillor, clergyman, headteacher, school liaison officer, youth leader or probation officer. The sponsor must justify the applicant's need. The latter is particularly important. The applicant should provide as much information on the form as possible. It is better to ask for a visit by a trustee if possible. A guide is available from the secretary. The trustees meet four times a year and applications must be received by the end of January, April, July and October; grants are given one month later.

Other information

Grants are also made for educational purposes.

Herefordshire

The Harley Charity (formerly The Honourable Miss Frances Harley Charity)

£100

Correspondent: Thomas Davies, Trustee, Elgar House, Holmer Road, Hereford HR4 9SF (01432 352222)

CC Number: 207072

Eligibility

(i) Church of England clergy and their widows/widowers who are in need and live primarily, but not exclusively, in the diocese of Hereford (ii) People who are blind, in need and are members of the Church of England. Usually grants are given to those people living within the area defined above

Types of grants

One-off grants, but individuals who receive a grant can reapply each year.

Annual grant total

In 2012/13 the charity had an income of £6,400 and a total expenditure of £116. We estimate that grants to individuals totalled £100.

Applications

In writing to the correspondent.

Other information

The charity also seeks to support Hereford Cathedral with upkeep and repairs, as well as other local Church of England churches and registered charities.

The Hereford Corn Exchange Fund

£1,000

Correspondent: Elton Edwards, Secretary, Casita, 7 Yew Tree Gardens, Kings Acre, Hereford HR4 0TH (01432 263040)

CC Number: 218570

Eligibility

People in Herefordshire who have been employed at one farm for over 30 years.

Types of grants

Grants of between £100 and £500 for the advancement of agriculture in the county of Herefordshire.

Annual grant total

In 2012/13 the fund had an income of £3,800 and a total expenditure of £4,300. The fund gives about £1,000 to individuals and £1,000 to agricultural organisations each year.

Applications

In writing to the correspondent in March/April for consideration in May.

The Hereford Society for Aiding the Industrious

£5,000

Correspondent: Sally Robertson, Secretary, 18 Venns Close, Bath Street, Hereford HR1 2HH (01432 274014 – Thursdays only; email: hsaialms@talktalkbusiness.net)

CC Number: 212220

Eligibility

People in need who live in Herefordshire (particularly Hereford city) and are trying to better themselves by their own efforts. The early history of the society involved aid to the 'industrious poor' and those who would not make an effort to help themselves were excluded. This is reflected today by priority being given to individuals who are trying to obtain training to get back to work, often as mature students. Grants will be considered when a person is required to fund a gap between formal education and training for a career. The society also considers applications from girl guides and boy scouts for assistance with the cost of camp, but need must be proved in all cases.

Types of grants

Grants or interest-free loans, of £50 to £1,000, according to need.

Annual grant total

In 2012/13 the society had assets of £1 million and an income of £107,000. It was not clear from the accounts the total amount given in grants/loans to individuals and we have estimated this to be around £5,000 for welfare purposes.

Applications

On a form available from the correspondent. Applicants are then interviewed by the secretary. The trustees usually meet on the third Monday of every month.

Other information

The society's main areas of activity are grants and loans to individuals and maintaining almshouses. Donations are also given to Herefordshire charities for specific projects rather than for running costs.

The Herefordshire Community Foundation (known as Herefordshire Foundation)

£2,500

Correspondent: Dave Barclay, Director, The Fred Bulmer Centre, Wall Street, Hereford, Herefordshire HR4 9HP (01432 272550; email: dave.barclay@herefordshire-cf.co.uk; website: www.herefordshirefoundation.org)

CC Number: 1094935

Eligibility

People in need who live in Herefordshire.

Types of grants

One-off and recurrent grants according to need.

Annual grant total

In 2012/13 the foundation had assets of £1.7 million and an income of £171,000. Our research suggests that approximately £5,000 is given each year to individuals.

Applications

HCF administers a number of different funds. These all have their specific application processes and criteria.

Applications should be addressed to 'The Herefordshire Foundation' and if a grant is awarded the applicant will be advised of which fund (or funds) it came from. It is rare for any of these funds to make an award of more than £1,000.

Applications for under £1,000 are welcomed as a 'free-format' letter but this of course should include some standard information such as contact details, what is the grant to be used for and when, a budget/costs and why the grant is needed. Contact the foundation if you wish to discuss details before you apply.

Other information

Grants are also made to organisations.

The Rathbone Moral Aid Charity

£5,000

Correspondent: Carol Thompson, Clerk, Herefordshire Community Council, PO Box 181, Hereford HR2 9YN (01981 250899)

CC Number: 222697

Eligibility

People who live in Herefordshire who are under 25 and in need of rehabilitation, 'particularly as a result of crime, delinquency, prostitution, addiction to drugs or drink, maltreatment or neglect'.

Types of grants

One-off and recurrent grants according to need.

Annual grant total

In 2013, the charity had an income of £5,500 and a total expenditure of £10,500. We estimate that the total amount of grants awarded to individuals was approximately £5,000.

Exclusions

No grants are given for nursery fees.

Applications

In writing to the correspondent. Individual applications are considered throughout the year. All individual applications must be supported by a welfare agency or a doctor, social worker, teacher or other professional.

Other information

Grants are also made to organisations.

Hereford

All Saints Relief-in-Need Charity

£2,100

Correspondent: Douglas Harding, Trustee, 6 St Ethelbert Street, Hereford HR1 2NR (01432 267821)

CC Number: 244527

Eligibility

Individuals in need who live in the city of Hereford, with a preference for those resident in the ancient parish of All Saints.

Types of grants

One-off grants. However, the charity typically prefers to give items rather than cash sums.

Annual grant total

In 2012/13 the charity had an income of £7,600 and a total expenditure of £4,400. We estimate that welfare grants to individuals totalled £2,100, with funding also awarded for educational purposes.

Applications

On a form available from the correspondent.

The Hereford Municipal Charities

£14,000

Correspondent: The Trustees, 147 St Owen Street, Hereford HR1 2JR (01432 354002; email: herefordmunicipal@btconnect.com)

CC Number: 218738

Eligibility

People in need who live in the city of Hereford.

Types of grants

One-off grants of amounts up to £200. Grants are given to help with household equipment, clothes, educational equipment, emergencies and so on.

Annual grant total

In 2013 the charity had an income of £307,000 and a total expenditure of £285,000. Most of the charity's expenditure is allocated to the running of its almshouses and we estimate that grants to individuals for social welfare purposes totalled around £14,000.

Exclusions

No grants towards debts or nursery fees.

Applications

On a form available from the correspondent; to be submitted directly by the individual or through a relevant third party. Applications are considered monthly.

Norton Canon

The Norton Canon Parochial Charities

£2,500

Correspondent: Mary Gittins, Administrator, Ivy Cottage, Norton Canon, Hereford HR4 7BQ (01544 318984)

CC Number: 218560

Eligibility

People in need who live in the parish of Norton Canon.

Types of grants

One-off and recurrent grants according to need.

Annual grant total

Grants total around £10,000 per year and are given to both individuals and organisations for educational and welfare purposes.

Applications

In writing to the correspondent at any time.

Leicestershire and Rutland

Ashby-de-la-Zouch Relief-in-Sickness Fund

£1,300

Correspondent: Leanne Cooper, Trust and Probate Executive, Crane and Walton, 30 South Street, Ashby-de-la-Zouch, Leicestershire LE65 1BT (01530 414111; fax: 01530 417022; email: leannecooper@craneandwalton.co.uk)

CC Number: 508621

Eligibility

People living in Ashby-de-la-Zouch and Blackfordby who are sick, convalescent, have a disability or are caring for ill people and require financial assistance.

Types of grants

Our research suggests that one-off grants in the range of £50 to £60 are given for various needs. Examples include hospital expenses, electrical goods, convalescence, clothing, holidays, travel expenses, medical equipment, furniture, disability equipment and help at home.

Annual grant total

In 2012/13 the fund had an income of £1,000 and an expenditure of £1,400, which is the highest in the past five years. Note that the annual expenditure tends to fluctuate significantly. We estimate the annual total of grants to be about £1,300.

Applications

In writing to the correspondent. Applications can be made at any time either directly by the individual or through a social worker, Citizens Advice or other welfare agency. Anybody who thinks they know someone who needs help is welcome to submit an application on their behalf. Candidates are asked to specify whether any other source of help has been approached.

W. C. Barnes Trust

£600

Correspondent: John Thornton, Trustee, The Old Rectory, Main Road, Wyfordby, Melton Mowbray, Leicestershire LE14 4RY (01664 564437)

CC Number: 500877

Eligibility

People in need who are sick and infirm and live in Melton Mowbray, Eye Kettleby or Great Dalby and have lived there for three years.

Types of grants

One-off grants for a range of needs, including wheelchairs, stairlifts (purchase and rental), household equipment for special needs, food, clothing, travel to hospital and treatment.

Annual grant total

In 2012/13, the trust had an income of £2,700 and a total expenditure of £1,400. We estimate that the total amount of grants awarded to individuals was approximately £600.

Applications

The trust welcomes an initial telephone call. Applications should be in writing to the correspondent either directly by the individual or through a doctor, church leader, social worker, Citizens Advice or other welfare agency. They are considered all year round.

Other information

The trust also awards grants to local organisations that support the sick or infirm.

The John Heggs Bates' Charity for Convalescents

£12,500

Correspondent: Barbara Amos, Administrator, 1 Mill Lane, Leicester LE2 7HU (01162 046620; email: barbara.amos@stwcharity.co.uk)

CC Number: 218060

Eligibility

'Necessitous convalescents' and their carers who reside in Leicester, Leicestershire and Rutland.

Types of grants

One-off grants of £100 to £600 for convalescence breaks.

Annual grant total

In 2013 the charity had an income of £13,600 and a total expenditure of £13,000. We estimate that grants to individuals totalled £12,500.

Applications

On a form available from: Leicester Charity Link, 20a Millstone Lane, Leicester LE1 5JN. Applications should be submitted through a social worker, Citizens Advice, doctor or church and are considered throughout the year.

The Brooke Charity

£2,500

Correspondent: Barbara Clemence, Trustee, Old Rectory Farm, Main Street, Brooke, Oakham, Leicestershire LE15 8DE (01572 770558)

CC Number: 221729

Eligibility

People in need who live in the parish of Brooke and the adjoining parishes of Oakham, Braunston, Ridlington and Morcott, with priority given to the sick, the elderly and children.

Types of grants

One-off grants to relieve financial difficulty, usually in the range of £50 to £250, and for items and services which will improve a person's daily life.

Annual grant total

In 2012/13 the charity had an income of £4,400 and a total expenditure of £5,100. We estimate that grants to individuals totalled £2,500, with funding also awarded to local organisations.

Applications

In writing to the correspondent. Applications can be submitted directly by the individual or, where applicable, through a social worker, Citizens Advice or other welfare agency. They are considered at any time.

The Elizabeth Clarke Relief-in-Need Fund and The Wigston Relief-in-Need Charity

£1,200

Correspondent: Michael Charlesworth, Trustee, 2 Midland Cottages, Wigston, Leicestershire LE18 2BU (01162 811245)

CC Number: 255015/217952

Eligibility

People in need who live in the urban district of Wigston.

Types of grants

One-off grants towards items, services or facilities to relieve general social welfare needs. Support can be given, for example, towards clothing, safety alarms, special chairs, wheelchairs, orthopaedic footwear, travel costs for medical treatment, bedding, spectacles and so on.

Annual grant total

At the time of writing (September 2014) the latest financial information available was from 2012. In 2012 between them the two funds had an income of around £3,200 and an expenditure of £2,600. We estimate that around £1,200 was awarded to individuals from both funds together.

Applications

In writing to the correspondent. Applications should be accompanied by a supporting letter from a social worker or other welfare agency, if possible.

Other information

These two trusts work closely together and often large grants are paid from both funds. However, grants from the Elizabeth Clarke Relief-in-Need Fund are more specifically given to those who live in any ward of Wigston, other than South Wigston.

Grants can also be made to organisations.

Coalville and District Relief-in-Sickness Fund

£200

Correspondent: Sue Clarke, Trustee, 6 Meadow Lane, Coalville, Leicestershire LE67 4DL (01530 834992)

CC Number: 512986

Eligibility

People who live in Coalville and neighbouring district. Support is given to individuals who are sick, infirm or have a disability, and require medical equipment or services not provided by the NHS or other statutory sources.

Types of grants

Our research suggests that one-off grants in the range of £100 to £1,000 are available towards, for example, medical needs, special mattresses, gas fires, washing machines, reconditioned computers, home alterations and so forth.

Annual grant total

In 2012/13 the fund had an income of £1,200 and a total expenditure of around £500. We estimate that grants to individuals totalled about £200. Note that the expenditure varies significantly each year.

Applications

In writing to the correspondent. Applications may be submitted directly by the individual and are generally considered at quarterly intervals.

Other information

The trust gives grants to both individuals and organisations.

Leicester and County Convalescent Homes Society (Leicester ARC)

£0

Correspondent: Lenore Headey, Charity Manager, 22 St Georges Way, Leicester LE1 1SH (01162 620617; email: enquiries@arcleicester.org; website: www.arcleicester.org)

CC Number: 1016951

Eligibility

People in need who are ill, have a disability or are receiving medical care and live in Leicester, Leicestershire and Rutland, and their dependents. Candidates should be on low income or in receipt of one of the following benefits: employment support/allowance; income support/carers allowance; job seekers (income based); disability living allowance/attendance allowance; pension tax credit; working tax credit; or personal budget.

Types of grants

Generally small grants to assist with medical needs with the aim of achieving a better quality of life, including the purchase or hire of a piece of equipment, rehabilitation, respite, specialist therapies, a period of 'quality' time away and so on. Consideration will be given to both short and long-term medically-related needs.

Annual grant total

At the time of writing (September 2014) the latest financial information available was from 2012. During the year no individual awards were made; however previously support has totalled under £1,000.

The trustees annual report from 2012 maintains that 'the charity, along with convalescence, respite and therapies is developing itself as a grant providing charity both for contributors and for individuals in need.'

Applications

Application should be made in writing marked 'for the attention of the grants committee'. They should be accompanied with supporting evidence from a doctor/occupational therapist. Our research suggests that in the case of powered/manual wheelchairs or other medical equipment no application is considered without an assessment from an occupational therapist or physiotherapist as to the best type of chair, make, model, price and adaptations (if any).

Further information on support available can also be requested on a form on the society's website.

Other information

The organisation also offers concessionary rates for therapies to individuals in receipt of one of the specified benefits and with a genuine medical need.

The Leicester Charity Link

£434,000 (3,008 grants)

Correspondent: James Munton, Director of Operations, 20a Millstone Lane, Leicester, Leicestershire LE1 5JN (01162 222200; fax: 01162 222201; email: info@charity-link.org; website: www.charity-link.org)

CC Number: 1078271

Eligibility

People in need who live in the city of Leicester and the vicinity, which includes the whole of Leicestershire and Rutland.

Types of grants

One-off grants and occasionally recurrent grants or pensions. The charity makes payments from its own funds, administers funds on behalf of other charities and puts potential beneficiaries into contact with funds and charities which may be able to help.

Grants are available for a wide range of needs, though the charity most commonly funds essential, everyday items such as beds, cookers and, in emergencies, food. Recent grants for larger items have included stairlifts and specialist wheelchairs.

Goods and services are received by the charity and delivered directly to applicants.

Annual grant total

In 2012/13 the charity held assets of £460,000 and had an income of £754,000. A total of 3,008 grants were awarded to individuals, amounting to £434,000.

Aside from making grants from its own funds, the charity also secured 297 awards totalling £177,000 for individuals and organisations from other donors.

Applications

The charity's website notes:

> We use a network of local organisations that are in the community working with individuals and families in need. Using organisations already in place keeps our overheads to a minimum, increases the efficiency of our services and ensures that we get the help to those who need it when they need it most.

Other information

The charity also makes small grants to organisations (4 grants totalling £475 in 2012/13).

The charity supports a food bank in conjunction with Leicester City Council, St Martin's House, Tomorrow Together and FareShare. Those working with vulnerable individuals or families wishing to access the food bank should telephone (01162 222200) or download an application form from the website.

The Leicester Freemen's Estate

£4,700 (8 grants)

Correspondent: Lynda Bramley, Administrator, Estate Office, 32 Freemen's Holt, Old Church Street, Leicester LE2 8NH (01162 834017; email: office@leicesterfreemen.com; website: www.leicesterfreemen.com)

CC Number: 244732

Eligibility

Needy freemen of Leicester and their widows who are elderly or infirm.

Types of grants

Monthly payments and Christmas hampers.

Annual grant total

In 2013 the charity held assets of £5.8 million and had an income of £238,000. Payments and Christmas hampers to three freemen and five widows totalled £4,700.

Applications

On a form available from the correspondent and including proof of status as a freeman/widow of a freeman. Applications can be submitted directly by the individual and are considered monthly. Beneficiaries' eligibility is reviewed annually.

Other information

The charity also provides accommodation for needy freemen and their widows. Application forms are available from the above address. Social events for residents and non-residents were arranged throughout the year.

Leicestershire Coal Industry Welfare Trust Fund

£14,000

Correspondent: Peter Smith, Trustee, Miners Offices Unit 12, The Springboard Centre, Mantle Lane, Coalville, Leicestershire LE67 3DW (01530 832085; email: leicesternum@ukinbox.com)

CC Number: 1006985

Eligibility

Miners and their dependents connected with the British coal mining industry in the Leicestershire area.

Types of grants

The fund aims to promote and improve applicants' health, social well-being and living conditions. Grants can be given towards holidays, special needs assistance, house repairs, heating systems, house conversions, electrical equipment and so on.

Annual grant total

At the time of writing (August 2014) the latest financial information available was from 2012. In 2012 the fund had an income of £11,500 and a total expenditure of £29,000. Note that both the income and the expenditure vary each year. We estimate the annual total of grants to individuals to be around £14,000.

Applications

In writing to the correspondent. Applications should include details of mining connections, residence in Leicestershire and dependence on the mineworker (in the case of children). The trustees meet throughout the year to discuss applications.

Other information

Grants are also given to organisations.

The Leicestershire and Rutland County Nursing Association

£39,000

Correspondent: Edward Cufflin, Treasurer, Brewin Dolphin, Permanent House, 31 Horsefair Street, Leicester LE1 5BU (01162 420700)

CC Number: 216594

Eligibility

Retired district nurses and people who are sick and in need, who live in Leicestershire or Rutland (excluding the city of Leicester). Priority is given to retired district nurses.

Types of grants

One-off grants up to £3,000 for any need. Recent grants have been given towards hospital costs, bedding and convalescence.

Annual grant total

In 2012/13 the association had assets of £1.4 million and a total income of £58,000. The grant total awarded to individuals was approximately £39,000.

Applications

In writing to the correspondent, directly by the individual in the case of retired district nurses or through Leicester Charity Link in other cases. Applications are considered in January and October.

Other information

The association also makes grants to organisations.

The Loughborough Welfare Trusts

£16,200

Correspondent: Lesley Cutler, Administrator, Bird Wilford and Sale Solicitors, 20 Churchgate, Loughborough LE11 1UD (07765934117; email: loughweltrsts@fsmail.net)

CC Number: 214654

Eligibility

People in need who live in Loughborough and Hathern.

Types of grants

One-off and recurrent grants are given to people on low income for decoration costs, second-hand fridges, holidays and cookers, for example. Grants are also made towards clothing for primary schoolchildren under the age of 11.

Annual grant total

In 2013 the trust had an income of £31,000 and a total expenditure of £30,000. Welfare grants to individuals totalled £16,200, of which more than £12,900 was distributed for relief-in-need purposes and £3,300 for relief in sickness.

Applications

In writing to the correspondent for consideration in January, March, May, July, September or November.

Other information

The trust administers Edgar Corah Charity, John Storer Education Foundation, The Reg Burton Fund, Loughborough Adult Schools, Herrick Charities, and The Loughborough Community Chest.

The Sir Andrew Martin Trust for Young People

£25,000

Correspondent: The Trust Administrator, Walkers Charnwood Bakery, 200 Madeline Road, Beaumont Leys, Leicester LE4 1EX (01162 340033; website: www.sirandrewmartintrust.org)

CC Number: 1042358

Eligibility

Young people in need living in the Leicestershire and Rutland areas.

Types of grants
One-off and recurrent.

Annual grant total
In 2012/13 the trust held assets of £842,000 and had an income of £116,000. Grants totalled £25,000 of which £13,000 was paid in grants to individuals.

Applications
In writing to the correspondent.

Other information
Grants are also made to organisations.

The Nicholson Memorial Fund (The Rosehill Trust)

£2,800

Correspondent: The Clerk to the Trustees, The Nicholson Memorial Fund (Rosehill Trust), 20a Millstone Lane, Leicester LE1 5JN (01162 222200; fax: 01162 222201; email: info@charity-link.org; website: www.charity-link.org)

CC Number: 1000860

Eligibility
Young people and children 'who are delinquent, deprived, neglected or in need of care' in Leicestershire or Rutland.

Types of grants
One-off grants according to need.

Annual grant total
In 2012/13 the trust had an income of £12,300 and total expenditure of £11,200. We estimate that welfare grants to individuals totalled £2,800, with funding also awarded to local organisations and for educational purposes.

Exclusions
One grant per two year period, except in exceptional circumstances.

Applications
On a form available from Leicester Charity Link website.

Other information
Leicester Charity Link, the administrator of this fund, provides a wide range of support and advice to people in need.

The Thomas Stanley Shipman Charitable Trust

£36,000

Correspondent: Andrew York, Secretary to the Trustees, 6 Magnolia Close, Leicester LE2 8PS (01162 835345; email: andrew_york@sky.com)

CC Number: 200789

Eligibility
People in need who live in the city and county of Leicester.

Types of grants
One-off and recurrent grants for living expenses and gifts at Christmas.

Annual grant total
In 2012/13 the trust held assets of £1.3 million and had an income of £55,000. Financial assistance for individuals was distributed as follows:

Leicester Charity Link	£15,000
Christmas gifts	£11,300
Grants and assistance to the elderly	£9,800

Individuals received a total of £36,000 from the trust, £15,000 of which was awarded in discretionary payments through Leicester Charity Link.

A further £15,400 was given to local organisations.

Applications
In writing to the correspondent either directly by the individual or, where applicable, via a relevant third party such as a social worker, Citizens Advice or other welfare agency, or through Leicester Charity Link. The trustees meet twice-yearly, normally in November and June. Applications should be submitted in mid-October and mid-April for consideration.

Other information
The trust does not usually provide educational grants due to lack of resources, and in light of its other objectives.

Barwell

Poor's Platt

£13,500

Correspondent: Jim Munton, Clerk to the Trustees, 20A Millstone Lane, Leicester LE1 5JN (01162 222200; website: barwell.leicestershireparishcouncils.org/parishcouncilgrantstoindividuals.html)

CC Number: 503580

Eligibility
People in need in the ancient parish of Barwell, Leicestershire.

Types of grants
One-off grants of between £50 and £500 are given according to need.

Annual grant total
At the time of writing (August 2014) the latest financial information available was from 2012. In 2012 the charity had an income of £24,000 and an expenditure of £29,000. We estimate that grants to individuals totalled about £13,500.

Applications
Applications can be made through the Leicester Charity Link using their application form (available to access from the Barwell parish council website) or in writing to the correspondent. Awards are considered quarterly, normally in March, June, September and December. The deadline for the submission is the 15th of the preceding month. Only one grant may be awarded in any 12 month period.

Other information
Grants are also available for various organisations, projects and schools in the area of benefit.

Cossington

Babington's Charity

£8,000

Correspondent: Helen McCague, Trustee, 14 Main Street, Cossington, Leicester, Leicestershire LE7 4UU (01509 812271)

CC Number: 220069

Eligibility
People in need in the parish of Cossington.

Types of grants
One-off and recurrent grants according to need.

Annual grant total
In 2012 the charity had an income of £28,000 and a total expenditure of £22,000. We have estimated the grant total to be around £21,000 with £16,000 going to individuals, of which £8,000 was awarded for social welfare purposes. The accounts for 2012 were the latest available at the time of writing (July 2014).

Applications
In writing to the correspondent.

Other information
The charity awards grants to individuals and organisations both for educational and social welfare purposes.

Great Glen

Great Glen Relief-in-Need Charity

£0

Correspondent: Major Gerald Hincks, Trustee, 19 Naseby Way, Great Glen, Leicester LE8 9GS (01162 593155)

CC Number: 231977

Eligibility

People in need (especially older people) who live in the parish of Great Glen and have been living there for a number of years.

Types of grants

One-off grants according to need. Older people receive grants in the form of vouchers at Christmas, at a rate of £15 per individual and £30 per couple.

Annual grant total

In 2013 the charity had an income of £2,000 and had no expenditure.

Applications

In writing to the correspondent. Applications are considered twice a year, usually in November and April.

Other information

In recent years the charity has also made grants to a local church project and to young people in the parish undertaking voluntary work abroad.

Groby

Thomas Herbert Smith's Trust Fund

£7,000

Correspondent: Andrew York, Administrator, 6 Magnolia Close, Leicester LE2 8PS (01162 835345; email: andrew_york@sky.com)

CC Number: 701694

Eligibility

People who live in the parish of Groby in Leicestershire.

Types of grants

One-off and recurrent grants ranging from £100 to £500.

Annual grant total

In 2012/13 the fund had an income of £15,900 and a total expenditure of £29,000. We estimate that grants made to individuals for social welfare purposes totalled around £7,000.

Applications

On a form available from the correspondent, for consideration throughout the year. Applications can be submitted either directly by the individual, or through a social worker, Citizens Advice or other third party.

Other information

The fund also makes grants to individuals and organisations for educational purposes.

Illston

Illston Town Land Charity

£6,700

Correspondent: John Tillotson, Administrator, Warwick House, 5 Barnards Way, Kibworth Harcourt, Leicester LE8 0RS (01162 792524)

CC Number: 246616

Eligibility

People in need who live in the town of Illston in Leicestershire.

Types of grants

Grants towards the costs of council tax charges.

Annual grant total

In 2012/13 the charity had an income of £7,200 and a total expenditure of £6,900. We estimate that welfare grants to individuals totalled £6,700.

Applications

In writing to the correspondent.

Keyham

Keyham Relief-in-Need Charity

£10,000

Correspondent: David Witcomb, Trustee, Tanglewood, Snows Lane, Leicester, Leicestershire LE7 9JS (01162 595663)

CC Number: 215753

Eligibility

People who live in the parish of Keyham (Leicestershire) and are in need. Applications from people who do not live in the area but have strong connections to residents in Keyham have previously been considered.

Types of grants

One-off grants according to need.

Annual grant total

In 2013 the charity had an income of £24,000 and a total expenditure of £21,000. We estimate that grants to individuals totalled £10,000.

Applications

In writing to the correspondent, to be submitted directly by the individual. If the applicant does not live in Keyham, information about their connection with residents should be provided with the application.

Other information

The charity's primary source of funding is rental income from the four cottages it owns. In 2010, two of the cottages underwent major refurbishment and at the time of writing, trustees are hoping to soon upgrade a third.

Leicester

The Leicester Aid-in-Sickness Fund

£13,000

Correspondent: Mark Dunkley, Clerk, Shakespeares, Two Colton Square, Leicester LE1 1QH (01162 545454; email: mark.dunkley@shakespeares.co.uk)

CC Number: 219785

Eligibility

People living in the city of Leicester, who are in poor health and financial need.

Types of grants

One-off grants, generally ranging between £20 and £125.

Annual grant total

In 2012/13 the fund had an income of £11,500 and a total expenditure of £13,300. We estimate that grants to individuals totalled £13,000.

Applications

In writing to the correspondent. Applications are usually considered quarterly.

The Leicester Indigent Old Age Society

£1,400

Correspondent: The Clerk to the Trustees, Leicester Indigent Old Age Society, 20a Millstone Lane, Leicester LE1 5JN (01162 222200; fax: 01162 222201; email: info@charity-link.org; website: www.charity-link.org/leicester-indigent-old-age)

CC Number: 208476

Eligibility

People aged 65 or over who are in need and live in the city of Leicester.

Types of grants

Pensions in payments of £10 per month to approximately 90 recipients. Grants are also made for coach trips and outings for older people living in Leicester.

Annual grant total

In 2012/13 the society had an income of £5,300 and a total expenditure of £2,900. We estimate that welfare grants to individuals totalled £1,400, with funding also awarded to organisations in Leicester 'who assist older people that are in need, hardship or distress', as noted on the Charity Link website

Applications

Applications should be made through Leicester Charity Link using an application form which can be found on the website.

Note the following statement from the charity's website: 'Due to pressure on funds help is only given once every two years unless there are exceptional circumstances.'

The Parish Piece Charity

£6,500

Correspondent: Revd Canon Barry Naylor, Trustee, St Martins House, 7 Peacock Lane, Leicester LE1 5PZ (email: magwill26@ntlworld.com)

CC Number: 215775

Eligibility

People in need who live in the parish of St Margaret in Leicester. Priority is usually given to older people and people with disabilities.

Types of grants

One-off grants and small pensions. Grants have been given for heating costs and electrical appliances.

Annual grant total

In 2012/13 the charity had an income of £10,600 and a total expenditure of £13,300. We estimate that welfare grants to individuals totalled £6,500, with funding also awarded to local organisations.

Applications

In writing to the correspondent or via Leicester Charity Link using their standard application form.

St Margaret's Charity

£3,700

Correspondent: Revd Canon Barry Naylor, Trustee, St Martins House, 7 Peacock Lane, Leicester LE1 5PZ (email: magwill26@ntlworld.com)

CC Number: 234626

Eligibility

People in need who live in the city of Leicester.

Types of grants

One-off grants, usually ranging from £25 to £100.

Annual grant total

In 2012/13 the charity had an income of £5,700 and a total expenditure of £7,700. We estimate that grants to individuals totalled £3,700, with funding also awarded to local organisations.

Applications

Applications must be made through a welfare organisation such as Leicester Charity Link.

Sir Edward Wood's Bequest Fund For Gentlewomen

£1,200

Correspondent: Andrew Norris, Trustee, 63 Carisbrooke Road, Leicester LE2 3PF (01162 704223; email: andrew.norris@brewin.co.uk)

CC Number: 220606

Eligibility

Women who are 55 years old or over, are either unmarried or widows, who have lived in the area administered by Leicester City Council for at least ten years, and who are members of a Protestant non-conformist church.

Types of grants

Pensions only of £400 a year, paid quarterly.

Annual grant total

In 2013/14 the fund had an income of £4,400 and a total expenditure of £1,400. We estimate that social welfare grants to individuals totalled £1,200, though expenditure for the fund tends to vary widely from year to year.

Applications

On a form available from the correspondent, either directly by the individual or through a third party. A reference from a church minister is also needed. There are only a limited number of pensions available and applications can only be considered when a vacancy arises.

Market Harborough

The Market Harborough and The Bowdens Charity

£39,000 (85 grants)

Correspondent: James Jacobs, Administrator, Steward, Godfrey Payton and Co., 149 St Mary's Road, Market Harborough, Leicester LE16 7DZ (01858 462467; email: admin@mhbcharity.co.uk; website: www.mhbcharity.co.uk)

CC Number: 1041958

Eligibility

People in need who have lived within Market Harborough area for at least six months. The guidance notes state: 'The charity prefers prevention to palliatives. It wishes to foster self-help and the participation of those intended to benefit; enable less advantaged people to be independent, gain useful skills and overcome handicaps; and encourage volunteer involvement.'

Types of grants

Grants are one-off and typically under £1,000.

Annual grant total

At the time of writing (August 2014) the latest financial information available was from 2012. In 2012 the charity had assets of £15.8 million and an income of £629,000. Grants totalling £39,000 were given to 85 individuals in need.

Exclusions

Applicants must have exhausted all other areas of assistance before applying to the charity. Individuals who have received a grant from the charity in previous 12 months will not normally be eligible for assistance.

Applications

Application forms are available from the correspondent or can be downloaded from the charity's website. They can be submitted either directly by the individual or through a third party, such as a social worker, Citizens Advice or other welfare agency, if applicable. In any case a supporting letter from a professional will be required. Potential applicants are invited to contact the correspondent directly for further guidance at 01858 581315.

Other information

Support is also given to individuals for educational purposes, to organisations, institutions and towards preservation of historical churches in the area.

Markfield

Jane Avery Charity – Markfield

£0

Correspondent: Revd Simon Nicholls, Trustee, The Rectory, 3a The Nook, Markfield, Leicestershire LE67 9WE (01530 242844)

CC Number: 231958

Eligibility

People in need who live in the ancient parish of Markfield.

Types of grants

Normally one-off grants of £25 to £300. Grants have included those towards holiday costs, nursery school fees, a wheelchair and house repairs.

Annual grant total

In 2012 the charity had an income of £1,200 and had no expenditure.

At the time of writing (August 2014) this was the most recent financial information available for the charity.

Exclusions

There are no grants available for educational purposes.

Applications

In writing to the correspondent. Applications can be submitted directly by the individual or through a social worker, Citizens Advice, other welfare agency, or through a third party such as a doctor, minister, neighbour or relative. They can be considered at any time.

Mountsorrel

Mountsorrel Relief-in-Need Charity

£68,000

Correspondent: Paul Blakemore, Educational Fund Secretary, KDB Accountants and Consultants Ltd, 21 Hollytree Close, Hoton, Loughborough LE12 5SE (01509 889369; website: mountsorrelunitedcharities.co.uk)

CC Number: 217615

Eligibility

People in need who live in the parish of Mountsorrel.

Types of grants

One-off grants towards electrical household goods, garden maintenance, decorating costs, carpets/flooring, Charnwood Piper Lifelines, mobility equipment, childcare expenses, hospital travel expenses and so on.

Annual grant total

In 2013, the charity had an income of £126,000 and a total expenditure of £130,000. We estimate that grants awarded to individuals totalled £68,000 based on previous grantmaking patterns. Grants are also awarded to organisations.

Applications

To apply, contact Carol Watts, Benefit Secretary (tel: 01162 375132 or 0753 460 4337), who will visit the applicant in their home and help them to complete the application form.

Other information

This charity is closely linked to the Mountsorrel United Charities (Charity Commission no. 1027652).

Oadby

The Oadby Educational Foundation

£0

Correspondent: Rodney Waterfield, Hon. Secretary and Treasurer, 2 Silverton Road, Oadby, Leicester LE2 4NN (01162 714507)

CC Number: 528000

Eligibility

People in need in the parish of Oadby only.

Types of grants

One-off and recurrent grants in the range of £50 and £200.

Annual grant total

In 2012 the foundation had assets of £1 million and an income of £46,000. £21,000 was given in educational grants and no grants for welfare were made during the year. These were the latest accounts available at the time of writing (July 2014).

Applications

In writing to the correspondent, to be submitted either through a social worker, Citizens Advice or other welfare agency, or directly by the individual. They are considered in March, June and October.

Other information

Grants are also made to organisations.

Queniborough

Alex Neale Charity

£3,700

Correspondent: Maurice Kirk, Administrator, 6 Ervin Way, Queniborough, Leicester LE7 3TT (01162 606851; email: mrakirk@btinternet.com)

CC Number: 260247

Eligibility

Older people in need who live in the parish of Queniborough.

Types of grants

Grants towards gas and electricity bills.

Annual grant total

In 2013, the charity had both an income and a total expenditure of £3,800. We estimate that the total amount of grants awarded to individuals was approximately £3,700.

Applications

The trustees publicise the grants, usually every two years, in The Queniborough Gazette. An application form is then available from the correspondent. The charity may ask for copies of fuel bills for the two years prior to application, and then a grant would be made towards the costs of these bills.

Quorn

The Quorn Town Lands Charity

£1,900

Correspondent: Trish Jonczyk, Clerk to the Trustees, 45 Leicester Road, Quorn, Loughborough, Leicestershire LE12 8BA (01509 412457; fax: 01162 350946; email: trish.jonczyk@btinternet.com; website: quorndon.com/townlands/index.php)

CC Number: 216703

Eligibility

People in need who live in the parish of Quorn.

Types of grants

One-off and recurrent grants usually in the range of £50 to £250. Grants given have included those for hospital expenses, convalescence, living costs, household bills, food, travel expenses and help in the home.

Annual grant total

In 2012/13 the charity had an income of £4,300 and a total expenditure of £3,900. We estimate that grants to individuals totalled £1,900, with funding also awarded to local organisations and clubs.

Applications

By completing the application form, which is available for both individuals and groups from the Quorn Village website, or in writing to the correspondent. Applications should be submitted directly by the individual or through a relevant third party. They are considered quarterly.

Other information

This charity consists of three different funds: Quorn Town Lands Charity, Quorn Aid in Sickness Fund and Quorn Education Fund.

Rutland

The Rutland Dispensary

£1,600

Correspondent: The Administrator, 31 Springfield Way, Oakham, Leicestershire LE15 6QA (01572756120; email: angelaandfrancis@talktalk.net)

CC Number: 230188

Eligibility

People who are poor, old or sick and live in Rutland.

Types of grants

One-off and recurrent grants, usually in the range of £100–£250. Support is mainly given to relieve medical needs not covered by the NHS.

Annual grant total

In 2013 the charity had an income of £3,100 and an expenditure of £1,800. We estimate the annual total of grants to be about £1,600.

Applications

In writing to the correspondent. Applicants should include details of any medical conditions and their general circumstances.

The Rutland Trust

£3,500

Correspondent: Richard Adams, Clerk, 35 Trent Road, Oakham, Rutland LE15 6HE (01572 756706; email: adams@apair.wanadoo.co.uk)

CC Number: 517175

Eligibility

People who have disabilities, live in Rutland and are in need.

Types of grants

One-off and recurrent grants ranging between £50 and £400, to buy equipment.

Annual grant total

In 2013 the trust had an income of £20,000 and a total expenditure of £14,000. Grants are also made for educational purposes and to organisations. We estimate grants awarded to individuals for social welfare purposes totalled around £3,500.

Applications

An initial telephone call is recommended.

Syston

The H. A. Taylor Fund

£14,000

Correspondent: The Clerk to the Trustees, H. A. Taylor Fund, 20a Millstone Lane, Leicester LE1 5JN (01162 222200; fax: 01162 222201; email: info@charity-link.org; website: www.charity-link.org)

CC Number: 516428

Eligibility

People in need who have been resident in the parish of Syston for at least one year.

Types of grants

One-off grants, usually ranging from £50 to £1,000, towards travel costs, furniture, clothing, fuel, household repairs, medical treatment, books and course fees, mobility aids and telephone and television expenses, for example.

Annual grant total

In 2012/13 the fund had an income of £24,000 and a total expenditure of £30,000. We estimate that grants to individuals totalled £14,000, with funding also awarded to organisations.

Exclusions

Applicants should not reapply within two years of receiving a grant, apart from in exceptional circumstances.

Applications

Application forms are available from Syston and District Volunteer Centre, Syston Health Centre and Syston Library or can be downloaded from the website. They can be submitted at any time, either through a third party or directly by the individual, and are considered every two months.

Wymeswold

The Wymeswold Parochial Charities

£2,000

Correspondent: Mrs J. Collington, 94 Brook Street, Wymeswold, Loughborough LE12 6TU (01509 880538)

CC Number: 213241

Eligibility

People in need who have lived in Wymeswold for the last two years.

Types of grants

Winter gifts to senior citizens, widows and widowers. One-off grants are also given to people who are ill.

Annual grant total

Grants awarded to individuals total about £4,000 a year. The charity also awards educational grants.

Applications

In writing to the correspondent at any time.

Lincolnshire

Addlethorpe Parochial Charity

£2,300

Correspondent: Maggie Boughton, Administrator, The Willows, Mill Lane, Addlethorpe, Skegness, Lincolnshire PE24 4TB (01754 760644)

CC Number: 251412

Eligibility

People who are sick, convalescent, disabled or infirm, and who live in the parish of Addlethorpe, or who previously lived in Addlethorpe and now live in an adjoining parish. Applicants must be either living on a low income, with limited savings or investments of less than £10,000, or have a disability or illness that renders them unable to work.

Types of grants

Most grants are in the form of solid fuel or electricity/gas cheques. One-off grants are given towards funeral expenses, household repairs and other necessities. Grants have also been given for hospital or doctor's visits. Grants of £60 are available, and may be given up to three times during the year.

Annual grant total

In 2012/13, the charity had an income of £3,200 and a total expenditure of £2,500. We estimate that the total amount of grants awarded to individuals was approximately £2,300.

Applications

In writing to the correspondent to be submitted either directly by the individual or a family member, through a third party such as a social worker, or through an organisation such as Citizens Advice or other welfare agency. Applicants must state that they are living on a reduced income and that savings/ investments are below £10,000. Applications are considered on an ongoing basis.

The Bishop of Lincoln's Discretionary Fund

£9,100

Correspondent: Revd Sally-Anne McDougall, Trustee, The Bishop's Office, The Old Palace, Minster Yard, Lincoln LN2 1PU

CC Number: 1022582

Eligibility

Ministers of the Church of England who live and work in the Diocese of Lincoln, and their dependents.

Types of grants

One-off grants of around £25 to £450 according to need. Grants are usually to assist sick clergy and their families and for holiday grants.

Annual grant total

In 2013 the fund had an income of £17,400 and a total expenditure of £9,300. We estimate that grants to individuals totalled £9,100.

Applications

In writing by the individual or one of the other local bishops to the Bishop of Lincoln. Applications are considered throughout the year.

Boston and District Sick Poor Fund

£1,100

Correspondent: Susan Ganley, Trustee, 65 Manor Gardens, Boston PE21 6JJ (01205 368977; email: rsharpe@home.modcomp.net)

CC Number: 500743

Eligibility

People in need through low income or sickness who live in Boston and the surrounding district.

Types of grants

One-off grants according to need.

Annual grant total

In 2013 the fund had an income of £5,100 and a total expenditure of £2,200. We estimate that social welfare grants to individuals totalled £1,100, with funding also awarded to organisations.

Applications

In writing to the correspondent.

Michael Cornish Charitable Trust

£200

Correspondent: Phillipa Cridland, Administrator, Wright Vigar Ltd, 15 Newland, Lincoln LN1 1XG (01522 531341; email: phillipa.cridland@wrightvigar.co.uk)

CC Number: 1107890

Eligibility

Children and young people who are in need with a preference for those who live in Lincolnshire.

Types of grants

One-off and recurrent grants according to need. Previous support has also included assistance for volunteers and sports activities. Individual grants are often of about £200.

Annual grant total

At the time of writing (September 2014) the latest financial information available was from 2012. In 2012 the trust had assets of £13 million and an income of £169,000. A total of £5,500 was awarded in community and individual grants, of which £200 was given through Raleigh Foundation for an individual. The annual total of grants to individuals varies each year.

Applications

In writing to the correspondent. The trustees meet quarterly.

Other information

The trust predominantly makes grants to organisations, especially in the Lincolnshire area and charities involving children or young people from disadvantaged backgrounds, although 'the trustees may consider grants to individuals for worthy causes in exceptional circumstances.'

The Charity of John Dawber

£13,000

Correspondent: Helen Newson, Administrator, Andrew and Co. Solicitors, St Swithin's Court, 1 Flavian Road, Lincoln LN2 1HB (01522 512123; email: helen.newson@andrew-solicitors.co.uk)

CC Number: 216471

Eligibility

People in need who live in the city of Lincoln and the parish of Bracebridge.

Types of grants

The charity has ceased making payments of annuities and Christmas grocery vouchers. They plan to make grants which will be of benefit to the community and are hoping to work with Lincoln City Council to address these needs.

Annual grant total

In 2012/13 the charity had assets of £1.4 million and an income of £40,000. During the year, charitable grant expenditure totalled £5,000.

Applications

In writing to the correspondent. There are no deadlines for applications.

Other information

The charity also makes grants to organisations that benefit people living in the beneficial area.

The Farmers' Benevolent Institution

£5,700

Correspondent: J. D. Andrew, Administrator, c/o Duncan and Toplis, 3 Castlegate, Grantham, Lincolnshire NG31 6SF (01476 591200; fax: 01476 591222; email: duncan.andrew@duntop.co.uk)

CC Number: 216042

Eligibility

People living within a 15-mile radius of Grantham who have 'been owners or occupiers of land, but who from losses or other untoward circumstances have become destitute'. Applicants must be over 60 if they have been a subscriber of the fund for ten years or more. Otherwise they should be over 65.

Types of grants

Annual payments of around £150 and a supplementary payment at Christmas.

Annual grant total

In 2012/13, the charity had an income of £4,700 and a total expenditure of £5,900. We estimate that the total amount of grants awarded to individuals was approximately £5,700.

Applications

In writing to the correspondent.

Hunstone's Charity

£16,000

Correspondent: Tony Bradley, Administrator, 58 Eastwood Road, Boston, Lincolnshire PE21 0PH (01205 364175)

CC Number: 214570

Eligibility

Gentlemen in need who live in Lincolnshire with preference for 'decayed gentlemen of the family of Edward Hunstone or of the several families of the Gedneys or of Robert Smith or of the Woodliffes and decayed gentlemen living in the county of Lincoln'. Particular mention is also made of retired clergymen, members of HM Forces, farmers, farm labourers or anyone connected with land, and people with disabilities.

Types of grants

Recipients receive £250 per year, paid in two instalments of £125 in April and October. The assistance will be given as long as the trustees consider necessary or until the death of the recipient.

Annual grant total

In 2013 the charity had an income of £30,000 and a total expenditure of £102,000 (2011: £21,000 and 2012: £29,000). Grants usually total in the region of £16,000. The accounts were not available to view and we have no information on the unusual increase in expenditure.

Exclusions

Grants are not given to women.

Applications

On a form available from the correspondent. Applications should be submitted either through a social worker, Citizens Advice or other welfare agency, or directly by the individual. They are considered in May each year and should be received by 30 April; urgent applications can be considered at other times. Two references are required with each application.

The Kitchings General Charity

£8,000

Correspondent: J. Smith, Secretary, 42 Abbey Road, Bardney, Lincoln LN3 5XA (01526 398505)

CC Number: 219957

Eligibility

People in need who live in the parish of Bardney (covers Stainfield, Apley, Tupholme and Bucknall).

Types of grants

One-off grants to relieve hardship or distress, such as for holidays/respite care for disabled people (mostly at a special home at Sandringham), specialised nursing equipment including wheelchairs, funeral expenses and household essential such as carpets, flooring and bedding. Grants are usually in the range of £200 and £500 but can be up to £2,000.

Annual grant total

In 2013 the charity had an income of £38,000 and made social welfare grants, including widows' pensions, totalling £16,000. We estimate that grants to individuals for social welfare purposes was around £8,000.

Applications

In writing to the correspondent directly by the individual; only basic details are required. Applications are considered in May, October and January.

Other information

The charity also gives grants to local schools and organisations, and to individuals for education.

The Lincoln General Dispensary Fund

£6,200

Correspondent: Michael Bonass, Administrator, Durrus, Scothern Lane, Dunholme, Lincoln LN2 3QP (01673 860660)

CC Number: 220159

Eligibility

People who are in poor health, convalescent or who have disabilities and live within the ten-mile radius of the Stonebow (Lincoln).

Types of grants

One-off grants up to around £250 to alleviate suffering or aid recovery. Our research tells us that past grants have been given for orthopaedic beds, alarm systems and recuperative holidays.

Annual grant total

In 2013 the fund had an income of £11,900 and a total expenditure of £12,700. We estimate that grants to individuals totalled £6,200. Funding was also given to local organisations.

Exclusions

No grants are given for building adaptations, debts already incurred or anything that could be provided by public funds.

Applications

On a form available from the correspondent, to be submitted through a recognised social or medical agency. Applications are considered throughout the year.

Lincolnshire Community Foundation

£4,000

Correspondent: Sue Fortune, Grants Manager, 4 Mill House, Moneys Yard, Carre Street, Sleaford, Lincolnshire NG34 7TW (01529 305825; email: lincolnshirecf@btconnect.com; website: www.lincolnshirecf.co.uk)

CC Number: 1092328

Eligibility

Generally, residents of Lincoln who are in need. However, different funds have different eligibility criteria attached. See types of grant section.

Types of grants

The Colin Batts' Family Trust

Grants of up to £500 are available to individuals and not for profit community groups to provide opportunities for young people. Mr Batts is keen to give a helping hand to families suffering hardship and improve the quality of life for their children. Grants are awarded for travel, competition fees and kit. Help can be given to children with disabilities who cannot participate in mainstream activities.

Be aware that, like other community foundations, schemes can open and close at very short notice. Check the website before applying.

Annual grant total

In 2012/13 the foundation had assets of £3.4 million and a total expenditure of £895,000. Grants for social welfare purposes made to individuals from the Colin Batts' Family Trust totalled just over £4,000.

Applications

On an application form available to download from the website.

Lincolnshire Police Charitable Fund

£31,000

Correspondent: Donna Grant, Administrator, 12 Newbury Road, Newark, Nottinghamshire NG24 2JL (01522 558303; email: charitable.fund@lincs.pnn.police.uk)

CC Number: 500682

Eligibility

People in need who are present or former employees of Lincolnshire Police Authority, and their dependents. Former employees of other Police Authorities who have retired and now live in Lincolnshire may also qualify for assistance.

Types of grants

One-off grants according to need.

Annual grant total

In 2012/13 the fund held assets of £150,000 and had an income of £37,000. Grants to individuals totalled more than £31,000 and were distributed as follows:

General cases	£17,800
Medical, travel and expenses	£10,500
Death grants	£1,200
Fruit, flowers and donations	£1,000
Christmas gifts	£900

A further £2,500 was awarded in grants to four organisations.

Applications

On a form available from the Welfare Officer. Applications can be submitted directly by the individual or, where applicable, through a social worker, Citizens Advice or other welfare agency.

The Tyler Charity for the Poor

£3,000

Correspondent: Mrs E. M. Bradley, Administrator, 22 Market Place, Gainsborough, Lincolnshire DN21 2BZ (01427 010761)

CC Number: 217594

Eligibility

People in need who live in the parishes of Morton and Thornock.

Types of grants

One-off and recurrent grants according to need.

Annual grant total

In 2012/13 the charity had an income of £1,000 and a total expenditure of £3,500. When compared to previous years this figure for expenditure is unusually high. We estimate that social welfare grants to individuals totalled £3,000, though it is likely that grants expenditure fluctuates each year.

Applications

In writing to the correspondent.

Willingham and District Relief-in-Sickness Charity

£3,000

Correspondent: J. Spencer, Secretary, 4 Church Road, Upton, Gainsborough DN21 5NS (01427 838385)

CC Number: 512180

Eligibility

People in need who live in the parishes of Corringham, Heapham, Kexby, Springthorpe, Upton and Willingham.

Types of grants

Grants of money or providing or paying for items, services or facilities which help those in need.

Annual grant total

In 2012 the charity had an income of £4,900 and an expenditure of £3,500. Grants totalled around £3,000.

These were the latest set of accounts available at the time of writing (August 2014).

Applications

In writing to the correspondent by 1 April or 1 October for meetings at the end of those months.

Barrow-upon-Humber

The Beeton, Barrick and Beck Relief-in-Need Charity

£4,000

Correspondent: Mrs A. Lawe, Administrator, Barrow Wold Farm, Deepdale, Barton-upon-Humber, North Lincolnshire DN18 6ED (01469 531928)

CC Number: 234571

Eligibility

People in need who are over 60 and live in the parish of Barrow-upon-Humber.

Types of grants

Christmas vouchers and one-off grants for a variety of purposes, such as travel costs to hospital.

Annual grant total

In 2012/13 the charity had an income of £4,700 and a total expenditure of £4,100. We estimate that grants to individuals totalled £4,000.

Applications

On a form available from the correspondent.

Barton-upon-Humber

The Barton-upon-Humber Relief-in-Sickness Fund

£1,300

Correspondent: Harold Ready, Administrator, Market Place, Barton-upon-Humber, North Lincolnshire DN18 5DD (01652 632215; email: mail@keithready.co.uk)

CC Number: 504255

Eligibility

People in the parish of Barton-upon-Humber who are suffering from ill-health, and their relatives/carers (in appropriate cases).

Types of grants

Discretionary grants are given for all kinds of need, but usually for medical aids and equipment.

Annual grant total

In 2012/13, the fund had an income of £2,400 and a total expenditure of £1,500. We estimate that the total amount of grants awarded to individuals was approximately £1,300.

Applications

In writing to the correspondent. The trustees discuss cases which are known personally to them, although written applications are equally welcome and are considered when received.

Blue Coat Charity

£13,000

Correspondent: Keith Ready and Co. Solicitors, Market Place, Barton-upon-Humber, North Lincolnshire DN18 5DD (01652 632215)

CC Number: 237891

Eligibility

People in need who live in Barton-upon-Humber.

Types of grants

One-off grants, usually of around £25 to £30, towards footwear, clothing, bedding and other essential items.

Annual grant total

In 2012/13 the charity had an income of £29,000 and a total expenditure of £21,000.

Applications

In writing to the correspondent. Unless urgent, applications are considered each November.

Other information

The charity is also known as the Charity of John Tripp.

Billingborough

Billingborough United Charities

£300

Correspondent: Neal Newnham, Trustee, Barbridge Farmhouse, Low Grounds, Swineshead, Boston, Lincolnshire PE20 3PG (01205 820448)

CC Number: 217451

Eligibility

People in need, hardship or distress who live in the civil parish of Billingborough.

Types of grants

Our research suggests that one-off grants of £40 are given according to need, including awards to people at Christmas.

Annual grant total

At the time of writing (September 2014) the latest financial information available was from 2012. In 2012 the charity had an income of £2,400 and an expenditure of £350, which is the lowest in the past five years. We estimate that grants totalled about £300, although the expenditure varies annually.

Exclusions

Payments are not made towards statutory liabilities, for example council tax, income tax or national insurance.

Applications

In writing to the correspondent. Applications can be made either directly by the individual or on their behalf by a vicar, churchwarden, school master, doctor, district nurse, friend, family member, social worker, Citizens Advice or other welfare agency. They are considered at any time.

Deeping

Deeping St James United Charities

£27,000

Correspondent: Julie Banks, Clerk, The Institute, 38 Church Street, Deeping St James, Peterborough PE6 8HD (01778 344707 (Tues/Thurs 9am-12pm); email: dsjunitedcharities@btconnect.com; website: www.dsjunitedcharities.org.uk)

CC Number: 248848

Eligibility

People in the parish of Deeping St James (including Frognall) who are in need, hardship or suffer from ill health, disability or are otherwise disadvantaged. There are no fixed income limits for applications.

Grants are also paid to widows over 60 who have lived in the parish for at least three years.

Types of grants

One-off and recurrent grants according to need are given for a variety of purposes such as clothing, hospital travel expenses, household equipment and repairs, white goods, carpets, bathroom conversions for older people, special equipment or services (for example foot care), pre-paying prescriptions, food, bills, heating installations or bereavement support. Interest free loans may also be made. In partnership with Deeping Men's Group funds are provided for mobility aid, such as wheelchairs, beds, hoists and so on.

St Thomas' Day charity awards grants of £25 each to widows. If you prefer to receive the original benefaction of a loaf of bread and a bucket of coal please let the trustees know in plenty of time so they can make arrangements.

Annual grant total

In 2013 the charity had assets of £2.6 million and an income of £99,000. Relief-in-need support totalled £21,000 and relief-of-sickness grants reached £2,500. Grants to 141 widows totalled around £3,400.

Applications

Application forms can be requested from the correspondent or collected from the Institute (see 'Correspondent'). Awards are generally considered at the start of March, June, September and December.

Application forms for St Thomas Day grants are available online, from the local post office or the correspondent. The awards are made on or around 21 December.

Other information

The charity is an amalgamation of a number of small charities from the local area. This charity also gives grants to individuals for welfare purposes and local organisations, groups, clubs or societies. Regular support is given to all three schools in Deeping St James for the benefit of their pupils.

Applicants are encouraged to get in touch with the charity via phone, email or by calling in to the office if they have any questions or need further assistance.

The charity is also funding counselling sessions with Citizens Advice for local residents. The sessions are held on a fortnightly basis at the Institute (to book an appointment call: 01780 763051).

Funding is also given for educational purposes.

Frampton

The Frampton Town Lands and United Charities

£2,800

Correspondent: Mark Hildred, Administrator, Moore Thompson, Bank House, Broad Street, Spalding, Lincolnshire PE11 1TB (01775 711333; fax: 01775 711307)

CC Number: 216849

Eligibility

People in need who have lived in the ancient parish of Frampton for at least five years. Preference is usually given to older people (aged over 65) and recently bereaved widows.

Types of grants

One-off grants towards electricity bills, Christmas gifts for older people and so on.

Annual grant total

In 2012/13 the charities had an income of £11,200 and an expenditure of £11,400. We estimate that welfare grants to individuals totalled £2,800, with funding also awarded to local organisations and for educational purposes.

Applications

In writing to the correspondent. Applications are normally considered in October.

Friskney

The Friskney United Charities

£400

Correspondent: Jacquie Scott, Secretary, Sigtoft Farm, Low Road South, Friskney, Boston PE22 8QH (01754 820554)

CC Number: 217282

Eligibility

Older people in need who live in Friskney, particularly those who have a connection with agricultural work.

Types of grants

Annual grants of 3CWT of coal and/or £10 each, classed as Christmas gifts.

Annual grant total

This charity's main purpose is the provision of housing for older people. Coal and charitable gifts given usually total around £400.

Applications

In writing to the correspondent. Applications are usually considered in

November. A list of applicants is produced by the trustees based upon their local knowledge.

Grimsby

Sir Alec Black's Charity

£3,100 (6 grants)

Correspondent: Stewart Wilson, Trustee, Wilson Sharpe and Co., 27 Osborne Street, Grimsby, North East Lincolnshire DN31 1NU (01472 348315; email: sc@wilsonsharpe.co.uk)

CC Number: 220295

Eligibility

Fishermen and dockworkers who are sick and poor, who live in the borough of Grimsby. Grants are also available to people employed by Sir Alec Black during his lifetime.

Types of grants

One-off and recurrent grants according to need.

Annual grant total

In 2012/13 the charity had an income of £100,000 and a total expenditure of £144,000. Grants to fishermen and dockworkers totalled £3,100 and grants to hospices totalled £119,000.

Applications

In writing to the correspondent. The trustees meet twice a year, in May and November, to consider applications.

Grimsby Sailors and Fishing Charity

£25,000

Correspondent: Duncan Watt, Charities Administrator, 1st Floor, 23 Bargate, Grimsby, South Humberside DN34 4SS (01472 347914; fax: 01472 347914; email: duncan.watt4@gmail.com)

CC Number: 500816

Eligibility

Primarily the children of Grimsby fishermen lost at sea or dying ashore while still fishermen. However, help may also be available to other beneficiaries living in Grimsby and the surrounding area, at the trustees' discretion.

Types of grants

Weekly and quarterly grants to support children of deceased fishermen while they are still in full-time education. Weekly grants are usually around £13 and quarterly grants range from £100 to £250.

Annual grant total

In 2013 the charity had assets of £4.3 million and an income of £544,000. The majority of the charity's expenditure is spent on providing and maintaining almshouses. Grants to individuals totalled £25,000.

Applications

On a form available from the correspondent or from the Port Missioner. Applications should be submitted directly by the individual or through an appropriate welfare agency. They are considered when received.

Other information

The Grimsby Fishermen's Dependents Fund transferred its funds to this charity and is now a subsidiary.

Haconby and Stainfield

Haconby Poor's Money and Others

£2,800

Correspondent: Sally Burton, Trustee, 36 Headland Way, Haconby, Bourne, Lincolnshire PE10 0UW (01778 571441; email: sally.burton@tiscali.co.uk)

CC Number: 218589

Eligibility

People in need who live in the parish of Haconby and Stainfield.

Types of grants

One-off and recurrent grants according to need. Grants have been given as Christmas gifts to people aged over 60, help with home alterations for disabled people, and towards funeral expenses and hospital travel costs.

Annual grant total

In 2013 the charity had an income of £3,600 and a total expenditure of £2,900. We estimate that grants to individuals totalled £2,800.

Applications

In writing to the correspondent. Applications can be submitted directly by the individual or through a third party such as a social worker, Citizens Advice, welfare agency or neighbour.

Kesteven

Committee For Kesteven Children in Need (KCIN)

£5,200

Correspondent: Alexandra Howard, Trustee, Nocton Rise, Lincoln LN4 2AF (01522 791217; email: enquiries@kcin.org; website: www.kcin.org)

CC Number: 700008

Eligibility

Children/young people up to the age of 16 who live in Kesteven (Lincolnshire) and are in need.

Types of grants

One-off and recurrent grants of up to £500. Examples of previous grants include clothing, educational holidays, days out, prams/pushchairs, beds/sheets, fireguards, second-hand washing machines, educational toys and playschool fees.

Annual grant total

In 2013 the charity had an income of £22,000 and a total expenditure of £11,400. Previously the majority of grants were made for welfare purposes with a small proportion given for educational needs. We estimate that welfare grants totalled about £5,200.

Applications

The charity acts purely on referrals from professionals, such as social workers, health visitors, teachers, education officers and similar. Applications should include the family situation, the age of the child and his/her special needs. Applications are considered throughout the year.

Other information

Organisations may also be helped. Individuals can be assisted towards educational causes.

A. L. Padley Charity Fund

£1,500

Correspondent: William Cursham, Trustee, Fraser Brown Solicitors, 84 Friar Lane, Nottingham NG1 6ED (01159 472541)

CC Number: 1062216

Eligibility

People living in Kesteven, Lincolnshire who are: couples wishing to get married where the man is 24 years or older and the woman is 21 years or older; pensioners; or people who have been experiencing prolonged illness.

Types of grants

One-off and recurrent grants according to need.

Annual grant total

In 2012/13 the fund had both an income and a total expenditure of £1,800. We estimate the total amount of grants to individuals to be £1,500.

Applications

The trustees ask applicants to write a short initial letter to see if their interests match those of the fund. Mark all correspondence with reference WECC.

Other information

Grants are also made to organisations.

Lincoln

The Lincoln Municipal Relief-in-Need Charities

£29,000

Correspondent: M. G. Bonass, Clerk, Durrus, Scothern Lane, Dunholme, Lincoln LN2 3QP (01673 860660; email: m.bonass213@btinternet.com)

CC Number: 213651

Eligibility

People in need who live in the city of Lincoln.

Types of grants

One-off grants up to £500 each according to need.

Annual grant total

In 2012/13 the charity held assets of £796,000 and had an income of £64,000. Grants to individuals totalled £29,000 and were distributed as follows:

Various individuals	£26,000
Quarterly payments	£3,000

Exclusions

No grants which will relieve public funds, contribute to the fabric of buildings or towards debts that have already been incurred. No recurrent grants.

Applications

Applications are generally only accepted through recognised social or medical agencies and are considered at any time. Requests for more than £500 must be approved at a quarterly trustee meeting.

Other information

Grants are occasionally made to organisations.

The Herbert William Sollitt Memorial Trust

£200

Correspondent: Jacqueline Smith, Secretary, 24 Sunfield Crescent, Birchwood, Lincoln LN6 0LL (01522 885006; email: jacq.smith@ntlworld.com)

CC Number: 1085018

Eligibility

Elderly widows and widowers who live in the city of Lincoln.

Types of grants

One-off grants towards, for example, household items, life line alarms, decoration, convalescent holidays, telephone installation and so on.

Annual grant total

In 2012/13 the trust had an income of £1,600 and an expenditure of about £400, which is the lowest in the past five years. We estimate that grants to individuals totalled £200. Previously the annual expenditure has fluctuated between £1,000 and £2,000.

Exclusions

Our research suggests that grants cannot be given to married people or people who live outside the area of benefit.

Applications

Application forms are available from the correspondent. They should be submitted through a social worker, Citizens Advice or other welfare agency and are considered on a regular basis.

Other information

Grants are made to both individuals and organisations.

Moulton

The Moulton Poor's Lands Charity

£8,000

Correspondent: Richard Lewis, Clerk, Maples and Son Solicitors, 23 New Road, Spalding, Lincolnshire PE11 1DH (01775 722261)

CC Number: 216630

Eligibility

People in need, generally older people, who live in the civil parish of Moulton.

Types of grants

Grants can be paid in cash or in kind. Relief-in-need grants are generally paid following a severe accident, unexpected loss or misfortune.

Annual grant total

In 2012 the charity had assets of £919,000 and an income of £31,000. During the year, £11,200 was awarded in grants, the majority of which we believe was to individuals for welfare purposes. We estimate that educational grants to individuals amounted to no more than £200. A total of £3,000 was awarded to two local primary schools.

At the time of writing (September 2014) this was the most recent financial information available.

Applications

In writing to the correspondent, usually through a trustee. Applications are considered in April and December.

Other information

The charity also manages almshouses, the rent from which makes up a small part of its income.

Navenby

The Navenby Town's Farm Trust

£3,000

Correspondent: Leonard Coffey, Secretary, 17 North Lane, Navenby, Lincoln LN5 0EH (01522 810273)

CC Number: 245223

Eligibility

People in need who live in the village of Navenby.

Types of grants

One-off grants according to need.

Annual grant total

About £12,000 a year is awarded to individuals and organisations. We estimate that around £3,000 is given to individuals for social welfare purposes.

Exclusions

No grants can be given outside the village.

Applications

On a form available from the correspondent, the village post office, or the local newsagents. Applications are considered in September. Urgent applications may occasionally be considered at other times. Unsolicited applications are not responded to.

Other information

Grants are also awarded for educational purposes.

South Holland

Spalding Relief-in-Need Charity

£18,000

Correspondent: Richard Knipe, Clerk and Solicitor, Dembleby House, 12 Broad Street, Spalding, Lincolnshire PE11 1ES (01775 768774; email: patrick.skells@chattertons.com)

CC Number: 229268

Eligibility

People in need who live in the area covered by the district of South Holland. Preference is given to residents of the urban district of Spalding and the parishes of Cowbit, Deeping St Nicholas, Pinchbeck and Weston.

Types of grants

The charity can provide one-off and recurrent grants in the range of £100 to £400. Support is given towards various items, services and facilities, including awards for furniture and domestic appliances, rent arrears and other debts, children's clothing and so on. Residents of the almshouses can be helped with the cost of TV licence.

Annual grant total

In 2013 the charity had assets of £1.3 million, an income of £49,000 and gave grants totalling over £32,000. The support can be broken down as follows:

- Individuals – £29,000
- Individuals, TV licences – £2,200
- Individuals, annual grants – £1,400

Exclusions

Grants are not intended to be made where support can be obtained from statutory sources.

Applications

Application forms can be requested from the charity. They can be submitted directly by the individual or assisted by a social worker/Citizens Advice/other welfare agency, if applicable. Grants are considered fortnightly.

Other information

Grants can also be awarded to organisations. Normally payments are made directly to suppliers.

This charity is connected with the Spalding Almshouse Charity (registered charity number 220077) and shares the same body of administration, the Spalding Town Husbands.

Spilsby

The Spilsby Poor Lands Charity

£3,100

Correspondent: Mrs J. Tong, Clerk, Rosedale Lodge, Ashby Road, Spilsby, Lincolnshire PE23 5DW (01790 752885)

CC Number: 220613

Eligibility

People of retirement age in need who have lived in Spilsby for at least five years.

Types of grants

Grants of up to £25 are made twice a year in June and December.

Annual grant total

In 2013, the charity had both an income and a total expenditure of £3,300. We estimate that the total amount of grants awarded to individuals was approximately £3,100.

Applications

On a form available from the correspondent. Applications must be submitted directly by the individual and are considered in June and December. Applicants must state how long they have lived in Spilsby.

Stickford

The Stickford Relief-in-Need Charity

£7,500

Correspondent: Katherine Bunting, Clerk, The Old Vicarage, Church Road, Stickford, Boston, Lincolnshire PE22 8EP (01205 480455)

CC Number: 247423

Eligibility

People in need who live in the parish of Stickford.

Types of grants

One-off and recurrent grants for relief-in-need purposes, towards school uniforms, and a Christmas bonus. Further grants are given towards bus services for older people, youth club outings and so on.

Annual grant total

In 2013 the charity had an income of almost £20,000 and an expenditure of £16,300. We estimate grants to individuals totalled around £15,000 with awards being made for both educational and social welfare purposes.

Applications

In writing to the correspondent. Applications should be submitted directly by the individual and are considered all year.

Surfleet

The Surfleet United Charities

£2,700

Correspondent: Leanne Barlow, Clerk, Crimond, Hedgefield Hurn, Gosberton, Spalding, Lincolnshire PE11 4JE (01775 750183)

CC Number: 215260

Eligibility

Retired people in need who have lived in the parish of Surfleet for over ten years (exceptions will be made on the age restriction in cases of extreme need).

Types of grants

Normally grants are given as Christmas gifts each year of £15 (individuals) and £25 (couples). Other one-off grants are available according to need.

Annual grant total

At the time of writing (August 2014) the latest financial information available was from 2012. In 2012 the charities had assets of £157,000 and an income of £40,000. Grants to the elderly and poor totalled £2,700.

Applications

In writing to the correspondent. Applications can be submitted directly by the individual and are normally considered in November.

Other information

The United Charities consist of Samuel Elsdale, Joseph Burton, the Poor's Land and Salt Marsh Allotment charities. In 2012 most of the charitable expenditure was allocated to the Surfleet Parish Council (£12,000).

Support is also given to vicar and churchwardens of the ecclesiastical Parish of Surfleet St Lawrence for the purchase of Old and New Testaments and other religious books to be distributed among the poor inhabitants of the parish.

Sutterton

The Sutterton Parochial Charity Trust

£6,700

Correspondent: Deirdre McCumiskey, 6 Hillside Gardens, Wittering, Peterborough PE8 6DX (01780 782668)

CC Number: 234839

Eligibility

People in need who live in the parishes of Sutterton and Amber Hill.

Types of grants

One-off grants of around £50.

Annual grant total

In 2012/13 the trust had both an income and a total expenditure of £13,500. We estimate that grants to individuals totalled £6,700, with funding also awarded to local organisations.

Applications

On a form available from the correspondent which can be submitted directly by the individual or a family member. Applications for Christmas grants should be received by the trust by the end of November for consideration in early December.

Sutton St James

The Sutton St James United Charities

£4,000

Correspondent: Keith Savage, Clerk to the Trustees, Lenton Lodge, 94 Wignals Gate, Holbeach, Spalding, Lincolnshire PE12 7HR (01406 490157; email: keithsavage@btinternet.com)

CC Number: 527757

Eligibility

People in need who live in the parish of Sutton St James.

Types of grants

One-off and recurrent grants according to need. Recent grants have been given for funeral expenses and to help people who have been evicted.

Annual grant total

In 2012/13 the charity had an income of £15,000 and a total expenditure of over £17,000. Grants are made to individuals and organisations for educational and welfare purposes. We estimate the amount awarded to individuals for social welfare purposes was around £4,000.

Applications

On a form available from the correspondent. Applications are only considered when all other available avenues have been explored.

Swineshead

The Swineshead Poor Charities

£5,000

Correspondent: Lynne Richardson, Administrator, 27 Sorrel Drive, Spalding, Lincolnshire PE11 3GN (01775 762977)

CC Number: 216557

Eligibility

People in need who live in the parish of Swineshead.

Types of grants

One-off and recurrent grants and loans according to need.

Annual grant total

In 2012/13 the charities had an income of £18,400 and a total expenditure of £10,800. We estimate that grants to individuals totalled £5,000, with organisations also receiving funding.

Applications

In writing to the correspondent.

Northamptonshire

Edmund Arnold's Charity (Poors Branch)

£1,900

Correspondent: Jane Forsyth, Clerk, 4 Grange Park Court, Roman Way, Grange Park, Northampton NN4 5EA (01604 876697)

CC Number: 260589

Eligibility

People in need who live in the parish of Nether Heyford, Northamptonshire, the ancient parish of St Giles in Northampton and the parish of Stony Stratford, Buckinghamshire.

Types of grants

One-off cash grants of between £50 and £400 for 'extra comforts'.

Annual grant total

In 2012 the charity had an income of £28,000 and a total expenditure of £29,000. At the time of writing (August 2014) this was the most recent financial information available for the charity and its accounts for the year were not yet available to view on the Charity Commission's website. In previous years social welfare grants to individuals have totalled £1,900.

Applications

On a form available on written request from the correspondent. Applications can be submitted either directly by the individual or through a third party such as a social worker, Citizens Advice or other welfare agency. They are considered in March/April and September/October.

Other information

The charity also makes grants to individuals through its Apprenticing and Educational Branch and to organisations.

St Giles Charity Estate

£21,000

Correspondent: The Grants Administrator, c/o Nicholas Rothwell House, 290 Harborough Road, Kingsthorpe, Northampton NN2 8LR (email: tonylains43@gmail.com (general enquiries))

CC Number: 202540

Eligibility

People in need who live within the borough of Northampton.

Types of grants

St Giles Charity makes one-off grants for the benefit of needy persons residing in Northamptonshire. Grants to individuals and families towards, for example, helping to fund individual household requirements such as carpets/washing machines and so on. Grants are always made for a specific purpose, not as a financial 'top up'.

The trustees state that the charity's funds are limited, and consequently the grants made are in the low to moderate category. Sometimes it may be necessary to offer a reserved contribution grant payable on condition that the balance needed can be raised from other sources.

Annual grant total

In 2012 the charity had assets of £3 million and an income of £625,000 most of which came from residents' fees. 100 grants were made totalling £43,000 and were given to both individuals and organisations. The charity's accounts for 2013 had been received at the Charity Commission but were not available to view.

Exclusions

Grants cannot be made in certain circumstances, for instance:

- Applications from, or on behalf of, persons residing outside Northampton
- For building projects, staffing costs, etc.
- For educational course fees, expenses, or materials
- For gap year projects, overseas expeditions, etc.
- For the repayment of debts, arrears of council tax or rent, or other payments to public bodies
- For funeral expenses

General funding grants are not made to other charities and organisations.

Applications

Information taken from the charity's website:

> Please note that the correspondent's address is for postal applications only – staff at Nicholas Rothwell House **cannot** deal with personal or telephone enquiries. General enquiries may be made by email to the charity administrator at: tonylains43@gmail.com
>
> Applicants may be asked to complete an application form available from the administrator, or downloaded from the charity website.
>
> Due to the quarterly cycle of meetings, applications can sometimes be held over for up to three months. However urgent cases may be dealt with between meetings, at the discretion of the trustees.

Applications by individuals and families, which **must** be supported by a social care agency or similar organisation, are considered by the charity's grants committee, which meets quarterly, usually in February, May, August, and November.

Other information

The charity's main activity is the provision of almshouses and the support of Nicholas Rothwell House, a specially designed and purpose-built complex dedicated to providing both short and long-term residential care.

Valentine Goodman Estate Charity

£6,200

Correspondent: John Stones, Administrator, Blaston Lodge, Blaston Road, Blaston, Market Harborough LE16 8DB (01858 555688)

CC Number: 252108

Eligibility

People in need who live in the parishes of Blaston, Bringhurst, Drayton, East Magna, Hallaton and Medbourne.

Types of grants

One-off or recurrent grants according to need.

Annual grant total

In 2012 the charity had an income of £16,200 and an expenditure of £6,500. Grants made totalled approximately £6,200.

These were the latest set of accounts available at the time of writing (August 2014).

Applications

In writing to the correspondent. Grants are distributed in February each year.

The Henry and Elizabeth Lineham Charity

£28,000

Correspondent: Angela Moon, Clerk to the Trustees, Hewitsons LLP, Elgin House, Billing Road, Northampton NN1 5AU (01604 233233; email: angelamoon@hewitsons.com)

CC Number: 205975

Eligibility

Women in need who are at least 55 and live in the borough of Northampton.

Types of grants

Annuities, currently £512 per annum, are paid half-yearly in June and December.

Annual grant total

In 2013 the charity held assets of £1.2 million and had an income of £49,000. During the year, individuals received £28,000 in annuities.

Applications

In writing to the correspondent. Beneficiaries are usually nominated by one of the trustees, mostly councillors or ex-councillors.

The Page Fund

£5,200 (5 grants)

Correspondent: Jane Forsyth, Clerk to the Trustees, Wilson Browne Solicitors, 4 Grange Park Court, Roman Way, Northampton NN4 5EA (01604 876697; fax: 01604 768606; email: jforsyth@wsqblaw.com)

CC Number: 241274

Eligibility

People in need who live in the borough of Northampton or within five miles of the Guild Hall and have done so for more than five years. Preference is given to older people, and to those with a sudden and unforeseen drop in income, for example widows following the death of a husband.

Types of grants

Pensions of around £1,000 per year for people who have experienced a reduction in income due to widowhood or old age.

Annual grant total

In 2012/13 the fund had assets of £786,000 and an income of £32,000. Grants totalled £27,000; of which £5,200 was distributed to five individuals.

A further £22,000 was awarded to 11 organisations.

Exclusions

Applicants must have lived in the Northampton area for at least five years.

Applications

On a form available from the correspondent. Applications can be submitted directly by the individual or through a social worker, Citizens Advice or other welfare agency. They are accepted at any time and are considered in May and November.

Sir Thomas White's Northampton Charity

£75,000

Correspondent: Angela Moon, Clerk to the Trustees, Hewitsons LLP, Elgin House, Billing Road, Northampton NN1 5AU (01604 233233; email: angelamoon@hewitsons.com)

CC Number: 201486

Eligibility

People between 21 and 34 years of age who live in the extended borough of Northampton.

Types of grants

Nine year interest-free loans for education, business start-up and household essentials and grants for education.

Annual grant total

In 2013 the charity had assets of £3.4 million and an income of £262,000. Interest-free loans and educational grants are available. 30 loans totalling £75,000 and £76,000 in student grants were made.

Applications

Apply in writing for a form in November, following a public notice advertising the grants.

Other information

Previously called Sir Thomas White's Loan Fund.

The Yelvertoft and District Relief-in-Sickness Fund

£4,700

Correspondent: Richard Atterbury, Trustee, Crick Lodge, Crick, Northampton NN6 7SN (01788 822247)

CC Number: 285771

Eligibility

People in need who live in the parishes of Yelvertoft, West Haddon, Crick, Winwick, Clay Coton and Elkington, who are sick, convalescent, infirm, or have disabilities.

Types of grants

Small one-off grants for wheelchairs, walkers and the like.

Annual grant total

In 2013 the fund had an income of £9,600 and a total expenditure of £5,100. We estimate that grants to individuals totalled £4,700.

Applications

In writing to the correspondent. Applications should be submitted directly by the individual, a relative or district nurse, and can be considered at any time.

Blakesley

The Blakesley Parochial Charities

£2,000

Correspondent: Derek Lucas, Administrator, Bradworthy, Main Street, Woodend, Towcester NN12 8RX (01327 860517)

CC Number: 202949

Eligibility

People in need who live in Blakesley.

Types of grants

One-off and recurrent grants according to need. Grants are given towards the fuel bills of older people and as pensions to widows.

Annual grant total

In 2013 the charity had an income of £6,700 and a total expenditure of almost £5,000. We estimate that grants awarded for social welfare purposes to individuals totalled around £2,000.

Applications

In writing to the correspondent. Applications are considered in December.

Other information

The charities also make grants for educational purposes.

Brackley

The Brackley United Feoffee Charity

£6,000

Correspondent: Rosemary Hedges, Administrator, 7 Easthill Close, Brackley, Northamptonshire NN13 7BS (01280 702420; email: caryl.billingham@tesco.net)

CC Number: 238067

Eligibility

People in need who live in Brackley.

Types of grants

The charity gives funding to a wide range of causes, including the distribution of Christmas donations to around 60 elderly residents of Brackley. Previous grants have included: help towards the cost of aids for people with disabilities, temporary accommodation for a couple following a serious house fire, the purchase of a new washing machine for a young mother of a child with disabilities, help with childcare for parents deemed vulnerable and a contribution towards the repair of the headstone of a young child.

Annual grant total

In 2012/13 the charity had an income of £34,000 and a total expenditure of over £26,000. We estimate grants to individuals for social welfare purposes to be around £6,000.

Applications

In writing to the correspondent, preferably by the individual or through a social worker, Citizens Advice or other welfare agency. Trustees meet every three to four months.

Other information

The charity awards grants to individuals and organisations for both educational and social welfare purposes.

Brington

The Chauntry Estate

£5,000

Correspondent: Rita Tank, Administrator, Walnut Tree Cottage, Main Street, Great Brington, Northampton NN7 4JA (01604 770809)

CC Number: 200795

Eligibility

Elderly people in need who live in the parish of Brington. Other funding, including educational grants, is available to those who have been resident in Brington for at least five years.

Types of grants

One-off grants to relieve sudden distress or illness, for example, towards travel expenses for visits to hospital, food, fuel and heating appliances, and aids not provided by health authorities. Educational grants are also available.

Annual grant total

In 2012/13 the charity had an income of £10,500 and an expenditure of £10,100. We estimate that welfare grants to individuals totalled £5,000, with additional grants afforded for educational purposes.

Applications

In writing to the correspondent.

Byfield

The Poors Allotment

£350

Correspondent: Pam Hicks, Administrator, 1 Edwards Close, Byfield, Daventry, Northamptonshire NN11 6XP

CC Number: 220321

Eligibility

People in need, hardship or distress who live in the parish of Byfield.

Types of grants

Our research suggests that generally one-off grants of £10–£100 are available towards household bills, travel expenses, dental costs, spectacles and other 'minor medical items'. Awards (usually to older people) are also given for Christmas expenses.

Annual grant total

At the time of writing (August 2014) the latest financial information available was from 2012. In 2012 the charity had both an income and a total expenditure of around £800. We estimate that welfare support totalled around £350.

Applications

Application forms are available from the correspondent. They can be submitted directly by the individual or through a relevant third party at any time for consideration in March, June, September and December.

Other information

The charity also makes grants for educational purposes.

Chipping Warden

Relief-in-Need Charity of Reverend William Smart (Chipping Warden Smarts Charity)

£900

Correspondent: Nigel Galletly, Trustee, 3 Allens Orchard, Chipping Warden, Banbury, Oxfordshire OX17 1LX (01295 660365)

CC Number: 239658

Eligibility

People in need who live in the parish of Chipping Warden, Northamptonshire. Preference is given to elderly people and young people in education.

Types of grants

One-off grants can be given according to need.

Annual grant total

At the time of writing (August 2014) the latest financial information available was from 2012. In 2012 the charity had an income of £4,100 and a total expenditure of £2,900. We estimate that welfare grants to individuals totalled around £900.

Exclusions

People outside the area of benefit cannot be supported.

Applications

In writing to the correspondent. Applications can be made either directly by the individual or through a third party, such as a social worker. They are considered at any time.

Other information

Grants can also be given to organisations and to support education.

Daventry

The Daventry Consolidated Charity

£4,000

Correspondent: Maggie Dowie, Administrator, 15 Astbury Close, Daventry, Northamptonshire NN11 4RL

CC Number: 200657

Eligibility

People in need who live in the borough of Daventry.

Types of grants

One-off grants for a specific need such as a special chair for a child with cerebral palsy, travel to hospital 45 miles from home and help with the costs of adaptations to a Motability vehicle.

Annual grant total

The 2012 accounts were the latest available at the time of writing (August 2014).

In 2012 the charity had an income of £10,000 and a total expenditure of £7,000. We estimate that the total amount of grants awarded to individuals was approximately £4,000.

Exclusions

There are no grants available towards debts or ongoing expenses.

Applications

In writing to the correspondent. The trustees meet three times a year in March, July and November. Applications must include financial circumstances and the specific purpose for the grant. Relevant information not included will be requested if required.

Other information

The charity also makes grants to organisations.

Desborough

The Desborough Town Welfare Committee

£2,600

Correspondent: Ann King, Hon. Secretary, 190 Dunkirk Avenue, Desborough, Kettering, Northamptonshire NN14 2PP (01536 763390)

CC Number: 235505

Eligibility

People who are older, sick or in need and living in Desborough.

Types of grants

One-off and recurrent grants, paid mainly at Christmas.

Annual grant total

In 2012/13 the committee had an income of £6,000 and an expenditure of £5,300. We estimate that grants to individuals totalled £2,600, with funding also awarded to local organisations.

Applications

In writing to the correspondent, for consideration within two to three months.

East Farndon

The United Charities of East Farndon

£2,800

Correspondent: Cameron Fraser, Trustee, Linden Lea, Main Street, Market Harborough, Northamptonshire LE16 9SJ (01858 464218; email: fraser_cameron@hotmail.com)

CC Number: 200778

Eligibility

Families in need who live in East Farndon.

Types of grants

One-off cash grants of up to £50 are provided for travel expenses to hospital, fuel grants towards electricity, disablity equipment, living costs and household bills.

Annual grant total

In 2013 the charity had an income of £7,800 and an expenditure of £5,600. We estimate that grants awarded to individuals for social welfare purposes totalled around £2,800.

Applications

In writing to the correspondent, directly by the individual or a family member for consideration as they are received.

Other information

Grants are also made for educational purposes.

Harpole

The Harpole Parochial Charities

£3,000

Correspondent: Mary Burt, Trustee, 16 Garners Way, Harpole, Northampton NN7 4DN (01604 831365)

CC Number: 202568

Eligibility

People in need who have lived in Harpole for more than seven years, with a preference for those over 65.

Types of grants

Recurrent grants ranging from £25 to £30.

Annual grant total

In 2013 this charity had an income of £7,000 and a total expenditure of £3,200.

Applications

On a form available from the correspondent including details of financial status, benefits and income. Applications can be submitted either directly by the individual or through a relative. They are considered in December and should be submitted in November.

Kettering

The Broadway Cottages Trust

£700 (26 grants)

Correspondent: Nina Wilson, Chair, Wilson Browne LLP, 41 Meadow Road, Kettering, Northants NN16 8TL (01536 041 004)

CC Number: 203763

Eligibility

People in need who live or have lived in or near Kettering.

Types of grants

One-off and recurrent grants according to need.

Annual grant total

In 2012/13 the trust held assets totalling £1 million and had an income of £55,000. Total charitable expenditure came to £24,000 of which £700 was made in grants to 26 individuals.

Applications

In writing to the correspondent.

Other information

The trust's main object is the provision of housing with affordable rents. It also makes grants to organisations which in 2012/13 totalled £3,900.

The Kettering Charities (Fuel Grants)

£6,000

Correspondent: Anne Ireson, Administrator, Kettering Borough Council, Council Offices, Bowling Green Road, Kettering NN15 7QX (01536 534398; email: anneireson@kettering.gov.uk)

CC Number: 207698

Eligibility

Widows, widowers and single people over the age of 60 who live alone in Kettering or Barton Seagrave and who are in receipt of retirement pension.

Types of grants

Grants of £25 towards winter fuel bills.

Annual grant total

In 2012/13 the charities had an income of £14,800 and a total expenditure of £12,200. We estimate that welfare grants to individuals totalled £6,000, with funding also awarded to individuals for educational purposes.

Applications

The charities place advertisements in local newspapers in November each year, after which an application form can be requested from the correspondent. Applications are considered in November. Applicants must include details of their income, marital status, age and address.

Other information

Educational grants are available for over 16s who live in Kettering and Barton Seagrave.

The Stockburn Memorial Trust Fund

£10,000

Correspondent: Mrs P. M. Reynolds, 70 Windermere Road, Kettering, Northamptonshire NN16 8UF (01536 524662)

CC Number: 205120

Eligibility

People in need who live in the borough of Kettering.

Types of grants

One-off grants according to need.

Annual grant total

In 2012/13 the trust had an income of £10,400 and a total expenditure of £10,200. We estimate that grants to individuals totalled £10,000.

Applications

In writing to the correspondent through a social worker, Citizens Advice or other welfare agency. Applicants should include details of their age, address, telephone number, financial situation and health circumstances.

Litchborough

The Litchborough Parochial Charities

£3,000

Correspondent: Maureen Pickford, Trustee, 18 Banbury Road, Litchborough, Towcester NN12 8JF (01327 830110)

CC Number: 201062

Eligibility

People in need who live in Litchborough.

Types of grants

Grants to assist the elderly with heating costs and widows' pensions.

Annual grant total

In 2012/13 the charities had an income of £6,200 and an expenditure of £6,100. We estimate that welfare grants totalled £3,000, with funding also awarded to individuals for educational purposes.

Applications

In writing to the correspondent.

Northampton

Coles and Rice Charity

£10,800

Correspondent: The Administrator, Wilson Browne Solicitors, 4 Grange Park Court, Roman Way, Northampton NN4 5EA (01604 876697)

CC Number: 238375

Eligibility

People in need who are over the age of 55 and have lived in the borough of Northampton for at least five years. However, the charity also makes one-off grants to younger people in need.

Types of grants

Annual pensions to elderly people around £200 paid in quarterly instalments. One-off grants of up to about £500 may be provided.

Annual grant total

At the time of writing (August 2014) the latest financial information was from 2012. In 2012 the charity had an income of £12,400 and an expenditure of £11,000. We estimate that around £10,800 was given in individual grants.

The charity has previously stated that there were about 30 beneficiaries receiving annual payments.

Applications

Application forms are available from the correspondent. They can be submitted either directly by the individual or through a social worker and are usually considered in March and November.

The John and Mildred Law Fund

£12,700

Correspondent: Jane Forsyth, Clerk to the Trustees, Wilson Browne, 4 Grange Park Court, Roman Way, Grange Park, Northampton NN4 5EA (01604 876697; email: jforsyth@qswblaw.com)

CC Number: 1121230

Eligibility

People in need who live in the borough of Northampton.

Types of grants

One-off grants of up to £1,000 according to need.

Annual grant total

In 2012/13 the fund held assets of £806,000 and had an income of £34,000. Grants to individuals and organisations totalled £25,000. A breakdown of distributions was not available in the fund's financial statements for the year; we estimate that grants to individuals totalled £12,700.

Applications

In writing to the correspondent. The trustees meet twice a year to consider applications in May and November.

The Northampton Municipal Church Charities

£50,000

Correspondent: Jane Forsyth, Clerk to the Trustees, Wilson Browne Solicitors, 4 Grange Park Court, Roman Way, Grange Park, Northampton NN4 5EA (01604 876697; email: jforsyth@qswblaw.com)

CC Number: 259593

Eligibility

People in need who live in the borough of Northampton.

Types of grants

People aged over 55 are eligible for payments of £85 a quarter and a Christmas voucher of £45. People of any age can receive one-off grants up to a maximum of £500.

Annual grant total

In 2012/13 the charity had an income of £242,000 and an expenditure of

£273,000. Grants to individuals for social welfare purposes usually total around £50,000.

Exclusions

The charity is unable to assist with debt.

Applications

On a form available from the correspondent, including details of the applicant's age, residence, income, assets and expenditure. Applications can be submitted either directly by the individual or through a third party such as a social worker, Citizens Advice or other welfare agency. They are considered on a regular basis.

Other information

The charity runs a sheltered housing scheme at St Thomas House in St Giles Street, Northampton. It is warden controlled and has 17 small flats for people over 55. The charity's income must firstly be used for maintaining St Thomas House, secondly for the benefit of residents, and thirdly for the relief-in-need of people who live in Northampton.

Pattishall

The Pattishall Parochial Charities

£11,200

Correspondent: Wendy Watts, Administrator, 59 Leys Road, Pattishall, Towcester NN12 8JY (01327 830583; website: pattishallparish.org.uk/parish-council/pattishall-charities/)

CC Number: 204106

Eligibility

People in need who have lived in the parish of Pattishall for at least three years. Preference is given to people who are over 65.

Types of grants

The 15 oldest applicants for the Widows' and Widowers' pension receive monthly payments of £30. Others can apply separately to receive grants for fuel at Christmas (currently £65 per household). Grants of between £15 and £500 are available for one-off needs within the community and have been given towards, for example, provision of a downstairs toilet and a contribution towards a child's playgroup fees.

Annual grant total

In 2013 the charities had an income of £12,100 and a total expenditure of £11,500. We estimate that pensions and grants to individuals totalled £11,200.

Applications

In writing to the correspondent, making sure to include details of the applicant's age, marital status and the length of time the applicant has been resident in the parish. Applications are usually considered in November for fuel grants, July for pensions, and throughout the year for other grants. Applications can be submitted either directly by the individual or by anybody who hears of a need. Receipts (copies will do) should be included for the cost of travel for hospital visits and estimates for the purchases of large equipment, for example wheelchairs.

Other information

The trust states that:

> Each year the charity clerk will advertise around Pattishall and on the website for new applicants. In an effort to help identify those who would benefit from a grant, members of the parish are requested to bring forward names to the attention of the clerk.

Roade

The Roade Feoffee and Chivall Charity

£16,000

Correspondent: Michael Dowden, Trustee, 67 High Street, Roade, Northampton NN7 2NW

CC Number: 202132

Eligibility

People in need who live in the ancient parish of Roade.

Types of grants

One-off grants usually ranging from £15 to £100. Previous grants have been given at Christmas time and for such things as travel expenses to visit relatives in hospital.

Annual grant total

In 2012 the charity had an income of £18,600 and a total expenditure of £17,400. We estimate that welfare grants to individuals totalled £16,000.

At the time of writing (August 2014) this was the most recent financial information available for the charity.

Applications

In writing to the correspondent, specifying the reason for the application.

Scaldwell

Scaldwell Relief-in-Need Charity (SRINC)

£900

Correspondent: S. K. Dodds-Smith, Administrator, The Old Barn, High Street, Scaldwell, Northampton NN6 9JS (01604 881950; email: d.doddssmith@btinternet.com)

CC Number: 205281

Eligibility

People in need who live in the parish of Scaldwell only.

Types of grants

One-off grants ranging from £50 to £250.

Annual grant total

In 2013/14 the charity had an income of £1,400 and a total expenditure of £1,800. We estimate that individual grants totalled about £900.

Applications

In writing to the correspondent. Applications can be submitted directly by the individual or a family member and are usually considered in November and February.

Other information

Support may also be given to organisations.

Wappenham

Wappenham Poor's Land Charity

£2,200

Correspondent: Mrs J. E. McNeil, Administrator, Primrose Cottage, Main Street, Abthorpe, Towcester, Northants NN12 8QN (01327 857744)

CC Number: 205147

Eligibility

People in need who live in the ecclesiastical parish of Wappenham.

Types of grants

The charity gives a small standard grant to pensioners in need. Grants are also given to widows, widowers and people who are sick or have disabilities and are in need of specific items.

Annual grant total

In 2012/13 the charity had an income of £650 and an expenditure of £2,400. Grants totalled approximately £2,200.

Applications

In writing to the correspondent.

Welton

Welton Village Hall (formerly The Welton Town Lands Trust)

£1,000

Correspondent: Carol Bertozzi, Trustee, 5 Well Lane, Welton, Daventry, Northamptonshire NN11 2JU (01327 702213; email: caroline@paddockend.com)

CC Number: 304449

Eligibility

People in need, irrespective of age, who have lived in the village of Welton for at least two years.

Types of grants

One-off grants to families. The amount varies according to the total number of applicants as it is divided in equal shares.

Annual grant total

In 2013/14 the charity had an income of £6,900 and a total expenditure of £4,700. Grants given to individuals totalled approximately £1,000.

Applications

On a form available from the correspondent.

Other information

The charity also makes grants to local schools and churches.

Nottinghamshire

The John and Nellie Brown Farnsfield Trust

£6,000

Correspondent: Alan Dodd, Trustee, Roan House, Crabnook Lane, Farnsfield, Newark NG22 8JY (01623 882574)

CC Number: 1078367

Eligibility

People in need who live in the Farnsfield, Edingley Halam and Southwell areas of Nottinghamshire.

Types of grants

Grants are given according to need.

Annual grant total

In 2012/13 the trust had an income of £5,100 and a total expenditure of £25,000. Grants are made to individuals and organisations for both educational and social welfare purposes. We estimate the grant total for the year made to individuals for social welfare purposes to be around £6,000.

Applications

In writing to the correspondent.

The Mary Dickinson Charity

£21,000

Correspondent: Nigel Cullen, Clerk to the Trustees, Freeth Cartwright LLP, Cumberland Court, 80 Mount Street, Nottingham NG1 6HH (01159 369369; fax: 01158 599600)

CC Number: 213884

Eligibility

Older people in need who live in the city or county of Nottingham. Preference is given to Christians.

Types of grants

Pensions are given to a fixed number of older people. One-off grants may also be available for emergency items such as replacing gas fires and safety alarm and telephone systems.

Annual grant total

In 2012 the charity had assets of £1.2 million and an income of £42,000. Pensions and grants to individuals amounted to £21,000. The 2012 accounts were the latest available at the time of writing (August 2014).

Applications

On a form available from the correspondent. Applications should be submitted through a doctor/member of the clergy or directly by the individual, supported by a reference from one of the aforementioned. Applications can be submitted all year round and are considered in March, June, September and December, although emergency cases can be considered at any time.

The Fifty Fund

£58,000

Correspondent: Craig Staten-Spencer, Administrator, Nelsons Solicitors, Pennine House, 8 Stanford Street, Nottingham NG1 7BQ (01159 895251)

CC Number: 214422

Eligibility

People in need who live in Nottinghamshire only.

Types of grants

Monthly payments and one-off grants to help with debts, household and white goods.

Annual grant total

In 2013 the fund had assets of £7.9 million and an income of £282,000. Grant expenditure totalled £58,000 and can be broken down as follows:

Payments to beneficiaries	£54,000
Summer gifts	£4,000

Exclusions

No grants are given for education, sponsorship, holidays, house moving costs, bonds or rents in advance.

Applications

Applications, in writing to the correspondent, can be submitted either by the individual or through a recognised referral agency (such as a social worker, Citizens Advice or doctor) or other third party. Applications are considered throughout the year.

Other information

Grants are also made to organisations (£140,000 in 2013). The accounts note that at trustee meetings, 'the level of income not utilised is considered and, if considered appropriate, funds are donated to charities with similar aims to The Fifty Fund on the basis that such funds are used to help individuals and families in need and who are resident in Nottinghamshire.'

The Charles Wright Gowthorpe Fund and Clergy Augmentation Fund

£7,600

Correspondent: Lloyds Bank plc, Lloyds TSB Private Banking Ltd, UK Trust Centre, 22–26 Ock Street, Abingdon, Oxfordshire OX14 5SW (01235 232700)

CC Number: 213852/1213853

Eligibility

The Gowthorpe Fund supports widows and other women in need who live within a 12-mile radius of the Market Square, Nottingham; and The Clergy Augmentation Fund generally supports clergymen and their widows who live within a 10-mile radius of St Peter's Church, Nottingham.

Types of grants

Grants typically of around £100, paid annually in December.

Annual grant total

In 2012/13 the Gowthorpe Fund had an income of £4,900 and a total expenditure of £5,100. In the same year, the Clergy Augmentation Fund had an income of £2,700 and a total expenditure of £2,800.

We estimate that combined grants from the funds totalled £7,600; around £4,900 from the Gowthorpe Fund, and £2,700 from the Clergy Augmentation Fund.

Applications

On a form available from local Church of England vicars, to be returned by the end of October. Do not write to the correspondent initially; only send the application form once it has been completed.

The John William Lamb Charity

£14,000

Correspondent: Nina Dauban, Chief Executive, Nottinghamshire Community Foundation, Pine House B, Southwell Road West, Rainworth, Mansfield NG21 0HJ (01623 620202; fax: 01623 620204; email: enquiries@nottscf.org.uk; website: www.nottscf.org.uk)

CC Number: 221978

Eligibility

People in need who have been living for at least one year within the city of Nottingham, or within 20 miles of the Nottingham Exchange, with a preference for older people.

Types of grants

Annuities are paid quarterly. One-off grants are also available.

Annual grant total

In 2012/13 the charity had assets of £961,000 and an income of £35,000. Annuities to individuals totalled £14,000 and were distributed as follows:

Annuities	27	£13,700
One-off grants	–	£300

Applications

In writing to the correspondent. Applicants will be visited by a member of the charity.

Other information

The charity is administered by Nottinghamshire Community Foundation.

The New Appeals Organisation for the City and County of Nottingham

£12,000

Correspondent: Phil Everett, Joint Chair, 4 Rise Court, Hamilton Road, Nottingham NG5 1EU (01159 609644 (answering service); email: enquiries@newappeals.org.uk; website: www.newappeals.org)

CC Number: 502196

Eligibility

People in need who live in the city and county of Nottingham.

Types of grants

One-off grants ranging from £50 to £2,000 to meet needs which cannot be met from any other source. For example, wheelchairs, white goods, flooring, beds and bedding, rise/recliner chairs, adapted vehicles, holidays, sensory stimulation equipment, computers and other electrical goods. Christmas gifts are also given to elderly and homeless people. Much of the money is raised for specific projects or people.

Annual grant total

In 2012/13 the organisation had an income of £61,000 and a total expenditure of £26,000. We estimate that £12,000 was given in grants to individuals, with funding also awarded to local schools and organisations.

Exclusions

The organisation does not usually help with debt arrears, building works, wages, educational costs, foreign travel for students or requests from outside Nottingham.

Applications

On a form available from the correspondent. Applications should ideally be made through a social worker, Citizens Advice, medical establishment or other welfare agency, although those submitted directly by the individual are considered. Applications are considered on the first Monday of each month.

The Nottingham Annuity Charity

£12,500

Correspondent: David Simmons, Administrator, c/o Nottingham Community Housing Association, Property Management Services, 12–14 Pelham Road, Sherwood Rise, Nottingham NG5 1AP (01158 443404; email: davids@ncha.org.uk)

CC Number: 510023

Eligibility

People in need who live in Nottinghamshire, with a preference for widows and unmarried women.

Types of grants

Regular yearly allowances of around £200 are paid in quarterly grants.

Annual grant total

In 2012/13 the charity had an income of £15,000 and a total expenditure of £12,700. We estimate that pensions totalled £12,500.

Applications

On a form available from the correspondent to be submitted either directly by the individual or through an appropriate third party such as a social worker, Citizens Advice or other welfare agency. Applications are usually considered quarterly.

The Nottingham Children's Welfare Fund

£1,800

Correspondent: Gwen Derry, Trustee, 37 Main Road, Wilford, Nottingham NG11 7AP (01159 811830)

CC Number: 215445

Eligibility

Children and young adults under 18, with priority given to children who live in Nottinghamshire, especially in Nottingham and especially those who have lost either or both of their parents.

Types of grants

One-off grants of around £50 to £75. Recent awards have been made for domestic appliances, furniture, furnishings, clothing, toys and contributions to school trips and family holidays.

Annual grant total

In 2012/13, the fund had an income of £2,200 and a total expenditure of £2,000. We estimate the total amount of grants awarded to individuals was approximately £1,800.

Applications

On a form available from the correspondent; to be submitted by social services, the probation service or another welfare agency or third party such as a teacher. Applications are usually considered four times a year.

The Nottingham General Dispensary

£20,000

Correspondent: Nigel Cullen, Clerk to the Trustees, Cumberland Court, 80 Mount Street, Nottingham NG1 6HH (01159 015558; fax: 01159 015500)

CC Number: 228149

Eligibility

People who are in poor health, convalescent or who have disabilities and live in the county of Nottinghamshire.

Types of grants

One-off grants ranging from £20 to £1,000 are given for a variety of needs including, home adaptations, mobility equipment, medical aids, hospital travel costs, computer equipment, holidays and respite breaks.

Annual grant total

In 2012/13 the charity had an income of £43,000 and a total expenditure of £47,000. We estimate that grants to individuals, paid either directly or through other organisations, totalled around £20,000. The charity usually sets aside an additional annual donation of £10,000 for the Nottingham Self Help Projects Funds.

Exclusions

No grants are given where funds are available from statutory sources. No recurrent grants are made.

Applications

In writing to the correspondent through a social worker, Citizens Advice, other welfare agency or a professional, for example, a doctor or teacher. Individuals can apply directly via an application form available from the correspondent but must include supporting medical evidence and details of the costs of the items or facilities needed. Applications are considered all year round, although requests for grants exceeding £1,000 may take longer.

Nottingham Gordon Memorial Trust for Boys and Girls

£15,400

Correspondent: Anna Chandler, Charity Administrator, Cumberland Court, 80 Mount Street, Nottingham NG1 6HH (01159 015562; fax: 01158 599652; email: anna.chandler@freeths.co.uk)

CC Number: 212536

Eligibility

Children and young people under the age of 25 who are in need, hardship or distress and live in Nottingham or the area immediately around the city. Preference can be given to individuals who are of the former Nottingham Gordon Memorial Home for Destitute Working Boys.

Types of grants

One-off grants are made for baby essentials, clothing, bedding, electrical goods (mainly cookers and washing machines), basic equipment for people who have disabilities, also family holidays and trips.

Annual grant total

At the time of writing (August 2014) the latest financial information available was from 2012. In 2012 the trust had assets of £1.1 million and an income of £46,000. A total of £36,000 was awarded to individuals, broken down as follows:

Educational grants	£8,200
Electrical goods	£6,500
Bed and bed linens	£5,500
Holiday/trips	£5,100
Baby items and equipment	£3,400

Applications

Application forms are available from the correspondent. They can be submitted through the individual's school, college, educational welfare agency, health visitor, social worker, probation officer or similar professional. Our research suggests that individuals, supported by a reference from their school/college, can also apply directly. The trustees meet twice a year, although applications can be considered all year round.

Other information

The trust also supports organisations in the Nottingham area and provides educational support for individuals.

The Nottinghamshire Miners' Welfare Trust Fund

£93,000

Correspondent: Donald Brookes, Secretary, CISWO, Welfare Offices, Berry Hill Lane, Mansfield, Nottinghamshire NG18 4JR (01623 625767; email: donald.brookes@ciswo.org.uk)

CC Number: 1001272

Eligibility

Members of the mining community in Nottinghamshire who are in need, and their dependents.

Types of grants

One-off and recurrent grants are given to improve health and living conditions. Recent grants have been given for bathroom alterations, mortgage repayments, stair lifts, wheelchairs, scooters, beds and bedding, furniture and replacement boilers. Holiday grants of £100 to £250 are also available.

Annual grant total

In 2013, the fund had assets of £3.5 million and an income of £124,000. Grants were made totalling £93,000 and were distributed as follows:

Personal welfare and hardship grants	£73,000
Holiday grants	£19,000
Convalescent grants	£1,000

Applications

On a form available from the correspondent, to be submitted directly by the individual or through a third party such as the Coal Industry Social Welfare Organisation (CISWO), Citizens Advice, social worker or similar welfare organisation. Applications are considered regularly throughout the year.

Other information

Grants are also made to organisations (£5,600 in 2013).

The Perry Trust Gift Fund

£9,400

Correspondent: Anna Chandler, Administrator, c/o Freeth Cartwright LLP, Cumberland Court, 80 Mount Street, Nottingham NG1 6HH (01159 015562)

CC Number: 247809

Eligibility

In order of preference: (a) people in need who have lived in the city of Nottingham for at least five years; (b) people in need who have lived in Nottinghamshire for at least five years. Grants are mainly given to older people with low incomes but some help is also available to younger people in need.

Types of grants

One-off grants up to £200 towards, for example, electric bills, clothing, living costs, household bills, food, furniture, disability equipment and help in the home.

Annual grant total

In 2012/13 the fund had an income of £11,400 and a total expenditure of £9,600. We estimate that grants to individuals totalled £9,400.

Applications

On a form available from the correspondent. Applications can be made through a third party such as a social worker, Citizens Advice or other welfare agency. Grants are made in either May or November. Successful applicants may apply again another year if necessary.

The Puri Foundation

£0

Correspondent: Nathu Ram Puri, Trustee, Environment House, 6 Union Road, Nottingham NG3 1FH (01159 013000)

CC Number: 327854

Eligibility

Individuals in need living in Nottinghamshire who are from India (particularly the towns of Mullan Pur near Chandigarh and Ambala). Employees/past employees of the Melton Medes Group Ltd, Blugilt Holdings or Melham Inc. and their dependents, who are in need, are also eligible. The foundation wants to support people who have exhausted state support and other avenues, in other words to be a 'last resort'.

Types of grants

One-off and recurrent grants according to need, for items such as furniture or clothes. The maximum donation is usually between £150 and £200.

Annual grant total

In 2012/13 the foundation had assets of £2.8 million and an income of £325,000. There were no grants to individuals made in that financial year. Grants to organisations totalled £278,000, of which £234,000 was given to an organisation operating in India.

Applications

In writing to the correspondent, either directly by the individual or through a social worker.

The Skerritt Trust

See entry on page 314

The West Gate Benevolent Trust

£60,000

Correspondent: Stephen Carey, Secretary, 17 Storcroft Road, Retford, Nottinghamshire DN22 7EG (01777 707677)

CC Number: 503506

Eligibility

People in need who live in Nottinghamshire.

Types of grants

One-off grants ranging from about £50 to £5,000. For example, recent grants have been given for washing machines, holidays and travel to visit relations in hospital.

Annual grant total

In 2012/13, the trust had an income of £57,000 and a total expenditure of £63,000. Grants awarded to individuals totalled approximately £60,000.

Applications

Applications cannot be made by individuals directly, but only through a third party such as a social worker or Citizens Advice.

Balderton

The Balderton Parochial Charity

£1,000

Correspondent: Louise Tetlaw, Administrator, 1 Birch Road, New Balderton, Newark, Nottinghamshire NG24 3DB (07818 081490; email: bpc@jimandlou.com)

CC Number: 217554

Eligibility

People in need who live in the parish of Balderton.

Types of grants

One-off grants according to need. Recent grants have been given for cookers, electric wheelchairs, cycle trailers and garden alterations.

Annual grant total

In 2012/13 the charity had an income of £2,000 and a total expenditure of £1,700. We estimate that around £1,000 was made in grants to individuals for social welfare purposes.

Exclusions

No donations for the relief of rates, taxes, fines or other public funds.

Applications

In writing to the correspondent either directly by the individual or through a social worker, Citizens Advice or other welfare agency. Applications are considered at any time.

Bingham

The Bingham Trust Scheme

£330

Correspondent: Gillian M. Bailey, Trustee, 20 Tithby Road, Bingham, Nottingham NG13 8GN (01949 838673)

CC Number: 513436

Eligibility

People under the age of 21 living in Bingham.

Types of grants

Grants in the range of £50 and £150 to help with expenses incurred in the course of education, religious and physical welfare and so on. They are made in January and early July each year.

Annual grant total

In 2012/13 the scheme had both an income and a total expenditure of £1,300. Grants seem to be made mainly for educational purposes.

Applications

Application forms are available from the correspondent. They can be submitted directly by the individual or a family member by 30 April and 31 October each year.

Bingham United Charities 2006 (formerly known as Bingham United Charities)

£3,200

Correspondent: Susan Lockwood, Administrator, 23 Douglas Road, Bingham, Nottingham NG13 8EL (01949 875453; email: lockwoodsue79@gmail.com)

CC Number: 213913

Eligibility

People in need who live in the parish of Bingham.

Types of grants

For a range of welfare purposes.

Annual grant total

In 2013/14 the charity had an income of £10,800 and an expenditure of £6,800. Grants totalled around £6,500 and were divided between welfare and education.

Exclusions

Applicants must live in Bingham and be able to show need, hardship or distress.

Applications

Application forms are available from the secretary. However applications supported by a professional, medical, or social care agency can often be dealt with more quickly.

Other information

Grants are also given to organisations and individuals for educational purposes.

Carlton in Lindrick

The Christopher Johnson and the Green Charity

£1,000

Correspondent: Robin Towle, Hon. Secretary and Treasurer, 135 Windsor Road, Carlton in Lindrick, Worksop, Nottinghamshire S81 9DH (01909 731069; email: 1cert@tiscali.co.uk)

CC Number: 219610

Eligibility

People in need who live in the village of Carlton in Lindrick.

Types of grants
One-off grants according to need.

Annual grant total
Grants usually total about £2,000 each year and are given for educational and welfare purposes.

Applications
In writing to the correspondent either directly by the individual, via a third party such as a social worker, doctor or district nurse or through Citizens Advice or other welfare agency. Applications are considered throughout the year.

Coddington

The Coddington United Charities

£6,200

Correspondent: Alasdair Morrison, Clerk to the Trustees, Alasdair Morrison and Partners, 26 Kirkgate, Newark, Nottinghamshire NG24 1AB (01636 700888; fax: 01636 700885)

CC Number: 1046378

Eligibility
People in need who live in the parish of Coddington.

Types of grants
One-off grants for individuals resident in the charity's almshouses and general relief in need.

Annual grant total
In 2013 the charities had an income of £16,600 and a total expenditure of £12,700. We estimate that grants to individuals totalled £6,200, with funding also awarded to local organisations.

Applications
In writing to the correspondent. Applications can be submitted at any time, either through a third party such as a social worker or Citizens Advice or directly by the individual.

Farndon

The Farndon Relief-in-Need Charity

£600

Correspondent: Gwen Palmer, Trustee, 112a Farndon Road, Newark, Nottinghamshire NG24 4SE (01636 688299; email: admin@invisiblecommunications.com)

CC Number: 215940

Eligibility
People in need who live in the parish of Farndon.

Types of grants
One-off grants, Christmas hampers and clothing vouchers.

Annual grant total
About £1,200 a year. Grants are given to both individuals and organisations.

Applications
In writing to the correspondent directly by the individual or through a third party such as Citizens Advice or a social worker. The trustees meet twice a year, usually in May and October. Emergency applications can be considered at other times.

Gotham

Doctor M. A. Gerrard's Gotham Old People's Benevolent Fund

£150

Correspondent: Judy Raven, Trustee, The Old Rectory, 33 Leake Road, Gotham, Nottingham NG11 0HW (01159 830863; email: gothamclerk@yahoo.co.uk)

CC Number: 244908

Eligibility
Older people in need who live, or have lived, in the parish of Gotham.

Types of grants
One-off grants according to need. Gifts in kind are also available.

Annual grant total
In 2013/14 this charity had an income of £1,100 and a total expenditure of £250. Although income has remained fairly static, expenditure has fallen each year over the past five years.

Applications
In writing to the correspondent, submitted directly by the individual or via a third party such as a social worker.

Other information
The fund also makes grants to organisations.

Hucknall

The Hucknall Relief-in-Need Charity

£1,000

Correspondent: Kenneth Creed, Administrator, 67 Glendon Drive, Hucknall, Nottingham NG15 6DF (01159 635929)

CC Number: 215974

Eligibility
People in need who live in Hucknall, with a preference for 'poor householders'.

Types of grants
One-off and recurrent grants according to need.

Annual grant total
Income averages between £3,000 to £4,000 per year and expenditure around £2,300 per year.

Exclusions
No grants for the relief of rates, taxes or other public funds.

Applications
In writing to the correspondent at any time. Individuals should apply through a social worker, minister of religion or similar third party.

Other information
The charity also makes grants to organisations.

Long Bennington and Foston

Long Bennington Charities

£4,600

Correspondent: Nicola Brown, Trustee, 61 Main Road, Long Bennington, Newark, Nottinghamshire NG23 5DJ (01400 282458)

CC Number: 214893

Eligibility
People in need who live in the parish of Long Bennington.

Types of grants
One-off grants according to need. Grants have previously been given for garden maintenance and disability aids.

Annual grant total
In 2013 the charity had an income of £7,300 and a total expenditure of £4,700. We estimate that welfare grants to individuals totalled £4,600.

Applications

In writing to the correspondent directly by the individual or through a third party.

Mansfield

The Brunts Charity

£12,000

Correspondent: H. Hawkins, Administrator, Brunts Chambers, 2 Toothill Lane, Mansfield, Notts NG18 1NJ (01623 623055)

CC Number: 213407

Eligibility

Older people over 60 who are in need and have lived in the former borough of Mansfield (as constituted in 1958) for at least five years.

Types of grants

Regular allowances in the form of small pensions. Christmas gifts are also available.

Annual grant total

In 2012/13 the charity had assets of £12.1 million and an income of £652,000. During the year £384 was given in pensions, £9,800 in Christmas gifts and £1,900 in other grants.

Applications

On a form available from the correspondent to be submitted directly by the individual. Applications are considered regularly.

Other information

The charity's main concern is the provision of almshouses for elderly residents in financial difficulty. It also makes grants to local organisations.

Newark

The Mary Elizabeth Siebel Trust

£74,000 (83 grants)

Correspondent: Frances Kelly, Administrator, Tallents Solicitors, 3 Middlegate, Newark, Nottinghamshire NG24 1AQ (01636 671881; fax: 01636 700148; email: frances.kelly@tallents.co.uk)

CC Number: 1001255

Eligibility

People over 60 years of age who are in poor health and live within a 12-mile radius of Newark Town Hall.

Types of grants

One-off grants ranging from £50 to £2,500. The trust aims to enable individual applicants to live in their own homes and as such provides help with, for example, the cost of stairlifts, essential home repairs, aids for people with disabilities, care at home, relief for carers and so on.

Annual grant total

In 2012/13 the trust had assets of £2.8 million, an income of £111,000 and a total expenditure of £124,000. Grants were made to 83 individuals totalling £74,000.

Applications

On a form available from the correspondent. Applications can be submitted at any time but must be endorsed by a recognised third party such as a doctor or social worker. Individuals are usually visited by the trust's assessor who will then make a recommendation to the trustees. The trustees meet every two months to consider applications.

Other information

Grants are also made to organisations (£7,500 in 2012/13).

Nottingham

Bilby's and Cooper's Relief-in-Need Charity

£500

Correspondent: The Trustees, Somersby Consulting Ltd, 100 Somersby Road, Woodthorpe, Nottingham NG5 4LT

CC Number: 215185

Eligibility

People in need who live in the city of Nottingham.

Types of grants

One-off grants ranging from £50 to £200.

Annual grant total

This charity generally awards around £500 in grants to individuals.

Applications

In writing to the correspondent either through a social worker, Citizens Advice or other welfare agency, or directly by the individual. Applications are considered at any time.

The Nottingham Aged Persons' Trust

£0

Correspondent: The Trustees, Nottingham City Council, Single Gateway Unit, Communities Courtyard, Wollaton Road, Nottingham NG8 2AD (01158763654; email: tracy.white@nottinghamcity.gov.uk)

CC Number: 242499

Eligibility

People in need, over 60 years of age, who live in the city of Nottingham and are in receipt of, or eligible for, the state retirement pension.

Types of grants

One-off grants ranging from £15 to £200 towards, for example, travel expenses to visit sick or older relatives; help for victims of crime; medical items; household costs.

Annual grant total

In 2012/13 the trust had no income and no expenditure. There has been no expenditure by this fund since before 2007.

Exclusions

Only one award per year will be made to any individual who makes a successful application.

Applications

On a form available from the correspondent. Applications can be submitted directly by the individual or family member. There are no deadlines.

The Skerritt Trust

£0 (1 grant)

Correspondent: Nigel Cullen, Administrator, Freeth Cartwright LLP, Cumberland Court, 80 Mount Street, Nottingham NG1 6HH (01159 015558)

CC Number: 1016701

Eligibility

Older people who live within ten miles of the market square in Nottingham.

Types of grants

Funding is given for house repairs and improvements to assist older people so that they can remain in their homes as long as possible.

Annual grant total

In 2012/13 the trust had assets of £2.1 million and an income of £86,000. Grants totalled £67,000, all of which was paid to institutions.

Applications

In writing to the correspondent through a social worker, Age Concern, day centre or similar third party. Applications are considered all year round.

St Peter's United Charities

£1,000

Correspondent: The Clerk, St Peter's Church Centre, St Peter's Square, Nottingham NG1 2NW (email: stpeterscharities@nottinghamchurches.org; website: www.nottinghamchurches.org/charities)

CC Number: 216737

Eligibility

Individuals in need living in the city of Nottingham or the surrounding districts of Greater Nottingham.

Types of grants

One-off grants of up to £100 for essential basic items that applicants are unable to afford for themselves, such as bedding, clothing, household items and furniture.

Annual grant total

In 2012 the charity had an income of £2,000 and a total expenditure of £1,100. Although our research tells us that around £1,800 is available each year for grants, we estimate that, during this year, social welfare grants to individuals totalled £1,000.

At the time of writing (August 2014) this was the most recent financial information available for the charity.

Applications

On the charity's application form (which can be downloaded from the website along with guidelines or requested by post or email), which must be submitted by a referrer such as a social worker, religious leader or staff of support organisations and not by the individual seeking assistance. Applications are considered upon receipt; a response can normally be expected within two weeks.

The Thorpe Trust

£14,600

Correspondent: Mandy Kelly, Administrator, Actons Solicitors, 20 Regent Street, Nottingham NG1 5BQ (email: mandy.kelly@actons.co.uk)

CC Number: 214611

Eligibility

Widows and unmarried women in need who live within a mile radius of Nottingham city centre. The recipients must be the widows or fatherless daughters of clergymen, gentlemen or professional people or of people engaged (otherwise than in a menial capacity) in trade or agriculture.

Types of grants

Recurrent grants according to need.

Annual grant total

In 2012/13 the trust had both an income and a total expenditure of £14,800. We estimate that grants to individuals totalled £14,600.

Applications

On a form available from the correspondent. Applications can be submitted directly by the individual or, where applicable, through a social worker, Citizens Advice or other welfare agency. They are considered once during the summer and at Christmas.

Warsop

The Warsop United Charities

£1,100

Correspondent: Jean Simmons, Trustee, Newquay, Clumber Street, Warsop, Mansfield, Nottinghamshire NG20 0LX

CC Number: 224821

Eligibility

People in need who live in the urban district of Warsop (Warsop, Church Warsop, Warsop Vale, Meden Vale, Spion Kop and Sookholme).

Types of grants

One-off grants for necessities and quarterly grants to about 60 individuals.

Annual grant total

In 2012 this charity had an income of £8,000 and total expenses of £2,200. We estimate grants for social welfare purposes to be around £1,100. These were the latest accounts available at the time of writing (July 2014).

Applications

In writing to the correspondent. The trustees meet three or four times a year.

Other information

Grants are also made for educational purposes.

Shropshire

The Ellen Barnes Charitable Trust

£5,000

Correspondent: Mark Woodward, Administrator, Crampton Pym and Lewis, 47 Willow Street, Oswestry, Shropshire SY11 1PR (01691 653301; fax: 01691 658699; email: info@crampton-pym-lewis.co.uk; website: www.crampton-pym-lewis.co.uk)

CC Number: 217344

Eligibility

People in need who live in Weston Rhyn and adjoining parishes.

Types of grants

Although the trust's income is mainly used to run six almshouses, one-off grants are considered.

Annual grant total

In 2013, the trust had an income of £23,000 and a total expenditure of £19,000. We estimate that the total amount of grants awarded to individuals was approximately £5,000.

Applications

In writing to the correspondent either directly by the individual or through a social worker, Citizens Advice, doctor or other welfare agency. Applications are considered throughout the year.

Other information

The trust's main activity is the provision of almshouses.

The Lady Forester Trust

£60,000 (117 grants)

Correspondent: Janet McGorman, Administrator, Willey Park, Broseley, Shropshire TF12 5JJ (01952 884318; fax: 01952 883680; email: ladyforesttrust@willeyestates.co.uk)

CC Number: 241187

Eligibility

Firstly, people who live in the ancient borough of Wenlock and then to the inhabitants of the county of Shropshire who are sick, convalescent, infirm or have a disability.

Types of grants

One-off grants for medical equipment, nursing care, travel to and from hospitals and other medical needs not otherwise available on the NHS.

Annual grant total

In 2013 the trust held assets of £4.9 million and had an income of £146,000. Grants to 117 individuals totalled almost £60,000.

Exclusions

No retrospective grants are made, nor are grants given for building repairs/alterations, home/garden improvements or household bills.

Applications

On a form available from the correspondent. Applications should be made through a doctor (or social services in exceptional circumstances) and are considered on a quarterly basis.

Other information

Grants are also made to local charitable organisations (£94,000 in 2013).

Dr Gardner's Charity for Sick Nurses

£600

Correspondent: Dr Leonard Hill, Trustee, Radbrook Stables, Radbrook Road, Shrewsbury SY3 9BQ (01743 236863; email: dr.lenhill@gmail.com)

CC Number: 218202

Eligibility

Nurses in need who live in Shropshire.

Types of grants

One-off grants, usually of up to about £300, to help sick nurses to convalesce or to have further help to enable them to return to work. Grants are made to individuals and organisations.

Annual grant total

In 2013 the charity had an income of £2,000 and a total expenditure of £2,300. We estimate that social welfare grants to individuals totalled £600. Grants are also given to individuals for educational purposes and to organisations.

Applications

On a form available from the correspondent. Applications can be submitted at any time either through a social worker, Citizens Advice or other welfare agency, or directly by the individual or a relevant third party.

Gibbons Charity

See entry on page 78

The Basil Houghton Memorial Trust

£5,400

Correspondent: Julia Baron, Trustee, c/o Community Council Building, The Creative Quarter, Shrewsbury Business Park, Shrewsbury SY2 6LG (01743 360641; email: houghton.trust@shropshire-rcc.org.uk)

CC Number: 1101947

Eligibility

People with learning disabilities who are in need and live in Shropshire.

Types of grants

One-off grants usually of no more than £250. Grants should be additional to any services provided by statutory bodies. Typically, grants have been made towards travel expenses, achieving individuals' goals, the provision of life-improving items and services, and as contributions towards holidays.

Annual grant total

In 2012/13 the trust had an income of £13,800 and a total expenditure of £11,100. We estimate that grants to individuals totalled £5,400, with funding also awarded to local organisations.

Exclusions

Applicants for individual grants must be resident in Shropshire.

Applications

On a form available from the correspondent. Trustees meet quarterly in March, June, September and December.

Other information

The trust was established with an endowment from Mrs Doris Houghton and named after her son, the late Basil Houghton of Shrewsbury, who himself had a learning disability.

The Oswestry Dispensary Fund

£300

Correspondent: Emyr Richard Lloyd, Administrator, Brown and Lloyd, The Albany, 37–39 Willow Street, Oswestry, Shropshire SY11 1AQ (01691 659194)

CC Number: 212212

Eligibility

People who are in poor health and financial difficulties and live in the borough of Oswestry and its surrounding district.

Types of grants

One-off grants, normally up to £300, for items such as medical equipment and care and second-hand television sets.

Annual grant total

Over the past number of years we believe grants to have averaged around £300 each year.

Applications

In writing to the correspondent either directly by the individual or via a relevant third party such as a social worker, Citizens Advice or other welfare agency.

The Shropshire Football Association Benevolent Fund

£500

Correspondent: Roy Waterfield, Chief Executive, New Stadium, Oteley Road, Shrewsbury, Shropshire SY2 6ST (01743 362769; email: roy.waterfield@shropshirefa.com)

CC Number: 505509

Eligibility

People in need who live in Shropshire, who are: (i) amateur and professional footballers; (ii) apprentices; (iii) coaches; (iv) managers; (v) any other official or employee of any football team; (vi) referees and referees' assistants and widows and orphans of other persons dependent wholly or partially on any of the above people.

Types of grants

One-off and recurrent grants according to need.

Annual grant total

In 2013 the fund had an income of £100 and a total expenditure of £1,300. This expenditure is unusually high when compared to previous years. We estimate that grants total on average around £500 each year.

Applications

Applications can be submitted at any time and should include details of present income, occupation and any dependents along with any other information which may be helpful.

The Shropshire Welfare Trust

£500

Correspondent: Dr Leonard Hill, Honorary Secretary, Radbrook Stables, Radbrook Road, Shrewsbury SY3 9BQ (01743 236863; email: dr.lenhill@gmail.com; website: www.shropshirewelfaretrust.co.uk)

CC Number: 218206

Eligibility

Patients and members of staff in specified hospitals in Shropshire who are in need. People with serious health problems or disabilities living in Shropshire are assisted with medically-related and disability-related expenses. Applicants will normally be on low income and have little or no savings.

Types of grants

Small, one-off grants, generally in the range of £50 to £300. Support can be given towards travel to and from hospital, convalescence, respite care, medical equipment, mobility aids and essential household necessities.

Annual grant total

In 2013 the charity had an income of £2,100 and an expenditure of £1,100. We estimate the annual total of grants to individuals to be around £500. Note that the charitable expenditure varies from year to year.

Exclusions

Grants are not normally made retrospectively, to cover debts or bills.

Applications

Application forms can be requested from the correspondent or downloaded from the charity's website. They can be submitted directly by the individual or through a social worker, Citizens Advice or similar agency. Candidates should provide any relevant information helping the trustees to assess their circumstances. Supporting letters from professional third parties would also help the application. The trustees normally meet in March and October but also as needed.

Other information

Occasionally grants are given to organisations with similar objects in Shropshire.

The St Chad's and St Alkmund's Charity

£800

Correspondent: Ann Matthews, Administrator, 40 Preston Street, Shrewsbury SY2 5PG (01743341894)

CC Number: 231383

Eligibility

People in need who have lived in the ecclesiastical districts of St Chad and St George, Shrewsbury, Astley, Kinnerley, Guilsfield, Great Ness, Annscroft, Oxon and Bicton for not less than five years immediately before their application.

Types of grants

One-off grants of up to £50 to help with the cost of clothes, linen, bedding, tools, medical or other aid in sickness, food or other articles in kind.

Annual grant total

In 2012/13 the charity had an income of £2,400 and a total expenditure of £1,700. We estimate that around £800 was given in grants to individuals for social welfare purposes.

Applications

On a form available from the correspondent. Applications should be submitted directly by the individual and they are considered at any time.

Other information

The charity also gives support to religious work of the Church of England and to promote education for people under 25.

The Thompson Pritchard Trust

£18,000

Correspondent: Dr Leonard Hill, Trustee, Radbrook Stables, Radbrook Road, Shrewsbury SY3 9BQ (01743 236863; email: dr.lenhill@gmail.com)

CC Number: 234601

Eligibility

Individuals who live in Shropshire and have medically-related and disability-related expenses and problems. Preference is given to those who have recently been discharged from hospital.

Types of grants

One-off grants up to £300 are given towards: medical equipment (and repairs); convalescent treatment; domestic equipment which affects health such as washing machine or fridge repairs; expenses incurred during illness, including treatment; and travel and occasional accommodation for relatives during major operations.

Annual grant total

In 2013 the trust had both an income and a total expenditure of £20,000. We estimate that grants to individuals totalled £18,000.

Exclusions

No recurrent grants or grants towards purchasing, repairing or maintaining buildings or to pay off debts.

Applications

On a form available from the correspondent. Applications for small grants can be submitted at any time either directly by the individual or through a relevant third party such as a social worker, Citizens Advice or other welfare agency. More advice is available from the trust.

Alveley

The Alveley Charity

£14,600

Correspondent: The Trust Administrator, MFG Solicitors LLP, Adam House, Birmingham Road, Kidderminster, Worcestershire DY10 2SH (01562 820181)

CC Number: 1026017

Eligibility

People in need who live in the parishes of Alveley and Romsley.

Types of grants

One-off grants according to need.

Annual grant total

In 2012/13 the charity had an income of £21,000 and a total expenditure of £14,900. We estimate that grants to individuals totalled £14,600.

Applications

In writing to the correspondent either directly by the individual, or through a social worker, Citizens Advice or other welfare agency.

Bridgnorth

The Bridgnorth Parish Charity

£0

Correspondent: Elizabeth Smallman, Clerk, 37 Stourbridge Road, Bridgnorth WV15 5AZ (01746 764149; email: eeesmallman@aol.com)

CC Number: 243890

Eligibility

People living in Bridgnorth parish, including Oldbury and Eardington, who are in need.

Types of grants

One-off grants according to need, including those towards playgroup fees, school visits, funeral expenses and heating costs.

Annual grant total

In 2013 the charity had an income of £4,100 but there was no expenditure. Note that the expenditure varies each year and in the past has fluctuated from £2,000 to £9,400.

Applications

In writing to the correspondent either directly by the individual or through a doctor, nurse, member of the local clergy, social worker, Citizens Advice or other welfare agency.

Other information

Grants are also made to organisations.

Hodnet

The Hodnet Consolidated Eleemosynary Charities

£3,000

Correspondent: Mrs S. W. France, Administrator, 26 The Meadow, Hodnet, Market Drayton, Shropshire TF9 3QF (01630 685907)

CC Number: 218213

Eligibility

People in need who live in Hodnet parish.

Types of grants

Grants include Christmas parcels for people of pensionable age.

Annual grant total

In 2012 the charities had an income of £4,000 and a total expenditure of £5,000. We estimate that grants awarded to individuals for social welfare purposes totalled around £3,000. The 2012 accounts were the latest available at the time of writing (August 2014).

Applications

In writing to the correspondent for consideration throughout the year. Applications can be submitted directly by the individual or through a social worker, Citizens Advice or other welfare agency.

Other information

This is essentially a relief-in-need charity that also gives money to students for books.

Hopesay

Hopesay Parish Trust

£500

Correspondent: David Evans, Trustee, Park Farm, The Fish, Hopesay, Craven Arms, Shropshire SY7 8HG (01588 660545; email: annedalgliesh@aol.com; website: www.2shrop.net/live/welcome.asp?id=3167)

CC Number: 1066894

Eligibility

People in need living in the parish of Hopesay, Shropshire. Priority may be given to young people under the age of 25.

Types of grants

One-off grants between £25 and £500 can be awarded according to need.

Annual grant total

In 2013 the trust had an income of £2,800 and an expenditure of £3,500. Grants usually total around £3,000 per year. In the past about 20 individuals a year have been supported. Most support is given for educational purposes, therefore we estimate that welfare support to individuals was of around £500.

Exclusions

Grants are not made where the funding is the responsibility of central or local government, whether or not the individual has taken up such provision. Retrospective applications are not considered.

Applications

Application forms are available from the correspondent or can be downloaded from the Hopesay Parish Council website. The application form covers the essential information required, and the trustees will ask for further details if necessary. Applications can be made at any time directly by the individual or by a third party, such as a parent/guardian, teacher/tutor, or through an organisation such as Citizens Advice or school.

Other information

The trust gives priority to educational grants. At the trustees' discretion, any surplus income may be applied for other charitable purposes but only within the parish.

Lilleshall

The Charity of Edith Emily Todd – Lilleshall Share

£6,800

Correspondent: Mary Ayres, Administrator, 4 Willmoor Lane, Lilleshall, Newport, Shropshire TF10 9EE (01952 606053)

CC Number: 215058

Eligibility

People over the age of 60 who are in need and who live in the ecclesiastical parish of Lilleshall.

Types of grants

Pensions of £15 a month with bonus payment at Christmas time.

Annual grant total

In 2012/13 the charity had an income of £7,700 and a total expenditure of £7,000. We estimate that grants to individuals totalled £6,800.

Applications

In writing directly by the individual to the correspondent. Applications are considered on receipt.

Shrewsbury

The Gorsuch, Langley and Prynce Charity

£25,000 (246 grants)

Correspondent: Pamela Moseley, Administrator, 116 Underdale Road, Shrewsbury SY2 5EF

CC Number: 247223

Eligibility

People in need who live in the parishes of Holy Cross (the Abbey) and St Giles in Shrewsbury.

Types of grants

One-off and recurrent grants usually ranging from £50 to £500. Grants have been given towards furniture, carpets, washing machines, cookers, fridges, baby clothes and cots.

Annual grant total

In 2012 the charity had assets of £919,000 and an income of £40,000. During the year the charity gave grants to 246 individuals and families, as well as to four local primary schools. The total of grants given was £30,000, although a breakdown of distribution was not available from the accounts. We estimate that grants to individuals and families totalled £25,000.

At the time of writing (August 2014) this was the most recent financial information available for the charity.

Applications

In writing to the correspondent through a social worker, healthcare professional, Citizens Advice or other welfare agency such as Home-Start. Applications should include details of the full the amount required and why it is needed. They are considered on a regular basis.

Staffordshire

Albrighton Relief-in-Need Charity

£2,100

Correspondent: David Beechey, Trustee, 34 Station Road, Albrighton, Wolverhampton WV7 3QG (01902 372779; email: dabeechey@blueyonder.co.uk)

CC Number: 240494

Eligibility

People in need who live in the parishes of Albrighton, Boningale, Boscobel and Donington. The charity aims to relieve temporary hardship.

Types of grants

One-off grants according to need. Grants could be given for clothing, household necessities, food, furniture, special medical and disability equipment, towards bereavement and funeral costs, travel expenses to people attending an interview and recuperative holiday costs. Examples of previous grants also include a specialised computer for a young man with severe disabilities, provision of family holidays and support towards travel expenses to young people. Our research indicates that Christmas hampers are also distributed.

Annual grant total

In 2013 the charity had an income of £3,900 and an expenditure of £2,300. We have estimated the annual total of grants to individuals to be around £2,100. Bear in mind that the expenditure tends to fluctuate quite widely.

Exclusions

Help is not given where the need can be addressed by statutory sources.

Applications

In writing to the correspondent. Applications can be made either directly by the individual or through a third party, such as a social worker, Citizens Advice, GP, district nurse or health visitor.

Other information

The charity is a merger of a number of ancient local charities.

The Burton on Trent Nursing Endowment Fund

£4,000

Correspondent: Marilyn Arnold, Administrator, East Staffordshire CVS, Voluntary Services Centre, Union Street, Burton-on-Trent DE14 1AA (01283 543414)

CC Number: 239185

Eligibility

People in need who live in the former county borough of Burton-on-Trent.

Types of grants

One-off grants towards, for example, chiropody treatment, bedding, removal costs, electric scooter batteries, fridges, freezers and childcare provision.

Annual grant total

In 2013 the fund had an income of £6,600 and a total expenditure of £8,200. We estimate that grants to individuals totalled £4,000, with funding also awarded to organisations.

Applications

On a form available from the correspondent. Applications can come directly via the individual or through a recognised referral agency (social worker, Citizens Advice, local GP and so on).

Consolidated Charity of Burton upon Trent

£50,000 (182 grants)

Correspondent: J. P. Southwell, Clerk, Dains LLP, 1st Floor, Gibraltar House, Crown Square, First Avenue, Burton-on-Trent (01283 527067; fax: 01283 507969; email: clerk@consolidatedcharityburton.org.uk; website: www.consolidatedcharityburton.org.uk)

CC Number: 239072

Eligibility

People who live in Burton upon Trent and the neighbouring parishes of Branston, Outwoods and Stretton and are in need by reason of youth, age, health, disability, financial hardship or other disadvantage.

Types of grants

One-off grants of up to £400 (£250 for applicants who have been living in the area for less than two years) for essential items, for example, electrical appliances, mobility aids, furniture, bedding, carpets and children's clothing.

Annual grant total

In 2013 the charity had assets of £12.3 million and an income of £497,000. A total of £89,000 was awarded to individuals during the year. Relief-in-need grants totalled £50,000 awarded to 182 individuals.

Exclusions

Grants are not awarded for the relief of debt. Only one item per applicant can normally be given.

Applications

Application forms are available from the charity's website or can be requested from the correspondent. They should be supported by evidence of the applicant's income and outgoings, quotes from recommended suppliers and a letter of support from an appropriate support worker or welfare agency.

The trustees meet regularly to consider grants.

Other information

The charity also runs 32 almshouses in the local area, makes grants to local organisations and to individuals for educational purposes. Grants to organisations totalled £55,000 in 2013.

The Baron Davenport Emergency Grant (North Staffordshire)

£5,000

Correspondent: Information and Advice Service, c/o Age UK, 83–85 Trinity Street, Hanley, Stoke-on-Trent ST1 5NA (01782 286809)

Eligibility

Women (widows, singles and divorcees) who have lived in north Staffordshire for at least ten years and are over the age of 60. Applicants must live alone and have a low income and little or no savings.

Types of grants

One-off grants for emergencies only.

Annual grant total

Grants usually total about £5,000 a year.

Applications

This fund is now administered by Age UK, North Staffordshire. Application should be made on a form available from the correspondent. Applications are considered upon receipt.

Other information

For information on Baron Davenport's Charity Trust, see entry in the Midlands general section.

The Baron Davenport Emergency Grant (Staffordshire)

£2,000

Correspondent: The Administrator, Stafford District Voluntary Services, 131–141 North Walls, Stafford ST16 3AD (01785 606670; email: office@sdvs.org.uk)

Eligibility

Widows, unmarried women, divorcees and women abandoned by their husbands, who are over 60 years old and have lived in Staffordshire for at least ten years. Help may be given to younger women in special circumstances.

Types of grants

One-off and recurrent grants of up to £250 towards electrical goods, clothing, living costs, household bills, food, medical equipment, furniture, disability equipment, help in the home and so on.

Annual grant total

Grants awarded to individuals total around £2,000.

Applications

Stafford District Voluntary Services (Support Staffordshire) now administers this fund. Applications should be made on a form to be submitted either directly by the individual or through an appropriate third party, such as a family member or welfare agency. Applications are usually considered upon receipt.

The North Staffordshire Coalfield Miners Relief Fund

£18,500

Correspondent: Susan Jackson, Administrator, c/o Coal Industry Social Welfare Organisation, 142 Queens Road, Penkhull, Stoke-on-Trent, Staffordshire ST4 7LH (01782 744996; fax: 01782 749117)

CC Number: 209616

Eligibility

Mineworkers or retired mineworkers who worked in the North Staffordshire coalfield (including Cheadle), and their widows or dependents. The mineworker must have suffered an industrial accident, a disease or died as a result of their duties.

Types of grants

One-off grants according to need.

Annual grant total
In 2012/13 the fund had an income of £3,600 and a total expenditure of £22,000.

Applications
In writing to the correspondent or by telephone either directly by the individual or via a third party such as a social worker, Citizens Advice or other welfare agency. Grants are given after a home visit. Applications are considered throughout the year.

Other information
Grants are also made to organisations.

Staffordshire Community Foundation

£48,000 (189 grants)

Correspondent: Sally Grieve, Grants Officer, Staffordshire Community Foundation, c/o BL157, Staffordshire University, Blackheath Lane, Stafford ST18 0AD (01785 353789; email: sally.grieve@staffsfoundation.org.uk; website: www.staffsfoundation.org.uk)

CC Number: 1091628

Eligibility
Visit the foundation's website for further information.

Types of grants
Grants vary

Annual grant total
In 2012/13 the foundation had an income of £940,000 and a total expenditure of £624,000. The fund gave approximately £577,000 to organisations and £48,000 to individuals.

Applications
There are five different grants available for individuals which are listed on the website under the 'Grants' tab. The forms for each may be returned by post or completed electronically and emailed to the community foundation. The form includes a reference section to be completed by a doctor, health visitor, local councillor or similar. Note that these funds are rarely open all year and usually tend to run in rounds.

Other information
The Malam Heath Endowment Fund was formed in 2011 by the merger of the Edward Malam Convalescent Fund and the Heath Memorial Trust Fund. The new fund is administered by the Staffordshire Community Foundation (a new entry in this book).

Grants are also made to organisations that will benefit individuals.

The Strasser Foundation

£5,000

Correspondent: The Trustees, c/o Knights Solicitors, The Brampton, Newcastle-under-Lyme, Staffordshire ST5 0QW (01782 619225)

CC Number: 511703

Eligibility
Individuals in need in the local area, with a preference for North Staffordshire.

Types of grants
Usually one-off grants for a specific cause or need, to help with the relief of poverty.

Annual grant total
In 2012/13 the foundation had both an income and a total expenditure of £21,000. We estimate that grants made to individuals for social welfare purposes totalled around £5,000.

Applications
In writing to the correspondent. The trustees meet quarterly. Applications are only acknowledged if an sae is sent.

Other information
The foundation also makes grants to individuals for education.

Church Eaton

Church Eaton Relief-in-Need Charity (Church Eaton Charities)

£8,200

Correspondent: Stephen Rutherford, Trustee, 5 Ashley Croft, Church Eaton, Stafford ST20 0BJ (01785 823958)

CC Number: 216179

Eligibility
People in need who have lived in the parish of Church Eaton for at least two years. In exceptional circumstances grants may be available to those living immediately outside the parish.

Types of grants
Support is generally given towards the heating costs or in provision of coal during the winter season. Grants are also available for other items, equipment or services, for example, TV licences, lifeline telephones and so on.

Annual grant total
At the time of writing (August 2014) the latest financial information available was from 2012. In 2012 the charity had an income of £10,200 and a total expenditure of £8,400. We estimate that grants totalled around £8,200.

Applications
In writing to the correspondent. Applications are considered upon receipt.

Enville

The Enville Village Trust

£2,600

Correspondent: Richard Jones, Trustee, Batfield House, Batfield Lane, Enville, Stourbridge, West Midlands DY7 5LF (01746 780350)

CC Number: 231563

Eligibility
People in need who live in the parish of Enville, with a preference for older people.

Types of grants
One-off grants ranging from £50 to £150. Grants may not always be given directly to individuals; sometimes they may be to provide a service to individuals, which they cannot themselves afford. Grants have been given for telephone installation/connection (including an emergency contact line), emergency medical help, optician bills for partially-sighted people, special dental treatment, travel to hospital, food parcels, clothing and fuel in winter.

Annual grant total
In 2012/13, the trust had an income of £3,600 and a total expenditure of £2,800. We estimate that the total award given to individuals was approximately £2,600.

Applications
In writing to the correspondent. Applications can be submitted either directly by the individual or through a social worker, the vicar of the parish church or the village welfare group. They are considered at any time.

Leek

The Carr Trust

£40,000

Correspondent: Alison Carp, Administrator, St Luke's Church of England, Fountain Street, Leek, Staffordshire ST13 6JS (01538 373306; email: stlukesleek@hotmail.co.uk)

CC Number: 216764

Eligibility
Residents of Leek, mainly older people, who are in need.

Types of grants
Mainly pensions, usually of around £20 a month towards items, services and facilities that will help to reduce need or hardship. One-off grants are also available and most beneficiaries receive a Christmas bonus.

Annual grant total
In 2013 the trust had an income of £25,000 and a total expenditure of £45,000. We estimate that grants to individuals totalled around £40,000.

Applications
In writing to the correspondent. An advert about the grants appears in a local paper in March each year. The trustees require details of the applicant's age, marital status, income, savings and details of any property owned.

Other information
The Carr Trust administers three charities – the Charity of Charles Carr, the Charity of Elizabeth Flint for the Poor and the Charity of William Carr.

Lichfield

The Lichfield Municipal Charities

£11,300 (34 grants)

Correspondent: Simon R. James, Clerk, Ansons Solicitors, St Mary's Chambers, 5 Breadmarket Street, Lichfield, Staffordshire WS13 6LQ (01543 263456; fax: 01543 250942; email: sjames@ansonsllp.com)

CC Number: 254299

Eligibility
Individuals in need who live in the city of Lichfield (as it was pre-1974).

Types of grants
One-off grants according to need.

Annual grant total
In 2013 the charity had assets of £2.1 million and an income of £74,000. Grants were made to 34 individuals totalling £11,300.

Applications
On a form available from the correspondent. The trustees meet four times a year in March, June, September and December.

Other information
Grants are also made to organisations (£6,000 in 2013).

Michael Lowe's and Associated Charities

£43,000 (222 grants)

Correspondent: Christopher Kitto, Administrator, Ansons LLP, 5–7 Breadmarket Street, Lichfield, Staffordshire WS13 6LQ (01543 267995)

CC Number: 214785

Eligibility
People in need who live in the city of Lichfield, particularly older people and those requiring help in an emergency.

Types of grants
One-off grants up to £600 for domestic items, special chairs, school uniforms, wheelchairs and so on. People who are over 70 and living on a low income can also apply for fuel grants. The trustees may require the recipient to make a contribution of 10% to the cost of any item provided. Gifts in the form of second-hand furniture are also distributed.

Annual grant total
In 2012/13 the charities held assets of £1.7 million and had an income of £100,000. Grants to individuals totalled £43,000 and were distributed as follows:

Other grants	89	£33,000
Fuel grants	133	£10,000

The charities spent a further £7,500 running the 'Furniture Transfer Scheme', which redistributes second-hand furniture to families recommended by local welfare agencies. Grants to organisations amounted to a further £15,300.

Applications
On a form available from the correspondent. Applications are considered on their own merits and individuals are usually interviewed before any grant is awarded. Beneficiaries of the 'Furniture Transfer Scheme' are usually recommended to trustees through a local welfare organisation. The trustees meet on average five times a year to consider grant applications, though special meetings may be called to deal with urgent requests.

Newcastle-under-Lyme

The Newcastle-under-Lyme United Charities

£3,000

Correspondent: Caroline Horne, Administrator, Civic Offices, Merrial Street, Newcastle-under-Lyme, Staffordshire ST5 2AG (01782 742232; email: caroline.horne@newcastle-staffs.gov.uk)

CC Number: 217916

Eligibility
People in need who live in the borough of Newcastle-under-Lyme (as it was before 1974).

Types of grants
Small donations are given at Christmas.

Annual grant total
In 2012/13 the charity had an income of £4,400 and a total expenditure of £3,200. We estimate that grants to individuals totalled £3.000.

Exclusions
No grants are given to older people living in sheltered housing.

Applications
In writing to the correspondent. Applications should be submitted either directly by the individual or via a friend or family member. They are considered in October each year. The circumstances of beneficiaries are assessed on an annual basis by the trustees.

Rugeley

Chetwynd's Charity

£700

Correspondent: Carl Bennett, Councillor, Sherwood, 17 East Butts Road, Rugeley WS15 2LU (01889 800727)

CC Number: 234806

Eligibility
Inhabitants of the ancient parish of Rugeley, Staffordshire who are in need.

Types of grants
One-off grants according to need.

Annual grant total
In 2013, the charity had an income of £3,700 and a total expenditure of £2,900. We estimate that the total amount of grants awarded to individuals for social welfare purposes was approximately £700. The charity also awards grants to organisations.

Applications
In writing to the correspondent.

Other information
The charity also awards separate grants for the advancement of education, training and cultural activities.

Stoke-on-Trent

Malam-Heath Fund

£11,000 (181 grants)

Correspondent: Sally Grieve, Grants Officer, Staffordshire Community Foundation, c/o BL157, Staffordshire University, Blackheath Lane, Stafford ST18 0AD (01785 353789; email: sally.grieve@staffsfoundation.org.uk; website: www.staffsfoundation.org.uk)

Eligibility
In order to qualify for a grant from the Malam-Heath Fund applicants must be aged over 18; be resident in Stoke-on-Trent, or a neighbouring area that identifies more with Stoke-on-Trent than other areas, such as Kidsgrove, Biddulph or Cheadle; be unable to finance the holiday themselves; and be in financial need of a holiday as part of recuperation or respite, or relief from a recent traumatic event.

Note that all payments will be made directly to the holiday company/hotel and that there will be no direct payments to applicants. It is unlikely that an individual would benefit from an award in consecutive years.

Types of grants
Awards are as follows: single person for one week holiday – £150; single person for two weeks holiday – £300; a couple for one week holiday – £300; and a couple for two weeks holiday – £600.

Annual grant total
In 2012/13 the fund had assets of £260,000, an income of £10,000 and awarded grants of approximately £11,000 to 181 individuals.

Applications
Applications can be downloaded as part of an application pack from Staffordshire Community Foundation's website.

Applications will be considered at quarterly panels, although the frequency of these panels may increase or decrease depending on demand. In any event, you should allow at least four weeks between the panel and the date of your holiday.

Other information
Since 2009, the Malam-Heath Fund has been administered by the Staffordshire Community Foundation. It was previously listed as a separate fund in this guide but has now been removed from the Central Register of Charities.

Tamworth

Beardsley's Relief-in-Need Charity

£5,900

Correspondent: Derek Tomkinson, Trustee, 'Torview', 95 Main Road, Wigginton, Tamworth, Staffordshire B79 9DU (01543 255612)

CC Number: 214461

Eligibility
People in need who live in the borough of Tamworth.

Types of grants
One-off grants and loans for health and welfare purposes.

Annual grant total
In 2012/13 the charity had an income of £12,300 and a total expenditure of £11,900. We estimate that grants to individuals totalled £5,900, with funding also awarded to local organisations.

Applications
In writing to the correspondent, either directly by the individual or, where applicable, through a social worker, Citizens Advice or other welfare agency.

The Rawlet Trust

£5,000

Correspondent: Christine Gilbert, Administrator, 47 Hedging Lane, Wilnecote, Tamworth B77 5EX (01827 288614; email: christine.gilbert@mail.com)

CC Number: 221732

Eligibility
People in need who live in the borough of Tamworth.

Types of grants
One-off and recurrent grants towards disability facilities, holidays, bibles for children and Home Link telephone expenses. Grants for educational purposes are also available for young people under the age of 25 who have parents resident in the area.

Annual grant total
In 2012/13 the trust had an income of £24,000 and an expenditure of £21,000. The trust was not required to submit accounts to the Charity Commission, but we estimate grants to individuals for social welfare purposes to have totalled £5,000. The trust also awarded funding for educational purposes, and to organisations.

Applications
On a form available from the correspondent, to be submitted either directly by the individual or through a third party such as a social worker or Citizens Advice. The clerk or one of the trustees will follow up applications if any further information is needed. The trustees meet in January, April, July and October to consider applications.

Tamworth Municipal Charity

£2,600

Correspondent: Anthony Goodwin, Trustee, Tamworth Borough Council, Marmion House, Lichfield Street, Tamworth, Staffordshire B79 7BZ (01827 709212)

CC Number: 216875

Eligibility
People in need who live in the borough of Tamworth.

Types of grants
One-off grants towards, for example, equipment, household items and hospital travel costs.

Annual grant total
In 2012 the charity had an income of £3,500 and an expenditure of £2,800. Grants totalled around £2,600.

2012 accounts were the most recent available at the time of writing (August 2014).

Applications
In writing to the correspondent.

Other information
Grants may also be given to organisations.

Trentham

Edith Emily Todd (The Todd Fund)

£1,000

Correspondent: Adam Bainbridge, Clerk to the Trustees, 67 Jonathan Road, Stoke-on-Trent ST4 8LP (01782 643567; email: yankee.echohotel@gmail.com)

CC Number: 209922

Eligibility
People in need who live in the parishes of St Mary and All Saints (Trentham) and St Mathias (Hanford).

Types of grants
Elderly people can receive recurrent pensions, which are reviewed twice a year. One-off and recurrent grants are

also offered to those in need towards items, services or facilities.

Annual grant total

In 2013/14 the charity had an income of £1,700 and an expenditure of £1,100. We estimate that grants to individuals totalled around £1,000.

Applications

In writing to the correspondent at any time. Applications can be submitted either directly by the individual or through a third party, such as a social worker, Citizens Advice or other welfare agency.

Tutbury

The Tutbury General Charities

£1,500

Correspondent: Jeanne Minchin, Administrator, 66 Redhill Lane, Tutbury, Burton-on-Trent, Staffordshire DE13 9JW (01283 813310)

CC Number: 215140

Eligibility

Only people in need who live in the parish of Tutbury.

Types of grants

One-off and recurrent grants according to need. All residents in the parish who are over 70 receive a birthday card. Vouchers for fuel or goods at a local store (usually under £20) are also given to about 200 people in need who live within the parish regardless of their age at Christmas. Special cases are considered on their merits by the trustees but applicants must live in the parish of Tutbury.

Annual grant total

In 2012/13 the charities had an income of £9,200 and an expenditure of £6,500. Grants are made for welfare and educational purposes to both individuals and organisations.

Applications

The charities have application forms, available from the correspondent, which should be submitted for consideration in November for Christmas vouchers. Inclusion in the birthday voucher scheme can be done at any time (all that is needed is the name, address and date of birth of the person).

Other information

The clerk of the charities states that details of the charities are well publicised within the village.

Warwick-shire

Sir Edward Boughton Long Lawford Charity

£25,000

Correspondent: Debbie Groves, Secretary, 17 Edinburgh Way, Long Lawford, Rugby, Warwickshire CV23 9AE

CC Number: 237841

Eligibility

People in need who live in the parish of Long Lawford or Rugby. Applicants for pensions must have lived in the parish for the last five years.

Types of grants

Pensions of £10 a month and Christmas bonuses of £40. One-off grants are awarded for various welfare purposes, including disability aids, TV licences and stairlifts. Small awards have also been made for swimming classes.

Annual grant total

In 2013 the charity had assets of £1.6 million and an income of £123,000. Grants to individuals totalled more than £25,000, of which £15,500 was given in pensions and Christmas bonuses, and £9,900 in 21 one-off grants.

A further £58,000 was given in grants to local schools and organisations.

Applications

On a form available from the correspondent, to be considered by the trustees every three months, usually February, May, August and November.

The Baron Davenport Emergency Grant (Leamington Spa, Kenilworth or Warwick)

£3,000 (21 grants)

Correspondent: Linda Price, Grants Administrator, c/o WCAVA – Warwick District Office, 4–6 Clemens, Leamington Spa, Warwickshire CV31 2DL (01926 477512; fax: 01926 315112; email: warwickinfo@wcava.org.uk; website: www.wcava.org.uk)

Eligibility

Widows, single women over 60, and occasionally, young single women who are in need. The children (aged under 25) of these individuals may also qualify for assistance. All beneficiaries must live alone apart from school aged children and have resided in the Midlands for at least ten years. The applicant's household income should not be more than £165 a week and savings should amount to no more than £6,000.

Types of grants

One-off grants of up to £150 can be given for cookers, bath lifts, baby equipment, carpets, telephone extensions, showers, pushchairs and so on.

Annual grant total

In 2012/13 grants were awarded to 21 women totalling £3,000.

Applications

Applications should be made by letter, including details of marital status, circumstances, financial situation and a supporting statement from a GP, social worker or similar professional. Grants will only be paid to individuals via the person supporting the applications. There may be an additional payment for those in receipt of certain benefits. Contact the correspondent for further information.

Applications should be marked confidential. Those from within the Warwick district should be sent to the correspondent. Other applicants should apply to their closest office in either Nuneaton or Bedworth: 72 High Street, Nuneaton, Warwickshire CV11 5DA or the Rugby office: 19 and 20 North Street, Rugby, Warwickshire CV21 2AG.

Other information

For information on Baron Davenport's Charity Trust, see entry in the Midlands general section.

The Baron Davenport Emergency Grant (North Warwickshire)

£500

Correspondent: The Manager, c/o North Warwickshire Citizens Advice, The Parish Rooms, Welcome Street, Atherstone, Warwickshire CV9 1DU (0844 855 2322; fax: 01827 721944; email: nwcab.advice@cabnet.org.uk; website: www.nwcab.org.uk)

Eligibility

(i) Widows, unmarried women and divorcees over 50 years old, and women abandoned by their partners; and (ii) children under the age of 25 whose mothers are in the first category, in the borough of North Warwickshire. Applicants must have been resident in the West Midlands for 10–15 years, be living alone (except where school age children are living with their mother) and have a bank, building society or Post Office account. The total income of the household should be no more than about £141 a week; this figure changes in line with state benefits.

Types of grants

One-off grants of between £150 and £200 for house repairs, furniture, school clothes, bedding, emergencies and so on. Pensions are also given of either £110 or £90 at each half-yearly distribution.

Annual grant total

Around £500 is awarded to individuals each year.

Applications

This fund is now administered by North Warwickshire Citizens Advice. Application should be made on a form available from the correspondent. Applications should be submitted through a social worker or welfare agency. They are considered throughout the year.

Other information

For information on Baron Davenport's Charity Trust, see entry in the Midlands general section.

The Baron Davenport Emergency Grant (Warwickshire)

£525

Correspondent: Pauline Dye, Administrator, Coventry Carers Centre, 3 City Arcade, Coventry CV1 3HX (02476 633788; email: contactus@coventrycarers.org.uk; website: www.coventrycarers.org.uk)

Eligibility

Widows, unmarried women (over 18) and children whose fathers are dead (under 21) who are in need. Applicants should not have savings over £1,000. Applicants must have lived within the old county boundaries of Warwickshire for at least ten years (this includes Coventry).

Types of grants

One-off grants for emergencies only, particularly unexpected domestic expenses, heavy funeral expenses or similar instances where state benefit is not available or undue delay would cause hardship. Grants are normally between £100 and £200.

Annual grant total

Grants awarded annually total between £500 and £1,000. In 2012/13 the administrators set aside £525 for awards. This information was taken from the annual report of Coventry Carers' Centre's 2012/13 annual report and accounts.

Applications

This fund is now administered by Coventry Carers' Centre. Application should be made in writing to the correspondent. Applications can be submitted through a social worker, Citizens Advice or other welfare agency; or directly by the individual. They are considered at any time.

Other information

For information on Baron Davenport's Charity Trust, see entry in the Midlands general section.

The Hatton Consolidated Charities

£4,500

Correspondent: M. H. Sparks, Clerk, Weare Giffard, 32 Shrewley Common, Shrewley, Warwick CV35 7AP (01926 842533)

CC Number: 250572

Eligibility

People in need who live in the parishes of Hatton, Beausale and Shrewley. Applications from outside these areas will not be considered.

Types of grants

One-off grants usually in the range of £50 to £500.

Annual grant total

In 2012/13 the charity had an income of £10,300 and an expenditure of £9,200. Grants are given for both educational and social welfare purposes and we estimate that the total of grants awarded to individuals for social welfare was around £4,500.

Exclusions

Grants are not given to schoolchildren.

Applications

In writing to the trustees or the correspondent.

Other information

Grants are also given to help students and young people starting work to help buy books and tools.

The South Warwickshire Welfare Trust

£8,700

Correspondent: Valerie Grimmer, Clerk, 62 Foxes Way, Warwick CV34 6AY (01926 492226; email: valerie.grimmer@sky.com)

CC Number: 235967

Eligibility

People who are sick and in need and live in Warwick district and the former rural district of Southam.

Types of grants

One-off grants of £25 to £400 for items, services or facilities to alleviate suffering or assist recovery for people who are sick, convalescent, infirm or have a disability. Grants are awarded towards holidays, cookers, carpets, white goods and home aids, for example.

Annual grant total

In 2013 the trust had an income of £9,500 and a total expenditure of £8,900. We estimate that grants to individuals totalled £8,700.

Exclusions

Grants are not repeated and are not given for relief of taxes or other public funds.

Applications

On an application form available from the correspondent to be submitted through a social worker, Citizens Advice or other welfare agency, or through a doctor, church official or similar third party. Applications are considered in January, April, July and October and should be submitted in the preceding months. Details of income/expenditure must be disclosed on the application form.

Warwick Combined Charity

£14,600 (29 grants)

Correspondent: Christopher Houghton, Administrator, c/o Moore and Tibbits Solicitors, 34 High Street, Warwick CV34 4BE (01926 491181; fax: 01926 402692; email: choughton@moore-tibbits.co.uk; website: www.warwickreliefinneed.org.uk)

CC Number: 256447

Eligibility

People in need who live in the town of Warwick.

Types of grants

One-off grants of up to £1,000 towards, for example, washing machines, beds, mattresses, vacuum cleaners, carpets, holidays and home repairs.

Annual grant total

In 2013 the charity had an income of £139,000 and a total expenditure of £131,000. Grants to 29 individuals totalled £14,600.

A further £85,000 was awarded in grants to 13 organisations.

Applications
On a form available from the correspondent or to download from the charity's website. Applications are normally submitted through social services or a similar welfare organisation and should be accompanied by a covering letter providing details of the applicant and the nature of the need. They are considered by the trustees at quarterly meetings.

Warwickshire Constabulary Benevolent Fund

£18,000

Correspondent: The Trustees, PO Box 4, Leek Wootton, Warwick CV35 7QB (01926 415000)

CC Number: 504560

Eligibility
Police officers of the Warwickshire Constabulary who regularly subscribe to the fund, retired members who take on honorary membership, and their immediate dependents.

Types of grants
One-off and recurrent grants and loans of up to £5,000 for individuals in financial difficulty. Help is also given to members attending a police convalescence home to assist with their travel costs and other expenditure.

Annual grant total
In the past grants to individuals have totalled around £18,000.

Applications
On a form available from the correspondent to be submitted either directly by the individual or through a work colleague, occupational health department or local NARPO secretary to the trustees or the force welfare department. Applications are considered on a regular basis.

Warwickshire Miners' Welfare Trust Fund Scheme

£9,400

Correspondent: David Thomas, Administrator, CISWO, 142 Queens Road, Stoke-on-Trent ST4 7LH (01782 744996; email: david.thomas@ciswo.org.uk)

CC Number: 519724

Eligibility
People who work or have worked within the coal mining industry in Warwickshire, and their dependents. Widows, widowers and relatives of the deceased miners are eligible to apply.

Types of grants
Our research suggests that one-off grants from £50 to £1,500 can be given towards convalescent holidays, hospital visits, electrical appliances (such as cookers and vacuum cleaners), carpets, beds and other furniture, wheelchairs, stair lifts, scooters and medical reports for industrial diseases.

Annual grant total
At the time of writing (August 2014) the latest financial information available was from 2012. In 2012 the fund had an income of £14,400 and a total expenditure of £18,900. We estimate that individual grants totalled around £9,400.

Exclusions
According to our research, death grants are not provided and support is not given to people who have received redundancy pay in the last ten years. Awards will not be given for any purpose for which the DWP will pay.

Applications
In writing to the correspondent. Applications can be submitted at any time directly by the individual or through a third party, for example, a social worker, Citizens Advice or other welfare agency. Candidates should include weekly income and medical proof from a doctor (if applicable).

Other information
Organisations in old coalfield areas are also supported.

Atherstone

The Charity of Priscilla Gent and Others

£800

Correspondent: M. L. R. Harris, Clerk, 42 King Street, Seagrave, Loughborough, Leicestershire LE12 7LY (01509 812366)

CC Number: 259461

Eligibility
People in need who live in Atherstone, Warwickshire.

Types of grants
One-off grants ranging from £50 to £250. Grants have included those to clear rent arrears and towards the cost of furniture and bedding, clothes, shoes (particularly for children), heaters and washing machines, travel expenses to hospital and short breaks for poor children and families.

Annual grant total
In 2013 the charity had an income of £5,900 and a total expenditure of £1,700. We estimate that grants to individuals totalled £800, with funding also awarded to local organisations.

Applications
Applications can be submitted in writing by the individual or through a recognised referral agency (such as a social worker, Citizens Advice or a doctor). They are considered in May and November. Emergency applications can be considered at other times.

Barford

The Barford Relief-in-Need Charity

£3,000

Correspondent: Terry Offiler, Administrator, 14 Dugard, Barford, Warwick CV35 8DX (01926 624153)

CC Number: 256836

Eligibility
People in need who live in the parish of Barford.

Types of grants
One-off cash grants and gifts in kind are given towards 'any reasonable need', including hospital expenses, electric goods, convalescence, living costs, household bills, holidays, travel expenses, medical equipment, nursing fees, furniture, disability equipment and help in the home.

Annual grant total
In 2013, the charity had an income of £12,400 and a total expenditure of £10,800. The charity makes grants to both individuals and organisations for educational and social welfare purposes. We estimate that grants to individuals for social welfare totalled around £3,000.

Exclusions
No loans are given.

Applications
In writing to the correspondent, directly by the individual or a family member. Applications are considered upon receipt. One of the trustees will visit to elicit all necessary information. Applications are usually considered in May and October.

Bedworth

The Henry Smith Charity (Bedworth)

£1,000

Correspondent: Lesley King, Administrator, Nuneaton and Bedworth Borough Council, Town Hall, Coton Road, Nuneaton, Warwickshire CV11 5AA (02476 376270; email: lesley.king@nuneatonandbedworth.gov.uk)

CC Number: 248109

Eligibility

Older people in need who live in Bedworth.

Types of grants

Small Christmas food vouchers to be used at a local shop.

Annual grant total

Grants usually total about £1,000 each year.

Applications

In writing to the correspondent before September, for consideration in December.

Other information

This charity is also known as the 'Consolidated Charity of Hammersley, Smith and Orton'.

Bilton and New Bilton

The Bilton Poor's Land and Other Charities

£6,000

Correspondent: Robin Walls, Trustee, 6 Scots Close, Rugby CV22 7QY (01788 810930)

CC Number: 215833

Eligibility

People in need who live in the ancient parish of Bilton (now part of Rugby). Preference is given to older people and those referred by social services.

Types of grants

One-off grants, generally of between £15 and £250.

Annual grant total

In 2012/13 the charity had an income of £21,500 and a total expenditure of £17,500. The charity makes grants to both individuals and organisations for social welfare and educational purposes. We estimate that grants to individuals for social welfare purposes totalled around £6,000.

Applications

In writing to the correspondent, by the individual or through a third party such as a minister, although often applications are forwarded by social services. They are considered three times a year.

Coleshill

Relief-in-Need Charity of Simon Lord Digby and Others

£1,300

Correspondent: Juliet Bakker, Administrator, The Vicarage, High Street, Coleshill, Birmingham B46 3BP (01675 462188; email: juliet.bakker@coleshillparishchurch.org.uk)

CC Number: 237526

Eligibility

People in extreme hardship who live in the parish of Coleshill.

Types of grants

One-off grants are given according to need. Our research shows that in the past grants have been made, for example, to an individual with multiple sclerosis towards the cost of electric reclining/rising chair and to a family of an eight year old with leukaemia for help with extra expenses.

Annual grant total

In 2013 the charity had an income of £6,900 and an expenditure of £2,800. We estimate the annual total of grants to individuals to be around £1,300.

Applications

In writing to the correspondent. Applications are usually decided in March and November, although decisions can be made more quickly in an emergency. They can be submitted directly by the individual or through a social worker, Citizens Advice or other welfare agency. Candidates are requested to provide as much detail as possible, including information about applications to other organisations/trusts.

Other information

Organisations may also be supported.

Grandborough

Grandborough Charity

£600

Correspondent: Michelle Johns, Administrator, 3 Hargrave Close, Grandborough, Rugby, Warwickshire CV23 8DS (01788 812945)

CC Number: 260425

Eligibility

People in need who live in the parish of Grandborough.

Types of grants

Small, one-off grants to help with optician's fees, hospital travel expenses and other general needs. Support is also available for older people at Christmas time.

Annual grant total

In 2012/13 the charity had an income of £900 and an expenditure of about £700. We estimate that grants totalled about £600.

Exclusions

Grants are not given when the need is covered by the state.

Applications

In writing to the correspondent. Applications can be made directly by the individual or a family member. They are considered on an ongoing basis. Candidates are required to provide evidence of expenditure.

Other information

Grants may also be given towards educational books for students.

Kenilworth

The Kenilworth Carnival Comforts Fund

£165

Correspondent: James Evans, Trustee, 7 Queens Road, Kenilworth, Warwickshire CV8 1JQ (01926 859161)

CC Number: 255027

Eligibility

People in need who live in Kenilworth.

Types of grants

Mainly one-off grants of £15 per person or £20 per couple, usually in the form of a grocery voucher redeemable at various shops in Kenilworth, hampers of food or bouquets of flowers. About 60 grants are given at Christmas, the rest are given throughout the year. Grants are not made to charities.

Annual grant total

In 2013 this charity had an income of £1,000 and a total expenditure of £165. Although the charity's income doubled this year from 2009, expenditure seems to be steadily decreasing.

Applications

In writing to the correspondent. Applications can be submitted directly by the individual or through a social worker, Citizens Advice, other welfare agency or a third party, for example, a friend or relative. They are considered bi-monthly from February.

The Kenilworth United Charities

£5,000

Correspondent: The Clerk to the Trustees, Damian J. Plant and Co., 29b Warwick Road, Kenilworth, Warwickshire CV8 1HN (01926 857741)

CC Number: 215376

Eligibility

People in need who live in the ancient parish of Kenilworth.

Types of grants

Generally grocery vouchers given to one-parent families. One-off grants have also been made towards white goods.

Annual grant total

The 2012 accounts were the latest available at the time of writing (August 2014).

In 2012, the charities had an income of £20,000 and a total expenditure of £15,500. We estimate that the total amount of grants awarded to individuals was approximately £5,000.

Applications

On a form available from the correspondent. Applications are considered quarterly, although urgent cases will receive special consideration.

Other information

The charities also fund almshouses and the CAB office in Kenilworth.

Leamington Spa

Leamington Relief-in-Sickness Fund

£3,000

Correspondent: Peter Byrd, Trustee, 2 Oakley Wood Cottages, Banbury Road, Bishops Tachbrook, Leamington Spa CV33 9QJ (01926 651789; email: peterandsuebyrd@hotmail.com)

CC Number: 216781

Eligibility

People suffering from ill-health and expectant mothers who live in the former borough of Leamington Spa and the neighbourhood, and are in need. People with disabilities or mental health problems are especially welcomed.

Types of grants

One-off grants only from around £25, including help with fuel debts, television licences, baby necessities, food for special diets, fares for visiting hospitals or sick relatives, replacing locks after a burglary, children's clothing, repairs to washing machines and so on.

Annual grant total

In 2012/13, the fund had an income of £4,100 and a total expenditure of £3,000.

Exclusions

Applicants can only receive one grant each year.

Applications

In writing through a social worker, Citizens Advice, health visitor, doctor, probation service, Mind or other welfare agency. Applications submitted by individuals will not be acknowledged or considered. Applications are considered throughout the year.

Napton-on-the-Hill

The Napton Charities

£1,000

Correspondent: Ross Ritchie, Trustee, Menin House, Vicarage Road, Napton, Southam, Warwickshire CV47 8NA (01926 811165; email: sid@flyheli.co.uk)

CC Number: 244051

Eligibility

People in need who live in the parish of Napton-on-the-Hill only.

Types of grants

One-off grants ranging from £30 to £35 mainly towards heating for older people (for gas, electricity, solid fuel, etc.) although other applications are considered, including clothing and living costs.

Annual grant total

In 2012/13 this charity had an income of £2,000 and a total expenditure of £1,300. The grants total each year is around £1,000.

Applications

On a form available from the correspondent. Applications can be submitted either directly by the individual or by a relative or friend with the consent of the individual. Proof of having lived in Napton for over a year is required.

Rugby

Rugby Relief-in-Need Charity

£2,900

Correspondent: Carol Davies, Clerk, 14 School Street, Long Lawford, Rugby, Warwickshire CV23 9AU (01788 544630)

CC Number: 217987

Eligibility

People in need who live in the ancient parish of Rugby, which includes the parishes of St Andrew's and St Matthew's.

Types of grants

Christmas vouchers to the elderly of the parish. Some one-off grants may be made in cases of emergency.

Annual grant total

In 2012/13 the charity had an income of £3,300 and a total expenditure of £3,100. We estimate that vouchers and social welfare grants to individuals totalled £2,900.

Applications

In writing to the correspondent. Applications are generally considered three or four times a year, although urgent cases can be considered at any time.

Stratford-upon-Avon

The Baron Davenport Emergency Grant (Stratford-upon-Avon)

£1,500

Correspondent: Helen Bowie-Simpson, Community Development Manager, Voluntary Action Stratford, Suite 3 Arden Court, Arden Street, Stratford-upon-Avon CV37 6NT (1789 298102; email: helen.bowie-simpson@vasa.org.uk; website: www.vasa.org.uk/funding/baron-davenports-charity)

Eligibility

Widows, unmarried and divorced women who are over the age of 60. Applicants must:

- Live alone
- Have a total household income of no more than £165 per week and less than £5,000 in savings
- Not be in receipt of low/high rate Attendance Allowance, middle/high rates of Disability Living Allowance, or Mobility (Car) Allowance
- Have lived in the Midlands area for at least five years

Types of grants

Small, one-off grants of up to £150 for emergencies only.

Annual grant total

Our research suggests that grants usually total about £1,500 annually.

Applications

Applications can be made directly to the correspondent but must include supporting evidence from a third party, such as a health visitor, social worker, doctor or other professional.

Other information

For information on Baron Davenport's Charity, see entry in the Midlands general section.

Mayor's Fund Society of Stratford-upon-Avon

£3,400

Correspondent: Ros Dobson, Trustee, 155 Evesham Road, Stratford-upon-Avon, Warwickshire CV37 9BP (01789 293749; email: themayorsfund@yahoo.com; website: www.themayorsfund.webs.com)

CC Number: 220136

Eligibility

Older people in need who live in the former borough of Stratford-upon-Avon.

Types of grants

One-off and recurrent grants are usually given in the form of grocery vouchers.

Annual grant total

In 2012/13, the fund had an income of £1,000 and a total expenditure of £3,600. We estimate that the total amount of grants awarded to individuals was approximately £3,400 which was paid to an average of 45 beneficiaries.

Applications

In writing to the correspondent. Applications can be submitted directly by the individual or through a social worker, Citizens Advice, other welfare agency or other third party such as a member of the clergy. They should include a general summary of income, other relief received (for example housing benefits) and financial commitments.

The Stratford-upon-Avon Municipal Charities – Relief in Need

£15,000

Correspondent: Ros Dobson, Clerk to the Trustees, 155 Evesham Road, Stratford-upon-Avon CV37 9BP (01789 293749; email: municharities@yahoo.co.uk; website: www.municipal-charities-stratforduponavon.org.uk)

CC Number: 214958

Eligibility

People in need, generally older people of state pensionable age, who have been living in the town of Stratford-upon-Avon for at least 18 months. People immediately outside the area of benefit may be supported in exceptional circumstances.

Types of grants

One-off and recurrent grants in the range of £100 and £500 towards essential living expenses. Support can be given for food, fuel, clothing, items of furniture and household equipment (such as bed, support chair, cooker, microwave, fridge, freezer or washing machine), mobility aids and unexpected household bills.

Annual grant total

At the time of writing (September 2014) the latest financial information available was from 2012. In 2012 the fund had an income of £56,000 (including a transfer from Charity of William Tyler). Grants from the Relief-in-Need fund totalled £31,000. We estimate that about £15,000 was awarded to individuals.

Exclusions

Grants are not given for the repayment of debts, rent and council tax arrears, rental deposits and where support is available from statutory sources.

Applications

Application forms are available from the correspondent. They should include details of the financial circumstances of the applicant (income and savings). When applying for financial assistance in connection with a specific health condition, applicants are asked to include a letter from a GP, occupational therapist, social worker or similar professional to support the application. Requests for help are considered throughout the year.

Candidates are encouraged to contact the correspondent to clarify any questions or discuss their case.

Other information

The Stratford-upon-Avon Municipal Charities is an amalgamation of seven different charities in the local area. A big part of the charitable activities is provision of almshouse accommodation. Welfare support is given from the Relief-in-Need fund. Educational grants are occasionally given.

Sutton Cheney

Sir William Roberts Relief-in-Need Charity

£1,500

Correspondent: Leon Angrave, Trustee, Lower Ambion House, 1 Lower Ambion Farm, Ambion Lane, Sutton Cheney, Nuneaton CV13 0AD

CC Number: 242296

Eligibility

People who live in the village of Sutton Cheney and are in need.

Types of grants

One-off grants, usually in the range of £150 to £200, for basic necessities only.

Annual grant total

In 2013 the charity had an income of £4,100 and a total expenditure of £4,400. We estimate that around £1,500 was made in grants to individuals for social welfare purposes.

Applications

In writing to the correspondent, or any of the trustees. Applications may be submitted directly by the individual at any time.

Other information

Grants are also made to organisations based in Sutton Cheney.

Thurlaston

The King Henry VIII Endowed Trust – Warwick

£1,300 (1 grant)

Correspondent: Jonathan Wassall, Clerk and Receiver, 12 High Street, Warwick CV34 4AP (01926 495533; email: jwassall@kinghenryviii.org.uk; website: www.kinghenryviii.org.uk)

CC Number: 232862

Eligibility

People who live in the former borough of Warwick. The area of benefit is roughly the CV34 postcode but exceptions apply so see the full list of eligible areas within the guidelines or contact the correspondent for clarification.

Types of grants

One-off grants can be given for general welfare purposes according to need. Awards are usually made only if a previous application to The Warwick Relief-in-Need Charity has been unsuccessful.

Grants are intended to be supplementary and applicants are expected to raise additional funds themselves. Payments are normally made upon submission of receipts.

Annual grant total

At the time of writing (July 2014) the latest financial information available was from 2012. In 2012 the trust had assets of £24 million and an income of £1.4 million. Two grants to individuals totalled £2,600, one of which we estimate to be for welfare purposes. In previous years individual awards were made to 20–30 persons totalling under £20,000. The money for charitable activities is generated from the permanent endowment.

Exclusions

Grants are not made where support should be provided by local or central government. Funding is not given retrospectively.

Applications

Application forms are available from the correspondent or from the trust's website. Applications should provide full details of the costs involved and the time schedule of the activity, where relevant. Awards are considered on a quarterly basis, usually in March, June, September and December. The closing dates for applications are the beginning of March/ June and the second half of August/ November. You will normally receive the outcome of your application within a week of the relevant meeting. In urgent cases applications can be 'fast-tracked' (emergency should be specified in the application).

Other information

The income is distributed to Anglican churches in Warwick (50%), Warwick Independent Schools Foundation for allocation in scholarships and bursaries (30%) and to organisations and individuals in the town for educational and welfare causes (20%). Town grants to various institutions and groups totalled £160,000, the foundation received £342,000 and the churches were awarded £565,000 in 2012.

The trust's guidelines note: 'where the trust believes that there are more suitable charities within the town to assess applications it will either forward the application directly to another charity or recommend that the applicant approaches them directly.'

Warwick

The Austin Edwards Charity

£5,000

Correspondent: Jackie Newton, Receiver, 26 Mountford Close, Wellesbourne, Warwick CV35 9QQ (01789 840135; website: www. austinedwards.org.uk)

CC Number: 225859

Eligibility

People living in the old borough of Warwick.

Types of grants

Grants ranging from £250 to £500 for relief-in-need purposes.

Annual grant total

In 2012/13 the charity had an income of £10,700 and a total expenditure of £10,200. We estimate that welfare grants to individuals totalled £5,000, with funding also awarded for educational purposes.

Applications

In writing to the correspondent. Applications are considered throughout the year.

Other information

The charity was named after Mr Austin Edwards who lived and worked in Warwick as a photographic manufacturer in the early years of the twentieth century. As a councillor of the borough of Warwick, he remained deeply interested in Warwickians and Warwick affairs generally. He gave generously to the Corporation of Warwick throughout his life.

Warwick Provident Dispensary

£1,000

Correspondent: Christopher Houghton, Managing Director, Moore and Tibbits, 34 High Street, Warwick CV34 4BE (01926 491181; email: choughton@ moore-tibbits.co.uk; website: www. warwickprovidentdispensary.org.uk)

CC Number: 253987

Eligibility

People in need who are in poor health, convalescent or have a disability and live in the town of Warwick.

Types of grants

One-off and recurrent grants according to need. The charity's website specifies: 'Help can be given to pay for [such] items, services or facilities which are calculated to alleviate the suffering or assist the recovery of [beneficiaries] but are not readily available to them from other sources.'

Annual grant total

In 2013 the charity had both an income and an expenditure of around £22,000. Previously grants to individuals have totalled around £1,000.

Applications

Application forms are available from the charity's website or upon request from the correspondent. They can be submitted directly by the individual or through a third party. A covering letter needs to be included.

Other information

The charity mainly makes grants to local organisations.

West Midlands

The Avon Trust

£1,000

Correspondent: Andrew Cashmore, Trustee, Trygva, Carthew Way, St Ives TR26 1RJ (01736 438347)

CC Number: 219050

Eligibility

Retired Methodist ministers and their dependents with some preference for those living in the West Midlands, and people in residential homes who live in the West Midlands.

Types of grants

One-off and recurrent grants according to need.

Annual grant total

In 2012/13 the trust had an income of £7,500 and a total expenditure of £2,800. As the trust predominantly focuses on funding religious organisations, we estimate that grants to individuals totalled around £1,000.

Applications

In writing to the correspondent. The trustees meet once a year in July but can consider applications at other times.

The Badley Memorial Trust

£41,000 (109 grants)

Correspondent: Christopher Williams, Administrator, 16 Manderville Gardens, Kingswinford DY6 9QW (01384 294019)

CC Number: 222999

Eligibility

People in need who are in poor health, convalescent or who have disabilities and live in the former county borough of Dudley (as constituted in 1953). In certain cases the present metropolitan boroughs of Dudley and Sandwell may be included.

Types of grants

One-off grants have been made towards medical aids, clothing, beds/bedding, heating appliances, domestic appliances, televisions, radios, fuel, respite holidays and adaptations for people with disabilities. Recurrent grants are only given in exceptional cases.

Payments are made directly via cheque to the providers of goods or services, no cash payments are made to applicants.

Annual grant total

In 2012/13 the trust held assets of £1.4 million and had an income of £58,000. A total of £41,000 was distributed in 109 grants to individuals.

Exclusions

Grants are not given to pay off debts or for educational fees.

Applications

On a form available from the correspondent to be submitted directly by the individual or, where applicable, through a social worker, Citizens Advice, other welfare agency or a third party such as a relative, doctor or member of the clergy. Applications are considered quarterly. Those of an urgent nature may be dealt with more quickly by an authorised trustee.

Other information

Although none were awarded in 2012/13, the trust also makes grants to organisations.

Birmingham Jewish Community Care

£850

Correspondent: The Grants Administrator, Bill Steiner Suite, 1 River Brook Drive, Birmingham B30 2SH (01214 593819; email: admin@bhamjcc.co.uk; website: www.bhamjcc.co.uk)

CC Number: 209078

Eligibility

Jewish people in need living in the West Midlands.

Types of grants

Mainly one-off grants ranging from £10 to £250. Grants have been given to a small number of clients at Jewish festivals and for school clothing, music lessons for a gifted child, holidays for disadvantaged children and travel expenses for visiting distant cemeteries and occasionally to pay household or car bills. There is also a kosher meals-on-wheels service. Regular payments are no longer made. Applicants must be prepared to update their circumstances before a second grant is made (other than in the case of regular telephone rental payment in some cases).

Annual grant total

In 2012/13 grants to needy people totalled £850.

Exclusions

Grants are not made for setting up businesses.

Applications

In writing to the correspondent, including information on length of residence in the area, other applications made and whether or not the applicant is in receipt of income support or support from other charities. Applications are considered monthly and may be submitted directly by the individual or through a social worker, Citizens Advice or other welfare agency or third party such as a rabbi. No grant is ever made without personal contact with someone from the charity's social work department.

Other information

The charity also runs a residential nursing home, Andrew Cohen House, at Stirchley in Birmingham.

The Thomas Bromwich Trust

£13,600

Correspondent: Revd Martin Rutter, The Vicarage, Church Road, Perry Barr, Birmingham B42 2LB (email: mcrutter@tesco.net)

CC Number: 214966

Eligibility

People in need living in Handsworth, Great Barr and Perry Barr.

Types of grants

One-off grants towards electric goods, clothing, household bills, food and help in the home.

Annual grant total

In 2012/13 the charity held assets of £889,000, had an income of £27,000 and a total expenditure of £15,000. Grants totalled £13,600.

Applications

In writing to the correspondent either directly by the individual or through a social worker, Citizens Advice or other welfare agency. Applications are considered at any time.

The Chance Trust

£1,500

Correspondent: Revd Iain Shelton, Trustee, 192 Hanover Road, Rowley Regis B65 9EQ (01215 591251; email: robertshelton954@hotmail.com; website: www.warleydeanery.co.uk)

CC Number: 702647

Eligibility

People in need in the rural deaneries of Warley and West Bromwich (the area covered by the southern parts of Sandwell borough).

Types of grants

One-off grants ranging from £50 to £400 can be given according to need.

Annual grant total

In 2012/13 the trust had an income of £2,900 and an expenditure of £1,900. We estimate that around £900 was given in welfare grants. Normally the trust spends around £2,500–£3,000 per year in grants to individuals for both educational and relief-in-need purposes.

Exclusions

Grants are not normally provided where statutory funding is available.

Applications

In writing to the correspondent. Applications should specify the need and the amount required. They are usually considered in January and July.

Other information

Support is also given for educational purposes.

The Coventry Freemen's Charity

£550,000 (2,769 grants)

Correspondent: David Evans, Administrator, Abbey House, Manor Road, Coventry CV1 2FW (02476 257317; email: john@foxevans.co.uk; website: www.foxevans.co.uk)

CC Number: 229237

Eligibility

Freemen and their dependents, as well as the widows, widowers and other former dependents of deceased freemen, who are in need and live within the existing boundary of the city of Coventry or within seven miles of St Mary's Hall, Coventry.

Types of grants

One-off and recurrent grants.

Annual grant total

In 2013 the charity had assets of £12.4 million and an income of £799,000. Grants totalled £550,000 and were distributed to 2,769 beneficiaries as follows:

Freemen and women	2,184	£434,000
Freemen's widows	574	£113,000
Special cases	12	£2,500

Grants for relief in need totalled almost £600.

Applications

On a form available from the correspondent directly by the individual.

Friends of the Animals

£211,000 (4,142 grants)

Correspondent: Martin Gomez, Treasurer, 17A Riverway, Newport PO30 5UX (01983 810375; email: fotaiow@hotmail.com; website: www.friendsoftheanimals.co.uk)

CC Number: 1000249

Eligibility

People who are in need and live on the Isle of Wight, in Portsmouth or the West Midlands.

Types of grants

Subsidised veterinary treatment, such as spaying, neutering, microchipping, inoculations and treatment of accidents.

Annual grant total

In 2012/13 the charity held assets of £125,000 and had an income of £428,000. A total of £211,000 was spent on vet's bills, with animals receiving 4,142 treatments.

Applications

Requests for assistance can be made by calling the head office on 01983 522511 (Tuesday to Saturday, 10am to 4pm) or by emailing. Include details of the area in which you live, a phone number and as much information about your enquiry as possible.

Other information

The charity's activities include the rehoming of animals and the provision of free advice and information on animal welfare, as well as loans of baskets, pens and other equipment to assist with animal care.

Friends of the Animals also supports the Farm Animal Rescue Sanctuary at Wolverton, which is home to more than 470 animals.

Grantham Yorke Trust

£10,500 (22 grants)

Correspondent: Christine Norgrove, Martineau, 1 Colmore Square, Birmingham B4 6AA (0870 763 2000; email: christine.norgrove@sghmartineau.com)

CC Number: 228466

Eligibility

People under 25 who were born in the old West Midlands Metropolitan County area (basically: Birmingham, Coventry, Dudley, Redditch, Sandwell, Solihull, Tamworth, Walsall or Wolverhampton).

Types of grants

One-off grants according to need.

Annual grant total

In 2012/13 the trust held assets of £6.5 million and had an income of £221,000. A total of £21,000 was made in 43 grants to individuals. We estimate the welfare grants total to be around £10,500.

Applications

On a form available from the correspondent. Applications should be submitted directly by the individual or via a relevant third party such as a social worker, Citizens Advice or other welfare agency, in February, May, August and November for consideration in the following month.

Other information

The trust also makes grants to organisations and to individuals for educational purposes.

The Harborne Parish Lands Charity

£32,000 (122 grants)

Correspondent: The Grants Administrator, 109 Court Oak Road, Birmingham B17 9AA (01214 261600; fax: 01214 282267; email: julie.boardman@hplc.org.uk; website: www.hplc.org.uk)

CC Number: 219031

Eligibility

People in need who live in the ancient parish of Harborne, which includes parts of Harborne, Smethwick, Bearwood and Quinton. A map of the old parish is available to view on the website and individuals are advised to check that they reside in the area of benefit before making an application.

Types of grants

One-off grants up to £700. Grants cover a wide range of needs, including furniture, aids and adaptations, clothing, and assistance with transport. Applications for carpets are only eligible if there is a health and safety issue and grants for washing machines are made only to families.

Annual grant total

In 2012/13 the charity held assets of £14.7 million and had an income of £1.3 million. Grants were made totalling £290,000 of which, £32,000 was awarded to individuals.

Exclusions

Grants are not made for help with statutory bills, such as taxes.

Applications

A short application form is available from the correspondent. Applications can be made at any time and must be submitted through a local agency or organisation, such as social services or Citizens Advice. Applications are not accepted directly from the applicant. All applicants are visited.

Other information

The charity also runs five almshouses with around 100 residents, most of whom are elderly.

The CB and AB Holinsworth Fund of Help

£4,200

Correspondent: Dave Boardman, Administrator, Room B41, The Council House, Victoria Square, Birmingham B1 1BB (01213 032020)

CC Number: 217792

Eligibility

People in need who live in or near to the city of Birmingham and are sick or convalescing.

Types of grants

One-off grants ranging from £50 to £300. Grants are given towards the cost of respite holidays, travelling expenses to and from hospital, clothing, beds and carpets.

Annual grant total

In 2012/13, the fund has an income of £6,500 and a total expenditure of £8,600. We estimate that the total amount of grants awarded to individuals was approximately £4,200.

Exclusions

Generally grants are not given for bills or debt repayments.

Applications

On a form available from the correspondent. Applications are considered throughout the year and should be submitted through a social worker, Citizens Advice or other welfare agency. Confirmation of illness is needed, for example a letter from a doctor, consultant or nurse.

Other information

Grants are also given to organisations.

The James Frederick and Ethel Anne Measures Charity

£7,500

Correspondent: Laura Reid, Clerk to the Trustees, Harris Allday, 2nd Floor, 33 Great Charles Street, Birmingham B3 3JN

CC Number: 266054

Eligibility

The following criteria apply:

1 Applicants must usually originate in the West Midlands
2 Applicants must show evidence of self-help in their application
3 Trustees have a preference for disadvantaged people
4 Trustees have a dislike for applications from students who have a full local authority grant and want finance for a different course or study
5 Trustees favour grants towards the cost of equipment
6 Applications by individuals in cases of hardship will not usually be considered unless sponsored by a local authority, health professional or other welfare agency

Types of grants

One-off or recurrent grants, usually between £50 and £500.

Annual grant total

In 2012/13 the charity had assets of £963,000 and an income of £36,000. Grants were made totalling £31,000. The charity gives to both individuals and organisations and we estimate grants to individuals for social welfare purposes to be around £7,500.

Applications

In writing to the correspondent. No reply is given to unsuccessful applicants unless an sae is enclosed.

The Newman Trust Homes

£16,500 (28 grants)

Correspondent: Judy Dyke, Trustee, Tyndallwoods Solicitors, 29 Woodbourne Road, Harborne, Birmingham B17 8BY (01216 932222; email: jdyke@tyndallwoods.co.uk)

CC Number: 501567

Eligibility

People who are in need, hardship or distress who live, or have formerly lived, in the city of Birmingham. Grants are primarily paid to benefit people who are older, people with housing difficulties and people living within the area of Handsworth and its immediate vicinity.

Types of grants

One-off and recurrent grants according to need.

Annual grant total

In 2012/13 the trust held assets totalling £780,000 and had an income of £42,000. Grants were made to 28 individuals totalling £16,500.

Exclusions

No funding for funerals.

Applications

Application forms are available from the trust. Applicants are encouraged to detail any additional information they believe may assist the trustees in their decision.

The Samuel Smith Charity, Coventry

£19,600

Correspondent: Richard Kenyon, Trustee, Four Winds, Dalehouse Lane, Kenilworth CV8 2JZ (02476 419622; email: delaroche37@gmail.com)

CC Number: 240936

Eligibility

People who live in Coventry and the ancient parish of Bedworth and are in need.

Types of grants

Pensions and one-off grants.

Annual grant total

In 2013 the charity had an income of £31,000 and a total expenditure of £24,000. Grants totalled £19,600 and were distributed as follows:

Pensions	£15,000
Payments in lieu of coal	£1,900
May gifts	£1,500
Christmas gifts to pensioners	£1,000
Bibles	£200

During the year, 36 pensioners received recurrent grants.

Applications

Applications can be made in writing to the correspondent, but most beneficiaries are referred by the charity's almoner. Trustees meet three times a year to consider applications.

The trustees' annual report from 2013 notes: 'Due to limited resources suitable applicants are added to the pensions list and receive a pension when a vacancy arises or funds become available.'

Other information

This charity has merged with Spencer's Charity – City of Coventry Warwickshire (charity no. 212935) which was removed from the central register of charities in August 2014. We are informed by the solicitor acting for both charities in the merger, that the charity will be renamed 'Samuel Smith's and Spencer's Charities' in the near future.

Birmingham

The Freda and Howard Ballance Trust

£2,300

Correspondent: Michael Stocks, Appeals Secretary and Trustee, Blackhams, Lancaster House, 67 Newhall Street, Birmingham B3 1NR (01212 330062; fax: 01212 339880; email: mstocks@blackhams.com)

CC Number: 513109

Eligibility

People in need who live in Birmingham.

Types of grants

One-off grants usually ranging from £50 to £200. Recent grants have been given for clothing, furniture and disability aids. A small amount is also available for educational items.

Annual grant total

In 2012/13, the trust had an income of £3,500 and a total expenditure of £4,800. We estimate that the total amount of grants awarded to individuals was approximately £2,300. The trust also awards grants to organisations for the relief of poverty.

Applications

On a form available from the correspondent. A letter giving brief details of the application is required before an application form is sent out. Applications can be made either directly by the individual or via a third party such as a charity, social worker or Citizens Advice. They are usually considered quarterly.

The Richard and Samuel Banner Trust

£4,100

Correspondent: Anne Holmes, Administrator, Veale Wasbrough Vizards LLP, Second Floor, 3 Brindley Place, Birmingham B1 2JB (01212 273705)

CC Number: 218649

Eligibility

Men and widows who are in need and live in the city of Birmingham.

Types of grants

Grants of up to £100, usually for clothing.

Annual grant total

In 2012/13 the trust had an income of £10,500 and a total expenditure of £8,400. We estimate that welfare grants totalled £4,100, with funding also awarded to individuals for educational purposes.

Applications

Applicants must be nominated by a trustee, doctor or the Council for Old People. Applications are considered on 1 November and grants are distributed immediately after this date.

Other information

The trust can also give apprenticeship grants to male students under 21, but this is done through certain colleges; applicants should not apply directly.

Friends of Home Nursing in Birmingham

£3,600

Correspondent: Mrs J. Burns, Hon. Treasurer, 46 Underwood Road, Handsworth Wood, Birmingham B20 1JS (01216 865565)

CC Number: 218182

Eligibility

Sick and older people who live in Birmingham city and who are patients nursed at home by the district nurse.

Types of grants

The charity provides goods, equipment and occasional monetary grants which are not available from other sources. In the past this has included digital thermometers, a dressing trolley, cameras and films for ulcer recordings, and part of the cost of holidays. Grants are usually one-off and range from £50 to £500. No grants are made for double glazing or electrical work.

Annual grant total

In 2012 the charity had an income of £9,700 and a total expenditure of £7,400. We estimate that welfare grants to individuals totalled £3,600, with funding also given for educational purposes.

At the time of writing (August 2014) this was the most recent financial information available for the charity.

Applications

In writing, via a district nurse, to the correspondent. Applications can be submitted at any time, for consideration in the spring and autumn. The charity has previously stated that if a real case of need occurs we deal with it as soon as possible.

The Charity of Jane Kate Gilbert

£450

Correspondent: David Boardman, Administrator, Committee Services, Room B25, Council House, Victoria Square, Birmingham B1 1BB (01213 032020; email: Mohammed.Majid@birmingham.gov.uk)

CC Number: 216800

Eligibility

People in need who are over 60 years of age and have lived in Birmingham for at least two years.

Types of grants

Small quarterly pensions with a possible Christmas bonus. One-off hardship payments up to a maximum of £100 may also be considered.

Annual grant total

In 2013 the charity had an income of £1,400 and an unusually low total expenditure of £476. We estimate that social welfare grants to individuals totalled £450.

Applications

On a form available from the correspondent to be submitted through a social worker, Citizens Advice or other welfare agency. Applications are usually considered in March and November.

The Handsworth Charity

£2,800

Correspondent: Dipali Chandra, Administrator, 109 Court Oak Road, Birmingham B17 9AA (email: info@handsworth-charity.com; website: www.handsworth-charity.com)

CC Number: 216603

Eligibility

People in need who live in the parish of Handsworth (now in Birmingham). A map of the beneficial area is available on the website.

Types of grants

One-off grants of up to £500 according to need. Grants are given towards essential household items such as bedding, carpets, cookers, fridges and for small property repairs.

Annual grant total

In 2013 the charity had an income of £23,000 and a total expenditure of £5,900. We estimate that grants to individuals totalled £2,800, with funding also awarded to organisations whose work benefits the residents of Handsworth.

Applications

Application forms are available to download from the website. Forms must be submitted through a recognised referral agency that is willing to act as a sponsor throughout the application process. The trustees meet three times a year, normally in mid-March, mid-July and mid-November. Applications should be received by the charity in the month before a meeting.

Note: Successful applicants are expected to provide receipts of items purchased with the grant awarded. Sponsoring agencies are expected to accept some responsibility in making sure the grant is spent on its intended purposes.

Charity of Harriet Louisa Loxton

£7,700

Correspondent: Maureen Morris, Administrator, 67 Sutton New Road, Erdington, Birmingham B23 6QT (01216 752501)

CC Number: 702446

Eligibility

People in need who live in Birmingham, particularly older people, children and individuals with disabilities.

Types of grants

Our research suggests that one-off grants can range from £100 to £2,000, although the average award is generally around £400. Examples of grants given have included: £500 to an older person with disabilities for a washing machine and drier; £100 for a vacuum cleaner for an older woman who was ill; £1,700 for central heating for a woman who was blind; and £500 towards an electric scooter for a man who was totally immobile.

Annual grant total

In 2012/13 the charity had assets of £1.5 million and an income of £31,000. A total of £7,700 was awarded in grants.

Exclusions

According to our research, grants are not available to pay off debts, relieve public funds or towards the community charge.

Applications

Application forms are available from the correspondent. The trustees normally meet four times a year to consider applications. Note that applications must be made by a social worker (or an equivalent agency) and may take some considerable time to process. Immediate decisions on applications cannot be given.

Other information

The fund was established from proceeds of the sale of Icknield, a property donated to the city by Harriet Louisa Loxton for use as a home for older people.

Organisations could also be supported at the approval by the advisory panel and general purposes committee.

The Sir John Middlemore Charitable Trust

£400

Correspondent: Teresa Soden, Company Secretary, 55 Stevens Avenue, Birmingham B32 3SD (email: office@middlemore.org.uk; website: www.middlemore.org.uk)

CC Number: 1102736

Eligibility

Disadvantaged children under the age of 16. Preference is given to south Birmingham, although the surrounding areas of the West Midlands may be considered.

Types of grants

Small, one-off grants up to £100. Things the trust will fund include: day trips, toys, outings (cinema, theatre, bowling, etc.), adventure camps, school trips, contributions towards modest holidays to support the child and contribution towards out of school activities.

Annual grant total

In 2012/13 the trust had assets of £1.4 million and an income of £67,000. During the year the trust made grants totalling £14,900. The fund for individuals accounts for only a small part of the trust's grantmaking, although a breakdown of the grants given to individuals and organisations was not available in the accounts. We estimate that grants to individuals totalled £400.

Exclusions

Household or similar items, clothing and equipment (such as child buggies, high chairs, safety equipment, etc.).

Applications

On an application form available to download from the trust's website or requested via email. The trust prefers completed applications to be submitted via email, though they also accept hard copies if this is not possible. Applications should be completed by a social, medical or educational professional known to the child. The trustees meet four times a year to consider applications. They will not enter into correspondence or telephone calls with applicants. Only successful applications are acknowledged.

Other information

The trust also funds the Middlemore Family Centre, which offers vulnerable families practical and emotional support, counselling and activities.

Sands Cox Relief-in-Sickness Charity

£3,300

Correspondent: Ann Andrew, Trustee, 12 Hayfield Gardens, Moseley, Birmingham B13 9LE

CC Number: 217468

Eligibility

People who live in Birmingham and are in need due to illness, disability or other difficulties.

Types of grants

One-off grants of up to £200 are available according to need.

Annual grant total

In 2012/13 the charity had an income of around £8,600 and an expenditure of £6,900. We estimate that individual grants totalled around £3,300.

Applications

In writing to the correspondent. Applications can be made either directly by the individual or through a responsible person, for example, a trustee, doctor or social services professional.

Other information

The charity also makes grants to local organisations.

The Yardley Great Trust

£32,000 (134 grants)

Correspondent: Karen Grice, Clerk to the Trustees, 31 Old Brookside, Yardley Fields Road, Stechford, Birmingham B33 8QL (01217 847889; fax: 01217 851386; email: enquiries@ygtrust.org.uk; website: www.ygtrust.org.uk)

CC Number: 216082

Eligibility

People living in the ancient parish of Yardley in the city of Birmingham. This includes the wards of Yardley, Acocks Green, Fox Hollies, Billesley, Hall Green and part of the wards of Hodge Hill, Shard End, Sheldon, Small Heath, Sparkhill, Moseley, Sparkbrook and Brandwood. (A map is produced by the trust outlining the beneficial area.)

Types of grants

One-off grants towards washing machines, fridges, cookers, clothing, beds and bedding and household furniture. Grants towards the purchase of carpets will only be considered in cases where the household has either: a child under ten years old; a disabled person; a person in receipt of a disability payment of some sort; or an old age pensioner.

Annual grant total

In 2013 the trust held assets of £8.5 million and had an income of £2.3 million. A total of 134 welfare grants to individuals amounted to £32,000.

A further £35,000 was awarded to other causes, including 21 grants to organisations.

Exclusions

No grants are given towards the relief of rates, taxes or for items that should be met by local authorities, health authorities or social services. No grants for educational purposes, home improvements (redecoration excepted) or school uniforms.

Applications

Applications can be made on a standard paper form or online via the website. Online applications require a password; those who do not have a password should at first contact the trust's office. Applications must be submitted through a Council Neighbourhood Office, Citizens Advice or other welfare agency. On occasion, a trustee or the clerk may visit an applicant to discuss their application further.

A full list of guidelines is available from the website. The trust welcomes enquiries.

Other information

The trust also provides second-hand furniture through a partner organisation, Ladywood Furniture Project and manages sheltered accommodation, care and nursing homes for elderly people.

Bushbury

The Bushbury United Charities

£4,000

Correspondent: The Administrator, Dallow and Dallow, 23 Waterloo Road, Wolverhampton, West Midlands WV1 4TJ (01902 420208)

CC Number: 242290

Eligibility

People in need living in the ancient parish of Bushbury.

Types of grants

Annual grants paid at Christmas.

Annual grant total

The 2012 accounts were the latest available at the time of writing (August 2014).

In 2012, the charities had an income of £7,000 and a total expenditure of £4,000. We estimate that the total amount of grants awarded to individuals was approximately £4,000.

Applications

In writing to the correspondent.

Castle Bromwich

The Mary Bridgeman Non-Ecclesiastical Charity

£750

Correspondent: Revd Gavin Douglas, 67 Chester Road, Castle Bromwich, Birmingham B36 9DP (0121 7478546; email: gavindouglas@yahoo.co.uk)

CC Number: 701557

Eligibility

People in need living in the ecclesiastical parishes of St Mary and St Margaret, and St Clement, Castle Bromwich.

Types of grants

One-off grants have in the past been used to meet the cost of heating bills or respite care.

Annual grant total

In 2013/14 the charity had an income of £3,300 and a total expenditure of £3,400. Grants are awarded to individuals and organisations for both educational and social welfare purposes. We estimate that social welfare grants to individuals totalled around £750.

Exclusions

Grants are not given if they will affect any statutory benefits.

Applications

In writing to the correspondent, directly by the individual or through a social worker, welfare agency or other third party such as a parent, partner or relative. Applications should include the applicant's income and expenditure. The trustees meet twice a year in May and November.

Other information

This entry is an amalgamation of three separate charity funds which are administered as one.

Coventry

The Children's Boot Fund

£8,000

Correspondent: Janet McConkey, Trustee, 123A Birmingham Road, Coventry CV5 9GR (02476 402837; email: martin_harban@btconnect.com)

CC Number: 214524

Eligibility

Schoolchildren in the city of Coventry, aged 4 to 16

Types of grants

Grants for school footwear for children in need. No other type of help is given. Grants are made directly to footwear suppliers in the form of vouchers.

Annual grant total

In 2012/13 the fund had an income of £7,500 and an expenditure of £16,000. We estimate grants to individuals for social welfare purposes in this accounting year totalled around £8,000.

Applications

Application forms are available from schools in the area and should be completed, verified and signed by the headteacher of the child's school. Applications are considered four times a year.

General Charity (Coventry)

£160,000

Correspondent: Victoria Tosh, Clerk to the Trustees, General Charities Office, Old Bablake, Hill Street, Coventry CV1 4AN (02476 222769; email: cov.genchar@btconnect.com)

CC Number: 216235

Eligibility

People in need living in the city of Coventry.

Types of grants

One-off grants in kind and recurrent grants, but not cash grants. Regular payments of around £45 a quarter can be given to a maximum of 650 pensioners over the age of 60.

Annual grant total

In 2013 the charity had an income of £880,000 and a total expenditure of £899,000. Full accounts were not available to view at the time of writing (August 2014); however in previous years grants to individuals for welfare purposes have totalled around £160,000. The support is normally distributed in pension allowances (about £90,000 a year), relief-in-need grants (about £65,000 a year) and the trustees' annual vouchers (about £7,500 a year), although the money available varies.

Exclusions

Our research suggests that regular cash grants are not given.

Applications

Applications should normally be made through social workers, probation officers, Citizens Advice or other welfare agencies.

Other information

The charity consists of the charities formerly known as The Relief-in-Need Charity, Sir Thomas White's Pension Fund and Sir Thomas White's Educational Fund. The trustees are also responsible for the administration of Lady Herbert's Homes and Eventide Homes Ltd providing accommodation for the elderly in the city of Coventry.

Most of the charity's assistance is given to organisations. Support is also given for educational purposes.

John Moore's Bequest

£3,000

Correspondent: Ian Cox, Administrator, Sarginsons, 10 The Quadrant, Coventry CV1 2EL

CC Number: 218805

Eligibility

People in need, generally older people, living in the city of Coventry.

Types of grants

Grants of up to £20 given in December.

Annual grant total

In 2012/13 the charity had and income of £4,800 and a total expenditure of £3,500. We estimate that around £3,000 was made in grants to individuals for social welfare purposes.

Applications

The charity's trustees each select around 25 recipients either directly or through local churches.

The Tansley Charity Trust

£4,800

Correspondent: Lara Knight, Administrator, Governance Services, Room 59, Council House, Earl Street, Coventry CV1 5RR (02476 833237)

CC Number: 505364

Eligibility

Women over 50 years old who are in poor health and live in the city of Coventry.

Types of grants

One-off grants up to £200. In the past, grants have been given towards the purchase of clothing, household items and the payment of bills.

Annual grant total

In 2012/13 the trust had an income of £6,300 and a total expenditure of £5,000. We estimate that grants to individuals totalled £4,800.

Exclusions

No grants for council tax or Inland Revenue payments.

Applications

On a form available from the correspondent. Applications can be submitted by the individual or through a recognised referral agency (such as a social worker, Citizens Advice or a doctor). Grants are considered twice a year.

The Tile Hill and Westwood Charities for the Needy Sick

£9,000

Correspondent: John Ruddick, Clerk, 4 Poundgate Lane, Coventry CV4 8HJ (02476 466917; email: john.ruddick@bttj.com)

CC Number: 220898

Eligibility

People who are both sick and in need and live in the parish of Westwood and parts of the parish of Berkswell, Kenilworth and Stoneleigh and elsewhere within a three and a half mile radius of 93 Cromwell Lane, Coventry.

Types of grants

One-off grants according to need. The charity is often able to provide assistance where a potential beneficiary 'falls between the cracks' of other providers.

Annual grant total

The 2012 accounts were the latest available at the time of writing (August 2014).

In 2012, the charity had an income of £21,000 and a total expenditure of £9,500. We estimate that the total amount of grants awarded to individuals was approximately £9,000.

Applications

In writing to the correspondent.

Harry Weston Memorial Fund

£1,500

Correspondent: The Administrator, 8 Eaton Road, Coventry CV1 2FF (02476 713942)

CC Number: 254183

Eligibility

Pensioners, aged 65–75, who are in financial difficulty (usually those on pension credit) and live in the city of Coventry.

Types of grants

One-off grants up to about £50, mainly towards the cost of television licences. The fund has also helped with the provision of reconditioned television sets and the cost of converting aerials for the digital TV switchover.

Annual grant total

The 2012 accounts were the latest available at the time of writing (August 2014).

In 2012, the fund had an income of £2,500 and a total expenditure of £1,500. We estimate that the total amount of grants awarded to individuals was approximately £1,500.

Applications

In writing to the correspondent either directly by the individual or through a third party such as a social worker, Citizens Advice, other welfare agency or a relative or neighbour. Applications must include information on the applicant's age, circumstances and date of TV licence renewal if relevant.

Doctor William MacDonald of Johannesburg Trust

£2,500

Correspondent: Jane Barlow, Trustee, Lord Mayor's Office, Council House, Earl Street, Coventry CV1 5RR (02476 833047)

CC Number: 225876

Eligibility

People in need who live in the city of Coventry.

Types of grants

One-off welfare grants, typically about £50; usually the maximum is £200.

Annual grant total

In 2012/13, the trust had an income of £3,200 and total expenditure of £2,500.

Exclusions

No grants for the relief of debt.

Applications

In writing to the correspondent. Applications can be submitted directly by the individual or through a third party such as a social worker.

Dudley

The Dudley Charity

£2,800

Correspondent: David Hughes, Trustee, 53 The Broadway, Dudley, West Midlands DY1 4AP (01384 259277; email: dudleycharity@hotmail.co.uk; website: www.dudleyrotary.org.uk/dudleycharity.html)

CC Number: 254928

Eligibility

People in need who live in the town of Dudley (as constituted prior to 1 April 1966) and its immediate surroundings, including Netherton.

Types of grants

One-off grants in the range of £100 to £250. Examples of the types of grants considered are: payments to relieve sudden distress; expenses for visiting people in hospitals or correctional facilities; assistance in meeting gas or electricity bills; the provision of furniture, bedding, clothing, food and other household appliances; the supply of tools, payment for training or equipment for recreational pursuits; respite care; contributions towards wheelchairs and scooters; and food for special diets, medical or other aids and nursing requisites or comforts. Weekly allowances may also be given for a limited period.

Annual grant total

In 2012/13 the charity had an income of £6,700 and a total expenditure of £5,700. We estimate that grants to individuals totalled £2,800, with funding also awarded to local organisations.

Applications

On a form available from the correspondent or from the charity's webpage. Applications can be submitted directly by the individual or through a third party such as a social worker. They are normally considered monthly.

Other information

The charity was formed in 1987 through the amalgamation of a number of small charities in Dudley. The charity's website notes: 'The earliest of these charities dates back to 1659 founded under the will of Jasper Cartwright that with two others became known as The Bread Charities.'

The Reginald Unwin Dudley Charity

£2,800

Correspondent: David Hughes, Trustee, 53 The Broadway, Dudley, West Midlands DY1 4AP (01384 259277; fax: 01384 259277; email: rududley@hotmail.com; website: www.dudleyrotary.org.uk/rududley.html)

CC Number: 217516

Eligibility

People in need who live in Dudley.

Types of grants

One-off grants of up to around £200. Since the charity began grantmaking in 1980, it has provided funding for items such as clothing, household appliances, respite holidays, funeral expenses, course fees, nebulizers, computers, software and wheelchairs, for example.

Annual grant total

In 2012/13 the charity had an income of £3,300 and a total expenditure of £2,900. We estimate that grants to individuals totalled £2,800.

Applications

On a form available from the correspondent or from the charity's page on the Dudley Rotary website. The application is more likely to succeed if accompanied with a supporting letter detailing the nature of the need for a grant.

Other information

The charity was originally established in 1904 by Reginald Unwin Dudley, who was a silk mercer in Dudley. 'Originally the charity was called The Reginald Unwin Dudley Highland Road Homes' and consisted of four houses for elderly residents, which were sold in 1980 when the charity was organised into its current form.

King's Norton

The King's Norton United Charities

£2,500

Correspondent: Canon Rob Morris, Trustee, The Rectory, 273 Pershore Road, Kings Norton, Birmingham B30 8EX (01214 590560; email: parishoffice@kingsnorton.org.uk; website: www.knuc.org.uk)

CC Number: 202225

Eligibility

The charity is able to assist only those who live within the boundary of the ancient parish of Kings Norton, formerly in Warwickshire and Worcestershire, now in Warwickshire and the West Midlands. This area includes the current Church of England parishes of Kings Norton, Cotteridge, Stirchley, parts of Bournville, Balsall Heath, Kings Heath, Moseley (St Anne's and St Mary's), Brandwood, Hazelwell, Highters Heath, Wythall, West Heath, Longbridge, Rubery and Rednal.

Types of grants

One-off and recurrent grants according to need.

Annual grant total

Grants usually total around £5,000 for welfare and educational purposes.

Applications

The charity's website states that grants are usually between £50 and £350 and are typically for one-off purchases of essential household items, for short-term bridging support or for educational needs such as help with fees or to cover unforeseen expenses. The trustees may consider making larger grants in specific cases.

The trustees prefer to receive requests for grants through organisations or agencies working on behalf of families or individuals in need. An organisation or individual applying on another's behalf will then be expected to take responsibility and to account for the correct use of the grant.

The trustees meet twice each year to consider grant requests and to distribute regular amounts to the discretionary funds of the incumbents of member parishes. Other selected organisations or agencies, based within the ancient parish of King's Norton and who assist in relieving genuine poverty or hardship, may also be awarded discretionary grants. Grant applications for smaller amounts (currently up to £250) may also be agreed and paid by the chair, vice-chair and treasurer on behalf of the main meeting.

Sandwell

The Fordath Foundation

£6,500

Correspondent: John Sutcliffe, Trustee, 33 Thornyfields Lane, Stafford ST17 9YS (01785 247035; email: fordath-foundation@ntlworld.com)

CC Number: 501581

Eligibility

People who are in need and live in the metropolitan borough of Sandwell. Preference is given to older people and those in poor health.

Types of grants

One-off grants to meet a specific expense. Grants are also available for educational needs.

Annual grant total

In 2013 the foundation had an income of £6,600 and a total expenditure of £6,700. We estimate that grants to individuals totalled £6,500.

Applications

Applications are usually only considered if they are made through Sandwell Social Services, Citizens Advice or a similar organisation. They should include brief details of the individual's circumstances. They are considered throughout the year, funds permitting.

George and Thomas Henry Salter Trust

£16,500 (50 grants)

Correspondent: J. Styler, Administrator, Lombard House, Cronehills Linkway, West Bromwich, West Midlands B70 7PL (01215 533286)

CC Number: 216503

Eligibility

People in need who live in the borough of Sandwell.

Types of grants

One-off grants, usually in the range of £50 to £1,000, towards clothing, household equipment and so on.

Annual grant total

In 2012 the trust had assets of £1.4 million and an income of £31,000. Relief-in-need grants totalled £16,500 and were made to 50 individuals.

These were the latest accounts available at the time of writing (July 2014).

Applications

On a form available from the correspondent.

Other information

Grants are also given to local organisations.

Stourbridge

The Palmer and Seabright Charity

£10,500

Correspondent: Susannah Griffiths, Administrator, c/o Wall, James and Chappell, 15–23 Hagley Road, Stourbridge, West Midlands DY8 1QW (01384 371622)

CC Number: 200692

Eligibility
Elderly people in need living in the parish of Stourbridge.

Types of grants
One-off and recurrent grants according to need.

Annual grant total
In 2013, this charity had assets of £268,000, an income of £48,000 and made grants totalling £18,800 (which includes £3,200 in Christmas gifts). We estimate grants to individuals for social welfare purposes to be around £10,500.

Applications
On a form available from the correspondent. Applications can be submitted either directly by the individual or a family member, through a third party such as a social worker or teacher, or through an organisation such as Citizens Advice or a school.

Chris Westwood Charity

£34,000

Correspondent: Martyn Morgan, Trustee, Talbots Solicitors, 63 Market Street, Stourbridge DY8 1AQ (01384 445850; email: martynmorgan@talbotssolicitors.co.uk; website: www.chriswestwoodcharity.co.uk)

CC Number: 1101230

Eligibility
Children and young people under the age of 25 in Stourbridge, and the surrounding areas (typically within a 50-mile radius), with physical disabilities.

Types of grants
Typical examples of support have included: special exercise equipment to assist in regaining and maintaining mobility; wheelchairs, special mobility chairs and lifting equipment; and contributions towards the cost of home modifications, to improve access, or provide specialised facilities that may be required.

Annual grant total
In 2012/13 the charity had an income of £58,000 and an expenditure of £67,000. All of this expenditure was given in financial assistance, in the form of 61 grants, with the charity spending no money on governance or accountancy costs. The charity makes grants to organisations as well as individuals. We estimate that welfare grants to individuals totalled £34,000.

Applications
In writing to the correspondent. Applications should detail: the name, age and address of the family and, where applicable, the school attended; background information and the reason for the request; a detailed quotation prepared after an assessment by the supplier; details of the financial position of the family; and details of any funds already raised. Applications should also be supported by a suitable professional person detailing the applicants medical condition and any advantages the proposed equipment purchase would bring. The charity aims to respond to requests within 48 hours. Grants are made by cheque paid directly to the supplier.

Sutton Coldfield

Sutton Coldfield Municipal Charities

£21,000 (28 grants)

Correspondent: Helen Kimmet, Administrator, Lingard House, Fox Hollies Road, Sutton Coldfield, West Midlands B76 2RJ (01213 512262; fax: 01213 130651; email: helen.kimmet@suttoncharitabletrust.org; website: www.suttoncoldfieldmunicipalcharities.com)

CC Number: 218627

Eligibility
People in need living in the Four Oaks, New Hall and Vesey wards of Sutton Coldfield.

Types of grants
One-off grants are given to individuals in the range of £100 and £1,500. Grants are given for special needs, for example, stair lifts, adapted bathrooms and mobility vehicles for people who are elderly or disabled, school clothing, building repairs and essential household equipment such as carpets, washing machine, cookers.

Annual grant total
In 2012/13 the charity had assets of almost £48 million and an income of £1.7 million. There were 28 grants to individuals in need, hardship or distress totalling £21,000, 3 grants for individual educational and personal needs totalling £1,500 and 278 school clothing grants totalling £9,500.

Exclusions
Grants are not given to people in receipt of benefits from other sources, for example social services, family, DWP and so on.

Applications
On a form available from the correspondent. Applications should be made directly by the individual or through a parent or carer. They are considered every month, except April, August and December. Telephone enquiries are welcomed.

Other information
The principal objective of the charities is the provision of almshouses, the distribution of funds and other measures for the alleviation of poverty and other needs for inhabitants and other organisations within the boundaries of the former borough of Sutton Coldfield.

Tettenhall

The Tettenhall Relief-in-Need and Educational Charity

£1,000

Correspondent: Peter Hughes, Trustee, 2 Perton Court Farm Cottages, Pattingham Road, Wolverhampton WV6 8DD (01902 762189; email: PPH.WOLVES@BTINTERNET.COM)

CC Number: 1002952

Eligibility
People in need who live in the parish of Tettenhall, as constituted on 22 June 1888.

Types of grants
Grants are given mainly for clothing and food and range from £25 to £50.

Annual grant total
In 2012/13 the charity had an income of £3,400 and a total expenditure of £2,800. We estimate that around £1,000 was given in grants to individuals for social welfare purposes.

Applications
In writing to the correspondent. Applications should be made through a social worker, Citizens Advice or other welfare agency, doctor or senior citizen's organisation. They should be submitted in October for consideration in November.

Other information
The charity also makes grants to organisations.

Walsall

W. J. Croft for the Relief of the Poor (commonly known as W. J. Croft Charity)

£2,000

Correspondent: Matthew Underhill, Scrutiny Officer, Legal and Democratic Services, Council House, Lichfield Street, Walsall WS1 1TW (01922 654369; email:

charities@walsall.gov.uk; website: cms.walsall.gov.uk/charities)

CC Number: 702795

Eligibility

Residents of the borough of Walsall.

Types of grants

The charity stresses that limited funds mean they can only offer small grants.

Annual grant total

In 2012/13, the charity had an income of £2,700 and a total expenditure of £2,000.

Exclusions

Property deposits, taxes, rent arrears, mortgage payments and utility bills.

Applications

On a form available to download from the Walsall council website or by telephoning the council to receive a copy by post.

Walsall Wood Allotment Charity

£18,000

Correspondent: Craig Goodall, Administrator, Democratic Services, Walsall Council, Council House, Lichfield Street, Walsall WS1 1TW (01922 654765; email: goodallc@walsall.gov.uk; website: www.walsall.gov.uk/charities)

CC Number: 510627

Eligibility

Residents of the borough of Walsall.

Types of grants

The remit of the charity is wide, but typically awards are made for items like clothing, white goods and furniture.

Annual grant total

In 2012/13 the charity had an income of £23,000 and an expenditure of £19,100. We estimate that grants to individuals totalled £18,000.

Exclusions

Property deposits, rent arrears, mortgage payments and utility bills.

Applications

On a form available to download from the Walsall council website or by contacting the council by telephone to request a copy. It is helpful, though not essential, to include evidence to outline the applicant's personal circumstances; for example, proof of income (wage slips, benefits letters or bank statements) or/and a letter of support from a professional familiar with the case. The charity requests, if applicable, that three quotations from reputable suppliers/contractors for any work required are included; however, the charity has its own suppliers for household and electrical items. Applications are considered at meetings which occur approximately six times a year.

The Blanch Woolaston Walsall Charity

£850

Correspondent: Matthew Underhill, Administrator, Constitutional Services, Walsall Council, The Civic Centre, Darwall Street, Walsall WS1 1TP (01922 652087; email: underhillm@walsall.gov.uk)

CC Number: 216312

Eligibility

People in need living in the borough of Walsall. Educational grants will only be given to those under 21 years of age. There is no age limit for relief-in-need grants.

Types of grants

One-off grants for school uniforms and small household items.

Annual grant total

In 2012/13 the charity had both an income and an expenditure of £1,800. Grants totalled approximately £1,700 and were split between educational and welfare purposes.

Exclusions

No grants are made for the payment of rates, taxes or other public funds.

Applications

On a form available from the correspondent. Applications are considered four times a year.

West Bromwich

The Charity of Jane Patricia Eccles

£500

Correspondent: David Coles, Trustee, 9 Highcroft Drive, Sutton Coldfield, West Midlands B74 4SX (01283 513065)

CC Number: 516953

Eligibility

Older women in need who live in Sandwell.

Types of grants

One-off grants in kind to meet specific needs, for example phone installation, showers and Braille reader machines for the blind.

Annual grant total

Grants average around £500 a year, though the actual grant figure tends to fluctuate quite widely.

Applications

In writing to the correspondent for consideration at any time. Applications can be submitted either directly by the individual or a family member, through a third party such as a social worker, or through an organisation such as Citizens Advice or other welfare agency. Applications must be made through, and include a letter of support from, a doctor, church minister or welfare agency.

Wolverhampton

The Power Pleas Trust

£8,600

Correspondent: Keith Berry, Trustee, 80 York Avenue, Wolverhampton WV3 9BU (01902 655962; email: keithoberry@hotmail.com; website: www.powerpleas.org)

CC Number: 519654

Eligibility

Mainly young people, under 18 years of age, with muscular dystrophy and similar diseases living in the Wolverhampton area.

Types of grants

Grants are given primarily towards the purchase and provision of outdoor electric powered wheelchairs and other aids.

Annual grant total

In 2012/13 the trust had an income of £25,000 and a total expenditure of £8,800. We estimate that grants to individuals totalled £8,600.

Applications

In writing to the correspondent directly by the individual or family member.

Worcestershire

The Astley and Areley Kings Sick Fund

£1,000

Correspondent: Mary Wood, Trustee, Muldoon, Areley Common, Stourport-on-Severn, Worcestershire DY13 0NG (01299 823619)

CC Number: 230709

Eligibility

People who suffer from ill health or have disabilities and who live in the parishes of St Peter Astley, St Bartholomew Areley Kings, St Michael and All Angels

Stourport-on-Severn and All Saints Wilden.

Types of grants

One-off grants are made towards specialist equipment for home-care, disability facilities and additional home support.

Annual grant total

In 2012/13 the fund had an income of £3,600 and a total expenditure of £1,900. We estimate that around £1,000 was made in grants to individuals for social welfare purposes.

Applications

In writing to the correspondent. Applications can be submitted either directly by the individual, or through a social worker, Citizens Advice or another third party. The trustees meet regularly throughout the year.

Other information

The fund also supports organisations.

The Baron Davenport Emergency Fund (Worcestershire)

£800

Correspondent: The Administrator, Community Action Malvern District, 28–30 Belle Vue Terrace, Malvern, Worcestershire WR14 4PZ (01684 892381; fax: 01684 575155; email: info@communityaction.org.uk)

CC Number: 501700

Eligibility

Divorcees over 55, young single women/women abandoned by their partners, fatherless children under 25 and widows. Applicants must have been resident in the West Midlands for at least ten years. Applicants are means-tested.

Types of grants

One-off grants ranging from £100 to £150 for emergencies only. Grants have been given towards telephone debt, removal expenses and electrical goods.

Annual grant total

Grants from this fund are generally around £800 a year.

Applications

This fund is now administered by Community Action Malvern District. Applications should be made on a form available from the correspondent. A personal income and expenditure breakdown must accompany all applications. Applications can be made through a social worker, Citizens Advice or other welfare agency, or directly by the individual or family member. They are considered on receipt.

John Martin's Charity

£143,000

Correspondent: John Daniels, The Clerk to the Trustees, 16 Queen's Road, Evesham, Worcester WR11 4JN (01386 765440; fax: 01386 765340; email: enquires@johnmartins.org.uk; website: www.johnmartins.org.uk)

CC Number: 527473

Eligibility

People resident in Evesham, Worcestershire. Applicants or a parent/guardian must have lived in the town for at least 12 months at the date of application.

Note: Applications may also be considered from residents in a number of designated villages close to Evesham if they are suffering from chronic ill health conditions.

Types of grants

Grants are available for the benefit of children, single parent families, people with disabilities and people who have fallen on hard times for a variety of circumstances beyond their control. Applications are subject to income assessment and will be considered for a variety of reasons including help with clothing, essential household items, medical and mobility equipment.'

Annual Heating Allowance – an annual award is currently made to assist those aged 60 and over in meeting their energy bills.

Annual grant total

In 2012/13 the charity had assets of £20.5 million and an income of £749,000. Grants exclusive of support and governance costs were made to individuals and organisations totalling £638,000 and were broken down as follows:

	Grants to individuals	Grants to organisations/ schools
Promotion of education	£266,000	£54,000
Relief in need	£143,000	£67,000
Health	£11,000	£20,000
Religious support	£8,500	£69,000

Exclusions

Support is not normally approved for the repayment of debts, rent or council tax arrears, nor are rental deposits provided. Grants are not considered unless all statutory benefits are being claimed.

Applications

On a form available from the correspondent or downloaded from the website, where criteria is also posted. Applications can be submitted directly by the individual or through a social worker, Citizens Advice or other welfare agency. They are considered twice monthly.

Other information

Grants are also made to organisations and to individuals for educational purposes. The charity has an informative website.

Pershore United Charity

£4,800

Correspondent: Cllr Christopher Parsons, Administrator, Town Hall, 34 High Street, Pershore, Worcestershire WR10 1DS (01386 561561; fax: 01386 561996)

CC Number: 200661

Eligibility

People in need who live in private or rented accommodation (not residential or nursing homes) in the parishes of Pershore and Pensham. Priority is given to older people and people in need who have lived in the town for several years.

Types of grants

Recurrent and occasionally one-off grants to help with heating costs at Christmas.

Annual grant total

In 2012/13 the charity had an income of £5,400 and a total expenditure of £9,500. We estimate that grants to individuals totalled £4,800, with funding also awarded to local organisations.

Applications

In writing to the correspondent. Applications are considered in October.

The Ancient Parish of Ripple Trust

£1,800

Correspondent: John Willis, Secretary, 7 Court Lea, Holly Green, Upton-upon-Severn, Worcestershire WR8 0PE (01684 594570; email: willis.courtlea@btopenworld.com)

CC Number: 1055986

Eligibility

People in need living in the parishes of Ripple, Holdfast, Queenhill and Bushley.

Types of grants

Small one-off cash grants are made. Ongoing Christmas grants can also be made to older people.

Annual grant total

In 2012/13 the trust had both an income and expenditure of around £13,000. Accounts were not required to be submitted to the Charity Commission due to the low income. The trust gives to both individuals and organisations and for both educational and welfare purposes. We estimate the grants for individuals totalled approximately £3,500 with £1,800 being awarded to people in need in the area of benefit.

Applications

In writing to the correspondent. Grants are considered at any time of year.

The Henry and James Willis Trust

£6,100

Correspondent: John Wagstaff, Clerk, The Laurels, 4 Norton Close, Worcester WR5 3EY (01905 355659)

CC Number: 201941

Eligibility

People who are convalescing and live in the city of Worcester.

Types of grants

One-off grants to allow convalescents to spend six weeks at the seaside or other health resort. Travel costs, accommodation and, in special cases, the cost of a carer are included. Patients are usually asked for a small weekly contribution.

Annual grant total

In 2012/13 the trust had an income of £7,000 and a total expenditure of £6,300. We estimate that grants to individuals totalled £6,100.

Applications

On a form available from the clerk. Applications can be submitted directly by the individual or, where applicable, through a social worker, Citizens Advice or other welfare agency.

The Worcestershire Cancer Aid Committee

£8,000

Correspondent: Anthony T. Atkinson, Trustee, c/o Kennel Ground, Gilberts End, Hanley Castle, Worcestershire WR8 0AS (01684 310408)

CC Number: 504647

Eligibility

People with cancer who live in the old county of Worcestershire.

Types of grants

One-off and recurrent grants and loans, including grants in kind to assist cancer patients in financial distress with home nursing, transport to hospital, specialist equipment and so on.

Annual grant total

In 2012/13 the committee had an income of £27,000 and a total expenditure of £17,100. At the time of writing (August 2014) the committee's accounts for the year were not yet available to view on the Charity Commission website. We estimate that social welfare grants to individuals totalled around £8,000, with funding also awarded to organisations.

Applications

Applicants must be referred by a medical professional, a hospice senior staff member or a social worker, etc. Applications are normally considered within one week.

Cropthorne

Randolph Meakins Patty's Farm and the Widows Lyes Charity

£1,500

Correspondent: Mrs J. Ayliffe, Orchard House, Main Street, Cropthorne, Pershore, Worcestershire WR10 3LT (01386 860011)

CC Number: 500624

Eligibility

People in need who live in the village of Cropthorne (Worcestershire).

Types of grants

As well as general welfare grants, Christmas parcels are also given.

Annual grant total

In 2012/13 the charity had an income of £4,200 and an expenditure of £3,300. Grants totalled approximately £3,000 which was divided between education and welfare purposes.

Applications

In writing to the correspondent.

Kidderminster

The Kidderminster Aid in Sickness Fund

£2,200

Correspondent: Rachel Summers, Clerk to the Trustees, c/o M. F. G. Solicitors, Adam House, Birmingham Road, Kidderminster DY10 2SH (01562 820181; email: rachel.summers@mfgsolicitors.com; website: kaisf.org.uk/)

CC Number: 210586

Eligibility

People who are sick, infirm, convalescent, or in need of rest or domestic help, or in financial need, and live in the borough of Kidderminster.

Types of grants

One-off grants typically ranging between £100 and £2,000 towards, for example, fuel expenses, equipment, furniture, beds and bedding.

Annual grant total

In 2012 the fund had an income of £15,500 and an expenditure of £4,500. We estimate grants to individuals to have totalled £2,200, with grants also awarded to organisations.

At the time of writing (August 2014) this was the most recent financial information available for the fund.

Applications

In writing to the correspondent or on a form available for download from the fund's website. Application forms must be accompanied by a Supporting Information form and can be considered at any time.

Worcester

Armchair

(254 grants)

Correspondent: Richard Hines, Manager, Grevis Cottage, Lower Dingle, Malvern WR14 4BQ (01905 456080; fax: 01905 456080; email: armchair@talktalkbusiness.net; website: www.armchairworcester.co.uk)

CC Number: 702078

Eligibility

People in need who have no savings and live in Worcester city (generally, within three mile radius).

Types of grants

The charity collects, recycles and provides good quality second-hand furniture at low cost (£25 per item in 2012/13) to families and individuals. Furniture provided includes beds, wardrobes, tables/chairs, TV stands and so on.

Annual grant total

In 2013/14 the charity had assets of £67,000, an income of £26,000 and a total expenditure of £25,000, all of which has been spent on the overheads required for the distribution of second-hand furniture – the charity's main activity.

During the year the charity received 966 donated items and delivered them to 254 people and families (on average four items each).

Exclusions

The charity cannot provide electrical goods, carpets, clothing, bedding, kitchen utensils and similar items.

Applications

Applications should be submitted through local authorities, a social worker, Citizens Advice or other welfare agency. They are considered all year round. If the need is urgent specify so in the application.

Other information

The trustees' annual report from 2013/14 notes that 'occasionally, gifts are collected from just outside the city but due to limited resources, the need to economise on fuel, and to achieve a low carbon footprint, all deliveries of household items are within the city boundary.'

The Mary Hill Trust

£5,000

Correspondent: Andrew Duncan, Clerk, 16 The Tything, Worcester WR1 1HD (01905 731731)

CC Number: 510978

Eligibility

People in need who live within the boundaries of the city of Worcester.

Types of grants

One-off grants ranging from £50 to £500.

Annual grant total

The 2012 accounts were the latest available at the time of writing (August 2014).

In 2012, the trust had an income of £8,500 and a total expenditure of £11,000. We estimate that the total amount of grants awarded to individuals was approximately £5,000. The trust also awards grants to organisations.

Applications

In writing to the correspondent either through a third party such as a social worker, Citizens Advice or other welfare agency, or directly by the individual. Applications from individuals are considered upon receipt. Applicants should include as many financial details as possible, for example income and weekly outgoings.

Mayor's Fund, Worcester

£500

Correspondent: Claire Chaplin, Administrator, Worcester City Council, Guildhall, High Street, Worcester WR1 2EY (01905 722005; email: claire.chaplin@worcester.gov.uk)

CC Number: 203691

Eligibility

People in need who live within the Worcester city boundary. People immediately outside the city boundaries may be supported in exceptional circumstances.

Types of grants

According to our research, usually one-off grants between £30 and £100 are given for items like school books and clothing, bedding, carpets, decorating materials, pushchairs and household appliances.

Annual grant total

In 2012/13 the fund had an income of £1,400 and an expenditure of almost £600. We estimate that about £500 was given in grants to individuals. Both figures vary each year.

Exclusions

Support is not given for course fees to students.

Applications

Application forms are available from the correspondent. They can be submitted by the individual or through a third party, such as a social worker, Citizens Advice or other welfare agency. Requests are normally considered in March, June, September and December.

The United Charities of Saint Martin

£2,600

Correspondent: Michael Bunclark, Administrator, 4 St Catherine's Hill, London Road, Worcester WR5 2EA (01905 355585)

CC Number: 200733

Eligibility

People in need who live in the parish of St Martin, Worcester.

Types of grants

One-off grants and pensions, according to need.

Annual grant total

In 2013 the charity had an income of £6,600 and a total expenditure of £5,300. We estimate grants awarded to individuals for social welfare purposes to be around £2,600. The charity also makes grants to individuals for educational purposes.

Applications

In writing to the correspondent.

Worcester Consolidated Municipal Charity (Worcester Municipal Charities)

£100,000 (464 grants)

Correspondent: Mary Barker, Administrator, Worcester Municipal Charities, Kateryn Heywood House, Berkeley Court, The Foregate, Worcester WR1 3QG (01905 317117; fax: 01905 619979; email: admin@wmcharities.org.uk; website: www.wmcharities.org.uk)

CC Number: 205299

Eligibility

People in need who live in the city of Worcester.

Types of grants

One-off grants of £20 to £1,000. Support is mainly given towards household essentials, such as white goods, carpets, electrical items, beds, baby necessities, clothing and so on, also funeral costs.

Annual grant total

In 2013 the charity had assets of £14.3 million and an income of £986,000. Grants to 464 individuals for welfare purposes totalled around £100,000.

Further 442 awards totalling £82,000 were made through the Discretionary Welfare Assistance Scheme, which the charity is acting as an agent for.

Note that a significant proportion of charity's income is spent in maintaining the almshouses.

Exclusions

Grants are not given where help is available from family/friends or statutory sources. Previous recipients of a grant from the charity are generally ineligible to apply again.

Applications

Applications have to be made through a social worker, Citizens Advice or other welfare agency. Candidates should have exhausted any statutory sources before applying to the charity. Application forms can be accessed online and are considered monthly. For specific deadlines see the charity's website.

Other information

The charity also provides grants to organisations and maintains almshouses in Worcester. In 2013 grants to organisations totalled £220,000.

Worcester Municipal Exhibitions Foundations (registered charity number 527570), administered by the same body of trustees, offers educational grants to individuals and organisations.

South West

General

Viscount Amory's Charitable Trust

£6,000

Correspondent: The Trust Secretary, The Island, Lowman Green, Tiverton, Devon EX16 4LA (01884 254899)

CC Number: 204958

Eligibility

People in need in the south west of England, with a preference for smaller charities and those operating in Devon (due to limited funds).

Types of grants

One-off and recurrent grants according to need.

Annual grant total

In 2012/13 the trust had assets of almost £12.5 million and an income of £390,000. The trust made 14 grants to individuals totalling £11,200, of which £6,000 was awarded for social welfare purposes. A further £369,000 was given to organisations.

Applications

In writing to the correspondent, for consideration every month.

Avon and Somerset Constabulary Benevolent Fund

£19,000

Correspondent: Caroline Peters, Administrator, Police Headquarters, PO Box 37, Valley Road, Portishead, Bristol BS20 8QJ (01275 816905; email: caroline.peters@avonandsomerset.police.uk)

CC Number: 1085497

Eligibility

Mainly serving and retired members of the Avon and Somerset Constabulary who are in need. Their dependents may also be supported.

Types of grants

One-off grants, ranging from £500 to £2,000, for equipment and house repairs, travel costs for hospital visits and holidays in extreme cases. Interest-free loans are also available to cover debts or other urgent needs.

Annual grant total

In 2012 the fund had assets of £887,000 and an income of £71,000. Grants and donations to individuals and organisations totalled £39,000. We estimate that welfare grants to individuals totalled £19,000.

At the time of writing (August 2014) these were the most recent accounts available for the fund.

Exclusions

No grants for private medical treatment, legal representation or private education.

Applications

Applications must be submitted with a report and recommendation by a force welfare officer. They can be considered at any time.

The Beckly Trust

£3,600

Correspondent: Stephen Trahair, Trustee, 10 South Hill, Stoke, Plymouth PL1 5RR (01752 675071)

CC Number: 235763

Eligibility

Children under 18 who live in the city of Plymouth or district of Caradon, Cornwall, who are sick or have a disability and are in need.

Types of grants

One-off grants of around £200 to £300.

Annual grant total

In 2012/13 the trust had an income of £9,600 and a total expenditure of £4,700. We estimate that grants to individuals totalled £3,600. Funding is occasionally also awarded to organisations.

Applications

In writing to the correspondent giving brief details of income and outgoings of the applicant's parent/guardian and a description of the child's need. Applications should be made preferably through a social worker, Citizens Advice or other welfare agency but can also be made directly by the individual or through another third party. They are considered on an ongoing basis.

Gloucestershire Football Association Benevolent Fund

£7,900

Correspondent: Tony Stone, Manager, Gloucestershire Football Association Ltd, Oaklands Park Stadium, Gloucester Road, Almondsbury, Bristol BS32 4AG (01454 615888; email: secretary@gloucestershirefa.com; website: www.gloucestershirefa.com/clubs-and-leagues/benevolent-fund)

CC Number: 249744

Eligibility

'Players of Clubs affiliated to the Gloucestershire Football Association and in membership of the Fund, and players of Representative League and County Teams, who may be injured whilst playing football in a recognised match.' The fund also helps affiliated referees who are injured whilst officiating at sanctioned matches. Applicants must be unable to work normally for at least two weeks before they will be considered eligible for a grant.

Types of grants

One-off and recurrent grants according to the nature of the accident and the applicant's personal circumstances. Grants may be awarded as a lump sum or in instalments.

Annual grant total

In 2013 the fund had an income of £6,800 and a total expenditure of £7,900. We believe that grants to individuals accounted for the fund's entire expenditure.

Applications

Forms are available from the correspondent or to download from the website. Applications must be made within 28 days of the injury unless there are exceptional circumstances. All forms must also include a report by a member of council and a medical certificate.

The Douglas Martin Trust

£26,000

Correspondent: David Evans, Trustee, 45 Burnards Field Road, Colyton, Devon EX24 6PE (01297 553007)

CC Number: 267876

Eligibility

People in need who live in southern England but only in cases personally known to the trustees. Unsolicited applications will not be responded to.

Types of grants

One-off grants typically up to £300 for items such as bedding, furniture, children's holidays, debt relief and educational grants.

Annual grant total

In 2012/13 the trust held assets of £532,000 and had an income of £45,000. A total of £26,000 was awarded in grants for individuals.

Exclusions

The trust can only support cases known to the trustees.

Applications

Applications will not be accepted unless applicants are known by the trustees or referred by an organisation known to the trustees. Organisations which have recently made successful referrals include various Citizens Advice, SAFE, Devon Development Education and String of Pearls Project.

The Pirate Trust

£9,000

Correspondent: Nicholas Lake, Pirate FM Ltd, Carn Brea Studios, Barncoose Industrial Estate, Redruth, Cornwall TR15 3XX (01209 314400; email: piratetrust@piratefm.co.uk)

CC Number: 1032096

Eligibility

People in need living within the Pirate FM 102 broadcast area (Cornwall, Plymouth and west Devon). Preference is given to people with disabilities.

Types of grants

One-off and recurrent grants mainly towards disability equipment.

Annual grant total

In 2012/13 the trust had an income of £4,200 and a total expenditure of £11,000. Grants are given to both individuals and organisations.

Applications

In writing to the correspondent at any time.

The Plymouth and Cornwall Cancer Fund

£12,000

Correspondent: Peter Harker, Trustee, Whiteford Crocker Solicitors, 28 Outland Road, Plymouth PL2 3DE (01752 220587; email: admin@pccf.org.uk; website: www.plymouthandcornwallcancerfund.org.uk)

CC Number: 262587

Eligibility

People in need who have cancer, or who have a dependent or relative with cancer, and live in the county of Cornwall and within a radius of 40 miles of Plymouth Civic Centre in Devon. Also in-patients or out-patients of any hospital controlled by Plymouth Hospital NHS Trust.

Types of grants

One-off grants between £30 and £500 to relieve hardship which is caused by cancer, for example, towards the cost of travel to hospital for patients and visitors, additional clothing, bed linen, stairlifts and telephone installations and bills.

Annual grant total

In 2012/13 the fund had an income of £52,000 and a total expenditure of £54,000. These accounts had been received at the Charity Commission but were not available to view online. We estimate that grants for social welfare purposes awarded to individuals were in the region of £12,000.

Applications

In writing to the correspondent at any time. Applicants should have exhausted all other potential sources of help before approaching the fund.

St Monica Trust (formerly known as St Monica Trust Community Fund)

£352,000 (707 grants)

Correspondent: Robert Whetton, Head of Finance, Cote Lane, Bristol BS9 3UN (01179 494006; email: info@stmonicatrust.org.uk; website: www.stmonicatrust.org.uk)

CC Number: 202151

Eligibility

People who have a physical disability or long-term physical health problem living in Bristol, South Gloucestershire, North Somerset or Bath and North East Somerset. Applicants must have a low income, limited savings and be over 40 years old.

Help is available to people who are in recovery from substance misuse or alcoholism, provided they have been drug or alcohol-free for at least six months and also have a physical disability or long-term physical health problem.

Types of grants

Gifts

One-off grants averaging around £300 but never exceeding £500 to help towards mobility aids, home/car adaptations, domestic appliances, furniture and flooring, bedding, clothing, health costs, communication aids, bills and debts.

This list is by no means exhaustive and gifts will be considered for anything that will make a positive difference to the applicant's everyday life.

Short-Term Grants

A period of monthly payments designed to help a person through a time of crisis. For example, help can be given for: debt relief; adjusting to a sudden loss of income; unexpected costs; and the extra costs involved when undergoing chemotherapy, interferon or similar treatments. Usually up to £25 each week is paid for anywhere between a couple of months up to a maximum of three years. Help is usually given for around six months.

Annual grant total

In 2012 the trust had assets of £218 million and an income of £24 million. Charitable expenditure totalled £23 million. Grants were made to 707 individuals (of 1,361 applications received) totalling £352,000 and can be categorised as follows:

Gifts	478	£222,000
Short-term grants	220	£116,000
Annuities	9	£14,000

Over 700 were helped directly through grants and more were helped through LinkAge.

This was the latest financial information available at the time of writing.

Exclusions

No help is given to people with mental health problems or people with a learning disability unless they also have a physical disability or long-term physical health problem. Help is not generally given to people who have more than £3,000 in savings.

Help will not be given for holidays; gardening; bankruptcy fees; funeral expenses; decorating labour costs; respite care and care home fees.

Applications

On a form available to download from the trust's website or by contacting the fund. If possible, applications should be submitted via a social worker, advice worker or a similar professional, although individuals can apply themselves. Depending on the request, a letter may be needed from an occupational therapist confirming the need for a particular item and why it is not available from statutory funds. Individuals should contact the trust if they are having any difficulties in filling out the form, and, if needed, a home visit can be arranged to help complete the application.

The trust expects you to have applied for statutory funding first, for example community care grants and disabled facilities grants, before applying. They may refer you to a relevant trade or forces benevolent fund before considering your application where possible. The trust's website also advises: 'If you own your own home and are asking for help with repairs or improvements, we would expect you to investigate equity release schemes and charitable interest free loans before you ask us for help.'

Other information

Grants are also made to organisations whose aim is to support a similar group of beneficiaries, with seven organisations receiving a total of £73,000 in 2012. The trust also provides sheltered housing and retirement accommodation; support services; and nursing and residential care.

Avon

The Anchor Society

£36,000 (116 grants)

Correspondent: Erica Planer, Administrator, 29 Alma Vale Road, Clifton, Bristol BS8 2HL (01179 734161; email: admin@anchorsociety.co.uk or info@anchorsociety.co.uk; website: www.anchorsociety.co.uk)

CC Number: 208756

Eligibility

Isolated people over the age of 55 who are in genuine immediate need and live in the Bristol and former Avon postcode area (BS).

Types of grants

One-off and regular grants as well as Christmas gifts, usually up to £500.

Annual grant total

In 2012/13 the society had assets of £3.9 million and an income of £123,000. Grants were made totalling £82,000, of which £36,000 was given to individuals: £10,900 to 18 regular annuitants and £25,000 in 98 one-off grants.

Exclusions

No grants to organisations or for debts, outstanding bills, funeral costs, respite, holidays or for ongoing care costs. Grants are not given for general living expenses, except for cases of extreme long-term hardship. The society will also not make a grant where family members, particularly children, can reasonably be expected to help their relative, especially with requests for building repairs.

Applications

Applications may be made in writing or by email (though email is preferred) and should include the following applicant details: name, address, age, what the grant is for, details of any disabilities, residential status – does the applicant live alone or with family who can assist financially, and financial circumstances – including income, housing costs and any other significant outgoings. Applicants should also indicate whether they rent or own their home and if they have applied to any other charities for help. The society aims to respond to all enquiries within a few days.

Other information

The society has also invested in the provision of a new form of day care for elderly people within the region through LinkAge, who it supports with an annual grant (£47,000 2012/13) and has close links with other welfare charities in the area. It has also invested in a number of housing projects the most recent one providing affordable housing for elderly people on a shared equity basis where necessary.

The Backwell Foundation

£800

Correspondent: David Pike, Trustee, Sedalia, Brockley Hall, Brockley Lane, Brockley, Bristol BS48 3AZ (01275 463261)

CC Number: 1086036

Eligibility

People in need who live in the civil parishes of Backwell and Brockley.

Types of grants

Small one-off and recurrent grants can be given according to need.

Annual grant total

In 2013 the foundation had an income of £1,000 and an expenditure of £900. We have estimated the annual total of grants to be around £800.

Applications

In writing to the correspondent. Applications made from outside the area of benefit are not acknowledged.

The Grateful Society

£73,000

Correspondent: June Moody, Administrator, 17 St Augustine's Parade, Bristol BS1 4UL (01179 291929; fax: 01179 253824; email: g-s.moody@btconnect.com; website: gratefulsociety.org)

CC Number: 202349

Eligibility

Ladies over 50 who have lived in Bristol and the surrounding area for at least ten years and would benefit from financial assistance, typically to pursue an independent life in their own home.

Grants may occasionally be given to men in reduced circumstances.

Types of grants

Regular allowances of £100 to £200 a year. One-off grants can be paid towards, for example, electrical goods, clothing, household bills, food, holidays, travel expenses, heating repairs, medical equipment, furniture and disability equipment.

Annual grant total

In 2013, the society had an income of £135,000 and total assets of £240,000. Total expenditure was £80,000. During the year annuities and gifts were paid to an average of 43 ladies totalling £37,000.

Applications

In writing to the correspondent; to be submitted directly by the individual or through a third party.

Other information

Grants may also be made to organisations with similar aims (£36,000 in 2013).

The Peter Hervé Benevolent Institution

£74,000

Correspondent: June Moody, Hon. Secretary and Treasurer, 17 St Augustine's Parade, Bristol BS1 4UL (01179 291929; email: g-s.moody@btconnect.com)

CC Number: 202443

Eligibility

People aged 60 and over who live within a 25-mile radius of Bristol city centre, own their own homes and have fallen on hard times.

Types of grants

Recurrent grants, averaging £200 a quarter, and one-off emergency grants of up to £300 towards, for example, the costs of a new boiler.

Annual grant total

In 2013 the charity held assets of £2.1 million and had an income of £97,000. Grants and annuities to individuals totalled £74,000 and were distributed as follows:

Regular gifts	£48,000
Emergency gifts	£23,000
Annuities	£2,500

There were 10 grants made to individuals totalling £2,800. There was no breakdown of whether the grants were for social welfare or educational purposes.

Exclusions

Grants are not given towards fuel bills.

Applications

On a form available from the correspondent or the website. Cash grants are never made directly to the individual; the grant is either paid via a third party such as social services, or the charity pays for the item directly and donates it to the individual. The trustees meet six times a year usually in January, March, May, July, September and November (exact dates available on the website) and applications should be submitted at least two weeks beforehand.

Other information

Grants were also made to schools and organisations totalling £17,700.

Bath

The Mayor of Bath's Relief Fund

£11,000

Correspondent: James Money-Kyrle, Director of Support Services, c/o St John's Hospital, 4–5 Chapel Court, Bath BA1 1SQ (01225 486400; email: james.money-kyrle@stjohnsbath.org.uk)

CC Number: 204649

Eligibility

People in need who live in Bath.

Types of grants

One-off grants ranging from £50 to £350 for carpets, second-hand furniture and appliances, school uniforms and bills. The fund states that its key aim is to ensure that children have 'clean clothes, hot food and a warm house.'

Annual grant total

In 2013 the fund had an income of £7,500 and a total expenditure of £11,500. We estimate that grants to individuals totalled £11,000.

Exclusions

No grants are given for tuition fees or rent arrears.

Applications

On a form available from local health visitors, social services or Citizens Advice. Applications should be submitted through one of these organisations or a similar third party and are considered throughout the year. Note: Grants are only made as a last resort for those who have already exhausted all other funding channels such as Social Security, social services and other local charities.

St John's Hospital (Bath)

£180,000 (535 grants)

Correspondent: James Money-Kyrle, Director of Support Services, St John's Hospital and Bath Municipal Charities, 4–5 Chapel Court, Bath BA1 1SQ (01225 486400; email: james.money-kyrle@stjohnsbath.org.uk; website: www.stjohnsbath.org.uk)

CC Number: 201476

Eligibility

People who live Bath and the surrounding area and are in need due to age, ill-health, disability, financial hardship or other circumstances. There are no age restrictions.

Types of grants

Grants can be made up of several payments but generally not for more than a total of £1,500 over three years. Support can be given towards clothing, white goods, rent arrears, utility bills, food, TV licenses, furniture, bedding, carpets, bankruptcy fees or counselling. Other requests may also be considered.

Annual grant total

In 2013 the charity awarded grants to 535 individuals totalling £180,000.

Exclusions

Grants are not given for:

- DWP loans
- Funeral expenses
- Magistrates court fines
- Deposits or rent in advance for accommodation
- Washing machines (unless there is a child in the family or there are medical grounds, in which case medical confirmation must be supplied)

Only one grant per individual/family is considered in any twelve-month period. No family or individual shall receive more than three grants within five years or up to a limit set by the trustees. The charity will not duplicate assistance available from statutory or other external agencies.

Applications

Applications can only be made through recognised local welfare agencies, such as Citizens Advice, Housing Advice Centre, health visitors, Developing Health and Independence (DHI), the Genesis Trust or others. There is an online system where applications can be made on behalf of the individual. Direct applications from those in need are not accepted.

Almondsbury

Almondsbury Charity

£1,400 (5 grants)

Correspondent: Peter Orford, Administrator, Shepperdine Road, Oldbury Naite, Oldbury-on-Severn, Bristol BS35 1RJ (01454 415346; email: peter.orford@gmail.com; website: www.almondsburycharity.org.uk)

CC Number: 202263

Eligibility

People in need in the old parish of Almondsbury.

Types of grants

One-off grants according to need, for instance for household appliances.

Annual grant total

In 2012/13 the charity had assets of £2.2 million and an income of £66,000.

Other information

The charity also provides almshouse accommodation for people over the age of 65 and grants to local organisations. In 2013 grants to 25 community organisations totalled £266,000.

Bath and North East Somerset

Combe Down Holiday Trust

£23,000 (214 grants)

Correspondent: The Administrator, c/o Combe Down Surgery, The Avenue, Combe Down, Bath BA2 5EG (01225 837181; email: ro@cdht.org.uk; website: www.cdht.org.uk)

CC Number: 1022275

Eligibility

People who have disabilities, their families and carers, who live in the Bath and North East Somerset area.

Types of grants

One-off grants averaging around £130 towards the cost of a holiday, short break or respite care.

Annual grant total

In 2012 the trust had assets of £935,000 and an income of £63,000. 214 holiday grants totalled £23,000.

At the time of writing (August 2014) this was the most recent financial information available for the trust.

Applications

On a form available from the correspondent, to be submitted directly by the individual or through a social worker, Citizens Advice or other welfare agency.

Other information

Note, specialised accommodation is usually booked months in advance, so applicants are advised to apply as early as possible to avoid disappointment.

Batheaston

Henry Smith's Charity (Longney)

£1,800

Correspondent: John Irons, Trustee, Spindle Berries, 48 Northend, Batheaston, Bath BA1 7ES (01225 852440; email: johnirons@dsl.pipex.com)

CC Number: 204620

Eligibility

People in need who live in Batheaston, particularly widows.

Types of grants

One-off grants for fuel costs.

Annual grant total

In 2013/14 the charity had both an income and an expenditure of £2,000. We estimate that grants to individuals were made totalling around £1,800.

Applications

In writing to the correspondent.

Other information

The charity distributes grants received from the main Henry Smith's Charity within its suggested guidance.

Bristol

Thomas Beames' Charity

£2,800

Correspondent: Philippa Drewett, Administrator, 1 All Saints Court, Bristol BS1 1JN (01179 665739)

CC Number: 245822

Eligibility

People in need who live in the ancient parish of St George with St Augustine, Bristol or the parishes of Christchurch with St George, St Stephen with St James or St John the Baptist with St Michael, Bristol. In exceptional cases, the charity may help people who live outside this area, who produce sufficient good reason why they should be treated as being resident within the parish.

Types of grants

Grants are made at the discretion of the trustees, towards, for example, bedding, food and electrical cookers.

Annual grant total

In 2012/13 the charity had an income of £6,900 and a total expenditure of £3,000. We estimate that grants to individuals totalled £2,800.

Applications

In writing to the correspondent including details of why help is needed. Applications are usually considered quarterly.

The Bristol Benevolent Institution

£366,000

Correspondent: Maureen Nicholls, Secretary, 45 High Street, Nailsea, Bristol BS48 1AW (01275 810365 (mobile 07968 434 274); email: admin@bristolbenevolent.org; website: bristolbenevolent.org/)

CC Number: 204592

Eligibility

Older people with small, fixed incomes and little or no capital. Applicants must be over 60 and have lived in Bristol for 15 years or more. People over the age of 55 who have chronic illness or severe disabilities are also eligible.

Types of grants

Mostly small recurrent grants paid quarterly, (at the time of writing) up to a maximum of £25 per week. One-off grants may also be made for specific needs.

People over the age of 70 who own their homes, free of mortgage, can apply for small interest-free loans to help supplement a low income or to help make essential repairs. Loans are repaid from the sale of the property upon the death of the beneficiary, or if the beneficiary sells their home. In the cases of couples, a loan can be transferred to the surviving spouse automatically.

Annual grant total

In 2013 the institution had an income of £421,000 and a total expenditure of £467,000. Grants totalled £366,000. Each quarter, the average number of grants received by individuals was 237.

During the year the trustees also awarded special grants for heating costs after a period of cold weather, and also in the summer and at Christmas.

Exclusions

The institution's website states that whilst it 'cannot give grants to people who own their own homes', it can offer interest-free loans to those homeowners over the age of 70.

Applications

Potential applicants should contact the secretary by phone, email or in writing. A visitor from the institution will then call to complete an application. Applications can be submitted directly by the individuals or through a third party such as a family member, a friend, a social worker or doctor, provided the individual concerned is notified and approves of the application.

Other information

BBI's accounts state that most of its beneficiaries 'have less than £80 per week for food and clothing after paying their rent, medical bills, heat, light, transport and other standing costs.'

The institution notes that although it gives financial assistance, 'we believe that the most valued assistance we give is friendship and advice, ably provided by our lady visitors.' Newsletters, visits and telephone calls help the institution keep in touch with its beneficiaries.

Bristol Charities

£226,000

Correspondent: Anne Anketell, Chief Executive, 17 Augustine's Parade, Bristol BS1 4UL (01179 300301; fax: 01179 253824; email: info@bristolcharities.org.uk; website: www.bristolcharities.org.uk)

CC Number: 1109141

Eligibility

People in need who have lived in Bristol for more than two consecutive years.

Types of grants

Grants are mainly in the form of vouchers which are used to purchase specific goods. Grants are considered for beds, carpets, clothing for school age children aged 5–15 (where more than one child in the family is at school, one voucher per child), white goods, essential furniture (second-hand or reconditioned), safety equipment, washing machines and starter packs.

In recent years, the trustees have introduced a 'retained ownership scheme' for items such as wheelchairs, electric wheelchairs and scooters, by which they are acquired for specific individuals but remain under the ownership of the charities, with the purpose of recycling the equipment should the original recipient no longer require it.

Annual grant total

In 2012/13 the charities had a consolidated income of £1.6 million and a total expenditure of £1.4 million. Grants to individuals totalled £226,000.

Exclusions

No grants for debts or rent arrears. Only one grant is given per applicant per year and there is a limit of three grants per person.

Applications

On a form available from the Bristol Charities website. All applicants require the support of a sponsor who should be a healthcare professional. Applications are considered daily.

Other information

The provision of accommodation for the elderly at four almshouse sites (Perrett House, Red Cross Mews, Manor House and John Foster's) is carried out through 'Orchard Homes', which is a registered provider. The charities also own and manage two day centres (Summerhill in St George and Henbury).

The Lord Mayor of Bristol's Christmas Appeal for Children

£59,000 (1,485 grants)

Correspondent: Bruce Simmonds, Hon. Treasurer, 3 Park Crescent, Frenchay, Bristol BS16 1PD (website: www.lordmayorofbristolappeal.co.uk)

CC Number: 288262

Eligibility

Children under 16 who are in need and who live in the city of Bristol.

Types of grants

One-off grants in the form of vouchers. Each child receives two vouchers; one worth £20 to be spent on food, and another worth £20 to be spent on either clothing or toys.

Annual grant total

In 2012/13 the charity held assets of £92,000 and had an income of £55,000. The total value of food, clothing and toy vouchers, awarded to approximately 1,485 children, amounted to £59,000.

Applications

Through a social worker, Citizens Advice, welfare agency or other third party such as a parent or a person who can confirm the individual's needs.

Other information

The Appeal originated in the 1920's, when it was known as the Lord Mayor's Fund, and the money raised was used to provide Christmas dinners and boots for poor children.

The Dolphin Society

£57,000

Correspondent: June Moody, Administrator, 17 Augustine's Parade, Bristol BS1 4UL (01179 291929; email: dolphinsociety@btconnect.com; website: dolphinsociety.org.uk)

CC Number: 203142

Eligibility

People in need and/or at risk through poor health, disability or financial difficulty and who live in Bristol. Preference is given to older people who need help in maintaining their independence and security in their own homes.

Types of grants

Help with telephone installations, smoke alarms, pendant alarms and security items such as external security boxes and door and window locks. Payments from the hardship fund can be used to help with home adaptations to enable people to continue to live in their homes while coping with increasing disability. One-off cash grants are given occasionally and can range from £10 to £1,000.

Annual grant total

In 2012/13 the society held assets of £186,000 and had an income of £138,000. We believe that charitable expenditure for individuals totalled £57,000 and was distributed as follows:

Pendant alarms/telephone installation	£29,000
Grants for disability equipment	£9,400
Home security	£9,400
Independent Living fund	£9,400

A further £5,200 was spent on the society's pilot i-Pad project, a door entry system and the Horfield Community Project.

Exclusions

No grants to applicants living outside the area of benefit.

Applications

On a form available from the correspondent. Applications can be submitted directly by the individual or family member or by an appropriate third party. There are no deadlines and applications are considered throughout the year.

Other information

In the future, the society hopes to continue its i-Pad project, which explores the role tablet computers can play in helping isolated older people to live independently in the community.

Extension and Special Fund (Unity Fund for the Elderly)

£7,400

Correspondent: David Rowcliffe, Trustee, 5 Bishop Road, Emersons Green, Bristol BS16 7ET (01179 561289)

CC Number: 1000421

Eligibility

Elderly people (generally over the age of 60) in the Bristol area who are in need, hardship or distress.

Types of grants

Our research suggests that one-off grants are available towards repairs, clothing, electric goods, household bills, medical equipment, furniture, disability equipment and so on.

Annual grant total

In 2013 the fund had an income of £13,900 and an expenditure of £13,000. We estimate that grants to individuals totalled about £7,400.

Applications

In writing to the correspondent. Applications should be submitted through a social worker, Citizens Advice or other welfare agency. They are considered at any time.

Other information

Grants are also made to organisations.

The Redcliffe Parish Charity

£4,000

Correspondent: Paul Tracey, Trustee, 18 Kingston Road, Nailsea, Bristol, North Somerset BS48 4RD (01275 854057; email: redcliffeparishclerk@mail.com)

CC Number: 203916

Eligibility

People in need who live in the city of Bristol.

Types of grants

One-off grants usually of £25 to £50. 'The trustees generally limit grants to families or individuals who can usually manage, but who are overwhelmed by circumstances and are in particular financial stress rather than continuing need.' Grants are typically given for electric goods, clothing, living costs, food, holidays, furniture and disability equipment.

Annual grant total

In 2012/13 the charity had an income of £9,600 and a total expenditure of £8,200. We have estimated social welfare grants to total around £4,000.

Exclusions

No grants for bankruptcy fees, debts in respect of Council Tax, rent arrears or credit debts.

Applications

In writing to the correspondent. Applications should be submitted on the individual's behalf by a social worker, doctor, health visitor, Citizens Advice or appropriate third party, and will be considered early in each month. Ages of family members should be supplied in addition to financial circumstances and the reason for the request.

Other information

Grants to schoolchildren occur as part of the charity's wider welfare work.

Wraxall Parochial Charities

£4,000

Correspondent: Mrs A. Sissons, Clerk to the Trustees, 2 Short Way, Failand, Bristol BS8 3UF (01275 392691)

CC Number: 230410

Eligibility

People living in the parish of Wraxall and Failand, Bristol who are in need due to hardship or disability.

Types of grants

One-off grants.

Annual grant total

In 2013 the charity had an income of £26,000 and a total expenditure of £18,000. We estimate grants to individuals for social welfare purposes totalled around £4,000.

Applications

In writing to the correspondent, directly by the individual. Applications are considered in February, June, September and November.

Other information

Grants are also made for educational purposes and to organisations.

Midsomer Norton

Ralph and Irma Sperring Charity

£23,000

Correspondent: E. Hallam, Administrator, Thatcher and Hallam Solicitors, Island House, Midsomer Norton, Bath BA3 2HJ (01761 414646; email: sperringcharity@gmail.com)

CC Number: 1048101

Eligibility

People in need who live within a five-mile radius of the Church of St John the Baptist in Midsomer Norton, Bath.

Types of grants

One-off and recurrent grants according to need.

Annual grant total

In 2012/13 the charity had assets of £6.1 million and an income of £331,000. Awards to local causes amounted to £94,000. The charity makes grants to both individuals and organisations although there is no stipulation as to how the income is divided. We have estimated the amount awarded to individuals for welfare purposes to be approximately £23,000.

Applications

In writing to the correspondent, to be considered quarterly.

North Somerset

Nailsea Community Trust Ltd

£1,500

Correspondent: Ann Tonkin, Administrator, 8 Blakeney Grove, Nailsea, Bristol BS48 4RG (website: www.nailseacommunitytrust.co.uk)

CC Number: 900031

Eligibility

People of any age or occupation who are in need due, for example, to hardship, disability or sickness, and who live in the town of Nailsea and the immediate area in North Somerset.

Types of grants

One-off grants, usually up to £500, towards items, services or facilities.

Annual grant total

This organisation makes grants to individuals and organisations for both social welfare and educational purposes. We estimate grants to individuals for educational purposes to be around £1,500.

Applications

On a form available from the correspondent. Applications can be submitted either directly by the individual or via a relevant third party such as a school, social worker or Citizens Advice. Applications are considered at meetings held every three months.

Charles Graham Stone's Relief-in-Need Charity

£7,700

Correspondent: John Gravell, Administrator, Easton Grey, Webbington Road, Cross, Axbridge BS26 2EL (01934 732266)

CC Number: 260044

Eligibility

People in need who live in the parishes of Churchill and Langford, North Somerset.

Types of grants

One-off grants of about £50 to £150 towards travel expenses to visit relatives in hospitals or nursing homes, help in the home, household bills or medical/ disability equipment.

Annual grant total

In 2013 the charity had an income of £4,300 and an expenditure of £9,400. Some support may also be given for educational purposes, therefore we estimate that grants to individuals for welfare needs totalled about £7,700.

Exclusions

Our research suggests that grants are not made for payment of national or local taxes or rates.

Applications

In writing to the correspondent. Candidates should provide a full explanation of their personal circumstances and submit requests for funding by the end of February or August for consideration in the following month.

Note that the charity does not welcome initial telephone calls.

Other information

Grants are also made to vocational students in the parishes.

Portishead

The Portishead Nautical Trust

£2,700

Correspondent: Liz Knight, Secretary, 108 High Street, Portishead, Bristol BS20 6AJ (01275 847463; fax: 01275 818871)

CC Number: 228876

Eligibility

People in need, usually under 25, who live in Portishead. Preference is given to people who are: homeless; unemployed; experiencing problems related to drug or solvent abuse; being ill-treated; being neglected, in the areas of physical, moral and educational well-being; or 'people who have committed criminal acts, or are in danger of doing so'.

Types of grants

Small grants and bursaries, 'where such a grant will enable a young person to realise their full potential'.

Annual grant total

In 2012/13 the trust had assets of £1.95 million and an income of £88,000. Grants totalled £57,000, most of which was given to a combination of local and regional organisations, with individuals receiving £5,500. We estimate that around £2,700 of this was given for welfare purposes.

Applications

On a form available from the correspondent. Applications must be supported by a sponsor, such as a welfare officer or health visitor. The trustees meet four times a year to consider applications.

South Gloucestershire

The Chipping Sodbury Town Lands

£23,000

Correspondent: Nicola Gideon, Administrator, Town Hall, 57–59 Broad Street, Chipping Sodbury, Bristol BS37 6AD (01454 852223; email: nicola.gideon@chippingsodburytownhall.co.uk; website: www.chippingsodburytownhall.co.uk)

CC Number: 236364

Eligibility

People in need who live in Chipping Sodbury or Old Sodbury.

Types of grants

One-off and recurrent grants according to need. Grants to help with winter heating bills, as well as for equipment for a variety of activities.

Annual grant total

In 2013 the charity had assets of £8.9 million, an income of £360,000 and gave grants totalling £127,000, of which £23,000 was given for welfare purposes.

Applications

In writing to the correspondent.

Stanton Prior

The Henry Smith Charity (Longnet Estate)

£1,500

Correspondent: Alistair Hardwick, Trustee, Church Farm, Stanton Prior, Bath BA2 9HT (01761 479625)

CC Number: 240003

Eligibility

People in need who have lived in Stanton Prior for more than three years. Preference is usually given to those living in rented accommodation.

Types of grants

One-off cash grants and gift vouchers.

Annual grant total

Grants usually total between £1,000 and £2,000 each year.

Applications

In writing to the correspondent, directly by the individual, for consideration by the trustees in November and December.

Thornbury

Thornbury Consolidated Charities (administered by Thornbury Town Trust)

£14,200

Correspondent: Margaret Powell, Clerk, 9 Elmdale Crescent, Thornbury, Bristol BS35 2JH (01454 281777; email: margaret.towntrust@googlemail.com)

CC Number: 238273

Eligibility

People in need who live in the parish of Thornbury. Beneficiaries are often of pensionable age or disabled but anyone in the parish can apply.

Types of grants

One-off grants of £110 (at the time of writing) to help with the extra expense of Christmas but they are also given at other times.

Annual grant total

In 2012 the charities had assets of £837,000 and an income of £38,000. Gifts to individuals totalled £15,700, of which we estimate around £14,200 was given solely for welfare purposes.

A further £2,800 was given to local groups.

At the time of writing (August 2014) this was the most recent financial information available for the charities.

Exclusions

Grants are not given where the need is covered by statutory authorities.

Applications

By letter to the correspondent. Applications can be submitted directly by the individual or through a social worker, Citizens Advice or other welfare agency and should include details of the applicant's income. They are considered in November for Christmas but applications for special needs can be made at any time.

Other information

The charities also own almshouses.

Cornwall

Blanchminster Trust

£34,000 (28 grants)

Correspondent: Jane Bunning, Clerk to the Trustees, Blanchminster Building, 38 Lansdown Road, Bude, Cornwall EX23 8EE (01288 352851; fax: 01288 352851; email: office@blanchminster.plus.com; website: www.blanchminster.org.uk)

CC Number: 202118

Eligibility

People who live in the parishes of Bude, Stratton and Poughill (the former urban district of Bude-Stratton).

Types of grants

Generally one-off grants up to a maximum of £25,000 for the relief of need, hardship or distress, for example for clothing, food, electrical goods, furniture, medical care and equipment, and travel to and from hospital.

Annual grant total

In 2013 the trust had assets of £10 million. It should be noted that this is in the form of investment property, only the surplus income from which is available for grant giving. In this accounting year, the charity had an income of £510,000 and made 28 social welfare grants totalling £34,000.

Applications

On a form available from the correspondent. Applications are considered monthly and should be submitted directly by the individual. Where possible the application should include a request for a specific amount and be supported with quotes for the costs needed and/or written support from a social worker or other welfare agency. Applications must include evidence of financial need.

Other information

Grants are also made to individuals for education and for community projects.

The Lizzie Brooke Charity

£18,500

Correspondent: Sheila Bates, Administrator, 13 Church Close, Lelant, St Ives TR26 3JX (01736 752383; email: michael@vickers13.co.uk)

CC Number: 254764

Eligibility

Older people, people who are sick and those in need who live in West Cornwall.

Types of grants

One-off grants ranging from £100 to £200 for the necessities of everyday living. Grants can be given towards electric goods, clothing, holidays, travel expenses, furniture and hospital expenses.

Annual grant total

In 2013 the charity had an income of £2,800 and a total expenditure of £19,000. We estimate that grants to individuals totalled £18,500.

Exclusions

Grants are not made to people living in other parts of Cornwall or for students for fees.

Applications

On a form available from the correspondent, to be completed by a sponsor. Applications should be submitted through a social worker, Citizens Advice or other welfare agency. They are considered at any time.

Cornwall Community Foundation

£25,000 (Around 45 grants)

Correspondent: The Grants Team, Suite 1, Sheers Barton, Lawhitton, Launceston, Cornwall PL15 9NJ (01566 779865 or 01566 779333; email: grants@cornwallfoundation.com; website: www.cornwallfoundation.com)

CC Number: 1099977

Eligibility

People in need living in Cornwall.

Types of grants

Usually one-off awards ranging from £50 to about £1,000 (depending on the fund). Grants have been made to alleviate poverty, hardship and distress, provide support in crisis or to help young people foster their talent.

A special emergency fund has also been established to help people affected by adverse weather conditions and flooding.

Annual grant total

In 2013 the foundation had an income of £1.1 million and a total expenditure of £854,000. Full accounts were not available to view at the time of writing (August 2014); however in previous years grants to individuals from various funds have totalled about £25,000 annually distributed amongst about 45 people.

Applications

Initial enquiries should be directed to the grants team to discuss which funds are available and further application procedure. Alternatively, a list of open grant schemes together with application forms and separate deadlines are available on the foundation's website. Note that, as with all community foundations, schemes are likely to open and close regularly, so check before applying.

Other information

Grants are mostly made to organisations, groups, clubs and community projects.

The Cornwall Retired Clergy, Widows of the Clergy and their Dependants Fund

£5,500

Correspondent: C. M. Kent, Administrator, Truro Diocesan Board Of Finance, Diocesan House, Truro, Cornwall TR1 1JQ (01872 274351; email: accountant@truro.anglican.org)

CC Number: 289675

Eligibility

Widows, widowers and dependents of deceased members of the clergy who live in, or have worked in, the diocese of Truro. Retired Anglican clergy who are in need and have links with Truro are also eligible for support.

Types of grants

Grants given are one-off and occasionally recurrent, according to need. Recent grants have ranged from £50 to £500 and included funding for dentist's fees, spectacles, travel to hospital and assistance with equipment for people with disabilities.

Annual grant total

In 2013, the fund had an income of £14,000 and a total expenditure of £6,000. We estimate that the total amount of grants awarded to individuals was approximately £5,500.

Exclusions

No grants for assistance with school or university fees.

Applications

In writing to the correspondent. Applications can be submitted directly by the individual or through a relative or a carer. They are usually considered monthly.

The Duke of Cornwall's Benevolent Fund

(1 grant)

Correspondent: Terry Cotter, Administrator, Duchy of Cornwall, 10 Buckingham Gate, London SW1E 6LA (020 7834 7346)

CC Number: 269183

Eligibility

People who are in need because of sickness, poverty or age. In practice funds are steered towards the South West England and areas related to Duchy lands, which are principally in Cornwall.

Types of grants

One-off and recurrent grants according to need.

Annual grant total

In 2012/13 the fund had assets of £3.7 million and an income of £396,000. Grants totalled £179,000. During the year one grant was made to an individual, although the amount awarded was not specified.

Applications

In writing to the correspondent. The trustees meet quarterly to consider grants.

Other information

The fund's main focus is on awarding grants to registered charities.

The United Charities of Liskeard

£1,000

Correspondent: A. J. Ball, Administrator, Tremellick, Pengover Road, Liskeard, Cornwall PL14 3EW (01579 343577)

CC Number: 215173

Eligibility

For the relief-in-need fund, people in need who live in the town of Liskeard (formerly the borough of Liskeard). For the relief-in-sickness fund, people in need who live in Liskeard, the parish of Dobwalls with Trewidland (formerly the parish of Liskeard) and the parishes of Menheniot and St Cleer.

Types of grants

One-off and recurrent grants according to need.

Annual grant total

In 2013 the charity had an income of £1,900 and a total expenditure of £1,400. We estimate that around £1,000 was made in grants to individuals for social welfare purposes.

Applications

In writing to the correspondent.

Gunwalloe

The Charity of Thomas Henwood

£7,000

Correspondent: Jennifer Moyle, Trustee, Homeleigh, Gunwalloe, Helston TR12 7QG (01326 564806)

CC Number: 206765

Eligibility

People who live in the parish of Gunwalloe and are unemployed, sick or retired and in need.

Types of grants

One-off or recurrent grants according to need, and grants for the provision of nurses and to assist people recovering from illness. Grants normally range from £60 to £100. All by periodic distribution. Income is also used to care for graves in the churchyard if no relatives are still alive.

Annual grant total

In 2013 the charity had an income of £8,400 and a total expenditure of £7,400. We estimate that grants to individuals totalled £7,000.

Applications

In writing to the trustees. Applications are considered in March and December.

Gwennap

Charity of John Davey

£12,400

Correspondent: E. T. Pascoe, Administrator, Tregenna Lodge, Crane, Camborne TR14 7QX (01209 718853)

CC Number: 232127

Eligibility

Ex-miners over 70 years of age and their widows who are in need and live in the ancient parish of Gwennap, near Redruth in Cornwall. Ex-miners should have worked underground in a mine for at least five consecutive years.

Types of grants

Quarterly grants of £10 to £40 for general living expenses.

Annual grant total

In 2012/13 the charity had an income of £10,800 and a total expenditure of £12,600. We estimate that grants to individuals totalled £12,400.

Applications

Initial telephone calls to the correspondent are welcome and application forms are available on request. Applications can be submitted directly by the individual or family member.

Helston

The Helston Welfare Trust

£700

Correspondent: Chris Dawson, Administrator, The Guildhall, Helston, Cornwall TR13 8ST (01326 572063; email: townclerk@helstontc.com)

CC Number: 1014972

Eligibility

People in need who live in the area administered by Helston Town Council (parish of Helston as constituted on 1 April, 1985)

Types of grants

Our research suggests that the trust gives one-off grants in kind. Essential electrical goods like cookers, refrigerators or furniture will be purchased on behalf of the individual.

Annual grant total

In 2013/14 the trust had an income of £2,700 and an expenditure of £800. Note that both figures tend to fluctuate. We estimate that during the year around £700 was given in grants to individuals.

Applications

In writing to the correspondent. Applications can be submitted directly by the individual or through a third party, such as a social worker or Citizens Advice. Details of need and the financial circumstances of the applicant should be included. Applications are considered upon receipt.

Devon

The Barnstaple and North Devon Dispensary Fund

£6,800

Correspondent: Christina Ford, Administrator, 17 Sloe Lane, Landkey, Barnstaple, Devon EX32 0UF (01271 831551; email: bandnddf@gmail.com)

CC Number: 215805

Eligibility

People in need who live in the North Devon parishes.

Types of grants

One-off grants towards coal and heating bills, convalescence, medical equipment and other costs, bedding, clothing, travel expenses and food.

Annual grant total

In 2013 the fund had an income of £11,800 and a total expenditure of £7,100. We estimate that grants to individuals amounted to £6,800.

Applications

In writing to the correspondent, preferably through a doctor, health visitor, social worker or other third party.

Bideford Bridge Trust

£20,000

Correspondent: P. R. Sims, Steward, 24 Bridgeland Street, Bideford, Devon EX39 2QB (01237 473122)

CC Number: 204536

Eligibility

People in need who live in Bideford and the immediate neighbourhood.

Types of grants

One-off grants ranging from £150 to £500.

Annual grant total

In 2012 the trust had assets of £15 million, an income of £1 million and made welfare grants totalling around £20,000. The accounts for 2012 were the latest available at the time of writing (July 2014). The majority of grants to individuals are given as education grants.

Exclusions

Grants are not given for computers for personal use.

Applications

On a form available from the correspondent, to be submitted at any time during the year by the individual, although a sponsor is usually required.

Edward Blagdon's Charity

£6,000

Correspondent: Joan McCahon, Clerk to the Trustees, Gunshot Cottage, Lower Washfield, Tiverton, Devon EX16 9PD (01884 253468)

CC Number: 244676

Eligibility

People in need who live in Tiverton and Washfield in Devon.

Types of grants

One-off grants only, ranging from £10 to £500. Grants may be given in monetary form directly to the individual, or through payment for the provision of suitable services/facilities.

Annual grant total

In 2012/13 the charity had an income of £16,800 and a total expenditure of £6,200. We estimate that grants to individuals totalled £6,000.

Applications

In writing to the correspondent directly by the individual or through a social worker, Citizens Advice or other welfare agency.

The Brownsdon and Tremayne Estate Charity (also known as the Nicholas Watts' Gift)

£12,900

Correspondent: Joan Stewart, Administrator, 17 Chapel Street, Tavistock, Devon PL19 8DX

CC Number: 203271

Eligibility

For the Brownsdon Fund, men in need who live in Devon, with a preference for Tavistock applicants, preferably owner/occupiers. For the Tremayne Estate Charity, people in need who live in Tavistock.

Types of grants

One-off grants of around £300. In addition to general relief-in-need, the trustees help towards the maintenance of homes owned by beneficiaries, for example, providing new carpets, grants towards the costs of roof repairs and occasionally supplying computers to people with disabilities.

Annual grant total

In 2012/13 the charity had an income of £21,000 and a total expenditure of £13,200. We estimate that grants to individuals totalled £12,900.

Exclusions

The charity does not assist with mortgage repayments.

Applications

On a form available from the correspondent. The trustees mainly advertise for applications in July, to be considered in September, but will also consider applications for emergencies at other times. Applications can be submitted directly by the individual.

Other information

The charity is known as Nicholas Watts' Gift and is made up of two different funds: the Brownsdon Fund and the Tremayne Estate Charity.

Cranbrook Charity

£1,200

Correspondent: Stephen Purser, Trustee, Venn Farm, Bridford, Exeter EX6 7LF (01647 252328; email: purseratvenn@hotmail.com)

CC Number: 249074

Eligibility

People in need who live in the parishes of Dunsford, Doddiscombesleigh and 'that part of the parish of Holcombe Burnell as in 1982 constituted part of the parish of Dunsford'. Promotion of education of people under 25 living in the area of benefit.

Types of grants

One-off and recurrent grants to those in need. Recently, grants of £80 have been given every six months for relief-in-need and educational purposes.

Annual grant total

In 2012/13 the charity had an income of £10,000 and a total expenditure of £5,400. We estimate grants to individuals for welfare purposes to be around £1,200.

Applications

In writing to the correspondent.

Other information

Grants are also made for educational purposes and to organisations as well as individuals.

The David Gibbons Foundation

£13,800 (25 grants)

Correspondent: Roger Dawe, Trustee, 14 Fore Street, Budleigh Salterton, Devon EX9 6NG (01395 445259; website: www.gibbonstrusts.org)

CC Number: 1134727

Eligibility

The elderly, sick and people with disabilities or those in need in Devon, with a preference for those from East Devon.

Types of grants

One-off grants according to need, typically ranging between £550 and £650.

Annual grant total

In 2012/13 the foundation held assets of £2.6 million and had an income of £102,000. Grants to 25 individuals totalled £13,800, with 48 organisations receiving a further £85,000.

Applications

On an application form which can be downloaded from the website and posted to the foundation. Applications must be supported by at least one letter from a professional third party such as a social worker, teacher, doctor, etc. Applications without a letter of support will not be considered. It is also helpful, but not essential, to include a copy of personal identification. All applications will be acknowledged by letter or email. The trustees usually meet in January, April, July and October; therefore, it may be three months before the success of an application is confirmed. All grants are paid by cheque and successful applicants should acknowledge receipt of the grant through the foundation's office address, or risk ineligibility for any future applications.

Note the following from the foundation's website: 'Do not send applications by Recorded Delivery post. Also ensure you have attached the correct stamps to cover the postage cost.'

Other information

The foundation was established by the will of Mr David Gibbons of Exmouth who passed away in February 2008.

Devonian Fund

£2,000

Correspondent: The Grants Administrator, The Factory, Leat Street, Tiverton EX16 5LL (01884 235887; fax: 01884 243824; email: grants@devoncf.com.; website: www.devoncf.com/apply-for-a-grant/devonian-fund)

CC Number: 1057923

Eligibility

People resident in Devon who are experiencing mobility or transport issues due to illness or disability.

Types of grants

Grants of £500 to £1,000 for items that relieve mobility problems, including specialised equipment or specialised transport such as accessible coaches or taxis.

Annual grant total

In 2012/13 the fund had an income of £15,700 and a total expenditure of £23,000. We estimate that grants to individuals totalled £2,000.

At least £21,000 was awarded in grants to organisations.

Exclusions

Grants for IT and associated equipment can only be made for up to £400.

Applications

Application forms are available to download from the Devon Community Foundation website. Applications must be made through a health care professional such as an occupational therapist, or a community group working with the individual. Applications can be made throughout the year.

Other information

This fund is administered by Devon Community Foundation.

The Dodbrooke Parish Charity (Dodbrooke Feoffees)

£12,000

Correspondent: Jane Balhatchet, Administrator, Springfield House, Ashleigh Road, Kingsbridge, Devon TQ7 1HB (01548 854321)

CC Number: 800214

Eligibility

People in need who live in the parishes of Dodbrooke and Kingsbridge.

Types of grants

One-off grants and pensions to older people.

Annual grant total

At the time of writing (August 2014) the latest financial information available was from 2012. In 2012 the charity had an income of £16,800 and a total expenditure of £25,000. We estimate the annual total of grants to individuals to be around £12,000.

Applications

In writing to the correspondent. Applications are normally considered in January, March, June and September.

Other information

The charity also makes grants to organisations, supports the parish church and rents property to local residents.

The Exeter Relief-in-Need Charity

£7,600

Correspondent: Martin King, Administrator, Exeter Municipal Charities, Chichester Mews, 22A Southernhay East, Exeter, Devon EX1 1QU (01392 201550; email: admin@exetermunicipalcharities.org.uk)

CC Number: 1002152

Eligibility

People in need who live in the city of Exeter.

Types of grants

One-off grants of between £50 and £150. Individuals can reapply in subsequent years for further support. Grants can be made towards household furniture, equipment, floor coverings, bedding, school uniforms and other clothing, essential travelling expenses, heating and lighting bills and so on.

Annual grant total

At the time of writing (August 2014) the latest financial information available was from 2012. In 2012 the charity had an income of £8,000 and a total expenditure of £7,800. We estimate that grants to individuals totalled around £7,600.

Exclusions

Grants cannot be made for debt repayment, interest on loans, rent, mortgage, or council tax arrears.

Applications

Application forms are available from the correspondent. They can be submitted directly by the individual, or through a social worker, Citizens Advice or other welfare agency. Applications should include details of the income (including benefits) and outgoings of the individual. Three references must normally be supplied. Candidates are invited for an interview with the trustees in February, May, August and November.

Other information

This charity is part of Exeter Municipal Charities.

The Heathcoat Trust

£413,000

Correspondent: Mrs C. J. Twose, Secretary, The Factory, Tiverton, Devon EX16 5LL

CC Number: 203367

Eligibility

People who are older, in poor health or financial need and live in Tiverton and the mid-Devon area. Applicants need to have a personal connection with either the John Heathcoat or the Lowman Companies.

Types of grants

One-off and recurrent grants according to need.

Annual grant total

In 2012/13 the trust had assets of £19.3 million and an income of £534,000. Grants made to individuals totalled £567,000 and were distributed as follows:

Consolidated grant	£284,000
Educational	£154,000
Death grants	£34,000
Hospital visiting	£29,500
Chiropody	£24,000
Opticians' charges	£20,000
Dentists' charges	£12,000
Communication grant	£5,000
Cases of hardship	£3,000
Employee sickness	£3,000

Applications
In writing to the correspondent.

Other information
Grants were also made to charitable organisations (£186,000 in 2012/13).

The Christopher Hill Charity

£600

Correspondent: Colin Bond, Trustee, Fortescue Crossing, Thorverton, Exeter EX5 5JN (01392 841512; email: colinbond008@btinternet.com)

CC Number: 203380

Eligibility
People in need who live in the former parish of Netherexe or in the surrounding parishes in Devon.

Types of grants
One-off grants according to need.

Annual grant total
Grants to individuals are in the region of £600 a year.

Applications
In writing to the correspondent. Applications can be submitted directly by the individual or through a third party such as Citizens Advice or a social worker. Applications are considered in December or anytime in urgent cases.

Other information
Grants are also given to organisations.

The Maudlyn Lands Charity

£2,000

Correspondent: Anthony Golding, Clerk to the Trustees, Blue Haze, Down Road, Tavistock, Devon PL19 9AG (01822 612983)

CC Number: 202577

Eligibility
People who live in the Plympton St Mary and Sparkwell areas and are in financial need.

Types of grants
One-off or recurrent grants, usually ranging between £250 and £500.

Annual grant total
In 2012 this charity had an income and expenditure of around £8,000. This is the most up to date information available at the time of writing (July 2014). We estimate the total awarded to individuals for social welfare purposes was around £2,000.

Applications
In writing to the correspondent. Applications are considered in November.

Other information
The charity also makes grants to local organisations.

Northcott Devon Foundation

£176,000 (934 grants)

Correspondent: Emma O'Loughlin, Administrator, 1b Victoria Road, Exmouth, Devon EX8 1DL (01395 269204; fax: 01395 269204; email: emma.pat@live.co.uk; website: www.northcottdevon.co.uk/home)

CC Number: 201277

Eligibility
People living in Devon who are in need as the result of illness, injury, bereavement or exceptional disadvantages.

Types of grants
One-off and recurrent grants up to £200 towards, for example, computers for children with physical disabilities, adaptations, repairs, holidays, clothing, furniture and wheelchairs.

Annual grant total
In 2012/13 the foundation held assets of £5.7 million and had an income of £199,000. A total of £176,000 was awarded in 934 grants to individuals.

A further £6,500 was awarded to organisations.

Exclusions
No grants towards long-term educational needs, funeral expenses or to relieve debts, council tax or other taxes.

Applications
On a form available from the correspondent or to download from the foundation's website. Applicants must be sponsored by a doctor, social worker, Citizens' Advice, health visitor, headteacher or a faith leader who is prepared to handle any grant on the applicant's behalf. The application must state the need for the grant, the applicant's income and expenditure, and must be accompanied by a supporting letter from the sponsor, complete with the sponsor's details. Any estimates should also be included. Cheques are made to the sponsor.

Note: applicants must have explored all statutory funding options with no success. Successful applicants must wait at least two years before reapplying.

Other information
The foundation was established in 1960 by George Northcott who relocated to Lympstone after World War ll.

South West Peninsula Football League Benevolent Fund (Millennium Benevolent Fund)

£1,700

Correspondent: Mark Hayman, Trustee, SCONICCA, 17 Nelson Place, Newton Abbot, Devon TQ12 2JH (01626 363376; email: phil@swpleague.co.uk; website: www.swpleague.co.uk)

CC Number: 1079397

Eligibility
People in need who live in the counties of Devon and Cornwall who are or were involved with or connected to the South West Peninsula Football League, and referees in the league. Grants are given to people who have disabilities, a serious illness, or have experienced a personal misfortune.

Types of grants
One-off and recurrent grants, generally ranging from £50 to £250. An example of support given in the past is an award made to a player with a depressed cheekbone fracture.

Annual grant total
In 2013/14 the fund had an income of £2,300 and an expenditure of £1,900. We estimate that grants to individuals totalled around £1,700.

Exclusions
Grants are not available to people with short-term injuries or anyone not considered to be 'in need'.

Applications
In writing to the correspondent. Applications can be made either directly by the individual or through a third party, for example, a social worker, Citizens Advice or the club secretary. Applications should include the individual's marital and employment status, number of children and length of incapacity. Supporting documentation may be required upon request. Our research indicates that the trustees meet to consider applications on the first Thursday in January, March, May, September and November, although emergency grants may be approved in between.

Tavistock, Whitchurch and District Nursing Association Trust Fund

£900

Correspondent: John Oliver, Administrator, 38 Priory Close, Tavistock, Devon PL19 9DJ (01822 612743; email: johnrica@johnrica.fsnet.co.uk)

CC Number: 200782

Eligibility

People in poor health who are in need and live in Tavistock, Whitchurch, Brentor, Mary Tavy and Peter Tavy, Lamerton, Tavistock Hamlets and part of the parish of Lydford.

Types of grants

One-off grants of up to about £100 to help with heating and water bills, travel to medical appointments, stair lifts and alarm systems to help people stay in their own homes and to assist carers in caring for spouses. Grants can occasionally be recurrent.

Annual grant total

In 2012/13, the fund had an income of £2,700 and a total expenditure of £1,800. We estimate that the total amount of grants awarded to individuals was approximately £900. The fund also awards grants to local organisations that benefit those in need.

Applications

In writing to the correspondent; to be submitted either directly by the individual or through a social worker, Citizens Advice or similar third party.

The Christine Woodmancy Charitable Foundation

£500

Correspondent: Jill Hill, Administrator, Thompson and Jackson, 4–5 Lawrence Road, Plymouth PL4 6HR (01752 665037; email: jill@thompsonandjackson.co.uk)

CC Number: 1012761

Eligibility

Children and young people under the age of 21 who live in the Plymouth area and are in need.

Types of grants

One-off grants to help maintain and educate young people in need.

Annual grant total

In 2012/13 the foundation had an income of £15,300 and a total expenditure of £12,800. However, in previous years grants have tended to be given mostly to organisations rather than individuals.

Applications

In writing to the correspondent, directly by the individual or via a social worker, Citizens Advice or other welfare agency. Applications should include background information and provide evidence of financial need.

Barnstaple

Barnstaple Municipal Charities (The Poor's Charity Section)

£350 (3 grants)

Correspondent: M. Steele, Secretary, 29 Carrington Terrace, Yeo Vale, Barnstaple, Devon EX32 7AF (01271 346354; email: barnstaplemunicipalcharities@msn.com)

CC Number: 204460

Eligibility

People in need who live in the parish of Barnstaple. People living within a five-mile radius may be considered.

Types of grants

One-off grants of about £100–£200 are available according to need.

Annual grant total

In 2012/13 the poor's charities fund had an income of over £700 and awarded grants totalling £350 to three individuals.

Applications

In writing to the correspondent. Applications are considered quarterly.

Other information

The main charity also provides almshouses and can fund certain educational costs.

Bridge Trust

£3,000

Correspondent: Peter Laurie, Clerk, The Bridge Trust, 7 Bridge Chambers, The Strand, Barnstaple EX31 1HB (01271 343995; email: chamberlain@barumbridgetrust.org; website: www.barumbridgetrust.org)

CC Number: 201288

Eligibility

People who live in the borough of Barnstaple, Devon, with a preference for people who have disabilities, older and young people. Area of benefit extends within a five-mile radius of the Guild Hall at Barnstaple.

Types of grants

Individuals are eligible for Samaritan Grants (emergency grants of up to £400) towards furniture or domestic appliances and Support or Development Grants (for example, towards attendance of a competition, voluntary work, sports, special educational needs or skills development).

Annual grant total

In 2013 the trust had assets of £4.8 million and an income of £322,000. Most of the charitable expenditure is allocated to organisations. We estimate that around £3,000 a year is available for individuals.

The Samaritan fund has £2,000 annually for distribution.

Exclusions

Recurrent grants are not given.

Applications

In writing to the correspondent. Applications must be made via a third party, such as social worker, Citizens Advice or other welfare agency at any time. Applications should provide full contact information (including telephone and email), the amount required, the purpose for which it is to be used and any additional supporting information. Payments are normally made to organisations or the supplier of items/services, not the applicant.

All applications for Support or Development Grants must be supported in writing by the sponsor (such as school/college or health professional).

Other information

The trust's main priority is the maintenance of 24 properties in Barnstaple and making grants to local organisations.

Brixham

John Mitchelmore's Charity

£1,500

Correspondent: Russell Postlethwaite, Trustee, The Tern, 38 Station Hill, Brixham, Devon TQ5 8BN (01803 851036; email: russelldenny@onetel.com)

CC Number: 235640

Eligibility

People who live in Brixham who are in need, for example due to hardship, disability or sickness.

Types of grants

One-off or recurrent grants according to need.

Annual grant total

In 2013, the charity had an income of £2,200 and a total expenditure of £3,400. We estimate that the total amount of grants awarded to individuals was approximately £1,500. The charity also awards grants to other local charities.

Applications

In writing to the correspondent.

Brixton

Brixton Feoffee Trust

£5,600

Correspondent: Sally Axell, Clerk, 15 Cherry Tree Drive, Brixton, Plymouth PL8 2DD (01752 880262; email: brixtonfeoffeetrust@googlemail.com; website: www.brixton-village.co.uk/feoffee.htm)

CC Number: 203604

Eligibility

People in need who live in the parish of Brixton, near Plymouth.

Types of grants

One-off and recurrent grants according to need. Recent grants have been given for disability aids, driving lessons, insurance costs on a Motability vehicle, pre-school costs and an orthopaedic chair.

Annual grant total

In 2012/13 the trust had assets of £1.2 million and an income of £37,000. Grants were made totalling £38,000, of which £5,600 was given to individuals, £12,000 to St Mary's Church and £20,000 to local organisations and initiatives.

Exclusions

The trust cannot give grants where the funds can be obtained from state sources.

Applications

In writing to the correspondent including as much detail as possible. Applications can be submitted directly by the individual or through a social worker, Citizens Advice or other welfare agency or third party. They are considered throughout the year.

Other information

The trust's scheme states that its net income should be shared equally between people in need in the parish of Brixton and a local church, St Mary's in Brixton, for its upkeep and maintenance. If any of the allotted money is unspent at the end of the financial year it is transferred to a third fund which is distributed to charitable schemes that benefit Brixton parish as a whole.

Budleigh Salterton

Budleigh Salterton Nursing Association

£800

Correspondent: Jenny Tilbury, Church Council Secretary, Hayes End, 1 Boucher Way, Budleigh Salterton, Devon EX9 6HQ (01395 442304; email: jenny@tilbury24.plus.com)

CC Number: 204219

Eligibility

People living in the Budleigh Salterton areas (including East Budleigh and Otterton) who are in poor health, convalescent, have disabilities or are caring for sick partners.

Types of grants

One-off grants according to need. Grants have been given for medical items, wheelchairs, raised beds, Propad cushions, mattress elevators, reclining chairs, stair lifts, audio cassettes, telephone extensions, transport costs to and from hospital and other facilities.

Annual grant total

In 2013/14 the association had an income of £4,800 and an expenditure of £1,600. We estimate that grants to individuals totalled around £800.

Applications

In writing to the correspondent. Applications can be submitted directly by the individual or through a social worker, Citizens Advice or other appropriate third party.

Other information

Grants may also be given to organisations.

The Fryer Recreational Trust

£50

Correspondent: The Administrator, 7 Coastguard Road, Budleigh Salterton, Devon EX9 6NU (01395 445945)

CC Number: 200632

Eligibility

People in need living in the local authority boundary of Budleigh Salterton, Devon.

Types of grants

One-off grants of £200 to £500 for recreation and leisure time occupation.

Annual grant total

In 2012/13 the trust had an income of £1,500 and an expenditure of £120. We estimate that about £50 was given to individuals. Note that the expenditure varies significantly each year.

Applications

In writing to the correspondent at any time. Applications can be submitted directly by the individual or through a social worker, Citizens Advice or other welfare agency.

Other information

Grants are also made to local organisations.

Cornwood

Reverend Duke Yonge Charity

£3,000

Correspondent: Janet Milligan, Administrator, 8 Chipple Park, Lutton, Ivybridge, Devon PL21 9TA

CC Number: 202835

Eligibility

People in need who live in the parish of Cornwood.

Types of grants

One-off and recurrent grants according to need. Recent grants have included help with playgroup attendance fees, a sit-in shower facility, a support chair and winter heating costs.

Annual grant total

In 2013 the charity had an income of £15,500 and a total expenditure of £12,000. We estimate that grants awarded to individuals for social welfare purposes totalled around £3,000.

Applications

In writing to the correspondent via the trustees, who are expected to make themselves aware of any need. Applications are considered at trustees' meetings.

Other information

Grants are also made for education purposes and to organisations.

Crediton

Crediton United Charities

£3,800

Correspondent: Mike Armstrong, Clerk, 5 Parr House, Lennard Road, Crediton EX17 2AP (01363 776529)

CC Number: 247038

Eligibility
People in need who have been resident in Crediton town and the parish of Crediton Hamlets for at least 12 months.

Types of grants
One-off grants of up to £300 towards, for example, nursery school costs, travel expenses, second-hand furniture, medical equipment, food, hospital expenses, electrical goods, household bills and disability equipment. 'General benefit tickets' of £5 each to buy food in local shops are also available from local health visitors.

The charity purchases goods and services from suppliers on behalf of beneficiaries whenever possible. Individuals generally do not receive payments directly.

Annual grant total
In 2012/13 the charities had both a combined income and a total expenditure of £36,000. The sum of £3,800 was awarded in 22 grants to individuals. 'General benefit tickets' were reimbursed to local traders totalling £55.

A further 4 grants were made to local organisations, amounting to £1,200.

Exclusions
Grants are not given towards house improvements or to repay existing debts.

Applications
On a form available from the correspondent. Applications can be submitted directly by the individual, or through a third party such as a social worker. Applications are considered on the first working Monday of every month and should be submitted before the end of the previous month. 'A supplementary letter is always useful'.

Other information
Crediton United Charities consists of the Crediton Relief-in-Need Charity, through which grants are made to individuals and organisations, and the Charity of Humphrey Spurway, which owns almshouses in the form of four flats and four bungalows.

Culmstock

Fuel Allotment Charity (formerly known as Culmstock Fuel Allotment Charity)

£1,500

Correspondent: Jennifer Sheppard, Administrator, Rexmead, Culmstock, Cullompton, Devon EX15 3JX (01823 680516; email: jenny@rexmead.eclipse.co.uk)

CC Number: 205327

Eligibility
People in need who live in the ancient parish of Culmstock.

Types of grants
Recurrent grants according to need for electricity and heating bills.

Annual grant total
In 2013/14 the charity had an income of £4,900 and an expenditure of £4,700. Grants usually total around £1,500.

Applications
In writing to the correspondent, directly by the individual.

Other information
Grants are also made for educational purposes.

Dartmouth

The Saint Petrox Trust Lands

£4,700

Correspondent: Hilary Bastone, Clerk/Treasurer, 30 Rosemary Gardens, Paignton, Devon TQ3 3NP (01803 666322; fax: 01803 666322; email: hilarybastone@hotmail.co.uk)

CC Number: 230593

Eligibility
People in need who live in the parish of Dartmouth and particularly within the ancient parish of St Petrox.

Types of grants
One-off grants of £100 to £500 to people affected by hardship through illness, homelessness, hospitalisation and so on for items including electrical goods, hospital expenses, household bills, travel expenses, medical equipment and furniture.

Annual grant total
In 2012/13 the trust had assets with a total book value of £705,000. However, according to the trustees' annual report for that year, the trust's properties and investment figures given in the accounts do not reflect the current market value which is much greater than the book value.

The trust had an income of £59,000 and grants totalled £4,700. There were no grants made during the year from the Ancient Buildings Scheme.

Exclusions
Recurring grants are not made.

Applications
In writing to the correspondent either directly by the individual or through a social worker, Citizens Advice, other welfare agency, or other third party on behalf of the individual. Applications should include details on the purpose of grant, proof of need and estimates of costs. They are considered in January, April, July and October.

Other information
The trustees recently stated that they would like to support more individuals in need. They have therefore widened the trust's beneficial area to cover the whole of the Parish of Dartmouth.

Grants are also given towards the upkeep of ancient buildings within the ancient parish of St Petrox (Ancient Buildings Scheme).

Exeter

Central Exeter Relief-in-Need Charity

£3,200

Correspondent: M. J. Richards, Trustee, 32 Oakley Close, Exeter EX1 3SB (01392 468531)

CC Number: 1022288

Eligibility
People in need who live in the parish of Central Exeter.

Types of grants
One-off grants usually of £50 to £150 for basic needs such as furniture, assistance with heating bills, children's clothing and mobility aids.

Annual grant total
In 2012/13, the charity had an income of £2,800 and a total expenditure of £3,400. We estimate that the total amount of grants awarded to individuals was approximately £3,200.

Exclusions
Grants are not made for educational and training needs.

Applications
In writing to the correspondent with the support of a social worker, health visitor or other welfare agency. Applications are considered in June and December.

Exeter Dispensary and Aid-in-Sickness Fund

£23,000 (121 grants)

Correspondent: Carol Cathcart, Hon. Secretary, Ridge Farm, Broadhembury, Honiton, Exeter EX14 3LU (01404 841401)

CC Number: 205611

Eligibility
People living in Exeter who are in poor financial circumstances and who are sick or have disabilities.

Types of grants

One-off grants for day-to-day needs including convalescence breaks, help with fuel or telephone bills, cooking or heating appliances, clothing, food, medical care, bedding, travel to and from hospitals and so on. The average such grant is £100. Larger grants are made towards medical appliances and aids.

Annual grant total

In 2013 the fund had assets of £910,000 and an income of £43,000. There were 121 grants made to individuals totalling £23,000.

Exclusions

Grants are not given for items which are available from public funds or for structural alterations to property.

Applications

Applications should be made through Citizens Advice, other welfare agency, a social worker or other third party such as a doctor. They should include brief details of the medical condition, the financial circumstances and the specific need. Applications are considered throughout the year for day-to-day needs and in March and November for medical appliances and so on.

Other information

Grants are also given to other organisations with similar objectives (2013: £21,000).

The Exeter Nursing Association Trust

£3,700

Correspondent: Helen Hiscox, Trustee, 1 Thompson Road, Exeter, Devon EX1 2UB (01392 211306)

CC Number: 202314

Eligibility

People in need who are receiving, or in need of, medical/nursing care, or needy employees or ex-employees of the association and the nursing profession, who live in the city and county of Exeter. Grants are also available to supplement nursing services of any kind, nursing amenities, educational facilities and any charity associated with nursing.

Types of grants

Providing and supplementing nursing services of any kind. One-off grants are also made.

Annual grant total

In 2012/13 the trust had an income of £9,100 and a total expenditure of £7,500. We estimate that grants to individuals totalled £3,700, with funding also awarded to charities associated with nursing.

Applications

In writing to the correspondent. Patients should write via their attending health visitor or district nurse; nurses should write via a senior nurse at Community Nursing Services Exeter Localities.

Exminster

Parish Lands (Exminster Feoffees)

£300

Correspondent: Raymond Adams, Trustee, 26 Exe View, Exminster, Exeter EX6 8AL (01392 833024; email: chris@chris-hodgson.co.uk)

CC Number: 212497

Eligibility

People in need living in the parish of Exminster, Devon.

Types of grants

According to our research, one-off grants and loans, usually of up to £200 each, are available. Grants have previously included cash grants and gifts in kind. About four to five grants are made each year.

Annual grant total

At the time of writing (September 2014) the latest financial information was from 2012. In 2012 the charity had an income of £1,300 and an expenditure of £700. We estimate that grants to individuals totalled around £300.

Applications

In writing to the correspondent. Applications can be submitted either directly by the individual or through a third party, such as a social worker, Citizens Advice or another welfare agency. They are normally dealt with within three weeks of receipt.

Other information

The charity gives to both individuals and organisations.

Exmouth

Exmouth Welfare Trust

£8,000

Correspondent: Lynne Elson, Trustee, 23 Hazeldene Gardens, Exmouth, Devon EX8 3JA (01395 264731)

CC Number: 269382

Eligibility

People living in the former urban district of Exmouth, comprising the parishes of Withycombe Raleigh and Littleham-cum-Exmouth who are convalescent, infirm, in need or have a disability. A fund is available for modest awards for those setting up home on a minimal budget.

Types of grants

One-off grants and gift vouchers, for example, towards dietary needs, childcare, respite costs, safety equipment, hospital expenses, electrical goods, convalescence, clothing, travel expenses, medical equipment, furniture, disability equipment and help in the home. Cheques will be payable to charities, suppliers, service providers and official departments. Payments will not be made personally to individuals.

Annual grant total

In 2012 the trust had an income of £17,800 and a total expenditure of £16,600. We estimate that social welfare grants to individuals totalled £8,000, with funding also awarded to organisations.

At the time of writing (August 2014) this was the most recent financial information available for the trust.

Exclusions

No grants for rents, rates, debts and outstanding liabilities.

Applications

On a form available from the correspondent, submitted through an independent third party (not a relative) such as a social worker, Citizens Advice, other welfare agency, or another professional or well experienced person with detailed knowledge. Applications are considered throughout the year.

Gittisham

Elizabeth Beaumont Charity

£4,000

Correspondent: Paula Land, Administrator, The Laurels, 46 New Street, Honiton, Devon EX14 1BY (01404 43431; email: paula.land@everys.co.uk)

CC Number: 202065

Eligibility

People in need who live in the parish of Gittisham, Devon.

Types of grants

Quarterly pensions and Christmas bonuses.

Annual grant total

In 2012/13 the charity had an income of £6,200 and a total expenditure of £4,100. We estimate that grants to individuals totalled £4,000.

Applications

In writing to the correspondent at any time throughout the year. Applications can be submitted directly by the individual or through a third party such as a social worker and should include details of income and any savings.

Great Torrington

The Great Torrington Town Lands Poors Charities

£9,000

Correspondent: Ian Newman, Administrator, Town Hall Office, High Street, Great Torrington, Devon EX38 8HN (01805 625738; email: greattorringtoncharities@btconnect.com)

CC Number: 202801

Eligibility

People in need who live in the former borough of Great Torrington.

Types of grants

Usually one-off grants according to need.

Annual grant total

In 2012/13 the charity had assets of £6.4 million, an income of £267,000. The total spent on charitable activities for this charity totalled £156,000 and we estimate grants to individuals for social welfare purposes to be around £9,000.

Applications

In writing to the correspondent, with all relevant personal information.

Other information

The main purpose of this charity is the provision of accommodation. Grants are provided for organisations with various purposes, pensioners, and those in need.

Highweek

Highweek Charities

£2,000

Correspondent: Lisa Hocking, Clerk and Collector, 4 Castlewood Avenue, Highweek, Newton Abbot, Devon TQ12 1NX (email: highweekcharities@hotmail.co.uk)

CC Number: 203004

Eligibility

People in need over the age of 65 who live in the ancient parish of Highweek.

Types of grants

One-off Christmas grants and other grants usually of around £50 to £60.

Annual grant total

In 2013 the charity had an income of £37,000 and a total expenditure of £27,000. Our research tells us that grants to individuals usually total around £2,000.

Applications

In writing to the correspondent, directly by the individual. Applications should be submitted in October, for consideration in November.

Other information

The charity's main priority is the management of almshouses in Highweek.

Holsworthy

Peter Speccott

£2,000

Correspondent: Denzil Blackman, Administrator, 8 Fore Street, Holsworthy, Devon EX22 6ED (01409 253262; email: denzilblackman@peterslaw.co.uk)

CC Number: 203987

Eligibility

People in need who live in Holsworthy or Holsworthy Hamlets and also in the parish of Black Torrington, Devon.

Types of grants

According to our research, grants and loans can be given to provide temporary relief for people facing unexpected loss or sudden destitution.

Annual grant total

At the time of writing (September 2014) the latest financial information was from 2012. In 2012 the charity had both an income and an expenditure of £2,100. We estimate the annual total of grants to be around £2,000. Note that this figure may vary each year.

Applications

In writing to the correspondent. The trust also advertises in local colleges, careers offices, social services and so on.

Honiton

Honiton United Charities

£5,000

Correspondent: Paula Land, Administrator, The Laurels, 46 New Street, Honiton, Devon EX14 1BY (01404 43431; email: paula.land@everys.co.uk)

CC Number: 200900

Eligibility

People in need who live in the borough of Honiton.

Types of grants

One-off and recurrent grants ranging from £50 to £100. Pensions are paid quarterly.

Annual grant total

In 2013 the charity had an income of £11,500 and a total expenditure of £10,100. We estimate that grants to individuals totalled £5,000, with organisations also receiving funding.

Exclusions

No grants to people living outside the beneficial area or for funding a gap year.

Applications

In writing to the correspondent including details of income and savings. Applications can be submitted directly by the individual or through a social worker, Citizens Advice or other welfare agency, and are considered throughout the year.

Litton Cheney

The Litton Cheney Relief-in-Need Trust

£2,200

Correspondent: Brian Prentice, Trustee, Steddings, Chalk Pit Lane, Litton Cheney, Dorchester DT2 9AN (01308 482535; email: bpprentice@gmail.com)

CC Number: 231388

Eligibility

People in need who live in the parish of Litton Cheney. Elderly people on limited income.

Types of grants

Grants are distributed once a year at the beginning of December. One-off emergency grants can be made at any time, for example, where there is a serious illness in the family or for heating and utility bills.

Annual grant total

In 2013 the trust had an income of £5,800 and an expenditure of £4,600. Grants totalled around £4,400 which were split between educational and welfare purposes.

Applications

In writing to the correspondent.

Ottery St Mary

The Non-Ecclesiastical Charity of Thomas Axe

£1,200

Correspondent: David Roberts, Administrator, 50 Claremont Field, Ottery St Mary EX11 1NP (01404 813961; email: david.coral683844@btinternet.com)

CC Number: 202725

Eligibility

Older people living in Ottery St Mary (the old Ottery St Mary Urban District Council area).

Types of grants

One-off grants ranging from £25 to £200 in 'marriage portions', and aids for the elderly and people with disabilities.

Annual grant total

In 2013 the charity had an income of £1,900 and a total expenditure of £1,300. We estimate that social welfare grants to individuals totalled £1,200.

Exclusions

Recurrent support cannot be given.

Applications

In writing to the correspondent directly by the individual. Applications are considered quarterly.

The Ottery Feoffee Charity

£100

Correspondent: John Akers, Clerk, 7 Broad Street, Ottery St Mary, Devon EX11 1BS (01404 812228; email: osmlaw@gilbertstephens.co.uk)

CC Number: 202095

Eligibility

People in need who live in the ancient parish of Ottery St Mary. Priority is usually given to older people and people with disabilities.

Types of grants

One-off grants according to need.

Annual grant total

In 2012 grants to individuals totalled just over £100.

The vast majority of this charity's funds are spent on the provision of 22 flats for people in need. So while the charity has the ability to apply up to one half of its income in grants, in reality, the costs associated with property upkeep mean that only a small amount is usually available for welfare grants.

At the time of writing (August 2014) this was the most recent financial information available for the charity.

Applications

In writing to the correspondent.

Other information

The charity also runs a small day centre.

Paignton

Paignton Parish Charity

£2,300

Correspondent: Revd Roger Carlton The Revd Prebendary, Trustee, The Vicarage, Palace Place, Paignton, Devon TQ3 3AQ (01803 551866)

CC Number: 240509

Eligibility

Poor people who are long-term residents of Paignton. In exceptional circumstances the trustees may decide to assist somebody who is resident outside Paignton.

Types of grants

Cash payments of £50 to £60 are given twice a year for use as the recipient wishes.

Annual grant total

In 2012/13 the charity had an income of £9,300 and a total expenditure of £4,900. We estimate that grants to individuals totalled £2,300, with funding also awarded to local organisations.

Exclusions

Payments are not made for living expenses.

Applications

On a form available from the correspondent. Applications are considered in May and November and should be submitted by the end of April and October respectively. They should include the applicant's age and length of residency in Paignton.

Plymouth

The Joseph Jory's Charity

£11,200

Correspondent: Jennifer Rogers, Administrator, c/o Wolferstans, 60–66 North Hill, Plymouth PL4 8EP (01752 292347)

CC Number: 235138

Eligibility

Widows over 50 who are in need and have lived in the city of Plymouth for the last seven years.

Types of grants

Small pensions, paid quarterly. Amounts vary according to available income.

Annual grant total

In 2013 the charity had an income of £12,600 and an expenditure of £11,400. We estimate that grants to individuals totalled £11,200.

Applications

The charity advertises locally when funds are available; because ongoing grants are made, funds only become available to new applicants when someone leaves the charity's list of beneficiaries. However, any new applications are kept on file.

The Ladies' Aid Society and the Eyre Charity

£10,200

Correspondent: Mrs J. M. Stephens, Administrator, Headland View, 14 Court Park, Thurlestone, Kingsbridge, Devon TQ7 3LX (01548 560891; email: r_john_venngrove@hotmail.com)

CC Number: 202137

Eligibility

Widows and unmarried women in need who live, or have lived, in Plymouth.

Types of grants

Pensions of around £100 are given quarterly to each recipient.

Annual grant total

In 2013 the charity had an income of £13,400 and a total expenditure of £10,400. We estimate that grants to individuals totalled £10,200.

Exclusions

Women who are divorced are not eligible for grants.

Applications

On a form available from the correspondent, to be submitted through a social worker, Citizens Advice, clergy, doctor, solicitor or similar third party. Before applying to the charity, the applicant should have obtained any statutory help they are entitled to.

Plymouth Charity Trust

£3,800

Correspondent: Samantha Easton, Trust Manager, Charity Trust Office, 41 Hele's Terrace, Prince Rock, Plymouth PL4 9LH (01752 663107; email: info@plymouthcharitytrust.org.uk)

CC Number: 1076364

Eligibility

People living in the city of Plymouth who are under the age of 25 and require financial assistance. In exceptional cases individuals who are otherwise qualified but reside outside the city of Plymouth, or are only temporarily resident there, may be supported at the trustees' discretion.

Types of grants

Grants are normally one-off and can be given towards a wide range of welfare needs of families with very limited income and to relieve sudden distress, sickness or infirmity. Awards range between £50 and £100 and can be given for household essentials, clothing, in Christmas gifts and so on. The trust usually makes the payment in the form of vouchers or credit at a relevant shop – payments are not made directly to the applicant.

Annual grant total

In 2012/13 the trust had assets of £2 million and an income of £361,000. Grants to individuals totalled around £4,700, consisting of donations (£1,500), Christmas vouchers (£1,800) and residents' outings subsidy (£1,300). We estimate that about £3,800 was awarded for welfare purposes.

Exclusions

Our research suggests that no grants are given to other charities, to clear debts or for any need that can be met by social services.

Applications

Application forms are available from the correspondent. Candidates should normally be referred through a third party, for example, a social worker, health professional or Citizens Advice. Applications are normally considered on the first Monday of every month.

Other information

The trust also gives grants to individuals for educational purposes and provides housing accommodation.

Sandford

Sandford Relief-in-Need Charity

£5,200

Correspondent: H. D. Edworthy, Administrator, 7 Snows Estate, Sandford, Crediton, Devon EX17 4NJ (01363 772550)

CC Number: 235981

Eligibility

People in need who live in Sandford parish. Support is mostly given to pensioners.

Types of grants

One-off grants, usually between £10 and £50, towards the repair of household utility items, bereavement expenses and fuel bills; also recurrent grants of £12 a month (to about 30 households). Christmas vouchers of £25 are also available.

Annual grant total

At the time of writing (August 2014) the latest financial information available was from 2012. In 2012 the charity had an income of £5,300 and an expenditure of £5,400. We have estimated the annual total of grants to be around £5,200.

Applications

Application forms can be requested from the correspondent. They can be submitted either directly by the individual or through a social worker, Citizens Advice, or other welfare agency. The trustees usually meet in March, September and November, but awards may also be considered outside these times.

Sidmouth

Sidmouth Consolidated Charities

£5,000

Correspondent: Ruth Rose, Administrator, 22 Alexandria Road, Sidmouth, Devon EX10 9HB (01395 513079; email: ruth.rose@eclipse.co.uk)

CC Number: 207081

Eligibility

People in need who live in Sidmouth, Sidford, Sidbury or Salcombe Regis.

Types of grants

One-off grants of up to £1,000 towards, for example, new cookers, washing machines and stairlifts, and to help with travel expenses to visit someone in hospital.

Annual grant total

In 2013 the charity had assets of £1.2 million, almost all of which was permanent endowment and unavailable for grant giving. The charity's income was £36,000 and £21,000 was spent in awarding grants to both individuals and organisations for educational and social welfare purposes. We estimate that grants to individuals for social welfare purposes was around £5,000.

Applications

In writing to the correspondent, either directly by the individual, or through a social worker, Citizens Advice or welfare agency. Applications are considered at monthly meetings.

Silverton

Silverton Parochial Charity

£9,000

Correspondent: Michelle Valance, Secretary to the Trustees, 9 Davis Close, Silverton, Devon EX5 4DL (01392 860408; email: secretary@silvertonparochialtrust.co.uk)

CC Number: 201255

Eligibility

People in need in the parish of Silverton.

Types of grants

One-off grants, with no minimum or maximum limit. Grants are towards anything that will help relieve hardship or need, such as alarms for people who are infirm, stair lifts, hospital travel costs, heating costs, medical equipment, children's clothing and wheelchairs.

Annual grant total

In 2012/13 the charity had an income of £29,000 and a total expenditure of £37,000. We estimate that grants to individuals for social welfare purposes totalled around £9,000.

Exclusions

No grants are made towards state or local authority taxes.

Applications

Application forms are available to download from the website. They can also be obtained from the Silverton Post Office or the Community Hall, or prospective beneficiaries can write to the correspondent. Completed forms can be submitted to the correspondent by the individual or by a carer or welfare department, and so on. The trustees will need details of the applicant's financial situation. Applications are considered monthly.

Other information

Grants are also made to organisations providing assistance to people in need who live in the parish and for educational purposes.

The charity has an informative website.

South Brent

Parish Lands (South Brent Feoffees)

£9,000

Correspondent: John Blackler, Clerk, Luscombe Maye, 6 Fore Street, South Brent TQ10 9BQ (01364 646180)

CC Number: 255283

Eligibility
Individuals who live or have lived in the parish of South Brent.

Types of grants
One-off or recurrent grants and Christmas gifts. Awards are generally in the range from £50 to £300 and can be for a variety of needs, including hospital transport/travel costs and special treatment where the family is in desperate need of help.

Annual grant total
In 2013 the charity had assets of around £58,000 and an income of £52,000. A total of £37,000 was given in grants. We estimate that welfare support to individuals totalled around £9,000.

Applications
Application forms can be requested from the correspondent. They can be submitted at any time either directly by the individual or through a third party, such as a family member, social worker, teacher, or an organisation, for example Citizens Advice or school.

Other information
Grants are also given to organisations and for educational purposes. The trustee's annual report from 2013 further specifies that one third of the income of the charity is to be applied for the upkeep of the parish church, one third for the benefit of deserving people in need living in the parish and one third to form the endowment of the Parish Lands Educational Foundation (to support the education and advancement in life of the parish children).

Sowton

Sowton In Need Charity

£500

Correspondent: Noel Waine, Administrator, Meadowsweet, Sowton, Exeter EX5 2AE (01392 368289; email: waine@pobroadband.co.uk)

CC Number: 204248

Eligibility
People in need who live in the parish of Sowton.

Types of grants
One-off grants for any specific educational or personal need. Grants have been given towards funeral expenses in the past.

Annual grant total
In 2013 the charity had an income of £1,800 and an expenditure of £1,500. We estimate that around £500 was made in grants to individuals for social welfare purposes.

Applications
In writing to the correspondent, to be submitted either directly by the individual or through a social worker, Citizens Advice, other welfare agency or any third party.

Other information
Grants are also given to organisations and to individuals for educational purposes.

Teignbridge

The Special People Fund

£700

Correspondent: Mervyn Nosworthy, Trustee, 5 Higher Drive, Dawlish EX7 0AS (01626 865221)

CC Number: 1110652

Eligibility
'Children who live in Teignbridge who have learning difficulties, or a disability, or are suffering emotional trauma arising from the breakdown of marriage or family life, or bereavement or social circumstances.'

Types of grants
Grants are given according to need.

Annual grant total
In 2012/13 the fund had an income of £2 and a total expenditure of £3,200. We estimate that social welfare grants to individuals totalled £700. Grants are also given to individuals for educational purposes and to organisations.

Applications
In writing to the correspondent.

Topsham

The Charity of John Shere and Others

£4,000

Correspondent: David Tucker, Trustee, 5 Elm Grove Gardens, Topsham, Exeter EX3 0EL (01392 873168; email: tucker-david@talktalk.net)

CC Number: 220736

Eligibility
People in need who live in the parish of Topsham.

Types of grants
One-off and recurrent grants in the range of £350 to £400 are given where assistance cannot be obtained from any other means. Other forms of financial assistance are available.

Annual grant total
In 2013 the charity had an income of £3,700 and a total expenditure of £4,200. We estimate that grants to individuals totalled £4,000.

Exclusions
Applicants must have lived in Topsham for at least three years.

Applications
On a form available from the correspondent. Applications can be submitted at any time either directly by the individual or through a third party such as a social worker.

Torbay

Mrs E. L. Blakeley-Marillier Charitable Fund

See entry on page 221

Torquay

The Annie Toll Bequest

£3,100 (7+ grants)

Correspondent: Keith Thompson, Trustee, Flat 6, Teneriffe, Warberry Road, Torquay TQ1 1SJ (01803 214291)

CC Number: 201197

Eligibility
Older women who live in Torquay and are in need, suffer from ill health or other hardship. Preference is given to women resident in ecclesiastical parish of St George and St Mary.

Types of grants
Recurrent grants of £400 a year and small, one-off payments for special needs, services or items, ranging from £100 to £300. Our research suggests that awards may be given towards the hire costs of equipment, for example a television.

Annual grant total
At the time of writing (August 2014) the latest financial information available was from 2012. In 2012 the charity had an income of £3,600 and an expenditure of £3,300. We estimate that grants totalled around £3,100. The charity states that currently seven individuals are receiving annual payments.

Applications
In writing to the correspondent. Applications can be made directly by the individual or through a third party, such as a social worker, Citizens Advice or other welfare agency, if applicable.

Dorset

Cole Anderson Charitable Foundation

£4,000

Correspondent: Martin Davies, Administrator, Rawlins Davy, Rowland House, Hinton Road, Bournemouth BH1 2EG (01202 558844; email: martin.davies@rawlinsdavy.com)

CC Number: 1107619

Eligibility

People in need who live in Bournemouth and Poole.

Types of grants

Grants for providing or paying for services or facilities.

Annual grant total

This foundation generally gives around £10,000 to individuals for educational and welfare purposes.

Applications

In writing to the correspondent.

Other information

The charity also awards grants to organisations.

The Beaminster Charities

£2,300

Correspondent: John Groves, Administrator, 24 Church Street, Beaminster, Dorset DT8 3BA (01308 862192; email: jan@hand-n-head.freeserve.co.uk)

CC Number: 200685

Eligibility

People in need who live in Beaminster, Netherbury and Stoke Abbott.

Types of grants

One-off grants in the range of £50 and £1,000. The trustees will consider any application. About 50 grants are made each year.

Annual grant total

In 2012 this charity had an income of £11,300 and a total expenditure of £9,600. We estimate that the total awarded to individuals for social welfare purposes was around £2,300. The latest accounts available at the time of writing (July 2014) were for year ending December 2012.

Applications

Applications can be submitted in writing to the correspondent by the individual or through a recognised referral agency such as social worker, Citizens Advice or doctor. The trustees meet throughout the year.

The Boveridge Charity

£2,800

Correspondent: Rosemary Hunt, Administrator, Brinscombe House, Lower Blandford Road, Shaftesbury, Dorset SP7 0BG (01747 852511)

CC Number: 231340

Eligibility

Poor people who are in need and have lived in the ancient parish of Cranborne (which includes the present parishes of Cranborne-cum-Boveridge, Wimborne St Giles, Alderholt, Verwood, Ferndown, West Parley and Edmondsham) for at least two years. People in need who live outside the beneficial area may also be supported in exceptional circumstances.

Types of grants

One-off grants ranging from £100 to £500. Small pensions are also available.

Annual grant total

In 2012/13 the charity had an income of £6,200 and an overall expenditure of £5,900. We estimate that grants to individuals totalled £2,800, with funding also awarded to local organisations.

Applications

In writing to the correspondent, submitted directly by the individual, through a third party such as a social worker or through an organisation such as Citizens Advice or other welfare agency. Applications are considered throughout the year and should contain details of the individual's annual income and capital, details of need, age and occupation.

The MacDougall Trust

£14,200

Correspondent: Diana Ginever, Administrator, 96 Scarf Road, Poole, Dorset BH17 8QL (01202676961; email: dginever@hotmail.com; website: www.macdougalltrust.com)

CC Number: 209743

Eligibility

People in need who live in Dorset.

Types of grants

One-off grants of up to £250 for all kinds of personal need. Only in exceptional circumstances will more than £250 be awarded, though the trust can contribute towards larger projects which will be jointly funded.

Annual grant total

In 2012/13 the trust had an income of £15,700 and a total expenditure of £14,400. We estimate that grants to individuals totalled £14,200.

Exclusions

Grants for education, sponsorship, childcare, debt, people living outside Dorset or to organisations.

Applications

On a form available from the correspondent or to download from the trust's website. Applications should be supported by a recognised agency such as Citizens Advice, a local GP, social services or a similar organisation. Forms should be returned to the administrative secretary. Applications are considered quarterly – usually in March, June, September and late November/early December – though urgent requests may be considered between meetings. For consideration at a quarterly meeting, applications should be received the month before.

Note: if the application is being made on behalf of a minor, then details of the whole family will need to be included.

The Pitt-Rivers Charitable Trust

£0

Correspondent: George Pitt-Rivers, Trustee, Hinton St Mary Estate Office, Sturminster Newton, Dorset DT10 1NA (01258 472623)

CC Number: 283839

Eligibility

People who live in rural Dorset, and North Dorset in particular, who are in need, for example, due to hardship, disability or sickness.

Types of grants

One-off grants, ranging from £100 and £1,000.

Annual grant total

In 2012/13 the trust had an income of £51,000 and a total expenditure of £47,000. No grants were made to individuals during the year.

Applications

In writing to the correspondent. No email or telephone applications will be accepted. Applications can be submitted directly by the individual or family member and are considered at any time.

St Martin's Trust

£1,700

Correspondent: Revd David Ayton, Trustee, 201 Kinson Road, Bournemouth BH10 5HB (01202 547054; email: davidj.ayton@ntlworld.com; website: www.stmartinsbooks.co.uk)

CC Number: 1065584

Eligibility

People who are in need, people who have disabilities and older people who live in Dorset.

Types of grants

One-off and recurrent grants according to need.

Annual grant total

In 2012/13 the trust had an income of £6,100 and a total expenditure of £6,900. We estimate that welfare grants to individuals totalled around £1,700.

Applications

In writing to the correspondent.

Note that the trust has informed us: 'Whilst we have made such grants in the past, our income has dropped significantly during the last year and we are unlikely to be able to make further grants for the foreseeable future.'

Other information

The trust also provided us the following information:

> St Martin's Bookshop is a charity bookshop staffed by volunteers in Bournemouth, England. St Martin's Trust is an ecumenical charity, founded in 1997 by a group of Christians who wanted to work together for the good of the local community. The funds raised from book sales are used to support local and other good causes including Michael House (a Bournemouth charity for the homeless).

Tollard Trust

See entry on page 18

The William Williams Charity

£42,000

Correspondent: Ian Winsor, Administrator, Stafford House, 10 Prince of Wales Road, Dorchester, Dorset DT1 1PW (01305 264573; email: enquires@williamwilliams.org.uk; website: www.williamwilliams.org.uk)

CC Number: 202188

Eligibility

People in need who live in the ancient parishes of Blandford, Shaftesbury or Sturminster Newton.

Types of grants

Grants of money or providing or paying for items, services or facilities which help those in need.

Annual grant total

In 2013 the charity had £7.9 million and an income of £307,000. Grants to 219 individuals totalled £140,000 with £98,000 given for education and £42,000 for welfare.

Applications

On a form available from the correspondent or the website along with guidelines.

Other information

Grants totalling £56,000 were made to 13 organisations.

Blandford Forum

Blandford Forum Charities

£500

Correspondent: Irene Prior, Administrator, Barnes Homes, Salisbury Road, Blandford Forum, Dorset DT11 7HU (01258 451810)

CC Number: 230853

Eligibility

Residents of Blandford Forum who are in need.

Types of grants

One-off grants according to need.

Annual grant total

In 2012/13 the relief-in-need charity had an income of £11,800 and made grants totalling £500. The grantmaking for welfare appears to be steadily declining.

Applications

In writing to the correspondent.

Other information

The Blandford Forum Charities include the Relief-in-Need fund, the Blandford Forum Almshouse Charity, Blandford Forum Apprenticing and Educational Foundation Charity and George Ryves Apprenticing Charity.

Charmouth

The Almshouse Charity

£900

Correspondent: Anthea Gillings, Administrator, Swansmead, Riverway, Charmouth, Bridport, Dorset DT6 6LS (01297 560465)

CC Number: 201885

Eligibility

People in need who, or whose immediate family, live in the parish of Charmouth.

Types of grants

One-off and recurrent grants, generally of £25 to £250. Grants have been given for hospital expenses, nursing fees, funeral expenses, special needs, health, sports and general living expenses. Grants can also be towards the total or part payment of the costs of equipment, such as electric chairs and cars, arthritic supports, shopping trolleys, washing machines and nebulisers. Annual grocery vouchers are given to selected people ranging from £40 to £60. The charity also makes interest-free loans.

Annual grant total

In 2013 the charity had an income of £3,800 and a total expenditure of £3,600.

Applications

In writing to the correspondent or other trustees. Applications can be submitted directly by the individual or through a third party such as a rector, doctor or trustee. They are usually considered at quarterly periods; emergencies can be considered at other times. Applications should include details of the purpose of the grant, the total costs involved, and an official letter or programme/itinerary.

Other information

Grants are also given to individuals for further and higher education and overseas voluntary work, and to youth clubs for specific purposes.

Christchurch

Legate's Charity

£5,000

Correspondent: Sarah Culwick, Administrator, 83 Brierley Road, Bournemouth BH10 6EG (01202 495273)

CC Number: 215712

Eligibility

People in need who live in the borough of Christchurch and the immediate surrounding area.

Types of grants

One-off grants for domestic items and clothes and small monthly allowances to help towards household bills. At the time of writing allowances stand at £8 per week for individuals and £10 per week for couples.

Annual grant total

In 2012 the charity had an income of £8,100 and a total expenditure of £5,200. We estimate that social welfare grants to individuals totalled around £5,000.

At the time of writing (August 2014) this was the most recent financial information available for the charity.

Applications

On a form available from the correspondent submitted either directly by the individual or through a friend, relative, social worker, Citizens Advice or other welfare agency.

Mayor's Goodwill Fund

£500

Correspondent: The Mayor's Secretary, Civic Offices, Bridge Street, Christchurch, Dorset BH23 1AZ (01202 495134; email: sroxby@christchurchandeastdorset.gov.uk)

CC Number: 263342

Eligibility

People in need who live in the borough of Christchurch.

Types of grants

One-off grants of grocery parcels, potted plants, sweets and chocolates.

Annual grant total

In 2012/13 the fund had an income of £800 and a total expenditure of £1,100. We estimate that grocery parcels, potted plants and sweets amounted to £500. Grants are also given to organisations for the provision of Christmas activities for people who are in need in the borough.

Applications

On a form available from the correspondent, to be submitted through a social worker, Citizens Advice, other welfare agency, friend, neighbour or clergy. Applications should include the applicant's name and address and details of their circumstances.

Corfe Castle

Corfe Castle Charities

£13,000 (22 grants)

Correspondent: Jenny Wilson, Clerk to the Trustees, The Spinney, Springbrook Close, Corfe Castle, Wareham, Dorset BH20 5HS (01929 480873)

CC Number: 1055846

Eligibility

People in need who live in the parish of Corfe Castle.

Types of grants

One-off grants or interest-free loans according to need. In recent years grants have been given to relieve sickness, infirmity or distress, including support for rental of emergency lifelines, help with recuperative hospital costs and payment of travel expenses for patients and visiting relatives in hospital.

Annual grant total

In 2012/13 the charity had assets of £3.2 million and an income of £241,000. There were 22 welfare grants made to individuals totalling almost £13,000.

Applications

On a form available from the correspondent, to be submitted directly by the individual. The trustees meet monthly, but emergency requests are dealt with as they arise.

Other information

Grants are also made to organisations.

Dorchester

Dorchester Relief-in-Need Charity

£1,000

Correspondent: Robert Potter, Trustee, 8 Mithras Close, Dorchester, Dorset DT1 2RF (01305 262041; email: robjoy1@talktalk.net)

CC Number: 286570

Eligibility

People in need who live in the ecclesiastical parish of Dorchester.

Types of grants

One-off grants according to need.

Annual grant total

In 2013/14 this charity had an income of £3,000 and a total expenditure of £1,700. We estimate grants to individuals for educational purposes totalled around £700 and for social welfare purposes £1,000.

Applications

Application forms are available from the correspondent and can be submitted through a social worker, health visitor, Citizens Advice or social services.

Shaftesbury

John Foyle's Charity

£3,000

Correspondent: Simon Rutter, Administrator, Cann Field House, Cann Common, Shaftesbury, Dorset SP7 8DQ (01747 851881; email: simonrutter@pwcr.co.uk)

CC Number: 202959

Eligibility

People in need who live in the town of Shaftesbury.

Types of grants

One-off and recurrent grants and loans, including those for educational toys for people who have disabilities, moving expenses, fuel, equipment, carpets and decoration. Around 15 grants a year are made ranging from £30 to £500.

Annual grant total

In 2013 the charity had an income of £6,500 and a total expenditure of £5,000. We estimate that the total amount of grants awarded to individuals was approximately £3,000. The charity also awards grants to organisations.

Exclusions

No grants for items/services that are the responsibility of the state.

Applications

In writing to the correspondent at any time. Applications can be submitted directly by the individual or through an appropriate third party and should show evidence of need, for example, benefit record, and proof of address. They can be submitted at any time, for consideration at the discretion of the trustees.

Wimborne Minster

Brown Habgood Hall and Higden Charity

£13,000

Correspondent: Hilary Motson, Administrator, White Oaks, Colehill Lane, Colehill, Wimborne, Dorset BH21 7AN (01202 886303; email: bhhh.charity@btinternet.com)

CC Number: 204101

Eligibility

Usually retired people on low income living in the ancient parish of Wimborne Minster, in Dorset.

Types of grants

One-off grants, but mainly quarterly payments. Grants are not usually for more than £200, and are mainly for smaller amounts. About 26 regular grants are given plus one-off grants.

Annual grant total

In 2013 the total income was £18,000 and total spending was £14,000. We estimate grants to individuals to be in the region of £13,000.

Applications

In writing to the correspondent either directly by the individual, through a social worker, Citizens Advice, other welfare agency or through another third party such as a doctor, health visitor or clergy. The applicant's full name, address, age and employment should be included.

Gloucester-shire

Barnwood House Trust

£125,000 (Around 350 grants)

Correspondent: Gail Rodway, Grants Manager, Ullenwood Manor Farm, Ullenwood, Cheltenham, Gloucestershire GL53 9QT (01452 611292; fax: 01452 634011; email: gail.rodway@barnwoodtrust.org; website: www.barnwoodtrust.org)

CC Number: 218401

Eligibility

People in need who live in Gloucestershire, have a long-term mental or physical disability that affects their quality of life, are on a low income and have little or no savings. Applicants are expected to seek statutory support first.

Types of grants

The trust's Wellbeing Fund offers one-off grants ranging from £50 to £750 to enable applicants live independently. Support can be given for the purchase of domestic appliances, holidays, personal items, home repairs and adaptations, disability-related equipment, mobility aids, respite care breaks, holidays, computers, clothes, selected bills and so on.

Annual grant total

In 2013 the trust had an income of £3.5 million and a total expenditure of £2.6 million. Full accounts were not available at the time of writing (August 2014); however each year around 700 individuals are supported totalling over £250,000. We estimate that wellbeing grants total about £125,000.

Exclusions

Grants are not made for:

- Funeral costs
- Medical equipment
- Private healthcare (for example, assessment, treatment or medication)
- Counselling or psychotherapy
- Top-up nursing home fees
- Private education or university tuition fees
- Council tax
- Court fines
- House purchase, rent deposits or rent in advance
- Regular payments to supplement income
- The needs of non-disabled dependents or carers
- Retrospective requests

Applications

Application forms can be downloaded from the trust's website or requested from the correspondent. All applications should be made through, or endorsed by, a social or healthcare professional (an occupational therapist, social worker, health visitor, district nurse or community psychiatric nurse). Wherever possible, the trust will visit applicants at home to discuss their needs in greater detail. The trust aims to provide an answer within ten working days of the home visit.

Other information

Small grants are made to local organisations with similar aims. The trust is also engaged in providing housing accommodation.

The trust's website specifies that the Opportunities Award offers individuals 'the chance to try something new that will enable them to move on to employment, volunteering or give them the ability to help others.'

Cheltenham Aid-in-Sickness and Nurses Welfare Fund (Gooding Fund)

£13,000

Correspondent: Patricia Newman, Administrator, Cheltenham Family Welfare Association, 21 Rodney Road, Cheltenham, Gloucestershire GL50 1HX (01242 522180; email: info@cheltenhamfamilywelfare.co.uk; website: www.cheltenhamfamilywelfare.co.uk)

CC Number: 205340

Eligibility

People in need who are engaged in domiciliary nursing in the Cheltenham area or retired nurses who were so engaged.

Types of grants

One-off and recurrent grants to those in need.

Annual grant total

In 2012/13 the fund had an income and a total expenditure of £14,900. We estimate that grants to individuals totalled £13,000.

Applications

On a form available from the correspondent. Applications should be submitted through a third party such as a health visitor, social worker or Citizens Advice.

The Fluck Convalescent Fund

£32,000 (146 grants)

Correspondent: Peter Sanigar, Administrator, c/o Whitemans Solicitors, Second Floor, 65 London Road, Gloucester GL1 3HT (01452 411601; fax: 01452 300922; email: info@whitemans.com)

CC Number: 205315

Eligibility

Women of all ages and children under 16 who live in the city of Gloucester and its surrounding area, and are in poor health or convalescing after illness or operative treatment.

Types of grants

One-off grants between £50 and £350 for recuperative holidays, clothing, bedding, furniture, fuel, food, household equipment, domestic help, respite care and medical or other aids.

Annual grant total

In 2012/13 the fund had assets of £1 million and an income of £42,000. Grants were made to 146 individuals totalling £32,000.

Exclusions

No grants are made for the repayment of debts or for recurrent payments such as rent and rates.

Applications

In writing to the correspondent through a 'responsible person' such as a social worker, medical professional or welfare organisation. Applications are considered throughout the year.

Gloucestershire Bowling Association Benevolent Fund

£300

Correspondent: Derek Severs, Administrator, 1 Wolfridge Ride, Alveston, Bristol BS35 3RA (01454 414179)

CC Number: 257886

Eligibility

Bowlers, ex-bowlers and their immediate dependents, who are in need and are present or past members of the association.

Types of grants

One-off and recurrent grants towards, for example, hospital visits.

Annual grant total

In 2012/13 the fund had an income of £200 and a total expenditure of £400.

We estimate that social welfare grants to individuals totalled £300.

Applications

In writing to the correspondent.

Sylvanus Lyson's Charity

£25,000 (60 grants)

Correspondent: A. Holloway, Administrator, Morroway House, Station Road, Gloucester GL1 1DW (01452 301903)

CC Number: 202939

Eligibility

Widows and dependents of the clergy of the Church of England in or retired from the diocese of Gloucester who are in need.

Types of grants

One-off grants according to need.

Annual grant total

In 2012/13 the charity had assets of £10 million and an income of £344,000. Individuals received 60 grants totalling £25,000.

Applications

In writing to the correspondent, directly by the individual, for consideration in March, July, September and November.

The Prestbury Charity (Prestbury United Charities)

£3,000

Correspondent: Brian Wood, Clerk, 2 Honeysuckle Close, Prestbury, Cheltenham, Gloucestershire GL52 5LN (01242 515941; email: puc.clerk@prestbury.net; website: www.prestbury.net/puc)

CC Number: 202655

Eligibility

People in need who live in the ecclesiastical parish of Prestbury and the adjoining parishes of Southam and Swindon village. Preference is given to the residents of Prestbury.

Types of grants

One-off grants according to need. Previously support has been given towards: heating costs for a person with disabilities; security lights for an elderly person; repairs and decorating costs; and assistance for single parent families.

Annual grant total

At the time of writing (August 2014) the latest financial information available was from 2012. In 2012 the charity had an income of £16,000 and an expenditure of £6,300. We have estimated the annual total of grants to individuals to be around £3,000.

Applications

In writing to the correspondent. Applications can be made directly by the individual or via a third party, such as a social worker, Citizens Advice or other welfare agency. Candidates should provide their home address, so that the charity can see that they live in the area of benefit.

Other information

Local organisations, groups and societies are also supported. The charity has an almshouse branch responsible for providing accommodation to those in need.

Bisley

The Ancient Charity of the Parish of Bisley

£3,800

Correspondent: Jane Bentley, Secretary, The Old Post Office, High Street, Bisley, Stroud GL6 7AA (01452 770756; email: bisleycharity.capb@gmail.com)

CC Number: 237229

Eligibility

People in need who live in the ancient parish of Bisley.

Types of grants

One-off grants according to need. Grants have included gifts of money to people who are sick and convalescing and have been awarded towards, for example, the costs of hospital visits, help with residential care and the support of young people pursuing work experience.

Annual grant total

In 2012/13 the charity had an income of £10,800 and a total expenditure of £7,700. We estimate that grants to individuals totalled £3,800, with organisations also receiving funding.

Exclusions

No grants towards the relief of rates or taxes. No recurrent gifts.

Applications

In writing to the correspondent.

Charlton Kings

Charlton Kings Relief-in-Need Charity

£1,500

Correspondent: Martyn Fry, Administrator, 7 Branch Hill Rise, Charlton Kings, Cheltenham GL53 9HN (01242 239903; email: martyn.fry@dsl.pipex.com)

CC Number: 204597

Eligibility

People in need who live in the parish of Charlton Kings or have a connection with the parish.

Types of grants

One-off grants of £50 to £1,000, according to need. In the past grants have been given towards travel expenses and medical equipment and can be used to help people to make a fresh start.

Annual grant total

In 2012/13 the charity had an income of £1,500 and a total expenditure of £6,100. We estimate that social welfare grants to individuals totalled £1,500. Grants are also awarded to individuals for educational purposes and to organisations.

Applications

In writing to the correspondent.

Cirencester

The Smith's Cirencester Poor Charity

£1,100

Correspondent: Maria Bell, Administrator, 7 Dollar Street, Cirencester, Gloucestershire GL7 2AS (01285 650000)

CC Number: 232383

Eligibility

People in need who have lived in the parish of Cirencester for the last three years.

Types of grants

One-off and recurrent grants towards disability aids, domestic appliances, furniture, heating bills and living expenses.

Annual grant total

In 2012/13 the charity had an income of £4,900 and a total expenditure of £2,300. We estimate that grants to individuals totalled £1,100, with local organisations also receiving funding.

Applications

Applicants should be referred through local agencies such as a medical practice or hospital, social services, Citizens Advice, or another voluntary or charitable organisation. Applications are usually considered quarterly.

Gloucester

United Charity of Palling Burgess and Others

£800

Correspondent: Margaret Churchill, Administrator, 30 Gambier Parry Gardens, Gloucester GL2 9RD (01452 421304)

CC Number: 236440

Eligibility

People in need who live in the Gloucester City Council administrative area, including people with disabilities, children and young people, and the elderly.

Types of grants

One-off cash grants and grants in kind up to a maximum value of £250.

Annual grant total

In 2012/13, the charity had an income of £1,900 and a total expenditure of £1,600. We estimate that half of the awards are given to individuals for general charitable purposes (£800) and the other half for educational purposes.

Applications

In writing to the correspondent. Applications should be submitted through a social worker, nurse, health visitor, minister of religion or similar third party and are considered twice a year in March and October. Applications should be submitted by the end of February and September respectively.

Minchinhampton

Albert Edward Pash Charitable Trust Fund

£600

Correspondent: Diana Wall, Clerk, Minchinhampton Parish Council, The Trap House, West End, Minchinhampton, Gloucestershire GL6 9JA (01453 731186; fax: 01453 731186; email: minchparish@btconnect.com)

CC Number: 278558

Eligibility

People who live in the civil parish of Minchinhampton, of any age or occupation, who are in need due, for example, to hardship, disability or sickness.

Types of grants

One-off grants according to need.

Annual grant total

A minimum of 25% of the income must be given towards hospital research each year, with the rest donated to individuals. In 2012/13 the charity had an income and expenditure of £800.

Applications

In writing to the correspondent, directly by the individual or family member. Applications should be received by 31 March for consideration in April.

Tewkesbury

Gyles Geest Charity

£9,000

Correspondent: M. Simmonds, Administrator, 10 Troughton Place, Tewkesbury GL20 8EA (01684 850697)

CC Number: 239372

Eligibility

People in need who live in the borough of Tewkesbury.

Types of grants

Grants usually average around £30 per household and are given as vouchers for use in local shops.

Annual grant total

In 2012/13 the charity had an income of £9,000 and a total expenditure of £9,200. We estimate that grants to individuals totalled £9,000.

Applications

On a form available from the correspondent, to be submitted directly by the individual or through a third party.

Other information

The charity has been in existence since 1551, when Gyles Geest established a fund for the poor of Tewkesbury.

Wotton-under-Edge

Edith Strain Nursing Charity

£600

Correspondent: Joan Deveney, Administrator, 85 Shepherds Leaze, Wotton-under-Edge, Gloucestershire GL12 7LJ (01453 844370)

CC Number: 204598

Eligibility

People who live in the town of Wotton-under-Edge and who are in need due to sickness or infirmity.

Types of grants

One-off and recurrent grants normally ranging between £50 and £100. Grants are not made where statutory money is available.

Annual grant total

Generally this charity has both an income and an expenditure of around £3,000 with approximately £600 paid to individuals who are in need due to sickness or infirmity.

Applications

In writing to the correspondent, either directly by the individual, or via a social worker, Citizens Advice or other welfare agency. An sae is required. Applications are usually considered in May and November.

Other information

Grants are also made to local organisations which care for people who are sick.

Somerset

J. A. F. Luttrell Memorial Charity

£5,000

Correspondent: Agnes Auld, Administrator, West Close, Church Road, Edington, Bridgwater, Somerset TA7 9JT (01278 722529)

CC Number: 201495

Eligibility

People in need who live in Edington, Catcott, Chilton Polden and Burtle.

Types of grants

One-off grants ranging from £25 to £500.

Annual grant total

In 2012/13, the charity had an income of £24,000 and a total expenditure of £21,000. We estimate that grants to individuals totalled £5,000, with funding also awarded to local organisations and to individuals for educational needs.

Applications

In writing to the correspondent, directly by the individual or a family member. Applications are considered in March and October and should be received by February and September respectively.

Other information

Grants are awarded to organisations which have the objective of supporting older people, environmental needs and cardiac rehabilitation.

The Nuttall Trust

£10,600

Correspondent: Nicholas Redding, Trustee, Barrington and Sons, 60 High Street, Burnham-on-Sea, Somerset TA8 1AG (01278 782371)

CC Number: 1085196

Eligibility

People in need who live in the parishes of Brent Knoll, East Brent, Mark and Lympsham in Somerset.

Types of grants

One-off grants according to need.

Annual grant total

In 2012/13 the trust had an income of £23,000 and an expenditure of £22,000. We estimate that grants to individuals totalled £10,600, with funding also awarded to local organisations.

Applications

In writing to the correspondent. Applications can be submitted directly by the individual or via a third party.

The Somerset Local Medical Benevolent Fund

£23,000

Correspondent: Dr Harry Yoxall, Secretary to the Trustees, Somerset LMC, The Crown Medical Centre, Crown Industrial Estate, Venture Way, Taunton TA2 8QY (01823 331428; email: lmcoffice@somersetlmc.nhs.uk; website: www.somersetlmc.co.uk)

CC Number: 201777

Eligibility

General medical practitioners who are practising or have practised in Somerset and their dependents who are in need.

Types of grants

One-off or recurrent grants according to need. Grants have included a contribution to the locum costs of a young GP undergoing a cardiac procedure and a donation towards the costs of a doctor absent from work to care for a sick relative. The trustees may also make a death-in-service payment to the dependents of any practising GP working in Somerset.

Annual grant total

In 2012/13 the fund had assets of £551,000 and an income of £27,000. Grants were distributed as follows:

Doctors and their dependents	£19,500
Doctors in distress (pastoral care)	£3,800
Donations to medical charities	£1,000

Grants to individuals totalled £23,000, with a further £1,000 awarded to medical charities.

Applications

In writing to the correspondent. Applications can be submitted directly by the individual or by any person on their behalf.

Bridgewater

The Tamlin Charity

£500

Correspondent: Richard Young, Clerk, 5 Channel Court, Burnham-on-Sea, Somerset TA8 1NE (01278 789859)

CC Number: 228586

Eligibility

Older people, generally those over 65, who are in need and live in Bridgwater.

Types of grants

Small quarterly pensions.

Annual grant total

In 2013 the charity had an income of £2,300 and an expenditure of around £600, which is the lowest in the past five years. We estimate that grants totalled about £500.

Applications

Application forms are available from the correspondent. They can be submitted directly by the individual or through a third party, such as a social worker, Citizens Advice or other welfare agency.

Cannington

The Cannington Combined Charity

£2,300

Correspondent: Betty Edney, Clerk to the Trustees, Down Stream, 1 Mill Close, Cannington, Bridgewater, Somerset TA5 2JA (01278 653026)

CC Number: 290789

Eligibility

People in need who live in the parish of Cannington. There is some preference for older people and those with disabilities.

Types of grants

Grants to meet regular or one-off bills where applicants cannot receive additional assistance from any other source. Other grants have been given towards a shower for a woman following major surgery, help with household expenses and travel expenses to a special school.

Annual grant total

In 2012/13, the charity had an income of £3,700 and a total expenditure of £4,700. We estimate that the total amount of grants awarded to individuals was approximately £2,300. The charity also awards grants to organisations and for educational purposes.

Applications

On a form available from the correspondent. Applications can be submitted directly by the individual or through a social worker, family member, doctor or similar third party. The trustees meet quarterly in January, April, August and November.

Draycott

Charity of John and Joseph Card (also known as Draycott Charity)

£3,800

Correspondent: Helen Dance, Administrator, Leighurst, The Street, Draycott, Cheddar, Somerset BS27 3TH (01934 742811)

CC Number: 203827

Eligibility

People in need who live in the hamlet of Draycott, near Cheddar, with a preference for those who receive a pension from the charity.

Types of grants

Pensions usually range up to £500 a year and are made to people of pensionable age on low incomes (i.e. basic pensions). One-off payments range up to £250 and can be made to people of all ages, for welfare and educational purposes.

Annual grant total

In 2012/13 the charity had an income of £4,300 and a total expenditure of £4,000. We estimate that grants to individuals totalled £3,800.

Exclusions

No grants to pay normal household bills.

Applications

For pensions apply on a form available from the correspondent and for hardship grants apply in writing. Applications for pensions are considered in November and hardship grants are considered at any time. Applications can be submitted directly by the individual or by a family member.

Ilchester

Ilchester Relief-in-Need and Educational Charity (IRINEC)

£4,000

Correspondent: Kaye Elston, Clerk, 15 Chilton Grove, Yeovil, Somerset BA21 4AN (01935 421208; website: www.ilchesterparishcouncil.gov.uk/Core/IlchesterPC/Pages/IRINEC_3.aspx)

CC Number: 235578

Eligibility

People in need who live in the parish of Ilchester only. Preference may be given to people over the age of 50.

Types of grants

One-off grants according to need are given for specific items or services.

Annual grant total

At the time of writing (August 2014) the latest financial information available was from 2012. In 2012 the charity had assets of £382,000 (mainly as a permanent endowment) and an income of £35,000. Relief in need grants totalled £4,000.

Exclusions

Grants are not available where support should be received from statutory sources.

Applications

Application forms can be requested from the correspondent. They should be submitted directly by the individual. Additional information can be obtained from the correspondent. The trustees consider grants at their monthly meetings. Evidence of financial need will be required.

Other information

Grants are also given for educational purposes. Organisations may be supported.

Pitminster

The Pitminster Charity

£3,000

Correspondent: Bryan Thomas, Trustee, Greencrest, Sellicks Green, Taunton, Somerset TA3 7SD (01823 421616)

CC Number: 281105

Eligibility

People who live or have recently lived in the parish of Pitminster and are in need.

Types of grants

One-off grants of at least £250 for items, services or facilities to reduce need. Funding has been given to assist with a hospital visit to a family member and to provide a personal alarm. Christmas gifts are given to those most in need.

Annual grant total

In 2012/13 the charity had an income of £5,700 and a total expenditure of £6,200. We estimate that welfare grants to individuals totalled £3,000, with funding also awarded to organisations and for educational purposes.

Applications

In writing to the correspondent. Applications can be submitted at any time directly by the individual or family member. Enclose an sae.

Other information

When funds permit, the trustees may also make grants towards the upkeep of recreation grounds or for other charitable purposes which will benefit the residents of Pitminster.

Porlock

The Henry Rogers Charity (Porlock Branch)

£2,200

Correspondent: Mrs C. M. Corner, Administrator, Tyrol, Villes Lane, Porlock, Minehead, Somerset TA24 8NQ (01643 862645; email: dennis.corner@talktalk.net)

CC Number: 290787

Eligibility

Older people who live in Porlock.

Types of grants

One-off grants and small monthly payments.

Annual grant total

In 2013 the charity had an income of £4,400 and a total expenditure of £2,400. We estimate that social welfare grants to individuals totalled £2,200.

At the time of writing (August 2014) the charity's Charity Commission record states that 12 pensioners are being assisted by the charity.

Applications

On a form available from the correspondent, to be submitted directly by the individual.

Rimpton

The Rimpton Relief-in-Need Charities

£700

Correspondent: John Spencer, Trustee, Field End House, Home Farm Lane, Rimpton, Yeovil, Somerset BA22 8AS (01935 850530)

CC Number: 239816

Eligibility

People in need who live in the parish of Rimpton only. Preference is generally given to older people.

Types of grants

One-off or recurrent grants according to need.

Annual grant total

Grants to individuals for welfare purposes usually total about £700 each year. Grants for education are also made.

Applications

On a form available from the correspondent, to be submitted either by the individual, a family member or through a third party.

Street

Charity of George Cox

£1,900

Correspondent: Susan Williams, Trustee, 61 The Whithys, Street, Somerset BA16 9PJ (01459 442390)

CC Number: 240491

Eligibility

People in need who live in the parish of Street.

Types of grants

One-off grants generally ranging from £50 to £100. Recent grants have been given for holidays; repair of domestic appliances such as washing machines and cookers; equipment for older people such as visual aids, second-hand furniture and carpets, and hospital travel costs. Grants are usually paid through the social services.

Annual grant total

In 2013, the charity had an income of £3,200 and a total expenditure of £3,800. We estimate that the total amount of grants awarded to individuals was approximately £1,900. The charity also awards grants to other charities or voluntary bodies.

Applications

In writing to the correspondent. Applications are usually submitted through a social worker, Citizens Advice or other welfare agency, or through one of the trustees or someone known to the trustees.

Other information

Grants are made to both organisations and individuals.

Taunton

The Taunton Aid in Sickness Fund

£6,500 (20 grants)

Correspondent: Ian Pinder, Clerk, A. C. Moles and Sons, Stafford House, Blackbrook Park Avenue, Taunton, Somerset TA1 2PX (01823 624450; email: www.tauntonaidinsicknessfund.co.uk)

CC Number: 260716

Eligibility

People in poor health who are in need and live within a four-mile radius of St Mary's Church, Taunton. Priority is given to those living in the former borough of Taunton and the parish of Trull.

Types of grants

One-off grants generally up to £200. Recent grants have been given towards holidays, travel costs, outings and entertainments, laundering, furniture, food for special diets, help with childcare costs, and many other benefits for those in poor health.

Annual grant total

In 2012/13 the fund held assets of £186,000 and had an income of £29,000. Grants were made to 20 individuals totalling £6,500.

Exclusions

There can be no grant payment for council tax, other taxes, other public funds or payment of debts. Grants cannot be made on a recurring basis.

Applications

On a form available from the correspondent. Applications should be completed and signed by a recognised referral agency such as social services or a local NHS trust. They should include details of any benefits received by the applicant and a summary of all applications made to other charities or other sources of help. Specific items of basic need should be costed and the actual amount required should be given. Applications can be made at any time.

Taunton Heritage Trust

£53,000 (286 grants)

Correspondent: Karen White, Clerk to the Trustees, Huish Homes, Magdalene Street, Taunton, Somerset TA1 1SG (01823 335348 (Mon-Fri, 9am-12pm); email: tauntonheritagetrust@btconnect.com; website: www.tauntonheritagetrust.org.uk)

CC Number: 202120

Eligibility

People who live in the Borough of Taunton Deane and are in conditions of need, hardship or distress. Applicants should not have had an application submitted on their behalf in the previous 12 months and should be eligible for/in receipt of housing benefit or another form of low income support.

Types of grants

One-off grants for specific items, for example, furniture, white goods, equipment for babies/children, household repairs/decoration, flooring, holidays, clothing, disability aids, garden equipment, bedding, counselling, computers and so on.

Annual grant total

In 2013 the trust had assets of £5.5 million and an income of £546,000. A total of £53,000 was awarded in about 286 grants for general purposes. Mostly towards furniture, white goods and household essentials.

Exclusions

Retrospective funding or replacement of statutory support (supplementary grants may be available) is not given. The trust cannot provide support towards school trips, school bags, stationery, course fees, course books, further/higher education expenses or payments for clearing debts.

Applications

Application forms are available on the trust's website or can be requested from the correspondent but must be completed by a recognised referral agency (such as a school, educational welfare agency, social services or Citizens Advice) on behalf of the candidate. They should be typed (not handwritten) and posted in four copies. The third party should verify that the applicant is in receipt of all statutory benefits to which they are entitled. Grants are considered on the first Wednesday of each month and all applications should be received by Friday preceding that date. Specific items must be itemised and costed (see further guidelines on the website).

Other information

The prime role of the charity is to provide sheltered accommodation for people over the age of 60. Grants are also made for educational purposes and to organisations.

Wiltshire

Malmesbury Community Trust

£800

Correspondent: Phil Rice, Clerk and Trustee, The First, Milbourne Lane, Milbourne, Malmesbury, Wiltshire SN16 9JH (01666 824007; email: philrice@lineone.net; website: malmesburyareacharitiestogether.weebly.com/)

CC Number: 1018458

Eligibility

People in need who live in Malmesbury and the surrounding area, with priority given to older residents.

Types of grants

Funds are allocated to individuals with the following priorities:

Priority 1 – A life threatening emergency. In such cases and immediate grant of up to £500 may be approved

Priority 2 – The elderly and other vulnerable individuals

Annual grant total

In 2013/14 the trust had an income of £143,000 and a total expenditure of £1,900. The income for the year was unusually high due to a substantial legacy left to the trust. We estimate that social welfare grants to individuals totalled around £800, with funding also awarded to organisations and projects in the community.

Applications

On an application form available from the correspondent.

Salisbury City Almshouse and Welfare Charities

£13,000 (43 grants)

Correspondent: Clerk to the Trustees, Trinity Hospital, Trinity Street, Salisbury SP1 2BD (01722 325640; fax: 01722 325640; email: clerk@almshouses.demon.co.uk; website: www.salisburyalmshouses.co.uk)

CC Number: 202110

Eligibility

People in need who live in Salisbury and district.

Types of grants

One-off grants of between £100 and £300, to meet all kinds of emergency or other needs that cannot be met from public funds. Grants can be towards, for example, essential items such as reconditioned cookers, washing machines, refrigerators, school clothing, shoes, moving costs, beds/bedding, holidays and wheelchairs.

Annual grant total

In 2013 the charities had assets of £13.7 million and an income of £1.6 million. Overall spending was £1.3 million. Welfare grants made to around 43 individuals totalled approximately £13,000. The charities usually have around £22,500 available for distribution each year.

Exclusions

No grants for debts. It is unusual for the trust to make more than one grant to an applicant in any one year.

Applications

Applications are considered in the second week of each month. Application forms should be submitted at least 15 days before and should be sponsored by a recognised professional who is fully aware of statutory entitlements and is capable of giving advice/supervision in budgeting and so on. Application forms, together with guidance notes, are available to download from the website or by contacting the clerk.

Other information

The charities' main concern is the maintenance of almshouses.

Wiltshire Ambulance Service Benevolent Fund

£2,500

Correspondent: Andrew Newman, Treasurer, 82 Dunch Lane, Melksham, Wiltshire SN12 8DX (07966 534713)

CC Number: 280364

Eligibility

Serving and retired members of the Wiltshire Ambulance Service and their dependents.

Types of grants

One-off and recurrent grants according to need.

Annual grant total

In 2012/13, the fund had an income of £17,700 and a total expenditure of £20,300. We estimate that the total amount of grants awarded to individuals was approximately £2,500.

Applications

Applicants should contact their station benevolent fund representative, who will then contact the chair on their behalf.

Other information

The fund also owns and supports three properties that provide convalescence.

Aldbourne

Aldbourne Poors' Gorse Charity

£2,000

Correspondent: Terence Gilligan, Administrator, Poor's Allotment, 9 Cook Road, Aldbourne, Marlborough, Wiltshire SN8 2EG (01672 540205; email: terrygilliganaldbourne@gmail.com)

CC Number: 202958

Eligibility

People in need who live in the parish of Aldbourne, with a preference for those over 65.

Types of grants

One-off grants towards fuel costs.

Annual grant total

In 2013 the charity had an income of £2,300 and a total expenditure of £2,300. We estimate that social welfare grants to individuals totalled £2,000.

Applications

In writing to the correspondent, directly by the individual, usually on the charity's invitation.

Ashton Keynes

The Ashton Keynes Charity

£1,600

Correspondent: Richard Smith, Trustee, Amberley, 4 Gosditch, Ashton Keynes, Swindon, Wiltshire SN6 6NZ (01285 861461)

CC Number: 205302

Eligibility

People in need who live in Ashton Keynes.

Types of grants

Grants to pensioners. In previous years as many as 180 individuals have benefited.

Annual grant total

In 2013 the trust had an income of £7,200 and a total expenditure of £6,600. We estimate that welfare grants to individuals totalled £1,600. Funding was also awarded to local organisations and to young people undertaking apprenticeships.

Applications

In writing to the correspondent.

Chippenham

Chippenham Borough Lands Charity

£16,000

Correspondent: Philip Tansley, Administrator, Jubilee Building, 32 Market Place, Chippenham, Wiltshire SN15 3HP (01249 658180; fax: 01249 446048; email: admin@cblc.org.uk; website: www.cblc.org.uk)

CC Number: 270062

Eligibility

People in need who are living within the parish of Chippenham at the date of application, and have been for a minimum of two years immediately prior to applying. People applying for mobility equipment will be asked to attend the Independent Living Centre in order for them to assess which equipment would be most appropriate.

Types of grants

One-off, and occasionally recurrent, grants and loans are made according to need. Recent grants have included help with living costs, mobility aids, domestic appliances, debt relief, travel passes, food vouchers, furniture and childcare.

Annual grant total

In 2012/13 this charity had assets of £13.2 million and an income of £436,000. Grants were given to 58 individuals totalling over £37,000. Grants are awarded to both individuals and organisations for educational, social welfare and other charitable purposes. We estimate total grants paid to individuals for social welfare purposes was around £16,000.

Exclusions

Grants are not given in any circumstances where the charity considers the award to be a substitute for statutory provision. The charity will not consider an application if a grant has been received within the past two years (or one year for mobility aids) unless the circumstances are exceptional. The charity does not make awards for the provision of carpets or Council Tax arrears.

Applications

On a form available from the correspondent. Once received the application will be looked at in detail by a welfare officer. It is possible that the charity will visit, or ask applicants to call in at this stage. Applications are considered every month and can be submitted directly by the individual or through a third party such as Citizens Advice, social worker or GP.

Other information

The charity was first established in 1554 when Queen Mary granted a Royal Charter to Chippenham. She gave Crown Land to the borough and the income was to be used to pay for two members of parliament and for the upkeep of the bridge over the River Avon. A full history of the charity can be found on its informative and helpful website.

East Knoyle

The East Knoyle Welfare Trust

£800

Correspondent: Sabrina Sully, Trustee, Old Byre House, Millbrook Lane, East Knoyle, Salisbury SP3 6AW

CC Number: 202028

Eligibility

People in need who live in the parish of East Knoyle.

Types of grants

One-off grants only, usually for heating bills.

Annual grant total

Grants awarded to individuals for social welfare purposes usually total around £800.

Applications

Applications to the correspondent or any other trustee by the end of May to receive fuel payments for the next winter.

Other information

Grants are also made for educational purposes.

Salisbury

Charity of William Botley

£6,300

Correspondent: Clerk to the Trustees, Trinity Hospital, Trinity Street, Salisbury, Wiltshire SP1 2BD (01722 325640; email: clerk@almshouses.demon.co.uk; website: www.salisburyalmshouses.co.uk)

CC Number: 268418

Eligibility

Women in need who live in the city of Salisbury.

Types of grants

One-off grants ranging from about £100 to £200, to meet all kinds of emergency and other needs which cannot be met from public funds. Recent grants have been made for second-hand white goods, clothing for mothers and children, carpets and floor coverings and holiday costs.

Annual grant total

In 2013, the charity had an income of £9,200 and a total expenditure of £6,400. We estimate that the total amount of grants awarded to individuals was approximately £6,300.

Exclusions

No grants for the payment of debts.

Applications

Application forms are available from the Salisbury City Almshouse and Welfare charity website. Applications are considered during the second week of every month and should be received at least two weeks prior to this. They should be submitted through a recognised professional such as a social worker.

Swindon

Community Foundation for Wiltshire and Swindon

£66,000 (317 grants)

Correspondent: The Grants Team, Ground Floor, Sandcliff House, 21 Northgate Street, Devizes SN10 1JX (01380 729284; email: info@wscf.org.uk; website: www.wscf.org.uk)

CC Number: 1123126

Eligibility

People in need living in Wiltshire and Swindon.

Types of grants

The foundation administers a number of funds that make welfare grants to individuals. Grants are given to older people who spend on average 10% of their income on fuel during winter. Grants of up to £200 are awarded towards, for example, paying fuel bills, purchasing oil or an oil heater, purchasing coal, topping up electricity meters or purchasing warm slippers and a blanket. Grants may also be awarded to those who have a disability or are suffering extreme hardship.

There are also funds for individuals with educational and training needs. These are the Personal Support Funds, the One Degree More Educational Fund and the Vocational Grants Fund. See the foundation's website for details.

Note: As with many community foundations, applications for open funds are subject to submission deadlines and changes in eligibility criteria. Refer to the website before pursuing an application.

Annual grant total

In 2012/13 the foundation held assets of £16.4 million and had an income of £6.75 million. A total of £179,000 was awarded in 395 grants to individuals, of these, 317 totalling £66,000 were awarded from the Surviving Winter fund.

A further £590,000 was received by 198 organisations.

Applications

Applications for assistance from the Surviving Winter Fund must be made through a recognised organisation, a list of which is available on the foundation's website. For applications for grants from other funds, visit the foundation's website to complete an expression of interest form.

Trowbridge

The Cecil Norman Wellesley Blair Charitable Trust

£8,000

Correspondent: Matthew Ridley, Administrator, 6 Middle Lane, Trowbridge BA14 7LG (01225 752289; email: redrum.ridley@gmail.com)

CC Number: 202446

Eligibility

People in need who live in the civil parish of Trowbridge. Preference is given to those in receipt of income support, job seekers allowance or pension credit.

Types of grants

Small, one-off grants, mainly in the form of vouchers for food, fuel and clothing.

Annual grant total

In 2012/13 the trust had an income of £8,400 and a total expenditure of £8,200. We estimate that welfare grants to individuals totalled £8,000.

Applications

The trust advertises the date of distribution each year in the local press – usually the first Friday in December. It issues vouchers via two distribution points and beneficiaries must go to those points and present proof that they are in receipt of statutory benefits.

Other information

In very exceptional circumstances, when there is surplus money, grants are also available for local charitable organisations.

Dr C. S. Kingston Fund

£1,500

Correspondent: Matthew Ridley, Administrator, Castle House, 6 Middle Lane, Trowbridge, Wiltshire BA14 7LG (01225 752289)

CC Number: 265423

Eligibility

People in need who live in the urban district of Trowbridge.

Types of grants

One-off grants according to need. In the past, grants have been given towards white goods, school uniforms and school trips for families not otherwise able to afford them.

Annual grant total

In 2012/13 the fund had an income of £5,200 and a total expenditure of £3,100. We estimate that grants to individuals totalled £1,500, with funding also awarded to organisations.

Applications

On a form available from the correspondent. Applications can be submitted directly by the individual, but are generally made through a social worker, doctor, Citizens Advice or other welfare agency.

Warminster

The Ernest and Marjorie Fudge Trust

£12,000

Correspondent: The Clerk, 12 Rock Lane, Warminster, Wiltshire BA12 7HD (email: jbiancoli@yahoo.co.uk; website: www.fudgetrust.co.uk)

CC Number: 298545

Eligibility

People in need who live in Warminster and surrounding areas, with a preference for people with learning difficulties.

Types of grants

One-off and recurrent grants according to need. Recent grants have been made for items such as mobility scooters, stairlifts and winter fuel payments.

Annual grant total

In 2012/13 the trust had assets of £1.3 million and an income of £53,000. A total of £46,000 was awarded to 17 individuals and 22 organisations. Grants are given for both educational and social welfare purposes. A breakdown of grants distributed was not available. We estimate that welfare grants to individuals totalled £12,000.

Applications

An application form is available to download from the website. Applications must be countersigned by a social worker, minister of religion, solicitor or some other professional person who is independent of the applicant. If you wish to discuss your application or eligibility before submitting a form, call the trust's chairperson Fran Pearson on 01985 213440 or fill out the contact form on the website.

Other information

The trust has an informative website.

Westbury

The Henry Smith Charity (Westbury)

£1,000

Correspondent: Bill White, Trustee, Pinniger Finch and Co., Solicitors, 35–37 Church Street, Westbury, Wiltshire BA13 3BZ (01373 823791; email: info@pinngerfinch.co.uk)

CC Number: 243888

Eligibility

People in need who live in Westbury and are aged over 40 years.

Types of grants

Grants of around £40 are given towards, for example, fuel, food and clothing.

Annual grant total

Grants usually total around £1,000 a year.

Applications

In writing to the correspondent.

South East

General

Anglia Care Trust

£500

Correspondent: Jane Simpson, Secretary, 65 St Matthew's Street, Ipswich, Suffolk IP1 3EW (01473 213140; email: admin@angliacaretrust.org.uk; website: www.angliacaretrust.org.uk)

CC Number: 299049

Eligibility

Offenders, ex-offenders, people who are at risk of offending, and their families, who live in East Anglia and are in need.

Types of grants

One-off grants towards rehabilitation. Grants usually range from £10 to £70 and can be given for furniture, moving into new accommodation, clothing for people seeking or starting work, basic equipment and other needs, as required. Sums of money are not usually paid direct but itemised bills will be met directly. If items can be reclaimed from either housing benefit or returnable deposit, this must be considered.

Applicants will usually already be supported by, or are known to, ACT and should have exhausted all possible sources of statutory funds.

Annual grant total

In 2012/13 the trust had assets of £1.1 million and an income of £1.4 million. The trustees' annual report from 2012/13 notes that 'grant giving is a very small part of the activities of the charity, supported from its current unrestricted reserves.' Generally grants to individuals total under £1,000.

Exclusions

Grants are not given towards payment of debts, fines, legal costs or hire purchases.

Applications

In writing to the correspondent. All applications must be supported by a probation officer or other professional person. The committees meet at least four times a year.

Other information

For this entry, the information relates to the money available from ACT. For more information on what is available throughout East Anglia, including advice and advocacy, housing services and other support, contact the correspondent and see the trust's website.

The Argus Appeal

£21,000

Correspondent: Elsa Gillio, Fundraising Co-ordinator, Argus House, Crowhurst Road, Hollingbury, Brighton BN1 8AR (01273 544465; email: elsa.gillio@theargus.co.uk; website: www.theargus.co.uk/argusappeal)

CC Number: 1013647

Eligibility

People in need, particularly older people and underprivileged children, who live in the Sussex area.

Types of grants

One-off and recurrent grants according to need and food parcels for older people. Past grants have been made to purchase computers for hospitalised children to enable them to continue with their school work and to purchase specially adapted trikes for four disabled children. More than 1,000 Christmas hampers and food vouchers were given to pensioners and low income families in 2012.

Annual grant total

In 2012 the charity held assets of £324,000 and had an income of £158,000. Grants to individuals totalled more than £21,000, of which £17,000 went towards the provision of food parcels for older people and people in need. The remaining £4,200 was given in 22 one-off grants and donations to families.

A further £43,000 was awarded to local organisations.

At the time of writing (August 2014) these were the most recent accounts available for the charity.

Applications

In writing to the correspondent including details on who you are, what you do, how much is needed, how it will be spent and what has been done so far to raise the necessary funds.

The Berkshire Nurses and Relief-in-Sickness Trust

£40,000 (135 grants)

Correspondent: Rosalind Pottinger, Honorary Secretary, 26 Montrose Walk, Calcot, Reading RG31 7YH (01189 010196)

CC Number: 205274

Eligibility

1. People in need through sickness or disability who live in the county of Berkshire and those areas of Oxfordshire formerly in Berkshire.

2. Nurses and midwives employed as district nurses in the county of Berkshire and those areas of Oxfordshire formerly in Berkshire and people employed before August 1980 as administrative and clerical staff by Berkshire County Nursing Association.

Types of grants

One-off grants only towards household accounts (excluding those below), holidays, some medical aids, special diets, clothing, wheelchairs, electronic aids for people with disabilities, hospital travel costs, prescription season tickets and so on. In 2012/13 grants ranged from £30.50 for train fares to £2,500 towards a powered wheelchair.

Annual grant total

In 2012/13 the trust held assets of £1.4 million and had an income of £64,000. A total of £40,000 was distributed in 135 grants to individuals

Exclusions

No grants for rent or mortgage payments, water rates, funeral bills, ongoing payments such as nursing home fees or any items thought to be the responsibility of statutory authorities.

Applications

On a form available from the correspondent. Applications should be made through a social worker, Citizens Advice or other welfare agency known to the trustees and supported by a member of the statutory authorities. They are considered as received and are not accepted directly from members of the public.

Other information

The trust states in its 2012/13 annual report that 'where funds allow, the trust has provided funding for local caring organisations, such as hospices and good neighbour schemes'.

The Chownes Foundation

£17,000

Correspondent: Sylvia J. Spencer, Secretary, The Courtyard, Shoreham Road, Upper Beeding, Steyning, West Sussex BN44 3TN (01903 816699)

CC Number: 327451

Eligibility

The elderly in mid-Sussex and former employees of Sound Diffusion plc who lost their pensions when the company went into receivership.

Types of grants

One-off and recurrent grants according to need.

Annual grant total

In 2012/13 the foundation had assets of £1.5 million and an income of £26,000. Grants were made to individuals totalling £33,000 broken down as £17,000 relief of poverty; and £16,000 other charitable activities.

Applications

The trustees prefer a one page document and will request further information if they require it.

Other information

The majority of the foundation's funds are committed to long-term support for poor and vulnerable beneficiaries, so only very few applications are successful.

The Derek and Eileen Dodgson Foundation

£20,000

Correspondent: Ian Dodd, Clerk to the Trustees, 8 Locks Hill, Portslade, Brighton and Hove BN41 2LB (01273 419802; email: ianwdodd@gmail.com)

CC Number: 1018776

Eligibility

People in need over 55, who live in East and West Sussex, with a strong preference for connections with Brighton and Hove.

Types of grants

On average 500 one-off grants or loans of up to £1,000 are made, mainly to older people. Most of the funds are given to local non-governmental organisations to pass on to individuals.

Annual grant total

In 2012/13 the foundation held assets of £2.1 million and had an income of £118,000. We estimate that social welfare grants to individuals amounted to around £20,000. Grants are also given for educational purposes and to organisations.

Applications

On a form available from the correspondent. Applications can be submitted either directly by the individual or through a social worker, Citizens Advice or other third party.

East Sussex Farmers' Union Benevolent Fund

£12,700

Correspondent: Gordon J. Fowlie, Trustee, Farthings, North Road, Ringmer, Lewes, West Sussex BN8 5JP (01273 812406)

CC Number: 271188

Eligibility

People in need who are farmers, farmworkers or their dependents, with priority for those who live in the county of East Sussex. When funds are available, eligible people living in Kent, Surrey and West Sussex may also be supported.

Types of grants

One-off and recurrent grants according to need.

Annual grant total

In 2012/13 the fund had assets of more than £1.4 million and an income of £36,000. Grants to individuals totalled £12,700 and were distributed as follows:

Grants and donations	£9,500
Hampers	£3,200

Applications

In writing or by telephone to the correspondent.

The Stanley Foster Charitable Trust

£1,000

Correspondent: John Graham, Trustee, 4 Meadowcroft, Bromley BR1 2JD (020 8402 1341)

CC Number: 1085985

Eligibility

People in need in south east England.

Types of grants

One-off grants up to £1,000 mainly for medical support.

Annual grant total

In 2012/13 the charity had both an income and total expenditure of £18,300. We estimate that around £1,000 was made in grants to individuals for social welfare purposes.

Applications

Grants are only made to individuals known to the trustees. The majority of grants are made to organisations.

Other information

The trust also makes grants to organisations.

The Hunstanton Convalescent Trust

£3,800

Correspondent: Fay Wilby, Trustee, 66 Collingwood Road, Hunstanton PE36 5DY (01485 533788)

CC Number: 218979

Eligibility

People who are on a low income, physically or mentally unwell and in need of a convalescent or recuperative holiday, with a preference for those living in Norfolk, Cambridgeshire and Suffolk.

Types of grants

Grants ranging from around £100 to £350 are given to provide or assist towards the expenses of recuperative holidays, including for carers. The trust can sometimes provide other items, services or facilities which will help the individual's recovery.

Annual grant total

In 2012/13 the trust had an income of £2,100 and a total expenditure of £4,000. We estimate that grants to individuals totalled £3,800.

Applications

On a form available from the correspondent, through a social worker, doctor or other welfare workers. Applications should be submitted at least one month before the proposed holiday.

The full board of trustees usually meet in January, June and September.

Jewish Care

£10,000

Correspondent: Simon Morris, Jewish Care, Amelie House, Maurice and Vivienne Wohl Campus, 221 Golders Green Road, London NW11 9DQ (020 8922 2151; email: info@jcare.org; website: www.jewishcare.org)

CC Number: 802559

Eligibility

Members of the Jewish faith who are older, mentally ill, visually impaired or physically disabled, and their families, who live in London and the south east of England.

Types of grants

Jewish Care (includes the former Jewish Welfare Board, Jewish Blind Society and the Jewish Home and Hospital at Tottenham) is the largest Jewish social work agency, providing a range of services, both domiciliary and residential. Financial assistance is not a normal part of the trust's work, though some such expenditure is inevitably associated with its social work service.

Annual grant total

In 2012/13 the trust had assets of £96 million, an income of £45 million and a total expenditure of £46 million, the majority of which went on the provision and administration of Jewish social services. In the past direct financial help was provided in the form of grants, however, despite requests to the charity we were unable to determine the value of these awards. We estimate them to total around £10,000 a year.

Exclusions

No help with burial expenses or education fees.

Applications

Initial contact should be made in writing or by contacting the helpline on 020 8922 2222.

The Elaine and Angus Lloyd Charitable Trust

£4,700 (5 grants)

Correspondent: Ross Badger, Administrator, 3rd Floor, North Side, Dukes Court, 32 Duke Street, St James's, London SW1Y 6DF (020 7930 7797; email: ross.badger@hhllp.co.uk)

CC Number: 237250

Eligibility

People 'whose circumstances are such they come within the legal conception of poverty', particularly those who require assistance due to ill-health or disability. Applications from South East England may be favoured.

Types of grants

One-off and recurrent grants according to need. Awards have ranged up to £2,000.

Annual grant total

In 2013/14 the trust had assets of £3 million and an income of £104,000. A total of £98,000 was paid in grants, of which awards to five individuals totalled £4,700.

Applications

In writing to the correspondent. The trustees meet regularly to consider grants.

Other information

The trust predominantly awards grants to organisations. Support may also be given for educational purposes.

The B. V. MacAndrew Trust

£3,800

Correspondent: Roger Clow, Trustee, 4th floor, Park Gate, 161–163 Preston Road, Brighton, East Sussex BN1 6AF (01273 562563)

CC Number: 206900

Eligibility

People in need who live in East and West Sussex.

Types of grants

One-off grants for a variety of needs including emergencies and household appliances.

Annual grant total

In 2012/13 the trust had an income of £8,600 and a total expenditure of £7,700. We estimate that grants to individuals totalled £3,800, with funding also awarded to local organisations.

Exclusions

The trust are unable to assist with bankruptcy fees or debts.

Applications

In writing to the correspondent at any time including the amount required and the name of the person the cheque is to be made out to. Applications can be made either through a third party such as a social worker or through an organisation such as Citizens Advice or other welfare agency. Applications are usually considered a month following receipt.

South East Water's Helping Hand

£100,000

Correspondent: Grants Team, Freepost RSHE-ARTT-AAUE, South East Water's Helping Hand, PO BOX 42, Peterborough PE3 8XH (01733 421060; fax: 01733 421020; email: helpinghand@southeastwater.co.uk; website: www.southeastwater.co.uk/helpinghand)

Eligibility

Domestic customers of South East Water who, through whatever difficulty, have found themselves in debt and unable to pay their water/sewerage charges.

Types of grants

Grants are initially made on a provisional basis: following the receipt of a provisional award, an applicant needs to demonstrate their commitment and ability to improve their financial sustainability and their ability to pay current and future water charges. After this period, if the applicant is judged to have taken these steps, their award will be confirmed and their debt to the company at the time of the provisional award will be cleared.

Annual grant total

In 2012/13 the parent company South East Water contributed a total of £157,000 to charitable causes, of which this fund received £111,000. We estimate that grants to individuals totalled around £100,000.

Applications

Applicants may apply online on the fund's website or by completing an application form which can be obtained via download or by telephoning the fund's application request line. Applicants must attach the relevant supporting documents, otherwise the fund will make contact before the assessment of an application begins. Such documents include: proof of income, relevant bills and evidence of any special circumstances such as disability. The application must be made in the account holders name.

Successful applicants (and those who have also successfully applied to the EOS Foundation) may not apply again. Unsuccessful applicants may reapply after six months.

Other information

The fund was founded by South East Water upon the dissolution of the EOS Foundation in April 2010 and is administered by Charis Grants.

Sussex Police Welfare Fund

£27,000

Correspondent: Lorna Stagg, Administrator, Sussex Police Headquarters, Malling House, Church Lane, Lewes, East Sussex BN7 2DZ (101 (or 01273 470101) ext. 540703; email: spct@sussex.pnn.police.uk; website: www.sussex.police.uk)

CC Number: 257564

Eligibility

Serving and retired Sussex police officers and their dependents who are in need.

Types of grants

One-off grants towards, for example, hospital travel and parking costs, emergency accommodation, essential household items, mobility problems and emergency childcare. Assistance is also given to facilitate mediation and initial legal advice.

Discretionary loans may be given to serving officers subscribing to the fund who are facing financial difficulties. Loans are repayable from salary at source per pay period. Any assistance agreed will usually be paid directly to the provider of a service requested by a member.

Annual grant total

In 2012 the fund had assets of £1.4 million and an income of £452,000. Grants were paid totalling £27,000. Though the fund's Charity Commission record states that it also makes grants to organisations, we estimate that all grants expenditure went to individuals.

Total loan help paid during the year amounted to £12,100.

At the time of writing (August 2014) this was the most recent financial information available for the fund.

Applications

By calling, emailing or writing to the fund. Your case will be dealt with by a trust adviser who will work with you to address your problems. If it is deemed appropriate they will prepare an anonymous application to the fund for financial assistance. The trust adviser then presents your application at a monthly meeting and advocates on behalf of the applicant. More urgent requests can be considered between the monthly meetings.

Other information

The fund employs two trust advisers who offer advice, information and practical support particularly to older members of the fund and those struggling with debt problems. The trust also owns a bungalow in Highcliffe, Christchurch, which is available to members in need of a recuperative break.

On 1 April 2012 the trust merged with the Sussex Police Staff Charitable Trust.

The Vokins Charitable Trust

£1,000

Correspondent: Trevor Vokins, Trustee, 56 Hove Park Road, Hove, East Sussex BN3 6LN (01273 556317)

CC Number: 801487

Eligibility

People in Brighton and Hove and East and West Sussex, particularly people with disabilities or those suffering from ill health.

Types of grants

One-off and recurrent grants according to need and mobility scooters to the less able-bodied.

Annual grant total

At the time of writing (August 2014) the latest financial information available was from 2012. In 2012 the trust had an income of £1,500 and a total expenditure of £2,000. We estimate that individual awards totalled around £1,000.

Applications

In writing to the correspondent.

Other information

Grants are also made to organisations.

The Wantage District Coronation Memorial and Nursing Amenities Fund

£3,300

Correspondent: Carol Clubb, Administrator, 133 Stockham Park, Wantage, Oxfordshire OX12 9HJ (01235 767355)

CC Number: 234384

Eligibility

People who are in poor health, convalescent or who have disabilities and live in the Wantage area of Oxfordshire.

Types of grants

One-off and recurrent grants typically ranging from around £20 to £100.

Annual grant total

In 2012/13 the fund had an income of £5,700 and a total expenditure of £3,500. We estimate that grants to individuals totalled £3,300.

Exclusions

No grants towards the relief of taxes, rates or other public funds, but grants may be applied in supplementing relief or assistance provided out of public funds.

Applications

In writing to the correspondent.

Whitton's Wishes (The Kathryn Turner Trust)

£50,000

Correspondent: Kathryn Turner, Trustee, Unit 3, Suffolk Way, Abingdon, Oxfordshire OX14 5JX (01235 527310; email: kathrynturnertrust@hotmail.co.uk)

CC Number: 1111250

Eligibility

Children, young people, the elderly and people with disabilities/special needs in the area of the old county of Middlesex. Grants can also be made in relieving the need, suffering and distress of members and former members of the armed services, their wives, husbands, widows, widowers and dependents.

Types of grants

Grants towards the costs of equipment and other support.

Annual grant total

In 2012 the trust had an income of over £201,000 and a total expenditure of nearly £200,000. Grants are made to organisations and individuals for both social welfare and educational purposes. We estimate grants to individuals totalled around £50,000. The 2012 accounts were the latest available at the time of writing.

Applications

In writing to the correspondent.

Other information

The trust's registered name is The Kathryn Turner Trust. The trust acknowledges that it relies on volunteers and youngsters working towards their Duke of Edinburgh Awards.

Bedfordshire

The Norah Mavis Campbell Trust

£0

Correspondent: Lynn McKenna, Administrator, Bedfordshire Borough Council, Borough Hall, Cauldwell Street, Bedford MK42 9AP (01234 228193; email: lynn.mckenna@bedford.gov.uk)

CC Number: 1073047

Eligibility

People who are elderly and in need who reside in the Bedford Borough Council area.

Types of grants

Grants are given according to need.

Annual grant total

In 2012/13 the trust had an income of £1,300 and a total expenditure of £0. There was no expenditure in the previous two financial years.

Applications

In writing to the correspondent.

Other information

The trust also provides additional benefits for residents at the Puttenhoe Home in Bedford.

Mary Lockington Charity

£4,150

Correspondent: Yvonne Beaumont, Administrator, Grove House, 76 High Street North, Dunstable, Bedfordshire LU6 1NF (01582 660008; email: dunstablecharity@yahoo.com)

CC Number: 204766

Eligibility

Individuals living in the parishes of Dunstable, Leighton Buzzard and Hockliffe who are in need, for example due to hardship, disability or sickness.

Types of grants

One-off grants towards items, services or facilities.

Annual grant total

In 2012/13 the charity had an income of £10,400 and a total expenditure of £8,300. We estimate the grant total to be £4,150 because the charity also gives grants to organisations that provide facilities for those in need.

Applications

In writing to the correspondent.

Other information

The charity also contributes to the upkeep of almshouses and makes grants to local organisations.

The Sandy Charities

£3,500

Correspondent: P. J. Mount, Clerk, Woodfines Solicitors, 6 Bedford Road, Sandy, Bedfordshire SG19 1EN (01767 680251; email: pmount@woodfines.co.uk)

CC Number: 237145

Eligibility

People who live in Sandy and Beeston and are in need.

Types of grants

One-off grants only ranging from £100 to £1,000, towards, for instance, motorised wheelchairs, decorating costs and children's clothing.

Annual grant total

In 2012/13 the charities had an income of £9,600 and a total expenditure of £14,800. We estimate the total amount awarded to individuals for social welfare purposes was around £3,500.

Applications

In writing to the correspondent who will supply a personal details form for completion. Applications can be considered in any month, depending on the urgency for the grant; they should be submitted either directly by the individual or via a social worker, Citizens Advice or other welfare agency.

Other information

Grants are also made to organisations and to individuals for educational purposes.

Bedford

Bedford Municipal Charities

£26,000

Correspondent: Lynn McKenna, Administrator, Bedford Borough Council, Committee Services, Borough Hall, Cauldwell Street, Bedford MK42 9AP (01234 228193; email: lynn.mckenna@bedford.gov.uk)

CC Number: 2005566

Eligibility

People in need who live in the borough of Bedford.

Types of grants

Pensions, grants towards fuel bills and other necessities, occasional one-off grants for special purposes and Christmas bonuses.

Annual grant total

In 2012/13 the trust held assets of £912,000 and had an income of £50,000. Grants to individuals totalled almost £26,000 and were distributed as follows:

Contingency grants	£21,300
Fuel grants	£1,900
Pensions	£1,400
Christmas distribution	£800
Church distribution	£300

A further £1,200 was awarded to various other charitable causes.

Applications

In writing to the correspondent. Applications can be submitted directly by the individual or through an appropriate third party. Individual applicants may be visited to assess the degree of need.

Clophill

Clophill United Charities

£3,900

Correspondent: Gillian Hill, Clerk, 10 The Causeway, Clophill, Bedford MK45 4BA (01525 860539)

CC Number: 200034

Eligibility

People who live in the parish of Clophill and are in need. Older people and individuals with disabilities are particularly supported.

Types of grants

One-off and recurrent grants are given according to need.

Annual grant total

In 2013 the charity had an income of £17,100 and a total expenditure of £15,900. We estimate that welfare grants to individuals totalled around £3,900.

Exclusions

Grants are not given where statutory funds are available.

Applications

Application forms can be obtained from the correspondent. The trustees normally meet every two months.

Other information

Grants are also made to organisations and to individuals for educational purposes.

Dunstable

Dunstable Poor's Land Charity

£4,200

Correspondent: Yvonne Beaumont, Administrator, Grove House, 76 High Street North, Dunstable, Bedfordshire LU6 1NF (01582 660008; email: dunstablecharity@yahoo.com)

CC Number: 236805

Eligibility

People, usually pensioners, who live in the parish of Dunstable.

Types of grants

Grants of around £20 each are made annually on Maundy Thursday mostly to older people on Income Support or other benefits.

Annual grant total

In 2012/13, the charity had an income of £5,900 and a total expenditure of £4,400. We estimate that the total amount of grants awarded to individuals was approximately £4,200.

Applications

By personal application to the trustees. Applicants must provide evidence of their income.

The Dunstable Welfare Trust

£200

Correspondent: Revd Richard Andrews, Trustee, The Rectory, 8 Furness Avenue, Dunstable LU6 3BN (01582 703271)

CC Number: 251859

Eligibility

People in need who live in the borough of Dunstable or in exceptional cases 'immediately' outside Dunstable. Preference is given to people who attend Church of England services.

Types of grants

One-off grants typically ranging from £50 to £100 for those in need.

Annual grant total

Grants average around £300 to 400 a year and are also given to individuals for educational purposes.

Exclusions

Grants are not given for relief of rates, taxes or other public funds. The trust may also give donations to organisations that provide services.

Applications

In writing to the correspondent through a social worker, Citizens Advice or other welfare agency or clergy. Applications are considered regularly.

Flitwick

The Flitwick Town Lands Charity

£4,000

Correspondent: David Empson, Trustee, 28 Orchard Way, Flitwick, Bedford MK45 1LF (01525 718145; email: Deflitwick8145@aol.com)

CC Number: 233258

Eligibility

People in need who live in the parish of Flitwick.

Types of grants

Usually one-off grants.

Annual grant total

In 2012/13 the charity had an income of £11,000 and total expenditure of £9,000. Grants are given for both education and welfare purposes.

Applications

On a form available from the correspondent.

Husborne Crawley

Husborne Crawley Charity Estate (formerly known as The Husborne Crawley Charities of the Poor)

£3,800

Correspondent: Rita Chidley, Administrator, 40 Leighton Street, Woburn, Milton Keynes MK17 9PH (01525 290802)

CC Number: 248497

Eligibility

People in need who live in the ancient parish of Husborne Crawley.

Types of grants

One-off grants according to need. Christmas gifts.

Annual grant total

In 2012 the charity had an income of £83,000 and assets of £92,000. Grants to individuals totalled £3,800. Grants were broken down as follows:

Christmas gifts	£1,600
Fuel allowances	£1,100
Other donations	£800
Death benefits	£300

These were the latest accounts available at the time of writing (September 2014).

Applications

In writing to the correspondent either directly by the individual or via a third party. Applications are considered throughout the year.

Other information

Grants are also made to the local Church. Grants are also given for educational purposes.

Kempston

The Kempston Charities

£1,000

Correspondent: Christine Stewart, Administrator, 15 Loveridge Avenue, Kempston, Bedford MK42 8SF (01234 302323)

CC Number: 200064

Eligibility

People in need who live in Kempston (including Kempston rural).

Types of grants

One-off grants according to need.

Annual grant total

In 2012 this charity had an income of £3,900 and a total expenditure of £3,700. Grants are awarded to individuals for both educational and social welfare purposes. Grants are also given to local schools and other local organisations. We estimate that the total grants given to individuals for social welfare purposes was around £1,000. The 2012 accounts were the latest available at the time of writing (August 2014).

Exclusions

No recurrent grants are made.

Applications

In writing to the correspondent. Applications should be made either directly by the individual or through a social worker, Citizens Advice or other welfare agency. They are considered in March, July and November.

Potton

Potton Consolidated Charity

£0

Correspondent: Dean Howard, Administrator, 69 Stotfold Road, Arlesey, Bedfordshire SG15 6XR (01462735220; email: pcc.clerk@hotmail.co.uk; website: www.potton-consolidated-charity.co.uk)

CC Number: 201073

Eligibility
People in need who live in the parish of Potton.

Types of grants
Grants are given according to need.

Annual grant total
In 2013/14 the charity had assets of £4 million and an income of £146,000. No welfare grants to individuals were made during the year.

Applications
Directly by the individual on a form available from the correspondent. Applications are considered in November and should be received by 31 October.

Other information
In 2013/14 grants were also made to organisations for education totalling £51,000. Welfare grants were also made to organisations totalling £20,000.

Ravensden

The Ravensden Town and Poor Estate

£5,700

Correspondent: Alison Baggott, Trustee, Westerlies, Church End, Ravensden, Bedford MK44 2RN (01234 771919; email: alisonbaggott@btinternet.com)

CC Number: 200164

Eligibility
Older people who are in need and live in the parish of Ravensden.

Types of grants
One-off and recurrent grants according to need.

Annual grant total
In 2013, the charity had an income of £3,700 and a total expenditure of £5,900. We estimate that the total amount of grants awarded to individuals was approximately £5,700.

Applications
In writing to the correspondent. Applications can be submitted directly by the individual. They are usually considered in November, although urgent cases can be responded to at any time.

Other information
This charity also gives grants to a local school.

Shefford

The Charity of Robert Lucas for the Poor and for Public Purposes

£1,000

Correspondent: Keith Bland, Administrator, 47 Lucas Way, Shefford, Bedfordshire SG17 5DX (01462 812870)

CC Number: 204345

Eligibility
People in need who live in the ancient township of Shefford.

Types of grants
One-off or recurrent grants for needs which cannot be met by statutory sources.

Annual grant total
In 2012 the charity had an income of £98,000 and a total expenditure of £121,500. Grants totalled £33,500. We estimate that around £1,000 was made in grants to individuals for social welfare purposes.

The 2012 accounts were the latest available at the time of writing.

Applications
In writing to the correspondent. Applications should be submitted directly by the individual and are considered every two months.

Other information
The charity primarily makes grants to organisations.

Berkshire

The Earley Charity

£11,500 (42 grants)

Correspondent: Jane Wittig, Clerk to the Trustees, The Liberty of Earley House, Strand Way, Lower Earley, Reading RG6 4EA (01189 755663; fax: 01189 752263; email: enquiries@earleycharity.org.uk; website: www.earleycharity.org.uk)

CC Number: 244823

Eligibility
People in need who have lived in Earley and the surrounding neighbourhood for at least six months. Applicants must be living in permanent accommodation and have UK citizenship or have been granted indefinite leave to remain in the UK.

In order to check whether you satisfy the geographical criterion see the map available on the website. If in doubt, get in touch with the correspondent to confirm.

Types of grants
One-off grants are given according to need to the elderly, carers and people with disabilities, individuals in need of housing, those in poor health or on low income and so on. Recent grants have been mainly given for household goods, such as washing machines, cookers, fridges/freezers, beds and bedding, other furniture, kitchen appliances, also mobility aids (wheelchairs, scooters) and sensory equipment. In the past support has been given towards gardening tools, specialist computer software, laptops, computers and counselling sessions. Grants normally do not exceed £400, but larger sums may be given for specialist medical or therapeutic equipment or essential building work and repairs.

Annual grant total
At the time of writing (August 2014) the latest financial information available was from 2012. In 2012 the charity had assets of £12.2 million and an income of £1.1 million. Grants to 42 individuals totalled £11,500.

Exclusions
Grants are not given to:

- Those who are planning to move out of the area of benefit
- People who have been awarded a grant within the last two years
- Individuals who have received 3 grants in the past
- Enter postgraduate education
- Pay for general living costs
- Cover repayment of debts
- Help with non-essential items
- Buy floor coverings and carpets (unless in very exceptional circumstances)

Applications
Application forms can be requested from the correspondent. They can be submitted either directly by the individual or through a social worker, Citizens Advice or other welfare agency. Applications for smaller grants (under £500) are considered eight times a year and for bigger awards (over £500) – quarterly. Meeting and deadline dates are published on the charity's website.

Other information
Grants are also made to organisations and local voluntary and community groups (£472,000 in 2012).

The charity's website notes that currently the main focus is on various community initiatives and projects aimed at older people.

The Finchampstead and Barkham Relief-in-Sickness Fund

£600

Correspondent: Gaynor Popplestone, Trustee, 11 Tickenor Drive, Finchampstead, Wokingham, Berkshire RG40 4UD (01189 736855; email: gaynorpopplestone@doctors.org.uk)

CC Number: 259206

Eligibility

People in need who are sick, convalescent, who have mental or physical disabilities, or who are infirm and who live in the parish of Finchampstead and Barkham.

Types of grants

One-off grants ranging from £100 to £1,000 towards the cost of, for example, electric goods, convalescence, clothing, living costs, household bills, food, holidays, travel expenses, medical equipment, nursing fees, furniture, equipment, help in the home and respite care.

Annual grant total

In 2012 the fund had an income of £3,300 and a total expenditure of £647. We estimate that social welfare grants to individuals totalled £600.

At the time of writing (August 2014) this was the most recent financial information available for the fund.

Exclusions

No grants for relief of rates or taxes. Grants cannot be repeated or renewed.

Applications

In writing to the correspondent including confirmation of eligibility. Applications can be made directly by the individual, through a social worker, Citizens Advice or other welfare agency or through a third party on behalf of the individual. Applications can be submitted throughout the year.

The Polehampton Charity

£1,700

Correspondent: Caroline White, Administrator, 65 The Hawthorns, Charvil, Reading RG10 9TS (01189 340852; email: thepolehamptoncharity@gmail.com; website: www.thepolehamptoncharity.co.uk)

CC Number: 1072631

Eligibility

People in need who live in Twyford and Ruscombe.

Types of grants

One-off grants of £100 to £250 for items such as clothing, domestic appliances, holidays, medical equipment, furniture and equipment for people who have disabilities.

Annual grant total

In 2013 the charity had an income of £97,000. The trustees annual report states: 'During the year, grants by the charity totalled £80,000. Of this, £46,500 went to local schools. The trustees made grants for books and equipment totalling £1,600, with £1,700 to individuals and £31,000 to local groups and organisations.'

Applications

Applications should be submitted either directly by the individual or a family member, through a third party such as a social worker or teacher, or through and organisation such as Citizens Advice or a school. Applications can be made at any time and are considered at trustee meetings.

Other information

Grants are also made to local schools and organisations.

Reading Dispensary Trust

£23,500 (137 grants)

Correspondent: Walter Gilbert, Clerk, 16 Wokingham Road, Reading RG6 1JQ (01189 265698; email: admin@rdt.btconnect.com)

CC Number: 203943

Eligibility

People in need who are in poor health, convalescent or who have a physical or mental disability or illness and live in Reading and the surrounding area (roughly within a seven-mile radius of the centre of Reading).

Types of grants

One-off grants of on average around £200, for a wide range of needs including beds and bedding, counselling, clothing and footwear, computer equipment and software, cooking equipment, course fees, food vouchers, furniture and carpets, glasses, instruments, holidays, travel, respite care, house and garden adaptations, repairs and redecoration, therapeutical assessments, play schemes, white goods and equipment, removals, baby and child equipment, disability and access equipment, play equipment and wheelchairs and scooters.

Annual grant total

In 2012 the trust had assets of £1.2 million and an income of £48,000. A total of £25,000 was awarded in 145 grants to individuals, most of which were given for social welfare purposes. During the year there were 5 grants awarded for course fees and books, and a further 3 grants for computer equipment and software. We estimate these grants to have totalled around £1,500.

At the time of writing (August 2014) this was the most recent financial information available for the trust.

Applications

On a form available from the correspondent. Applications should be submitted directly by the individual or through a social worker, Citizens Advice or other third party. They are considered on a monthly basis.

Other information

Grants are also made to organisations although the trust focuses on grants to individuals.

The Slough and District Community Fund

£4,600

Correspondent: David Nicks, Trustee, 7 Sussex Place, Slough SL1 1NH (01753 577475; email: dave.nicks@btinternet.com)

CC Number: 201598

Eligibility

People who are in need and live in Slough, New Windsor and Eton.

Types of grants

One-off grants according to need. Grants are typically awarded for household essentials, clothing, food and fuel costs, child and baby expenses and the like.

Annual grant total

In 2013 the fund had an income of £4,200 and a total expenditure of £4,800. We estimate that grants to individuals totalled £4,600.

Applications

On a form available from the correspondent.

Other information

This trust was formed by the amalgamation of 'All Good Causes' and 'The Slough Nursing Fund'.

The Wokingham United Charities

£2,500

Correspondent: P. Robinson, Clerk, 66 Upper Broadmoor Road, Crowthorne, Berkshire RG45 7DF (01344 351207; email: peter.westende@btinternet.com)

CC Number: 1107171

Eligibility
People in need who live in the civil parishes of Wokingham, Wokingham Without, St Nicholas, Hurst, Ruscombe and that part of Finchampstead known as Finchampstead North.

Types of grants
One-off grants towards household items, utility arrears and clothing.

Annual grant total
Grants for individuals in 2012/13 totalled around £5,000. We estimate grants awarded for social welfare purposes to be around £2,500.

Exclusions
The charity is unable to fund items that are the obligation of the state or local authority.

Applications
On a form available from the correspondent or website. Applications can be submitted directly by the individual although most often, grants are delivered through a social worker, school liaison officer or similar third party.

Other information
Wokingham United Charities 'is an amalgamation of some 21 Wokingham local charities – which date back to being some of the oldest charities in England.'

The organisation's Almshouse Charity runs a sheltered accommodation for elderly people in the area. The charity's almshouses at Westende are made up of 27 two person flats and any income generated is reinvested into the property for the benefit of residents.

The organisation has an informative website.

Binfield

The Muir Family Charitable Trust

£7,800

Correspondent: The Trustees, SG Hambros Trust Company Ltd, Norfolk House, 31 St James's Square, London SW1Y 4JR (020 7597 3065)

CC Number: 255372

Eligibility
Older people who are in need.

Types of grants
One-off and recurrent grants ranging from £300 to £1,500.

Annual grant total
In 2012/13 the trust had an income of £8,700 and a total expenditure of £15,800. We estimate that grants to individuals totalled £7,800, with funding also awarded to organisations based across the country.

Applications
In writing to the correspondent.

Other information
The trust is also known by its registered name 'The Fritillary Trust'.

Datchet

The Datchet United Charities

£3,900

Correspondent: Anita Goddard, Administrator, 25 High Street, Datchet, Slough SL3 9EQ (01759 541933)

CC Number: 235891

Eligibility
People in need who live in the ancient parish of Datchet.

Types of grants
Grants of £15 to £1,500 are given for clothing, fuel bills, living costs, food, holidays, travel expenses and household bills. Christmas vouchers are also distributed.

Annual grant total
In 2012/13 the charity had assets of £806,000 and an income of £29,900. Grants to individuals totalled £3,900 and were distributed as follows:

Christmas vouchers	£2,900
Family assistance	£1,000

An additional £11,000 was awarded to local organisations.

The charity also spent £4,800 as part of its 'People to Places' transport scheme.

Applications
In writing to the correspondent either directly by the individual or through a social worker, Citizens Advice or other welfare agency. All applicants will be visited by a social worker.

Other information
The organisation owns a day centre which local groups are able to use free of charge. Loans of medical equipment are also available.

Hedgerley

The Tracy Trust

£12,000

Correspondent: Jim Cannon, Trustee, 21 Ingleglen, Farnham Common, Slough, Bucks SL2 3QA (01753 643930; email: cannassoc@msn.com)

CC Number: 803103

Eligibility
People of a pensionable age who are in need and live in the parish of Hedgerley.

Types of grants
One-off grants towards medical and welfare needs such as spectacles, chiropody, hospital travel costs, aid alarms, TV licenses, stairlifts and so on.

Annual grant total
In 2012/13 the trust had an income of £25,000 and a total expenditure of £13,600. We estimate that £12,000 was given in grants to individuals.

Applications
In writing to the correspondent.

Newbury

The Newbury and Thatcham Welfare Trust

£2,500

Correspondent: Jacqui Letsome, Administrator, Volunteer Centre West Berkshire, 1 Bolton Place, Northbrook Street, Newbury, Berkshire RG14 1AJ (07917 414376; email: ntwt@hotmail.com; website: www.newburyandthatchamwelfaretrust.org)

CC Number: 235077

Eligibility
People in financial need who are sick, disabled, convalescent or infirm and live in the former borough of Newbury as constituted on 31 March 1974 and the parishes of Greenham, Enborne, Hamstead Marshall, Shaw-cum-Donnington, Speen and Thatcham.

Types of grants
One-off grants up to £250. Grants given include those for medical aids, food, holidays, respite care, travel, special equipment, TV licences, furniture and appliances.

Annual grant total
In 2012 the trust had an income of £2,900 and a total expenditure of £2,600. This was the most recent financial information available at the time of writing.

Exclusions
Grants are not given towards housing or rent costs and debts.

Applications
By application form submitted either through a social worker, Citizens Advice or other welfare agency or through a third party on behalf of an individual such as a doctor, health visitor or other health professional. They can be considered at any time.

Reading

St Laurence Relief-in-Need Trust

£3,100 (2 grants)

Correspondent: Jason Pyke, Treasurer, Vale and West, Victoria House, 26 Queen Victoria Street, Reading RG1 1TG (01189 573238)

CC Number: 205043

Eligibility

People in need or hardship who live in the ancient parish of St Laurence in Reading. Surplus money can be given to people living in the county borough of Reading.

Types of grants

One-off and annual grants are awarded according to need. Our research suggests that the minimum grant is £100.

Annual grant total

At the time of writing (September 2014) the latest financial information available was from 2012. In 2012 the trust held assets of £124,000 and an income of £57,000, mainly from related Church Lands and John Johnson's Estate Charities. Grants to two individuals totalled £3,100.

Exclusions

Grants are not made to students for training and research purposes or to people not resident in the area of benefit.

Applications

In writing to the correspondent. Applications can be made directly by the individual or through a third party (such as a social worker or Citizens Advice), including details of required help and the place of residence. Requests are considered twice a year, usually in April and November.

Other information

The trust gives predominantly to organisations (£56,000 to 38 institutions in 2012).

Sunninghill

Sunninghill Fuel Allotment Trust

£4,500

Correspondent: Ruth Fettes, Administrator, Sunninghill and Ascot Parish Council, The Courtyard, High Street, Ascot, Berkshire SL5 7JF (email: ruthfettes@hotmail.com)

CC Number: 240061

Eligibility

People in need who live in the parish of Sunninghill.

Types of grants

One-off grants ranging from about £100 to £1,000. Recent awards have been made to relieve sudden distress, to purchase essential equipment or household appliances and to cover utility bills.

Annual grant total

In 2012/13, the trust had an income of £79,000 and a total expenditure of £93,000. Grants to individuals totalled £4,500.

Applications

In writing to the correspondent either directly by the individual or through a third party such as a social worker, Citizens Advice or similar welfare agency. The trustees meet four times a year to consider applications, though urgent cases may be dealt with between meetings. Applicants should be prepared to provide documentary evidence of their difficulties and circumstances.

Other information

The majority of the trust's charitable giving is to organisations.

Buckinghamshire

1067 Trust Fund

£1,500

Correspondent: David Tracey, Trustee, Uplands, New Road, Bourne End, Buckinghamshire SL8 5BY (01628 528699; email: tracey@brantridge.net)

CC Number: 294975

Eligibility

People in need who live in the parishes of Wooburn, Little Marlow, Flackwell Heath, Hedsor, Bourne End and Loudwater (south of the A40) in the area of Wycombe, Buckinghamshire.

Types of grants

One-off grants in the approximate range of £30 to £500. Previously grants were broken down as follows: Equipment (£309); Rent (£120); Utilities (£112); Hamper and Medicine (£82); and Other (£10).

Annual grant total

In 2013/14 the fund had an income of £20 and a total expenditure of £1,700. We estimate that around £1,500 was made in grants to individuals for social welfare purposes.

Applications

In writing to the correspondent. Applications should be made either through a social worker, Citizens Advice or other welfare agency or directly by the individual or a third party on behalf on an individual. Applications can be submitted at any time for consideration in March, June, September or December. Emergency applications can be considered at any time.

The Amersham United Charities

Correspondent: C. Atkinson, Clerk to the Trustees, 25 Milton Lawns, Amersham, Buckinghamshire HP6 6BJ (01494 723416)

CC Number: 205033

Eligibility

Persons who are in need of financial assistance and are resident in the parishes of Amersham and Coleshill, Buckinghamshire.

Types of grants

One-off grants to relieve persons who are in need, hardship or distress.

Annual grant total

Although no grants have been made in recent years, the correspondent has stated that the charity is open to applications from individuals for relief in need and education.

Applications

In writing to the correspondent.

Other information

The main work of the charity is the administration and management of 13 almshouses.

The Iver Heath Sick Poor Fund

£2,100

Correspondent: John Shepherd, Trustee, Loch Luichart, Bangors Road North, Iver SL0 0BN (01753 651398)

CC Number: 231111

Eligibility

People who are sick, convalescing, physically or mentally disabled or infirm and who live in the Iver Heath ward of the parish of Iver and part of the parish of Wexham.

Types of grants

Usually one-off grants for clothing, medical needs, home help, fuel, lighting, chiropody and other necessities, although recurrent grants will be considered.

Annual grant total
In 2013 the fund had an income of £4,500 and a total expenditure of £2,200. We estimate that social welfare grants to individuals totalled £2,100.

Applications
In writing to the correspondent. Applications are considered twice a year in spring and autumn, although in emergencies they can be considered at other times.

Paradigm Foundation

Correspondent: Manjit Nanglu, Executive Facilitator, Paradigm Housing Group, Glory Park Avenue, Wooburn Green, High Wycombe, Buckinghamshire HP10 ODF (01628 811784; website: www.paradigmfoundation.org.uk)

CC Number: 1156204

Eligibility
Individuals in times of crisis living in an area in which Paradigm works (South East and East Midlands – see the Paradigm Group website for details).

Types of grants
Grants of up to £1,000.

Annual grant total
This is the new charitable foundation of the Paradigm Housing Group. At the time of writing (July 2014) no accounts had yet been filed with the Charity Commission.

Applications
Applications can be made online via the foundation's website. Application forms may also be downloaded and sent by post.

Other information
The foundation also makes grants to organisation working with the community in the local areas where it operates.

The Stoke Mandeville and Other Parishes Charity

£30,000

Correspondent: Caroline Dobson, Administrator, 17 Elham Way, Aylesbury HP21 9XN (01296 431859; email: smandopc@gmail.com)

CC Number: 296174

Eligibility
People in need who live in the parishes of Stoke Mandeville, Great and Little Hampden and Great Missenden. Most of the funding is given to the residents of Stoke Mandeville.

Types of grants
The charity offers annual Christmas grants to people over the age of 70, support towards senior railway cards and other one-off grants to people who have a disability, for example towards wheelchairs or stair lifts.

Annual grant total
In 2013 the charity had assets of £1.8 million and an income of £96,000. Welfare grants totalled about £30,000, comprising £9,500 in Christmas grants, £3,300 in senior railcards and £17,400 in other grants.

Applications
On a form available from the correspondent. Grants are normally considered in January, April, July and October.

Other information
The charity gives grants to individuals for education and can also support organisations.

Town Lands

£2,300

Correspondent: Julian Barrett, Trustee, South Cottage, 18 Broughton Road, Salford, Milton Keynes MK17 8BH (01908 583494)

CC Number: 256465

Eligibility
People in need who live in the parish of Hulcote and Salford.

Types of grants
Grants can be made to relieve any social welfare need of people in hardship and distress. Grants are usually one-off and range from £60 to £200. Older people and children can also receive Christmas gifts.

Annual grant total
At the time of writing (August 2014) the latest financial information available was from 2012. In 2012 the charity had an income of £7,700 and an expenditure of £9,600. We estimate that welfare support to individuals totalled around £2,300.

Applications
In writing to the correspondent. Applications can be submitted directly by the individual or through any other parishioner.

Other information
Grants are also made to organisations supporting the community.

Tyringham Pension Fund for the Blind

£1,100

Correspondent: Vanessa Jones, Trustee, 6 St Faiths Close, Newton Longville, Milton Keynes MK17 0BA (01908 643816)

CC Number: 210332

Eligibility
People in need who are blind or partially sighted and live in Newport Pagnell and Wolverton.

Types of grants
According to our research, the fund offers pensions of around £100 per year.

Annual grant total
In 2012/13 the fund had an income of £5,300 and an expenditure of £1,300. We estimate that support to individuals totalled around £1,100.

Applications
Applications should not be made directly to the fund. Individuals should contact Buckinghamshire Association for the Blind (tel. 01296 487556), who will approach the trust on their behalf.

Wooburn, Bourne End and District Relief-in-Sickness Charity

£12,000

Correspondent: Dorothea Heyes, 11 Telston Close, Bourne End, Buckingham SL8 5TY (01628 523498)

CC Number: 210596

Eligibility
People who live in the parishes of Wooburn, Bourne End, Hedsor or parts of Little Marlow who are sick, convalescent, physically or mentally disabled or infirm.

Types of grants
One-off grants and gift vouchers in the range of £50 to £400 for telephone installation, help with nursing costs, convalescence, holidays, home help and other necessities. All items for which a grant is requested must have a direct connection with the applicant's illness.

Annual grant total
In 2012 the charity had an income of £24,000 and a total expenditure of £14,000. This was the latest information at the time of writing (July 2014)

Exclusions
No recurrent grants are given.

Applications
In writing to the correspondent through a doctor, health visitor, priest or other third party. Applications are considered throughout the year and should contain details of the nature of illness or disability.

Other information
Grants are also made to organisations.

Aylesbury

Elizabeth Eman Trust

£49,000

Correspondent: Neil Freeman, Clerk, Horwood and James LLP, 7 Temple Square, Aylesbury, Buckinghamshire HP20 2QB (01296 487361; email: enquiries@horwoodjames.co.uk; website: www.emans.co.uk)

CC Number: 215511

Eligibility
Due to the expansion of the trust both men and women living in Aylesbury Vale are eligible, however, priority is still given to people born in Aylesbury.

Types of grants
Allowances of £111 per quarter, paid at the end of March, June, September and December. Grants are for life.

Annual grant total
At the time of writing (September 2014) the latest financial information available was from 2012. In 2012 the charity had assets of £639,000 and an income of £61,000. Annuities to 119 pensioners totalled £49,000.

Applications
Applications can be made online through the trust's website. Alternatively, potential applicants can print out the form or request one from the correspondent. Applicants will be informed about the outcome of their application in about a month following the submission.

Thomas Hickman's Charity

£24,000

Correspondent: John Leggett, Clerk, Parrott and Coales, 14–16 Bourbon Street, Aylesbury, Buckinghamshire HP20 2RS (01296 318500; email: doudjag@pandcllp.co.uk)

CC Number: 202973

Eligibility
People who live in Aylesbury town and are in need, hardship or distress.

Types of grants
One-off grants according to need.

Annual grant total
In 2013 the charity had assets of £18.6 million and an income of £635,000. Grants were made to 95 individuals totalling £48,000. We estimate that grants for welfare purposes totalled at least £24,000.

Applications
Application forms can be requested from the correspondent. They should be submitted either directly by the individual or through a third party, such as a family member, social worker, school or Citizens Advice. The trustees meet on a regular basis and applications are considered as they arise.

Other information
The charity provides almshouses to the elderly, supports individuals for educational purposes and makes grants to organisations. Awards to institutions totalled £49,000 and almshouse expenditure reached £270,000.

Calverton

Unknown Donor (Calverton Apprenticing Charity)

£700

Correspondent: Karen Phillips, Administrator, 78 London Road, Stony Stratford, Milton Keynes MK11 1JH (01908 563350; email: karen.phillips30@yahoo.co.uk)

CC Number: 239246

Eligibility
People in need who have lived in the parish of All Saints, Calverton. Preference is given to people over the age of 65 and widows.

Types of grants
Grants, generally in the range of £100 to £150, can be awarded for essential items, such as clothing, medical equipment, nursing fees, furniture, heating and so on.

Annual grant total
In 2013/14 the charity had an income of £2,200 and a total expenditure of £2,800. We estimate that welfare grants to individuals totalled around £700. Our research suggests that grants for welfare purposes usually total around £1,000 annually.

Applications
Application forms can be requested from the correspondent. They can be submitted directly by the individual or a family member.

Other information
The charity also makes grants to organisations and to individual for educational purposes.

Cheddington

Cheddington Town Lands Charity

£2,000

Correspondent: Stuart Minall, 10 Hillside, Cheddington, Leighton Buzzard LU7 0SP (01296 661987)

CC Number: 235076

Eligibility
People in need who live in Cheddington.

Types of grants
One-off and recurrent grants according to need.

Annual grant total
In 2012/13 the charity's income was £13,000 and total expenditure £17,000. One third of the charity's income is paid to the parish church and the remaining income divided between local organisations and individuals for welfare and educational purposes. We estimate welfare grants to be around £2,000.

Applications
In writing to the correspondent, directly by the individual or a family member.

Other information
The charity also gives to community organisations and individuals for educational purposes.

Emberton

Emberton United Charity

£2,500

Correspondent: Warwick Clarke, Trustee, Old Pits, West Lane, Emberton, Olney, Bucks MK46 5DA (01234 713174)

CC Number: 204221

Eligibility
Older people in need who live in the parish of Emberton.

Types of grants
One-off and recurrent grants, usually of up to £350.

Annual grant total

In 2013 the charity had an income of £38,000 and a total expenditure of £38,500. Grants awarded to individuals for social welfare purposes totalled £2,500.

Applications

In writing to the correspondent, directly by the individual.

Other information

Grants are also given for educational purposes.

Great Linford

Great Linford Relief in Need Charity

£500

Correspondent: Michael Williamson, Trustee, 2 Lodge Gate, Great Linford, Milton Keynes MK14 5EW (01908 605664)

CC Number: 237373

Eligibility

People in need who live in the parish of Great Linford.

Types of grants

One-off grants of up to £200. Grants have been given towards educational activities and to assist with the cost of sheltered housing.

Annual grant total

Grants for individuals usually total about £500 each year.

Applications

On a form available from the charity. Applications can be submitted either directly by the individual or through a social worker, Citizens Advice, other welfare agency or a third party such as a relative, teacher or carer. Applications are usually considered in January, June and September.

High Wycombe

The High Wycombe Central Aid Society

£3,400 (59 grants)

Correspondent: Stuart Allen, Secretary, Central Aid, West Richardson Street, High Wycombe, Buckinghamshire HP11 2SB (01494 535890; fax: 01494 538256; email: office@central-aid.org.uk; website: www.central-aid.org.uk)

CC Number: 201445

Eligibility

People in need, usually older people and those in receipt of benefits, who live in the old borough of High Wycombe. The society will also help ex-service personnel and their dependents.

Types of grants

Mainly one-off grants in kind and gift vouchers to a maximum of £100. Recent grants have been given for food, clothing and furniture.

Annual grant total

In 2012/13 the society had assets of £409,000 and an income of £161,000. Grants totalled £3,400 and were distributed to 59 families through the society's furniture warehouse.

Exclusions

No grants towards council tax.

Applications

In writing to the correspondent including details of income, savings, family situation and a quote for the goods needed along with any relevant supporting documents. Applications can be submitted through a social worker, Citizens Advice or other welfare agency and are considered on a monthly basis.

Other information

Up to 190 people over the age of 50 use the Pensioners Pop-In each week. The society also runs an SSAFA office, through which £30,000 was raised for ex-service personnel in 2012/13.

The society has a second-hand furniture warehouse and clothes and soft furnishings store (Tel: 01494 443459, Email: furniture@central-aid.org.uk).

Hitcham

Hitcham Poor Lands Charity

£2,200

Correspondent: Donald Cecil Lindskog, Trustee, Little Orchard, Poyle Lane, Burnham, Slough SL1 8JZ (01628 605652)

CC Number: 203447

Eligibility

People in need who live in the parishes of Hitcham, Burnham and Cippenham.

Types of grants

Gifts in kind including furniture, white goods and school uniforms. Grants are available towards the costs of school trips and carer's holidays. Around 300 Christmas parcels are distributed each year.

Annual grant total

In 2012/13 the charity had an income of £7,100 and a total expenditure of £4,600. We estimate that grants to individuals totalled £2,200, with funding also awarded to local organisations.

Applications

In writing to the correspondent. Applications can be submitted directly by the individual or through a third party such as Citizens Advice or a social worker. There are no deadlines for applications and they are considered frequently.

Other information

The trust supports The Burnham Righthouse Project and Thames Hospice Care, which operate in the local area.

Radnage

Radnage Charity

£4,600

Correspondent: Ian Blaylock, Clerk to the Trustees, Hilltop, Green End Road, Radnage, High Wycombe, Buckinghamshire HP14 4BY (01494 483346)

CC Number: 201762

Eligibility

People in need who live in the parish of Radnage.

Types of grants

One-off and recurrent grants of around £50 to £200. Grants have been given towards food and hospital visits.

Annual grant total

In 2013 the charity had an income of £10,000 and a total expenditure of £10,100. We estimate that grants to individuals totalled £4,600, with local organisations also receiving funding.

Applications

In writing to the correspondent either directly by the individual or, where applicable, through a social worker, Citizens Advice or other third party.

Other information

The charity also contributes to the upkeep of the village's twelfth-century parish church.

Stoke Poges

Stoke Poges United Charity

£1,500

Correspondent: Anthony Levings, Clerk, The Cedars, Stratford Drive, Wooburn Green, High Wycombe HP10 0QH (email: anthony@levings123.wanadoo.co.uk)

CC Number: 205289

Eligibility

People in need who live in the parish of Stoke Poges and the surrounding area, including parts of the parish of Slough Borough – Stoke wards. Preference is given to widows and people who are sick.

Types of grants

According to our research, grants of £30 to £1,500 can be given for clothing, food, household necessities, medical care and equipment.

Annual grant total

In 2013 the charity had an income of £46,000 and an expenditure of £6,300. At the time of writing (September 2014) full accounts were not available. We estimate that about £1,500 was given in welfare support to individuals.

Applications

In writing to the correspondent. Applications should be submitted either directly by the individual or through a third party, such as a social worker, Citizens Advice or other welfare agency.

Other information

Organisations may also be supported.

Stony Stratford

The Ancell Trust

£1,500

Correspondent: Karen Phillips, Secretary, 78 London Road, Stony Stratford, Milton Keynes MK11 1JH (01908 563350; email: karen.phillips30@hotmail.co.uk)

CC Number: 233824

Eligibility

People in need in the town of Stony Stratford.

Types of grants

Grants are given to students for books and are occasionally made to individuals for welfare purposes and to organisations.

Annual grant total

In 2012/13 the trust had an income of £10,000 and a total expenditure of £7,500. Accounts were not required to be submitted to the Charity Commission due to the low income. We estimate the grant total to be around £7,000 with approximately £3,500 paid to organisations, around £2,000 paid to individuals for educational purposes and £1,500 to individuals in welfare grants.

Applications

In writing to the correspondent at any time.

Other information

The charity owns the sports ground in Stony Stratford which provides cricket, football, bowls, croquet and tennis facilities.

Wolverton

Catherine Featherstone

£4,000

Correspondent: Karen Phillips, Secretary, 78 London Road, Stony Stratford, Milton Keynes, Buckinghamshire MK11 1JH (01908 563350; email: karen.phillips20@yahoo.co.uk)

CC Number: 242620

Eligibility

People in need who live in the ancient parish of Wolverton.

Preference is given to persons who attend church regularly.

Types of grants

One-off and recurrent grants ranging from £150 to £500. Recent grants have been given for household bills, food, medical and disability equipment, electrical goods, living costs and home help.

Annual grant total

In 2013, the charity had an income of £9,700 and a total expenditure of £8,000. We estimate that the total amount of grants awarded to individuals was approximately £4,000. The charity also awards grants to organisations and other voluntary bodies.

Applications

On a form available from the correspondent, to be submitted either directly by the individual or through a social worker, Citizens Advice or other welfare agency. Applications are considered in March, July and October.

Cambridgeshire

The Farthing Trust

£8,600

Correspondent: Joy Martin, Trustee, PO Box 277, Cambridge CB7 9DE

CC Number: 268066

Eligibility

People in need, with a priority given to those either personally known to the trustees or recommended by those personally known to the trustees.

Types of grants

One-off and recurrent grants are given to meet 'charitable causes' in the UK and overseas.

Annual grant total

In 2012/13 the trust had assets of £2.9 million and an income of £62,000. Grants totalled £166,000, the majority of which was awarded to Christian churches and causes worldwide. Welfare grants to individuals totalled £8,600 of which, £1,500 was distributed in the UK and £7,100 overseas.

Applications

In writing to the correspondent. Applications can be submitted directly by the individual or through a social worker, Citizens Advice or other welfare agency. They are considered quarterly. Note applicants will only be notified of a refusal if an sae is enclosed.

The trust has previously stated that it is only able to accept about one in every one hundred of the applications it receives; therefore, success is unlikely unless a personal contact with a trustee is established.

Other information

Grants are also available to individuals for educational needs.

The Leverington Town Lands Charity

£17,200

Correspondent: Rosemary Gagen, Clerk to the Trustees, 78 High Road, Gorefield, Wisbech, Cambridgeshire PE13 4NB (01945 870454; email: levfeoffees@aol.com)

CC Number: 232526

Eligibility

People in need who live in the parishes of Leverington, Gorefield and Newton.

Types of grants

One-off grants towards, for example, glasses, new teeth or household appliances.

Annual grant total

In 2012/13 the charity held assets of £972,000 and had an income of £44,000. One-off grants to individuals totalled £17,200.

Applications

On a form available from the correspondent. Applications are considered in May and November.

The Upwell (Cambridgeshire) Consolidated Charities

£3,500

Correspondent: Ronald Stannard, Administrator, Riverside Farm, Birchfield Road, Nordelph, Downham Market, Norfolk PE38 0BP (01366 324217; email: ronstannard@waitrose.com)

CC Number: 203558

Eligibility

People in need who are over 65 (unless widowed) and live in the parish of Upwell (on the Isle of Ely) and have done so for at least five years.

Types of grants

Grants, which in previous years have ranged between £10 to £40, are given at Christmas.

Annual grant total

In 2013 the charities had an income of £6,000 and a total expenditure of £3,800. We estimate that grants to individuals totalled £3,500.

Applications

In writing to the correspondent. Applications should be submitted directly by the individual and are considered in November.

Cambridge

The Cambridge Community Nursing Trust

£5,000

Correspondent: Jan Young, Trustee, 38 Station Road West, Whittlesford, Cambridge CB22 4NL (01223 840259; email: enquiries@cambridgecommunitynursingtrust.co.uk; website: www.cambridgecommunitynursingtrust.co.uk)

CC Number: 204933

Eligibility

People in need who live in the boundaries of the city of Cambridge.

Types of grants

Grants of up to around £300 are given to provide extra care, comforts and special aids which are not available from any other source.

Annual grant total

The 2012 accounts were the latest available at the time of writing (August 2014).

In 2012, the trust had an income of £11,000 and a total expenditure of £10,000. We estimate that the total amount of grants awarded to individuals was approximately £5,000.

Applications

In writing to the correspondent. Applications are considered as received. The correspondent is happy to speak to potential applicants over the telephone before an application is submitted.

Chatteris

Feoffee Charity (Poor's Land)

£1,900

Correspondent: Brian Hawden, Administrator, Brian Hawden and Co. Solicitors, The Coach House, Chatteris, Cambridgeshire PE16 6PX (01354 692133; email: b.hawden@sky.com)

CC Number: 202150

Eligibility

People who are 'poor and needy' and have lived in Chatteris for at least ten years.

Types of grants

Grants of around £25 given annually in January.

Annual grant total

In 2012/13, the charity had an income of £4,200 and a total expenditure of £3,800. We estimate that the total amount of grants awarded to individuals was approximately £1,900. The charity also awards grants to organisations.

Applications

In writing to the correspondent, or upon recommendation of a trustee.

Downham

The Downham Feoffee Charity

£500

Correspondent: Jo Howard, 35 Fieldside, Ely, Cambridgeshire CB6 3AT (01353 665774; email: downhamfeoffees@hotmail.co.uk)

CC Number: 237233

Eligibility

People in need who live in the ancient parish of Downham.

Types of grants

One-off and recurrent grants according to need.

Annual grant total

In 2012/13 the charity had assets of £4.15 million and an income of £79,000. Grants to individuals totalled £500.

The charity gave an additional £8,000 in educational grants and £3,500 to public organisations, although its main focus is the provision of housing and allotments.

Applications

In writing to the correspondent.

Other information

The charity owns 20 houses and 200 acres of agricultural land.

Elsworth

The Samuel Franklin Fund Elsworth

£16,900

Correspondent: Serena Wyer, Administrator, 5 Cowdell End, Elsworth, Cambridge CB23 4GB (01954 267156; email: serena.wyersff@gmail.com)

CC Number: 228775

Eligibility

People who live in the parish of Elsworth and suffer from poverty, hardship or illness. Preference is given to older people, children and people with disabilities.

Types of grants

Our research suggests that one-off or recurrent grants, generally of £10 to £1,000, can be given according to need. Support can be provided towards hospital expenses, convalescence, household bills, medical equipment, nursing fees, disability equipment and home help. Christmas grants are also given.

Annual grant total

In 2013 the fund had assets of £137,000 and an income of £34,000. During the year support was provided to 32 beneficiaries totalling £17,900. We estimate that support for general welfare needs totalled around £16,900.

Applications

In writing to the correspondent. Applications should provide brief details of assistance required.

Other information

Grants are also made to local organisations and for educational purposes.

Ely

Thomas Parson's Charity

£2,000

Correspondent: The Clerk, Hall Ennion and Young, 8 High Street, Ely, Cambridgeshire CB7 4JY (01353 662918; fax: 01353 662747; email: john@heysolicitors.co.uk; website: www.thomasparsonscharity.org.uk)

CC Number: 202634

Eligibility

People in need who live in the city of Ely.

Types of grants

One-off and occasionally recurrent grants to relieve financial hardship and towards medical needs.

Annual grant total

In 2012/13 the charity had an income of £260,000 and a total expenditure of £191,000. At the time of writing (May 2014), the charity's accounts were not available to view on the Charity Commission website. We estimate that grants to individuals totalled around £2,000.

Applications

In writing to the correspondent. Applications can be submitted either directly by the individual, or through a social worker, Citizens Advice or other welfare agency. Applicants should include as much detail about their financial situation and their need for the grant as is possible. Applications are considered monthly.

Other information

The charity's primary activity is the management of its 27 almshouses in Ely, more details of which are available on the website.

Grantchester

The Grantchester Relief in Need Charity

£6,500

Correspondent: Allen Wheelwright, Trustee, 39 Green End, Comberton, Cambridge CB23 7DY

CC Number: 202175

Eligibility

People in need who live in the ancient parish of Grantchester.

Types of grants

One-off grants according to need.

Annual grant total

In 2013 the charity had an income of £7,700 and a total expenditure of £26,500. We estimate that welfare grants to individuals totalled £6,500, with funding also awarded to local organisations and to individuals for educational purposes.

Applications

In writing to the correspondent.

Hilton

Hilton Town Charity

£1,500

Correspondent: Phil Wood, Administrator, 1 Sparrow Way, Hilton, Huntingdon, Cambridgeshire PE28 9NZ (01480 830866; email: phil.n.wood@btinternet.com)

CC Number: 209423

Eligibility

People who live in the village of Hilton (Cambridgeshire). Applicants of any age or occupation who are experiencing hardship due to unforeseen circumstances, disability or sickness.

Types of grants

One-off grants can be given according to need.

Annual grant total

In 2013 the charity had an income of £4,500 and a total expenditure of £5,300. We estimate that welfare grants to individuals totalled around £1,500.

Applications

In writing to the correspondent.

Other information

Grants are also available for organisations which serve the direct needs of the village.

Ickleton

The Ickleton United Charities (Relief-in-Need Branch)

£5,800

Correspondent: John Statham, Trustee, 35 Abbey Street, Ickleton, Saffron Walden, Essex CB10 1SS (01799 530258)

CC Number: 202467

Eligibility

People in need who live in the Parish of Ickleton, Cambridgeshire.

Types of grants

One-off grants of around £40 towards fuel costs and necessities, and gift vouchers at Christmas. The charity often pays for 'Lifelines' for those who require them.

Annual grant total

In 2013 the charity had an income of £9,500 and a total expenditure of £6,000. We estimate that grants to individuals totalled £5,800.

Applications

In writing to the correspondent to be submitted directly by the individual.

Other information

Some of the charities in Ickleton date back to the Middle Ages; a fact given away by names such as Town Housen, Lettice Martin's Bequest, and The Charity of Richard Swan. When they were amalgamated in 1970, the organisations were arranged into two separate funds: The Relief in Need charity, which makes grants; and The Gertrude Homes Charity, which runs three almshouses for people with close associations with the village.

Landbeach

Rev Robert Masters Charity for Widows

£600

Correspondent: Ms J. Russell, Trustee, 2 Flint Cottages, Flint Lane, Ely Road, Waterbeach, Cambridge CB25 9PG (01223 441769; email: jrussell3@btinternet.com)

CC Number: 265254

Eligibility

People in need who live in the parish of Landbeach, with a preference for widows.

Types of grants

One-off and recurrent grants according to need.

Annual grant total

Grants total around £600 each year.

Applications

In writing to the correspondent.

Other information

The charity also gives to organisations.

Little Wilbraham

The Johnson, Bede and Lane Charitable Trust

£1,000

Correspondent: Linda Stead, Trustee, 76 High Street, Little Wilbraham, Cambridge CB21 5JY (01223 813794; email: lindastead9@googlemail.com)

CC Number: 284444

Eligibility

People in need who live in the civil parish of Little Wilbraham.

Types of grants

Our research indicates that one-off grants, usually between £50 and £150, can be given for a wide range of welfare needs.

Annual grant total

In 2012/13 the trust had an income of £4,400 and a total expenditure of £4,100. We estimate that around £1,000 was awarded in welfare grants to individuals.

Applications

In writing to the correspondent. Applications can be made directly by the individual or through a third party, such as a social worker, Citizens Advice or a neighbour. Applications are considered on an ongoing basis.

Other information

Grants are also made to organisations and for educational purposes.

Pampisford

Pampisford Relief-in-Need Charity

£3,000

Correspondent: Dennis Beaumont, Clerk, 4 Hammond Close, Pampisford, Cambridge CB22 3EP (01223 833653)

CC Number: 275661

Eligibility

People in need who live in the parish of Pampisford, particularly children and young people, older people and individuals who have a disability. In exceptional circumstances support may be given to otherwise eligible candidates who live immediately outside the parish.

Types of grants

Christmas gifts or individual grants of up to £250 for items, services or other specific requirements. Contributions are also made for the improvement of village amenities, which can then be enjoyed by the parishioners, particularly the elderly, the young and people with disabilities.

Annual grant total

In 2013 the charity had an income of £14,500 and an expenditure of £14,000. About £3,000 is available each year for individuals.

Applications

In writing to the correspondent. Applications can be made directly by the individual at any time.

Other information

Half of the charity's income goes to the Pampisford Ecclesiastical Charity. Other organisations may also be supported.

Peterborough

The Florence Saunders Relief-in-Sickness Charity

£3,800

Correspondent: Paula Lawson, Stephenson House, 15 Church Walk, Peterborough PE1 2TP (01733 343275; email: paula.lawson@stephensonsmart.com)

CC Number: 239177

Eligibility

People in need who are in poor health, convalescent, or who have disabilities and live in the former city of Peterborough.

Types of grants

One-off grants typically range between £100 and £500, and have been awarded to assist with hospital expenses, convalescence, holidays, travel expenses, electrical goods, medical equipment, furniture, disability equipment and help in the home.

Annual grant total

In 2012/13 the charity had an income of £6,900 and a total expenditure of £7,600. We estimate that grants to individuals totalled £3,800, with funding also awarded to local organisations.

Exclusions

No grants are given for the repayment of debts.

Applications

In writing to the correspondent to be submitted either directly by the individual or, where applicable, through a third party such as a family member, social worker or other welfare agency. Applications are considered at trustees' meetings, usually held three times per year.

Sawston

John Huntingdon's Charity

£11,500 (140 grants)

Correspondent: Jill Hayden, Charity Manager, John Huntingdon House, Tannery Road, Sawston, Cambridge CB2 3UW (01223 492492; email: office@johnhuntingdon.org.uk)

CC Number: 1118574

Eligibility

People in need who live in the parish of Sawston in Cambridgeshire.

Types of grants

Grants can be given for essential household items such as cookers, beds or fridges, TV licences, holidays, household bills, food, clothing, travel expenses, medical equipment, debts, transport costs, and nursery/playgroup fees.

Annual grant total

In 2013 the charity had assets of £8.4 million which mainly represents permanent endowment and is not available for grant giving. It had an income of £363,000 and a total expenditure of £335,000. Grants to individuals totalled £23,500 and we estimate that those awarded for welfare purposes totalled £11,500.

Applications

On an application form available from Sawston Support Services at the address above or by telephone. Office opening hours are 9am to 2pm Monday to Friday.

Other information

The charity provides almshouses for those in financial need in the area of benefit. It also gives grants for educational purposes.

Stetchworth

The Stetchworth Relief-in-Need Charity

£1,000

Correspondent: Judith Mahoney, Administrator, 26 High Street, Stetchworth, Newmarket, Suffolk CB8 9TJ (01638 508336)

CC Number: 245790

Eligibility

People in need who live in the parish of Stetchworth and have done so for at least two years.

Types of grants

One-off grants according to need. Grants have been given towards, for example, electricity bills, fuel, groceries (through an account at the local community shop), transport to hospital and educational needs.

Annual grant total

In 2012/13 the charity had an income of £2,600 and a total expenditure of £2,100. We estimate that social welfare grants to individuals totalled £1,000, with funding also awarded to individuals for educational purposes.

Applications

On a form available from the correspondent or the Ellesmere Centre, Stetchworth which should include details of income, expenditure and any other applications for help, rebates or discounts. Applications are considered at any time. The charity says: 'we welcome information from anyone who knows someone in need'.

Other information

Grants are available at any time of the year, although many of the elderly applicants tend to apply for a Christmas bonus in December. Whilst it is not the policy of the charity to give Christmas bonuses, it is happy to be used in this way.

Swaffham Bulbeck

Swaffham Bulbeck Relief-in-Need Charity

£3,000

Correspondent: Cheryl Ling, Administrator, 43 High Street, Swaffham Bulbeck, Cambridge CB25 0HP (01223 811733)

CC Number: 238177

Eligibility

People in need who live in the parish of Swaffham Bulbeck.

Types of grants

One-off and annual grants.

Annual grant total

In 2012 the charity had both an income and expenditure of £7,700. It makes grants to individuals, as well as organisations. Grants to individuals totalled approximately £3,000.

These were the latest accounts available at the time of writing (September 2014).

Applications

In writing to the correspondent.

Swavesey

Thomas Galon's Charity

£2,200

Correspondent: Linda Miller, Clerk, 21 Thistle Green, Swavesey, Cambridge CB24 4RJ (01954 202982; email: thomasgaloncharity@swavesey.org.uk; website: www.swavesey.org.uk/thomas_galon_charity)

CC Number: 202515

Eligibility

People in need who live in the parish of Swavesey. Preference is given to those who are over 70, single or widowed; married couples when one partner reaches 70; and widows and widowers with dependent children up to 18 years old.

Types of grants

An annual gift, to be agreed in November, for people in need. One-off grants for hospital travel expenses, fuel costs and other needs.

Annual grant total

In 2013 the charity had an income of £8,900 and a total expenditure of £4,600. We estimate that grants to individuals totalled £2,200, with funding also awarded to local organisations.

Exclusions

No grants for capital projects such as buildings.

Applications

In writing to the correspondent for consideration in November. Grants will be delivered in December.

Walsoken

The United Walsoken and Baxter Charities

£9,000

Correspondent: Derek Mews, Clerk, 7 Pickards Way, Wisbech, Cambridgeshire PE13 1SD (01945 587982)

CC Number: 205494

Eligibility

Older people in need who have lived in the parish of Walsoken for at least two years.

Types of grants

Small one-off grants and gifts in kind.

Annual grant total

The 2012 accounts were the latest available at the time of writing (August 2014).

In 2012, the charity had an income of £9,000 and a total expenditure of £9,000. We estimate that the total amount of grants awarded to individuals was approximately £9,000.

Applications

In writing to the correspondent, directly by the individual.

Whittlesey

The Whittlesey Charity

£720

Correspondent: Phil Gray, Administrator, 33 Bellamy Road, Oundle, Peterborough PE8 4NE (01832 273085)

CC Number: 1005069

Eligibility

People in need who live in the ancient parishes of Whittlesey Urban and Whittlesey Rural only.

Types of grants

Small annual cash grants, plus the occasional one-off grant.

Annual grant total

In 2013 welfare grants totalled £720.

Applications

In writing to the correspondent. Applications are considered in February, May and September, but urgent applications can be dealt with at fairly short notice. Note, the trust will not respond to ineligible applicants.

Other information

The charity makes grants to organisations and individuals, for relief in need, educational purposes, public purposes and it also makes grants to churches.

Whittlesford

The Charities of Nicholas Swallow and Others

£3,400

Correspondent: Nicholas Tufton, Clerk, 11 High Street, Barkway, Royston, Hertfordshire SG8 8EA (01763 848888)

CC Number: 203222

Eligibility

People in need who live in the parish of Whittlesford (near Cambridge) and adjacent area.

Types of grants

One-off cash grants at Christmas; help can also be given towards hospital travel and educational costs.

Annual grant total

In 2012/13 the charity had assets of £651,000 and an income of £59,000. Grants totalling £3,400 were made to individuals for social welfare purposes.

Applications

In writing to the correspondent directly by the individual.

Other information

The principal activity of this charity is as a housing association managing bungalows and garages.

Wisbech

Elizabeth Wright's Charity

£3,000

Correspondent: Dr Iain Mason, Trustee, 13 Tavistock Road, Wisbech, Cambs PE13 2DY (01945 588646; email: Eliz.wrightcharity1725@gmail.com)

CC Number: 203896

Eligibility

People who live in the parishes of St Peter and Paul and St Augustine, Cambridgeshire.

Types of grants

One-off grants for essential items to offset hardship or cope with long-term illness.

Annual grant total

The latest financial information available at the time of writing (August 2014) was from 2012. In 2012 the charity had an income of £38,000 and an expenditure of £33,000. Previously grants to individuals for welfare purposes have totalled around £3,000.

Applications

In writing to the correspondent. Applications can be submitted directly by the individual at any time. The trustees usually meet quarterly.

Other information

Grants are also given for educational purposes and to local organisations.

East Sussex

The Catharine House Trust

£29,000 (108 grants)

Correspondent: Richard Palim, Administrator, Ridge Cottage, New Cut, Westfield, Hastings, East Sussex TN35 4RL

CC Number: 801656

Eligibility

Older individuals and people in poor health who live in the borough of Hastings.

Types of grants

One-off grants of up to £400. Funding is available for medical equipment and treatment; household goods when they are essential for maintaining health (but not general furniture); respite breaks for the client or carer; and relevant courses for instruction.

Annual grant total

In 2012/13 the trust had an income of £38,000 and an expenditure of £29,000. Individuals received 108 welfare grants, amounting to £29,000.

Exclusions

Usually only one application is accepted per person.

Applications

In writing to the correspondent, supported by a written statement from a medical professional or social worker. Most applications are made through NHS trusts, local authority social services departments and other charities.

Hart Charitable Trust

£1,100 (6 grants)

Correspondent: Michael Bugden, Gaby Hardwicke, 2 Eversley Road, Bexhill-on-Sea, East Sussex TN40 1EY (01424 730945)

CC Number: 801126

Eligibility

People in need who live in East Sussex.

Types of grants

One-off grants, usually of around £75, are given towards clothing, bedding, travel and most other needs. Small amounts are also given to meet immediate needs.

Annual grant total

In 2012/13 the trust had assets of £692,000 and an income of £29,000. Grants were made to six individuals totalling £1,100 – this is down sharply on 2010/11 when grants to 203 individuals totalled almost £19,000. However, the trust also makes grants to organisations – the major beneficiary, Relief(Hastings Are Community Trust), received £15,000 for onward distribution in small grants to individuals.

Applications

On a form available from the correspondent, to be submitted through a third party such as a social worker, Citizens Advice or other welfare agency.

The Hastings Area Community Trust

£39,000 (397 grants)

Correspondent: Anthony Bonds, Administrator, Bolton Tomson House, 49 Cambridge Gardens, Hastings, East Sussex TN34 1EN (01424 718880; website: reliefhastings.moonfruit.com/#/about-us/4547780748)

CC Number: 1002470

Eligibility

People in need who are under 60 and live in Hastings and St Leonards-on-Sea who are on a very low income and have children, or who have medical reasons for not working.

Types of grants

One-off grants mainly in the form of payments to suppliers for essential household needs, including white goods, beds, fuel costs, clothing and baby items.

Annual grant total

In 2012/13 the trust held assets of £539,000 and had an income of £57,000. Grants to 397 individuals totalled £39,000.

Exclusions

No grants for carpets, curtains or televisions.

Applications

On a form available from the correspondent. Applications can only be accepted from a recognised referral agency (such as a social worker, Citizens Advice or recognised advice agency) and are considered throughout the year. The trust encourages applicants who wish to telephone to leave a message on the answer phone if there is no reply as messages are listened to daily.

Other information

The trust also provides accommodation and administration services to other local charities and organisations.

The Mrs A. Lacy Tate Trust

£10,500

Correspondent: The Trustees, Heringtons Solicitors, 39 Gildredge Road, Eastbourne, East Sussex BN21 4RY (01323 411020)

CC Number: 803596

Eligibility

People in need who live in East Sussex.

Types of grants

One-off and recurrent grants according to need.

Annual grant total

In 2012/13 the trust had assets of £686,000 and an income of £56,000. Grants were made to 75 individuals totalling £21,000. We estimate that grants to individuals for social welfare purposes were around £10,500.

Applications

In writing to the correspondent.

Other information

Grants are also made to individuals for educational purposes and to organisations.

Battle

The Battle Charities

£2,000

Correspondent: Timothy Roberts, Administrator, 1 Upper Lake, Battle, East Sussex TN33 0AN (01424 772401; email: troberts@heringtons.net)

CC Number: 206591

Eligibility

People in need who live in Battle and Netherfield, East Sussex.

Types of grants

Grants are usually made towards fuel and children's clothing, and range from £50 to £200.

Annual grant total

In 2013, the charity had an income of £3,000 and a total expenditure of £3,000. We estimate that the total amount of grants awarded to individuals was approximately £2,000.

Applications

In writing to the correspondent. Applications can be sent directly by the individual or family member, through an organisation such as Citizens Advice or through a third party such as a social worker. Full details of the applicant's circumstances are required.

Brighton and Hove

The Brighton District Nursing Association Trust

£5,000

Correspondent: Anthony Druce, Hon. Secretary, Fitzhugh Gates, 3 Pavilion Parade, Brighton BN2 1RY (01273 686811; fax: 01273 676837; email: anthonyd@fitzhugh.co.uk)

CC Number: 213851

Eligibility

People in need who are in poor health, convalescent or who have a disability and live in the county borough of Brighton and Hove.

Types of grants

One-off grants of up to £250 for items in respect of medical treatment and for convalescence; some limited allowances for nurses may also be available.

Annual grant total

The 2012 accounts were the latest available at the time of writing (August 2014).

In 2012, the trust had assets of £2 million and an income of £61,000. Total expenditure was £58,000 and grants awarded to individuals totalled approximately £5,000.

Applications

In writing to the correspondent; preferably supported by a doctor or health visitor. Applications are considered quarterly, though emergency grants may be awarded between meetings in urgent cases.

The Brighton Fund

£15,000

Correspondent: Mary Grealish, Administrator, Brighton and Hove City Council, Central Accounting, Room 201, Kings House, Grand Avenue, Hove (01273 291259; website: www.brighton-hove.gov.uk)

CC Number: 1011724

Eligibility

Usually people over 60 who are in need who live in Brighton and Hove administrative boundary.

Types of grants

One-off cash grants according to need including those for household items, medical equipment and subsistence. Christmas gifts of £20 in the form of gift vouchers.

Annual grant total

In 2012/13 the fund had an income of £46,000 and a total expenditure of £32,000. Grants are awarded to individuals for both educational and social welfare purposes. We estimate grants made for social welfare purposes to be around £15,000.

Applications

On a form, available from the correspondent or the website, to be submitted either through an organisation such as Citizens Advice or a school or through a third party such as a social worker or teacher. Applications are considered upon receipt.

The Mayor of Brighton and Hove's Welfare Charity

£5,200

Correspondent: Michael Hill, Administrator, Selborne Centre, 5 Selborne Place, Hove, East Sussex BH3 3ET (01273 779432; email: hill.michael4@sky.com)

CC Number: 224012

Eligibility

Individuals in need living in the old borough of Hove and Portslade.

Types of grants

One-off grants up to a maximum of £250.

Annual grant total

In 2012/13 the trust had an income of £3,300 and a total expenditure of £5,400. We estimate that grants to individuals totalled £5,200.

Exclusions

No retrospective grants are made.

Applications

On a form available from the correspondent along with full guidelines. Applications should be submitted directly by the individual or a relevant third party, for example, a friend, carer or professional (social worker, health visitor). Grants are considered bi-monthly, in January, March, May, July, September and November. No money is given directly to the applicant, but rather directly to settle invoices. The committee will only consider one grant for each applicant and successful applicants should not reapply.

Eastbourne

The Mayor's Poor Fund, Eastbourne

£1,500

Correspondent: Robert Cottrill, Chief Executive, Eastbourne Borough Council, Town Hall, Grove Road, Eastbourne, East Sussex BN21 4UG (01323 415002; email: robert.cottrill@eastbourne.gov.uk)

CC Number: 210664

Eligibility

People living in the borough of Eastbourne who are in need of temporary financial assistance due to illness, unemployment or similar circumstances.

Types of grants

One-off grants, generally ranging between £25 and £100.

Annual grant total
In 2012/13 the fund received no income but had an expenditure of £1,600. Bear in mind that both figures vary each year. We estimate that grants to individuals totalled around £1,500.

Applications
In writing to the correspondent. Applicants are asked to include all the relevant information to help their case. Applications are usually submitted through a social worker or health visitor but individuals can apply directly if they wish.

The Doctor Merry Memorial Fund

£3,000

Correspondent: Ronald Pringle, Friston Corner, 3 Mill Close, East Dean, Eastbourne, East Sussex BN20 0EG (01323 423319; email: ronpringle@hotmail.com)

CC Number: 213449

Eligibility
People who are ill and who live in the Eastbourne Health Authority area.

Types of grants
One-off grants for nursing home care and medical equipment.

Annual grant total
In 2012/13 the fund had an income of £6,600 and a total expenditure of £6,100. We estimate that grants to individuals totalled £3,000, with funding also awarded to local organisations.

Applications
Individuals should apply via their doctor on a form available from the correspondent. Applications are considered throughout the year.

Other information
The fund was established in 1922 as commemoration to a Dr Merry, who died of exhaustion whilst caring for the people of Eastbourne during a flu epidemic.

Hastings

William Shadwell Charity

£4,500

Correspondent: C. R. Morris, Administrator, 4 Barley Lane, Hastings TN35 5NX (01424 433586)

CC Number: 207366

Eligibility
People in need who are sick and live in the borough of Hastings.

Types of grants
One-off and recurrent grants.

Annual grant total
In 2013 the charity had an income of £8,400 and a total expenditure of £9,200. We estimate that grants to individuals totalled £4,500, with funding also awarded to local organisations.

Exclusions
No grants are given for the payment of debt, taxes and so on.

Applications
In writing to the correspondent to be submitted in March and September for consideration in April and October, but urgent cases can be considered at any time. Applications can be submitted directly by the individual or through a third party.

Mayfield

The Mayfield Charity

£1,000

Correspondent: Brenda Hopkin, Administrator, Appletrees, Alexandra Road, Mayfield, East Sussex TN20 6UD (01435 873279)

CC Number: 212996

Eligibility
People in need who live in the ancient parish of Mayfield.

Types of grants
One-off grants of £50 to £500 according to need. Grants have been given towards hospital travel, clothing, equipment for people who have disabilities, purchase of aids and Christmas gifts for older people.

Annual grant total
In 2012 the charity had an income of £4,000 and a total expenditure of £4,500. We estimate that around £1,000 was given in grants to individuals for social welfare purposes.

The 2012 accounts are the latest available at the time of writing.

Exclusions
Grants are not made for religious or political causes.

Applications
In writing to the correspondent at any time either directly by the individual or a family member, through a third party such as a social worker or teacher, or through an organisation such as Citizens Advice or a school. Proof of need should be included where possible.

Other information
The charity also makes grants to individuals for educational purposes.

Newick

The Newick Distress Trust

£2,000

Correspondent: Geoffrey Clinton, Trustee, 3 High Hurst Close, Newick, Lewes, East Sussex BN8 4NJ (01825 722512)

CC Number: 291954

Eligibility
People in need who live in the village of Newick (East Sussex) and the surrounding area.

Types of grants
One-off or recurrent grants towards, for example, heating bills in very cold weather, school uniforms required due to a change of school and other basic living costs. The trust notes that most often requests for assistance come from people experiencing reduction in income due to bereavement, ill-health, unemployment, marital breakdown or other unexpected circumstances.

Annual grant total
In 2013 the trust had an income of £1,600 and an expenditure of £2,200. We estimate that around £2,000 was given in individual grants. The total amount awarded each year can vary depending on the number of requests.

Exclusions
Applications from people living outside the village are not accepted.

Applications
In writing to the correspondent or one of the trustees. The trustees meet twice a year and as necessary.

Rotherfield

Henry Smith (Rotherfield Share)

£1,800

Correspondent: Trevor Thorpe, Trustee, 82 Fermor Way, Crowborough TN6 3BJ (01892 664245; email: rotherfieldpc@yahoo.co.uk; website: www.rotherfieldparishcouncil.co.uk)

CC Number: 235516

Eligibility
People in need who live in the ancient parish of Rotherfield (Rotherfield and Crowborough civil parishes).

Types of grants

One-off and recurrent grants according to need. Grants have recently been awarded to help with the transport costs of regular hospital visits and the purchase of a mobility scooter.

Annual grant total

In 2013 the charity had an income of £1,800 and a total expenditure of £3,800. We estimate that grants to individuals totalled £1,800, with funding also awarded to local organisations.

Applications

In writing to the correspondent to be submitted either directly by the individual, through a third party such as a social worker, or through an organisation such as Citizens Advice or other welfare agency. Applications are considered upon receipt.

Rye

Rye Relief In Need Charity

£250

Correspondent: The Trustees, Rye Town Council, Town Hall, Market Street, Rye, East Sussex TN31 7LA (01797 223902; email: townhall@ryetowncouncil.gov.uk; website: www.ryetowncouncil.gov.uk)

CC Number: 1075806

Eligibility

People who live in Rye who are in need.

Types of grants

One-off grants according to need. Recent grants have been given for removal costs and debt relief.

Annual grant total

In 2012/13 the charity had an income of £1,900 and an expenditure of £600. We estimate that around £250 was made in grants to individuals for social welfare purposes.

Applications

On a form available from the correspondent or to download from the website. Applications may be made at any time and are generally considered within two months of submission.

Warbleton

Warbleton Charity

£500

Correspondent: John Leeves, Administrator, 4 Berners Court Yard, Berners Hill, Flimwell, Wadhurst, East Sussex TN5 7NE (01580 879248)

CC Number: 208130

Eligibility

People in need who live in the parish of Warbleton. Preference is usually given to older people.

Types of grants

One-off grants according to need. Recent awards have been made for fuel and Christmas hampers.

Annual grant total

In 2013 the charity had an income of £2,700 and a total expenditure of £2,000. We estimate that around £500 was made in grants to individuals for social welfare purposes.

Applications

In writing to the correspondent either directly by the individual or through a third party. Applications are considered on a regular basis.

Other information

Grants are also made for educational purposes.

Essex

Colchester Blind Society

£4,000

Correspondent: Marilyn Theresa Peck, Trustee, Kestrels, Harwich Road, Beaumont, Clacton-on-Sea, Essex CO16 0AU (01255 862062)

CC Number: 207361

Eligibility

People who are blind or sight impaired and live in the borough of Colchester.

Types of grants

One-off or recurrent grants according to need.

Annual grant total

In 2012/13 the society had an income of £6,800 and a total expenditure of £4,200. We estimate that grants to individuals totalled £4,000.

Applications

In writing to the correspondent.

The Colchester Catalyst Charity

£175,000

Correspondent: Peter Fitt, Trustee, 7 Coast Road, West Mersea, Colchester CO5 8QE (email: info@colchestercatalyst.co.uk; website: www.colchestercatalyst.co.uk)

CC Number: 228352

Eligibility

People in north east Essex who are living with a disability or sickness.

Types of grants

One-off and recurrent grants for respite care and specialist therapy. Funding is also given towards wheelchairs, mobility scooters and other mobility aids, special beds, pressure relieving mattresses and cushions, computers for specific needs and communication aids. Grants are paid directly to the supplier or an appropriate registered charity. Where appropriate, a loan or part-funding of an item may be awarded.

Annual grant total

In 2012/13 the charity had an income of £352,000 and a total expenditure of £336,000. Grants to individuals totalled £175,000 and were distributed as follows:

Respite care	£109,000
Special individual needs	£66,000

A further £107,000 was awarded to organisations.

Exclusions

Funding will not be given for items already purchased or where there is an obligation for provision by a statutory authority. The charity states that it does not take responsibility for the insurance, maintenance and repairs of any items funded. Grants towards replacement vehicles will only be considered where evidence of a replacement fund is available.

Applications

On a form available directly from the correspondent or to download from the charity's website. Applications should include supporting statements, professional assessments by an appropriate professional practitioner (GP, occupational therapist, district nurse) and any quotes or estimates. The charity may request further professional assessments before a grant is made.

Other information

Applications for respite care and counselling are administered through the charity's partners, a full list of which is available on the website.

Essex Police Support Staff Benevolent Fund

£3,600

Correspondent: Barry Faber, Trustee, Essex Police Headquarters, PO Box 2, Chelmsford, Essex CM2 6DA (01245 452597)

CC Number: 269890

Eligibility

People in need who work or worked full-time or part-time for Essex Police Authority, and their dependents.

Types of grants

One-off grants or loans for essential needs such as travel expenses for hospital visits and unforeseen bills such as car repairs.

Annual grant total

In 2012/13, the fund had an income of £6,500 and a total expenditure of £3,800. We estimate that the total amount of grants awarded to individuals was approximately £3,600.

Exclusions

No grants towards medical treatment.

Applications

Individuals should apply via the benevolent fund representative of their division or subdivision of Essex Police Authority. Applications are considered quarterly, although this can be sooner in emergencies.

Help-in-Need Association (HINA)

£4,000

Correspondent: The Trustees, Students Union Building, St Bartholomew's and Royal London, School of Medicine and Dentistry, Stepney Way, London E1 2AD (email: applications@blhina.org; website: blhina.org/)

CC Number: 285585

Eligibility

Individuals in need living in Tower Hamlets, the City of London, Hackney, Newham, Waltham Forest, Redbridge, Barking and Dagenham, Havering or Essex.

Types of grants

One-off grants of up to £175 each for a specified purpose.

Annual grant total

The 2011/12 accounts were the latest available at the time of writing (August 2014).

In 2011/12, the association had an income of £8,000 and a total expenditure of £8,000. We estimate that the total amount of grants awarded to individuals was approximately £4,000. The association also awards grants to organisations.

Applications

Online application form on the fund's website. Applications must be submitted via a third party such as a social worker, GP, support worker, etc., who should also include a supporting letter and any relevant supporting documentation. Additional documents may be uploaded along with the application form.

Kay Jenkins Trust

£2,700

Correspondent: Diana Tritton, Trustee, Hole Farm House, Great Leighs, Chelmsford, Essex CM3 1QR (01245 361204; email: dstritton@yahoo.com)

CC Number: 241344

Eligibility

People in need, especially older or disabled people, who live in Great and Little Leighs.

Types of grants

One-off, mainly small, grants to help with household expenditure, medical aids and equipment. Occasionally up to £1,000 is given for a large item. No loans are made.

Annual grant total

In 2012/13, the charity had an income of £12 but a total expenditure of £2,700. We assume that most of this was taken from the trust's reserves.

Applications

In writing to the correspondent directly by the individual or through a relative. Grants are considered throughout the year.

Braintree

Braintree United Charities (The Thorn Charities (General))

£1,600

Correspondent: The Administrator, Smith Law Partnership, Gordon House, 22 Rayne Road, Braintree, Essex CM7 2QW (01376 321311; fax: 01376 559239; email: lawyers@slpsolicitors.co.uk)

CC Number: 212131

Eligibility

People in need who live in the parishes of St Michael's and St Paul's, Braintree. Beneficiaries will usually be those in receipt of an old age pension.

Types of grants

One-off and recurrent grants ranging from £50 to £100. Annual grants are given at Christmas to people in need who are registered with the charity.

Annual grant total

In 2012/13 the charity had an income of £3,800 and a total expenditure of £3,400. We have estimated the annual total of grants to individuals to be around £1,600.

Exclusions

Loans are not normally made.

Applications

Application forms are available from the correspondent. They can be submitted either directly by the individual or through a third party, such as a social worker, Citizens Advice or other welfare agency. Requests are considered twice a year, usually in May and October and should be received by April and September, respectively.

Other information

Grants are also made to organisations working for the benefit of local people.

Broomfield

Broomfield United Charities

£2,200

Correspondent: Brian Worboys, Trustee, 5 Butlers Close, Chelmsford CM1 7BE (01245 440540; email: brian@theworboys.freeserve.co.uk)

CC Number: 225563

Eligibility

People in need who live in the civil parish of Broomfield.

Types of grants

One-off grants according to need and vouchers at Christmas.

Annual grant total

In 2012/13 the charities had an income of £5,900 and an expenditure of £4,400. We estimate that grants to individuals totalled £2,200, with funding also awarded to local organisations.

Applications

In writing to the correspondent directly by the individual for consideration at any time.

Chigwell and Chigwell Row

The George and Alfred Lewis (of Chigwell) Memorial Fund

£1,500

Correspondent: Elizabeth Smart, Trustee, 16 Forest Terrace, High Road, Chigwell, Essex IG7 5BW (020 8504 9408)

CC Number: 297802

Eligibility

People in need and widows of those who served in HM Forces or the Merchant Service during the Second World War and were living in the parishes of

Chigwell and Chigwell Row at the time of their enlistment.

Types of grants

One-off grants to help people who are in need due to family illness, old age, domestic emergencies and so on.

Annual grant total

In 2013, the fund had an income of £2,300 and a total expenditure of £1,700. We estimate that the total amount of grants awarded to individuals was approximately £1,500.

Applications

In writing to the correspondent. Applications can be made either directly by the individual or through a third party on behalf of the individual, such as a spouse or child, and should include as much detail of personal circumstances as is deemed appropriate. Applications are considered at any time.

Dovercourt

Henry Smith's Charity (Ancient Parish of Dovercourt)

£2,400

Correspondent: Janet Elliot, Administrator, 20 Kilmaine Road, Dovercourt, Harwich, Essex CO12 4UZ (01255 503020)

CC Number: 246792

Eligibility

People in need who live in the ancient parish of Dovercourt and the parish of Harwich Peninsula.

Types of grants

The charity does not normally give direct grants. It prefers to provide goods or to contribute towards the total cost of items/services or fuel expenses. Help can be given for domestic items, clothing, bedding, food, disability aids, TV licence costs and other needs. Our research suggests that one-off payments may be of up to £100.

Annual grant total

In 2012/13 the charity had an income of £2,000 and a total expenditure of £2,600. We estimate that support to individuals totalled around £2,400.

Applications

In writing to the correspondent for consideration at any time. Applications should contain family details and be submitted through a third party, such as Citizens Advice or other welfare agency, or a priest who can recommend the applicant. After receiving a letter, the trustees usually visit the applicant.

East Bergholt

The East Bergholt United Charities

£500

Correspondent: Greta Abbs, Administrator, 31 Fiddlers Lane, East Bergholt, Colchester CO7 6SJ (01206 299822)

CC Number: 208194

Eligibility

People in need who live in East Bergholt.

Types of grants

One-off grants according to need. If no cases of hardship are brought to the attention of the trustees, they usually give £20 each at Christmas to 10 to 20 older people who are known to have small incomes. These are not given to the same person two years running, although additional help can be given if needed.

Annual grant total

The main purpose of this charity is the provision and maintenance of almshouses. Grants to individuals are usually under £500.

Applications

In writing to the correspondent, although most cases are brought to the attention of the trustees. Applications can be submitted directly by the individual or by a relative at any time. Proof of the financial situation of the applicant is required.

East Tilbury

East Tilbury Relief-in-Need Charity

£0

Correspondent: Reginald F. Fowler, Treasurer, 27 Ward Avenue, Grays, Essex RM17 5RE (01375 372304)

CC Number: 212335

Eligibility

People in need who live in the parish of East Tilbury.

Types of grants

One-off and recurrent grants have been given towards hospital visits and children in need.

Annual grant total

In 2013 the charity had an income of £8,100 and had no expenditure during this financial year.

Applications

In writing to the correspondent, to be considered in November.

Other information

The charity also makes grants to organisations operating in the local area.

Halstead

Helena Sant's Residuary Trust Fund

£2,300

Correspondent: Malcolm Willis, Trustee, Greenway, Church Street, Gestingthorpe, Halstead, Essex CO9 3AX (01787 469920)

CC Number: 269570

Eligibility

People in need who live in the parish of St Andrew with Holy Trinity, Halstead who have at any time been a member of the Church of England.

Types of grants

One-off cash grants according to need.

Annual grant total

In 2013 the fund had an income of £5,500 and a total expenditure of £4,800. As half of the fund's charitable expenditure goes towards religious and other charitable work in the parish, we estimate that grants to individuals totalled around £2,300.

Exclusions

Grants are not given to pay rates, taxes or public funds.

Applications

In writing to the correspondent directly by the individual, through an organisation such as Citizens Advice or through a third party such as a social worker. Applications are considered at any time.

Harlow

The Harlow Community Chest

£5,600

Correspondent: Chris Sheldrick, Trustee, c/o K. P. Dispatch, Joseph House, Harolds Road, Harlow, Essex CM19 5BJ (email: harlowcommunitychest@virginmedia.com)

CC Number: 252764

Eligibility

Individuals and families in financial need, particularly where a small financial contribution will help to prevent a spiral of debt. Applicants must live in Harlow.

Types of grants

One-off grants. Grants have been made for payment of outstanding utility bills for people with special needs, clothing (for unemployed young people attending a job interview, for example), household items, funeral expenses, removal costs, lodging deposits and nursery fees. Small emergency grants are also available.

Annual grant total

In 2012/13 the charity had an income of £5,600 and a total expenditure of £5,700. We estimate that grants to individuals totalled £5,600.

Exclusions

No grants for housing rents or rates. Only one main grant to an individual/ family can be made in any one year.

Applications

On a form available from the correspondent to be submitted through a recognised referral agency such as a social worker, welfare organisation or doctor. Applications are considered on a monthly basis. Emergency payments can be made between meetings.

Hutton

Ecclesiastical Charity of George White

£2,300

Correspondent: Reverend Robert Wallace, Trustee, c/o St Peter's Parish Office, Claughton Way, Hutton, Brentwood, Essex CM13 1JS (01277 262864; email: dawn_shaxon@btconnect.com; website: www.huttonchurch.org.uk)

CC Number: 208601

Eligibility

People in need who live in the parish of All Saints with St Peter, Hutton. Particular favour is given to children, young adults and older people. The usual length of residency is seven years.

Types of grants

Pensions and one-off grants usually in the range of £100 and £400 towards necessary living expenses.

Annual grant total

In 2013 the charity had an income of £3,200 and a total expenditure of £2,800. We estimate that grants to individuals totalled £2,300.

Applications

In writing to the correspondent at any time. Applications can be submitted either directly by the individual, through a third party such as a social worker, or through an organisation such as Citizens Advice or other welfare agency. They are considered at any time.

Other information

The charity also makes grants towards the repair of the church fabric in the two local parish churches.

Saffron Walden

The Saffron Walden United Charities

£14,000

Correspondent: Jim Ketteridge, Clerk to the Trustees, c/o Community Hospital, Radwinter Road, Saffron Walden, Essex CB11 3HY (01799 526122)

CC Number: 210662

Eligibility

People in need who live in Saffron Walden including the hamlets of Little Walden and Sewards End.

Types of grants

One-off grants in kind and gift vouchers. A range of help is considered including, for example, electrical goods, convalescence, clothing, household bills, food, holidays, travel expenses, furniture, disability equipment and nursery fees.

Annual grant total

In 2013 the charity had assets of £1.1 million and an income of £48,000. Grants to individuals totalled £14,000.

Exclusions

No grants for credit card debt.

Applications

In writing to the correspondent either directly by the individual, through a third party such as a social worker, or through an organisation such as Citizens Advice or other welfare agency. Applications are considered as they arrive.

Springfield

The Springfield United Charities

£6,500

Correspondent: Nick Eveleigh, Administrator, Civic Centre, Duke Street, Chelmsford, Essex CM1 2YJ (01245 606606)

CC Number: 214530

Eligibility

Individuals in need living in the parish of Springfield.

Types of grants

One-off grants according to need.

Annual grant total

In 2012/13 the charity had an income of £18,000 and a total expenditure of £7,400. We estimate that around £6,500 was made in grants to individuals for social welfare purposes.

Applications

In writing to the correspondent.

Thaxted

Thaxted Relief-in-Need Charities

£5,300

Correspondent: Michael Hughes, Secretary, Yardley Farm, Walden Road, Thaxted, Essex CM6 2RQ (01371 830642; email: michaelbhughes@hotmail.co.uk)

CC Number: 243782

Eligibility

People in need who live in the parish of Thaxted.

Types of grants

One-off and recurrent grants according to need.

Annual grant total

In 2013, the charity had an income of £27,000 and a total expenditure of £22,000. The total grants awarded to individuals was £5,300.

Applications

In writing to the correspondent.

Other information

The main priority for the charity is to maintain its almshouses. A small number of grants are also made to local organisations.

Hampshire

The Alverstoke Trust

£500

Correspondent: Jane Hodgman, Administrator, 5 Constable Close, Gosport, Hampshire PO12 2UF (02392589822)

CC Number: 239303

Eligibility

People in need who live in the parish of Alverstoke. In exceptional circumstances people resident in the borough of Gosport can be supported.

Types of grants

One-off grants, usually of up to £200, can be given according to need.

Annual grant total

In 2013 the trust had an income of £1,800 and a total expenditure of £1,200. We estimate that welfare support totalled around £500.

Exclusions

Our research indicates that the trust does not make loans, grants to other charities or recurring awards.

Applications

In writing to the correspondent. Applications can be made by individuals directly or through a third party, such as Citizens Advice, a social worker or welfare agency, if applicable. Awards can be considered at any time.

Bordon Liphook Haslemere Charity

£70,000

Correspondent: Sue Nicholson, Administrator, Room 29, The Forest Centre, Pinehill Road, Bordon, Hampshire GU35 0TN (01420 477787; email: info@blhcharity.co.uk; website: www.blhcharity.co.uk)

CC Number: 1032428

Eligibility

People in need who live in North-East Hampshire and South-West Surrey.

Types of grants

One-off grants of between £50 and £3,000 can be awarded. The trustees consider a wide range of applications including heating and rent arrears.

Annual grant total

In 2013 the charity had an income of £148,000 and a total expenditure of £111,000. The accounts for 2013 had been received at the Charity Commission but had not been published online. Based on previous research we estimate that grants to individuals for social welfare purposes in the year 2013 was in the region of £70,000.

Applications

On a form available from the correspondent or to download from the website. Applications can be made either directly by the individual or through a social worker, Citizens Advice, other welfare agency, health visitor or district nurse. Applications are considered monthly and the charity reserves the right to commission a case worker's report.

Other information

The charity raises money through its three charity shops – Bordon Care, Haslemere Care and Liphook Care and provides support to both individuals and organisations.

Dibden Allotments Fund

£166,000 (1,092 grants)

Correspondent: Valerie Stewart, Administrator, 7 Drummond Court, Prospect Place, Hythe, Southampton SO45 6HD (02380 841305; email: dibdenallotments@btconnect.com; website: daf-hythe.org.uk)

CC Number: 255778

Eligibility

People in need who live in the parishes of Hythe, Dibden, Marshwood and Fawley.

Types of grants

One-off grants according to need, for the relief of hardship or distress. Grants to individuals can take many forms, for example it could be vouchers for food, clothes or household items, or the supply of white goods or furniture.

Annual grant total

In 2012/13 the fund had assets of £9.1 million and an income of £349,000. There were 1092 welfare grants given to individuals totalling £166,000. These included 692 grants totalling £21,000 for the Shoe Vouchers Scheme and 144 grants totalling almost £36,000 for the Garden Support Scheme. 256 general grants were made for individuals in need and totalled £110,000.

Applications

On a form available on the fund's website, where its criteria, guidelines and application process are also posted. It is helpful to supply a supporting statement from a 'professional' such as a health or social worker, midwife or teacher.

Other information

7 grants were also made for educational purposes totalling £2,400. Grants are also made to charitable and voluntary organisations.

The Farnborough (Hampshire) Welfare Trust

£2,000

Correspondent: M. R. Evans, Administrator, Bowmarsh, 45 Church Avenue, Farnborough, Hampshire GU14 7AP (01252 542726; email: evans.bowmarsh@ntlworld.com)

CC Number: 236889

Eligibility

People in need who live in the urban district of Farnborough, Hampshire.

Types of grants

One-off and recurrent grants mainly to older people at Christmas. Grants are generally between £20 and £50.

Annual grant total

The 2012 accounts were the latest available at the time of writing (August 2014).

In 2012, the trust had an income of £3,500 and a total expenditure of £2,000. We estimate that the total amount of grants awarded to individuals was approximately £2,000.

Applications

In writing to the correspondent; to be submitted either directly by the individual or by a third party. Applications are usually considered in early December.

Hampshire Ambulance Service Benevolent Fund

£11,500

Correspondent: Terence Forgham, Trustee, 8 Ashley Gardens, Chandler's Ford, Eastleigh, Hampshire SO53 2JH (02380 269600)

CC Number: 1041811

Eligibility

Serving and retired members of Hampshire Ambulance Service/South Central Ambulance Service NHS Trust and their dependents.

Types of grants

One-off grants according to need.

Annual grant total

In 2012/13 the fund had an income of £9,000 and a total expenditure of £11,700. We estimate that welfare grants to individuals totalled £11,500.

Applications

In writing to the correspondent.

The Hampshire Constabulary Welfare Fund

£77,000

Correspondent: Paul Robertson, Trustee, Hampshire Constabulary Welfare Fund, Federation House, 440 The Grange, Romsey Road, Romsey SO51 0AE (02380 674397; email: hampshire@polfed.org; website: www.hampshirepolfed.org.uk/services/welfare.htm)

CC Number: 291061

Eligibility
Members, pensioners and civilian employees of the Hampshire Constabulary and their dependents. Assistance may also be available to special constables injured during police duty.

Types of grants
One-off and recurrent grants or loans to help support people experiencing family crisis or recovering from injury or illness. Past grants have been given towards stair-lifts, bath-lifts, wheelchairs, respite holidays and general living costs.

Annual grant total
In 2012/13 the fund held assets of £500,000 and had an income of £258,000. Grants were distributed as follows:

Assistance and grants	£37,000
Widows and children's Christmas gifts	£30,000
Loans now written off as grants	£27,000
Gifts to sick members, wreaths and donations	£10,200

Grants to individuals totalled more than £77,000, with loans from previous years now converted to grants amounting to another £27,000.

Applications
Via an application form available to download from the Hampshire Police Federation website. Applicants are requested to provide at least two quotes for grants above £2,000 and one quote for amounts below £2,000. If a grant is for medical purposes, applicants should provide as much relevant information as possible, such as medical reports, occupational therapy reports and other supporting information. Details of any other agencies or charities that have been approached for funding must be provided. Applications are considered on a regular basis and eligible applicants may be contacted for further information. Urgent applications can be fast-tracked.

Other information
The fund also donates to other charities which support police officers. In 2012/13 the Police Convalescent Home received £150,000 from the fund.

Hampshire Football Association Benevolent Fund

£4,600

Correspondent: Robin Osborne, Chair, Winklebury Football Complex, Winklebury Way, Basingstoke, Hampshire RG23 8BF (01256 853000)

CC Number: 232359

Eligibility
People in need who have been injured whilst playing football, and others who have 'done service' to the game of football. Applicants must be playing for a team affiliated with Hampshire Football Association.

Types of grants
One-off and recurrent grants, usually ranging from £50 to £1,000 according to need.

Annual grant total
In 2013 the fund had an income of £3,800 and a total expenditure of £4,800. We estimate that grants to individuals totalled £4,600.

Applications
The club secretary must apply to Hampshire Football Association or the Area Benevolent Officer for an application form on behalf of the applicant. The application should be completed by the applicant and endorsed by the secretary of the club.

A doctor's certificate clearly stating the nature of the injury and probable period of incapacitation must accompany each application. Completed application forms should be returned to the county office or the Area Benevolent Officer.

The Kingsclere Welfare Charities

£2,500

Correspondent: Roy Forth, Administrator, PO Box 7721, Kingsclere RG20 5WQ (07796423108; email: kclerecharities@aol.co.uk)

CC Number: 237218

Eligibility
People in need who live in the parishes of Ashford Hill, Headley and Kingsclere.

Types of grants
The provision or payment for items, services or facilities such as medical equipment, expenses for travel to hospital and grants to relieve hardship. Grants are mostly one-off, but recurrent grants can be considered. They range from around £100 to £2,500.

Annual grant total
In 2013 the charity had an income of £6,000 and a total expenditure of £2,900. We estimate that grants to individuals would be around £2,500.

Applications
In writing to the correspondent. Applications are considered in February, April, June, September and November.

Open Sight

£2,000

Correspondent: Stacey Allen, Administrator, 25 Church Road, Eastleigh, Hampshire SO50 6BL (02380 646378; email: info@opensight.org.uk; website: www.opensight.org.uk)

CC Number: 1055498

Eligibility
People who are visually impaired, in need and live in Hampshire, excluding the cities of Portsmouth and Southampton.

Types of grants
One-off grants of up to £500 each to aid independent living for eligible people, such as towards special equipment, aids to daily living, holiday costs and costs incurred when moving into independent living.

Annual grant total
In 2012/13, the charity had assets of £420,000 and an income of £240,000. Total expenditure was approximately £545,000 and grants awarded to individuals totalled £41,000.

Exclusions
No grants are given for educational purposes or to groups.

Applications
On a form available from the correspondent. Applications can be made directly by the individual or through a third party (as long as it is signed by the individual). The charity encourages a supporting statement from the individual. Applications are usually processed within five weeks.

Other information
The charity's main activities are service delivery and community outreach.

The charity also administers the Scale Trust (see separate entry for further information).

The Portsmouth Victoria Nursing Association

£17,000

Correspondent: Susan Resouly, Secretary, Southlands, Prinsted Lane, Prinsted, Emsworth, Hampshire PO10 8HS (01243 373900; email: portsmouth.victoria.nursing@gmail.com)

CC Number: 203311

Eligibility
People in need who are sick and live in the areas covered by the Portsmouth City Primary Care Trust, the Fareham

and Gosport Primary Care Trust and the East Hampshire Primary Care Trust.

Types of grants

One-off grants of up to £750 towards medical equipment, household essentials, special clothing and respite care.

Annual grant total

In 2013 the association's income was £51,000 and total spending was £45,000. Past practice indicates that grants of around £17,000 would have been made for patients welfare.

Exclusions

Items that should be provided by the NHS.

Applications

All applications must be made through the community nursing staff and help is confined to those on whom the nurses are in attendance. Referrals are made by the district nurses on a form which is considered by the committee at monthly meetings.

Other information

Assistance is also given to the community nurses of the area to improve the care they give to their patients.

The Earl of Southampton Trust

£17,700

Correspondent: Sue Boden, Clerk to the Trustees, 24 The Square, Titchfield, Hampshire PO14 4RU (01329 513294; email: earlstrust@yahoo.co.uk; website: eost.org.uk/)

CC Number: 238549

Eligibility

People in need who live in the ancient parish of Titchfield (now subdivided into the parishes of Titchfield, Sarisbury, Locks Heath, Warsash, Stubbington and Lee-on-the-Solent). Groups catering for people in need are sometimes considered.

Types of grants

One-off grants in the range of £25 and £1,000 towards motorised wheelchairs, stairlifts, specialist furniture for people who have disabilities, respite care, household equipment, redecoration, home help, childminding, holiday activities, legal fees, respite holidays and so on.

Annual grant total

In 2012/13 the trust had assets of £1.6 million and an income of £99,000. A total of £27,000 was awarded in 55 grants, the majority of which were awarded for social welfare purposes which totalled £17,700. Grants for school canopies totalled £5,600 and we estimate that grants for school uniforms totalled around £500. During the year, no grants were made towards tuition fees.

Exclusions

The trust will not supply items or services which should be provided for by the state.

Applications

In writing to the correspondent through a social worker, Citizens Advice, other welfare agency or third party (for example, doctor, district nurse, clergy or councillor). Applications must include details of medical/financial status. Applications are considered on the last Tuesday of every month, although in the event of extreme urgency requests can be fast tracked between meetings. Forms are available to download from the website.

Other information

The trust runs almshouses and a day centre for old people.

The Sway Welfare Aid Group

£14,000

Correspondent: Jeremy Stevens, Treasurer, Driftway, Mead End Road, Sway, Lymington, Hampshire SO41 6EH (01590 682843; email: info@swaghants.org.uk; website: www.swaghants.org.uk)

CC Number: 261220

Eligibility

Individuals and families in need who live in the parish of Sway and its immediate neighbourhood.

Types of grants

One-off grants towards: household equipment; rent (to avoid eviction); bereavement costs; hospital travel costs; heating bills; essential decorating costs and home repairs; insulation; reasonable recreational equipment; and disability aids. Help may also be given towards training courses and school trips.

Annual grant total

In 2012/13 the charity had an income of £17.800 and expenditure of £17,600.

Applications

In writing to the correspondent or by personal introduction.

Other information

The charity runs a lunch club for people living on their own. It also has a team of volunteer drivers that can help local residents who have difficulty in getting to, for example, hospital appointments.

Twyford and District Nursing Association

£12,300

Correspondent: Giselle Letchworth, Trustee, Sunnyside, High Street, Twyford, Winchester SO21 1RG (01962 712158; email: giselleletchworth@btinternet.com)

CC Number: 800876

Eligibility

People who are in need and live in the parishes of Twyford, Compton and Shawford, Colden Common and Owslebury, in the county of Hampshire.

Types of grants

One-off grants according to need. In the past, awards have been given for: electrical goods; convalescence; clothing; travel expenses; medical equipment; nursing fees; furniture; disability equipment; and help in the home.

Annual grant total

In 2013 the association had an income of £8,000 and a total expenditure of £12,500. We estimate that grants to individuals totalled £12,300.

Exclusions

The association cannot offer long-term care.

Applications

On a form available from the correspondent. Applications are usually made through the medical practices in the area (mainly the Twyford Practice) and people can also apply through the social services, a doctor or community nurse, or if they do not have a direct medical contact, directly to the correspondent or through a relevant third party.

Winchester Charity for the Sick (Winchester Welfare Charities)

£100

Correspondent: Dave Shaw, Principal Democratic Services Officer, Winchester Council, City Offices, Colebrook Street, Winchester, Hampshire SO23 9LJ (01962 848221; email: dshaw@winchester.gov.uk)

CC Number: 810159

Eligibility

People who are in need or distress, sick, convalescing, infirm or have a disability and live in Winchester and its immediate surroundings.

Types of grants

Our research suggests that the charity provides winter fuel payments in December and emergency grants throughout the year. These one-off grants (typically of £25–£50) have been given towards repairs to an electric wheelchair, special shoes for people with disabilities, repairs to a washing machine and so on. Help can also be offered for furniture, bedding, clothing, food, fuel and nursing requirements.

Annual grant total

In 2012/13 the charity had an income of almost £700 and an expenditure of about £100. The charitable expenditure varies; however, we estimate that grants to individuals also totalled around £100.

Applications

Recipients of Christmas vouchers are nominated by the trustees and local agencies. Applications for emergency payments should be made through a social worker, Citizens Advice or similar third party.

Other information

A leaflet is available from the correspondent.

The Winchester Rural District Welfare Trust

£700

Correspondent: Susan Lane, Trustee, Witts Cottage, Oxford Road, Sutton Scotney, Winchester, Hampshire SO21 3JG (01962 760858)

CC Number: 246512

Eligibility

People in need who live in the former Winchester rural district. This includes the parishes of Bighton, Bramdean, Compton, Headbourne Worthy and Abbot's Barton, Hursley, Itchen Valley, King's Worthy, Micheldever, Old Alresford, Owslebury, Sparsholt, Twyford, Wonston, Beauworth, Bishop's Sutton, Cheriton, Chilcomb, Crawley, Itchen Stoke and Ovington, Kilmeston, Littleton, New Alresford, Northington, Oliver's Battery and Tichborne. It does not include the city of Winchester.

Types of grants

One-off grants towards, for example, bedding, clothing, special food, fuel and heating appliances, telephone, nursing requirements, house repairs, hospital travel costs and convalescent care. Support may also be given to students seeking employment and other educational needs.

Annual grant total

In 2012/13, the trust had an income of £3,700 and a total expenditure of £2,900. We estimate that the total amount of grants awarded to individuals was approximately £700. The trust also awards grants to organisations and for educational purposes.

Applications

In writing to the correspondent, to be submitted through a social worker, Citizens Advice or other welfare agency.

Other information

This trust was formed by merging the endowments of 26 charities in 25 parishes in the Winchester rural district.

Brockenhurst

Groome Trust

£500

Correspondent: Patricia Dunkinson, Administrator, Belmont, Burford Lane, Brockenhurst SO42 7TN (01590 622303)

CC Number: 204829

Eligibility

People in need who live in the parish of Brockenhurst.

Types of grants

One-off grants towards talking books for the blind, lifelines for people living alone, Christmas gifts to nursing home residents and food vouchers for older people at Christmas.

Annual grant total

In 2013 the trust had an income of £7,000 and a total expenditure of £6,500. We estimate that the total amount of grants awarded to individuals was around £500. The trust mainly awards grants to local organisations.

Applications

In writing to the correspondent, although often the applicant is known to the trustees. Applications are considered as received.

Fareham

The Fareham Welfare Trust

£11,200

Correspondent: Anne Butcher, Clerk, 44 Old Turnpike, Fareham, Hampshire PO16 7HA (01329 235186)

CC Number: 236738

Eligibility

People in need who live in the ecclesiastical parishes of St Peter and Paul, St John and Holy Trinity, all in Fareham. Preference is given to widows in need.

Types of grants

One-off and recurrent grants up to around £250 a year. Grants have been given for clothing, furniture, food, cookers, washing machines and other essential electrical items.

Annual grant total

In 2012/13 the trust had an income of £12,100 and a total expenditure of £11,400. We estimate that grants to individuals totalled £11,200.

Applications

Applications should be submitted through a recognised referral agency (such as a social worker, health visitor, Citizens Advice or a doctor) or a trustee. They are considered throughout the year. Details of the individual's income and circumstances must be included.

Gosport

Thorngate Relief-in-Need and General Charity

£3,000

Correspondent: Kay Brent, Administrator, 16 Peakfield, Waterlooville PO7 6YP (02392 264400; email: kay.brent@btinternet.com)

CC Number: 210946

Eligibility

People in need who live in Gosport.

Types of grants

One-off grants mostly between £100 and £500.

Annual grant total

In 2012/13 the charity had an income of £8,800 and a total expenditure of £12,300. Grants are made for both welfare and educational purposes. We estimate grants for social welfare purposes for individuals to be around £3,000.

Exclusions

No grants are made towards legal expenses.

Applications

On a form available from the correspondent. Applications can be made either directly by the individual or through a social worker, Citizens Advice, Probation Service or other welfare agency.

Other information

Grants are also given to organisations.

Hawley

The Hawley Almshouse and Relief-in-Need Charity

£8,200

Correspondent: The Secretary, Trustees' Office, Ratcliffe House, Hawley Road, Blackwater, Camberley, Surrey GU17 9DD (01276 33515; website: www.hawleyalmshouses.org.uk/relief-in-need)

CC Number: 204684

Eligibility

People in need who live in the area covered by Hart District Council and Rushmoor Borough Council. Beneficiaries are generally women aged 60 or over and men aged 65 or over.

Types of grants

Generally one-off grants for needs that cannot be met from any other source. Examples of grants made in recent years include: funding towards school trips for low income families; one-off help with utility bills; rent deposits; purchase of special equipment for disabled people; and contributions to specialist medical assessments. The charity's website states: 'the trust only has a limited amount of funds and therefore the trustees are not able to help with every request received.'

Annual grant total

In 2012/13 the charity had assets of £1.7 million and an income of £123,000. Grants to individuals totalled £8,200.

Applications

An initial contact form can be completed on the website by the individual or by an appropriate third party such as a social worker or close family member. It should include a brief summary of the problem and how a grant may be able to help. The charity will then make contact to discuss the applicant's situation and whether they qualify.

Other information

The charity also provides warden-operated individual accommodation for elderly people in the area.

Isle of Wight

The Broadlands Home Trust

£7,500

Correspondent: Mrs M. Groves, Administrator, 2 Winchester Close, Newport, Isle of Wight PO30 1DR (01983 525630; email: broadlandstrust@btinternet.com)

CC Number: 201433

Eligibility

Widows of pensionable age who are in need and live on the Isle of Wight.

Types of grants

Pensions of around £450 a year and Christmas boxes of between £50 and £100. General relief-in-need grants may occasionally be given.

Annual grant total

In 2012/13 the trust had an income of £11,800 and a total expenditure of £9,600. It gives grants for both educational and social welfare purposes and we estimate the total given in social welfare grants to be around £7,500.

Exclusions

No grants for married women or graduates.

Applications

On a form available from the correspondent, to be submitted either directly by the individual or a family member. Applications are considered quarterly in January, April, July and October.

Mary Pittis for Widows

£2,000

Correspondent: Anthony Holmes, Administrator, 62–66 Lugley Street, Newport, Isle of Wight PO30 5EU (01983 524431)

CC Number: 262018

Eligibility

Widows who are aged 60 or over, live on the Isle of Wight and express Christian (in practice, Protestant) beliefs. Applicants must be known to the minister and have some connection with the church detailed on the application form. Preference is given to the candidates who were born in the Isle of Wight.

Types of grants

One-off grants ranging from £50 to £200 towards essential household equipment, semi-medical items (such as easy-lift armchairs), alarm systems and so on.

Annual grant total

At the time of writing (August 2014) the latest financial information available was from 2012. In 2012 the charity had an income of £11,000 and an expenditure of £2,100. We estimate the annual total of grants to be £2,000.

Applications

Application forms are available from the correspondent. Applicants should provide details of the church attended and the minister of that church. Submissions can be made directly by the individual, through a welfare agency or by a minister of religion on behalf of the candidate. Request can be considered at any time.

Lyndhurst

The Lyndhurst Welfare Charity

£1,000

Correspondent: A. G. Herbert, Trustee, 59 The Meadows, Lyndhurst, Hampshire SO43 7EJ (02380 283895)

CC Number: 206647

Eligibility

People in need who live in the parish of Lyndhurst.

Types of grants

Grants are normally one-off and are made towards items, services or facilities, such as household items, respite care and counselling. Grants usually range between £50 and £500.

Annual grant total

In 2012/13 the charity had an income of £5,000 and a total expenditure of £2,200.

Applications

Applicants should telephone or write to the correspondent, either directly themselves, or through a social worker, Citizens Advice or other welfare agency. Applications are usually considered in April and October, but emergency applications can be considered in between those times.

Other information

Grants are also made to organisations.

New Forest

The New Forest Keepers Widows Fund

£12,000

Correspondent: Richard Mihalop, Administrator, 17 Ferndale Road, Marchwood, Southampton SO40 4XR (02380 861136)

CC Number: 1016362

Eligibility

Retired keepers or widows and children of deceased keepers who are in need and live in the New Forest.

Types of grants

One-off and recurrent grants ranging from £50 to £2,500.

Annual grant total

In 2012/13 the fund had an income of £14.200 and a total expenditure of £14,000.

Applications

In writing to the correspondent directly by the individual or family member. Applications can be submitted at any time.

Portsmouth

The Isaac and Annie Fogelman Relief Trust

£9,300

Correspondent: Mr S. J. Forman, Trustee, Torrington House, 47 Holywell Hill, St Albans, Hertfordshire AL1 1HD (01727 885560)

CC Number: 202285

Eligibility

People of the Jewish faith aged 40 and over who live in Portsmouth and worship at the Portsmouth Jewish Synagogue.

Types of grants

One-off and recurrent grants according to need.

Annual grant total

In 2012/13 the trust had an income of £7,800 and a total expenditure of £9,400. We estimate that grants to individuals totalled £9,300.

Applications

In writing to: The Secretary, Portsmouth and Southsea Hebrew Congregation, The Thicket, Elm Grove, Southsea PO5 2AA. Applications are considered quarterly.

The Montagu Neville Durnford and Saint Leo Cawthan Memorial Trust

£16,000

Correspondent: Toni Shaw, Administrator, Hampshire and Isle of Wight Community Foundation, Dame Mary Fagan House, Chineham Court, Lutyens Close, Basingstoke, Hampshire RG24 8AG (01256 776127; email: info@hantscf.org.uk; website: www.hantscf.org.uk)

CC Number: 1100417–1

Eligibility

People over 60 who are in need and who live in the city of Portsmouth. Preference was given to ex-naval personnel and their dependents/widows.

Types of grants

Annual grants.

Annual grant total

This trust is now administered by Hampshire and the Isle of Wight Community Foundation (registered charity no. 1100417). Visit: www.hantscf.org.uk/philanthropy/fund-holders.aspxt for details. We believe that the trust is now held as part of the foundation's endowment funds under the Portsmouth City Community First Fund which holds 'moribund funds for the benefit of people in Portsmouth' (annual accounts 2012). The accounts for 2012 were the latest available for the community foundation at the time of writing (August 2014). Based on previous information held, we estimate that yearly total grants would be in the region of £16,000.

Applications

Application forms are available from the correspondent. Grants are made to the RNBT and Age UK in November, for redistribution.

The Lord Mayor of Portsmouth's Charity

£22,000

Correspondent: Toni Shaw, Administrator, Dame Mary Fagan House, Chineham Court, Lutyens Close, Basingstoke, Hampshire RG24 8AG (01256 776127; email: info@hantscf.org.uk; website: www.hantscf.org.uk)

CC Number: 1100417–2

Eligibility

Contact the correspondent for current details. Formerly this charity funded individuals in need who lived in the City of Portsmouth, or former residents who lived in Havant, Waterlooville, Fareham or Droxford.

Types of grants

One-off grants with average grants of around £200.

Annual grant total

This is now a linked charity to the Hampshire and Isle of Wight Community Foundation, however, we could not find any information in the foundation's accounts for this particular charity. In the past we know that the charity awarded around £22,000 in grants.

Applications

In writing to the correspondent.

Other information

Grants are also made to local organisations.

E. C. Roberts Charitable Trust (Roberts Trust)

£4,000

Correspondent: Revd Wendy Kennedy, Administrator, First Floor, Peninsular House, Wharf Road, Portsmouth PO2 8HB (02392 899668; email: wendy.kennedy@portsmouth.anglican.org)

CC Number: 1001055

Eligibility

Children in need who live in the city of Portsmouth, with a preference for those who are orphans, blind or have a disability.

Types of grants

One-off or recurrent grants according to need, including clothing and other essentials.

Annual grant total

In 2013 the trust had an income of £10,200 and an expenditure of £8,000. We estimate that about £4,000 was given in grants to individuals. Note that the expenditure varies significantly each year and in the past five years has fluctuated from £0 to £36,000.

Applications

In writing to the correspondent. Applications can be submitted either directly by the individual or through a third party, for example, a social worker, Citizens Advice or other welfare agency. Requests for assistance are considered upon receipt.

Other information

Organisations may also be supported.

Ryde

Ryde Sick Poor Fund (Greater Ryde Benevolent Trust)

£7,700

Correspondent: Rachel McKernan, Administrator, 29 John Street, Ryde PO33 2PZ (01983 812552; email: rachel.mckernan@btinternet.com)

CC Number: 249832

Eligibility

People who live in the former borough of Ryde (Isle of Wight) and are on low income and have health problems.

Types of grants

Small, one-off grants only.

Annual grant total

At the time of writing (August 2014) the latest financial information available was from 2012. In 2012 the fund had an income of £7,500 and a total expenditure of £7,900. We estimate that grants totalled around £7,700.

Exclusions

Our research indicates that the fund is unable to provide recurrent grants.

Applications

In writing to the correspondent.

Southampton

The Southampton (City Centre) Relief-in-Need Charity

£7,600

Correspondent: Valerie Warren, Trustee, 4 Morley Close, Burton, Christchurch BH23 7LA (01202 481984; email: valeriewarren@yahoo.com)

CC Number: 255617

Eligibility

People in need who live in the ecclesiastical parish of Southampton (in practice, the city centre).

Types of grants

One-off grants usually ranging from £50 to £100. The charity supplies a leaflet detailing the types of grants it can give.

Annual grant total

In 2013 the charity had an income of £9,400 and a total expenditure of £7,700. We estimate that grants to individuals totalled £7,600.

Exclusions

No grants towards rent, debts or council tax.

Applications

In writing to the correspondent submitted through a social worker, Citizens Advice, health visitor or other welfare agency. Applications are considered quarterly, usually in March, June, September and December; those made directly by the individual will not be considered.

Southampton and District Sick Poor Fund and Humane Society (Southampton Charitable Trust)

£5,100

Correspondent: Katy Norris, Administrator, c/o BDO LLP, Arcadia House, Maritime Walk, Southampton SO14 3TL (email: katy.norris@bdo.co.uk)

CC Number: 201603

Eligibility

People who are sick and poor and live in Southampton and the immediate surrounding area. Grants and certificates are also awarded to people for saving or attempting to save someone from drowning or other dangers.

Types of grants

Our research suggests that one-off grants, usually ranging from £50 to £250, are available for bedding, food, fuel and specialist equipment to alleviate an existing condition or to assist with day-to-day living.

Annual grant total

At the time of writing (August 2014) the latest financial information available was from 2012. In 2012 the society had an income of £11,500 and a total expenditure of £10,400. We estimate that around £5,100 was awarded in grants to individuals.

Applications

In writing to the correspondent. Applications should, preferably, be submitted through a social worker, Citizens Advice or other welfare agency. The trustees usually meet twice a year, but applications can be dealt with outside these meetings. Candidates must clearly demonstrate that they are both sick and poor (such as evidence of Income Support or other state benefits).

Other information

Grants may also be made to organisations.

Hertfordshire

The Bowley Charity for Deprived Children

£10,800

Correspondent: Pam Hill, Trustee, c/o HCC, Brindley Way, Hemel Hempstead HP3 9BF (email: pam.hill@hertfordshire.gov.uk; website: www.bowleycharity.btck.co.uk)

CC Number: 212187

Eligibility

Disadvantaged children up to 16 years (or 18 if in full-time education) who live in South West Hertfordshire.

Types of grants

Small one-off grants up to £300 for cookers, beds, bedding, prams, cots and other essential household items. Grants are also given for clothing and shoes for children. Grants should primarily benefit children, rather than adults, and usually come in the form of Argos vouchers.

Annual grant total

In 2012/13 the charity had an income of £10,800 and a total expenditure of £11,000. We estimate that grants to individuals totalled £10,800.

Exclusions

Trustees will not normally fund flooring, living room furniture, holidays, school uniform, outings or school trips.

Applications

On a form available to download from the charity's website or from the correspondent. Applications should be made through a social worker, Citizens Advice or other welfare agency. The trustees meet quarterly in March, June, September and December to consider grants. See the website for closing dates for applications.

The Hertfordshire Charity for Deprived Children

£8,400

Correspondent: Ralph Paddock, Administrator, 86 Ware Road, Hertford SG13 7HN (01992 551128; email: ralphiegerry@btopenworld.com)

CC Number: 200327

Eligibility

Disadvantaged children up to the age of 17 living in Hertfordshire (excluding the Watford area).

Types of grants

One-off grants generally for holidays (not overseas), clothing (such as school or cub/brownie uniforms or general clothing), bedding, furniture and other household items (such as cookers, or washing machines, where this would improve the quality of life for the child). Grants usually range between £30 and £300.

Annual grant total

In 2012/13 the charity had an income of £8,200 and an expenditure of £8,600. We estimate that grants to individuals totalled £8,400.

Applications

On a form available from the correspondent. Applications should be made through a health visitor, social worker, probation officer or similar third party. Trustees normally meet in May and November, but applications can be considered between meetings and can be approved on the agreement of two trustees.

Hertfordshire Community Foundation

£84,000 (523 grants)

Correspondent: Caroline Langdell, Fund Manager, Foundation House, 2–4 Forum Place, Off Fiddlebridge Lane, Hatfield, Hertfordshire AL10 0RN (01707 251351; fax: 01707 251133; email: caroline.langdell@hertscf.org.uk; website: www.hertscf.org.uk)

CC Number: 299438

Eligibility

People who live in Hertfordshire and are in need. Eligibility criteria varies depending on which fund is being applied to. See Hertfordshire Community Foundation's website for more details of funds that are currently accepting applications.

Types of grants

In 2012/13 the average grant for individuals was £161. The type of grant available varies according to the fund; see the foundation's website for details.

Annual grant total

In 2012/13 the foundation held assets of £7.5 million and had an income of £1.5 million. A total of £703,000 was awarded in grants through the various funds administered by the foundation, the majority of which were to local organisations. Grants to individuals totalled more than £84,000. Of this, £34,000 was given to 200 families from the Hertfordshire Children's Fund and a further £50,000 was distributed to 323 individuals and families from the Warm Homes/Healthy People Fund.

Applications

Please see the foundation's website for more details on open funds and how to make an application.

Other information

The foundation administers 90 funds which provide grants to organisations and to individuals.

The Hertfordshire Convalescent Trust

£24,500

Correspondent: Janet Bird, Administrator, 140 North Road, Hertford SG14 2BZ (01992 587544; fax: 01992 582595; email: janet_l_bird@hotmail.com)

CC Number: 212423

Eligibility

People in need who are convalescing following an operation or period of ill health, chronically sick, terminally ill or children with special needs and their carers. Families suffering from domestic violence or relationship breakdown may also be eligible for assistance. Applicants must live in Hertfordshire.

Types of grants

One-off grants in the range of £300 to £500 for traditional convalescence in a nursing home or for respite breaks and recuperative holidays in hotels and caravans.

Annual grant total

In 2012 the trust had assets of £508,000 and an income of £32,900. Grants totalled £24,500. The 2012 accounts were the latest available at the time of writing (August 2014).

Exclusions

There are no grants available for equipment or transport costs.

Applications

On a form available from the correspondent. Applications should be sponsored by a health professional, social worker or member of the clergy. They are considered throughout the year.

Other information

The annual report for 2012 states that: 'In excess of 120 adults and children throughout the county of Hertfordshire were able to take a holiday during the year due to receiving a grant from the trust. Grants to each family or individual averaged between £450 and £500.'

The Ware Charities

£4,500 (11 grants)

Correspondent: Susan Newman, Administrator, 3 Scotts Road, Ware, Hertfordshire SG12 9JG (01920 461629; email: suedogs@hotmail.com)

CC Number: 225443

Eligibility

People in need who live in the area of Ware Town Council, the Parish of Wareside and the Parish of Thundridge.

Types of grants

Grants are made towards items or services not readily available from any other source.

Annual grant total

In 2012/13 the charity had assets of £1.2 million and an income of £62,000. Grants made totalled £30,000 of which £21,000 went to organisations which provide or undertake services or facilities to people residing in Ware who are in need, hardship or distress and £9,000 went to individuals for social welfare or educational purposes.

Applications

In writing to the correspondent at any time, to be submitted directly by the individual or a family member. Applications must include brief details of the applicant's income and savings and be supported and signed by a headteacher, GP, nurse or social worker.

Other information

Grants are also made to local organisations.

Buntingford

Buntingford Relief-in-Need Charity

£15,000

Correspondent: Eunice Woods, Trustee, 38 Hare Street Road, Buntingford, Hertfordshire SG9 9HW (01763 271974)

CC Number: 262264

Eligibility

Older people on state registered pensions who have lived in the parish of Buntingford for at least ten years. Other people in need within the parish may also be helped.

Types of grants

Our research suggests that £20 per household is given in early December towards the cost of fuel.

Annual grant total

At the time of writing (September 2014) the latest financial information available was from 2011. In 2011 the charity had an income of £9,500 and a total expenditure of £124,000, which is exceptionally high. Both figures vary from year to year. In the past grants to individuals have totalled around £15,000.

Applications

In writing to the correspondent.

Other information

Organisations may also be assisted.

Dacorum

The Dacorum Community Trust

£49,000

Correspondent: The Grants and Finance Officer, The Hub Dacorum, Paradise, Hemel Hempstead HP2 4TF (01442 231396; email: admin@dctrust.org.uk; website: www.dctrust.org.uk)

CC Number: 272759

Eligibility

People in need who live in the borough of Dacorum.

Types of grants

Generally one-off grants up to £500 towards domestic equipment; disability equipment; clothes and shoes; funeral expenses; respite breaks and holidays for families; debt relief; and the costs involved in making homes habitable and safe for young and old.

Annual grant total

In 2012/13 the trust had assets of £136,000 and received an income of £107,500. There were 673 grants made totalling £65,000. Direct grants totalled £41,000 and gifts in kind were costed at £23,000. We have estimated the educational grants total to be around £15,000 and welfare grants/gifts in kind to total £49,000.

Exclusions

Grants are not normally given for the costs of further or mainstream education and only in exceptional circumstances for gap-year travel.

Applications

On a form available from the correspondent or to download from the website. Applications can be submitted by the individual, through a recognised referral agency (such as Social Services or Citizens Advice) or through an MP, GP or school. Applications are considered in March, June, September and December. The trust asks for details of family finances. A preliminary telephone call is always welcome.

Other information

This trust also gives to organisations.

Harpenden

The Harpenden Trust

£45,000 (794 grants)

Correspondent: Dennis Andrews, Trustee, The Trust Centre, 90 Southdown Road, Harpenden AL5 1PS (01582 460457; email: admin@theharpendentrust.org.uk; website: www.theharpendentrust.org.uk)

CC Number: 1118870

Eligibility

People in need who live in the 'AL5' postal district of Harpenden, with a preference for younger and older people.

Types of grants

One-off grants for up to £200 are made, for example, for large unexpected bills, essential household items and children's food and clothing. Grants towards the cost of utility bills are available to pensioners on a low income. Educational grants may also be made.

Annual grant total

In 2012/13 the trust had assets of £4 million and an income of £217,500. Grants were made to 794 individuals totalling £58,500 and were distributed as follows:

General grants	543	£30,000
Utilities grants	71	£13,300
Youth grants	121	£13,300
Christmas parcels	180	£1,700

Grants for educational purposes benefited 121 children and totalled £13,300. The remaining £45,000 was given to individuals for welfare purposes. A further £45,500 was given to organisations.

Exclusions

Grants are not given to individuals living outside Harpenden.

Applications

In writing to the correspondent, either directly by the individual or, if applicable, through a third party such as a social worker or Citizens Advice.

Other information

The Harpenden Trust was founded in 1948 by Dr Charles Hill 'remembered by some as the gravel-voice Radio Doctor during WW2.' It now runs its own centres in Southdown Road and at the High Street Methodist Church. The trust organises weekly coffee mornings, coach trips and a Christmas parcel scheme for pensioners, as well as outings for children. The trust publishes and sells its own annual calendar, 50 of which it donates to around a dozen local charities for selling purposes.

The trust has an informative website.

Hatfield

Hatfield Broad Oak Non-Ecclesiastical Charities

£2,600

Correspondent: Martin Gandy, Administrator, Carters Barn, Cage End, Hatfield Broad Oak, Bishop's Stortford, Hertfordshire CM22 7HL (01279 718316)

CC Number: 206467

Eligibility

People in need who live in Hatfield Broad Oak.

Types of grants

One-off and recurrent grants ranging from £20 to £25.

Annual grant total

In 2013 the charity had an income of £7,000 and a total expenditure of £5,600. We estimate that grants to individuals totalled around £2,600.

Applications

In writing to the correspondent directly by the individual or family member.

Other information

The charity's Charity Commission record states that it also assists with housing accommodation.

Wellfield Trust

£12,500

Correspondent: Jeanette Bayford, Administrator, Birchwood Leisure Centre, Longmead, Hatfield, Hertfordshire AL10 0AN (01707 251018; email: wellfieldtrust@aol.com; website: www.wellfieldtrust.co.uk)

CC Number: 296205

Eligibility

People in need who are on a low income and who have lived in the parish of Hatfield for six months.

Types of grants

One-off grants of £100 to £500 towards a range of welfare needs. The trust also loans motorised scooters.

Annual grant total

In 2012/13 grants to individuals totalled £15,500, with a further £1,700 given towards projects.

The majority of grants are given for welfare purposes which we estimate to be around £12,500 with approximately £3,000 awarded in educational grants.

Exclusions

Grants are not made for council tax arrears, rent or funeral costs.

Applications

On a form available from the correspondent or to download from the website, only via a third party such as social services or Citizens Advice. Most of the local appropriate third parties also have the application form. Applications are considered monthly and should be received by the first Monday of every month.

Other information

The trust also gives to organisations, has a room at a local leisure centre which can be hired free of charge to charitable organisations and a scooter loan scheme. It has a helpful and informative website.

Letchworth Garden City

The Letchworth Civic Trust

£1,100 (3 grants)

Correspondent: Sally Jenkins, Administrator, 66 Highfield, Letchworth Garden City, Hertfordshire SG6 3PZ (01462 686919; email: letchworthct@gmail.com; website: letchworthct.org.uk)

CC Number: 273336

Eligibility

People who have lived in Letchworth Garden City for two years or more.

Types of grants

One-off grants and occasionally loans in the range of £50 to £500. Bursaries are sometimes available to exceptionally talented musicians, athletes and swimmers. Disability individuals with mobility problems can also apply for grants.

Annual grant total

In 2012/13 the trust had assets of £644,000 and an income of £72,000. Grants to individuals totalled £48,000 including three grants for educational purposes and medical support totalling £1,100.

Applications

On forms available from the website. Applications are considered in January, March, June, September, October and December and can be submitted by the individual or a third party such as a headteacher, social worker, probation officer or police officer.

Other information

Grants are also made to schoolchildren and students, and to groups and societies, but not religious or political groups.

In a typical year about 200 grants are given to individuals, mainly for young people.

Watford

The Watford Health Trust

£18,800

Correspondent: Ian Scleater, Trustee, Allways, 23 Shepherds Road, Watford WD18 7HU (01923 222745; email: ian@scleater.co.uk)

CC Number: 214160

Eligibility

People in need who are in poor health, convalescent or who have a disability and live in the borough of Watford and the surrounding neighbourhood.

Types of grants

One-off and recurrent grants to assist recovery or improve quality of life. During 2012/13 grants ranged from less than £100 to more than £2,000.

Annual grant total

In 2012/13 the trust had an income of £27,000 and a total expenditure of £23,000. During the year, individuals received £18,800 in grants. A further £2,400 was returned to the trust unspent.

Applications

In writing to the correspondent. Grants are generally made through official bodies or practices familiar with the applicant's needs.

Wormley

The Wormley Parochial Charity

£3,500

Correspondent: Carol Proctor, Trustee, 5 Lammasmead, Broxbourne, Hertfordshire EN10 6PF

CC Number: 218463

Eligibility

People in need who live in the parish of Wormley as it was defined before 31 March 1935, particularly those who are elderly, sick or newly bereaved.

Types of grants

Grants towards (i) transport to or from hospital, either as a patient or visitor; (ii) Christmas vouchers to spend locally for food and other necessities for people who are in need, sick, frail, elderly, bereaved and so on; (iii) one-off grants for people with special needs.

Annual grant total

In 2012 this charity had an income of £15,000 and a total expenditure of nearly £7,000. We estimate that grants for individuals for social welfare purposes totalled around £3,500. The accounts for 2012 were the latest available at the time of writing (July 2014).

Exclusions

The charity does not give loans.

Applications

In writing to the correspondent, either directly by the individual, or through a social worker, Citizens Advice, welfare agency or a third party such as a friend who is aware of the situation. Applications are considered in April and October.

Kent

The Appleton Trust (Canterbury)

£5,400 (4 grants)

Correspondent: Mark Spraggins, Administrator, Diocesan Board of Education, Diocesan House, Lady Wootton's Green, Canterbury, Kent CT1 1NQ (01227 459401)

CC Number: 250271

Eligibility

People in need connected with the Church of England in the diocese of Canterbury.

Types of grants

One-off grants normally ranging between £100 and £500. The trust also makes loans to members of the clergy, local parishioners and widows of clergymen for items such as cars, computer equipment and equity loans.

Annual grant total

At the time of writing (August 2014) the latest financial information available was from 2012. In 2012 the trust had assets of £802,000 and an income of £33,000. Grants were made to four individuals totalling £5,400.

Exclusions

Our research suggests that grants are not given for further education.

Applications

In writing to the correspondent. Applications should be submitted directly by the individual or a church organisation. They are considered every two months.

Other information

Organisations connected to the Church of England in Canterbury Diocese are also supported (three grants totalling £4,500 in 2012).

The Coleman Trust

£46,000

Correspondent: Peter Sherred, Clerk, Bradleys, 15–21 Castle Street, Dover CT16 1PU (01304 204080)

CC Number: 237708

Eligibility

People who live in Dover and the immediate neighbourhood and are sick, convalescing, or living with a mental or physical disability.

Types of grants

One-off grants according to need. In the past, grants have been given for periods in residential care and nursing homes, disability aids, telephone facilities and convalescent holiday breaks.

Annual grant total

In 2013 the trust had assets of £1.2 million (almost all of which represented permanent endowment and was not available for grant giving). It had an income of £61,000 and a total expenditure of £54,000. Grants to individuals totalled £46,000.

Exclusions

No grants for furniture, home repairs or debts.

Applications

Applications should be made through a social worker, Citizens Advice, welfare agency, doctor or consultant and sent to Barbara Godfrey, Welfare Officer, 41 The Ridgeway, River, Dover, Kent CT16 1RT.

Headley-Pitt Charitable Trust

£5,500

Correspondent: Thelma Pitt, Administrator, Old Mill Cottage, Ulley Road, Kennington, Ashford, Kent TN24 9HX (01233 626189; email: thelma.pitt@headley.co.uk)

CC Number: 252023

Eligibility

Individuals in need who live in Kent with a preference for Ashford. There is also a preference for older people.

Types of grants

One-off grants, usually in the range of £100 to £300.

Annual grant total

In 2012/13 the trust had assets of £2.4 million and an income of £79,000. Grants made to individuals totalled £11,000. We estimate that grants made to individuals for welfare purposes totalled around £5,500.

Applications

In writing to the correspondent, either directly by the individual or through a third party.

Other information

Grants are also made to organisations and to individuals for educational purposes.

Kent Community Foundation

Correspondent: Grants Team, Office 23, Evegate Park Barn, Evegate, Ashford, Kent TN25 6SX (01303 814500; email: admin@kentcf.org.uk; website: www.kentcf.org.uk)

CC Number: 1084361

Eligibility

People who live in Kent and are in need. Eligibility criteria varies depending on which fund is being applied to. See the Kent Community Foundation website for details of funds that are currently accepting applications.

Types of grants

The type of grant available varies according to fund; see the foundation's website for details.

Annual grant total

In 2012/13 the foundation held assets of £11 million and had an income of £4.2 million. During the year grants totalled £1.8 million, the vast majority of which we believe was given to organisations. We were unable to obtain a figure for welfare grants to individuals but believe they account for only a small portion of the grant total.

Applications

See the foundation's website for details of open funds and how to make an application.

Other information

The Kent Community Foundation administers a number of funding schemes for both organisations and individuals. See the foundation's informative website for more details.

The Kent County Football Association Benevolent Fund

£1,100

Correspondent: Keith Masters, Chief Executive, Invicta House, Cobdown House, London Road, Ditton, Aylesford, Kent ME20 6DQ (01622 791850; email: info@kentfa.com; website: www.kentfa.com)

CC Number: 273118

Eligibility

Players and others directly connected with affiliated bodies or within the jurisdiction of the association who may be injured whilst playing football or who may be incapacitated through illness definitely attributable to participation in the game.

Types of grants

One-off grants according to need.

Annual grant total

In 2013 the fund had an income of £4,300 and a total expenditure of £1,200. We estimate that social welfare grants to individuals totalled £1,100.

Applications

On a form available from the correspondent.

The Kent Fund for Children

£10,000

Correspondent: The Trustees, 3rd Floor, Invicta House, County Hall, Maidstone, Kent ME14 1XX (01622 694845; website:www.kenttrustweb.org.uk)

Eligibility

Children and young people up to the age of 21, who are in need and live in Kent county council area. The fund is keen to support children and young people who have not had the opportunities that most children and young people enjoy, either because they have physical or learning disabilities, a sensory impairment, or difficult social circumstances.

Types of grants

One-off grants usually up to £500. Grants must be of direct benefit to the child or young person. The fund is particularly keen to enable children and young people to pursue activities, hobbies and interests which cannot be financed through usual sources, i.e. local authorities, schools and community groups and where applicants show self-help through fundraising. Grants may be for equipment for personal development, or to allow the opportunity to learn new skills, or being involved in an expedition or outing.

Annual grant total

Grants usually total around £10,000 per year.

Applications

In writing to the correspondent. Applications must be made on behalf of individuals by a charity, an organised group, society or professional. This includes schools, youth, and community groups and so on.

Note: The fund is heavily over-subscribed at present, so unsolicited applications are likely to be rejected.

Other information

Formerly known as The Kent Children's Trust.

Kent Nursing Institution

£2,000

Correspondent: Canon R. B. Stevenson, Trustee, Michaelmas Cottage, Stan Lane, West Peckham, Maidstone, Kent ME18 5JT (01732 842245)

CC Number: 211227

Eligibility

People in need who are sick, convalescent, disabled or infirm and live in west Kent.

Types of grants

One-off grants ranging between £200 and £500. Grants have been given to relieve hardship caused by family illness (for example, hospital visiting costs) and to assist with payments for specialist equipment to relieve discomfort (special beds, ultrasound matching, etc.).

Annual grant total

In 2013 the institution had an income of £5,700 and a total expenditure of £4,300. We estimate that grants to individuals totalled £2,000, with local organisations also receiving funding.

Exclusions

The institution does not assist with debt or bankruptcy fees.

Applications

In writing to the correspondent either directly by the individual or through a social worker, doctor, priest, Citizens Advice or other welfare agency. Applications are usually considered in March and October.

Littledown Trust

£9,800

Correspondent: P. G. Brown, Trustee, Littledown Farmhouse, Lamberhurst Down, Lamberhurst, Tunbridge Wells TN3 8HD (01892 890867)

CC Number: 1064291

Eligibility

People in need, with a preference for the elderly and disadvantaged or disabled children and adults who live in Kent or Devon.

Types of grants

One-off and recurrent grants according to need, ranging between £100 and £500.

Annual grant total

In 2012/13 the trust had an income of £20,000 and an unusually high total expenditure also of £20,000. We estimate that grants to individuals totalled £9,800, with funding also awarded to organisations in Devon and Kent.

Applications

In writing to the correspondent, or through Citizens Advice, a social worker or another relevant third party.

The Lord Mayor of Canterbury's Christmas Gift Fund

£18,000

Correspondent: Jennifer Sherwood, Administrator, MHA MacIntyre Hudson, 31 St George's Place, Canterbury, Kent CT1 1XD (01227 464991; website: www.christmasgiftfund.co.uk/about.php)

CC Number: 278803

Eligibility

People in need who live in Canterbury and the surrounding area comprised in the former district of Bridge Blean. Preference is given to older people and to families with young children.

Types of grants

Food parcels (worth approximately £25 each) and toy vouchers are distributed before Christmas.

Annual grant total

In 2012/13 the fund had an income of £19,700 and a total expenditure of £18,600. We estimate that Christmas gifts to individuals – including 500 grocery parcels – totalled £18,000.

Applications

A list is compiled over the year from local doctors, clergy, Age UK, direct applications and other sources. Direct applications should be made in writing to the correspondent. Gifts are delivered in person by volunteers.

Other information

The fund's website describes how it 'was set up 60 years ago by members of the business community, who approached the then Mayor, suggesting that they might launch an appeal to give parcels to the elderly and needy at Christmas time. In that first year the appeal raised between £200 and £300.'

The Dorothy Parrott Trust Fund

£2,400

Correspondent: Gina Short, Administrator, 10 The Landway, Kemsing, Sevenoaks TN15 6TG (01732 760263)

CC Number: 278904

Eligibility

People in need who live in the area administered by Sevenoaks Town Council and adjoining parishes. Young children and older people are given preference.

Types of grants

Usually one-off grants ranging from £25 to £100 according to need. Previously grants have been given towards a fridge, a school outing for the child of a single parent, house decoration, boots, ballet shoes, a mattress for twins and project trips such as Operation Raleigh.

Annual grant total

Grants to individuals for social welfare purposes average around £2,400 per year.

Applications

Either direct to the correspondent or through a social worker, Citizens Advice or similar third party, including a general history of the family. Applications are considered on the last Monday of January, April, July and October.

Other information

Grants may also be made to local organisations.

Sir Thomas Smythe's Charity

£19,000

Correspondent: Charities Administrator, The Skinners' Company, Skinners' Hall, 8 Dowgate Hill, London EC4R 2SP (020 7236 5629; email: charitiesadmin@skinners.org.uk; website: www.skinnershall.co.uk)

CC Number: 210775

Eligibility

People who are elderly or disabled and live within the 26 parishes of Tonbridge and Tunbridge Wells in their own home, either as a tenant or an owner-occupier. Most successful applicants are in receipt of a combination of benefits, disability allowances or state retirement pension, but each case will be examined individually.

Types of grants

Quarterly pensions (£640 per annum in 2012/13) are distributed personally by a trustee. Pension levels are reviewed every April. One-off crisis grants are typically made for items not covered by benefits, for example, unexpected household repairs or the replacement of domestic appliances.

Annual grant total

In 2012/13 the charity held assets of £1.3 million and had an income of £31,000. Pensions to individuals totalled £19,000.

Exclusions

Grants are not made to people in residential care and cannot be given to cover funeral costs or debt repayments.

Applications

Applications are only recommended via local trustees. For contact details of your local trustee, contact the charity's administrator. Trustees meet twice yearly in April and October.

Note: in 2012/13 no new applications for pensions were considered 'partly because funds were fully committed'. Furthermore, at the time of writing (August 2014) the charity's webpage states that: 'Funds are fully committed at present'.

Other information

The Sir Thomas Smythe's Charity was founded in the will of Sir Thomas Smythe in 1625.

The charity has an informative website.

Borden

The William Barrow's Charity

£42,000

Correspondent: Stuart Mair, Administrator, George Webb Finn, 43 Park Road, Sittingbourne, Kent ME10 1DY (01795 470556; email: stuart@georgewebbfinn.com)

CC Number: 307574

Eligibility

People in need who live in the ancient ecclesiastical parish of Borden or have lived in the parish and now live nearby. There is a preference for people of 60 years or over and disabled people.

Types of grants

One-off grants and twice-yearly allowances may be given for pensions, disability and medical equipment, travel expenses, convalescence and living costs. Grants typically range from £350 to £500.

Annual grant total

In 2013 the charity had assets of £6.1 million and an income of £217,000. Grants to individuals from the eleemosynary fund totalled £42,000 and were distributed as follows:

Grants to pensioners	£25,000
Grants to students	£16,600
Other grants	£400
Age Concern vouchers	£200

Individuals also received £8,700 in grants from the educational fund, from which a further £33,000 was awarded in 'school grants'.

Applications

On a form available from the correspondent. Applications are considered in January, April, July and October.

Other information

The charity works in close cooperation with Age UK.

Canterbury

The Canterbury United Municipal Charities

£1,500

Correspondent: Aaron Spencer, Furley Page, Solicitors, 39–40 St Margaret's Street, Canterbury, Kent CT1 2TX (01227 863140; email: aas@furleypage.co.uk)

CC Number: 210992

Eligibility

People in need who have lived within the boundaries of what was the old city of Canterbury for at least two years.

Types of grants

One-off and recurrent grants and pensions. Annual pensions of £100 are given to about 20 needy older people. Also at Christmas, vouchers/tokens of £25 are given for: clothing for children aged 6 to 16 (30 children); and people who are elderly and in need (120 adults).

Annual grant total

In 2012 this charity had an income of £9,100 and a total expenditure of £6,400. We estimate that the total awarded to individuals for social welfare purposes was around £1,500. The latest accounts available at the time of writing (July 2014) were for year ending December 2012.

Applications

In writing to the correspondent through the individual's school/college/educational welfare agency or directly by the individual. Applications are considered on an ongoing basis and should include a brief statement of circumstances and proof of residence in the area.

Other information

Grants are also given for educational purposes and to organisations with similar objects.

Streynsham's Charity

£20,500

Correspondent: The Clerk to the Trustees, PO Box 970, Canterbury, Kent CT1 9DJ (0845 094 4769)

CC Number: 214436

Eligibility

People who live in the ancient parish of St Dunstan's.

Types of grants

One-off grants, up to a maximum of about £300.

Annual grant total

In 2012 grants awarded to individuals for educational purposes totalled £3,500. Grants to individuals for social welfare purposes totalled £20,500 and organisations were awarded £5,600. The latest accounts available at the time of writing (July 2014) were for year ending December 2012.

Applications

In writing to the correspondent. Applications should be made directly by the individual. They are usually considered in March and October but can be made at any time and should include an sae and telephone number if possible.

Chatham

Chatham District Masonic Trust

£90

Correspondent: John Knight, Administrator, 42 The Everglades, Hempstead, Gillingham, Kent ME7 3PY (01634 300755; email: CDMTchatham@hotmail.com)

CC Number: 1040230

Eligibility

Freemasons and their widows and children, living in Chatham.

Types of grants
One-off and recurrent grants according to need.

Annual grant total
In 2012/13 the trust had assets of £35,000, an income of £26,000 and a total expenditure of £18,000. One donation of £85 was made, although it was not specified whether an individual or an organisation has been supported. In previous years individual grants have rarely been made.

Applications
In writing to the correspondent.

Other information
The principal activity of the trust is the running of the Masonic Centre at Manor Road, Chatham.

Folkstone

Folkestone Municipal Charities

£78,000

Correspondent: Michael A. Cox, Administrator, Romney House, Cliff Road, Hythe CT21 5XA (01303 260144; email: gillyjc@btinternet.com)

CC Number: 211528

Eligibility
People in need who live in the borough of Folkestone and have done so for at least five years. Preference is usually given to older people and single parent families.

Types of grants
Pensions and one-off relief in need grants. Previous grants have been given for telephone installation, help after a burglary, loss of a purse/wallet, shoes for disadvantaged children, gas/electricity bills, beds/bedding, prams, clothing and household repairs. Relief in need payments, whenever possible, are made directly to the supplier.

Annual grant total
In 2012/13 the charity held assets of £2.9 million and had an income of £109,000. Grants and pensions totalled £78,000 and were distributed as follows:

Pensions	£50,000
Relief in need	£28,000

Other charitable causes received a further £8,800 in grants and donations.

Applications
On a form available from the correspondent. Applications should be submitted through a third party such as a social worker, Citizens Advice or similar welfare agency. They are considered on a monthly basis, though urgent requests can be dealt with between meetings.

Fordwich

The Fordwich United Charities

£2,000

Correspondent: Dr Roger Green, Trustee, 15 Water Meadows, Fordwich, Canterbury, Kent CT2 0BF (01227 713661; email: rogergreen@fordwich.net)

CC Number: 208258

Eligibility
People in need or with disabilities living in Fordwich.

Types of grants
One-off grants mostly given towards household bills.

Annual grant total
In 2013 the charity had an income of £15,700 and an expenditure of £8,400. It gives to individuals and organisations for both educational and social welfare purposes. We estimate grants awarded to individuals for social welfare purposes to be around £2,000.

Applications
In writing to: M R Clayton, Ladywell House, Fordwich, Canterbury CT2 0DL. The deadline for applications is 1 September and a decision will be made within a month.

Gillingham

The Dobson Trust

£1,500

Correspondent: Margaret Taylor, Resources, Medway Council, Gun Wharf, Dock Road, Chatham, Kent ME4 4TR (01634 332144; email: margaret.taylor@medway.gov.uk)

CC Number: 283158

Eligibility
People in receipt of a state pension or over the age of 60 who are in financial need and live in the former borough of Gillingham.

Types of grants
One-off grants according to need. Recent grants ranged from £70 for audio books to £2,500 for a replacement boiler. Grants are generally given to help cover exceptional outgoings or unexpected bills, such as to repair or replace an essential domestic appliance or piece of furniture; specialist equipment associated with disability or impairment; or the costs associated with the death of a partner (excluding funeral costs).

Annual grant total
In 2012/13, the trust had an income of £1,800 and a total expenditure of £3,500. We estimate the grants total for individuals to be £1,500. The trust also awards grants to local organisations providing welfare for the elderly.

Applications
On a form available from the correspondent. Applications can be submitted at any time and the trustees meet about four times a year.

Godmersham

Godmersham Relief in Need Charity

£2,500

Correspondent: David T. Swan, Administrator, Feleberge, Canterbury Road, Bilting, Ashford, Kent TN25 4HE (01233 812125)

CC Number: 206278

Eligibility
People in need who live in the ancient parish of Godmersham.

Types of grants
One-off grants according to need, towards items, services or facilities.

Annual grant total
In 2013 the charity had an income of £6,500 and a total expenditure of £5,400. Grants are given for both educational and relief-in-need purposes.

Applications
In writing to the correspondent, either directly by the individual or through a third party.

Gravesham

William Frank Pinn Charitable Trust

£166,000 (1,659 grants)

Correspondent: Trust Officer, HSBC Trust Company (UK) Ltd, 10th Floor Norwich House, Nelson Gate, Commercial Road, Southampton SO15 1GX (02380 722224)

CC Number: 287772

Eligibility
People of pensionable age who live in the Borough of Gravesham. Priority is given to those on lower incomes.

Types of grants

One-off grants averaging £100 are made for specific purposes only, mainly for household expenses and clothing.

Annual grant total

In 2012/13 the trust held assets of £6.2 million and had an income of £265,000. A total of £166,000 was awarded in 1659 grants to individuals.

Exclusions

No more than two grants may be made to any household per calendar year.

Applications

On a form available from the correspondent. Applications should be submitted directly by the individual and are considered as received.

Other information

This trust was formed from the estate of Mr William Frank Pinn who died on 18 June 1983.

Hayes

Hayes (Kent) Trust

£4,100 (10 grants)

Correspondent: Andrew Naish, Administrator, 2 Warren Wood Close, Bromley BR2 7DU (020 8462 1915; email: hayes.kent.trust@gmail.com)

CC Number: 221098

Eligibility

People in need who live in the parish of Hayes.

Types of grants

One-off grants in the region of £75 to £1,500 are given according to need.

Annual grant total

In 2012/13, the trust had assets of £966,000 and an income of £45,000. A total of £4,100 was awarded in ten welfare grants to individuals:

Relief in Need	9	£3,400
Relief in Sickness	1	£700

The trust also granted £10,500 to five welfare organisations. Educational grants to five individuals and eight organisations totalled a further £18,500.

Applications

In writing to the correspondent. Applications should include the full name of the applicant, postal address in Hayes (Kent), telephone number and date of birth. Applications can be made either directly by the individual, or through a third party such as a social worker, Citizens Advice or other welfare agency.

Herne Bay

The Herne Bay Parochial Charity

£500

Correspondent: Susan Record, Clerk, 39 William Street, Herne Bay, Kent CT6 5NR (01227 367355)

CC Number: 1069542

Eligibility

People in need who live in Herne Bay. Applicants preferably should be on income support or in receipt of similar financial assistance.

Types of grants

Both one-off and regular grants during the year and at Christmas. The usual grant to individuals consists of:

(i) a monthly voucher of around £6 which can be exchanged at certain shops or the local council office (ii) a cash grant of £20 at Christmas (iii) a cash grant of £10 in February towards fuel (iv) a cash grant of £10 in November towards fuel.

The charities may make a £10 Christmas grant to several other individuals. Examples of other grants are to purchase a particular necessary item such as providing a telephone or to clear a debt, for example.

Annual grant total

In 2012 the charity had an income of £1,600 and a total expenditure of £1,200. We estimate that donations to individuals totalled around £500, with grants also given to organisations who help people in need.

At the time of writing (August 2014) this was the most recent financial information available for the charity.

Applications

In writing to the correspondent through a social worker, Citizens Advice or other welfare agency or directly by the individual or some relevant third party. Applications are normally considered in April and October and ideally should be received in the preceding month. The charities have to be satisfied that the applicant is financially in need, such as by providing supporting evidence of low income through wage slips or a benefit award letter. Particulars of what the grant is required for should be included.

Hothfield

The Thanet Charities

£4,900

Correspondent: Pat Guy, Administrator, Garden House, Bethersden Road, Hothfield, Ashford, Kent TN26 1EP (01233 612449)

CC Number: 213093

Eligibility

People in need who live in the parish of Hothfield.

Types of grants

Small monthly payments to elderly residents of Hothfield village. There are also a limited number of hardship grants available for individuals in need. These come in the form of one-off monetary payments or through the provision of services/facilities.

Annual grant total

In 2012/13, the charity had an income of £6,500 and a total expenditure of £5,600. We estimate that grants to individuals totalled £4,900.

The charity also makes a yearly payment to the Thanet Educational Foundation.

Applications

In writing to the correspondent.

Hythe

Anne Peirson Charitable Trust

£4,500

Correspondent: Ina Tomkinson, Trustee/Secretary, Tyrol House, Cannongate Road, Hythe, Kent CT21 5PX (01303 260779)

CC Number: 800093

Eligibility

People who live the parish of Hythe and are in need, due for example to hardship, disability or sickness. Support is primarily given for educational needs but grants for emergency needs will be made if financial hardship is demonstrated.

Types of grants

One-off grants ranging from £100 to £600. Recent grants were made towards nursery school fees, special needs for people with children who have disabilities, household goods and so on.

Annual grant total

In 2013 the trust had an income of £13,200 and a total expenditure of £18,000. Grants are awarded to individuals and organisations for both educational and social welfare purposes. We estimate the amount given to individuals for social welfare purposes was around £4,500.

Exclusions

No grants are made where statutory support is available.

Applications

In writing to the correspondent via either Citizens Advice, a social worker, health visitor, school headteacher or other third party. Grants are considered on an ongoing basis.

Leigh

The Leigh United Charities

£42,000

Correspondent: Sally Bresnahan, Administrator, 3 Oak Cottages, High Street, Leigh, Tonbridge TN11 8RW (01732 838544; email: sally@bresnahan.co.uk)

CC Number: 233988

Eligibility

People in need who live in the ancient parish of Leigh.

Types of grants

One-off grants according to need.

Annual grant total

In 2012/13 the charity had an income and an expenditure of £49,000. Grants to individuals totalled £42,000, of which £33,000 was distributed in Leigh and more than £9,000 in Hildenborough.

Exclusions

No payment for rates.

Applications

In writing to the correspondent directly by the individual. Applications are considered throughout the year.

Other information

The charity also makes grants to organisations and in 2012/13 awarded a total of £2,500 to Leigh Primary School.

Maidstone

The Edmett and Fisher Charity

£8,000

Correspondent: Robin Rogers, Administrator, 72 King Street, Maidstone, Kent ME14 1BL (01622 698000)

CC Number: 241823

Eligibility

People in need who are aged over 60 and live in the former borough of Maidstone (as it was before April 1974).

Types of grants

One-off and recurrent grants according to need. Christmas gifts have also been distributed in previous years.

Annual grant total

In 2012/13 the charity had an income of £9,100 and a total expenditure of £8,500. We estimate that grants to individuals totalled £8,000.

Applications

On a form available from the correspondent to be submitted directly by the individual. Applications are usually considered twice a year.

The Maidstone Relief-in-Need Charities

£800

Correspondent: Debbie Snook, Administrator, Maidstone Borough Council, Maidstone House, King Street, Maidstone ME15 6JQ (01622 602030)

CC Number: 210539

Eligibility

People in need, hardship or distress who live in the former borough of Maidstone.

Types of grants

One-off grants of up to around £300. Grants given include those for hospital expenses, electrical goods, convalescence, clothing, household bills, food, travel expenses, medical equipment, nursing fees, furniture, disability equipment and help in the home.

Annual grant total

In 2012/13 the charity had an income of £4,100 and a total expenditure of £1,700. We estimate that social welfare grants to individuals totalled £800, with funding also awarded to organisations.

Applications

Applications must be made through a social worker, health visitor, doctor or similar third party on a form available from the correspondent.

Margate

Margate and Dr Peete's Charity

£2,500

Correspondent: Dorothy Collins, Administrator, 31 Avenue Gardens, Cliftonville, Margate, Kent CT9 3AZ (01843 226173)

CC Number: 212503

Eligibility

People in need who live in the former borough of Margate (as constituted before 1974).

Types of grants

One-off and recurrent grants generally in the range of £50 to £250.

Annual grant total

In 2012/13 the charity had an income of £7,500 and a total expenditure of £5,100. We estimate that welfare grants totalled £2,500, with funding also awarded to individuals for educational purposes.

Applications

On a form available from the correspondent, to be submitted either directly by the individual or, where applicable, through a social worker, Citizens Advice or other welfare agency.

Other information

The charity was established in 1907 following the death of a Dr Thomas Peete, who left his entire estate – a total of £50,000 – to the Margate Philanthropic Institution. Since then, the charity has supported many of Margate's neediest residents.

Rochester

Cliffe-at-Hoo Parochial Charity

£2,600

Correspondent: Paul Kingman, Clerk, 52 Reed Street, Cliffe, Rochester, Kent ME3 7UL (01634 220422; email: paul.kingman@btopenworld.com)

CC Number: 220855

Eligibility

People in need who live in the ancient parish of Cliffe-at-Hoo.

Types of grants

One-off grants according to need. For example, grants towards household bills and nursing fees.

Annual grant total

In 2012/13 the charity had an income of £7,900 and a total expenditure of £5,600. We estimate that around £2,600 worth of grants were given for social welfare purposes.

Applications

In writing to the correspondent, to be submitted directly by the individual or a family member, or through a third party such as a social worker or Citizens Advice.

The William Mantle Trust

£3,700

Correspondent: Jane Rose, Administrator, Administrative Offices, Watt's Almshouses, Maidstone Road, Rochester, Kent ME1 1SE (01634 842194; email: wattscharity@btconnect.com)

CC Number: 248661

Eligibility

People in need who are over 60 and were either born in that part of Rochester which lies to the south and east of the River Medway, or have at any time lived in that part of the city for a continuous period of at least 15 years.

Types of grants

Recurrent grants, typically of around £65 per person, per month.

Annual grant total

In 2012/13 the trust had an income of £9,300 and a total expenditure of £3,800. We estimate that grants to individuals totalled £3,700.

Applications

On a form available from the correspondent. Applications should be submitted directly by the individual or through a third party on their behalf. They are considered on a regular basis.

Richard Watts and The City of Rochester Almshouse Charities

£73,000 (122 grants)

Correspondent: Jane Rose, Clerk, The Office, Watts Almshouses, Maidstone Road, Rochester, Kent ME1 1SE (01634 842194; fax: 01634 409348; email: jane.rose@richardwatts.org.uk; website: www.richardwatts.org.uk)

CC Number: 212828

Eligibility

People in need who live in the city of Rochester and urban Strood.

Types of grants

The charity offers regular four weekly pension payments to retired people in the area of benefit and one-off grants to people of any age towards a wide variety of needs, including clothing, electrical goods, travel expenses, medical equipment, furniture, disability equipment and subsidised home help. In kind grants can also be made. Awards are usually in excess of £50.

Annual grant total

In 2013 the charity had assets of £20.4 million and an income of £1.1 million. Grants to individuals for welfare needs totalled £12,600, broken down as follows:

- Helpline: 9 grants totalling £1,300
- Children and family: 26 grants totalling £7,800
- Elderly: 3 grants totalling £1,300
- Others: 6 grants totalling £2,200

Additionally, pensions were provided to 78 individuals totalling £60,000.

Note that most of the charity's expenditure is spent in maintaining the almshouses.

Applications

Application forms can be requested from the correspondent and can be submitted at any time directly by individuals. Grants are considered on a regular basis and candidates will be interviewed before the final decision is reached.

Other information

The charity also runs almshouses and supports organisations which benefit the local community. In 2013 grants to institutions for purposes, other than educational, totalled £4,700.

Grants are also given to schools and individuals for educational purposes as well.

Sevenoaks

The Kate Drummond Trust

£2,000

Correspondent: David Batchelor, Trustee, The Beeches, Packhorse Road, Sevenoaks, Kent TN13 2QP (01732 451584)

CC Number: 246830

Eligibility

People in need who live in Sevenoaks, preference is given to young people.

Types of grants

The majority of grants are one-off.

Annual grant total

In 2012/13 the trust had an income of £7,500 and a total expenditure of £7,000. We estimate grants to individuals for educational purposes totalled around £1,500 and for social welfare purposes around £2,000.

Applications

In writing to the correspondent, with an sae if a reply is required.

Other information

This trust also gives grants to organisations.

Tunbridge Wells

Miss Ethel Mary Fletcher's Charitable Bequest

£5,500

Correspondent: Trust Administrator, Thomson, Snell and Passmore, Ref 1295, 3 Lonsdale Gardens, Tunbridge Wells TN1 1NU (01892 510000)

CC Number: 219850

Eligibility

Older people in need who live in the Tunbridge Wells area.

Types of grants

One-off and recurrent grants towards, for example, fuel bills, clothing, medical treatment, food and other necessary comforts.

Annual grant total

In 2012/13 the bequest had an income of £10,700 and a total expenditure of £11,200. We estimate that grants to individuals totalled £5,500, with organisations also receiving funding.

Applications

In writing to the correspondent through a social worker, Citizens Advice or other welfare agency. At times when funds are already committed, consideration will only be given to those with exceptional circumstances.

Wilmington

The Wilmington Parochial Charity

£8,000

Correspondent: Regina Skinner, Administrator, 101 Birchwood Road, Dartford DA2 7HQ (01322 662342)

CC Number: 1011708

Eligibility

People in need, living in the parish of Wilmington, who are receiving a statutory means-tested benefit, such as Income Support, Housing Benefit or help towards their council tax.

Types of grants

Recurrent grants are available as follows: grocery vouchers of £30, cash grants of

£10 at Christmas and heating grants of £60 at Easter.

Annual grant total

Welfare grants to individuals total about £8,000 a year.

Applications

Applications should be submitted by the individual, or through a social worker, Citizens Advice or other welfare agency. The trustees meet in February and November. Urgent applications can be considered between meetings in exceptional circumstances.

Other information

Grants are also given to local schools at Christmas and to individuals for education.

Norfolk

The Blakeney Twelve

£11,000

Correspondent: Christopher Scargill, Trustee, 24 Kingsway, Blakeney, Holt NR25 7PL (01263 741020)

CC Number: 276758

Eligibility

Individuals who are older, infirm or disabled and who live in the parish of Blakeney, Morston and surrounding district.

Types of grants

One-off and recurrent grants, donations of coal and the payment of insurance.

Annual grant total

In 2012/13 the charity had an income of £14,500 and a total expenditure of £11,400. We estimate that grants to individuals totalled £11,000.

Applications

In writing to the correspondent.

The Calibut's Estate and the Hillington Charities

£3,300

Correspondent: William J. Tawn, Trustee/Chair, 2 Wheatfields, Hillington, King's Lynn, Norfolk PE31 6BH (01485 600641)

CC Number: 243510/243511

Eligibility

People in need, usually over the age of 65, who live in Hillington or East Walton.

Types of grants

One-off and recurrent grants, generally ranging from £25 to £100.

Annual grant total

In 2013 the charity had an income of £3,300 and a total expenditure of £3,300. We estimate that expenditure consisted entirely of grants made to individuals.

Income from the charity is divided evenly, with the trustees of the Parish of East Walton receiving one half for distribution to individuals in need, and the trustees of the Parish of Hillington receiving the other.

Exclusions

Owner occupiers are not eligible for support.

Applications

In writing to the correspondent to be submitted directly by the individual. Applications are considered in November.

Anne French Memorial Trust

£60,000

Correspondent: Christopher Dicker, Administrator, Trustee Training and Support Ltd, Hill House, Ranworth, Norwich NR13 6AB (01603 270356; email: cdicker@hotmail.co.uk)

CC Number: 254567

Eligibility

Members of the Anglican clergy in the diocese of Norwich.

Types of grants

Holiday and other relief-in-need grants as well as training costs for clergy and young people.

Annual grant total

In 2012/13 the trust had assets of £6.8 million and an income of £251,000. Grants to individuals totalled approximately £60,000 and were broken down as follows:

Gifts to clergy	£41,000
Youth and training	£14,400
Training of the clergy	£4,200

Applications

In writing to the correspondent.

Other information

The charity has a close association with the Bishop of Norwich Fabric Fund Trust and the Norwich Diocesan Board of Finance Ltd.

The King's Lynn and West Norfolk Borough Charity

£9,000

Correspondent: Kathleen Moorhouse, Administrator, 1 Cedar Court, Rareridge Lane, Bishops Waltham, Hampshire SO23 1DX (01489896366; email: katebeale@hotmail.com)

CC Number: 243864

Eligibility

People who live in the borough of King's Lynn and West Norfolk and are in need, hardship or suffer from illness or disability.

Types of grants

One-off grants of up to £300 are available towards, for example, furniture, beds, washing machines, carpets, bedding, cookers, electric scooters and other essentials.

Annual grant total

In 2013 the charity had an income of £11,100 and an expenditure of £9,200. We estimate that the annual total of grants was around £9,000.

Exclusions

Grants are not given to relieve public funds.

Applications

Application forms are available from the correspondent. They should be submitted through a social worker, Citizens Advice or other welfare agency. Requests are usually considered in March, June, September and December and should be received in the preceding month.

The Saham Toney Fuel Allotment and Perkins Charity

£2,900

Correspondent: Jill Glenn, Administrator, Orchard House, 1 Cressingham Road, Ashill, Thetford, Norfolk IP25 7DG (01760 441738; email: jill@glenn8530.freeserve.co.uk)

CC Number: 211852

Eligibility

People in need who have lived in Saham Toney, Saham Hills or Saham Waite for at least two years.

Types of grants

Recurrent grants of between £40 and £120, to help with the cost of fuel.

Annual grant total
In 2013 the charity had an income of £5,000 and a total expenditure of £3,000. We estimate that grants to individuals totalled £2,900.

Applications
On a form available from the correspondent, to be submitted directly by the individual, giving details of dependents and income. Applications should be submitted in May for consideration in June.

The Shelroy Trust

£12,000

Correspondent: Norfolk Community Foundation, St James Mill, Whitefriars, Norwich NR3 1TN (01603 623958)

CC Number: 327776

Eligibility
Residents of East Norfolk and Norwich, with a preference for Christians, older people and people with disabilities.

Types of grants
One-off grants, ranging from £200 to £500 to cover a specific need.

Annual grant total
In 2012/13 the trust had an income of £29,000 and a total expenditure of £27,000. Grants to individuals for relief-in-need totalled around £12,000.

Exclusions
The trust does not assist with bankruptcy costs.

Applications
In writing to the correspondent at any time. Individuals applying for grants must provide full information and two referees are required. Applications can be made directly by the individual or through a social worker, Citizens Advice or other third party. They are considered at the trustees' quarterly meetings in March, June, September and December. The trust is not able to reply to unsuccessful applicants unless an sae is provided.

Other information
Grants are also made to organisations.

The Southery, Feltwell and Methwold Relief-in-Need Charity

£800

Correspondent: Maureen Sharman, Trustee, 2a Church Lane, Southery, Downham Market PE38 0NE (01366 377571; email: RMS165@HOTMAIL.CO.UK)

CC Number: 268856

Eligibility
People in need who live in the parishes of Southery, Feltwell and Methwold.

Types of grants
One-off grants in the range of £25 to £100. Grants are often given towards the costs of travel to and from hospital.

Annual grant total
In 2013/14 the charity had an income of £1,300 and a total expenditure of £800. We estimate that around £800 was made in grants to individuals for social welfare purposes.

Applications
In writing to the correspondent. Applications are to be submitted by a third party such as a parishioner or committee member, and must be received by the application deadline of 31 March.

Witton Charity

£200

Correspondent: Beryl Lodge, Trustee, The Old Chapel, Chapel Road, Witton, North Walsham NR28 9UA (01692 650546)

CC Number: 1009959

Eligibility
Pensioners and other people in need who live in Witton and Ridlington.

Types of grants
Grants of coal twice a year and food parcels at Christmas.

Annual grant total
In the past five years total expenditure has fluctuated between £4 and £264. In 2013 we estimate that grants to individuals totalled £200.

Applications
In writing to the correspondent.

Banham

The Banham Parochial Charities

£4,800

Correspondent: Brian Harper, Trustee, 6 Pound Close, Banham, Norwich NR16 2SY (01953 887008)

CC Number: 213891

Eligibility
People in need who live in the parish of Banham.

Types of grants
One-off grants according to need. Grants have been given towards such things as heating bills, fuel, clothing and 'illness needs'

Annual grant total
In 2012 the charity had both an income and a total expenditure of £9,900. We estimate that social welfare grants to individuals totalled £4,800, with grants also awarded to individuals for educational purposes.

At the time of writing (August 2014) this was the most recent financial information available for the charity.

Applications
In writing to the correspondent. Applications can be considered at any time.

Barton Bendish

The Barton Bendish Poor's Charity

£1,000

Correspondent: Jocelyn Keshet-Price, Administrator, Hill Farm House, Boughton Long Road, Baton Bendish, King's Lynn, Norfolk PE33 9DN

CC Number: 211638

Eligibility
Widows and people in need who live in Barton Bendish, including Eastmoor.

Types of grants
One-off grants of about £40 to help with fuel expenses during the winter and towards travel to hospitals and funeral expenses.

Annual grant total
In 2012/13 the charity had an income of £1,200 and a total expenditure of £1,500. We estimate that around £1,000 was made in grants to individuals for social welfare purposes.

Applications
In writing to the correspondent at any time throughout the year.

Beeston

The Beeston Fuel Charity (Fuel Allotment)

£1,000

Correspondent: Bryan Leigh, Administrator, Dawn Meadow, Fakenham Road, East Bilney, Norfolk NR20 4H (01362 861112; email: bryan.leigh@btinternet.com)

CC Number: 213779

Eligibility

People over 65 years old who are in need and have lived in the parish of Beeston for at least five years.

Types of grants

Fuel grants of between £20 and £25 given at Christmas.

Annual grant total

In 2013/14 the charity had an income of £1,600 and a total expenditure of £1,300. We estimate that around £1,000 was made in grants to individuals for social welfare purposes.

Applications

In writing to the correspondent for consideration in December. Application deadlines are in November.

Burnham Market

The Harold Moorhouse Charity

£7,500

Correspondent: Christine Harrison, Trustee, 30 Winmer Avenue, Winterton-on-Sea, Great Yarmouth, Norfolk NR29 4BA (01493 393975; email: haroldmoorhousecharity@yahoo.co.uk)

CC Number: 287278

Eligibility

Individuals in need who live in Burnham Market in Norfolk only.

Types of grants

One-off grants are made ranging from £50 to £200 for heating, medical care and equipment, travel to and from hospital, educational equipment and school educational trips.

Annual grant total

This charity gives around £15,000 each year for both educational and welfare purposes.

Applications

In writing to the correspondent. Applications should be submitted directly by the individual in any month.

Buxton with Lammas

Picto Buxton Charity

£8,300

Correspondent: Stephen Pipe, Administrator, Beam End, Mill Street, Buxton, Norwich NR10 5JE (01603279823)

CC Number: 208896

Eligibility

People in need who live in the parish of Buxton with Lamas.

Types of grants

One-off and recurrent grants of £100 to £200 towards household bills, food, living expenses and so on.

Annual grant total

In 2012/13 the charity had an income of £29,000 and a total expenditure of £10,300. We estimate that around £8,300 was given in grants to individuals for welfare purposes.

Applications

In writing to the correspondent directly by the individual or a family member, or through a third party such as a social worker or teacher. Applications are considered at any time.

Other information

Educational help for needy families is also available. Grants are also made to organisations or groups within the parish boundary.

Diss

Diss Parochial Charity

£6,200 (25+ grants)

Correspondent: Sylvia Grace, Honorary Clerk, 2 The Causeway, Victoria Road, Diss IP22 4AW (01379 650630)

CC Number: 210154

Eligibility

People in need who live in the town and parish of Diss.

Types of grants

One-off grants ranging between £30 and £200 are made for a range of welfare purposes, including bereavement support (£150 each), funeral expenses and Christmas gifts.

Annual grant total

In 2013 the charity had assets of £633,000 and an income of £30,000. Awards to individuals totalled £2,800 with further £3,300 being paid in 25 bereavement grants and £600 in bereavement Christmas gifts. Previously the majority of grants have been welfare-related, with a couple of awards made for educational purposes.

Applications

In writing to the correspondent. Applications can be made directly by the individual or through a third party, for example DWP, Citizens Advice, Diss Health Centre or Diss Town Hal. Applications are considered upon receipt.

Other information

The charity also supports local organisations and maintains almshouses.

Downham Market and Downham West

Downham Aid in Sickness

£500

Correspondent: Philip Reynolds, Trustee, 39 Bexwell Road, Downham Market PE38 9LH (01366 383385; email: p.reynolds@fsbdial.co.uk)

CC Number: 258153

Eligibility

People who are sick, convalescent or infirm and live in the district of Downham Market or the parish of Downham West.

Types of grants

One-off and recurrent grants according to need.

Annual grant total

Expenditure for the charity is around £1,000 per year. It gives grants to both individuals and organisations.

Applications

In writing to the correspondent for consideration in May and November. Applications can be submitted directly by the individual or through a social worker, Citizens Advice or other welfare agency.

The Hundred Acre Charity – Dolcoal

£6,700

Correspondent: Ronald Stannard, Administrator, Riverside Farm, Birchfield Road, Nordelph, Downham Market PE38 0BP (01366 324217)

CC Number: 208301

Eligibility

People in need who live in Downham Market, Downham West, Stow Bardolph and Wimbotsham.

Types of grants

Fuel and food vouchers.

Annual grant total

In 2013 the charity had an income of £7,600 and a total expenditure of £6,900. We estimate that grants to individuals totalled £6,700.

Applications

In writing to the correspondent, after local advertisements are placed in shops in the village. Applications can be submitted directly by the individual and are usually considered at the end of November.

East Dereham

The East Dereham Relief-in-Need Charity

£2,000

Correspondent: Derek Edwards, Administrator, Lansdown House, 3 Breton Close, Dereham NR19 1JH (01362 695835; email: dae.air-arch@talktalk.net)

CC Number: 211142

Eligibility

People in need who live in East Dereham.

Types of grants

One-off and recurrent grants ranging from £35 to £100 including payments of coal and clothing vouchers.

Annual grant total

In 2012/13 the charity had an income of £9,000 and a total expenditure of £4,200. We estimate that grants to individuals totalled £2,000, with funding also awarded to local organisations.

Applications

On a form available from the correspondent, submitted either directly by the individual or through a social worker, Citizens Advice or other welfare agency.

East Tuddenham

The East Tuddenham Charities

£1,000

Correspondent: Janet Guy, Administrator, 7 Mattishall Road, East Tuddenham, Dereham, Norfolk NR20 3LP (01603 880523)

CC Number: 210333

Eligibility

People in need who live in East Tuddenham.

Types of grants

Christmas grants for fuel and occasional one-off grants.

Annual grant total

Grants are made to individuals usually totalling around £2,000 a year, mostly for welfare purposes.

Applications

In writing to the correspondent.

Other information

The main activity of this charity is the provision of almshouse accommodation.

Feltwell

Edmund Atmere (Feltwell) Charity

£3,000

Correspondent: Edmund Lambert, Trustee, Hill Farm, Feltwell, Thetford, Norfolk IP26 4AB (01842 828156)

CC Number: 270226

Eligibility

People, generally aged over 70 or who have a disability (except in special cases of dire need) who have lived in Feltwell for at least ten years. Grants have been made to people with multiple sclerosis or a similar condition and children who are sick.

Types of grants

One-off grants in the range of £10 to £250.

Annual grant total

In 2013, the charity had an income of £3,500 and a total expenditure of £3,000. We estimate that the total amount of grants awarded to individuals was approximately £3,000.

Applications

In writing to the correspondent. Applications can be submitted between 1 October and 1 November either directly by the individual or through a relevant third party. Applications are considered in November.

Sir Edmund Moundeford Charity

£9,800

Correspondent: Barry Hawkins, Administrator, The Estate Office, 15 Lynn Road, Downham Market, Norfolk PE38 9NL (01366 387180)

CC Number: 1075097

Eligibility

Individuals in need who live in Feltwell.

Types of grants

Fuel grants.

Annual grant total

In 2012 the charity had assets of £3.5 million and an income of £120,000. Grants to individuals for fuel totalled £9,800 and educational grants awarded to individuals totalled £2,400. Accounts for 2012 were the latest available at the time of writing (August 2014).

Applications

In writing to the correspondent.

Other information

The main purpose of this charity is the provision of almshouse accommodation.

Foulden

The Foulden Parochial Charities

£500

Correspondent: Robin Orrow, Trustee, Foulden Watermill, Foulden, Thetford, Norfolk IP26 5AG (01366 328001)

CC Number: 213885

Eligibility

People in need who live in Foulden.

Types of grants

One-off and recurrent grants according to need.

Annual grant total

In 2013 both the income and expenditure of this charity was in the region of £500.

Applications

In writing to the correspondent, directly by the individual or through a welfare agency. Applications are considered when necessary.

Garboldisham

The Garboldisham Parish Charities

£1,500

Correspondent: P. Girling, Treasurer, Sandale, Smallworth Common, Garboldisham, Diss, Norfolk IP22 2QW (01953 681646; email: pandw6@btinternet.com)

CC Number: 210250

Eligibility

People in need who live in the parish of Garboldisham. Generally, this is covered by the Relief-in-Need Fund, although widows and those over 65 who have lived in the parish of Garboldisham for over two years may qualify for allowances given by the Fuel Allotment Charity.

Types of grants

One-off and recurrent grants in the range of £30 to £600. Grants in kind are also made.

Annual grant total

In 2013/14 the charity had both an income and an expenditure of £6,000. We estimate that grants awarded to individuals for social welfare purposes totalled around £1,500.

Applications

Applications can be submitted directly by the individual, including specific details of what the grant is required for. They are usually considered in July and December.

Other information

The charity also makes grants to individuals for educational purposes and to organisations.

Gayton

Gayton Fuel Allotment

£1,500

Correspondent: Annmarie Parker, Administrator, Journeys End, Wormegay Road, Blackborough End, King's Lynn, Norfolk PE32 1SG (01553 841464; email: annmarieparker@talktalk.net)

CC Number: 243082

Eligibility

People in need, hardship or distress who live in the administrative parish of Gayton, which includes the village of Gayton Thorpe (Norfolk).

Types of grants

One-off and recurrent grants from £25 are given according to need.

Annual grant total

In 2013/14 the charity had both an income and an expenditure of £1,600. We have estimated the annual total of grants to individuals to be around £1,500.

Exclusions

Only in exceptional circumstances otherwise qualifying applicants who live outside the area of benefit (or are resident in Gayton only temporary) may be supported.

Applications

In writing to the correspondent. Applications can be submitted directly by the individual or a family member.

Gayton Relief-in-Need Charity (Gayton Poors)

£1,500

Correspondent: Barry Steer, Secretary, 12 St Marys Court, Gayton, Northampton NN7 3HP (01604 858886; email: barrywendysteer@yahoo.co.uk; website: www.gayton-northants.co.uk/organisations/charities/index.html)

CC Number: 201685

Eligibility

People in need who live in the parish of Gayton. In exceptional circumstances assistance may be given to individuals resident immediately outside the parish.

Types of grants

One-off grants usually ranging from £10 to £100.

Annual grant total

In 2013/14 the charity had an income of £3,300 and an expenditure of £3,100. We estimate that grants to individuals totalled around £1,500.

Applications

Application forms are available from the correspondent. The trustees meet twice a year. Our research also suggests that applications could be made through the vicar of Gayton Church.

The chair of trustees, David Coppock (tel. 01604859645) 'is happy to offer general advice about an application and/or assist with the completion of an application form.'

Other information

Grants to organisations are also made.

Gaywood

The Gaywood Poors' Fuel Allotment Trust

£3,800

Correspondent: Marjorie Lillie, Trustee, 'Edelweiss', Station Road, Hillington, King's Lynn, Norfolk PE31 6DE (01485 600615)

CC Number: 209364

Eligibility

Elderly people who are in need and live in the parish of Gaywood in Norfolk.

Types of grants

Grants to help with fuel costs.

Annual grant total

In 2012/13 the trust had an income of £4,200 and a total expenditure of £4,000. We estimate that grants to individuals totalled £3,800.

Applications

In writing to the correspondent through social services.

Harling

Harling Combined Trust

£1,000

Correspondent: David Gee, Clerk, Hanworth House, Market Street, East Harling, Norwich NR16 2AD (01953 717652; fax: 01953 717611; email: gee@harlingpc.org.uk)

CC Number: 211117

Eligibility

People in need living in Harling. In exceptional cases, grants may be made to people resident immediately outside the parish.

Types of grants

Principally one-off grants to assist with the purchase of fuel and heating costs; however other needs may also be addressed.

Annual grant total

In 2013/14 the trust had an income of £2,600 and an expenditure of £2,000. The grant total varies each year, depending on applications received, but usually is under £1,000.

Applications

Application forms are available from the correspondent. They can be submitted at any time together with a brief financial statement.

Other information

The trust was previously known as Fuel Allotment.

Grants are also made to organisations.

The trust has previously noted:

> In spite of ongoing publicity, the continuing paucity of applications caused the trustees some concern but, apart from remaining alert to cases of potential need, they felt that there was little else they could do to encourage people to come forward for assistance.

Hilgay

Hilgay United Charities (Non-Ecclesiastical Branch) (formerly known as The Hilgay Feoffee Charity)

£500

Correspondent: A. Hall, Administrator, Windrush, Church Road, Ten Mile Bank, Downham Market, Norfolk PE38 0EJ (01366 377127; email: hilgay.feoffees@aol.com)

CC Number: 208898

Eligibility

People in need who live in the parish of Hilgay.

Types of grants

One-off and recurrent grants according to need, including fuel vouchers and help towards costs of an apprenticeship or training.

Annual grant total

In 2013 the charity had an income of £24,000 and an expenditure of almost £24,000. In the past, grants to individuals have generally totalled around £2,000 with 75% for education, training and apprenticeships and the remainder for general grants.

Applications

In writing to the correspondent, directly by the individual.

Other information

The charity also makes grants to local schools.

Little Dunham

The Little Dunham Relief-in-Need Charity

£1,600

Correspondent: Susan Nally, Administrator, Beech Cottage, Burrows Hole Lane, King's Lynn, Norfolk PE32 2DP (01760 336864)

CC Number: 241875

Eligibility

People in need who live in the parish of Little Dunham.

Types of grants

One-off grants according to need.

Annual grant total

In 2012/13, the charity had an income of £5,600 and a total expenditure of £3,200. We estimate that the total amount of grants awarded to individuals was approximately £1,600.

Applications

The trustees usually depend on their local knowledge, but also consider direct approaches from village residents.

Other information

Grants may be given to the local primary school, church and community organisations.

Lyng

The Lyng Heath Charity

£500

Correspondent: Peter Dilloway, Trustee, Woodstock Bungalow, Etling Green, Dereham, Norfolk NR20 3EY (01362 691243; email: parish.pete@tiscali.co.uk)

CC Number: 206756

Eligibility

People in need who have lived in the parish of Lyng for at least one year.

Types of grants

One-off and recurrent grants between £30 and £40, primarily for fuel in winter.

Annual grant total

In 2013/14 the charity had an income of £1,200 and a total expenditure of £1,100. We estimate that social welfare grants to individuals totalled £500. Grants are also occasionally made to village organisations.

Applications

On a form available from the correspondent or any member of the committee at any time. Applications can be submitted directly by the individual and are usually considered in November.

Marham Village

The Marham Poor's Allotment

£24,000

Correspondent: Wendy Steeles, Trustee, Jungfrau, The Street, Marham, Kings Lynn, Norfolk PE33 9JQ (01760 337286)

CC Number: 236402

Eligibility

People of a pensionable age who are in need and live in Marham Village.

Types of grants

One-off vouchers usually of around £35 for food and fuel, to be spent in local shops.

Annual grant total

In 2012/13 the allotment had an income of £30,000 and a total expenditure of £29,000. Welfare grants to individuals totalled almost £24,000 and were distributed as follows:

Food vouchers	£14,600
Fuel vouchers	£8,900

A further £250 was given towards hospital travel assistance.

Applications

In writing to the correspondent. Applications are considered in October and vouchers distributed in November.

Northwold

The Northwold Combined Charities and Edmund Atmere Charity

£4,000

Correspondent: Helaine Wyett, Administrator, Pangle Cottage, Church Road, Wretton, King's Lynn PE33 9QR (01366 500165)

CC Number: 270227

Eligibility

People in need who live in the parish of Northwold.

Types of grants

One-off grants according to need. Aids for people with disabilities are also loaned by the charity.

Annual grant total

In 2013 the charity had an income of £2,500 and a total expenditure of £4,000. We estimate that the total amount of grants awarded to individuals was approximately £4,000.

Applications

In writing to the correspondent directly by the individual.

Norwich

Benevolent Association for the Relief of Decayed Tradesmen, their Widows and Orphans

£4,100

Correspondent: Nicholas Saffell, Administrator, c/o Brown and Co., The Atrium, St George's Street, Norwich, Norfolk NR3 1AB (01603 629871; fax: 01603 616199; email: nick.saffell@brown-co.com)

CC Number: 209861

Eligibility

People who are in need and live in Norwich or the parishes of Costessey, Earlham, Hellesdon, Catton, Sprowston, Thorpe St Andrew, Trowse with Newton and Cringleford. Preference is given to those who have carried on a trade in the area of benefit and their dependents.

Types of grants

One-off and recurrent grants according to need.

Annual grant total

In 2012/13 the association had an income of £5,100 and a total expenditure of £4,300. We estimate that grants to individuals totalled £4,100.

Exclusions

The association does not assist with bankruptcy fees.

Applications

In writing to the correspondent.

Norwich Consolidated Charities

£287,000 (310 grants)

Correspondent: Norma Dupres, Grants Officer, 1 Woolgate Court, St Benedicts Street, Norwich NR2 4AP (01603 621023; email: info@

norwichcharitabletrusts.org.uk; website: www.norwichcharitabletrusts.org.uk)

CC Number: 1094602

Eligibility

People on low incomes who are permanent residents of the city of Norwich. Grants are generally only made to those with dependents, unless the application is supported by a social worker.

Types of grants

One-off grants for welfare needs typically in the range of £50 to £500. Grants given include those for carpets, cookers, beds, bankruptcy applications and debt relief orders.

The trustees are increasingly focusing on ways of using the grants programme as part of a preventative strategy. This includes the provision of free legal advice and targeting grants at debt prevention and relief.

Annual grant total

In 2013 the charity held assets of £29.3 million and had an income of £1.9 million. Grants totalled £720,000, of which grants to individuals amounted to £170,000 and grants to residents of Doughty's almshouses £117,000.

A further £433,000 was awarded to organisations, including £50,000 to Age UK Norwich towards the provision of outreach services.

Applications

On a form available from the correspondent to be submitted either through a social worker, Citizens Advice, other welfare agency or directly by the individual. Ring or write to the office to confirm eligibility.

Generally, applicants will be asked to attend an interview or will be visited by the Grants Officer.

Other information

The main activity of the charity is the provision of almshouses, these are: Doughty's, which acts as a residence for elderly people, and Bakery Court, which is run by the charity Julian Support, whose residents have mental health problems.

Norwich Town Close Estate Charity

£106,000

Correspondent: David Walker, Clerk to the Trustees, 1 Woolgate Court, St Benedicts Street, Norwich NR2 4AP (01603 621023; email: david.walker@norwichcharitabletrusts.org.uk; website: www.norwichcharitabletrusts.org.uk)

CC Number: 235678

Eligibility

Freemen of Norwich and their families who are in need.

Types of grants

One-off grants, for example towards decorating costs, house repairs, carpets, spectacles and dental work. Grants are occasionally given for holiday costs. Small regular pensions have also been made to older people.

Annual grant total

In 2012/13 the charity had assets of £21 million, an income of £844,000 and grants were made totalling £166,000. Grants were broken down as follows:

Pensions	£100,000
Education	£61,000
Relief in need	£3,100
TV licence fees	£2,800

Applications

On a form available from the correspondent. Applications are considered throughout the year. Applicants living locally will usually be required to attend an interview.

Old Buckenham

United Eleemosynary Charity (Old Buckenham Charities)

£2,200

Correspondent: Jenny Sallnow, Administrator, Arianne, Attleborough Road, Old Buckenham, Attleborough, Norfolk NR17 1RF (01953 860166)

CC Number: 206795

Eligibility

People in need who live in Old Buckenham, Norfolk. Preference for pensioners (over 65) but other groups are also considered.

Types of grants

Normally recurrent grants of coal or cash in lieu for those without coal fires, although other needs may also be addressed. Grants are usually £50 or equivalent and distributed yearly in early December. Cases considered to be of exceptional need may be given more. There is a reserve of money to help those in emergencies throughout the year.

Annual grant total

In 2013 the charity had an income of £2,600 and an expenditure of £2,400. We estimate that around £2,200 was given in grants to individuals.

Applications

Application forms are available from the correspondent, following posted notices around the parish each autumn. Requests are usually considered in early November and can be submitted either directly by the individual or through a third party, such as any of the trustees. Any relevant evidence of need is helpful, but not essential.

Pentney

The Pentney Charity

£5,600

Correspondent: Emma Greeno, Administrator, 19 Westfields, Narborough, King's Lynn, Norfolk PE32 1SX (email: emmagreeno@aol.com)

CC Number: 212367

Eligibility

People over 65 who have lived in the parish of Pentney for the last two years are eligible for fuel grants. Other people in need may also apply for help.

Types of grants

One-off grants of £50 to £150 for fuel costs, travel to and from hospital, funeral expenses, medical expenses, disability equipment, clothing and household bills.

Annual grant total

In 2012/13 the charity had an income of £13,200 and a total expenditure of £11,800. We estimate that grants to individuals totalled £5,600, with funding also awarded to local organisations.

Exclusions

No grants are given where help is available from the social services.

Applications

In writing to the correspondent either directly by the individual; through a social worker, Citizens Advice or other welfare agency; or by a third party on behalf of the individual, for example a neighbour or relative. Applications are usually considered twice a year.

Saham Toney

The Ella Roberts Memorial Charity for Saham Toney

£800

Correspondent: Rosemary Benton, Treasurer, 36 Richmond Road, Saham Toney, Thetford, Norfolk IP25 7ER (01953 881844)

CC Number: 1025909

Eligibility
People in need who are older, sick or who have disabilities and live in Saham Toney.

Types of grants
One-off cash grants to cover half of the cost of dentures, glasses, physiotherapy or dental treatment, up to a maximum of £100 per application.

Annual grant total
In 2012/13 the charity had an income of almost £1,000 and a total expenditure of about £800. We estimate that grants to individuals totalled around £800.

Applications
On a form available from the correspondent, to be submitted directly by the individual or a family member. Applications are considered on receipt.

Saxlingham

The Saxlingham United Charities

£4,000

Correspondent: Jane Turner, 4 Pitts Hill Close, Saxlingham, Nethergate NR15 1AZ (01508 499623)

CC Number: 244713

Eligibility
People in need aged 70 or over who have lived in the village of Saxlingham, Nethergate for five or more years.

Types of grants
Recurrent grants for coal and electricity of £50 to £100 and one-off grants for widows and widowers.

Annual grant total
In 2012/13 the charity had an income of £5,000 and a total expenditure of £8,300. Grants are made for welfare and educational purposes. We estimate grants for social welfare purposes were in the region of around £4,000.

Applications
In writing to the correspondent. Applications can be submitted directly by the individual and are usually considered in October.

Shipdham

The Shipdham Parochial and Fuel Allotment

£0

Correspondent: Helen Crane, Meadow Bank, Carbrooke Lane, Shipdham, Thetford, Norfolk IP25 7RP (01362 821440; email: hscmeadowbank@yahoo.co.uk)

CC Number: 206339

Eligibility
People in need who live in Shipdham.

Types of grants
One-off grants generally ranging from £50 to £350.

Annual grant total
In 2012/13 the charity had an income of £18,000 and no expenditure. No grants were made.

Applications
On an application form available from the correspondent. Applications are usually considered quarterly.

Other information
The charity also makes grants to organisations.

South Creake

The South Creake Charities

£2,000

Correspondent: Sarah Harvey, Administrator, Byanoak, Leicester Road, South Creake, Fakenham, Norfolk NR21 9PW (01328 823391)

CC Number: 210090

Eligibility
People in need who live in South Creake.

Types of grants
Mostly recurrent annual grants towards fuel of between £35 and £100 per year. No grants are given to people in work.

Annual grant total
In 2012/13 the charity had an income of £5,000 and a total expenditure of £3,500. Grants are given for both educational and social welfare purposes. We estimate that grants awarded to individuals for social welfare purposes totalled around £2,000.

Applications
In writing to the correspondent. Applications should be submitted directly by the individual and are considered in November; they should be received before the end of October.

Other information
Grants can also be given to schools and playgroups.

Swaffham

Swaffham Relief in Need Charity

£2,000

Correspondent: Richard Bishop, Town Clerk, The Town Hall, Swaffham, Norfolk PE37 7DQ (01760 722922; fax: 01760 720469; email: reliefinneed@swaffhamtowncouncil.gov.uk; website: swaffhamtowncouncil.gov.uk/)

CC Number: 1072912

Eligibility
People in need who have lived in Swaffham for at least 12 months. In exceptional circumstances, the trustees may decide to aid someone who is resident outside Swaffham or only temporary resident in the area.

Types of grants
Grants have been given for a number of reasons, for example to provide school uniforms, disability access facilities or mobility scooters, central heating, to relieve long-term debt and to provide basic home start-up facilities.

Annual grant total
In 2012/13 the charity had an income of £11,300 and a total expenditure of £8,800. We estimate that £4,000 was awarded in grants to individuals for both educational and social welfare purposes. The charity also grants money to organisations.

Exclusions
Typically, an applicant is eligible for one grant per three years. The charity will not fund forms of assistance which may be provided by the state.

Applications
On an form available from the correspondent. The charity may arrange a visit to the applicant as part of the application process and may contact a GP, a vicar or priest, or a care worker familiar with the applicant's situation. The trustees meet six times a year to consider applications.

Other information
Information on the charity is available via the Swaffham Town Council website.

Swanton Morley

Charity of Thomas Barrett

£1,900

Correspondent: Nicholas Saffell, Administrator, Brown and Co., The Atrium, St George's Street, Norwich NR3 1AB (01603 629871)

CC Number: 207494

Eligibility

Older people, children and young people in need who live in Swanton Morley.

Types of grants

One-off and recurrent grants according to need.

Annual grant total

In 2012/13, the charity had an income of £4,000 and a total expenditure of £3,700. We have estimated the total of grants awarded to individuals to be £1,900. The charity also awards grants to organisations.

Applications

In writing to the correspondent directly by the individual. Applications are considered in June and December.

Other information

The charity gives out a portion of its moiety income towards the maintenance and repair of the parish church.

Walpole

The Walpole St Peter Poor's Estate

£1,800

Correspondent: Edward Otter, Administrator, 1 Sutton Meadows, Leverington, Wisbech, Cambridgeshire PE13 5ED (01945 665018)

CC Number: 233207

Eligibility

Older people over 65 who are in need and live in the old parishes of Walpole St Peter, Walpole Highway and Walpole Marsh.

Types of grants

One-off grants for welfare.

Annual grant total

In 2012 the charity had both an income and an expenditure of £3,800. Grants for welfare totalled around £1,800.

These were the latest set of accounts available at the time of writing (August 2014).

Applications

In writing to the correspondent. Applications should be submitted directly by the individual and are considered in November.

Other information

Grants are also made to college or university students for books.

Watton

The Watton Relief-in-Need Charity

£1,900

Correspondent: Derek Smith, Administrator, 39 Dereham Road, Watton, Norfolk IP25 6ER (01953 884044; email: derekismith@talktalk.net)

CC Number: 239041

Eligibility

People in need who live in Watton.

Types of grants

One-off grants according to need. Recent grants have been given towards medical equipment, funeral expenses, clothing, carpets, kitchen and household expenses and to older people at Christmas time.

Annual grant total

In 2012/13, the charity had an income of £4,800 and a total expenditure of £3,900. We estimate that the total amount of grants awarded to individuals was approximately £1,900.

Applications

In writing to the correspondent either directly by the individual or via a social worker, Citizens Advice, welfare agency or through a friend or neighbour. Applications are usually considered quarterly.

Other information

Grants are also made to organisations with similar objects.

Welney

Bishop Land Charity

£800

Correspondent: Pat Copeman, Administrator, 1 Chestnut Avenue, Welney, Wisbech, Cambridgeshire PE14 9RG (01354 610226; email: g8sww@aol.com)

CC Number: 200801

Eligibility

People in need (men over 65 years and women over 60 years) who live in the parish of Welney.

Types of grants

According to our research, grants of around £12 per person are given each year.

Annual grant total

In 2013/14 the charity had an income of £1,000, which has been about the same for the past five years. A total of around £900 was spent on charitable activities and we estimate that about £800 was distributed in grants.

Applications

Applications should be made by personal attendance or a signed note, to St Mary's Church (Welney) on the second Saturday of December.

Other information

The charity owns approximately 12 acres of land which is let and the income is used to make payments to the elderly residents of the village at Christmas.

Marshall's Charity

£9,900

Correspondent: Lynda Clarke-Jones, Clerk to the Trustees, The Barn, Main Street, Littleport, Cambridgeshire CB6 1PH (01353 860449; email: littleportpc@btconnect.com)

CC Number: 202211

Eligibility

Widows in need who live in the parish of Welney.

Types of grants

Grants of £125 paid quarterly.

Annual grant total

In 2013 the charity held assets of £1.5 million and had an income of £55,000. Quarterly payments to individuals totalled £9,900.

Applications

In writing to the correspondent. The list of recipients is reviewed quarterly.

Other information

William Marshall was a lawyer from London who in 1661, following an illness from which he was nursed back to health by the people of Welney, bequeathed land to be held in trust for their benefit.

> The original intention of William Marshall was that the income was to be used for assisting poor widows, apprenticing poor children and repairing the church, the bridge over the Old Bedford River and the roads within Welney. Over the years, as the income of the Charity increased, the Trustees were granted permission to use the income for other purposes. These included the building of a school, a new church and almshouses in 1847/48. The Charity now supports many other village facilities including, among others, the Parish Hall and the Playing Field.

Woodton

Woodton United Charities

£2,000

Correspondent: Peter Moore, Trustee, 6 Triple Plea Road, Woodton, Bungay, Suffolk NR35 2NS (01508 482375; email: peter.bmoore@btinternet.com)

CC Number: 207531

Eligibility

People in need who live in the parish of Woodton. The charity is particularly interested in supporting pensioners and people with disabilities or their carers.

Types of grants

One-off and recurrent grants of £20–£300 are given according to need. Annual grants are made to older people and people with disabilities. Contributions can also be made towards funeral expenses.

Annual grant total

In 2013 the charity had an income of £5,100 and a total expenditure of £4,300. We estimate that welfare grants totalled around £2,000.

Applications

In writing to the correspondent. Applications can be made directly by the individual, including full details and the nature of the need. Applications can be submitted at any time.

Other information

Grants are also given for educational purposes.

Oxfordshire

The Appleton Trust (Abingdon)

£2,500

Correspondent: David Dymock, Administrator, 73 Eaton Road, Appleton, Abingdon, Oxfordshire OX13 5JJ (01865 863709; email: appleton.trust@yahoo.co.uk)

CC Number: 201552

Eligibility

People who live in Appleton with Eaton and are in need or suffer from sickness, disability or other hardship.

Types of grants

One-off and recurrent grants in the range of £50 to £100 can be given towards various needs, including fuel and bereavement costs.

Annual grant total

In 2013 the trust had an income of £6,000 and a total expenditure of £5,200. We estimate that individual grants totalled around £2,500.

Applications

In writing to the correspondent. Applications can be made either directly by the individual or through an appropriate third party.

Other information

Grants are also given to local organisations and for educational purposes to former pupils of Appleton Primary School.

The Bampton Welfare Trust

£3,900

Correspondent: David Pullman, Administrator, Mill Green Cottage, Bampton, Oxon OX18 2HF (01993 850589; email: david@dpullman.plus.com)

CC Number: 202735

Eligibility

People who live in the parishes of Bampton, Aston, Lew and Shifford, of any occupation, who are in need. Preference is given to children, young people and older people.

Types of grants

One-off grants which can be repeated in subsequent years at the discretion of the trustees. Past grants have included food vouchers for families awaiting benefit payment, heating allowance for older people in need and assistance in purchasing a washing machine for a single parent with multiple sclerosis.

Annual grant total

In 2013 the trust had an income of £10,500 and a total expenditure of £8,000. We estimate that grants to individuals totalled £3,900, with organisations also receiving funding.

Applications

Applicants are advised to initially discuss their circumstances with the correspondent, who will advise the applicant on what steps to take. This initial contact can be made directly by the individual, or by any third party, at any time. The trustees meet twice a year.

The Banbury Charities

£46,000 (329 grants)

Correspondent: Nigel Yeadon, Administrator, 36 West Bar, Banbury OX16 9RU (01295 251234)

CC Number: 201418

Eligibility

People in need who live within the former borough of Banbury.

Types of grants

One-off and recurrent grants towards living costs, household essentials and appliances, bedding, fuel and domestic help.

Annual grant total

In 2013 the charities had assets of £5.6 million and an income of £1.6 million. Grants were made to 329 individuals for both education and welfare purposes at an average of £279 per grant, totalling approximately £46,000 for welfare purposes.

Applications

In writing to the correspondent. Applicants are encouraged to obtain a letter of support from their social worker, carer or other person in authority to give credence to their application.

Other information

Banbury Charities is a group of eight registered charities. These are as follows: Bridge Estate Charity; Countess of Arran's Charity; Banbury Arts and Educational Charity; Banbury Almshouses Charity; Banbury Sick Poor Fund; Banbury Welfare Trust; Banbury Poor Trust; and Banbury Recreation Charity.

The Bartlett Taylor Charitable Trust

£3,600 (9 grants)

Correspondent: Gareth Alty, Trustee, John Welch and Stammers, 24 Church Green, Witney, Oxfordshire OX28 4AT (01993 703941; email: galty@johnwelchandstammers.co.uk)

CC Number: 285249

Eligibility

People in need who live in Oxfordshire.

Types of grants

Relief-in-need grants range from £250 to £800 and medical support can be of around £500. Loans may also be considered.

Annual grant total

In 2012/13 the trust had assets of £2 million and an income of £79,000. Grants to 11 individuals totalled £4,000, of which one was a medical grant (£500) and eight relief-in-need (£3,600) grants. Further £350 was awarded in two educational grants.

Applications

In writing to the correspondent. The trustees meet bi-monthly.

Other information

Grants are also made to organisations and national or, preferably, local charities (£41,000 in 2012/13).

The trust states that educational grants are not made routinely.

The Burford Relief-in-Need Charity

£2,400

Correspondent: Ruth Reavley, Administrator, 124 High Street, Burford OX18 4QR (01993 823957; email: Ruth-reavley@lineone.co.uk)

CC Number: 1036378

Eligibility

People in need who live within seven miles of the Tolsey, Burford.

Types of grants

One-off grants towards hospital expenses, electrical goods, travel costs, convalescence, medical equipment and disability aids.

Annual grant total

In 2013 the charity had an income of £13,600 and a total expenditure of £4,900. We estimate that welfare grants to individuals totalled £2,400, with funding also awarded to individuals for educational needs.

Applications

In writing to the correspondent either directly by the individual or, where applicable, through a social worker, Citizens Advice or other welfare agency. Applications should include the individual's full name, address, age, and the number of years they have lived in Burford or their connection with Burford. Receipts are required for grants towards the cost of equipment. Applications are usually considered on a quarterly basis but urgent cases can be dealt with quickly.

Ducklington and Hardwick with Yelford Charity

£3,800

Correspondent: Joyce Parry, Administrator, 16 Feilden Close, Ducklington, Witney, Oxfordshire OX29 7XB (07993 705121)

CC Number: 237343

Eligibility

People in need or hardship who live in the villages of Ducklington, Hardwick and Yelford.

Types of grants

One-off grants of up to £200 can be given towards heating, transport costs, assistance with playgroup fees, furniture, funeral expenses, conversion of rooms for people who are older or have disabilities, provision of telephones, spectacles, school holiday assistance, help with rent arrears and other needs.

Annual grant total

In 2013 the charity had an income of £2,700 and an expenditure of £5,000. We estimate that welfare support to individuals totalled around £3,800.

Applications

In writing to the correspondent. The trustees meet in March and November but applications can be made at any time.

Other information

Grants are also made to organisations, clubs, schools and so on.

The Faringdon United Charities

£2,500

Correspondent: Vivienne Checkley, Administrator, Bunting and Co., 7 Market Place, Faringdon, Oxfordshire SN7 7HL (01367 243789; fax: 01367 243789)

CC Number: 237040

Eligibility

People in need who live in the parishes of Faringdon, Littleworth, Great and Little Coxwell, all in Oxfordshire.

Types of grants

One-off grants towards clergy expenses for visiting the sick, domestic appliances, holidays, travel expenses, medical and disability equipment, furniture and food and so on.

Annual grant total

In 2012/13 the charity had an income of £13,500 and total expenditure of £9,000. Grants are awarded to individuals and organisations for both educational and social welfare purposes. We estimate the total awarded to individuals for social welfare purposes was around £2,500.

Exclusions

Grants cannot be given for nursing/retirement home fees or the supply of equipment that the state is obliged to provide.

Applications

In writing to the correspondent throughout the year. Applications can be submitted either through Citizens Advice, a social worker or other third party, directly by the individual or by a third party on their behalf, for example a neighbour, parent or child.

The Lockinge and Ardington Relief-in-Need Charity

£5,000

Correspondent: Mrs A. Ackland, Administrator, c/o Lockinge Estate Office, Ardington, Wantage, Oxfordshire OX12 8PP (01235 833200; email: aackland@lockinge-estate.co.uk)

CC Number: 204770

Eligibility

People in need who live in the parish of Lockinge and Ardington. Help is given when government sources are not available or adequate.

Types of grants

One-off and recurrent grants between £30 and £60.

Annual grant total

In 2012/13 the charity had an income of £4,800 and a total expenditure of £5,200. We estimate that grants to individuals totalled £5,000.

Applications

In writing to the correspondent directly by the individual. Applications are considered in March, July and November although urgent cases can be considered at any time.

Ellen Rebe Spalding Memorial Fund

£2,000

Correspondent: Tessa Rodgers, Secretary, PO Box 85, Stowmarket IP14 3NY (website: www.spaldingtrust.org.uk)

CC Number: 209066–1

Eligibility

As specified by the fund's website, its objectives are:

> To help disadvantaged women and children to adjust more easily to the

pressure of modern life, and to promote those conditions of society that will enable people of different cultures and faiths to understand and appreciate one another.

Types of grants

Grants are at the discretion of trustees and are administered monthly throughout the year. Grants are only distributed to those who intend to further the objectives of the fund.

Annual grant total

Grants awarded from this fund to individuals for social welfare purposes generally total in the region of £2,000.

Applications

Applications should be made through Oxfordshire social services.

Other information

The Ellen Rebe Spalding Memorial Fund is a linked charity to the larger Spalding Trusts. While a small amount is given in welfare grants through the Ellen Rebe fund, the majority of the Spalding Trusts' funds are spent on educational grants.

The Thame Welfare Trust

£6,000

Correspondent: John Gadd, Administrator, 2 Cromwell Avenue, Thame, Oxfordshire OX9 3TD (01844 212564; email: johngadd4@gmail.com)

CC Number: 241914

Eligibility

People in need who live in Thame and immediately adjoining villages.

Types of grants

One-off grants of amounts up to £1,000, where help cannot be received from statutory organisations. Recent grants have been given towards a single parent's mortgage repayments and a wheelchair for a person who has disabilities.

Annual grant total

In 2012/13 the trust had an income of £18,500 and a total expenditure of £24,000. Grants are made to organisations and individuals for relief-in-need and educational purposes. We have estimated the welfare grants total to be around £6,000.

Applications

In writing to the correspondent, mainly through social workers, probation officers, teachers, or a similar third party but also directly by the applicant.

The Peter Ward Charitable Trust

£2,000

Correspondent: A. J. Carter and Co., 22b High Street, Witney, Oxfordshire OX28 6RB (01993 703414; fax: 01993 778052; email: ajc@ajcarter.com)

CC Number: 258403

Eligibility

People in need who live in Oxfordshire.

Types of grants

One-off and recurrent grants according to need.

Annual grant total

In 2012/13, the trust had an income of £10,200 and a total expenditure of £28,000, the majority of which was made in grants to organisations known to the trustees.

Applications

In writing to the correspondent, although unsolicited applications are not encouraged.

Bletchington

The Bletchington Charity

£2,500

Correspondent: Sue Green, Administrator, Causeway Cottage, Weston Road, Bletchington, Kidlington, Oxon OX5 3DH (01869 350895)

CC Number: 201584

Eligibility

People in need who live in the parish of Bletchington, in particular people who are elderly or infirm.

Types of grants

Grants to people who are elderly and infirm at Christmas and Easter towards fuel bills and other needs. Help is given for travel, chiropody and television licences. Otherwise one-off grants for social welfare, education and relief-in-sickness according to need.

Annual grant total

In 2012 the charity had an income of £11,000 and a total expenditure of just under £10,000. This was the most up to date information available at the time of writing (July 2014). We estimate grants to individuals for social welfare purposes totalled around £2,500.

Applications

Generally grants are given as the trustees see a need, but applications can be made in writing to the correspondent by the individual or by a social worker, doctor or welfare agency.

Other information

The charity also seeks to support any educational, medical and social needs that will benefit the village community as a whole.

Eynsham

Eynsham Consolidated Charity

£2,800 (28 grants)

Correspondent: Robin Mitchell, Clerk to the Trustees, 20 High Street, Eynsham, Witney, Oxfordshire OX29 4HB (01865 880665; email: robinmitchell255@gmail.com; website: eynsham-pc.gov.uk/a-z_club_detail.asp?ClubID=140)

CC Number: 200977

Eligibility

People in need who live in the ancient parish of Eynsham (which covers Eynsham and part of Freeland). The website provides a map marking the area of benefit. In exceptional circumstances grants can be made to people living immediately outside the parish; in practice, residents from most of Freeland may apply.

Types of grants

One-off grants, generally ranging from £50 to £200, can be given for specific items (glasses, furniture, washing machines, cookers, paint, school clothing or special equipment for people with disabilities), services (an insurance premium, heating costs or other utility bills, urgent debts, electric rewiring and so on) and for 'general expenses in a sudden financial crisis caused by matrimonial problems, bereavement' or other unforeseen difficulties. The charity notes that where the cost of providing the necessary help will be high help may be given in conjunction with other welfare organisations.

Most awards are made to elderly people in winter.

Annual grant total

In 2013 the charity had an income of £5,600. Grants to 28 individuals totalled £2,800. There usually is a maximum of around £3,000 to be distributed in grants each year.

Exclusions

Grants are not made to help with the payment of rates, taxes or other public charges. Support is not given on a recurrent basis or through personal loans.

Applications

In writing to the correspondent. Applications can be made directly by the individual or on their behalf by a neighbour, friend, family member and so on. Candidates should include details of what the grant is for, the costs involved and their personal circumstances. The trustees meet four times a year, usually in February, May, August or September and November, although urgent requests can be dealt with in between the meetings.

Other information

This charity also gives grants to organisations helping people in the local area.

Great Rollright

The Great Rollright Charities

£2,600

Correspondent: Paul Dingle, Administrator, Tyte End Cottage, Tyte End, Great Rollright, Chipping Norton, Oxfordshire OX7 5RU (01608 737676)

CC Number: 242146

Eligibility

People who are in need and live in the ancient parish of Great Rollright.

Types of grants

One-off grants towards, for example, fuel payments and to older people at Christmas.

Annual grant total

In 2012/13 the charity had an income of £11,200 and a total expenditure of £10,500. We estimate that welfare grants to individuals totalled £2,600, with funding also awarded to local organisations and for educational purposes.

Exclusions

No grants are given for the relief of rates, taxes or other public funds.

Applications

In writing to the correspondent.

Henley-on-Thames

The John Hodges Charitable Trust

£2,800

Correspondent: Julie Griffin, Administrator, 3 Berkshire Road, Henley-On-Thames RG9 1ND (01491 572621; email: juliegriffin2004@googlemail.com)

CC Number: 304313

Eligibility

People in need living in the Parish of St Mary the Virgin, Henley-On-Thames and the surrounding area.

Types of grants

One-off and recurrent grants towards, for example, white goods, carpets and flooring, clothing, mobility aids, bankruptcy fees and heating bills.

Annual grant total

In 2013/14 the trust had an income of £13,300 and a total expenditure of £5,700. We estimate that grants to individuals totalled £2,800, with funding also awarded to organisations.

Applications

In writing to the correspondent.

Oxford

The City of Oxford Charity

£72,000 (267 grants)

Correspondent: David Wright, Administrator, 11 Davenant Road, Oxford OX2 8BT (01865 247161; email: enquiries@oxfordcitycharities.fsnet.co.uk; website: www.oxfordcitycharities.org)

CC Number: 239151

Eligibility

People who have lived in the city of Oxford for at least three years and who are in need and hardship. Priority is given to children and people who are elderly, or have a disability or a medical condition.

Types of grants

The charity can offer one-off relief-in-need grants, generally of up to £600, towards various welfare needs, such as furniture to people moving home, household appliances, washing machines, recuperation holidays for people with disabilities or medical problems and/or their carers, baby equipment, wheelchairs and mobility scooters and so on. Support is also available towards the payment of bankruptcy court fees.

Annual grant total

In 2013 the charity had assets of £5.3 million, an income of £342,000 and made grants totalling £87,000. Relief-in-need grants to 236 persons/organisations totalled £65,000 and bankruptcy support to 31 individuals amounted to £7,200.

A major part of the charity's expenditure is spent in maintaining the almshouses.

Applications

Application forms can be downloaded from the charity's website or requested from the correspondent. They can be submitted through welfare services/other organisations or by individuals directly. All applications have to be supported by a letter from a social worker/health visitor/similar professional commenting on the circumstances of the family and the need for a grant. The trustees meet every six weeks to consider applications. Candidates are required to specify exactly what the money is for and the costs involved, as applications without exact costings will be delayed.

Other information

The charity is an amalgamation of a number of charities working for the benefit of the people of Oxford city. It also gives grants to organisations, can support local schools, assists individuals for educational needs, and maintains almshouses in the local area.

The Stanton Ballard Charitable Trust

£0

Correspondent: The Secretary, PO Box 81, Oxford OX4 4ZA

CC Number: 294688

Eligibility

Individuals in need who live in the city of Oxford and the immediate area.

Types of grants

Small one-off grants according to need.

Annual grant total

In 2012/13 the trust had assets of £2.7 million and an income of £107,000. Grants were made totalling £32,000, most of which was given to Oxfordshire based charities and voluntary organisations.

Applications

On an application form available from the correspondent on receipt of an sae. Applications should be made through social services, probation officers or other bodies and are considered approximately five times a year.

Sibford Gower

The Town Estate Charity

£2,500

Correspondent: Jean White, Trustee, Whitts End, Sibford Gower, Banbury, Oxfordshire OX15 5RT (01295 780529)

CC Number: 253440

Eligibility

People in need who live in the civil parish of Sibford Gower.

Types of grants
One-off and recurrent grants.

Annual grant total
This charity generally gives up to around £5,000 a year to individuals for social welfare purposes. The accounts available show that for the past two years the trustees have awarded £2,500 in this way. The charity owns land held on trust as permanent endowment.

Applications
In writing to the correspondent, to be considered at the twice-yearly trustees' meeting.

Other information
Grants are also given to organisations.

Souldern

The Souldern United Charities

£2,200

Correspondent: Carol Couzens, Trustee, 2 Cotswold Court, Souldern, Bicester, Oxfordshire OX27 7LQ (01869 346694)

CC Number: 1002942

Eligibility
People in need who live in the parish of Souldern.

Types of grants
One-off and recurrent grants according to need.

Annual grant total
In 2012/13 the charity had an income of £10,900 and a total expenditure of £8,900. We estimate that welfare grants to individuals totalled £2,200, with funding also awarded to local organisations and for educational purposes.

Applications
In writing to the correspondent.

Other information
The charity also provides housing.

Steventon

The Steventon Allotments and Relief-in-Need Charity

£2,500

Correspondent: Patrina Effer, Administrator, 19 Lime Grove, Southmoor, Abingdon, Oxfordshire OX13 5DN (01865 821055; email: info@sarinc.org.uk)

CC Number: 203331

Eligibility
People in need who live in Steventon.

Types of grants
One-off grants for the provision of food, fuel and personal items such as clothing, repair or replacement of faulty domestic equipment or furniture, loans of electric wheelchairs, provision of special equipment to chronically sick people and grants or loans for unforeseen difficulties. Priority is given to assist young people in obtaining independent housing, to set up home within the community in which they were raised. Large loans will need to be secured as a percentage of a second mortgage.

Annual grant total
In 2013 the charity had an income of £120,000 and a total expenditure of £93,000. Grants made to individuals for social welfare purposes usually total between £2,000 and £3,000.

Applications
In writing to the correspondent. The charity advertises regularly in the local parish magazine. Applications should include full details of income and expenditure, and will be treated in strictest confidence.

Other information
Educational grants are also made.

Wallingford

Wallingford Relief in Need Charity

£4,500

Correspondent: Andrew Rogers, Town Clerk, 9 St Martin's Street, Wallingford, Oxfordshire OX10 0AL (01491 835373; email: wallingfordtc@btconnect.com)

CC Number: 292000

Eligibility
People in need who live in the former borough of Wallingford.

Types of grants
One-off grants for necessities including the payment of bills, shoes, cookers, fridges and so on. Payments are made to local suppliers; cash grants are not made directly to the individual.

Annual grant total
Grants average around £6,500 and we estimate that grants awarded for social welfare purposes is generally around £4,500.

Applications
On a form available from the correspondent, submitted either directly by the individual or through a local organisation. The trustees meet about every three months, although emergency cases can be considered. Urgent cases may require a visit by a trustee.

Other information
The charity also gives grants for educational purposes; however, the majority of grants are given for relief in need.

Wheatley

The Wheatley Charities

£3,000

Correspondent: R. F. Minty, Trustee, 24 Old London Road, Wheatley, Oxford OX33 1YW (01865 874676)

CC Number: 203535

Eligibility
Residents of Wheatley, Oxford who are in need.

Types of grants
One-off and recurrent grants according to need.

Annual grant total
In 2012 the charity had an income of £4,500 and a total expenditure of £6,400. We estimate that grants to individuals for social welfare purposes totalled around £3,000. The accounts for 2012 were the latest available at the time of writing (July 2014).

Applications
In writing to the correspondent.

Other information
Educational grants are also made.

Suffolk

The Cranfield Charitable Trust

£600 (3 grants)

Correspondent: Sarah Price, Trustee, Townsend House, 22 Lucas Lane, Ashwell, Hertfordshire SG7 5LN (01462 742386)

CC Number: 263518

Eligibility
People who live in East Anglia and are in need.

Types of grants
One-off grants ranging from £90 to £1,500.

Annual grant total
In 2012/13 the trust had an income of £29,000 and a total expenditure of £38,000. Welfare grants to three individuals totalled £600.

The trust also awarded 3 grants amounting to £3,200 to individuals for educational purposes, and a further £8,400 to 27 charitable organisations.

Applications

In writing to the correspondent.

The Martineau Trust

£28,000

Correspondent: Roger Lay, Clerk, 5 Princethorpe Road, Ipswich, Suffolk IP3 8NY (01473 724951; email: clerk@martineautrust.org.uk; website: www.martineautrust.org.uk)

CC Number: 206884

Eligibility

People living in Suffolk who have incurred expenses as a result of an illness or disability.

Types of grants

The trust makes approximately 100 one-off grants a year. These may cover the whole cost of an item or be a contribution to a larger sum. Grants have been made towards new wheelchairs; transport costs for parents visiting children in hospital; clothing for a cancer patient; a bath lift; a gas cooker for a family affected by a disability; and a new bed and mattress for a cancer patient. Further examples are available on the trust's website.

Annual grant total

The trust has an annual grant budget of around £20,000, although this is not always entirely distributed: in 2012/13 the trust had a total expenditure of £31,000.

Exclusions

Grants are not normally made for: holidays and 'breaks' for families, childcare costs, alternative treatment therapies such as acupuncture, normal household running expenses, repayment of debts, retrospective grants or for anything not relating to an illness or disability.

Applications

On a form available from the correspondent or to download from the website. Applications must be completed by a suitable third party, such as a social worker, health visitor, nurse, doctor or charity welfare officer.

The Mills Charity

£6,400

Correspondent: The Clerk, PO Box 1703, Framlingham, Suffolk IP13 9WW (01728 724370; email: info@themillscharity.co.uk; website: www.themillscharity.co.uk)

CC Number: 207259

Eligibility

Individuals in need who live in Framlingham or are very closely associated with the town.

Types of grants

One-off grants towards hospital expenses, electrical goods, living costs, household bills, travel expenses, medical equipment, furniture and disability equipment.

Annual grant total

In 2012/13 the charity had assets of £7.5 million and an income of £179,000. Payments for relief in need totalled £6,400.

Applications

In writing to the correspondent. Applications should outline the need and why it has arisen and preferably include a supporting letter from a professional or other suitable referee. They are normally considered every two months.

Other information

The charity also provides and maintains almshouses.

Aldeburgh

Aldeburgh United Charities

£1,700

Correspondent: Lindsay Lee, Administrator, Moot Hall, Market Cross Place, Aldeburgh IP15 5DS (01728 452158; email: aldeburghtc@moothall1.fsnet.co.uk)

CC Number: 235840

Eligibility

People in need who live in the town of Aldeburgh. The charity describes its current beneficiaries as 'senior citizens, people in specific sensitive situations, young and young minded people and people in the development stage of life's experience.'

Types of grants

One-off and recurrent grants according to need.

Annual grant total

In 2013 the charity had an income of £6,900 and an expenditure of £3,500. We estimate that around £1,700 was given in grants to individual during the year.

Applications

In writing to the correspondent.

Other information

The charity is a combination of various charities in Aldeburgh, some hundreds of years old. Grants may also be given to organisations.

Brockley

The (Brockley) Town and Poor Estate (formerly known as The Brockley Town and Poor Estate)

£1,000

Correspondent: Jane Forster, Trustee, Brooklands, Chapel Lane, Brockley, Bury St Edmunds, Suffolk IP29 4AS (01284 830558; email: binnybops@btinternet.com)

CC Number: 236989

Eligibility

People in need who live in Brockley village.

Types of grants

In previous years recurrent grants of £65–£70 have been given, usually as rebates on electricity bills paid directly to the suppliers.

Annual grant total

In 2013 the charity had an income of £2,600 and a total expenditure of £2,100. Grants are made for educational and welfare purposes and totalled around £2,000.

Applications

In writing to the correspondent, to be submitted directly by the individual or through relatives or family friends.

Bungay

Henry Smith's Charity (Bungay Charities)

£1,000

Correspondent: Peter Morrow, Administrator, 11 Wharton Street, Bungay, Suffolk NR35 1EL (01986 893148)

CC Number: 210362

Eligibility

People in need who live in the parish of Bungay.

Types of grants

One-off grants of about £200 can be given to meet a wide range of needs. Our research suggests that older people can receive help, for example, for telephone installation, heating costs or travel to hospital, children from needy families can receive grants to pay for school trips or clothing and single parents can be given grants to help pay for furniture, washing machines and so on.

Annual grant total

In 2012/13 the charity had an income of £3,100 and an expenditure of £2,000. We estimate that about £1,000 was given in grants to individuals.

Applications

In writing to the correspondent.

Other information

Grants may also be made to organisations.

Carlton and Calton Colville

Carlton Colville Fuel or Poors' Allotment

£12,000

Correspondent: Keith Vincent, Trustee, 23 Wannock Close, Carlton Colville, Lowestoft, Suffolk NR33 8DW (01493 852411)

CC Number: 242083

Eligibility

People in need who live in the ancient parish of Carlton Colville. Preference is given for older people who only receive the basic state pension and have limited savings.

Types of grants

Recurrent grants for fuel and heating costs.

Annual grant total

At the time of writing (August 2014) the latest financial information available was from 2012. In 2012 the charity had an income of £15,900 and a total expenditure of £14,500. We have estimated that around £12,000 was given in grants to individuals.

Applications

Application forms are available from the correspondent. They can be submitted directly by the individual or through a social worker, Citizens Advice or other welfare agency.

Other information

If there are any funds remaining after heating costs have been covered for those in need, support can also be given to help in other instances of financial hardship, illness or disability, and to organisations working for the benefit of people in the local area.

Chediston

United Charities Town and Poor's Branch

£3,800

Correspondent: David Mantell, Administrator, Rosecroft Farm, Chediston Green, Chediston, Halesworth, Suffolk IP19 0BB (01986 785440; email: dpmantell@gmail.com; website: www.chediston.suffolk.gov.uk)

CC Number: 206742

Eligibility

People in need who live in the civil parish of Chediston.

Types of grants

One-off and recurrent grants according to need ranging from £5 to £100. Grants are given for alarm systems for older people, hospital transport and as Christmas gifts to all pensioners and children in full-time education.

Annual grant total

In 2012/13, the charity had an income of £4,000 and a total expenditure of £3,800.

Applications

In writing to the correspondent. Applications are considered throughout the year, although mainly in November. The charity has no formal application procedure as requests are usually made personally to the trustees.

Chelsworth

The Chelsworth Parochial Charity

£1,000

Correspondent: Alison Russell, Trustee, Tudor Cottage, 70 – 72 The Street, Chelsworth, Ipswich, Suffolk IP7 7HU (01449 740438)

CC Number: 210224

Eligibility

People in need who live in the parish of Chelsworth.

Types of grants

One-off grants or payment for items, services and facilities that will reduce the person's need, hardship or distress.

Annual grant total

In 2013 the charity's income and expenditure was around £1,000 and this is generally the amount the trustees award annually in grants to individuals.

Applications

In writing to the correspondent. The charity stated in early 2006 that it is 'solely for residents' and they will not accept any unsolicited applications.

Corton

Corton Poors' Land Trust

£5,000

Correspondent: Claire Boyne, Administrator, 48 Fallowfields, Lowestoft NR32 4XN (01502 733978; email: claire.murray4@tesco.net)

CC Number: 206067

Eligibility

People in need who live in the ancient parish of Corton.

Types of grants

Grants are given for various needs and in Christmas gifts for older people. Previously support has included funding for chiropody treatment, taxi fares to hospital, payment for home alarm installation and rent.

Annual grant total

In 2012/13 the trust had an income of £19,400 and a total expenditure of £11,000. We estimate that grants to individuals totalled around £5,000.

Applications

In writing to the correspondent. Applications can be submitted at any time directly by the individual or by an appropriate third party.

Other information

The trust also maintains almshouses and makes grants to organisations which carry out the charity's aims within the area of benefit.

Dennington

The Dennington Consolidated Charities

£1,500

Correspondent: Peter Lamb, Administrator, 2 The Coach House, The Square, Dennington, Woodbridge, Suffolk IP13 8AB (01728 638897; email: peterlamb54@googlemail.com)

CC Number: 207451

Eligibility

People in need who live in the village of Dennington.

Types of grants

One-off and recurrent grants according to need towards, for example, travel expenses for hospital visiting of relatives, telephone installation for emergency help calls for people who are elderly and infirm, and Christmas grants to older people. Grants usually range from £50 to £250.

Annual grant total

In 2012 the charity had an income of £14,900 and a total expenditure of £6,200. We estimate that social welfare grants to individuals totalled £1,500. Grants are also given for educational purposes and to organisations.

At the time of writing (September 2014) this was the most recent financial information available for the charity.

Exclusions

The charity does not make loans, nor does it make grants where public funds are available unless they are considered inadequate.

Applications

In writing to the correspondent. Applications are considered throughout the year and a simple means test questionnaire may be required by the applicant. Grants are only made to people resident in Dennington (a small village with 500 inhabitants). The charity does not respond to applications made outside this specific geographical area.

Dunwich

The Dunwich Town Trust

£14,100

Correspondent: Angela Abell, Trustee, The Old Forge, St James Street, Dunwich, Saxmundham, Suffolk IP17 3DU (01728 648107; email: dtchairman@btinternet.com; website: www.dunwichtowntrust.org)

CC Number: 206294

Eligibility

People in need who live in the parish of Dunwich.

Annual grant total

In 2013 the trust had assets of £2.5 million and an income of £97,000. Grants to individuals for social welfare purposes totalled £14,100 and were awarded as follows:

Contact care alarms	£1,950
Winter grants	£9,500
Education grants	£0 (2012: £3,400)
General relief	£2,750
Unrestricted fund	£0 (2012: £60,000)

Applications

Write to the correspondent requesting an application form.

Other information

Formerly known as 'Dunwich Pension Charity'. The trust makes grants to both individuals and organisations.

Earl Stonham

Earl Stonham Trust

£1,500

Correspondent: Sam Wilson, College Farm, Forward Green, Stowmarket, Suffolk IP14 5EH (01449 711497; email: sam_wilson@talk21.com)

CC Number: 213006

Eligibility

People in need who live in the parish of Earl Stonham.

Types of grants

One-off grants up to a maximum of £200.

Annual grant total

In 2012/13 the trust had an income of £8,000 and an expenditure of £6,800. Grants can be made for educational and welfare needs and for both individuals and organisations. We estimate that grants to individuals for social welfare purposes totalled around £1,500.

Applications

In writing to the correspondent, to be submitted either by the individual or through a social worker, Citizens Advice or other third party. Applications are considered in March, June, September and December.

Framlingham

The Florence Pryke Charity

£300

Correspondent: Sally Butcher, Trustee, 90 Station Road, Framlingham, Woodbridge IP13 9EE (01728 723365)

CC Number: 262319

Eligibility

People in need who live in the ecclesiastical parish of Framlingham.

Types of grants

One-off grants ranging from £30 to £50 towards, for example, hospital travel costs and medical care.

Annual grant total

Grants total around £600 a year.

Applications

In writing to the correspondent either directly by the individual or through a relevant third person. Applications are considered monthly.

Other information

The charity also gives grants to organisations.

Gisleham

Gisleham Relief in Need Charity

£2,500

Correspondent: Elizabeth Rivett, Trustee, 2 Mill Villas, Black Street, Gisleham, Lowestoft, Suffolk NR33 8EJ (01502 743189; email: elizabethrivett@hotmail.co.uk)

CC Number: 244853

Eligibility

People in need who live in the parish of Gisleham.

Types of grants

One-off and recurrent grants according to need, but usually averaging about £50. Recent grants have been given for household bills, travel expenses and disability aids.

Annual grant total

In 2012/13, the charity had an income of £3,400 and a total expenditure of £2,800. We estimate the grant total given to individuals was approximately £2,500.

Applications

In writing to the correspondent; to be submitted directly by the individual. Applications are considered at any time.

Other information

A luncheon club for older people is held at the local school once a month during term time. Those that are deemed not able to pay are paid for by the charity.

Gislingham

The Gislingham United Charity

£2,000

Correspondent: Robert Moyes, Administrator, 37 Broadfields Road, Gislingham, Eye, Suffolk IP23 8HX (01379 788105; email: r.moyes1926@btinternet.com)

CC Number: 208340

Eligibility

People in need who live in Gislingham.

Types of grants

Usually one-off grants according to need. For example, the cost of hospital travel for older people, playgroup fees or specific items or equipment.

Annual grant total

In 2013 the charity had an income of £16,500 and an expenditure of £9,000. We estimate that grants to individuals for social welfare purposes totalled around £2,000.

Applications

In writing to the correspondent directly by the individual or verbally via a trustee.

Other information

Grants are awarded to individuals and organisations for both educational and social welfare purposes.

Halesworth

The Halesworth United Charities

£1,000

Correspondent: Janet Staveley-Dick, Clerk, Hill Farm, Primes Lane, Blyford, Halesworth, Suffolk IP19 9JT (01986 872340)

CC Number: 214509

Eligibility

People in need who live in the ancient parish of Halesworth.

Types of grants

One-off grants according to need. Recent examples include travel abroad for educational purposes, medical equipment or tools needed for a trade.

Annual grant total

Grants usually total between £2,000 and £3,000.

Applications

In writing to the correspondent, directly by the individual or through a social worker, Citizens Advice or other welfare agency. Applications can be submitted at any time for consideration in January, July and December, or any other time if urgent.

Other information

Grants are also made to individuals for educational purposes and to organisations.

Ipswich

John Dorkin's Charity

£6,000

Correspondent: Jay Harvey, Trustee, Kerseys Solicitors, 20 Back Hamlet, Ipswich, Suffolk IP3 8AJ (email: office@johndorkincharityipswich.co.uk; website: www.johndorkincharityipswich.co.uk)

CC Number: 209635

Eligibility

People in need who live in the ancient parish of St Clement's, Ipswich (broadly speaking the south-eastern sector of Ipswich bounded by Back Hamlet/Foxhall Road and the River Orwell). Preference for the widows and children of seamen.

Types of grants

One-off cash grants of about £200 towards electrical goods, clothes, holidays, furniture and disability equipment.

Annual grant total

The 2012 accounts were the latest available at the time of writing (August 2014).

In 2012, the charity had an income of £12,000 and a total expenditure of £11,500. We estimate that the total amount of grants awarded to individuals was approximately £6,000. The charity also awards grants to organisations.

Exclusions

No grants to applicants resident outside the beneficial area.

Applications

In writing to the correspondent at any time, giving details of financial circumstances. Applications can be submitted through a third party such as a social worker, or through an organisation such as Citizens Advice or other welfare agency, and are considered twice a year.

Mrs L. D. Rope's Third Charitable Settlement

£503,000 (2,159 grants)

Correspondent: The Grants Administrator, Crag Farm, Boyton, Woodbridge, Suffolk IP12 3LH (01473 333288)

CC Number: 290533

Eligibility

People in need who live in east Suffolk, particularly in the parish of Kesgrave and the areas around it, including Ipswich.

Types of grants

One-off grants or vouchers according to need. Grants may be given for items such as food, clothing, household appliances, carpet, or for essential applications (possibly visa compliance or bankruptcy protection). The average amount for grants in east Suffolk during 2012/13 was £225.

Annual grant total

In 2012/13 the charity had both an income and a charitable expenditure of £1.4 million. During this financial year, 2,159 grants were awarded to individuals totalling £503,000. The majority of these grants were distributed to people living in the charity's local area of east Suffolk (£415,000 in 1,842 grants), with the remainder received by individuals living in other parts of East Anglia.

The charity also awarded grants to organisations to the sum of £690,000, almost half of which was given to overseas causes.

Exclusions

Grants are not given for individuals working overseas, debt relief, health/palliative care or educational fees. Only in exceptional cases will more than one grant be awarded to the same individual or family in any one year.

Applications

In writing to the correspondent preferably through a social worker, Citizens Advice or another agency with whom the charity works. Apply in a concise letter, saying what is needed and how the charity may be able to help. It helps to include details of household income (including benefits), expenses, and a daytime telephone number.

Note: though unsolicited requests are carefully reviewed, the charity awarded no grants for unsolicited requests in 2012/13 and states in its accounts that 'relatively few unsolicited requests meet our objectives.'

Kirkley

Kirkley Poor's Land Estate

£15,700

Correspondent: Lucy Walker, Administrator, 4 Station Road, Lowestoft, Suffolk NR32 4QF (01502 514964; email: kirkleypoors@gmail.com; website: kirkleypoorslandestate.co.uk/)

CC Number: 210177

Eligibility

Individuals in need who live in the parish of Kirkley.

Types of grants

One-off grants ranging from £50 to £300. Vouchers of £20 are also available to pensioners each winter to help towards the cost of groceries.

Annual grant total

In 2012/13 the charity had assets of £2 million and an income of £87,000. Grants were made totalling £62,000 and were distributed as follows:

Grants to individuals (education)	£5,700
Grocery voucher scheme	£15,700
Grants to organisations	£41,000

Applications

In writing to the correspondent.

Lakenheath

George Goward and John Evans

£3,500

Correspondent: Laura Williams, Administrator, 8 Woodcutters Way, Lakenheath, Brandon, Suffolk IP27 9JQ (01842 860445)

CC Number: 253727

Eligibility

People who are in need, hardship or distress and live in the parish of Lakenheath, Suffolk.

Types of grants

One-off grants in the range of £25 to £300 can be given according to need.

Annual grant total

At the time of writing (August 2014) the latest financial information available was from 2012. In 2012 the charity had an income of £37,000 and a total expenditure of £16,000. We estimate that grants to individuals for welfare purposes totalled around £3,500.

Exclusions

Help is not normally given for the relief of public funds.

Applications

In writing to the correspondent. Applications can be submitted either directly by the individual or through a third party, such as a family member, social worker, teacher, or an organisation, for example, Citizens Advice. Applications should generally be submitted by February and August for consideration in March and September, respectively. Candidates should provide brief details of their financial situation and include receipts for the items purchased.

Other information

One eighth of the charity's income is allocated to Soham United Charities. Grants are also made to other organisations, local primary, secondary, nursery and Sunday schools, and to individuals for educational purposes.

Lowestoft

The Lowestoft Church and Town Relief in Need Charity

£900

Correspondent: John Loftus, Clerk, 148 London Road North, Lowestoft, Suffolk NR32 1HF (01502 718700; fax: 01502 718709)

CC Number: 1015039

Eligibility

People in need who have lived in the area of the old borough of Lowestoft for at least three years.

Types of grants

On average ten one-off grants ranging from £50 to £500 for items and services such as childcare costs, clothing, debt relief, furniture, help for disabled people and help with funeral costs, for example.

Annual grant total

In 2012/13 the charity had an income of £7,900 and a total expenditure of £1,900. We estimate that grants to individuals totalled £900, with funding also awarded to local organisations.

Applications

In writing to the correspondent, directly by the individual. Applications are considered throughout the year.

The Lowestoft Fishermen's and Seafarers' Benevolent Society

£33,000

Correspondent: H. G. Sims, Secretary, 10 Waveney Road, Lowestoft, Suffolk NR32 1BN (01502 565161; fax: 01502 514382; email: lowestoftfpo@tiscali.co.uk; website: fsd.suffolk.gov.uk/kb5/suffolk/fsd/organisation.page?id=gRkUDSP_dqM)

Eligibility

Widows, children and dependents of fishermen and seamen lost at sea from Lowestoft vessels, who are in need.

Types of grants

Recent one-off grants have been made for funeral costs, mobility aids and household adaptations.

Annual grant total

Grants generally total between £30,000 and £36,000 a year. Both monthly payments and one-off grants are made.

Applications

In writing to the correspondent.

Other information

Details given on: www.suffolk.gov.uk/.

Melton

The Melton Trust

£3,000

Correspondent: Revd Michael Hatchett, Trustee, Melton Rectory, Station Road, Melton, Woodbridge IP12 1PX (01394 380279; email: meltontrust.suffolk@googlemail.com)

CC Number: 212286

Eligibility

People living in Melton who are in need, hardship or distress.

Types of grants

One-off and recurrent grants according to need.

Annual grant total

In 2012 the trust had an income of £10,700 and an expenditure of £3,700. Grants totalled approximately £3,000.

These were the latest set of accounts available at the time of writing (August 2014).

Mendlesham

Mendlesham Town Estate Charity

£7,000

Correspondent: Shirley Furze, Clerk, Beggars Roost, Church Road, Mendlesham, Stowmarket, Suffolk IP14 5SF (01449 767770)

CC Number: 207592

Eligibility

People who are in need and live in the parish of Mendlesham (Suffolk), particularly the elderly and those who are suffering from sickness or hardship.

Types of grants

One-off grants can be given towards, for example, heating, hospital visiting and associated special needs, including bereavement costs.

Annual grant total

At the time of writing the latest financial information available was from 2012. In 2012 the charity had an income of £15,100 and an expenditure of £14,200. We estimate that individual grants totalled around £7,000.

Applications

In writing to the correspondent. Applications can be submitted directly by the individual or through a third party, such as a social worker or Citizens Advice.

Other information

Grants are also made to the Church Estate Charity for the upkeep of St Mary's Church.

Mildenhall

The Mildenhall Parish Charities

£13,000

Correspondent: Vincent Coomber, Clerk, 22 Lark Road, Mildenhall, Bury St Edmunds IP28 7LA (01638 718079)

CC Number: 208196

Eligibility

Pensioners, widowers and widows in need who live in the parishes of Mildenhall and Beckrow.

Types of grants

The majority of the charity's giving is achieved through annual payments of £10 per person. One-off cash grants up to £500 towards travelling expenses to hospital, assistance to persons preparing to enter into a trade or profession and subscriptions to homes or hostels for infirm or homeless persons are also available.

Annual grant total

In 2013 the charity had an income of £15,400 and total expenditure of £15,600. Grants of around £13,000 were made.

Applications

In writing to the correspondent either directly by the individual or through a recognised third party. Applications are considered three times a year.

Pakenham

The Pakenham Charities for the Poor

£2,800

Correspondent: Christine Cohen, Clerk, 5 St Mary's View, Pakenham, Bury St Edmunds IP31 2ND (01359 232965)

CC Number: 213314

Eligibility

People in need who live in Pakenham.

Types of grants

Annual fuel grants and one-off payments of around £20 to £1,250 for particular needs. In the past, grants have been awarded for alarms for people who are elderly, disability equipment, medical equipment, hospital expenses, clothing and travel expenses.

Annual grant total

In 2013 the charity had an income of £6,100 and a total expenditure of £5,700. We estimate that grants to individuals totalled £2,800, with funding also available for organisations which benefit residents of Pakenham.

Applications

In writing to the correspondent either directly by the individual, through a third party such as a social worker, or through an organisation such Citizens Advice or other welfare agency. Applications are considered in early December and should be received by 30 November.

Reydon

The Reydon Trust

£12,400

Correspondent: H. C. A. Freeman, Administrator, 22 Kingfisher Crescent, Reydon, Southwold, Suffolk IP18 6XL (01502 723746; email: h_freeman1@sky.com)

CC Number: 206873

Eligibility

People in need who live in the parish of Reydon.

Types of grants

One-off grants towards hospital expenses, clothing, food, travel costs and disability equipment. Vouchers are also given as gifts at Christmas time.

Annual grant total

In 2012/13 the trust had assets of £664,000 and an income of £26,000. There was a considerable increase in grants during this financial year, with the trust donating £72,000 to various charitable causes. We estimate that one-off welfare grants to individuals totalled £10,000, with a further £2,400 gifted in Christmas vouchers. Funding was also awarded to local organisations and for educational purposes.

Applications

In writing to the correspondent. Applications can be submitted either directly by the individual, through a third party such as a social worker or via a doctor or health centre. They are considered upon receipt.

Risby

The Risby Fuel Allotment

£2,900

Correspondent: Penelope Wallis, Trustee, 3 Woodland Close, Risby, Bury St Edmunds IP28 6QN (01284 81064)

CC Number: 212260

Eligibility

People in need who live in the parish of Risby.

Types of grants

Annual grants, primarily to buy winter fuel, although also for other needs.

Annual grant total

In 2012/13 the charity had an income of £3,700 and a total expenditure of £3,500. Grants are given primarily for relief-in-need purposes and fuel costs. We estimate that social welfare grants to individuals totalled around £2,900.

Applications

In writing to the correspondent. Applications made outside the specific area of interest (the parish of Risby) are not acknowledged.

Stanton

The Stanton Poors' Estate Charity

£5,800

Correspondent: Susan Buss, Treasurer, 3 Shepherds Grove Park, Stanton, Bury St Edmunds, Suffolk IP31 2AY (01359 250388)

CC Number: 235649

Eligibility

People in need who live in the parish of Stanton and are in receipt of means-tested benefits. Grants can be made in special cases of need or hardship outside these criteria at the trustees' discretion.

Types of grants

Grants generally range between £40 and £90, although larger applications may be considered. Applications are considered for both full and part-funding.

Annual grant total

In 2012/13 the charity had an income of £4,400 and a total expenditure of £6,000. We estimate that grants to individuals totalled £5,800.

Applications

In writing to the correspondent, for consideration in November.

Stowmarket

The Stowmarket Relief Trust

£54,000

Correspondent: Colin Hawkins, Administrator, Kiln House, 21 The Brickfields, Stowmarket, Suffolk IP14 1RZ (01449 674412; email: colinhawkins08@aol.com)

CC Number: 802572

Eligibility

People in need who live in the town of Stowmarket and its adjoining parishes including the parish of Old Newton with Dagworth.

Applicants must have approached all sources of statutory funding. People on Income Support will normally qualify. People in full-time paid employment will not normally qualify for assistance, but there are possible exceptions. People with substantial capital funds are also ineligible.

Types of grants

Normally one-off, but recurrent grants have been given in special circumstances. Recent grants have been made for the purchase and repair of white goods; payment of modest arrears (rent, council tax, electricity, gas, water and telephone charges); payment of bankruptcy fees and debt relief orders; repayments resulting from the overpayment of state benefits; carpets and floor coverings; beds, bedding and household furniture; electric wheelchairs and riser/recliner chairs; living/household expenses; car repairs; medical aids; and clothing and footwear. Grants generally range from about £15 to £700, although in exceptional circumstances awards may exceed £1,000.

Annual grant total

In 2012/13 the trust had assets of £1.4 million most of which represents a permanent endowment and is not available for grant giving. It had an income of £70,000. Grants were made to 195 individuals totalling £54,000. A further £1,000 was awarded to an organisation.

Applications

On a form available from the correspondent. Applications should be submitted through a third party such as a social worker, probation officer, Citizens Advice or doctor. Applications are considered at trustee meetings held three times a year, though urgent cases can be dealt with between meetings.

Stutton

The Charity of Joseph Catt

£3,500

Correspondent: Keith Bales, Trustee, 34 Cattsfield, Stutton, Ipswich, Suffolk IP9 2SP (01473 328179)

CC Number: 213013

Eligibility

People in need who live in the parish of Sutton only.

Types of grants

One-off grants and loans to help with fuel, hospital travel expenses, convalescent holidays, household goods and clothing.

Annual grant total

In 2012 this charity had an income of £9,900 and a total expenditure of £14,600. We estimate that grants for individuals for social welfare purposes totalled around £3,500. The accounts for 2012 were the latest available at the time of writing (July 2014).

Applications

Applications can be submitted by the individual, or through a recognised referral agency (such as a social worker, Citizens Advice or a doctor) and are considered monthly. They can be submitted to the correspondent, or any of the trustees at any time, for consideration in May and November.

Other information

The charity also supports local almshouses.

Sudbury

Sudbury Municipal Charities

£1,800

Correspondent: Adrian Walters, Clerk, Longstop Cottage, The Street, Lawshall, Bury St Edmunds IP29 4QA (01284 828219; email: a.walters@sclc.entadsl.com)

CC Number: 213516

Eligibility

Older people (generally those over 70) who are in need and live in the borough of Sudbury.

Types of grants

Ascension Day and Christmas gifts, usually in the range of £10 to £30. Grants for special cases of hardship are also available.

Annual grant total

In 2013, the charity had an income of £3,400 and a total expenditure of £3,700. We estimate that the total amount of grants awarded to individuals was approximately £1,800.

Applications

Grants are usually advertised in the local newspaper when they are available.

Other information

The charity also make grants to local organisations.

Walberswick

The Walberswick Common Lands

£3,900

Correspondent: Jayne Tibbles, Administrator, Lima Cottage, Walberswick, Southwold, Suffolk IP18 6TN (01502 724448; website: walberswick.onesuffolk.net/walberswick-common-lands-charity/)

CC Number: 206095

Eligibility

People in need who live in Walberswick.

Types of grants

Grants include quarterly payments to individuals and grants of £35 to £1,200 towards gardening, telephone rental and television licence payments, household items, access adaptations, travel expenses and Christmas cash and vouchers. Personal loans are also available.

Annual grant total

In 2013 the charity had assets of £125,000, an income of £72,000 and total expenditure of £78,000. Educational grants to individuals totalled almost £1,500. Grants for social welfare purposes awarded to individuals totalled £3,900 and grants to organisations £26,000.

Applications

In writing to the correspondent through a social worker, Citizens Advice or other welfare agency, or directly by the individual or through a relative or neighbour. Applications are considered in February, April, June, August, October and December.

Surrey

Banstead United Charities

£1,600

Correspondent: Michael Taylor, Administrator, 6 Garratts Lane, Banstead SM7 2DZ (01737 355827)

CC Number: 233339

Eligibility

People in need who live in the wards of Banstead village, Burgh Heath, Kingswood, Nork, Preston, Tadworth and Tattenhams (Surrey).

Types of grants

One-off grants, usually up to £500. Our research suggests that awards have been given towards funeral expenses, equipment for people with disabilities, travel for hospital treatment and rehabilitation, children's clothing, living expenses and towards minor educational needs.

Annual grant total

At the time of writing (September 2014) the latest financial information available was from 2012. In 2012 the charity had an income of £3,500 and a total expenditure of £3,400. We estimate that grants to individuals totalled about £1,600.

Applications

In writing to the correspondent. Applications can be submitted directly by the individual or through a social worker, Citizens Advice or other welfare agency. They are considered throughout the year.

Other information

Grants are also made to organisations.

John Beane's Eleemosynary Charity (Guildford)

£22,000

Correspondent: Brian France, Administrator, 4 Henderson Avenue, Guildford GU2 9LP (01483 504180)

CC Number: 242309

Eligibility

People in need who live in the administrative county of Surrey.

Types of grants

One-off or recurrent grants according to need. Grants have been made for furniture, bedding, clothing, removal expenses and electrical appliances.

Annual grant total

In 2012/13 the charity had an income of £24,000 and an expenditure of £22,000. We estimate that £22,000 was awarded in grants to individuals.

Applications

On a form available from the correspondent, to be submitted through a social worker, health visitor, Citizens Advice or other welfare agency.

Other information

The charity was founded in 1772 on the death of the Reverend John Beane, who left in trust certain assets 'to be applied, interalia to the relief of the needy in Dorking and Guildford.'

The Bookhams, Fetcham and Effingham Nursing Association Trust

£3,800

Correspondent: Jenny Peers, Trustee, 1 Manor Cottages, Manor House Lane, Bookham, Leatherhead, Surrey KT23 4EW (01372 456752; email: j.peers@tiscali.co.uk)

CC Number: 265962

Eligibility

People in need who are sick, convalescent, disabled or infirm who live in Great Bookham, Little Bookham, Fetcham and Effingham.

Types of grants

Grants of between £100 and £1,500 for items, services or facilities which will alleviate the discomfort or assist the recovery of such people, where these facilities are not available from any other sources.

Annual grant total

In 2012/13 the trust had an income of £7,700 and a total expenditure of £7,800. We estimate that grants to individuals totalled £3,800, with funding also awarded to local organisations.

Applications

Applications should be referred through medical or social services, not directly from the public.

Lady Noel Byron's Nursing Association

£1,000

Correspondent: J. R. Miles, Trustee, Postboys, Cranmore Lane, West Horsley, Leatherhead, Surrey KT24 6BX (01483 284141; email: maganddave@tiscali.co.uk)

CC Number: 237970

Eligibility

People in need of medical or welfare assistance who live in the parishes of East and West Horsley.

Types of grants

One-off or recurrent grants according to need for medical or welfare related purposes only. This has included grants towards holidays, equipment and such like.

Annual grant total

In 2012/13 the charity had both an income and a total expenditure of £1,700. Our research tells us that social welfare grants to individuals usually total around £1,000 each year.

Applications

In writing to the correspondent. Applications can be made directly by the individual or through a social worker, other welfare agency or third party. They are considered at any time.

Other information

Grants are also made to organisations.

The Churt Welfare Trust

£2,000

Correspondent: Mrs E. Kilpatrick, Trustee, Hearn Lodge, Spats Lane, Headley Down, Bordon, Hampshire GU35 8SU (01428 712238)

CC Number: 210076

Eligibility

People in need who live in the parish of Churt and its neighbourhood.

Types of grants

One-off grants in the range of £10 to £1,000. Grants have been given towards: winter fuel bills for the elderly; equipment, furnishings and comforts for the physically or mentally ill; specialist equipment or household assistance for the terminally or temporarily ill; travel or holiday arrangements; medical expenses; taxi or transport costs for the elderly or for long distance medical appointments; and household repairs and maintenance.

Annual grant total

In 2012/13 the trust had an income of £11,500 and a total expenditure of £8,100. We estimate that grants to individuals totalled £2,000, with funding also awarded to local organisations and to individuals for educational purposes.

Exclusions

The trust cannot renew or commit to repeat grants.

Applications

In writing to the correspondent.

The Cranleigh and District Nursing Association

£400

Correspondent: Jennifer Henderson, Trustee, 14 Dukes Close, Cranleigh, Surrey GU6 7JU (01483 274162)

CC Number: 200649

Eligibility

People in need who are sick and poor and live in the parishes of Cranleigh and Ewhurst.

Types of grants
One-off grants ranging from £25 to £500. Recent grants have been made towards carpets, phone rental, MedicAlert bracelets, chiropody, hospital visits and pavement vehicles.

Annual grant total
In 2013, the association had an income of £2,200 and a total expenditure of £500. We estimate that the total amount of grants awarded to individuals was approximately £400.

Applications
In writing to the correspondent through a social worker, Citizens Advice or other welfare agency.

The Dempster Trust

£4,300

Correspondent: Peter Jeans, Trustee, 21 Broomleaf Road, Farnham GU9 8DG (01252 721075)

CC Number: 200107

Eligibility
People in need, hardship or distress who live in Farnham and the general neighbourhood.

Types of grants
One-off grants or help for limited periods only. In the past, grants have been given towards nursing requisites, to relieve sudden distress, travelling expenses, fuel, television and telephone bills, clothing, washing machines, televisions, radios, alarm systems and so on. Grants usually range from £50 to £500.

Annual grant total
In 2012/13 the trust had an income of £11,500 and an expenditure of £8,800. We estimate that grants to individuals totalled £4,300, with funding also awarded to local organisations.

Exclusions
Help is not given towards rent, rates or house improvements.

Applications
On a form available from the correspondent to be submitted through a doctor, social worker, hospital, Citizens Advice or another welfare agency. Applications can be considered at any time.

The Ewell Parochial Trusts

£28,000

Correspondent: Miriam Massey, Clerk and Treasurer, 19 Cheam Road, Ewell, Epsom KT17 1ST (020 8394 0453; email: mirimas@globalnet.co.uk)

CC Number: 201623

Eligibility
People in need who live, work or are being educated in the ancient ecclesiastical parish of Ewell and the domain of Kingswood.

Types of grants
One-off or recurrent grants according to need.

Annual grant total
In 2013 the trusts had an income of £46,000 and a total expenditure of £41,000. We estimate that welfare grants to individuals totalled around £28,000. Grants are also given to organisations and for educational purposes.

Applications
In writing to the correspondent. Applications which do not meet the eligibility criteria will not be acknowledged.

The Godstone United Charities

£6,600

Correspondent: Patricia Bamforth, Administrator, Bassett Villa, Oxted Road, Godstone, Surrey RH9 8AD (01883 742625; website: www.godstonepc.org.uk)

CC Number: 200055

Eligibility
People in need who live in the old parish of Godstone (Blindley Heath, South Godstone and Godstone Village).

Types of grants
Food vouchers are usually given in December and March. One-off grants are also available.

Annual grant total
In 2012/13 the charity had an income of £6,500 and a total expenditure of £6,800. We estimate that grants to individuals totalled £6,600.

Applications
In writing to the correspondent; either directly by the individual, through a relevant third party or, where applicable, via a social worker, Citizens Advice or other welfare agency. Applications should include relevant details of income, outgoings, household composition and the reason for the request. All grants are paid directly to the supplier.

Other information
The charities may also assist with educational needs.

Richmond Charities Almshouses (formerly known as The Henry Smith Charity (Richmond)

£2,000

Correspondent: Catherine Rumsey, Administrator, The Richmond Charities, 8 The Green, Richmond, Surrey TW9 1PL (020 8948 4188; email: info@richmondcharities.org.uk)

CC Number: 200431

Eligibility
People experiencing hardship or distress who lived in Richmond upon Thames for at least five years.

Types of grants
One-off grants up to £250. Recently the greatest number of grants have been made to unemployed single parents, towards children's clothing and fuel bills.

Annual grant total
Grants usually total around £2,000 per year.

Applications
In writing to the correspondent, from referring bodies such as social services, health authority or Citizens Advice. Applications are considered at trustees' meetings in February, March, May, June, September, November and December.

The Henry Smith Charity (Ash and Normandy)

£1,800

Correspondent: Alan Coomer, Administrator, 84 Queenhythe Road, Jacob's Well, Guildford, Surrey GU4 7NX (01483 300103; email: alancoomer@yahoo.co.uk)

CC Number: 240485

Eligibility
People in need who live in Ash and Normandy.

Types of grants
One-off or recurrent grants according to need.

Annual grant total
In 2013/14 the charity had an income of £3,600 and a total expenditure of £3,700. We estimate that grants to individuals totalled £1,800, with funding also awarded to local organisations.

Applications
In writing to the correspondent, either directly by the individual or through a social worker, Citizens Advice or other welfare agency. Applications are normally considered as they arrive.

The Henry Smith Charity (Eastbrook Estate)

£2,100

Correspondent: Ron Howard, Trustee, 4 Cholmley Terrace, Portsmouth Road, Thames Ditton, Surrey KT7 0XX (email: ron_286@yahoo.co.uk)

CC Number: 200123

Eligibility
Widows or people over 60 who are in need, of good character and have lived in the parishes of Long Ditton and Tolworth for the past five years.

Types of grants
Grants to be spent on heating fuel, clothing and electricity bills at named retailers.

Annual grant total
Grants usually total around £2,100 a year.

Applications
In writing to the correspondent. Applications are considered in December and January and must include details of the applicant's age and length of residence in the parish.

The Henry Smith Charity (Frimley)

£1,600

Correspondent: Jane Sherman, Democratic Services Manager, Surrey Heath Borough Council, Surrey Heath House, Knoll Road, Camberley, Surrey GU15 3HD (01276 707302; email: committee.services@surreyheath.gov.uk)

CC Number: 236367

Eligibility
People in need who live in the former parish of Frimley (Frimley, Frimley Green, Camberley and Mytchett).

Types of grants
One-off grants normally ranging from £100 to £200 towards clothing, bedding, furniture, disability equipment and electrical goods.

Annual grant total
In 2013/14 the charity had an income of £2,000 and a total expenditure of £1,800. We estimate that social welfare grants to individuals totalled £1,600, though expenditure tends to vary each year.

Applications
In writing to the correspondent through a social worker, Citizens Advice or other welfare agency.

The Henry Smith Charity (I. Wood Estate)

£22,000

Correspondent: Bernard Fleckney, Committee Section Manager, Committee Section, Runnymede Borough Council, Civic Offices, Station Road, Addlestone KT15 2AH (01932 425620)

CC Number: 233531

Eligibility
People over 60 who are in need and live in Chertsey, Addlestone, New Haw and Lyne, Surrey.

Types of grants
Recurrent fuel vouchers which can be used as part-payment of fuel bills.

Annual grant total
In 2012/13 the charity had an income of £21,000 and a total expenditure of £22,000. We estimate that grants to individuals also totalled £22,000.

Applications
In writing to the correspondent either through a social worker, Citizens Advice or other third party or directly by the individual. Applications can be considered at any time during the year.

The Henry Smith Charity (Puttenham and Wanborough)

£2,000

Correspondent: David Knapp, Administrator, Walnut Tree Close, Guildford, Surrey GU1 4UX (01483 887766; fax: 01483 887750; email: dsk@hartbrown.co.uk)

Eligibility
People in need who live in Puttenham and Wanborough parishes.

Types of grants
One-off grants for needy people who do not have an income other than pensions.

Annual grant total
The charity receives around £2,000 a year, allocated by Henry Smith's (General Estate) Charity.

Exclusions
Grants are not given to people who are working or who own their house.

Applications
In writing to the correspondent.

Other information
Grants are also given for the benefit of the parish as a whole.

The Henry Smith Charity (Send and Ripley)

£4,900

Correspondent: Geoffrey A. Richardson, Trustee, Emali, 2 Rose Lane, Ripley, Surrey GU23 6NE (01483 225322)

CC Number: 200496

Eligibility
People in need who live in Send and Ripley, and have done so for five years.

Types of grants
One-off grants of around £30 at Christmas to 50 or 60 elderly people in Send and a similar number in Ripley. Other grants according to need are also available from any remaining funds, primarily for the elderly and those with disabilities.

Annual grant total
In 2012/13 the charity had an income of £4,900 and a total expenditure of £5,000. We estimate that grants to individuals totalled £4,900.

Applications
In writing to the correspondent. Applications can be submitted directly by the individual or, where applicable, through a social worker, Citizens Advice or any other welfare agency or third party on behalf of the individual. Applications are considered as they arrive.

The Surrey Association for Visual Impairment

£1,300

Correspondent: Bob Hughes, Chief Executive, Rentwood, School Lane, Fetcham, Leatherhead, Surrey KT22 9JX (01372 377701; fax: 01372 360767; email: info@sightforsurrey.org.uk; website: www.surreywebsight.org.uk)

CC Number: 1121949

Eligibility
People who are blind or partially-sighted and who live in the administrative county of Surrey.

Types of grants
Small one-off grants are given when absolutely necessary. Grants are usually to help pay for equipment required to overcome a sight problem or a sudden domestic need. Applications from service users for small, interest-free loans are also occasionally considered.

Annual grant total
In 2012/13 the association had assets of £898,000 and an income of £1.6 million. Grants to individuals totalled £1,300, with local clubs receiving a further £700.

A budget of £5,000 is set aside each year for grants to individuals, clubs and classes.

Applications
On a form available from the correspondent. Applications can be submitted at any time by the individual or through a social worker, welfare agency, club or any recognised organisation for blind or partially-sighted people.

Other information
The association's main focus is the provision of services, advice, IT training and information for visually impaired people. It runs a resource centre equipped with a wide range of aids and equipment as well as a home visiting scheme and outreach groups. The association has a successful children's services division and also provides support for those struggling to navigate the benefits system.

Windlesham United Charities

£4,000 (62 grants)

Correspondent: Carol Robson, Clerk to the Trustees, 4 James Butler Almshouses, Guildford Road, Bagshot, Surrey GU19 5NH (01276476158)

CC Number: 200224

Eligibility
Mainly the elderly and people with disabilities who are in need and have lived in the parishes of Bagshot, Lightwater and Windlesham (Surrey) for at least two years.

Types of grants
One-off grants, mainly in the form of small heating grants.

Annual grant total
At the time of writing (August 2014) the latest financial information available was from 2012. In 2012 the charity had assets of £325,000 and an income of £49,000. Grants to individuals totalled about £4,000 and were distributed to 62 people in Bagshot, Lightwater and Windlesham to cover fuel expenses.

Applications
In writing to the correspondent at any time.

Other information
Windlesham United Charities consists of four separate funds: R E Cooper Educational Fund, The Duchess of Gloucester Educational Fund, Windlesham Poors Allotments and Windlesham United Charities. The charity also maintains allotments for the poor.

The Witley Charitable Trust

£1,700

Correspondent: Daphne O'Hanlon, Trustee, Triados, Waggoners Way, Grayshott, Hindhead, Surrey GU26 6DX (01428 604679)

CC Number: 200338

Eligibility
Children and young people (normally under the age of 20) and older people (normally aged over 60) who are in need and who live in the parishes of Witley, Milford and small part of Brook.

Types of grants
One-off, modest grants ranging from £25 to £300. Support can be given towards telephone, electricity and gas debts (up to about £150, usually paid via social services), for medical appliances not available through the NHS, in Christmas gifts, food hampers or vouchers, and towards other needs.

Annual grant total
At the time of writing (August 2014) the latest financial information available was from 2012. In 2012 the trust had an income of £5,500 and an expenditure of £3,500. We estimate that around £1,700 was awarded in welfare grants.

Exclusions
The trust does not give loans or support for items which should be provided by statutory services.

Applications
In writing to the correspondent. Applications should be submitted through nurses, doctors, social workers, clergy, Citizens Advice and so on but not directly by the individual. Awards are usually considered in early February and September, although emergency applications can be considered throughout the year.

Other information
Grants are also given for educational needs.

The Wonersh Charities

£5,000

Correspondent: Anna Pritchard, Administrator, 8 Hullmead, Shamley Green, Guildford, Surrey GU5 0UG (01483 894191; email: wonershuc@gmail.com)

CC Number: 200086

Eligibility
Older people and people with a disability who live in the parishes of Wonersh, Shamley Green and Blackheath.

Types of grants
Cash grants are given at Christmas. One-off grants are also available.

Annual grant total
In 2012/13 the charity had an income of £5,500 and a total expenditure of £5,300. We estimate that grants to individuals totalled £5,000.

Applications
In writing to the correspondent preferably through a third party such as Citizens Advice, trustee of the charity, local clergy or other organisation. Applications are usually considered in early July and early December.

Abinger

The Abinger Consolidated Charities

£6,000

Correspondent: Caroline Sack, PCC Secretary, The Rectory, Abinger Lane, Abinger Common, Dorking, Surrey RH5 6HZ (01306 737160)

CC Number: 200124

Eligibility
People in need who live in the ancient parish of Abinger.

Types of grants
One-off or recurrent grants according to need.

Annual grant total
In 2012/13, the charity had an income of £14,500 and a total expenditure of £11,000. We estimate that the total amount of grants awarded to individuals was approximately £6,000. The charity also awards grants to organisations.

Applications
In writing to the correspondent.

Ashford

Ashford Relief in Need Charities

£1,800

Correspondent: Peter Harding, Administrator, 8 Portland Road, Ashford TW15 3BT (01784 241257; email: pjlr_2000@yahoo.co.uk)

CC Number: 231441

Eligibility

People in need who live in the ancient parishes of Ashford and Laleham.

Types of grants

One-off grants according to need.

Annual grant total

In 2012/13, the charity's total income was £8,900 and total expenditure was £3,800. We estimate that the total amount of grants awarded to individuals was £1,800. The charity also awards grants to organisations with similar objectives.

Applications

In writing to the correspondent. Applications can be made either directly by the individual, or through a third party such as a social worker, Citizens Advice or relative.

Betchworth

Betchworth United Charities

£5,000

Correspondent: Andrea Brown, Clerk, 15 Nutwood Avenue, Brockham, Betchworth, Surrey RH3 7LT (01737 843806; email: anthonybrown7lt@btinternet.com)

CC Number: 200299

Eligibility

People in need who live in the ancient parish of Betchworth.

Types of grants

One-off grants usually ranging from £60 to £250. The majority of funding is given for welfare purposes but a small amount is also available for educational needs under the Margaret Fenwick fund.

Annual grant total

In 2012 the charity had an income of £260 and a total expenditure of £11,800. We estimate that social welfare grants to individuals totalled £5,000. Grants are also awarded to organisations and to individuals for educational purposes.

At the time of writing (August 2014) this was the most recent financial information available for the charity.

Applications

In writing to the correspondent to be submitted by a third party, such as a doctor, minister or social worker. Applications are considered at trustee meetings.

Bisley

The Henry Smith Charity (Bisley)

£2,000

Correspondent: Alexandra Gunn, Trustee, 213 Guildford Road, Bisley, Woking, Surrey GU24 9DL (email: sandy213@ntlworld.com)

CC Number: 200157

Eligibility

People in need who live in Bisley.

Types of grants

Grants to assist with food costs are distributed twice a year.

Annual grant total

In 2013 this charity's income was £2,500 and its total expenditure was £2,000.

Applications

On a form available from the correspondent to be submitted directly by the individual.

Bletchingley

The Bletchingley United Charities

£6,100

Correspondent: Mrs C. A. Bolshaw, Administrator, Cleves, Castle Street, Bletchingley, Surrey RH1 4QA (01883 743000; email: chrisbolshaw@hotmail.co.uk)

CC Number: 236747

Eligibility

People in need, hardship or distress who live in the parish of Bletchingley.

Types of grants

One-off and recurrent grants in the range of £20 to £200 towards medical items, welfare support, gas and electricity. Grants are also given for equipment such as cookers, fridges and freezers.

Annual grant total

In 2012/13 the charity had an income of £11,100 and a total expenditure of £12,400. We estimate that grants to individuals totalled £6,100, with funding also awarded to local organisations.

Exclusions

Grants are not given for rates, taxes or other public funds.

Applications

In writing to the correspondent. Applications can be submitted either directly by the individual, through a third party such as a social worker, or where applicable, through an organisation such as Citizens Advice or other welfare agency. They are considered throughout the year.

Bramley

The Henry Smith Charity (Bramley)

£1,600

Correspondent: Kathy Victor, Clerk, Bramley Village Hall, Hall Road, Bramley, Guildford GU5 0AX (01483 894138; email: bramleyparish@gmail.com; website: www.bramleyparish.co.uk)

CC Number: 200128

Eligibility

People in need who live in the parish of Bramley, Surrey.

Types of grants

One-off grants according to need.

Annual grant total

In 2012/13 the charity had an income of £3,600 and a total expenditure of £3,300. We estimate that grants to individuals totalled £1,600, with funding also awarded to local organisations.

Applications

In writing to the correspondent; there are no application forms. The letter should contain as much information as possible about why support is required.

Other information

This charity is also known as the 'Smiths Charity'.

Byfleet

The Byfleet United Charity

£255,000 (96 grants)

Correspondent: Christopher Russell, Clerk to the Trustees, 10 Stoop Court, Leisure Lane, West Byfleet, Surrey KT14 6HF (01932 340943; email: buc@byfleetunitedcharity.org.uk)

CC Number: 200344

Eligibility

People in need who have lived in the ancient parish of Byfleet or West Byfleet area for at least a year (normally three years) immediately prior to their application.

Types of grants

Monthly pensions and one-off grants towards essential household items, for example, cookers, heaters, vacuum cleaners and also for nursery school fees.

Annual grant total

At the time of writing (August 2014) the latest financial information available was from 2012. In 2012 the charity had assets of £5.9 million and an income of £493,000. Grants were made to 96 individuals totalling around £48,000 and a further £207,000 was paid in pensions.

Exclusions

People outside the area of benefit or resident there temporary can only be assisted in exceptional circumstances.

Applications

In writing to the correspondent. Applications can be made directly by the individual or through a third party, such as a social worker, Citizens Advice, local GP or church. Candidates are usually visited and assessed.

Other information

The charity gives money to local organisations who work in a similar field (£9,800 to five organisations in 2012). It also operates a sheltered housing complex of 24 flats available to people over the age of 55 who are in real need. During the year accommodation was provided to 27 individuals.

This charity is an amalgamation of smaller trusts, including the Byfleet Pensions Fund.

Capel

The Henry Smith Charity (Capel)

£2,000

Correspondent: Mrs J. Richards, Administrator, Old School House, Coldharbour, Dorking, Surrey RH5 6HF (01306 711885)

Eligibility

People in need who have lived in Beare Green, Capel and Coldharbour, usually for at least five years.

Types of grants

Mostly Christmas vouchers for older people redeemable at several local stores. The vouchers are usually £20 for couples and £15 for single people.

Annual grant total

Grants usually total about £2,000 each year.

Applications

In writing to the correspondent directly by the individual or a family member. Applications should be received by 1 November and are considered in December.

Charlwood

John Bristow and Thomas Mason Trust

£700

Correspondent: Marie Singleton, Trust Secretary, 3 Grayrigg Road, Maidenbower, Crawley RH10 7AB (01293 883950; email: trust.secretary@jbtmt.org.uk; website: www.jbtmt.org.uk)

CC Number: 1075971

Eligibility

People who are in need who live in the parish of Charlwood as constituted on 17 February 1926, including Hookwood and Lowfield Heath.

Types of grants

One-off and recurrent grants and loans are given according to the need. Support for illness and disability and recreation and leisure.

Annual grant total

In 2013 the trust had assets of £2.7 million representing mainly endowment funds with only £85,000 being unrestricted. The trust had an income of £95,000 and made grants totalling almost £93,000, of which £500 went to individuals for educational purposes and almost £700 to individuals for social welfare purposes. The remainder was awarded to organisations.

Applications

On a form available from the correspondent or to download from the website. Applications can be submitted directly by the individual or through a third party. They will normally be considered within two weeks but can be dealt with more quickly in urgent cases.

Smith and Earles Charity

£2,400

Correspondent: Jeanette Gillespie, Administrator, The Birches, Ifield Road, Charlwood, Horley, Surrey RH6 0DR (01293 862129; email: gillespie2@btinternet.com)

CC Number: 200043

Eligibility

People with disabilities or those over 65 and in need who have lived in the old parish of Charlwood for at least five years.

Types of grants

One-off and recurrent grants of up to £80.

Annual grant total

In 2013 the charity had an income of £6,300 and a total expenditure of £4,900. We estimate that grants to individuals totalled £2,400.

Applications

On a form available from the correspondent. Applications for one-off (usually larger) grants should be submitted through a recognised referral agency (such as a social worker, Citizens Advice or other welfare agency). Applications for recurrent grants can be submitted directly by the individual. They are considered in November. Details of any disability or special need should be given.

Other information

Help is also given towards the hiring of halls for meetings for older people, hospices and school requirements.

Cheam

Cheam Consolidated Charities

£3,400

Correspondent: Nola Freeman, Trustee, St Dunstan's Church, Church Road, Cheam, Surrey SM3 8QH (020 8641 1284)

CC Number: 238392

Eligibility

People in need who live in Cheam. Preference is given to older people.

Types of grants

One-off and recurrent grants, of £50 to £200.

Annual grant total

In 2013 the charity had an income of £4,900 and a total expenditure of £6,800. We estimate that grants to individuals totalled £3,400, with funding also awarded to organisations.

Applications

In writing to the correspondent, usually for consideration at the start of May and November. Applications can be made either directly by the individual, or via a social worker, Citizens Advice or other welfare agency.

Chessington

Chessington Charities

£2,000

Correspondent: Mrs L. Roberts, Administrator, St Mary's Centre, Church Lane, Chessington, Surrey KT9 2DR

CC Number: 209241

Eligibility

People in need who live in the parish of St Mary the Virgin, Chessington. Applicants must have lived in the parish for at least one year.

Types of grants

Grants are usually one-off in the range of £30 to £250. Donations include those given to older people (with low income) at Christmas and for items such as special food, furniture, medical equipment, electrical goods and clothing.

Annual grant total

In 2013 the charity had both an income and total expenditure of almost £8,000.

Exclusions

Grants are not given 'as a dole' or to pay debts. Applicants must live in the Parish of St Mary the Virgin, which excludes those who live in the rest of the Chessington postal area.

Applications

On a form available from the correspondent to be submitted either directly by the individual or through a social worker, Citizens Advice or other agency. Other applications are considered throughout the year. A home visit will be made by a trustee to ascertain details of income and expenditure and to look at the need. Applications for Christmas grants for older people must be received by 1 November and are distributed in this month.

Other information

Grants are also given to local organisations which help older people or people with disabilities. Educational grants are also made to individuals.

Chobham

The Chobham Poor Allotment Charity

£10,500

Correspondent: Elizabeth Thody, Administrator, 46 Chertsey Road, Windlesham GU20 6EP (01276 475396)

CC Number: 200154

Eligibility

People in need who live in the ancient parish of Chobham, which includes the civil parishes of Chobham and West End.

Types of grants

The majority of grants are given in the form of vouchers, ranging between £30 and £50, as payment towards goods in local shops. Awards are also made towards stair lifts, electric scooters, school trips and school uniforms.

Annual grant total

In 2012/13 the charity had assets of £422,000 and an income of £45,500. Grants to individuals totalled more than £10,500 and were distributed as follows:

Annual distribution	£8,500
Other (mobility)	£1,500
Individuals (general)	£600

A further £4,700 was awarded to local organisations.

Applications

On a form available from the correspondent. Applications should be submitted directly by the individual for consideration at any time.

Other information

The trust also manages almshouses and an area of allotment land.

Henry Smith Charity (Chobham)

£8,000

Correspondent: Elizabeth Thody, 46 Chertsey Road, Windlesham, Surrey GU20 6EP

CC Number: 200155

Eligibility

People in need who live in the ancient parish of Chobham (roughly the current civil parishes of Chobham and West End) in Surrey.

Types of grants

One-off grants, usually in the form of vouchers worth £20 to £30, to be used to purchase goods from local shops.

Annual grant total

In 2012/13 the charity had an income of £8,500 and a total expenditure of £8,200. We estimate that grants to individuals totalled £8,000.

Applications

On a form available from the correspondent.

Other information

The origins of this charity date back to 1642.

Crowhurst

Crowhurst Relief-in-Need Charities

£600

Correspondent: Mrs Edwards, Trustee, 1 Lankester Square, Oxted, Surrey RH8 0LJ (01883 712874)

CC Number: 200315

Eligibility

People in need who live in Crowhurst, Surrey.

Types of grants

One-off grants according to need. Recent grants of £100 to £250 have been given to help with fuel bills and travel to or from hospital.

Annual grant total

In 2012/13 the charity had an income of £2,500 and a total expenditure of £2,400. We estimate that social welfare grants to individuals totalled £600. Grants are also given to organisations and for educational purposes.

Applications

On a form available from the correspondent.

Dunsfold

The Henry Smith Charity (Dunsfold)

£2,000

Correspondent: Celeste Lawrence, Dunsfold Parish Clerk, Council Office, Unit 3, The Orchard, Chiddingfold Road, Dunsfold GU8 4PB (01483 200980; email: dunsfoldparishclerk@btconnect.com)

Eligibility

People in need who live in Dunsfold and who have done so for the past five years.

Types of grants

Grocery vouchers for about £40 to £50, exchangeable in the village store.

Annual grant total

Grants usually total around £2,000.

Applications

In writing to the correspondent. Applications are considered in December.

East Horsley

Henry Smith's Charity (East Horsley)

£800

Correspondent: Nicholas Clemens, Clerk, East Horsley Parish Council Office, Kingston Avenue, East Horsley, Surrey KT24 6QT (01483 281148; email: henrysmithcharity@easthorsley.net)

CC Number: 200796

Eligibility

People in need who have lived in East Horsley for at least two years and have disabilities or are in need.

Types of grants

One-off or recurrent grants according to need.

Annual grant total

Each year the trust receives an amount allocated by Henry Smith's (General Estate) Charity which is divided according to need between welfare and educational grants.

Applications

In writing to the correspondent through a third party such as a social worker, teacher or vicar. Applications are considered in December.

Effingham

The Henry Smith Charity (Effingham)

£2,600

Correspondent: The Clerk, Effingham Parish Council, The Parish Room, 3 Home Barn Court, The Street, Effingham, Leatherhead KT24 5LG (01372 454911; email: clerk2009@effinghamparishcouncil.gov.uk)

CC Number: 237703

Eligibility

People in need who live in Effingham.

Types of grants

One-off grants and gift vouchers, generally of £50 to £100; many grants are given at Christmas.

Annual grant total

In 2012/13 the charity had an income of £1,700 and a total expenditure of £2,800. We estimate that grants to individuals totalled £2,600.

Applications

In writing to the correspondent. Applications are considered monthly.

Egham

The Egham United Charity

£6,000

Correspondent: The Secretary, 33 Runnemede Road, Egham, Surrey TW20 9BE (01784 472742; email: eghamunicharity@aol.com; website: www.eghamunitedcharity.org)

CC Number: 205885

Eligibility

People in need who have lived in Egham, Englefield Green (West and East), Hythe or Virginia Water for at least five years.

Types of grants

One-off grants according to need. Grants are awarded towards, for example, fuel bills, household essentials, mobility aids and for school uniforms, trips and travel fares. Payments are made directly to the supplier/provider (in the case of settling bills) or to the sponsoring agency for distribution.

Annual grant total

In 2013 the charity had an income of £21,000 and a total expenditure of £12,500. We estimate that grants to individuals totalled £6,000, with funding also awarded for educational purposes.

Exclusions

No recurrent grants or loans. No funding to cover services which should be provided by central or local authorities (though 'top-up' of partial provision may be considered).

Applications

On a form available to download from the website. Applications should be submitted through an appropriate third party such as Citizens Advice or a social worker. Ideally applications should include quotations for goods or services required. Applications are only ever considered at trustee meetings which are held every six weeks. Applicants may occasionally be visited.

Other information

The charity has an informative website.

Epsom

Epsom Parochial Charities

£1,200

Correspondent: John Steward, Trustee, 26 Woodcote Hurst, Epsom, Surrey KT18 7DT (email: vanstonewalker@ntlworld.com)

CC Number: 200571

Eligibility

People in need who live in the ancient parish of Epsom.

Types of grants

One-off grants ranging from £100 to £500 according to need. Grants given include those for clothing, food, medical care and equipment and household appliances.

Annual grant total

In 2012 the charity had an income of £83,000 and assets of £1.6 million. Grants were made to individuals for education and welfare purposes totalling approximately £2,400.

These were the latest accounts available at the time of writing (August 2014)

Applications

On a form available from the correspondent.

Other information

Grants are also made for education. The charity also provides residential accommodation through its three almshouses.

The Henry Smith Charity (Ewell)

Correspondent: The Administrator, 19 Cheam Road, Ewell, Epsom, Surrey KT17 1ST

Eligibility

People in need who live, work or are being educated in the ancient ecclesiastical parish of Ewell and the liberty of Kingswood.

Types of grants

One-off or recurrent grants according to need.

Annual grant total

According to our research, the trust receives about £12,000 each year, allocated by Henry Smith's (General Estate) Charity.

Applications

In writing to the correspondent. Applications which do not meet the criteria will not be acknowledged.

Esher

The Henry Smith Charity (Esher)

£2,000

Correspondent: Gill Barnett, Administrator, 24 Pelhams Walk, Esher KT10 8QD (01372 465755; email: gill@gillmikebarnett.plus.com)

Eligibility

People in need who live in the ancient parish of Esher.

Types of grants

Annual grants to a number of elderly/low income families.

Annual grant total

The trust has an income of about £2,000, allocated by Henry Smith's (General Estate) Charity, all of which is given in grants.

Applications

In writing to the correspondent through a social worker, Citizens Advice or other third party. Details of the applicant's financial circumstances should be included.

Guildford

The Guildford Poyle Charities

£30,000 (212 grants)

Correspondent: Janice Bennett, Manager, 208 High Street, Guildford GU1 3JB (01483 303678; fax: 01483 303678; email: admin@guildfordpoylecharities.org; website: www.guildfordpoylecharities.org)

CC Number: 1145202

Eligibility

People in need who live in the borough of Guildford as constituted prior to 1 April 1974 and part of the ancient parish of Merrow. A map showing the beneficial area can be viewed on the website.

Types of grants

Mainly one-off grants ranging between £100 and £300 for electrical appliances, kitchen items, second-hand furniture, household items, baby equipment, clothing, second-hand computers and holiday playschemes, for example. Christmas food vouchers are also available to families. Grants for carpets are only considered in special circumstances. Grants are in the form of cheques or vouchers for suppliers with which the charities have arrangements or a cheque made out to the referral agency.

Annual grant total

In 2013 the charity held assets of £4.2 million and had an income of £205,000. A total of 212 grants were awarded to individuals, amounting to £30,000.

A further £93,000 was given in 25 grants to organisations.

Exclusions

Grants are usually not made to pay for basic items such as food, rent and utility bills. No help is given towards debt or arrears.

Applications

On a form available from the correspondent or to download from the website. Applications can be submitted at any time through a social worker, Citizens Advice or other welfare agency. Individuals may apply directly, though the charities state that an application has more chance of being successful if it is supported by a letter from a health or welfare professional who is familiar with the individual's circumstances. They are considered every two to three weeks and decisions are confirmed in writing.

The charity's office welcomes enquiries.

Other information

The charity is also known as the Henry Smith's or The Poyle Charity.

Applications for school uniforms are now handled through the Home School Link Worker (HSLW) attached to your child's school. Approach them for more details.

The Mayor of Guildford's Christmas and Local Distress Fund

£5,700

Correspondent: Kate Foxton, Civic Secretary, Guildford Borough Council, Millmead House, Millmead, Guildford, Surrey GU2 4BB (01483 444031; fax: 01483 444444; email: civicsecretary@guildford.gov.uk.)

CC Number: 258388

Eligibility

People in need who live in the borough of Guildford, with a preference for the elderly and people living with disabilities.

Types of grants

One-off grants of up to £150. There are no specific restrictions on what can be applied for and the purpose of the grant is defined in the application form. Grants are also made for Christmas events.

Annual grant total

In 2012/13 the trust had an income of £4,500 and a total expenditure of £5,900. We estimate that grants to individuals totalled £5,700.

Applications

On a form available for download from the Guildford Borough Council website, to be submitted through a social worker, Citizens Advice, local GP or other relevant third party. Applications are usually considered in January, April, July and October.

Hascombe

The Henry Smith Charity (Hascombe)

£2,000

Correspondent: Beverley Weddell, Hascombe Parish Clerk, Lock House Lodge, Knightons Lane, Dunsfold GU8 4NU (01483 200314; email: clerk@hascombeparishcouncil.co.uk)

Eligibility

People in need, generally older people who live in Hascombe.

Types of grants

Small grants to Hascombe residents only.

Annual grant total

Usually grants total around £2,000.

Applications

In writing to the correspondent.

Headley

The Henry Smith Charity (Headley)

£5,000

Correspondent: Anthony Vine-Lott, Administrator, Broom Cottage, Crabtree Lane, Headley, Epsom KT18 6PS (01372 374728; email: tony.vinelott@btinternet.com)

Eligibility

People in need who live in the parish of Headley.

Types of grants

One-off and recurrent grants are available to help with, for example, groceries and hospital travel.

Annual grant total

Grants usually total about £5,000 each year.

Applications

In writing to the correspondent or any trustee, giving the reasons for the application.

Horne

The Henry Smith Charity (Horne)

£6,800

Correspondent: Pamela Bean, Hon. Secretary, Yew Tree Cottage, Smallfield Road, Horne, Horley RH6 9JP (01342 843173)

CC Number: 201988

Eligibility

Older people and people in need who live in the ancient parish of Horne.

Types of grants

One-off grants are the norm, although recurrent grants can be considered.

Annual grant total

In 2012/13 the charity had an income of £7,600 and a total expenditure of £7,000. We estimate that grants to individuals amounted to around £6,800.

Exclusions

Group applications are not accepted.

Applications

On a form available from the correspondent. Applications can be submitted either directly by the individual or through a social worker and should include details of the applicant's level of income. They are normally considered twice a year (notices are posted around the parish).

Kingston upon Thames

The Charities of Ann Savage

£1,000

Correspondent: Christopher Ault, Trustee, 18 Woodbines Avenue, Kingston upon Thames KT1 2AY (020 8546 8155)

CC Number: 237108

Eligibility

People in need who live in the borough of Kingston upon Thames.

Types of grants

Mainly recurrent grants.

Annual grant total

Grants to individuals are generally around £1,000 a year. When funds allow, the charity donates half of its income to the local church.

Applications

The trustees usually support individuals known via their contacts at All Saints Parish Church in Kingston upon Thames. It is unlikely that grants would be available to support unsolicited applications.

Leatherhead

Leatherhead United Charities

£10,000 (50–60 grants)

Correspondent: David Matanle, Clerk to the Trustees, Homefield, Forty Foot Road, Leatherhead, Surrey KT22 8RP (01372 370073; email: luchar@btinternet.com)

CC Number: 200183

Eligibility

People in need who live in the area of the former Leatherhead urban district council (Ashtead, Bookhams, Fetcham and Leatherhead). Preference is given to residents of the parish of Leatherhead as constituted on 27 September 1912.

Types of grants

One-off grants in the range of £100 and £750 are given for general relief of need. Pensions are also available.

Annual grant total

At the time of writing (July 2014) the latest accounts were not available to view. In 2013 the charity had an income of £298,000 and a total expenditure of £233,000. In the past grants to individuals have totalled around £20,000 a year distributed in 50–60 awards. We estimate that grants for social welfare purposes totalled around £10,000.

Applications

Application forms can be requested from the correspondent. Our research suggests that they should be submitted through a recognised referral agency, such as a social worker, Citizens Advice or a doctor. Candidates should also provide details of their/their family income and include names of two referees. Awards are considered throughout the year.

Other information

Grants are also made to organisations.

The residents of Mole Valley district council are offered sheltered housing and associated services.

Leigh

The Henry Smith Charity (Leigh)

£5,000

Correspondent: Mrs J. Sturt, Administrator, 12 Knoll Road, Dorking RH4 3EW (01306 881547; email: notman-janesturt@hotmail.co.uk)

CC Number: 237335

Eligibility

People in need who live in Leigh, Surrey.

Types of grants

The trust has a list of all people over 65; each receives support at Christmas in the form of food vouchers, or help with household bills. Gifts may also be given at Easter in the years when the trust receives more income. Help is also given to other residents of Leigh, who are in need.

Annual grant total

In 2012/13 the charity had an income of £5,100 and a total expenditure of £5,200. We estimate that grants to individuals totalled £5,000.

Applications

In writing or by telephone to the correspondent, or through a third party.

Newdigate

The Henry Smith Charity (Newdigate)

£5,000

Correspondent: Diana Salisbury, Parish Councillor, 'Langholm', Village Street, Newdigate, Dorking, Surrey RH5 5DH (website: newdigate.atspace.com/benefact.htm)

Eligibility

People in need who live in the parish of Newdigate.

Types of grants

One-off grants for a variety of needs. Grants are typically made to help residents with bereavement, health needs and special educational requirements. In addition, just after Christmas each year the Charity hosts a special lunch provided in the village hall for all residents over 65 years old.

Annual grant total

Grants usually total around £5,000 per year.

Applications

In writing to the correspondent to be submitted directly by the individual.

Nutfield

Smith's Charity-Parish of Nutfield

£1,200

Correspondent: Kenneth Rolaston, Trustee, 7 Morris Road, South Nutfield, Redhill RH1 5SB (01737 823348; email: smithsnutfield@aol.com)

CC Number: 255839

Eligibility

People in need who live in the parish of Nutfield.

Types of grants

Small one-off and recurrent grants. Vouchers for local shops are given.

Annual grant total

In 2012/13 the charity had an income of £5,100 and a total expenditure of £5,000. We estimate that welfare grants to individuals totalled £1,200. Funding was also awarded to individuals for educational purposes and to organisations providing services for children and older people.

Applications

In writing to the correspondent, to be submitted either directly by the individual or by any of the trustees. Applications are usually considered in December.

Ockley

Ockley United Charities (Henry Smith Charity)

£7,400 (51 grants)

Correspondent: Tim Pryke, Trustee, Danesfield, Stane Street, Ockley, Dorking RH5 5SY (01306 711511)

CC Number: 200556

Eligibility

People in need who live in Ockley (primarily older people living in sheltered accommodation provided by Ockley Housing Association or rented housing).

Types of grants

Recurrent annual cash gifts of £110. Assistance is also given to local families for nursery fees.

Annual grant total

In 2012/13 the charity had an income of £8,800 and a total expenditure of £7,600. We estimate that grants to individuals totalled £7,400.

During the year, 51 parishioners benefitted from annual gifts.

Applications

In writing to the correspondent. Applications should include details of income, housing and need. They are considered on a regular basis.

Oxted

The Oxted United Charities

£4,800

Correspondent: C. J. Berry, Trustee, Robinslade, Wilderness Road, Oxted, Surrey RH8 9HS (01883 714553)

CC Number: 200056

Eligibility

People in need who live in the parish of Oxted.

Types of grants

One-off grants, generally in the range of £20 to £500. In the past, grants have been given for clothing, food, education, utility bills, television licences, furniture and floor covering.

Annual grant total

In 2012/13 the charity had an income of £6,100 and a total expenditure of £5,000. We estimate that grants to individuals totalled £4,800.

Applications

In writing to the correspondent. Applications are considered at any time and should be submitted directly by the individual or, where applicable, through a social worker, Citizens Advice or other welfare agency.

Pirbright

The Pirbright Relief-in-Need Charity

£1,200

Correspondent: Philip Lawson, Administrator, Stanemore, Rowe Lane, Pirbright, Woking GU24 0LX (01483 472842)

CC Number: 238494

Eligibility

People in need, hardship or distress who live in the parish of Pirbright.

Types of grants

One-off grants for a variety of items, services or facilities that will reduce the need, hardship or distress of the individual, including buying or renting medical equipment to use at home.

Annual grant total

In 2012/13, the charity had an income of £3,000 and a total expenditure of £3,300.

The trust also awards grants to organisations that provide items, services or facilities to individuals in need. We approximate that £1,200 is awarded to individuals directly.

Exclusions

Grants will not be given for taxes, rates or any other public funds. The trustees must not commit themselves to repeating or renewing any grant.

Applications

In writing to the correspondent or any of the trustees.

Shottermill

Shottermill United Charities (Henry Smith and Others)

£1,000

Correspondent: Hilary Bicknell, Administrator, 7 Underwood Road, Haslemere, Surrey GU27 1JQ (01428 651276)

CC Number: 200394

Eligibility

People in need who live in the parish of Shottermill, Surrey.

Types of grants

Grants usually ranging from £40 to £50 according to need. The charity distributes grocery vouchers at Christmas.

Annual grant total

In 2012/13 the charity had an income of £3,200 and a total expenditure of £2,300. We estimate that around £1,000 was made in grants to individuals for social welfare purposes.

Applications

In writing to the correspondent. Applications can be submitted directly by the individual or through a social worker, Citizens Advice or other welfare agency or third party. They are considered at any time, but particularly at Christmas.

Other information

The charity also gives grants to organisations.

Staines

The Staines Parochial Charity

£3,400

Correspondent: Carol Davies, Honorary Clerk to the Trustees, 191 Feltham Hill Road, Ashford, Middlesex TW15 1HJ (01784 255432)

CC Number: 211653

Eligibility

Older people over the age of 60 who live in the parish of Staines; people who are unable to work; people caring for a person with disabilities and occasionally other people in need who live in the area of the former urban district of Staines.

Types of grants

One-off grants according to need to alleviate hardship or distress, for example, the payment of gas or electricity bills. Grants usually range from £80 to £100.

Annual grant total

In 2012/13 the charity had an income of £5,100 and a total expenditure of £3,500. We estimate that grants to individuals totalled £3,400.

Exclusions

No grants to individuals living outside the beneficial area.

Applications

On a form available from the correspondent including evidence of need, hardship or distress. Applications can be submitted either directly by the individual, through a social worker, Citizens Advice, welfare agency or other third party. The application must be sent via a trustee who must countersign the application. Applications are normally considered in September.

Stoke D'Abernon

Jemima Octavia Cooper for the Poor (Stoke D'Abernon Charities)

£3,300

Correspondent: Ron Stewart, Trustee, Old Timbers, Manor Way, Oxshott, Leatherhead, Surrey KT22 0HU (07785 272590; email: ronandjackie@tecres.net)

CC Number: 200187

Eligibility

People in need who live in the ancient parish of Stoke D'Abernon (which includes part of Oxshott).

Types of grants

One-off and recurrent grants according to need. Grants are made at Christmas and are of around £50 on average. Occasionally smaller distributions are made in the summer.

Annual grant total

In 2013/14 the charity had an income of £2,800 and an expenditure of £3,500. We estimate that around £3,300 was awarded in grants to individuals.

Applications

Applications can be made formally in writing; however, in practice many applications are made informally by word of mouth given the small size and catchment area of the charity. If a formal application is to be made the trustees prefer email, where possible.

Thursley

Anthony Smith and Others

£1,100

Correspondent: Revd Peter Muir, Trustee, Yew Cottage, Dye House Lane, Thursley, Godalming GU8 6QA (01252 702360; email: peter.muir@thursleychurch.org.uk)

CC Number: 239259

Eligibility

People in need, including those who are sick, disabled, elderly, single parents and bereaved young people, who live in the parish of Thursley in Surrey.

Types of grants

One-off and recurrent grants according to need ranging from £100 to £300.

Annual grant total

In 2012/13, the trust had an income of £2,500 and a total expenditure of £2,400. We estimate the total amount of grants awarded to individuals was £1,100. The trust also awards grants to organisations.

Applications

In writing to the correspondent. Applications can be submitted directly by the individual or through an organisation such as Citizens Advice, or through a third party such as a social worker. Applications are considered in November each year.

Other information

The charities are the Charities of Anthony Smith and Henry Smith.

West Clandon

Henry Smith Charity West Clandon

£2,600

Correspondent: Stephen Meredith, Trustee, 11 Bennett Way, West Clandon, Guildford GU4 7TN

CC Number: 200165–1

Eligibility

People in need, mainly older people, who have lived in the parish of West Clandon for at least five years.

Types of grants

One-off cash grants.

Annual grant total

In 2012 the charity had an income of £3,000 and an expenditure of almost £3,000. Grants totalled around £2,600.

These were the latest accounts available at the time of writing (August 2014).

Applications

In writing to the correspondent. The deadline for applications is 31 October. Grants are usually distributed during December.

West Molesey

The Henry Smith Charity (West Molesey)

£1,600

Correspondent: Revd Peter Tailby, Administrator, 518 Walton Road, West Molesey, Surrey KT8 2QF (020 8979 3846; email: ptailby@supanet.com)

Eligibility

People in need who live in West Molesey.

Types of grants

Small one-off grants, usually under £50.

Annual grant total

Our research tells us that social welfare grants to individuals usually total around £1,600.

Applications

In writing to the correspondent. Applications can be submitted directly by the individual or through a social worker, Citizens Advice or other welfare agency.

Weybridge

Weybridge Land Charity

£34,000 (277 grants)

Correspondent: Howard Turner, Clerk to the Trustees, Little Knowle, Woodlands, Send, Woking GU23 7LD (01483 211728)

CC Number: 200270

Eligibility
People in need who live in Weybridge.

Types of grants
Emergency grants for food, clothing, household appliances and furniture, for example. Christmas grants (including fuel payments for the elderly) which in 2013 ranged between £50 – £260.

Annual grant total
In 2013 the charity held assets of £1.8 million and had an income of £65,000. A total of 277 grants were made to individuals, amounting to £34,000. Of these, 23 grants totalling £6,500 were given in emergency payments to individuals who had been referred to the charity by various welfare agencies, and the remaining 254 were Christmas gifts.

Exclusions
No funding towards credit card or debt relief.

Applications
Applications for emergency grants must be recommended to the charity by the Citizens Advice, North Surrey Primary Care Trust or another approved agency. Direct applications from individuals are not considered. Application forms for Christmas grants are available during September and October at the Weybridge Day Centre and Public Library and should be returned before 31 October for payments in the first week in December.

Woking

The Henry Smith Charity (Woking)

£5,800

Correspondent: David Bittleston, Trustee, Pin Mill, Heathfield Road, Woking, Surrey GU22 7JJ (01483 828621)

CC Number: 232281

Eligibility
People in need who live in the ancient parish of Woking.

Types of grants
One-off grants only.

Annual grant total
In 2012/13 the trust had both an income and an expenditure of £6,000. We estimate that grants to individuals totalled £5,800.

Exclusions
Grants are not given for the relief of rates, taxes and other public funds.

Applications
In writing to the vicar of the parish, either directly by the individual or, where applicable, through a social worker, Citizens Advice or other welfare agency. Successful grants are distributed by the vicars of each of the seven parishes in the area.

Worplesdon

Worplesdon United Charities

£2,500

Correspondent: Eric Morgan, Trustee, 21 St Michael's Avenue, Fairlands, Guildford, Surrey GU3 3LY (01483 233344)

CC Number: 200382

Eligibility
People in need who live in the parish of Worplesdon.

Types of grants
Grants of around £80 to buy coal, clothing or groceries at Christmas.

Annual grant total
In 2012/13, the charity had an income of £2,700 and a total expenditure of £2,600. We estimate that the total amount of grants awarded to individuals was approximately £2,500.

Applications
Applications should be made after the distribution is advertised within the parish (normally in October/November each year). Emergency grants can be considered at any time.

Wotton

The Henry Smith Charity (Wotton)

£4,000

Correspondent: Rosemary Wakeford, Secretary, 2 Brickyard Cottages, Hollow Lane, Wotton, Dorking, Surrey RH5 6QE (01306 730856)

CC Number: 240634

Eligibility
People in need who live in the ancient parish of Wotton.

Types of grants
One-off grants ranging from £100 to £500. Grants have in the past been given to older people of the parish towards fuel and lighting bills and holidays, young people taking part in schemes such as The Duke of Edinburgh Award which will enhance their job prospects, and help towards the cost of independent projects or travel costs.

Annual grant total
The 2012 accounts were the latest available at the time of writing (August 2014).

In 2012 the charity had an income of £6,000 and a total expenditure of £4,000. We estimate that the total amount of grants awarded to individuals was approximately £4,000.

Applications
In writing to the correspondent. Applications are considered in March and September. They can be submitted directly by the individual or through a third party.

West Sussex

Ashington, Wiston, Warminghurst Sick Poor Fund

£7,500

Correspondent: Rod Shepherd, Trustee, Sheen Stickland, 7 East Pallant, Chichester, West Sussex PO19 1TR

CC Number: 234625

Eligibility
People in need – typically those who are ill – firstly those who live in the villages of Ashington, Wiston and Warminghurst, and secondly those who live in West Sussex.

Types of grants
One-off grants according to need. Most grants are for equipment that will make an ill individual's life easier though trustees award grants towards anything that will improve their wellbeing. The average grant is £300.

Annual grant total
In 2013 the fund had an income of £834 and a total expenditure of £7,800. We estimate that grants to individuals totalled £7,500.

Applications
On a form available from the correspondent. Applications can be submitted directly by the individual or a relevant third party.

Sussex County Football Association Benevolent Fund

£5,300

Correspondent: Michael Brown, Trustee, 10 Hillcrest, Brighton BN1 5FN (01273 708587; website: www.sussexfa.com)

CC Number: 217496

Eligibility

Members of Sussex county FA clubs and their relatives or dependents.

Types of grants

One-off or recurrent grants to support players and officials affiliated to Sussex County FA who have suffered a football-related injury and, as a result, find themselves in financial hardship.

Annual grant total

In 2012/13 the fund had an income of £12,900 and a total expenditure of £5,500. We estimate that grants to individuals totalled £5,300.

Exclusions

Claims for one week's incapacity should only be submitted in very exceptional circumstances as they are not considered necessitous.

Applications

On forms available from the correspondent. Requests for applications must be received by the secretary within 14 days of the injury and then completed and returned within a further 28 days.

Applications must include a full disclosure of financial and general circumstances alongside a medical certificate.

The West Sussex County Nursing Benevolent Fund

£6,800

Correspondent: Rod Shepherd, Trustee, Sheen Stickland LLP, 7 East Pallant, Chichester PO19 1TR

CC Number: 234210

Eligibility

Nurses who are or have been engaged in community nursing in West Sussex and are in financial need. Beneficiaries must also be in poor health, convalescing or have disabilities. The fund may also assist general or specialist nurses, both retired and serving, if such a need arises.

Types of grants

One-off and recurrent grants according to need. Gifts are also distributed at Christmas.

Annual grant total

In 2013 the fund had an unusually low income of £154 and an expenditure of £7,000. We estimate that grants to individuals totalled £6,800.

Applications

On a form available from the correspondent. Applications can be submitted directly by the individual, or through a third party such as a social worker, Citizens Advice or other welfare agency.

Crawley

Crawley and Ifield Relief in Sickness Fund

£2,200

Correspondent: Roger Gibson, Trustee, 7 Priestcroft Close, Crawley RH11 8RL (01293 520752; email: roger.gibson7@talktalk.net)

CC Number: 254779

Eligibility

People in need who are sick, disabled, convalescent or infirm and live within a three-mile radius of the church of St John Crawley.

Types of grants

One-off grants according to need.

Annual grant total

In 2013 the fund had an income of £2,900 and a total expenditure of £2,400. We estimate that grants to individuals totalled £2,200.

Applications

In writing to the correspondent.

Horsham

Innes Memorial Fund

£3,000

Correspondent: James Innes, Trustee, Innes Memorial Fund, Campfield Lodge, Leith Hill, Dorking RH5 6LX (01306 713192)

CC Number: 212936

Eligibility

People who are poor, sick and in need and who live in Horsham.

Types of grants

One-off grants are given towards wheelchairs, cookers, alarms, domestic help, school uniforms, holidays, disability equipment, travel expenses and chiropody costs. On average ten grants are made a year ranging between £100 and £250.

Annual grant total

In 2012/13, the fund had an income of £17,200 and total expenditure of £18,400. Expenditure on individual grants tends to be quite low as the fund mainly supports the Roffey Institute and other local charities.

Applications

In writing to the correspondent, to be submitted through a doctor or social worker.

Midhurst

The Pest House Charity

£800

Correspondent: Tim Rudwick, Clerk, 31 Pretoria Avenue, Midhurst, West Sussex GU29 9PP (01730 812489; email: timrudwick@yahoo.co.uk)

CC Number: 227479

Eligibility

People living in the parish of Midhurst who are in need and/or have ill-health.

Types of grants

According to our research, one-off grants in the range of £60 to £500 are given towards various needs. In the past support has been given towards transport and holiday costs.

Annual grant total

In 2013 the charity had an income of £12,700 and a total expenditure of £13,200. Our research suggests that the majority of the expenditure is used to maintain the charity's properties. Previously, grants to individuals have totalled around £800.

Exclusions

Requests from outside the parish will not be accepted.

Applications

In writing to the correspondent. Applications can be made either directly by the individual or through a social worker, Citizens Advice or other welfare agency. They are usually considered in April and October and should be received in the preceding month.

Other information

Grants are also made to other organisations and occasionally to a local school.

Wisborough Green

The Elliott Charity

£500

Correspondent: Helen Vause, Trustee, Upfield's Stores, School Road, Wisborough Green, Billinghurst, West Sussex RH14 0DT (01403 700567)

CC Number: 216197

Eligibility

People who are older or who have disabilities, live in the parish Wisborough Green and are in need.

Types of grants

One-off or recurrent grants according to need, usually ranging between £200 and £500.

Annual grant total

Our research tells us that grants to individuals usually total around £500 a year.

Applications

In writing to the correspondent. Applications can be submitted directly by the individual or through a social worker, Citizens Advice or other welfare agency.

Other information

Grants are also made to community causes, including an annual donation to the Village Minibus Association.

London

General

The Arsenal Foundation

£4,200

Correspondent: Svenja Geissmar, Director and Trustee, Highbury House, 75 Drayton Park, London N5 1BU (020 7704 4000; fax: 020 7704 4001)

CC Number: 1145668

Eligibility

People in need including those injured whilst playing sport, or their dependents, who live in Greater London, with a preference for Islington and Hackney. The charity also supports the provision of recreational activities to those in need.

Types of grants

Grants and loans according to need.

Annual grant total

In 2012/13 the foundation had assets of £1.3 million and an income of £2.1 million. Grants to individuals totalled £8,300 and are given for both social welfare and educational purposes. We estimate social welfare grants to individuals to have totalled £4,200.

A further £492,000 was also given in grants to organisations.

Applications

In writing to the correspondent.

Other information

The foundation has also supported Save the Children's international campaigns to provide emergency disaster relief and educational and recreational opportunities for disadvantaged children in China, West Java and Syria.

Benevolent or Strangers' Friend Society

£800

Correspondent: Chris Linford, Trustee, Room 403, 1 Central Buildings, Westminster, London SW1H 9NH (020 7222 8010; email: chris.linford@methodistlondon.org.uk)

CC Number: 239385

Eligibility

People in need, particularly 'strangers not entitled to parochial relief', that is, people who have exhausted all other possible sources of funding. Beneficiaries must live in London, mainly inner London.

Types of grants

One-off and recurrent grants in the range of £50 and £150 are distributed through certain Methodist ministers.

Annual grant total

In 2012/13 the society had an income of £2,500 and an expenditure of £900. We estimate the annual total of grants to be around £800.

Applications

Applications should not be made to the society since it does not make grants directly to individuals. It allocates funds to certain Methodist ministers living in most areas of inner London and some areas of outer London, who in turn distribute the funds to individuals in need of whom they become aware.

BlindAid

£22,000 (90 grants)

Correspondent: Sue O'Hara, Chief Executive, Lantern House, 102 Bermondsey Street, London SE1 3UB (020 7403 6184; fax: 020 7234 0708; email: enquiries@blindaid.org.uk; website: www.blindaid.org.uk)

CC Number: 262119

Eligibility

Blind and partially sighted people aged 18 and over who live on a permanent basis in one of the 12 central London boroughs or the City of London and who are in receipt of means tested benefits, with a preference for those registered blind/partially sighted.

Types of grants

One-off grants typically up to £500 towards: computer equipment; equipment and gadgets, including talking clocks, big button phones, colour detectors, talking mobile phones and talking microwaves; and domestic items.

Annual grant total

In 2012 the trust had assets of £4.5 million and an income of £488,000. Grants to 90 individuals totalled £22,000 and were broken down as follows:

General purpose	£12,100
Small grants	£7,500
Holiday grants	£2,000

A further £15,700 was awarded in grants to organisations.

At the time of writing (August 2014) this was the most recent financial information available for the trust.

Exclusions

BlindAid does not make grants for the following purposes: payment of outstanding debts; non-essential furniture or home goods; payment of council tax or mortgage/rent arrears; legal fees for insolvency/bankruptcy; utility bills or other household bills (including Internet connection); deposit payments for rented or leased accommodation; garden fencing or clearing; home modifications/adaptations; educational or occupational training; medical treatment/alternative therapies; funeral expenses; removal expenses; motor vehicle purchase or maintenance; fines or arrears; pest control; fixtures or fittings (including carpets, curtains and blinds); or holidays.

Applications

Online application process; or on a form available to download or from the correspondent. Applications should be made through a third party such as a social worker or through an organisation such as Citizens Advice or other welfare agency. A supporting letter may be attached to explain the background to the case, though is not mandatory. the trust tries to process applications within 28 days. A full list of guidelines is available to download from the website.

Only one application per person/household can be considered in any two year period.

Note: The trust is no longer able to offer grants towards holidays.

Other information

BlindAid's core service is a home-visiting service which provides company and conversation and aims to lessen isolation in the community, on which it spends almost half its income. It also offers telephone support for those who choose not to have a visit, as well as advice, information and links to other appropriate organisations. The charity also supports small local organisations helping visually impaired people such as social clubs.

Formerly known as The Metropolitan Society for the Blind.

Brentford and Chiswick Relief in Need and Sick Poor Persons Fund

£450

Correspondent: Julie Cadman, Clerk, c/o St Paul's Church, St Paul's Road, Brentford, Middlesex TW8 0PN (020 8568 7442; email: clerk@brentfordchiswickmc.org.uk; website: https://sites.google.com/site/brentfordchiswickmc/)

CC Number: 211860/209811

Eligibility

People in need who live in Brentford and Chiswick.

Types of grants

One-off grants typically ranging from £150 to £300 per individual. Examples of things for which grants may been given from the Relief in Need Charity are: special needs; sudden distress; expenses for visiting people in hospital; utility bills; furniture; bedding; clothing; food; fuel; heating appliances and expenses.

The Sick Poor Persons Fund gives grants to help alleviate the suffering or to assist the recovery of people who are sick, convalescent, disabled or infirm.

Annual grant total

In 2012/13 the relief in need fund had an income of £850 and a total expenditure of £930. In the same financial year the Sick Poor Persons fund had an income of £440 and had no expenditure. We estimate that social welfare grants to individuals from the relief in need charity totalled £450. Both funds make grants to organisations as well as to individuals.

Exclusions

No grants for items which should be provided by a statutory authority.

Applications

On an application form available to download from the funds' website. The form must be signed by a professional person such as a vicar, social worker, teacher or doctor and sent to the clerk by email. The trustees meet quarterly to consider applications.

Other information

Brentford and Chiswick Merged Charities consists of the Brentford and Chiswick Relief in Need Charity, the Brentford and Chiswick Sick Poor Persons' Fund and a third charity, the Need and Taylor's Educational Charity.

The Charity of Sir Richard Whittington

£233,000 (202 grants)

Correspondent: Mahvish Inayat, Grants Officer, Worshipful Company of Mercers, Mercers' Hall, Ironmonger Lane, London EC2V 8HE (020 7776 7235; email: mahvishi@mercers.co.uk; website: www.mercers.co.uk/grants-elderly-individuals)

CC Number: 1087167

Eligibility

Elderly London residents who are on a low income. Applicants must be over the age of 60, although priority will be given to older and more frail applicants.

Types of grants

Regular grants of £1,140, paid quarterly, mainly for essential household goods.

Annual grant total

In 2013 the charity held assets of £78.4 million and had an income of £2.8 million. Grants to 202 elderly individuals totalled £233,000.

A further £297,000 was awarded to organisations.

Applications

Application forms may be requested by contacting the correspondent. The application must be submitted by an appropriate agency, such as social services, a registered charity, member of the clergy, etc., who must also provide a reference. This is followed by a home visit from a member of the Mercers' Company. The charity welcomes enquiries.

Note the following from the charity's website: 'our list of beneficiaries is currently full, so we are adding new applicants to a waiting list for future consideration.'

Other information

The following information is taken from the charity's annual report:

> The Charity of Sir Richard Whittington is the amalgamation of both The Charity of Sir Richard Whittington and Lady Mico's Almshouse Charity.
>
> The Charity of Sir Richard Whittington was founded in 1424 under the will of Richard Whittington (1354–1423) who was Mayor of London four times and Master of the Mercers' Company three times.
>
> Lady Mico's Almshouses were founded under the bequest of Lady Jane Mico, widow of Sir Samuel Mico, Alderman and Mercer. In 1690 almshouses for eight elderly women were built opposite St Dunstan's Church, Stepney.

The charity still owns almshouses at Whittington College, Felbridge, Surrey and at Stepney, London.

Cripplegate Foundation

£55,000

Correspondent: Kristina Glenn, Director, 13 Elliott's Place, London N1 8HX (020 7288 6940; email: grants@cripplegate.org.uk; website: www.cripplegate.org)

CC Number: 207499

Eligibility

Residents of the Borough of Islington who are facing exceptional hardship. The Resident Support Scheme targets those 'most at risk and vulnerable'. Residents who can apply for a budgeting loan or short-term benefit advance are encouraged to do so before applying to the Resident Support Scheme. Applicants must also be in receipt of specified benefits. Full details of eligibility criteria are available from the Cripplegate Foundation website.

Types of grants

The RSS may be able to assist with, for example: payments for the purchase of essential household items; payments towards a shortfall in rent caused by the bedroom tax, for example; payments for removal expenses; help with living expenses for those affected by crisis or disaster; help managing a council tax bill. In the case of a crisis or disaster, assistance can be given in the form of grocery vouchers, clothing or to connect or maintain access to gas or electricity supplies. The scheme does not make cash payments and the form of payment varies depending on the type of assistance.

Annual grant total

In 2013, the foundation had assets of £35 million and a total income of £2.3 million. The annual total for grants to individuals was £55,000.

Exclusions

The scheme cannot fund: clothing (except when someone is fleeing their home rapidly, is in a case of disaster such as a flood/fire, or needs help to start work); minor structural repairs;

furniture and household items (for those living in private rented furnished accommodation or those placed in furnished temporary accommodation where these are the responsibility of the landlord); specialist disability equipment, adaptations or recliner chairs; wheelchairs or mobility scooters; debts; or funeral expenses.

Note: If your benefits have stopped as a result of a sanction you are encouraged to apply for a hardship payment and seek advice to challenge the decision. Every application is individually assessed but the existence of a sanction alone will not automatically lead to an award under the scheme.

Applications

Applications for the Resident Support Scheme can only be made online through designated access points, a list of which is available from the Cripplegate website. Usually only one application needs to be made to receive assistance from any of the funds.

Other information

From 2 April 2013 Cripplegate Foundation joined with Islington Council to deliver the new Resident Support Scheme (RSS), which brought together a number of different funds to help those facing exceptional hardship. These are: discretionary housing payments; Localised Welfare Assistance (previously Discretionary Social Fund, administered by the DWP); Islington Council's new welfare provision for council tax relief in exceptional circumstances; and Cripplegate Foundation's former Grants to Resident's Scheme.

Financial assistance is only one way in which the scheme offers support to those most in need. The scheme also aims to help improve the long-term circumstances of the residents it assists, through benefit checks and referrals to specialist services in the fields of money advice, education or employment opportunities, for example. More details are available from the website.

The Edmonton Aid-in-Sickness and Nursing Fund

£8,600

Correspondent: David M. Firth, Hon. Secretary, 9 Crossway, Bush Hill Park, Enfield EN1 2LA (020 8127 1949)

CC Number: 210623

Eligibility

People in need who are in poor health and live in the old borough of Edmonton (mainly N9 and N18).

Types of grants

One-off grants usually up to £300. In the past, grants have been awarded towards clothing, furniture, household necessities, convalescence, household bills and debts and medical equipment not covered by NHS provision.

Annual grant total

In 2012/13 the fund had an income of £7,700 and a total expenditure of £8,800. We estimate that grants to individuals amounted to £8,600.

Exclusions

The trust will not subsidise public funds, therefore applicants should have sought help from all public sources before approaching the trust.

Applications

In writing to the correspondent either directly by the individual or through social services, Citizens Advice or other welfare agency. Applications can be received at any time.

Emanuel Hospital

£66,000 (50 grants)

Correspondent: Clerk to the Trustees, Emanuel Hospital Charitable Trust, Town Clerk's Office, Corporation of London, PO Box 270, Guildhall, London EC2P 2EJ (020 7332 1399; website: www.cityoflondon.gov.uk)

CC Number: 206952

Eligibility

Needy persons of 60 years of age or older who have lived in the London boroughs of Kensington and Chelsea, Hillingdon or Westminster for at least two years.

Types of grants

Pensions of around £1,200 a year are paid in monthly instalments along with a Christmas 'bonus' of £125 per person. One-off grants are also available for essential household items.

Annual grant total

In 2012/13 the charity had assets of £2.1 million and an income of £55,000. Grants were made totalling £66,000, of which £65,000 was given in pensions to 49 beneficiaries and £800 in one one-off grant.

Applications

Application forms can be obtained from the City of London website and should be returned along with evidence of income such as benefit award notices, a copy of your birth certificate and two written testimonials confirming your eligibility and need for assistance, at least one of which must be from someone other than a friend or relative.

Applications should be submitted directly by the individual.

Other information

The charity publicises its activities and details of pension vacancies in local papers, through welfare agencies and churches within the beneficial areas.

The Fund for the Forgotten

£23,000

Correspondent: Alexandra Taliadoros, Foundation Director, 203 Larna House, 116 Commercial Street, London E1 6NF (020 3651 4706; email: info@beattiefoundation.com; website: www.beattiefoundation.com/fundfortheforgotten/index.htm)

CC Number: 1142892

Eligibility

People facing social injustice and inequality in the Midlands and London.

Types of grants

One-off grants of £500 – £1,000 'will be awarded to individuals facing injustice or inequality against their dignity, freedom or sanctuary.' Grants may help with everyday living costs and purchasing essential household items, for example.

Annual grant total

In 2012/13 the Jack and Ada Beattie Foundation had an income of £109,000 and charitable expenditure totalled £83,000. The accounts show that gifts and donations totalled £23,000 and we have taken this to represent money from the 'Fund for the Forgotten'.

Applications

Initial applications are made by sending a proposal, via email, summarising your situation, the injustice/inequality you face and how it is aligned to the foundation's objectives and values. You should also explain how support from the foundation can help you.

If your proposal is successful you will be invited to submit an application form, which can be downloaded from the website. Applications must be accompanied by two references and identity documentation.

Other information

The fund is part of the registered charity, The Jack and Ada Beattie Foundation.

The Hampton Fuel Allotment Charity

£774,000 (2,253 grants)

Correspondent: Mrs J. Price, Grants Manager, 15 High Street, Hampton, Middlesex TW12 2SA (020 8941 7866; fax: 020 8979 5555; website: www.hfac.co.uk)

CC Number: 211756T

Eligibility

People who are in poor health or financial need and live in the ancient parish of Hampton. Priority is given to applicants from Hampton but grants may also be made to those living in the remainder of the former borough of Twickenham. Applicants must either work part time or be on a low wage; in receipt of state benefits; in receipt of help with rent or council tax; or have children who receive free school meals.

Types of grants

One-off grants are given for heating costs (the average grant given for 2012/13 was £389) and other household essentials such as fridges, cookers, washing machines, wheelchairs and special medical equipment. Grants are made directly to the supplier and, in the case of fuel grants, credited to the applicant's account.

Annual grant total

In 2012/13 the charity had an income and a total expenditure of £2 million. Grants to individuals in need totalled £774,000 and were distributed as follows:

Fuel grants	1,792	£698,000
Essential equipment and furniture	312	£66,000
'Careline' telephone equipment	149	£11,000

A further £855,000 was awarded in 72 grants to organisations.

Exclusions

The charity is unlikely to support: private and further education; building adaptations; holidays (except in cases of severe medical need); decorating costs, carpeting or central heating; anything which will replace statutory funds.

Applications

On a form available to download from the website, the charity's office or from the Greenwood Centre, Twickenham Citizens Advice or the White House. Applications should be submitted by post either directly by the individual or by a third party. Applications for fuel grants are considered every two months. Those for essential household items are reviewed weekly and should be verified through a letter of support from a welfare professional such as a social worker or housing officer. If this is not possible, the charity will visit the applicant at home.

Note the following from the charity's most recent accounts: 'We no longer accept new applications for 'careline' units.'

Other information

The charity also offers school journey grants for children in their penultimate or final year of junior school 'to enable them to participate in the school journey arranged before they transfer to secondary school.' Interested parties should at first discuss this with the child's school. More details are available on the charity's informative website.

The Hornsey Parochial Charities

£25,000

Correspondent: Lorraine Fincham, Administrator, PO Box 22985, London N10 3XB (020 8352 1601; fax: 020 8352 1601; email: hornseypc@blueyonder.co.uk)

CC Number: 229410

Eligibility

People in need who live in the ancient parish of Hornsey in Haringey and Hackney.

Types of grants

Grants to residents in need of essential items such as clothing, bedding, household equipment and for the cost of heating lighting.

Annual grant total

In 2013 the charity had assets of £1.6 million and an income of £51,000. Grants to individuals averaged £500 and totalled approximately £25,000. Grants ranged from £145 to £960 in the year.

Applications

Individuals can write requesting an application form which, on being returned, can usually be dealt with within a month.

Other information

Grants are also made for educational purposes.

Grants to individuals for welfare purposes have been estimated at £25,000 as approximately £50,000 was given in grants to both organisations and individuals but no further breakdown was available.

Mary Minet Trust

£13,400

Correspondent: The Trustees, PO Box 53673, London SE24 4AF (07906 145 199; email: admin@maryminettrust.org.uk)

CC Number: 212483

Eligibility

People who are living with a disability, sickness or infirmity and reside in the boroughs of Southwark or Lambeth.

Types of grants

One-off grants towards convalescence holidays, disability aids, medical equipment and household items such as washing machines, fridges, cookers, essential furniture, carpets, clothing, beds and bedding.

Annual grant total

In 2012/13 the trust had an income of £16,100 and a total expenditure of £13,600. We estimate that grants to individuals totalled £13,400.

Applications

Applications for individuals are invited from sponsoring organisations, social workers, housing officers and other involved professionals. Applications should be made on the trust's application form, available by contacting the trust by email or telephone. Payments are made to the sponsoring organisation to ensure that the money is spent appropriately, and are paid by BACS transfer. Applications from families and friends, interested persons or the individual in need will be considered only in exceptional circumstances and supporting information will be required. Applications are considered quarterly.

The Lilian Eveleigh Nash Foundation

£8,500

Correspondent: NatWest Trust Services, 5th Floor, Trinity Quay 2, Avon Street, Bristol BN2 0PT (0551 657 7371)

CC Number: 1043563

Eligibility

Women in need in the area comprising the Dioceses of London, Southwark and Chelmsford.

Types of grants

One-off grants for the provision of permanent accommodation, maintenance, holidays and so on.

Annual grant total

In 2012/13 the foundation held assets of £143,000 and had an income of £26,000.

Grants to individuals and organisations totalled £23,000. We estimate that of this, £8,500 was distributed in welfare grants to individuals.

Applications

In writing to the correspondent.

Other information

The foundation committee is formed of the Anglican Bishops of the Dioceses of London, Chelmsford and Southwark.

Arthur and Rosa Oppenheimer Fund

£1,100

Correspondent: Arthur Oppenheimer, Trustee, 27 Hove Park Villas, Hove BN3 6HH (01273 770094)

CC Number: 239367

Eligibility

Jewish people who are sick or disabled and live in London. Preference is given to older people.

Types of grants

One-off grants to those in need and recurrent grants over a longer period to cover nursing care for patients in their own homes. The fund also provides support for the provision of kosher food and other amenities.

Annual grant total

In 2013, the fund had an income of £3,200 and a total expenditure of £2,300. We estimate that the total amount of grants awarded to individuals was approximately £1,100. The fund also awards grants to organisations and other voluntary bodies.

Applications

In writing to the correspondent, either directly by the individual, or via a social worker, Citizens Advice or other third party.

Port of London Authority Police Charity Fund

£8,000

Correspondent: Chair to the Board of Trustees, 14 Bedford Close, Rayleigh, Essex SS6 7QR (01268 777061)

CC Number: 265569

Eligibility

Former officers who have served in the port authority's police force, and their dependents.

Types of grants

One-off grants are given to help with unforeseen bills, household items, holidays and so on.

Annual grant total

In 2012/13 the fund had an income of £2,000 and a total expenditure of £8,200. We estimate that grants to individuals totalled £8,000.

Applications

In writing to the correspondent, clearly stating the need for financial assistance. Applications are considered at quarterly meetings, or sooner if the need is urgent.

Positive East

£3,000

Correspondent: Alastair Thomson, Director of Finance, The Stepney Centre, 159 Mile End Road, London E1 4AQ (020 7791 2855 (Helpline); email: talktome@positiveeast.org.uk; website: www.positiveeast.org.uk)

CC Number: 1001582

Eligibility

People affected by HIV who live and/or receive treatment in East London and are in need of short-term financial assistance to cover basic needs.

Types of grants

Grants of up to £25 each, up to a maximum of £50 in a year, with six months between each application. Each individual has a 'lifetime limit' of £150, after which access to the fund will be closed to them. Grants are given for one-off, HIV related expenses, child expenses such as school uniforms or medical treatment, utility bills, the cost of travel to an essential appointment and basic necessities such as food or clothing.

Annual grant total

In 2012/13 the charity held assets of £608,000 and had a consolidated income of £1.7 million. Around £3,000 is allocated each year for emergency hardship grants.

Exclusions

Grants are not given for: legal costs; non-essential travel or travel outside London; funeral costs; ongoing non-HIV related treatment; household goods; and credit card or other debts.

Applications

On a form available from the correspondent. Applications can only be made through Positive East staff and are only available to registered members of the trust (new service users will need to fill in a registration form). Forms can be submitted at any time but applicants should note that the fund is a limited resource and will not be topped up again until the end of the financial year.

Before any grant is awarded proof will be required that the individual is not eligible for any other financial assistance. Equally, if the person has been the victim of a crime, a crime reference number should be included in the application.

Other information

Positive East is a charity formed from the merger between the London East AIDS Network (LEAN) and the Globe Centre in 2005.

The charity provides a range of services for people affected by HIV including: counselling; support groups; employability services and training; and advice and information on HIV, living with the disease and health and wellbeing. A full list of services run by the charity, all of which are 'impartial and confidential', is available on its informative website.

The Saint George Dragon Trust

£6,500

Correspondent: Di Emmerson, Trustee, 12 Lindsay Close, Epsom, Surrey KT19 8JJ (07779 636677; email: di.emmerson1@gmail.com)

CC Number: 275674

Eligibility

People in need who live in Greater London and are moving, or have recently moved, from supported housing into independent accommodation.

Types of grants

One-off grants ranging from £100 to £400 for buying essential household equipment and furniture. Small grants of £50 to £100 are also available for the purchase of essential items following move-on. Applicants should not be eligible for a Community Care grant or support from the Social Fund and have only minimal resources. (A rare exception may be where a very low Community Care grant has been awarded – see Applications section.)

Annual grant total

In 2012/13 the trust had an income of £3,400 and a total expenditure of £6,700. We estimate that grants to individuals totalled £6,500.

Exclusions

Grants are not made to students or to 'able young people'.

Applications

In writing, through a social, housing or welfare worker. Applications should be typed wherever possible and should be made on the headed notepaper of the organisation through which the application is being made. Guidance can be obtained by emailing: SGDT@barraball.com.

The Sheriffs' and Recorders' Fund

£150,000 (1,088 grants)

Correspondent: The Secretary, c/o Central Criminal Court, Old Bailey, Warwick Square, London EC4M 7BS (020 7248 3277; email: secretary@srfund.net; website: www.srfund.org.uk)

CC Number: 221927

Eligibility

People on discharge from prison, and families of people imprisoned. Applicants must live in the Greater Metropolitan area of London.

Types of grants

One-off grants towards clothing, household items, furnishings, beds and bedding, white goods, carpets, baby needs and so on.

Annual grant total

In 2012/13 the fund had assets of £1.3 million and an income of £245,000. Grants were made to 1,193 individuals totalling £166,500. There were 1,088 grants totalling £150,000 made for welfare purposes.

Applications

On a form available from the correspondent, submitted through probation officers or social workers. They are considered throughout the year.

Other information

Grants are also made for educational purposes and for special projects.

Society for the Relief of Distress (SRD)

£14,000

Correspondent: Caroline Armstrong, Honorary Treasurer, 21 Harstwood Road, London W12 9NE (website: www.reliefofdistress.org.uk)

CC Number: 207585

Eligibility

People in need who live in the inner London boroughs (Camden, Greenwich, Hackney, Hammersmith and Fulham, Islington, Kensington and Chelsea, Lambeth, Lewisham, Southwark, Tower Hamlets, Wandsworth, Westminster and the City of London).

Types of grants

One-off grants, usually of £25 to £100, for 'any cases of sufficient hardship or distress, whether mental or physical.' Grants may be given towards essential household items, clothing and similar needs. Payments are made to the applicant body, not the individual.

Annual grant total

At the time of writing (September 2014) the latest financial information available was from 2012. In 2012 the society had an income of £15,400 and an expenditure of £14,500. We estimate that about £14,000 was awarded in grants.

Exclusions

Grants are very rarely given towards holidays, funeral expenses or debts.

Applications

Applications must be made through a social worker, Citizens Advice, registered charity, NHS, church or similar organisation. Requests submitted by individuals will not be considered. Grants are considered throughout the year, normally on the third Wednesday of each month (except August). There is no formal application form, instead the following information needs to be supplied: name, address and date of birth of the individual; a concise summary of personal circumstances and financial position (including benefits received); particular items needed or expenses to be incurred; other sources of funding secured or applied to; and any other relevant or special circumstances.

The South London Relief-in-Sickness Fund

£6,000

Correspondent: Ozu Okere, Administrator, Room 111, Town Hall, Wandsworth High Street, London SW18 2PU (020 8871 6035; fax: 020 8871 6036; email: ookere@wandsworth.gov.uk)

CC Number: 210939

Eligibility

People in need through sickness, disability or infirmity who live in the boroughs of Lambeth and Wandsworth.

Types of grants

One-off grants up to £200, towards, for example, furniture, furnishings, clothing, holidays and medical equipment.

Annual grant total

In 2013 the fund had an income of £13,300 and a total expenditure of £12,700. We estimate that grants to individuals totalled £6,000, with funding also awarded to organisations.

Exclusions

No grants towards taxes or debts.

Applications

In writing to the correspondent through a social worker, Citizens Advice or other welfare agency. Applications are considered quarterly (normally March, June, September and December). They should include details of the applicant's name, address, age, family composition, disability/illness, source of income and benefits, purpose of the grant, whether any other funding has been applied for and whether any applications have been made to the fund before.

The Spanish Welfare Fund

£6,000

Correspondent: Robert Rouse, Administrator, 9 Bridle Close, Surbiton Road, Kingston upon Thames, Surrey KT1 2JW (020 8546 1817)

CC Number: 273177

Eligibility

People of Spanish nationality and their dependents in need who live in the UK

Types of grants

One-off and recurrent grants according to need.

Annual grant total

The 2012 accounts were the latest available at the time of writing (August 2014).

In 2012 the fund had an income of £8,500 and a total expenditure of £6,000. We estimate that the total amount of grants awarded to individuals was approximately £6,000.

Applications

In writing to the correspondent.

St John Southworth Fund

£25,000

Correspondent: Mary Gandy, Grants Administrator, Department of Pastoral Affairs, Vaughan House, 46 Francis Street, London SW1P 1QN (020 7798 9063; fax: 020 7798 9077; email: sjsfadmin@rcdow.org.uk; website: www.rcdow.org.uk/stjohnsouthworth)

CC Number: 233699

Eligibility

Generally individuals in need within the thirty-three London boroughs. Eligibility is restricted to young people up to 18 years of age and those over 65 in the dioceses of Southwark and Brentwood.

More specifically, the panel administers six linked funds under the St John Southworth Fund banner. Guidance notes available on the website detail the exact criteria for each fund and applicants should ensure that they meet the criteria for at least one of these funds.

Types of grants
One-off grants of around £500 to assist those in poverty, in danger of homelessness, with disabilities, and so on.

Annual grant total
In 2012 this fund awarded a total of 122 grants to the value of £263,000. Of these 72 went to organisations and projects. 50 grants were given directly to individuals and families suffering hardship. We estimate the amount to be around £25,000. The latest figures at the time of writing (August 2014) were for the year 2012.

Applications
On a form available from the correspondent or to download from the website. Applications need to include details of two referees. Applications can be made at any time and the grants panel meets quarterly each year. Applications need to be received at least three weeks before the panel meeting. Meeting and deadline dates are available on the website. Emergency grants of up to £250 may be given between meetings.

Note the following statement from the fund: 'In the case of applications from individuals, the panel is particularly interested in applications which are supported by third party organisations and where the referee is someone willing to act in the role of third party for any grant awarded.'

Other information
Note: The website www.rcdow.org.uk states:

> Established in 2007, the St John Southworth Fund has supported the work of parishes, organisations and projects across a range of issues including poverty, homelessness, old age and infirmity and children with disabilities or in danger of deprivation; it also gives grants direct to individuals.
>
> The Fund is not a separate charity but is part of Westminster Diocese. It was created by the amalgamation of a large number of existing legacies and trusts held within the Diocese, some dating back as far as the 19th century. However, with the creation of Caritas Westminster as the social action agency for the Diocese, the St John Southworth Fund now comes under the Caritas umbrella. Its operational procedures are therefore being changed to address poverty and deprivation more effectively in partnership with the ongoing development of Caritas Westminster.
>
> While these changes are taking place, grant giving has been suspended and no new applications are currently being accepted. Further information about the changes and when applications may re-open will be given [on the fund's website] as soon as they are known.

Barnet

The Mayor of Barnet's Benevolent Fund

£8,600

Correspondent: Ken Argent, Grants Manager, London Borough of Barnet, Building 4, North London Business Park, Oakleigh Road South, London N11 1NP (020 8359 2020; email: ken.argent@barnet.gov.uk; website: www.barnet.gov.uk/info/930094/grants_for_individuals/262/grants_for_individuals)

CC Number: 1014273

Eligibility
People, who are on an income-related statutory benefit, have lived in the London borough of Barnet for at least a year and are in need, hardship or distress. Children, young people, the elderly and individuals with disabilities are particularly supported.

Types of grants
Small, one-off grants of up to £200 are given towards essential household items, appliances (for example, cooker, refrigerator or washing machine), furnishing or equipping new property, children and baby necessities, clothing items where there is an exceptional need, small one-off debts (such as telephone bills), the cost of school uniforms and for any other necessities arising from an unforeseen financial crisis. Up to two awards per applicant are provided.

Annual grant total
In 2012/13 the fund had an income of £11,800 and a total expenditure of £11,600. Both figures are the highest in the past five years. Nevertheless, the income and the expenditure vary each year. Most support is given in relief-in-need grants, therefore we estimate that welfare support to individuals totalled around £8,600.

Applications
In writing to the correspondent via post or email. Applications can be submitted directly by the individual or through a third party, such as a social worker, health visitor or an advice agency. Candidates should provide full details of their name, address, contact number, confirmation of residence in the borough, number and ages of the family members, family income, proof of entitlement to a benefit, summary of the applicant's circumstances, details of support requested, a quotation for any items required and information on other sources of funding approached. Consideration takes about a month. Payments are not made to the applicant directly, but to the service provider or supplier of the items/facilities.

Other information
Grants are also given for educational purposes.

The Finchley Charities

Correspondent: Jean Field, Office Manager, 41A Wilmot Close, East Finchley, London N2 8HP (020 8346 9464; fax: 020 8346 9466; email: info@thefinchleycharities.org; website: www.thefinchleycharities.org)

CC Number: 206621

Eligibility
People in need who live in the former borough of Finchley.

Types of grants
One-off grants only.

Annual grant total
In 2013 the charity had an income of £1.2 million and a total expenditure of £926,000. Full accounts were not available to view at the time of writing (September 2014); however our research suggests that grantmaking to individuals is sporadic and often limited to modest sums.

Exclusions
Grants are not made for educational purposes.

Applications
In writing to the correspondent either directly by the individual or through a social worker, Citizens Advice or other welfare agency. Applications must include details of the amount being asked for and the reason for the application.

Other information
The charity's main concern is the provision of 156 flats for people in Finchley aged 55 and over who have insufficient funds to purchase their own property and have been resident in the London borough of Barnet for at least five years.

Awards are made to local churches and organisations helping people in the area of benefit.

Jesus Hospital Charity

£7,700

Correspondent: Simon Smith, Administrator, Ravenscroft Lodge, 37 Union Street, Barnet EN5 4HY (020 8440 4374; email: info@jesushospitalcharity.org.uk; website: www.jesushospitalcharity.org.uk)

CC Number: 1075889

Eligibility
People in need who live in the former district of Barnet, East Barnet and Friern Barnet.

Types of grants
One-off grants between £100 and £1,000 towards, for example, lifeline rentals, winter clothing, shoes, food vouchers, fridges/freezers, beds, gas cookers and utensils for single parent families and couples living on low incomes; and holidays for people with disabilities.

Annual grant total
In 2013 the charity held assets of more than £11 million and had an income of £621,000. Relief in need grants to individuals totalled £7,700, of which £6,600 was given to residents of the charity's almshouses and £1,100 to other individuals.

A further £19,500 was given in grants to organisations.

Applications
On a form which can be downloaded from the charity's website. Applications are considered by trustees who meet every other month. Applicants may be visited by the clerk.

Other information
The charity maintains 54 almshouses in the Chipping Barnet and Monken Hadley area.

Eleanor Palmer Trust

£8,000

Correspondent: Fred Park, The Clerk to the Trustees, 106b Wood Street, Barnet, Hertfordshire EN5 4BY (020 8441 3222; fax: 020 8364 8279; email: info@eleanorpalmertrust.org.uk; website: www.eleanorpalmertrust.org.uk)

CC Number: 220857

Eligibility
People in need who live in the former urban districts of Chipping Barnet and East Barnet, This includes those living within the postal codes of EN4, EN5 N11 and N14. Applicants must have lived within the area for at least two years prior to the submission of your application.

Types of grants
One-off grants up to £1,000 towards, for example, carpets, furniture and clothing. Items or services are purchased directly from the supplier. No cash grants are made.

Annual grant total
In 2012/13 the trust held assets of £4.5 million and had an income of £1.5 million. Grants from the trust's relief in need fund totalled almost £26,000:

Relief in need (organisations)	£17,700
Relief in need (individuals)	£8,000

Other grants amounting to £9,100 were awarded to elderly residents of homes managed by the trust.

Exclusions
No grants available towards educational purposes, bankruptcy fees, medical costs, taxes or debts.

Applications
On an application form available from the trust's website. Applications are considered every two months. Applications should include details of the applicant's circumstances and income, the items or service required, and details of any other local charities to which the applicant has applied for assistance. The clerk visits applicants in order to assess need if this has not been done recently by a local charity.

Other information
The trust is named after Eleanor Palmer and was founded through the charitable bequest she made in 1558, just months before Queen Elizabeth I was crowned Queen of England.

The trust concentrates on running almshouses and a residential home for older people.

The Valentine Poole Charity

£40,000

Correspondent: Victor Russell, Clerk, The Forum Room, Ewen Hall, Wood Street, Barnet, Hertfordshire EN5 4BW (020 8441 6893; email: vpoole@btconnect.com)

CC Number: 220856

Eligibility
People in need who live in the former urban districts of Barnet and East Barnet (approximately the postal districts of EN4 and EN5).

Types of grants
One-off grants are given towards essential items such as household goods, children's clothing, travel and food. Pensions of £80 to £100 a month are also made to older people.

Annual grant total
In 2013 the charity had assets of £629,000 and an income of £68,000. The trustees' annual report states that 32 families received a Christmas grant which totalled £1,900; payment of pensions totalled £19,500; and almost £21,000 was spent on relief in need and advancement in life purposes. We consider the majority of these latter payments would have been for social welfare purposes and have estimated advancement in life grants to have been around £2,000. In this year there were no grants awarded to organisations.

Applications
On a form available from the correspondent for consideration in March, July and November. Applications should be submitted by a social worker, Citizens Advice or other third party or welfare agency, not directly by the individual.

Bexley

The Bexley Mayor's Benevolent Fund

£2,000

Correspondent: Dave Easton, Mayors Office, London Borough of Bexley, Civic Offices, Broadway, Bexleyheath, Kent DA6 7LB (020 3045 3678; email: mayors.office@bexley.gov.uk)

Eligibility
People in need who live in the borough of Bexley.

Types of grants
Grants, usually in the range of £50 to £100, for a variety of needs (for example towards an electric wheelchair for an individual with disabilities and to buy new clothes for an older person whose home had been damaged in a fire). There can be an immediate response in emergency cases.

Annual grant total
An exact grant total figure was not available but is usually around £2,000 per year.

Applications
In writing to the correspondent. In practice, many applications are referred by the council's social services department who also vet all applications from individuals. Applications can be submitted at any time.

Samuel Edward Cook for Poor

£600

Correspondent: The Administrator, Barclays Bank Trust Company Ltd, Osborne Court, Gadbrook Park, Rudheath, Northwich CW9 7UE (01606 313195)

CC Number: 220274

Eligibility
People in need who live in Bexleyheath only.

Types of grants
According to our research, one-off grants in the range of £50–£300 are given to individuals and families towards household essentials, holidays and so on.

Annual grant total
In 2012/13 the charity had an income of £800 and an expenditure of £700. We estimate that grants totalled around £600. The total expenditure usually averages around £800.

Applications
In writing to the correspondent. Applications can be made directly by the individual. Our research indicates that allocation of funds is at the discretion of the Minister of Trinity Baptist Church.

The John Payne Charity

£300

Correspondent: Bill Price, Clerk, Foster's Primary School, Westbrooke Road, Welling, Kent DA16 1PN (020 8317 8142)

CC Number: 210999

Eligibility
Older people who live in the ancient parish of East Wickham.

Types of grants
One-off grants of up to £100, mostly towards gas, electricity and water bills.

Annual grant total
In 2013 the charity had an income of £2,900 and a total expenditure of £1,200. We estimate that social welfare grants to individuals totalled £300. Grants are also given to organisations and for educational purposes.

Applications
In writing to the correspondent, to be submitted through a social worker, Citizens Advice, Age UK or a similar agency. They are usually considered in March and October. Financial details such as sources of income, rent and other bills are required.

Other information
Our research tells us that grants were made to the British Polio Fellowship to be given as grants for holiday relief for carers.

Brent

The Kingsbury Charity

£1,000

Correspondent: Philomena Hughes, Administrator, 29 Bowater Close, London NW9 0XD (020 8205 9712)

CC Number: 205797

Eligibility
People in need who live in the ancient parish of Kingsbury.

Types of grants
One-off grants according to need. Most of the charity's expenditure is on almshouses. Grants to individuals have previously included £100 towards the cost of a trip to Lourdes for a terminally-ill woman, and £100 to help a family with a six-year-old child with leukaemia.

Annual grant total
Grants to individuals usually total around £1,000.

Applications
In writing to the correspondent, either directly by the individual or through a social worker, Citizens Advice, other welfare agency or other third party. They are considered every six weeks.

Other information
The charity's main area of activity is the maintenance of almshouses, it also makes grants to organisations.

The Wembley Samaritan Fund

£800

Correspondent: Jack Taylor, Administrator, c/o Sudbury Neighbourhood Centre, 809 Harrow Road, Wembley, Middlesex HA0 2LP (020 8908 1220)

CC Number: 211887

Eligibility
People in need who live in the electoral wards of Wembley (Tokyngton, Alperton, Sudbury, Sudbury Court and Wembley Central). The charity is particularly aimed at children.

Types of grants
One-off grants mostly for school uniforms, warm clothing, nursery equipment and the costs of school outings.

Annual grant total
In 2013 this charity had an income of £3,500 and a total expenditure of £1,600. We estimate grants to individuals for social welfare purposes in this financial year was around £800.

Applications
By telephone or in writing to the correspondent.

Bromley

Bromley Relief-in-Need Charity

£2,000

Correspondent: M. Cox, Clerk, Lavender House, 11 Alexandra Crescent, Bromley, Kent BR1 4ET (020 8460 5242)

CC Number: 262591

Eligibility
People in need who live in the ancient borough of Bromley, though there is some discretion to make grants within the wider area of the modern borough of Bromley.

Types of grants
One-off grants of up to £150. Twice-yearly seasonal grants are also available.

Annual grant total
The 2012 accounts were the latest available at the time of writing (August 2014).

In 2012, the charity had an income of £2,500 and a total expenditure of £1,000. We estimate that the total amount of grants awarded to individuals was approximately £1,000.

Applications
Only through social services or a similar welfare agency or Citizens Advice, doctor, health worker, headteacher and so on.

Camden

Hampstead Wells and Campden Trust

£269,000

Correspondent: Sheila Taylor, Director, 62 Rosslyn Hill, London NW3 1ND (020 7435 1570; email: grant@hwct.co.uk; website: www.hwct.org.uk)

CC Number: 1094611

Eligibility
People who are sick, convalescent, disabled, infirm or in conditions of need, hardship or distress and who live in the former metropolitan borough of Hampstead. Grants to individuals, whether one-off payments or pensions, can only be made to residents of the

former Metropolitan Borough of Hampstead (the area of benefit). A temporary stay in Hampstead, or in hospital in the area is not in itself a sufficient qualification.

Types of grants

In addition to pensions, grants are given for a range of purposes including holidays, clothing, help with debts, removals and transport, furniture, gas, electric, fuel, TV and telephone bills and medical purposes. Kitchen starter packs and birthday and Christmas hampers are also given.

Annual grant total

In 2012/13 the trust had assets of £1.3 million, an income of over £552,000 and gave grants to 3,176 individuals totalling £197,000, including eight education grants totalling £2,000. 93 pensions totalling over £72,000 were also awarded.

Applications

Applications should normally be sponsored by a statutory or voluntary organisation, or by a person familiar with the circumstances of the case such as a social worker, doctor or clergyman. Applications for pensions are made on a form available from the correspondent. Applications for one-off grants can be made in writing and should include the client's name, date of birth, occupation, address and telephone number, details of other household members, other agencies and charities applied to, result of any application to the Social Fund, household income, and details of any savings and why these savings cannot be used. Decisions are usually made within two weeks.

Other information

The trust also assists organisations or institutions providing services and facilities for the relief of need or distress. Grants are also made to individuals for educational purposes although this only makes up a small proportion of funding.

Refer to the trust's website which at the time of writing (July 2014) was in the process of being updated.

St Andrew Holborn Charities

£60,000

Correspondent: Alison Shaw, Administrator, 5 St Andrew Street, London EC4A 3AB (020 7583 7394; email: info@standrewholborn.org.uk; website: www.standrewholborn.org.uk)

CC Number: 1095045

Eligibility

People in need resident in a defined area of Holburn (applicants should call or check the website for confirmation of the beneficial area).

Types of grants

One-off grants of up to £500 towards household appliances, furnishing and clothing and so on. Annual awards of £650 a year are available for the long-term sick, older retired people, widows or widowers with children and people living with disabilities.

Annual grant total

In 2012 the charity had assets of £8.8 million and an income of £225,000. Grants totalled around £60,000.

These were the latest accounts available at the time of writing (July 2014).

Exclusions

No grants for holidays unless in exceptional circumstances.

Applications

On a form available from the correspondent or to download from the trust's website.

Other information

This charity is the result of an amalgamation of three trusts: The City Foundation, The Isaac Duckett Charity and The William Williams Charity. Grants are also given to organisations.

The St Pancras Welfare Trust

£24,000 (164 grants)

Correspondent: John Knights, Secretary to the Trustees, PO Box 51764, London NW1 1EA (020 7267 8428; fax: 020 7267 8428; email: thesecretary@spwt.org.uk; website: www.spwt.org.uk)

CC Number: 261261

Eligibility

People in need or who are sick, convalescent, disabled or infirm who live in the old Metropolitan Borough of St Pancras (postal districts NW5, most of NW1, parts of N6, N19 NW3 and WC1). If you are unsure of whether you live in a qualifying area the trust's website has a street directory on their website. Applicants must have the support of a sponsoring agency. The trust does not accept direct applications.

Types of grants

One-off grants, typically between £100 and £300, for a wide range of needs. Grants may be in the form of cash or vouchers.

Annual grant total

In 2012/13 the trust held assets of £718,000 and had an income of £48,000. Individuals received 164 grants totalling £24,000. The trust's grantmaking activities benefitted in all 818 individuals, the majority of whom were children.

Of 194 applications received by the trust, 114 were made through referral agencies and the remaining 80 through the trust's winter/Christmas voucher programme; of these, 24 were ineligible and only six were not supported.

Exclusions

No grants are made for educational purposes, computers, utility bills, statutory payments or rent arrears.

Applications

On an application form available from the trust's website, with an accompanying cover letter. The trustees will only consider applications made through statutory bodies such as social services or community organisations like Citizens Advice. Applications are considered in March, June, September and December and should be received two weeks prior to the meeting.

Other information

The trust occasionally makes small grants of less than £1,000 to local organisations.

Stafford's Charity

£73,000 (128 grants)

Correspondent: Charlotte Maizels, Grants Officer, 5 St Andrew Street, London EC4A 3AB (020 7583 7394; fax: 020 7583 3488; email: stafford@standrewholborn.org.uk; website: www.standrewholborn.org.uk/charities)

CC Number: 206770

Eligibility

People in need who have lived in the Holborn locality, centred on the ancient parish of St Andrew Holborn now comprising of the guild church of St Andrew Holborn and the parishes of St George the Martyr, Queen Square and St Alban the Martyr Holborn for at least three years.

Annual payments are made to the long-term sick and those with a chronic illness on a low income: less than £75 (single person/£120 (couple) per week.

Types of grants

Pensions for people in financial need who suffer from chronic medical problems and who are sick and disabled. One-off grants of up to £500 are also available to people on a low income for kitchen appliances, furnishings, carpets, medical equipment, clothing, redecoration costs and so on.

Annual grant total
In 2012 the charity had assets of £6.4 million and an income of £202,000. Annual awards were given to 95 people and totalled £62,000 and 33 grants were given to individuals which totalled £11,000.

Accounts had been received by the Charity Commission but were not available to view at the time of writing (September 2014).

Applications
On a form available to download from the website or from the correspondent. Applications can be submitted at any time. All applicants are visited by the grants officer.

Other information
Grants are also made to organisations (£26,000 in 2012).

City of London

The Aldgate Freedom Foundation

£8,400

Correspondent: Michael Sonn, Administrator, 140 Hall Lane, Upminster, London RM14 1AL (01708 222482)

CC Number: 207046

Eligibility
Older people, generally aged over 65, who are in need and live in the parish of St Botolph's without Aldgate or the area to the boundary of the Portsoken ward.

Types of grants
Our research suggests that one-off and recurrent grants of £200 a year, plus a £30 Christmas gift, are available.

Annual grant total
At the time of writing (August 2014) the latest financial information available was from 2012. In 2012 the foundation had assets of £1.3 million and an income of £61,000. Grants to individuals, including Christmas bonuses, totalled £8,400.

Applications
Application forms are available from the correspondent. They can be submitted directly by the individual, through a social worker, Citizens Advice or through a councillor or an alderman. Details of income/capital/expenditure and length of residence in the parish must also be included. Requests for support can be considered at any time.

Other information
Grants are also given to organisations or hospitals within the city and towards the maintenance of St Botolph's church.

The Hyde Park Place Estate Charity (Civil Trustees)

£11,000

Correspondent: Shirley Vaughan, Clerk, St George's Hanover Square Church, The Vestry, 2a Mill Street, London W1S 1FX (020 7629 0874; website: www.stgeorgeshanoversquare.org)

CC Number: 212439

Eligibility
People in need who are residents of the borough of Westminster.

Types of grants
One-off grants in the range of £50 and £500 to individuals and families for all kinds of need, including educational.

Annual grant total
In 2012/13 the charity had assets totalling £11.9 million, an income of £439,000 and made grants totalling £154,000 for the relief of hardship, the relief of sickness and the advancement of education, of which £132,000 went to organisations and £22,000 to 160 individuals. We estimate that grants to individuals for social welfare purposes was around £11,000.

Exclusions
Refugees and asylum seekers are not eligible.

Applications
All applications should be made through a recognised third party/organisation and include a case history and the name, address and date of birth of the applicant. Applications are considered on an ongoing basis.

The Mitchell City of London Charity

£16,800 (25 grants)

Correspondent: Lucy Jordan, Clerk to the Trustees, Ash View, High Street, Orston, Nottingham NG13 9NU (0845 600 1558; email: mitchellcityoflondon@gmail.com)

CC Number: 207342

Eligibility
Men over 65 and women over 60 who are in need and who live or work, or have lived or worked, in the City of London for at least five years. Widows of men so qualified may also apply.

Types of grants
Pensions of £300 a year are paid in quarterly sums of £75. Gifts are also given at Christmas (£125) and on the Queen's birthday (£75).

Annual grant total
In 2012/13 the charity held assets of £1.9 million and had an income of £76,000. Pensions and welfare grants totalled £16,800, to the benefit of 25 older individuals.

Applications
On a form available from the correspondent including details of the applicant's income and expenditure. Applications can be submitted directly by the individual or through an organisation such as Citizens Advice. They are considered in March, June, September and November.

Other information
The charity is one half of the Mitchell City of London Charity and Educational Foundation. The Educational Foundation also makes grants.

Croydon

Croydon Relief in Need Charities

£12,000 (1 grant)

Correspondent: Mr W. B. Rymer, Clerk to the Trustees, Elis David Almshouses, Duppas Hill Terrace, Croydon CR40 4BT (020 8774 9382; email: billrymer@croydonalmshousecharities.org.uk; website: www.croydonalmshousecharities.org.uk)

CC Number: 810114

Eligibility
Residents of the London Borough of Croydon who are in conditions of need, hardship or distress (including ill health).

Types of grants
One-off grants according to need.

Annual grant total
The 2012 accounts were the latest available at the time of writing (August 2014).

In 2012, the charity had an income of £200,000 and a total expenditure of £220,000. During the year, only one grant of £12,000 was awarded to an individual in respect of the Sequal Trust.

Applications
In writing to the correspondent.

Other information
This trust mainly makes grants to organisations.

Ealing

Acton (Middlesex) Charities

£2,000

Correspondent: Revd David Brammer, The Rectory, 14 Cumberland Park, London W3 6SX (020 8992 8876; email: acton.charities@virgin.net; website: www.actoncharities.co.uk)

CC Number: 312312

Eligibility

People in need between the ages of 18 and 25 who have lived in the former ancient parish of Acton for at least five years.

Types of grants

One-off grants for the purchase of domestic items or other needs. Payments are made directly to suppliers.

Annual grant total

In 2013 the charities had an income of £9,200 and a total expenditure of £8,000. We estimate that grants awarded to individuals for social welfare purposes totalled around £2,000.

Applications

On a form available from the correspondent, by referral from clergy, doctors, health visitors or other professional people.

Other information

The charities also gives grants towards education and the arts, supporting individuals and local schools and carnivals.

The Ealing Aid-in-Sickness Trust

£2,800

Correspondent: Anita Sheehan, Administrator, c/o William Hobbayne Community Centre, St Dunstans Road, London W7 2HB (020 8810 0277; email: hobbaynecharity@btinternet.com)

CC Number: 212826

Eligibility

People in need, who live in the old metropolitan borough of Ealing (this includes Hanwell, Ealing, Greenford, Perivale and Northolt but not Southall or Acton), who are incurring extra expense due to long or short-term illness.

Types of grants

One-off grants according to need.

Annual grant total

In 2012/13 the trust had an income of £2,200 and a total expenditure of £3,100. Both figures are unusually high when compared to those from previous years. We estimate that social welfare grants to individuals totalled £2,800, though the actual figure for grants expenditure is likely to fluctuate each year.

Applications

On a form available from the correspondent. Applications should be made through a third party such as a social worker or an organisation such as Citizens Advice.

The Eleemosynary Charity of William Hobbayne

£5,200 (44 grants)

Correspondent: Anita Sheehan, Administrator, The William Hobbayne Centre, St Dunstan's Road, London W7 2HB (020 8810 0277; email: hobbaynecharity@btinternet.com)

CC Number: 211547

Eligibility

People in need who live in the civil parish of Hanwell. Only in exceptional circumstances will grants be made to people who live outside this area.

Types of grants

One-off grants for clothing, furniture and domestic appliances. Grants are paid directly to the sponsors or suppliers.

Annual grant total

In 2012/13 the charity held assets of £3.1 million and had an income of £149,000. Welfare grants to 44 individuals totalled £5,200, with 18 local organisations receiving a further £31,000.

Applications

On a form available from the correspondent, to be submitted through a sponsoring organisation such as a local health centre, church, outreach organisation or social services. Applications are considered on a monthly basis although urgent cases can be dealt with more quickly.

Other information

The charity owns the William Hobbayne Centre which runs activities and events for local people over the age of 50. It also has an outreach worker who, aside from encouraging grant applications, organises Christmas toy collections in more affluent parts of Hanwell for redistribution to families with difficult financial circumstances.

Enfield

The Old Enfield Charitable Trust

£175,000 (Over 200 grants)

Correspondent: Karen Wellings, Administrator, The Old Vestry Office, 22 The Town, Enfield, Middlesex EN2 6LT (020 8367 8941; email: enquiries@toect.org.uk; website: www.toect.org.uk)

CC Number: 207840

Eligibility

People in need, hardship or distress who live in the ancient parish of Enfield.

Types of grants

One-off grants to help with unexpected expenses. Support is given towards clothing, replacing/providing household goods, beds, furniture, carpets, special needs of people who have a disability or chronical illness. In exceptional circumstances help can be given for bills, debts and so on.

Around 150 regular quarterly grants are also made to people on a low income in financial need.

Annual grant total

In 2012/13 the trust had an income of £632,000 and a total expenditure of £645,000. At the time of writing (August 2014) full accounts were not available to view. Normally over 200 grants are given to individuals for welfare needs each year totalling around £175,000.

Exclusions

The trust will not provide support where local authority or central government should be assisting. Our research suggests that grants are not normally given to people who are homeless.

Applications

Application forms are available upon request from the correspondent. They can be submitted either directly by the individual or through social services, probation service, hospitals, clinics or clergy. Applicants who write directly are visited and assessed. Grants are distributed either directly to individuals or through a welfare agency or suitable third party. Applications are considered on a monthly basis.

Other information

Community grants are also made to organisations. The trust also administers Ann Crowe's and Wright's Almshouse Charity which owns 10 Almshouses that are let to needy people already resident in the Ancient Parish of Enfield.

Greenwich

Greenwich Charities of William Hatcliffe and The Misses Smith

£10,000

Correspondent: Tina Stanley, 12 Westcombe Park Road, London SE3 7RB

CC Number: 227721

Eligibility

People over the age of 55 who live within a five-mile radius of the almshouses operated by the charity.

Types of grants

One-off grants to help older people remain independent in their own homes and Christmas grants of £100 to almshouse residents.

Annual grant total

In 2011/12 the charity had an income of £153,000 and a total expenditure of £99,000. Grants totalled £10,000 – £1,000 in Christmas gifts and the remainder in one-off grants. This was the latest financial information available at the time of writing.

Applications

In writing to the correspondent. The 2011/12 accounts note that 'applicants are referred to the charity by Age UK and other relevant local agencies, and applications are beginning to come through, though the take-up remains unacceptably slow.'

Other information

The charity also provides almshouse accommodation for elderly residents in the ancient parish of East Greenwich.

The Greenwich Charity

£3,200

Correspondent: Raymond Crudington, Grant Saw Solicitors, Norman House, 110–114 Norman Road, London SE10 9EH (020 8858 6971)

CC Number: 1074816

Eligibility

People in need who live in Greenwich.

Types of grants

One-off and recurrent grants according to need.

Annual grant total

In 2012/13 the trust had an income of £7,000 and a total expenditure of £6,500. We estimate that grants to individuals totalled £3,200, with funding also awarded to local organisations.

Applications

In writing to the correspondent.

The Woolwich and Plumstead Relief-in-Sickness Fund

£6,200

Correspondent: Dave Lucas, Administrator, Royal Borough of Greenwich, The Woolwich Centre, 35 Wellington Street, Woolwich, London SE18 6HQ (020 8921 5261; email: dave.lucas@royalgreenwich.gov.uk)

CC Number: 212482

Eligibility

People in need who have a physical illness or disability and live in the parishes of Woolwich and Plumstead. When funds allow, applications may be accepted from people living in the borough of Greenwich.

Types of grants

One-off grants ranging between £50 and £500 towards meeting a specific need or a contribution towards the total cost.

Annual grant total

In 2012/13 the fund had an income of £12,100 and a total expenditure of £12,500. We estimate that grants to individuals totalled £6,200, with funding also awarded to local organisations.

Exclusions

No grants to help with debts, utility bills, recurrent expenditure, structural works or rent. Support for recurring items is not usually provided.

Applications

On a form available from the correspondent either directly by the individual or through a health visitor, district nurse, social services or other welfare agency. The application should include the applicant's income and expenditure; a supporting letter from a health professional confirming the diagnosis and the resulting problems; and the reason why a grant is needed. Applications can be dealt with as and when received.

Hackney

Hackney Benevolent Pension Society

£5,200

Correspondent: Frances Broadway, Trustee, 39 Sydner Road, London N16 7UF (020 7254 6145)

CC Number: 212731

Eligibility

People who are older and in need, and who have lived in Hackney for at least seven years.

Types of grants

Gifts of around £30 are given to pensioners at Christmas, on their birthday and at the society's annual general meeting in November. Payments are delivered in person through home visits.

Annual grant total

In 2012/13 the society had an income of £5,500 and a total expenditure of £5,400. We estimate that grants to individuals totalled £5,200.

Applications

In writing to the correspondent.

The Hackney Parochial Charities

£25,000

Correspondent: Benjamin Janes, Clerk to the Trustees, The Trust Partnership, 6 Trull Farm Buildings, Trull, Tetbury GL8 8SQ (01285 841900; email: office@thetrustpartnership.com)

CC Number: 219876

Eligibility

People in need who live in the former metropolitan borough of Hackney (as it was before 1970).

Types of grants

The charity states that grants to individuals are usually made for the purchase of clothing and essential household equipment, although grants can be given for many other welfare purposes, such as bedding, furniture and medical and travel expenses for hospital visits. Grants have also been given for holidays for widows with small children and single parent families and for gifts at Christmas for children in need.

Grants are one-off, generally of £100 to £250, although individuals can apply annually.

Annual grant total

In 2012/13 the charity had assets of £5.4 million and an income of £187,000, of which at least £58,000 was distributed in grants to organisations. We have estimated the grants for individuals for welfare purposes to be approximately £25,000.

Exclusions

No grants for statutory charges, rent, rates, gas, electricity or telephone charges.

Applications

In writing to the correspondent. Grants for individuals will be considered by the trustees by email on a monthly or bi-monthly basis.

Other information

In 2008 the charity took over the administration of Hackney District Nursing Association.

The Lolev Charitable Trust

£3.9 million

CC Number: 326249

Eligibility

People who are sick or in need who live in Hackney and the surrounding area.

Types of grants

The trust's annual report states: 'Assistance is given according to circumstances and available finance.'

Note: see 'Other information'.

Annual grant total

In 2012 the trust had assets of £7,100 and had an income of £4.2 million. Grants to individuals totalled £3.9 million. A further £250,000 was made in grants to organisations.

At the time of writing (August 2014) this was the most recent financial information available for the trust.

Applications

Applications by individuals must be accompanied by a letter of recommendation by the applicant's minister or other known religious leader.

Note: See other information.

Other information

At the time of writing this was the only information available for the trust. We were unable to contact the correspondent for more details. Potential applicants are advised to write to the correspondent to confirm eligibility criteria and the types of grants available before submitting an application.

Hammersmith and Fulham

Dr Edwards' and Bishop King's Fulham Charity

£134,000

Correspondent: The Clerk to the Trustees, Percy Barton House, 33–35 Dawes Road, London SW6 7DT (020 7385 9387; fax: 020 7610 2856; email: clerk@debk.org.uk; website: www.debk.org.uk)

CC Number: 1113490

Eligibility

People in need who are on low incomes and live in the old Metropolitan borough of Fulham. This constitutes all of the SW6 postal area and parts of W14 and W6.

Types of grants

One-off grants according to need are made towards essential items of daily living including kitchen appliances, beds, furniture and clothing (including school uniforms). Grants for other things such as floor coverings, decorating materials, baby items, and disability aids are also considered.

Annual grant total

In 2012/13 grants to individuals totalled £136,000 with most grants being awarded for relief-in-need purposes. We could not find a figure for how much was awarded to individuals for social welfare purposes but we do know from the charity's accounts that 1% of the total grant spend was given for education. We have used this figure as that given to individuals as the breakdown of organisations given in the accounts does not appear to include any educational grants. The total given in social welfare grants is therefore around £134,000.

Exclusions

Grants are not normally given to people who are homeowners. Arrears on utility bills are not paid, nor are grants given retrospectively. The trust will only give cash grants if they are to be administered by an agency.

Applications

Application forms are available from the correspondent or on the charity's website. Applications must be submitted in hard copy either directly by the individual or through a third party. Though, it is important to note that individuals applying directly for a grant will be visited at home by the grants administrator.

The committee which considers relief-in-need applications, including educational grant applications, meets ten times a year, roughly every four to five weeks. The charity suggests that applications be submitted around two to three weeks before the next meeting.

Other information

In April 2006 the activities, assets and liabilities of the Dr Edwards' and Bishop King's Fulham Charity (No. 247630) were transferred to the charitable company, of which it became a subsidiary and was renamed the Dr Edwards and Bishop King's Fulham Endowment Fund (No. 1113490 – 1). The fund continues to give money to both individuals and organisations, with its main responsibility being towards the relief of poverty rather than assisting students.

Fulham Benevolent Society

£3,700

Correspondent: Angela Rogers, Trustee, 4 Maltings Place, London SW6 2BT (020 7736 6128)

CC Number: 207938

Eligibility

Elderly people, young children and people with special needs who are in need of temporary financial assistance, and live in the metropolitan borough of Fulham.

Types of grants

One-off and recurrent grants according to need.

Annual grant total

In 2012/13 the society had an income of £9,100 and a total expenditure of £7,500. We estimate that grants to individuals totalled £3,700, with funding also awarded to local organisations.

Applications

In writing to the correspondent. Applications should be submitted through a third party such as social services, Citizens Advice, general practitioner or minister of religion.

Haringey

The Tottenham District Charity

£69,000

Correspondent: Carolyn Banks, Secretary, 7th Floor, River Park House, 225 High Road, London N22 8HQ (email: charities@virginmedia.com; website: www.tottenhamdistrictcharity.org.uk)

CC Number: 207490

Eligibility

People in need, especially the elderly, who have lived in the urban district of Tottenham (as constituted on 28 February 1896, which is largely the postal districts of N15 and N17) for at least three years prior to applying.

Types of grants

One-off grants and pensions. Grants of up to £400 are available towards, for example: basic household furniture or items; white goods; clothing; hospital visits; indirect educational expenses such as transport costs; recuperative holidays; or home decoration or repairs. Lifetime pensions totalling £260 a year (two payments of £130) are awarded to people over the age of 65.

Annual grant total

In 2012/13 the charity held assets of £2.4 million and had an income of £104,000. Grants to individuals totalled £69,000 and were distributed as follows:

Pensions	£48,000
Grants	£21,000

Exclusions

No grants for bills or debts.

Applications

On a form available from the correspondent or to download from the charity's website. Applications should be submitted through, or with the support of, an organisation such as social services, the Citizens Advice, or other welfare agency. Applications for grants should include information and costs of the specific items required (website, catalogue page, etc.). The charity aims to make decisions on applications within a month. Organisations supporting successful applicants are required to find suitable shops that will accept the charity's cheque. The charity does not normally make cheques out to individuals directly unless proof of purchase has been submitted.

Harrow

Mayor of Harrow's Charity Fund

£3,000

Correspondent: Nana Asante, Councillor, c/o Independent Labour Group Office, Middlesex Suite North, PO Box 2, Civic Centre, Station Road, Harrow HA1 2UH (020 8424 1154)

CC Number: 219034

Eligibility

People in need who live in the borough of Harrow.

Types of grants

One-off grants usually up to a maximum of £150 are given for basic items such as beds, food, heating appliances, cookers, clothing and so on. Grants are also given towards holidays/school trips for children.

Annual grant total

In 2012/13, the fund had an income of £5,800 and a total expenditure of £3,400. We estimate that the total amount of grants awarded to individuals was approximately £3,000.

Applications

On a form available from the correspondent. Most applications come through a social worker, Citizens Advice or other welfare agency, although this does not preclude individuals from applying directly. Applications are considered at any time. Applicants must demonstrate that the individual/family is experiencing financial hardship and that the grant will alleviate ill health or poverty or improve essential living conditions. Grants are paid directly to the supplier or through a third party.

Hillingdon

The Harefield Parochial Charities

£2,900

Correspondent: John Ross, Chair, 11 Burbery Close, Harefield, Uxbridge UB9 6QP (01895 823058; fax: 01895 823644; email: hpc@harefieldcharities.co.uk; website: www.harefieldcharities.co.uk)

CC Number: 210145

Eligibility

People in need who live in the ancient parish of Harefield, especially those who are older or in poor health.

Types of grants

The trustees state in their annual report from 2012 that grantmaking is minimal and usually limited to coal allocation grants made each Christmas by cheques to elderly residents. Occasionally modest support may be given for clothing, food, furniture, convalescence, home help, educational needs, hospital travel expenses, medical equipment and disability aids.

Annual grant total

At the time of writing (September 2014) the latest financial information available was from 2012. In 2012 the charity had assets of £1.5 million and an income of £128,000. Grants were made totalling £3,100. We estimate that about £2,900 was given in welfare support. Most of the charity's expenditure is allocated for the almshouses.

Applications

In writing to the correspondent. Applications can be made directly by the individual or through a social worker, Citizens Advice or other welfare agency.

Other information

The charity also provide alms accommodation for older women and families in need. People entering a trade or undertaking apprentices are also supported.

The Hillingdon Partnership Trust

£10,000

Correspondent: John Matthews, Chief Executive, Room 22–25, Building 219, Epsom Square, Eastern Business Park, London Heathrow Airport, Hillingdon, Middlesex TW6 2BW (020 8897 3611; email: johnmatthewshpt@lineone.net; website: www.hillingdonpartnershiptrust.com)

CC Number: 284668

Eligibility

People in need who live in the borough of Hillingdon.

Types of grants

Occasional one-off grants or gifts of equipment, furniture, clothes and toys. Partners have also donated hampers around Christmas time. The 2012/13 accounts note that the trust does not have the resources to act as a typical grantmaking body, but instead:

> Channels appeals to its business supporters on behalf of needy organisations and, exceptionally, individuals, and our business partners may then provide funds for an applicant. Occasionally, we may meet a need by arranging the purchase of necessary items and arranging delivery direct to an

applicant, using funds held in reserve or generated through a number of fundraising activities.

Annual grant total

In 2012/13 the trust had an income of £217,000 and a total expenditure of £224,000. Cash contributions and in kind gifts totalled £210,000, the majority of which was awarded to local organisations. We estimate that individuals benefitted from gifts in kind to the value of £10,000.

Applications

On a form available from the correspondent.

Other information

The trust is a formal grouping of businesses and people in business who have come together as volunteers, either as representatives of local companies or as individuals. Essentially, the trust acts as a broker between business and the community and tries to match projects in need of funding with a company wishing to sponsor a local activity. As such, grantmaking to individuals is only a small part of the trust's overall activities.

Uxbridge United Welfare Trusts

£60,000 (151 grants)

Correspondent: J. Duffy, Grants Officer, Trustee Room, Woodbridge House, New Windsor Street, Uxbridge UB8 2TY (07912 270937; email: grants.officer@uuwt.org; website: www.uuwt.org)

CC Number: 217066

Eligibility

People in need due to financial circumstances, health problems, age and so on who live in or have a very strong connection with the Uxbridge area. The area of benefit covers Cowley, Harefield, Hillingdon, Ickenham and Uxbridge.

Types of grants

One-off grants can be given for services or specific goods, such as furniture, household equipment, clothing, baby equipment, help with fuel bills and so on.

Annual grant total

At the time of writing (August 2014) the latest financial information available was from 2012. In 2012 the trust had assets of £6.4 million and an income of £583,000. Grants and awards totalled £78,000. Relief in need grants amounted to £60,000 distributed to 151 individuals.

Exclusions

Our research suggests that grants are not given for rent or rates. Funding is not available where help could be obtained from the statutory sources.

Applications

Application forms can be requested from the correspondent. They can be submitted directly by the individual or through a social worker, Citizens Advice or educational welfare agency, if applicable. Awards are considered each month. A trained member of staff will visit applicants for an interview to better assess their case.

Other information

Grants are also awarded for educational purposes and may be given to support organisations. The trust also runs almshouses. In 2012 a total of £136,000 was spent in almshouse expenses.

Islington

Richard Cloudesley's Charity

£90,000

Correspondent: Melanie Griffiths, Director, Office 1.1, Resource for London, 365 Holloway Road, London N7 6PA (020 7697 4094; email: info@richardcloudesleyscharity.org.uk; website: www.richardcloudesleyscharity.org.uk)

CC Number: 205959

Eligibility

People in need who are sick or disabled and live in the ancient parish of St Mary's Islington (roughly the modern borough, excluding the area south of the Pentonville and City Roads). A map of the area of benefit is available on the charity's website.

Types of grants

One-off grants, for a wide range of purposes, with the aim of relieving poverty and distress for those who are sick and poor.

Annual grant total

In 2012/13 the charity held assets of £37.6 million and had an income of £1.4 million. Welfare grants made to individuals via Cripplegate Foundation totalled £90,000.

In addition, £81,000 was committed for the Interim Welfare Grants Programme 2013/14, for grants which will be delivered by Cloudesley Trusted Partners.

Exclusions

No help for debts, education, computers, childcare, funeral expenses or for money that has been stolen.

Applications

Applications should be made to one of the charity's Welfare Grants Programme Trusted Partner organisations. The charity does not currently accept direct applications but can give further information and refer individuals to the appropriate partner agency.

Other information

Since 2 April 2013 there has been a new local scheme in place in Islington to help residents called the Resident Support Scheme, with a budget of approximately £3 million. Details of the scheme are available on the Cripplegate Foundation website (www.cripplegate.org) and from Islington Council (www.islington.gov.uk).

In light of this and ongoing changes to welfare benefits, Richard Cloudesley's Charity is carrying out a review of its grant programme to find the best way to offer support to individuals and complement the Resident Support Scheme.

Lady Gould's Charity

£22,000 (57 grants)

Correspondent: Andrew Couch, Clerk, Bircham Dyson Bell, 50 Broadway, Westminster, London SW1H 0BL (020 7783 3769; fax: 020 7222 3480; email: andycouch@bdb-law.co.uk; website: www.ladygouldscharity.org)

CC Number: 234978

Eligibility

People in need who live in Highgate (i.e. the N6 postal district and part of the N2, N8 N10 and N19 districts). A reference map and street index is available on the website. Most grantees are in receipt of income support and housing benefit, though the charity may also consider applications from people earning under £10,000 a year.

Types of grants

One-off grants generally ranging from £200 to £400, though more is available in exceptional circumstances. Grants are given for clothing, furniture, furnishings, baby necessities and white goods. Grants to help towards debts and holidays are available but will only be given in very needy cases. It is possible that more than one grant will be awarded during the accounting year.

Annual grant total

In 2013 the charity made grants totalling £22,000 to 57 applicants.

During the year the average grant was £389 per person.

Exclusions

Grants are rarely made for educational or recreational purposes or for debt relief.

Applications

On a form available to download from the website. Applications should be accompanied by a supporting statement from a social worker, GP or other recognised body. If this is not possible attach evidence of your entitlement to benefits, such as a housing benefit letter. Applications can be submitted directly by the individual or through a third party such as a social worker, Citizens Advice or other welfare agency. They are considered at any time.

Dame Alice Owen's Eleemosynary Charities

£600

Correspondent: The Clerk, The Worshipful Company of Brewers, Brewers' Hall, Aldermanbury Square, London EC2V 7HR (020 7600 1801)

CC Number: 215543

Eligibility

Widows in need who are over 50 and have lived in the parishes of St Mary, Islington and St James, Clerkenwell for at least seven years.

Types of grants

Recurrent grants including pensions.

Annual grant total

In 2012 the charity had an income of £1,700 and a total expenditure of £1,300. This was the latest financial information available at the time of writing. We estimate that social welfare grants to individuals totalled £600, with funding also awarded to organisations.

Applications

In writing to the correspondent.

The St Sepulchre (Finsbury) United Charities

£39,000

Correspondent: Elias Poli, Administrator, Smithfield Accountants LLP, 117 Charterhouse Street, London EC1M 6AA (020 7253 3757)

CC Number: 213312

Eligibility

People over 45 who are in need who live in the old London Borough of Finsbury.

Types of grants

Quarterly pensions and one-off grants.

Annual grant total

In 2012/13 the charity held assets of £2.7 million and had an income of £78,000. Grants totalled £25,000, of which we believe £10,100 was given to several organisations operating within the charity's catchment area. Quarterly pensions amounted to £24,000.

Applications

In April 2013 the charity joined the new Islington Resident Support Scheme, which is delivered through a partnership between Cripplegate Foundation and Islington Council. Applications to the scheme can only be made online through a designated access point. See the Cripplegate Foundation website (cripplegate.org) for a list of access points and more details on the scheme.

Kensington and Chelsea

The Campden Charities

£876,000

Correspondent: Christopher Stannard, Clerk, Studios 3&4, 27a Pembridge Villas, London W11 3EP (020 7243 0551 Grants officer: 020 7313 3797; website: www.campdencharities.org.uk)

CC Number: 1104616

Eligibility

Individuals applying for funding must:

- Be living in the former parish of Kensington
- Have been living continuously in Kensington for two years or more
- Are a British or European citizen or have indefinite leave to remain in Britain
- Be renting their home

Working age members of the family must also in receipt of an out-of-work benefit or on a very low income.

Annual grant total

In 2012/13 welfare grants totalled £876,000, the majority of which was given to 'retired beneficiaries'. £92,000 was given in grants to families of working age for goods and services to assist them towards financial independence.

Exclusions

The charity will not give funding for:

- Direct payment of council tax or rent
- Debt repayments
- Fines or court orders
- Foreign travel or holidays
- Career changes
- Personal development courses
- Postgraduate studies
- Computers
- Individuals whose immediate goal is self-employment
- Goods and services catered for by central government

Applications

Preliminary telephone enquiries are welcomed. Specific application forms are available for social work organisations seeking pensions or charitable relief for individuals in the parish. Applications are considered by the case committee, the education committee or the board of trustees as appropriate. Each of these meets monthly (except during August).

Applicants should also be willing for a grants officer to visit them at home.

Other information

The charity also makes grants to organisations and individuals for educational purposes.

The Kensington and Chelsea District Nursing Trust

£35,000 (120 grants)

Correspondent: The Trustees, 13b Hewer Street, London W10 6DU (020 8969 8117; email: kcdnt@tiscali.co.uk)

CC Number: 210931

Eligibility

People who are older and frail and people who are physically or mentally ill who are in need and have lived for at least two years in the borough of Kensington and Chelsea.

Types of grants

One-off grants up to £1,000 for domestic appliances, medical and nursing aids and equipment, beds, bedding and other furniture and clothing. Up to 60 heating allowances of £100 are also made.

Annual grant total

In 2012/13 this trust had an income of £77,000 and total expenditure of £67,000. Accounts for the year had been received at the Charity Commission but were not available to view online. The trust awards grants to both individuals and organisations for social welfare purposes and in the past has given more to individuals. We estimate that grants to individuals in this year totalled around £35,000.

Exclusions

Grants are not given for payment of salaries, rents, court orders or fines.

Applications

On a form available from the correspondent. Applications must be submitted through a social worker, Citizens Advice or other welfare agency and are considered each month.

Kingston upon Thames

The Hampton Wick United Charity

£5,000

Correspondent: Roger Avins, Clerk to the Trustees, Hunters Lodge, Home Farm, Redhill Road, Cobham, Surrey KT11 1EF (01932 596748)

CC Number: 1010147

Eligibility

People in need who live in Hampton Wick and most of South Teddington, within the parishes of St John the Baptist, Hampton Wick and St Mark, South Teddington.

Types of grants

One-off grants (with the possibility of future reapplication).

Annual grant total

We have no current information on the grant giving of this charity. We know that previously over £20,000 a year was awarded to individuals in educational and welfare grants. Grants are also awarded to organisations. We estimate the amount given to individuals for social welfare purposes is around £5,000.

Applications

In writing to the correspondent. The trustees normally meet three times a year to consider applications.

The Kingston upon Thames Association for the Blind

£11,100

Correspondent: Della Murphy, KAB Office, Kingston Association for the Blind, Adams House, Dickerage Lane, New Malden, Surrey KT3 3SF (020 8605 0060; email: kingstonassoc@btconnect.com; website: www.kingstonassociationforblind.org)

CC Number: 249295

Eligibility

Blind and partially sighted people who live in the royal borough of Kingston upon Thames.

Types of grants

One-off grants of £50 to £2,000 towards the cost of holidays, travel expenses, white goods, furniture, household repairs, computers and aids like 'Easy Reader'.

Annual grant total

In 2012/13 the association held assets of £228,000 and had an income of £85,000. Grants to individuals totalled £11,100, with organisations receiving a further £3,700.

Applications

On a form available to download from the website or from the office. If the applicant is not in receipt of income support, housing benefit, or family credit they will need to provide detailed financial circumstances. Applications are considered every other month from January onwards.

Other information

The association runs various initiatives specifically designed to improve the lives of blind and partially sighted people. This includes: the Eye Buddy home visiting scheme; exercise programmes such as the Tandem Scheme, Walking Buddies and Running Buddies; and a talking newspaper. It also supports other groups for visually impaired people in the local area.

Lambeth

The Clapham Relief Fund

£7,900 (38 grants)

Correspondent: Shirley Cosgrave, Clerk to the Trustees, PO Box 37978, London SW4 8WX (020 7627 0306; email: enquires@claphamrelieffund.org; website: claphamrelieffund.org/)

CC Number: 1074562

Eligibility

People in need who live in Clapham. A map of the area of benefit is available on the website.

Types of grants

One-off grants under £500 towards domestic appliances, beds and bedding, redecoration, clothing and convalescent holidays, for example. Recurrent grants can be made for a limited period to meet a particular need. Christmas gifts may also be distributed. Cheques cannot normally be made out to individuals, but rather to sponsors, or, if this is not possible, to the supplier on receipt of an estimate or page from a catalogue.

Annual grant total

In 2013 the fund had an income of £25,000 and a total expenditure of £28,000. Grants to individuals totalled £7,900. Of 38 grants awarded during the year, 36 were one-off grants and the remaining two were Christmas distributions.

A further £13,000 was awarded to organisations which benefit residents of Clapham.

Exclusions

No grants will be given where sufficient help is available from public sources. Support will only be given to permanent residents of Clapham. Grants are not usually given for debts and living expenses.

Applications

On a form available to download from the website. Applications should include details of monthly income and outgoings and verification by a sponsor. They can be submitted either directly by the individual, through a welfare agency or by a third party such as a district nurse, charitable agency worker, parish priest or doctor. They are considered at trustee meetings held four times a year, usually in March, June, September and December. Application forms should be submitted during the last week of the month before meetings. Emergency grants of up to £300 can be awarded between meetings.

Lewisham

The Deptford Pension Society

£5,500

Correspondent: Mike Baker, Administrator, 144 Farnaby Road, Shortlands, Bromley BR1 4BW (020 8402 0775; email: mjpbaker@hotmail.co.uk)

CC Number: 219232

Eligibility

People over the age of 60 in receipt of supplementary benefits who have lived in the former London borough of Deptford for at least seven years.

Types of grants

Pensions of £15 per month (with a bonus payment in December) to around 30 individuals.

Annual grant total

In 2013 the society had an income of £7,200 and a total expenditure of £5,700. We estimate that grants to individuals totalled £5,500.

Applications

On a form available from the correspondent, for consideration bi-monthly. Applications can be submitted either directly by the individual or a family member, through a third party such as a social worker, or through an organisation such as Citizens Advice or other welfare agency. The application form must be signed by the individual.

Sir John Evelyn's Charity

£13,300

Correspondent: Colette Saunders, Clerk, Clerk's Office, Armada Court Hall, 21 Macmillan Street, Deptford, London SE8 3EZ (020 8694 8953)

CC Number: 225707

Eligibility

People in need who are in receipt of state benefits and live in the ancient parish of St Nicholas and St Luke (Deptford, South East London).

Types of grants

Grants for various needs, for example, household equipment or recuperative holidays. Pensioners are awarded regular payments as well as grants for holidays and outings.

Annual grant total

In 2012 the charity had assets of £2.5 million and an income of £75,000. Grants to individuals totalled around £13,300, broken down as follows:

Payment to pensioners	£6,900
Pensioner outings and holidays	£5,300
Miscellaneous grants to individuals	£1,100

This was the latest financial information available at the time of writing.

Applications

Application forms are available from the correspondent. They are considered every two months.

Other information

Organisations and community projects are also supported.

The Lee Charity of William Hatcliffe

£25,000 (48 grants)

Correspondent: Gordon Hillier, Oakroyd, Bowers Place, Crawley Down, Crawley, West Sussex RH10 4HY (01342 713153; email: gandbhillier@tiscali.co.uk)

CC Number: 208053

Eligibility

People in need in Lewisham, with preference to those living in the ancient parish of Lee, who are in need, hardship or distress.

Types of grants

Regular allowances.

Annual grant total

In 2012 the trust had assets of £143,000 and an income of £31,000. Grants were made to 48 individuals totalling £25,000. This was the latest information at the time of writing (July 2014).

Applications

In writing to the correspondent. Many applications come via partner agencies in Lewisham.

Other information

Grants are also made to organisations. During the year grants totalled £32,000 to 12 organisations.

Lewisham Relief in Need Charity

£4,400

Correspondent: The Clerk, Clerk's Office, Lloyd Court, Slagrove Place, London SE13 7LP (020 8690 8145)

CC Number: 1025779

Eligibility

People in need, including those who are who are older, disadvantaged or who have disabilities and who live in the ancient parish of Lewisham, which does not include Deptford or Lee.

Types of grants

Small one-off grants for specific purposes rather than general need, including those for clothing, household bills, travel expenses, furniture, disability equipment and legal fees. Christmas grants of £25 are also made to older people.

Annual grant total

In 2012/13 the charity had assets of £969,000 and an income of £122,000. Grants and gifts to individuals totalled £4,400.

Exclusions

No grants are made where statutory assistance is available.

Applications

In writing to the correspondent either directly by the individual, through a third party such as a social worker, or through an organisation such as Citizens Advice or other welfare agency. Applications should include as much supporting information as possible to enable the trustees to make informed decisions about why the individual is in need. Applications are considered throughout the year.

Other information

The charity is primarily engaged in providing sheltered accommodation for the elderly at its almshouse, Lloyd Court. It also makes grants to small organisations aiding the people of Lewisham.

Merton

The Wimbledon Guild

£19,000

Correspondent: Jane Platts, Head of Social Welfare, 30–32 Worple Road, Wimbledon, London SW19 4EF (020 8946 0735; email: info@wimbledonguild.co.uk; website: www.wimbledonguild.co.uk)

CC Number: 200424

Eligibility

Individuals in need who live primarily in Wimbledon but also in the borough of Merton.

Types of grants

Small one-off grants (averaging around £300) according to need towards kitchen equipment, children's clothing, household bills, exam entrance fees, mobility scooter batteries and so on. The guild also distributes gifts in kind, including furniture, food and Christmas toys. Grants will not normally be given to anyone who has been a recipient in the previous year.

Annual grant total

In 2012/13 the guild had assets of £6.7 million and an income of £2.9 million. We could not find a figure in the accounts, but the website states that grants were made to individuals totalling £19,000.

Applications

On a form available from the correspondent or to download from the website. Applications are considered every other month. Upcoming meeting dates can be found on the website. Applications must be received a week before the date of each meeting, except when applying for an emergency food grant.

Other information

The guild also runs clubs, classes and a furniture recycling service.

Newham

Mary Curtis' Maternity Charity

£1,200

Correspondent: Eileen Da-Silva, Administrator, 14 Farm Close, Dagenham, Essex RM10 9TX (020 3740

8114; email: eileen.da-silva@aston-mansfield.org.uk)

CC Number: 235036

Eligibility

Pregnant women or mothers with children under one. Applicants must live in Newham and can be asylum seekers or pregnant underage.

Types of grants

One-off grants ranging from £50 to £100 towards, for instance, cots, pushchairs and baby clothes.

Annual grant total

In 2012/13, the charity had an income of £2,100 and a total expenditure of £1,400. We estimate that the total amount of grants awarded to individuals was approximately £1,200.

Applications

In writing to the correspondent, through a doctor, vicar, teacher, midwife or social worker. Applications are considered every month and should include details about the area in which the individual lives and how many children she is responsible for.

Redbridge

The Ethel Baker Bequest

£4,500

Correspondent: Revd Charles Neil Spencer, Trustee, 18 Chestnut Walk, Woodford Green IG8 0TE (020 8530 4916)

CC Number: 270274

Eligibility

People in need who live in the parish of Woodford Baptist Church in the London borough of Redbridge. In the case of any excess income, applications from those living outside the area who have attended or are connected with the church will be considered.

Types of grants

One-off and recurrent grants according to need.

Annual grant total

In 2012/13 the charity had an income of £1,500 and a total expenditure of £4,500. We estimate that grants to individuals accounted for all expenditure during the year.

Applications

In writing to the correspondent, although the charity states that its funds are already allocated.

Richmond upon Thames

The Barnes Workhouse Fund

£17,900 (63 grants)

Correspondent: Miranda Ibbetson, Administrator, PO Box 665, Richmond, Surrey TW10 6YL (020 8241 3994; email: mibbetson@barnesworkhousefund.org.uk; website: www.barnesworkhousefund.org.uk)

CC Number: 200103

Eligibility

People in need who live in the ancient parish of Barnes (in practice SW13).

Types of grants

Grants of up to £350, for example to provide items such as carpets, domestic appliances, furniture, children's clothing and school trips and assistance with the costs of medical needs not available from the National Health Service. Grants are also made for bills and bankruptcy orders

Annual grant total

In 2013 the fund had assets of £9.4 million most of which represented permanent endowment and is therefore not available for grant giving. It had an income of £615,000. Grants were made to 23 individuals for education totalling £9,400; to individuals for social welfare purposes £17,900; and to organisations £191,000.

Exclusions

Grants are not generally made to people who are homeless, as the scheme requires applicants to be resident in Barnes.

Applications

Applications can be submitted through a recognised referral agency (such as social worker, health visitor, housing association, Citizens Advice or doctor) on a form available from the correspondent. Applications are considered upon receipt.

Other information

Grants are also made to organisations and for educational purposes.

The Hampton and Hampton Hill Philanthropic Society

£3,000

Correspondent: Joan Barnett, Trustee, Waverley, Old Farm Road, Hampton, Middlesex TW12 3RL (020 8979 0395)

CC Number: 208992

Eligibility

People in need in St Mary's and All Saints', Hampton and St James, Hampton Hill.

Types of grants

Grants of about £200 each are made to people who have suddenly come into financial need.

Annual grant total

In 2012/13, the society had an income of £900 and a total expenditure of £3,000. Priority is given to making grants to individuals, with any surplus funds left over donated to local organisations.

Applications

In writing to the correspondent.

The Petersham United Charities

£800

Correspondent: Canon Tim Marwood, The Clerk, The Vicarage, Bute Avenue, Richmond, Surrey TW10 7AX (020 8940 8435)

CC Number: 200433

Eligibility

People in need who live in the ecclesiastical parish of Petersham, Surrey.

Types of grants

Pensions and grants, usually of around £75 to £500, including Christmas and birthday gifts. Grants may also be given towards heating and disability equipment.

Annual grant total

In 2012 the charity had an income of £5,000 and a total expenditure of £3,000. We estimate that social welfare grants to individuals totalled £800. Grants are also given for educational purposes and to organisations.

At the time of writing (August 2014) this was the most recent financial information available for the charity.

Applications

In writing to the correspondent. Applications are considered in January, April, July and October and can be submitted either directly by the individual or through a social worker, Citizens Advice or other welfare agency.

The Richmond Aid-in-Sickness Fund

£4,100

Correspondent: Catherine Rumsey, Secretary, 8 The Green, Richmond, Surrey TW9 1PL (020 8948 4188; email: info@richmondcharities.org.uk; website: www.richmondcharities.org.uk)

CC Number: 200434

Eligibility

People in need who live in the borough of Richmond.

Types of grants

One-off grants up to £250 towards, for example, fuel costs, extra bedding, nightwear and the costs of special equipment.

Annual grant total

In 2013 the fund had an income of £6,100 and a total expenditure of £4,300. We estimate that grants to individuals totalled £4,100.

Applications

Applications should be submitted through social services, Citizens Advice or other organisations such as Richmond Community Mental Health Resource Centre. Payments are received in February, May, August and November.

The Richmond Parish Lands Charity

£139,000

Correspondent: The Clerk to the Grants Committee, The Vestry House, 21 Paradise Road, Richmond, Surrey TW9 1SA (020 8948 5701; fax: 020 8332 6792; website: www.rplc.org.uk)

CC Number: 200069

Eligibility

People who are in need and have lived in the TW9 TW10 or SW14 areas of Richmond for at least six months prior to application and have no other possible sources of help. Older people must be in receipt of a means tested benefit to qualify for a winter heating grant.

Types of grants

Crisis grants of up to £250, mostly for household goods, bills, debts, food and clothing. Grants of £60 towards heating bills are available to older people.

Annual grant total

The charity is a grant maker and housing provider. In 2012/13 it had assets of £69.3 million and an income of £3.5 million. It made grants to over 1,000 individuals totalling £269,000. Grants for welfare purposes totalled £139,000.

Applications

Contact the correspondent or visit the charity's website for further information.

Crisis Grants are made to individuals in extreme need following a referral from local agencies such as Richmond Borough support teams or the Citizens Advice.

The RPLC distributes over 700 payments to pensioners who are in receipt of benefits in January each year to assist with energy bills. Cheques are usually made payable to the relevant energy company.

Forms for people interested in applying for winter fuel payments are distributed through local agencies including GP surgeries.

There are two charities which are also administered by the Richmond Parish Lands Charity:

The Barnes Relief in Need Charity (BRINC) – cc.no 200318
The charity's website states that 'BRINC and the RPLC use the same application forms. Forms are held by referral agencies such as health agencies or local charities including the Citizens Advice Bureau. Applications from individuals are not accepted.'

The Bailey and Bates Trust – cc.no 312249
Grants are made for relief-in-need purposes for individuals living in the postcode area SW14. Contact the correspondent for further details of how to apply. However, note that charitable expenditure for this trust has been particularly low since 2005.

Other information

Grants are also made to organisations. The charity has an informative website.

The Richmond Philanthropic Society

£16,200

Correspondent: Catherine Rumsey, Clerk to the Trustees, 8 The Green, Richmond, Surrey TW9 1PL (020 8948 4188; email: info@richmondcharities.org.uk; website: www.richmondcharities.org.uk)

CC Number: 212941

Eligibility

People in need who live in the borough of Richmond, including Kew, Petersham and Ham (postcodes TW9 and TW10).

Types of grants

Small one-off grants up to £250 for white goods, prams, beds and bedding, TV licences, rent arrears and fuel bills. Christmas hampers are distributed to elderly people who have been recommended by care workers and district nurses.

Annual grant total

In 2013 the society had an income of £15,700 and a total expenditure of £17,000. We estimate that grants to individuals totalled £16,200.

Exclusions

No grants are given for educational purposes or for the payment of council tax. There are no cash grants available.

Applications

Applications should be made through Citizens Advice, social services, district nurses, health visitors or other established third parties and are considered regularly.

Other information

Richmond Charities took over the administration of the society in October 2010.

In previous years, the society has also chosen to award grants to organisations, to help reach as many individuals as possible through specific projects.

Southwark

The Camberwell Consolidated Charities

£45,000 (125 grants)

Correspondent: Janet McDonald, Administrator, London Borough of Southwark, Level 2, Hub 5, PO Box 64529, London SE1P 5LX (020 7525 7511; email: janet.mcdonald@southwark.gov.uk)

CC Number: 208441

Eligibility

Primarily older people in need who have lived in the former parish of Camberwell for at least two years. Priority is given to those whose income is on or around the minimum state pension.

Types of grants

Annual pensions, the rates of which vary each year (in 2012/13 pensions stood at £352 per person or £530 per couple). Hardship grants are also available for emergency items.

Annual grant total

In 2012/13 the charities held assets of £1.1 million and had an income of £47,000. Payments to 125 individuals totalled £45,000, all but £80 of which was awarded in pensions to elderly people.

Applications

On a form available from the correspondent. Vacancies are advertised in the local press and by social services, Age UK and so on.

Rotherhithe Consolidated Charities

£82,000

Correspondent: John Clarke, Administrator, Amwell House, 19 Amwell Street, Hoddeson, Hertfordshire EN11 8TS (01992 444466; email: johnc@hbaccountants.co.uk)

CC Number: 211980

Eligibility

Recurrent grants are made primarily to widows who are in need and have lived in the ancient parish of Rotherhithe for at least ten years. Help is also given for the general benefit of those in need who live in the parish.

Types of grants

One-off grants for relief in need, Christmas donations and the provision of holidays. Annual pensions are also provided to widows in need.

Annual grant total

In 2012 the charity had assets of almost £4.2 million and an income of £95,000. Grants totalled nearly £83,000 and were broken down as follows:

Holidays	£53,000
Stipend grants	£28,000
Christmas donations	£1,400
Other donations	£150

These were the latest set of accounts available at the time of writing (August 2014).

Applications

In writing to the correspondent.

Other information

Grants are also made to organisations (£5,800 in 2012).

Southwark Charities

£7,400

Correspondent: Chris Wilson, Clerk to the Trustees, Charities Office, Edward Edwards House, Nicholson Street, London SE1 0XL (020 7593 2000; email: clerk@southwarkcharities.org.uk; website: www.southwarkcharities.co.uk)

CC Number: 1137760

Eligibility

Older people in need who have lived in the former metropolitan borough of Southwark for at least five years.

Types of grants

Quarterly pensions, a Christmas bonus and one-off grants towards the cost of holidays.

Annual grant total

In 2013 this charity had assets of £21 million, an income of £652,000 and awarded grants to individuals for pensions and holidays totalling £7,400. There are currently 177 people receiving pensions.

Applications

In writing to the correspondent, either directly by the individual, via a third party or through a social worker, Citizens Advice or other welfare agency.

Other information

The charity's main objective is the maintenance of a number of almshouses for the benefit of older people who are in financial difficulties. The assets of the charity therefore bear no relation to the amount available for grant giving.

The Mayor of Southwark's Common Good Trust (The Mayor's Charity)

£6,000 (37 grants)

Correspondent: Eric Bassett, Treasurer, 90 Sunnywood Drive, Haywards Heath RH16 4PB (01444 412812; email: eric.bassett@btinternet.com)

CC Number: 280011

Eligibility

People in need who live in the borough of Southwark and the immediate surrounding area.

Types of grants

One-off grants, averaging around £160 each, for essential kitchen items, medical equipment, clothing, furniture and household items.

Annual grant total

In 2012/13 the trust had an income of £30,000 and a total expenditure of £30,500. The following information was taken from the trustees' report for the year: 'During the year, over £6,000 was expended on 37 individual applicants either directly by the provision of required items, or through administration by other local organisations.'

The trust also awarded funding to ten organisations that provide services and facilities for the elderly.

Applications

In writing to the correspondent. Applications can be made either directly by the individual or, where applicable, through a social worker, Citizens Advice or other third party such as a family member, MP or doctor. Applications should include full details of family/financial/health background and details of other sources of funds, including whether a previous application has been made to this trust. Trustees may visit applicants to assess needs and to determine the best course of action.

Other information

The trust works alongside local community groups.

The United Charities of St George the Martyr

£163,000

Correspondent: Paul Leverton, Clerk, Marshall House, 66 Newcomen Street, London SE1 IYT (020 7407 2994; email: stgeorge@marshalls.org.uk)

CC Number: 208732

Eligibility

Older people in need in the parish of St George the Martyr (in north Southwark SE1).

Types of grants

Pensions and Christmas parcels. Pensions currently total £150 per annum. One-off grants according to need, usually of up to £300, towards kitchen equipment, furnishing, flooring, mobility aids, accompanied transport to medical and dental treatments, easy-fitting slippers and shoes, and illuminated magnifying lenses. The charity also funds holidays and outings for its beneficiaries.

Annual grant total

In 2013 the charity held assets of £7.6 million and had an income of £321,000. Financial assistance for individuals totalled £163,000 and were distributed as follows:

Pensioner holiday costs	£86,000
Pensions	£32,000
Pensioner trips and outings	£23,000
Christmas hampers and parties	£16,300
Grants	£3,000
Relief in need	£3,000
Sundry purchases for pensioners	£60

Applications

In writing to the correspondent. The charity has previously stated that its grants and pensions are fully committed but that any new applications will be kept on file.

Other information

The charity also has a welfare visitor, who is able to visit beneficiaries and potential beneficiaries in their own homes.

St Olave's United Charity, incorporating the St Thomas and St John Charities

£297,000

Correspondent: Angela O'Shaughnessy, 6–8 Druid Street, off Tooley Street, London SE1 2EU (020 7407 2530; email: st.olavescharity@btconnect.com)

CC Number: 211763

Eligibility

People in need who live in Bermondsey (part SE1 and all SE16).

Types of grants

Individuals over the age of 70 can receive a birthday gift of £100 a year and a further grant towards holidays once every year or every two years. Depending on additional income, other one-off grants can be made for a wide variety of needs, including clothes, musical instruments and holidays.

Annual grant total

In 2012/13 the charity had assets of almost £13.8 million and an income of £381,000. Social welfare grants to individuals totalled over £297,000.

Applications

Applications should be made in writing to the correspondent and are considered four times a year.

Other information

Grants are also made to organisations and to individuals for education purposes. In this accounting year, the trustees awarded almost £27,000 in educational grants.

The Emily Temple West Trust

£200

Correspondent: The Administrator, c/o Marshall House, 66 Newcomen Street, London SE1 1YT (020 7407 2967; email: catherine@newcomencollett.org.uk)

CC Number: 210077

Eligibility

People under the age of 19, or their parents, who are in need and live in the metropolitan borough of Southwark.

Types of grants

According to our research, one-off cash grants ranging from £150 to £500 are available towards, for example, clothing, footwear, food, toys, recreational activities, convalescence and so on.

Annual grant total

In 2013 the trust had an income of £3,300 and an expenditure of around £500. We estimate that about £200 was given in grants to individuals. Note that the expenditure varies each year.

Applications

Application forms are available from the correspondent. They can be completed directly by individuals or their parents as well as through a third party, such as a church, social services, advice centre and so on. Requests for assistance are normally considered in May and November.

Other information

Grants are given to both individuals and organisations.

Sutton

Sutton Nursing Association

£11,000

Correspondent: John Helps, 28 Southway, Carshalton SM5 4HW (020 8770 1095; email: sna@skingle.co.uk)

CC Number: 203686

Eligibility

People who are in poor health, require financial assistance and live in the London borough of Sutton or the surrounding area.

Types of grants

One-off grants of up to £500 for domestic items, specialised equipment (such as phones or buggies), furniture, beds, holiday expenses (including insurance), gym sessions, rent arrears, respite care, carpets, disability and other medical aids, computer equipment, clothing and school uniforms, Christmas gifts and so on.

Annual grant total

At the time of writing (August 2014) the latest financial information available was from 2012. In 2012 the association had an income of £21,000 and a total expenditure of £23,000. Grants are mainly made through various organisations. We estimate that support to individuals totalled around £11,000.

Exclusions

Recurrent grants and matters relating to ongoing liabilities are not considered.

Applications

Applications are normally made through a social worker, Citizens Advice or other welfare agency. They are considered on a bi-monthly basis and should include as much information as possible, including estimated costs, funds available from other sources secured or applied to and the ability of the individual to contribute.

Other information

The association also makes grants to the community nursing services, hospitals and local organisations.

Tower Hamlets

Bishopsgate Foundation

£43,000 (55 grants)

Correspondent: Geoff Wilson, Director of Finance and Admin, 230 Bishopsgate, London EC2M 4QH (020 7392 9253; email: enquiries@bishopsgate.org.uk; website: www.bishopsgate.org.uk)

CC Number: 1090923

Eligibility

Pensioners over the age of 60 who live and work, or have lived or worked, in the parishes of St Botolph's without Bishopsgate; Christchurch, Spitalfields; and St Leonard's, Shoreditch – all within the borough of Tower Hamlets.

Types of grants

Recurrent grants of around £180 per quarter plus a Christmas bonus.

Annual grant total

In 2012/13 the foundation held assets of £22.8 million and had an income of £2.3 million. Pensions to 55 individuals totalled £43,000, with local charitable organisations receiving a further £40,000.

Applications

On a form available from the correspondent. Applications can be submitted either directly by the individual or, where applicable, through a social worker, Citizens Advice or other welfare agency. There are no deadlines and applications are considered as and when a vacancy arises.

Other information

The foundation's principal activity is the running of the Bishopsgate Institute and library. As well as making top-up pension grants, it runs monthly lunches, a Christmas lunch and day trips for elderly individuals, and offers funding for local organisations.

The Henderson Charity

£20,000

Correspondent: Philip Hendry, Administrator, Flat 8, Masters Lodge, Johnson Street, London E1 0BE (020 7790 1793; email: philipehendry@gmail.com)

CC Number: 1012208

Eligibility

Older people who live in the hamlet of Ratcliff and the parish of St George's-in-the-East, Stepney. Applicants must be longstanding residents of the beneficial area and there is a maximum income requirement.

Types of grants

Small pensions of around £20 a month.

Annual grant total

In 2012/13 the charity had an income of £20,000 and a total expenditure of £21,000. We estimate that grants to individuals amounted to £20,000.

Applications

Vacancies are normally advertised locally through social services and appropriate welfare agencies. When a pension is available, application forms can be obtained from social services or the correspondent.

The Ratcliff Pension Charity

£11,300

Correspondent: Adrian Carroll, Clerk, Cooper's Hall, 13 Devonshire Square, London EC2M 4TH (020 7247 9577; fax: 020 7377 8061; email: clerk@coopers-hall.co.uk; website: www.coopers-hall.co.uk)

CC Number: 234613

Eligibility

People in financial need who live in the London borough of Tower Hamlets, with a preference for older people living in the Stepney area.

Types of grants

One-off and recurrent grants according to need.

Annual grant total

In 2012/13 the charity had assets of £537,000 and an income of £46,000. Grants to individuals totalled £11,300 and were distributed as follows:

Individuals in need	16	£9,500
Contingency Fund	–	£1,800

A further £34,000 was awarded in grants to 32 organisations.

Applications

In writing to the correspondent. For emergency grants from the Contingency Fund, applications must be made through a social worker, or another welfare agency.

Stepney Relief-in-Need Charity

£11,000

Correspondent: Mrs J. Partleton, Clerk to the Trustees, Rectory Cottage, 5 White Horse Lane, Stepney, London E1 3NE (020 7790 3598)

CC Number: 250130

Eligibility

People in need who live within the old Metropolitan Borough of Stepney.

Types of grants

One-off grants of £100 to £500 will be considered for a variety of needs, including household items, clothing, holiday where individuals will benefit from a short break, convalescence costs following discharge from hospital, hospital travel, mobility aids and so on.

Annual grant total

In 2012/13 the charity had both an income and total expenditure of £22,800. Grants are given to individuals for both social welfare and educational purposes. We estimate the total awarded for social welfare purposes was around £11,000.

Exclusions

No grants are made towards the repayment of loans, rent, council tax or utility bills.

Applications

An application form is available from the correspondent and may be submitted either directly by the individual or through a relative, social worker or other welfare agency. The trustees usually meet four times a year, but some applications can be considered between meetings at the chair's discretion.

Miss Vaughan's Spitalfields Charity

£1,100

Correspondent: Philip Whitehead, Administrator, 45 Quilter Street, Bethnal Green, London E2 7BS (020 7729 2790)

CC Number: 262480

Eligibility

People in need who live in the ecclesiastical parishes of Christchurch with All Saints in Spitalfields, St Matthew in Bethnal Green and St Leonard in Shoreditch.

Types of grants

Originally clothing and support was given to poor mechanics and weavers in Spitalfields who were unable to work. Now grants are given to individuals and families who are convalescing, unemployed or who have disabilities and also to large families on a low income.

Annual grant total

In 2012/13 the charity had an income of £1,300 and a total expenditure of £1,200. We estimate that social welfare grants to individuals totalled £1,100.

Applications

In writing to a member of the clergy from any of the eligible parishes.

Wandsworth

The Wandsworth Combined Charity

£13,000

Correspondent: R. J. Cooles, 179 Upper Richmond Road West, East Sheen, London SW14 8DU (020 8876 4478; fax: 020 8878 5686)

CC Number: 210269

Eligibility

People in need who live in the London borough of Wandsworth. The current funding themes for welfare are to relieve poverty or need of the elderly, to provide education or training to help residents irrespective of age, to become better equipped to enter the world of work and to tackle crime and anti-social behaviour, particularly amongst those who feel marginalised

Types of grants

One-off grants up to £1,500 may be made.

Annual grant total

In 2012/13 the charity had an income of £11,400 and a total expenditure of £15,000.

Exclusions

The grant cannot be used to fund work that is the responsibility of statutory agencies, statutory organisations, such as local authorities and schools, purely commercial ventures, political campaigns or concerns, religious organisations where the activities benefit only those of a particular faith, individuals, spending that has already taken place.

Applications

In writing to the correspondent, to be submitted as part of a scheme by constituted voluntary or community groups or registered charities.

Other information
Grants are made to organisations working in the local area.

Westminster

The Charity of A. J. G. Cross

£7,000

Correspondent: Michael Horsley, Administrator, 4 Chester Square, London SW1W 9HH (020 7730 8889)

CC Number: 210466

Eligibility
People who are sick and in need and live in South Westminster (i.e. south of Oxford Street).

Types of grants
One-off grants up to £150 for purposes including heating costs, clothing, holidays and furnishings.

Annual grant total
In 2012/13 the charity had both an income and a total expenditure of £7,300. We estimate that grants to individuals totalled £7,000.

Exclusions
No grants are given towards arrears.

Applications
On a form available from the correspondent to be submitted through a third party such as a social worker. The charity does not deal directly with the individual.

St Giles-in-the-Fields and Bloomsbury United Charity

£3,000 (9 grants)

Correspondent: Pam Nicholls, Clerk to the Trustees, The Rectory, 15A Gower Street, London WC1E 6HW (020 7323 1992; email: pam.nicholls@london.anglican.org; website: www.stgilescharities.org.uk)

CC Number: 1111908

Eligibility
People in need who live in the ancient parishes of St Giles in the Fields and St George's Bloomsbury. A map of the area of benefit is available on the website. In exceptional cases, the trustees may assist an individual outside the area of benefit.

Types of grants
One-off grants, usually up to £500, towards the purchase of white goods, furniture, bedding, clothing, medical equipment and to cover the costs of restorative holidays.

Annual grant total
In 2012 the charity had an income of £78,000 and assets of £1.7 million. Grants totalled £3,000 and were made to nine individuals.

The charity's latest set of accounts have been received by the Charity Commission but have not yet been uploaded onto its website (September 2014).

Applications
On a form available to download from the website. Completed forms should be returned via email to the clerk to the trustees and a signed, hard copy must also be provided. Applications are considered at trustees' meetings, which take place four times a year, normally in January, April, July and October. Applications should ideally be received least two weeks in advance of the meeting. Meeting dates are published on the website. In urgent cases, grants may be considered between meetings.

Other information
The charity also provides almshouse accommodation for eight females over 60 in the Covent Garden area.

The St Marylebone Health Society

£2,000

Correspondent: David Dunbar, Administrator, 31 Llanvanor Road, London NW2 2AR (020 8455 9612; email: dgldunbar@aol.com)

CC Number: 248984

Eligibility
Families with children of school age and under who live in the former borough of St Marylebone in the city of Westminster i.e. east of Edgware Road and north of Oxford Street in NW8 NW1 or W1.

Types of grants
One-off grants for beds, bedding, household equipment, children's equipment, clothing and so on. Grants average between £300 and £400. Christmas grants are made in the form of grocery vouchers.

Holidays and outings for parents and their children are also supported. The applicant should have lived in the beneficial area for two years.

Annual grant total
In 2012 the society had an income of £0 and a total expenditure of £5,000. We estimate that around £2,000 was made in grants to individuals for social welfare purposes.

The 2012 accounts were the latest available at the time of writing.

Exclusions
Overseas holidays and families without children cannot be funded. Grants are not given to adults not caring for children, to assist older people or to students. Cash grants are rarely given.

Applications
Through a social worker, educational welfare officer or health visitor using the application form available from the correspondent. Holiday applications should be made by February if possible; other applications at any time.

Strand Parishes Trust

£37,000 (161 grants)

Correspondent: Frank Brenchley-Brown, Clerk to the Trustees, 169 Strand, London WC2R 2LS (020 7836 3205; email: sptwestminster@aol.com)

CC Number: 1121754

Eligibility
People who live and/or work in the London borough of the City of Westminster, with preference for the parish of St Clement Danes and St Mary le Strand.

Types of grants
One-off grants and pensions.

Annual grant total
In 2012 the charity had assets of £5.8 million, the majority of which represented permanent endowment and is not available for grant giving. It had an income of £233,000. Pensions were made to 54 individuals totalling £18,100 and a further £18,500 was given in grants to 107 individuals. The 2012 accounts were the latest available at the time of writing (August 2014).

Exclusions
No grants for expeditions, electives, non-residents of Westminster or asylum seekers.

Applications
On a form available from the correspondent. Applications must be made through a sponsoring organisation i.e. social services or Citizens Advice.

Other information
The Isaac Duckett's Charity, St Mary le Strand Charity and St Clement Danes Parochial Charities were amalgamated with other charities to form the Strand Parishes Trust.

Grants are also made to organisations (£86,000 in 2012).

The United Charities of St Paul's, Covent Garden

£4,000

Correspondent: Maggie Rae, Flat 9, 19 Henrietta Street, London WC2E 8QH (020 7379 6080; email: mrae@clintons.co.uk)

CC Number: 209568

Eligibility

People in need who live in the city of Westminster.

Types of grants

One-off grants ranging from £50 to £120. Grants can be paid directly or through hospitals, health authorities, family service units or an early intervention service.

Annual grant total

In 2012/13 the charity had an income of £4,500 and a total expenditure of £5,600. We estimate that grants to individuals totalled £4,000, with funding also occasionally awarded to organisations.

Exclusions

Tuition fees and holidays are not funded.

Applications

In writing to the correspondent.

The Waterloo Parish Charity for the Poor

£2,500

Correspondent: Eileen Hamilton, Trustee, 2 Secker Street, London SE1 8UF (020 7450 4601; email: admin@stjohnswaterloo.org)

CC Number: 251594

Eligibility

People in need, hardship or distress who live in the parish of Waterloo, St John with St Andrew. Preference may be given to people resident in the area of the former ecclesiastical parish of St John the Evangelist, Lambeth.

Types of grants

According to our research, small grants ranging from £25 to £100 can be given for living expenses and domestic items.

Annual grant total

In 2012/13 the charity had an income of £1,400 and an expenditure of £2,700. We estimate that around £2,500 was given in grants. Note that the expenditure varies each year.

Applications

Application forms can be requested from the correspondent. They can be submitted either by the individual or through a social worker, Citizens Advice or similar third party and are considered quarterly.

Westminster Almhouses Foundation

£114,000

Correspondent: Cristina O'Halloran, Administrator, 7 Allandale Place, Orpington, Kent BR6 7TH (020 7828 3131; email: cristina@westminsteralmshouses.com; website: www.westminsteralmshouses.com)

CC Number: 226936

Eligibility

People in need who live in the London Borough of Westminster. Limited support is available to those living elsewhere in Greater London and to women living elsewhere in the UK.

Types of grants

One-off grants averaging around £360, as well as pensions. Grants are typically offered for help in obtaining cookers, washers, microwaves, as well as children's clothing and equipment.

Annual grant total

In 2012 the foundation had assets of £22.4 million and an income of £713,000. Pensions and grants totalled £114,000.

These were the latest accounts available at the time of writing (September 2014).

Applications

On an application form available from the correspondent. Forms must detail your request, current circumstances and how this award will help you towards self-sufficiency. Decisions are made quickly once all the necessary information is acquired.

Other information

The foundation also makes educational grants.

The Westminster Amalgamated Charity

£39,000 (254 grants)

Correspondent: Julia Moorcroft, Grants Administrator, School House, Drury Lane, London WC2B 5SU (020 7395 9460; fax: 020 7395 9479; email: wac@3chars.org.uk; website: www.w-a-c.org.uk)

CC Number: 207964

Eligibility

People in need who live, work or study in the old City of Westminster (the former Metropolitan Borough of Westminster) or those who have previously lived or worked in the area for a total of five years or more.

Note: the old City of Westminster is that area covered by Westminster Council which is situated south of Oxford Street.

Types of grants

One-off grants ranging from £100 to £350 towards: clothing; essential household items (furniture, white goods, kitchen equipment); holidays for individuals aged 60 and over (taken in the UK only); and decorating and flooring costs. Payments will be made to the sponsor or a designated retailer.

Annual grant total

In 2012 the charity had assets of £6.4 million, most of which represents permanent endowment and is not available for grant giving. It had an income of £273,000. Grants to 254 individuals (259 applications considered) totalled nearly £39,000 and were distributed as follows:

Discretionary	£14,900
Household	£14,400
Clothing	£6,700
Holidays and fares	£2,700
Other	£20

Grants to 42 organisations totalled almost 181,000.

The 2012 accounts were the latest available at the time of writing (August 2014).

Exclusions

No grants for: TVs; CD/DVD players; mobile phones; computers/software; educational needs; holidays abroad; debt repayment or fees. No retrospective grants.

Applications

On a form available from the correspondent or to download from the website. Applications must be submitted through a recognised referral agency such as Social Services, Citizens Advice, hostel worker, etc.; and be accompanied by a supporting statement. The supporting statement should include all of the details which explain the individual's need, for example: family circumstances; medical, domestic or behavioural issues; the extent of your agency's involvement with the applicant and why assistance is sought. Applications will usually take four to six weeks to process.

Other information

The charity regularly publishes and updates the amount of money available for distribution on its website.

Advice organisations

The following section lists the names and contact details of voluntary organisations that offer advice and support to individuals in need. The list is split into two sections: 'Welfare' and 'Illness and disability'. Each section begins with an index before listing the organisations by category.

The listings are a useful reference guide to organisations that individuals can contact to discuss their situation and receive advice and support. These organisations will have experience in tackling the sorts of problems that other individuals have faced, and will know the most effective and efficient ways of dealing with them. They may also be able to arrange for people to meet others in a similar situation. As well as providing advice and support, many of the organisations will be happy to help individuals submit applications to the trusts included in this guide. They may also know of other sources of funding available.

Some organisations included in this list have their own financial resources available to individuals. We have marked these with an asterisk (*). This list should not be used as a quick way of identifying potential funding – the organisations will have criteria and policies that may mean they are unable to support all the needs under that category and the guide will include many more potential sources of funding than there are organisations here.

Some organisations have local branches, which are better placed to have a personal contact with the individual and have a greater local knowledge of the need. We have only included the headquarters of such organisations, which will be happy to provide details for the relevant branches.

It is helpful for the organisations listed if any request for information includes a sae.

This list is by no means comprehensive and should only be used as a starting point. It only contains organisations that have a national remit and does not include organisations that provide general advice and support solely to members of a particular religion, country or ethnic group. For further details of groups, look for charitable and voluntary organisations in your local phone book, or contact your local council for voluntary service (CVS) (sometimes called Voluntary Action) which should be listed in the phone book.

The following general welfare section includes 'Benefit and grants information' and 'Debt and financial advice', which may be of particular relevance during these difficult economic times.

There is also a separate section 'Service and regimental funds' (see page 149), which details where support and advice for ex-service men and women and their families in need can be sought.

Welfare

General

Advice NI, 1 Rushfield Avenue, Belfast BT7 3FP (tel: 02890 645919; email: info@adviceni.net; website: www.adviceni.net). For information on sources of advice and support in Northern Ireland.

National Association of Citizens Advice Bureaux (NACAB), Myddelton House, 115–123 Pentonville Road, London N1 9LZ (tel: 020 7833 2181 [admin only]; email: info@nacab.org.uk; website: www.nacab.org.uk). For details of your local Citizens Advice office please see the website. Online advice is also available on a range of topics from the Citizens Adviceguide website: www.adviceguide.org.uk.

The Salvation Army, Territorial Headquarters, 101 Newington Causeway, London SE1 6BN (tel: 020 7367 4500; email: info@salvationarmy.org.uk; website: www.salvationarmy.org.uk)

Samaritans, Freepost RSRB-KKBY-CYJK, Chris, PO Box 90 90, Stirling FK8 2SA (tel: 020 8394 8300; 24-hour helpline: 0845 790 9090; see phone book for local number; email: admin@samaritans.org (general) jo@samaritans.org (helpline); website: www.samaritans.org)

Benefit and grants information

The Association of Charity Organisations (ACO), 2nd Floor, Acorn House, 314–320 Grays Inn Road, London WC1X 8DP (tel: 020 7255 4480; email: info@aco.uk.net; website: www.aco.uk.net)

Child Benefit, PO Box 1, Newcastle upon Tyne NE88 1AA (helpline: 0300 200 3100 [8am–8pm Monday to Friday and until 4pm Saturday]; textphone: 0300 200 3103; email: Online contact form; website: www.hmrc.gov.uk/childbenefit)

Child Maintenance Options, (tel: 0800 988 0988 [Mon–Fri, 8am–8pm and Sat 9am–4pm]; textphone: 0800 988 9888; website: www.cmoptions.org). Contact can also be made through an online live chat feature or by using online form.

Child Trust Fund, Child Trust Funds have been withdrawn. Information about Child Trust Funds can only be given through the company which holds your child's trust fund. You can find out who that is by using the online form on the HMRC website. See www.hmrc.gov.uk/tools/childtrustfundclaim/ctfaccount.htm.

Gov.uk, general information on money, tax and benefits (website: www.gov.uk)

Disability Benefits Centre, Warbreck House, Warbreck Hill, Blackpool, Lancashire FY2 0YE (Disability Living Allowance helpline: 0345 712 3456 [Mon–Fri, 8am–6pm]; Attendance Allowance helpline: 0345 605 6055; Personal Independence Payment (PIP) helpline: 0345 850 3322; to make a new claim for a PIP: 0800 917 2222; textphone: 0345 722 4433; website: www.gov.uk/browse/benefits/disability)

Jobseekers (Benefit claim line: 0800 055 6688 [Mon–Fri, 8am–6pm]; textphone: 0800 023 4888; website: www.gov.uk/jobseekers-allowance overview). You may also make a claim online.

Pension Credit Claim Line; (tel: 0800 991 234 [Mon–Fri, 8am–6pm]; textphone: 0800 169 0133; website: www.gov.uk/pension-credit/overview) See the website for information on local offices.

Tax Credits helpline, Tax Credit Office, Preston PR1 4AT; (tel: 0345 300 3900 [8am–8pm Monday-Friday, 8am – 4pm Saturday]; textphone 0345300 3909; website: www.hmrc.gov.uk/taxcredits)

Veterans Agency, Ministry of Defence, Norcross, Thornton Cleveleys, Lancashire FY5 3WP; (Veterans helpline: 0808 191 4218 [Mon–Thurs, 7:30am–6:30pm and Fri 7:30am–5:00pm] Out of hours calls will be taken by Combat Stress or Samaritans, using same number; email: veterans-uk@mod.uk; website: www.veterans-uk.info)

Winter Fuel Payments, Winter Fuel Payment Centre, Mail Handling Site A, Wolverhampton WV98 1LR; (helpline: 0845 915 1515 [Mon–Fri, 8:00am–6:00pm]; textphone: 0845 606 0285; website: www.gov.uk/winter-fuel-payment.

Bereavement

Cruse Bereavement Care, PO Box 800, Richmond upon Thames, Surrey TW9 1RG; (tel: 020 8939 9530; helpline: 0844 477 9400; email: info@cruse.org.uk or helpline@cruse.org.uk; website: www.cruse.org.uk)

Natural Death Centre, In The Hill House, Watley Lane, Twyford, Winchester SO21 1QX; (tel: 01962 712690; email: rosie@naturaldeath.org.uk; website: www.naturaldeath.org.uk)

Survivors of Bereavement by Suicide (SOBS), The Flamsteed Centre, Albert Street, Ilkeston, Derbyshire DE7 5GU; (tel: 01159 441117; helpline: 0844 561 6855 [9am–9pm daily]; email: sobs.support@hotmail.com; website: www.uk-sobs.org.uk)

Children

Child Bereavement UK, Clare Charity Centre, Wycombe Road, Saunderton, Buckinghamshire HP14 4BF; (tel: 01494 568900; email: support@childbereavement.org.uk; website: www.childbereavement.org.uk)

Winston's Wish, 3rd Floor, Cheltenham House, Clarence Street, Cheltenham, Gloucestershire GL50 3JR; (tel: 01242 515157; helpline: 0845 203 0405 [Mon–Fri,9am–5pm, and Wed evening 7pm–9.30pm]; email: info@winstonswish.org.uk; website: www.winstonswish.org.uk)

Parents

Child Death helpline, York House, 37 Queen Square, London WC1N 3BH; (tel: 020 7813 8416 [admin]; helpline: 0800 282 986 or from mobiles 0808 800 6019 [Mon, Thurs and Fri, 10am–1pm; Tues–Wed, 10am–4pm; and every evening 7pm–10pm]; email: contact@childdeathhelpline.org; website: www.childdeathhelpline.org.uk)

The Compassionate Friends, 14 New King Street, Deptford, London SE8 3HS; (tel: 0845 120 3785; helpline: 0845 123 2304 [10am–4pm and 7pm–10pm daily]; Northern Ireland helpline: 02887 788016 [10am–4pm and 7pm–9.30pm daily]; email: info@tcf.org.uk or helpline@tcf.org.uk; website: www.tcf.org.uk)

The Lullaby Trust, 11 Belgrave Road, London SW1V 1RB (tel: 020 7802 3200; helpline: 0808 802 6868 [Mon–Fri 10am–5pm; Weekends and public holidays 6pm–10pm]; email: office@lullabytrust.org.uk or support@lullabytrust.org.uk; website: www.lullabytrust.org.uk)

Stillbirth and Neonatal Death Society (SANDS), 28 Portland Place, London W1B 1LY (tel: 020 7436 7940; helpline: 020 7436 5881 [Mon–Fri, 9.30am–5.30pm and Tues and Thurs, 6pm–10pm]; email: support@uk-sands.org [general information] or helpline@uk-sands.org; website: www.uk-sands.org)

Carers

Carers UK, 20 Great Dover Street, London SE1 4LX; (tel: 020 7378 4999; The Carers UK Adviceline: 0808 808 7777 [Mon–Fri, 10am–4pm]; email: advice@carersuk.org; website: www.carersuk.org)

Leonard Cheshire Disability, 66 South Lambeth Road, London SW8 1RL; (tel: 020 3242 0200; website: www.leonardcheshire.org). Contact can also be made by completing an online enquiry form.

Children and young people

Action for Children, 3 The Boulevard, Ascot Road, Watford WD18 8AG (tel: 01923 361500; email: ask.us@actionforchildren.org.uk; website: www.actionforchildren.org.uk)

Catch 22, 27 Pear Tree Street, London EC1V 3AG (tel: 020 7336 4800; email: using the online form on website; website: www.catch-22.org.uk)

ChildLine, 42 Curtain Road, London EC2A 3NH (tel: 020 7825 2500; 24-hour advice helpline: 08001111; website: www.childline.org.uk). A personal inbox can be set up on the site which will allow you to send emails to Childline and save replies in similar way to a normal email service. Alternatively, send a message without signing in through the 'send Sam a message' function. You can also chat online with a ChildLine counsellor.

Coram Children's Legal Centre, Riverside Office Centre, Century House North , North Station Road, Colchester CO1 1RE (tel: 01206 714650 [general]; Child Law Advice Line: 0808 802 0008 [Mon–Fri, 8am–8pm]; Civil Legal Advice Education Law Line: 0845 345 4345 [Mon–Fri, 9am–8pm and Sat, 9am–12:30pm]; Migrant Children's Project Advice Line: 020 7636 8505 [Tues–Thurs, 10am–4pm]) email: info@coramclc.org.uk; website: www.childrenslegalcentre.com)

The Children's Society, Edward Rudolf House, Margery Street, London WC1X 0JL (tel: 0300 303 7000; email: supportercare@childrenssociety.org.uk; website: www.childrenssociety.org.uk)

Get Connected, PO BOX 7777, London W1A 5PD; (tel: 020 7009 2500; helpline: 0808 808 4994 [1pm–11pm daily]; text: 80849; email: only by using online form [general enquiries]; website: www.getconnected.org.uk). There is also a Webchat service available between 1pm and 11pm every day accessible through the website.

National Youth Advocacy Service, Egerton House, Tower Road, Birkenhead, Wirral CH41 1FN (tel: 01516 498700; helpline: 0808 808 1001 [Mon–Fri 9am–8pm, Sat 10am–4pm]; email: main@nyas.net or help@nyas.net; website: www.nyas.net)

NSPCC, Weston House, 42 Curtain Road, London EC2A 3NH (tel: 020 7825 2500 [Mon–Fri 9am–5pm]; helpline for adults concerned about a child: 0808 800 5000; ChildLine: 08001111; email: only by using online form; website: www.nspcc.org.uk)

Save the Children UK, 1 St John's Lane, London EC1M 4AR (tel: 020 7012 6400; email: supporter.care@savethechildren.org.uk; website: www.savethechildren.org.uk)

The Who Cares? Trust, Kemp House, 152–160 City Road, London EC1V 2NP (tel: 020 7251 3117; email: mailbox@thewhocarestrust.org.uk; website: www.thewhocarestrust.org.uk)

Youth Access, 1–2 Taylors Yard, 67 Alderbrook Road, London SW12 8AD (tel: 020 8772 9900 [Mon–Fri 9:30am–1pm and 2pm–5:30pm]; email: admin@youthaccess.org.uk; website: www.youthaccess.org.uk; for an online directory of information, advice and support services for young people)

Bullying

The Anti-bullying Alliance, National Children's Bureau, 8 Wakely Street, London EC1V 7QE (website: www.anti-bullyingalliance.org; details of the regional offices are available on the website)

Kidscape, 2 Grosvenor Gardens, London SW1W 0DH (tel: 020 7730 3300; helpline: 0845 120 5204 [please note the helpline is only for parents, guardians or friends who are concerned about a child being bullied]; email: info@kidscape.org.uk; website: www.kidscape.org.uk)

Young People Leaving Care, Catch22, National Care Advisory Service (NCAS), 27 Pear Tree Street, London EC1V 3AG; (tel: 020 7336 4824; email: ncas@catch-22.org.uk; website: www.leavingcare.org)

Debt and financial advice

Age UK Money Matters, provides a range of advice on topics such as pensions, tax, financial management, consumer issues and benefits (website: www.ageuk.org.uk/money-matters; Age UK Advice: 0800 169 6565)

Business Debtline, (tel: 0800 197 6026 [Mon–Fri, 9am–5:30pm]; website: www.businessdebtline.org). The debtline does not provide advice by letter or email.

Gamblers Anonymous (GANON), (website: www.gamblersanonymous.org.uk; they advertise three types of meetings please check their website for further details.)

GamCare, 2nd Floor, 7–11 St John's Hill, London SW11 1TR (tel: 020 7801 7000; helpline: 0808 802 0133 [8am–midnight daily]; email: info@gamcare.org.uk; website: www.gamcare.org.uk)

The Money Advice Service, Holborn Centre, 120 Holborn, London EC1N 2TD (tel: 0300 500 5000; typetalk: 18001 0300 500 5000 [Mon–Fri, 8am–8pm, Sat 9am–1pm]; email: enquiries@moneyadviceservice.org.uk; website: www.moneyadvice.org.uk; an online chat facility is also available.)

National Debtline, Tricorn House, 51–53 Hagley Road, Edgbaston, Birmingham B16 8TP (helpline: 0808 808 4000 [Mon–Fri, 9am–9pm and Sat 9.30am–1pm]; website: www.nationaldebtline.co.uk). Contact can also be made by completing an online enquiry form.

StepChange Debt Charity, Wade House, Merrion Centre, Leeds LS2 8NG (helpline: 0800 138 1111 [Mon–Fri 8am–8pm and Sat 8am–4pm]; email: by using online form; website: www.stepchange.org).

TaxAid, 304 Linton House, 164–180 Union Street, London SE1 0LH (tel: 020 7803 4950 [advice agencies only]; helpline: 0345 120 3779; website: www.taxaid.org.uk). Contact can also be made by completing an online enquiry form.

TPAS (Pensions Advisory Service), 11 Belgrave Road, London SW1V 1RB (tel: 020 7630 2250; pensions advice: 0845 601 2923; helpline for women: 0845 600 0806; helpline for self-employed: 0845 602 7021; email: by using online form; website: www.pensionsadvisoryservice.org.uk). An online chat facility for legal advice is also available from Mon–Fri 9am–5pm and Tuesdays between 7pm–9 pm.

Families

Home-Start UK, Home-Start Centre, 8–10 West Walk, Leicester LE1 7NA (tel: 01162 587900; freephone: 0800 068 6368 Mon–Fri, 8am–8pm, Sat 9am–12pm; email: info@home-start.org.uk; website: www.home-start.org.uk)

Housing

Shelter, 88 Old Street, London EC1V 9HU (tel: 0300 330 1234; helpline: 0808 800 4444; email: only by using online enquiry form; website: www.shelter.org.uk)

Homes and Communities Agency, Arpley House, 110 Birchwood Boulevard, Birchwood, Warrington WA3 7QH (tel: 0300 1234 500; email: mail@homesandcommunities.co.uk; website: www.homesandcommunities.co.uk)

Legal

Advice Services Alliance (ASA), Tavis House (Floor 7), 1 – 6 Tavistock Square, London WC1H 9NA (tel: 07904 377460; email: by using online form; website: www.asauk.org.uk) Please note: ASA does not give advice to the general public.

Bar Pro Bono Unit, 48 Chancery Lane, London WC2A 1JF (tel: 020 7092 3960 [Mon–Fri 10am–4pm]; email: enquiries@barprobono.org.uk and emails can also be sent using the online form; website: www.barprobono.org.uk)

Civil Legal Advice, (helpline: 0345 345 4 345 [Mon–Fri, 9am–8pm and Sat 9am–12.30pm]; email: by using online form; website: www.gov.uk/civil-legal-advice). An online chat facility for legal advice is also available.

Law Centres Network, Floor 1, Tavis House, 1–6 Tavistock Square, London WC1H 9NA (tel: 020 3637 1330 [please note: this is not an advice line but LCN's office line]; email: by using online enquiry form; website: www.lawcentres.org.uk). See the website for information on your local law centre.

LGBT

The Lesbian and Gay Foundation (LGF), 5 Richmond Street, Manchester M1 3HF (helpline: 0845 330 3030 [6pm–10pm daily]; email: info@lgf.org.uk; website: www.lgf.org.uk)

Stonewall, Tower Building, York Road, London SE1 7NX (Office (admin): 020 7593 1850; Info Line: 0800 050 2020 [Mon– Fri, 9.30am–5.30pm]; email: info@stonewall.org.uk; website: www.stonewall.org.uk)

Missing people

Missing People, 284 Upper Richmond Road West, London SW14 7JE; (helpline: 116 000; text: 116 000; email: 116000@missingpeople.org.uk [if you're missing and want to talk about your situation] or report@missingpeople.org.uk/use the online enquiry form [to report someone missing]; website: https://www.missingpeople.org.uk)

Offenders and ex-offenders

APEX Trust, Tontine House, 24 Church Street, St. Helens, Merseyside WA10 1BD; (tel: 01744 612898; email: sthelens@apextrust.com)

National Association for the Care and Rehabilitation of Offenders

(NACRO), Park Place, 10–12 Lawn Lane, London SW8 1UD (tel: 020 7840 7200; Resettlement Advice Service: 020 7840 1212; email: helpline@nacro.org.uk; website: www.nacro.org.uk)

Prisoners Abroad, 89–93 Fonthill Road, Finsbury Park, London N4 3JH (tel: 020 7561 6820; helpline: 0808 172 0098; email: info@prisonersabroad.org.uk; website: www.prisonersabroad.org.uk)

UNLOCK; Maidstone Community Support Centre, 39–48 Marsham Street, Maidstone, Kent ME14 1HH (tel: 01622 230705 [office/admin]; helpline: 01634 247350 [Mon–Fri 10am–4pm]; text: 07824 113848; Skype: unlock.helpline; email: advice@unlock.org.uk, emails can also be sent using the online form; website: www.unlock.org.uk)

Families of offenders

Offenders' Families helpline, c/o Family Lives CAN Mezzanine 49–51 East Road London N1 6AH (helpline: 0808 808 2003 [Mon–Fri, 9am–8pm and Sat–Sun 10am–3pm]; email: info@offendersfamilieshelpline.org.uk. Information sheets are available on request by post or can be downloaded from the website: www.offendersfamilieshelpline.org.uk)

Partners of Prisoners and Families Support Group, POPS 1079 Rochdale Road, Blackley, Manchester M9 8AJ (tel: 01617 021000; helpline: 0808 808 2003 [Mon–Fri, 9am–8pm and Sat–Sun 10am–3pm]; email: mail@partnersofprisoners.co.uk or by using the online form; website: www.partnersofprisoners.co.uk)

Prisoners' Families and Friends Service, 20 Trinity Street, London SE1 1DB (tel: 020 7403 4091; helpline: 0808 808 3444; email: info@pffs.org.uk or by using the online enquiry form; website: www.pffs.org.uk)

Women offenders and ex-offenders

Creative and Supportive Trust (CAST), Unit 1 Lysander Mews, Lysander Grove, Upper Holloway, London N19 3QP (tel: 020 7281 9928; mobile: 07435967990; email: info@castwomen.org.uk; website: www.castwomen.org.uk)

Older people

Friends of the Elderly, 40–42 Ebury Street, London SW1W 0LZ (tel: 020 7730 8263; email: enquiries@fote.org.uk or by using the online form; website: www.fote.org.uk)

Age UK, Tavis House, 1–6 Tavistock Square, London WC1H 9NA (helpline: 0800 169 6565 [Mon–Fri, 9am–4pm]; email: contact@ageuk.org.uk or by using online form; website: www.ageuk.org.uk)

The Age and Employment Network, Headland House, 308–312 Grays Inn Road, London WC1X 8DP (tel: 020 7837 4762; email: info@taen.org.uk; website: www.taen.org.uk)

Parenting

Home-Start UK, Home-Start Centre, 8–10 West Walk, Leicester LE1 7NA (tel: 01162 587900; freephone: 0800 068 6368 [Mon–Fri, 8am–8pm, Sat 9am–12pm]; email: info@home-start.org.uk; website: www.home-start.org.uk)

Family Lives, CAN Mezzanine, 49–51 East Road, London N1 6AH (tel: 020 7553 3080; 24-hour helpline: 0808 800 2222; website: www.familylives.org.uk). Contact can also be made by using the online chat support service.

Twins and Multiple Births Association (TAMBA), Lower Ground Floor and The Studio, Hitherbury House, 97 Portsmouth Road, Guilford, Surrey GU2 4YF (tel: 01483 304442; helpline: 0800 138 0509 [10am–1pm and 7pm–10pm daily]; email: asktwinline@tamba.org.uk; website: www.tamba.org.uk/home)

Abduction

Reunite (National Council for Abducted Children), P.O Box 7124, Leicester LE1 7XX (tel: 01162 555345; Advice line: 01162 556234; email: reunite@dircon.co.uk; website: www.reunite.org)

Adoption and fostering

British Association for Adoption and Fostering (BAAF), Saffron House, 6–10Kirby Street, London EC1N 8TS (tel: 020 7421 2600; email: mail@baaf.org.uk; website: www.baaf.org.uk)

Adoption UK, Linden House, 55 The Green, South Bar Street, Banbury OX19 9AB (tel: 01295 752240; helpline: 0844 848 7900 [Mon–Fri, 10am–4pm]; online contact form also available; website: www.adoptionuk.org.uk)

After Adoption, Unit 5 Citygate, 5 Blantyre Street, Manchester M15 4JJ (tel: 01618 394932; Action Line: 0800 056 8578; email: information@afteradoption.org.uk; website: www.afteradoption.org.uk)

Fostering Network, 87 Blackfriars Road, London SE1 8HA (tel: 020 7620 6400; Fosterline: England – 0800 040 7675, Wales – 0800 316 7664, Scotland – 01412 041400, Northern Ireland – 02890 705056; email: info@fostering.net; website: www.fostering.net)

National Association of Child Contact Centres, 1 Heritage Mews, High Pavement, Nottingham NG1 1HN (tel: 0845 450 0280 or 01159 484557 from mobiles [call for information on nearest centre]; email: contact@naccc.org.uk; website: www.naccc.org.uk)

Post-Adoption Centre, 5 Torriano Mews, Torriano Avenue, London NW5 2RZ (tel: 020 7284 0555; Advice line: 020 7284 5879 [Mon, Tues & Fri, 10am–4pm, Wed 10am–1pm then 5pm–7pm and Thurs 2pm–7pm]; email: using online form; website: www.pac.org.uk)

Childcare

Family and Childcare Trust, The Bridge, 81 Southwark Bridge Road, London SE1 0NQ (tel: 020 7940 7510; email: info@familyandchildcaretrust.org.uk; website: www.familyandchildcaretrust.org)

Family Rights Group, Second Floor, The Print House, 18 Ashwin Street, London E8 3DL (tel: 020 7923 2628; advice line: 0808 801 0366 [Mon–Fri, 9.30am–3pm]; textphone: 18001 0808 801 0366; email: using the online contact form; website: www.frg.org.uk)

Divorce

Both Parents Forever, 39 Cloonmore Avenue, Orpington, Kent BR6 9LE (helpline: 01689 854343 [8am–9pm daily])

Families Need Fathers, 134–146 Curtain Road, London EC2A 3AR (helpline: 0300 0300 363 [7am–midnight daily]; email: fnf@fnf.org.uk; website: www.fnf.org.uk)

National Family Mediation, 4 Barnfield Hill, Exeter, Devon EX1 1SR (tel: 0300 4000 636; email: using the online contact form; website: www.nfm.org.uk)

NCDSW (National Council for the Divorced and Separated and Widowed), 68 Parkes Hall Road, Woodsetton, Dudley DY1 3SR (tel: 07041 478120; email: secretary@ncdsw.org.uk; website: www.ncdsw.org.uk)

CAFCASS (Children and Family Court Advisory and Support Service), 3rd Floor, 21 Bloomsbury Street, London WC1B 3HF (tel: 0300 456 4000; email: webenquiries@cafcass.gsi.gov.uk or telephoneenquiries@cafcass.gsi.gov.u-k; website: www.cafcass.gov.uk)

Pregnancy

ARC (Antenatal Results and Choices), 345 City Road, London EC1V 1LR (tel: 020 7713 7356; helpline: 0845 077 2290 or 020 7713 7486 from a mobile [Mon–Fri, 10am–5.30pm]; email: info@arc-uk.org or online using the contact form; website: www.arc-uk.org)

British Pregnancy Advisory Service (BPAS), 20 Timothys Bridge Road, Stratford Enterprise Park, Stratford upon-Avon, Warwickshire CV37 9BF (tel: 03457 30 40 30; Advice line: 03457 30 40 30 or 01789 416569 from mobiles; email: info@bpas.org; website: www.bpas.org)

Brook, 50 Featherstone Street, London EC1Y 8RT (tel: 020 7284 6040 [admin]; email: admin@brook.org.uk; website: www.brook.org.uk). You may also use the Ask Brook facility to ask questions via email or text 07717 989023.

Disability Pregnancy and Parenthood International (DPPI), 336 Brixton Road, London SW9 7AA (tel: 020 7263 3088; helpline: 0800 018 4730 [Tues–Thurs 10.30am–2.30pm; email: info@dppi.org.uk; website: www.dppi.org.uk)

National Childbirth Trust, Alexandra House, Oldham Terrace, London W3 6NH (helpline: 0300 330 0700 [8am–midnight daily]; website: www.nct.org.uk; email: enquiries@nct.org.uk). Contact can also be made by completing an online enquiry form.

Grandparents

Grandparents Association, Moot House, The Stow, Harlow, Essex CM20 3AG (tel: 01279 428040 [admin]; helpline: 0845 434 9585 [Mon–Fri, 10am–4pm]; email: advice@grandparents-association.org.uk; website: www.grandparents-association.org.uk)

Mothers

Mothers Apart from their Children (MATCH), BM Box No. 6334, London WC1N 3XX (email: enquiries@matchmothers.org; website: www.matchmothers.org)

Mumsnet, (email: contactus@mumsnet.com; website: www.mumsnet.com)

Single parents

Gingerbread, 520 Highgate Studios, 53–79 Highgate Road London NW5 1TL (tel: 020 7428 5420 [admin]; helpline: 0808 802 0925 [Mon, 10am–6pm, Tues, Thurs and Fri 10am–4pm and Wed 10am–1pm and 5pm–7pm]; website: www.gingerbread.org.uk). Contact can also be made by completing an online enquiry form.

One Space, for information, advice and links to online support groups (website: www.onespace.org.uk)

Poverty

Care International, 9th Floor, 89 Albert Embankment, London SE1 7TP (tel: 020 7091 6000; website: www.careinternational.org.uk). Contact can also be made by completing an online enquiry form.

Counselling, 5 Pear Tree Walk, Wakefield, West Yorkshire WF2 0HW (website: www.counselling.ltd.uk)

Family Action, 501–505 Kingsland Road, London E8 4AU (tel: 020 7254 6251; grants service: 020 7241 7459 [Tues, Wed and Thurs 2pm–4pm]; email: info@family-action.org.uk; website: www.family-action.org.uk). Contact can also be made by completing an online enquiry form.

Law Centres Network, Floor 1, Tavis House, 1–6 Tavistock Square, London WC1H 9NA (tel: 020 3637 1330 [admin]; an online enquiry form is also available for non-legal advice; website: www.lawcentres.org.uk). See the website for information on your local law centre.

The Trussell Trust, Unit 9 Ashfield Trading Estate, Ashfield Road, Salisbury SP2 7HL (tel: 01722 580180; email: enquiries@trusselltrust.org; website: www.trusselltrust.org). You can also use the sites search facility to find your nearest foodbank.

Refugees and asylum seekers

Asylum Aid, Club UnionHouse, 253–254 Upper Street, London N1 1RY (tel: 020 7354 9631; advice line: 020 7354 9264 [Tues 1pm–4pm]; email: info@asylumaid.org.uk; website: www.asylumaid.org.uk)

Migrant Help, Charlton House, Dour Street, Dover, Kent CT16 1AT (tel: 01304 203977; email: mhl@migranthelpline.org; website: www.migranthelp.org)

Refugee Action, Victoria Charity Centre, 11 Belgrave Road, London SW1V 1RB (tel: 020 7952 1511; asylum advice: 0808 800 0630 [Mon–Fri 8.30am–7pm]; website: www.refugee-action.org.uk). See the website for a list of local offices.

Refugee Council, PO Box 68614, London E15 9DQ; (tel: 020 7346 6700 [head office]; website: www.refugeecouncil.org.uk. Please visit the website for signposting to a specific service)

Refugee Support Centre, 47 South Lambeth Road, London SW8 1RH (tel: 020 7820 3606; email: rsctherapy47@hotmail.com).

Relationships

Albany Trust Counselling, 239A Balham High Road, London SW17 7BE (tel: 020 8767 1827; email: albanytrustoffice@gmail.com; website: www.albanytrust.org.uk)

Family Planning Association, 50 Featherstone Street, London EC1Y 8QU (tel: 020 7608 5240; email: general@fpa.org.uk; website: www.fpa.org.uk)

Relate (National Marriage Guidance) Premier House, Carolina Court, Lakeside, Doncaster DN4 5RA (tel: 0300 100 1234; email: using the online contact form; website: www.relate.org.uk; there is also a Live Chat service available on the website)

Social isolation

The Farming Community Network, Manor Farm, West Haddon,

Northampton NN6 7AQ (helpline: 0845 367 9990 [7am–11pm daily]; email: using the online contact form; website: www.fcn.org.uk)

The Single Concern Group, P.O. Box 40, Minehead TA24 5YS (tel: 01643 708008; helpline: 01643 708008 [Office Hours])

Squatters

Advisory Service for Squatters (ASS), Angel Alley, 84b, Whitechapel High Street, London E1 7QX (tel: 020 3216 0098; email: advice@squatter.org.uk; website: www.squatter.org.uk)

Victims of accidents and crimes

Abuse

NSPCC, Weston House, 42 Curtain Road, London EC2A 3NH (tel: 020 7825 2500; helpline: 0808 800 5000; email: help@nspcc.org.uk; website: www.nspcc.org.uk)

Action on Elder Abuse (AEA), PO Box 60001, Streatham SW16 9BY (tel: 020 8835 9280; helpline: 0808 808 8141; email: enquires@elderabuse.org.uk or using the online contact form; website: www.elderabuse.org.uk)

The Clinic for Boundaries, 49–51 East Road, London N1 6AH (tel: 020 3468 4194; email: info@professionalboundaries.org.uk; website: www.professionalboundaries.org.uk)

Crime

Victim Support, Octavia House, 50 Banner Street, London EC1Y 8ST (tel: 020 7336 1730; Supportline: 0845 303 0900 [weekdays 8am–8pm and Sat–Sun, 9am–7pm]; email: supportline@victimsupport.org.uk; website: www.victimsupport.org). For details on the regional offices please see the website.

Disasters

Disaster Action, No.4, 71 Upper Berkeley Street, London W1H 7DB (tel: 01483 799066; email: pameladix@disasteraction.org.uk; website: www.disasteraction.org.uk)

Domestic violence

Broken Rainbow, PO Box 68947, London E1W 9JJ (tel: 0845 260 5560 [admin]; helpline: 0300 999 5428 [Mon and Thurs 10am–8pm, Tues and Wed 10am–5pm]; email: mail@broken-rainbow.org.uk or help@brokenrainbow.org.uk; website: www.brokenrainbow.org.uk) They also have an online chat service.

Mankind, Flook House, Belvedere Road, Taunton, Somerset TA1 1BT (tel: 01823334244; helpline: 01823 334244 [Mon–Fri, 10am–4pm and 7pm–9pm]; email: admin@mankind.org.uk; website: www.mankind.org.uk)

Men's Advice Line and Enquiries (MALE), (helpline: 0808 801 0327 [Mon–Fri, 9am–5pm]; email: info@mensadviceline.org.uk; website: www.mensadviceline.org.uk)

National Centre for Domestic Violence, PO Box 999 Guildford Surrey GU1 9BH (24-hour helpline: 0844 804 4999; minicom: 18001 08009702070; text: 'NCDV' to 60777 for call back; email: office@ncdv.org.uk; website: www.ncdv.org.uk)

Women's Aid Federation, PO BOX 3245, Bristol BS2 2EH (tel: 01179 444411 [admin]; national 24-hour helpline: 0808 200 0247; email: info@womensaid.org.uk or helpline@womensaid.org.uk; website: www.womensaid.org.uk). For details on the regional offices please see the website.

Medical accidents

Action for Victims of Medical Accidents (AVMA), 117 High Street, Croydon, London CR0 1QG (tel: 020 8688 9555 [admin only]; helpline: 0845 123 2352 [Mon–Fri, 10am–5pm]; email: advice@avma.org.uk; website: www.avma.org.uk)

Rape

Rape Crisis Centre, BCM Box 4444, London WC1N 3XX (helpline: 0808 802 9999 [12pm–2.30pm and 7pm–9.30pm daily); email: rceinfo@rapecrisis.org.uk; website: www.rapecrisis.org.uk). See website for contact information on local rape crisis centres.

Women Against Rape (WAR) and Black Women's Rape Action Project, Crossroads Women's Centre, 25 Wolsey Mews NW5 2DX (tel: 020 7482 2496 [Mon–Fri, 1.30pm–4pm]; email: war@womenagainstrape.net or bwrap@dircon.co.uk; website: www.womenagainstrape.net)

Road accidents

RoadPeace, Shakespeare Business Centre, 245a Cold Harbour Lane, Brixton, London SW9 8RR (tel: 020 7733 1603; helpline: 0845 450 0355 [Mon–Fri, 9am–5pm]; email: info@roadpeace.org or helpline@roadpeace.org; website: www.roadpeace.org)

Work issues

Employment Tribunals Enquiry Line, PO Box 10218 Leicester LE1 8EG (Public Enquiry Line: 0300 123 1024; minicom: 01509 221564; website: www.justice.gov.uk/tribunals/employment). See website for the contact details of local employment tribunals.

Public Concern at Work, 3rd Floor, Bank Chambers, 6–10 Borough High Street, London SE1 9QQ (tel: 020 3117 2520; Whistleblowing Advice Line: 020 7404 6609; email: whistle@pcaw.org.uk; website: www.pcaw.org.uk)

Women

Refuge, Fourth Floor, International House, 1 St Katharine's Way, London E1W 1UN (tel: 020 7395 7700 (general); 24-hour helpline: 0808 200 0247; email: info@refuge.org.uk; website: www.refuge.org.uk)

Women and Girls Network, PO Box 13095, London W14 0FE (tel: 020 7610 4678; Advice Line: 0808 801 0660 [Mon–Fri 10am–4pm, Wed 6pm–8pm]; Sexual Violence Helpline: 0808801066 [Please see website for opening times]; email: website: www.wgn.org.uk; an online contact facility is also available)

Women's Health Concern, Spracklen House, Dukes Place, Marlow, Buckinghamshire SL7 2QH (tel: 01628 890199; email and telephone advice is available for a small fee please check the website for more details; website: www.womens-health-concern.org)

Illness and disability

Disability (general)

Action Medical Research, Vincent House, Horsham, West Sussex RH12 2DP (tel: 01403 210406; email: info@action.org.uk; website: www.action.org.uk)

Contact a Family, 209–211 City Road, London EC1V 1JN (tel: 020 7608 8700; helpline: 0808 808 3555 [Mon–Fri 9.30am–5pm]; email: info@cafamily.org.uk or by using online enquiry form; website: www.cafamily.org.uk)

Disabled Living Foundation (DLF), Ground Floor, Landmark House, Hammersmith Bridge Road, London W6 9EJ (tel: 020 7289 6111; helpline: 0300 999 0004 [Mon–Fri, 10am–4pm]; email: helpline@dlf.org.uk; website: www.dlf.org.uk)

Disabled Parents' Network, Poynters House, Poynters Road, Dunstable, Bedfordshire LU5 4TP (helpline and general enquiries: 07817 300103; email: by using online enquiry form; website: www.disabledparentsnetwork.org.uk)

Disabilities Trust, 32 Market Place, Burgess Hill, West Sussex RH15 9NP (tel: 01444 239123; email: info@thedtgroup.org; website: www.thedtgroup.org)

Disability Rights, Ground Floor, CAN Mezzanine, 49–51 East Rd, London N1 6AH (tel: 020 7250 8181; there are a number of different advice lines for different issues, see the website for more information, Independent Living Advice Line: 0300 555 1525 [Mon–Fri, 9am–1pm]; email: enquiries@disabilityrightsuk.org or independentliving@disabilityrightsuk.org; website: www.disabilityrightsuk.org)

Disability Law Service (DLS), C/O Real, First floor, Jack Dash House, 2 Lawn House Close, London E14 9YQ (tel: 020 7791 9800 (Option 5); email: advice@dls.org.uk; website: www.dls.org.uk)

Disability Pregnancy and Parenthood International (DPPI), 336 Brixton Road, London SW9 7AA (helpline: 0800 018 4730 [Tues–Thurs 10.30am–2.30pm; email: info@dppi.org.uk; website: www.dppi.org.uk)

I CAN's, Unit 31, Angel Gate (Gate 5), Goswell Road, London EC1V 2PT (tel: 0845 225 4073; email: info@ican.org.uk; website: www.ican.org.uk)

* Jewish Care, Amélie House, Maurice and Vivienne Wohl Campus, 221 Golders Green Road, London NW11 9DQ (tel: 020 8922 2000; helpline: 020 8922 2222 [Mon–Fri 8.30am–5.30pm]; email: helpline@jcare.org; website: www.jewishcare.org)

Kids, 7–9 Elliott's Place, London N1 8HX (tel: 020 7359 3635; email: by using the online contact form; website: www.kids.org.uk)

PHAB England, Summit House, 50 Wandle Road, Croydon CR0 1DF (tel: 020 8667 9443; email: info@phab.org.uk; website: www.phab.org.uk)

Queen Elizabeth's Foundation (QEF), Leatherhead Court, Woodlands Road, Leatherhead, Surrey KT22 0BN (tel: 01372 841100; email: by using online contact form; website: www.qef.org.uk)

RESPOND, 3rd Floor, 24–32 Stephenson Way, London NW1 2HD (tel: 020 7383 0700; helpline: 0808 808 0700 [Thurs 10am–4pm]; email: wvhelpline@respond.org.uk; website: www.respond.org.uk)

Addiction

Addaction, 67–69 Cowcross Street, London EC1M 6PU (tel: 020 7251 5860; email: info@addaction.org.uk or by using online contact form; website: www.addaction.org.uk)

Tacade (Advisory Council on Alcohol and Drug Education), Old Exchange Building, 6 St Ann's Passage, King Street, Manchester M2 6AD (tel: 01618 366850; email: by using online contact form; website: www.tacade.com)

Ageing

Age UK, Tavis House, 1–6 Tavistock Square, London WC1H 9NA (helpline: 0800 169 6565 [Mon–Fri, 9am–4pm]; email: by using online contact form; website: www.ageuk.org.uk)

* Independent Age, 18 Avonmore Road, London W14 8RR, (tel: 020 7605 4200; advice line: 0800 319 6789 [Mon–Fri, 10am–4pm]; email:

advice@independentage.org; website: www.independentage.org)

AIDS/HIV

National Aids Trust, New City Cloisters, 196 Old Street, London EC1V 9FR (tel: 020 7814 6767; email: info@nat.org.uk; website: www.nat.org.uk)

Terrence Higgins Trust, 314–320 Grays Inn Road, London WC1X 8DP (tel: 020 7812 1600; advice and support: 0808 802 1221 [Mon–Fri, 10am–8pm]; email: info@tht.org.uk; website: www.tht.org.uk)

Alcohol

Al-Anon Family Groups UK and Eire (AFG), 57B Great Suffolk Street, London SE1 OBB (helpline: 020 7403 0888 [10am–10pm daily]; email: enquiries@al-anonuk.org.uk; website: www.al-anonuk.org.uk)

Alcohol Concern, 25 Corsham Street, London N1 6DR (tel: 020 7566 9800; email: by using online contact form; website: www.alcoholconcern.org.uk)

Alcoholics Anonymous (AA), General Service Office, PO Box 1, 10 Toft Green, York YO1 7NJ (tel: 01904 644026; helpline: 0845 769 7555; email: help@alcoholics-anonymous.org.uk; website: www.alcoholics-anonymous.org.uk)

Drinkline, helpline: 0300 123 1110 [Mon–Fri 9am–8pm, Sat–Sun 11am–4pm]

Foundation 66, (Now a subsidiary of Pheonix Futures Group) ASRA House, 1 Long Lane, London SE1 4PG (tel: 020 7234 9940; email: info@foundation66.org.uk; website: www.foundation66.org.uk)

Turning Point, Standon House, 21 Mansell Street, London E1 8AA (tel: 020 7481 7600; email: info@turningpoint.co.uk; website: www.turning-point.co.uk)

Allergy

Action Against Allergy, PO Box 278, Twickenham TW1 4QQ (tel: 020 8892 4949; helpline: 020 8892 2711; email: aaa@actionagainstallergy.freeserve.co.uk or by using the online contact form; website: www.actionagainstallergy.co.uk)

Allergy UK, Planwell House, LEFA Business Park, Edgington Way Sidcup, Kent DA14 5BH (helpline: 01322 619898 [Mon–Fri 9am–5pm]; email: info@allergyuk.org; website: www.allergyuk.org; a live chat facility is also available on the website)

Alopecia areata and alopecia androgenetica

Alopecia UK, 39 Wykeham Drive, Baskingstoke RG23 8HW (tel: 020 8333 1661; email: see website for details; website: www.alopeciaonline.org.uk)

Alzheimer's disease

* Alzheimer's Society, Devon House, 58 St Katharine's Way, London E1W 1LB (tel: 020 7423 3500; helpline: 0300 222 1122 [Mon–Fri, 9am–5pm; Sat–Sun, 10am–4pm]; email: by using online contact form; website: www.alzheimers.org.uk)

Angelmann syndrome

ASSERT (Angelman Syndrome Support Education and Research), PO Box 4962, Nuneaton CV11 9FD (helpline: 0300 999 0102; email: assert@angelmanuk.org; website: www.angelmanuk.org)

Ankylosing spondylitis

National Ankylosing Spondylitis Society (NASS), Unit 0.2, One Victoria Villas, Richmond, Surrey TW9 2GW (tel: 020 8948 9117; email: admin@nass.co.uk; website: www.nass.co.uk)

Arthritis/rheumatic diseases

Arthritis Care, Floor 4, Linen Court, 10 East Road, London N1 6AD (tel: 020 7380 6500; helpline: 0808 800 4050 [Mon–Fri, 10am–4pm]; email: info@arthritiscare.org.uk or helplines@arthritiscare.org.uk; website: www.arthritiscare.org.uk)

Arthritis Research UK, Copeman House, St Mary's Gate, Chesterfield S41 7TD (tel: 0300 790 0400; email: enquiries@arthritisresearchuk.org or by using online contact form; website: www.arthritisresearchuk.org)

Arthrogryposis

Arthrogryposis Group (TAG), PO Box1199, Spalding, Lincolnshire PE11 9EY (helpline: 0800 028 4447; email: info@taguk.org.uk or by using online contact form; website: www.tagonline.org.uk)

Asthma

Asthma UK, 18 Mansell Street, London E1 8AA (tel: 020 7786 4900; Advice line: 0800 121 6244 [Mon–Fri, 9am–5pm]; email: info@asthma.org.uk; website: www.asthma.org.uk)

Ataxia

* Ataxia UK, Lincoln House, Kennington Park, 1–3 Brixton Road, London SW9 6DE (tel: 020 7582 1444; helpline: 0845 644 0606 [Mon–Thurs, 10.30am–2.30pm]; email: helpline@ataxia.org.uk; website: www.ataxia.org.uk)

Autism

National Autistic Society (NAS), 393 City Road, London EC1V 1NG (tel: 020 7833 2299; helpline: 0808 800 4104 [Mon–Fri, 10am–4pm]; email: nas@nas.org.uk; website: www.autism.org.uk)

Back pain

Back Care, 16 Elmtree Road, Teddington, Middlesex TW11 8ST (tel: 020 8977 5474; helpline: 0845 130 2704; email: by using online helpline enquiry form; website: www.backcare.org.uk)

Behçet's syndrome

Behçet's Syndrome Society, 8 Abbey Gardens, Evesham, Worcester WR11 4SP (tel: 0845 130 7328; helpline: 0845 130 7329; email: info@behcetsdisease.org.uk; website: www.behcets.org.uk)

Blind/partially sighted

CALIBRE (Cassette Library of Recorded Books), Aylesbury, Buckinghamshire HP22 5XQ (tel: 01296 432339; email: enquiries@calibre.org.uk; website: www.calibre.org.uk)

International Glaucoma Association (IGA), Woodcote House, 15 Highpoint Business Village, Henwood, Ashford, Kent TN24 8DH (tel: 01233 648164; helpline: 01233 648170; email: info@iga.org.uk; website: www.iga.org.uk)

Listening Books, 12 Lant Street, London SE1 1QH (tel: 020 7407 9417; email: info@listening-books.org.uk; website: www.listening-books.org.uk)

National Federation of the Blind of the UK, Sir John Wilson House,

215 Kirkgate, Wakefield WF1 1JG (tel: 01924 291313; email: nfbuk@nufbk.org or by using online enquiry form; website: www.nfbuk.org)

Partially Sighted Society, 1 Bennetthorpe, Doncaster DN2 6AA (tel: 0844 477 4966; email: reception@partsight.org.uk; website: www.partsight.org.uk)

* Royal National Institute for the Blind (RNIB), 105 Judd Street, London WC1H 9NE (helpline: 0303 123 9999 [Mon–Thurs, 8.45am–5.30pm]; email: helpline@rnib.org.uk; website: www.rnib.org.uk)

RP Fighting Blindness, PO Box 350, Buckingham MK18 5GZ (tel: 01280 821334; helpline: 0845 123 2354; email: info@rpfightingblindness.org.uk or helpline@rpfightingblindness.org.uk; website: www.rpfightingblindness.org.uk)

Voluntary Transcribers' Group, 8 Segbourne Road, Rubery, Birmingham B45 9SX (tel: 01214 534268; email: braillist@btinternet.com)

Bone marrow

Anthony Nolan Trust, 2 Heathgate Place, 75–87 Agincourt Road, London NW3 2NU (tel: 0303 303 0303; email: by using online contact form; website: www.anthonynolan.org.uk)

Bowel disorders

National Advisory Service for Parents of Children with a Stoma (NASPCS), 51 Anderson Drive, Darvel, Ayrshire KA17 0DE (tel: 01560 322024)

Children with Crohn's and Colitis (CICRA) Parkgate House, 356 West Barnes Lane, Motspur Park, Surrey KT3 6NB (tel: 020 8949 6209; email: support@cicra.org or by using online contact form; website: www.cicra.org)

National Association for Colitis and Crohn's Disease (NACC), 4 Beaumont House, Sutton Road, St Albans, Hertfordshire AL1 5HH (tel: 01727 830038; helpline: 0845 130 2233 [Mon–Fri, 10am–1pm] and 0845 130 3344 [Mon–Fri 1–3pm and 6.30–9pm]; email: info@CrohnsAndColitis.org.uk; website: www.crohnsandcolitis.org.uk)

Brain injury

British Institute for Brain-Injured Children (BIBIC), Old Kelways, Somerton Road, Langport, Somerset TA10 9SJ (tel: 01458 253344; email: info@bibic.org.uk; website: www.bibic.org.uk)

Brittle bones

* Brittle Bone Society, Grant-Paterson House, 30 Guthrie Street, Dundee DD1 5BS (tel: 01382 204446; email: bbs@brittlebone.org or by using online enquiry form; website: www.brittlebone.org)

Burns

British Burn Association, Royal College of Surgeons of England, 35–43 Lincoln's Inn Fields, London WC2A 3PE (tel: 020 7869 6923; email: by using the online contact form; website: www.britishburnassociation.org)

Children's Burns Trust, 2 Grosvenor Gardens, London SW1W 0DH (tel: 020 7881 0902; email: info@cbtrust.org.uk or by using online contact form; website: www.cbtrust.org.uk)

Cancer and leukaemia

Action Cancer, 1 Marlborough Park South, Belfast BT9 6XS (tel: 02890 803344; email: info@actioncancer.org; website: www.actioncancer.org)

* CLIC Sargent Cancer Care for Children, Horatio House, 77–85 Fulham Palace Road, London W6 8JA (tel: 0300 330 0803; email: by using online enquiry form; website: www.clicsargent.org.uk)

* Leukaemia Care Society, 89 Blackpole Road, Worcester, Worcestershire WR3 8TJ (tel: 01905 755977; 24-hour helpline: 0808 801 0444; email: care@leukaemiacare.org.uk; website: www.leukaemiacare.org.uk; online chat facility also available)

* Macmillan Cancer Relief, 89 Albert Embankment, London SE1 7UQ (tel: 020 7840 7840; helpline: 0808 808 0000; email: by using online enquiry form; website: www.macmillan.org.uk).

Marie Curie Foundation, 89 Albert Embankment, London SE1 7TP (tel: 0800 716 146; email: supporter.relation@mariecurie.org.uk; website: www.mariecurie.org.uk)

Tak Tent Cancer Support Flat 5, 30 Shelley Court, Gartnavel Complex Glasgow G12 0YN (tel: 01412 110122; website: www.taktent.org.)

Tenovous Cancer Head Office, Gleider House, Ty Glas Road, Llanishen, Cardiff CF14 5BD (tel: 02920 768850; helpline: 0808 808 1010 [Mon–Fri 8am–8pm]; email: post@tenovus.com or by using their 'ask the nurse' facility online; website: www.tenovus.org.uk)

Cerebral palsy

SCOPE, 6 Market Road, London N7 9PW (tel: 020 7619 7100; helpline: 0808 800 3333 [Mon–Fri 8am–5pm]; email: helpline@scope.org.uk; website: www.scope.org.uk)

Chest/lungs

British Lung Foundation, 73–75 Goswell Road, London EC1V 7ER (tel: 020 7688 5555; helpline: 03000 030 555; email: helpline@blf.org.uk or by using online enquiry form; website: www.blf.org.uk)

Child growth

Child Growth Foundation, 21 Malvern Drive, Sutton Coldfield B76 1PZ (helpline: 020 8995 0257 [Mon–Fri 9.30am–4pm]; email: info@childgrowthfoundation.org; website: www.childgrowthfoundation.org)

Cleft lip/palate disorder

Cleft Lip and Palate Association (CLAPA), 1st Floor, Green Man Tower, 332B Goswell Road, London EC1V 7LQ (tel: 020 7833 4883; email: info@clapa.com or by using online contact form; website: www.clapa.com)

Charcot-Marie-Tooth disease

CMT International United Kingdom, 98 Broadway, Southbourne, Bournemouth BH6 4EH (tel: 0800 652 6316; helpline: 0800 652 6316 [Mon, Thurs and Fri 9am–4pm, Tues and Wed 9am–1pm] email: info@cmtuk.org.uk; website: www.cmt.org.uk)

Coeliac disease

Coeliac UK, 3rd Floor, Apollo Centre, Desborough Road, High Wycombe HP11 2QW (tel: 01494 437278; helpline: 0845 305 2060; email: by using online contact form; website: www.coeliac.org.uk).

Colostomy

Colostomy Association (CA), Enterprise House, 95 London Street, Reading, Berkshire RG1 4QA (tel: 01189 391537; 24-hour helpline: 0800 328 4257; email: cass@colostomyassociation.org.uk or by using online enquiry form; website: www.colostomyassociation.org.uk)

Cot death

Compassionate Friends, 14 New King Street, Deptford, London SE8 3HS (helpline: 0845 123 2304; or 02887 788016 in Northern Ireland [Mon–Fri 10am–4pm, 7pm–10pm]; email: helpline@tcf.org.uk; website: www.tcf.org.uk)

The Lullaby Trust (formerly Foundation for the Study of Infant Deaths), 11 Belgrave Road, London SW1V 1RB (tel: 020 7802 3200; helpline: 0808 802 6868; email: office@fsid.org.uk or support@fsid.org.uk; website: www.lullabytrust.org.uk)

Counselling

British Association for Counselling and Psychotherapy, 15 St John's Business Park, Lutterworth LE17 4HB, (tel: 01455 883300; email: bacp@bacp.co.uk; website: www.bacp.co.uk)

Samaritans, The Upper Mill, Kingston Road, Ewell KT17 2AF (tel: 020 8394 8300; 24-hour helpline: 0845 790 9090; see phone book for local number; email: admin@samaritans.org (general) jo@samaritans.org (helpline); website: www.samaritans.org)

SupportLine, PO Box 2860, Romford, Essex RM7 1JA (tel: 01708 765222; helpline: 01708 765200; email: info@supportline.org.uk; website: www.supportline.org.uk)

Craniosynostosis orcraniostenosis

Headlines Craniofacial Support, 8 Footes Lane, Frampton, Cottrell, Bristol BS36 2JQ (tel: 01454 850557; helpline: 01454 850557; email: info@headlines.org.uk; website: www.headlines.org.uk)

Crohn's disease

Children with Crohn's and Colitis (CICRA) Parkgate House, 356 West Barnes Lane, Motspur Park, Surrey KT3 6NB (tel: 020 8949 6209; email: support@cicra.org or by using online contact form; website: www.cicra.org)

National Association for Colitis and Crohn's Disease (NACC), 4 Beaumont House, Sutton Road, St Albans, Hertfordshire AL1 5HH (tel: 01727 830038; helpline: 0845 130 2233 [Mon–Fri, 10am–1pm] and 0845 130 3344 [Mon–Fri 1–3pm and 6.30–9pm]; email: info@crohnsandcolitis.org.uk; website: www.crohnsandcolitis.org.uk)

Crying/restless babies

The CRY-SIS Helpline, BM CRY-SIS, London WC1N 3XX (sae required); (helpline: 0845 122 8669 [9am–10pm daily]; website: www.cry-sis.org.uk)

Cystic fibrosis

Butterfly Trust, Swanston Steading, 109/3B Swanston Road, Edinburgh EH10 7DS (tel: 01314 455590; email: info@butterflytrust.org.uk; website: www.butterflytrust.org.uk)

* Cystic Fibrosis Trust, 11 London Road, Bromley, Kent BR1 1BY (tel: 020 8464 7211; support helpline: 0300 373 1000; email: enquiries@cysticfibrosis.org.uk; website: www.cysticfibrosis.org.uk)

Deafblind

Deafblind UK, National Centre for Deafblindness, John and Lucille Van Geest Place, Cygnet Road, Hampton, Peterborough PE7 8FD (tel: 01733 358100; helpline: 0800 132 320; textphone: 0800 132 320; email: info@deafblind.org.uk or by using online contact form; website: www.deafblind.org.uk)

* Sense, 101 Pentonville Road, London N1 9LG (tel: 0300 330 9250; textphone: 0300 330 9252; email: info@sense.org.uk; website: www.sense.org.uk)

Deafness/hearing difficulties

Action on Hearing Loss, 19–23 Featherstone Street, London EC1Y 8SL (tel: 020 7296 8000; text: 020 7296 8001; information line: 0808 808 0123 [voice] 0808 808 9000 [text]; email: informationonline@hearingloss.org.uk; website: www.actionhearingloss.org.uk)

British Deaf Association (BDA), 3rd Floor, 356 Holloway Road, London N7 6PA (tel: 020 7697 4140; email: bda@bda.org.uk; website: www.bda.org.uk)

The Guide Dogs for the Blind Association, Burghfield Common, Reading RG7 3YG (tel: 01189 835555; email: guidedogs@guidedogs.org.uk; website: www.guidedogs.org.uk)

Hearing Dogs for Deaf People, The Grange, Wycombe Road, Saunderton, Buckinghamshire HP27 9NS (tel and minicom: 01844 348100; email: info@hearingdogs.org.uk; website: www.hearingdogs.org.uk)

* National Deaf Children's Society, Ground Floor South, Castle House, 37–45 Paul Street, London EC2A 4LS (tel: 020 7490 8656; minicom: 020 7490 8656; helpline: 0808 800 8880; email: ndcs@ndcs.org.uk or helpline@ndcs.org.uk; website: www.ndcs.org.uk)

Royal Association for Deaf People (RAD), Century House South, Riverside Office Centre, North Station Road, Colchester, Essex CO1 1RE (tel: 0845 688 2525; minicom: 0845 688 2527; email: info@royaldeaf.org.uk; website: www.royaldeaf.org.uk)

Dental health

British Dental Association, 64 Wimpole Street, London W1G 8YS (tel: 020 7935 0875; email: enquiries@bda.org website: www.bda.org)

British Dental Health Foundation (BDHF), Smile House, 2 East Union Street, Rugby, Warwickshire CV22 6AJ (tel: 01788 546365; helpline: 0845 063 1188; email: helpline@dentalhealth.org; website: www.dentalhealth.org).

Depression

Befrienders Worldwide, c/o The Samaritans, Upper Mill, Kingston Road, Ewell, Surrey KT17 2AF (tel: 0845 790 9090; minicom: 0845 790 9192; email: info@befrienders.org; website: www.befrienders.org)

Depression Alliance, 20 Great Dover Street, London SE1 4LX (tel: 0845 123 2320; email: info@

depressionalliance.org; website: www.depressionalliance.org)

Depression UK, c/o Self Help Nottingham, Ormiston House, 32–36 Pelham Street, Nottingham NG1 2EG (tel: 01912 399630; email: info@depressionuk.org; website: www.depressionuk.org)

Bipolar UK, 11 Belgrave Road, London SW1V 1RB (tel: 020 7391 6480; email: info@bipolaruk.org.uk; website: www.bipolaruk.org.uk)

Samaritans, The Upper Mill, Kingston Road, Ewell KT17 2AF (tel: 020 8394 8300; 24-hour helpline: 0845 790 9090; see phone book for local number; email: admin@samaritans.org (general) jo@samaritans.org (helpline); website: www.samaritans.org)

Diabetes

Diabetes Foundation, Macleod House, 10 Parkway, London NW1 7AA (tel: 020 7424 1000; website: www.diabetesfoundation.org.uk)

Diabetes UK, 10 Parkway, London NW1 7AA (tel: 0345 123 2399; helpline: 0345 123 2399 [Mon–Fri 9am–7pm]; email: info@diabetes.org.uk or careline@diabetes.org.uk; website: www.diabetes.org.uk)

Disfigurement

Disfigurement Guidance Centre, PO Box 7, Cupar, Fife KY15 4PF (tel: 01337 870281)

Let's Face It, 72 Victoria Avenue, Westgate-on-Sea, Kent CT8 8BH (tel: 01843 833724; email: chrisletsfaceit@aol.com; website: www.lets-face-it.org.uk)

Down's syndrome

Down's Syndrome Association, Langdon Down Centre, 2a Langdon Park, Teddington Middlesex TW11 9PS (helpline: 0333 1212 300 [Mon–Fri 10am–4pm]; email: info@downs-syndrome.org.uk; website: www.downs-syndrome.org.uk)

Drugs

ADFAM National, 25 Corsham Street, London N1 6DR (tel: 020 7553 7640; email: admin@adfam.org.uk; website: www.adfam.org.uk)

Cocaine Anonymous UK, Talbot House, 204–226 Imperial Way, Rayners Lane, Harrow HA2 7HH (helpline: 0800 612 0225 or 0300 11 2285 [10am–10pm daily]; email: helpline@cauk.org.uk or wtf@cauk.org.uk; website: www.cauk.org.uk)

DrugScope, 4th Floor, Asra House, 1 Long Lane, London SE1 4PG (tel: 020 7234 9730; email: info@drugscope.org.uk; website: www.drugscope.org.uk)

Early Break, Annara House, 7–11 Bury Road, Radcliffe M26 2UG (Bury: 01617 233880; East Lancashire: 01282 604022; email: info@earlybreak.co.uk; website: www.earlybreak.co.uk)

Families Anonymous, Doddington and Rollo Community Association, Charlotte Despard Avenue, Battersea, London SW11 5HD (helpline: 0845 120 0660 or 020 7498 4680; website: www.famanon.org.uk)

FRANK (National Drugs Helpline), (24-hour helpline: 0300 123 6600; text: 82111; website: www.talktofrank.com). Contact can also be made via an online chat facility from 2pm–6pm.

Narcotics Anonymous (NA), 202 City Road, London EC1V 2PH (tel: 020 7251 4007; helpline: 0300 999 1212; website: www.ukna.org)

Turning Point, Standon House, 21 Mansell Street, London E1 8AA (tel: 020 7481 7600; email: info@turning-point.co.uk or by using online contact form; website: www.turning-point.co.uk)

Dyslexia

British Dyslexia Association, Unit 8, Bracknell Beeches, Old Bracknell Lane, Bracknell RG12 7BW (tel: 0333 405 4555; helpline: 0333 405 4567 [Mon–Fri, 10am–12.30pm and 1pm–4pm (but not on Wed)]; email: helpline@bdadyslexia.org.uk; website: www.bdadyslexia.org.uk)

Dyslexia Action, Dyslexia Action House, 10 High Street, Egham, Surrey TW20 9EA (tel: 0300 303 8357; email: info@dyslexiaaction.org.uk or by using online contact form; website: www.dyslexiaaction.org.uk)

Dyspraxia

Dyspraxia Foundation, 8 West Alley, Hitchin, Hertforshire SG5 1EG (tel: 01462 455016; helpline: 01462 454986 [Mon–Fri, 9am–5pm]; email: dyspraxia@dyspraxiafoundation.org.uk; website: www.dyspraxiafoundation.org.uk)

Dystonia

Dystonia Society, Second Floor, 89 Albert Embankment, London SE1 7TP (tel: 020 7793 3651; helpline: 020 7793 3650; email: info@dystonia.org.uk; website: www.dystonia.org.uk)

Eating disorders

Eating Disorders Association (Beat), Wensum House, 103 Prince of Wales Road, Norwich NR1 1DW (tel: 0300 123 3355; helpline: 0845 634 1414 [Mon–Fri, 1.30pm–4.30pm and Mon and Wed 5.30pm–8.30pm]; Youth helpline: 0845 634 7650 [Mon–Fri, 1.30pm–4.30pm and Mon and Wed 5.30pm–8.30pm]; email: help@b-eat.co.uk or fyp@b-eat.co.uk (youth); website: www.b-eat.co.uk)

Eczema

National Eczema Society, Hill House, Highgate Hill, London N19 5NA (tel: 020 7281 3553; helpline: 0800 089 1122 [Mon–Fri, 8am–8pm]; email: info@eczema.org or helpline@eczema.org; website: www.eczema.org)

Endometriosis

National Endometriosis Society, Suites 1&2, 46 Manchester Street, London W1U 7LS (tel: 020 7222 2781; Crisis helpline: 0808 808 2227 [opening times vary depending on volunteer availability, see website for details]; email: admin@endometriosisuk.org or by using online contact form; website: www.endometriosis-uk.org.uk)

Epidermolysis bullosa

Dystrophic Epidermolysis Bullosa Research Association (DEBRA), Debra House, 13 Wellington Business Park, Dukes Ride, Crowthorne, Berkshire RG45 6LS (tel: 01344 771961; email: debra@debra.org.uk; website: www.debra.org.uk)

Epilepsy

Epilepsy Action, New Anstey House, Gateway Drive, Yeadon, Leeds LS19 7XY (tel: 01132 108800;

helpline: 0808 800 5050 [Mon–Thurs 9am–4.30pm; Fri 9am–4pm]; text: 07537 410044; email: epilepsy@epilepsy.org.uk or helpline@epilepsy.org.uk; website: www.epilepsy.org.uk)

The National Society for Epilepsy, Chesham Lane, Chalfont St Peter, Buckinghamshire SL9 0RJ (tel: 01494 601300; helpline: 01494 601400 [Mon–Fri, 9am–4pm, Wed 9am–8pm]; website: www.epilepsysociety.org.uk)

Feet

Sole-Mates, Goodlass House, Goodlass Rd, Hunts Cross L24 9HJ (tel: 07872 961663; email: enquiries@sole-mates.eu; website: sole-mates.eu)

Growth problems

Child Growth Foundation, 21 Malvern Drive, Sutton Coldfield B76 1PZ (tel: 020 8912 0722; helpline: 020 8995 0257; email: info@childgrowthfoundation.org; website: www.childgrowthfoundation.org)

Restricted Growth Association (RGA), PO Box 99, Lyndney GL15 9AW (tel: 0300 111 1970; email: office@restrictedgrowth.co.uk; website: www.restrictedgrowth.co.uk)

Guillain Barré syndrome

Guillain Barré & Associated Inflammatory Neuropathies (GAIN), Ground Floor, Woodholme House, Heckington Business Park, Station Road, Heckington, Sleaford NG34 9J (tel: 01529 469910; helpline: 0800 374 803; email: admin@gbs.org.uk; website: www.gaincharity.org.uk)

Haemophilia

* Haemophilia Society, First Floor, Petersham House, 57a Hatton Garden, London EC1N 8JG (tel: 020 7831 1020; helpline: 0800 018 6068; email: info@haemophelia.org.uk; website: www.haemophilia.org.uk)

Head injury

Headway – National Head Injuries Association Ltd, Bradbury House, 190 Bagnall Road, Old Basford, Nottingham, Nottinghamshire NG6 8SF (tel: 01159 240800; helpline: 0808 800 2244; email: enquiries@headway.org.uk or helpline@headway.org.uk; website: www.headway.org.uk)

Heart attacks/heart disease

British Heart Foundation, Greater London House, 180 Hampstead Road, London NW1 7AW (tel: 020 7554 0000; helpline: 0300 330 3311; website: www.bhf.org.uk). Contact can also be made by completing an online enquiry form.

HeartLine Association, 32 Little Heath, London SE7 8HU (tel: 03300224466; email: admin@heartline.org.uk; website: www.heartline.org.uk)

Hemiplegia

Hemi-Help, 6 Market Road, London N7 9PW (tel: 0845 120 3713, helpline: 0845 123 2372 [Mon–Fri, 10am–1pm during term time]; email: support@hemihelp.org.uk or helpline@hemihelp.org.uk; website: www.hemihelp.org.uk)

Herpes

Herpes Viruses Association (SPHERE), 41 North Road, London N7 9DP (helpline: 0845 123 2305; email: info@herpes.org.uk; website: www.herpes.org.uk)

Hodgkin's disease

Lymphoma Association, PO Box 386, Aylesbury, Buckinghamshire HP20 2GA (helpline: 0808 808 5555 [Mon–Fri 9am-5pm]; email: information@lymphomas.org.uk; website: www.lymphomas.org.uk). Contact can also be made by completing an online enquiry form.

Huntington's disease

* Huntington's Disease Association, Suite 24, Liverpool Science Park ic1, 131 Mount Pleasant Liverpool L3 5TF (tel: 01513 315444; email: info@hda.org.uk; website: www.hda.org.uk)

Hyperactive children

Hyperactive Children's Support Group, 71 Whyke Lane, Chichester, West Sussex PO19 7PD (tel: 01243 539966 Mon–Fri, 2.30–4.30pm; email: hacsg@hacsg.org.uk; website: www.hacsg.org.uk). If writing, the Group requests that you enclose a large sae.

Hypertension

Coronary Artery Disease Research Association (CORDA), Royal Brompton Hospital, Sydney Street, London SW3 6NP (tel: 020 7349 8686)

Incontinence

Association for Continence Advice (ACA), Fitwise Management Ltd, Blackburn House, Redhouse Road, Seafield, Bathgate, West Lothian EH47 7AQ (tel: 01506 811077; email: aca@fitwise.co.uk; website: www.aca.uk.com)

Industrial diseases

Mesothelioma UK, Glenfield Hospital, Groby Road, Leicester LE3 9QP (helpline: 0800 169 2409; email: mesothelioma.uk@uhl-tr.nhs.uk; website: www.mesothelioma.uk.com)

Repetitive Strain Injury Association (RSIA), c/o Keytools Ltd, 2 Swangate, Charnham Park, Hungerford, Berkshire RG17 0YX (email: rsia@rsi.org.uk; website: www.rsi.org.uk)

Infantile hypercalcaemia

Williams Syndrome Foundation, 161 High Street, Tonbridge, Kent TN9 1BX (tel: 01732 365152; email: enquiries@williams-syndrome.org.uk; website: www.williams-syndrome.org.uk)

Infertility

Infertility Network UK, Charter House, 43 St Leonards Road, Bexhill-on-Sea, East Sussex TN40 1JA (helpline: 0800 008 7464; email: admin@infertilitynetworkuk.com; website: www.infertilitynetworkuk.com)

Irritable bowel syndrome

The IBS Network 5, Unit 1.12 SOAR Works, 14 Knutton Road, Sheffield S5 9NU (tel: 01142 723253; email: info@ttheibsnetwork.org; website: www.theibsnetwork.org)

Kidney disease

* British Kidney Patient Association (BKPA), 3 The Windmills, St Mary's Close, Turk Street, Alton GU34 1EF (tel: 01420 541424; helpline: 01420 541424; email: info@britishkidney-pa.co.uk; website: www.britishkidney-pa.co.uk)

National Kidney Federation, The Point, Coach Road, Shireoaks, Worksop, Notts S81 8BW (helpline: 0845 601 0209; email: helpline@

kidney.org.uk; website: www.kidney.org.uk)

Learning disability

Mencap, Mencap National Centre, 123 Golden Lane, London EC1Y 0RT (tel: 020 7454 0454; helpline: 0808 808 1111; email: help@mencap.org.uk; website: www.mencap.org.uk)

Limb disorder

*British Limbless Ex-Servicemen's Association (BLESMA), 185–187 High Road, Chadwell Heath, Romford RM6 6NA (tel: 020 8590 1124; email: ChadwellHeath@blesma.org; website: www.blesma.org)

Limbless Association, Unit 10, Waterhouse Business Centre, 2 Cromar Way, Chelmsford CM1 2QE (tel: 01245 216670; helpline: 0800 644 0185; email: enquiries@limbless-association.org; website: www.limbless-association.org)

Reach – The Association for Children with Hand or Arm Deficiency, Pearl Assurance House, Brook Street, Tavistock, Devon PL19 0BN (tel: 0845 130 6225; email: reach@reach.org.uk; website: www.reach.org.uk). Contact can also be made by completing an online contact form.

STEPS (A National Association for Families of Children with Congenital Abnormalities), Wright House, Crouchley Lane, Lymm, Cheshire WA13 0AS (helpline: 01925 750271; email: info@steps-charity.org.uk; website: www.steps-charity.org.uk)

Literacy/learning difficulties

National Institute of Adult Continuing Education (NIACE), Chetwynd House, 21 De Montfort Street, Leicester LE1 7GE (tel: 01162 044200; email: enquiries@niace.org.uk; website: www.niace.org.uk)

Liver disease

British Liver Trust, 2 Southampton Road, Ringwood BH24 1HY (tel: 01425 481320; information line: 0800 652 7330; email: info@britishlivertrust.org.uk; website: www.britishlivertrust.org.uk)

Lowe Syndrome Trust (UK Contact Group) (LSA) 77 West Heath Road, London NW3 7TH (tel: 020 7794 8858; email: lowetrust@gmail.com; website: www.lowetrust.com)

Lupus

Lupus UK, St James House, Eastern Road, Romford RM1 3NH (tel: 01708 731251; email: headoffice@lupusuk.org.uk; website: www.lupusuk.org.uk)

Raynaud's and Scleroderma Association, 112 Crewe Road, Alsager, Cheshire ST7 2JA (tel: 01270 872776; freephone: 0800 917 2494; email: info@raynauds.org.uk; website: www.raynauds.org.uk)

Marfan syndrome

Marfan Association UK, Rochester House, 5 Aldershot Road, Fleet, Hampshire GU51 3NG (tel: 01252810472; email: contactus@marfan-association.org.uk; website: www.marfan-association.org.uk)

Mastectomy

Breast Cancer Care (BCC), 5–13 Great Suffolk Street, London SE1 0NS (tel: 0845 092 0800; helpline: 0808 800 6000 [Mon–Fri, 9am–5pm and Sat 10am–2pm]; email: info@breastcancercare.org.uk; website: www.breastcancercare.org.uk)

Ménière's disease

Ménière's Society, The Rookery, Surrey Hills Business Park, Wotton, Dorking, Surrey RH5 6QT (tel: 01306 876883; helpline: 0845 120 2975; email: info@menieres.org.uk; website: www.menieres.org.uk)

Meningitis

Meningitis Now, Fern House, Bath Road, Stroud, Gloucestershire GL5 3TJ (tel: 01453 768000; 24-hour helpline: 0808 801 0388; email: info@meningitisnow.org or helpline@meningitisnow.org; website: www.meningitisnow.org)

Menopause

The Daisy Network Premature Menopause Support Group, PO Box 183, Rossendale, Lancashire BB4 6WZ (email: daisy@daisynetwork.org.uk; website: www.daisynetwork.org.uk)

Mental health

CARE (Self Unlimited), 13 & 14 Nursery Court, Kibworth Business Park, Harborough Road, Leicester LE8 0EX (tel: 01162 793225; email: info@selfunlimited.co.uk; website: www.selfunlimited.co.uk; online contact form also available)

Mental Health Foundation, Colechurch House, 1 London Bridge Walk, London SE1 2SX (tel: 020 7803 1100; email: mhf@mhf.org.uk; website: www.mentalhealth.org.uk). Note that MHF does not offer a help or advice line and should not be contacted unless specific information on its work is required or you wish to collaborate with the foundation in a professional capacity. Its website advises that other organisations such as The Samaritans, however, can offer emotional support. The Samaritans can be contacted by calling 0845 790 9090 or by emailing jo@samaritans.org.

Mind (National Association for Mental Health), 15–19 Broadway, Stratford, London E15 4BQ (tel: 020 8519 2122; Mind information line: 0300 123 3393; email: info@mind.org.uk; website: www.mind.org.uk)

SANE (The Mental Health Charity), 1st Floor, Cityside House, 40 Adler Street, London E1 1EE (tel: 020 7375 1002; helpline: 0845 767 8000; email: info@sane.org.uk; website: www.sane.org.uk; an online contact support service is also available)

Metabolic disorders

CLIMB (Research Trust for Metabolic Diseases in Children), Climb Building, 176 Nantwich Road, Crewe CW2 6BG (tel: 0845 241 2173 or 0800 652 3181; email: info.svcs@climb.org.uk; website: www.climb.org.uk)

Migraine

Migraine Action Association (formerly British Migraine Association), Fourth Floor, 27 East Street, Leicester LE1 6NB (tel: 01162 758317; email: info@migraine.org.uk; website: www.migraine.org.uk). Contact can also be made by completing an online enquiry form.

Migraine Trust, 52–53 Russell Square, London WC1B 4HP (tel: 020 7631 6970; email: info@migrainetrust.org; website: www.migrainetrust.org)

Miscarriage

The Miscarriage Association, 17 Wentworth Terrace, Wakefield, West Yorkshire WF1 3QW (tel: 01924

200795; helpline: 01924 200799 [Mon–Fri, 9am–4pm]; email: info@miscarriageassociation.org.uk; website: www.miscarriageassociation.org.uk)

Tommy's, Nicholas House, 3 Laurence Pountney Hill, London EC4R 0BB (tel: 020 7398 3400; Advice line: 0800 014 7800; email: info@tommys.org; website: www.tommys.org)

Motor neurone disease

* Motor Neurone Disease Association (MND), PO Box 246, Northampton NN1 2PR (tel: 01604 250505; helpline: 0845 762 6262; email: enquiries@mndassociation.org or mndconnect@mndassociation.org; website: www.mndassociation.org)

Multiple sclerosis

* Multiple Sclerosis Society, MS National Centre, 372 Edgware Road, London NW2 6ND (tel: 020 8438 0700; helpline: 0808 800 8000 [Mon–Fri, 9am–9pm]; email: infoteam@mssociety.org.uk or helpline@mssociety.org.uk; website: www.mssociety.org.uk). Contact can also be made by using the online form.

Muscular dystrophy

Muscular Dystrophy Campaign, 61A Great Suffolk Street, London SE1 0BU (tel: 020 7803 4800; helpline: 0800 652 6352; email: info@muscular-dystrophy.org; website: www.muscular-dystrophy.org)

Myasthenia gravis

Myasthenia Gravis Association, The College Business Centre, Uttoxeter New Road, Derby DE22 3WZ (tel: 01332 290219; helpline: 0800 919 922; email: mga@mga-charity.org; website: www.myaware.org)

Myotonic dystrophy

Myotonic Dystrophy Support Group, 19–21 Main Road, Gedling, Nottingham NG4 3HQ (tel: 01159 875869; helpline: 01159 870080; email: contact@mdsguk.org; website: www.mdsguk.org)

Narcolepsy

Narcolepsy Association (UK), PO Box 26865, Kirkaldy KY2 9BX (tel: 0845 450 0394; email: info@narcolepsy.org.uk; website: www.narcolepsy.org.uk)

Neurofibromatosis

The Neuro Foundation, HMA House, 78 Durham Road, London SW20 0TL (tel: 020 8439 1234; minicom: 020 8481 0492; helpline: 07866 946334 Tuesday and Wednesday ONLY; email: info@nfauk.org; website: www.nfauk.org)

Organ donors

British Organ Donor Society (BODY), Balsham, Cambridge CB21 4DL (tel: 01223 893636; email: body@argonet.co.uk; website: body.orpheusweb.co.uk)

Osteoporosis

National Osteoporosis Society, Camerton, Bath BA2 0PJ (tel: 01761 471771; helpline: 0845 450 0230; email: info@nos.org.uk; website: www.nos.org.uk).

Paget's disease

National Association for the Relief of Paget's Disease, 323 Manchester Road, Walkden, Worsley, Manchester M28 3HH (tel: 01617 994646; nurse helpline: 07713 568197; email: helpline@paget.org.uk; website: www.paget.org.uk)

Parkinson's disease

* Parkinson's Disease Society of the United Kingdom, 215 Vauxhall Bridge Road, London SW1V 1EJ (tel: 020 7931 8080; helpline: 0808 800 0303 weekdays [9am–8pm (last call taken at 7.45pm) and Saturdays 10am–2pm]; email: hello@parkinsons.org.uk; website: www.parkinsons.org.uk)

Perthes' disease

Perthes Association, PO Box 773, Guildford GU1 1XN (tel: 01483 447122; helpline: 01483 306637; email: admin@perthes.org.uk; website: www.perthes.org.uk). Contact can also be made by completing an online enquiry form.

Phobias

Anxiety UK (National Phobics Society), Zion Community Resource Centre, 339 Stretford Road, Hulme, Manchester M15 4ZY (tel: 01612 267727: helpline: 0844 477 5774; email: support@anxiety.org.uk; website: www.anxietyuk.org.uk). Contact can also be made by completing an online enquiry form.

Pituitary disorders

Pituitary Foundation, 86 Colston Street, Bristol BS1 5BB (tel: 0845 450 0376; support line: 0845 450 0375 [Mon–Fri 10am–4pm]; Endocrine Nurse helpline: 0845 450 0377 [Mondays 6pm–9pm and Thursdays 9am–1pm]; email: helpline@pituitary.org.uk; website: www.pituitary.org.uk).

Poliomyelitis

British Polio Fellowship, Eagle Point, The Runway, South Ruislip, Middlesex HA4 6SE (tel: 0800 018 0586; email: info@britishpolio.org.uk; website: www.britishpolio.org.uk)

Post-natal

Association for Post-Natal Illness, 145 Dawes Road, Fulham, London SW6 7EB (tel: 020 7386 0868 [Mon–Fri, 10am–2pm]; email: info@apni.org; website: www.apni.org)

Prader-Willi syndrome

Prader-Willi Syndrome, Craegmoor Administration Office, Unit 59, Innovation Centre, Highfield Drive, Churchfields, St Leonards-on-Sea, East Sussex TN38 9UH (tel: 01424 858949; website: www.praderwillisyndrome.org.uk)

Pre-eclampsia

Pre-Eclampsia Society, c/o Dawn James, Rhianfa, Carmel, Caernarfon LL54 7RL (tel: 01286 882685; email: dawnjames@clara.co.uk; website: www.pre-eclampsiasociety.org.uk)

Psoriasis

Psoriasis Association, Dick Coles House, 2 Queensbridge, Northampton NN4 7BF (tel: 01604 251620; helpline: 0845 676 0076; email: mail@psoriasis-association.org.uk; website: www.psoriasis-association.org.uk)

Raynaud's and Scleroderma Association, 112 Crewe Road, Alsager, Cheshire ST7 2JA (tel: 01270 872776; freephone: 0800 917 2494; email: info@raynauds.org.uk; website: www.raynauds.org.uk)

Retinitis pigmentosa

RP Fighting Blindness, PO Box 350, Buckingham MK18 5GZ (tel: 01280 821334; helpline: 0845 123 2354; email: info@rpfightingblindness.org.uk or helpline@rpfightingblindness.org.uk; website: www.rpfightingblindness.org.uk)

Rett syndrome

Rett Syndrome Association UK, Langham House West, Mill Street, Luton LU1 2NA (tel: 01582 798910; helpline: 01582 798911; email: info@rettuk.org or support@rettuk.org; website: www.rettuk.org)

Reye's syndrome

National Reye's Syndrome Foundation of the UK (NRSF), 15 Nicholas Gardens, Pyrford, Woking, Surrey GU22 8SD (tel: 01932 346843; website: www.reyessyndrome.co.uk). Contact can also be made using by completing the online contact form.

Sacoidosis

SILA (Sacoidosis and Interstitial Lung Association), c/o Department of Respiratory Medicine, 1st Floor, Cheyne Wing, King's College Hospital, Denmark Hill SE5 9RS (tel: 020 7237 5912; website: www.sila.org.uk). The best way to contact the association is by completing the online contact form.

Schizophrenia

Rethink, 15th Floor, 89 Albert Embankment, London SE1 7TP (general enquiries telephone: 01215 227007; Advice Service: 0300 5000 927; email; info@rethink.org or advice@rethink.org; website: www.rethink.org). The Advice Team can be contacted Mon–Fri 10am–2pm, except on bank holidays. Note that Rethink cannot deal with emergency or crisis issues. See the website for a list of emergency contact details.

Scoliosis

Scoliosis Association (UK) (SAUK), 4 Ivebury Court, 325 Latimer Road, London W10 6RA (tel: 020 8964 5343; helpline: 020 8964 1166; email: info@sauk.org.uk; website: www.sauk.org.uk)

Seasonal affective disorder

SAD Association (SADA), PO Box 332, Wallingford OX10 1EP (email: contact@sada.org.uk; website: www.sada.org.uk). If writing, the Association asks that you include an sae.

Sickle cell disease

Sickle Cell Society (SCS), 54 Station Road, London NW10 4UA (tel: 020 8961 7795; email: info@sicklecellsociety.org; website: www.sicklecellsociety.org). Contact can also be made by completing an online enquiry form.

Sjögren's syndrome

British Sjögren's Syndrome Association (BSSA), PO Box 15040, Birmingham B31 3DP (tel: 01214 780222; helpline: 01214 781133 [Mon–Fri, 9.30am–4pm]; website: www.bssa.uk.net)

Sleep disorders

British Snoring and Sleep Apnoea Association (BSSAA), Chapter House, 33 London Road, Reigate RH2 9HZ (tel: 01737 245638; email: info@britishsnoring.co.uk; website: www.britishsnoring.co.uk)

Smoking

Fag Ends (Roy Castle Lung Cancer Foundation), The Roy Castle Centre, 4–6 Enterprise Way, Wavertree Tech Park, Liverpool, Merseyside L13 1FB (helpline: 0800 195 2131 [Mon–Fri, 9.30am–8pm]; website: www.royalcastle.org/how-we-can-help/Prevention/Stop-Smoking).

QUIT (National Society of Non-Smokers), 4 Sovereign Close, St Katharine's & Wapping, London E1W 3HW (tel: 020 7553 2100; helpline: 0800 002 200; website: www.quit.org.uk).

Solvent abuse

Re-Solv, 30a High Street, Stone, Staffordshire ST15 8AW (tel: 01785 817885; helpline: 01785 810762; email: information@re-solv.org; website: www.re-solv.org)

Speech and language difficulties

Association for All Speech-Impaired Children (AFASIC), 1st Floor, 20 Bowling Green Lane, London EC1R 0BD (tel: 020 7490 9410; helpline: 0845 355 5577; email: info@afasic.org.uk; website: www.afasic.org.uk). You can also contact the helpline by completing an online enquiry form.

British Stammering, 15 Old Ford Road, London E2 9PJ (tel: 020 8983 1003; helpline: 0845 603 2001 or 020 8880 6590 [for a geographic number]; email: mail@stammering.org or info@stammering.org [helpline]); website: www.stammering.org). The helpline is open 2pm–5pm on Monday, Tuesday, Wednesday and Thursday.

Royal Association for Deaf People (RAD), Century House South, Riverside Office Centre, North Station Road, Colchester, Essex CO1 1RE (tel: 0845 688 2525; minicom: 0845 688 2527; email: info@royaldeaf.org.uk; website: www.royaldeaf.org.uk)

Speakability, 240 City Road, London EC1V 2PR, (tel: 020 7261 9572; helpline: 0808 808 9572 [Tues–Thurs 11am–3pm, answerphone all other times]; email: speakability@speakability.org.uk; website: www.speakability.org.uk)

Spina bifida

SHINE, 42 Park Road, Peterborough PE1 2UQ (tel: 01733 555988; email: info@shinecharity.org.uk; website: www.shinecharity.org.uk). Contact can also be made by completing an online enquiry form.

Spinal injuries

Spinal Injuries Association, SIA House, 2 Trueman Place, Oldbrook, Milton Keynes MK6 2HH (tel: 0845 678 6633; counselling: 0800 980 0501 [Mon–Fri, 9.30am–4.30pm]; email: sia@spinal.co.uk; website: www.spinal.co.uk)

Stress

Coronary Artery Disease Research Association (CORDA), Royal Brompton Hospital, Sydney Street, London SW3 6NP (tel: 020 7349 8686)

Stroke

Stroke Information Service, Stroke Association, Life After Stroke Centre, Church Lane, Bromsgrove, Worcestershire B61 8RA, (helpline:

0303 303 3100; textphone: 18001 0303 303 3100; email: info@stroke.org.uk website: www.stroke.org.uk)

Thalassaemia

United Kingdom Thalassaemia Society (UKTS), 19 The Broadway, Southgate Circus, London N14 6PH (tel: 020 8882 0011; email: office@ukts.org; website: www.ukts.org)

Thrombocytopenia with absent radii

TAR Syndrome Support Group, for further information contact Susy Edwards (email: SusyEdwards@hotmail.co.uk; website: www.ivh.se/TAR)

Tinnitus

Action on Hearing Loss
19–23 Featherstone Street, London EC1Y 8SL (tel: 020 7296 8000; text: 020 7296 8001; information line: 0808 808 0123 [voice] 0808 808 9000 [text]; email: informationonline@hearingloss.org.uk; website: www.actionhearingloss.org.uk)

British Tinnitus Association (BTA), Ground Floor, Unit 5, Acorn Business Park, Woodseats Close, Sheffield S8 0TB (tel: 01142 509933; helpline: 0800 018 0527; minicom: 01142 585694; email: info@tinnitus.org.uk; website: www.tinnitus.org.uk)

Tourettes syndrome

Tourettes Action, Kings Court, The Meads Business Centre, 19 Kingsmead, Farnborough, Hampshire GU14 7SR (tel: 01276 482903; helpline: 0300 777 8427; website: www.tourettes-action.org.uk). Contact can also be made by completing the online contact form.

Tracheo-oesophagealfistula

Aid for Children with Tracheotomies (ACT), Lammas Cottage, Stathe, Bridgwater, Somerset TA7 0JL. For further information contact Amanda Saunders (tel: 01823 698398; email: support@actfortrachykids.com; website: www.actfortrachykids.com)

Tracheo-Oesophageal Fistula Support Group (TOFS), St George's Centre, 91 Victoria Road, Netherfield, Nottingham NG4 2NN (tel: 01159 613092; email: info@tofs.org.uk; website: www.tofs.org.uk)

Tranquillizers

Tasha Foundation, 112 High Street, Brentford, Middlesex TW8 8AT (tel: 020 8560 4583; email: enquiries@tasha-foundation.org.uk; website: www.tasha-foundation.org.uk)

Tuberous sclerosis

Tuberous Sclerosis Association (website: www.tuberous-sclerosis.org). See the website for a list of staff contacts or to complete the online contact form.

Turner syndrome

Turner Syndrome Support Society, 12 Simpson Court, 11 South Avenue, Clydebank Business Park, Clydebank G81 2NR (tel: 01419 528006; helpline: 0300 111 7520; email: turner.syndrome@tss.org.uk, website: www.tss.org.uk)

Urostomy

Urostomy Association, 4 Demontfort Way, Uttoxeter ST14 8XY (tel: 01889563191; email: secretary.ua@classmail.co.uk; website: www.urostomyassociation.org.uk)

Williams syndrome

Williams Syndrome Foundation, 161 High Street, Tonbridge, Kent TN9 1BX (tel: 01732 365152; email: enquiries@williams-syndrome.org.uk; website: www.williams-syndrome.org.uk)

Index

What else can DSC do for you?

Let us help you to be the best you possibly can be. DSC equips individuals and organisations with expert skills and information to help them provide better services and outcomes for their beneficiaries. With the latest techniques, best practice and funding resources all brought to you by our team of experts, you will not only boost your income but also exceed your expectations.

Publications

With over 100 titles, we produce fundraising directories and research reports, as well as accessible 'how to' guides and best practice handbooks, all to help you help others.

Training

The voluntary sector's best-selling training – 80 courses covering every type of voluntary sector training.

In-house Training

All DSC courses are available on your premises, delivered by expert trainers and facilitators. We also offer coaching, consultancy, mentoring and support.

Conferences and Fairs

DSC conferences are a fantastic way to network with voluntary sector professionals whilst taking part in intensive, practical training workshops.

Funding Websites

DSC's funding websites provide access to thousands of trusts, grants, statutory funds and corporate donations. You won't get more funders, commentary and analysis anywhere else. Demo our sites ***free*** *today.*

Trust**funding**.org.uk
Government**funding**.org.uk
Company**giving**.org.uk
Grantsfor**individuals**.org.uk

Visit our website today and see what we can do for you:

www.**dsc.org.uk**

Or contact us directly: publications@dsc.org.uk

@DSC_Charity
For top tips and special offers